Tulsian's

QUICK REVISION for FINANCIAL ACCOUNTING

[For ICWA Intermediate : Paper 5]

CA (Dr.) P.C. TULSIAN

M.Com., Ph.D., FCA, PGDFM

Additional Director (Former)
Board of Studies
The Institute of Chartered Accountants of India, New Delhi
Head
Department of Commerce
Ramjas College, University of Delhi
DELHI
Recipient of an Award for 'Exemplary Services contributed to the cause of Profession' by The Institute of Chartered Accountants of India, New Delhi

CA BHARAT TULSIAN

Chartered Accountant

Manager, KPMG
Alumnus of Sri Ram College of Commerce (SRCC), University of Delhi, DELHI
Recipient of an Award for the 'Best Article on Foreign Exchange' in All India by The Institute of Chartered Accountants of India, New Delhi

S. CHAND
PUBLISHING

S Chand And Company Limited

(ISO 9001 Certified Company)

S Chand And Company Limited

(ISO 9001 Certified Company)

Head Office: Block B-1, House No. D-1, Ground Floor, Mohan Co-operative Industrial Estate, New Delhi – 110 044 | Phone: 011-66672000

Registered Office: A-27, 2nd Floor, Mohan Co-operative Industrial Estate, New Delhi – 110 044 Phone: 011-49731800

www.**schandpublishing.com**; e-mail: **info@schandpublishing.com**

Branches

Chennai : Ph: 23632120; chennai@schandpublishing.com
Guwahati : Ph: 2738811, 2735640; guwahati@schandpublishing.com
Hyderabad : Ph: 40186018; hyderabad@schandpublishing.com
Jalandhar : Ph: 4645630; jalandhar@schandpublishing.com
Kolkata : Ph: 23357458, 23353914; kolkata@schandpublishing.com
Lucknow : Ph: 4003633; lucknow@schandpublishing.com
Mumbai : Ph: 25000297; mumbai@schandpublishing.com
Patna : Ph: 2260011; patna@schandpublishing.com

First Edition 2015

ISBN: 978-93-856-7612-3 **Product Code:** H8FAC44ACCN10ENAA16O

PRINTED IN INDIA

By Vikas Publishing House Private Limited, Plot 20/4, Site-IV, Industrial Area Sahibabad, Ghaziabad – 201 010 and Published by S Chand And Company Limited, A-27, 2nd Floor, Mohan Co-operative Industrial Estate, New Delhi – 110 044.

Preface

The book adopts a fresh and novel approach to the study of **QUICK REVISION FOR FINANCIAL ACCOUNTING** for the students of Paper 5: ICWA Intermediate Examination (Group-I). It has been written in a teach yourself style strictly following a student-friendly approach, and is essentially meant to serve as a tutor at home.

Two important Questions which usually arise in the mind of every student are:

1. What Minimum to Revise to Maximise the Marks?

2. What to Revise One Day Before Examination?

Tulsian's Quick Revision provides Answers to above Two Questions by providing the following contents:

SECTION 1 :	**VERY SHORT ANSWER QUESTIONS**	**[WEIGHTAGE 20 MARKS]**
SECTION 2 :	**GAAP AND ACCOUNTING SYSTEMS**	**[WEIGHTAGE 8 MARKS]**
SECTION 3 :	**PREPARATION OF ACCOUNTS**	**[WEIGHTAGE 24 MARKS]**
SECTION 4 :	**CONTROL OF ACCOUNTING SYSTEMS**	**[WEIGHTAGE 8 MARKS]**
SECTION 5 :	**ACCOUNTING IN SERVICE SECTOR**	**[WEIGHTAGE 8 MARKS]**
SECTION 6 :	**ACCOUNTING FOR SPECIAL TRANSACTIONS**	**[WEIGHTAGE 16 MARKS]**
SECTION 7 :	**ACCOUNTING FOR BANKING, INSURANCE AND ELECTRICITY COMPANIES**	**[WEIGHTAGE 16 MARKS]**
SECTION 8 :	**TULSIAN'S MODEL TEST PAPERS**	
SECTION 9 :	**ICWA EXAMINATION PAPERS**	

IMPORTANT NOTES FOR STUDENTS

DON'TS

1. DO NOT IGNORE THEORY.
2. DO NOT IGNORE "ACCOUNTING STANDARDS".
3. DO NOT DO THE AUDIT OF ANSWERS.
4. DO NOT LEAVE ANY TOPIC OF THE SYLLABUS UNCOVERED. DO NOT THINK OF ANY TOPIC AS UNIMPORTANT.
5. DO NOT LEAVE ANY QUESTION OF THE PAPER UNATTEMPTED.
6. AVOID SHORTCUTS.

DO'S

1. DO ALL VERY SHORT ANSWER QUESTIONS TO HAVE CONCEPTUAL UNDERSTANDING OF VARIOUS TOPICS.
2. PREPARE ALL THE TOPICS OF THE SYLLABUS.
3. SOLVE THE PRACTICAL QUESTIONS USING PAPER & PENCIL.
4. ATTEMPT ALL TULSIAN'S MODEL TEST PAPERS.
5. ATTEMPT ICWA EXAMINATION PAPERS OF AT LEAST LAST 3 ATTEMPTS [UNDER THE SAME SYLLABUS] IMMEDIATELY PRECEDING YOUR ATTEMPT.
6. COMPARE YOUR ANSWERS WITH THE MODEL ANSWERS AND NOTE THE VARIATIONS, IF ANY, AS TO THE ACCURACY AND PRESENTATION—Find out the reasons for the variations. Take the corrective action to rectify the variations. Mark those parts of Questions where you committed the error(s) with highlighter. Revise such Highlighted Items Daily so as to prevent the occurrence of the error in the next examination.

We are confident that these features would make this book an invaluable asset to the students who can brush up their knowledge quickly.

CA (Dr.) P.C. Tulsian
pctulsian@gmail.com
CA Bharat Tulsian
bharattulsian88@gmail.com

Acknowledgements

We wish to express our sincere thanks to several individuals who have been a source of inspiration and support personally and professionally including Dr. R. P. Tulsian, Dr. M. M. Goyal, Dr. S. C. Garg, Dr. Tanushree Jain, Ms. Madhu Aggarwal, Dr. Rajeev Goyal, Dr. S.N. Gupta, Dr. S.S. Lamba, Dr. Sarita Jain, Dr. Usha Jain, Dr. V. K. Aggarwal, Dr. V. P. Bansal, Dr. Vibha Jain, Dr. Savita Gopal, Dr. S.C. Gupta, Dr. S.P. Gupta, Dr. Naresh Gupta, Dr. Amit Singhal, Dr. J.B. Gupta, Dr. Madhu Gupta, Dr. Sushma Aggarwal, Dr. Renu Gupta, Dr. Manju Gupta, Dr. C.P. Gupta, Dr. S. Z. H. Zaidi. CA M.K. Aggarwal, CA S.K. Aggarwal, CA N.D. Gupta, CA Naveen Gupta, CA Anil Jindal, CA Madhu Sudan Goyal, CA Vinod Aggarwal, CA Sunil Gupta, CA Arun Jain, CA Virender Aggarwal, CA. S.K. Gupta, CA Ishwar Khemka, CA Prem Bansal, CA Ashish Gupta, CA M.K. Sharda, CA Rajeev Rastogi, CA Atul Gupta, CA Kuldeep Bhardwaj, CA Neeraj Chabra, CA Kishore Paul, CA Pradeep Narang, CA S.K. Gupta, CA R. Devarajan, CA Tapas Dutta, CA Arnav Chakrabarty, CA Seema Gupta, CA Shilpa Aggarwal, CA Vishal Pandey, Ms. Nidhi Singh, Dr. N.N. Sen Gupta, Prof. J.P. Sharma, CA Pallavi, CA Antima Jain, CA Piyush Tulsian, CA Swati Tulsian, CA Piyush and CA **Prarthana Mittal.**

Special word of thanks is also due to our favourite students **Piyush, Pranav, Arushi and Aman Mittal** who provided incisive comment and useful feedback.

We must conclude that this book would not have been possible without the support, encouragement and prodding of our family members. Many thanks to them.

Any criticisms or suggestions for further improvement of the book will be gratefully acknowledged and appreciated.

CA (Dr.) P.C. Tulsian
pctulsian@gmail.com

CA Bharat Tulsian
bharattulsian88@gmail.com

Syllabus

PAPER 5: FINANCIAL ACCOUNTING

SECTION A: GENERALLY ACCEPTED ACCOUNTING PRINCIPLES & ACCOUNTING SYSTEMS [10 MARKS]

1. **Accounting Process**
   (a) Theoretical framework (meaning, scope and usefulness of Accounting; Accounting principles, concepts and convention)
   (b) Accounting Life Cycle (ALC) – From Investment of Capital (Cash) to Realization of Revenue (Cash)
   (c) Capital and Revenue transactions- capital and revenue expenditures, capital and revenue receipts
   (d) Measurement, valuation and accounting estimates Double entry system, books of prime entry, subsidiary books, cash book, ledgers, trial balance
   (e) Rectification of errors, opening entries, transfer entries, adjustment entries, closing entries
2. **Accounting Standards**
   (a) AS-1: Disclosure of Accounting Policies
   (b) AS-2: Valuation of Inventories
   (c) AS-4: Contingencies and Events Occurring after the Balance Sheet Date
   (d) AS-5: Net Profit or Loss for the Period, Prior Period Items and Changes in Accounting Policies
   (e) AS-10: Accounting for Fixed Assets
   (f) AS-11: The Effects of Changes in Foreign Exchange Rates
   (g) AS-15: Employee Benefits
   (h) AS-16: Borrowing Costs
3. **Reconciliation Statements**
   (a) Bank Reconciliation Statements
   (b) Stock Reconciliation Statements
   (c) Receivables/Payables Reconciliation Statement

SECTION B: PREPARATION OF ACCOUNTS [30 MARKS]

4. **Accounting for Depreciation, Depletion, Amortization and Impairment of Assets**
   (a) Depreciation Policy, Depletion, Amortization and Impairment of Assets
   (b) Depreciation Accounting (AS – 6); Impairment of Assets (AS -28)
   (c) Methods, computation and accounting treatment
5. **Preparation of Financial Statements :**
   (a) Of Profit-making organizations:
   (i) Preparation of Profit & Loss Account and Balance Sheet
   (ii) Preparation of Cash Flow Statement (AS – 3)
   (iii) Accounting treatment of bad debts, reserve for bad and doubtful debts, provision for discount on debtors and provision for discount on creditors
   (b) Of Not-for-Profit organizations :
   (i) Preparation of Receipts and Payments Account
   (ii) Preparation of Income and Expenditure Account
   (iii) Balance Sheet

(c) Under single entry system including conversion of single entry into double entry system :

(i) Concept of single entry system, conversion of single entry system into double entry system of accounting

(ii) Application of accounting ratios for preparation of accounts under single entry system

6. Partnership

(a) Past adjustments and guarantee, profit & loss appropriation account

(b) Admission, Retirement, Death, Treatment of Joint Life Policy

(c) Dissolution of partnership firms including piece meal distribution

(d) Amalgamation of partnership firms, Conversion of partnership firm into a company and sale of partnership firm to a company

7. Royalty and Hire Purchase

(a) Accounting from the point of view of various parties

(b) Possession and repossession in case of default in payments

8. Branch and Departmental Accounts

(a) Branch Accounts-Debtors system, Stock & Debtors system, Foreign Branch

(b) Departmental Accounts: Trading Account; Profit & Loss Account

(c) Calculation of net profit of various departments and allocation of expenses on the basis of suitable base, treatment of shortages, treatment of unrealized profit

(d) Preparation of General Profit & Loss Account and Balance Sheet

SECTION C : CONTROL OF ACCOUNTING SYSTEMS [10 MARKS]

9. Self-Balancing Ledger and Sectional Balancing Ledgers

(a) Self- Balancing Ledgers

(b) Sectional Balancing Ledgers

SECTION D: ACCOUNTING IN SERVICE SECTOR [10 MARKS]

10. Accounting for Service Sectors

(a) Revenue Recognition (AS-9)

(b) Construction Companies (AS 7), Project Accounting

(c) Service sectors such as Software, ITES, Telecommunication, Entertainment, Hospital, Educational Institutions

SECTION E: ACCOUNTING FOR SPECIAL TRANSACTIONS [20 MARKS]

11. Accounting for Special Transactions

(a) Bills of Exchange, Consignment, Joint venture, Sale of goods on approval or return basis, Account Current

(b) Investment Accounts (AS – 2, 13)

(c) Insurance Claim (Loss of Stock and Loss of profit)

SECTION F: ACCOUNTING FOR BANKING, INSURANCE AND ELECTRICITY COMPANIES [20 MARKS]

12. Banking, Electricity and Insurance Companies

(a) Accounts of a Banking Company (as per Banking Companies Regulation Act)

(b) Accounts of an Electricity Company (as per Electricity Act)

(c) Accounts of Insurance Companies (as per Insurance Act) including Stock Valuation

Contents

PAPER-5 : FINANCIAL ACCOUNTING

VERY SHORT ANSWERS QUESTIONS

SECTION A: GENERALLY ACCEPTED ACCOUNTING PRINCIPLES & ACCOUNTING SYSTEMS [10 MARKS]

SECTION B: PREPARATION OF ACCOUNTS [30 MARKS]

SECTION C : CONTROL OF ACCOUNTING SYSTEMS [10 MARKS]

SECTION D: ACCOUNTING IN SERVICE SECTOR [10 MARKS]

SECTION E: ACCOUNTING FOR SPECIAL TRANSACTIONS [20 MARKS]

SECTION F: ACCOUNTING FOR BANKING, INSURANCE AND ELECTRICITY COMPANIES [20 MARKS]

TULSIAN'S MODEL TEST PAPERS

EXAMINATION PAPERS

PAPER – 5: FINANCIAL ACCOUNTING

VERY SHORT ANSWER QUESTIONS WITH ANSWERS

(10 Questions Carrying 2 Marks Each)

STRUCTURE OF QUESTION 1 [BASED ON DECEMBER 2014 EXAMINATION]

TOPIC	NO. OF VERY SHORT ANSWER QUESTIONS	WEIGHTAGE
1. Generally Accepted Accounting Principles & Accounting Systems	1	$1 \times 2 = 2$
2. Preparation of Accounts	3	$3 \times 2 = 6$
3. Control of Accounting Systems	1	$1 \times 2 = 2$
4. Accounting in Service Sector	1	$1 \times 2 = 2$
5. Accounting for Special Transactions	2	$2 \times 2 = 4$
6. Accounting for Banking, Insurance and Electricity Companies	2	$2 \times 2 = 4$
Total	10	20

This Page has been intentionally left blank

VERY SHORT ANSWER QUESTIONS

[10 QUESTIONS OF 2 MARKS EACH]

INTRODUCTION TO ACCOUNTING

QUESTION 1: What is meant by Accounting?

ANSWER:

1. Accounting is the process of identifying, measuring and communicating economic information to permit informed judgements and decisions by users of information.
2. Accounting is an information system which communicates the accounting information to the users (whether internal *or* external) to enable them to make reasoned decisions.

QUESTION 2: List the activities covered under Accounting.

ANSWER:

1. Identifying
2. Measuring
3. Recording
4. Classifying
5. Summarising
6. Analysing
7. Interpreting
8. Communicating

QUESTION 3: What is meant by Transaction?

ANSWER: A transaction is an exchange in which each participant receives *or* sacrifices value (e.g., Purchase of Raw Material).

QUESTION 4: What is meant by an Event?

ANSWER: An Event (whether internal *or* external) is a happening of consequence to an entity (e.g., use of raw material for production).

QUESTION 5: What is meant by an Entity?

ANSWER: An entity means an economic unit that performs economic activities (e.g., TATA Steels, Birla Industries Ltd., Reliance Industries Ltd.).

QUESTION 6: What is meant by Identifying?

ANSWER: Identifying is concerned with the ascertainment of financial transactions and events of a specific entity.

QUESTION 7: What is meant by Recording?

ANSWER: It is concerned with the recording of identified and measured financial transactions in an orderly manner, soon after their occurrence in the proper books of account.

QUESTION 8: What is meant by Classifying?

ANSWER: It is concerned with the classification of the recorded transactions so as to group the transactions of similar type at one place. This function is performed by maintaining the ledger in which different accounts are opened to which related transactions are brought to one place by posting. ***For Example***, All purchases of goods for cash *or* on credit on different dates are brought to Purchases Account.

QUESTION 9: What is meant by Summarising?

ANSWER: It is concerned with the summarization of the classified transactions in a manner useful to the users. This function involves the preparation of Financial Statements such as Income Statement, Balance Sheet, Cash Flow Statement.

QUESTION 10. What is meant by Analysing?

ANSWER: It is concerned with the establishment of relationship between the various items *or* group of items taken from Income Statement *or* Balance Sheet *or* both. Its purpose is to identify the financial strengths and weaknesses of the enterprise. It provides the basis for interpretation.

QUESTION 11: What is meant by Interpreting?

ANSWER: It is concerned with explaining the meaning and significance of the relationship so established by the analysis.

QUESTION 12: What is meant by Communicating?

ANSWER: It is concerned with the transmission of summarised, analysed and interpreted information to the users to enable them to make reasoned decisions.

QUESTION 13: What is meant by Accountancy?

ANSWER: Accountancy refers to a systematic knowledge of accounting. It explains 'why to do' and 'how to do' of various aspects of accounting. It tells us why and how to prepare the books of accounts and how to summarize the accounting information and communicate it to the interested parties.

QUESTION 14: What is Book-keeping?

ANSWER: Book-keeping is a part of accounting and is concerned with record keeping *or* maintenance of books of accounting which is often routine and clerical in nature. It only covers the following four activities:

1. Identifying the transactions
2. Measuring the identified transactions in a common measuring unit
3. Recording the identified and measured transactions in Proper Books of Accounts
4. Classifying the recorded transactions in the ledger

QUESTION 15. What is an Accounting Cycle?

ANSWER: An Accounting Cycle is a complete sequence beginning with the recording of the transactions and ending with the preparation of the Financial Statements.

QUESTION 16: List the sequential steps involved in an Accounting Cycle.

ANSWER:

Step 1	Journalising	Record the transactions in the Journal.
Step 2	Posting	Transfer the transactions (recorded in the Journal), in the respective accounts opened in the Ledger.
Step 3	Balancing	Ascertain the difference between the total of debit amount column and the total of credit amount column of a ledger account.
Step 4	Trial Balance	Prepare a list showing the balances of each and every account to verify whether the sum of the debit balances is equal to the sum of the credit balances.
Step 5	Income Statement	Prepare Trading and Profit & Loss Account to ascertain the profit *or* loss for the accounting period.
Step 6	Position Statement (i.e., Balance Sheet)	Prepare the Balance Sheet to ascertain the financial position as at the end of accounting period.

QUESTION 17: Name any four users of Accounting Information.

ANSWER:

I. Internal Users

1. Management
2. Employees

II. External Users

1. Short-term Creditors
2. Long-term Creditors
3. Investors(Present & Potential)
4. Tax Authorities
5. Government and their agencies

QUESTION 18: List the primary objectives of Accounting.

ANSWER:

1. To maintain Systematic Accounting Records
2. To ascertain Financial Performance
3. To ascertain Financial Position
4. To communicate the Information to the Users

QUESTION 19: List any two advantages of Accounting.

ANSWER:

1. Facilitates to Replace Memory
2. Facilitates to comply with Legal Requirements
3. Facilitates to ascertain Financial Performance
4. Facilitates to ascertain Financial Position
5. Facilitates the users to take decisions
6. Facilitates a Comparative Study
7. Assists the Management
8. Facilitates Control over Assets
9. Facilitates the Settlement of Tax Liability
10. Facilitates the Ascertainment of Value of Business
11. Facilitates Raising Loans
12. Acts as Legal Evidence

QUESTION 20: List any two limitations of Accounting.

ANSWER:

1. Ignores the qualitative elements
2. Not free from bias
3. Ignores the price level Changes
4. Estimated position and not real position
5. Danger of window dressing

QUESTION 21: State any two branches of accounting.

ANSWER: (a) Financial Accounting (b) Cost Accounting (c) Management Accounting.

QUESTION 22: Briefly Explain the branches of accounting.

ANSWER:

Financial Accounting	Financial Accounting is the process of identifying, measuring and communicating accounting information to permit informed judgements and decisions by the users of accounting
Cost Accounting	It is the process of accounting and controlling the cost of a product, operation *or* function.
Management Accounting	It is the application of accounting techniques for providing information for the purpose of planning, controlling and decision making.
Social Responsibility Accounting	It is the process of identifying, measuring and communicating the social effects of business decisions to permit informed judgements and decisions by the users of information.
Human Resource Accounting	It is the process of identifying, measuring and communicating the investments made in human resources of an enterprise to permit informed judgements and decisions by the users of accounting.

QUESTION 23: Explain the term 'Business Transaction'.

ANSWER: A Business transaction is an exchange in which each participant receives *or* sacrifices value (***For Example***, Purchase of Raw Material for cash *or* on credit). It involves exchange of goods *or* services on cash *or* credit basis. It is an economic event that relates to a business entity involving transfer of money *or* money's worth.

QUESTION 24: Explain the term 'Account'.

ANSWER: An account is a summary of relevant transactions at one place relating to a particular head. It records not only the amount of transaction but also their effect and direction.

QUESTION 25: Explain the term 'Assets'.

ANSWER: Assets refer to tangible objects *or* intangible rights of an enterprise which carry probable future benefits. In other words, an asset is a resource controlled by the enterprise as a result of past events and from which future economic benefits are expected to flow to the enterprise. These assets may broadly be classified as follows:

1. **Current Assets** — Current assets are those assets which are held:–
   (i) in the form of cash, *or*
   (ii) for their conversion into cash, *either* within the Operating Cycle Period *or* within the 12 Months Period from the date of Balance Sheet, *or*
   (iii) for their consumption in the production of goods *or* rendering of services in the normal course of business.

   For Example, 1. Current Investments, 2. Inventories, 3. Trade Receivables, 4. Cash and Cash Equivalents, 5. Short-term Loans and Advances, 6. Other Current Assets

   Liquid Assets (or Quick Assets) – Liquid Assets represent the Current Assets other than Stock and Prepaid Expenses.

   Liquid Assets = Current Assets – Stock & Prepaid Expenses

2. **Non-Current Assets** — Non-Current Assets refer to those assets which are held for the purposes of producing *or* providing goods *or* services and those that are not held for resale in the normal course of business. ***For Example***, 1. Fixed Assets, 2. Non-Current Investments 3. Long-Term Loans and Advances, 4. Other Non-Current Assets

   Fixed assets may be classified as follows:

   (i) **Tangible Fixed Assets** — Refer to those fixed assets which have physical existance. ***For Example***, Land and Building, Plant and Machinery and Furniture and Fixtures.

   (ii) **Intangible Fixed Assets** — Refer to those fixed assets which do not have physical existance. ***For Example***, Goodwill, Patent, Trademarks, Copyrights and the like.

3. **Fictitious Assets:** Fictitious Assets *either* represent Accumulated Losses *or* Deferred Revenue Expenses not yet written off till the date of Balance Sheet.

QUESTION 26: How to determine whether an asset is a Current Asset *or* Fixed Asset?

An asset is classified *either* as a Current Asset *or* as a Fixed Asset on the basis of the purpose for which an asset is held in the hands of user.

ANSWER: The following table summarises the circumstances when a particular asset is treated as Current in one case and Fixed in another case:

Asset	When treated as Current Asset	When treated as Fixed Asset
1. Land	In case of Land Developers & Property Dealers.	In case of other persons.
2. Buildings	In case of Builders & Property Dealers.	In case of other persons.
3. Furniture	In case of Furniture Manufacturers and Furniture Dealers.	In case of other persons.
4. Motor Vehicles	In case of Motor Vehicles Manufacturers and Dealers.	In case of other persons.
5. Shares & Debentures	In case of Dealer in Securities.	In case of other persons.
6. Plant & Machinery	In case of Plant & Machinery Manufacturers and Dealers.	In case of other persons.

QUESTION 27: Explain the term 'Liabilities'.

ANSWER: Liabilities refer to the financial obligations of an enterprise other than owner's funds. Liabilities may be broadly classified as follows:

I. LIABILITIES ON THE BASIS OF PERIOD

1. **Current Liabilities** – Current liabilities refer to those liabilities which are expected to be settled *either* within the Operating Cycle Period *or* within the 12 Months Period from the date of the Balance Sheet.

   For Example, 1. Short-Term Borrowings, 2. Trade Payables, 3. Other Current Liabilities, 4. Short-Term Provisions.

2. **Non-Current Liabilities** – Non-Current Liabilities refer to those liabilities which are expected to be settled after 12 months from the date of Balance Sheet *or* after Operating Cycle which ever is latter. ***For Example***, 1. Long-term Borrowings, 2. Other Long term Liabilities, 3. Long-term Provisions.

II. LIABILITIES ON THE BASIS OF SOURCE

1. **Internal Liabilities:** Internal Liabilities refers to the financial obligations of an enterprise towards owners.

2. **External Liabilities:** External Liabilities refer to the financial obligations of an enterprise towards outsiders.

QUESTION 28: Explain the term 'Capital'.

ANSWER: Capital refers to the amount invested in an enterprise by the proprietor (in case of proprietorship) *or* partners (in case of a partnership concern). This amount is increased by the amount of profits earned and amount of additional capital introduced and is decreased by the amount of losses incurred and the amount withdrawn (whether in the form of cash *or* kind). It represents the owner's claim on the assets of the enterprise. It is also known as Owner's Equity *or* Net Assets *or* Net Worth.

Since the liability holders have a definite and prior claim against the assets, the capital is also called a residual of assets over liabilities and may be expressed as follows:

Capital = Assets – Liabilities

Thus, Capital is the excess of Assets over External Liabilities.

QUESTION 29: Explain the term 'Drawings'.

ANSWER: The term 'Drawings' refer to the total amount of cash *or* goods *or* any other asset withdrawn by the proprietor (in case of a proprietorship enterprise) *or* partner (in case of a partnership enterprise) for personal use. ***For Example***, If Cash of ₹ 10,000 and Goods costing ₹ 5,000 are withdrawn by a proprietor, ₹ 15,000 is called as the amount of drawings.

QUESTION 30: Explain the term 'Goods'.

ANSWER: Goods refer to the items in which the enterprise deals in. ***For Example***, Cars purchased by a Car Dealer, Tables & Chairs purchased by a Furniture Dealer.

QUESTION 31: Explain the term 'Purchases'.

ANSWER: The term 'Purchases' refers to the total amount of goods obtained by an enterprise for resale *or* for use in the production of goods *or* rendering of services in the normal course of business. The purchases may be for cash *or* on credit.

For Example, in case 100 units are purchased @ ₹ 2 per unit for cash, ₹ 200 is called as the amount of cash purchase. In case 200 units are purchased @ ₹ 3 per unit from Ram on credit, ₹ 600 is called as the amount of credit purchase.

QUESTION 32: Explain the term 'Purchases Returns'.

ANSWER: The term 'Purchase Returns' refers to the total amount of goods returned by an enterprise to the Suplier. ***For Example***, in case 50 units (Purchased @ ₹ 3 per unit) are returned to Ram, ₹ 150 is called as the amount of purchase returns.

QUESTION 33: Explain the term 'Sales'.

ANSWER: The term 'Sales' refers to the amount for which the goods are sold *or* services are rendered. The sales may be for cash *or* on credit. ***For Example***, in case 60 units are sold @ ₹ 5 per unit for cash, ₹ 300 is called as the amount of cash sales in case 120 units are sold @ ₹ 6 per unit to Shyam on credit, ₹ 720 is called as the amount of credit sales.

QUESTION 34: Explain the term 'Sales Returns'.

ANSWER: The term 'Sales Returns' refers to the total amount of goods returned by a customer to the enterprise. ***For Example***, in case 50 units (Sold @ ₹ 6 per unit) are returned by Shyam (customer), ₹ 300 is called as the amount of sales returns.

QUESTION 35: Explain the term 'Stock (or Inventory *or* Merchandise)'.

ANSWER: The term 'Stock' refers to tangible property held for sale in the ordinary course of business *or* for consumption in the production of goods *or* services for sale. It includes Stock of Raw Materials, Semi-Finished goods and Finished Goods. ***For Example***, in case 40 units out of 100 units (purchased @ ₹ 2 per unit) remained unsold, ₹ 80 is called as the Cost of Stock. The stock may be Opening Stock *or* Closing Stock. Opening Stock means the unsold goods at the beginning of the Current Accounting Period. Closing Stock means the Unsold Goods at the end of the Current Accounting Period.

QUESTION 36: Explain the term 'Trade Receivables'.

ANSWER: The term 'Trade Receivables' include Trade Debtors and Bills Receivables.

QUESTION 37: Explain the term 'Trade Debtors'.

ANSWER: The term 'Trade Debtor' refers to the person from whom the amounts are due for goods sold *or* services rendered on credit basis. ***For Example***, in case 60 units are sold to Mr X @ ₹ 5 per unit on credit, Mr X is a Trade Debtor of the business.

QUESTION 38: Explain the term 'Bills Receivables'.

ANSWER: A bill of exchange is an unconditional order in writing given by the creditor to the debtor to pay on demand *or* at a fixed *or* determinable future time, a certain sum of money to *or* to the order of a specified person *or* to the bearer. This bill of exchange is known as Bills Receivable for the creditor.

QUESTION 39: Explain the term 'Trade Payables'.

ANSWER: The term 'Trade Payables' include Trade Creditors and Bills Payables.

QUESTION 40: Explain the term 'Trade Creditors'.

ANSWER: The term 'Trade Creditor' refers to the person to whom the amounts are due for goods purchased *or* services rendered on credit basis. ***For Example***, in case 100 units are purchased @ ₹ 2 per unit from Mr Y on credit, Mr Y is a Trade Creditor of the business.

QUESTION 41: Explain the term 'Bills Payables'.

The Bill of Exchange is known as Bills Payable for the Debtors.

QUESTION 42: Explain the term 'Expenses'.

ANSWER: Expenses are decrease in economic benefits during an accounting period in the form of (a) Outflow *or* Depletion of Assets *or* (b) Incurrence of Liabilities, that result in decrease in internal equity other than those relating to distribution to Equity Participants.

Example I: Purchase of Goods for Cash involves outflow of Cash.

Example II: Purchase of Goods on Credit involves increase in Creditors.

Example III: Discount Allowed to Customers involves decrease in Assets.

QUESTION 43: Explain the term 'Income'.

ANSWER: Income is increase in economic benefits during an accounting period in the form of (a) Inflow of Assets, *or* (b) Decrease of Liabilities, that result in increase in internal equity other than those relating to Investment by Equity Participants.

Note: Equity Participants means —

(a) Proprietor in case of sole proprietorship
(b) Partners in case of a partnership firm
(c) Shareholders in case of a company

Example I: Trading Commission received involves inflow of Cash.

Example II: Discount Received from Creditors involves decrease in Creditors.

QUESTION 44: Explain the term 'Net Profit'.

ANSWER: Net Profit means the excess of Revenue & Gains Over its related Expenses & Losses during an accounting period. It increases Owners' Equity.

Net Profit = (Revenue & Gain) – (Expenses & Loss)

QUESTION 45: Explain the term 'Gains'.

ANSWER: Gains are increases in equity (i.e., Net Assets) from incidental transaction of an entity and from all other transactions and other events and circumstances affecting the entity during the accounting period except those that result from revenues *or* investment by equity participants. These gains may be operating *or* non-operating.

Example I: Profit on sale of marketable securities is usually considered as operating gain.

Example II: Profit on sale of a fixed asset is usually considered as non-operating gain.

Example III: Increase in Equity due to Profit on sale of goods is not considered as Gain because it is due to Revenue.

: Increase in Equity due to increase in Capital is not gain because it is due to increase in Capital.

QUESTION 46: Explain the term 'Losses'.

ANSWER: Losses are decreases in equity (i.e., Net Assets) from incidental transactions of an entity and from all other transactions and other events and circumstances affecting the entity during the accounting period except those result from expenses *or* distribution to equity participants. These losses may be operating *or* non-operating.

Example I: Loss *or* Sale of marketable securities, losses on writing down inventory from Cost to Market Value, writing off Bad Debts are considered as operating losses.

Example II: Loss on Sale of a Fixed Asset, Losses from disposal of segments of enterprises, Losses on Foreign Currency Devaluations are usually considered as Non-Operating Losses.

QUESTION 47: Explain the term 'Discount'.

ANSWER: Discount is an incentive to promote Sales (i.e. Trade Discount) *or* prompt payment by the debtors (i.e. Cash Discount).

QUESTION 48: Explain the term 'Trade Discount'.

ANSWER: Trade Discount is a reduction granted by a supplier from the list price of goods *or* services on business considerations (such as quantity bought, trade practices, etc.,) other than for prompt payment.

Example — If 10 Gold Rings are sold at the list price of ₹ 50,000 each subject to trade discount of 10%. In this case trade discount will be calculated as given on below:

10 Gold Rings @ ₹ 50,000	₹ 5,00,000
Less: Trade Discount @ 10%	₹ 50,000
Amount Payable as per Invoice	₹ 4,50,000

QUESTION 49: Explain the term 'Cash Discount'.

ANSWER: Cash Discount is a reduction granted by a supplier from the invoice price in consideration of immediate payment *or* payment within a stipulated period.

Example — If in the above example, terms of payable are 2%, 30 Days, it means buyer will get 2%

cash discount if he makes payment within 30 days. In case the purchaser makes the payment within 30 days, the cash discount will be calculated as under:

Amount Payable as per Invoice	₹ 4,50,000
Cash Discount @ 2%	₹ 9,000
Cash paid within 30 days	₹ 4,41,000

QUESTION 50: Explain the term 'Cost'.

ANSWER: The term 'Cost' may be defined as noun *or* as a verb as follows:

(a) **As a noun** — The amount of expenditure (actual *or* notional) incurred on a specified thing *or* activity.

(b) **As a verb** — To ascertain the cost of specified thing *or* activity.

ICA, India defines Cost as "mesurement, in monetary terms, of the amount of resource used for the purpose of production of goods *or* rendering services"

The work 'Cost' can rerely stand on its own and should be qualified as to its limitation (e.g., historical, variable, fixed etc.) and should be related to a particular thing *or* activity (e.g., a given quantity *or* unit of produced *or* services performed).

QUESTION 51: Explain the term 'Voucher'.

ANSWER: Voucher is a documentary evidence in support of a business transaction.

For Example, in case of Cash Purchases, Cash memos and in case of Credit Purchases, Purchase Invoices are Vouchers. The vouchers act as source documents on the basis of which transactions are recorded in the books of accounts.

QUESTION 52: Explain the term 'Revenue'.

ANSWER: The term 'revenue' refers to the amount charged for the goods sold *or* services rendered, *or* permitting others to use enterprise's resources yielding Interest, Royalty, and Dividend. ***For Example***, Sales, Commission earned, Interest earned, Royalty earned, Dividend earned.

QUESTION 53: Explain Expenditure, Expense and Asset.

ANSWER:

Expenditure	Expenditure is the cost incurred in acquiring of asset *or* service in the form of outflow *or* depletion of asset *or* incurrence of liability. It may be expired *or* unexpired.
Expense	Expense (or Expired Cost) is that portion of expenditure which has been consumed during current accounting period. It may be utilized cost *or* lost cost.
Asset	Unexpired Cost (Asset) is that portion of expenditure which has not been consumed during current accounting period.

QUESTION 54: State the Meaning of Double Entry System of Book-keeping.

ANSWER:

1. Double Entry System of Book-keeping refers to a system of accounting under which both the aspects (i.e., Debit *or* Credit) of every transaction are recorded in the accounts involved.
2. Dual Aspect — Two fold aspect of a transaction is called dual aspect *or* duality of a transaction. This duality is the basis of double entry records.
3. As the name implies, the entry made for each transaction is composed of two parts — one for debit and another for credit. The double entry system may be compared with the Newton's law of motion, viz to every action there is always an equal and contrary reaction.
4. Every debit has equal amount of credit. So the total of all debits must be equal to the total of

all credits.

5. The terms debit and credit used today have their origin from the terms — Debito and Credito as used by Luca fra Pacioli in his book.
6. Account — The individual record of a person *or* thing *or* an item of income *or* an expense is called an account.

QUESTION 55: State any two Advantages of Double Entry System.

ANSWER:

1. It facilitates the accuracy of ledger accounts through the device of trial balance.
2. It facilitates the ascertainment of Financial Performance.
3. It facilitates the ascertainment of Financial Position.
4. It facilitates the comparability of Financial Statements.

QUESTION 56: State any two bases *or* systems of accounting.

ANSWER: (a) Cash basis (b) Accrual basis (c) Hybrid

QUESTION 57: What is Accrual Basis of Accounting?

ANSWER: Accrual Basis of Accounting is a method of recording transactions by which Revenue, Costs, Assets and Liabilities are recognised during the accounting period in which they accrue/arise.

QUESTION 58. What is Cash Basis of Accounting?

ANSWER: Cash Basis of Accounting is a method of recording transactions by which Revenues, Costs, Assets and Liabilities are recognised during the accounting period in which Actual Receipts *or* Actual Payments take place.

QUESTION 59. What is Hybrid Basis of Accounting?

ANSWER: It is a combination of both Cash Basis of Accounting and Accrual Basis of Accounting. Under the hybrid basis of accounting, Incomes are recorded on Cash basis (i.e., during the accounting period in which they are received irrespective of when they accrue) and Expenses are recorded on Accrual Basis, (i.e., during the accounting period in which they arise irrespective of when they are paid).

QUESTION 60. Which basis of Accounting is recognised under the Companies Act, 2013?

ANSWER: Accrual Basis of Accounting is recognised under the Companies Act, 2013.

QUESTION 61. Name the basis of Accounting under which Prepaid Expenses are adjusted.

ANSWER: Prepaid Expenses are adjusted under the Accrual Basis of Accounting.

QUESTION 62. Name the basis of Accounting under which Outstanding Expenses are adjusted.

ANSWER: Outstanding Expanses are adjusted under the Accrual Basis of Accounting.

QUESTION 63. Name the basis of Accounting under which Accrued Incomes are adjusted.

ANSWER: Accrued Incomes are adjusted under the Accrual Basis of Accounting.

QUESTION 64: Name the basis of Accounting under which Unaccrued Incomes are adjusted.

ANSWER: Unaccrued Incomes are adjusted under the Accrual Basis of Accounting.

QUESTION 65: PRARTHANA PESTISIDES supplies you the following information about his incomes and expenses for the financial year 2013–2014:

Particulars	₹	Particulars	₹
Expenses paid	75,000	Income received	2,03,000
Expenses paid in advance	38,000	Income received in advance	25,000
Expenses not yet paid	23,000	Income earned but not received	22,000
Loans taken	1,00,000	Loans given	20,000
Compute the Net Income on:	(i) Cash basis, (ii) Accrual basis, (iii) Hybrid basis.		

ANSWER:

COMPUTATION OF INCOME

Particulars	On Cash basis ₹	On Accrual basis ₹	On Hybrid basis ₹
A. Total Revenue:			
(a) Income received	2,03,000	2,03,000	2,03,000
(b) Income received in advance	—	(25,000)	—
(c) Income not yet received	—	22,000	—
	2,03,000	2,00,000	2,03,000
B. Total Expenditure:			
(a) Expenses paid	75,000	75,000	75,000
(b) Expenses paid in advance	—	(38,000)	(38,000)
(c) Expenses not yet paid	—	23,000	23,000
	75,000	60,000	60,000
C. Income for the year	1,28,000	1,40,000	1,43,000

Note: Loans taken and Loan given are not considered while calculating Income because these represent Capital Receipts and Capital Payments respectively.

QUESTION 66. TULSIAN Cloth Agency provides you the following information for the year 2013–2014:

Cash sales	₹ 1,00,000	
Credit sales	₹ 9,00,000	(out of which ₹ 8,00,000 collected)
Cash purchases	₹ 80,000	
Credit purchases	₹ 6,50,000	(out of which ₹ 6,00,000 paid)
Expenses paid	₹ 75,000	
Expenses paid in advance	₹ 38,000	
Outstanding expenses	₹ 23,000	
Closing stock at end	Nil	
Compute the Net Income on		
(i) Cash basis, (ii) Accrual basis, (iii) Hybrid basis.		

ANSWER:

COMPUTATION OF INCOME

Particulars	On Cash basis ₹	On Accrual basis ₹	On Hybrid basis ₹
A. Total Revenue:			
(a) Cash sales	1,00,000	1,00,000	1,00,000
(b) Credit sales			
(i) Collected	8,00,000	8,00,000	8,00,000
(ii) Outstanding	—	1,00,000	—
Total Revenue	**9,00,000**	**10,00,000**	**9,00,000**
B. Total Expenditure:			
(a) Cash purchases	80,000	80,000	80,000
(b) Credit purchases			
(i) Paid	6,00,000	6,00,000	6,00,000
(ii) Outstanding	—	50,000	50,000
(c) Expenses			
(i) Paid	75,000	75,000	75,000
(ii) Paid in advance	—	(38,000)	(38,000)
(iii) Outstanding	—	23,000	23,000
	7,55,000	7,90,000	7,90,000
C. Income	1,45,000	2,10,000	1,10,000

CAPITAL AND REVENUE RECEIPTS & EXPENDITURE

QUESTION 1: State the Meaning and Accounting Treatment of Capital Expenditure.

ANSWER:

1. Meaning	It is an expenditure which is incurred: (a) to acquire *or* bring into existence an asset, or (b) to acquire *or* bring into existence an advantage *or* benefit of an enduring nature, or (c) to increase the productivity *or* earning capacity.
2. Benefits	It normally yields benefits beyond current accounting period.
3. Accounting Treatment	It is debited to the Respective Asset Account which appears on the Assets side of the Balance Sheet.
4. Examples	(a) Cost of Land and Building (b) Cost of Plant and Machinery (c) Cost of Furniture and Fixtures

QUESTION 2: State the meaning and Accounting Treatment of Revenue Expenditure.

ANSWER:

1. Meaning	It is an expenditure which is incurred: (a) to maintain the productivity *or* earning capacity of a business. (b) to carry out operating activities in the normal course of business.
2. Benefits	It normally does not yield benefits beyond current accounting period.
3. Accounting Treatment	It is debited to Respective Expense Account which appears on the debit side of Trading A/c (If Direct Expense) *or* P&L A/c (If Indirect Expense).
4. Examples	(a) Depreciation on Land & Building (b) Rent of Machines (c) Repairs of Building (d) Insurance of Building

QUESTION 3: State the meaning and Accounting Treatment of Deferred Revenue Expenditure.

ANSWER:

1. Meaning	According to the Guidance note on 'Terms used in Financial Statements', issued by ICAI 'Deferred revenue expenditure is the expenditure for which payment has been made *or* a liability has been incurred but which is carried forward on the presumption that it will be of benefit over a subsequent period *or* periods'. In short, it refers to that expenditure which is, for the time being, deferred from being charged to income. Such suspension of 'charging off' operation may be due to the nature of expenses and the benefit expected therefrom.
2. Example	Heavy advertising to launch a new product is a deferred revenue expenditure since the benefit from it will be availed over the next 3 to 5 years.
3. Accounting Treatment	Normally such expenditure should be written off over a period of 3 to 5 years. The written off portion is debited to P&L Account and unwritten off portion is shown on the Assets Side of Balance Sheet.

QUESTION 4: State the Meaning and Accounring Treatment of Capital Receipts.

ANSWER:

1. Meaning	Capital receipts refer to those receipts which are not revenue in nature.
2. Accounting Treatment	These are credited to the respective account of capital nature.
3. Examples	(a) Sale of Land and Building by a person other than a dealer in real estate. (b) Raising of Loan by a person other than one engaged in the business of finance/banking. (c) Raising of Capital.

QUESTION 5. State the Meaning and Accounring Treatment of Revenue Receipts.

ANSWER:

1. Meaning	Revenue receipts refer to those receipts which arise in the normal course of business.
2. Accounting Treatment	These are credited to Respective Revenue Account which appears in the Income Statement.
3. Examples	(a) Sale of Land and Building by a dealer in real estate. (b) Sale of Securities by a dealer in securities

QUESTION 6: Give any two examples of Deferred Revenue Expenditure.

ANSWER: (a) Heavy Advertisement Cost (b) Plastic Paint of Building.

ACCOUNTING PRINCIPLES

QUESTION 1: Name the Accounting Standard which states the Fundamental Accounting Assumptions.

ANSWER: The Accounting Standard (AS-1) 'Disclosure of Accounting Policies' issued by Institute of Chartered Accountants of India (ICAI).

QUESTION 2: State the Fundamental Accounting Assumptions.

ANSWER:

1. Going Concern
2. Consistency
3. Accrual

QUESTION 3: What is Going Concern Assumption?

ANSWER:

1. The enterprise is normally viewed as a going concern, i.e. as continuing operations for the foreseeable future.
2. It is assumed that the enterprise has *neither* the intention nor the necessity of liquidation *nor* curtailing materially its scale of operations.
3. If an enterprise is not a going concern, valuation of its assets and liabilities on historical cost becomes irrelevant and as a consequence its profit/loss may not give reliable information.

QUESTION 4: What is Consistency Assumption?

ANSWER:

1. It is assumed that accounting policies are consistent from one period to another.
2. This adds the virtue of comparability to accounting data.
3. If comparability is lost, the relevance of accounting data for users' judgement and decision making is gone.

QUESTION 5: What is Accrual Assumption?

ANSWER:

1. Revenues and costs are accrued, that is, recognised as they are earned *or* incurred (and not as money is received *or* paid) and recorded in the financial statements of the periods to which they relate.

2. This assumption is the core of accrual accounting system.
3. For companies it is mandatory to keep accounts on accrual basis under the Companies Act, 2013.

QUESTION 6: What is meant by Accounting Principles?

ANSWER: Basic Principles of accounting are essentially, the general decision rules which govern the development of accounting techniques. These principles guide how transactions should be recorded and reported.

QUESTION 7: What is meant by Generally Accepted Accounting Principles (GAAP)?

ANSWER: Generally Accepted Accounting Principles may be defined as those rules of action *or* conduct which are derived from experience and practice and when they prove useful, they become accepted as principles of accounting.

QUESTION 8: What is the Accounting Entity Principle?

ANSWER: According to Accounting Entity Principle, a business is treated as a separate entity that is distinct from its owner(s), and all other accounting entities and hence a distinction should be made between (i) personal transactions and business transactions, and (ii) transactions of one business entity and those of another business entity. ***For Example***, in case of a proprietary concern, though the legal entity of the business and its proprietor is the same, for the purpose of accounting, they are to be treated as separate from each other.

QUESTION 9: What is the Money Measurement Principle?

ANSWER: According to Money Measurement Principle, only those transactions which are capable of being expressed in terms of money are included in the accounting records.

QUESTION 10: What is Accounting Period Principle?

ANSWER: According to Accounting Period Principle, the economic life of an enterprise is artificially split into periodic intervals which are known as accounting periods, at the end of which an Income Statement and Position Statement are prepared to show the Financial Performance and Position.

QUESTION 11: Name the exception to Consistency Principle.

ANSWER: Prudence Principle (or Conservatism Principle)

QUESTION 12: What is Prudence Principle (or Conservatism Principle)?

ANSWER: According to 'Prudence Principle', the principle of 'anticipate no profit but provide for all probable losses' should be applied. In other words, the Prudence Principle of conservatism requires that in the situation of uncertainty and doubt, the business transactions should be recorded in such a manner that the profits and assets are not overstated and the losses and liabilities are not understated.

QUESTION 13: State any two applications of Prudence Principle.

ANSWER:

1. Valuation of Stock-in-trade at a lower of Cost *or* Net Realiable Value
2. Making the Provisions for Doubtful Debts and Discount on Debtors

QUESTION 14: What is the Full Disclosure Principle? State any one application of this principle.

ANSWER: According to Full Disclosure Principle, the financial statements should act as means of conveying and not concealing.The financial statements must disclose all the relevant and reliable information which they purport to represent, so that the information may be useful for the users.

EXAMPLE: The practice of appending notes to the financial statements has developed as a result of the principle of full disclosure.

QUESTION 15: Name the exception to Full Disclosure Principle.

ANSWER: Materiality Principle

QUESTION 16: What is the Materiality Principle?

ANSWER: According to the 'Materiality Principle', all relatively relevant items, the knowledge of which might influence the decision of the users of the financial statements, should be disclosed in the financial statements.

QUESTION 17: What is the Cost Principle?

ANSWER: According to Cost Principle, an asset is ordinarily recorded in the accounting records at the price paid to acquire it at the time of its acquisition and the cost becomes the basis for the accounts during the period of acquisition and subsequent accounting periods.

QUESTION 18: What is the Matching Principle?

ANSWER: According to Matching Principle, the expenses incurred in an accounting period should be matched with the revenues recognised in that period,

It means, if revenue is recognised on all goods sold during a period, cost of those goods sold should also be charged to that period. It is wrong to recognise revenue on all sales, but charge expenses only on such sales as are collected in cash till that period.

QUESTION 19: What is the Duality Principle?

ANSWER: According to Duality Principle, Two fold aspects of a transaction (i.e., one for Debit and another for Credit) should be the basis of accounting.

QUESTION 20: Name the Accounting Principle applied in Classification of assets as Current Assets and Fixed Assets.

ANSWER: Going Concern Principle

QUESTION 21: Name the Accounting Principle applied in Appending Notes to the Financial Statements.

ANSWER: Full Disclosure Principle

QUESTION 22: Name the Accounting Principle applied in Accounting of a small calculator as an expense and not as an asset.

ANSWER: Materiality Principle

QUESTION 23: Name the Accounting Principle applied in following the WDV Method of depreciating a particular asset year after year.

ANSWER: Consistency Principle

QUESTION 24: Name the Accounting Principle applied in Valuation of Stock at lower of Cost *or* Net Realisable Value.

ANSWER: Prudence Principle

QUESTION 25: Name the Accounting Principle applied in Making Provision for Doubtful Debts.

ANSWER: Prudence Principle

QUESTION 26: Personal transactions are distinguished from business transactions in accordance with which Accounting Principle?

ANSWER: Accounting Entity Principle

QUESTION 27: The economic life of an enterprise is artificially split into periodic intervals in accordance with which Accounting Principle?

ANSWER: Accounting Period Principle

QUESTION 28: The Financial Statements must disclose all the relevant and the reliable information in accordance with which Accounting Principle?

ANSWER: Full Disclosure Principle

QUESTION 29: Accounting Practices should be followed on a horizontal basis from one accounting period to another period in accordance with which Accounting Principle?

ANSWER: Consistency Principle

QUESTION 30: When Stock is valued at cost in one accounting period and at lower of Net Realisable Value in another accounting period, which Accounting Principle conflicts with which Accounting Principle?

ANSWER: Prudence Principle conflicts with the Consistency Principle

QUESTION 31: State whether Revenues are matched with expenses *or* Expenses are matched with Revenues in accordance with the Matching Principle.

ANSWER: Expenses are matched with Revenues

QUESTION 32. Name the Accounting Principle which ignores the non-monetary facts *or* attributes.

ANSWER: Money Measurement Principle

QUESTION 33: Name the Accounting Principle which treats all rupees alike, whether it is a rupee of 1950 *or* 2013.

ANSWER: Money Measurement Principle

QUESTION 34: State the Meaning and two Examples of Accounting Policy.

ANSWER:

Meaning	Accounting Policy refers to accounting principles and methods of applying those principles adopted by enterprise in the preparation of financial statements.
Examples	1. Accounting Policy for Providing Depreciation 2. Accounting Policy for Valuation of Inventories

QUESTION 35: State the Qualitative Characteristics of Accounting Information

ANSWER:

1. Understanding
2. Relevance
3. Reliability
4. Comparability

QUESTION 36: Comment in brief on any two of the following naming the principles of accounting on which these statement are based :

(a) Balance sheet is not a valuation statement.

(b) Advance received from a supplier is not taken as income or sales.

(c) Calibre or quality of management team is not directly disclosed on the Balance sheet.

ANSWER:

Balance" sheet is not a Valuation Statement	This statement is based on '**Cost Concept**' which says that an asset is recorded in the books of account at the price paid for it and not at its market value e.g. if a computer valued ₹ 1 lac is purchased from a friend for ₹ 60,000 then the computer is recorded in the books at ₹ 60,000 and all future transactions are based on ₹ 60,000. So assets are valued at cost or book value and not the market value. Items which have no cost are ignored. Goodwill appears in the books only when the firm has purchased this for a price. So balance sheet is not a valuation statement.
Advance received from a supplier is not taken as income or sales	This statement is based an **Accrual Concept**. This concept applies to both revenue and expenses. Accrual Concept says that revenue is recognised when sale is complete or servicesare rendered and it is immaterial whether the cash is received or not. This concept makes the distinction between the receipt of cash and right to receive cash. So any advance received from a supplier is not treated as sales. Because income is associated with the changes in owner's equity and that it is not necessarily related to changes in cash.
Calibre or quality of management team is not directly disclosed on the Balance Sheet	This statement is based on '**Money Measurement Concept**' which says that only those transactions are recorded into business which can be expressed or measured in terms of money. So the quality of management, efficient staff, death of a partner or director, dispute between purchase manager and sales manager are not recorded in the books of accounts at all.

QUESTION 37: "Revenue is recognised when a sale transaction is made or when services are rendered". State there exceptions to this general rule.

ANSWER: Generally revenue is recognised when a sale transaction is made or when services are rendered. But there are certain exceptions to this rule:

1. First, in case of long-term contracts revenue is recognised before completion of the job.
2. Second, when Cash basis of accounting is followed revenue is recognised when it is received in cash.
3. Third, Under hire-purchase transactions – revenue is recognised in proportion to the instalments over price.
4. Fourth, in case of gold mining revenue is recognised at the point of production itself.

QUESTION 38: Attempt any two of the following (Answer need not exceed 50 words each):

(i) The proprietor has withdrawn some goods from the business for his personal use. Is it compulsory to record it in the books of the firm? Give reasoning.

(ii) The life of business is assumed to be indefinite (going concern concept), yet companies prepare their accounts annually. What is the basis?

(iii) You started a business on 1st April, 2004 (financial year closes on 31st March, 2005). Salaries for March, 2005 were paid on 7th April, 2005. Monthly salaries bill amounts to ₹ one lac. How much amount would be shown in 2004-05 P & L A/c and on what basis?

ANSWER:

(i) Yes, it is compulsory to record in the books of the firm withdrawl of goods by proprietor from the business for his personal use as per Business Entity Concept. As per this concept, a business is treated as a separate entity that it is distinct from its owner.

(ii) Accounting Period Concept is the base of preparing final accounts annually.

(iii) As per Accrual basis of Accounting we record ₹ 12,00,000 as salaries in Profit & Loss Account for the year ended 31st March, 2005,

QUESTION 39: "Accounting principles become Generally Accepted Accounting Principles (GAAP) when they satisfy certain norms." What are those norms ? Explain.

ANSWER: Accounting principles become Generally Accepted Accounting Principles (GAAP) when they satisfy the following three norms :

1. **Relevance.** A principle is relevant to the extent it results in information that is meaningful and useful to those who use the accounting information.
2. **Objectivity.** The principle must have objectivity. A principle is objective to the extent the information is not influenced by the personal bias or judgement of those who provide it. The accounting information must be reliable. There must be some way of ascertaining the correctness of the information provided, it means that accounting information should be variable.
3. **Feasibility.** A principle is feasible to the extent it can be implemented without undue complexity or cost. Thus the principle must be practicable.

ACCOUNTING EQUATION

QUESTION 1: What is Accounting Equation?

ANSWER: An accounting equation is a Statement of Equality between Total Assets and Total Equities and is expressed as follows:

Total Assets = Total Equities

or

Assets = Internal Equity + External Equity

or

Assets = Capital + Liabilities

QUESTION 2: State whether Earnings increase *or* decrease Owner's Equity.

ANSWER: Increase

QUESTION 3: State whether Withdrawl of Cash for personal use increase *or* decrease Owner's Equity.

ANSWER: Decrease

QUESTION 4: State whether Withdrawl of Goods for personal use increase *or* decrease Owner's Equity.

ANSWER: No Change since Owner's Equity decreases by drawings but increases by reduction in purchases.

QUESTION 5: State whether Additional Capital increase *or* decrease Owner's Equity.

ANSWER: Increase

ANSWER:

(a) According to Traditional Approach

(i) Personal Accounts –6, 7, 8, 9, 10, 11, 12, 16, 17

(ii) Real Accounts –5, 13

(iii) Nominal Accounts –1, 2, 3, 4, 14, 15,

(b) According to Accounting Equation Approach *or* Modern Approach

(i) Assets Accounts –5, 6, 10, 11, 13, 16

(ii) Liabilities Account –7, 9, 12, 17

(iii) Capital Accounts –8

(iv) Revenue Accounts –3, 4, 14

(v) Expenses Account –1, 2, 15

QUESTION 5: What is meant by the term 'Debit'?

ANSWER: Basically debit means to enter an amount of transaction on the left side of an account. Debit in relation to Assets Accounts and Expenses Accounts represents an increase but in relation to Liabilities Accounts, Capital Accounts and Revenue Accounts represents a decrease.

QUESTION 6: What is meant by the term 'Credit'?

ANSWER: Basically credit means to enter an amount of transaction on the right side on an account. Credit in relation to Assets Accounts and Expenses Accounts represents a decrease but in relation to Liabilities Accounts, Capital Account and Revenue Accounts represents an increase.

QUESTION 7: State the Origin of Debit and Credit.

ANSWER: The terms of debit and credit have their origin from the terms debito and credito as used by *lucafrapacioli.*

QUESTION 8: What is a Journal?

ANSWER: A Journal is a book in which transactions are recorded in the order in which they occur i.e., in chronological order. A Journal is called a book of prime entry (also called of original entry) because all business transactions are entered first in this book.

QUESTION 9: What is Journalising?

ANSWER: The process of recording a transaction in a journal is called Journalising.

QUESTION 10: What is Journal Entry?

ANSWER: An entry made in the journal is called a 'Journal Entry'.

QUESTION 11: Which column in a Journal is not filled at the time of journalising?

ANSWER: The 'Ledger Folio column' is filled in at the time of posting into the ledger and not at the time of journalising.

QUESTION 12: What is Narration?

ANSWER: Narration is a brief explanation of the transaction.

QUESTION 13: State any two Advantages of Journal.

ANSWER:

1. Chronological Record	Journal is a chronological record in the sense that it records the transactions in the order in which they occur.
2. Explanation of Transaction	Each journal entry in the journal carries narration which gives a brief explanation of the transaction.
3. Recording of both aspects	Both the aspects (i.e., debit and credit) of a transaction are recorded in the journal. Since the amounts recorded in both debit amount column and credit amount column must be equal, the possibility of committing error is reduced and the detection of errors, if any, committed becomes easy.

QUESTION 14: State any two Limitations of Journal.

ANSWER:

1. **Time and Cost Consuming** — The system of recording all the transactions in a journal requires (i) the writing down of the name of the account involved as many times as the transactions occur; and (ii) an individual posting of each account debited and credited and hence involves the repetitive journalising and posting labour.
2. **Delay** — Such a system does not provide the information on prompt basis.
3. **No Internal Check** — Such a system does not facilitate the installation of an internal check system since the journal can be handled by only one person.
4. **Bulky and Voluminous** — The journal becomes bulky and voluminous.

QUESTION 15: What is done to overcome the shortcomings of the use of the journal only as a book of original entry?

ANSWER: The journal is sub-divided into special journals.

QUESTION 16: List any two differences between Trade Discount and Cash Discount.

ANSWER:

Basis of Distinction	Trade Discount	Cash Discount
1. Meaning	It is a reduction granted by a supplier from the List Price of goods *or* services on business considerations (such as quantity bought, trade practices, etc.,) other than for prompt payment.	A reduction granted by a supplier from the Invoice Price in consideration of immediate payment *or* payment within a credit period allowed.
2. Purpose	It is allowed to promote the sales *or* as a trade practices.	It is allowed to encourage the prompt payment.
3. Time when allowed	It is allowed on purchase of goods.	It is allowed on immediate payment *or* payment within a specified period.
4. Disclosure in the Invoice	It is shown by way of deduction in the invoice itself.	It is not shown in the invoice.
5. Ledger Account	Trade Discount Account is not opened in the ledger.	Cash Discount Account is opened in the ledger.
6. Variation	It may vary with the quantity purchased.	It may vary with the period within which the payment is made.

QUESTION 17: Name the book in which accounts are opened.

ANSWER: Ledger

QUESTION 18: What is a Ledger?

ANSWER: A Ledger is a principal book which contains all the accounts (Assets Accounts, Liabilities Accounts, Capital Accounts, Revenue Accounts, Expenses Accounts) to which the transactions recorded in the books of original entry are transferred.

QUESTION 19: What is the object of preparing an Account?

ANSWER: The object of preparing an account is to ascertain the net effect of various transactions during a given period on a particular account.

QUESTION 20: Why is the Ledger called the Book of Final Entry?

ANSWER: The ledger is called the 'Book of Final Entry' because the ledger is the ultimate destination of all transactions.

QUESTION 21: Enumerate the forms in which a ledger may be kept.

ANSWER: A ledger may be kept in the form of bound books, loose leaf sheets *or* CDs *or* RCDs *or* DBDs *or* PAN Drive (in case computer is used) *or* any other like device.

QUESTION 22: Enumerate any five utilities of ledger.

ANSWER:

1. It provides complete information about all accounts in one book.
2. It enables to ascertain what the main items of revenues are.
3. It enables to ascertain what the main items of expenses are.
4. It enables to ascertain what the assets are and of what values.
5. It enables to ascertain what the liabilities are and of what amounts.
6. It facilitates the preparation of Final Accounts.

QUESTION 23: What is Posting?

ANSWER: Posting is the process of transferring the transactions recorded in the books of original entry in the concerned accounts opened in the ledger.

QUESTION 24: What is the necessity of Posting?

ANSWER: It is necessary to post all journal entries into various accounts in the ledger because posting helps us to know the net effect of various transactions during a given period on a particular account.

QUESTION 25: What is a Compound Entry?

ANSWER: When more than two accounts are involved in a transaction and the transaction is recorded by means of a single journal entry instead of passing several journal entries, such single journal entry is termed as 'Compound Journal Entry'. It may be recorded in the following three ways:

(a) by debiting one account and crediting two *or* more accounts; or

(b) by debiting two *or* more accounts and crediting one account; or

(c) by debiting several accounts and crediting several accounts.

QUESTION 26: What is an Opening Entry?

ANSWER: Opening Entry is a journal entry by means of which previous accounting period's balances of various assets, liabilities and capital are brought forward in the books of current accounting period.

QUESTION 27: How is an Opening Entry recorded in a Journal?

ANSWER: The procedure of posting an opening entry is same as in case of an ordinary journal entry except that in case of an account which has been debited, the words To balance b/f are recorded in the 'Particulars column' on the debit side and in case of an account which has been credited, the words By balance b/f are recorded in the 'Particulars column' on the credit side.

QUESTION 28: What is balancing of an Account?

ANSWER: The process of ascertaining the difference between the total of debits and total of credits appearing in an account, is known as 'Balancing of an account'.

QUESTION 29: What is Balance of an Account?

ANSWER: Balance of an account is the difference between the total of debits and total of credits appearing in an account. It may be a debit balance *or* a credit balance *or* a nil balance depending upon whether the debit *or* the credit side total is higher.

QUESTION 30: What is the significance of Balancing?

ANSWER: Balancing an Account is Necessary to ascertain the Net Effect of all transactions Posted To that account during a given period.

QUESTION 31: Name the type of Accounts which are Balanced.

ANSWER: (a) Personal Accounts (b) Real Accounts

QUESTION 32: Name the type of accounts which are never balanced but are closed.

ANSWER: Nominal Accounts.

QUESTION 33: Give any two examples of representative personal accounts.

ANSWER: (a) Outstanding Salaries A/c (represents employee) (b) Prepaid Rent A/c (represents landlord)

QUESTION 34: Why is a journal called a book of original entry?

ANSWER: Journal is called a book of original entry because all the business transaction are first recorded chronologically in journal.

QUESTION 35: Give one example of Adjusting Entry.

ANSWER:

Prepaid Insurance A/c Dr.

To Insurance Premium A/c

(Being prepaid insurance adjusted)

QUESTION 36: When is a transaction said to be a cash transaction?

ANSWER: A transaction is said to be a cash transaction when the word 'Cash' is used *or* name of party is not used.

SUBSIDIARY BOOKS – CASH BOOK

QUESTION 1: Why is a Journal sub-divided?

ANSWER: The Journal is sub-divided into special journals because of the following limitations of use of Journal only as a book of original entry:

(a) The system of recording all the transactions in a journal requires (i) the writing down of the name of the account involved as many times as the transactions occur; and (ii) an individual posting of each account debited and credited and hence involves the repetitive journalising and posting labour.

(b) Such a system does not provide the information on prompt basis.

(c) Such a system does not facilitate the installation of an internal check system since the journal can be handled by only one person.

(d) The journal becomes bulky and voluminous.

QUESTION 2: How is a Journal sub-divided?

ANSWER: The journal is sub-divided in such a way that a separate book is used for each category of transactions which are repetitive in nature and are sufficiently large in number.

QUESTION 3: What is a Special Journal?

ANSWER: Special Journals refer to the journals which are used to record the specific transactions of similar nature. Special Journals are also known as Subsidiary Books *or* Day Books.

QUESTION 4: List any four Special Journals.

ANSWER:

1. Purchases Book
2. Sales Book
3. Purchase Returns Book
4. Sales Returns Book
5. Journal Proper

QUESTION 5: State any two advantages of using Special Journals.

ANSWER:

1. **Facilitates division of work:** The accounting work can be divided among many persons.
2. **Permits the installation of Internal Check System:** The accounting work can be divided in such a manner that the work of one person is automatically checked by another person. With the use of internal check, the possibility of occurrence of error/fraud may be avoided.
3. **Permits the use of specialised skill:** The accounting work requiring specialised skill may be assigned to a person possessing the required skill. With the use of a specialised skill, prompt, economical and more accurate supply of accounting information may be obtained.
4. **Time and labour saving in journalising and posting:** For instance, when Sales Book is kept, the name of Sales Account will not be required to be written down in the Journal as many times as the sales transactions and at the same time, Sales Account will not be required to be posted again and again since only a periodic total of Sales Book is posted to the Sales Account.

QUESTION 6: What is a Cash Book?

ANSWER: A Cash Book is a special journal which is used for recording all Cash Receipts and Cash Payments.

QUESTION 7: Explain that the Cash book is a journal as well as a ledger account.

ANSWER: The Cash Book is a book of Original Entry (or Prime Entry) since transactions are recorded for the first time from the source documents. The Cash Book is a ledger in the sense that it is designed in the form of a Cash Account and records Cash Receipts on the debit side and Cash Payments on the credit side. Thus, the Cash Book is both a Journal and a Ledger.

QUESTION 8: List the various types of Cash Books.

ANSWER:

1. Single Column Book
2. Cash Book with Discount Column
3. Cash Book with Bank & Discount Column
4. Petty Cash Book

QUESTION 9: What is a Single Column Cash Book?

ANSWER: Single Column Cash Book has one amount column on each side. All Cash Receipts are recorded on the debit side and all Cash Payments on the credit side. In fact, this book is nothing but a Cash Account. Hence, there is no need to open Cash Account in the ledger.

QUESTION 10: Can there be a credit balance in a Simple Cash Book? State with reason.

ANSWER: No, because Cash Payments can never exceed Cash Receipts.

QUESTION 11: Name the account which is not opened in the ledger in the case of a Single Column Cash Book.

ANSWER: Cash Account.

Reason: Single Column Cash Book serves the purpose of Cash Account.

QUESTION 12. What is a Cash Book with Discount Column?

ANSWER: Cash Book with Discount Column has two amount columns (one for Cash and another for Discount) on each side. All Cash Receipts and Cash Discount allowed are recorded on the debit side and all Cash Payments and Cash Discount received are recorded on the credit side.

QUESTION 13: Can there be a credit balance in a Cash Book with Discount Column? State with reason.

ANSWER: No, because Cash Payments can never exceed Cash Receipts.

QUESTION 14: Name the account which is not opened in the ledger in the case of a Cash Book with Discount Column.

ANSWER: Cash Account.

Reason: Cash Book with Discount Column serves the purpose of Cash Account.

QUESTION 15: What is a Three Column Cash Book?

ANSWER: Three Column Cash Book has three amount columns (one for Cash, one for Bank and one for Discount) on each side. All Cash Receipts, Deposits into Bank and Cash Discount allowed are recorded on the debit side and all Cash Payments, Withdrawals from Bank and Cash Discount received are recorded on the credit side. In fact, a three-column Cash Book serves the purpose of Cash Account. Hence, there is no need to open these two accounts in the ledger.

QUESTION 16: Can there be a Credit Balance in a Three Column Cash Book? State with reason.

ANSWER: Yes, because Payments through bank can exceed Deposits into bank in case Bank Overdraft facility is available and is availed by the customer.

QUESTION 17: Name the accounts which are not opened in the ledger in the case of a Three Column Cash Book.

ANSWER: Cash Account and Bank Account.

Reason: Three Column Cash Book serves the purpose of Cash Account and Bank Account. Cash column serves the purpose of a Cash Account. Bank column serves the purpose of a Bank Account.

QUESTION 18: If the total of Bank Column on credit side exceeds the total of Bank Column on debit side, what does it indicate?

ANSWER: Bank Overdraft

QUESTION 19: Which discount is recorded in the discount column of a Cash Book?

ANSWER: Cash Discount

QUESTION 20: Which discount is recorded on the debit side of a Cash Book?

ANSWER: Cash Discount allowed

QUESTION 21: Which discount is recorded on the credit side of a Cash Book?

ANSWER: Cash Discount received

QUESTION 22: Can the total of Discount Allowed Column exceed the total of Discount Received Column?

ANSWER: Yes, because your Discount Policy may not be the same as that of your Creditors.

QUESTION 23: Are the discount Columns of Cash Book balanced?

ANSWER: 'Discount Columns' are merely totalled and never balanced.

QUESTION 24: How are the discount columns of a Cash Book posted in the ledger?

1. Posting in the 'Discount Allowed Account' and 'Discount Received Account' are made only for the totals and not for the individual transactions.
2. The total of discount allowed column on the debit side is posted to the debit of the 'Discount Allowed A/c' in the ledger by writing To Sundries as per Cash Book in the particulars column.
3. The total of discount received column on the credit side is posted to the credit of the 'Discount Received A/c' in the ledger by writing By Sundries as per Cash book in the particulars column.

QUESTION 25: What is a Contra Entry?

ANSWER: Contra Entry is an Entry of which both the debit and credit aspects are simultaneously recorded in the Cash Book itself.

QUESTION 26: Give two examples of Contra Entry.

ANSWER:

1. Cash deposited into the Bank
2. Cash withdrawn from the Bank

QUESTION 27: How is Contra Entry distinguished from other entries?

ANSWER: Contra Entry is marked with letter 'C' in Ledger Folio Column.

QUESTION 28: Why is the sign 'c' recorded in the folio column of a Three column cash book?

ANSWER: In case of a contra entry, the sign 'C' is recorded in the folio column of both the sides of the cash book to indicate that the both the aspects of the transaction have been recorded and it requires no posting to the ledger.

QUESTION 29: What is a Petty Cash Book?

ANSWER: Petty Cash Book is the book which is used to record the payment of Petty Cash Expenses.

QUESTION 30: Who is Petty Cashier?

ANSWER: Petty Cashier is the person who is authorised to make payments of Petty Cash Expenses and to record them in Petty Cash Book.

QUESTION 31: Explain the meaning of Imprest System of Petty Cash.

ANSWER: Meaning of Imprest *or* **Float** — The amount which the Head Cashier hands over to the Petty Cashier in order to meet the Petty Cash Expenses of a given period, is known as 'Imprest' *or* 'Float'.

Imprest System of Petty Cash — Under imprest system, the Chief Cashier makes the reimbursement of the amount spent by the Petty Cashier and the Petty Cashier again has the same amount of Petty Cash at the end as in the beginning.

QUESTION 32: Explain the method of posting the Petty Cash Book.

ANSWER: All the heads of expenses (including miscellaneous) are totalled periodically (usually monthly) and such periodic totals are individually posted to the debit side of the concerned ledger accounts in the ledger by writing 'To Sundries as per Petty Cash Book' in the particulars column. The ledger folio number is written under every total amount of expense to indicate that the entry has been posted in the ledger. In the folio column of the ledger account, the page number of the Petty Cash Book is written.

QUESTION 33: State the name and side of the account to which Total of Discount Column on the credit side of the Cash Book would be posted.

ANSWER: Discount Received A/c – Cr. side

QUESTION 34: State the name and side of the account to which Cash received from a Customer for goods sold on credit would be posted.

ANSWER: Customer's Account – Cr. side,

QUESTION 35: State the name and side of the account to which Cash paid to a Supplier for goods bought on credit would be posted.

ANSWER: Supplier's A/c – Dr. side

QUESTION 36: State the name and side of the account to which Cash paid for purchase of furniture would be posted.

ANSWER: Furniture Account – Dr. side

QUESTION 37: State the name and side of the account to which Cash received for sale of old furniture would be posted.

ANSWER: Furniture Account – Cr. side

QUESTION 38: State the name and side of the account to which a Sale to Ram for Cash would be posted.

ANSWER: Sales Account – Cr. side

QUESTION 39: State the name and side of the account to which a Purchase from Shyam for Cash would be posted.

ANSWER: Purchases Account – Dr. Side

SUBSIDIARY BOOKS (OTHER THAN CASH BOOK)

QUESTION 1: What is a Purchase Book?

ANSWER: Purchases book (also known as Invoice book/Bought book) is one of the subsidiary books which is used to record the Credit Purchases of merchandise (i.e., the goods in which the enterprise deals in).

QUESTION 2: Name the Source Document which is used for recording entries in a Purchases Book.

ANSWER: Purchase Invoices received from the Suppliers.

QUESTION 3: How would you post a Purchases Book?

ANSWER:

Posting of Individual Amount	Posting of Periodic Total
Individual amounts are daily posted to the credit of Suppliers' Accounts by writing 'By Purchases A/c' in the particulars column.	Periodic total is posted to the debit of Purchases Account by writing 'To Sundries as per Purchases Book' in the particulars column.

QUESTION 4: What is a Sales Book?

ANSWER: Sales Book (also known as Day Book/Sales Journal) is one of the subsidiary books which is used to record the Credit Sales of Merchandise.

QUESTION 5: Name the Source Document which is used for recording entries in a Sales Book.

ANSWER: Sales Invoices issued to the Customers.

QUESTION 6: How would you post a Sales Book?

ANSWER:

Posting of Individual Amount	Posting of Periodic Total
Individual amounts are daily posted to the debit of Customers' Accounts by writing 'To Sales A/c' in the particulars column.	Periodic total is posted to the credit of Sales Account by writing 'By Sundries as per Sales Book' in the particulars column.

QUESTION 7: What is a Purchases Returns Book?

ANSWER: Purchases Returns Book (also known as Return Outwards Book/Journal) is one of the subsidiary books which is used to record the Returns of merchandise purchased on credit.

QUESTION 8: Name the Source Document which is used for recording entries in a Purchase Returns Book.

ANSWER: Debit Notes issued to the Suppliers *or* Credit Notes received from the Suppliers.

QUESTION 9: What is a Debit Note?

ANSWER: A Debit Note is a document prepared by the purchaser to inform the supplier that his account has been debited with the amount mentioned and for the reasons stated therein. Debit Note contains the date of return, name of the supplier to whom the goods have been returned, details of the goods returned, reasons for returning the goods. Each debit note is serially numbered.

QUESTION 10. How would you post a Purchases Returns Book?

ANSWER:

Posting of Individual Amount	Posting of Periodic Total
Individual amounts are daily posted to the debit of Suppliers' Accounts by writing 'To Purchases Returns A/c' in the particulars column.	Periodic total is posted to the Credit of Purchases Returns Account by writing 'By Sundries as per Purchases Returns Book' in the particulars column.

QUESTION 11: What is a Sales Returns Book?

ANSWER: Sales Returns Book (also known as Returns Inward Book/Journal) is one of the subsidiary books which is used to record the Returns of merchandise sold on credit.

QUESTION 12: Name the Source Document which is used for recording entries in a Sales Returns Book.

ANSWER: Credit Notes issued to the Customers *or* Debit Notes issued by the Customers.

QUESTION 13: What is a Credit Note?

ANSWER: A Credit Note is a document prepared by the seller to inform the buyer that his account has been credited with the amount mentioned and for the reasons stated therein. Credit Note contains the date of return of goods, the name of the customer who has returned the goods, details of goods received back and the amount of such goods. Each credit note is serially numbered.

QUESTION 14: How would you post a Sales Returns Book?

ANSWER:

Posting of Individual Amount	Posting of Periodic Total
Individual amounts are daily posted to the Credit of Customers' Accounts by writing 'By Sales Returns A/c' in the particulars column.	Periodic total is posted to the debit of Sales Returns Account by writing 'To Sundries as per Sales Returns Book' in particulars column.

QUESTION 15: State any two points of difference between Debit Note and Credit Note.

ANSWER:

Debit Note	Credit Note
It is prepared by Purchaser.	It is prepared by Seller.
Contents	**Contents**
(a) Date of return	(a) Date of return
(b) Name of supplier to who returned	(b) Name of customer who returned
(c) Details of goods returned	(c) Details of goods returned
(d) Reasons for returning goods	(d) Reason for returning goods

QUESTION 16: What is Journal Proper?

ANSWER: Journal Proper is a residuary book in which those transactions are recorded which cannot be recorded in any other subsidiary book such as (a) Cash Book, (b) Purchases Book, (c) Sales Book, (d) Purchases Returns Book, (e) Sales Returns Book, (f) Bills Receivable Book, and (g) Bills Payable Book.

QUESTION 17: Give any two examples of entries which appear in Journal Proper.

ANSWER:

1. Opening Entry
2. Closing Entries
3. Transfer Entries
4. Adjusting Entries
5. Rectifying Entries

QUESTION 18: What is the purpose of Opening Entry?

ANSWER: An Opening Entry is passed in the journal to bring the previous accounting period's balances of various assets, liabilities and capital in the books of current accounting period.

QUESTION 19: What is the purpose of Closing Entries?

ANSWER: Closing Entries are passed in the journal to close the nominal accounts by transferring them to the Trading and Profit and Loss Account. These are needed at the end of the accounting year, when the final accounts are prepared.

QUESTION 20: What is the purpose of Transfer Entries?

ANSWER: Transfer Entries are passed in the journal to transfer an amount from one account to another account, i.e., Transfer of Total Drawings from Drawings A/c to Capital A/c.

QUESTION 21: What is purpose of Adjusting Entries?

ANSWER: Adjusting Entries are passed in the journal to bring into the books of accounts certain unrecorded items like closing stock, depreciation on fixed assets, outstanding and prepaid items. These are needed at the time of preparing the final accounts.

QUESTION 22: What is the purpose of Rectifying Entries?

ANSWER: Rectifying Entries are passed in the journal to rectify the various errors committed while posting, totalling, balancing, etc.

QUESTION 23: Name the book of original entry in which a Credit purchase of Furniture worth ₹ 5,000, by M/s Delhi Furniture is recorded.

ANSWER: Purchases Book

QUESTION 24: Name the book of original entry in which a second hand motor car purchased on credit from M/s Delhi Motors for ₹ 50,000, by M/s Delhi Furniture is recorded.

ANSWER: Journal Proper

QUESTION 25: Name the book of original entry in which a Cash Purchase of Furniture worth ₹ 5,000, by M/s Delhi Furniture is recorded.

ANSWER: Cash Book

QUESTION 26: Name the book of original entry in which a second hand motor car purchased for cash from M/s Delhi Motors for ₹ 50,000, by M/s Delhi Furniture is recorded.

ANSWER: Cash Book

QUESTION 28: Name the book of original entry in which a Credit Sale of Furniture worth ₹ 5,000, by M/s Delhi Furniture is recorded.

ANSWER: Sales Book

QUESTION 29. Name the book of original entry in which a second hand motor car sold on credit to M/s Delhi Motors for ₹ 50,000, by M/s Delhi Furniture is recorded.

ANSWER: Journal Proper

QUESTION 30. Name the book of original entry in which a Cash Sale of Furniture worth ₹ 5,000, by M/s Delhi Furniture is recorded.

ANSWER: Cash Book

QUESTION 31: Name the book of original entry in which a second hand motor car sold for cash to M/s Delhi Motors for ₹ 50,000, by M/s Delhi Furniture is recorded.

ANSWER: Cash Book

QUESTION 32. Name the book of original entry in which a Return of Furniture purchased on credit for ₹ 5,000, by M/s Delhi Furniture is recorded.

ANSWER: Purchase Returns Book

QUESTION 33. Name the book of original entry in which a Return of second hand motor car purchased on credit from M/s Delhi Motors for ₹ 50,000, by M/s Delhi Furniture is recorded.

ANSWER: Journal Proper

QUESTION 34. Name the book of original entry in which a Return of Furniture purchased for a Cash ₹ 5,000, by M/s Delhi Furniture is recorded.

ANSWER: Cash Book

QUESTION 35: Name the book of original entry in which a Return of second hand motor car purchased for cash from M/s Delhi Motors for ₹ 50,000, by M/s Delhi Furniture is recorded.

ANSWER: Cash Book

QUESTION 36: Name the book of original entry in which a Return of Furniture sold on credit for ₹ 5,000, by M/s Delhi Furniture is recorded.

ANSWER: Sales Returns Book

QUESTION 37. Name the book of original entry in which a Return of second hand motor car sold on credit to M/s Delhi Motors for ₹ 50,000, by M/s Delhi Furniture is recorded.

ANSWER: Journal Proper

QUESTION 38. Name the book of original entry in which a Return of Furniture sold for a Cash ₹ 5,000, by M/s Delhi Furniture is recorded.

ANSWER: Cash Book

QUESTION 39. Name the book of original entry in which a Return of second hand motor car sold for cash to M/s Delhi Motors for ₹ 50,000, by M/s Delhi Furniture is recorded.

ANSWER: Cash Book

QUESTION 40. Name the book of Original Entry wherein an allowance of 10% was offered for a large quantity sales order of ₹ 1,00,000 will be recorded.

ANSWER: Trade Discount is not recorded at all in any of the books of Original Entry.

QUESTION 41. Name the book of Original Entry wherein an allowance of 10% was offered for an early cash payment of of ₹ 1,00,000 will be recorded.

ANSWER: Cash Book

QUESTION 42. Name the book of Original Entry in which goods withdrawn by the proprietor for personal use are recorded.

ANSWER: Journal Proper

QUESTION 43. Name the book of Original Entry in which Goods given as charity are recorded.

ANSWER: Journal Proper

QUESTION 44. Name the book of Original Entry in which Goods distributed as free samples are recorded.

ANSWER: Journal Proper

QUESTION 45. Name the book of Original Entry in which Goods stolen in transit are recorded.

ANSWER: Journal Proper

QUESTION 46. Name the book of Original Entry in which Goods destroyed by fire are recorded.

ANSWER: Journal Proper

QUESTION 47: Name the book of Original Entry in which Goods stolen by an employee are recorded.

ANSWER: Journal Proper

QUESTION 48. Name the book of Original Entry in which Goods used in making of Furniture are recorded.

ANSWER: Journal Proper

QUESTION 49. Name the book of Original Entry in which commencement of business with Furniture ₹ 50,000 is recorded.

ANSWER: Journal Proper

QUESTION 50: Name the book of Original Entry in which Bad Debts written off ₹ 50,000 are recorded.

ANSWER: Journal Proper

QUESTION 51: Name the book of Original Entry in which Opening Entry is recorded.

ANSWER: Journal Proper

QUESTION 52: Name the book of Original Entry in which Closing Entry is recorded.

ANSWER: Journal Proper

QUESTION 53: Name the book of Original Entry in which Outstanding Salary is recorded.

ANSWER: Journal Proper

QUESTION 54. Name the book of Original Entry in which Prepaid Salary is recorded.

ANSWER: Journal Proper

QUESTION 55: Name the book of Original Entry in which Accrued Interest is recorded.

ANSWER: Journal Proper

QUESTION 56: Name the book of Original Entry in which Interest received in advance is recorded.

ANSWER: Journal Proper

QUESTION 57: Name the book of Original Entry in which Rectifying the error of a credit purchase of goods worth ₹ 10,000 recorded as credit sale to Mr Lele, discovered two months later is recorded.

ANSWER: Journal Proper

QUESTION 58: Name the book of Original Entry wherein Empty crates, charged earlier to a customer, now received back from him will be recorded.

ANSWER: Journal Proper if immediate payment is not made. Cash Book if immediate payment is made.

QUESTION 59. State the nature of balance of a Purchases Account?

ANSWER: Debit

QUESTION 60: State the nature of balance of a Sales Account?

ANSWER: Credit

QUESTION 61: State the nature of balance of a Purchase Returns Account?

ANSWER: Credit

QUESTION 62. State the nature of balance of a Sales Returns Account?

ANSWER: Debit

QUESTION 63. Name the book in which entries are recorded on the basis of Invoices received.

ANSWER: Purchases Book

QUESTION 64. Name the book in which entries are recorded on the basis of Invoices sent out.

ANSWER: Sales Book

QUESTION 65. Name the book in which entries are recorded on the basis of debit notes issued.

ANSWER: Purchases Returns Book

QUESTION 66. Name the book in which entries are recorded on the basis of credit notes issued.

ANSWER: Sales Returns Book

QUESTION 67. Name the book of Original Entry wherein each of the following will be recorded:

(a) **Goods sold for cash were returned by a customer but cash was not given immediately.**
(b) **Goods sold on Credit were returned by a customer and cash was given immediately.**
(c) **Goods received from the manufacturer for distribution among the customers as free samples.**

ANSWER:

(a) Journal Proper
(b) Sales Returns Book & Cash Book
(c) Journal Proper

TRIAL BALANCE

QUESTION 1: What is a Trial Balance?

ANSWER: Trial Balance is a statement which shows *either* the balances *or* Total Amounts of Debit Items and Credit Items of all the accounts in the Ledger and the Cash and Bank Balances.

QUESTION 2: State with reason whether a Trial Balance is an account.

ANSWER: No. A Trial Balance is a Statement and not an Account.

QUESTION 3: State with reason whether a Trial Balance is prepared for a particular period.

ANSWER: No. A Trial Balance is prepared on a particular date and not for a particular period.

QUESTION 4: State any two objectives of a Trial Balance.

ANSWER:

1. **To ascertain the Arithmetical Accuracy of ledger accounts** – A tallied trial balance indicates that equal debits and credits have been recorded in the ledger accounts.
2. **To help in locating Errors** – An untallied trial balance indicates that some error(s) has (have) been committed.
3. **To facilitate the preparation of Financial Statements** – A trial balance can directly be used for preparing the financial statements and there is no need to refer to the ledger.

QUESTION 5: State any one limitation of a Trial Balance.

ANSWER: A tallied trial balance does not necessarily ensure that –

(a) all transactions have been correctly recorded (i.e., Correct Book, Correct Account, Correct Amount)

(b) all Entries/Total (e.g. Total of Purchases Book etc.) have been correctly posted in the ledger, (i.e., posting to correct account on correct side with correct amount.)

QUESTION 6: Is a tallied Trial Balance a conclusive proof of the accuracy of the books of accounts?

ANSWER: No. A tallied Trial Balance is not a conclusive proof of the accuracy of the books of accounts since certain types of errors remain even when the Trial Balance tallies. The following errors do not affect the Trial balance at all.

(a) Error of Principle,

(b) Compensating error,

(c) Error of Complete Omission,

(d) Error of Recording in the books of original entry, and

(e) Posting a correct amount in the wrong account but on the correct side.

QUESTION 7: Name two methods of preparing a Trial Balance.

ANSWER:

1. Balance Method
2. Total Amount Method.

QUESTION 8: What is Balance Method of preparing a Trial Balance?

ANSWER: Under Balance method, the Balances of all the accounts (including Cash and Bank Account) are incorporated in the trial balance. It may be noted that a trial balance by this method can be prepared only when all the ledger accounts have been balanced.

QUESTION 9: What is Total Amount Method of preparing a Trial Balance?

ANSWER: Under Total Amount method, the total amount of debit items and credit items in each ledger account are incorporated in the trial balance. It may be noted that a trial balance by this method can be prepared immediately after the completion of posting from the books of original entry to the ledger.

RECTIFICATION OF ERRORS

QUESTION 1: What is meant by Error of Omission?

ANSWER: Error of Omission arises when a transaction is completely *or* partially omitted to be —

(i) Recorded in the books of accounts, or

(ii) Posted to the ledger

QUESTION 2: What is meant by Error of Complete Omission?

ANSWER: Error of Complete Omission arises when any transaction is not recorded in the books of original entry at all *or,* the transaction is recorded in General Journal (or Journal Proper) but is not posted in the ledger at all. This error does not affect the trial balance. Example: Goods sold on credit to Shyam not recorded in the Sales Book.

QUESTION 3: What is meant by Error of Partial Omission?

ANSWER: An error of omission other than an error of complete omission is called an error of partial omission. This error affects the trial balance. Example: A Credit Sale of Goods to Shyam recorded in Sales Book but omitted to be posted in Shyam's Account.

QUESTION 4: What is meant by Error of Commission?

ANSWER: Error of Commission arises due to wrong recording, wrong casting, wrong carry forward, wrong posting, wrong balancing etc.,

QUESTION 5: What is meant by Error of Recording?

ANSWER: Error of Recording arises when any transaction is incorrectly recorded in the books of original entry. This error does not affect the trial balance.

Example: Goods sold on credit to Shyam recorded in the Purchases Book.

QUESTION 6: What is meant by Error of Casting?

ANSWER: Error of Casting arises when a mistake is committed in totalling. This error affects the trial balance. Example: Sales Book is totalled as ₹ 500 instead of ₹ 5,000.

QUESTION 7: What is meant by Error in Carrying Forward?

ANSWER: Error in Carrying Forward arises when a mistake is committed in carrying forward a total of one page on the next page. This error affects the trial balance. Example: Total of Sales Book is carried forward as ₹ 100 instead of ₹ 1,000.

QUESTION 8: What is meant by Error of Posting?

ANSWER: Error of Posting arises when information recorded in the books of original entry is incorrectly entered in the ledger. This error may *or* may not affect the trial balance. Example I: A Credit Sale of Goods of ₹ 1,000 to Shyam posted in Ram's Account. Example II: A Credit Sale of Goods of ₹ 1,000 to Shyam posted as ₹ 100.

QUESTION 9: What is meant by Compensating Errors?

ANSWER: Compensating Errors arise when two *or* more errors are committed in such a way that the net effect of these errors on the debits and credits of accounts involved is nil. In other words, compensating errors refer to such a group of errors wherein the effect of one error is compensated by the effect of other error *or* errors. These errors do not affect the agreement of the trial balance but may *or* may not affect the figure of net profit.

Example — If the total of Purchases Book is posted in the ledger as ₹ 1,000 instead of ₹ 100 and at the same time Ram's A/c is credited in the ledger as ₹ 1,000 instead of ₹ 100, as a result of these errors, there is an excess credit of ₹ 900 in Ram's Account and an excess debit of ₹ 900 in Purchases Account. Thus, these two errors nullify the effects of each other. The first error will increase the figure of Purchases and consequently will reduce the figure of Profit.

QUESTION 10: What is meant by Error of Principle?

ANSWER: Error of Principle arises when the transaction is recorded ignoring the distinction between the capital item and revenue item. In other words, this error involves an incorrect allocation of expenditure *or* receipt between Capital and Revenue. The correct allocation between Capital and Revenue is of paramount importance because any incorrect allocation would disturb the final results as disclosed by the Financial Statements.

Effect — It may lead to Under/Over stating of Incomes *or* Assets *or* Liabilities. This error does not affect the Trial Balance.

Example, if Freight paid for bringing a new machinery is posted to Freight A/c, this error will increase the figure of freight and reduce the figure of depreciation and as a result, the figure of net profit shall be changed by the net effect (i.e., the difference between the amount of freight and amount of depreciation).

QUESTION 11: What is a Suspense Account?

ANSWER: A Suspense Account is an account in which the amount of difference in the trial balance is put till such time that errors are located and rectified.

QUESTION 12: What is the purpose of opening of a Suspense Account?

ANSWER: The purpose of opening of a Suspense Account is to avoid delay in the preparation of financial statements.

QUESTION 13: How is a Suspense Account opened?

ANSWER: The difference in the trial balance is transferred on the credit side of the Suspense Account (if the debit side of the trial balance exceeds the credit side) *or* on the debit side of the Suspense Account (if the credit side of the trial balance exceeds the debit side). Thus, the difference is put on the shorter side.

QUESTION 14: When is a Suspense Account closed?

ANSWER: When the errors affecting the Suspense Account are located, they are rectified with the help of the Suspense Account. When all the errors affecting the trial balance are located and rectified, the Suspense Account automatically stands balanced and closed.

QUESTION 15: What does the Balance of Suspense Account indicate? How is this Balance of Suspense Account treated?

ANSWER: The balance of Suspense Account merely represents the net effect of errors which are still to be located and rectified. Such balance will be shown in the Balance Sheet on the assets side (if debit balance) *or* on the liabilities side (if credit balance).

QUESTION 16: List two Examples of Errors not Affecting the Trial Balance.

ANSWER:

1. Error of Recording in the books of original entry
2. Error of Principle
3. Compensating errors

QUESTION 17: What is a Rectifying Entry?

ANSWER: Rectifying Entry is the entry which is passed to rectify an error.

QUESTION 18: How are Two Sided Errors of Omission rectified?

ANSWER: Two sided errors of omission in the books of original entry are rectified simply by the passing the journal entry which was to be passed at the time of transaction but was omitted to be passed.

QUESTION 19: How are Two Sided Errors of Commission rectified?

ANSWER: Two sided errors of commission are rectified by passing a journal entry giving the appropriate debit and credit to the Respective Accounts which were affected by the error.

QUESTION 20: List Two Examples of Errors affecting the Trial Balance.

ANSWER:

1. Error of casting
2. Error in carrying forward
3. Error in totalling *or* balancing of an account

QUESTION 21: How are One Sided Errors of Commission rectified before transferring the difference in the Trial Balance to the Suspense Account?

ANSWER: One sided errors of Commission are rectified by Debiting/Crediting the "Respective Account" with the required amount alongwith an explanatory note in the "Particulars column".

QUESTION 22: How are One Sided Errors of Commission rectified after transferring the difference in the Trial Balance to the Suspense Account but before the preparation of the Financial Statements?

ANSWER: One sided errors of Commission are rectified by passing a Journal Entry with the help of Respective Account(s) (affected by the error) and Suspense Account.

QUESTION 23: State the effect of rectification of error on profit/loss.

ANSWER:

1. If a nominal account is debited in a rectifying entry, Profit will be decreased *or* loss will be increased.
2. If a nominal account is credited in a rectifying entry, Profit will be increased *or* loss will be decreased.

QUESTION 24: How are Errors rectified after the preparation of the Financial Statements?

ANSWER: After the preparation of final accounts, the errors affecting the nominal accounts (e.g., Sales A/c, Purchases A/c, Expense A/c) are rectified with the help of Profit and Loss Adjustment Account.

QUESTION 25: Why are Errors affecting the nominal accounts rectified with the help of Profit and Loss Adjustment Account after the preparation of the Financial Statements? How is the balance of Profit and Loss Adjustment Account treated?

ANSWER: Errors affecting the nominal accounts rectified with the help of Profit and Loss Adjustment Account after the preparation of the Financial Statements so that current year's profit/loss may not be affected as a result of rectification of such errors.

The balance of Profit and Loss Adjustment Account is transferred to the Capital Account in case of proprietorship/partnership concerns.

QUESTION 26: Is a tallied Trial Balance a conclusive proof of the accuracy of the ledger accounts?

or

If a Trial Balance tallies, can it be concluded that there are no errors?

ANSWER: A tallied Trial Balance is not a conclusive proof of the accuracy of the ledger accounts since the following errors which do not affect the Trial Balance may still remain there.

1. Error of Complete Omission
2. Error of Recording in the books of original entry
3. Error of Posting involving the posting to wrong account on correct side with correct amount
4. Compensating errors
5. Error of Principle

QUESTION 27: If the Trial Balance does not tally at the end of the accounting period even after all the reasonable steps to locate the errors have been taken, what step would you suggest to proceed further?

ANSWER: Open the Suspense Account and transfer the difference in the trial balance on the credit side of the Suspense Account (if the debit side of the trial balance exceeds the credit side) *or* on the debit side of the Suspense Account (if the credit side of the trial balance exceeds the debit side). Thus, the difference is put on the shorter side.

QUESTION 28. A transaction is recorded in a wrong book of original entry with wrong amount, will it affect the trial balance? State with reasons.

ANSWER: No. Reason: Error of Recording has the same effect on both the Debit and Credit aspects of a transaction.

QUESTION 29. A transaction is recorded in a correct book of original entry(other than Journal Proper) but not posted in the ledger at all, will it affect the Trial Balance? State with reasons.

ANSWER: Yes. Reason: Such Error of Posting has not the same effect on both the Debit and Credit aspects of a transaction as posting has been done in one Account and not in other Account.

QUESTION 30. A transaction is recorded correctly in Journal Proper but not posted in the ledger at all, will it affect the Trial Balance? State with reasons.

ANSWER: No. Reason: Such Error of Posting has the same effect on both the Debit and Credit aspects of a transaction as posting has not been done in both the Accounts.

QUESTION 31: The total of the debit side and credit side of the Trial Balance of Mr Rajinder Singh Yusuf prepared (on half yearly basis) as on September 30, were ₹ 16,350 and ₹ 10,000 respectively. The difference was put in the Suspense Account. On October 2, an examination of the books revealed that the total of Purchases Returns Book was carried forward as ₹ 1,220 insteadof ₹ 1,120. Calculate the balance of Suspense Account after the rectification of the errors located.

ANSWER: (₹ 16,350 – ₹ 10,000) + (₹ 1,220 – ₹ 1,120) = ₹ 6,450

QUESTION 32: A cash sale of Goods to X ₹17,000 posted as ₹ 71,000. Pass the Rectifying Entry.

ANSWER:

Date	Particulars		Dr.(₹)	Cr.(₹)
	Sales A/c	Dr.	5,400	
	To Suspense A/c (Being the posting to X's A/c, now rectified)			5,400

QUESTION 33: A credit sale of Goods to Y ₹17,000 posted as ₹ 71,000. Pass the Rectifying Entry.

ANSWER:

Date	Particulars		Dr.(₹)	Cr.(₹)
	Suspense A/c	Dr.	5,400	
	To X (Being the posting to X's A/c, now rectified)			5,400

QUESTION 34: A credit sale of Furniture to Z for ₹17,000 posted as ₹ 71,000. Pass the Rectifying Entry.

ANSWER:

Date	Particulars		Dr.(₹)	Cr.(₹)
	Furniture A/c	Dr.	5,400	
	To Z (Being error in posting, now rectified)			5,400

QUESTION 35: Bills Receivable from Henry of ₹ 16,000 posted to the credit of Bills Payable Account and also credited to Henry with ₹ 1,600. Pass the Rectifying Entry.

ANSWER:

Date	Particulars		Dr.(₹)	Cr.(₹)
	Bills Payable A/c	Dr.	16,000	
	Bills Receivable A/c	Dr.	16,000	
	To Suspense A/c			17,600
	To Henry (Being a B/R received from Henry wrongly posted to the credit of B/P& Henry, now rectified)			14,400

QUESTION 36: Discounts received of ₹ 14,200 had been debited to Discount Allowed as ₹ 14,020. Pass the Rectifying Entry.

ANSWER:

Date	Particulars		Dr.(₹)	Cr.(₹)
	Suspense A/c	Dr.	28,220	
	To Discount Allowed A/c			14,020
	To Discount Received A/c (Being Discount Received wrongly posted to Discount Allowed A/c, now rectified)			14,200

QUESTION 37: A credit sale of goods of ₹ 423 to Krishan entered in the purchases book as ₹ 432 and posted therefrom to the credit of Kishan as ₹ 423. Pass the Rectifying Entry.

ANSWER:

Date	Particulars		Dr.(₹)	Cr.(₹)
	Krishan	Dr.	423	
	Kishan	Dr.	423	
	Suspense A/c	Dr.	9	
	To Sales A/c			423
	To Purchases A/c (Being sale recorded as purchase with wrong amount and wrong posting therefrom, now rectified)			423

QUESTION 38: Goods (Cost ₹ 423, Sale Price ₹ 432) taken by Ganesh, the proprietor for his personal use recorded in the sales book. Pass the Rectifying Entry.

ANSWER:

Date	Particulars		Dr.(₹)	Cr.(₹)
	Sales A/c	Dr.	432	
	Drawings A/c	Dr.	423	
	To Ganesh's Capital A/c			432
	To Purchases A/c (Being the goods taken by proprietor for his personal use recorded in sales book, now rectified)			432

QUESTION 39: Materials from store of ₹ 10,000 and Wages ₹ 4,000 had been used in making tools and implements for use in own factory, but no adjustments were made in the books. Pass the Rectifying Entry.

ANSWER:

Date	Particulars		Dr.(₹)	Cr.(₹)
	Tools & Implements A/c	Dr.	14,000	
	To Purchases A/c			10,000
	To Wages A/c (Being materials and wages used in making tools, omitted to be adjusted, now adjusted)			4,000

QUESTION 40: A credit purchase of old machinery from Sohan for ₹ 17,000 was entered in the Purchases Book as purchase from Mohan for ₹ 71,000. ₹ 3,000 paid as repairing charges on the reconditioning of a newly purchased second hand Machinery debited to General Expenses Account. Pass the Rectifying Entry.

ANSWER:

Date	Particulars		Dr.(₹)	Cr.(₹)
	Mohan	Dr.	71,000	
	Machinery A/c	Dr.	20,000	
	To Sohan			17,000
	To Purchases A/c			71,000
	To General Expenses A/c			3,000
	(Being dishonour of a B/Riwrongly debited to Bills Receivable A/c now rectified)			

QUESTION 41: A discounted Bill of Exchange receivable for ₹ 16,000 returned by the firm's bank had been credited to the Bank Account and debited to Bills Receivable Account. A cheque was received later from the Customer for ₹ 16,000 and duly paid. Pass the Rectifying Entry.

ANSWER:

Date	Particulars		Dr.(₹)	Cr.(₹)
	Customer	Dr.	16,000	
	To Bills Receivable A/c			16,000
	To Wages A/c			4,000
	(Being materials and wages used in making tools, omitted to be adjusted, now adjusted)			

QUESTION 42: Bills payable worth ₹ 3,000 accepted in favour of Murari, was passed through bills receivable book with ₹ 300 and Murari's account was debited with ₹ 3,000. Pass the Rectifying Entry.

ANSWER:

Date	Particulars		Dr.(₹)	Cr.(₹)
	Suspense A/c	Dr.	3,300	
	To B/R A/c			300
	To B/P A/c			3,000
	(Being B/P recorded in B/R Book but Murari's A/c correctly posted, now rectified)			

ACCOUNTING STANDARDS

APPLICABILITY OF ACCOUNTING STANDARDS

QUESTION 1: List the criteria to be applied for rating an enterprise as Level-I enterprise for the purpose of compliance of Accounting Standard in India.

ANSWER: Enterprises which fall in any one *or* more of the following categories, at any time during the accounting period, are classified as Level I enterprises:

1. Enterprises, whose equity *or* debt securities are listed *or* is in the process of being listed in India *or* outside India.
2. Banks (including co-operative banks), Insurance companies and Financial Institutions.
3. All commercial, industrial and business reporting enterprises, whose turnover for the immediately preceding accounting period on the bases of audited financial statements exceeds ₹ 50 crores. Here turnover does not include other income.
4. All commercial, industrial and business reporting enterprises whose total borrowings including public deposits exceeds ₹ 10 crores, at any time during the accounting period.
5. Holding and subsidiary companies of any of the above enterprises at any time during the accounting period.

QUESTION 2: What are the issues, with which Accounting Standards deal?

ANSWER: Accounting Standards deal with the issues of

1. Recognition of events and transactions in the financial statements,
2. Measurement of these transactions and events,
3. Presentation of these transactions and events in the financial statements in a manner that is meaningful and understandable to the reader, and
4. Disclosure requirements which should be there to enable the public at large and the stakeholders and the potential investors in particular, to get an insight into what these financial statements are trying to reflect and thereby facilitating them to take prudent and informed business decisions.

AS-1

QUESTION 3: When can a company change its accounting policy?

ANSWER: A change in accounting policy should be made in the following conditions:

(i) If the change is required by some statue *or* for compliance with an Accounting Standard.

(ii) Change would result in more appropriate presentation of the financial statement.

Change in accounting policy may have a material effect on the items of financial statement. ***For Example***, if depreciation method is changed from straight-line method to written-down value method, *or* if cost formula used for inventory valuation is changed from weighted average to FIFO, *or* if interest is capitalized which was earlier not in practice, *or* if proportionate amount of interest is changed to inventory which was earlier not the practice, all these may increase *or* decrease the net profit. Unless the effect of such change in accounting policy is quantified, the financial statements may not help the users of accounts. Therefore, it is necessary to quantify the effect of change on financial statement items like assets, liabilities, profit/loss.

QUESTION 4: Mention six areas in which different accounting policies are followed by companies.

ANSWER:

(i) Methods of Depreciation, Depletion and Amortisation.

(ii) Treatment of Expenditure during construction.

(iii) Valuation of Inventories.

(iv) Treatment of Goodwill.

(v) Valuation of Investments.

(vi) Valuation of Fixed Assets.

QUESTION 5: What are the three fundamental accounting assumptions recognised by Accountig Standard (AS) I? Briefly describe each one of them.

ANSWER:

1. **Going Concern:** The financial statements are normally prepared on the assumption that an enterprise will continue its operations in the foreseeable future and n*either* there is intention, nor there is need to materially curtail the scale of operations.
2. **Consistency:** The principle of consistency refers to the practice of using same accounting policies for similar transactions in all accounting periods unless the change is required (i) by a statute, (ii) by an accounting standard *or* (iii) for more appropriate presentation of financial statements.
3. **Accrual basis of accounting:** Under this basis of accounting, transactions are recognised as soon as they occur, whether *or* not cash *or* cash equivalent is actually received *or* paid.

AS-2

QUESTION 6: What are the items that are to be excluded in determination of the cost of inventories as per AS-2?

ANSWER: Items that are to be excluded in determination of the cost of inventories as per para 13 of AS 2 on 'Valuation of Inventories' are:

(1) Abnormal Amounts of wasted materials, labour *or* other production costs.

(2) Storage Costs unless those costs are necessary in the production process prior to a further production stage.

(3) Administrative Overheads that do not contribute to bringing the inventories to their present location and condition; and

(4) Selling and Distribution Costs.

QUESTION 7: What is meant by Accounting Estimate? Give two examples for accounting estimate.

ANSWER: As a result of the uncertainties in business activities, many financial statement items cannot be measured with precision but can only be estimated. This is called accounting estimates. On account of such uncertainties, management makes various estimates and assumptions of assets, liabilities, income and expenses as on the date of preparation of financial statements. This process of estimation involves judgments, which is based on the latest information available.

Examples of estimation in some fields are:

(i) Estimation of useful life of depreciable assets.

(ii) Estimation of provision to be made for bad and doubtful debts.

AS-3

QUESTION 8: What is meant by Cash and Cash Equivalent as per AS?

ANSWER: As per AS 3 'Cash Flow Statements', the term 'Cash' and 'Cash equivalents' mean the following:

Cash	It includes cash on hand and demand deposits with banks.

Cash Equivalents	It means short-term, highly liquid investments that are readily convertible into known amounts of cash and which are subject to insignificant risk of changes in value. Cash equivalents are held for the purpose of meeting short-term cash commitments rather than for investment *or* other purposes. For an investment to qualify as a cash equivalent, it must be readily convertible to a known amount of cash and be subject to an insignificant risk of changes in value. Therefore, an investment normally qualifies as a cash equivalent only when it has a short maturity of, say, three months *or* less from the date of acquisition.

QUESTION 9: Garden Lid. acquired fixed assets viz. plant and machinery for ₹ 20 lakhs. During the same year it sold its furniture and fixtures for ₹ 5 lakhs. Can the company disclose, net cash outflow towards purchase of fixed assets in the cash flow statement as per AS-3?

ANSWER:

PROVISION OF AS 3

As per Para 21 of AS 3 (Revised) 'Cash Flow Statements', an enterprise should report separately major classes of gross cash receipts and gross cash payments arising from investing and financing activities, except to the extent that cash flows described in paragraphs 22 and 24 are reported en a net basis. Acquisition and disposal of fixed assets is not prescribed in para 22 and 24 of the standard.

ADVICE

Hence, the company cannot disclose net cash flow in respect of acquisition of plant and machinery and disposal of furnitures and fixtures.

QUESTION 10: Intelligent Ltd., a non financial company has the following entries in its Bank Account. It has sought your advice on the treatment of the same for preparing Cash Flow Statement.

1. **Loans and Advances given to the following and interest earned on them:**
   - **(a) to suppliers**
   - **(b) to employees**
   - **(c) to its subsidiaries companies**
2. **Investment made in subsidiary Smart Ltd. and dividend received**
3. **Dividend paid for the year**
4. **TDS on interest income earned on investments made**
5. **TDS on interest earned on advance given to suppliers**
6. **Insurance claim received against loss of fixed asset by fire**

   Discuss in the context of AS 3 Cash Flow Statement.

ANSWER:

1. Loans and advances given and interest earned	
(a) to supliers	Operating Cash flow
(b) to employees	Operating Cash flow
(c) to its subsidiary companies	Investing Cash flow
2. Investment made in subsidiary company and dividend received	Investing Cash flow
3. Dividend paid for the year	Financing Cash Outflow
4. TDS on interest income earned on investments made	Investment Cash Outflow

5. TDS on interest earned on advance given to suppliers	Operating Cash Outflow
6. Insurance claim received against loss of fixed asset by fire	Extraordinary item to be shown under a separate heading as 'Cash inflow from Operating activities'.

AS-4

QUESTION 11: What is meant by Events occurring after the balance sheet date?

ANSWER: Events occurring after the balance sheet date are those significant events, both favourable and unfavourable, that occur between the balance sheet date and the date on which the financial statements are approved by the Board of Directors in the case of a company, and, by the corresponding approving authority in the case of any other entity.

QUESTION 12: State the Accounting Treatment of Events occurring after the Balance Sheet Date.

ANSWER:

Nature of Events occurring after the Balance Sheet Date	Accounting Treatment
1. Events that provide additional evidence to assist the estimation of amounts relating to conditions existing at the balance sheet date.	Assets and Liabilities should be adjusted.
2. Events that indicate that the fundamental accounting assumption of going concern (i.e., the continuance of existence or substratum of the enterprise) is not appropriate.	Assets and Liabilities should be adjusted.
3. Dividend proposed or declared by the enterprise after the Balance Sheet Date	Dividend should be adjusted.
4. Other events occurring after the Balance Sheet Date that represent material changes and commitments affecting the financial position of the enterprise.	Disclosure should be made in the report of Approving Authority.

QUESTION 13: State the Disclosure Requirements as to Events occurring after the Balance Sheet Date.

ANSWER:

1. Nature of the Event
2. An Estimate of the financial effect, or a statement that such an estimate cannot be made.

AS-5

QUESTION 14: When can an item qualify to be a prior period item as per AS 5?

ANSWER: According to para 16 of AS 5 on 'Net Profit *or* Loss for the Period, Prior Period Items and Changes in Accounting Policies', prior period items refers to those income *or* expenses, which arise in the current period as a result of errors *or* omissions in the preparation of financial statements of one *or* more prior periods. The term does not include other adjustments necessitated by circumstances, which though related to prior periods, are determined in the current period e.g., arrears payable to workers in current period as a result of revision of wages with retrospective effect.

QUESTION 15: Explain the provisions of AS-5 regarding accounting treatment of prior period items.

ANSWER: As per AS-5, prior period items are income *or* expenses, which arise, in the current period as a result of errors *or* omission in the preparation of financial statements of one *or* more prior periods. The term does not include other adjustments necessitated by circumstances, which though related to prior periods, are determined in the current period. Example: arrears payable to workers in current period as a result of retrospective revision of wages.

The nature and amount of prior period items should be separately disclosed in the statement of profit and loss in manner that their impact on current profit *or* loss can be perceived.

As per para 19 of AS-5, prior period items are normally included in determination of net profit *or* loss for the current profit, they can be added (or deducted as the case may be) from the current profit. An alternative approach is to show such items in the statement of profit *or* loss after determination of current net profit *or* loss. In *either* case, the objective is to indicate the effect of such items on the current profit *or* loss.

QUESTION 16: Give two examples on each of the following items:

- **(i) Change in Accounting Policy**
- **(ii) Change in Accounting Estimate**
- **(iii) Extra Ordinary Items**
- **(iv) Prior Period Items.**

ANSWER:

(i) Examples of Changes in Accounting Policy:
   a. Change of Depreciation method from WDV to SLM and vice-versa.
   b. Change in Cost formula in measuring the cost of inventories.

(ii) Examples of Changes in Accounting Estimates:
   a. Change in estimate of provision for doubtful debts on sundry debtors.
   b. Change in estimate of useful life of fixed assets.

(iii) Examples of Extraordinary items:
   a. Loss due to earthquakes/fire/strike
   b. Attachment of property of the enterprise by government

(iv) Examples of Prior period items:
   a. Applying incorrect Rate of Depreciation in one *or* more prior periods.
   b. Omission to account for Income *or* Expenditure in one *or* more prior periods.

AS-6

QUESTION 17: Mention four assets, in respect of which AS 6 (revised) is not applicable.

ANSWER; AS-6 on 'Depreciation Accounting', is not applicable in respect of following assets:

(1) Forest, Plantations and similar Regenerative Natural Resources.
(2) Wasting Assets including expenditure on the exploration for and extraction of Minerals, Oils, Natural Gas and similar Non-Regenerative Resources.
(3) Expenditure on Research and Development.
(4) Goodwill.
(5) Livestock.
(6) Land unless it has limited useful life for the enterprise.

QUESTION 18: What are depreciable assets as per Accounting Standard-6? Explain why AS-6 does not apply to Land.

ANSWER: As per AS 6 'Depreciation Accounting', depreciable assets are the assets which

(i) are expected to be used during more than one accounting period; and

(ii) have a limited useful life: and

(iii) are held by an enterprise for use in the production *or* supply of goods and services, for rental to others, *or* for administrative purposes and not for the purpose of sale in the ordinary course of business.

AS 6 does not apply to 'land' as land is considered to have unlimited useful life. Therefore, it is not appropriate to charge depreciation on land.

AS-7

QUESTION 19: What are the types of construction contracts?

ANSWER: Construction contracts may be formulated in a number of ways. Some general types of contracts are given below: -

(i) Fixed Price Contracts	The contractor agrees to fixed contract price, or a fixed rate per unit of output, which in some cases is subject to cost escalation clauses;
(ii) Cost Plus Contracts	The contractor is reimbursed for allowable or otherwise defined costs, and is also allowed a percentage of these costs or a fixed fee.
(iii) Mixed Types of Contracts	These types of construction contracts may contain characteristics of both of fixed price contracts and cost plus contracts.
(iv) Real Estate Project	Some real estate projects indicate significant characteristics of construction contracts. These real estate projects then are subject to this standard.

QUESTION 20: What is Expected Loss? What should be the treatment of Expected Loss?

ANSWER:

MEANING OF EXPECTED LOSS

Expected loss is the excess of total contract cost over total contract revenue.

TREATMENT OF EXPECTED LOSS

When it is probable that expected loss shall occur, it should be recognized as an expense immediately irrespective of

(i) Whether or not work has commenced on the contract;

(ii) Whether or not the outcome of contract can be estimated reliably;

(iii) The stage of completion of contract activity;

(iv) The amount of profit expected on other contracts not treated as single contracts (i.e. segmented from single contract).

QUESTION 21: Explain Contract Costs as per Accounting Standard-7 related to 'Construction Contracts'

ANSWER: As per para 15 of AS-7 "Construction Contracts (revised 2002)", contract cost should comprise:

(a) costs that relate directly to the specific contract;

(b) costs that are attributable to contract activity in general and can be allocated to the contract; and

(c) such other costs as are specifically chargeable to the customer under the terms of the contract.

AS-9

QUESTION 22: Define the term ' Revenue'as per AS – 9.

ANSWER:

Revenue is the gross inflow of cash, receivables or other consideration arising in the course of the ordinary activities of an enterprise from:

1. the sale of goods,
2. the rendering of services, and
3. the use by others of enterprise resources yielding interest, royalties and dividends

Note: *In an agency relationship, the revenue is the amount of commission and the not the gross inflow of cash, receivables or other consideration.*

QUESTION 23: When should revenue from sale of goods be recognized?

ANSWER:

Revenue from sale of goods should be recognized when:

1. The seller of goods has transferred to the buyer the property in the goods for a price or all significant risks and rewards of ownership have been transferred to the buyer and the seller retains no effective control of the goods transferred to a degree usually associated with ownership;
2. No significant uncertainty exists regarding the amount of the consideration that will be derived from the sale of goods.
3. At the time of performance it is reasonable to expect ultimate collection (i.e. there is a reasonable certainty of ultimate collection).

QUESTION 24: When should revenue from service transactions be recognized?

ANSWER: Revenue from service transactions should be recognized when

1. No significant uncertainty exists regarding the amount of the consideration that will be derived from the rendering the service.
2. At the time of performance it is reasonable to expect ultimate collection.

QUESTION 25: When and on what basis should revenue from from Interest, Royalties and Dividends be recognized?

ANSWER:

WHEN SHOULD REVENUE BE RECOGNIZED?

Revenue arising from the use by others of enterprise resources yielding interest, royalties and dividends should only be recognized **when no significant uncertainty as to measurability or collectability exists.**

BASIS OF REVENUE RECOGNISION

Cases	Basis of Revenue Recognision
(i) Interest	**On a time proportion basis** taking into account the amount outstanding and the rate applicable.
(ii) Royalties	**On an accrual basis** in accordance with the terms of the relevant agreement.
(iii) Dividends from	When the owner's **right to receive** investment in payment is **established** (i.e. the Date of declaration of Final Dividend & ate of Payment of Interim Dividend)

Notes:

(i) *Revenue arising from the use by others of enterprise resources yielding interest, royalties and dividends should only be recognized when no significant uncertainty as to measurability or collectability exists.*

(ii) *When interest, royalties and dividends from foreign countries require exchange permission and uncertainty in remittance is anticipated, revenue recognition may need to be postponed.*

QUESTION 26: Y Ltd. used certain resources of X Ltd. In return X Ltd. receives ₹ 10 lakhs and ₹ 15 lakhs as interest and royalties respectively, from Y Ltd. during the year. State on what basis X Ltd. should recognize their revenue, as per AS-9.

ANSWER: As per AS-9 on 'Revenue Recognition', interest of ₹ 10 lakhs received in the year should be recognized on the time proportion basis taking into account the amount outstanding and the rate applicable; whereas royalty of ₹ 15 lakhs received in the same year should be recognized on accrual basis as per the terms of relevant agreement.

AS-10

QUESTION 27: What is the treatment of expenses incurred?

(a) upto the date of commencement of commercial production

(b) between the date at which a project is ready to commence commercial production and the date at which commercial production actually begins

(c) after the date of commencement of commercial production

ANSWER:

TREATMENT OF EXPENDITURE

1. Expenditure incurred upto the date of commencement of commercial production	Should be capitalized
2. Expenditure incurred between the date at which the project becomes ready to commence commercial production and the date at which commercial production actually begins	Should be treated as Revenue/Deferred Revenue Expenditure.
3. Subsequent Expenditures	Should be capitalized only if they increase the future benefits from the existing asset beyond its previously assessed standard of performance

QUESTION 28: How should first revaluation of asset be accounted for?

ANSWER:

1. Surplus should be credited to Revaluation Reserve.
2. Deficiency should be charged to Profit & Loss A/c.

QUESTION 29: How should the subsequent revaluation be accounted for?

ANSWER:

1. Surplus to the extent of decrease arising on revaluation previously charged to Profit & Loss A/c should be credited to Profit & Loss A/c and remaining surplus should be credited to Revaluation Reserve.
2. Deficiency to the extent of increase arising on revaluation previously credited to Revaluation Reserve should be reversed or utilized and remaining deficiency should be charged to Profit & Loss A/c

QUESTION 30: Explain the Disclosture Requirements for Fixed Assets as per 'AS-10'?

ANSWER: As per AS-10 following information should be disclosed in the financial statements:

1. Gross and net book values of fixed assets at the beginning and at the end of an accounting period showing additions, disposals, acquisitions and other movements.
2. Expenditure incurred on account of fixed assets in the course of construction *or* acquisition; and
3. Revalued amounts substituted for historical costs of fixed assets, the method adopted to compute the revalued amounts, the nature of indices used the year of any appraisal made, and whether an external valuer was involved, in case where fixed assets are stated at revalued amounts.

AS-13

QUESTION 31: State the meaning and accounting treatment of Current Investments.

ANSWER:

Meaning	A current investment is an investment that is by its nature readily realizable and is intended to be held for not more than one year from the date on which such investment is made.
Carrying	These should be carried **at the lower of cost and fair value** determined amount *either* on an individual investment basis *or* by category of investment, but not an overall (or global) basis.
Reduction & Reversal	Any reduction to fair value and any reversals of such reductions should be debited or credited to the Profit and Loss Statement.

QUESTION 32: State the meaning and accounting treatment of Long-term Investments.

ANSWER:

Meaning	A long-term investment is an investment other than a current investment.
Carrying	These should be carried **at cost**. However, provision for diminution Amount shall be made to recognize a decline, other than temporary, in the value of the investments, such reduction being determined and made for each investment individually.
Reduction	Any reduction in the carrying amount and any reversals of & Reversal such reductions should be charged or credited to the Profit and Loss Statement.

QUESTION 33: Mention two categories of investments defined by AS-13 and also state their valuation principles.

ANSWER: As per para 7 and 8 of AS 13 'Accounting for Investments', there are two categories of investments, viz., Current Investments and Long Term Investments. According to para 14 of the standard, the carrying amount for current investments is the lower of cost and fair value whereas para 17 states that Long Term Investments are valued at cost less permanent diminutions in value of investment. For current investments, para 16 of the standard states that, any reduction to fair value and any reversals of such reductions are included in the profit and loss statement.

AS-16

QUESTION 34: State the meaning of Qualifying Asset. Name the Assets that are not considered as qualifying assets.

ANSWER:

Meaning	A qualifying asset is an asset that necessarily takes a substantial period of time (**ordinarily, a period of 12 months**) to get ready for its intended use or sale. Examples of qualifying assets are manufacturing plants, power generation facilities, inventories that require a substantial period of time to bring them to a saleable condition and investment properties.
Assets that are not considered as qualifying assets	1. Other investments and those inventories that are routinely manufactured or otherwise produced in large quantities on a repetitive basis over a short period of time. 2. Assets that are ready for their intended use or sale when acquired,

QUESTION 35: State the treatment of Borrowing Costs in case of Specifically borrowed funds.

ANSWER: The amount of borrowing costs eligible for capitalization on that asset should be determined as the actual borrowing costs incurred on that borrowing during the period less any income on the temporary investment of those borrowings.

QUESTION 36: State the treatment of Borrowing Costs in case of General borrowed funds.

ANSWER: The amount of borrowing costs eligible for capitalization should be determined by applying a capitalization rate to the expenditure on that asset. The capitalization rate should be the weighted average of the borrowing costs applicable to the borrowings of the enterprise that are outstanding during the period, other than borrowings made specifically for the purpose of obtaining a qualifying asset.

Note: *The amount of borrowing costs capitalized during a period should not exceed the amount of borrowing costs incurred during that period.*

QUESTION 37: State the Relevant Period for Capitalization of Borrowing Costs.

ANSWER:

Case	Relevant Period
1. When all the activities necessary to prepare the qualifying asset for its intended use or sale are in progress	Capitalization of borrowing costs should continue during the period in which active development is in progress.
2. When all the activities necessary to prepare the qualifying asset for its intended use or sale are interrupted.	Capitalization of borrowing costs should be suspended during extended periods in which active development is interrupted.
3. When all the activities necessary to prepare the qualifying asset for its intended use or sale are complete	Capitalization of borrowing costs should cease completion of active development.

QUESTION 38: State the Disclosure Requirements as per AS-16.

ANSWER:

1. The accounting policy adopted for borrowing costs; and
2. The amount of borrowing costs capitalized during the period.

QUESTION 39: Briefly indicate the items which are included in the expressions "Borrowing Cost" as per AS-16.

ANSWER: Borrowing costs are interest and other costs incurred by any enterprise in connection with the borrowing of funds. Borrowing cost may include:

(a) Interest and commitment charges on bank borrowings and other short term and long term borrowings.

(b) Amortisation of discounts *or* premiums relating to borrowings.

(c) Amortisation of ancillary costs incurred in connection with the arrangement of borrowings.

(d) Finance charges in respect of assets required under finance leases *or* under other similar arrangements; and

(e) Exchange differences arising from foreign currency borrowings to the extent that they are regarded as an adjustment to interest costs.

BANK RECONCILIATION STATEMENT

QUESTION 1: What is a Bank Pass Book *or* Bank Statement?

ANSWER: Bank Pass Book (also known as Bank Statement) is merely a copy of the Customer's Account in the books of a bank.

QUESTION 2: If the Cash Book shows a credit balance. What will the Bank Pass Book indicate?

ANSWER: Bank Pass Book will indicate a debit balance.

QUESTION 3: If the Cash Book shows a debit balance, what will the Bank Pass Book indicate?

ANSWER: Bank Pass Book will indicate a credit balance.

QUESTION 4: In case of Bank overdraft, state the nature of balance as per Bank Pass Book.

ANSWER: Bank Pass Book will indicate a debit balance.

QUESTION 5: Who prepares the Bank Statement?

ANSWER: Bank Statement is prepared by the Bank.

QUESTION 6: For what period a Bank Statement is prepared?

ANSWER: Bank Statement is prepared for a particular period and not on a particular date.

QUESTION 7: What is a Bank Reconciliation Statement?

ANSWER: Bank Reconciliation Statement is a statement which reconciles the bank balance as per Cash Book with the balance as per Bank Pass Book (or Statement), by showing all causes of differences between the two.

QUESTION 8: State the Purpose of Bank Reconciliation Statement.

ANSWER: Bank Reconciliation Statement is prepared to reconcile the bank balance as per Cash Book with the balance as per Bank Pass Book (or Bank Statement) by showing all causes of differences between the two and to take necessary follow-up action.

QUESTION 9: Is a Bank Reconciliation Statement an account?

ANSWER: No

QUESTION 10: Who prepares the Bank Reconciliation Statement?

ANSWER: Bank Reconciliation Statement is prepared by the Bank Customer i.e. Account Holder.

QUESTION 11: For what period a Bank Reconciliation Statement is prepared?

ANSWER: Bank Reconciliation Statement is prepared on a particular date and not for a particular period.

QUESTION 12: What records are necessary for preparing a Bank Reconciliation Statement?

ANSWER: 1. Cash Book 2. Bank Pass Book

QUESTION 13: Give any two points of difference between Bank Reconciliation Statement and a Bank Statement.

ANSWER:

Basis of Distinction	Bank Statement	Bank Reconciliation Statement
1. Who prepares	It is prepared by the bank.	It is prepared by the bank customer i.e., account holder.
2. Object	It is prepared to inform the customer about all transactions which have taken place during the period covered by the Statement.	It is prepared to reconcile the bank balance as per cash book with the bank balance shown by the Bank Statement.
3. Timing When Prepared	It is prepared for a particular period.	It is prepared on a particular date.
4. Necessity	It is compulsory for the bank to prepare it.	It is not compulsory.

QUESTION 14: State any five causes of disagreement between the balances shown by the Cash Book and Pass Book.

ANSWER:

1. Cheques issued but not yet presented for payment,
2. Cheques deposited but not yet collected by Bank,
3. Bank charges and interest on overdraft debited in Pass Book only,
4. Interest allowed in Pass Book only,
5. Direct Payment by a customer into the bank but not yet recorded in Cash Book,
6. Direct Payment made by a Bank under the standing instructions of the customer but not yet recorded in Cash Book,
7. Bills Receivable directly collected by Bank,
8. Cheque deposited for collection, returned dishonoured and recorded in Pass Book only,
9. Discounted Bills dishonoured but not yet recorded in Cash Book,
10. Errors in Cash Book (e.g. Cheques/Cash Deposited but not recorded),
11. Errors in Pass Book e.g. Cheques/Cash presented recorded in another customer's account.

QUESTION 15: The bank statement shows an overdrawn balance of ₹ 2,000. A cheque for ₹ 500 drawn in favour of a creditor has not yet been presented for payment. When the creditor presents the cheque for payment, What will be the bank balance?

ANSWER: ₹ 2,500 (overdrawn).

QUESTION 16: A debit balance of ₹ 1,000 has been brought forward as a credit balance of ₹ 100 on the next page in the Pass Book. What should be added/subtracted to the balance as per Pass Book is order to ascertain the balance as per Cash Book?

ANSWER: ₹ 1,100 should be subtracted from the balance as per Pass Book is order to ascertain the balance as per Cash Book.

QUESTION 17: Out of Cheques of ₹ 20,500 received from the customers on 27th March, cheques amounting to ₹ 750 were collected on 7th April, a cheque for ₹ 1,000 entered in Cash Book but omitted to be banked on 31st March, a cheque for ₹ 16,000 deposited into bank but omitted to be recorded in Cash Book and was collected by the bank on 30th March, a cheque deposited of ₹ 112 was recorded as ₹ 121 in the Cash Book as if there is no Bank Column therein and one cheque for ₹ 792 was recorded twice in the Cash Book. Credit Balance as per Cash Book on 31st March was ₹ 9,570.Calculate the Balance as per Pass Book on 31st March. Also Calculate the Bank Balance to be taken to the Balance Sheet.

ANSWER: Balance as per Pass Book = ₹ 9,570 + ₹ 750 + ₹ 1,000 – ₹16,000 – ₹ 112 + ₹ 792

= ₹ 4,000

Bank Balance to be taken to the Balance Sheet = ₹ 9,570 – ₹16,000 – ₹ 112 + ₹ 792 = ₹ 5,750

QUESTION 18: Out of Cheques of ₹ 20,500 issued to Creditors on 27th March, cheques amounting to ₹ 750 were presented on 7th April, a cheque for ₹ 1,000 entered in Cash Book but omitted to be sent to a Creditor till 31st March, a cheque for ₹ 16,000 issued to Creditors but omitted to be recorded in Cash Book and were paid by the bank on 30th March, a cheque issued of ₹ 112 was recorded as ₹ 121 in the Cash Book as if there is no Bank Column therein and one cheque for ₹ 792 was recorded twice in the Cash Book. Credit Balance as per Cash Book on 31st March was ₹ 9,570.Calculate the Balance as per Pass Book on 31st March. Also Calculate the Bank Balance to be taken to the Balance Sheet.

ANSWER: Balance as per Pass Book = ₹ 9,570 – ₹ 750 – ₹ 1,000 + ₹16,000 + ₹ 112 – ₹ 792

= ₹ 23,140

Bank Balance to be taken to the Balance Sheet = ₹ 9,570 + ₹16,000 + ₹ 112 – ₹ 792 = ₹ 24,890

QUESTION 19: A bill receivable for ₹ 5200 previously discounted (Discount ₹ 200) with the bank had been dishonoured but advice was received on 1st April. A bill for ₹ 1,00,000 was retired/paid by the bank under a rebate of ₹ 1500 but the full amount of the bill was credited in the bank column of the Cash Book.A cheque of ₹ 1,080 credited in the Pass Book on March 28 being dishonoured is debited again in the Pass Book on 1st April. There was no entry in the Cash Book about the dishonour of the cheque until 15th April. A cheque of ₹ 17,270 drawn on his Saving Deposit Account has been shown as drawn on Current Account in Cash Book. Credit Balance of Current Account as per Cash Book on 31st March was ₹ 9,570. Calculate the Balance as per Pass Book on 31st March. Also Calculate the Bank Balance to be taken to the Balance Sheet.

ANSWER: Balance as per Pass Book = ₹ 9,570 + ₹ 5,200 – ₹ 1500 – ₹ 17,270 = ₹ 4,000

Bank Balance to be taken to the Balance Sheet = ₹ 9,570 + ₹ 5,200 – ₹ 1500 – ₹ 17,270 = ₹ 4,000

QUESTION 20: The debit balance of ₹ 15,121 as on the previous day was brought forward as a credit balance of ₹ 15,112 in the Cash Book,the payment side of the Cash Book (Bank column) was under cast by ₹ 1000.and a cash discount allowed of ₹ 1120 was recorded as ₹ 1210 in the Bank Column. Credit Balance of as per Cash Book on 31st March was ₹ 9,570. Calculate the Balance as per Pass Book on 31st March. Also Calculate the Bank Balance to be taken to the Balance Sheet.

ANSWER: Balance as per Pass Book = ₹ 9,570 + ₹ 1,000 + ₹ 1,210 – ₹ 30,233 = ₹ 18,453

Bank Balance to be taken to the Balance Sheet = ₹ 9,570 + ₹ 1,000 + ₹ 1,210 – ₹ 30,233 = ₹ 18,453

QUESTION 21: Balance as per Pass Book of Shri Krishan is ₹ 10,000. Bank collected a cheque of ₹ 500 on behalf of Shri Krishan but wrongly credited it to Shri Kishan's A/c (another customer).Bank recorded a Cash deposit of ₹ 1,589 as ₹ 1,598. Withdrawal column of the Pass Book undercast by ₹ 100. The credit balance of ₹ 15,121 as on page 5 of the Pass Book was recorded on page 6 as the debit balance of ₹ 15,112. The payment of a cheque of ₹ 350 was recorded twice in the Pass Book.The Pass Book showed a credit for a cheque of ₹ 50,000 deposited by Shri Kishan (another customer of the Bank). Calculate the Balance as per Cash Book on 31st March. Also Calculate the Bank Balance to be taken to the Balance Sheet.

ANSWER:

Bank Overdraft as per Cash Book = ₹ 10,000 + ₹ 500 + ₹ 30,233 + ₹ 350 – ₹ 9 – ₹ 100 – ₹ 50,000
= ₹ 9,026

Bank Overdraft to be taken to the Balance Sheet
= ₹ 10,000 + ₹ 500 + ₹ 30,233 + ₹ 350 – ₹ 9 – ₹ 100 – ₹ 50,000 = ₹ 9,026

STOCK RECONCILIATION STATEMENT

QUESTION 1: The stock was physically verified on 24th March and was valued at ₹ 2,00,000. Goods are normally sold by the trader at a profit of 25% on cost. After stock taking the following transactions have taken place till 31st March. Sales of ₹ 2,21,600 which includes:

(i) Sales of ₹ 10,800 at 20% more than the normal selling price.

(ii) Sales of ₹ 10,800 at 10% less than the normal selling price.

Required: Determine the value of stock to be taken to the Balance Sheet of PCT Ltd. as at 31st March.

ANSWER:

STATEMENT SHOWING THE VALUATION OF STOCK AS AT 31ST MARCH

Particulars	₹
A. Value of Stock as at 24th March	2,00,000
B. *Less:* Cost of Goods sold	
Normal Sales [80% of (₹ 2,21,600 – 10,800 – 10,800]	(1,60,000)
Abnormal Sales [80% of (10,800 × 100/120)]	(7,200)
[80% of (10,800 × 100/90)]	(9,600)
C. Value of Stock as at 31st March	23,200

QUESTION 2: The stock was physically verified on 24th March and was valued at ₹ 2,00,000. Goods are normally sold by the trader at a profit of 25% on cost. On 21st March goods of the sale value of ₹ 1,00,000 were sent on sale *or* return basis to a customer, the period of approval being two weeks. He returned 20% of the goods and approved 80% of the remaining on 31st March. Determine the value of stock to be taken to the Balance Sheet of PCT Ltd. as at 31st March.

ANSWER:

STATEMENT SHOWING THE VALUATION OF STOCK AS AT 31ST MARCH

Particulars	₹
A. Value of Stock as at 24th March	2,00,000
B. *Add:* Cost of Goods sent on approval and received back	

[20% of ₹ 1,00,000 – 20% of ₹ 20,000]	16,000
Cost of Goods sent on approval and still with customer	
[20% of 80% of ₹ 1,00,000 – 20% of ₹ 16,000]	12,800
C. Value of Stock as at 31st March	2,28,800

QUESTION 3: The stock was physically verified on 24th March and was valued at ₹ 2,00,000. Goods are normally sold by the trader at a profit of 25% on cost. On 27th March goods of the sale value of ₹ 1,00,000 were sent on sale *or* return basis to a customer, the period of approval being two weeks. He returned 20% of the goods and approved 80% of the remaining on 31st March. Determine the value of stock to be taken to the Balance Sheet of PCT Ltd. as at 31st March.

ANSWER:

STATEMENT SHOWING THE VALUATION OF STOCK AS AT 31ST MARCH

Particulars	₹
A. Value of Stock as at 24th March	2,00,000
B. *Less:* Cost of those goods sent on approval which have been approved	
[80% of ₹ 1,00,000 – 20% of ₹ 64,000]	(51,200)
C. Value of Stock as on 31st March	1,48,800

QUESTION 4: The Stock was physically verified on 7th April and was valued at ₹ 2,00,000. Goods are normally sold by the trader at a profit of 25% on cost. On 27th March goods of the sale value of ₹ 1,00,000 were sent on sale *or* return basis to a customer, the period of approval being two weeks. He returned 20% of the goods and approved 80% of the remaining on 6th April. Determine the value of stock to be taken to the Balance Sheet of PCT Ltd. as at 31st March.

ANSWER:

STATEMENT SHOWING THE VALUATION OF STOCK AS AT 31ST MARCH

Particulars	₹
A. Value of Stock as at 7th April	2,00,000
B. *Add:* Cost of Goods Sent on approval and still with the customer	
[80% of ₹ 1,00,000 – 20% of ₹ 80,000]	64,000
C. Value of Stock as at 31st March	2,64,000
Note: 20% of the goods is already included in given stock of 7th April.	

QUESTION 5: The Stock was physically verified on 7th April and was valued at ₹ 2,00,000. Goods are normally sold by the trader at a profit of 25% on cost. On 1st April. goods of the sale value of ₹ 1,00,000 were sent on sale *or* return basis to a customer, the period of approval being two weeks. He returned 20% of the goods and approved 80% of the remaining on 6th April. Determine the value of stock to be taken to the Balance Sheet of PCT Ltd. as at 31st March.

ANSWER:

STATEMENT SHOWING THE VALUATION OF STOCK AS AT 31ST MARCH

Particulars	₹
A. Value of Stock as at 7th April	2,00,000
B. *Add:* Cost of Goods Sent on approval and still with the customer	

	[80% of ₹ 1,00,000 – 20% of ₹ 80,000]	64,000
C.	Value of Stock as at 31st March	2,64,000
	Note: 20% of the goods is already included in given stock of 7th April.	

QUESTION 6: Determine the value of stock as per books of BT Ltd at 31st March from the following information:

(a) The cost of stock as per physical verification as on 24th March amounted to ₹ 2,00,000.

(b) Purchases as per Purchase Book after stock taking till 31st March amounted to ₹ 2,00,000 and included the following:

(i) ₹ 10,000 for goods received till 23rd March

(ii) ₹ 20,000 for goods received on 1st April.

(c) Sales as per Sales Book after stock taking, till 31st March amounted to ₹ 2,00,000 and included the following:

(i) ₹ 10,000 for goods delivered till 23rd March

(ii) ₹ 20,000 for goods delivered on 1st April.

(d) Goods are sold by the trader at a profit of 25% on Cost.

ANSWER:

STATEMENT SHOWING THE VALUATION OF STOCK AS AT 31ST MARCH

	Particulars	₹
A.	Stock as per physical verification as at 24th March	2,00,000
B.	*Add:* Cost of goods purchased after stock taking till 31st March (whether *or* not received)	1,90,000
	[₹ 2,00,000 – ₹ 10,000 (being already received)]	
C.	*Less:* Cost of goods sold after stock taking till 31st March (whether *or* not delivered) [80% of (₹ 2,00,000 – ₹ 10,000) (being already delivered)]	(1,52,000)
D.	Stock as per Books as at 31st March	2,38,000

QUESTION 7: Determine the cost of physical stock as at 31st March in Previous Question

ANSWER:

STATEMENT SHOWING THE COST OF PHYSICAL STOCK AS AT 31ST MARCH

	Particulars	₹
A.	Stock as per physical verification as at 24th March	2,00,000
B.	*Add:* Cost of Goods purchased and received after stock taking till 31st March [₹ 2,00,000 – ₹ 10,000 (being already received) – ₹ 20,000 (being not yet received)]	1,70,000
C.	*Less:* Cost of goods sold and delivered after stock taking till 31st March [80% of ₹ 2,00,000 – ₹ 10,000 being already delivered – ₹ 20,000 (being not yet delivered)]	(1,36,000)
D.	Cost of Physical Stock in hand as at 31st March	2,34,000

ACCOUNTING FOR DEPRECIATION

QUESTION 1: Define Depreciation.

ANSWER:

1. According to the Institute of Chartered Accountants in England and Wales, 'Depreciation represents that part of the cost of a fixed asset to its owner which is not recoverable when the asset is finally out of use by him. Provision against this loss of capital is an integral cost of conducting the business during the effective commercial life of the asset and is not dependent on the amount of profit earned'.
2. Depreciation is the permanent and continuous decrease in the book value of a Fixed Depreciable Asset due to use, effluxion of time, obsolescence, expiration of legal rights *or* any other cause.
3. Comprehensively, the term 'Depreciation' covers Depletion, Amortisation and Obsolescence,

QUESTION 2: Define Depletion.

ANSWER: The term 'Depletion' refers to the physical deterioration by the exhaustion of natural resources (ore-deposits in mines, oil wells, quarries, timber stands etc.).

QUESTION 3: Define Amortisation.

ANSWER: The term 'Amortisation' refers to the economic deterioration by the expiration of intangible assets (patents, copyrights, goodwill etc.)

QUESTION 4: Define Obsolescence.

ANSWER: The term 'Obsolescence' refers to the economic deterioration by (a) invention of improved technique *or* equipment (b) market decline due to change in taste and fashion etc. (c) inadequacy of existing plant to meet the increased business.

QUESTION 5: Define Depreciation Accounting.

ANSWER: According to the American Institute of Certified Public Accountants (AICPA), 'Depreciation Accounting is a system of accounting which aims to distribute cost *or* the basic value of tangible capital assets less salvage (if any), over the estimated useful life of the unit (which may be group of assets) in a systematic and rational manner. It is a process of allocation and not of valuation'.

QUESTION 6: List any two causes of depreciation.

ANSWER:

1. Physical wear and tear
2. With the passage of time
3. Changes in economic environment
4. Expiration of legal rights

QUESTION 7: Is depreciation affected by fluctuations? State with reasons.

ANSWER: Depreciation is not the result of fluctuations in the value of fixed assets since, the fluctuation is concerned with the market price of the fixed asset whereas the depreciations is concerned with the historical cost.

QUESTION 8: List any two objectives for providing depreciation.

ANSWER:

1. To ascertain the true financial performance
2. To ascertain the true financial position

3. To ascertain the true cost of production
4. To accumulate funds for replacement of assets
5. To Comply with legal provisions if any, Applicable.

QUESTION 9: List the factors determining the amount of depreciation.

ANSWER:

1. Historical Cost
2. Expected Useful Life
3. Estimated Residual Value

QUESTION 10: List the two methods of recording depreciation.

ANSWER:

1. By Charging to Asset Account.
2. By Creating Provision for Depreciation/Accumulated Depreciation Account.

QUESTION 11: List any two methods for providing depreciation.

ANSWER:

1. Straight Line Method (SLM) and
2. Written Down Value Method (WDV).

QUESTION 12: What is Straight Line Method of providing depreciation?

ANSWER: Under the straight line method, a fixed and equal amount in the form of depreciation, according to a fixed percentage on the original cost, is written off during each accounting period over the expected useful life of the asset.

QUESTION 13: State any two merits of the Straight Line Method.

ANSWER:

1. It is easy to understand.
2. It is easy to calculate the amount and rate of depreciation.
3. Under this method, the book value of the asset becomes zero *or* equal to its scrap value at the expiry of its useful life.

QUESTION 14: State any two demerits of the Straight Line Method.

ANSWER:

1. The total charge (i.e., depreciation plus repairs and renewals) in later years is more as compared to that in earlier years since, the amount of repairs and renewals goes on increasing as the asset grows older whereas the amount of depreciation remains constant year after year.
2. It does not take into consideration the interest on the capital invested in the asset.
3. It does not provide for the replacement of the asset on the expiry of its useful life.

QUESTION 15: For which type of assets is the Straight Line Method considered suitable?

ANSWER: This method is suitable for those assets in relation to which (a) repair charges are less, and (b) the possibility of obsolescence is less. This method is suitable for furniture, patent, copyright, trademark, lease etc.

QUESTION 16: Enumerate any two examples of assets for which the Straight Line Method is considered suitable.

ANSWER: This method is suitable for furniture, patent, copyright, trademark, lease etc.

QUESTION 17: What is Written Down Value Method?

ANSWER: Under the Written Down Value method, depreciation according to a fixed percentage calculated upon the original cost (in the first year) and written down value, (in subsequent years) of an asset, is written off during each accounting period over the expected useful life of the asset. Under this method, the rate of depreciation remains constant year after year whereas the amount of depreciation goes on decreasing.

QUESTION 18: State any two merits of the Written Down Value Method.

ANSWER:

1. The total charge (i.e., depreciation plus repairs renewals) remains almost uniform year after year, since in earlier years the amount of depreciation is more and the amount of repairs and renewals is less, whereas in later years the amount of depreciation is less and the amount of repairs & renewals is more.
2. This method is logical in the sense that as the asset grows older, the amount of depreciation also goes on decreasing.

QUESTION 19: State any two demerits of the Written Down Value Method.

ANSWER:

1. It is difficult to calculate the rate of depreciation.
2. It does not take into consideration the interest on capital invested in the asset.
3. It does not provide for the replacement of the asset on the expiry of its useful life.
4. It takes a very long time to write an asset down to its break-up value, unless a very high rate is used.

QUESTION 20: For which type of assets, is the Written Down Value Method considered suitable?

ANSWER: This method is suitable for those assets in relation to which (a) the amount of repairs and renewals goes on increasing as the asset grows older (b) the possibilities of obsolescence are more.

QUESTION 21: Enumerate any two examples of assets for which the Written Down Value Method is considered suitable.

ANSWER: This method is suitable for plant and machineries, building etc.

QUESTION 22: List any two points of difference between Straight Line Method and Written Down Value Method.

Basis of Distinction	Straight Line Method	Written Down Value Method
1. Basic of Calculation	Depreciation is calculated at a fixed percentage on the original cost.	Depreciation is calculated at a fixed percentage on original cost (in first year) and on written down value (in subsequent years).
2. Amount of Depreciation	The amount of depreciation remains constant.	The amount of depreciation goes on decreasing.
3. Total Charge (i.e., depreciation plus repairs and renewals)	Total charge in later years is more as compared to that in earlier years since the amount of repairs and renewals goes on increasing as the asset grows older, whereas the amount of depreciation remains constant year after year.	Total charge remains almost uniform year after year, since in earlier years the amount of depreciation is more and the amount of repairs and renewals is less whereas in later years, the amount of depreciation is less and the amount of repairs & renewals is more.

4. Book Value	The book value of the asset becomes zero or equal to its scrap value.	The book value of the asset does not become zero.
5. Suitability	This method is suitable for those assets in relation to which (a) repair charges are less (b) the possibility of obsolescence is less.	This method is suitable for those assets in relation to which (a) the amount of repairs & renewals goes on increasing as the asset grows older and (b) the possibilities of obsolescence are more.
6. Calculation – Easy or Difficult	It is easy to calculate the rate of depreciation.	It is difficult to calculate the rate of depreciation.

QUESTION 23: What method of providing depreciation would you consider suitable for

(a) **Lease,**

(b) **Machinery**

(c) **Furniture**

(d) **Computers**

(e) **Copyright**

(f) **An air-cooler (second-hand) bought for ₹ 8,000 expected to last for two years with a nil scrap value.**

ANSWER: Straight Line Method: (a), (c), (e), (f). Written Down Value Method, (b), (d)

QUESTION 24: What is meant by Provision?

ANSWER: The term 'provision' refers to any of the following amounts:

(a) The amount written off *or* retained by way of providing for depreciation, renewals *or* diminution in value of assets; or

(b) The amount retained by way of providing for any known liability of which the amount cannot be determined with substantial accuracy.

QUESTION 25: Give any two examples of Provisions.

ANSWER:

1. Provision for Depreciation,
2. Provision for Doubtful Debts,
3. Provision for Taxation

QUESTION 26: State the Objective of Provision.

ANSWER: Provision is created to cover a loss in the value of assets, *or* a loss *or* expenses, the amount of which cannot be determined with substantial accuracy.

QUESTION 27: State the Objective of Provision for Doubtful Debts.

ANSWER: A provision for doubtful debts is created to cover the loss of possible bad debts by means of a predetermined percentage of net debtors (i.e., debtors less bad debts) with a view to bring in a certain element of certainty in the amount of bad debts charged for each accounting period.

QUESTION 28: State the Objective of Provision for Discount on Debtors.

ANSWER: Provision for Discount on Debtors is created to provide for discount likely to be allowed on good debtors (i.e., Sundry Debtors less additional bad debts given outside the Trial Balance and the provision for doubtful debts).

QUESTION 29: State the Accounting Treatment of Provision.

ANSWER: Provision is a charge against the profits and is created by debiting Profit & Loss Account.

QUESTION 30: State the Disclosure of Provision.

ANSWER: Provision is shown *either* on assets side by way of deduction from the respective asset in relation to which it has been created (e.g. Provision for Depreciation is shown by way of deduction from the Respective Fixed Asset, Provision for Doubtful Debt is shown by way of deduction from Debtors) *or* on the liabilities side under the sub-head 'Provisions' e.g. Provision for tax.

QUESTION 31: What is meant by Reserve?

ANSWER: The term 'reserve' refers to the profits retained in the business not having any of the attributes of a 'provision'. If however, the provision exceeds the amount which is required to meet the loss *or* the liability, the excess is to be treated as reserve. In other words, reserve means accumulated *or* undistributed profits.

QUESTION 32: Give any two examples of Reserves.

ANSWER:

1. General Reserve,
2. Contingency Reserve,
3. Debenture Redemption Reserve,
4. Investment Fluctuation Reserve.
5. Workmen Compensation Reserve.

QUESTION 33: State the Objectives of Reserve.

ANSWER: The objectives of creating the reserve includes the following:-

1. To strengthen the financial position of the concern,
2. To provide funds for the modernization and/or expansion of existing plant *or* acquisition of a new plant,
3. To equalize the dividend during the periods of inadequate profits,
4. To comply with legal requirements e.g. Debenture Redemption Reserve, Capital Redemption Reserve under the Companies Act 1956, Investment Allowance Reserve, Development Allowance Reserve, Foreign Project Allowance Reserve under the Income Tax Act, 1961,
5. To meet unforeseen abnormal losses.

QUESTION 34: What is meant by Revenue Reserve?

ANSWER: Revenue Reserves are those reserves which are created out of profits available for distribution by way of dividend. Revenue Reserves may be classified into two categories as under:

(i) **General reserve** — General Reserve is that reserve which is not created for a specific purpose. Examples of such reserves include General Reserve, Contingency Reserve etc.

(ii) **Specific reserve** — Specific reserve is that reserve which is created for a specific purpose. Examples of such reserves include Dividend Equalization Reserve, Debenture Redemption Reserve, Investment Fluctuation Reserve.

QUESTION 35: What is meant by Capital Reserve?

ANSWER: Capital reserves are those reserves which are not created out of operating profits.

QUESTION 36: Give any two examples of Capital Reserve.

ANSWER:

1. Profit on sale of fixed assets,
2. Profit on revaluation of fixed asset,
3. Profit on sale of the whole undertaking *or* a part of it.

QUESTION 37: List any one point of difference between Revenue Reserve and Capital Reserve.

ANSWER: Revenue reserve refers to the amounts which are free for distribution by way of dividend. Capital reserve refers to the amounts which are not free for distribution by way of dividend.

QUESTION 38: List any two points of difference between Provision and Reserve.

ANSWER:

Basis of Distinction	Provision	Reserve
1. Purpose	It is created for a particular purpose and can only be used for that particular purpose.	It need not necessarily be created for a particular purpose. e.g., General reserve is not for any particular purpose.
2. Charge Vs. Appropriation	It is a charge against the profit and is required to be created irrespective of the amount of profit.	It is an appropriation out of profit and can be created only if profits have been earned.
3. Disclosure in Income Statement	It is shown on the debit side of P & L A/c.	It is shown on the debit side of P & L Appropriation A/c.
4. Disclosure in Balance Sheet	Usually a provision is shown by way of deduction from the amount of the items for which the it is created. e.g. Provision for Doubtful Debts.	Reserve is shown as a separate item under the head Reserves and Surplus on the liabilities side of the Balance Sheet.
5. Investment outside the business	There is **no** question of investment of the amount of provisions.	The amount of a reserve **can be** invested outside the business.
6. Utilisation for Dividends	It **cannot be** utilised for distribu tion by way of dividends.	It **can be** utilised for distribution by way of dividends.
7. Legal Necessity	It is made mainly because of legal necessity.	It is a matter of financial prudence.
8. Examples	1. Provision for Tax 2. Provision for Doubtful Debts	1. General Reserve 2. Contingency Reserve

QUESTION 39: How would you compute the profit *or* loss on sale of a fixed asset?

ANSWER:

Step 1: Book Value as on date of Sale = Original Cost – Total Depreciation till date of sale

Step 2: Profit = Sale Proceeds – Book Value as on date of sale *or*
Loss = Book Value as on date of sale – Sale Proceeds

QUESTION 40: CAS Ltd. imported a machine on 01.10.2013 for ₹ 1,28,000, paid customs duty and freight ₹ 64,000 and incurred erection charges ₹ 48,000. Another local machinery costing ₹ 80,000 was purchased on 01.04.2014. On 1st Oct 2015, a portion of the imported machinery (value one-third) got out of order and was sold for ₹ 27,840. Depreciation is to be calculated at 20% p.a.on SLM basis. Calculate the profit/ loss on sale of machine.

ANSWER:

Loss on sale of machine = [(₹ 1,28,000 +₹ 64,000 +₹ 48,000) × 1/3] – [₹ 80,000 × 20% × 2] – ₹ 27,840

= ₹ 20,160

QUESTION 41: On 01.04.2012 Purchased 10 second hand Machines for ₹ 9,00,000. Incurred ₹ 70,000 towards freight & insurance, ₹ 20,000 towards carriage inward, Residual Value ₹ 4,09,600, Useful life 4 years. On 01.01.2013 Incurred ₹ 7,000 towards Repairs and ₹ 3,000 on installation of machines and commenced the commercial production. 01.01.2014 Incurred ₹ 10,000 towards Repairs and ₹ 12,000 towards Annual Insurance Premium. On 01.01.2015, Sold one machine for ₹ 50,000. Depreciation is to be provided as per WDV basis. Calculate the Profit/ Loss on sale of machine.

ANSWER:

WDV rate of Depreciation = 1 – [4√₹ 4,09,600/₹ 10,00,000] = 20%

Cost of machine sold = [(₹ 9,00,000 + ₹ 70,000 +₹ 20,000+ ₹ 7,000+ ₹ 3,000) × 1/10] = = ₹ 1,00,000

Loss on sale of machine = [(₹ 1,00,000 x95% × 80% × 85%)] – ₹ 50,000 = ₹ 14,600

QUESTION 42: Glass, Cutlery etc.: Balance b/f on 01.04.2014 is ₹ 28,000. Glass, Cutlery, etc. purchased on Ist April during the year ₹ 16,000. Depreciation is to be charged on the above assets as follows — 1/5th of their values is to be written off in the year of purchase and 2/5th in each of the next 2 years. Of the stock of Glass, Cutlery, etc. as on 01.04.2014, 1/2 was one year old and 1/2 was 2 years old. Calculate the Depreciation for 3rd year and the Closing Balance in Glass, Cutlery A/c at the end of 3rd year.

ANSWER: Depreciation for 3rd year = 50% of ₹ 14,000 + ₹14,000 + ₹ 3,200 = ₹ 24,200

Closing Balance in Glass, Cutlery A/c at the end of 3rd year = ₹ 28,000 + ₹ 16,000 – ₹ 24,200

= ₹ 19,800

QUESTION 43: On 1 April 2012, X Ltd. purchased a machinery for ₹ 12,00,000. On 1 Oct. 2014, a part of the machinery purchased on 1 April 2012 for ₹ 80,000 was sold for ₹ 45,000 and a new machinery at a cost of ₹ 1,58,000 was purchased and installed on the same date. The company has adopted the method of providing 10% p.a. depreciation on the written down value basis. Calculate the Closing Balance of 'Provision for Depreciation Account' as at 31.03.2015.

ANSWER:

Depreciation on machinery sold = ₹ 80,000 – [₹ 80,000 × 90% × 90% × 95%] = ₹ 18,440

Depreciation on old machinery (other than sold)

= (₹ 12,00,000 – ₹ 80,000) – [₹ 11,20,000 × 90% × 90% × 90%] = ₹ 3,03,520

Depreciation on new machinery = ₹ 1,58,000 – [₹ 1,58,000 × 95%] = ₹ 7,900

Closing Balance of 'Provision for Depreciation Account' as at 31.03.2015 = ₹ 3,03,520 + ₹ 7,900

= ₹ 3,11,420

QUESTION 44: On 1.4.2014 the balance of Machinery Account ₹ 5,17,000. It was discovered during 2014-2015 that ₹ 25,000 being repairs to machinery incurred on 30 June, 2012 had been capitalized. After rectification and depreciation @ 20% p.a. on reducing balances, Calculate the balance of Machinery Account as at 31.03.2015.

ANSWER: Book Value of repairs to machinery as at 1.4.2014 = ₹ 25,000 × 85% × 80% = ₹ 17,000

Balance of Machinery Account(after rectification) as at 1.4.2014 = ₹ 5,17,000 – ₹ 17,000 = ₹ 5,00,000

Balance of Machinery Account(after rectification) as at 31.03.2015 = ₹ 5,00,000 – [₹ 5,00,000 × 20%]

= ₹ 4,00,000

QUESTION 45: On 1.04.2014, the balance of Machinery Account ₹ 4,71,200. It was discovered during 2014-2015 that ₹ 50,000 being the cost of Generator purchased on 1st Oct, 2011 had been written off to Stores. After rectification and depreciation @ 20% p.a. on reducing balances, Calculate the balance of Machinery Account as at 31.03.2015.

ANSWER: Book Value of Generator as at 1.4.2014 = ₹ 50,000 × 90% × 80% × 80% = ₹ 28,800

Balance of Machinery Account(after rectification) as at 1.4.2014 = ₹ 4,71,200 + ₹ 28,800 = ₹ 5,00,000

Balance of Machinery Account(after rectification) as at 31.03.2015 = ₹ 5,00,000 – [₹ 5,00,000 × 20%]
= ₹ 4,00,000

QUESTION 46: Bharat Ltd. which depreciates its machinery at 10% p.a. straight line basis, had on 1st April 2014 ₹ 28,000 to the debit of Machinery Account. On 31st March 2015, the company decided to change the method of depreciation to diminishing balance method with effect from 1st April, 2011 being the date of purchase of machine and the rate of depreciation remaining the same. There was no purchase/sale of machine after1st April, 2011. Pass the necessary journal entry on account of change in method of depreciation.

ANSWER:

Cost as on 1.4.2014 = ₹ 28,000/.70 = ₹ 40,000

A. Total Depreciation under Old Method = ₹ 40,000 – ₹ 28,000 = ₹ 12,000

B. Total Depreciation under New Method = ₹ 40,000 – [₹ 40,000 × 90% × 90% × 90%] = ₹ 10,840

C. Excess Depreciation to be written back ₹ 1,160

JOURNAL ENTRY TO ADJUST EXCESS DEPRECIATION

Machinery A/c	Dr. ₹1,160	
To Profit and Loss A/c		₹ 1,160
(Being the Excess Depreciation written back on a/c of change in method of Depreciation)		

QUESTION 47: Bharat Tushar Ltd. which depreciates its machinery at 10% p.a. on diminishing balance method, had on1st April 2014 ₹ 29,160, to the debit of Machinery Account. On 31st March 2015, the company decided to change the method of depreciation to Straight Line Method with effect from 1st April 2011 being the date of purchase of machine and the rate of depreciation remaining the same. There was no purchase/sale of machine after1st April, 2011. Pass the necessary journal entry on account of change in method of depreciation

ANSWER:

Cost as on 1.4.2014 = ₹ 29,160/(.90 ×. 90 ×. 90) = ₹ 40,000

A. Total Depreciation under Old Method = ₹ 40,000 – ₹ 29,160 = ₹ 10,840

B. Total Depreciation under New Method = ₹ 40,000 × 10% × 3 = ₹ 12,000

C. Short Depreciation to be provided = ₹ 1,160

JOURNAL ENTRY TO ADJUST SHORT DEPRECIATION

Profit and Loss A/c	Dr. ₹ 1,160	
To Machinery A/c		₹ 1,160
(Being the Short Depreciation provided on a/c of change in method of Depreciation)		

QUESTION 48: Tulsian Ltd. purchased a machinery for ₹ 9,00,000 on 1 April 2011 and incurred ₹ 1,00,000 towards freight, insurance, carriage inwards and installation charges. It was estimated that the machinery will have a scrap value of ₹ 71,800 at the end of its useful life which is 4 years. It was decided to institute a sinking fund for the purpose of accumulating

sufficient funds to replace the machinery at the end of its useful life and to invest in some readily convertible securities yielding 10% interest p.a. Reference to the table shows that ₹ 1 p.a. at 10% compound interest amounts to ₹ 4.641 in 4 years. Investments are to be made in the bonds of ₹ 100 each available at par. Calculate the annual amount to be charged to Profit and Loss Account.

ANSWER:

	₹
A. Original Cost	9,00,000
B. *Add:* Capital Expenditure	1,00,000
C. *Less:* Estimated scrap value	71,800
D. Depreciate Cost (A + B – C)	9,28,200
E. Value of annuity per ₹ 1	4,641
F. Annual amount to be charged (D/E)	2,00,000

QUESTION 49: A lease is purchased on 1st April, 2011 for 4 years at a cost of ₹ 40,000. It is proposed to depreciate the lease by the annuity method charging interest @ 5% p.a. A reference to the annuity table shows that to depreciate ₹ 1 by annuity method over 4 years charging interest at 5% p.a. one must write off a sum of ₹ 0.2820. ₹ 4,000 would also be refunded after 4 years. Calculate the Annual Depreciation Charge as per Annuity Method.

ANSWER:

CALCULATION OF ANNUAL DEPRECIATION CHARGE

A Cost of Lease paid	₹	40,000
B *Less:* Refundable amount	₹	4,000
C Depreciable amount (A – B)	₹	36,000
D Annuity Factor @ 5% interest for 4 years	₹	0.2820
E Fixed Depreciation Charge (C × D)	₹	10,142
F Interest on Salvage @ 5% on ₹ 2,000 for a year	₹	200
G Annual Depreciation Charge (E + F)	₹	10,352

QUESTION 50: Tulsian Ltd. acquired a lease right for 10 years of a mine on 1.1.2014 on a lumpsum payment of ₹ 9,00,000 to the landlord. It was estimated by the expert that the coal deposit of the mine was 40,00,000 tonnes, 75% of which could be raised within time period allowed. Tulsian Ltd. decided to depreciate the lease on Depletion Method. The sales and stocks (in tonnes) were as under:

Year	2014	2015
Sales	30,000	62,000
Closing Stock	10,000	8,000

Calculate the Depreciation for the year 2014 & 2015.

ANSWER:

1. Depreciation per tonne = Total Cost/Total Expected Outputwithin Lease Period
   = ₹ 9,00,000/75% of 40,00,000 = ₹ 9,00,000/30,00,00
   = ₹ 0.30 per tonne
2. Annual raisings = Sales + Closing Stock – Opening Stock
   For 2014: 30,000 + 10,000 – 0 = 40,000, For 2015: 62,000 + 8,000 – 10,000 = 60,000

3. Depreciation for the year 2014 = 40,000 × ₹ 0.30 per tonne = ₹ 12,000
4. Depreciation for the year 2015 = = 60,000 × ₹ 0.30 per tonne = ₹ 18,000

QUESTION 51: Tulsian Ltd. purchased a machine for ₹ 2,20,000 on 1st January, 2014 and incurred ₹ 40,000 towards freight, insurance, carriage inwards and installation charges. It was estimated that the machinery will have a scrap value of ₹ 20,000 at the end of its useful life which is 10 years of 12,000 hours each. Tulsian Ltd. decided to depreciate the machines on 'Machine Hour Rate Method'. The machine hours during the year 2014 were 6,000. Calculate the Depreciation for the year 2014.

ANSWER:

1. Calculation of Rate of depreciation per Machine Hour

   Machine Hour Rate = (Cost of Acquisition – Scrap Value)/Life of the asset (in Hours)

   = ₹ 2,00,000 – ₹ 20,000/10 × 12,000 = ₹ 2 per hour
2. Depreciation for the year 2014 = 6,000 × ₹ 2 per hour = ₹ 12,000

QUESTION 52: On 1st April 2014, Tulsian Ltd. purchased a machinery for ₹ 2,00,000 and incurred ₹ 14,000 towards freight and insurance, ₹ 2,000 towards carriage inwards and ₹ 4,000 towards installation charges. It was established that the machinery will have a scrap value of ₹ 20,000 at the end of its useful life which is 4 years. Calculate the Depreciation for the year 2015 according to the Double Declining Method.

ANSWER:

1. Rate of Depreciation 200%/n = 200%/4 = 50%
2. Depreciation for the year 2015 = 50% [(₹ 2,00,000 + ₹ 14,000 + ₹ 2,000 + ₹ 4,000) – 50%]
   = ₹ 1,10,000

QUESTION 53: On 1st April 2015, Tulsian Ltd. purchased a machinery for ₹ 2,00,000 and incurred ₹ 14,000 towards freight and insurance, ₹ 2,000 towards carriage inwards and ₹ 4,000 towards instalation charges. It was established that the machinery will have a scrap value of ₹ 20,000 at the end of its useful life which is 4 years. Determine the Amount of Depreciation for the year 2015 according to the Sum of Years' Digits Method.

ANSWER:

1. Rate of Depreciation = Number of Years Life Remaining/Sum of Years Digits × 100

   Sum of Years' Digits = n (n + 1)/2 = 4 (4 + 1)/2 = 20/2 = 10

   1st Year = 4/10 × 100 = 40%

   2nd Year = 3/10 × 100 = 30%

   3rd Year = 2/10 × 100 = 20%

   4th Year = 1/10 × 100 = 10%
2. Calculation of the Amount of Depreciation p.a.

   = Number of Years Life Remaining/Sum of Years Digits × (Original Cost – Scrap Value)

   Depreciation for the year 2015 = 40% [(₹ 2,00,000 + ₹ 14,000 + ₹ 2,000 + ₹ 4,000) – ₹ 20,000]
   = ₹ 80,000

QUESTION 54: On 1st April, 2015, the value of loose tools was ₹ 20,000 and during the year ₹ 10,000 worth of tools were purchased and ₹ 2,000 realised by way of sale of scrapped loose tools. At the end of the year, the loose tools are considered to be worth only ₹ 12,000. Calculate the amount to be charged to Profit & Loss Account.

ANSWER:

AMOUNT TO BE CHARGED TO PROFIT AND LOSS ACCOUNT

	Particulars			₹
A	Opening Balance of Loose tools			20,000
B	*Add:* Purchased during the year			10,000
C	*Less:*	(a) Sale of scrapped Loose tools	2,000	
		(b) Closing Balance of Loose tools (at revalued figure)	12,000	14,000
D	Depreciation to be charged to Profit & Loss Account (A + B – C)			16,000

PREPARATION OF FINANCIAL STATEMENTS OF PROFIT-MAKING ORGANIZATIONS

QUESTION 1: What is meant by Financial Statements?

ANSWER: The Financial Statements are historical documents which show the organised summaries of detailed information about the Financial Performance of an enterprise for an accounting period and Financial Position at the end of an accounting period.

QUESTION 2: Name the two basic Financial Statements.

ANSWER:

1. Income Statement
2. Balance Sheet.

QUESTION 3: State the meaning of An Income Statement.

ANSWER: An Income Statement is a Statement of Revenue from Operations, other Incomes and Expenses during a given accounting period. It indicates the Financial Performance of an enterprise for an accounting period.

QUESTION 4: State the meaning of Balance Sheet.

ANSWER: A Balance Sheet is a Statement of Assets (Current and Non-Current), Liabilities (Current and Non-Current) and Capital indicating the Financial Position of an enterprise at a given date.

QUESTION 5: State any two objectives of Financial Statements.

ANSWER:

1. To provide information about the Financial Performance of an enterprise.
2. To provide information about the Financial Position of an enterprise.

QUESTION 6: What is a Trading Account?

ANSWER: Trading Account is one of the Financial Statements which shows the result of buying and selling of goods and/or services during an accounting period.

QUESTION 7: What is the purpose of Trading Account?

ANSWER: Trading Account is prepared to ascertain the Gross Profit *or* Gross Loss of an enterprise during the accounting period.

QUESTION 8: How does the matching principle apply to Trading Account?

ANSWER: The basis for the preparation of Trading Account is the matching of Selling Prices of goods and services with the Cost of Goods Sold and Services rendered.

QUESTION 9: What does the Balance of a Trading Account indicate?

ANSWER:

1. The Credit Balance of a Trading Account indicates Gross Profit.
2. The Debit Balance of a Trading Account indicates Gross Loss.

QUESTION 10: What is Gross Profit?

ANSWER: Gross Profit means excess of Operating Revenues over Direct Operating Expenses.

QUESTION 11: How is the balance of Trading Account treated?

ANSWER:

1. The Credit Balance of a Trading Account (i.e., Gross Profit) is transferred on the credit side of Profit and Loss Account.
2. The Debit Balance of a Trading Account (i.e., Gross Loss) is transferred on the debit side of Profit and Loss Account.

QUESTION 12. State any two items which are shown by way of deduction from the Purchases in the Trading Account.

ANSWER:

1. Goods distributed as free samples
2. Goods withdrawn for personal use
3. Abnormal Loss of Goods

QUESTION 13: What is a Profit and Loss Account?

ANSWER: The Profit and Loss account is one of the Financial Statements which shows the Financial Performance of an enterprise during an accounting period.

QUESTION 14: What is the purpose of a Profit and Loss Account?

ANSWER: The Profit and Loss Account is prepared to ascertain the Net Profit earned *or* Net Loss incurred by the an enterprise during an accounting period.

QUESTION 15: What does the Balance of a Profit and Loss Account indicate?

ANSWER:

1. The Credit Balance of a Profit and Loss Account indicates Net Profit.
2. The Debit Balance of a Profit and Loss Account indicates Net Loss.

QUESTION 16: What is Net Profit?

ANSWER: Net Profit means the excess of all Revenue (whether operating *or* non-operating) over Expenses & Losses (whether operating *or* non-operating).

QUESTION 17: How is the balance of Profit & Loss Account treated?

ANSWER:

1. The Credit Balance of a Profit & Loss Account (i.e., Net Profit) is transferred on the credit side of Capital Account.
2. The Debit Balance of a Profit & Loss Account (i.e., Net Loss) is transferred on the debit side of Capital Account.

QUESTION 18: What is Operating Profit?

ANSWER: Operating Profit means the excess of Operating Revenues over Operating Expenses & Losses. It arises as a result of carrying out Operating Activities.

QUESTION 19: What are Operating Activities?

ANSWER: Operating Activities are the Principal Revenue Producing activities of the enterprise and other activities that are not investing *or* financial activities. ***For Example*** — Sales and Purchases of buildings by Builders and Property dealers are operating activities. Granting loans to third parties by them are investing activities. Taking loans from third parties by them are financing activities.

QUESTION 20: List any two points of difference between a Trading Account and a Profit and Loss Account.

ANSWER:

Basis of Distinction	Trading Account	Profit & Loss A/c
1. Purpose	Trading Account is prepared to ascertain the Gross Profit *or* Gross Loss of an enterprise during the accounting period.	The Profit and Loss Account is prepared to ascertain the Net Profit *or* Net Loss of an enterprise during an accounting period.
2. Closure	Trading Account is closed by transferring its balance to the Profit and Loss Account.	Profit and Loss Account is closed by transferring its balance to the Capital Account

QUESTION 21: What is the difference between Gross Profit and Net Profit?

ANSWER:

1. Gross Profit = Operating Revenues – Direct Operating Expenses
2. Net Profit = All Revenue (whether Operating *or* Non-Operating) – Expenses & Losses (whether Operating *or* Non-Operating)

QUESTION 22: What is the difference between Gross Profit and Operating Profit?

ANSWER:

1. Gross Profit = Operating Revenues – Direct Operating Expenses
2. Operating Profit = Operating Revenues – All Operating Expenses (whether Direct *or* Indirect)

QUESTION 23: What is the difference between Operating Profit and Net Profit?

ANSWER:

1. Operating Profit = Operating Revenues – All Operating Expenses (whether Direct *or* Indirect)
2. Net Profit = All Revenue (whether Operating *or* Non-Operating) – Expenses & Losses (whether Operating *or* Non-Operating)

QUESTION 24: What are Closing Entries?

ANSWER: Closing Entries are passed in the journal for closing the Nominal Accounts by transferring them to the Trading and Profit and Loss Account. These are needed at the end of the accounting year, when the final accounts are prepared.

QUESTION 25: Why is it wrong to head the Trading and Profit & Loss Account on 31st March, 2013?

ANSWER: Trading and Profit & Loss Account is prepared for a particular period and not at a particular point of time.

QUESTION 26: How do you close a Profit and Loss Account?

ANSWER: Profit & Loss Account is closed by transferring its balance to the Capital Account.

QUESTION 27. State the nature of all incomes, expenditures and losses shown in the Trading and Profit & Loss Account.

ANSWER: Revenue

QUESTION 28. State Whether Operating *or* Non-Operating items are shown in the Trading Account.

ANSWER: Operating items

QUESTION 29. State Whether Operating *or* Non-Operating items are shown in the Profit & Loss Account.

ANSWER: Both Operating and Non-Operating items

QUESTION 30. Name the Non-Cash but Operating item which is shown in the Profit & Loss Account.

ANSWER: Depreciation

QUESTION 31: What is a Balance Sheet?

ANSWER: A Balance Sheet is a Statement of Assets (Current and Non-Current), Liabilities (Current and Non-Current) and Capital indicating the Financial Position of an enterprise at a given date.

QUESTION 32: List any two characteristics of a Balance Sheet.

ANSWER:

1. A Balance Sheet is only a Statement and not an Account. It has no debit side *or* credit side. The headings of the two sides are 'Assets' and 'Liabilities'.
2. A Balance Sheet is prepared at a particular point of time and not for a particular period. The information contained in a Balance Sheet is true only at that particular point of time at which it is prepared.

QUESTION 33: What is the purpose of a Balance Sheet?

ANSWER:

1. To ascertain the Nature and Value of Assets of a business.
2. To ascertain the Nature and Amount of Liabilities of a business.
3. To find out the Financial Solvency of an enterprise. An enterprise is considered to be a solvent if its assets exceed its external liabilities.

QUESTION 34: What is meant by Assets?

ANSWER: An asset is a resource:

(a) which is controlled by an enterprise as a result of past events; and
(b) from which future economic benefits are expected to flow to the enterprise.

QUESTION 35: What is meant by Liabilities?

ANSWER: A liability is a present obligation of the enterprise arising from past events, the settlement of which is expected to result in an outflow from the enterprise of resources embodying economic benefits.

QUESTION 36: What is meant by Fixed Assets?

ANSWER: Fixed assets are those assets which are held for the purposes of producing *or* providing goods *or* services and those which are not held for resale in the normal course of business.

QUESTION 37: What is meant by Tangible Fixed Assets?

ANSWER: A Tangible Asset is an identifiable non-monetary asset, with physical substance, which is held for use in the production *or* supply of goods *or* services, *or* for rental to others, *or* for administrative purposes. e.g., Land & Building, Plant & Machinery, Furniture & Fixture, Motor Vehicles.

Note: Non-monetary assets are assets other than monetary assets. Monetary Assets are money held and assets to be received in fixed *or* determinable amounts of money ***For Example*** Cash, Debtors, Bills Receivable, Investments held to maturity since their amount on maturity is determined, etc.

QUESTION 38: What is meant by Intangible Fixed Assets?

ANSWER: An Intangible Asset is an identifiable non-monetary asset, without physical substance, which is held for use in the production *or* supply of goods *or* services, *or* for rental to others, *or* for administrative purposes. e.g., Goodwill, Patents, Trade Marks.

Note: Non-monetary assets are assets other than monetary assets. Monetary Assets are money held and assets to be received in fixed *or* determinable amounts of money ***For Example*** Cash, Debtors, Bills Receivable, Investments held to maturity since their amount on maturity is determined, etc.

QUESTION 39: List any two points of difference between Tangible Assets and Intangible Assets.

Basis of Distinction	Tangible Assets	Intangible Assets
1. Physical identity	These assets have physical identity.	These assets do not have physical identity.
2. Depreciation or Amortisation	Fixed tangible assets are depreciated.	Intangible assets are amortized.
3. Fixed vs. Current	Tangible assets can be Fixed Asset or Current Asset.	Intangible assets usually fall in the category of Fixed Assets.
4. Acceptance in security	Lenders accept such assets as security.	Lenders usually do not accept such assets as security for a loan given.
5. Risk of loss due to fire	These assets may be lost due to fire.	These assets cannot be lost due to fire.

QUESTION 40: What is meant by Investments?

ANSWER: Investments are assets held by an enterprise for earning income by way of Dividends, Interest, and Rentals, for capital appreciation, *or* for other benefits to the investing enterprise. e.g., Investment in Shares, Investment in Debentures & Bonds, Investment in Immovable Properties.

QUESTION 41: What is meant by Current Assets?

ANSWER: Current assets are those assets which are held–

(i) in the form of cash e.g., Cash in hand and Cash at Bank,

(ii) for their conversion into Cash normally within an operating cycle *or* 12 months from the date of Balance Sheet e.g., Stock of Finished Goods, Debtors, Bills Receivable, Accrued Income,

(iii) for their consumption in the production of Goods *or* rendering of services in the normal course of business e.g., Stock of Raw Materials, WIP.

QUESTION 42: List any two points of difference between Fixed Assets and Current Assets.

ANSWER:

Basis of Distinction	Fixed Assets	Current Assets
1. Purposes of holding	These are the assets which are held for the purpose of producing or providing Goods or Services and those which are not held for resale in the normal course of business.	These are the assets which are held – (a) in the form ot Cash or Cash equivalents (b) for their conversion into cash normally within an operating cycle or 12 months from Balance Sheet date (c) for their consumption in the production of goods or rendering of services in the normal course of business.
2. Valuation	Fixed assets are valued **at cost less depreciation**.	These assets are valued **at cost or market price *whichever* is *lower***.
3. Subject to change	These assets are usually **not** subject to change.	These assets **are** usually subject to change.
4. Pledge	These assets **cannot** be pledged.	These assets **can be** pledged.
5. Fixed vs. Floating charge	**Fixed** charge can be created on these assets.	**Floating** charge can be created on these assets.
6. Nature of Profit on Sale	Profit on sale of these assets is of **capital** nature.	Profit on sale of these assets is of **revenue** nature.
7. Revaluation reserve in case of appreciation in the value	In case of appreciation in the value of such assets, revaluation reserve **can be created.**	In case of appreciation in the value of such assets, revaluation reserve **cannot be created.**
8. Source of finance	These assets are financed out of **long-term funds**.	These assets are mainly financed out of **short-term funds**.

QUESTION 43: Give any two examples of Wasting Assets.

ANSWER: (a) Mines (b) Oil wells.

QUESTION 44: Give any two examples of Fictitious Assets.

ANSWER: (a) Preliminary Expenses (b) Debit balance of P&L A/c.

QUESTION 45: List any two points of difference between Wasting Assets and Fictitious Assets.

ANSWER:

Basis of Distinction	Wasting Assets	Fictitious Assets
1. Meaning	Wasting Assets are those assets which are subject to physical deterioration by the exhausation of natural resources	Truly speaking, Fictitious Assets are not assets at all. These merely represent an unwritten off amount of some items, which are to be written off in future as per manage-ment's accounting policy.

2. Examples	1. Ore Deposits in mires 2. Oil wells 3. Ouarries 4. Timber stands	1. Dr. Balance of P&L A/c 2. Advertisement Expenditure Surpluse A/c 3. Discount in issue of shares/ Debantures A/c 4. Preliminary Exp. 5. Underwriting Commission
3. Depletion or writing off	Wasting assets are gradually depleted.	Fictitious assets are written off.
4. Disclosure	These are shown under the head 'Fixed Assets'.	These are shown after the head 'Current Assets, Loans & Advances'.
5. Acceptance in security	Lenders accept such assets as security for a loan given.	Lenders do not accept such assets as security for a loan given.

QUESTION 46: What is meant by Long term Liabilities?

ANSWER: Long term Liability refers to that liability which is expected to be settled after 12 months from the date of a Balance Sheet e.g., loan from a financial institution, Debentures.

QUESTION 47: What is meant by Current Liabilities?

ANSWER: Current Liability refers to that liability which is expected to be settled normally within an operating cycle *or* 12 months from the date of a Balance Sheet e.g., Bills Payables, Trade Creditors, Outstanding Expenses, Bank Overdraft, Installments of Loan and Deposits payable within 12 months from the date of Balance Sheet.

QUESTION 48: What is meant by Capital?

ANSWER: Capital is the Excess of Assets over External Liabilities. It refers to the amount invested in an enterprise by the proprietor (in case of a proprietorship concern) *or* partners (in case of a partnership concern), which is increased by the amount of profit earned and is decreased by the losses incurred and the amount withdrawn (whether in the form of cash *or* kind).

QUESTION 49: hat is meant by Drawings?

ANSWER: Drawings represent the amount withdrawn by the proprietor whether in the form of Cash *or* kind. Drawings are shown by way of deduction from the amount of capital in the Balance Sheet.

QUESTION 50: What is meant by Contingent Asset?

ANSWER: A Contingent Asset is a possible asset that arises from past events the existence of which will be confirmed only by the occurrence *or* non-occurrence of one *or* more uncertain future events not wholly within the control of the enterprise.

QUESTION 51: What is meant by Contingent Liability?

ANSWER: A Contingent Liability is a possible obligation that arises from past events and the existence of which will be confirmed only by the occurrence *or* non-occurrence of one *or* more uncertain future events not wholly within the control of the enterprise.

QUESTION 52: Give any two examples of Contingent Liabilities.

ANSWER:

(a) Bills discounted but not yet matured.

(b) Arrears of Dividend on Cummulative Preference Shares.

QUESTION 53: List any two points of difference between Contingent Liability and Other Liability.

Basis of Distinction	Contingent Liability	Other Liability
1. Meaning	It is an obligation which may or may not arise depending on the happening or non-happening of an uncertain future event.	These are financial obligations of an enterprise other than owners' equity.
2. Disclosure	It is disclosed by way of foot note to the Balance Sheet.	These are disclosed on the liabilities side of the Balance Sheet.
3. Example	1. Bills discounted but not yet matured 2. Arrears of dividend on Cum-Pref-Shares	1. Creditors for Goods 2. Outstanding Expenses

QUESTION 54: What is meant by Grouping of Assets and Liabilities?

ANSWER: The term 'Grouping' means putting together items of a similar nature under a common heading. ***For Example***, under the heading 'Trade Creditors' the balances of the ledger accounts of all the suppliers from whom goods have been purchased on credit, will be shown.

QUESTION 55: What is meant by Marshalling of Assets and Liabilities?

ANSWER: The term 'Marshalling' refers to the order in which the various Assets and Liabilities are shown in the Balance Sheet.

QUESTION 56: Enumerate the ways in which a Balance Sheet may be marshalled.

ANSWER: The assets and liabilities can be shown *either* in the order of liquidity *or* in the order of permanency.

QUESTION 57: What is meant by Liquidity Order of Assets and Liabilities?

ANSWER:

1. The assets are arranged in the order of their liquidity, i.e., the most liquid asset (e.g., Cash-in-hand), is shown first. The least liquid asset (e.g., goodwill) is shown last. The least liquid asset does not mean an asset which cannot be encashed.
2. The liabilities are arranged in the order of their urgency of payment, i.e., the most urgent payment to be made (e.g., short-term creditors), is shown first. The least urgent payment to be made (e.g., long-term creditors) is shown last.

QUESTION 58: What is meant by Permanency Order of Assets and Liabilities?

ANSWER:

1. The assets are arranged in the order of their permanence i.e., the least liquid asset (e.g., goodwill) is shown first and the most liquid asset (e.g., Cash-in-hand) is shown last.
2. The least urgent payment to be made (e.g., owners) is shown first and the most urgent payment to be made (e.g., short-term creditors) is shown last.

QUESTION 59: Why is it wrong to head the Balance Sheet for the year ended 31st March, 2013?

ANSWER: A Balance Sheet is prepared at a particular point of time and not for a particular period.

QUESTION 60: At what price should the closing stock be valued and why?

ANSWER: Current Assets are usually valued at Cost *or* Net Realizable Value (i.e., Realizable Value less Realization Expenses) whichever is less on the basis of Prudence (or Conservatism) Principle.

QUESTION 61: At what price should the fixed assets be valued and why?

ANSWER: Fixed assets are usually valued at cost less depreciation as per Cost Principle.

QUESTION 62: Why is it necessary to take into account the Closing Stock in preparing a Trading Account?

ANSWER: To match the correct Cost of Goods sold with the Selling Prices of Goods sold as per Matching Principle.

QUESTION 63: State the journal entry to open Closing Stock account for current year.

ANSWER:

Stock A/c Dr.

To Trading A/c

(Being the closing stock taken into A/c)

QUESTION 64: State the effect of undervaluation of Closing Stock on Gross Profit.

ANSWER: Gross Profit will decrease.

QUESTION 65: State the effect of overvaluation of Closing Stock on Gross Profit.

ANSWER: Gross Profit will increase.

QUESTION 66: Name the Principle involved in the valuation of inventory.

ANSWER: Prudence (or Conservatism) Principle

QUESTION 67: Name the principle involved in the valuation of Fixed Assets.

ANSWER: Cost Principle

QUESTION 68: Name the principle involved in the classification of Assets as fixed and current.

ANSWER: Going Concern Principle

QUESTION 69: What balance does a Nominal Account normally reflect?

ANSWER: A nominal account reflects a debit balance.

QUESTION 70: What balance does a Real Account normally reflect?

ANSWER: A real account reflects a debit balance.

QUESTION 71: What balance does a Personal Account normally reflect?

ANSWER: A personal account may reflect a debt balance *or* credit balance.

QUESTION 72: What type of balance may a Bank Account show?

ANSWER: Bank Account may show debit balance *or* credit balance (in case overdraft facility is availed of)

QUESTION 73: What type of balance may a Cash Account show?

ANSWER: Cash Account can show only debit balance because one can not spend in cash more than what he has in hand.

QUESTION 74: What does the Debit Balance of Returns Account indicate?

ANSWER: Sales Returns

QUESTION 85: What does the Credit Balance of a Returns Account indicate?

ANSWER: Purchase Returns

QUESTION 76: What does the Debit Balance of a Discount Account indicate?

ANSWER: Discount Allowed

QUESTION 77: What does the Credit Balance of a Discount Account indicate?

ANSWER: Discount Received

QUESTION 78: How would you treat the Wages & Salaries appearing in the Trial Balance while preparing Final Accounts?

ANSWER: Wages & Salaries shall be shown on the debit side of Trading Account.

QUESTION 79: How would you treat the Salaries & Wages appearing in the Trial Balance while preparing Final Accounts?

ANSWER: Salaries & Wages shall be shown on the debit side of Profit & Loss Account.

QUESTION 80. How will you deal with the Drawings appearing in a Trial Balance of a proprietor?

ANSWER: It will be shown by way of deduction from the Capital in the Balance Sheet only and not in the Income Statement.

QUESTION 81. How will you deal with the Income Tax paid appearing in a Trial Balance of a Proprietor?

ANSWER: It will be shown by way of deduction from the Capital in the Balance Sheet only and not in the Income Statement.

QUESTION 82: How do you close a Nominal Account?

ANSWER: A nominal account is closed by transferring it to the Income Statement.

QUESTION 83: How do you close a Manufacturing Account?

ANSWER: A Manufacturing Account is closed by transferring cost of goods manufactured on the debit side of Trading Account.

QUESTION 84: State the Accounting Principles behind making adjustments at the time of preparing the Final Accounts.

ANSWER:

1. Revenue Recognition Principle which requires that generally the revenue should be recognized in the period in which the sale is deemed to have taken place.
2. Matching Principle which requires that the expenses should be recognized in the same period as associated Revenues. Expenses recognition is tied to revenue recognition. Let the Expenses follow the Revenue.

QUESTION 85: What is an 'Adjusting Entry'?

ANSWER: Adjusting Entries are passed in the journal to adjust the unrecorded items like closing stock, depreciation on fixed assets, outstanding and prepaid items into the books of accounts. These are usually needed at the time of preparing the final accounts.

QUESTION 86: What is 'Outstanding Expense'?

ANSWER: Outstanding Expenses refer to those Expenses which have been incurred but not paid during the current accounting period.

QUESTION 87: What is an 'Prepaid Expense'?

ANSWER: Prepaid Expenses refer to those Expenses which have been paid during the current accounting period but the benefit of which will accrue in the subsequent accounting period *or* periods.

QUESTION 88: What is an 'Accrued Income'?

ANSWER: Accrued Income refers to that Income which has been earned but not received during the current accounting period.

QUESTION 89: What is an 'Unaccrued Income'?

ANSWER: Unaccrued Income refers to that Income which has been received but not earned during the current accounting period.

QUESTION 90: How will you deal with the Closing Stock appearing in a Trial Balance of a proprietor?

ANSWER: It will be shown as a Current Asset on the Assets side of the Balance Sheet only and not in the Trading Account.

QUESTION 91: How will you deal with the Outstanding Salary appearing in a Trial Balance of a proprietor?

ANSWER: It will be shown as a Current Liability on the Liabilities side of the Balance Sheet only and not in the Income Statement.

QUESTION 92: How will you deal with the Prepaid Rent appearing in a Trial Balance of a proprietor?

ANSWER: It will be shown as a Current Asset on the Assets side of the Balance Sheet only and not in the Income Statement.

QUESTION 93: How will you deal with the Accrued Interest appearing in a Trial Balance of a proprietor?

ANSWER: It will be shown as a Current Asset on the Assets side of the Balance Sheet only and not in the Income Statement.

QUESTION 94: How will you deal with the Unaccrued Interest appearing in a Trial Balance of a proprietor?

ANSWER: It will be shown as a Current Liability on the Liabilities side of the Balance Sheet only and not in the Income Statement.

QUESTION 95: How will you deal with the Depreciation Account appearing in a Trial Balance of a proprietor?

ANSWER: It will be shown only on the debit side of Profit & Loss Account as a separate item and not in the Balance Sheet.

QUESTION 96: How will you deal with the Bad Debts if no Provision for Doubtful Debts is appearing in the Trial Balance of a Proprietor?

ANSWER: It will be shown only on the debit side of Profit & Loss Account as a separate item and not in the Balance Sheet.

QUESTION 97: How will you deal with the Bad Debts if Provision for Doubtful Debts is appearing in the Trial Balance of a Proprietor?

ANSWER: It will be shown only on the debit side of Provision for Doubtful Debts Account.

QUESTION 98: How will you deal with the Discount Allowed if no Provision for Discount on Debtors is appearing in the Trial Balance of a Proprietor?

ANSWER: It will be shown only on the debit side of Profit & Loss Account as a separate item and not in the Balance Sheet.

QUESTION 99: How will you deal with the Discount Allowed if Provision for Discount on debtors is appearing in the Trial Balance of a Proprietor?

ANSWER: It will be shown only on the debit side of Provision for Discount on Debtors Account.

QUESTION 100: Give the Journal Entry for taking closing stock into account.

ANSWER:

Closing Stock A/c Dr

To Trading A/c

QUESTION 101: Give the Journal Entry for Bad Debts Recovered.

ANSWER:

Cash/Bank A/c Dr

To Bad Debts Recovered A/c

QUESTION 102: Opening Stock ₹ 40,000, Purchases ₹ 3,60,000, Closing Stock ₹ 1,30,000, Net Sales ₹ 3,80,000, Carriage inward ₹ 6,000, Freight inward ₹ 4,000, Wages and salaries ₹ 50,000, Returns inward ₹ 20,000, Returns outward ₹ 40,000. Freight outward ₹ 600. Market value of closing stock was ₹ 1,20,000. Calculate the Gross Profit.

ANSWER: Gross Profit = ₹ 3,60,000 – [₹ 40,000 +₹ 3,60,000 + ₹ 6,000 +₹ 4,000 + ₹ 50,000 – ₹ 40,000 – ₹ 1,20,000] = ₹ 60,000

QUESTION 103: Adjusted Purchases ₹ 6,63,600, Sales ₹ 7,44,000, Cost of Closing Stock ₹ 50,400, Market value of closing stock was ₹ 40,000, Freight & Cartage Inward ₹ 3,600, Wages ₹ 2,400, Freight & Cartage outward ₹ 1,800. Calculate the Gross Profit.

ANSWER Gross Profit = ₹ 7,44,000 – [₹ 6,63,600 + ₹ 3,600 + ₹ 2,400] = ₹ 74,400

QUESTION 104: Cost of Goods Sold ₹ 6,69,600, Sales ₹ 7,44,000, Closing Stock ₹ 50,400. Market value of closing stock was ₹ 40,000. Freight & Cartage Inward ₹ 3,600, Wages ₹ 2,400. Calculate the Gross Profit.

ANSWER: Gross Profit = ₹ 7,44,000 – ₹ 6,69,600 = ₹ 74,400

QUESTION 105: Sales ₹ 1,00,000, Cost of Goods sold ₹ 80,000, Closing stock, ₹ 10,000, Operating expenses ₹ 5,000, freight Inward ₹ 1,000, Freight outward ₹ 3,000. Calculate the Operating Profit.

ANSWER: Operating Profit = ₹ 1,00,000 – ₹ 80,000 – ₹ 5,000 = ₹ 15,000

QUESTION 106: Opening Stock ₹ 1,00,000, Sales ₹ 5,00,000, Gross Profit @ 25% on sales, Purchases ₹ 5,00,000, Calculate the Closing Stock.

ANSWER: Closing Stock = [₹ 1,00,000 + ₹ 5,00,000] – [₹ 5,00,000 × 75%] = ₹ 2,25,000

QUESTION 107: Opening Stock ₹ 1,00,000, Sales ₹ 5,00,000, Gross profit @ 25% on cost, Purchases ₹ 5,00,000. Calculate the Closing Stock.

ANSWER: Closing Stock = [₹ 1,00,000 + ₹ 5,00,000] – [₹ 5,00,000 × 80%] = ₹ 2,00,000

QUESTION 108: H's Trial Balance contains the following information:

Bad debts ₹ 3,000,Discount allowed ₹ 3,000, Provision for discount on debtors ₹ 3,200, Provision for Doubtful Debts ₹ 13,500,Sundry Debtors ₹ 55,000.

Additional Bad Debts ₹ 4,000, Additional Discount allowed ₹ 1,000. At the end of the year, it is desired to maintain a provision for Doubtful Debts at 10% and Provision for Discount on Debtors at 2%. At what figure Sundry Debtors will appear in the Balance Sheet?

ANSWER:

Sundry Debtors = (₹ 55,000 – ₹ 4,000 – ₹ 1,000) – (₹ 50,000 × 10%) – (₹ 45,000 × 2%) = ₹ 44,100

QUESTION 109: H's Trial Balance contains the following information:

Bad debts ₹ 3,000,Discount allowed ₹ 3,000, Provision for discount on debtors ₹ 3,200, Provision for Doubtful Debts ₹ 13,500,Sundry Debtors ₹ 55,000.

Additional Bad Debts ₹ 4,000, Additional Discount allowed ₹ 1,000. At the end of the year, it is desired to maintain a provision for Doubtful Debts at 10% and Provision for Discount on Debtors at 2%. At what figure these items will appear in the Profit & Loss A/c?

ANSWER:

1. Profit & Loss A/c to be cr. with Excess Provision for Doubtful Debts ₹ 1,500
2. Profit & Loss A/c to be dr. with Short Provision for Discount on Debtors ₹ 1,700

QUESTION 110: I's Trial balance contains 12% Bank loan ₹ 40,000, Interest paid ₹ 3,800. At what figure these items will appear in the Profit & Loss A/c?

ANSWER: Profit & Loss A/c to be Dr. with Interest ₹ 4,800,

QUESTION 111: Following are the extracts from the Trial Balance of Mr. Tulsian as at 31st March, 2015:

Particulars	₹	Particulars	₹
Purchases	5,25,000	Sales	6,30,000
Trade Debtors	2,67,000	Capital Account(Opening Balance)	5,19,000
Income Tax Paid	10,000		

Additional Information:

1. **Closing Stock: Cost ₹ 1,50,000,Market Value 80%,Realisable Expenses 5%**
2. **Goods costing ₹ 20,000 (Sale Price ₹ 25,000) were taken by the proprietor for his personal use but not recorded.**
3. **Goods costing ₹ 30,000 (Sale Price ₹ 37,500) were distributed as free samples but not recorded.**
4. **On 31st March Goods costing ₹ 10,000 (Sale Price ₹ 12,500) were destroyed by fire it was fully insured but the insurance company admitted the claim to the extent of 60% only.**
5. **On 31st March, Goods for ₹ 50,000 were sent to a customer on 'Sale *or* Return' basis at a profit of 25% on cost and recorded as actual sales.**

Required: Show how these items will appear in the Financial Statements for the year ended 31st March, 2015

ANSWER:

AN EXTRACT OF TRADING AND PROFIT AND LOSS ACCOUNT OF MR. TULSIAN

Dr. *for the year ended 31st March, 2015* Cr.

Particulars		₹	Particulars		₹
To Purchases *Less:* Goods for personal use *Less:* Free Samples *Less:* Goods destroyed by fire	5,25,000 20,000 30,000 10,000	4,65,000	By Sales *Less:* Goods sent on approval By Closing stock *Add:* Cost of Stock with customer	6,30,000 50,000 1,14,000 40,000	5,80,000 1,54,000
To Loss of Stock by fire		4,000			
To Sales Promotion Expenses		30,000			

AN EXTRACT OF BALANCE SHEET OF MR. TULSIAN AS AT 31ST MARCH, 2015

Liabilities		₹	Assets		₹
Capital Account:			Closing Stock	1,14,000	
Opening Balance	5,19,000		*Add:* Stock with Customers	40,000	1,54,000
Less: Goods for personal use	20,000		Trade Debtors	2,67,000	
Less: Income Tax	10,000	4,89,000	*Less:* Good sent on approval basis	50,000	2,17,000
			Insurance Company (claim)		6,000

QUESTION 112: Following are the extracts from the Trial Balance of Mr. Tulsian as at 31st March, 2015:

Particulars	₹	Particulars	₹
Sales	**6,30,000**	**Provision for Doubtful Debts**	**10,000**
Trade Debtors	**2,67,000**	**Provision for Discount on Debtors**	**1,800**
Bad Debts	**3,000**	**Bad Debt recovered**	**2,500**
Discount Allowed	**2,000**	**Salaries and Wages**	**11,200**

Additional Information:

1. **Closing Stock: Cost ₹ 1,50,000,Market Value 80%,Realisable Expenses 5%**
2. **Write off further ₹ 4,000 as bad. Additional discount of ₹ 1,000 given to debtors. Maintain Provision for discount on Debtors@ 2%. Maintain a Provision for Doubtful debts @ 10%. Debtors also include Shyam for dishonoured bill of ₹ 10,000. Half the amount of Shyam's bills is irrecoverable. Remuneration of ₹ 2,000 paid to Sh. B. Barua, a temporary employee, stands debited to his personal account.**
3. **On 31st March, Goods for ₹ 50,000 were sent to a customer on 'Sale *or* Return' basis at a profit of 25% on cost and recorded as actual sales.**

Required: Show how these items will appear in the Financial Statements for the year ended 31st March, 2015

ANSWER:

AN EXTRACT OF TRADING AND PROFIT AND LOSS ACCOUNT OF MR. TULSIAN

Dr. *for the year ended 31st March, 2015* Cr.

Particulars	₹	Particulars		₹
		By Sales *Less:* Goods sent on approval	6,30,000 50,000	 5,80,000

			By Closing stock	1,14,000	
			Add: Cost of Stock with customer	40,000	1,54,000
To Bad Debts	3,000		By Bad Debt recovered		2,500
Add: Further Bad Debts	4,000				
Add: New Provision	20,000				
Less: Old Provision	10,000	17,000			
To Discount Allowed	2,000				
Add: Further Discount Allowed	1,000				
Add: New Provision	3,600				
Less: Old Provision	1,800	3,800			
To Salaries & Wages	11,200				
Add: Salary to Barua	2,000	13,200			

AN EXTRACT OF BALANCE SHEET OF MR. TULSIAN AS AT 31ST MARCH, 2015

Liabilities	₹	Assets		₹
		Closing Stock	1,14,000	
		Add: Stock with Customers	40,000	1,54,000
		Trade Debtors	2,67,000	
		Less: Good sent on approval basis	50,000	
		Less: Further Bad debts [₹ 4,000 + ₹ 5,000 (Shyam)]	9,000	
		Less: Further Discount Allowed	1,000	
		Less: Salary to Mr B. Barua	2,000	
			2,05,000	
		Less: Provision for doubtful debts @ 10% (on ₹ 2,05,000 – ₹ 5,000)	20,000	
			1,85,000	
		Less: Provision for Discount @ 2% (on ₹ 1,85,000 – ₹ 5,000)	3,600	1,81,400

Note: No provision for discount on Debtors is required on Shyam's balance.

QUESTION 113: Following are the extracts from the Trial Balance of Mr. Tulsian as at 31st March, 2015:

Particulars	₹	Particulars	₹
Building	**60,000**	**Furniture and Fittings**	**30,000**
Plant and Machinery	**2,10,000**	**Wages & Salaries**	**23,500**

Additional Information:

1. **Wages include a sum of ₹ 4,000 spent on the erection of a cycle shed for employees and customers.**
2. **A machine costing ₹ 1,90,000 was purchased on 1st July 2014. Wages₹ 10,000 paid for its erection have been debited to Wages Account.**
3. **A furniture costing ₹ 45,000 was purchased on 1st July 2014 but it was not recorded in the books as no payment was made of it. Wages ₹ 5,000 paid for its erection have been debited to Wages Account.**
4. **Provide for depreciation on Plant & Machinery @ 10% p.a. Write 10% off the Furniture & Fixtures. Depreciate Buildings by 5%.**

Required: Show how these items will appear in the Financial Statements for the year ended 31st March, 2015

ANSWER:

AN EXTRACT OF TRADING AND PROFIT AND LOSS ACCOUNT OF MR. TULSIAN

Dr. *for the year ended 31st March, 2015* Cr.

Particulars		₹	Particulars	₹
To Wages	23,500			
Less: Erection of a Cycle shed	4,000			
Less: Erection of Machine	10,000			
Less: Installation of Furniture	5,000	4,500		
To Depreciation on New Plant & Machinery [₹ 2,00,000 × 10/100 × 9/12]		15,000		
To Depreciation on Old Plant & Machinery [₹ 20,000 × 10/100 × 12/12]		2,000		
To Depreciation on Furniture [₹ 80,000 × 10/100 × 12/12]		8,000		
To Depreciation on Buildings [₹ 64,000 × 5/100 × 12/12]		3,200		

AN EXTRACT OF BALANCE SHEET OF MR. TULSIAN AS AT 31ST MARCH, 2015

Liabilities	₹	Assets		₹
Supplier of Furniture	45,000	**Fixed Assets:**		
		Plant and machinery	20,000	
		Add: Purchased	1,90,000	
		Add: Installation charges	10,000	
		Less: Depreciation	17,000	2,03,000
		Furniture & Fixtures	30,000	
		Add: Purchased	45,000	
		Add: Installation charges	5,000	
		Less: Depreciation	8,000	72,000
		Building	60,000	
		Add: Erection of a cycle shed	4,000	
		Less: Depreciation	3,200	60,800

Note: Depreciation on furniture has been charged for the full year because a flat rate of 10% (and not 10% p.a.) has been given, whereas depreciation on machinery has been charged for 9 months from 1st July to 31st Mar.

PREPARATION OF FINANCIAL STATEMENTS OF NOT-FOR-PROFIT ORGANIZATIONS

QUESTION 1: What is meant by a Not-for-profit organisation?

ANSWER: Not-for-Profit organisations refer to those organisations which:

(a) are formed for the purpose of promoting commerce, art, science, religion, charity *or* any other useful object,

(b) intend to spend their income in promoting their objectives, and
(c) prohibit the payment of any dividend to their members.

QUESTION 2: List any two Examples of Not-for-Profit Organisations.

ANSWER:

1. Govt. Schools
2. Charitable Hospitals,
3. Temples, Churches, Gurudwaras, Masjids
4. Professional Bodies (e.g. The Institute of Chartered Accountants of India, The Institute of Cost Accountants of India, The Institute of Company Secretaries of India).
5. Red Cross Society

QUESTION 3: State any two differences between A Profit seeking organisation and a Not-for-profit organization.

ANSWER:

Basis of Distinction	Profit seeking organisation	Not-for-profit organization
1. Primary Motive	The primary motive of such an entity is to earn profit.	The primary motive of such an entity is to provide services.
2. Owner's Fund Vs. Capital Fund	Interest of owners is known as Owner's Fund which represents the owner's investments *plus* accumulated reserves and surplus.	Interest of members is known as Capital Fund which represents the accumulated surplus of subscriptions, donations and net Income from activities carried on by such an entity.
3. Net Result of activities	The net result of the activities of such an entity is known as the profit/loss.	The net result of the activities of such an entity is known as the surplus/deficit.
4. Accounting Statements	The accounting statements of such type of entity include: (a) a Manufacturing A/c (b) a Trading A/c; (c) a Profit and Loss A/c; (d) a Balance Sheet.	The accounting statements of such an entity includes: (a) a Receipts and Payments A/c; (b) an Income and Expenditure A/c (c) a Trading A/c; (d) a Balance Sheet.

QUESTION 4: List any two books which are generally kept by every not-for-profit organization.

ANSWER:

(1) Cash book with *or* without Analysis Column
(2) Members' Register
(3) Register of Assets

QUESTION 5: List any three major sources of Income of a Not-for-profit organization.

ANSWER:

1. Membership Subscription
2. General Donations
3. Special Donations

QUESTION 6: Do Not-for-profit organisations have trading activities?

ANSWER: Not-for-profit organisations may *or* may not have trading activities. If trading activities are carried on by such entities, then the profit arising therefrom is used for the purposes of promoting the objectives for which such entities were formed. ***For Example***, if a sports club also runs a restaurant, the profit of such a restaurant is used to promote the service objectives. It may be noted that the restriction is on the application of income and not on the earning of income by not-for-profit organisations.

QUESTION 7: What is meant by Receipts & Payments Account?

ANSWER: Receipts & Payments Account is an asset account which shows all receipts and payments (whether Capital *or* Revenue *or* whether relating to previous, current *or* following accounting year) alongwith Cash and Bank Balance in the beginning and at the end of an accounting period.

QUESTION 8: State the basis of accounting on which Receipts & Payments Account is prepared in case of a Not-for-profit organization.

ANSWER: Cash basis of accounting

QUESTION 9: State any one difference between a Receipts & Payments Account and a Cash Book.

ANSWER: The 'Receipts & Payment Account' shows the classified summary of transactions of a Cash Book for a partcular period whereas Cash Book shows the daily cash transactions.

QUESTION 10: State with reason whether Receipts & Payments Account records only those receipts and payments which relate to current accounting period.

ANSWER: Receipts & Payments Account records all Receipts and Payments (Whether Capital *or* Revenue *or* whether relating to previous, current *or* following accounting year).

QUESTION 11: State with reason whether Receipts and Payments Account records all capital receipts and capital payments.

ANSWER: Receipts & Payments Account records all Receipts and Payments (whether Capital *or* Revenue *or* whether relating to previous, current *or* following accounting year).

QUESTION 12: State with reason whether Receipts and Payments Account records all revenue receipts and revenue payments.

ANSWER: Receipts & Payments Account records all Receipts and Payments (whether Capital *or* Revenue *or* whether relating to previous, current *or* following accounting year).

QUESTION 13: State with reason whether Non-cash items are shown in Receipts and Payments Account.

ANSWER: No.Non-cash items (e.g. Depreciation) are not shown in Receipts and Payments Account because these do not involve any cash flow.

QUESTION 14: What is Membership Subscription?

ANSWER: Subscriptions are the amounts paid by the members of such entity to maintain their membership. Subscriptions may be paid periodically (usually on yearly basis) *or* as a lump sum for lifetime membership.

QUESTION 15: State the accounting treatment of Subscription.

ANSWER: These are treated as Revenue Receipts and hence are credited to Income & Expenditure Account.

QUESTION 16: What is Life Membership Subscription?

ANSWER: Life Membership Subscription is a lump sum payment for lifetime membership.

QUESTION 17: State the accounting treatment of Life Membership Subscription.

ANSWER: These are treated as Capital Receipts and hence are added to the Capital Fund in the Balance Sheet

QUESTION 18: What is Entrance Fee?

ANSWER: Entrance Fee (or Admission Fee) is an initial amount payable at the time of seeking admission by a person who intends to become a member of a club, association, *or* society.

QUESTION 19: State the accounting treatment of Entrance Fee.

ANSWER:

1. If treated as a Revenue Receipt and is credited to Income & Expenditure Account.
2. If treated as a Capital Receipt and is added to the Capital Fund in the Balance Sheet.

QUESTION 20: What is meant by Donations?

ANSWER: Donations represent the amount donated by any person (whether member *or* outsider) to the organisation for a general *or* specific purpose.

QUESTION 21: What is meant by Legacies?

ANSWER: Legacies represent the donations which are given under a will on the death of a donor.

QUESTION 22: What is meant by General Donations and Legacies?

ANSWER: General Donations and Legacies refer to those Donations and Legacies which are given without any direction for their use.

QUESTION 23: State the accounting treatment of General Donations and Legacies received during the year.

ANSWER: These donations & legacies are treated as Revenue Receipts and hence, are credited to Income & Expenditure Account.

QUESTION 24: What is meant by Specific Donations and Legacies?

ANSWER: Specific Donations and Legacies refer to those Donations and Legacies which are given for a specific purpose.

QUESTION 25: State the accounting treatment of Specific Donations and Legacies received during the year.

ANSWER: These donations & legacies are treated as capital receipts and hence, are credited to a 'Special Fund Account' (e.g., Prize Fund,Tournament Fund, Building Fund) maintained for the purpose.

QUESTION 26: What does Prize Fund represent?

ANSWER: Prize Fund represents an amount accumulated for meeting Prize Expenses.

QUESTION 27: What does Tournament Fund represent?

ANSWER: Tournament Fund represents an amount accumulated for meeting Tournament Expenses.

QUESTION 28: What does Building Fund represent?

ANSWER: Building Fund represents an amount accumulated for meeting Building Expenses.

QUESTION 29: State the accounting treatment of Interest on Prize Fund Investments received during the year.

ANSWER: Interest on Prize Fund Investments is added to Prize Fund.

QUESTION 30: State the accounting treatment of Prize Expenses incurred during the year if Prize fund is maintained.

ANSWER: Prize Expenses are deducted from Prize Fund.

QUESTION 31: How would you account for the Cost of prizes purchased for distribution if a 'Prize Fund' is not maintained?

ANSWER: Cost of prizes will be debited to Income & Expenditure Account.

QUESTION 32: How would you account for Expenses incurred on Sports Activities if a 'Sports Fund' is maintained?

ANSWER: Sports Activities Expenses will be deducted from Sports Fund.

QUESTION 33: How would you account for Scholarship granted to students out of funds provided by Government?

ANSWER: Scholarship granted will be deducted from Scholarship Fund.

QUESTION 34: How would you account for Donations received for construction of an auditorium by a club?

ANSWER: Donations received for construction of an auditorium by a club are credited to a Auditorium Fund Account.

QUESTION 35: How would you account for the Cost of construction of a building if 'Building Fund' is maintained?

ANSWER: Cost of construction of a building is deducted from 'Building Fund' and is added to Capital Fund.

QUESTION 36: What is meant by an 'Income & Expenditure Account'?

ANSWER: An Income and Expenditure Account is a final account like Profit & Loss Account, which shows the classified summary of revenue incomes, revenue expenses and losses for current accounting period along with surplus (i.e., the excess of income over expenditure) *or* deficit (i.e., excess of expenditure over income) which is transferred to the Capital Fund.

QUESTION 37: State the basis of accounting on which Income & Expenditure Account is prepared in case of a Not-for-profit organization.

ANSWER: Accrual basis of accounting

QUESTION 38: State any two differences between an Income & Expenditure Account and a Profit & Loss Account.

ANSWER:

Basis of Distinction	Income & Expenditure A/c	Profit & Loss A/c
1. Object	The main object of Income and Expenditure Account is to ascertain excess of income over expenditure *or* excess of expenditure over income.	The main object of Profit and Loss Account is to ascertain Net Profit *or* Net Loss.

2. Who prepares?	This account is prepared by non-profit organisations.	This account is prepared by trading institutions.
3. Basis of Preparation	This account is prepared on the basis of Receipts and Payments Account and other information.	This account is prepared on the basis of trial balance.
4. Balance	The balance of this account represents Surplus *or* Deficit	The balance of this account represents Net Profit *or* Net Loss.

QUESTION 39: State any two differences between a Receipts & Payments Account and an Income & Expenditure Account.

ANSWER:

Basis of Distinction	Receipts & Payments A/c	Income & Expenditure A/c
1. Nature of Account	It is a **real** account.	It is a **nominal** account.
2. Period to which items relate	It records the receipts and payments whether they relate to **previous**, **current** or **following** accounting periods.	It records only those incomes, expenses and losses which relate to **current** accounting period.
3. Nature of items recorded—Revenue Vs. Capital.	It records all the receipts and payments **whether of capital or revenue nature.**	It records the incomes, expenditures and losses of **revenue nature.**
4. Non-cash Items	Non-cash items are **not shown** in this account.	Non-cash items such as depreciation, bad debts, etc., are **shown.**
5. Items of Debit side	It is debited with all the **sums received.**	It is debited with the **expenses and losses.**
6. Items of Credit side	It is credited with all the **sums paid out.**	It is credited with the **incomes.**
7. Closing balance	Closing balance represents **cash or bank balance (or bank overdraft) at the end** of the accounting period.	Its closing balance represents either **net surplus or net deficit.**
8. Treatment of closing balance	Its closing balance is **carried forward** in the same account of the **next period.**	Its closing balance is transferred to the **Capital Fund** in the Balance Sheet.
9. Opening balance	Opening balance represents **cash or bank balances (or Bank Overdraft) in the beginning** of the accounting period.	It has **no** opening balance.
10. Basic Structure	It is **basically a summarised Cash Book.**	It is **like a Profit & Loss Account.**
11. Object	It is prepared to present a summary of cash transactions during an accounting period.	It is prepared to ascertain the net results of all the transactions during an accounting period.

QUESTION 40: State the accounting treatment of Interest on General Fund Investments received during the year.

ANSWER: Interest on General Fund Investments is treated as Revenue Receipt and hence is credited to Income & Expenditure Account.

QUESTION 41: State the accounting treatment of Sports Material consumed during the year.

ANSWER: Amount of Sports Material consumed is debited to Income & Expenditure Account.

QUESTION 42: State the accounting treatment of Sale of Old Sports Materials already w/o during the year.

ANSWER: It is credited to Income & Expenditure Account.

QUESTION 43: State with reason whether Income and Expenditure Account records all incomes received and expenditures paid during the current year.

ANSWER: No. Income and Expenditure Account records all Revenue Incomes (whether received *or* not) and Revenue Expenditures (whether paid *or* not) relating to current year only.

QUESTION 44. State with reason whether Income and Expenditure Account records all revenue incomes received and revenue expenditures paid during the current year.

ANSWER: No. Income and Expenditure Account records all Revenue Incomes (whether received *or* not) and Revenue Expenditures (whether paid *or* not) **relating to current year only.**

QUESTION 46. State with reason whether Income and Expenditure Account records all revenue receipts and revenue payments relating to current year.

ANSWER: No. Income and Expenditure Account records all Revenue Incomes (whether received *or* not) and Revenue Expenditures (whether paid *or* not) relating to current year only.

QUESTION 48: State with reason whether Income and Expenditure Account records Revenue Incomes and Revenue Expenditures relating to previous *or* following year.

ANSWER: No. Income and Expenditure Account records all Revenue Incomes (whether received *or* not) and Revenue Expenditures (whether paid *or* not) relating to current year only.

QUESTION 49. State with reason whether Non-Cash items are shown in Income & Expenditure Account.

ANSWER: Yes. Non-Cash items (e.g. Depreciation) are shown in Income & Expenditure Account as per Matching Principle.

QUESTION 50: State any two items which appear in the Receipts & Payments Account but are not shown in the Income & Expenditure Account.

ANSWER:

1. Opening Cash and Bank Balances
2. Closing Cash and Bank Balances
3. Capital Receipts (e.g. Special Donations, Sale Proceeds of Fixed Assets), Entrance Fees and Life Membership Fees to the extent Capitalised)
4. Capital Payments (e.g. Purchase of Fixed Assets)
5. Expenses paid for the previous year(s) *or* following year(s)
6. Incomes received for the previous year(s) *or* following year(s).

QUESTION 51: State any two items which appear in the Income & Expenditure Account but are not shown in the Receipts & Payments Account.

ANSWER:

1. Depreciation
2. Loss on Sale of Asset
3. Outstanding Expenses for the current year

4. Accrued Incomes for the current year
5. Surplus (i.e., Excess of Income over Expenditure)
6. Deficit (i.e., Excess of Expenditure Over Income)

QUESTION 52: What is Fund Based Accounting?

ANSWER:

Meaning	Fund based accounting essentially involves preparation of financial statements fundwise. Separate ledgers are maintained for each fund. Fund ledgers are self-balancing in nature. A fund may be created for purchase, *or* construction of fixed assets *or* for any specific activities of the organisations *or* for both. Not-for-profit organisations, particularly educational institutions, sometimes maintain separate account *or* fund for specific activities of the organisation such as sports prizes, refreshments, and presentation of information in financial statements is made fund wise. In such cases, contribution and donations for specific activities, income from and expenses on those activities are not recorded in Income and Expenditure Account but are directly adjusted in Specific Fund Account.
Example	A Building Fund may be created with a view to purchase, *or* construct buildings. All receipts in connection with the purchase *or* construction of buildings are to be credited to the Building Fund. Any capital expenditure incurred for the purpose of construction *or* acquisition of building is debited to Building Fund. When building is ultimately acquired *or* constructed, the asset is recognised in the General Balance Sheet and consequently that portion of the Building Fund which has been utilised for the acquisition *or* construction of the building is transferred to General Fund. Depreciation on assets can be charged only after its completion *or* acquisition. In the same way, separate funds may be created for equipments, major repairs to fixed assets and for other developmental activities.

QUESTION 53: Explain the accounting treatment of donation received for specific purpose in the case of charitable society.

ANSWER: Donations may have been raised *either* for meeting some revenue *or* capital expenditure; those intended for the first mentioned purpose are credited directly to the income and Expenditure Account but others, if the donors have declared their specific intention, are credited to special fund account and in the absence thereof, to the Capital Fund Account. If any investments are purchased out of a special fund *or* an asset is acquired therefrom, these are disclosed separately. Any income received from such investments *or* any donations collected for a special purpose are credited to an account indicating the purpose and correspondingly the expenditure incurred in carrying out the purpose of the fund is debited to this account. On no account any such expense is charged to the income and Expenditure Account. The term 'Fund' is strictly applicable to the amounts collected for a special purpose when these are invested, e.g. Scholarship Fund, Prize Fund etc. In other cases, when the amounts collected are not invested in securities *or* assets distinguishable from those belonging to the institution, the word "Fund need not be used".

QUESTION 54: How will you deal with the following items while preparing the Income and Expenditure Account for the year ending on 31st December, 2015 and the Balance Sheet as on that date'?

Subscription outstanding as on 31.12.2014: ₹ 9,500 (including ₹ 500 for 2013) Subscription received in advance as on 31.12.2014: ₹ 3,000 (including ₹ 200 for 2016)

Subscription received during 2015: for 2013 ₹ 400, for 2014 ₹ 8,900, for 2015 ₹ 1,34,400, for 2016 ₹ 4,000, for 2017 ₹ 1,200.

Subscription outstanding as on 31.12.2015: ₹ 7,000.

Calculate Subscription Income for the year 2015.

ANSWER

SUBSCRIPTION ACCOUNT

Dr. Cr.

Particulars	₹	Particulars	₹
To Outstanding subscription A/c (Beg.)	9,500	By Advance Subscription A/c (Beg.)	3,000
To Income & Expenditure A/c (b.f.)	1,44,000	By Bank A/c	1,48,900
To Advance Subscription (end)	5,400	By Outstanding Subscription A/c	7,000
	1,58,900		1,58,900

QUESTION 55: How will you show the following items in Income & Expenditure Account for the year ended 31st Dec 2015 and the Opening & Closing Balance Sheets of a Club?

(a) Subscription received (including the ₹ 600 for 2014) ₹ 4,000

(b) Arrears of Subscription: 2014 ₹ 660, 2015 ₹ 800

ANSWER:

INCOME & EXPENDITURE ACCOUNT

for the year ending 31st December, 2015

Dr. Cr.

		By Subscription	4,200

BALANCE SHEET AS AT 31.12.2015

Liabilities	₹	Assets	₹
		Arrears of Subscriptions: 2014 60 2015 800	860

BALANCE SHEET AS AT 31.12.2014

		Arrears of Subscriptions	660

QUESTION 56: How will you show the following items in Income & Expenditure Account for the year ended 31st March 2015 and the Opening & Closing Balance Sheets of a Club?

		31.3.2014	31.3.2015
(a)	Subscription in arrears	₹ 2,000	₹ 1,800
	Subscription in advance	₹ 1,300	₹ 1,100

(b) Subscription received (including ₹ 600 of arrears from previous years) ₹ 21,000

(c) Subscription arrears of previous year written off ₹ 400.

ANSWER:

INCOME & EXPENDITURE ACCOUNT

for the year ended 31st March, 2015

Dr. Cr.

To Subscription (w/o)	400	By Subscription	21,400

BALANCE SHEET AS AT 31.3.2015

Subscription in advance	1,100	Subscription in arrears	1,800

BALANCE SHEET AS AT 31.3.2014

Subscription in advance	1,300	Subscription in arrears	2,000

Working Note:

SUBSCRIPTION ACCOUNT

To O/s Subscription A/c	2,000	By Advance Subscription A/c	1,300
To Income & Expenditure A/c	21,400	By Cash/Bank A/c	21,000
To Advance Subscription A/c	1,100	By Income & Expenditure A/c	400
		By o/s Subscription A/c	1,800
	24,500		24,500

QUESTION 57: How will you disclose the following items in Receipts & Payments Account and Final Accounts of a Club for the year ended 31st March 2015?

	31.3.2014	31.3.2015
Advance Subscription	**₹ 1,500**	**₹ 1,000**
Outstanding subscription	**₹ 3,000**	**₹ 5,000**

The Club had 300 Members on 31st March 2015 as per Register of Members. No fresh members were admitted during the year but 10 members left the club on 1st October, 2014.

Subscription payable – ₹ 15 per month.

ANSWER:

RECEIPTS AND PAYMENTS ACCOUNT

for the year ended 31st March, 2015

Dr. Cr.

To Subscription Received	52,400		

INCOME & EXPENDITURE ACCOUNT

for the year ended 31st March, 2015

Dr. Cr.

	₹		₹
		By Subscriptions for 1st Half year 310 × 15 × 6 = 27,900 for 2nd Half Year 300 × 15 × 6 = 27,000	54,900

BALANCE SHEETS

Liabilities	as at 31.3.2014 ₹	as at 31.3.2015 ₹		as at 31.3.2014 ₹	as at 31.3.2015 ₹
Advance Subscription	1,500	1,000	Outstanding Subscription	3,000	5,000

SUBSCRIPTION ACCOUNT

Dr. Cr.

Particulars	₹	Particulars	₹
To Outstanding Subscription A/c (Beg.)	3,000	By Advance Subscription A/c (Beg.)	1,500
To Income & Expenditure A/c	54,900	By Cash A/c (b.f.)	52,400
To Advance Subscription A/c (end)	1,000	By Outstanding Subscription A/c (end)	5,000
	58,900		58,900

QUESTION 58: How will you show the following items in the Financial Statements Account of a club for the year ended 31st March 2015?

(a) **Rates and Taxes paid ₹ 300, At March 31, 2015, the rates and taxes were prepaid to the following 31st Jan., the yearly charge being ₹ 300.**

(b) **Telephone charges paid ₹ 1,500, A quarter's charge for telephone is outstanding, the amount accrued being ₹ 300. The charge for each quarter is same for both 2013-2014 and 2014-2015.**

ANSWER:

INCOME & EXPENDITURE ACCOUNT FOR THE YEAR ENDED 31ST MARCH, 2015

Dr. Cr.

Expenditure		₹	Income	₹
To Rates & Taxes:				
Paid:	300			
Less: Prepaid at end	250			
Add: Prepaid in beg.	250	300		
To Telephone charges:				
Paid:	1,500			
Less: O/s in beginning (b. f)	600			
Add: O/s at end	300	1,200		

BALANCE SHEET AT 31.3.2015

Liabilities	₹	Assets	₹
O/s Telephone Charges	300	Prepaid Rates & Taxes	250

BALANCE SHEET AT 31.3.2014

Liabilities	₹	Assets	₹
O/s Telephone Charges	600	Prepaid Rates & Taxes	250

QUESTION 59: How will you deal with the following items in the final accounts of a club for the year ended 31st March 2015?

(a) **Entrance Donation received during 2014-2015 ₹ 1,00,000**

(b) **Entrance Donation received pending membership ₹ 1,00,000 as on 1.4.2014**

(c) **A sum of ₹ 20,000 received is October 2014 as Entrance Donation from an applicant was to be refunded as he had not fulfilled the requisite membership qualifications. The refund was made on 3.6.2015.**

(d) **50% of entrance denoation was to be capitalized. There was no pending membership as on 31.3.2015.**

ANSWER:

Particulars	₹
A. Entrance fees received in advance as at beg. of the year	1,00,000
B. *Add:* Entrance fees received during the year	1,00,000
C. *Less:* Entrance fees refundable in respect of ineligible member	20,000
	1,80,000
D. *Less:* 50% capitalized and to be added to Capital Fund	90,000
E. 50% Revenue Income and to be credited to Income & Expenditure A/c	90,000

INCOME & EXPENDITURE ACCOUNT FOR THE YEAR ENDED 31ST MARCH 2015

Dr. Cr.

Expenditure	₹	Income	₹
		By Entrance Donation	90,000

CLOSING BALANCE SHEET AS AT 31.3.2015

Dr. Cr.

Liabilities	₹	Assets	₹
Capital Fund:			
Opening Balance			
+ Entrance Donation	90,000		
Entrance Donation refundable	20,000		

OPENING BALANCE SHEET AS AT 31.3.2014

Liabilities	₹	Assets	₹
Entrance Donation received in advance	1,00,000		

QUESTION 60: Prizes awarded ₹ 2,00,000, Prize Fund as at 31.3.2014 ₹ 12,00,000, Donations for prizes received during the year 2014-2015 ₹ 2,80,000, 10% Prize Fund Investments as at 31.3.2014 ₹ 12,00,000. Interest received on Prize Fund Investments ₹ 60,000. Capital Fund as at 31.32012 ₹ 90,00,000. How will you disclose these items in Balance Sheet as at 31.3.2015?

ANSWER:

AN EXTRACT OF BALANCE SHEET AS AT 31ST MARCH, 2015

Liabilities		₹	Assets	₹
Capital Fund:		90,00,000	10% Prize Fund Investments	12,00,000
Prize Fund:			Accrued Interest on 10%	
Opening Balance	12,00,000		Prize Fund Investments	60,000
Add: Donations	2,80,000		Prize Fund Bank Balance	1,40,000
Add: Interest	1,20,000			
Less: Prizes awarded	(2,00,000)	14,00,000		

QUESTION 61: Expenditure on Building ₹ 2,00,000, Building Fund as at 31.3.2014 ₹ 12,00,000, Donations for building received during the year 2014-2015 ₹ 2,80,000, 10% Building Fund Investments as at 31.3.2014 ₹ 12,00,000. Interest received on Building Fund Investments ₹ 60,000. Capital Fund as at 31.3.2014 ₹ 90,00,000. How will you disclose these items in Balance Sheet as at 31.3.2015?

ANSWER:

AN EXTRACT OF BALANCE SHEET AS AT 31ST MARCH, 2015

Liabilities		₹	Assets	₹
Capital Fund:			Building	2,00,000
Opening Balance	90,00,000		10% Building Fund Investments	12,00,000
Add: Transferred from			Accured Interest on 10%	
Building fund	2,00,000	92,00,000	Building Fund Investments	60,000
Building Fund:			Building Fund Bank Balance	1,40,000
Opening Balance	12,00,000		[₹ 2,80,000 + ₹ 60,000 – ₹ 2,00,000]	
Add: Donations	2,80,000			
Add: Interest	1,20,000			
Less: Transferred to Capital Fund	(2,00,000)	14,00,000		

QUESTION 62: How will you show the following items in Income and Expenditure Account and the Balance Sheets of a club?

(A) TRIAL BALANCE

Particulars	Dr.(₹)	Cr.(₹)
Capital Fund		**15,60,000**
Prize Fund		**2,00,000**
Tournament Fund		**3,00,000**
General Reserve Fund		**2,00,000**
Interest Received on Investments		**77,000**

(b) **Investments were made against the various funds commonly.**

(c) **Prizes awarded ₹ 20,000. Tournament Expenses ₹ 30,000.**

ANSWER:

Dr. **INCOME & EXPENDITURE ACCOUNT** Cr.

Expenditure	₹	Income	₹
		By Interest on Investments [₹ 77,000 × 2,00,000/₹ 7,00,000]	22,000

BALANCE SHEET

Liabilities		₹	Assets		₹
General Reserve Fund:		2,00,000	Investments:		
Prize Fund:			Prize Fund	2,00,000	
Opening Balance	2,00,000		Tournament Fund	3,00,000	
Add: Interest on PFI	22,000		General Fund	2,00,000	7,00,000
Less: Cost Prizes					
awarded	(20,000)	2,02,000			
Tournament Fund:					
Opening Balance	3,00,000				
Add: Interest on TFI	33,000				
Less: Tournament Exp.	(30,000)	3,03,000			

QUESTION 63: How will you deal with the following items in the final accounts of a club?

(a) **Donation received for building and Library Room ₹ 2,00,000.**

(b) **Donation to the extent of ₹ 25,000 were utilized for the purchase of Library Books, balance was still untillized.**

(c) **Depreciation @ 10% p.a. was to be provided for the whole year.**

ANSWER:

Dr. **INCOME & EXPENDITURE ACCOUNT** Cr.

Expenditure	₹	Income	₹
To Depreciation on Books	2,500		

BALANCE SHEET AS AT...

Liabilities	₹	Assets		₹
Capital Fund:		Library Books	25,000	
Opening Balance		*Less:* Depreciation	(2,500)	22,500
Add: T/f from Library Fund	25,000			
Building & Library Fund:				
Donation received	2,00,000			
Less: Utilized & t/f to capital fund	25,000			
	1,75,000			

QUESTION 64: How will you deal with the following items while preparing the Income and Expenditure Account for the year ending on March 31, 2015 and a Balance Sheet as on that date?

	As at 1.4.2014 ₹	As at 31.3.2015 ₹
Amount due to Suppliers of Sports Materials	15,000	9,750
Advances to Suppliers of Sports Materials	5,000	3,750
Stock of Sports Materials	15,000	2,000

During 2014-2015, the payment made to the suppliers of Sports Materials was ₹ 44,000. Cash purchases amounted to 20% of total purchases.

ANSWER:

AN EXTRACT OF INCOME AND EXPENDITURE ACCOUNT

Dr. *for the year ended 31st March, 2015* Cr.

Expenditure	₹	Income	₹
To Sports Materials consumed	63,000		

AN EXTRACT OF BALANCE SHEET AS AT 31ST MARCH, 2015

Liabilities	₹	Assets	₹
Creditors for Sports Materials	9,750	Advance for Sports Materials	3,750
		Stock of Sports Materials	2,000

Working Notes:

Dr. **(I) CREDITORS FOR SPORTS MATERIALS ACCOUNT** Cr.

Particulars	₹	Particulars	₹
To Balance b/d	5,000	By Balance b/d	15,000
To Bank A/c	44,000	By Stock of Sports Materials A/c	40,000
To Balance c/d	9,750	(Credit purchases)	
		(Balancing figure)	
		By Balance c/d	3,750
	58,750		58,750

Dr. **(II) STOCK OF SPORTS MATERIALS ACCOUNT** Cr.

Particulars	₹	Particulars	₹
To Balance b/d	15,000	By Income and Expenditure A/c	
To Creditor for Sports Materials	40,000	(Sports Materials consumed)(B.F)	**63,000**
To Bank A/c (cash purchases)	10,000	By Balance c/d	2,000
[₹ 40,000 × 25%]			
	65,000		65,000

QUESTION 65: Bharat Club provides you the following information:

Stock in Restaurant on 31.3.2014 ₹ 3,900, and on 31.3.2015 ₹ 4,500, Restaurant Takings ₹ 3,61,600, Restaurant Purchases ₹ 2,04,800, Wages (including ₹ 50,000 for Restaurant) ₹ 92,300,

Fuel ₹ 17,700, China Glass Cutlery on 31.3.2014 ₹ 2,500, Depreciation @ 20% is to be provided on China Glass Cutlery. Cost of Boarding Expenses – Restaurant Staff ₹ 20,000, Other Staff ₹ 7,500.

Required: Show how will you deal with the above items while preparing Restaurant Trading Account, Income & Expenditure Account and Balance Sheet.

ANSWER:

RESTAURANT TRADING ACCOUNT

Dr. *for the year ended 31st March, 2015* Cr.

Particulars	₹	Particulars	₹
To Opening Stock	3,900	By Restaurant Takings	3,61,600
To Purchases	2,04,800	By Closing Stock	4,500
To Wages	50,000	By Cost of Boarding Expenses	27,500
To Fuel	17,700		
To Depreciation on China			
Glass Cutlery	500		
To Boarding Exp of Restaurant Staff	20,000		
To Surplus transferred to Income & Expenditure A/c	96,700		
	3,93,600		3,93,600

AN EXTRACT OF INCOME & EXPENDITURE ACCOUNT

Dr. *for the year ended 31st March, 2015* Cr.

Expenditure	₹	Income	₹
To Wages	42,300	By Profit from Restaurant	96,700
To Boarding Exp. of other staff	7,500		

AN EXTRACT OF BALANCE SHEET AS AT 31ST MARCH, 2015

Liabilities	₹	Assets	₹	
		Restaurant Stock		4,500
		China Glass Cutlery	2,500	
		Less: Depreciation @ 20%	(500)	2,000

QUESTION 66: How will you show the following items in final accounts of a club for the year ended 31.3.2015?

Glass cutlery etc. as at 1.4.2014 ₹ 2,000.

Glass cutlery etc. purchased during 2014-2015 ₹ 1,000.

1/5 of the value of Glass cutlery etc. is to be written off in the year of purchases and 1/2 of the balance in each of the next two years. Of the stock of glass, cultery etc. as on 1.4.2014 one half was a year old and the other half two years old.

ANSWER:

INCOME & EXPENDITURE ACCOUNT

Dr. *for the year ended 31st March, 2015* Cr.

To Depreciation on Glass etc.	1,700		

BALANCE SHEET AS AT 31ST MARCH, 2015

Liabilities	₹	Assets		₹
		Glass, Cultery etc.	3,000	
		Less: Depreciation	(1,700)	1,300

Working Note: *Depreciation on glass, cutlery etc. has been calculated as follows:*

On Purchase in 2012 – 2013 (2/5 of 2,500)	1,000
On Purchase in 2013 – 2014 (2/5 of 1,250)	500
On Purchase in 2014 – 2015 (1/5 of 1,000)	200
	1,700

QUESTION 67: How will you treat the following items in final accounts of a club?

(a) Payment for New Car (less Sale Proceeds of Old Car ₹ 6,000 as on 1.4.2014) ₹ 25,200.

(b) Car (as on 1.4.2014) ₹ 24,380

(c) Depreciation on Car (as on 1.4.2014) ₹ 20,580

(d) Rate of Depreciation on car 15% p.a. for the whole year.

ANSWER:

1. Profit on Sale of Car = Sale Proceeds – W.D.V.
   = ₹ 6,000 – (₹ 24,380 – ₹ 20,580) = ₹ 2,200
2. Depreciation on Car = 15% of (₹ 25,200 + ₹ 6,000) = ₹ 4,680

Dr. INCOME & EXPENDITURE ACCOUNT FOR THE YEAR ENDED 31ST MARCH 2015 Cr.

Expenditure	₹	Income	₹
To Dep. on car	4,680	By Profit on Sale of Car	2,200

BALANCE SHEET AS AT 31.3.2015

Liabilities	₹	Assets		₹
		Car	31,200	
		Less: Depreciation	(4,680)	26,520

BALANCE SHEET AS AT 31.3.2014

Liabilities	₹	Assets		₹
		Car	24,380	
		Less: Depreciation	(20,580)	3,800

QUESTION 68: How will you disclose the following items in Receipts and Payments Account for the year ended on 31st March 2015 and Balance Sheet as at 31.3.2014 & 31.3.211?

(a)	**As per Income & Expenditure A/c**	
	Depreciation on Furniture	**₹ 450**
	Profit on Sale of old furniture (on 1.4.2014)	**₹ 1,000**
	Depreciation on Sports Equipment	**₹ 1,000**
(b)	**Furniture as on 1.4.2014**	**₹ 5,000**
	Sport Equipment as on 1.4.2014	**₹ 6,000**
(c)	**New Furniture of ₹ 9,000 was purchased on credit but not entered in books.**	
(d)	**Sports Equipment as on 31.3.2015**	**₹ 9,000**

ANSWER:

Dr. RECEIPTS & PAYMENTS ACCOUNT FOR THE YEAR ENDED 31ST MARCH 2015 Cr.

Receipts	₹	Payments		₹
To Sale of Furniture		By Sports Equipment		
(5,000 + 1,000)	6,000	Depreciation	1,000	
		Closing Balance	9,000	
		Op. balance	(6,000)	4,000

CLOSING BALANCE SHEET AS AT 31.3.2015

Liabilities	₹	Assets		₹
Creditors for Furniture	9,000	Furniture	9,000	
		Less: Depreciation	(450)	8,550
		Sports Equipment		
		Opening Balance	6,000	
		+ Purchases	4,000	
		– Depreciation	(1,000)	9,000

OPENING BALANCE SHEET AS AT 31.3.2014

Liabilities	₹	Assets	₹
		Furniture	5,000
		Sports Equipments	6,000

QUESTION 69: Following are the extracts of Trial Balance as at 31st March, 2015:

Particulars	Dr (₹)	Cr (₹)
Furniture	**40,000**	
Sale of Old Furniture (on 30.9.2014)	**—**	**8,000**

Furniture costing ₹ 15,000 was purchased on 1.10.2014. The Book value of the Furniture sold was ₹ 20,000 on 1.4.2014. Depreciation is to be charged @ 10% p.a. on Furniture.

Required: How will you show the above items in final accounts of a club for the year ended 31st March 2015?

ANSWER:

INCÒME & EXPENDITURE ACCOUNT

Dr. *for the year ended 31st March, 2015* Cr.

To Depreciation Furniture	2,250		
To Loss on Sale of Furniture	11,000		

BALANCE SHEET AS AT 31ST MARCH, 2015

Labilities	₹	Assets		₹
		Furniture	20,000	
		Less: Depreciation	(1,250)	18,750

Since Sale of old furniture for ₹ 8,000 appears in the Trial Balance, if means, no accounting effect has yet been given in respect of Furniture Account.

Opening Balance of furniture as at 1.4.2015 = ₹ 40,000 – ₹ 15,000 = ₹ 25,000

Book Value of Unsold Old Furniture = ₹ 25,000 – ₹ 20,000 = ₹ 5,000

After passing the rectifying entry the Furniture Account will appear as under:

Dr. **FURNITURE ACCOUNT** **Cr.**

Particulars	₹	Particulars	₹
To Balance (Unadjusted given)	40,000	By Depreciation on old furniture	
		(20,000 × 10/100 × 6/12)	1,000
		By Sale of Furniture A/c	8,000
		By Income & Expenditure A/c (Loss)	11,000
		By Depreciation A/c	
		On Old Furniture of ₹ 5,000	500
		On New Furniture of ₹ 15,000	750
		By Balance c/d	18,750
	40,000		40,000

QUESTION 70: If in the previous question no entry has yet been passed for purchase of furniture. How shall your ANSWER be changed?

ANSWER:

INCOME & EXPENDITURE ACCOUNT

Dr. *for the year ended 31st March, 2015* Cr.

To Depreciation on Furniture	3,750		
To Loss on Sale of Furniture	11,000		

BALANCE SHEET AS AT 31ST MARCH, 2015

Liabilities	₹	Assets		₹
		Furniture	35,000	
		Less: Depreciation	(2,750)	32,250

QUESTION 71: How will you treat the following items in the Income & Expenditure Account for the year ended 31st March 2015 and the Opening & Closing Balance Sheet of a Club?

(a) **At 31.3.2014 the club owned the following assets for the number of years indicated.**
Furtniture (12 years old) **₹ 1,000 (Cost)**
Furtniture (5 years old) **₹ 800 (Cost)**

(b) **Furniture purchased on 1.10.2014** **₹ 900**

(c) **Rate of Depreciation on Furniture @ 10% p.a. on original cost.**

ANSWER:

Dr. INCOME & EXPENDITURE ACCOUNT FOR THE YEAR ENDED 31ST MARCH 2015 Cr.

Expenditure		₹	Income	₹
To Depreciation on Furniture:				
on 6 years old	80			
on 1/2 year old	45	125		

BALANCE SHEET AS AT 31.3.2015

Liabilities	₹	Assets		₹
		Furniture		
		13 years old		Nil
		6 years old	800	
		Less: Depreciation	(480)	320
		1/2 years old	900	
		Less: Depreciation	(45)	855

BALANCE SHEET AS AT 31.3.2014

Liabilities	₹	Assets		₹
		Furniture		
		12 years old		Nil
		5 years old	800	
		Less: Depreciation	(400)	400

QUESTION 72: How will you disclose the following items in Receipts and Payment Account for the year ended 31.3.2015 and Balance Sheet as at 31.3.2015?

(a) **Affiliation fees to association as per Income and Expenditure ₹ 1,200.**

(b) **The club was admitted as a member on 1.10.2014 when it paid subscription till 30.9.2015.**

ANSWER:

Dr. RECIPTS AND PAYMENTS ACCOUNT FOR THE YEAR ENDED 31.3.2015 Cr.

		By Affiliation fees	2,400

BALANCE SHEET AS AT 31.3.2015

		Prepaid Affiliation Fees	1,200

QUESTION 73: How will you deal with the following items in the final accounts of a club?

(a) Purchase of investments made ₹ 6,000.

(b) Interest on investments received ₹ 100.

(c) 8% interest has accrued on investments for 5 months.

ANSWER:

Dr. **INCOME & EXPENDITURE ACCOUNT** **Cr.**

Expenditure	₹	Income	₹
		By Interest on Investments	
		Received + Accrued	300
		[100 + (6,000 × 8% × 5/12)]	

CLOSING BALANCE SHEET AS AT...

Liabilities	₹	Assets	₹
		Investments	6,000
		Accrued Interest	200

QUESTION 74: How will you deal with the following items in the final accounts of a club? Purchase of Books and Periodicals (including ₹ 19,000 for purchase of books) ₹ 29,000. Rate of Depreciation on Books 10%.

ANSWER:

Dr. **INCOME & EXPENDITURE ACCOUNT** **Cr.**

Expenditure	₹	Income	₹
To Periodicals (29,000–19,000)	10,000		
To Dep. on Books	1,900		

CLOSING BALANCE SHEET AS AT...

Liabilities	₹	Income		₹
		Books	19,000	
		Less: Dep.	(1,900)	17,100

QUESTION 75: How will you deal with the following items in the final accounts of a club? Payment for Billiard Table during current year ₹ 8,000. Billiard Table costing ₹ 30,000 was purchased during the last year and ₹ 22,000 was paid for it.

ANSWER:

OPENING BALANCE SHEET AS AT...

Liabilities	₹	Assets	₹
Creditors for Billiard Table	8,000	Billiard Table	30,000

CLOSING BALANCE SHEET AS AT...

Liabilities	₹	Assets	₹
		Billiard Table	30,000

QUESTION 76: The following is the extract of Receipts and Payments Account for the year ended 31st March, 2015.

Receipts	₹	Payments	₹
		By Postage Expenses	200

Unused Stamps as on 31.3.2014 ₹ 50 and on 31.3.2015 ₹ 25.

Required: How will you show the above items in final accounts of a club for the year ended?

ANSWER:

INCOME & EXPENDITURE ACCOUNT

Dr. *for the year ended 31st March, 2015* Cr.

To Postage Expenses:				
Cash	200			
Add: Stamps in beg.	50			
Less: Stamps at end	(25)	225		

BALANCE SHEET AS AT 31ST MARCH, 2015

Liabilities	₹	Assets	₹
		Postage Stamps	25

QUESTION 77: The following is the extract of Receipts and Payments Account for the year ended 31st March, 2015.

Receipts	₹	Payments	₹
To Balance b/d:		By Postage Expenses	200
Stamps	50	By Balance c/d:	
		Stamps	25

Required: How will you show the above items in final Accounts of a club for the year ended 31st March 2015?

ANSWER:

INCOME & EXPENDITURE ACCOUNT

Dr. *for the year ended 31st March, 2015* Cr.

To Postage Expenses:				
Cash	175			
Stamps used (50 – 25)	25	200		

BALANCE SHEET AS AT 31ST MARCH, 2015

Liabilities	₹	Assets	₹
		Postage Stamps	25

QUESTION 78: How will you deal with the following items in the Opening & Closing Balance Sheets of a club?

	1.4.2014	31.3.2015
Bank Balance	**₹ 16,760**	**₹ 6,920**
Cheques issued but not presented for payment for printing	**₹ 180**	**₹ 60**

ANSWER:

BALANCE SHEET AS AT 31.3.2014

Liabilities	₹	Assets	₹
		Bank Balance	16,760

BALANCE SHEET AS AT 31.3.2015

Liabilities	₹	Assets	₹
		Bank Balance	6,920

Note: No adjustment has been made for cheques issued but not yet presented because bank balances as per cash book are given.

QUESTION 79: How will you deal with the following items in the final accounts of a club?

	1.4.2014	31.3.2015
Bank Balance as per Pass Book	**₹ 16,760**	**₹ 6,920**
Cheques issued but not presented for payment for printing	**₹ 180**	**₹ 60**

ANSWER:

BALANCE SHEET AS AT 31.3.2014

Liabilities	₹	Assets	₹
		Bank Balance	16,580

BALANCE SHEET AS AT 31.3.2015

Liabilities	₹	Assets	₹
		Bank Balance	6,860

QUESTION 80: Following is the Receipts & Payments Accounts for the year ended 31st March, 2015.

Receipts	₹	Payments	₹
To Balance as per Pass Book	**8,230**	**By Honorarium of Secretary**	**4,800**
To Cash Overspent	**20**	**By Printing & Stationary**	**470**
		By Balance as per Pass Book	**3,480**

Unpresented cheques being payment on printing on 1.4.2014 ₹ 90, and on 31.3.2015 ₹ 30.

Cash Overspent represents amount of honorarium to the treasurer not drawn due to shortage of fund. But the total salary payable to him for the year was already included in ₹ 4,800.

Required: How will you show the above items in final accounts of a club for the year ended 31st March, 2015?

ANSWER:

INCOME & EXPENDITURE ACCOUNT

Dr. *for the year ended 31st March, 2015* Cr.

Expenditure		₹	Income	₹
To Honorarium to Secretary		4,800		
To Printing & Stationary				
Paid as per Pass Book	470			
Add: Unpresented				
Ch. at end	30			
Less: Unpresented				
Ch. at beg.	(90)	410		

BALANCE SHEET AS AT 31ST MARCH, 2015

Liabilities	₹	Assets		₹
Outstanding Liabilities for	20	Bank Balance as per Cash Balance		
Honorarium of Secretary		as per Pass Book	3,480	
		Less: Unpresented ch. at end	(30)	3,450

PREPARATION OF FINANCIAL STATEMENTS UNDER SINGLE ENTRY SYSTEM

QUESTION 1: What is meant by incomplete accounting records?

ANSWER: Incomplete accounting records are those accounting records which, at present, are not complete according to double entry principles.

QUESTION 2: State any two reasons for maintaining incomplete records.

ANSWER:

1. The businessman may be ignorant of the separate legal entity assumption;
2. The businessman may be ignorant of the double entry accounting principles;
3. The businessman may not intentionally maintain proper accounts to evade taxation;
4. Destruction of the books of accounts due to fire, flood etc.

QUESTION 3: State any two defects *or* limitations of incomplete records.

ANSWER:

1. Arithmetical accuracy of the accounts can not be checked because no agreed trial balance can be prepared.
2. True profits/losses can not be ascertained because Trading and Profit & Loss Account cannot be prepared.
3. True financial position cannot be ascertained because Balance Sheet cannot be prepared.
4. It is difficult to conduct the audit of such records.
5. It is difficult to operate internal control system.
6. It is difficult to operate internal check system.

7. It is difficult to exercise control over assets.
8. It is difficult to detect fraud.
9. Such records are not recognised by the Courts, Sales Tax and Income Tax Authorities.

QUESTION 4: Give two points of difference between Single Entry System and Double Entry System.

ANSWER:

Basis of Distinction	Double Entry System	Single Entry System
1. Assumptions and principles	It is based on certain assumptions and principles.	It is not based on certain assumptions and principles.
2. Both aspects of all transactions	Both the aspects of all transactions are recorded.	Both the aspects of all transactions are not recorded.
3. Nature of accounts maintained	All types of accounts—Personal, Real & Nominal, are maintained.	Usually, Cash and Personal accounts are maintained.
4. Trial Balance	Arithmetical accuracy of the records cannot be checked since Trial Balance cannot be prepared.	Arithmetic accuracy of the records cannot be checked since Trial Balance cannot be prepared.

QUESTION 5: Enumerate the names of two methods of ascertaining profit *or* loss from incomplete records.

ANSWER:

1. Statement of Affairs Method
2. Final Accounts Method

QUESTION 6: What is meant by a Statement of Affairs?

ANSWER: Statement of Affairs which looks like a Balance Sheet is prepared on the basis of some ledger Accounts and estimates.

QUESTION 7: How can Opening capital be ascertained from incomplete records?

ANSWER: Opening Capital can be ascertained by preparing a Statement of Affairs at the beginning of the accounting period.

QUESTION 8: How can Closing Capital be ascertained from incomplete records?

ANSWER: Closing Capital can be ascertained by preparing a Statement of Affairs at the end of the accounting period.

QUESTION 9: Give two points of difference between Statement of Affairs and a Balance Sheet.

ANSWER:

Basis of Distinction	Statement of Affairs	Balance Sheet
1. Basis of preparation	It is prepared on the basis of some ledger accounts and estimates.	It is prepared on the basis of ledger accounts.
2. Balance of Capital Account	Balance of Capital Account is arrived at as a balancing figure.	Balance of Capital Account is taken from the ledger

3. Omission ofAssets/ Liabilities	Omission of an asset *or* liability cannot traced.	Omission of an asset *or* liability can be be easily traced because of non-agreement of both the sides of Balance Sheet.
4. Estimated Vs True Financial Position	It shows only the estimated financial position.	It shows the true financial position.

QUESTION 10: Give a format of Statement of Affairs.

ANSWER:

STATEMENT OF AFFAIRS OF... AS AT...

Liabilities	₹	Assets	₹
Sundry Creditors	xxxx	Cash in Hand	xxxx
Bills Payable	xxxx	Cash at Bank	xxxx
Outstanding Expenses	xxxx	Sundry Debtors	xxxx
Bank Overdraft	xxxx	Bills Receivable	xxxx
Capital (Balancing figure)	xxxx	Stock in trade	xxxx
		Prepaid Expenses	xxxx
		Fixed Assets	xxxx
	xxxx		xxxx

QUESTION 11: How can the profit *or* loss of a trader be ascertained with the help of a Statement of Affairs?

ANSWER:

Step 1: Ascertain Closing Capital by preparing a Statement of Affairs at the end of the accounting period.

Step 2: *Add:* the Amount of Drawings (whether in cash *or* in kind) to the Closing Capital (calculated as per Step 1).

Step 3: Deduct the Amount of Additional Capital introduced from the Closing Capital (calculated as per Step 1).

Step 4: Ascertain Opening Capital by preparing a Statement of Affairs at the beginning of the accounting period.

Step 5: Ascertain Profits *or* Loss by deducting Opening Capital from the Adjusted Closing Capital.

Note: Adjusted Closing Capital = Closing Capital + Drawings – Additional Capital.

Step 6: Make Adjustment for items not yet adjusted while calculating Closing Capital e.g., Depreciation, Outstanding/Prepaid Expenses, Provision for Doubtful Debts Interest on Capital and Salary of the proprietor *or* partner(s).

QUESTION 12: On 1.7.2014, Nikita Mittal commenced her business with ₹ 5,00,000. On 1.10.2014 she sold her private investments (Cost ₹ 50,000, Face value ₹ 40,000) at 125% of face value and brought the proceeds into her business. Her drawings were ₹ 1,000 p.m. Goods costing ₹ 11,000 were taken by her for personal use. On 31.3.2015, Capital before adjustments ₹ 7,00,000, Outstanding Expenses ₹ 21,000 and Prepaid Expenses ₹ 4,000.Provide Interest on Capital @ 12% p.a and for group incentive to staff @5% on Net Profit after charging such incentive and interest on capital. Calculate the Profit/Loss for the year ended 31st March,2015.

ANSWER:

STATEMENT OF PROFIT OR LOSS FOR THE YEAR ENDING ON 31.3.2015

	Particulars				₹
A.	Capital at the end				7,00,000
B.	*Add:* Drawings during the year [Cash (₹ 1,000 × 9) + Goods of ₹ 11,000]				20,000
C.	*Less:* Additional capital introduced during the year [₹ 40,000 + 25% of ₹ 40,000]				(50,000)
D.	Adjusted Capital at the end (A + B – C)				6,70,000
E.	*Less:* Capital in the beginning				(5,00,000)
F.	Profit subject to adjustments (D – E)				1,70,000
G.	*Less:*	Adjustments			
		Outstanding Expenses		(21,000)	
		Prepaid Expenses		4,000	
		Interest on Capital			
		(12% × 5,00,000 × 9/12)	45,000		
		(12% × 50,000 × 6/12)	3,000	(48,000)	65,000
H.	Net Profit before Group Commission for the year [F – G]				1,05,000
I.	*Less:* Group Commission [₹ 1,05,000× 5/105]				(5,000)
J.	Net Profit [H – I]				1,00,000

QUESTION 13: Calculate Cash Sales, Gross Credit Sales, Cash Purchases and Gross Credit Purchases from the following information:

(a) Uniform Rate of Gross Profit – 20%.

(b) Gross Profit for the year ended 31.03.2014 – ₹ 80,000.

(c) Cash Sales 33-1/3% of Net Credit Sales, Sales Returns – 1/7th of Gross Credit Sales.

(d) Cash Purchases – 20% of Net Credit Purchases, Purchases. Returns 1/7th of Gross Credit Purchases.

(e) His sales for the year ended 31st March, 2015 were 20% higher than the previous year's.

(f) On 1st April, 2014 the stock level was raised by ₹ 48,000 and stock was maintained at this new level all throughout the year.

(g) Stock as at 31.3.2014 ₹ 60,000

ANSWER:

1. **Calculation of Cash Sales and Credit Sales during the current year:**	₹
A. Previous year's Total Sales (Gross Profit/GP Ratio) (₹ 80,000/.20)	4,00,000
B. *Add:* Increase in Sales during current year @ 20%	80,000
C. Current year's Total Sales (A + B)	4,80,000
D. *Less:* Cash Sales @ 25% of Net Sales (₹ 4,80,000 × 25%)	1,20,000
E. Net Credit Sales (C – D)	3,60,000
F. *Add:* Sales Returns (₹ 3,60,000 × 1/6)	60,000
G. Gross Credit Sales (E + F)	4,20,000

2. **Calculation of Cash and Credit Purchases during the current year:**	₹
A. Current year's Total Sales	4,80,000
B. *Less:* Gross Profit @ 20%	96,000
C. Cost of Goods Sold (A – B)	3,84,000
D. *Add:* Closing Stock	1,08,000
E. *Less:* Opening Stock	60,000
F. Total Purchases (C + D – E)	4,32,000
G. *Less:* Cash Purchases (₹ 4,32,000 × 1/6)	72,000
H. Net Credit Purchases	3,60,000
I. *Add:* Purchase Returns (₹ 3,60,000 × 1/6)	60,000
J. Gross Credit Purchases	4,20,000

QUESTION 14: Calculate Cash Sales, Gross Credit Sales, Cash Purchases and Gross Credit Purchases from the following information:

1. **Uniform Rate of Gross Profit – 20%.**
2. **Terms of Credit: Debtors – 2 months.**
3. **Cash Sales 33-1/3% of Net Credit Sales, Sales Returns – 1/7th of Gross Credit Sales.**
4. **Cash Purchases – 20% of Net Credit Purchases, Purchases Returns 1/7th of Gross Credit Purchases.**
5. **His sales for the year ended 31st March, 2015 were 20% higher than the previous year's.**
6. **On 1st April, 2014 the stock level was raised by ₹ 48,000 and stock was maintained at this new level all throughout the year.**
7. **Stock as at 31.3.2014 ₹ 60,000, Trade Debtors as on 31.03.2014: ₹ 50,000.**

ANSWER:

1. **Calculation of Cash Sales, Credit Sales and Closing Debtors during the current year:**	₹
A. Previous year's credit sales (Closing debtors × 12/2) (₹ 50,000 × 12/2)	3,00,000
B. *Add:* Previous year's Cash Sales (₹ 3,00,000 × 1/3)	1,00,000
C. Previous year's Total Sales [A + B]	4,00,000
D. *Add:* Increase in sales during current year @ 20%	80,000
E. Current year's total sales [C + D]	4,80,000
F. *Less:* Cash Sales @ 25% [₹ 4,80,000 × 25%]	1,20,000
G. Net Credit Sales [E – F]	3,60,000
H. *Add:* Sales Returns [₹ 3,60,000 × 1/6]	60,000
I. Gross Credit Sales [G + H]	4,20,000
J. Closing Debtors [Net Credit Sales × 2/12] (₹ 3,60,000 × 2/12)	60,000
2. **Calculation of Cash and Credit Purchases during the current year:**	₹
A. Current year's Total Sales	4,80,000
B. *Less:* Gross Profit @ 20%	96,000
C. Cost of Goods Sold (A – B)	3,84,000
D. *Add:* Closing Stock	1,08,000
E. *Less:* Opening Stock	60,000

F. Total Purchases (C + D – E)	4,32,000
G. *Less:* Cash Purchases (₹ 4,32,000 × 1/6)	72,000
H. Net Credit Purchases	3,60,000
I. *Add:* Purchase Returns (₹ 3,60,000 × 1/6)	60,000
J. Gross Credit Purchases	4,20,000

QUESTION 15: Calculate Cash Sales, Gross Credit Sales, Cash Purchases and Gross Credit Purchases from the following information:

1. **Uniform Rate of Gross Profit – 20%.**
2. **Terms of Credit: Creditors – 1 month.**
3. **Cash Sales 25% of Net Credit Sales, Sales Returns – 1/7th of Gross Credit Sales.**
4. **Cash Purchases – 20% of Net Credit Purchases, Purchases Returns 1/7th of Gross Credit Purchases.**
5. **His sales for the year ended 31st March, 2015 were 20% higher than the previous year's.**
6. **On 1st April, 2014 the stock level was raised by ₹ 48,000 and stock was maintained at this new level all throughout the year.**
7. **Stock as at 31.3.2013 ₹ 60,000. Stock as at 31.3.2014 ₹ 60,000. Trade Creditors as on 31.03.2014: ₹ 25,000.**

ANSWER:

1. **Calculation of Cash Purchases, Credit Purchases and Closing Creditors during the current year:**	₹
A. Previous year's credit purchases (Closing creditors × 12/1) (₹ 25,000 × 12/1)	3,00,000
B. *Add:* Previous year's Cash Purchases (₹ 3,00,000 × 20%)	60,000
C. Previous year's Total Purchases [A + B]	3,60,000
D. *Add:* Opening Stock	60,000
E. *Less:* Closing Stock	60,000
F. Cost of goods Sold	3,60,000
G. *Add:* Gross Profit @ 25%	90,000
H. Total Sales for previous year	4,50,000
I. *Add:* Increase in Sales @ 20%	90,000
J. Current Year's Total sales	5,40,000
K. *Less:* Cash sales @ 25%	1,08,000
L. Net Credit Sales	4,32,000
M. *Add:* Sales Returns	72,000
N. Gross Credit Sales	5,04,000
2. **Calculation of Cash Purchases, Credit Purchases and Closing Creditors**	
A. Total Sales	5,40,000
B. *Less:* G.P.	1,08,000
C. Cost of goods sold	4,32,000
D. *Add:* Closing stock	1,08,000
E. *Less:* Opening stock	60,000

F. Current year's total Purchases	4,80,000
G. *Less:* Cash Purchases	80,000
H. Net Credit Purchases	4,00,000
I. Closing Creditors (4,00,000 × 1/12)	33,333.33

QUESTION 16: Calculate Cash Sales, Gross Credit Sales, Cash Purchases and Gross Credit Purchases from the following information:

1. **Stock as on 1st April 2013 was ₹ 20,000.**
2. **Rate of Gross Profit – No Change.**
3. **Terms of Credit: Debtors – 2 months, Creditors – 1 month.**
4. **Cash Sales % of Net Credit Sales, Sales Returns – 1/7th of Gross Credit Sales.**
5. **Cash Purchases – 20% of Net Credit Purchases, Purchases. Returns 1/7th of Gross Credit Purchases.**
6. **His sales for the year ended 31st March, 2015 were 20% higher than the previous year's.**
7. **On 1st April, 2014 the stock level was raised by ₹ 48,000 and stock was maintained at this new level all throughout the year.**
8. **Trade Debtors as on 31.03.2014: ₹ 50,000.**
   Trade Creditors as on 31.03.2014: ₹ 25,000.
   Stock as at 31.3.2014: ₹ 60,000

ANSWER:

1. **Calculation of Gross Profit Ratio during Previous Year**	₹
A. Credit Sales[₹ 50,000 × 12/2]	3,00,000
B. Cash Sales[₹ 3,00,000 × 1/3%]	1,00,000
C. Total Sales [A + B]	4,00,000
D. Credit Purchases [₹ 25,000 × 12/1]	3,00,000
E. Cash Purchases [₹ 3,00,000 × 20%]	60,000
F. Total Purchases [D + E]	3,60,000
G. *Add:* Opening Stock	20,000
H. *Less:* Closing Stock	(60,000)
I. Cost of Goods sold [F + G – H]	3,20,000
J. Gross Profit [C – I]	80,000
K. Gross Profit Ratio [(Gross Profit/Sales) × 100]	20%
2. **Calculation of Cash & Credit Sales and Closing Debtors during Current Year**	
A. Total Sales during Previous Year	4,00,000
B. *Add:* Increase in volume @20%	80,000
C. Total Sales during Current Year	4,80,000
D. Cash Sales [₹ 4,80,000 × 25%]	1,20,000
E. Credit Sales [C – D]	3,60,000
F. Closing Debtors [₹ 3,60,000 × 12/2]	60,000
3. **Calculation of Cash & Credit Purchases and Closing Creditors during Current Year**	

A. Total Sales during Current Year	4,80,000
B. *Less:* Gross Profit	96,000
C. Cost of Goods sold during Current Year	3,84,000
D. *Less:* Opening Stock	(60,000)
E. *Add:* Closing Stock	1,08,000
F. Total Purchases during Current Year	4,32,000
G. *Less:* Cash Purchases [₹ 4,32,000/6]	(72,000)
H. Credit Purchases	3,60,000
I. Closing Creditors [₹ 3,60,000 × 12/1]	30,000

QUESTION 17: Opening B/R nil, Closing B/R ₹ 5,000. During the year, of the Bills drawn (₹ 1,00,000).

(a) Some bills were endorsed in favour of creditors. Out of these endorsed bills, bills for ₹ 25,000 were dishonoured.

(b) Bills amounting to ₹ 25,000 were discounted at a discount of 2% of which a bill for ₹ 12,500 was dishonoured.

(c) Out of these dishonoured bills, drawees of bills of ₹ 18,750 became insolvent and paid 50% only by means of a bank draft.

(d) Bills amounting to ₹ 10,000 were discharged by drawees before maturity at a rebate of 2% by means of a bank draft.

(e) Bills amounting to ₹ 10,000 were collected at maturity by means of bank draft.

Required: Prepare Bills Receivable Account.

ANSWER:

Dr. **BILLS RECEIVABLE ACCOUNT** Cr.

Particulars	₹	Particulars	₹
To Debtors A/c (B/R Drawn)	1,00,000	By Creditors A/c (Endorsed B/R) (b.f.)	50,000
		By Bank A/c	24,500
		By Discounting Charges A/c	500
		By Bank A/c	9,800
		By Rebate Allowed	200
		By Bank A/c	10,000
		By Balance c/d	5,000
	1,00,000		1,00,000

ACCOUNTING FOR PARTNERSHIP – FUNDAMENTALS

QUESTION 1: What is Partnership?

ANSWER: According to Sec. 4 of The Indian Partnership Act, 1932, the term 'Partnership' is "the relation between two *or* more persons who have agreed to share the profits of a business carried on by all *or* any of them acting for all."

QUESTION 2: List any two characteristics of a partnership.

ANSWER:

1. At least two persons
2. Agreement
3. Business
4. Sharing of Profits
5. Mutual Agency.

QUESTION 3: What is meant by the term 'Firm'?

ANSWER: The persons who have entered into a partnership with one another are collectively called a 'Firm'.

QUESTION 4: What is meant by the term 'Firm Name'?

ANSWER: The name under which the business of the firm is carried on is called the 'Firm Name'.

QUESTION 5: What is meant by the term 'Partners'?

ANSWER: The persons who have entered into a partnership with one another are individually called 'Partners'.

QUESTION 6: What is the maximum limit of partners in case of a partnership for a banking business?

ANSWER: 50

QUESTION 7: What is the maximum limit of partners in case of a partnership for a non-banking business?

ANSWER: 50

QUESTION 8: State the nature of liability of Partners.

ANSWER: Joint & Several i.e. Partners are liable for firm's debts jointly with other partners and also individually in their own capacity. Net Private Assets of a Partner (i.e. Private Assets – Private Debts) can be used to pay off Firm's Debts in case Firm's Assets are less than Firm's Debts. Thus, Partners have Unlimited Liability.

QUESTION 9: What is meant by Unlimited Liability of a partner?

ANSWER: Unlimited Liability of a partner means that Partners are liable for firm's debts jointly with other partners and also individually in their own capacity. Net Private Assets of a Partner (i.e. Private Assets – Private Debts) can be used to pay off Firm's Debts in case Firm's Assets are less than Firm's Debts.

QUESTION 10: X and Y jointly purchased a building and contributed capital equally to convert the building into a hotel. They let it out on a rent of ₹ 1,00,000 per annum and share the rental income equally. State giving reason whether X and Y are partners.

ANSWER: X and Y are regarded as co-owners and not partners.

Reason: X and Y do not have mutual agency relationship.

QUESTION 11: Is a Sleeping Partner liable to the acts of other partners?

ANSWER: Yes, A Sleeping Partner is liable to the acts of other partners because of mutual agency relationship.

QUESTION 12: Would a "charitable dispensary" run by 8 members be deemed a partnership firm? Give reason in support of your answer.

ANSWER: 'Charitable dispensary' run by 8 members cannot be deemed a partnership because: there is n*either* business nor sharing of profits.

QUESTION 13: The following differences have arisen among X, Y and Z. State who is correct in each case:

(a) X used ₹ 3,00,000 belonging to the firm and made a profit of 50%, Y and Z want that X should return ₹ 4,50,000 to the firm but X wants to return ₹ 3,00,000 only.

(b) Y used ₹ 3,00,000 belonging to the firm and suffered a loss of ₹ 1,00,000. He wants to return ₹ 2,00,000 only.

(c) X and Y want to purchase goods from W. Z does not agree?

(d) Y and Z want to admit W as partner. X does not agree?

ANSWER:

(a) X must pay ₹ 4,50,000 because every partner has duty to pay to the firm the personal profits earned by him from the use of firm's property.

(b) Y must pay ₹ 3,00,000 because every partner has duty to bear the personal loss incurred by him from the use of firm's property.

(c) Goods may be purchased from W because every partner has an implied authority to purchase and sell the Goods.

(d) W cannot be admitted as a partner because every partner has the right to prevent the admission of a new partner without the consent of all the existing partners [Sec. 31].

QUESTION 14: What is 'Partnership Deed'?

ANSWER: 'Partnership Deed' is a written document which contains the terms and conditions of partnership agreed upon by all the partners. The deed is required to be duly signed by all the partners.

QUESTION 15: List any two contents of a Partnership Deed.

ANSWER: 1. Name of Firm, 2. Names and Addresses of all partners, 3. Name and Place of business, 4. Date of Commencement of Partnership, 5. Capital Contribution of each partner.

QUESTION 16: Is it essential to have an agreement to form a partnership?

ANSWER: Yes. An agreement is one of the essential elements of a partnership as per Sec. 4 of The Indian Partnership Act, 1932.

QUESTION 17: Is it essential to have an agreement in writing to form a partnership?

ANSWER: No since an agreement to form a partnership may be implied *or* express (Oral *or* written).

QUESTION 18: Why is it necessary to have Partnership Deed?

OR

What advantages does a firm perceive in having a partnership deed?

ANSWER:

1. To Settle the dispute and misunderstanding with regard to the terms and conditions of partnership
2. To regulate the Rights, Duties and Liabilities of each Partner.

QUESTION 19: State two elements of the partnership deed.

ANSWER: Two elements of partnership deed are:

1. It is a written document containing the terms and conditions agreed upon by all the partners.
2. In case of any misunderstanding *or* dispute among the partners it acts as an evidence in the court of law.

QUESTION 20: X and Y are partners in a firm having no partnership deed. X and Y have contributed ₹ 1,00,000 and ₹ 2,00,000 respectively as capitals. Y wants that profit should be distributed in the ratio of capitals but X does not agree to this. State giving reason who is correct in this case.

ANSWER: X is correct. Reason: In the absence of partnership deed Profits are to be shared equally.

QUESTION 21: X and Y are partners in a firm having no partnership deed. Y has advanced ₹ 10,000 as loan to the firm. He claims interest at the usual interest charged by banks. The rate of interest is 13% p.a. X does not want to give any interest. State giving reason who is correct in this case.

ANSWER: Both X and Y are not correct. Reason: In the absence of partnership deed a partner who has provided loan to firm, is entitled to claim an interest on his loan @ 6% p.a. Hence, Y is entitled to claim an interest on his loan of ₹ 10,000 @ 6% p.a.

QUESTION 22: X and Y are partners in a firm having no partnership deed. Y has advanced ₹ 10,000 as loan to the firm. He claims interest at the rate of 6% p.a. X does not want to give any interest since there is a Net Loss of ₹ 50,000 during the current year. State giving reason who is correct in this case.

ANSWER: Y is correct. Reason: In the absence of partnership deed a partner who has provided loan to firm, is entitled to claim an interest on his loan @ 6% p.a. even in case of losses. Hence, Y is entitled to claim an interest on his loan of ₹ 10,000 @ 6% p.a.

QUESTION 23: X and Y are partners in a firm having no partnership deed. X spends twice the time that Y devotes to business. X claims that he should get a salary of ₹ 6,000 per month for his extra time spent. Y does not want to give any salary. State giving reason who is correct in this case.

ANSWER: Y is correct. Reason: In the absence of partnership deed a partner is not entitled to claim any remuneration. Hence, X is not entitled to any salary.

QUESTION 24: X and Y are partners in a firm having no partnership deed. X and Y have contributed ₹ 1,00,000 and ₹ 5,00,000 respectively as capitals. Y claims interest @ 6%p.a. on excess capital of ₹ 4,00,000. X does not want to give any interest. State giving reason who is correct in this case.

ANSWER: X is correct. Reason: In the absence of partnership deed a partner is not entitled to claim any interest on his capital.

QUESTION 25: X and Y are partners in a firm having no partnership deed. X made a drawing of ₹ 10,000. Y wants that an interest @ 6% p.a. should be charged on X's drawings of ₹ 10,000 but X does not agree to this. State giving reason who is correct in this case.

ANSWER: X is correct. Reason: In the absence of partnership deed no Interest is to be charged on Drawings of a partner.

QUESTION 26: X and Y are partners in a firm having no partnership deed. X desires that Y should not participate in the conduct of firm's business but Y does not agree to this. State giving reason who is correct in this case.

ANSWER: Y is correct. Reason: In the absence of partnership deed Every partner is entitled to participate in the conduct of firm's business as per Sec. 12(a) of The Indian Partnership Act, 1932.

QUESTION 27: A, B and C are partners decided that no interest on drawings is to be charged to any partner. But after one year 'C' wants that interest on drawings should be charged to every partner. State how 'C' can do this.

OR

A, B and C decided that interest on capitals will be provided to each partner @ 5% p.a. But after one year C wants that no interest on capital is to be provided to any partner. State how 'C' can do this?

ANSWER: He can only do this if it is agreed by all partners (i.e. by changing partnership deed).

QUESTION 28: X, Y and Z decided that interest any partner's loan to firm should be allowed @ 10% p.a. But after one year, Z wants that no such interest should be provided. Can he do so?

ANSWER: He can only do this if it is agreed by all partners (i.e. by changing partnership deed).

QUESTION 29: Can a partner be exempted from sharing the losses in a firm? If yes, under what circumstances?

ANSWER: Yes, if all partners agree that one *or* more of them shall not bear the losses.

QUESTION 30: How can the terms of a partnership be changed?

ANSWER: The terms of a partnership can be changed by the consent of all the partners.

QUESTION 31: A partnership deed provides for the payment of interest on capital but there was a loss instead of profits during the year. At what rate will the interest on capital be allowed?

ANSWER: No interest on capital will be allowed.

QUESTION 32: A partnership deed provides for the distribution of profits but is silent as to the distribution of a loss, how such a loss is normally distributed?

ANSWER: Such a loss is normally distributed in the agreed ratio among the partners (other than minor partner).

QUESTION 33: What share of profit would a "Sleeping partner" Who has contributed 75% of the Total Capital get in the absence of a deed?

ANSWER: In the absence of a partnership deed sleeping partner will get equal share of profits.

QUESTION 34: What share of profit would a partner who has not contributed to the Total Capital of the firm get in the absence of a Partnership deed?

ANSWER: In the absence of a partnership deed, such partner will get an equal share of profits.

QUESTION 35: In the absence of a Partnership deed, At what rate is a working partner entitled for remuneration?

ANSWER: In the absence of a partnership deed no partner (whether working *or* not) is not entitled for any remuneration.

QUESTION 36: Is Registration of a Firm optional *or* compulsory?

ANSWER: Registration of a Firm is optional but not compulsory.

QUESTION 37: State the methods according to which Partners' Capital Accounts are maintained.

ANSWER:

1. Fixed Capital Accounts Method.
2. Fluctuating Capital Accounts Method.

QUESTION 38: List any one difference between Fixed Capital Account and Fluctuating Capital Account.

ANSWER:

1. Fixed Capital Account can never have a Debit Balance but Fluctuating Capital Account can have a Debit Balance.
2. Current Account is opened alongwith Fixed Capital Account and not with Fluctuating Capital Account.

QUESTION 39: Under which capital method, the Current Accounts are maintained?

ANSWER: Fixed Capital Accounts Method.

QUESTION 40: Under which capital method, the Current Accounts are not maintained?

ANSWER: Fluctuating Capital Accounts Method.

QUESTION 41: List any one difference between Partner's Capital Account and Current Account.

ANSWER: Capital Account shows the transactions relating to introduction *or* withdrawal of Capital whereas Current Account shows the other transactions like Interest on Capital, Drawings, Salary, Commission, Share of Profit/loss.

QUESTION 42: List any two items that may appear on the debit side of a Capital Account of a partner when the capitals are fluctuating.

ANSWER: Withdrawal of Capital, Closing Balance, Drawings, Interest on Drawings, Share of Loss.

QUESTION 43: List any two items that may appear on the debit side on a Partner's Fixed Capital Account.

ANSWER: Withdrawal of Capital, Closing Balance.

QUESTION 44: List any two items that may appear on the credit side of a Partner's Fixed Capital Account.

ANSWER: Opening Balance, Additional Capital.

QUESTION 45: List any two items that may appear on the credit side of a capital account when the capitals are fluctuating.

ANSWER: Additional Capital, Interest on Capital, Salary, Commission, Share of Profit.

QUESTION 46: List any two items which may appear on the debit side of a Partner's Current Account.

ANSWER: Drawings, Interest on Drawings, Share of Loss.

QUESTION 47: List any two items which may appear on the credit side of a Partner's Current Account.

ANSWER: Interest on Capital, Salary, Commission, Share of Profit.

QUESTION 48: State any two circumstances in which the fixed capital of a partner may change.

ANSWER: Withdrawal of Capital, Additional Capital.

QUESTION 49: If Patners' Capitals are fixed, where will you record Capital withdrawn and Share of Profit?

ANSWER: Capital withdrawn: on the debit side of a Partner's Fixed Capital Account. Share of Profit: on the credit side of a Partner's Current Account.

QUESTION 50: If Partners' Capitals are fixed, where will you record Additional Capital introduced and Drawings?

ANSWER: Additional Capital introduced: on the credit side of a Partner's Fixed Capital Account. Drawings: on the debit side of a Partner's Current Account.

QUESTION 51: Why is it that the Capital Account of a partner does not show a "Debit Balance" inspite of regular and consistent losses year after year?

ANSWER: All transactions relating to loss *or* profit, drawings, salaries etc. are shown in the Current Account and not in the Capital Account which always shows a credit balance in case of fixed capitals.

QUESTION 52: If Partners' Capitals are fixed, where will you record Interest on Capital and Interest on Drawings?

ANSWER: Interest on Capital: on the credit side of a Partner's Current Account. Interest on Drawings: on the debit side of a Partner's Current Account.

QUESTION 53: State the purpose of allowing Interest on Drawings of a Partner.

ANSWER: In case the profit sharing ratio differs from Drawings ratio, the Interest on Drawings compensates those partners who make Drawings less than the proportionate Drawings as per profit sharing ratio.

QUESTION 54: If a fixed amount is withdrawn on the first day of every month of calendar year, for what period the interest on the total amount of drawings will be calculated?

ANSWER: 6.5 Months

QUESTION 55: How will you calculate interest on the drawings of equal amounts on the 15th day of every month of a calendar year?

ANSWER: 6 Months

QUESTION 56: If a fixed amount is withdrawn on the last day of every month of calendar year, for what period the interest on the total amount of drawings will be calculated?

ANSWER: 5.5 Months

QUESTION 57: If a fixed amount is withdrawn on the first day of every quarter of calendar year, for what period the interest on the total amount of drawings will be calculated?

ANSWER: 7.5 Months

QUESTION 58: If a fixed amount is withdrawn on the last day of every quarter of calendar year, for what period the interest on the total amount of drawings will be calculated?

ANSWER: 4.5 Months

QUESTION 59: It the dates of drawings made during the year are not given, for what period the interest @ 10% p.a. on the total amount of drawings will be calculated?

ANSWER: 6 Months

QUESTION 60: If the dates of drawings made during the year are not given, for what period the interest @ 10% on the total amount of drawings will be calculated and why?

ANSWER: 12 Months because the Rate is 10% and not 10% p.a.

QUESTION 61: How would you calculate intereston drawings of equal amounts drawn in the middle of every month?

ANSWER: Interest on Drawings = Total Drawings ×

QUESTION 62: How would you calculate interest on drawings of equal amounts drawn on the 1st day of every month?

ANSWER: Interest on Drawings = Total Drawings ×

QUESTION 63: How would you calculate interest on drawings of equal amounts drawn on the last day of every month?

ANSWER: Interest on Drawings = Total Drawings ×

QUESTION 64: Name the method of calculating interest on drawings if different amounts are withdrawn at different dates.

ANSWER: Product Method

QUESTION 65: How would you calculate interest on drawings on unequal amounts drawn at unequal monthly intervals?

ANSWER: Interest on Drawings = Total Product ×

QUESTION 66: List any one difference between Drawings against Profits and Drawings against Capital.

ANSWER: Drawings against Profits are not considered for calculating Interest on Capital, and Drawings against Capital are considered for calculating Interest on Capital.

QUESTION 67: State the purpose of allowing Interest on Capital of a Partner.

ANSWER: In case the profit sharing ratio differs from capital ratio, the interest on capital compensates those partners who contribute capital more than the proportionate capital as per profit sharing ratio.

QUESTION 68: X and Y started business on 1st April, 2012 with Capitals of ₹ 2,50,000 and ₹ 1,50,000 respectively. On 1st Oct. 2012, they decided that their capitals should be ₹ 2,00,000 each. The necessary adjustments in the capitals were made by introducing *or* withdrawing cash. Interest on capital is allowed at 8% p.a. Calculate the Interest on X's Capital on March 31, 2013.

ANSWER: Interest on X's Capital:

On ₹ 2,50,000 for 6 months = ₹ 2,50,000 × 8/100 × 6/12 = ₹ 10,000

On ₹ 2,00,000 for 6 months = ₹ 2,00,000 × 8/100 × 6/12 = ₹ 8,000

Total Interest = ₹ 10,000 + ₹ 8,000 = ₹ 18,000

QUESTION 69: X and Y started business on 1st April, 2012 with Capitals of ₹ 2,50,000 and ₹ 1,50,000 respectively. On 1st Oct. 2012, they decided that their capitals should be ₹ 2,00,000 each. The necessary adjustments in the capitals were made by introducing *or* withdrawing cash. Interest on capital is allowed at 8% p.a. Calculate the Interest on Y's Capital on March 31, 2013.

ANSWER: Interest on Y's Capital:

On ₹ 1,50,000 for 6 months = ₹ 1,50,000 × 8/100 × 6/12 = ₹ 6,000

On ₹ 2,00,000 for 6 months = ₹ 2,00,000 × 8/100 × 6/12 = ₹ 8,000

Total Interest = ₹ 6,000 + ₹ 8,000 = ₹ 14,000.

QUESTION 70: X and Y are partners sharing the profits and losses in the ratio of 2: 3 with capitals of ₹ 20,000 and ₹ 10,000 respectively. The partnership deed is silent as to the Interest on Capital and the trading profits for the year are ₹ 1,500. State giving reason how much amount of Interest on Capital will be allowed.

ANSWER: Nil because In the absence of partnership deed no Interest on Capital is to be allowed.

QUESTION 71: X and Y are partners sharing the profits and losses in the ratio of 2: 3 with capitals of ₹ 20,000 and ₹ 10,000 respectively. The partnership deed provides for Interest on Capital @ 6% p.a. and the trading loss for the year are ₹ 1,500. State giving reason how much amount of Interest on Capital will be allowed.

ANSWER: Nil because no Interest on Capital is to be allowed in case of a loss as the partnership deed is silent as to the treatment of interest on Capital as a charge *or* appropriation.

QUESTION 72: X and Y are partners sharing the profits and losses in the ratio of 2: 3 with capitals of ₹ 20,000 and ₹ 10,000 respectively. The partnership deed provides for Interest on Capital @ 6% p.a and the trading profits for the year are ₹ 2,100. State giving reason how much amount of Interest on Capital will be allowed.

ANSWER: Interest on X's Capital = ₹ 20,000 × 6/100 ×12/12 = ₹ 1,200,

Interest on Y's Capital = ₹ 10,000 × 6/100 ×12/12 = ₹ 600

QUESTION 73: X and Y are partners sharing the profits and losses in the ratio of 2: 3 with capitals of ₹ 20,000 and ₹ 10,000 respectively. The partnership deed provides for Interest on Capital @ 6% p.a. and the trading profits for the year are ₹ 1,500. State giving reason how much amount of Interest on Capital will be allowed.

ANSWER: Since the amount of available profits is less than the total amount of interest on capital, the available profits have been distributed in the ratio of interest claims of X and Y i.e. ₹ 1,200: ₹ 600.

Interest on X's Capital = ₹ 1,500 × 1,200/1,800 = ₹ 1,000, Interest on Y's Capital = ₹ 1,500 × 600/1,800 = ₹ 500

QUESTION 74: X and Y are partners sharing the profits and losses in the ratio of 2: 3 with capitals of ₹ 20,000 and ₹ 10,000 respectively. The partnership deed provides for Interest on Capital @ 6% p.a. even if it involves the firm in loss and the trading loss for the year are ₹ 2,100. State giving reason how much amount of Interest on Capital will be allowed.

ANSWER: Interest on X's Capital = ₹ 20,000 × 6/100 ×12/12 = ₹ 1,200

Interest on Y's Capital = ₹ 10,000 × 6/100 ×12/12 = ₹ 600

Reason: The partnership deed provides for Interest on Capital even if it involves the firm in loss.

QUESTION 75: A partner has given a loan of ₹ 20,000 to firm on 1st July. The Partnership deed is silent as to the interest on partner's loan. State giving reason how much amount of Interest on Loan will be allowed on 31st March.

ANSWER: Interest on Partner's Loan = ₹ 20,000 × 6/100 × 9/12 = ₹ 900

Reason: When the partnership deed is silent, as per the Indian Partnership Act, 1932, interest on partner's loan is to be allowed @ 6% p.a.

QUESTION 76: A partner has given a loan of ₹ 20,000 to firm on 1st July. The Partnership deed is silent as to the interest on partner's loan. State giving reason how much amount of Interest on Loan will be allowed if the loss before any interest for the year ended 31st March amounted to ₹ 500.

ANSWER: Interest on Partner's Loan = ₹ 20,000 × 6/100 × 9/12 = ₹ 900

Reason: When the partnership deed is silent, as per the Indian Partnership Act, 1932, interest on partner's loan is to be allowed @ 6% p.a. even if there are losses.

QUESTION 77: State giving reason to which account Interest on Partner's Loan is debited if Partners' Capitals are fixed.

ANSWER: Interest on Partner's Loan is debited to Profit & Loss Account since it is a charge against the Profits and not an appropriation out of profits.

QUESTION 78: State giving reason to which account Interest on Partner's Loan is credited if Partners' Capitals are fixed.

ANSWER: Interest on Partner's Loan is credited to Partner's Loan Account since it is a gain to a partner in the capacity of a lender and not in the capacity of a Partner.

QUESTION 79: State giving reason to which account Rent paid to a partner for the use of his premises is debited.

ANSWER: Rent paid to a partner is debited to Profit & Loss Account since it is a charge against the Profits and not an appropriation out of profits.

QUESTION 80: State giving reason to which account Rent paid to a partner for the use of his premises is credited if Partners' Capitals are fixed.

ANSWER: Rent paid to a partner is to be credited to Partner's Current Account since Partners' Capitals are fixed.

QUESTION 81: What is Profit & Loss Appropriation Account?

ANSWER: Profit & Loss Appropriation Account is merely an extension of the Profit & Loss Account and is credited with Net Profits and Interest on Drawings and debited with Interest on Capitals, salary *or* Commission to Partners if provided under the terms of partnership agreement and its balance is transferred to the Partners' Capital (or Current) Accounts in their agreed profit sharing ratio.

QUESTION 82: Why is Profit & Loss Appropriation Account prepared?

ANSWER: After ascertaining the Net Profit as per Profit & Loss Account, usually the Profit & Loss Appropriation Account is prepared to show the Distribution of Net Profit among the partners.

QUESTION 83: For What Purposes the balance available in Profit & Loss Appropriation Account may be used?

ANSWER: The balance in Profit & Loss Appropriation Account may be used:

1. To provide for Interest on Capital of Partners (if Partnership Deed so provides).
2. To provide for Salary *or* Commission to Partners (if Partnership Deed so provides).
3. To transfer the Profits to General Reserve *or* Specific Reserve.
4. To distribute the Profits among the Partners in their profit sharing ratio.

QUESTION 84: List any two items appearing on the debit side of Profit & Loss Appropriation Account.

ANSWER: Interest on Capital, Salary to a partner, Commission to a partner, Share of Profit.

QUESTION 85: List any two items appearing on the credit side of Profit & Loss Appropriation Account.

ANSWER:

1. Net Profit for the year
2. Interest on Drawings.

QUESTION 86: List any one difference between Profit & Loss Account and Profit & Loss Appropriation Account.

ANSWER: Profit & Loss Account is prepared to ascertain Net Profit whereas Profit & Loss Appropriation Account is prepared to show the Distribution of Net Profit among the partners.

QUESTION 87: List any one difference between Profit & Loss Appropriation Account and Profit & Loss Adjustment Account.

ANSWER: Profit & Loss Appropriation Account is prepared to show the Distribution of Net Profit among the partners whereas Profit & Loss Adjustment Account is prepared to show the effect of revaluation of assets and liabilities at the time of reconstitution of partnership. (i.e. Change in Profit Sharing Ratio, Admission,Retirement and Death of a Partner).

QUESTION 88: Do all forms of business organisations prepare a Profit and Loss Appropriation Account?

ANSWER: No, there is no need to prepare Profit & Loss Appropriation A/c in case of sole proprietorship concerns. It is prepared in case of partnership firms.

QUESTION 89: State giving reason whether the interest on loan given by a Partner to the firm be paid if there are losses?

ANSWER: Yes since Interest on Loan is a charge against the Profits.

QUESTION 90: State giving reason to which account Interest on Partner's Loan is debited and credited if Partners' Capitals are fixed.

ANSWER: Interest on Partner's Loan is debited to Profit & Loss Account since it is a charge against the Profits and not an appropriation out of profits. Interest on Partner's Loan is credited to Partner's Loan Account since it is a gain to a partner in the capacity of a lender and not in the capacity of a Partner.

QUESTION 91: State giving reason to which account Interest on Partner's Capital is debited and credited if Partners' Capitals are fixed.

ANSWER: Interest on Partner's Capital is debited to Profit & Loss Appropriation Account since it is an appropriation out of profits and not a charge against the Profits. Interest on Partner's Capital is to be credited to Partner's Current Account since Partners' Capitals are fixed.

QUESTION 92: State giving reason to which account Salary & Commission to a Partner is debited and credited if Partners' Capitals are fixed.

ANSWER: Salary & Commission to a Partner is debited to Profit & Loss Appropriation Account since it is an appropriation out of profits and not a charge against the Profits. Salary & Commission to a Partner is to be credited to Partner's Current Account since Partners' Capitals are fixed.

QUESTION 93: State giving reason to which account Interest on Partner's Drawings is debited and credited if Partners' Capitals are fixed.

ANSWER: Interest on Partner's Drawings is credited to Profit & Loss Appropriation Account since it is an adjustment so as to justify the appropriate distribution of profits. Interest on Partner's Drawings is to be debited to Partner's Current Account since Partners' Capitals are fixed.

QUESTION 94: State giving reason to which account Rent paid to a partner for the use of his premises is debited and credited if Partners' Capitals are fixed.

ANSWER: Rent paid to a partner is debited to Profit & Loss Account since it is a charge against the Profits and not an appropriation out of profits. Rent paid to a partner is to be credited to Partner's Current Account since Partners' Capitals are fixed.

QUESTION 95: What Journal Entry is passed to transfer 10% of profits (₹ 2,75,000) to General Reserve?

ANSWER:

Date	Particulars		Dr. (₹)	Cr. (₹)
	Profit & Loss Appropriation A/c	Dr.	27,500	
	To General Reserve			27,500
	[Being 10% of Profit t/f to General Reserve]			

QUESTION 96: X, Y and Z entered into a partnership on 1st Oct. 2013 to share the profits and losses in the ratio of 5: 3: 2. The total capital was fixed at ₹ 18,00,000 to be contributed by X, Y and Z in the ratio of 4: 3: 2. X granted a loan of ₹ 1,00,000 on 1st Jan. 2014. The partnership deed provided for Interest on Capital @ 10% p.a. Interest on Drawings @12% p.a. salary to Y @ ₹ 6,000 p.m. and salary to Z @ ₹ 6,000 per quarter. Y's Drawings during the period ended 31st March, 2014 were ₹ 50,000. The profits of the firm for the period ended 31st March, 2014 before providing for any Interest and Salary were ₹ 2,16,000 prepare Profit & Loss Appropriation Account.

ANSWER:

PROFIT AND LOSS APPROPRIATION ACCOUNT

Dr. *for the year ended 31st March, 2014* **Cr.**

Particulars	₹	Particulars		₹
To Interest on Capital:		By Net Profit as per P & L A/c		
X's Current A/c	40,000	Profit before Interest	2,16,000	
Y's Current A/c	30,000	*Less:* Interest on Loan	1,500	2,14,500
Z's Current A/c	20,000	(₹1,00,000 × 6/100 × 3/12)		
To Salary:		By Interest on Drawings:		
Y's Current A/c [₹ 6,000 × 6]	36,000	Y's Current A/c		1,500
Z's Current A/c [₹ 6,000 × 2]	12,000	(₹50,000 × 12/100 × 3/12)		
To Profit t/f to:				
X's Current A/c	39,000			
Y's Current A/c	23,400			
Z's Current A/c	15,600			
	2,16,000			2,16,000

QUESTION 97: X, Y and Z are partners. Their fixed capitals as on 31st March, 2014 were: X ₹ 50,000, Y ₹ 1,00,000 and Z ₹ 1,50,000. Profits for the year 2013–2014 amounting to ₹ 60,000 were distributed. Interest on Capital was credited @ 12% p.a. instead of 10% p.a. Pass the necessary adjusting entry.

ANSWER:

STEP 1 → ADJUSTMENT TABLE

Particulars	X ₹	Y ₹	Z ₹	Total ₹
I. Interest on Capital already credited @ 12%	6,000	12,000	18,000	36,000
II. Amount that should have been credited by way of:				

Interest on capital @ 10%	5,000	10,000	15,000	30,000
Share of Profit [(₹ 36,000 – ₹ 30,000) in ratio of 1: 1: 1]	2,000	2,000	2,000	6,000
	7,000	12,000	17,000	36,000
III. Difference [I – II]	(1,000)	—	1,000	—

STEP 2 → ADJUSTING JOURNAL ENTRY

Date	Particulars		L.F.	Dr. (₹)	Cr. (₹)
	Z's Current A/c	Dr.		1,000	
	To X's Current A/c				1,000
	(Being the interest on capital wrongly provided, now adjusted)				

QUESTION 98: P, Q and R were partners in a firm sharing profits in the ratio of 1: 2: 2. After division of the profits for the year ended 31.3.2014 their capitals were: P ₹ 1,50,000; Q ₹ 1,80,000 and R ₹ 2,10,000. During the year they withdrew ₹ 20,000 each. The profit of the year was ₹ 60,000. The partnership deed provided that interest on capital will be allowed @ 10% p.a. While preparing the final accounts, interest on partners' capital was not allowed.

Required: You are required to calculate the capital of P, Q and R as on 1.4.2013 and pass the necessary adjustment entry for providing interest on capital.

ANSWER:

STEP 1 → CALCULATION OF OPENING CAPITALS

Particulars	P (₹)	Q (₹)	R (₹)	Total
A. Closing Capitals	1,50,000	1,80,000	2,10,000	5,40,000
B. *Add:* Drawings	20,000	20,000	20,000	20,000
C. *Less:* Share of Profit	12,000	24,000	24,000	60,000
D. Opening Capitals	1,58,000	1,76,000	2,06,000	5,00,000

STEP 2 → ADJUSTMENT TABLE

Particulars	P (₹)	Q (₹)	R (₹)	Total
I. Share of Profit already credited	12,000	24,000	24,000	60,000
II. Amount which should have been Credited:				
(a) Interest on Capital @ 10%	15,800	17,600	20,600	54,000
(b) Share of Profit	1,200	2,400	2,400	6,000
	17,000	20,000	23,000	60,000
III. Difference [I – II]	–5,000	4,000	1,000	–

STEP 3 → ADJUSTING JOURNAL ENTRY

Date	Particulars		L.F.	Dr. (₹)	Cr. (₹)
	Q's Capital A/c	Dr.		4,000	
	R's Capital A/c	Dr.		1,000	
	To P's Capital A/c				5,000
	(Being the omission of interest on capital rectified)				

QUESTION 99: X, Y and Z are partners sharing profits and losses in the ratio of 3: 2: 1. After the final accounts have been prepared, it was discovered that interest on drawings @ 5% p.a. has not been taken into consideration. The drawings of the Partners were: X ₹ 15,000; Y ₹ 12,600; Z ₹ 12,000. Pass the necessary adjusting journal entry.

ANSWER:

Step 1: Calculation of Interest on Drawings:

Since date of drawings are not given, interest will be charged for 6 months.

X: ₹ 15,000 × 5/100 × 6/12 = ₹ 375

Y: ₹ 12,000 × 5/100 × 6/12 = ₹ 315

Z: ₹ 12,000 × 5/100 × 6/12 = ₹ 300

₹ 990

STEP 1 → ADJUSTMENT TABLE

Particulars		X ₹	Y ₹	Z ₹	Total ₹
I. Interest on Drawings	(Dr.)	375	315	300	990
II. Divisions of ₹ 990 in 3: 2: 1	(Cr.)	495	330	165	990
III. Difference [I – II]		Cr. 120	Cr. 15	Dr. 135	—

STEP 2 → ADJUSTING JOURNAL ENTRY

Date	Particulars		L.F.	Dr. (₹)	Cr. (₹)
	Z's Capital A/c	Dr.		135	
	To X's Capital A/c				120
	To Y's Capital A/c				15
	(Being the Adjustment of omission of Interest on drawings)				

QUESTION 100: State the meaning of Guarantee of Minimum Profit.

ANSWER: Guarantee of minimum profit means assurance to give a minimum amount of Profit. The guarantee may be provided by one *or* some *or* all of the partners in an existing profit sharing ratio *or* in some other agreed ratio. If in any year, the actual Share of Profit of a Guaranteed Partner is less than the Guaranteed Amount, then the deficiency (i.e., excess of Guaranteed Amount over Actual Share of Profit) is borne by the Guaranteeing Partners in their agreed ratio.

QUESTION 101: A and B are partners sharing profits in the ratio of 3: 2. C was admitted for 1/6th share of profit with a minimum guaranteed amount of ₹ 10,000. At the close of the first financial year the firm earned a profit of ₹ 54,000. Find out the share of profit which A, B and C will get.

ANSWER: A's Share = (₹ 54,000 – ₹ 10,000) × 3/5 = ₹ 26,400;

B's Share = ₹ 54,000 – ₹ 10,000) × 2/5 = ₹ 17,600;

C's Share = ₹ 10,000.

QUESTION 102: A, B and C entered into a partnership on 1st Oct., 2013 to share profits and losses in the ratio of 3: 2: 1. A, however, personally guaranteed that C's share of profit would not be less than ₹ 30,000 p.a. The profits for the period ended 31st March, 2014 were ₹ 1,20,000. Calculate Deficiency to be charged to A.

ANSWER: C's Actual Share = ₹ 1,20,000 × 1/6 = ₹ 20,000

Guaranteed Amount for half year = ₹ 30,000 × 6/12 = ₹ 15,000. Since Actual Share (₹ 20,000) exceeds the Guaranteed Amount, no Deficiency is to be charged to A.

QUESTION 103: A, B and C entered into a partnership on 1st Oct., 2013 to share profits and losses in the ratio of 3: 2: 1. A, however, personally guaranteed that C's share of profit would not be less than ₹ 30,000 p.a. The loss for the period ended 31st March, 2014 were ₹ 1,20,000. Calculate Deficiency to be charged to A.

ANSWER: C's Actual Share of Loss = ₹ 1,20,000 × 1/6 = ₹ 20,000

Guaranteed Amount of Profit for half year = ₹ 30,000 × 6/12 = ₹ 15,000

Deficiency = Guaranteed Amount – (– ₹ 20,000)

= ₹ 15,000 + ₹ 20,000 = ₹ 35,000

QUESTION 104: A, B and C entered into a partnership on 1st April, 2013 to share profits and losses in the ratio of 3: 2: 1. A, however, personally guaranteed that C's share of profit after charging interest on capitals @ 5% p.a would not be less than ₹ 30,000 p.a. The capital contributions were A– ₹ 3,00,000; B– ₹ 2,00,000 and C–₹ 1,00,000. The profits for the period ended 31st March, 2014 were ₹ 1,20,000. Calculate Deficiency to be charged to A.

ANSWER:

Profit after charging interest on capitals = ₹ 1,20,000 – (₹ 6,00,000 × 5/100)

= ₹ 90,000

C's Actual Share = ₹ 90,000 × 1/6 = ₹ 15,000

Deficiency = Guaranteed Amount – ₹ 15,000 = ₹ 30,000 – ₹ 15,000 = ₹ 15,000

QUESTION 105: A, B and C entered into a partnership on 1st Oct., 2013 to share profits and losses in the ratio of 3: 2: 1. A, however, personally guaranteed that C's share of profit after charging interest on capitals @ 5% p.a would not be less than ₹ 30,000 p.a. The capital contributions were A–₹ 3,00,000; B–₹ 2,00,000 and C–₹ 1,00,000. The profits for the period ended 31st March, 2014 were ₹ 1,20,000. Calculate Deficiency to be charged to A.

ANSWER: Profit after charging interest on capitals = ₹ 1,20,000 – (₹ 6,00,000 × 5/100 × 6/12)

= ₹ 1,05,000

C's Actual Share = ₹ 1,05,000 × 1/6 = ₹ 17,500

Guaranteed Amount for half year = ₹ 30,000 × 6/12 = ₹ 15,000. Since Actual Share (₹ 17,500) exceeds the Guaranteed Amount, no Deficiency is to be charged to A.

QUESTION 106: X, Y and Z entered into partnership on 1st Oct., 2013 to share profits and losses in the ratio of 5: 3: 2. They contributed ₹ 8,00,000, ₹ 6,00,000 and ₹ 4,00,000 respectively as there capitals. Partners are entitled to interest on capital @ 10% per annum and salary to Y @ ₹ 6,000 per month and commission of ₹ 12,000 to Z respectively as per the provisions of the partnership deed. X's share of profit (excluding interest on capital but including salary) is guaranteed at a not less than of ₹ 50,000 p.a. Y's share of profit, including interest on capital but excluding salary, is guaranteed at not less than ₹ 1,10,000 p.a. Any deficiency arising on that account shall be met by Z. The profits of the firm for the year ended 31st March, 2014 amounted to ₹ 2,16,000. Prepare Profit & Loss Appropriation Account for the year ended on 31st March, 2014.

ANSWER:

PROFIT & LOSS APPROPRIATION ACCOUNT

Dr. *for the year ending on 31st March, 2014* **Cr.**

Particulars	₹	Particulars	₹
To Interest on Capital:		By Profit before appropriations	2,16,000

Particulars	₹	Particulars	₹
X 40,000			
Y 30,000			
Z 20,000	90,000		
To Salary:			
Y (₹ 6,000 × 6)	36,000		
To Commission to Z	12,000		
To Net Profit transferred to:			
X (₹ 78,000 × 5/10)	39,000		
Y (₹ 23,400 + ₹ 1,600)	25,000		
Z (₹ 15,600 – ₹ 1,600)	14,000		
	2,16,000		2,16,000

Note: Y's Deficiency = ₹ 55,000 – (₹ 23,400 + ₹ 30,000) = ₹ 1,600

QUESTION 107: Rehman, Suleman and Hanuman were partners in a firm sharing profits in the ratio of 7: 2: 1 respectively. Their fixed capitals were as follows: Rehman ₹ 3,00,000; Suleman ₹ 2,00,000 and Hanuman ₹ 1,00,000. The partnership deed provided for the following for the division of profit:

(i) 10% of the trading profits will be transferred to Reserve Account.

(ii) Hanuman was guaranteed a profit of ₹ 50,000. Any loss because of guarantee to Hanuman will be shared by Rehman and Suleman equally.

The trading profit of the firm for the year ended 31.3.2015 was ₹ 2,00,000.

Prepare the 'Profit and Loss Appropriation Account' for the year ended 31.3.2015.

ANSWER:

Step 1 : Hanuman's Actual Share of Profit = 1/10 of ₹ 1,80,000 = ₹ 18,000

Step 2 : Deficiency = Guaranteed amount – ₹ 18,000 = ₹ 50,000 – ₹ 18,000 = ₹ 32,000

Step 3 : Deficiency is to be borne by Rehman and Suleman in the ratio of 1: 1 as follows:

Deficiency to be borne by Rehman = 1/2 × ₹ 32,000 = ₹ 16,000

Deficiency to be borne by Suleman = 1/2 × ₹ 32,000 = ₹ 16,000

STEP 4 → PROFIT AND LOSS APPROPRIATION ACCOUNT

for the year ending on 31st March, 2015

Dr. Cr.

Particulars		₹	Particulars	₹
To Reserve A/c		20,000	By Profit & Loss A/c	2,00,000
To Profit t/f to:				
To Rehman's Current A/c (7/10 × ₹ 1,80,000)	1,26,000			
Less: Deficiency borne (1/2 × ₹ 32,000)	(16,000)	1,10,000		
To Suleman's Current A/c (2/10 × ₹ 1,80,000)	36,000			
Less: Deficiency borne (1/2 × ₹ 32,000)	(16,000)	20,000		

To Hanuman's Current A/c (1/10 × ₹ 1,80,000)	18,000			
Add: Deficiency recovered from				
Rehman	16,000			
Suleman	16,000	50,000		
		2,00,000		2,00,000

QUESTION 108: X, Y and Z entered into a partnership on 1st April 2013 to share profits in the ratio of 2: 1: 1. It was provided in the deed that Z's share of profit will not be less than ₹ 70,000 per annum. The loss for the year ended 31st March, 2015 was ₹ 2,00,000 before allowing interest ₹ 9,000 on X's Loan which is due for the current year.

Prepare Profit and Loss Appropriation Account for the year ended 31st March, 2015.

ANSWER:

PROFIT & LOSS APPROPRIATION ACCOUNT

Dr. *for the year ending on 31st March, 2015* **Cr.**

Particulars		₹	Particulars	₹
To Net Loss	2,00,000		By Loss t/f to:	
Add: Interest on Loan	9,000	2,09,000	X's Capital A/c (2,79,000 × 2/3)	1,86,000
To Z's Capital A/c (guaranteed)		70,000	Y's Capital A/c (2,79,000 × 1/3)	93,000
		2,79,000		2,79,000

QUESTION 109: Define Goodwill.

ANSWER: Goodwill is the value of reputation of a firm in respect of the profits expected in future over and above the normal profits earned by other similar firms belonging to the same industry. Such excess of future profits over the normal profits is known as super profits.

QUESTION 110: State the nature of Goodwill.

ANSWER: Goodwill is regarded as an intangible asset.

QUESTION 111: List any two factors affecting goodwill of a partnership firm.

ANSWER:

1. Quality of Products,
2. After Sales Service,
3. Efficiency of Management
4. Profitability

QUESTION 112: State any two circumstances when there is a need to revalue goodwill.

ANSWER:

1. On a Change in profit-sharing ratio amongst the existing partners;
2. On Admission of a new partner
3. On Retirement *or* Death of a partner.

QUESTION 113: State any two methods of valuation of goodwill.

ANSWER:

1. Average Profits Method,

2. Super Profits Method,
3. Capitalisation Method.

QUESTION 114: What is meant by number of years' purchase?

ANSWER: Number of years' purchase means the number of years during which the Purchaser of Goodwill expects that the profits due to goodwill are likely to be available in future.

QUESTION 115: What is meant by 'Super Profit'?

ANSWER: Super Profits = Average Future Maintainable Profits – Normal Profits

QUESTION 116: List any one difference between Average Profits and Super Profits.

ANSWER: Average Profit is the average of the profits of past few years whereas Super Profit is the excess of Average Profits over Normal Profits.

QUESTION 117: How does the factor 'Quality of Products' affect the goodwill of a firm?

ANSWER: Better Quality of Production increases customor satisfaction which increases sales and profits. Higher profits lead to higher value of goodwill.

QUESTION 118: How does the factor 'location' affect the goodwill of a firm?

ANSWER: Location factor enhances better business and sales which leads to higher profits which leads to higher value of goodwill.

QUESTION 119: How does the factor Efficiency of Management affect the goodwill of a firm?

ANSWER: A well-managed firm usually enjoys the advantages of high productivity and cost efficiency. This leads to higher profit which leads to higher value of goodwill.

QUESTION 120: How does the market situation affect the value of goodwill of a firm?

ANSWER: The monopoly condition *or* limited competition enables the concern to earn high profits which leads to higher value of goodwill.

QUESTION 121: How does the nature of business affect the value of goodwill of a firm?

ANSWER: A firm which produces high value added products *or* having a stable demand is able to earn more profits and therefore has more goodwill.

QUESTION 122: What is meant by Average Capital Employed?

ANSWER: Average Capital Employed = (Opening Capital Employed + Closing Capital Employed)/2

QUESTION 123: What is meant by Normal Rate of Return?

ANSWER: Normal Rate of Return refers to the rate of return normally earned by an average firm belonging to the same industry.

QUESTION 124: Give the formula for calculation of Normal Profits.

ANSWER: Normal Profit = Average Capital Employed × Normal Rate of Return

QUESTION 125: Give the formula for calculation of Super Profits.

ANSWER: Super Profits = Average Future Maintainable Profits – Normal Profits

QUESTION 126: Enumerate two main steps involved in valuing the Goodwill by according to Super Profits Method.

ANSWER:

1. Average Capital Employed = (Opening Capital Employed + Closing Capital Employed)/2
2. Normal Profit = Average Capital Employed × Normal Rate of Return
3. Super Profits = Average Future Maintainable Profits – Normal Profits
4. Goodwill = Super Profits × No. of Years' Purchase

QUESTION 127: Give the formula for calculation of Goodwill by Capitalisation of Super Profits.

ANSWER: Goodwill = Super Profits × 100/ Normal Rate of Return

QUESTION 128: Give the formula for calculation of Goodwill by Capitalisation of Average Profits.

ANSWER: Goodwill = Capitalised Value – Net Assets

Notes:

1. Capitalised Value = Average Profits × 100/ Normal Rate of Return
2. Net Assets = All Assets (other than goodwill, fictitious assets and non-trade investments) at their current values less Outsiders' Liabilities.

QUESTION 129: A firm's result of operations during the years I, II, III and IV were Profit ₹ 2,00,000, Profit ₹ 4,10,000, ₹ 2,20,000 and ₹ 4,70,000 respectively. Calculate goodwill of the firm based on four years' purchase of average profits of last three years.

ANSWER:

1. Average Profits = (₹ 4,10,000 – ₹ 2,20,000 + ₹ 4,70,000)/3 = ₹ 2,20,000
2. Goodwill = Average Profits × No. of years purchases
   = ₹ 2,20,000 × 4 = ₹ 8,80,000

QUESTION 130: Average Profits ₹ 1,20,000, Capital Employed ₹ 4,00,000, Normal Rate of Return 15%. Calculate the value of goodwill on the basis of two years' purchase of Super Profits.

ANSWER:

1. Normal Profit = (₹ 4,00,000 × 15/100) = ₹ 60,000
2. Super Profit = Average Profit – Normal Profit = ₹ 1,20,000 – ₹ 60,000 = ₹ 60,000
3. Goodwill = Super Profit × No. of years purchases = ₹ 60,000 × 2 = ₹ 1,20,000

QUESTION 131: Average Profits ₹ 1,20,000, Capital Employed ₹ 4,00,000, Normal Rate of Return 15%. Calculate the value of goodwill on the basis of Capitalisation of Super Profits.

ANSWER:

1. Normal Profit = (₹ 4,00,000 × 15/100) = ₹ 60,000
2. Super Profit = Average Profit – Normal Profit = ₹ 1,20,000 – ₹ 60,000 = ₹ 60,000
3. Goodwill = Super Profits × = ₹ 60,000 × 100/15 = ₹ 4,00,000

QUESTION 132: Average Profits ₹ 1,20,000, Capital Employed ₹ 4,00,000, Normal Rate of Return 15%. Calculate the value of goodwill on the basis of Capitalisation of Average Profits.

ANSWER:

1. Capitalised Value = Average Profits × 100/ Normal Rate of Return
   = ₹ 1,20,000 × 100/15 = ₹ 8,00,000
2. Goodwill = Capitalised Value – Net Assets = ₹ 8,00,000 – ₹ 4,00,000 = ₹ 4,00,000

QUESTION 133: Average Profits ₹ 2,20,000, Capital Employed ₹ 4,00,000, Normal Rate of Return 15%. The remuneration of all the partners during this period is estimated to be ₹ 1,00,000 per annum. Calculate the value of goodwill on the basis of two years' purchase of Super Profits.

ANSWER:

1. Average Profits for Goodwill = ₹ 2,20,000 – ₹ 1,00,000 (Partners' Remuneration)
   = ₹ 1,20,000
2. Normal Profit = (₹ 4,00,000 × 15/100) = ₹ 60,000
3. Super Profit = Average Profit – Normal Profit = ₹ 1,20,000 – ₹ 60,000 = ₹ 60,000
4. Goodwill = Super Profit × No. of years purchases = ₹ 60,000 × 2 = ₹ 1,20,000

QUESTION 134: Average Profits ₹ 2,20,000, Capital Employed ₹ 4,00,000, Normal Rate of Return 15%. The remuneration of all the partners during this period is estimated to be ₹ 1,00,000 per annum. Calculate the value of goodwill on the basis of Capitalisation of Super Profits.

ANSWER:

1. Average Profits for Goodwill = ₹ 2,20,000 – ₹ 1,00,000 (Partners' Remuneration)
   = ₹ 1,20,000
2. Normal Profit = (₹ 4,00,000 × 15/100) = ₹ 60,000
3. Super Profit = Average Profit – Normal Profit = ₹ 1,20,000 – ₹ 60,000 = ₹ 60,000
4. Goodwill = Super Profits × × 100/ Normal Rate of Return = ₹ 60,000 × 100/15 = ₹ 4,00,000

QUESTION 135: Average Profits ₹ 2,20,000, Capital Employed ₹ 4,00,000, Normal Rate of Return 15%. The remuneration of all the partners during this period is estimated to be ₹ 1,00,000 per annum. Calculate the value of goodwill on the basis of Capitalisation of Average Profits.

ANSWER:

1. Average Profits for Goodwill = ₹ 2,20,000 – ₹ 1,00,000 (Partners' Remuneration)
   = ₹ 1,20,000
2. Capitalised Value = Average Profits × 100/ Normal Rate of Return
   = ₹ 1,20,000 × 100/15 = ₹ 8,00,000
3. Goodwill = Capitalised Value – Net Assets = ₹ 8,00,000 – ₹ 4,00,000 = ₹ 4,00,000

QUESTION 136: From the following calculate the value of firm's goodwill:

(a) Goodwill of the firm will be valued at 2 years' purchase of 3 years' normal average profits of the firm.

(b) The profits of the previous three years were as follows:

Foe the year ended 31.3.2011 Profit ₹ 20,000 (includes insurance claim received of ₹ 40,000) For the year ended 31.3.2012 Loss ₹ 80,000 (includes voluntary retirement compensation paid ₹ 1,10,000) For the year ended 31.3.2013 Profits ₹ 1,05,000 (includes a profit of ₹ 25,000 on the sale of Assets)

ANSWER:

STATEMENT SHOWING THE CALCULATION OF GOODWILL

Particulars	For the year ending on		
	31.3.2013	**31.3.2009**	**31.3.2010**
A. Profit (loss)	20,000	(80,000)	1,05,000
B. *Add:* (less): Abnormal items	(40,000)	1,10,000	(25,000)

C. Net Profit (loss)	(20,000)	30,000	50,000
D. Average Profits = [(₹ 20,000) + ₹ 30,000 + ₹ 80,000)]3 = ₹ 30,000			
E. Firm's Goodwill = ₹ 30,000 × 2 = ₹ 60,000			

QUESTION 137: In the previous question calculate the value of firm's goodwill if goodwill is to be valued at 3 years purchases of super profits. Normal Rate of Return will be 18% on Fixed Capital (i.e., ₹ 1,00,000)

ANSWER:

Super Profit = Average Profits – Normal Profits
= ₹ 30,000 – (18% of ₹ 1,00,000) = ₹ 12,000

Firm's a Goodwill = ₹ 12,000 × 3 = ₹ 36,000

QUESTION 138: X and Y are partners. They are entitled for 9% interest on their capital contributions. The firm allowed ₹ 54,000 towards interest on capital to partners. Calculate the capital contribution of each partner if interest on X's capital is ₹ 13,500 more than the interest on Y's capital.

ANSWER:

Let interest on Y's capital 'x' then interest on X's capital will be x + 13500

Total interest = x + 13500 + x = 54000

or x = (54,000 – 13,500)/2 = 20,250

Interest on X's capital (x + 13500) = 20250 + 13500 = ₹ 33750 and her capital
= 33750/9% = ₹ 3,75,000

Interest on Y's capital (x) = ₹ 20250 and his capital = 20250/9% = ₹ 2,25,000

RECONSTITUTION OF PARTNERSHIP – CHANGE IN PROFIT SHARING RATIO

QUESTION 1: What is meant by Reconstitution of a Firm?

ANSWER: Reconstitution of a Firm means any change in existing agreement of partnership. As a result, the existing agreement comes to an end and a new agreement comes into existence and the firm continues.

QUESTION 2: State any two occasions on which reconstitution of partnership firm can take place.

ANSWER:

1. Change in the Profit Sharing Ratio of existing partners.
2. Admission of a new partner
3. Retirement of an existing partner
4. Death of a partner

QUESTION 3: What is meant by Change in Profit Sharing Ratio?

ANSWER: Change in profit sharing ratio implies increase in share of profit of one *or* more partners and decrease in share of profit of one *or* more partners.

QUESTION 4: State with reason whether the Change in Profit Sharing Ratio amounts to Dissolution of partnership.

ANSWER: Change in Profit Sharing Ratio amounts to DISSOLUTION of partnership because existing agreement comes to an end and a new agreement comes into existence.

QUESTION 5: State any two circumstances when there is a need to change the profit sharing ratio.

ANSWER:

1. When the partners decide to change the profit sharing ratio.
2. When a new partner is admitted.
3. When a partner retires.
4. When a partner dies.

QUESTION 6: State any two matters that need adjustments at the time of change in profit sharing ratio.

ANSWER:

1. Adjustment of Goodwill,
2. Adjustment of Profit/Loss arising from the Revaluation of Assets and Liabilities,
3. Adjustment of Accumulated Profits, Reserves and Losses

QUESTION 7: Define New Profit Sharing Ratio.

ANSWER: The ratio in which the partners decide to share the future profits and losses, is known as New Profit Sharing Ratio.

New Share = Old Share + Acquired Share

QUESTION 8: Define Sacrificing Ratio.

ANSWER: The ratio in which the partners have agreed to sacrifice their shares in profit in favour of other partner *or* partners, is known as sacrificing ratio. This ratio is calculated by taking out the difference between Old Profit Shares and New Profit Shares. Sacrifice of a Partner = Old Share – New Share

QUESTION 9: Define Gaining Ratio. How is it calculated?

ANSWER: The ratio in which the partners acquire additional share of profit from other partner *or* partners is called as gaining ratio. This ratio is calculated by taking out the difference between New Profit Share and Old Profit Share. Gain of a Partner = New Share – Old Share

QUESTION 10: Why is it necessary to adjust Goodwill at the time of change in profit sharing ratio? Or State the need for treatment of goodwill on change in profit sharing ratio.

ANSWER: Whenever there is a change in profit sharing ratio, the Gaining Partner (i.e., the partner whose share has increased as a result of change) is required to compensate the Sacrificing Partner (i.e., the partner whose share has decreased as a result of change).

QUESTION 11: Why are Assets and Liabilities revalued at the time of change in profit sharing ratio?

ANSWER: Assets and Liabilities are revalued at the time of change in profit sharing ratio so that the profit/loss on account of such revaluation upto the date of change in profit sharing ratio may be ascertained and adjusted in the partners' capital accounts in their old profit sharing ratio.

QUESTION 12: State the ratio in which the partners share the profit *or* loss on revaluation of assets & liabilities in case of change in profit sharing ratio.

ANSWER: Old Profit Sharing Ratio

QUESTION 13: Why is it necessary to distribute Accumulated Reserves, Profits & Losses at the time of change in profit sharing ratio?

ANSWER: It is necessary to distribute Accumulated Reserves, Profits & Losses at the time of change in profit sharing ratio so that such profits/losses upto the date of change in profit sharing ratio may be ascertained and adjusted in the partners' capital accounts in their Old Profit Sharing Ratio.

QUESTION 14: State the ratio in which the partners share all the accumulated profits, reserves, losses & fictitious assets in case of change in profit sharing ratio.

ANSWER: Old Profit Sharing Ratio

QUESTION 15: X, Y and Z who are presently sharing profits & losses in the ratio of 5: 3: 2, decide to share future profits & losses in the ratio of 2: 3: 5. Give the journal entry to distribute 'Workman Compensation Reserve' of ₹ 60,000 at the time of change in profit sharing ratio, when there is no claim against it.

ANSWER:

JOURNAL

Date	Particulars		L.F.	Dr. (₹)	Cr. (₹)
	Workman Compensation Reserve A/c	Dr.		60,000	
	To X's Capital A/c				30,000
	To Y's Capital A/c				18,000
	To Z's Capital A/c				12,000
	(Being the WCR t/f to partners in their old profit sharing ratio)				

QUESTION 16: X, Y and Z who are presently sharing profits & losses in the ratio of 5: 3: 2, decide to share future profits & losses in the ratio of 2: 3: 5. Give the journal entry to distribute 'Workman Compensation Reserve' of ₹ 60,000 at the time of change in profit sharing ratio, when there is claim of ₹ 40,000 against it.

ANSWER:

JOURNAL

Date	Particulars		L.F.	Dr. (₹)	Cr. (₹)
	Workman Compensation Reserve A/c	Dr.		60,000	
	To X's Capital A/c				10,000
	To Y's Capital A/c				6,000
	To Z's Capital A/c				4,000
	To Workman Compensation Claim A/c				40,000
	(Being the liability for Workman Compensation Claim created and surplus WCR t/f to partners in their old profit sharing ratio)				

QUESTION 17: X, Y and Z who are presently sharing profits & losses in the ratio of 5: 3: 2, decide to share future profits & losses in the ratio of 2: 3: 5. Give the journal entry to distribute 'Investment Fluctuation Reserve' of ₹ 4,000 at the time of change in profit sharing ratio, when Investments (market value ₹19,000) appear at ₹ 20,000.

ANSWER:

JOURNAL

Date	Particulars		L.F.	Dr. (₹)	Cr. (₹)
	Investment Fluctuation Reserve A/c	Dr.		4,000	
	To X's Capital A/c				1,500
	To Y's Capital A/c				900
	To Z's Capital A/c				600
	To Investments A/c				1,000
	(Being the value of Investments brought up to market value and surplus IFR t/f to partners in their old profit sharing ratio)				

QUESTION 18: X, Y and Z who are presently sharing profits & losses in the ratio of 5:3:2, decide to share future profits & losses equally. The goodwill of the firm has been valued at ₹ 1,80,000. Goodwill already appearing in the books is at ₹ 30,000. Show the necessary accounting treatment.

ANSWER:

JOURNAL

Date	Particulars		L.F.	Dr. (₹)	Cr. (₹)
	Y's Capital A/c [₹ 30,000 × 3/10]	Dr.		9,000	
	Z's Capital A/c [₹ 30,000 × 2/10]	Dr.		6,000	
	To Goodwill A/c				30,000
	(Being the existing goodwill w/o in old ratio on change in profit sharing ratio.)				
	Y's Capital A/c [₹ 1,80,000 × 1/30]	Dr.		6,000	
	Z's Capital A/c [₹ 1,80,000 × 4/30]	Dr.		24,000	
	To X's Capital A/c [₹ 1,80,000 × 5/30]				30,000
	(Being the adjustment made for goodwill on change in the profit sharing ratio)				

Working Note:

CALCULATION OF GAIN/LOSS

	X	Y	Z
New Shares	1/3	1/3	1/3
Old Shares	5/10	3/10	2/10
Difference	–5/30	1/30	4/30
	Sacrificing partner	Gaining partner	Gaining partner

QUESTION 19: X, Y and Z were sharing profits and losses in the ratio of 5: 3: 2. They decided to share future profits and losses in the ratio of 2: 3: 5 with effect from 1st April, 2015. They decided to record the effect of the following, without affecting their book values: Profit & Loss A/c ₹ 48,000, Advertisement Suspense A/c ₹ 12,000. Pass the necessary Journal entry.

ANSWER:

JOURNAL

Date	Particulars	L.F.	Dr. (₹)	Cr. (₹)
2015 April 1	Z's Capital A/c(₹36,000 × 3/10) Dr. To X's Capital A/c(₹36,000 × 3/10) (Being the adjustment for Profits & Advertisement Suspense on change in profit-sharing ratio)		10,800	10,800

Note: X's Sacrifice = 5/10 – 2/10 = 3/10, Y's Gain = 3/10 – 3/10 = nil, Z's Gain = 2/10 – 5/10 = (3/10)

QUESTION 20: X, Y and Z are partners in a firm sharing profits & losses in the ratio of 5:3:2. They decide to share future profits & losses in the ratio of 2:3:5 with effect from 1st April, 2015. The Land (having book value of ₹ 1,00,000) was found undervalued by ₹ 5,00,000. The Stock (having book value of ₹ 4,00,000) was found overvalued by ₹ 3,00,000. Pass the necessary single adjusting entry without affecting the existing figures.

ANSWER:

ADJUSTING JOURNAL ENTRY

Date	Particulars	L.F.	Dr. (₹)	Cr. (₹)
2015 April 1	Z's Capital A/c(₹2,00,000 × 3/10) Dr. To X's Capital A/c(₹2,00,000 × 3/10) (Being the adjustment made for change in the values of Assets on change in profit-sharing ratio)		60,000	60,000

Note: X's Sacrifice = 5/10 – 2/10 = 3/10, Y's Gain = 3/10 – 3/10 = nil, Z's Gain = 2/10 – 5/10= (3/10)

Net Effect of Adjustments to be made = ₹ 5,00,000 – ₹ 3,00,000 = ₹ 2,00,000.

RECONSTITUTION OF PARTNERSHIP – ADMISSION OF A PARTNER

QUESTION 1: What is meant by Admission of a Partner?

ANSWER: Admission of a partner is one of the modes of reconstituting the firm under which old partnership comes to an end and a new one between all partners (including incoming partner) comes into existence.

QUESTION 2: How can a partner admitted?

ANSWER: According to the Sec 31(1) of Indian Partnership Act, 1932, a person can Admitted be admitted as a new partner only with the consent of all the existing partners unless otherwise agreed upon.

QUESTION 3: X and Y are partners in a firm. They do not have any partnership deed. X wants to introduce his son, Z as third partner into the firm. Y objects. Who is correct in this case?

ANSWER: Y can object since as per Sec 31(1) of Indian Partnership Act, 1932, a person can be admitted as a new partner only with the consent of all the existing partners unless otherwise agreed upon.

QUESTION 4: State the two Financial Rights acquired by a new partner.

1. Right to Share the Assets of the firm;
2. Right to Share the Future Profits of the firm.

QUESTION 5: State any two Adjustments required on admission of a partner.

ANSWER:

1. Adjustment in Profit Sharing Ratio,
2. Adjustment of Goodwill,
3. Adjustment of Profit/Loss arising from the Revaluation of Assets and Liabilities,
4. Adjustment of Accumulated Profits, Reserves and Losses

QUESTION 6: Why does a new partner bring in the Capital into the firm?

ANSWER: A New Partner bring in the Capital into the firm to acquire the Right to Share the Assets of the firm.

QUESTION 7: Why does a new partner bring in Goodwill into the firm?

ANSWER: A New Partner brings in Goodwill into the firm to acquire the Right to Share the Future Profits of the firm.

QUESTION 8: State any one purpose for admitting a new partner in a firm.

ANSWER:

1. To have more Financial Resources for expansion and growth.
2. To have more Managerial Skills for efficient management.

QUESTION 9: State the other Right acquired by a new partner besides the Right to Share the Future Profits of the firm.

ANSWER: Right to Share the Assets of the firm;

QUESTION 10: State the other Right acquired by a new partner besides the Right to Share the Assets of the firm.

ANSWER: Right to Share the Future Profits of the firm.

QUESTION 11: Define New Profit Sharing Ratio in case of admission of a partner.

ANSWER: The ratio in which all partners (including incoming partner) share the Future Profits and Losses is known as the New Profit Sharing Ratio.

QUESTION 12: Why is it necessary to calculate New Profit Sharing Ratio even for old partners when a new partner is admitted?

ANSWER: When a new partner is admitted, he acquires his share in profits from the old partners. This reduces the old partners' shares in profits hence, profit sharing ratio for old partners have to be calculated.

QUESTION 13: Unless given otherwise, what will be the New Profit Sharing Ratio of Old Partners in case of admission of a partner?

ANSWER: Unless agreed otherwise, it is presumed that the new partner acquires his share in profits from the old partners in their old profit sharing ratio and the old partners continue to share the remaining profit in their old ratio and hence the New Profit Sharing Ratio of Old Partners will be the same as their Old Profit Sharing Ratio.

QUESTION 14: Define Sacrificing Ratio.

ANSWER: The ratio in which the Old Partners have agreed to sacrifice their shares in profit in favour of a new partner is called the Sacrificing Ratio. This ratio is calculated by taking out the difference between Old Profit Share and the New Profit Share.

QUESTION 15: Why is Sacrificing Ratio calculated in case of admission of a partner calculated?

ANSWER: Sacrificing Ratio is calculated to determine the amount of compensation to be paid by the incoming partner to the sacrificing partners.

QUESTION 16: State any two circumstances in which sacrificing ratio may be applied.

ANSWER:

1. When there is change in profit sharing ratio.
2. When a new partner is admitted.

QUESTION 17: Unless given otherwise, what will be the ratio of sacrifice in case of admission of a partner?

ANSWER: Unless agreed otherwise it is presumed that the old partners sacrifice in their old profit sharing ratio and hence, Sacrificing Ratio of Old Partners will be the same as their Old Profit Sharing Ratio.

QUESTION 18: Pawan and Jayshree are partners. Bindu is admitted for 1/4th share. What is ratio in which Pawan and Jayshree will sacrifice their share of profit in favour of Bindu?

ANSWER: Pawan and Jayshree will sacrifice their share of profit in their Old Profit Sharing Ratio in favour of Bindu.

QUESTION 19: A and B are partners sharing profits in the ratio of 3:2. They admit C, a new partner who acquires 1/5th of his share from A and 4/25th share from B. Calculate the new profit sharing ratio and sacrificing ratio.

ANSWER :

Step 1: Calculation of Share of Incoming Partner

Since C acquires 1/5th of his share from A, it means he acquires 4/5th (i.e. 1–1/5th) of his share from B.

If 4/5th shares = 4/25

1 share = 4/25 × 5/4 =1/5

Step 2: Calculation of New Shares

Share acquired by C : from A = 1/5 × 1/5 = 1/25, from B = 4/25

A's New Share = 3/5 – 1/25 = 14/25, B's New Share = 2/5 – 4/25 = 6/25

Step 3: New Profit Sharing Ratio of A, B and C = 14/25 : 6/25 : 5/25 = 14 : 6 : 5

Step 4: Sacrificing Ratio of A and B = 1/25 : 4/25 = 1 : 4

QUESTION 20: X and Y are sharing profits and losses in the ratio of 5: 3. They admit Z and decide that the profit sharing ratio between Y and Z shall be the same as existing between X and Y. Calculate the new profit sharing ratio and the sacrificing ratio.

ANSWER :

As the Ratio of X and Y is 5 : 3, Ratio of Y and Z should be 5: 3. Since Y's share is 60% of X's share, Z's share should also be 60% of Y's share. Thus, Z's share is 60% of 3 = 1.8 New Ratio of X, Y & Z = 5 : 3 : 1.8 *or* 25: 15 : 9

CALCULATION OF SACRIFICING RATIO

Particulars	X	Y
(a) Their existing shares	5/8	3/8
(b) Their new shares	25/49	15/49
(c) Difference [(a) – (b)]	5/8 – 25/49 = 45/392	3/8 – 15/49 = 27/392
(d) Sacrificing Ratio of X & Y = 45/392: 27/392 = 5: 3		

QUESTION 21: Why is it necessary to adjust Goodwill at the time of admission of a partner?

Or

State the need for treatment of goodwill on admission of a partner.

ANSWER: A New partner is required to compensate the partner (s) who has (have) made the sacrifice of share of profit in his favour.

QUESTION 22: State the ratio in which the old partners share New Partner's share of goodwill.

ANSWER: Old Partners share New Partner's share of goodwill in their Sacrificing Ratio.

QUESTION 23: A and B are partners in a firm sharing profits and losses equally. They admitted C as a partner for 1/5th share of profit. C brought into partnership "Book Debts" amounting to ₹ 20,000 (less provision for Doubtful Debts of 5%), the Goodwill of his connections valued at ₹ 40,000 and the balance amount in cash, borrowed from his friend D, so as to take his Capital of ₹ 1,20,000. Required: Show the Journal Entry in the books of the firm.

ANSWER:

JOURNAL

Date	Particulars		L.F.	Dr. (₹)	Cr. (₹)
	Sundry Debtors A/c	Dr.		20,000	
	Goodwill A/c	Dr.		40,000	
	Cash A/c	Dr.		61,000	
	To Provision for Doubtful Debts A/c				1,000
	To C's Capital A/c				1,20,000
	(Being the amount brought in by C towards capital)				

QUESTION 24: A and B are in partnership sharing profits and losses in the ratio of 3: 1. They admit C for one third share of the profits. As between themselves, A and B agree to share future profits and losses equally. C brings in ₹ 5,000 in cash and Machinery worth ₹ 6,000 out of his share of ₹ 15,000 for goodwill. Pass the necessary journal entries.

ANSWER:

JOURNAL

Date	Particulars		L.F.	Dr. (₹)	Cr. (₹)
	Cash A/c	Dr.		5,000	
	Machinery A/c	Dr.		6,000	
	To C's Capital A/c				11,000
	(Being the amount brought in by C towards goodwill)				

	C's Capital A/c Dr. To A's Capital A/c (Being the goodwill credited to sacrificing partner)		15,000	15,000
	B's Capital A/c [₹ 45,000 × 1/12] Dr. To A's Capital A/c (Being the adjustment made on account of change in profit sharing ratio. B loses 1/12th of profit and hence B compensates A for this loss in share of profit thus, 1/12th of ₹ 45,000, ₹ 3,750) (Firm's goodwill ₹ 15,000 × 3/1 = 45,000)		3,750	3,750

Working Note: *Calculation of Sacrificing Ratio*

Let the total Share be = 1, C's Share = 1/3, Remaining Share = 1 – 1/3 = 2/3

A's New Share = 1/2 × 2/3 = 2/6, B's New Share = 1/2 × 2/3 = 2/6

A's Sacrifice = 3/4 – 1/3 = 5/12, B's Gain = 1/4 – 1/3 = 1/12

QUESTION 25: X and Y share profits & losses in the ratio of 5: 3. Z is admitted for 3/10th share of profits half of which was gifted by X and the remaining share was taken by Z equally from X and Y. The goodwill of the firm is valued at ₹ 21,600. Z brings in his requisite share of firm's goodwill. The profit for the first year of new partnership amounts to ₹ 24,000. Pass the necessary journal entries to adjust goodwill and to distribute profits.

ANSWER:

JOURNAL

Date	Particulars	L.F.	Dr. (₹)	Cr. (₹)
	Cash A/c [₹ 21,600 × 3/20] Dr. To Z's Capital A/c (Being the amount of goodwill brought in by Z for purchased share of profit i.e. 3/20)		3,240	3,240
	Z's Capital A/c Dr. To X's Capital A/c [₹ 3,240 × 1/2] To Y's Capital A/c [₹ 3,240 × 1/2] (Being the goodwill credited to sacrificing partners in their sacrificing ratio of 1:1)		3,240	1,620 1,620
	Profit and Loss A/c Dr. To X's Capital A/c [₹ 24,000 × 4/10] To Y's Capital A/c [₹ 24,000 × 3/10] To Z's Capital A/c [₹ 24,000 × 3/10] (Being the profit credited to all partners in their new profit sharing ratio of 4: 3: 3)		24,000	9,600 7,200 7,200

Working Note:

CALCULATION OF NEW PROFIT SHARING RATIO

Particulars	X	Y
A Their old shares	5/8	3/8
B Share gifted by X	1/2 of 3/10 = 3/20	—
C Share acquired by Z	1/2 of 3/20 = 3/40	1/2 of 3/20 = 3/40
D Their new shares [A – B – C]	16/40	12/40
E New Ratio of X, Y & Z = 16/40: 12/40: 12/40 = 16: 12: 12 = 4: 3: 3.		

QUESTION 26: How is the amount of Hidden Goodwill calculated?

ANSWER: When the value of the goodwill of the firm is not specifically given, the value of goodwill has to be inferred on the basis of the Net Worth of the firm as follows:

		₹
A.	Net Worth (including goodwill) on the basis of capital brought in by Incoming Partner	
	(Incoming Partner's Capital × Reciprocal of share of Incoming Partner)	xxx
B.	*Less:* Net Worth (excluding goodwill) of the reconstituted firm (including Incoming Partner's Capital)	xxx
C.	Value of Goodwill (A – B)	xxx

Note: Net Worth = Sundry Assets – Outsiders' Liabilities
or, = Capitals of Partners + Net Accumulated Profits & Reserves (if any)

QUESTION 27: A and B are partners with capitals of ₹ 13,000 and ₹ 9,000 respectively. They admit C as partner with 1/5th share in the profit of the firm. C brings ₹ 8,000 as his capital. Calculate C's share of goodwill.

ANSWER:

1. Hidden Goodwill = (8,000 × 4/1) – (₹ 13,000 + ₹ 9,000) = ₹ 10,000,
   C's share of goodwill = ₹ 10,000 × 1/5 = ₹ 2,000

QUESTION 28: A and B are partners in a firm. They admit C as a partner with 1/4th share in the profits of the firm. Chetan brings ₹ 2,00,000 as his share of capital. The value of the total assets of the firm is ₹ 5,40,000 and outside liabilities are valued at ₹ 1,00,000 on that date. Calculate C's share of goodwill.

ANSWER:

1. Hidden Goodwill = (2,00,000 × 4/1) – (₹ 5,40,000 – ₹ 1,00,000 + ₹ 2,00,000) = ₹ 1,60,000,
2. C's Share of goodwill = ₹ 1,60,000 × 1/4 = ₹ 40,000

QUESTION 29: A and B are partners with capitals of ₹ 5,000 each. They admit C as a partner with 1/4th share in the profits of the firm. C brings ₹ 8,000 as his share of capital. The Profit and Loss Account showed a credit balance of ₹ 4,000 as on date of admission of C. Give the necessary journal entry to record goodwill.

ANSWER:

JOURNAL

Date	Particulars		L.F.	Dr. (₹)	Cr. (₹)
	C's Capital A/c [₹ 10,000 × 1/4]	Dr.		2,500	
	To A's Capital A/c				1,250
	To B's Capital A/c				1,250
	(Being the share of C in the hidden goodwill adjusted through capital accounts by crediting sacrificing partners in their sacrificing ratio)				

Note: Hidden Goodwill = – (₹ 5,000 + ₹ 5,000 + ₹ 4,000 + ₹ 8,000) = ₹ 10,000

QUESTION 30: From the following calculate the value of firm's goodwill:

(a) C a new partner is unable to bring in cash for his share of goodwill, partners.

(b) C brings ₹ 25,000 as his capital for 1/6th share in future profits.

(c) Capitals given of A & B are ₹ 44,000 and ₹ 36,000 respectively.

ANSWER:

Total Capital of New Firm (₹ 25,000 × 6/1)	₹ 1,50,000
Less: Combined Capital of A, B & C [₹ 44,000 + ₹ 36,000 + ₹ 25,000]	₹ 1,05,000
Hidden Goodwill	₹ 45,000

QUESTION 31: Why is it necessary to revalue Assets & Liabilities at the time of admission of a partner?

ANSWER: At the time of admission of a partner, the assets and liabilities are revalued so that the profit *or* loss on revaluation upto the date of admission of new partner may be ascertained and adjusted in the Old Partners' Capital Accounts in their Old Profit Sharing Ratio and the Incoming Partner may not be affected by such profit *or* loss because such profit *or* loss loss relates to pre-admission period and hence belongs to Old Partners and not to Incoming Partner.

QUESTION 32: Why is Profit *or* Loss on Revaluation not transferred to the Incoming Partner' Capital account?

ANSWER: Profit *or* Loss on Revaluation is not transferred to the Incoming Partner' Capital account because such profit *or* loss relates to pre-admission period and hence belongs to Old Partners and not to Incoming Partner.

QUESTION 33: State the ratio in which the Old Partners share gain *or* loss arising from revaluation of assets and liabilities at the time of admission of a partner.

ANSWER: At the time of admission of a partner Old Partners share gain *or* loss arising from revaluation of assets and liabilities in their Old Profit Sharing Ratio.

QUESTION 34: What is Revaluation Account?

ANSWER: Revaluation Account is a Nominal Account which is credited with increase in the value of assets and decrease in the amount of liabilities (it is a gain) and debited with decrease in the value of assets and increase in the amount of liabilities (it is a loss).

QUESTION 35: State the other name of Revaluation Account.

ANSWER: Profit & Loss Adjustment Account

QUESTION 36: State the nature of Revaluation Account.

ANSWER: Revaluation Account is a Nominal Account.

QUESTION 37: Why is Revaluation Account prepared? State any two reasons.

ANSWER: Revaluation Account is prepared:

1. To ascertain the Profit/Loss arising on account of Revaluation of Assets and Liabilities.
2. To record the effect of Revaluation of Assets & Liabilities so as to show the Assets & Liabilities at their revalued figures.

QUESTION 38: How is the balance of Revaluation Account dealt with?

ANSWER: The balance of Revaluation Account is transferred to the Partners' Capital accounts in their Old Profit Sharing Ratio.

QUESTION 39: At what figures, the assets and liabilities appear in the books of reconstituted firm in case a "Revaluation Account" is prepared?

ANSWER: When Revaluation Account is prepared, the Assets and Liabilities appear in the Balance Sheet of new firm at their Revised (Revalued) Figures.

QUESTION 40: At what figures, the assets and liabilities appear in the books of reconstituted firm in case a "Revaluation Account" is not prepared?

ANSWER: When Revaluation Account is not prepared, the Assets and Liabilities appear in the Balance Sheet of new firm at their Old Figures.

QUESTION 41: At what figures, the assets and liabilities appear in the books of reconstituted firm in case a "Revaluation Account" is not prepared?

ANSWER: When Revaluation Account is not prepared, the Assets and Liabilities appear in the Balance Sheet of new firm at their Old Figures.

QUESTION 42: State whether the Revaluation Account will be debited *or* credited on decrease in Provision for doubtful debts?

ANSWER: Credited.

QUESTION 43: State whether the Revaluation Account will be debited *or* credited on recovery of Bad debts already written off?

ANSWER: Credited.

QUESTION 44: State whether the Revaluation Account will be debited *or* credited when some Debtors proved Bad if Provision for doubtful debts is not maintained?

ANSWER: Debited.

QUESTION 45: State whether the Revaluation Account will be debited *or* credited when some Debtors proved Bad if Provision for doubtful debts is maintained?

ANSWER: N*either* Debited nor credited.

QUESTION 46: X and Y are partners in a firm sharing profits in the ratio of 3:2. They admitted Z as a new partner and fixed the new profit sharing ratio as 3:3:2. At the time of admission of Z, Debtors and Provision for Doubtful Debts appeared at ₹ 38,000 and ₹ 4,000 respectively. All Debtors are good. Pass the necessary journal entries.

ANSWER:

JOURNAL

Date	Particulars		L.F.	Dr. (₹)	Cr. (₹)
	Provision for Doubtful Debts A/c	Dr.		4,000	
	To Revaluation A/c				4,000
	(Being the excess Provision for Doubtful Debts t/f to Revaluation A/c)				
	Revaluation A/c	Dr.		4,000	
	To X's Capital A/c				2,400
	To Y's Capital A/c				1,600
	(Being the Profit on Revaluation t/f to partners in their old profit sharing ratio)				

QUESTION 47: X and Y are partners in a firm sharing profits in the ratio of 3:2. They admitted Z as a new partner and fixed the new profit sharing ratio as 3:3:2. At the time of admission of Z, Debtors and Provision for Doubtful Debts appeared at 8,000 and ₹ 4,000 respectively. ₹ 3,000 of the debtors proved bad. A provision of 5% is to be created on Sundry Debtors for doubtful debts. Pass the necessary journal entries.

ANSWER:

JOURNAL

Date	Particulars		L.F.	Dr. (₹)	Cr. (₹)
	Bad Debts A/c	Dr.		3,000	
	To Debtors A/c				3,000
	(Being the Bad Debts w/o)				
	Provision for Doubtful Debts A/c	Dr.		3,000	
	To Bad Debts A/c				3,000
	(Being the Bad Debts t/f to Provision for Doubtful Debts A/c)				
	Revaluation A/c	Dr.		750	
	To Provision for Doubtful Debts A/c				
	[5% (₹ 38,000 – ₹ 3,000)] – [(₹ 4,000 – ₹ 3,000)]				750
	(Being the short Provision for Doubtful Debts created)				
	X's Capital A/c	Dr.		450	
	Y's Capital A/c	Dr.		300	
	To Revaluation A/c				750
	(Being the Loss on Revaluation t/f to partners in their old profit sharing ratio)				

QUESTION 48: X and Y are partners in a firm sharing profits in the ratio of 3:2. They admitted Z as a new partner and fixed the new profit sharing ratio as 3:3:2. At the time of admission of Z, Stock (Book Value ₹ 50,000) is to be reduced by 40% and Furniture (Book Value ₹ 30,000) is to be reduced to 40%. Pass the necessary journal entries.

ANSWER:

JOURNAL

Date	Particulars		L.F.	Dr. (₹)	Cr. (₹)
	Revaluation A/c A/c	Dr.		38,000	
	To Stock A/c				20,000
	To Furniture A/c				18,000
	(Being the decrease in value of assets recorded)				
	X's Capital A/c	Dr.		22,800	
	Y's Capital A/c	Dr.		15,200	
	To Revaluation A/c				38,000
	(Being the Loss on Revaluation t/f to partners in their old profit sharing ratio)				

QUESTION 49: X and Y are partners in a firm sharing profits in the ratio of 3:2. They admitted Z as a new partner and fixed the new profit sharing ratio as 3:3:2. At the time of admission of Z, Investments appeared at ₹ 40,000. Half of the Investments to be taken over by X and Y in their profit sharing ratio at book value. Remaining Investments were valued at ₹ 25,000. Pass the necessary journal entries.

ANSWER:

JOURNAL

Date	Particulars		L.F.	Dr. (₹)	Cr. (₹)
	X's Capital A/c	Dr.		12,000	
	Y's Capital A/c	Dr.		8,000	
	To Revaluation A/c				20,000
	(Being the Investments taken over by partners)				
	Investments A/c	Dr.		5,000	
	To Revaluation A/c				5,000
	(Being the increase in value of assets recorded)				
	Revaluation A/c	Dr.		5,000	
	To X's Capital A/c				3,000
	To Y's Capital A/c				2,000
	(Being the Profit on Revaluation t/f to partners in their old profit sharing ratio)				

QUESTION 50: X and Y are partners in a firm sharing profits in the ratio of 3:2. They admitted Z as a new partner and fixed the new profit sharing ratio as 3:3:2. At the time of admission of Z, Unaccounted Accrued Income of ₹ 1,000 be provided for. A debtor whose dues of ₹ 5,000 were written off as bad debts paid ₹ 4,000 in full settlement.There is a liability of ₹ 5,000 included in Sundry Creditors that is not likely to arise.Pass the necessary journal entries.

ANSWER:

JOURNAL

Date	Particulars		L.F.	Dr. (₹)	Cr. (₹)
	Unaccounted Accrued Income A/c	Dr.		1,000	
	Bank A/c (Bad Debts Recovered)	Dr.		4,000	
	Creditors A/c	Dr.		5,000	
	To Revaluation A/c				10,000
	(Being the increase in value of assets & decrease in value of liabilities recorded)				
	Revaluation A/c	Dr.		10,000	
	To X's Capital A/c				6,000
	To Y's Capital A/c				4,000
	(Being the Profit on Revaluation t/f to partners in their old profit sharing ratio)				

QUESTION 51: X and Y are partners in a firm sharing profits in the ratio of 3:2. They admitted Z as a new partner and fixed the new profit sharing ratio as 6:9:5. At the time of admission of Z, Patents (Book Value ₹ 10,000) found overvalued by ₹ 8,500 and Stock (Book Value ₹ 30,000) to be written up to ₹ 31,000. Debtors and Provision for doubtful debts appeared at ₹ 65,000 and ₹ 5,000 respectively. All Debtors are good. There is a liability of ₹ 500 included in Sundry Creditors that is not likely to arise. Unaccounted Accrued Income of ₹ 1,000 to be provided for. A debtor whose dues of ₹ 5,000 were written off as bad debts paid 80% in full settlement. A claim of ₹ 3,000 on account of workmen's compensation to be provided for. Workmen's Compensation Fund appeared at ₹ 12,000. Half of the Investments (Total Book Value ₹ 50,000) to be taken over by X and Y in their profit sharing ratio at book value. Remaining Investments were valued at ₹ 20,000.Prepare the Revaluation Account.

ANSWER:

Dr. **REVALUATION ACCOUNT** Cr.

Particulars	₹	Particulars		₹
To Patents	8,500	By Sundry Creditors		500
To Investments	5,000	By Accrued Income		1,000
		By Bad Debts Recovered		4,000
		By Stock		1,000
		By Provision for Doubtful Debts		5,000
		By Loss on Revaluation t/f to:		
		X's Capital A/c	1,200	
		Y's Capital A/c	800	2,000
	13,500			13,500

QUESTION 52: Why is it necessary to distribute Accumulated Reserves, Profits & Losses at the time of admission of a partner?

ANSWER: At the time of admission of a partner, any Reserves, Accumulated Profits/Losses upto the date of admission of a partner are transferred to Old Partners' Capital Accounts (if capitals are fluctuating) *or* Current Accounts (if capitals are fixed) in their old profit sharing ratio since the Reserves, Accumulated Profits/Losses relate to pre-admission period and hence belong to the Old Partners and not to the New partner.

QUESTION 53: Why are Accumulated Reserves, Profits & Losses not transferred to the Incoming Partner' Capital account?

ANSWER: Accumulated Reserves, Profits & Losses are not transferred to the Incoming Partner' Capital account because such profits *or* losses relate to pre-admission period and hence belongs to Old Partners and not to Incoming Partner.

QUESTION 54: State the ratio in which the Old Partners share Accumulated Reserves, Profits & Losses at the time of admission of a partner.

ANSWER: At the time of admission of a partner Old Partners share Accumulated Reserves, Profits & Losses in their Old Profit Sharing Ratio.

QUESTION 55: Give the journal entry to distribute 'Workman Compensation Reserve' of ₹ 60,000 at the time of admission of Z, when there is no claim against it. The firm has two partners X and Y.

ANSWER:

JOURNAL

Date	Particulars		L.F.	Dr. (₹)	Cr. (₹)
	Workman Compensation Reserve A/c	Dr.		60,000	
	To X's Capital A/c				30,000
	To Y's Capital A/c				30,000
	(Being the WCR t/f to partners in their old profit sharing ratio)				

QUESTION 56: Give the journal entry to distribute 'Workman Compensation Reserve' of ₹ 60,000 at the time of admission of Z, when there is claim of ₹ 40,000 against it. The firm has two partners X and Y.

ANSWER:

JOURNAL

Date	Particulars		L.F.	Dr. (₹)	Cr. (₹)
	Workman Compensation Reserve A/c	Dr.		60,000	
	To X's Capital A/c				10,000
	To Y's Capital A/c				10,000
	To Workman Compensation Claim A/c				40,000
	(Being the liability for Workman Compensation Claim created and surplus WCR t/f to partners in their old profit sharing ratio)				

QUESTION 57: Give the journal entry to distribute 'Investment Fluctuation Reserve' of ₹ 4,000 at the time of admission of Z, when Investments (market value ₹ 19,000) appear at ₹ 20,000. The firm has two partners X and Y.

ANSWER:

JOURNAL

Date	Particulars		L.F.	Dr. (₹)	Cr. (₹)
	Investment Fluctuation Reserve A/c	Dr.		4,000	
	To X's Capital A/c				1,500
	To Y's Capital A/c				1,500
	To Investments A/c				1,000
	(Being the value of Investments brought up to market value and surplus IFR t/f to partners in their old profit sharing ratio)				

QUESTION 58: Give the journal entry to distribute 'General Reserve' of ₹ 4,000 at the time of admission of Z, when 25% of General Reserve is to be be transferred to Provision for Doubtful Debts. The firm has two partners X and Y.

ANSWER:

JOURNAL

Date	Particulars		L.F.	Dr. (₹)	Cr. (₹)
	General Reserve A/c	Dr.		4,000	
	To X's Capital A/c				1,500
	To Y's Capital A/c				1,500
	To Provision for Doubtful Debts A/c				1,000
	(Being 25% of General Reserve t/f to Provision and the Balance t/f to partners in their old profit sharing ratio)				

QUESTION 59: If new partner has to bring proportionate capital which is not given, how can it be worked out?

ANSWER:

Step 1: Total Capital = Total Adjusted Old Capitals of Old Partners × Reciprocal of proportion of Share of Old Partners

Step 2: New Partner's Proportionate Capital = Total Capital × Proportion of Share of New Partner

QUESTION 60: A and B are in partnership with ₹ 30,000 and ₹ 20,000 as their respective capitals. They admitted C as a partner for 1/6 share in profits. You are required to calculate the amount of C's share in the capital of the firm if he is asked to bring in capital in proportion to his profit sharing ratio.

ANSWER: Let Total Capital be X

X = ₹ 30,000 + ₹ 20,000 + 1/6 X,

X – 1/6 X = ₹ 50,000,

X = ₹ 50,000 × 6/5 = ₹ 60,000,

C's Capital = ₹ 60,000 × 1/6 = ₹ 10,000

QUESTION 61: A and B who are in partnership sharing profits and losses in the ratio of 3: 2 admit C for 1/5 share in profits. The capitals of A and B after adjustments are ₹ 60,000 and ₹ 40,000 respectively. C is to bring 20% of the total capital of the new firm. Calculate C's Capital.

ANSWER: Let Total Capital be X

Thus, X = Adjusted Old Capitals of old partners + Incoming Partners' Capital

X = ₹ 60,000 + ₹ 40,000 + 1/5 X

X–1/5 X = ₹ 1,00,000, X = ₹ 1,00,000 × 5/4 = ₹ 1,25,000

Thus, C's proportionate capital = 1/5 of ₹ 1,25,000 = ₹ 25,000

QUESTION 62: A and B who are in partnership sharing profits and losses in the ratio of 3: 2 admit C for 1/5 share in profits. The capitals of A and B after adjustments are ₹ 60,000 and ₹ 40,000 respectively. C is to bring 25% of the total capital of A and B. Calculate C's Capital.

ANSWER: C's proportionate capital = 25/100 × (₹ 60,000 + ₹ 40,000) = ₹ 25,000

QUESTION 63: A and B who are in partnership sharing profits and losses in the ratio of 3: 2 admit C as a partner who contributes ₹ 25,000 as capital for 1/5th share of profits B. The capitals of A and B after adjustments are ₹ 65,000 and ₹ 35,000 respectively.The capital accounts of old partners are to be adjusted on the basis of the proportion of C's capital to his share in the business. Calculate the amount of actual cash to be paid off *or* brought in by the old partners for the purpose.

ANSWER: Total Capital of the new firm = ₹ 25,000 × 5/1 = ₹ 1,25,000

A's New Capital = ₹ 1,25,000 × 12/25 = ₹ 60,000

B's New Capital = ₹ 1,25,000 × 8/25 = ₹ 40,000

CALCULATION OF CASH TO BE BROUGHT IN (CASH TO BE PAID)

Particulars	A	B
(a) New Capital	₹ 60,000	₹ 40,000
(b) Adjusted Old Capital	₹ 65,000	₹ 35,000
(c) Cash to be brought in (Cash to be paid)	(₹ 5,000)	₹ 5,000

QUESTION 64: A and B are in partnership sharing profits and losses in the ratio of 3: 2. The capitals of A and B remaining after adjustments are ₹ 80,000 and ₹ 60,000 respectively. They admit C as a third partner who has to contribute sufficient capital to acquire a 1/5th share of the total capital of the new firm equally from both the partners A and B. Calculate the capital to be brought in by C.

ANSWER: A's New share = 3/5 – 1/10 = 5/10, B's New Share = 2/5 – 1/10 = 3/10

Thus, New Profit Sharing Ratio = 5: 3: 2

Step 1: Total Adjusted Old Capitals of Old Partners = ₹ 80,000 + ₹ 60,000 = ₹ 1,40,000

Step 2: Total Capital of the reconstituted firm = ₹ 1,40,000 × 5/4 = ₹ 1,75,000

Alternative Method – Let us assume, the total capital of new firm be X

X = ₹ 80,000 + ₹ 60,000 + 1/5X *or,* X – 1/5X = ₹ 1,40,000

X = ₹ 1,40,000 × 5/4 = ₹ 1,75,000

Step 3: Proportionate Capital of Incoming Partner = ₹ 1,75,000 × 1/5 = ₹ 35,000

QUESTION 65: From the following, calculate the additional cash to be brought in by partners:

(a) C (a new partner) brings goodwill ₹ 6,000, Furniture ₹ 2,800, Stock ₹ 13,600

(b) Adjusted capitals of A and B are ₹ 36,200 and ₹ 53,200 respectively.

(c) **Capital Accounts are to be adjusted as to be equal. For this purpose additional cash should be brought in by the partner *or* partners concerned.**

ANSWER:

Let us take highest capital of partner (i.e. B) as base.

A is required to bring in ₹ 17,000 (i.e. ₹ 53,200 – ₹ 36,200)

C is required to bring in ₹ 39,800 (i.e. ₹ 53,200 – ₹ 22,400)

QUESTION 66: From the following, calculate the excess cash to be withdrawn by partners:

(a) **C (a new partner) brings goodwill ₹ 6,000, Furniture ₹ 2,800, Stock ₹ 13,600**

(b) **Adjusted Capitals of A and B are ₹ 36,200 and ₹ 53,200 respectively.**

(c) **Capital Accounts are to be adjusted as to be equal. For this purpose excess cash should be withdrawn by the partner *or* partners concerned.**

ANSWER:

Let us take lowest capital of partner (i.e. C) as base.

A should withdraw ₹ 13,800 (i.e. ₹ 36,200 – ₹ 22,400)

B should withdraw ₹ 30,800 (i.e. ₹ 53,200 – ₹ 22,400)

RECONSTITUTION OF PARTNERSHIP – RETIREMENT/DEATH OF A PARTNER

QUESTION 1: What is meant by Retirement of a Partner?

ANSWER: Retirement of a partner is one of the modes of reconstituting the firm under which an old partnership comes to an end and a new one between the remaining partners (i.e., partners other than the outgoing partner) comes into existence. However, the firm continues its business.

QUESTION 2: How can a partner retire from the firm?

ANSWER: A partner may retire:

1. with the consent of all other partners (whether implied *or* expressed);
2. in accordance with an express agreement by the partners; or
3. by giving notice in writing, to all other partners of his intention to retire in case of partnership at will

QUESTION 3: Is a Retiring Partner liable for firm's acts before his retirement?

ANSWER: Retiring Partner continues to be liable to the third party unless he discharges himself for the same by Novation (i.e., by tripartite agreement between him, third party and the continuing partners).

QUESTION 4: Is a Retiring Partner liable for firm's acts after his retirement'?

ANSWER: Retiring Partner continues to be liable to third party until public notice of his retirement is given by himself *or* any of the other partners. But he will not be liable to any third party if the latter deals with the firm without knowing, that the former was a partner.

QUESTION 5: State any two effects of retirement of a partner.

1. An old partnership comes to an end and a new one between the remaining partners (i.e., partners other than the outgoing partner) comes into existence.
2. The combined share of remaining partners increases.

QUESTION 6: State any two matters that need adjustments at the time of retirement of a partner.

1. Adjustment in Profit Sharing Ratio,
2. Adjustment of Goodwill,
3. Adjustment of Profit/Loss arising from the Revaluation of Assets and Liabilities,
4. Adjustment of Accumulated Profits, Reserves and Losses,

QUESTION 7: Define New Profit Sharing Ratio in case of retirement of a partner.

ANSWER: The ratio in which the remaining partners (i.e., partners other than an outgoing one) decide to share the future profits and losses, is known as New Profit Sharing Ratio.

New Share = Old Share + Acquired Share

QUESTION 8: What will be the new profit sharing ratio of the remaining partners in the absence of any specific future ratio, in the event of retirement *or* death of a partner?

ANSWER: Unless agreed otherwise, New Profit Sharing Ratio of the remaining partners is same as their Old Profit Sharing Ratio because it is presumed that the remaining partners acquire the outgoing partner's share in their old profit sharing ratio so that the remaining partners continue to share the future profits in their old ratio.

QUESTION 9: Why is it necessary to calculate New Profit Sharing Ratio at the time of retirement of a partner?

ANSWER: When a partner retires, remaining partners gain the share of profits of the retiring partner. This increases the remaining partners' shares of profits. Hence, it becomes necessary to calculate new profit sharing ratio of remaining partners.

QUESTION 10: Define Gaining Ratio in case of retirement of a partner. How is it calculated?

ANSWER: The ratio in which the remaining partners acquire the outgoing (retired *or* deceased) partner's share is called as gaining ratio. This ratio is calculated by taking out the difference between New Profit Share and Old Profit Share. Gain of a Partner = New Share – Old Share

QUESTION 11: Why is Gaining Ratio in case of retirement of a partner calculated?

ANSWER: Gaining Ratio is calculated to determine the amount of compensation to be paid by each of the Gaining partners to the Outgoing Partner.

QUESTION 12: Unless given otherwise, what will be the Gaining Ratio in case of retirement of a partner?

ANSWER: Unless agreed otherwise it is presumed that, the Continuing Partners gain in their old profit sharing ratio and hence their Gaining Ratio is same as their Old Profit Sharing Ratio.

QUESTION 13: Give the two circumstances in which Gaining Ratio may be applied.

ANSWER:

(a) When there is change in profit sharing ratio.

(b) When a partner retires/dies.

QUESTION 14: Give any two points of differences between Sacrificing Ratio and Gaining Ratio.

ANSWER:

1. **Meaning:** Sacrificing Ratio is the ratio in which the old partners have agreed to sacrifice their shares in profit in favour of new partner. Gaining Ratio is the ratio in which the continuing partners acquire the outgoing (retired *or* deceased) partners share.
2. **How to calculate?** Sacrificing Ratio is calculated by taking out the difference between Old Share and New Share. Gaining Ratio is calculated by taking out the difference between New Share and Old Share.

QUESTION 15: A, B and C are partners in a firm sharing profits in the ratio of 3: 2: 1. B died. C the son of B, is of the opinion that he is the rightful owner of his father's share of profit, and the profits of the firm be shared between A and C equally. A does not agree. Settle the dispute between A and C according to Indian Partnership Act.

ANSWER: C is not correct, NR 3: 1

QUESTION 16: Why a retiring/deceased partner is entitled to a share of goodwill of the firm?

ANSWER: When an existing partner of a firm decides to retire from the firm, the remaining partner(s) will gain in future profits. The remaining partner who gains by acquiring an additional right to share future profits must compensate the outgoing partner who sacrifices by foregoing his right to share future profits.The amount of compensation must be equal to the proportionate value of firm's goodwill. Thus,

Outgoing Partner's = Value of Firm's Goodwill × Share of Profit Sacrificed Share of Goodwill

QUESTION 17: State the ratio in which the Retiring Partner's share of goodwill is debited to Remaining Partners.

ANSWER: Retiring Partner's share of goodwill is debited to Remaining Partners in the Gaining Ratio.

QUESTION 18: A Retiring Partner is entitled to which share of Firm's Goodwill?

ANSWER: His Share of Profit in the Firm.

QUESTION 19: X, Y and Z share profits and losses in the ratio of 4: 3: 2 respectively. Y retires and X and Z decide to share future profits & losses in the ratio of 5: 3. Then immediately W is admitted for 3/10th share of profits half of which was gifted by X and the remaining share was taken by W equally from X and Z. The Goodwill of the firm is valued at ₹ 21,600. W brings in the required amount of goodwill. The profit for the year after W's admission was ₹ 24,000. Give the necessary journal entries to adjust goodwill and to distribute profits.

ANSWER:

JOURNAL

Date	Particulars		L.F.	Dr. (₹)	Cr. (₹)
	X's Capital A/c	Dr.		3,900	
	Z's Capital A/c	Dr.		3,300	
	To Y's Capital A/c				7,200
	(Being Y's share of goodwill adjusted in the capital accounts of gaining partners in their gaining ratio of 13: 11)				
	Cash A/c	Dr.		3,240	
	To W's capital A/c				3,240
	(Being the amount of goodwill brought in by W for purchased share of profit (i.e. 3/20)				
	W's Capital A/c	Dr.		3,240	
	To X's Capital A/c				1,620
	To Z's Capital A/c				1,620
	(Being the goodwill credited to sacrificing partners in their sacrificing ratio of 1: 1)				

	Profit & Loss A/c Dr. To X's capital A/c To Z's Capital A/c To W's Capital A/c (Being the profit credited to all partners in their new profit sharing ratio of 4: 3: 3)		24,000	 9,600 7,200 7,200

QUESTION 20: Why is it necessary to revalue Assets & Liabilities at the time of retirement of a partner?

ANSWER: At the time of retirement of a, partner, the assets and liabilities are revalued so that the profit/loss on revaluation upto the date of retirement/death of a partner may be ascertained and adjusted in All partners' capital accounts in their old profit sharing ratio becasue such profit *or* loss on revaluation relates to pre-retirement period.

QUESTION 21: State the ratio in which the partners share profit *or* loss on revaluation of assets and liabilities at the time of retirement of a partner.

ANSWER: At the time of retirement of a partner profit *or* loss revaluation of assets and liabilities is transferred to the Capital Accounts of all partners (including Retiring Partner) in their Old Profit Sharing Ratio.

QUESTION 22: X, Y, & Z share profits and losses in the ratio of 5: 3: 2 respectively. Y retires and X & Z decide to share future profits & losses in the ratio of 3: 5. At the time of retirement of Z, Debtors and Provision for Doubtful Debts appeared at ₹ 38,000 and ₹ 4,000 respectively. All Debtors are good. Pass the necessary journal entries.

ANSWER:

JOURNAL

Date	Particulars	L.F.	Dr. (₹)	Cr. (₹)
	Provision for Doubtful Debts A/c Dr. To Revaluation A/c (Being the excess Provision for Doubtful Debts t/f to Revaluation A/c)		4,000	 4,000
	Revaluation A/c Dr. To X's Capital A/c To Y's Capital A/c To Z's Capital A/c (Being the Profit on Revaluation t/f to partners in their old profit sharing ratio)		4,000	 2,000 1,200 800

QUESTION 23: X, Y, & Z share profits and losses in the ratio of 5: 3: 2 respectively. Y retires and X & Z decide to share future profits & losses in the ratio of 3: 5. At the time of retirement of Z, Debtors and Provision for Doubtful Debts appeared at ₹ 38,000 and ₹ 4,000 respectively. ₹ 3,000 of the debtors proved bad. A provision of 5% is to be created on Sundry Debtors for doubtful debts. Pass the necessary journal entries.

ANSWER:

JOURNAL

Date	Particulars		L.F.	Dr. (₹)	Cr. (₹)
	Bad Debts A/c	Dr.		3,000	
	To Debtors A/c				3,000
	(Being the Bad Debts w/o)				
	Provision for Doubtful Debts A/c	Dr.		3,000	
	To Bad Debts A/c				3,000
	(Being the Bad Debts t/f to Provision for Doubtful Debts A/c)				
	Revaluation A/c	Dr.		750	
	To Provision for Doubtful Debts A/c				
	[5% (₹ 38,000 – ₹ 3,000)] – [(₹ 4,000 – ₹ 3,000)]				750
	(Being the Short Provision for Doubtful Debts created)				
	X's Capital A/c	Dr.		375	
	Y's Capital A/c	Dr.		225	
	Z's Capital A/c	Dr.		150	
	To Revaluation A/c				750
	(Being the Loss on Revaluation t/f to partners in their old profit sharing ratio)				

QUESTION 24: X, Y, & Z share profits and losses in the ratio of 5: 3: 2 respectively. Y retires and X & Z decide to share future profits & losses in the ratio of 3: 5. At the time of retirement of Z, Stock (Book Value ₹ 50,000) is to be reduced by 40% and Furniture (Book Value ₹ 30,000) is to be reduced to 40%. Pass the necessary journal entries.

ANSWER:

JOURNAL

Date	Particulars		L.F.	Dr. (₹)	Cr. (₹)
	Revaluation A/c A/c	Dr.		38,000	
	To Stock A/c				20,000
	To Furniture A/c				18,000
	(Being the decrease in value of assets recorded)				
	X's Capital A/c	Dr.		19,000	
	Y's Capital A/c	Dr.		11,400	
	Z's Capital A/c	Dr.		7,600	
	To Revaluation A/c				38,000
	(Being the Loss on Revaluation t/f to partners in their old profit sharing ratio)				

QUESTION 25: X, Y, & Z share profits and losses in the ratio of 5: 3: 2 respectively. Y retires and X & Z decide to share future profits & losses in the ratio of 3: 5. At the time of retirement of Z, Investments appeared at ₹ 40,000. Half of the Investments to be taken over by partners in their profit sharing ratio at book value. Remaining Investments were valued at ₹ 25,000. Pass the necessary journal entries.

ANSWER:

JOURNAL

Date	Particulars		L.F.	Dr. (₹)	Cr. (₹)
	X's Capital A/c	Dr.		10,000	
	Y's Capital A/c	Dr.		6,000	
	Z's Capital A/c	Dr.		4,000	
	To Revaluation A/c (Being the Investments taken over by partners)				20,000
	Investments A/c	Dr.		5,000	
	To Revaluation A/c (Being the increase in value of assets recorded)				5,000
	Revaluation A/c	Dr.		5,000	
	To X's Capital A/c				2,500
	To Y's Capital A/c				1,500
	To Z's Capital A/c (Being the Profit on Revaluation t/f to partners in their old profit sharing ratio)				1,000

QUESTION 26: X, Y, & Z share profits and losses in the ratio of 5: 3: 2 respectively. Y retires and X & Z decide to share future profits & losses in the ratio of 3: 5. At the time of retirement of Z, Unaccounted Accrued Income of ₹1,000 be provided for. A debtor whose dues of ₹ 5,000 were written off as bad debts paid ₹ 4,000 in full settlement. There is a liability of ₹ 5,000 included in Sundry Creditors that is not likely to arise. Pass the necessary journal entries.

ANSWER:

JOURNAL

Date	Particulars		L.F.	Dr. (₹)	Cr. (₹)
	Unaccounted Accrued Income A/c	Dr.		1,000	
	Bank A/c (Bad Debts Recovered)	Dr.		4,000	
	Creditors A/c	Dr.		5,000	
	To Revaluation A/c (Being the increase in value of assets & decrease in value of liabilities recorded)				10,000
	Revaluation A/c	Dr.		10,000	
	To X's Capital A/c				5,000
	To Y's Capital A/c				3,000
	To Z's Capital A/c (Being the Profit on Revaluation t/f to partners in their old profit sharing ratio)				2,000

QUESTION 27: Why is it necessary to distribute Accumulated Reserves, Profits & Losses at the time of retirement of a partner?

ANSWER: At the time of retirement of a partner, all reserves, accumulated profits *or* losses upto the date of retirement/death of a partner are transferred to the Capital Accounts of all the partners (including outgoing partner) in their old profit sharing ratio so that the due share of an outgoing partner in the reserves, accumulated profits/losses gets adjusted in his Capital Account (or Current Account) because such reserves, profits/losses relate to pre-retirement period.

QUESTION 28: State the ratio in which the partners share all the accumulated profits, reserves, losses and fictitious assets at the time of retirement of a partner.

ANSWER: At the time of retirement of a partner all Partners (including Retiring Partner) share Accumulated Reserves, Profits & Losses in their Old Profit Sharing Ratio.

QUESTION 29: Give the journal entry to distribute 'Workman Compensation Reserve' of ₹ 60,000 at the time of retirement of Sajjan, when there is no claim against it. The firm has three partners Rajat, Sajjan and Kavita.

ANSWER:

JOURNAL

Date	Particulars		L.F.	Dr. (₹)	Cr. (₹)
	Workman Compensation Reserve A/c	Dr.		60,000	
	To Rajat's Capital A/c				20,000
	To Sajjan's Capital A/c				20,000
	To Kavita's Capital A/c				20,000
	(Being the WCR t/f to partners in their old profit sharing ratio)				

QUESTION 30: Give the journal entry to distribute 'Workman Compensation Reserve' of ₹ 70,000 at the time of retirement of Sajjan, when there is claim of ₹ 25,000 against it. The firm has three partners Rajat, Sajjan and Kavita.

ANSWER:

JOURNAL

Date	Particulars		L.F.	Dr. (₹)	Cr. (₹)
	Workman Compensation Reserve A/c	Dr.		70,000	
	To Rajat's Capital A/c				15,000
	To Sajjan's Capital A/c				15,000
	To Kavita's Capital A/c				15,000
	To Workman Compensation Claim A/c				25,000
	(Being the liability for Workman Compensation Claim created and surplus WCR t/f to partners in their old profit sharing ratio)				

QUESTION 31: Give the journal entry to distribute 'Investment Fluctuation Reserve' of ₹ 4,000 at the time of admission of Z, when Investments (market value ₹19,000) appear at ₹ 20,000. The firm has three partners X, Y and Z.

ANSWER:

JOURNAL

Date	Particulars		L.F.	Dr. (₹)	Cr. (₹)
	Investment Fluctuation Reserve A/c	Dr.		4,000	
	To X's Capital A/c				1,000
	To Y's Capital A/c				1,000
	To Z's Capital A/c				1,000
	To Investments A/c				1,000
	(Being the value of Investments brought up to market value and surplus IFR t/f to partners in their old profit sharing ratio)				

QUESTION 32: Give the journal entry to distribute 'General Reserve' of ₹ 4,000 at the time of retirement of Z when 25% of General Reserve is to be be transferred to Provision for Doubtful Debts. The firm has three partners X, Y and Z.

ANSWER:

JOURNAL

Date	Particulars		L.F.	Dr. (₹)	Cr. (₹)
	General Reserve A/c	Dr.		4,000	
	To X's Capital A/c				1,000
	To Y's Capital A/c				1,000
	To Z's Capital A/c				1,000
	To Provision for Doubtful Debts A/c				1,000
	(Being 25% of General Reserve t/f to Provision and the Balance t/f to partners in their old profit sharing ratio)				

QUESTION 33: X, Y and Z are partners in a firm sharing profits in the ratio of 3: 2: 1. X retires from the firm. Y and Z agree that the capital of the new firm shall be fixed at ₹ 2,10,000 in the profit-sharing ratio. The capital accounts of Y and Z after all adjustments on the date of retirement showed balances of ₹ 1,45,000 and ₹ 63,000 respectively. State the amount of actual cash to be brought in *or* to be paid to the partners.

ANSWER: Total Capital of New Firm = ₹ 2,10,000 (Given)

CALCULATION OF ACTUAL CASH TO BE PAID OFF OR BROUGHT IN

Particulars	Y	Z
I. New Capital (₹ 2,10,000 in the ratio of 2: 1)	₹ 1,40,000	₹ 70,000
II. Adjusted Old Capital	₹ 1,45,000	₹ 63,000
III. Cash to be brought in (paid off) (I – II)	(₹ 5,000)	₹ 7,000

QUESTION 34: X, Y and Z are partners in a firm sharing profits in the ratio of 3: 2: 1. X retires from the firm. Y and Z agree that the capital of the new firm shall be the same as before retirement in the new profit sharing ratio which will be 3: 2. The capital accounts of X,Y and Z after all adjustments on the date of retirement showed balances of ₹ 32,000, ₹ 1,45,000 and ₹ 63,000 respectively. The capital accounts of X,Y and Z before any adjustment on the date of retirement showed balances of ₹ 2,000, ₹ 1,61,000 and ₹ 77,000 respectively. State the amount of actual cash to be brought in *or* to be paid to the partners.

ANSWER: Total Capital of New Firm = Total Capital of Old Firm = ₹ 2,000 + ₹ 1,61,000 + ₹ 77,000
= ₹ 2,40,000

CALCULATION OF ACTUAL CASH TO BE PAID OFF OR BROUGHT IN

Particulars	Y	Z
I. New Capital (₹ 2,40,000 in the ratio of 3: 2)	₹ 1,44,000	₹ 96,000
II. Adjusted Old Capital	₹ 1,45,000	₹ 63,000
III. Cash to be brought in (paid off) (I – II)	(₹ 1,000)	₹ 33,000

QUESTION 35: Naresh, David and Ashlam are partners sharing profits in the ratio of 5: 3: 7. Naresh retires from the firm. David and Ashlam decided to share future profits in the ratio of 2: 3. The adjusted capital accounts of David and Ashlam showed the balances of ₹ 33,000 and ₹ 70,500 respectively. The total amount to be paid to Naresh is ₹ 90,500. This amount is to be paid by David and Ashlam in such a way that their capitals become proportionate to their new profit sharing ratio. State the amount of actual cash to be brought in *or* to be paid to the partners.

ANSWER:

1. Total Capital of New Firm = Adjusted Capitals of All Partners
   = ₹ 33,000 + ₹ 70,500 + ₹ 90,500 = ₹ 1,94,000

CALCULATION OF ACTUAL CASH TO BE PAID OFF OR BROUGHT IN

Particulars	David	Ashlam
(a) New Capital (₹ 1,94,000 in the ratio of 2: 3)	₹ 77,600	₹ 1,16,400
(b) Adjusted Old Capital	₹ 33,000	₹ 70,500
(c) Cash to be brought in (a – b)	₹ 44,600	₹ 45,900

QUESTION 36: A, B & C were partners sharing profits and losses in the ratio of 5: 3: 2 respectively. B retired on 31st March when the Capitals of A, B and C after all necessary adjustments stood at ₹ 43,200, ₹ 36,600 and ₹ 11,200 respectively. The cash and bank balance on 31st March amounted to ₹ 4,000. B was to be paid through cash brought in by A and C in such a way as to make their capitals proportionate to their new profit sharing ratio of 3: 2. Calculate the amount of cash to be paid off *or* to be brought in by the continuing partners assuming that a minimum Cash & Bank Balance of ₹ 3,000 was to be maintained.

ANSWER:

(i) Calculation of Total Capital of the firm after B's retirement	
(a) Adjusted Old Capital of A	₹ 43,200
(b) Adjusted Old Capital of C	₹ 11,200
(c) Shortage of Cash to be brought in by A & C in order to make payment to 'B' (₹ 36,600 – ₹ 1,000)	₹ 35,600
	₹ 90,000

(ii) Calculation of Actual Cash to be paid off *or* brought in by A & C.		
(a) New Capital (₹ 90,000 in the ratio of 3: 2)	₹ 54,000	₹ 36,000
(b) Adjusted Old Capital	₹ 43,200	₹ 11,200
(c) Cash to be brought in (a – b)	₹ 10,800	₹ 24,800

QUESTION 37: How will you compute the amount due to a Retiring Partner?

ANSWER:

Particulars	₹
Opening Balance of Capital	xxx
Add: Share of Goodwill	xxx
Add: Share of Profits up to date of retirement	xxx
Add: Share of Reserves	xxx
Add: Share of Profit on Revaluation of Assets and Liabilities	xxx
Add: Share of Unrecorded Surrender Value of Individual Life Policies of All Partners	xxx
Add: Interest on Capital & Salary up to date of retirement	xxx
Less: Share of Existing Goodwill written off	(xxx)
Less: Share of Loss up to date of retirement	(xxx)
Less: Share of Accumulated Losses	(xxx)
Less: Share of Loss on Revaluation of Assets and Liabilities	(xxx)
Less: Drawings up to date of retirement	(xxx)
Less: Interest on Drawings up to date of retirement	(xxx)
Amount Due to a Retiring Partner	(xxx)

QUESTION 38: State any two items of deduction that may have to be made while computing the amount payable to a Retiring Partner.

ANSWER:

1. Share of Existing Goodwill written off
2. Share of Loss up to date of retirement
3. Share of Accumulated Losses
4. Share of Loss on Revaluation of Assets and Liabilities
5. Drawings up to date of retirement
6. Interest on Drawings up to date of retirement

QUESTION 39: How can the amount due to the Retiring Partner be settled?

ANSWER: The amount due is *either* paid off immediately *or* is transferred to Retiring Partner's Loan A/c which is paid in instalments with *or* without interest as per agreement.

QUESTION 40: Give Journal Entry for discharging Retiring Partner's Claim.

ANSWER:

Retiring Partner's Capital A/c Dr.

To Investment/ Asset A/c [with Agreed Value of Asset (if any) given to a Retiring Partner]

To Bills Payable A/c (if B/E is accepted)

To Cash/ Bank A/c (if some immediate payment is made)

To Retiring Partner's Loan A/c (if amount is transferred to Loan A/c)

QUESTION 41: A, B and C are in partnership sharing profits and of 5: 3: 2 respectively. 'A' retires from the firm as on 1st January, 2011 when his Capital Account shows a net credit balance of ₹ 82,100 after the necessary adjustments. 'A' is to be paid ₹ 22,100 in cash immediately on retirement and the balance in three equal annual instalments together with interest @ 5% p.a. on diminishing balance. Show the necessary ledger accounts.

ANSWER:

Dr. **A'S CAPITAL ACCOUNT** Cr.

Particulars	₹	Particulars	₹
To Bank A/c	22,100	By Balance b/d (Net amount due)	82,100
To A's Loan A/c	60,000		
	82,100		82,100

Dr. **A'S LOAN ACCOUNT** Cr.

Date	Particulars	₹	Date	Particulars	₹
31.12.11	To Bank A/c	23,000	01.01.11	By A's Capital A/c	60,000
	To Balance c/d	40,000	31.12.11	By Interest A/c	3,000
		63,000			63,000
31.12.12	To Bank A/c	22,000	01.01.12	By Balance b/d	40,000
	To Balance c/d	20,000	31.12.12	By Interest A/c	2,000
		42,000			42,000
31.12.13	To Bank A/c	21,000	01.01.13	By Balance b/d	20,000
			31.12.13	By Interest A/c	1,000
		21,000			21,000

Working Note: Amount of Instalment = (₹ 82,100 — ₹ 22,100)/3 = ₹ 20,000

QUESTION 42: State two basis for determination of Profits from the date of last Balance Sheet to the date of death/retirement.

ANSWER:

1. On Time Basis,
2. On Sales Basis

QUESTION 43: X, Y and Z are partners sharing profits as 2: 2: 1 respectively. The firm's books are closed on 31st December every year. On 28th February, 2012, X died. It is not possible to prepare final accounts for calculations of profits to the date of death. Suggest the ways to Y and Z for ascertaining profits.

ANSWER:

1. On Time Basis,
2. On Sales Basis

QUESTION 44: Name the account which is usually considered to adjust the Share of Profits up to date of death of the deceased partner.

ANSWER: Profit & Loss Suspense Account

QUESTION 45: Why is Profit & Loss Suspense Account prepared?

ANSWER: Profit & Loss Suspense Account is prepared to adjust the Deceased Partner's Share of Profits up to date of death of the partner.

QUESTION 46: Name the account which is maintained in the books when the retired partner *or* executor of deceased partner's Loan Account keeps the money in the firm as additional finance?

ANSWER:

1. Loan from Retired Partner Account
2. Deceased Partner's Executors' Loan Account

QUESTION 47: What is the nature of the amount due to an outgoing partner?

ANSWER: Loan Account which represents an External Liability of the firm.

QUESTION 48: When is 'Partner's Executors' Account prepared?

ANSWER: Partner's Executor's Account is prepared at the time of death of a partner.

QUESTION 49: Why is 'Partner's Executors' Account prepared?

ANSWER: Partner's Executor's Account is prepared at the time of death of a partner so as to make the payment of deceased partner's share to his/her executors.

QUESTION 50: How will you compute the amount due to a Deceased Partner?

ANSWER:

Particulars	₹
Opening Balance of Capital	xxx
Add: Share of Goodwill	xxx
Add: Share of Profits up to date of death	xxx
Add: Share of Reserves	xxx
Add: Share of Profit on Revaluation of Assets and Liabilities	xxx
Add: Interest on Capital & Salary up to date of death	xxx
Less: Share of Existing Goodwill written off	(xxx)
Less: Share of Loss up to date of death	(xxx)
Less: Share of Accumulated Losses	(xxx)
Less: Share of Loss on Revaluation of Assets and Liabilities	(xxx)
Less: Drawings up to date of death	(xxx)
Less: Interest on Drawings up to date of death	(xxx)
Amount Due to Deceased Partner	xxx

QUESTION 51: Prepare a Format of Deceased Partner's Capital Account.

ANSWER:

Dr. **DECEASED PARTNER'S CAPITAL ACCOUNT** Cr.

Particulars	₹	Particulars	₹
To Goodwill A/c [Existing Goodwill w/o]	xxx	By Gaining Partner's Capital A/c (Share of Goodwill)	xxx
To Drawings	xxx	By Balance b/d	xxx
To Interest on Drawings	xxx	By P & L Suspense A/c	xxx
To Undistributed Losses	xxx	(Share of Profits)	
To Revaluation A/c	xxx	By Reserves (Share of Reserves)	xxx
(Share of Loss on Revaluation)		By Interest on Capital A/c	xxx
To Deceased Partner's Executors' A/c	xxx	By Revaluation A/c	xxx
[Balancing Figures]		[Share of Profit on Revaluation]	
	xxx		xxx

QUESTION 52: P, R and S are in the partnership sharing profits in the ratio of 4: 3: 1 respectively. It is provided in the partnership deed that, on the death of any partner, his share of goodwill is to be valued at half of the profits credited to his account during the previous four completed years. R dies on 1st January, 2013. The firm's profits for the last four years I: ₹ 1,20,000. II: ₹ 80,000, III: ₹ 40,000, IV: ₹ 80,000. Determine the amount that should be credited to R in respect of his share of goodwill.

ANSWER:

A. Total profits of the firm for 4 years = ₹ 1,20,000 + ₹ 80,000 + ₹ 40,000 + ₹ 80,000 = ₹ 3,20,000

B. R's share in four years' profits = ₹ 3,20,000 × 3/8 = ₹ 1,20,000

C. R's share of goodwill = ₹ 1,20,000 × 1/2 = ₹ 60,000.

QUESTION 53: A, B and C are in partnership sharing profits in the ratio of 4: 3: 1. B died on 30th June 2013.The firm's profits for various years were-2008 (Profits ₹ 6,48,888), 2009 (Profits ₹ 1,60,000), 2010 (Profits ₹ 20,000), 2011 (Losses ₹ 20,000), 2012 (Profits ₹ 80,000), 2013 (Profits ₹ 1,00,000). A and C decided to share future profits in the ratio of 3: 2. Goodwill is to be valued at three years' purchase of average profits of three years upto the date of death. Pass a Journal Entry to adjust Goodwill.

ANSWER:

A. Average Profits, of three years upto date of death comprise the profits earned from 1st July 2010 to 30th June 2013 = (50% of ₹ 20,000 – ₹ 20,000 + ₹ 80,000 + 50% of ₹ 1,00,000)/3 = ₹ 40,000

B. Firm's Goodwill = ₹ 40,000 × 3 = ₹ 1,20,000

C. B's share of Goodwill = ₹ 1,20,000 × 3/8 = ₹ 45,000

JOURNAL ENTRY

Date	Particulars	L.F.	Dr. (₹)	Cr. (₹)
	A's Capital A/c Dr.		12,000	
	C's Capital A/c		33,000	

	To B's Capital A/c (Being the B's share of goodwill credited to B and debited to A and C in their gaining ratio of 4: 11)			45,000

Working Note:

CALCULATION OF GAINING RATIO

Particulars	A	C
Their New Shares	3/5	2/5
Their Old Shares	4/8	1/8
Difference	4/40	11/40
Gaining Ratio of A & C = 4:11		

QUESTION 54: X, Y and Z were partners sharing profits & losses in the ratio of 3: 2: 1 respectively. X died on 31st March, 2013. Give the necessary Journal entry to record X's share of profit in each of the following alternative cases:

Case (a) If the partnership deed provided that the share of profit till the date of death be estimated at the sum calculated on the average of the last three completed years' profits. The book showed the profits for the calendar years as under: 2008–₹ 5,000; 2009–₹ 5,000; 2010 ₹ 8,000; 2011–₹ 7,600 & 2012–₹ 9,000.

Case (b) If the partnership deed provided that the share of profit till the date of death be estimated at the sum calculated on the sales till the date of death by applying the ratio of Net Profit to Sales for the last accounting year. Sales from 1.1.2013 to 31.3.2013 amounted to ₹ 30,000. Sales and Net Profit for the year 2012 amounted to ₹ 3,60,000 and ₹ 54,000 respectively.

ANSWER:

Case (a)

Particulars	₹
A. Total Profits for last three years (₹ 8,000 + ₹ 7,600 + ₹ 9,000)	24,600
B. Average Profits (₹ 24,600/3)	8,200
C. Estimated Profits for the period from 1.1.2013 to 31.3.2013 (₹ 8,200 × 3/12)	2,050
D. Share of X (₹ 2,050 × 3/6)	1,025

JOURNAL ENTRY

Date	Particulars	L.F.	Dr. (₹)	Cr. (₹)
	Profit & Loss Suspense A/c Dr. To X's capital A/c (Being X's share of Profit recorded)		1,025	 1,025

Case (b)

Particulars	₹
A. Estimated Profits for the period from 1.1.2013 to 31.3.2013 = × 54,000	4,500
B. Share of X (₹ 4,500 × 3/6)	2,250

JOURNAL ENTRY

Date	Particulars		L.F.	Dr. (₹)	Cr. (₹)
	P&L Suspense A/c	Dr.		2,250	
	To X's Capital A/c				2,250
	(Being X's share of profit recorded)				

QUESTION 55: A, B and C are partners in a firm whose book are closed on 31st March each year. A dies on 30th June 2013 and according to the agreement, the share of profits of a deceased partner up to the date of the death is to be calculated on the basis of the average profit for the last 5 years. The net profits for the last 5 years have been:I—₹ 14,000; II—₹ 18,000; III—₹ 16,000; IV—₹ 10,000 (loss) and V—₹ 16,000. Pass the necessary Journal Entry to record A's share of the profits up to the date of death.

ANSWER:

1. Average Profits = (₹ 14,000 + ₹ 18,000 + ₹ 16,000 – ₹ 10,000 + ₹ 16,000)/5 = ₹ 10,800
2. Deceased Partner's Share of Profit = ₹ 10,800 × 3/12 × 1/3 = ₹ 900

JOURNAL

Date	Particulars		L.F.	Dr. (₹)	Cr. (₹)
	Profit & Loss Suspense A/c	Dr.		900	
	To A's Capital A/c				900
	(Being the Deceased Partner's Share of Profit recorded)				

QUESTION 56: X, Y and Z were sharing profit in the ratio of 3: 3: 4. X died on June 30th 2013. X's share of profit *or* loss till the date of her death was to be calculated on the basis of sales. Sales for the year ended 31st March, 2013 amounted to ₹ 4,00,000 and that from 1st April to 30th June 2013 to ₹ 1,50,000. The profit for the year ended 31st March, 2013 was ₹ 1,00,000. Calculate X's share of profit *or* loss.

ANSWER: Share of Profit = ₹ 1,00,000 × 1,50,000/4,00,000 × 3/10 = ₹ 11,250

QUESTION 57: Can an Retiring Partner *or* Legal Representative of a Deceased Partner share in the subsequent profits?

ANSWER: If the amount due to the Retiring Partner *or* Legal Representative of a Deceased Partner is not settled and the business is carried on the Retiring Partner *or* Legal Representative of a Deceased Partner at his option is entitled to receive *either* interest @ 6% p.a. till the amount is paid off *or* a share of the profit which has been earned by using the amount due to him. [Section 37].

QUESTION 58: A, B and C were partners sharing profits and losses in the ratio of 2: 2: 1. C retired on 1st Oct, 2014 on which date the capitals of A, B and C after all necessary adjustments stood at ₹ 5,00,000, ₹3,00,000 and 2,00,000 respectively. A and B continued to carry on the business for six months without settling the accounts of C. During the period of six months from 1st Oct, 2014, a profit of ₹ 1,00,000 is earned by the use of the firm's property. State which of the two options available u/s 37 of the Indian Partnership Act 1932 should be exercised by C.

ANSWER:

(i) Share in the subsequent profits attributable to the use of his property = [2,00,000/(5,00,000 + 3,00,000 + 2,00,000)] × 1,00,000 = ₹ 20,000

(ii) Interest @ 6% p.a. on the use of his property = ₹ 2,00,000 × 6/12 × 6/100 = ₹ 6,000
C should exercise option (i) since the amount payable to him under this option is more as compared to the amount payable to him under option (ii).

DISSOLUTION OF PARTNERSHIP

QUESTION 1: What is meant by 'Dissolution'?

ANSWER: The term 'DISSOLUTION' stands for discontinuation. Under the Indian Partnership Act, 1932, the DISSOLUTION may be *either* of partnership *or* of a firm.

QUESTION 2: What is 'Dissolution of Partnership?

ANSWER: DISSOLUTION of partnership refers to the change in the existing relations of the partners. The firm continues its business. It may take place on admission/retirement/ death/expulsion/insolvency of a partner *or* on change in the profit sharing ratio.

QUESTION 3: What is 'Dissolution of a Firm?

ANSWER: DISSOLUTION of a firm means the DISSOLUTION of partnership between all the partners of the firm alongwith the termination of firm's business.

QUESTION 4: Does the Dissolution of a Firm necessarily mean the Dissolution of Partnership?

ANSWER: Yes because old partnership between all the partners of the firm comes to an end forever.

QUESTION 5: State any two differences between Dissolution of Partnership and Dissolution of a firm.

ANSWER:

Basis of Distinction	Dissolution of Partnership	Dissolution of Firm
1. Termination of business	The business is **not terminated.**	The business of the firm is **closed**.
2. Settlement of assets and liabilities	Assets and liabilities are **revalued** and new balance sheet is drawn.	Assets are **realized** and liabilities are paid off.
3. Account to determine Profit/Loss	**Revaluation Account** is prepared to determine the profit/ loss on revaluation.	**Realisation Account** is prepared to determine the profit/ loss on realization.
4. Court's Intervention	Court **does not** intervene because partnership is dissolved by mutual agreement.	A firm **can be** dissolved by the court's order.
5. Economic Relationship	Economic relationship between the partners **changes**.	Economic relationship between the partners **comes to an end forever**.
6. Closure of books	It **does not require** closure of books because the business is not terminated	All books of accounts are **closed**.

QUESTION 6: List any two circumstances under which a partnership is dissolved.

ANSWER:

1. When the partners decide to change the profit sharing ratio.
2. When a new partner is admitted.
3. When a partner retires.
4. When a partner dies.

QUESTION 7: List any two circumstances under which a firm is dissolved.

ANSWER:

1. on the insolvency of all the partners *or* all except one partner;
2. on business becoming unlawful.
3. When any one of the partners gives a notice in writing to other partners in case of partnership at will
4. A Court may dissolve a firm on grounds of Insanity of a partner.
5. A Court may dissolve a firm on grounds of Permanent incapacity of a partner.

QUESTION 8: List any two circumstances under which a firm is compulsorily dissolved without order of court.

ANSWER:

1. on the insolvency of all the partners *or* all except one partner;
2. on business becoming unlawful.

QUESTION 9: List any two grounds on which a Court may dissolve a firm.

ANSWER: A court may dissolve a firm on any of the following grounds:

(a) Insanity of a partner,
(b) Permanent incapacity of a partner,
(c) Misconduct of/by a partner,
(d) Persistent breach of agreement by a partner,
(e) Transfer of interest by a partner,
(f) Improbability of carrying on the business except at a loss,
(g) any other ground on which court is satisfied

QUESTION 10: List any two circumstances under which a firm is dissolved on the happening of certain contingencies Subject to contract between the partners.

ANSWER: Subject to contract between the partners. A firm is dissolved by:

(i) the expiry of the term for which the firm was formed;
(ii) the completion of the venture(s) for which the firm was formed;
(iii) the death of a partner;
(iv) the adjudication of a partner as insolvent.

QUESTION 11: What is meant by 'Dissolution by Notice?

ANSWER: A Firm is dissolved when any one of the partners gives a notice in writing to other partners in case of partnership at will

QUESTION 12: State the Treatment of Losses as per Sec 48 of the Indian Partnership Act, 1932.

ANSWER: Losses including deficiencies of capital are to be paid in the following manner:

(a) First out of profits;
(b) Then out of capital;
(c) Lastly by partners individually in their profit-sharing ratio.

QUESTION 13: State the Application of Assets as per Sec 48 of the Indian Partnership Act, 1932.

ANSWER: The assets of the firm (including the sums, if any, contributed by the partners to make up the deficiencies of capital) shall be applied in the following manner and order:

(a) First to pay off firm's debts due to the third parties;

Note: Secured Creditors are to be paid off first out of the proceeds of secured assets before anything is paid to Unsecured Creditors.

(b) Then to pay off Loans from Partners.

(c) Then to pay off Capitals of Partners.

(d) Lastly the Surplus, (if any), shall be divided among the partners in their profit-sharing ratio. [Sec. 48 (b)]

QUESTION 14: List any two points of differences between Firm's Debts and Private Debts.

ANSWER:

Basis of Distinction	Firm's Debts	Private Debts
1. Who incurs	Firm's debts are incurred by the firm.	Private debts are incurred by a partner in the individual capacity of a household and not in the capacity of a partner of a firm.
2. Who is liable	For firm's debts, all partners are jointly and severally liable.	For private debts, only the concerned partner is liable.
3. Application of firm's property	For firm's debts, firm's Property shall be applied first.	For private debts, only the share of concerned partner in the excess of firm's property over firm's debts can be applied.
4. Application of private property	For firm's debts, only the excess of partner's private property over his private debts can be applied.	For private debts, private property shall be applied first.

QUESTION 15: What is the nature of liability of the partners?

ANSWER: Jointly and Severally. i.e. Unlimited.

QUESTION 16: List the order of payment in case of DISSOLUTION of Firm.

ANSWER:

1. Secured Creditors
2. Unsecured Creditors
3. Loans from Partners
4. Capitals of Partners.
5. Surplus, (if any), shall be divided among the partners in their profit-sharing ratio.

QUESTION 17: Is the loan from an outsider having priority as to repayment over the repayment of loan from a partner?

ANSWER: Yes as per Sec. 48.

QUESTION 18: Is the loan from a partner having priority as to the repayment over the repayment of any part of the capital?

ANSWER: Yes as per Sec. 48.

QUESTION 19: All the partners want to dissolve the firm. Y, a partner wants that his loan of ₹ 16,000 must be paid off before the payment of capitals to the partners. But X, another partner wants that capitals must be paid before the payment of Y's loan. Decide.

ANSWER: Y is correct as per Sec. 48.

QUESTION 20: All the partners want to dissolve the firm. Y, a partner wants that his loan of ₹ 16,000 must be paid off before the payment of Mrs. X's loan.. But X, another partner wants that Mrs. X's loan must be paid before the payment of Y's loan. Decide.

ANSWER: X is correct as per Sec. 48.

QUESTION 21: What is Realisation Account'?

ANSWER: Realisation Account is a Nominal Account which is debited with book values of all the recorded assets and payments of liabilities and is credited with book values of all the recorded liabilities and realized values of assets. The balance of Revaluation Account is transferred to all the Partners' Capital accounts in their Profit Sharing Ratio.

QUESTION 22: Why is the Realisation Account prepared?

ANSWER: The object of Realisation Account is to close the books of account of a dissolved firm and to compute the net effect of realisation of various assets and payments of various liabilities.

QUESTION 23: State any two differences between Realisation Account and Revaluation Account.

ANSWER:

Basis of Distinction	Revaluation Account	Realisation Account
1. **Meaning**	It records the **effect of revaluation of assets and liabilities.**	It records the **realisation of various assets and payments of various liabilities.**
2. **Purpose**	It is prepared **to determine the net Profit/loss on revaluation.**	It is prepared **to determine the net profit/loss on realisation.**
3. **When prepared**	It Is prepared **at the time of constitution of partnership** (e.g., on admission of a new partner on retirement/death of a partner).	It is prepared **at the time of dissolution of the firm.**
4. **Transfer of Balance**	Its balance is transferred only to **old partners' capital accounts.**	Its balance is transferred **to all partners' capital accounts.**
5. **Basis of entries relating to the assets and liabilities**	Entries relating to assets and liabilities are made on the basis of **difference between the book values and revalued figures.**	Entries relating to assets and liabilities are made on the basis of their **book values and actual payments.**
6. **Effect of entries on accounts relating to assets and liabilities**	As a result of entries passed in this account, the **accounts** of assets and liabilities revalued, are **not closed**.	As a result of entries passed in this account, the **accounts** of assets and liabilities are **closed**.
7. **Preparation of account during the life time of the firm**	This account may be required to be prepared **at a number of occasions** during the lifetime of a firm.	This account is prepared only **once during the lifetime of a firm.**

QUESTION 24: List any five items which are usually not transferred to Realisation Account.

ANSWER:

1. Fictitious Assets,
2. Cash Balance, Bank Balance,
3. Current Account (Debit Balance) of a Partner
4. Capital Account (Debit Balance) of a Partner
5. Partner's Loan/Advance
6. Accumulated Profits & Reserves (e.g., Credit Balance in P & L A/c, General Reserve)

QUESTION 25: State the ratio in which the partners share profit *or* loss on realisation of various assets and payments of various liabilities.

ANSWER: Profit Sharing Ratio.

QUESTION 26: What journal entry will you pass when an Unrecorded Furniture worth ₹ 15,000 is taken over by X, a partner at ₹ 10,000 on the DISSOLUTION of a firm?

ANSWER:

JOURNAL

Date	Particulars		Dr. (₹)	Cr.(₹)
	X's Capital A/c To Realisation A/c (Being the Unrecorded Furniture taken over by Y)	Dr.	10,000	10,000

QUESTION 27: What journal entry will you pass when an Unrecorded Liability of ₹ 15,000 is settled at ₹ 10,000 and paid by X, a partner on the Dissolution of a firm?

ANSWER:

JOURNAL

Date	Particulars		Dr. (₹)	Cr.(₹)
	Realisation A/c To X's Capital A/c (Being the Unrecorded Liability taken over by Y)	Dr.	10,000	10,000

QUESTION 28: What journal entry will you pass when a Machine having a book value of ₹ 15,000 is given away to W, a firm's creditor of ₹ 22,000 at an agreed valuation of ₹ 12,000 towards full & final payment of his dues?

ANSWER: No journal entry may be passed.

QUESTION 29: What journal entry will you pass when a Machine having a book value of ₹ 15,000 is given away to W, a firm's creditor of ₹ 22,000 at an agreed valuation of ₹ 12,000 towards partial payment of his dues?

ANSWER:

JOURNAL

Date	Particulars		Dr. (₹)	Cr.(₹)
	Realisation A/c To X's Capital A/c (Being the balance of a Creditors paid)	Dr.	10,000	10,000

QUESTION 30: What journal entry will you pass when X, a partner agrees to pay the Realisation Expenses of ₹ 10,000 on behalf of the firm?

ANSWER:

JOURNAL ENTRIES

Date	Particulars		Dr. (₹)	Cr.(₹)
	Realisation A/c To Cash/Bank A/c (Being the Realisation Expneses paid by X on firm's behalf)	Dr.	10,000	 10,000

QUESTION 31: What journal entry will you pass when the firm pays actual Realisation Expenses of ₹ 10,000 on behalf of X, a partner who has to bear the expenses?

ANSWER:

JOURNAL ENTRIES

Date	Particulars		Dr. (₹)	Cr.(₹)
	X's Capital A/c To Cash/Bank A/c (Being the Realisation Expneses paid on X's behalf)	Dr.	10,000	 10,000

QUESTION 32: If a Loan from X, a partner of ₹ 11,000 appears on the liabilities side of the Balance Sheet of the firm and the X's Capital Account has a debit balance of ₹ 1,000, What journal entry will you pass on payment of such a loan?

ANSWER:

JOURNAL ENTRIES

Date	Particulars		Dr. (₹)	Cr.(₹)
	Loan from X A/c To Capital A/c To Cash/Bank A/c [Being X's Loan of ₹ 1,000 t/f to his capital A/c and the balance paid]	Dr.	11,000	 1,000 10,000

QUESTION 33: To which account the balance in Current Account is transferred?

ANSWER: Capital Account.

QUESTION 34: X, a partner of a dissolved film was to get as his remuneration 1% of value of assets realised other than cash and 10% of the amount distributed to the partners. Sundry assets (including Cash ₹ 1,000) realised ₹ 1,01,000. Creditors to be paid ₹ 45,000. Calculate X's remuneration.

ANSWER: Assets realised other than cash = ₹ 1,01,000 – ₹ 1,000 = ₹ 1,00,000

Commission on Assets realised = 1% of ₹ 1,00,000 = ₹ 1,000

Cash available for Partners & Commission based on cash distribution to partners = ₹ 1,01,000 – ₹ 45,000 – ₹ 1,000 = ₹ 55,000

Commission based on Cash distribution = ₹ 55,000 × 5/105 = ₹ 5,000

Hence Total Remuneration = ₹ 1,000 + ₹ 5,000 = ₹ 6,000

QUESTION 35: State the ratio in which the partners share the accumulated profits, reserves, losses and fictitious assets.

ANSWER: Profit Sharing Ratio.

QUESTION 36: A, B, C and D were the partners in a firm sharing profits in the ratio of 3:3:2:2. The firm was dissolved on 31.03.2015. Tangible Fixed Assets, Trade Creditors and Machinery Replacement Reserve were transferred to Realisation Account at ₹ 80,000, ₹ 70,000 and ₹ 20,000 respectively. Half the Trade Creditors accepted half the Net Tangible Fixed Assets at ₹ 24,000 [being 20% less than the book value], an unrecorded furniture of ₹ 2,000 at a discount of 50% and the balance in cash in full settlement of their claims after allowing a discount of ₹ 2,000; Remaining Trade Creditors accepted the Remaining Tangible Fixed Assets at an agreed valuation of 110% after allowing a discount of ₹ 4,000 and the Balance was paid by them in Cash.Pass necessary journal entries in the books of the firm.

ANSWER:

JOURNAL

Date	Particulars	L.F.	Dr. (₹)	Cr. (₹)
	Realisation A/c Dr. To Bank A/c (Being the payment made to creditors (i.e. ₹ 35,000 – ₹ 24,000 – ₹ 1,000 – 2,000)		8,000	8,000
	Bank A/c Dr. To Realisation A/c (Being the Net Tangible Fixed Assets realized (i.e. ₹ 35,000 – ₹ 32,000 – ₹ 5,000)		2,000	2,000

QUESTION 37: A, B, C and D were the partners in a firm sharing profits in the ratio of 3:3:2:2. The firm was dissolved on 31.03.2015. Sundry Debtors and Provision for doubtful debts were transferred to Realisation Account at ₹ 50,000 and ₹ 8,500 respectively. 60% of Sundry Debtors realized 34% less; B is to take over 40% of the balance of Sundry Debtors at 70%. Further, he is to be allowed ₹ 800 to cover future losses and the remaining debtors (if any) were sold to a debt collecting agency at 70%.Pass necessary journal entries in the books of the firm.

ANSWER:

JOURNAL

Date	Particulars	L.F.	Dr. (₹)	Cr. (₹)
	Bank A/c Dr. To Realisation A/c (Being the 60% of Sundry Debtors realized [i.e. ₹ (60% of 50,000 × 66%)]		19,800	19,800
	B's Capital A/c Dr. To Realisation A/c [Being some Sundry Debtors taken over by B (i.e. 40% of 20,000 × 70% – ₹ 800)]		4,800	4,800

	Bank A/c To Realisation A/c (Being the some Sundry Debtors sold to agency [i.e. ₹ (60% of 20,000 × 70%)]	Dr.	8,400	 8,400

QUESTION 38: A, B, C and D were the partners in a firm sharing profits in the ratio of 3:3:2:2. The firm was dissolved on 31.03.2015. Stock and Bank overdraft were transferred to Realisation Account at ₹ 25,000 and ₹ 15,000 respectively. Stock was taken over by the banker against Bank overdraft, and it realised 80%. Bank paid back ₹ 4,000 after recovering its overdraft and interest due thereon.Pass necessary journal entries in the books of the firm.

ANSWER:

JOURNAL

Date	Particulars	L.F.	Dr. (₹)	Cr. (₹)
	Bank A/c Dr. To Realisation A/c (Being the stock proceeds recievd from the Banker)		4,000	 4,000

QUESTION 39: A, B, C and D were the partners in a firm sharing profits in the ratio of 3:3:2:2. The firm was dissolved on 31.03.2015. A joint life policy was transferred to Realisation Account at ₹ 90,000. The Joint Life Policy was surrendered to the insurance company. The company paid a sum of ₹ 4,000 after deducting an amount of ₹ 6,500 towards loan and interest thereon by B against the policy. Pass necessary journal entries in the books of the firm.

ANSWER:

JOURNAL

Date	Particulars	L.F.	Dr. (₹)	Cr. (₹)
	Bank A/c Dr. B's Capital A/c Dr. To Realisation A/c (Being the JLP realised)		4,000 6,500	 10,500

QUESTION 40: A, B, C and D were the partners in a firm sharing profits in the ratio of 3:3:2:2. The firm was dissolved on 31.03.2015. A Debtor whose debt of ' 5,000 was written off as bad in the previous year paid 40% in full settlement. Pass necessary journal entries in the books of the firm.

ANSWER:

JOURNAL

Date	Particulars	L.F.	Dr. (₹)	Cr. (₹)
	Bank A/c Dr. To Realisation A/c (Being the Bad Debt already w/o recovered)		2,000	 2,000

QUESTION 41: A, B, C and D were the partners in a firm sharing profits in the ratio of 3:3:2:2. The firm was dissolved on 31.03.2015. There was one unrecorded asset estimated at ₹ 40,000, half of which was handed over at an agreed valuation of 60% to an unrecorded liability of ₹ 64,000 in settlement of claim of ₹ 32,000 and remaining half was taken over by B at an a greed valuation of 62%. Pass necessary journal entries in the books of the firm.

ANSWER:

JOURNAL

Date	Particulars		L.F.	Dr. (₹)	Cr. (₹)
	B's Capital A/c To Realisation A/c [Being an unrecorded asset taken over by B (i.e. 62% of ₹ 20,000)]	Dr.		12,400	12,400
	Realisation A/c To Bank A/c (Being the remaining unrecorded liability paid)	Dr.		32,000	32,000

QUESTION 42: A, B, C and D were the partners in a firm sharing profits in the ratio of 3:3:2:2. The firm was dissolved on 31.03.2015. B was appointed to realise the assets and to pay off the liabilities. He was entitled to receive ₹ 2,000 as remuneration for completing the dissolution work and was to bear the realisation expenses. The expenses of realisation ₹ 1,500 were paid by B out of his private funds. Pass necessary journal entries in the books of the firm.

ANSWER:

JOURNAL

Date	Particulars		L.F.	Dr. (₹)	Cr. (₹)
	Realisation A/c To B's Capital A/c (Being the remuneration due to B)	Dr.		2,000	2,000

QUESTION 43: A, B, C and D were the partners in a firm sharing profits in the ratio of 3:3:2:2. The firm was dissolved on 31.03.2015. There was a bill for ₹ 21,000 under discount.The bill was received from Z. Z proved insolvent and a first and final dividend of 60% was received from his estate. Pass necessary journal entries in the books of the firm.

ANSWER:

JOURNAL

Date	Particulars		L.F.	Dr. (₹)	Cr. (₹)
	Realisation A/c To Bank A/c (Being the payment of dishonoured discounted B/R)	Dr.		21,000	21,000
	Bank A/c To Realisation A/c (Being a first and final dividend of 60% received from the estate of Z)	Dr.		12,600	12,600

QUESTION 44: A, B, C and D were the partners in a firm sharing profits in the ratio of 3:3:2:2. The firm was dissolved on 31.03.2015. Prepaid Insurance of ₹ 3,000 and Goodwill of ₹ 5,000 were transferred to Realisation Account but no other additional information was given with regard to these two items.Pass necessary journal entries in the books of the firm.

ANSWER:

JOURNAL

Date	Particulars	L.F.	Dr. (₹)	Cr. (₹)
	No Journal Entry is required since there is no realisation.			

QUESTION 45: A, B, C and D were the partners in a firm sharing profits in the ratio of 3:3:2:2. The firm was dissolved on 31.03.2015. Employee's Provident Fund of ₹ 5,000 and Mrs. B's Loan of 3,000 were transferred to Realisation Account. Pass necessary journal entries in the books of the firm.

ANSWER:

JOURNAL

Date	Particulars	L.F.	Dr. (₹)	Cr. (₹)
	Realisation A/c Dr. To Bank A/c (Being the EPF & Mrs. B's Loan paid)		8,000	8,000

QUESTION 46: A, B, C and D were the partners in a firm sharing profits in the ratio of 3:3:2:2. The firm was dissolved on 31.03.2015. Other Assets of ₹ 51,000 were transferred to Realisation Account. These Assets realized at a loss of 2% on Net collection.Pass necessary journal entries in the books of the firm.

ANSWER:

JOURNAL

Date	Particulars	L.F.	Dr. (₹)	Cr. (₹)
	Bank A/c Dr. To Realisation A/c (Being the Other Assets realized (i.e. ₹ 51,000 – ₹ 51,000 × 2/102)		50,000	50,000

QUESTION 47: B was entitled to receive 5% commission on the amount finally paid to other partners as capital. He was to bear the expenses of realisation. A's loan was ₹ 10,000. Total cash available ₹ 23,100 towards loan, capital and commission. A's capital balance ₹ 8,000, B's Capital Balance ₹ 5,100, Realisation Expenses ₹ 500. How will you disclose these items in Capital Account and Cash Account?

ANSWER:

Dr. **CAPITAL ACCOUNTS OF PARTNERS** **Cr.**

Particulars	A	B	Particulars	A	B
To B's Capital (Commission) (8,000 × 5/105)	381		By Balance b/d	8,000	5,100

To Cash A/c	7,619	5,481	By A's Capital A/	381	
	8,000	5,481		8,000	5,481

Dr. **CASH ACCOUNT** Cr.

To Balance b/d	23,100		By A's Loan	10,000	
			By A's Capital A/c	7,619	
			By B's Capital A/c	5,481	
	23,100			23,100	

QUESTION 48: It was found that an investment not recorded in the books was worth ₹ 2,250, half of which was handed over to an unrecorded liability of ₹ 3,750 in settlement of his claim of ₹ 1,875 and remaining half was sold in the market, which realised ₹ 975. How will you disclose these items in Realisation Account?

ANSWER:

Dr. **REALISATION ACCOUNT** Cr.

Particulars		Particulars	
To Cash/Bank A/c Unrecorded Liability	1,875	By Cash/Bank A/c Unrecorded Investments (₹ 3,750 – ₹ 1,875)	975

QUESTION 49: Ram, Rahim and Auntony were sharing profits in the ratio of 3: 2: 1. Assets t/f to Realsiation Account ₹ 22,13,400, realised ₹ 23,25,000. Auntony whose capital balance was ₹ 1,20,000 agreed to receive ₹ 1,50,000 in full satisfaction of his rights, title and interest in the firm. How will you disclose these items in Realisation Account?

ANSWER:

Dr. **REALISATION ACCOUNT** Cr.

Particulars		Particulars	
To Sundry Assets To Auntony's Capital A/c (₹ 1,50,000 – ₹ 1,20,000)	22,13,400 30,000	By Cash/Bank A/c Unrecorded Investments (₹ 3,750 – ₹ 1,875)	23,25,000 975
To Profit on Realisation t/f to:			
Ram	48,960		
Rahim	32,640		
	23,45,000		23,25,000

QUESTION 50: W paid a premium to other partners of the firm at the time of his admission to the firm, with a condition that the will not be dissolved before expiry of five years. The firm is dissolved after three years. W claims refund to premium.

(i) List the criteria for the calculation of the amount of refund.

(ii) Also list any two conditions when no claim in this respect will arise.

ANSWER: If the firm is dissolved before the term expires, as is the case, W being a partner who has paid premium on admission will have to be repaid/refunded. The criteria for calculation of refund amount are:

(i) Terms upon which admission was made,

(ii) The time period for which it was agreed that the firm will not be dissolved.
(iii) The time period for which the firm has already been in existence.

No claim for refund will arise if:

(i) The firm is dissolved due to death of a partner,
(ii) If the Dissolution of the firm is basically because of misconduct of W.
(iii) If the Dissolution is through an agreement and such agreement does not have a stipulation for refund of premium.

PARTNERSHIP – INSOLVENCY, PIECEMEAL DISTRIBUTION, SALE ETC.

QUESTION 1: Explain Garner v/s Murray rule applicable in the case of partnership firms. State, when is this rule not applicable.

ANSWER: In the case of Dissolution of a partnership firm due to insolvency, Garner vs Murray rule is applicable at the time of any partner becoming insolvent. It requires—

1. That the solvent partners should bear the loss arising due to insolvency of a partner in their capital ratio after making adjustments for past accumulated reserves, profits *or* losses, drawings, interest on drawings/capitals, remuneration to partners etc., to the date of Dissolution but before making adjustment for profit *or* loss on realization in case of fluctuating capital. In case of fixed capital no such adjustments are required.
2. That the solvent partners should bring in cash equal to their respective shares of the loss on realization.

Non-Applicability: This rule is not applicable when:

1. When the solvent partner has a debit balance in the capital account.
2. Only one partner is solvent.
3. All partners are insolvent.
4. The partnership deed provides for a specific method to be followed in case of insolvency of a partner, then the conditions given in the deed would prevail.

QUESTION 2: A, B and C are partners; A became insolvent on 15.4.2010. The capital account balance of partner B is on the debit side. Partner B is solvent. Should partner B bear the loss arising on account of the insolvency of partner A?

ANSWER: According to Garner vs Murray Rule, if a solvent partner is having a debit balance in his capital account, then he cannot be called upon to bear the loss on account of the insolvency of the other partner. Hence, 'B' needs not bear the loss due to insolvency of partner 'A'.

QUESTION 3: Following is the Balance Sheet of A,B,C and D who were sharing in the ratio of 3:3:2:2 as at 31st March, 2015, when they decided to dissolve the firm:

Liabilities	₹	Assets	₹
Trade Creditors	1,21,000	Sundry Assets	1,70,000
A's Capital	60,000	C's Capital	48,000
B's Capital	49,000	D's Capital	18,000
General Reserve	20,000	B's Drawings	4,000
		Profit & Loss A/c	10,000
	2,50,000		2,50,000

C is insolvent but ₹ 11,100 is realized from his estate. Sundry Assets realized 80%. Realization Expenses ₹ 2,000. State who will bear C's deficiency and in which ratio.

ANSWER:

CALCULATION OF CAPITAL RATIO

	A ₹	B ₹
Capital	60,000	49,000
Less: B's Drawings	–	(4,000)
Less: Share of Debit balance of Profit & Loss A/c	(3,000)	(3,000)
Add: Share of General Reserve	6,000	6,000
	63,000	48,000

C's deficiency is to be borne by A and B in the ratio of 63,000: 48,000 *or* 21: 16.

D will not bear C's deficiency since he had a debit balance in his Caoital Account.

QUESTION 4: Following is the Balance Sheet of A,B,C and D who were sharing in the ratio of 3:3:2:2 as at 31st March, 2015, when they decided to dissolve the firm:

Liabilities	₹	Assets	₹
Trade Creditors	1,21,000	Sundry Assets	1,70,000
A's Capital	60,000	C's Capital	48,000
B's Capital	49,000	D's Capital	18,000
General Reserve	20,000	B's Drawings	4,000
		Profit & Loss A/c	10,000
	2,50,000		2,50,000

After preparing the Balance Sheet as at 31st March, it was discovered that purchases amounting to ₹ 10,000 in March, were not recorded in books, though the goods were received during March. C is insolvent but ₹ 11,100 is realized from his estate. Sundry Assets realized 86%. Realization Expenses ₹ 2,200. State who will bear C's deficiency and in which ratio.

ANSWER:

CALCULATION OF CAPITAL RATIO

	A ₹	B ₹
Capital	60,000	49,000
Less: B's Drawings	–	(4,000)
Less: Share of Debit balance of Profit & Loss A/c [10,000 + 10,000 (Ommited purchases)]	(6,000)	(6,000)
Add: Share of General Reserve	6,000	6,000
	60,000	45,000

C's deficiency is to be borne by A and B in the ratio of 60,000: 45,000 *or* 4: 3.

D will not bear C's deficiency since he had a debit balance in his Caoital Account.

QUESTION 5: Following is the Balance Sheet of A,B,C and D who were sharing in the ratio of 3:3:2:2 as at 31st March, 2015, when they decided to dissolve the firm:

Liabilities	₹	Assets	₹
Trade Creditors	1,21,000	Sundry Assets	1,70,000
A's Capital	60,000	C's Current	78,000
B's Capital	45,000	D's Current	33,000
C's Capital	30,000	Profit & Loss A/c	10,000
D's Capital	15,000		
General Reserve	20,000		
	2,91,000		2,91,000

After preparing the Balance Sheet as at 31st March, it was discovered that purchases amounting to ₹ 10,000 in March, were not recorded in books, though the goods were received during March. C is insolvent but ₹ 11,100 is realized from his estate. Sundry Assets realized 86%. Realization Expenses ₹ 2,200. State who will bear C's deficiency and in which ratio.

ANSWER: C's deficiency is to be borne by A, B, C and D in the ratio of their fixed capitals i.e. 60,000: 45,000: 30,000: 15,000 *or* 4: 3: 2: 1.

QUESTION 6: A, B, C and D who were sharing profits & losses in the ratio of 3: 3: 2: 2 decided to dissolve the firm. B was appointed to realise the assets and pay off the liabilities. He was entitled to receive 5% commission on the amount finally paid to other partners as capital. He was to bear the expenses on realisation which amounted to ₹ 1,500.The Capital Account balances of A, B, C and D (before adjusting P & L A/c (Dr. balance) ₹ 10,000 and Loss on Realisation ₹ 36,000] were as follows:

A	B	C	D
₹ 63,000	₹ 48,000	₹ 46,000 (Dr.	₹ 16,000 (Dr.)

The private position of the partners was as follows:

Particulars	A	B	C	D
Private Estate	1,00,000	2,00,000	3,00,000	4,00,000
Private Liabilities	10,000	20,000	2,88,900	30,000

Required: Prepare the Capital Accounts of Partners (Apply Garner Vs Murray Rule)

ANSWER:

Dr. **PARTNERS' CAPITAL ACCOUNTS** **Cr.**

Particulars	A ₹	B ₹	C ₹	D ₹	Particulars	A ₹	B ₹	C ₹	D ₹
To Balance b/d	—	—	48,000	18,000	By Balance b/d	60,000	45,000	—	—
To Realisation A/c	10,800	10,800	7,200	7,200	By Bank A/c	10,800	10,800	11,100	25,200
To C's Capital	25,200	18,900	—	—	By A's Capital	—	—	25,200	—

To B's Capital	1,143	—	—	—	By B's Capital	—	—	18,900	—
To Bank A/c	33,657	27,243	—	—	By C's Capital	–	1,143	—	—
	70,800	56,943	55,200	25,200		70,800	56,943	55,200	25,200

Notes:

(i) C's deficiency has been debited to A and B in the ratio of 60,000: 45,000 *or* 4: 3.

(ii) D will not bear any portion of the loss due to C's insolvency since he had a debit balance in his capital account to begin with.

(iii) The amount due to A, before commission payable to B is ₹ 24,000, ignoring the amount brought in by him on account of his share of the loss on realisation. The commission is 5/105 of ₹ 24,000.

(iv) It has been assumed that the realisation expenses have been met by B out of his private funds.

QUESTION 7: What is Piecemeal payment method under Partnership Dissolution? Briefly explain the two methods followed for determining the order in which the payments are made?

ANSWER: Generally, the assets sold upon Dissolution of partnership are realised only in small instalments over a period of time. In such circumstances the choice is *either* to distribute whatever is collected *or* to wait till whole amount is collected. Usually, the first cource is adopted. In order to ensure that the distributed cash amongst the partners is in proportion to their interest in the partnership concern *either* of the two methods described below may be followed for determining the order in which the payment should be made.

(i) Maximum Loss Each instalment realised is considered to be the final payment i.e. Method outstanding assets and claims are considered worthless and partners' accounts are adjusted on that basis each time when a deposit is made following *either* Garner Vs. Murray rule *or* the profit sharing ratio rule.

(ii) Highest Relative According to this method, the partner who has the higher relative capital, Capital Method that is, whose capital is greater in proportion to this profit sharing ration is first paid off. This method is also called as proportionate capital method.

QUESTION 8: X, Y and Z who were sharing the profit & losses in the ratio of 2: 3: 5 decided to dissolve the firm when their capitals were ₹ 18,00,000, ₹ 9,00,000 and ₹ 3,00,000 respectively, Reserves were ₹ 10,00,000 and Cash ₹ 60,000. Sundry Assets Realised ₹ 7,70,000 and Expenses on Realisation ₹ 30,000. Prepare the Statement showing the distribution of cash among the partners according to (a) Maximum Method (b) Proportionate Capital Method.

ANSWER:

STATEMENT SHOWING THE DISTRIBUTION OF CASH AMONG THE PARTNERS

Particulars	Total ₹	X ₹	Y ₹	Z ₹
A. Balance Due	40,00,000	20,00,000	12,00,000	8,00,000
B. Maximum Loss (₹ 40,00,000 – ₹ 8,00,000)	(32,00,000)	(6,40,000)	(9,60,000)	(16,00,000)
		13,60,000	2,40,000	(8,00,000)
C. Deficiency of Z Charged to X and Y in 20:12	(5,00,000)	(3,00,000)	8,00,000	
		8,60,000	(60,000)	—

D. Deficiency of Y charged to X		(60,000)	60,000	—
E. Cash paid	8,00,000	8,00,000	—	—
F. Balance Due (A – D)	32,00,000	12,00,000	12,00,000	8,00,000

(I) STATEMENT SHOWING THE CALCULATION OF HIGHEST RELATIVE CAPITALS

Particulars	X	Y	Z
A. Capitals (including Reserves)	20,00,000	12,00,000	8,00,000
B. Profit Sharing Ratio (PSR)	2	3	5
C. Actual Capital / PSR	10,00,000	4,00,000	1,60,000
D. Proportionate Capitals taking Z's capital as base capital	3,20,000	4,80,000	8,00,000
E. Surplus Capitals (A–D)	16,80,000	7,20,000	—
F. Profit Sharing Ratio (PSR)	2	3	—
G. Surplus Capitals / PSR	8,40,000	2,40,000	—
H. Revised Proportionate Capital Taking Y's capital base capital	4,80,000	7,20,000	—
I. Revised Surplus Capital (E–H)	12,00,000	—	—

DISTRIBUTION AS PER PROPORTIONATE CAPITAL METHOD

Particulars	X	Y	Z
Capitals (including Reserver)	20,00,000	12,00,000	8,00,000
Less: Amount paid	(8,00,000)	–	–
Balance Due	12,00,000	12,00,000	8,00,000

QUESTION 9: X, Y, Z who were sharing profits & losses in the ratio of 2: 3: 5 respectively decided to dissolve the firm when their capitals were ₹ 5,25,000, 6,75,000 and ₹ 8,00,000. Z agreed to take over investments of ₹ 6,00,000 at ₹ 4,40,000. Other Assets realised ₹ 7,80,000. Expenses on Realisation ₹ 20,000. Prepare the Statement showing the distribution of cash among the partners as per Maximum Loss Method.

ANSWER:

STATEMENT SHOWING THE DISTRIBUTION OF CASH AMONG PARTNERS

(ACCORDING TO MAXIMUM LOSS METHOD)

Particulars	Total (₹)	X (₹)	Y (₹)	Z (₹)
A. Balance Due	20,00,000	5,25,000	6,75,000	8,00,000
Maximum Loss (₹ 20,00,000 – ₹ 7,60,000 – ₹ 4,40,000)	(8,00,000)	(1,60,000)	(2,40,000)	(4,00,000)
B. Balance Due	12,00,000	3,65,000	4,35,000	4,00,000
C. Cash brought in by Z	40,000	40,000	(₹ 4,40,000 – ₹ 4,00,000)	
D. Cash Paid to X and Y and Asset to Z	(12,40,000)	(3,65,000)	(4,35,000)	(4,40,000)
E. Balance Due [A + C – D]	8,00,000	1,60,000	2,40,000	4,00,000

QUESTION 10: A, B and C who were sharing the profit & losses of a firm in the ratio of 5: 4: 3 respectively, formed a ABC (Private) Ltd. Their capital balances after adjustments are ₹ 79,000, ₹ 61,000 and ₹ 30,000 respectively. Equity shares of ₹ 10 each are to be issued to the partners at par in such numbers to ensure that by reason of their share holding alone, they will have the same rights of sharing profits & losses as they had in the firm. Balance, if any in their capital Accounter, will be settled by giving 7% Pref. Shares at par. Prepare statement showing the numbers of shares of each class to be issued by the company to each of the partners to settle their accounts.

ANSWER:

STATEMENT SHOWING THE NUMBER AND CLASSES OF SHARES ISSUED TO THE PARTNERS

Particulars	A	B	C
Closing Capital Balance (After Adjustments)	79,000	61,000	30,000
Proportionate Capitals Taking C's Capital as base	50,000	40,000	30,000
Surplus Capital	29,000	21,000	—
Equity Shares of ₹ 10 each to be issued for Proportionate Capitals	50,000	40,000	30,000
7% Pref. Share for Surplus Capitals	29,000	21,000	—

QUESTION 11: P, Q and R were carrying on business in partnership sharing profits & losses in the ratio of 5: 4: 3 respectively. The trial balance showed the balances:

Particulars	**P**	**Q**	**R**
Capital Accounts	**₹ 63,000**	**₹ 42,000**	**₹, 21,000**
Drawings Accounts	**₹ 20,000**	**₹ 20,000**	**₹ 15,000**

Interest on Capital accounts @ 5% p.a. on the amount standing to the credit of partner's Capital Account at the beginning of the year was not provided before preparing the above Trial Balance. On 31st March, they formed a Private Limited Co. with an authorised share capital of ₹ 2,00,000 in shares of ₹ 10 each to be divided in different classes to take over the business of partnership. Before transferring the business, the partners wish to draw from the partnership their profit to such an extent that the Bank balance is reduced to ₹ 50,000. For this purpose, sufficient profits of the year are to be retained in profit sharing ratio.

Required: Calculate the amount of additional drawings to be made.

ANSWER:

CALCULATION OF ADDITIONAL DRAWINGS

Drawings (already made: ₹ 55,000, plus those to be made ₹ 38,300, (i.e. ₹ 88,300 – 50,000), are ₹ 93,300. Of these, ₹ 6,300 is for interest. The remaining ₹ 87,000 is to be drawn by the partners in the ratio of 5: 4: 3.

STATEMENT SHOWING THE CALCULATION OF ADDITIONAL DRAWINGS

Particulars	P ₹	Q ₹	R ₹
A. Total Drawings (excluding interest) (Ratio 5: 4: 3)	36,250	29,000	21,750
B. *Add:* Interest on Capital	3,150	2,100	1,050

	39,400	31,100	22,800
C. *Less:* Amount already drawn	(20,000)	(20,000)	(15,000)
D. Additional Drawings to be made (A + B – C)	19,400	11,100	7,800

QUESTION 12: Firm X & Co. conlsists of partners A and B sharing Profits and Losses in the rato of 3:2. The firm Y & Co. consists of partners B and C sharing Profits and Losses in the ratio of 5:3. On 31st March, 2006 it was decided to amalgamate both the firms and form a new firm XY & Co., wherein A, B and C would be partners sharing Profits and Losses in the ratio of 4:5:1. Goodwill of X & Co., was valued at ₹ 75,000. Goodwill of Y & Co. was valued at ₹ 40,000. Goodwill account not to be opened in the books of the new firm but adjusted through the Capital accounts of the partners. You are required to Show, how the Goodwill value is adjusted amongst the partners.

ANSWER:

ADJUSTMENT FOR RAISING AND WRITING OFF OF GOODWILL

Raised in old profit sharing ratio	Total Written off in new ratio 4: 5: 1	Difference		X & Co. (3: 2)		Y & Co. (5: 3)	
₹	₹	₹		₹		₹	
45,000	—	45,000	Cr.	46,000	Dr.	1,000	Dr.
30,000	25,000	55,000	Cr.	57,500	Dr.	2,500	Dr.
—	15,000	15,000	Cr.	11,500	Dr.	3,500	Cr.
75,000	40,000	1,15,000		1,15,000		Nil	

QUESTION 13: In case of sale of a firm to a company, in which ratio the shares received from purchasing company should be divided among the partners?

ANSWER: In the ratio of final claims (i.e., balances of Capital Accounts after making all adjustments) of the partners.

ACCOUNTING FOR HIRE PURCHASE

QUESTION 1: State the Meaning of Hire Purchase Agreement.

ANSWER: Hire Purchase agreement means an agreement under which goods are let on hire and under which the hirer has an option to purchase them in accordance with the terms of the agreement and includes the agreement under which:

1. Possession of goods is delivered by the owner thereof to a person on condition that such person pays the agreed amount, in periodical instalments;
2. The property in the goods (i.e. ownership of goods) is to pass to such a person on the payment of the last instalment; and
3. Such a person has a right to terminate the agreement at any time before the property so passes.

QUESTION 2: Explain the term 'Hirer'.

ANSWER: A 'Hirer' means a person who obtains *or* has obtained possession of the goods from an owner under a hire purchase agreement.

QUESTION 3: Explain the term 'Hire Vendor'.

ANSWER: Hire Vendor means a person who delivers *or* has delivered the possession of goods to the hirer under a hire purchase agreement.

QUESTION 4: Explain the term 'Cash Price'.

ANSWER: Cash Price means the price at which the goods may be purchased by the hirer for cash.

QUESTION 5: Explain the term 'Down Payment'.

ANSWER: Down Payment means an initial payment payable by the hirer at the time of entering into a hire purchase agreement.

QUESTION 6: Explain the term 'Hire Purchase Price'.

ANSWER: Hire Purchase Price means the total sum payable by the hirer under a hire purchase agreement in order to complete the purchase of *or* acquisition of property in the goods to which the agreement relates and includes any sum so payable by the hirer under the hire purchase agreement by way of deposit *or* other initial payment. In the form of an equation, hire purchase price may be shown as follows:

Hire Purchase Price = Cash Price + Interest

QUESTION 8: Explain the term 'Hire Purchase Charges'.

ANSWER: Hire Purchase Charges means the difference between hire purchase price and the cash price as stated in the Hire Purchase Agreement. These hire purchase charges are popularly known as 'Interest'.

QUESTION 10: State the Meaning of Instalment Purchase Agreement.

ANSWER: Instalment Purchase Agreement means an agreement of sale under which:

1. The property in the goods (i.e. ownership of goods) is to pass to the buyer immediately on the signing of the contract of sale.
2. The buyer has no right to terminate the contract unless the seller defaults.
3. The seller has right only to sue for price if the buyer fails to pay any instalment (s). He can not take back the goods from the purchaser.
4. The buyer may dispose off the goods and give good title to the bona-fide purchaser.

QUESTION 11: Name the Method of Accounting followed under Instalment Purchase.

ANSWER: Accounting for Instalment Purchase is done on the basis of Interest Suspense Method. Under this method, both the seller and buyer make the entries with full value and keep the unaccrued amount of interest in "Interest Suspense Account', from which a sum equivalent to the interest accrued is transferred to the Interest account periodically as and when accrued.

QUESTION 12: State any two distinctions between Hire Purchase Agreement and Instatement Purchase Agreement.

ANSWER:

Hire Purchase Agreement	Instalment Purchase	Agreement
1. Act governing	It is governed by Hire Purchase Act 1972.	It is governed by the Sale of Goods Act 1930.
2. Nature of Contract	It is an agreement of hiring.	It is an agreement of sale.

3. Passing of Title (ownership)	The title to goods passes on last payment.	The title to goods passes immediately as in the case of usual sale.
4. Right to Return goods	The hirer may return goods without further payment, except for accrued instalment.	Unless seller defaults, goods are not returnable.
5. Seller's right to repossess	The seller may take possession of the goods if hirer is in default.	The seller can sue for price if the buyer is in default. He cannot take possession of the goods.
6. Right to Dispose off	Hirer cannot hire out, sell, pledge *or* assign entitling transferee to retain possession as against the hire vendor.	The buyer may dispose off the goods and give good title to the bonafide purchaser.
7. Responsibility for Risk of Loss	The hirer is not responsible for risk of loss of goods if he has taken reasonable precaution because the ownership has not yet transferred.	The buyer is responsible for risk of loss of goods because of the ownership has transferred.
8. Name of Parties involved	The parties involved are called Hirer and Hire vendor.	The parties involved are called buyer and seller.
9. Relationship between parties involved	The relationship between hirer and hire vendor is that of Bailee and Bailor.	The relationship between the buyer and seller is that of a debtor and creditor till last instalment is paid.
10. Component other than Cash Price	Component other than Cash Price included in Instalment is called Hire charges.	Component other than Cash price included in Instalment is called Interest.
11. Method of Accounting	1. Sales Method for goods of substantial sales values 2. Stock Methods for Goods of small sales values	Interest Suspense Method.

QUESTION 13: Cash Price—₹ 10,00,000, Cash Down Payment—20%, Four annual equal instalments of ₹ 2,50,000 each to be paid at the end of each year. Compute the payment of interest pertaining to each accounting year assuming (a) that the sales were made at the beginning of the year, and (b) that the sales were made uniformly throughout the year.

ANSWER:

(a) If the Sales were made at the beginning of the year

Step 1: Hire Purchase Price = Down Payment + Instalments

= ₹ 2,00,000 + ₹ 10,00,000 = ₹ 12,00,000

Step 2: Total Interest = H.P. Price – Cash Price

= ₹ 12,00,000 – ₹ 10,00,000 = ₹ 2,00,000

Step 3:

CALCULATION OF RATIO OF HPP OUTSTANDING IN THE BEGINNING OF EACH YEAR

A Year	B Outstanding H.P.P., in the Beginning of each year	C Instalment Paid	D = B – C Outstanding H.P.P. at the end of each year
I	10,00,000	2,50,000	7,50,000
II	7,50,000	2,50,000	5,00,000
III	5,00,000	2,50,000	2,50,000
IV	2,50,000	2,50,000	Nil

Ratio of outstanding H.P.P. at the beginning of each year = 100: 75: 50: 25 *or* 4: 3: 2: 1

Step 4: Calculation of Interest for each year

Interest for 1st year — ₹ 2,00,000 × 4/10 = ₹ 80,000

Interest for 2nd year — ₹ 2,00,000 × 3/10 = ₹ 60,000

Interest for 3rd year — ₹ 2,00,000 × 2/10 = ₹ 40,000

Interest for 4th year — ₹ 2,00,000 × 1/10 = ₹ 20,000

(b) If the sales were made uniformly throughout the year, If the sales take place uniformly throughout the year, the average period over which the price will remain unpaid in the first year will be only six months.

CALCULATION OF INTEREST PERTAINING TO EACH YEAR

A Year Ended on	B Amount Used	C Period of Use	D = B × C Product	E Ratio	F = ₹ 2,00,000 × E/300 Amount of Interest for Each Accounting Year
31.12.2013	10,00,000	6	60,00,000	60	40,000
31.12.2009	10,00,000	6	60,00,000		
	7,50,000	6	45,00,000	105	70,000
31.12.2010	7,50,000	6	45,00,000		
	5,00,000	6	30,00,000	75	50,000
31.12.2011	5,00,000	6	30,00,000		
	2,50,000	6	15,00,000	45	30,000
31.12.2012	2,50,000	6	15,00,000	15	10,000
			Total	300	2,00,000

QUESTION 14: Cash Down Payment—₹ 1,58,500, Four Instalments of ₹ 2,21,900, ₹ 2,06,050, ₹ 1,90,200 & ₹ 1,74,350 at the end of the Ist year, 2nd year, 3rd year and 4th year respectively. Payment of cash price in each instalment—Uniform. Compute the amount of Interest.

ANSWER: Difference between any two successive instalments represents the least amount of interest charged in the last year i.e. ₹ 2,21,900 – ₹ 2,06,050 = ₹ 15,850

Thus, Interest for 3rd year = Least amount of Interest × 2 = 31,700

Thus, Interest for 2nd year = ₹ 15,850 × 3 = 47,550

Thus, Interest for 1st year = ₹ 15,850 × 4 = 63,400

Thus, allocation of instalment between cash price and interest is as under:

Instalment (₹)	Interest (₹)	Cash Price (₹)
2,21,900	63,400	1,58,500
2,06,050	47,550	1,58,500
1,90,200	31,700	1,58,500
1,74,350	15,850	1,58,500
7,92,500	1,58,500	6,34,000

Total Cash Price = ₹ 6,34,000 + ₹ 1,58,500 = ₹ 7,92,500

QUESTION 15: Down Payment 20%, Balance in four annual instalments of ₹ 2,80,000, ₹ 2,60,000, ₹ 2,40,000 and ₹ 2,20,000 commencing from the end of a year from the date of down payment, Rate of Interest 10% p.a. Calculate Cash Price.

ANSWER:

COMPUTATION OF CASH PRICE AND PERIODIC INTEREST

A Instalment No.	B Closing Balance at the End After the Payment of Instalment	C Instalment Amount	D = B + C Closing Balance at the end before the Payment of Instalment	E = D*R/ (100 + R) Interest D* 10/110	F = D – E Opening Balance
IV	—	2,20,000	2,20,000	20,000	2,00,000
III	2,00,000	2,40,000	4,40,000	40,000	4,00,000
II	4,00,000	2,60,000	6,60,000	60,000	6,00,000
I	6,00,000	2,80,000	8,80,000	80,000	8,00,000

Let the Cash Price be 'X'

X = ₹ 8,00,000 + 20% of 'X' (i.e. down payment)

0.8X = ₹ 8,00,000

X = ₹ 8,00,000/.8 = ₹ 10,00,000

QUESTION 16: Down Payment 20%, Balance in four annual instalments of ₹ 1,84,000, ₹ 1,63,000, ₹ 1,42,000 and ₹ 1,21,000 commencing from the end of a year from the date of down payment. Rate of Interest 20% p.a. at half yearly rest. Calculate Cash Price.

ANSWER:

Principal	₹	100
Add: Interest @ 20% p.a. for 1st half year	₹	10
Principal & Interest at the end of 1st half year	₹	110
Add: Interest @ 20% p.a. for second half year	₹	11
Principal & Interest at the end of second half year	₹	121

Thus, every payment of ₹ 121 includes an interest of ₹ 21.

COMPUTATION OF CASH PRICE AND PERIODIC INTEREST

A Instalment No.	B Closing Balance at the End After the Payment of Instalment	C Instalment Amount	D = B + C Closing Balance at the end before the Payment of Instalment	E = D*R/(100 + R) Interest D* 21/121	F = D – E Opening Balance
IV	—	1,21,000	1,21,000	21,000	1,00,000
III	1,00,000	1,42,000	2,42,000	42,000	2,00,000
II	2,00,000	1,63,000	3,63,000	63,000	3,00,000
I	3,00,000	1,84,000	4,84,000	84,000	4,00,000

Let the Cash Price be 'X'

X = ₹ 4,00,000 + 20% of X (i.e., down payment)

0.8 X = ₹ 4,00,000

X = ₹ 4,00,000/0.8 = ₹ 5,00,000

QUESTION 17: Down Payment 20%, Balance in three yearly instalments of ₹ 1,63,000, ₹ 1,42,000 and ₹ 1,21,000 commencing from the end of a year form the date of down payment, Rate of Interest 20% p.a. compounded half yearly. Calculate Cash Price.

ANSWER:

Principal = 100

Add: Interest @ 20% p.a. for the 1st half year = 10

Principal interest at the end of 1st half year = 110

Add: Interest @ 20% p.a. for the 2nd half year = 11

Principal of interest at the end of year = 121

Thus, every payment of ₹ 121 includes an interest of ₹ 21.

COMPUTATION OF CASH PRICE AND PERIODIC INTEREST

A Instalment No.	B Closing Balance at the End After the Payment of Instalment	C Instalment Amount	D = B + C Closing Balance at the end before the Payment of Instalment	E = D*R/(100 + R) Interest D* 21/121	F = D – E Opening Balance
III	—	1,21,000	1,21,000	21,000	1,00,000
II	1,00,000	1,42,000	2,42,000	42,000	2,00,000
I	2,00,000	1,63,000	3,63,000	63,000	3,00,000

Let Cash Price be 'X'

X = ₹ 3,00,000 + 20% of X (i.e. down payment)

0.8X = ₹ 3,00,000

X = ₹ 3,00,000/0.8 = ₹ 3,75,000.

QUESTION 18: 40% Cash Down Payment and the balance in three instalments of ₹ 1,63,000 on 31.12.2012, ₹ 1,20,000 on 31.12.2013 and ₹ 1,10,000 on 31.12.2014. The rate of interest charged by the vendor is 10% p.a. compounded annually. Calculate the Cash Price.

ANSWER:

COMPUTATION OF CASH PRICE AND PERIODIC INTEREST

A Instalment No.	B Closing Balance at the End After the Payment of Instalment	C Instalment Amount	D = B + C Closing Balance at the end before the Payment of Instalment	E = D*R/(100 + R) Interest D* 10/110	F = D – E Opening Balance
III	Nil	1,10,000	1,10,000	10,000	1,00,000
II	1,00,000	1,20,000	2,20,000	20,000	2,00,000
I	2,00,000	1,63,000	3,63,000	33,000	3,30,000
	3,30,000	—	3,30,000	30,000	3,00,000

Let Cash Price be X

X = ₹ 3,00,000 + 40% of X

0.6X = ₹ 3,00,000

X = ₹ 3,00,000/0.6 = ₹ 5,00,000

QUESTION 19: On 1.1.2012, X Ltd. purchased from Y Ltd. 5 Machines for ₹ 10,00,000. X Ltd. writes off depreciation @20% p.a. on the original cost. On X Ltd.'s failure to pay the instalment due on 31.12.2014, after negotiations on 1.1.2015 Y Ltd. agreed to leave two machines with X Ltd. adjusting the value of the other three machines against the amount due. The machines being valued at cost less 40% p.a. depreciation on W.D.V. basis, Y Ltd. after spending ₹ 6,000 on repairs of these machines sold one of such machines for ₹ 70,000 on 30th June 2015.

Required: Calculate the Loss on Default in the books of Hire Purchaser and Loss on Sale of Goods Repossessed in the Books of Hire Vendor.

ANSWER:

LOSS ON DEFAULT

1. Book value of Goods Repossessed = Cost – Depreciation till Repossession = [₹ 2,00,000 × 3] – [₹ 6,00,000 × 20% × 2]	₹ 2,40,000
2. Agreed value of Goods Repossessed	
A. Cost [₹ 2,00,000 × 3]	₹ 6,00,000
B. *Less:* Depreciation for 1st year [40% of ₹ 6,00,000]	(₹ 2,40,000)
C. Book value in the beginning of 2nd year	₹ 3,60,000
D. *Less:* Depreciation for 2nd year [40% of ₹ 3,60,000]	(₹ 1,44,000)
E. Book Value at the end of 2nd year	₹ 2,16,000
3. Loss on default = Book value – Agreed value = ₹ 3,60,000 – ₹ 2,16,000	₹ 1,44,000
4. Loss on Sale of Goods Repossessed Total Cost = Agreed Value of Goods Repossessed + Repairs = ₹ 1,80,000 + ₹ 6,000 = ₹ 1,86,000 Profit on Sale = Sale Proceeds – Cost = ₹ 70,000 – (₹ 1,86,000 × 1/3)	₹ 8,000

ACCOUNTING FOR ROYALTIES

QUESTION 1: What is meant by Royalty?

ANSWER: Royalty is a periodic payment for the use of a certain property by the person who uses the property to the person who allows the use of property. The person who pays royalty is known as tenent *or* lessee and the person to whom royalty is paid is known as landlord *or* lessor. ***For Example***, in case of mining, the right to extact some mineral such as stone, oil, coal etc. is allowed by the landlord to the lessee.

QUESTION 2: State the meaning of minimum rent (or dead rent).

ANSWER: Minimum rent is a guaranteed amount which the lessee has to pay in the absense *or* inadequancy of the output *or* sales on which the royalty is based.

QUESTION 3: Should minimum rent already fixed be reduced proportionate to the period of strike when there is a general strike?

ANSWER: Yes unless otherwise provided in the royalty agreement.

QUESTION 4: State the meaning of Short Working (or Redeemable Dead Rent).

ANSWER: Short Working is the excess of minimum Rent over the Actual Royalties based on actual output/sales.

QUESTION 5: State the meaning of Surplus Working.

ANSWER: Short Working is the excess of Actual Royalties based on actual output/sales over the minimum Rent.

QUESTION 6: State the meaning of Short Working Recoupment Clause.

ANSWER: Short Working Recoupment Clause enables the tenant to recover the short working out of the royalties of the subsequent periods when there is surplus working.

QUESTION 7: State the meaning of Short Working Lapsed *or* Written Off.

ANSWER: It is the amount of short working which could not be recovered by lessee within the stipulated period of recoupment. It is written off to the Profit & Loss Account.

QUESTION 8: State the nature of Royalty Account. How is it closed?

ANSWER: Royalty Account is a nominal account.

In the books of Lessee	In the books of Lessor
Manufacturing A/c / P & L A/c Dr To Royalty Payable A/c	Royalty Receivable A/c Dr To P & L A/c

QUESTION 9: Give the Accounting Entries in the Books of the Landlord/Lessor where a minimum rent exists with right to recoup short workings.

ANSWER:

WHERE THE ACTUAL ROYALTY IS LESS THAN THE MINIMUM RENT

1. Lessee Account Dr. To Royalty Receivable Account To Royalty Suspense Account/ **Or** Shortworkings Allowable A/c	[Minimum rent] [Actual Royalties for the period] [Short fall in Royalties]

2. Bank Account Tax Deducted at source To Lessee Account	Dr. Dr.	[Net amount paid] [Tax deducted at source] [Minimum rent]
3. Royalties Receivable Account To Profit & Loss Account	Dr.	 [Transfer]

WHERE THE ACTUAL ROYALTY IS MORE THAN THE MINIMUM RENT

1. Royalty Suspense Account/ **Or** Short workings Allowable A/c To Lessee Account	Dr.	 [Recoupment of Short workings, if any]
2. Bank Account Tax Deducted at source To Lessee Account	Dr. Dr.	[Net amount paid] [Tax deducted at source]
3. Royalties Receivable Account To Profit & Loss Account	Dr.	 [Transfer]
4. Royalty Suspense Account/ **Or** Short workings Allowable A/c To Profit and Loss Account	Dr.	 [Short workings, which can not be recouped]

QUESTION 10: Tulsian Ltd provides you the following information:

Short Working B/f [₹ 6,000 for 2012, ₹ 10,000 for 2013]

Royalty @ ₹ 100 per unit produced subject to Minimum Rent of ₹ 1,00,000.

Sales of 2015: 950 units and Closing Stock: for 2014 300 units, for 2015 50 units

In the event of strike, the minimum rent would be taken pro-rata on the basis of actual numbers of working days but in the event of lockout, the lessee would be enjoy a concession in respect of minimum rent of 50% of the period of lockout. There was strike for 73 days and lockout for 4 months during the year 2015. Recoumpent of short working of each year is allowed during the next 3 years subject to maximum of ₹ 5,000 p.a.Calculate the Actual Payment and Short Working C/F.

ANSWER: Minimum Rent for 2015 = 1,00,000 – [(1,00,000 × 73/365) + (1,00,000 × 2/12)] = 63,333

ANALYSIS OF ROYALTY PAYABLE AND SHORT WORKINGS

A Year	B Output (Units)	C = B X Rate Actual Royalty	D Minimum Rent	E = D – C Short Working	F Short Working Recouped	G = C + E – F Actual Payment	H Short Working W/O	$I_n = I_{n-1} + E - F -$ H Short Working C/F
2015	700	70,000	63,333	—	5,000	65,000	1,000	10,000

ACCOUNTING FOR BRANCHES

QUESTION 1: Why goods are marked on invoice price by the head office while sending goods to the branch?

ANSWER: Goods are marked on invoice price to achieve the following objectives:

1. To keep secret from the branch manager, the cost price of the goods and profit made, so that the branch manager may not start a rival and competitive business with the concern; and
2. To have effective control on stock i.e stock at any time must be equal to opening stock plus goods received from head office minus sales made at branch.
3. To dictate pricing policy to its branches, as well as save work at branch because prices have already been decided.

QUESTION 2: State the Accounting Treatment of the following under (a) Debtors Method and (b) Stock and Debtors Method:

(i) **Normal Loss**
(ii) **Abnormal Loss**
(iii) **Insurance Claim**
(iv) **Goods Returned by Branch Customers directly to Head Office**
(v) **Cash Remitted by Branch Customers directly to Head Office**

ANSWER:

ACCOUNTING TREATMENT UNDER DEBTORS METHOD

Item	Accounting Treatment under Debtors Method
1. Normal Loss	Normal loss does not appear in the Branch Account since the Closing Stock appears at the adjusted figure.
2. Abnormal Loss	Abnormal loss does not appear in the Branch Account since the Closing Stock appears at the adjusted figure.
3. Insurance Claim	Insurance Claim is shown on the credit side of Branch Account either by way of Increased Closing Cash/Bank Balance or remittance to H.O.or Insurance Co. as a debtor at the end on the credit side of Branch Account. Cash A/c/BankA/c/ Insurance Co Dr. To Branch A/c
4. Goods Returned by Branch Customers directly to Head Office	These are treated like goods returned by Branch to H.O. and thus, the Cost/Invoice price (as the case may be) of these goods is shown on credit side of Branch Account. (i) Goods sent to Branch A/c Dr. [Invoice Price] To Branch A/c (ii) Branch A/c Dr. [Loading] To Goods sent to Branch A/c
5. Cash Remitted by Branch Customers directly to Head Office	It is treated like cash remitted by Branch to H.O. and is shown on credit side of Branch Account. Cash A/c/Bank A/c Dr. To Branch A/c

ACCOUNTING TREATMENT UNDER STOCK AND DEBTORS METHOD

Item	Accounting Treatment under Stock and Debtors Method
1. Normal Loss	Branch Adjustment A/c Dr. [Invoice Price] To Branch Stock A/c

2. Abnormal Loss	Branch Adjustment A/c Branch Profit & Loss A/c To Branch Stock A/c	Dr. Dr.	[Loading] [Cost] [Invoice Price]
3. Insurance Claim	Branch Cash A/c/ Insurance Co. To Branch Profit & Loss A/c	Dr.	
4. Goods Returned by Branch Cust omers directly to Head Office	(i) Goods sent to Branch A/c To Branch Debtors A/c (ii) Branch Adjustment A/c To Goods sent to Branch A/c	Dr. Dr.	[Invoice Price] [Loading]
5. Cash Remitted by Branch Customers directly to Head Office	Cash A/c To Branch Debtors A/c	Dr.	

QUESTION 3: How will you disclose the following under Stock & Debtors Method:

(a) **Goods are sent to Branch (at cost to HO) ₹ 5,24,000, Goods received by Branch till end of accounting year ₹ 7,71,000.**

(b) **Goods returned by credit customers directly to H.O. ₹ 3,000**

(c) **Cash remitted by Credit Customers directly to H.O. ₹ 40,000**

(d) **Agreed Allowance to Customers off Selling Price ₹ 1,000 (already taken into account while invoicing)**

(e) **Branch Debtors' cheques returned dishonoured (not yet recorded) ₹ 5,000.**

(f) **Loss of Goods at Branch through pilferage is estimated at 1% of goods received.**

(g) **Loss of Goods in transit (at invoice price) ₹ 6,000 against which a claim of ₹ 3,500 was received.**

(h) **Surplus Stock of ₹ 15,000.**

Note: Goods are invoiced by H.O. at cost plus 50%.

ANSWER:

Dr. **AN EXTRACT OF BRANCH STOCK ACCOUNT** **Cr.**

Particulars	₹	Particulars	₹
To Goods sent to Branch A/c	7,86,000	By Branch Adjustment A/c	1,000
[₹ 5,24,000 + 50%]		(Agreed Allowance)	
To Balance Adjustment A/c	15,000	By Branch Adjustment A/c	7,710
[Surplus]		[1% of ₹ 7,71,000]	
		By Branch Adjustment A/c	2,000
		[Load on AL]	
		By P & L A/c	4,000
		[Cost of Abnormal loss]	
		By Goods-in-Transit	15,000

Dr. **AN EXTRACT OF BRANCH DEBTORS ACCOUNT** Cr.

Particulars	₹	Particulars	₹
To Bank A/c (Ch. Dish)	5,000	By Goods sent to Branch A/c	3,000
		By Cash A/c	40,000

Dr. **AN EXTRACT OF BRANCH ADJUSTMENT ACCOUNT** Cr.

Particulars	₹	Particulars	₹
To Branch Stock A/c (Agreed Allowance)	1,000	By Goods sent to Branch A/c [Loading] [(₹ 7,86,000 – ₹ 3,000) 50/150]	2,61,000
To Branch Stock A/c (Normal Pilferage)	7,710	By Branch Stock A/c (Surplus)	15,000
To Branch Stock A/c (Abnormal Loss)	2,000		

Dr. **AN EXTRACT OF BRANCH PROFIT & LOSS ACCOUNT** Cr.

Particulars	₹	Particulars	₹
To Loss in Transit [₹ 4,000 – ₹ 3,500]	500		

QUESTION 4: Tulsian Ltd with its Head office in Delhi invoices goods to its Branch at Mumbai at 20% less than the catalogue price which is cost plus 50% with instructions that cash sales are to be made at invoice price and credit sales at catalogue price less discount at 15% on prompt payments. Provison is to be made for discount to be allowed to debtors, at year end on the basis of year's trend of prompt payments.

Opening Stock at Branch at its cost	**₹ 12,000**
Opening Branch Debtors	**₹ 10,000**
Goods Sent to Branch (at cost to H.O)	**₹ 1,40,000**
Goods received by Branch till close of the year	**₹ 1,38,000**
Cash Sales	**₹ 46,000**
Credit Sales	**₹ 1,00,000**
Cash received from Debtors	**₹ 85,635**
Discount Allowed to Debtors	**₹ 13,365**
Stock lost by fire (at Cost)	**₹ 2,500**

Required: Calculate the Provision for Discount on Debtors, Closing Stock at Branch and Branch Stock Reserve in respect of unrealized profit.

ANSWER:

COMPUTATION OF PROVISION FOR DISCOUNT ON DEBTORS

(a) Prompt paying debtors who availed of discount = ₹ 13,365 × 100/15 = 89,100

(b) Total debtors who made payment during the year = ₹ 13,365 + 85,635 = ₹ 99,000

(c) Proportion of prompt payers to those who made payment = (89,100/99,000) × 100 = 90%

(d) Likely Prompt paying debtors included in Closing Debtors = 90% of ₹ 11,000 = ₹ 9,900

(e) Provision for Discount on the Closing Balance = 15% of ₹ 9,900 = ₹ 1,485

CALCULATION OF CLOSING STOCK AT BRANCH

	Particulars	₹
A.	Opening Stock	12,000
B.	*Add:* Goods received	1,38,000
C.	*Less:* Invoice Price of Cash Sales	(46,000)
	Invoice Price of Credit Sales [₹ 1,00,000 × 120/150]	(80,000)
	Abnormal Loss [₹ 2,500 + 20%]	(3,000)
D.	Closing Stock at Branch in hand	21,000
E.	Closing Stock in transit [₹ 1,68,000 – ₹ 1,38,000]	30,000
F.	Total Branch Stock	51,000
	Branch Stock Reserve = ₹ 51,000 × 20/120 = ₹ 8,500	

ACCOUNTING FOR FOREIGN BRANCH

QUESTION 1: State the Meaning of Foreign Branch.

ANSWER: A Branch outside the home country in which Head office is situated is known as a foreign branch. It may be noted that the accounting principles which apply to a home branch (i.e., Inland Branch), also apply to a foreign branch after converting the trial balance of the foreign branch in the home currency.

QUESTION 2: State the Meaning of Integral Foreign Operations (IFO).

ANSWER: A foreign operation, the activities of which are an integral part of those of the reporting enterprise is known as Integral Foreign Operations (IFO). [e.g. Foreign Branch]

QUESTION 3: State the Meaning of Non-Integral Foreign Operations (NIFO).

ANSWER: A foreign operation, that is not an integral part of the reporting enterprise. is known as Non-Integral Foreign Operations (NIFO). [e.g. Foreign Branch/Subsidiary]

QUESTION 4: What are the indicators of Non-Integral Foreign Operation (NFO)?

ANSWER: The indicators of a Non-Integral Foreign Operation are:

1. **Autonomy:** While the reporting enterprise may control the foreign operation, the activities of the foreign operation are carried out with a significant degree of autonomy from those of the reporting enterprise,
2. **Transaction Pattern:** Transactions with the reporting enterprise are not a high proportion of the foreign operation's activities,
3. **Financing:** The activities of the foreign operation are financed mainly from its own operations *or* local borrowings rather than from the reporting enterprise,
4. **Expenditure in Local Currency:** Cost of Labour, Material and other components of the foreign operation's products *or* services are primarily paid *or* settled in the local currency rather than in the reporting currency.
5. **Sales Pattern:** The foreign operation's sales are mainly in currencies other then the reporting currency.
6. **Effect of Cash Flows:** Cash Flows of the reporting enterprise are insulated from the day-to-day activities of the foreign operation rather than being directly affected by the activities of the foreing operation.

7. **Prices of products:** Sales Prices for the foreign operation's products are not primarily responsive on a short-term basis to changes in exchange rates but are dtermined more by local com petitiion *or* local government regulation, and
8. **Local Market:** There is an active local sales market for the foreign operation's products, although there might be significant amounts of exports.

   The appropriate classification for each operation can be established from factual information and proper judgment, based on the indicators listed above

QUESTION 5: State the Treatment of Exchange Difference arising on Translation of Financial Statements.

ANSWER:

Integral Foreign Operations [IFO]	Non-Integral Foreign Operations [NIFO]
Recognised as Income *or* Expense in the period which they arise.	Accumulated in Foreign Currency Translation Reserve until the disposal of Net Investment

QUESTION 6: Distinguish between Integral and Non Integral Foreign Operations as per AS 11.

ANSWER:

Basis of Comparison	Integral Foreign Operations [IFO]	Non-Integral Foreign Operations [NIFO]
1. Meaning	A foreign operation, the activities of which are an integral part of those of the reporting enterprise [*e.g.* Foreign Branch]	A foreign operation that is not an integral foreign operation [*e.g.*Foreign Subsidiary]
2. Treatment of Exchange Difference arising on translation	Recognised as Income *or* Expense in the period which they arise.	Accumulated in Foreign Currency Translation Reserve until the disposal of Net Investment
3. Exchange Rate To Be Used For Reporting		
(a) Opening Stock if carried at historical cost	Actual Exchange Rate as on the date of purchase	Opening Rate
(b) Closing Stock if carried at historical cost	Actual Exchange Rate as on the date of purchase	Closing Rate
(c) Non-Monetary Items (excluding Stocks) carried at Historical [*e.g.* Fixed Assets]	Actual Exchange Rate as on the date of purchase	Closing Rate
(d) Depreciation if asset is carried at historicalcost	Actual Exchange Rate as on the date of purchase	Closing Rate

QUESTION 7: State the Items for which the same translation rate is used for Integral and Non Integral Foreign Operations as per AS 11.

ANSWER:

Basis of Comparison	Integral Foreign Operations [IFO]	Non-Integral Foreign Operations [NIFO]
(a) Monetary Items [e.g. Cash, Debtors, Creditors, Prepaid Exp., O/s Exp.,	Closing Rate	Closing Rate
(b) Contingent Liability	Closing Rate	Closing Rate
(c) Other Revenue Items [e.g. Purchases, Sales, Interest, Expenses]	Actual Exchange Rate	Actual Exchange Rate
(d) Remittances	Actual Exchange Rate	Actual Exchange Rate
(e) Goods received from HO/ Sent to HO	Taken at amounts recorded in H.O.Books	Taken at amounts recorded in H.O.Books
(f) Balance in HO A/c in Branch Books	Taken at amounts recorded in H.O.Books	Taken at amounts recorded in H.O.Books

QUESTION 8: State the Option available to Companies for Treatment of Exchange Difference as per Para 46A of The Companies (Accounting Standards) Rules, 2012.

ANSWER:

1. Long-term Foreign Currency Loans relating to Depreciable Assets	Exchange Difference should be debited(in case of Exchange Loss) *or* credited (in case of Exchange Profit) to **Respective Asset A/c.**
2. Long-term Foreign Currency Loans relating to Non-Depreciable Assets like land	1. Exchange Difference should be debited(in case of Exchange Loss) *or* credited (in case of Exchange Profit) to **Foreign Currency Monetary Items Translation Difference A/c.** 2. Such Exchange Difference should be transferred to Profit & Loss A/c in equal proportion over reporting periods ending on March 31,2020. **Note:** The Dr. *or* Cr. Balance of FCMITD A/c should be shown on the Equity & Liabilities side of the Balance Sheet under the head **'Reserves & Surplus'.**
Note: Once Option as per Para 46A is exercised,it is irrevocable. If Option as per Para 46A is not exercised, the Exchange Difference is transferred to Profit & Loss A/c.	

QUESTION 9: Explain "Monetary Item" as per Accounting Standard 11. How are foreign currency monetary items to be recognized at each Balance Sheet date? Classify the following as monetary or non-monetary item:

(i) Share Capital (ii) Trade Receivables (iii) Investments (iv) Fixed Assets

ANSWER:

1. As per AS 11 'The Effects of Changes in Foreign Exchange Rates', Monetary items are money held and assets and liabilities to be received or paid in fixed or determinable amounts of money.
2. Foreign currency monetary items should be reported **using the closing rate** at each balance sheet date. However, in certain circumstances, the closing rate may not reflect with reasonable

accuracy the amount in reporting currency that is likely to be realised from, or required to disburse, a foreign currency monetary item at the balance sheet date. In such circumstances, the relevant monetary item should be reported in the reporting currency at the amount which is likely to be realised from or required to disburse, such item at the balance sheet date.

Share capital	Non-monetary
Trade receivables	Monetary
Investments	Non-monetary
Fixed assets	Non-monetary

QUESTION 10: On 31st March, 2015, the following ledger balances have been extracted from the books of Washington branch office:

Ledger Accounts	$
Building	180
Opening Stock	26
Cash and Bank Balances	57
Purchases	96
Sales	110
Commission receipts	28
Debtors	46
Creditors	65

You are required to convert above Ledger balances into Indian Rupees. Use the following rates of exchange:

	₹ per $
Opening rate	46
Closing rate	50
Average rate	48
For fixed assets	42

ANSWER:

CONVERSION OF LEDGER BALANCES (IN DOLLARS) INTO RUPEES

	$ Ruees	Rate per $	Amount in
Building	180	42	7,560
Opening Stock	26	46	1,196
Cash and bank balances	57	50	2,850
Purchases	96	48	4,608
Sales	110	48	5,280
Commission receipts	28	48	1,344
Debtors	46	50	2,300
Creditors	65	50	3,250

QUESTION 11: Tulsian Limited, an Indian company has a branch at New York (USA). The trial balance of the Branch as at 31st March, 2015 is as follows:

Particulars	US $	
	Dr.	Cr.
Fixed Assets	51,200	
Opening Stock	22,400	
Purchases/Sales	96,000	1,66,400
Goods Sent from HO	32,000	
Carriage Inward	400	
Branch Expenses	4,800	
Head Office Account	—	45,600
Sundry Debtors/Creditors	9,600	6,800
Cash and Bank	2,400	
	2,18,800	2,18,800

The following further information's are given:

(1) Expenses outstanding $ 400.

(2) Depreciate Fixed Assets @ 10% p.a. at written down value.

(3) The Head Office sent goods to Branch for ₹ 15,80,000

(4) The head Office shown an amount of ₹ 20,50,000 due from Branch.

(5) Closing Stock $ 21,500.

(6) There were no transit items either at the start or at the end of the year.

(7) On April 1,2013 when the fixed assets were purchased the rate of exchange was ₹ 43 to one $. On April, 1, 2014, the rate was ₹ 47 per $. On March 31, 2015 the rate was ₹ 50 per $. Average Rate during the year was ₹ 45 to one $.

Required: Assuming that the Branch is an Integral foreign operation of the Indian Company. Calculate the Difference in Exchange and show its Accounting Treatment as per AS 11.

ANSWER:

TRIAL BALANCE (IN RUPEES) OF NEW YORK (USA) BRANCH AS ON 31ST MARCH, 2015

Particulars	Dr. US $	Cr. US $	Conversion Rate	Dr. ₹	Cr. ₹
Fixed Assets	46,080		43	19,81,440	
Depreciation on Fixed Assets	5,120		43	2,20,160	
Opening Stock	22,400		47	10,52,800	
Purchases	96,000		45	43,20,000	
Sales		1,66,400	45		74,88,000
Goods sent from H.O.	32,000			15,80,000	
Carriage inward	400		45	18,000	
Branch Expenses (4,800 + 400)	5,200		45	2,34,000	
Outstanding Expenses		400	50		20,000
Head Office A/c		45,600			20,50,000

Trade debtors	9,600		50	4,80,000	
Trade creditors		6,800	50		3,40,000
Cash & bank	2,400		50	1,20,000	
Exchange gain (bal. fig.)					1,08,400
	2,19,200	2,19,200		1,00,06,400	1,00,06,400
Closing Stock	21,500		50	10,75,000	

Accounting Treatment of Difference in Exchange: Difference in Exchange [e.g. 1,08,400] will be credted to the Statement of Profit & Loss.

QUESTION 12: Assuming that the Branch in Previous QUESTION is a Non-Integral foreign operation of the Indian Company, Calculate the Difference in Exchange and show its Accounting Treatment as per AS 11.

ANSWER:

TRIAL BALANCE (IN RUPEES) OF NEW YORK (USA) BRANCH AS ON 31ST MARCH, 2015

Particulars	Dr. US $	Cr. US $	Conversion rate	Dr. ₹	Cr. ₹
Fixed Assets	46,080		50	23,04,000	
Depreciation on Fixed Assets	5,120		50	2,56,000	
Opening Stock	22,400		47	10,52,800	
Purchases	96,000		45	43,20,000	
Sales		1,66,400	45		74,88,000
Goods sent from H.O.	32,000			15,80,000	
Carriage inward	400		45	18,000	
Branch Expenses (4,800 + 400)	5,200		45	2,34,000	
Outstanding Expenses		400	50		20,000
Head Office A/c		45,600			20,50,000
Trade debtors	9,600		50	4,80,000	
Trade creditors		6,800	50		3,40,000
Cash & bank	2,400		50	1,20,000	
Exchange gain (bal. fig.)					4,66,800
	2,19,200	2,19,200		1,03,64,800	1,03,64,800
Closing Stock	21,500		50	10,75,000	

Accounting Treatment of Difference in Exchange : Difference in Exchange [e.g. 4,66,800] will be credted to Foreign Currency Translation Reserve which will be shown in the balance Sheet.

ACCOUNTING FOR DEPARTMENTS

QUESTION 1: How is the Stock Reserve in respect of Unrealised Profit included in Closing Stock of each Deptt Calculated?

ANSWER: = Transfer Price of Unsold Stock of Transferee Deptt. × Gross Profit of the Transferor Deptt / Net Sales of the Transferor Deptt

QUESTION 2: Give a Journal Entry to record the Stock Reserve in respect of Unrealised Profit included in Closing Stock of each Deptt Calculated.

ANSWER:

Profit and Loss A/c Dr.
To Stock Reserve A/c
(Being the provision made for unrealised profit included in closing stock)

QUESTION 3: X Ltd. provides you the following information:

	Stock as on 1.4.2015	Purchases (for ₹ 1,00,000)	Sales
Department A	120 units	1000 Units	1020 units @ ₹ 20.00
Department B	80 units	2000 Units	1920 units @ ₹ 22.50
Department C	152 units	2400 Units	2496 Units @ ₹ 25.00

The rate of gross profit is the same in each case.

Required: Prepare Departmental Trading Account for the year 2014–2015.

ANSWER:

Dr. DEPARTMENTAL TRADING ACCOUNT FOR THE YEAR ENDING ON MARCH 31, 2013 Cr.

Particulars	A Dept. ₹	B Dept. ₹	C Dept. ₹	Total ₹	Particulars	A Dept. ₹	B Dept. ₹	C Dept. ₹	Total ₹
To Op. Stock	1,920	1,440	3,040	6,400	By Sales	20,400	43,200	62,400	1,26,000
To Purchases	16,000	36,000	48,000	1,00,000	By Cl. Stock	1,600	2,880	1,120	5,600
To Gross profit	4,080	8,640	12,480	25,200					
	22.000	46,080	63,520	1,31,600		22,000	46,080	63,520	1,31,600

Working Notes:

1. Closing Stock of Deptt. A = Opening Stock + Purchases – Sales = 120 + 1,000 –1,020 = 100
2. Closing Stock of Deptt. B = 80 + 2,000 – 1,920 = 160
3. Closing Stock of Deptt. C = 152 + 2,400 – 2,496 = 56
4. The rate of gross profit: Assuming all the purchases are sold,the sale proceeds would be:

Particulars	₹
A. 1,000 units @ ₹ 20.00	20,000
B. 2,000 units @ ₹ 22.50	45,000
C. 2,400 units @ ₹ 25.00	60,000
	1,25,000

5. Gross Profit = Sales – Cost = ₹ 1,25,000 – ₹ 1,00,000 = ₹ 25,000
   Gross Profit Ratio = (₹ 25,000/1,25,000) × 100 = 20%
   Profit and Cost for each article:

Particulars	Profit (₹)	Cost (₹)
A. 20% of ₹ 20.00	4.00	16.00
B. 20% of ₹ 22.50	4.50	18.00
C. 20% of ₹ 25.00	5.00	20.00

QUESTION 4: Goods are transferred from Deptt. P to Deptt. Q at a price 50% above Cost. If Closing Stock of Dept Q is ₹ 27,000. Compute the amount of stock Reserve.

ANSWER: Stock Reserve = ₹ 27,000 × 50/150 = ₹ 9,000.

QUESTION 5: X Ltd., has two departments A and B. From the following particulars, Calculate Stock Reserve.

Particulars	A ₹	B ₹
Opening Stock (at cost)	20,000	12,000
Purchases	92,000	68,000
Sales	1,40,000	1,12,000
Wages	12,000	8,000
Carriage	2,000	2,000
Closing Stock:		
(i) Purchased goods	4,500	6,000
(ii) Finished goods	24,000	14,000
Purchased goods transferred:		
by B to A	10,000	
by A to B		8,000
Finished goods transferred:		
by A to B	35,000	
by B to A		40,000
Return of finished goods:		
by A to B	10,000	
by B to A		7,000

You are informed that purchased goods have been transferred mutually at their respective departmental purchase cost and finished goods at departmental market price and that 20% of the finished stock (closing) at each department represented finished goods received from the other department. Profit of Deptt. A and Deptt B are ₹ 38,500 and ₹ 46,000 respectively.

ANSWER:

1. Calculation of Net Sales (including transfers)

	Dept A ₹	Dept B ₹
(a) Sales	1,40,000	1,12,000
(b) *Add:* Transfer	35,000	40,000
(c) *Less:* Returns	7,000	10,000
(d) Net Sales plus Transfer	1,68,000	1,42,000

2. Unrealised Profit on Closing Stock: Dept. A: 4,800 × 46,000/1,42,000 = ₹ 1,555
Dept. B: 2,800 × 38,500/1,68,000 = ₹ 642.

SELF-BALANCING LEDGERS AND SECTIONAL BALANCING LEDGERS

QUESTION 1: What is Sectional Balancing System?

ANSWER: Under Sectional Balancing System, only the total account for each of the subsidiary ledgers is opened in the General Ledger and no Control Account/Adjustment Account/Self Balancing Account is opened in the subsidiary ledger. A trial balance can be prepared only of General Ledger and not of Debtors' Ledger *or* Creditors' Ledger since the double entry is completed in respect of General Ledger and not in respect of Debtors' Ledger and Creditors' Ledger.

QUESTION 2: What is Self Balancing System?

ANSWER: A Self Balancing Ledger System implies a system of ledger keeping under which–

(a) Separate ledger (e.g. Debtors ledger, Creditors ledger) are maintained for different nature of transactions.

(b) A General Ledger Adjustment Account is opened in each subsidiary ledger in order to make each such ledger self-balancing.

(c) A Control Account/Adjustment Account is opened for each subsidiary ledger in the General Ledger in order to complete the double entry.

(d) The accuracy of individual balances in each ledger is checked by comparing the total of their balances with the balance of the Control Account.

(e) Usually the following accounts are maintained:

Ledger	Accounts Opened in the Ledger
(i) Debtors' Ledger	(a) Personal accounts of all Trade Debtors, (b) General Ledger Adjustment Account.
(ii) Creditors' Ledger	(a) Personal accounts of all Trade Creditors, (b) General Ledger Adjustment Account.
(iii) General Ledger	(a) Personal accounts (other than those of Trade Debtors & Creditors), (b) All Real Accounts, (c) All Nominal Accounts, (d) Debtors' Ledger Adjustment Account, (e) Creditors' Ledger Adjustment Account.

QUESTION 3: What does General Ledger Adjustment show?

ANSWER: General Ledger Adjustment Account in the Debtors Ledger shows a summary of all transactions of the Debtors Ledger in a reverse manner and similarly, General Ledger Adjustment Account in the Creditors Ledger shows a summary of all transactions of the Creditors Ledger in a reverse manner.

QUESTION 4: Give one example of a Company which follows Self Balancing System.

ANSWER: In case of Banking Companies, separate ledgers are maintained each for Saving Bank Account Holders, Current Account Holders, Borrowers, Fixed Depositors.

QUESTION 5: What are the advantages of Self Balancing System?

ANSWER:

(1) It facilitates the quick detection of errors with the minimum efforts.

(2) It fixes the responsibility of ledger keeper, as to the balancing of the ledger under his/her

charge and the person responsible for the mistake can be called upon to work overtime to locate it. Errors are localized.

(3) It facilitates the preparation of interim accounts without personal ledgers having to be balanced.

(4) It facilitates the ascertainment of the figures of total debtors and creditors readily.

QUESTION 6: What is the difference between the Sectional and Self-balancing system?

ANSWER:

Basis of Distinction	Sectional Balancing System	Self Balancing System
1. Trial Balance	Only one trial balance is prepared in General Ledger.	Separate trial balance is prepared in each ledger.
2. Nature of Total Debtors/Creditors Account	Total Debtors account and Total Creditors account are memorandum accounts and are not the part of double entry system.	Adjustment accounts are the parts of double entry system.
3. Arithmetical Accuracy	Arithmetical accuracy of Sales Ledger and Bought Ledger can be checked by preparing Total Debtors Account and Total Creditors Account.	Arithmetical accuracy of each ledger can be checked by preparing trial balance of each ledger.
4. Where opened	Total Debtors Account and Total Creditors Account are opened in General Ledger	Adjustment accounts are opened in General Ledger, Sales Ledger and bought ledger.

QUESTION 7: How will you show the following items in General Ledger Adjustment Account in Debtors Ledger and General Ledger Adjustment Account in Creditors Ledger:

		₹
(a)	Transfer from Debtors' Ledgers to Creditors' Ledger	1,100
(b)	Transfer from Creditors' Ledger to Debtors' Ledger	1,900
(c)	B/R endorsed to Creditors	4,000
(d)	Endorsed Bills dishonoured	1,000
(e)	Bad Debts written off (after deducting bad debts recovered ₹ 300)	2,200
(f)	Provision for Doubtful Debts	550
(g)	Provision for Discount on Debtors	1,000
(h)	Reserve for Discount on Creditors	2,000
(i)	Cash Sales	3,000
(j)	Cash Purchases	4,000
(k)	Bill Receivable Collected on maturity	5,000
(l)	Bills Receivable discounted	6,000
(m)	Bills Payable matured	7,000
(n)	Discount allowed	1,500
(o)	Discount received	600
(p)	Allowances from Creditors	3,200

(q) Discount allowed to debtors ₹ 500 was recorded as discount received from creditors.

(r) Closing Debtors Balance (as per General Ledger Adjustment Account) ₹ 60,000 (Cr.)

(s) Closing Creditors ₹ 30,000 (Dr)

ANSWER:

Dr. GENERAL LEDGER ADJUSTMENT ACCOUNT (IN DEBTORS LEDGER) Cr.

Particulars	₹	Particulars	₹
To Debtors Ledger Adjustment A/c:		By Debtors Ledger Adjustment A/c:	
Discount Allowed (₹ 1,500 + ₹ 500)	2,000	Endorsed B/R dish.	1,000
Bad Debts (2,200+300)	2,500		
T/f from Drs Ledger to Crs. Ledger	1,100		
T/f from Cr. Ledger to Drs. Ledger	1,900		
To Balance c/d (60,000 – 500)	59,500		

Dr. GENERAL LEDGER ADJUSTMENT ACCOUNT (IN CREDITORS LEDGER) Cr.

Particulars	₹	Particulars	₹
To Creditors Ledger Adjustment A/c:		By Creditors Ledger Adjustment A/c:	
Endorsed B/R Dish.	1,000	T/f from Drs. Ledger to Crs. Ledger	1,100
		T/f from Crs. Ledger to Drs. Ledger	1,900
		B/R Endorsed to Crs.	4,000
		Discount received (₹ 600–₹ 500)	100
		Allowances	3,200
		By Balance c/d (30,000 + 500)	30,500

Notes:

(i) The following items do not appear in GLA Account (in Debtors Ledger)

1. Cash Sales
2. Provision for Doubtful Debts
3. Provision for Discount on Debtors
4. Bad Debts Recovered
5. Bills Receivable matured/collected on maturity
6. Bills Receivable discounted
7. Bills Receivable endorsed

(ii) The following items do not appear in GLA Account (in Creditors Ledger)

1. Cash Purchases
2. Reserve for Discount on Creditors
3. Bills Payable matured / discharged

QUESTION 8: X Ltd. maintains three Debtors Ledgers viz. (A-J) Debtors Ledger, (K-P) Debtors Ledger and (Q-Z) Debtors Ledger. Debtors list include ₹ 5,000 owed by Miss Kansal who became Mrs. Bansal after marriage. Give the necessary journal entries for transfer assuming Self Balancing System.

ANSWER:

JOURNAL

Date	Particulars		Dr. (₹)	Cr.(₹)
	Mrs. Bansal (In A-J Debtors' Ledger) To Miss Kansal (In K-P Debtors' Ledger) (Being transfer of A/c of Miss Kansal to A-J Debtors' Ledger)	Dr.	5,000	 5,000
	General Ledger Adjustment A/c (In K-P Debtors' Ledger) To (K-P) Debtors' Ledger Adjustment A/c (In G.L.) (Being reduction in total K-P Debtors)	Dr.	5,000	 5,000
	(A-J) Debtors' Ledger Adjustment A/c (In G.L.) To General Ledger Adjustment A/c (In A-J Debtors' Ledger) (Being increase in (A-J) Debtors)	Dr.	5,000	 5,000

AS – 9 REVENUE RECOGNITION

QUESTION 1: Y Co. Ltd., used certain resources of X Co. Ltd. In return X Co. Ltd. received ₹ 10 lakhs and ₹ 15 lakhs as interest and royalties respectively from Y Co. Ltd. during the year 2014-2015. You are required to state whether and on what basis these revenue can be recognised by X Co. Ltd.

ANSWER: As per AS-9 on Revenue Recognition, revenue arising from the use by other of enterprise resources yielding interest and royalties should only be recognised when no significant uncertainty as to measurability or collectability exists. These revenues are recognised on the following bases:

(i) **Interest:** on a time proportion basis taking into amount outstanding and the rate applicable.

(ii) **Royalties:** on an accrual basis in accordance with the terms of the relevant agreement.

QUESTION 2: AQ Ltd., an investment company is finalizing its account for the Financial Year ending 2015 in the month of August 2015.

How will the following incomes be accounted for in the books of AQ Ltd.?

(1) X Ltd., has declared interim dividend which has not been received till 31-3-2015 but received on 25-4-2015.

(2) Y Ltd., has declared dividend on 8th May 2015 for the year ending 31-3-2015 which has been approved by the shareholders of the company on 30th June 2015.

(3) Z Ltd., a subsidiary of AQ Ltd., has declared dividend for the year ended 31-3-2015 on 25th May 2015 the AGM for which is to be held on September 2015.

ANSWER:

PROVISION OF AS-9

As per AS 9 "Revenue Recognition", dividends from investment in shares is recognized in the statement of Profit and Loss only when the owner's right to receive the payment is established.

ADVICE

(i) Since interim dividend was declared by X Ltd. before 31st March 2015 it means that the dividend had been vested (acrrued) to the shareholders of AQ Ltd. in the year 2014-2015.

Therefore, though it is received on 25.4.2015 (before finalization of accounts) yet it should be recognized in the financial statements for the year ended 31st March, 2015.

(ii) Dividend declared by Y Ltd and approved by the shareholders of AQ Ltd. after balance sheet date but before finalization of accounts will be accounted for 2015-2016 as the right to receive dividend will arise when the AGM will approve the dividend i.e. on 30th June 2015. Since right to receive the dividend was not established on or before 31st March, 2015, it will not be accounted for in the books for the year ended 31st March, 2015.

(iii) Dividend declared by Z Ltd. will be approved in the AGM to be held on 30th September, 2015. Before that right to receive dividend cannot be established. Hence it will not be accounted for in the financial year ended on 31st March, 2015.

QUESTION 3: On 25th September, 2015, Planet Advertising Limited obtained advertisement rights to World Cup Hockey Tournament to be held in Nov./Dec., 2015 for ₹ 520 lakhs.

They furnish the following information:

1. **The company obtained the advertisements for 70% of available time for ₹ 700 lakhs by 30th September, 2015.**
2. **For the balance time they got bookings in October, 2015 for ₹ 240 lakhs.**
3. **All the advertisers paid the full amount at the time of booking the advertisements.**
4. **40% of the advertisements appeared before the public in Nov. 2015 and balance 60% appeared in the month of December, 2015.**

You are required to calculate the amount of profit/loss to be recognized for the month November and December, 2015 as per Accounting Standard-9.

ANSWER:

PROVISION OF AS 9

As per AS 9 in a transaction involving the rendering of services, performance should be measured either under the completed service contract method or under the proportionate completion method, whichever relates the revenue to the work accomplished. Further, appendix to AS 9 states that revenue from advertising should be recognized when the service is completed. The service as regards advertisement is deemed to be completed when the related advertisement appears before the public.

ADVICE

In the given QUESTION, 40% of the advertisement appeared before the public in November, and balance 60% in December.

CALCULATION OF TOTAL PROFIT

	₹ in lakhs
Advertisement for 70% of available time obtained by 30th September, 2013	700
Advertisement for 30% of available time obtained in by October, 2013	240
Total	940
Less: Cost of advertisement rights	(520)
Profit	420

The profit amounting ₹ 420 lakhs should be apportioned in the ratio of 40:60 for the months of November and December, 2015. Thus, the company should recognise ₹ 168 lakhs (i.e. ₹ 420 lakhs × 40%) in November, 2015 and rest ₹ 252 lakhs (i.e. ₹ 420 lakhs × 60%) in December, 2015.

AS – 7 CONSTRUCTION CONTRACTS

QUESTION 1: PRARTHANA and PIYUSH Ltd, a firm of contractors provides the following details for the year ended 31st March, 2013:

Particulars	(₹ in lakhs)
Total Contract Price	**₹ 1,000 lacs**
Work Certified	**500**
Work not Certified	**105**
Estimated further Cost to Completion	**495**
Progress Payment Received	**400**
To be Received	**140**

Required: Show the relevant disclosures under AS-7.

ANSWER:

PROVISION OF AS-7

1. As per AS-7 when the outcome of a construction contract can be estimated reliably, contract revenue and contract costs associated with the construction contract should be recognised as revenue and expenses respectively by reference to stage of completion of the contract activity at the reporting date.
2. As per AS-7 an expected loss on the Construction contract should be recognized as an expense immediately irrespective of (i) whether or not the work has commenced on the contract; or (ii) the stage of completion of the contract: or (iii) the amount of profits expected to arise in other contracts.

ADVICE

A. Work Certified	500
B. Work Not Certified	105
C. Cost incurred till date/ Contract Expense[A+B]	605
D. Estimated Additional Cost	495
E. Estimated Total Cost [C+D]	1100
F. Contract Price	1000
G. Total Expected Loss [E – F]	100
H.% of Completion [(C/E)X 100]	55%
I. Contract Revenue to be recognised as Turnover [Contract Price × % of Completion]	550
J. Loss for the current year[I – C]	55
K. Expected Loss to be recognized immediately as per para 35 of AS 7[G – J]	45

DISCLOSURES AS PER AS-7

Particulars	₹ Lakhs
Contract Revenue	550
Contract Expenses	(605)
Provision for Expected Loss	(45)

Progress Billings[Progress Payment Received +To be Received]	540
Retentions (billed but not received from Contractee)	140
Gross amount due to customers[605-100-540]	35

ACCOUNTING FOR BILLS OF EXCHANGE

QUESTION 1: What is a Promissory Note?

ANSWER: A Promissory Note is an unconditional undertaking in writing given by the Debtor to the Creditor to pay on demand *or* at a fixed *or* determinable future time, a certain sum of money to *or* to the order of a specified person *or* to the bearer.

QUESTION 2: Name the parties to a Promissory Note.

ANSWER:

1. **The Maker** — The person who makes *or* draws the promissory note is called the maker.
2. **The Payee** — The person to whom the payment is to be made, is called the payee.

QUESTION 3: Can the Maker and Payee be the same? State with reason.

ANSWER: No, because Maker cannot promise to pay himself.

QUESTION 4: What is a Bill of Exchange?

ANSWER: A bill of exchange is an unconditional order in writing given by the Creditor to the Debtor to pay on demand, *or* at a fixed *or* determinable future time, a certain sum of money to *or* to the order of a specified person *or* to the bearer.

QUESTION 5: Name the parties to a Bill of Exchange?

ANSWER:

1. **Drawer** — The person who draws the bill is called the drawer. In other words, he is the person who grants credit.
2. **Drawee** — The person on whom the bill is drawn for its acceptance by him is called the drawee. In other words, he is the person to whom the credit is granted.
3. **Payee** — The person in whose favour the bill is drawn is called the payee. The payee may be a third party *or* the drawer himself.

QUESTION 6: Can the Drawer and Payee be the same? State with reason.

ANSWER: Yes, in case of Bill of Exchange because Drawer may order Drawee to pay himself.

QUESTION 7: Give any two advantages of a Bill of Exchange.

ANSWER:

1. **Evidence of Indebtedness** — It acts as an evidence of indebtedness since it is acknowledgement of debt.
2. **Source of Finance** — It acts as a source of finance since it can be discounted before the due date.
3. **Means of Remittance** — It acts as a means of remittance since money can be transferred easily from one place to another by means of a bill.
4. **Device of Discharging a Debt** — It acts as a device of discharging a debt since it is a negotiable instrument.

QUESTION 8: Distinguish between a Bill and a draft of a bill.

ANSWER: A bill is called a draft before its acceptance by a drawee. After the acceptance of a draft, the draft becomes a bill.

QUESTION 9: When is a Bill called draft?

ANSWER: Before its Acceptance.

QUESTION 10: What is meant by Acceptance of a Bill?

ANSWER: When the drawee puts his signature on the draft received from the drawer, such an act of putting the signature on the draft is traditionally called acceptance of a bill and technically called acceptance of a draft. After the acceptance of a draft, the draft becomes a bill.

QUESTION 11: Give any two points of difference between a Bill of Exchange and a Promissory Note.

ANSWER:

Basis of Distinction	Bill of Exchange	Promissory Note
1. No. of Parties	There are three parties—Drawer, Drawee and Payee and Payee.	There are two parties—Maker and Payee.
2. Promise/order	It contains an unconditional order given by a Creditor to a Debtor.	It contains an unconditional promise given by a debtor to a creditor.
3. Nature of Liability	The liability of the drawer is secondary and conditional.	The liability of the maker is primary and absolute.
4. Acceptance	It requires an acceptance to become a valuable instrument.	It does not require any acceptance since it is a valuable instrument right from the beginning.
5. Same identity of payer and payee	The drawer and payee may be the same person.	The maker and payee cannot be the same person.
6. Payable to bearer	It can be payable to the bearer.	It cannot be payable to bearer. It cannot be drawn as payable to bearer on demand.
7. Protest for Dishonour	It requires the protesting for dishonour.	It does not require any protesting.
8. Notice of Dishonour	Notice of dishonour must be given to all persons (including drawer) liable to pay.	Such notice is not required to be given to the maker.

QUESTION 12: What is term of a bill?

ANSWER: The term of a bill of exchange means the period for which a bill is drawn.

It may be of any duration. Usually the term does not exceed 90 days from the date of the bill.

QUESTION 13: When does the term of the bill after sight begin?

ANSWER: When a bill is drawn after sight, the term of the bill begins to run from the date of 'sighting', i.e., when the bill is accepted.

QUESTION 14: When does the term of the 'Bill after date' begin?

ANSWER: When a bill is drawn 'after date', the term of the bill begins to run from the date of drawing the bill.

QUESTION 15: State one basic difference between Bill at sight and Bill after sight.

ANSWER: Bill at sight is the bill payable on demand whereas the bill after sight is the bill payable after a fixed specified period.

QUESTION 16: State one basic difference between Bill after date and Bill after sight.

ANSWER: The term of a bill commences from the date of drawing a bill in case of a bill after date but from the date of acceptance in case of a bill after sight.

QUESTION 17: What is due date of a bill?

ANSWER: The date on which the term of the bill expires is called as 'Due Date of the bill'.

QUESTION 18: What is date of maturity of a bill?

ANSWER: The date which comes after adding three days to the due date of a bill, is called the date of maturity.

QUESTION 19: What are Days of Grace? Are all Bills of Exchange entitled to Days of Grace?

ANSWER: Days of Grace refer to extra number of days allowed for payment of a bill after its due date. No. Every instrument payable other than on demand is entitled to three days of grace.

QUESTION 20: When will payment be made if due date falls on Good Friday?

ANSWER: The payment is to be made on preceding working day i.e. on Thursday.

QUESTION 21: When will payment be made if the last day of grace is public holiday and the second day of grace is Sunday?

ANSWER: The payment is to be made on preceding working day i.e. Saturday.

QUESTION 22: What is meant by 'Discounting of a Bill'?

ANSWER: An act of selling of a bill to a bank *or* some other person to obtain payment for it before its maturity, is called as discounting of a bill. The purchaser of the bill usually charges the discount in terms of interest for the unexpired term of the bill. Such a discount is an expense for the Seller and a Gain for the Purchaser.

QUESTION 23: What is meant by 'Endorsement of a Bill'?

ANSWER: An endorsement means the writing of a person's name on the face *or* back of a negotiable instrument *or* on a slip of paper (called allonge) annexed thereto for the purpose of negotiation. The person who endorses the instrument is called the endorser. The person to whom the instrument is endorsed is called the endorsee.

QUESTION 24: What is meant by 'Dishonour of a Bill'?

ANSWER:

1. A Bill of Exchange (excluding cheques) may be dishonoured by (a) non-acceptance *or* by (b) non-payment.
2. It is to be noted that a Promissory Note *or* Cheque can be dishonoured by non-payment only.
3. When a bill is dishonoured by non-acceptance, no accounting entry is passed in the books of Drawer and Drawee.

QUESTION 25: What entry would be passed on dishonour of a bill endorsed in favour of a creditor?

ANSWER:

Drawee's A/c	Dr.	[Total]
To Endorsee's A/c		[Bill Amount + Noting Charges]
(Being the amount of dishonoured bill and Noting Charges debited to the Drawee)		

QUESTION 26: What entry would be passed on dishonour of a bill sent to the bankers for collection?

ANSWER:

Drawee's A/c	Dr.	[Total]
To Bill sent for Collection A/c		[Bill Amount]
To Bank A/c		[Noting Charges]
(Being the amount of dishonoured bill and Noting Charges debited to the drawee)		

QUESTION 27: What is Noting?

ANSWER: Noting is the recording of the fact of dishonour by a Notary Public. Such noting must be made within a reasonable time after dishonour.

QUESTION 28: List any two Contents of Noting.

ANSWER: Noting must specify (a) the date of dishonour, (b) the reason, if any, assigned for such dishonour (c) Noting Charges charged by Notary.

QUESTION 29: Who pays noting charges in the first instance and who ultimately bears noting charges?

ANSWER: In the first instance, whosoever is the holder of the bill at the time of dishonour, pays the noting charges. Ultimately, noting charges are borne by the drawee.

QUESTION 30: From which party Noting Charges are recoverable?

ANSWER: The amount of noting charges is recoverable from the party who is responsible for dishonour.

QUESTION 31: State the treatment of Noting Charges in the books of the Drawer.

ANSWER: The Drawee's Account is always debited with the total amount, i.e., the amount of the dishonoured bill plus the amount of Noting Charges (if any, incurred).

QUESTION 32: State the treatment of Noting Charges in the books of the Drawee.

ANSWER: The Drawer's Account is always credited with the total amount, i.e., the amount of the dishonoured bill plus the amount of Noting Charges (if any, incurred).

QUESTION 33: What is Protesting?

ANSWER: Protest is the formal certificate given by the Notary Public. This certificate is based on the noting.

QUESTION 34: Shyam's acceptance for ₹ 4,500, due this day, returned dishonoured, Noting charges ₹ 10. Record in the Journal of Ram.

ANSWER:

JOURNAL OF RAM

Date	Particulars		L.F.	Dr. (₹)	Cr. (₹)
	Shyam	Dr.		4,510	
	To Bills Receivable A/c				4,500
	To Cash A/c				10
	(Being B/R dishonoured, noting changes being ₹ 10)				

QUESTION 35: Shyam's acceptance for ₹ 4,500, discounted for ₹ 4,400, returned dishonoured, Noting charges ₹ 10. Record in the Journal of Ram.

ANSWER:

JOURNAL OF RAM

Date	Particulars		L.F.	Dr. (₹)	Cr. (₹)
	Shyam	Dr.		4,510	
	To Bank A/c				4,510
	(Being discounted B/R dishonoured, noting changes being ₹ 10)				

QUESTION 36: Shyam's acceptance for ₹ 4,500, endorsed in favour of Mohan, returned dishonoured, Noting charges ₹ 10. Record in the Journal of Ram.

ANSWER:

JOURNAL OF RAM

Date	Particulars		L.F.	Dr. (₹)	Cr. (₹)
	Shyam	Dr.		4,510	
	To Mohan A/c				4,510
	(Being endorsed B/R dishonoured, noting changes being ₹ 10)				

QUESTION 37: Shyam's acceptance for ₹ 4,500, sent to the Bank for collection, returned dishonoured, Noting charges ₹ 10. Record in the Journal of Ram.

ANSWER:

JOURNAL OF RAM

Date	Particulars		L.F.	Dr. (₹)	Cr. (₹)
	Shyam	Dr.		4,510	
	To Bills sent for Collection A/c				4,500
	To Bank A/c				10
	(Being B/R sent for Collection dishonoured, noting changes being ₹ 10)				

QUESTION 38: What is meant by the term 'Renewal of a Bill'?

ANSWER:

1. Cancellation of the original bill and drawing a fresh bill for another period on a request from the drawee is called Renewal of a Bill.
2. In case of Renewal of a Bill, the interest for the extended period is *either* paid in cash *or* is included in the amount of the New Bill.

QUESTION 39: State the treatment of the amount which remains unpaid by the drawee In case of insolvency of the Acceptor of a bill.

ANSWER:

1. In the books of Drawer, Such amount is debited to Bad debts Account.
2. In the books of Drawee, Such amount is transferred to the Deficiency Account.

QUESTION 40: Murli's acceptance for ₹ 20,000 renewed for three months, plus interest at 5% p.a. Record in the Journal of Ram.

ANSWER:

JOURNAL OF RAM

Date	Particulars		L.F.	Dr. (₹)	Cr. (₹)
	(i) Murli	Dr.		20,000	
	To Bills Receivable A/c				20,000
	(Being the old bill cancelled)				
	(ii) Murli	Dr.		250	
	To Interest A/c				250
	(Being interest due for 3 months)				
	(iii) Bills Receivable A/c	Dr.		20,250	
	To Murli				20,250
	(Being B/R renewed)				

QUESTION 41: Our acceptance to P to for ₹ 900 renewed for 3 months on the condition that ₹ 300 is paid in cash immediately and the remaining balance to carry interest @ 12% p.a. Record in the Journal of Ram.

ANSWER:

JOURNAL OF RAM

Date	Particulars		L.F.	Dr. (₹)	Cr. (₹)
	Bills Payable A/c	Dr.		900	
	Interest A/c	Dr.		18	
	To P				918
	(Being the original Bills Payable cancelled and interest charged for renewal of the same)				
	P A/c	Dr.		918	
	To Cash A/c				300
	To Bills Payable A/c				618
	(Being P was paid off partly in cash and partly through fresh acceptance)				

QUESTION 42: What is meant by 'Retirement of a Bill'?

ANSWER: Making the payment of a bill before the date of maturity is called Retirement of a bill.

QUESTION 43: What is meant by Rebate?

ANSWER:

1. An interest allowed by the holder of the bill to the Drawee at an agreed rate of interest for the unexpired period of the bill as a consideration for premature payment is known as Rebate.
2. Such rebate on retirement of a bill is an Income for the Drawee and is an Expense for the Payee.

QUESTION 44: Our acceptance for ₹ 20,000 retired one month before the due date at a discount of 12% p.a. Record in the Journal of Ram.

ANSWER:

JOURNAL OF RAM

Date	Particulars		L.F.	Dr. (₹)	Cr. (₹)
	Bills Payable A/c	Dr.		20,000	
	To Rebate on Bill A/c				200
	To Cash A/c				19,800
	(Being B/P retired @ 12% p.a. one month ago)				

QUESTION 45: What is Bills Receivable Book?

ANSWER: Bills Receivable Book is one of the subsidiary books which is used to record the details of Bills Receivable in favour of a person who is maintaining the Bills Receivable Book.

QUESTION 46: What is Bills Payable Book?

ANSWER: Bills Payable Book is one of the subsidiary books which is used to record the details of bills payable accepted by the person who is maintaining the Bills Payable Book.

QUESTION 47: State the Meaning of Accommodation Bills.

ANSWER: Accommodation Bills refer to those bills which are drawn, accepted *or* endorsed without any consideration.

QUESTION 48: State the Purpose of Accommodation Bills.

ANSWER: Accommodation Bills are drawn and accepted to meet the financial needs of the drawer/ drawee/both temporarily.

QUESTION 49: How is the Proceeds of the Accommodation Bills shared?

ANSWER: On discounting of Accommodation Bills, proceeds may be shared by drawer and drawee in an agreed ratio.

QUESTION 50: How is the Discount Charges of Accommodation Bills shared?

ANSWER: Each party bears the Discounts Charges of Accommodation Bills in the proportion in which it shares the proceeds of the bills unless otherwise agreed.

QUESTION 51: Can the drawer recover in case of Dishonour of Accommodation Bills?

ANSWER: On dishonour of Accommodation Bills, drawer cannot file suit against the drawee because drawee is not liable to drawer.

QUESTION 52: How are the Accounting Entries passed in case of Accommodation Bills

ANSWER: The accounting entries in case of Accommodation Bills are made in the usual manner as in case of trade bills.

QUESTION 53: Distinguish between Trade Bills and Accommodation Bills.

ANSWER:

Basis of Distinction	Trade Bills	Accommodation Bills
1. **Purpose**	These bills are drawn to settle a business transaction.	These bills are drawn to meet the financial needs of the drawer/ drawee/both temporarily.
2. **Consideration**	These bills are accepted for a consideration.	These bill are accepted without any consideration.
3. **Role**	These bills act as an evidence of indebtedness.	These bills act as a source of finance.
4. **Sharing of Proceeds of the Bill**	On discounting of such bills, proceeds remain with the holder.	On discounting of such bills, proceeds may be shared by drawer and drawee in an agree ratio.
5. **Recovery in case of dishonour**	On dishonour of such bills, drawer can file a suit against the drawee, because drawee is liable to drawer.	On dishonour of such bill, drawer cannot file suit against the drawee because drawee is not liable to drawer.

QUESTION 54: X draws on Y a bill for ₹ 2,00,000 on 1st April for 3 months. Y accepts the bill and sends it to X who gets it discounted for ₹ 1,95,000. X immediately remits ₹ 97,500 to Y. On due date, X being unable to remit the amount due accepts a bill for ₹ 1,20,000 for 2 months which is discounted by Y for ₹ 1,17,600. Y sends ₹ 7,800 to X out of the same. How much discount will be borne by X at the time of remittance of ₹ 7,800?

ANSWER: Proportionate Discount to be borne by X = (₹ 2,400 × ₹ 1,07,800/ ₹ 1,17,600) = ₹ 2,200

ACCOUNTING FOR CONSIGNMENT

QUESTION 1: What is Consignment?

ANSWER: Consignment means the transaction of sending goods by one person to another, who is to sell those goods on behalf of the first person.

QUESTION 2: State the features of consignment.

ANSWER:

1. The relationship between Consignor and Consignee is that of Principal and Agent.
2. Only the possession of goods and not the ownership of goods is transferred to the Consignee.
3. Risk of goods remains with the Consignor because ownership of goods remain with the Consignor.

4. Consignee is entitled to reimbursement of expenses incurred by him on behalf of the Consignor as per agreement.
5. Consignee is entitled to an agreed remuneration.
6. The profit/loss on sale of goods sent on Consignment belongs to the Consignor.

QUESTION 3: Who is consignor?

ANSWER: The person who sends the goods is known as 'Consignor'.

QUESTION 4: Who is consignee?

ANSWER: The person to whom the goods are sent is known as 'Consignee'.

QUESTION 5: State the Nature of Relationship between Consignor & Consignee.

ANSWER: The legal relationship between these two persons is that of principal and agent.

QUESTION 6: What is Outward/Inward Consignment?

ANSWER: The Consignment is an 'Outward Consignment' for the person who sends the goods for sale and an 'Inward Consignment' for the person who receives the goods for sale. Example: If 'X' sends goods to 'Y' for sale on his behalf, Here, 'X' is known as Consignor *or* Principal and 'Y' is known as Consignee *or* Agent. It is an Outward Consignment for X and an Inward Consignment for Y.

QUESTION 7: Distinguish between Consignment and Sale.

ANSWER

Basis of Distinction	Consignment	Sale
1. Nature of Relationship	The relation between the Consignor and the consignee is that of principle and agent.	The relation between the seller and the buyer is that of creditor and debtor.
2. Ownership and possession of goods	Only the possession and not the ownership is transferred to the consignee.	Both the possession and ownership are transferred.
3. Risk of goods	Risk remains with the Consignor because ownership remains with the Consignor.	Risk remains with the buyer since ownership remains with him.
4. Proforma Invoice/Invoice	Consignor prepares only a proforma invoice.	Seller prepares a sales invoice.
5. Subject matter of dealing	Only movable properly may be its subject matter.	Any property may be its subject matter.
6. Who bears expenses	Expenses incurred by consignee are borne by Consignor.	Expenses incurred after sale by buyer are borne by him and not by seller.
7. Profit/Loss belongs to	Profit/Loss on sale of belongs to Consignor.	After the sale is complete, the profit/loss belongs to buyer.
8. Return of Goods	Goods are returnable if they are not sold by the consignee.	Goods once sold are not returnable.
9. Account Sales	Account Sales has to be submitted by the consignee to the Consignor from time to time.	No Account Sale is required to be submitted by the Buyer to the Seller.

10. **Treatment of Unsold Goods**	Unsold goods with the Consignee is be treated as stock of the Consignor.	The seller has nothing to do with the goods which could not be resold. Unsold Goods with the buyer is treated as Stock of the Buyer.

QUESTION 8: What is Proforma Invoice?

ANSWER: A proforma invoice looks like an invoice but is really not one. the object of the proforma invoice is only to convey information to the Consignee regarding quantity, varieties and prices of goods sent and expenses incurred and not to make him liable like a trade debtor.

QUESTION 9: Who Prepares Proforma Invoice?

ANSWER: When the Consignor sends the goods to the Consignee, he prepares only a Proforma Invoice and not an Invoice.

QUESTION 10: What is an Account Sales?

ANSWER: An Account Sales is a statement sent by the Consignee to the Consignor periodically.

QUESTION 11: State the Contents of Account Sales.

ANSWER: An Account Sales contains the information like (i) Sales made (ii) Expenses incurred on behalf of Consignor (iii) Commission earned (iv) An Advance (if any) given (v) the balance due to the principal.

QUESTION 12: How does an Account Sales differ from Sales Account ?

ANSWER: An Account Sales is a statement sent by the consignee to the consignor periodically. It contains the information like (i) Sales made (ii) Expenses incurred on behalf of Consignor (iii) Commission earned (iv) An Advance (if any) given (v) the balance due to the principal. An Account Sales is different from Sales Account (which provides only the summary of sales made for cash and on credit).

QUESTION 13: What is Del-credere Commission?

ANSWER: It is allowed to the consignee only when he undertakes the risk of bad debts arising out of credit sales.

QUESTION 14: Howt is Del-credere Commission calculated?

ANSWER: It is calculated at an agreed rate *either* on total sales (if no agreement) *or* credit sales (if agreement provides).

QUESTION 15: What is Over-riding Commission?

ANSWER: Over-riding commission is an extra commission allowed over and above the normal commission is generally offered:

(i) when the agent is required to put in hard work in introducing a new product in the market,
(ii) where he is entrusted with the work of supervising the performance of other agents in a particular area,
(iii) for effecting for sales at prices higher than the price fixed by the Consignor.

QUESTION 16: How is Over-riding Commission calculated?

ANSWER: Depending upon the terms of agreement it may be calculated on the actual total sales *or* on the difference between Actual total sales and Sales at special selling price *or* invoice price. However, in the absence of any such agreement, over-riding commission should be allowed on the difference between the actual total sales and sales at specified selling price and ordinary commission should be allowed on total sales at specified sales price.

QUESTION 17: Distinguish between Ordinary Commission and Del-Gredere Commission.

ANSWER:

Basis of Distinction	Ordinary Commission	Delcredere Commission
1. When allowed?	It is allowed to all the consignees for all the consignments for selling goods.	It is allowed to the consignee only when he undertakes the risk of bad debts arising out of credit sales.
2. Guarantee	In return of this commission, consignee guarantees only the proceeds of cash sales	In return of this commission, consignee guarantees the proceeds of cash sales and credit sales.
3. How to Calculate?	It is calculated at an agreed rate on the total sales.	It is calculated at an agreed rate *either* on total sales (if no agreement) *or* credit sales (if agreement provides).

QUESTION 18: Mr X sent 250 units costing ₹ 10,000 each to Mr Y. The goods were to be sold so as to yield a gross profit of 20% on sales. Mr Y sold 150 units @ ₹ 14,200 per unit on credit and 75 units @ ₹ 14,000 for cash. Mr Y was entitled to an ordinary commission of 5%, del-credere commission of 2% on sales and an over-riding commission of 25% of any surplus realised. Calculate the commission due to Mr Y.

ANSWER: Since over-riding commission as % of surplus has been given, other commission have been calculated on sales at specified selling price otherwise Mr Y will get unnecessarily ordinary commission and delcredere commission on surplus realised also.

A. Actual Total Sales = (150 × ₹ 14,200) + (75 × ₹ 14,000)	=	₹ 31,80,000
B. Total Sales at Specified Selling Price = (150 + 75) ₹ 12,500	=	₹ 28,12,500
C. Surplus [A – B]	=	₹ 3,67,500
Ordinary Commission = 5% of ₹ 28,12,500	=	₹ 1,40,625
Del-Credere Commission = 2% of ₹ 28,12,500	=	₹ 56,250
Over-riding Commission = 25% of ₹ 3,67,500	=	₹ 91,875
Total Commission	=	₹ 2,88,750

QUESTION 19: X sent out goods costing ₹ 80,000 to Y so as to show 20% profit on invoice price. 40% goods were lost in transit. 60% of the goods received by consignee was sold at 25% above invoice price. Rate of commission is 10% on sales at invoice price plus 50% of the surplus over invoice price. Calculate the commission due to Y.

ANSWER: Invoice Price of Goods sold = 60% (₹ 1,00,000 – 40%) = ₹ 36,000

Surplus over invoice price = ₹ 36,000 × 25% = ₹ 9000

Commission = (36,000 × 10/110) + (9,000 × 50/100) = ₹ 8,100

QUESTION 20: X sent goods to B at 125% of cost which is invoice price. The Rate of Commission is 10% on sales at IP and 25% of any surplus realized above IP. 10% of the goods sent out on consignment, invoice value of which is ₹ 12,500 were destroyed. 75% of the total consignment is sold by B at ₹ 1,00,000. What will be the amount of commission payable to B?

ANSWER: Invoice Price of Goods Sent = ₹ 12500/10% = ₹ 125000

Invoice Price of Goods Sold = ₹ 12500 × 75% = ₹ 93750

Surplus = ₹1,00,000 – ₹ 93,750 = ₹ 6,250

Commission = (10% of ₹ 93,750) + (25% of ₹ 6,250) = ₹ 10,937.50

QUESTION 21: X sent out goods costing ₹ 80,000 to Y so as to show 20% profit on invoice price. 40% goods were lost in transit. 60% of the goods received were sold half at invoice price and the balance at 25% above the invoice price. Rate of Commission is 10% on sales at invoice price plus 50% of gross sales less all commission exceeds the invoice price. Calculate the commission due to Y.

ANSWER: Sale at invoice price = ₹ 36,000 × 50/100 = ₹ 18,000

Sale at 25% above invoice price = ₹ 36,000 × 50/100 × 25/100 = ₹ 22,500

Surplus over invoice price = ₹ 36,000 × 50/100 × 25% = ₹ 4,500

Let total Comission be X

X = (₹ 36,000 × 10/100) + 50% [₹ 40,500 – X – ₹ 36,000)

= ₹3,600 + 2,250 – 0.5X

1.5 X = ₹ 5,850

X = ₹ 5,850/1.5 = ₹ 3,900

QUESTION 22: Mr X sent 250 units costing ₹ 10,000 each to Mr Y. The goods were to be sold so as to yield a gross profit of 20% on sales. Mr Y sold 150 units @ ₹ 14,200 per unit on credit and 75 units @ ₹ 14,000 for cash. Mr Y entitled to a commission of ₹ 500 per unit sold plus one forth of the amount by which the gross sale proceeds less total commission thereon exceeded a sum calculated at the specified selling price.Calculate the commission due to Y.

ANSWER: Fixed Commission @ ₹ 500 = 225 × ₹ 500 = ₹ 1,12,500

Let the total Commission be X

Variable Commission = 1/4 [(₹ 31,80,000 – X) – (225 × ₹ 12,500)]

X – ₹ 1,12,500 = 1/4 [₹ 31,80,000 – X – ₹ 28,12,500]

X – ₹ 1,12,500 = 1/4 (₹ 3,67,500 – X)

X – ₹ 1,12,500 = 91,875 – 1/4 X

X – 1,12,500 = 91,875 –. 25 X

1.25 X = 2,04,375 X = ₹ 2,04,375/1.25 = ₹ 1,63,500

QUESTION 23: What is meant by Non-recurring Expenses in Consignment?

ANSWER: Non-recurring expenses refer to those expenses which are incurred in order to bring the inventories to their present location and condition, whereas recurring expenses refer to those expenses which cannot be considered as relating to putting the inventories in their present location and condition.

QUESTION 24: Give two examples of Non-recurring Expenses in Consignment.

ANSWER:

1. Consignor's Expenses	(i) Carriage outward (ii) Freight (iii) Insurance charges (iv) Packing
2. Consignee's Expenses	(i) Clearing charges (ii) Custom duty, Octroi, etc. (iii) Carriage inward/transport charges upto godown

QUESTION 25: Give two examples of recurring expenses in Consignment.

ANSWER:

(i) Warehouse charges

(ii) Insurance charges

(iii) Office & Administration Expenses

QUESTION 26: Forwarding and Insurance charges ₹ 50,000 incurred by Consignor, Expenses incurred by Consignee: Landing & Clearing ₹ 1,400, Godown Rent ₹ 2,000, Unloading Expenses ₹ 2,800, Selling & Distribution Expenses ₹ 1,500, Transport Charges upto godown ₹ 5,600, Advertisement & Insurance ₹ 1,200, Establishment Costs ₹ 4,000.Calculate the amount of expenses to be considered while valuing the consignment stock.

ANSWER: = 50,000 + 1,400 + 2,800 + 5,600 = ₹ 59,800

QUESTION 27: Distinguish between normal loss and abnormal loss in consignment.

ANSWER:

Basis of Distinction	Normal Loss	Abnormal Loss
1. Avoidable vs. Unavoidable	It is an unavoidable loss.	It is an avoidable loss.
2. Causes	It is caused due to the inherent feature of the goods e.g. evaporation, normal leakage/spoilage.	It is usuallly cause by fire, theft, abnormal spoilage/pilferage etc.
3. Part of Cost	It is treated as a part of cost.	It is not treated as a part of cost.
4. Valuation	Its value is not calculated separately.	Its value is calculated in the same manner as value of unsold stock.
5. Treatment	Its value is adjusted by inflating the cost per unit as under. Effective cost per unit = Total Cost/(Total Qty. – Normal Loss Qty.)	Its value is credited to the Consignment Account in order to calculate the normal profit/loss on consignment.
6. Journal Entry	No journal entry is passed to account for such loss.	The following journal entry is passed to account for such a loss: P&L A/c Dr. [irrecovered loss] Insurance Co. Dr. [Clain admitted] To Consignment A/c [Total Loss]

QUESTION 28: Cost of goods lost by fire ₹ 5,000, Insurance Co. paid a claim of 80%. In this case Consignment Account will be credited with what amount?

ANSWER: ₹ 5,000

QUESTION 29: Who prepares Consignment Account and Why?

ANSWER: The Consignor prepares a Consignment Account relating to each Consignment in order to ascertain the profit *or* loss on each consignment.

QUESTION 30: State the Nature of Consignment Account.

ANSWER: Consignment Account is a Nominal Account like Trading and Profit & Loss Account.

QUESTION 31: State any four Items with which Consignment Account is debited.

ANSWER: Consignment Account is debited with:

1. The Cost of goods consigned,
2. Expenses incurred by Consignor,
3. Expenses incurred by Consignee,
4. Commission due to Consignee.

QUESTION 32: State any four Items with which Consignment Account is credited.

ANSWER: Consignment Account is credited with:

1. Sale Proceeds,
2. Abnormal Loss,
3. Closing Stock and
4. The Cost of Goods Returned by Consignee.

QUESTION 33: How is Consignment Account closed?

ANSWER: Consignment Account is closed by transferring the Profit Or Loss to the Profit & Loss Account.

QUESTION 34: Why is consignee not debited as a debtor at the time of sending goods to him?

ANSWER: Consignee is not debited as a debtor at the time of sending goods to him since the goods have not been sold to him, merely possession has been transferred. he becomes indebted to the consignee when he sells the goods.

QUESTION 35: State the Journal entry to be passed to account for (i) receipt of goods from consignor (ii) expenses incurred by consignor (iii) abnormal loss/normal loss in his godown *or* in transit (iv) bill receivables discounted by the consignor (v) return of goods by consignee (vi) unsold stock lying with him.

ANSWER: No entry is passed in the books of consignee.

QUESTION 36: What is loading? Name the items that involve loading. Why is it necessary to eliminate loading?

ANSWER: The difference between the Invoice Price (IP) and the Cost Price (CP) is called 'loading'. Items that involve loading: Opening Stock, Goods Sent on Consignment, Goods Returned by Consignee, Closing Stock. When goods are sent at invoice price, to ascertain correct profit/loss on consignment, the items recorded at invoice price should be brought down to Cost price level.

QUESTION 37: How will you deal with the following in Consignment Accounts:

1. **Discount charges of Bills Receivable,**
2. **Non-realisation of book-debts due to the insolvency of Customer,**
3. **Non-realisation of book debts due to the dispute.**
4. **Goods returned by consignee,**
5. **Expenses in forwarding goods returned by consignee**

ANSWER:

1. Discount charges on discounting a Bill Receivable accepted by Consignee are debited to Profit & Loss Account.

2. Non-realisation of book-debts due to the insolvency of Customer is borne by Consignee if del-credare commission is allowed *or* Consignor in other cases.
3. Non-realisation of book-debts due to the dispute is borne by Consignor.
4. Defective Goods returned by consignee are credited to Consignment Account.
5. Expenses in forwarding goods returned by consignee are debited to Consignment Account.

QUESTION 38: Mr X provides you the following information:

1. **Good sent by Mr X to his agent Mr Y—10,000 Units @ ₹ 20 per unit**
2. **Mr X's Forwarding and Insurance Expenses—₹ 50,000**
3. **Agent took delivery and brought the goods to his godown after incurring expenses @ Re 1 per unit**
4. **Goods sold by Agent—7,300 units @ ₹ 30**
5. **Agent's Commission—5%**

Calculate the amount of Closing Stock ilf owing to fall in market price, the value of normal stock is to be reduced by 10%

ANSWER:

STATEMENT SHOWING THE CALCULATION OF UNSOLD STOCK

Particulars	Units	₹
A. Cost of Goods Sent	10,000	2,00,000
B. Consignor's Expenses	—	50,000
C. Total Cost of Goods Sent (A + B)	10,000	2,50,000
D. *Add:* Consignee's Non-recurring Expenses	—	10,000
E. Cost of Goods received by Consignee	10,000	2,60,000
F. Cost of Unsold Stock [₹ 2,60,000 × 2,700/10,000]	2,700	70,200
G. *Less:* 10%		₹ 7,020
H. Value of Closing Stock to be brought into accounts		₹ 63,180

QUESTION 39: Mr X provides you the following information:

1. **Good sent by Mr X to his agent Mr Y—10,000 Units @ ₹ 20 per unit**
2. **Mr X's Forwarding and Insurance Expenses—₹ 50,000**
3. **Agent took delivery and brought the goods to his godown after incurring expenses @ ₹ 1 per unit**
4. **Goods sold by Agent—7,300 units @ ₹ 30**
5. **Agent's Commission—5%**

Calculate the amount of Closing Stock ilf owing to depression in the market, a special trade discount of 10% is to be allowed to sell normal stock.

ANSWER:

STATEMENT SHOWING THE CALCULATION OF COST OF UNSOLD STOCK

Particulars	Units	₹
A. Cost of Goods Sent	10,000	2,00,000
B. Consignor's Expenses	—	50,000
C. Total Cost of Goods Sent (A + B)	10,000	2,50,000

D. *Add:* Consignee's Non-recurring Expenses	—	10,000
E. Cost of Goods received by Consignee	10,000	2,60,000
F. Cost of Unsold Stock [₹ 2,60,000 × 2,700/10,000]	2,700	70,200

(ii) Net Realizable Value

A. Gross Realizable Value (2,700 × ₹ 30 × 90%) ₹ 72,900

B. *Less:* Realization Exp. (Agent's Commission) [5% of ₹ 72,900] ₹ 3,645

C. Net Realizable Value [A – B] ₹ 69,255

(iii) Value of Closing Stock to be brought into accounts (at Cost *or* NRV whichever is lower) ₹ 69,255

QUESTION 40: 2000 kg of apples are consigned to a wholesaler, the cost being ₹ 3 per kg plus ₹ 800 of freight, it is known that a loss of 15% is unavoidable. Calculate the cost per kg.

ANSWER: Cost per kg = [(2000 kg × ₹ 3) + ₹ 800]/(2000 kg – 300 kg) = ₹ 4

QUESTION 41: X sent out 1000 units to Y at an invoice price of ₹ 125 each calculated at a profit of 25% profit on cost. X incurred ₹ 20,000. 1/5th of the goods were lost in transit. Y incurred ₹ 4,000 towards transportation upto godown and ₹ 5,000 as godown rent. 3/5th of goods received were sold by Y. 1/5th of balance goods were destroyed in consignee's godown due to fire. Calculate the cost of abnormal loss in transit and godown.

ANSWER: Cost of abnormal loss in transit = [(1000 × ₹ 100) + ₹ 20,000] × 200/1000 kg = ₹ 24,000

Cost of abnormal loss in godown = [(64 × ₹ 100) + (₹ 20,000 × 64/1000) + (₹ 4,000 × 64/800)]/(1000 kg – 300 kg) = ₹ 8,000

QUESTION 42: X sent out 1000 units to Y at an invoice price of ₹ 125 each calculated at a profit of 25% profit on cost. X incurred ₹ 20,000. 1/5th of the goods were lost in transit. Y incurred ₹ 4,000 towards transportation upto godown and ₹ 5,000 as godown rent. 3/5th of goods received were sold by Y. 1/5th of balance goods were destroyed in consignee's godown due to fire. Calculate the amount of stock reserve.

ANSWER: = 320 × ₹ 25 = ₹ 8,000

QUESTION 43: X sent out goods at invoice value of ₹ 2,50,000 to Y at 25% profit on cost price. Consignor's exp. ₹ 25,000, Consignee's Expenses–Non recurring ₹ 17,500, Selling expenses ₹ 2,500. 1/10th of the goods were lost in transit. 9/10th of the balance goods were sold. Calculate the cost of consignment stock.

ANSWER: ₹ 18,000 + (₹ 25,000 × ₹ 18,000/₹ 2,00,000) + (₹ 17,500 × ₹ 18,000/₹ 1,80,000) = ₹ 22,000

QUESTION 44: X sent out goods at invoice value of ₹ 2,50,000 to Y at 25% profit on cost price. Consignor's exp. ₹ 25,000, Consignee's Expenses–Non-recurring ₹ 17,500, selling expenses ₹ 2,500. 1/10th of the goods were lost in transit. 9/10th of the balance goods were sold. Calculate the amount of stock reserve on consignment stock.

ANSWER: = ₹ 18,000 × 25% = ₹ 4,500

QUESTION 45: Good sent by X to Y—10,000 Units @ ₹ 20 per unit, X's Forwarding and Insurance Expenses—₹ 50,000, 2% of goods sent were lost in transit(Insurance Co. paid 80% of loss). Expenses incurred by Y:Unloading charges ₹ 4,900, clearing custom and octroi charges ₹ 3,900, Carriage Inward ₹ 1,000, Storage & other expenses ₹ 11,850. 50% Goods received were sold by Y so as to yield a gross profit of 20% on sales.50% the balance goods were taken over by Y at an average cost. X drew a bill on Y for an amount equivalent to 80% of original cost of goods. X got it discounted at ₹ 1,50,000. Y's Commission:10%. Calculate the amount of Profit on Consignment.

ANSWER:

CALCULATION OF UNSOLD STOCK

Particulars	Units	₹
A. Cost of Goods Sent	10,000	2,00,000
B. X's Expenses	–	50,000
C. Total Cost of Goods Sent (A + B)	10,000	2,50,000
D. *Less:* Cost of Goods fully damaged-in-transit	200	5,000
E. Cost of goods reached the city of Y (C – D)	9,800	2,45,000
F. *Add:* Y's Non-Recurring expenses	–	9,800
G. Cost of Goods received by Y [E + F]	9,800	2,54,800
H. Cost of Unsold Stock in hand [₹ 2,54,800 × 2450/9,800]	2,450	63,700
I. Cost of Stock taken over by Y [₹ 2,54,800 × 2450/9,800]	2,450	63,700

Particulars	₹
Sales(4,900 × ₹ 32.50)	1,59,250
Closing Stock	63,700
Cost of Stock taken over by Y	63,700
Cost of Goods fully damaged-in-transit	5,000
	2,91,650
Less:	
Cost of Goods Sent	200000
X's Expenses	50,000
Y's Expenses	21,650
Y's Commission	15,925
	2,87,575
Profit on Consignment	4,075

QUESTION 46: Calculate the value of unsold consignment stock and abnormal loss from the following information:

Goods consigned: 10,000 units @ ₹ 20 per unit;

Freight and Insurance expenses incurred by Consignor: ₹ 47,500

Expenses incurred by Consignee: Unloading charges ₹ 4,900 clearing custom and octroi charges ₹ 3,900, Carriage Inward ₹ 1,000, Storage expenses ₹ 1,450, Office & Adm. Expenses ₹ 5,000, Selling, and Distribution Expenses ₹ 10,000, Bad debts ₹ 1,625.

Goods sold by Consignee: 2500 units @ ₹ 25 per unit for cash and 5000 units @ ₹ 32.50 credit.

100 units of goods sent were lost in transit.

100 units of goods are still in transit.

100 units of goods lost by fire in Consignee's godown.

100 units of goods lost in the godown of Consignee due to inherent nature of goods.

ANSWER:

STATEMENT SHOWING THE CALCULATION OF ABNORMAL LOSS AND UNSOLD STOCK

Particulars	Units	₹
A. Cost of Goods sent	10,000	2,00,000
B. Expenses incurred by Consignor	–	47,500
C. Total Cost of Goods Sent (A + B)	10,000	2,47,500
D. *Less:* Cost of Goods not reached the city of Consignee		
(a) Cost of Goods lost-in-transit (2,47,500 × 100/10,000)	100	2,475
(b) Cost of Goods still-in-transit (2,47,500 × 100/10,000)	100	2,475
E. Cost of Goods reached the city of Consignee (C – D)	9,800	2,42,550
F. *Add:* Non-recurring Expenses incurred by Consignee		
[₹ 4,900 + ₹ 3,900 + ₹ 1,000]	–	9,800
G. Cost of Goods received by Consignee (E + F)	9,800	2,52,350
H. *Less:* Cost of Goods lost in Consignee's Godown	100	2,575
[₹ 2,52,350 × 100/9,800]		
I. *Less:* Expected Normal Loss (in Units)	100	–
J. Cost of Goods available for sale (G – H – I)	9,600	2,49,775
K. Cost of Unsold Stock [₹ 2,49,775 × 2,100/9,600]	2,100	54,638
L. Total Cost of Unsold Stock		57,113

QUESTION 47: X invoiced goods to Y at 25% profit on cost. 40% of goods were lost in transit. 60% of goods received were sold by consignee at 25% above the invoice price. Rate of commission is 10% on sales at invoice price plus 50% of the surplus over invoice price. The amount of commission earned by consignee is ₹ 8,100. Calculate the cost of goods sent on consignment ?

ANSWER: Let Invoice price of Goods Sold = X

Total Commission = (10% of X) + (50% of 0.25X) = ₹ 8,100

8,100 =. X + 125X

X = ₹ 8,100/0.225 = ₹ 36,000

Cost of Goods Sold = ₹ 36,000/125% = ₹ 28,800

Cost of Goods received = ₹ 28,800/60% = ₹ 48,000

Cost of Goods Sent = ₹ 48,000/60% = ₹ 80,000

ACCOUNTING FOR JOINT VENTURE

QUESTION 1: What is Joint Venture?

ANSWER: Joint Venture may be described as a temporary partnership between two *or* more persons without the use of the firm name, for a limited purpose. In other words, under Joint Venture, two *or* more persons agree to undertake a particular venture (e.g. Joint consignment of goods, Joint construction of a building, Joint underwriting of a particular issue of shares *or* debentures) and to share the profits and losses thereof in an agreed ratio (if agreement is silent on this point, then in equal ratio).

QUESTION 2: Who are 'Joint Venturers' *or* 'Co-Venturers'?

ANSWER: The persons who have so agreed to undertake a Joint Venture are known as 'Joint Venturers' *or* 'Co-Venturers'.

QUESTION 3: State the Life of Joint Venture.

ANSWER: Such limited partnership automatically expires on the completion of the venture for which it was formed.

QUESTION 4: State the Similarities between Joint Venture and Partnership.

ANSWER:

1. At least 2 persons are required in both joint venture and partnership.
2. Business is carried on for profit in both joint venture and partnership.

QUESTION 5: State the methods of recording the Joint Venture transactions.

ANSWER:

Method I Separate set of Books Method Recording of all Joint Venture transactions in a separate set of books (i.e. not belonging to any of the Co-Venturers)

Method II Recording of all Joint Venture transactions only by one of the Co-Venturers in his own books of account.

Method III Recording of all Joint Venture transactions in the books of all Co-Venturers.

Method IV Memorandum Joint Venture Account Method Recording of the partial Joint Venture transactions concerning him only by each of the Co-Venturers in his own books of account.

QUESTION 6: Name the Accounts which are opened in Separate set of Books Method.

ANSWER:

1. Joint Bank Account which is personal account in nature, is used to record Cash and Bank transactions;
2. Co-Venturers' Accounts which are personal in nature, are used to record their dealings with the Joint business and to ascertain the amount due to/from them;
3. Joint Venture Account which is nominal in nature, is used to calculate the profit/loss on joint venture.

QUESTION 7: Name the Accounts which are opened in Recording in the books of one Co-venturer Method.

ANSWER

1. Joint Venture Account to ascertain profit/loss on Joint Venture
2. Personal Accounts of other Co-Venturers to record the Joint Venture transactions effected by other Co-Venturers and to ascertain the amount due to/from other Co-Venturer(s).

QUESTION 8: Write a short note on Memorandum Joint Venture Account Method.

ANSWER

1. Each Co-Venturer records only those joint venture transactions which are effected by him with the help of a personal account designed as 'Joint Venture with....(Name of the other Co-Venturer). .. Account'. It is debited with the purchases/supplies made and expenses incurred by the Venturer. It is credited with the sales effected and unsold stock taken over by the Venturer.
2. Each Co-Venturer sends a periodic statement of joint venture transactions effected by him only, to the other Co-Venturers.

3. Each Co-Venturer on the receipt of the aforesaid statement, prepares Memorandum Joint Venture Account in order to ascertain the profit/loss on Joint Venture transactions. Since this account is in fact not a part and parcel of double entry system the word 'Memorandum' is prefixed. This account can be compared with 'Joint Venture Account', as follows:
4. Each Co-Venturer makes a Journal entry for his share of profit/loss in his books of account.
5. Each Co-Venturer settles the balances of 'Joint Venture with....Account' *either* by paying (if Cr. Balance) *or* receiving Cash (if Dr. Balance).
   (i) Both these accounts are debited with the same items.
   (ii) Both these accounts are credited with the same items.
   (iii) Both these accounts show profit/loss on Joint Venture.
   (iv) All the items posted in Joint Venture Account have their corresponding debits/credits in the books of accounts, whereas it is not so in the case of 'Memorandum Joint Venture Accounts.

QUESTION 9: How will you deal with the following in Joint Venture Accounts:

1. **Discount on discounting a Bills Receivable.**
2. **Loss of goods due to fire.**

ANSWER

1. Discount on discounting a Bills Receivable is debited to Joint Venture Account.
2. The loss of goods due to fire is not credited to Joint Venture Account

QUESTION 10: Distinguish between Partnership and Joint Venture.

ANSWER:

Basis of Distinction	Partnership	Joint Venture
1. Scope	It is not limited to a specific venture.	It is limited to a specific venture.
2. Persons involved	The persons carrying on business are individually called partners.	The persons carrying on business are called co-venturers.
3. Ascertainment of Profit/loss	The profits/losses are ascertained on an annual basis.	The profits/losses are ascertained at the end of specific venture (if venture continues for a short period) *or* an interim basis annually (if venture continues for a longer period). No specific Act is there.
4. Act governing	Partnership firms are governed by Indian Partnership Act, 1932.	The doctrine of implied authority is not applicable to co-venturers.
5. Doctrine of Implied Authority	The doctrine of implied authority is applicable to partners.	The co-venturers have such freedom.
6. Freedom to run competition	The partners do not have such freedom.	There is no need for firm name.
7. Name	A partnership firm always has a name.	There is no need for a separate set of books.
8. Separate Set of Books	Separate set of books have to be maintained.	The accounts can be maintained even in one of the Coventurer's books only.
9. Admission of Minor	A minor can be admitted to the benefits of the firm.	A minor cannot be a co-venturer as he is incompetent to contract.

QUESTION 11: Distinguish between Joint Venture and Consignment.

ANSWER:

Basis of Distinction	Joint Venture	Consignment
1. Nature of Relationship	The relation between coventurers is that of co-owners.	The relation between the consignor and the consignee is that of Principal and Agent.
2. Ownership & Risk of Goods	Both these remain with co-venturers.	Both these remain with the consignor.
3. Account Sales	No Account Sales is sent by one co-venturer to another Co-venturer.	An Account Sale is prepared and submitted by the consignee to his consignor.
4. Profit & Loss on transactions	Profit & losses are shared by the co-venturers in an agreed ratio.	Profit & losses are shared only by the consignor and not by the consignee.
5. Subject-Matter of Dealing	Any movable *or* immovable property may be its subject matter.	Only movable property may be its subject matter.
6. No. of Persons	In a venture, there may be two *or* more persons.	In a consignment, there are two persons—Consignor and Consignee.
7. Methods of Recording	There are four methods of recording.	There is only one method of recording.

QUESTION 12: There are two co-venturers — X & Y. X is recording all Joint Venture transactions in his books of account. Discount charges on discounting a Bill Receivable accepted by Y are debited to which Account?

ANSWER: Joint Venture Account

QUESTION 13: There are two Co-venturers — X and Y. X and Y are recording their own joint venture transactions in their respective books of account. In the books of X, Discount Charges on discounting a Bill Receivable accepted Y are debited to which Account?

ANSWER: Y's Account

QUESTION 14: The share of profit of the Co-venturer maintaining all the Joint Venture transactions in his books is debited to which Account?

ANSWER: Joint Venture Account

QUESTION 15: The share of Profit of the co-venturer maintaining only his own transaction is debited to which Account?

ANSWER: Other Co-Venturer's Personal Account

QUESTION 16: Cost of Goods lost by fire ₹ 5,000, Insurance Co. paid a claim of 80%. In this case Joint Venture Account will be credited with what amount?

ANSWER: ₹ 4,000

QUESTION 17: Closing Stocks with X ₹ 26,400, with Y ₹ 60,000. How will the Stock be shown in the books of X who is recording all joint venture transactions?

ANSWER: Stock of ₹ 60,000 will be shown as closing credit balance in Y's Account as 'To Balance c/d'

QUESTION 18: Closing Stocks: with X ₹ 26,400, with Y ₹ 60,000. How will the Stock be shown in the books of X who is recording his own joint venture transactions?

ANSWER: Stock of ₹ 26,400 will be shown as closing debit balance in Joint Venture with Y account as by Balance c/d.

QUESTION 19: A and B enter into a joint venture sharing profit and losses in the ratio 3:2. A purchased goods costing ₹ 2,00,000. B sold 95% goods for ₹ 2,50,000. A is entitled to get 1% commission on purchase and B is entitled to get 5% commission on sales. A drew a bill on B for an amount equivalent to 80% of original cost of goods. A got it discounted at ₹ 1,50,000. Calculate B's share of profit.

ANSWER:

Particulars	₹
Sales	250000
Closing Stock(5%of 200000)	10000
	260000
Less:	
Purchases	200000
A's Commission	2000
B's Commission	12500
Discount Charges	10000
	224500
Net Profit	35500
B's Share of Profit(35500x2/5)	14200

QUESTION 20: X and Y enter into a joint venture sharing profit and losses in the ratio 3:2.1. Good sent by X to Y—10,000 Units @ ₹ 20 per unit, X's Forwarding and Insurance Expenses—₹ 50,000, 2% of goods sent were lost in transit(Insurance Co. paid 80% of loss). Expenses incurred by Y:Unloading charges ₹ 4,900, clearing custom and octroi charges ₹ 3,900, Carriage Inward ₹ 1,000, Storage & other expenses ₹ 11,850. 50% Goods received were sold by Y so as to yield a gross profit of 20% on sales.50% the balance goods were taken over by Y at an average cost. X drew a bill on Y for an amount equivalent to 80% of original cost of goods. X got it discounted at ₹ 1,50,000. Calculate the amount of Profit on Joint Venture.

ANSWER:

CALCULATION OF UNSOLD STOCK ETC.

Particulars	Units	₹
A. Cost of Goods Sent	10,000	2,00,000
B. X's Expenses	–	50,000
C. Total Cost of Goods Sent (A + B)	10,000	2,50,000
D. *Less:* Cost of Goods fully damaged-in-transit	200	5,000
E. Cost of goods reached the city of Y (C – D)	9,800	2,45,000
F. *Add:* Y's non-recurring expenses	–	9,800
G. Cost of Goods received by Y [E + F]	9,800	2,54,800
H. Cost of Unsold Stock in hand [₹ 2,54,800 × 2450/9,800]	2,450	63,700
I. Cost of Stock taken over by Y [₹ 2,54,800 × 2450/9,800]	2,450	63,700

CALCULATION OF PROFIT ON JOINT VENTURE

Particulars	₹
Sales(4,900 × ₹ 32.50)	1,59,250
Closing Stock	63,700
Cost of Stock taken over by Y	63,700
Insurance Claim(5,000 × 80%)	4,000
	2,90,650
Less:	
Cost of Goods Sent	200000
X's Expenses	50,000
Y's Expenses	21,650
Discount Charges	10000
	2,81,650
Profit on Joint Venture	9,000

SALE OF GOODS ON APPROVAL OR RETURN BASIS

QUESTION 1: What is meant by Goods sent on 'approval' *or* 'on sale *or* return' basis? When the sale will take place in respect of such goods?

ANSWER: Goods sent on 'approval' *or* 'on sale *or* return' basis mean the delivery of the goods to the customers with the option to retain *or* return them within a specified period. According to Sec. 24 of the Sale of Goods Act, 1930, in respect of such goods, the sale will take place *or* the property in the goods pass to the buyer:

(i) When he signifies his approval *or* acceptance to the seller;

(ii) When he does some act adopting the transaction; e.g. pledging such goods

(iii) If he does not signify his approval *or* acceptance to the seller but retains the goods without giving notice of rejection, on the expiry of the specified time (if a time has been fixed) *or* on the expiry of a reasonable time (if no time has been fixed).

QUESTION 2: List the Methods of Accounting for Goods Sent on approval.

ANSWER:

1. Ordinary Sale Method,
2. Multicolumn Journal Method and
3. Separate Day Books Method.

QUESTION 3: Briefly explain the Ordinary Sale Method of Accounting for Goods Sent on approval.

ANSWER:

1. When the transactions are few, the goods sent on 'approval' *or* 'on sale *or* return' basis are treated as an ordinary sale (although theoretically it is incorrect to describe as such).
2. If, at the year-end, goods are still lying with customers and the specified time has not yet expired, the original entry for sales is cancelled.
3. Like an ordinary closing stock, such goods are considered as stock lying with customers on behalf of seller and are valued at cost *or* net realisable value whichever is lower.

4. Journal Entries The journal entries which are passed under this method are given on next page:

JOURNAL ENTRIES TO BE PASSED UNDER ORDINARY SALE METHOD

1. When goods are sent on 'approval' 'or on sale *or* return' basis	Sundry Debtors A/c Dr. To Sales A/c	[With Invoice Price]
2. When such goods are returned within the specified time	Sales Returns A/c Dr. To Sundry Debtors A/c	[With Invoice Price]
3. When the customers take the delivery of such goods at a price lower than the invoice price	Sales A/c Dr. To Sundry Debtors A/c	[With Difference]
4. At the year end		
(i) When such goods are still lying with customers at year end and the specified time limit has not yet expired	Sales A/c Dr. To Sundry Debtors A/c	[With Invoice Price]
(ii) When such goods are brought into final accounts as closing stock at cost *or* net realizable value whichever is lower	Stock with Customers(on Sale *or* Return basis) A/c Dr. To Trading A/c	[With Cost *or* NRV whichever is lower]

Tutorial Notes:

1. Alternatively, Debtors' Suspense Account may be credited in place of Sundry Debtors Account in Entry (d)
2. In the beginning of next accounting period, entry (d) should be reversed. No entry is required to be passed when such goods are retained by the customers on a subsequent date in the next accounting period.

QUESTION 4: Where a large number of articles are sent out on a sale *or* return basis, Which books are maintained under Separate Day Books Methiod?

ANSWER:

1. Sale on Approval Day Book (Like an ordinary Sales Day Book)
2. Sale on Approval Inward Day Book (Like an ordinary Sales Inward Day Book)
3. Sales on Approval Ledger

QUESTION 5: What does the credit balance of the Sale on Approval Total Account at the close of the accounting period represent?

ANSWER: The credit balance of the Sale on Approval Total Account at the close of the accounting period represents the value of goods sent out but n*either* sold nor returned. Such goods are considered as stock lying with the customers on behalf of seller and are valued at 'Cost *or* Net Realisable Value whichever is lower'. Such goods are brought into final accounts by passing the following adjusting entry:

Stock with Customers (on Sale *or* Return basis) A/c Dr. To Trading A/c	[With cost *or* Net Realisable Value whichever is lower]

QUESTION 6: X sent goods at a sale price of ₹ 60,000 at a profit of cost plus 20% toY on sale *or* return basis. On 31st March these were lying with customer and no consent was received from Y.The stock with customers account will be shown at what amount?

ANSWER: = ₹ 60,000 – 1/6 of ₹ 60,000 = ₹ 50,000.

QUESTION 7: X sent some goods costing ₹ 10,500 at a profit of 25% on sale to Y on sale *or* return basis. B returned goods (having sale price of ₹ 3,200). At the end of the accounting period, the remaining goods were n*either* returned nor were approved by him. The stock on approval will be shown in the balance sheet at what amount?

ANSWER: = ₹ 10,500 – (₹ 3,200 – 25% of ₹ 3,200) = ₹ 8,100.

ACCOUNT CURRENT

QUESTION 1: What is Account Current?

ANSWER:

Meaning	Account Current is a running statement in the form of a ledger account showing the transactions between two parties during a given period together with the interest due *or* payable.
Heading	The heading of this statement is written as under: "—(Name of Receiving Party)—In Account Current with—(Name of Sending Party)—" to—(date) ***For Example***, if X sends the Account Current to Y, it will be headed as "Y in Account Current with X'. If Y sends the Account Current to X, it will be headed as — X in Account Current with Y'.
Who Sends	Account Current is usually sent by (a) a banker to its customer (b) a lender to its borrower (c) a supplier to its customer (d) an agent to its principal (e) a co-venturer to another co-venturer.

QUESTION 2: What is Red Ink Interest?

ANSWER: In case of transactions the due date of which falls after the date of closing the account, the product must be written *either* as negative product on the same side *or* as positive product on the opposite side (i.e. the side other than that on which the transaction appears). Traditionally, such product was used to be written in 'Red Ink' and interest on such 'Red Ink Product' was used to be called as "Red Ink Interest".

QUESTION 3: Define Average Due Date. List out the various instances when Average Due Date can be used.

ANSWER: Average Due Date is a break-even date on whcih the net amount payable can be settled without causing loss of interest *either* to the borrower *or* the lender. Few instances where average due date can be used:

(i) Calculation of interest on drawings made by the properietors *or* partners of a business firm at several points of time.

(ii) Settlement of accounts between a principal and an agent.

(iii) Settlement of contra accounts, taht is, A and B sell goods to each other on different dates.

QUESTION 4: On 20th Dec. Mr. X drew a Bill after sight of ₹ 1,00,000 for 1 month upon Mr. Y who accepted the same on 23rd Dec. Calculate the date of maturity of bill.

ANSWER: 25th Jan. since 26th Jan being a republic Day is a public holiday.

QUESTION 5: On 31st Dec. 2014. Mr. X drew a Bill after date of ₹ 1,00,000 for 2 months upon Mr Y who accepted the same on 5th Jan. 2015. Calculate the date of maturity of bill.

ANSWER: 3rd March 2015, i.e., 28th Feb + 3 days of grace

QUESTION 6: Mr. A advanced ₹ 30,000 to Mr. B on 1st April. The amount is repayable in 6 equal monthly instalments commencing from 1st May. Compute the average due date for the loan.

ANSWER:

$$\text{Average} = \frac{\text{Date of loan} + \text{Sum of months from the date of lending to repayment}}{\text{No. of instalments}}$$

= 1.4.2013 + 3.5 months = 16th July 2013

QUESTION 7: Average due Date 6th May, Amount Due ₹ 20,000, Calculate the interest @15% p.a. payable on 30th June:

ANSWER:

No. of Days from 6th May to 30th June = 55

Interest = ₹ 20,000 × = ₹ 452.05

QUESTION 8: Mr. X owed ₹ 4,000 on 1st Jan 2013 to Mr. Y. On 13th March, Mr. X accepted a Bill of ₹ 2,000 drawn by Mr. X for 1 month. Interest is to be calculated @10% p.a. Ascertain the amount to be paid if they agree to settle by one single payment on 15th March 2013.

ANSWER:

MR. X IN ACCOUNT CURRENT WITH MR. Y

Dr. (INTEREST UPTO 15TH MARCH, 2013 @ 10% P.A.) Cr.

Date	Particulars	₹	Days	Product	Date	Particulars	₹	Days	Product
2013					2013				
Jan. 01	To Balance b/d	4,000	74	2,96,000	Mar. 13	By B/R A/c	2,000	(32)	(64,000)
Mar. 15	To Interest A/c		99		Mar. 15	By Balance of Product (amount to be paid)			3,60,000
		4,099		2,96,000			4,099		2,96,000

INVESTMENT ACCOUNTS (AS – 13)

QUESTION 1: State the Provisions of AS – 13.

ANSWER:

Basis of Comparision	Current Investment	Long-Term Investment
1. Meaning	A Current Investment is an investment that is by its nature readily realizable and is intended to be held for not more than 1 year from the date of making such Investment.	Long-Term Investment is an Investment other than Current Investment.
2. Valuation	At lower of cost *or* fair value	At Cost

3. Reduction in Carrying Amount	Charged to Statement of Profit & Loss	Permament Reduction in Carrying Amount is Charged to Statement of Profit & Loss
4. Reversal of Reduction	Revesed in Statement of Profit & Loss	Revesed in Statement of Profit & Loss if reason for reduction no longer exists.

QUESTION 2: How will you deal with the following while preparing Investment Account?

(a) Dividend for Pre-acquistion period

(b) Sale of Rights

ANSWER:

(a) The dividend for the pre-acquisition period is treated as a capital receipt and hence entered in Cost column of Investment Account on the credit side.

(b) The price realised by sale of rights is entered on the credit side in the Dividend/Income column of the Investment Account as per AS-13.

QUESTION 3: How will you calculate the profit/loss on sale of Bonus shares?

ANSWER:

Profit/Loss on sale of Bonus shares = Sale Proceeds – Average Cost of Bonus Shares

Average Cost of Bonus Shares

$$= \text{Cost of Original Shares} \times \frac{\text{No. of Bonus Shares}}{\text{No. of Original Shares + No. of Bonus Shares}}$$

QUESTION 4: From the following information, calculate the profit *or* loss on sale of debentures and the value of closing balance of debentures if method of valuation is (a) FIFO (b) LIFO and (c) Weighted Average:

1.4.2015	**Balance: 100, 12% Debentures of ₹ 100 each @ ₹ 95**
5.4.2015	**Purchased: 150, 12% Debentures of ₹ 100 each @ ₹ 90 Ex.**
6.4.2015	**Sold: 200, 12% Debentures of ₹ 100 each @ ₹ 93 Ex.**

ANSWER:

Particulars	FIFO	LIFO ₹	Weighted Average ₹
A. Sale Proceeds of 200 Debentures	18,600	18,600	18,600
B. *Less:* Cost of 200 Debentures			
FIFO [100 × ₹ 95) + (100 × ₹ 90)]	18,500	—	—
LIFO: [(150 × ₹ 90) + (50 × ₹ 95)]	—	18,250	—
Weighted Average	—	—	18,400
C. Profit [A – B]	100	350	200
D. Value of Closing Balance			
FIFO: 50 × ₹ 90	4,500	—	—
LIFO: 50 × ₹ 95	—	4,750	—
Weighted Average:	—	—	4,600

INSURANCE CLAIM (LOSS OF STOCK AND LOSS OF PROFIT)

QUESTION 1: State the meaning of insurance contracts, insuer, insured, premium.

ANSWER: Insurance contracts are contracts of indemnity whereby one party, called the insurer, undertakes to indemnify the loss suffered by the other party, called the insured, on the happening of some unforeseen event in consideration of a fixed sum of money, called the Premium.

QUESTION 2: When does the liability insurer arise?

ANSWER: The liability of the insurer to indemnify the loss suffered by the insured arises only on the happening of the event for which the policy is taken out.

QUESTION 3: What is the extent of liability of Insurer?

ANSWER: The liability of the insurer is limited to the amount of loss actually suffered by the insured *or* the policy amount (i.e. known as Sum Insured) whichever is less. However, in case of under-insurance, (i.e. when the actual value of the property insured is greater than the insured value of the property) the liability of the insurer is limited to that proportion of the loss which the insured value bears to the actual value of the property insured if an Average Clause is included in the insurance policy.

QUESTION 4: What is 'Average Clause' in an Insurance Policy?

ANSWER:

1. **Significance:** In order to discourage Under-Insurance (i.e. where the sum insured is less than the actual insurable value), fire insurance policies often include an average clause.
2. **Calculation:** The amount of claim according to the average clause (if inserted in the of Claim contract of insurance) will be calculated as follows:

   Amount of Claim = (Actual Loss suffered/Actual Insurable Value) × Amount of Policy

   where, Actual Insurable Value = Estimated Value of Stock as at the date of fire.

   Actual Loss suffered = Estimated Value of Stock as at the date of loss – Value of Salvaged Stock.

QUESTION 5: State the purpose of taking loss of profit insurance policy.

ANSWER: The loss of profit insurance is designed to afford protection against such consequential loss following fire, viz

(i) Loss on account of standing charges,
(ii) Net profits before taxation, and
(iii) Increased cost of working.

QUESTION 6: From the following, calculate the amount of claim:

(a) Book value of Normal Stock ₹ 54,600
(b) Current value of Abnormal Stock ₹ 3,450
(c) Stock to the value of ₹ 8,700 was salvaged out of which one third was handed over to the Insurance Co.
(d) Sum Insured ₹ 50,000
(e) Fire Fighting expenses ₹ 2,750

ANSWER:

STATEMENT OF CLAIM

Particulars		₹
A. Estimated Value of Stock As at date of fire		
(a) Book-Value of Normal Items	₹ 54,600	
(b) Current Value of Abnormal Items	₹ 3,450	58,050
B. Value of Salvaged Stock [₹ 8,700 – ₹ 2,900 (handed over)]		5,800
C. Estimated Value of Stock Lost by fire (A–B)		52,250
D. Fire fighting expenses		2,750
		55,000
E. Amount of claim by applying Average clause:		47,373

QUESTION 7: From the following information, compute the amount of claim under loss of Stock Policy:

Sum Inssured ₹ 50,000	**Stock as on 1.1.2014**	**₹ 73,500**
Accounting Year Calender Year	**Stock as on 31.12.2014**	**₹ 79,600**
Damage Due to fire on 30-6-2015	**Purchases during 2014**	**₹ 3,98,000**
G.P. Ratio Uniform from year to year	**Sales during 2014**	**₹ 4,87,000**
Value of Salvaged Stock ₹ 5,800		
Purchases from 1.1.2015 to 30.6.2015 ₹ 1,62,000		
Sales from on 1.1.2015 to 30.6.2015 ₹ 2,31,200		

In valuing the stock at 31st December, 2014, ₹ 2,300 had been written off certain stock which was poor selling line, it having a cost of ₹ 6,900. A portion of these goods were sold in March, 2015 at a loss of ₹ 250 on original cost of ₹ 3,450. The remainder of this stock was now estimated to be worth its original cost for the purpose of claim. Subject to above exception, gross profit had remained at an uniform rate throughout the year value of stock as at date of fire.

ANSWER:

STATEMENT OF CLAIM

Particulars		₹
A. Estimated Value of Stock As at date of fire		
(a) Book-Value of Normal Items	₹ 54,600	
(b) Current Value of Abnormal Items	₹ 3,450	58,050
B. Value of Salvaged Stock		5,800
C. Estimated Value of Stock Lost by fire (A–B)		52,250
D. Amount of claim by applying Average clause: $\text{Loss suffered} \times \frac{\text{Sum Insured}}{\text{Actual Insurable Value}} = ₹52,250 \times \frac{₹50,000}{₹58,050}$		45,004

Working Notes:

(I) TRADING ACCOUNT FOR THE YEAR ENDING ON 31ST DEC., 2014

Particulars	₹	Particulars	₹
To Opening Stock	73,500	By Sales	4,87,000
To Purchases	3,98,000	By Closing Stock Valued	₹ 79,600
To Gross Profit (b.f)	97,400	*Add:* w/o ₹ 2,300	81,900
	5,68,900		5,68,900

(II) MEMORANDUM TRADING ACCOUNT FOR THE PERIOD FROM 01.01.2013 TO 30.06.2015

Particulars	Normal Items ₹	Abnormal Items ₹	Total Items ₹	Particulars	Normal Items ₹	Abnormal Items ₹	Total Items ₹
To Opening Stock	75,000	4,600	79,600	By Sales	2,28,000	3,200	2,31,200
To Purchases	1,62,000	—	1,62,000	By Closing Stock	54,600	2,300	56,900
To Gross Profit @ 20%	45,600	900	46,500	By Gross Loss	—	—	—
	2,82,600	5,500	2,88,100		2,82,600	5,500	2,88,100

QUESTION 8: From the following, Calculate the Gross Profit lost during the claim period:

(a) **Gross Profit Ratio for the last accounting year 24.5%**

(b) **Net Profit Ratio for the last accounting year 8%**

(c) **Turnover from 1.4.2014 to 31.3.2015 ₹ 40,00,000**

(d) **Turnover from 1.3.2014 to 31.7.2014 ₹ 20,00,000**

(e) **Turnover from 1.3.2015 to 31.7.2015 ₹ 8,00,000**

(f) **Of the standing charges 1/7th have not been insured.**

(g) **Dislocation period from 1.3.2015 to 31.7.2015**

(h) **Special circumstances clause in the policy provided for the increase of turnover by 10%**

ANSWER:

Step 1 Agreed G.P. Ratio

Total Standing Charges = G.P. – NP = (24.5% of ₹ 40,00,000) – (8% of ₹ 40,00,000)
= ₹ 9,80,000 – ₹ 3,20,000 = ₹ 5,60,000

Insured Standing Charges = ₹ 5,60,000 – 1/7 of ₹ 5,60,000 = ₹ 4,80,000

$$\text{G.P. Ratio} = \frac{\text{Net Profit} + \text{Insured Standing Charges}}{\text{Turnover of Last Accounting year}} \times 100$$

Step 2 Turnover Lost during Claim Period

A. Turnover for the corresponding claim period in the preceding year	₹ 20,00,000
B. *Add:* Agreed Increase	₹ 2,00,000
C. *Less:* Actual Turnover during the claim period	(₹ 8,00,000)
D. Turnover lost in claim period (A + B – C)	₹ 14,00,000

Step 3 Gross Profit lost = Turnover lost during the claim period × Agreed G.P. Ratio
= ₹ 14,00,000 × 20% = ₹ 2,80,000

QUESTION 9: Calculate the Net Claim for the increased Cost of working from the following information:

Agreed G.P. Ratio 20%, Net Profit for the last accounting year 2,40,000, Standing Charges (out of which ₹ 80,000 have not been insured) ₹ 5,60,000, actual turnover during claim period ₹ 8,00,000. During the claim period, 50% of the total turnover of this period was maintained by incurring the additional expenses amounting to ₹ 1,50,000 and there was a saving in insured standing charges of 6.25% and in uninsured standing charges of ₹ 10,000. Turnover during 12 months preceding the date of fire ₹ 30,00,000. Agreed Increase 20%.

ANSWER:

1. Adjusted Turnover = ₹ 30,00,000 + 20% of ₹ 30,00,000 = ₹ 36,00,000
2. Net Claim for the increase cost of Working

A. Gross claim for Increased Cost of Working (being the least of the following three amounts) ₹ 80,000

1. Actual Expenses ₹ 1,50,000
2. Proportionate Increased Cost of Working

$$= \text{Increased Cost of Working} \times \frac{\text{Gross Profit on Adjusted Turnover}}{\text{Gross Profit as above + Unisured Standing Charges}}$$

3. Maximum saving of liability of the insurer = Reduction in Turnover avoided through Increased Cost of Working × Agreed G.P. Ratio

= ₹ 4,00,000 × 20% = ₹ 80,000

B. *Less:* Saving In Insured Standing Charges (₹ 4,80,000 × 6.25%) ₹ 30,000

C. Net Claim for Increased Cost of Working (A – B) ₹ 50,000

QUESTION 10: Calculate the amount of claim if sum insured is (a) ₹ 10,00,000 and (b) ₹ 7,50,000 from the following data:

Date of fire 1.3.2015	
Turnover from 1.3.2014 to 28.2.2015	**₹ 44,00,000**
Turnover lost during Claim period	**₹ 14,00,000**
Agreed G.P. Ratio 20%	
Special Circumstances Clause provides for the increase in turnover by 10%	
Net Claim for increased Cost of working	**₹ 50,000**

ANSWER:

(a) If the Sum Insured is ₹ 10,00,000

Sum Insurable = Adjusted Turnover during 12 months immediately preceding the date of fire × Agreed G.P. Ratio

= (₹ 44,00,000 + 10% of ₹ 44,00,000) × 20%

= ₹ 48,40,000 × 20% = ₹ 9,68,000

Since Sum Insured exceeds the Sum Insurable, Average Clause will not apply at all and hence the amount of claim will be calculated as under:

Total claim = Gross Profit on turn over lost during claim period + Net Claim for the increased cost of working

= ₹ 2,80,000 (i.e., 20% of ₹ 14,00,000) + ₹ 50,000 = ₹ 3,30,000

(b) If the Sum Insured is ₹ 7,50,000

Since Sum Insured is less than the Sum Insurable, the average clause will apply as under:

$$\text{Net Claim} = \text{Total Claim} \times \frac{\text{Sum Insured}}{\text{Sum Insurable}} = \frac{₹3,30,000 \times ₹7,50,000}{₹9,68,000} = ₹2,55,682$$

FINANCIAL STATEMENTS OF A BANKING COMPANIES

QUESTION 1: State the objectives of Capital Adequacy Norms. State the Minimum Capital Adequacy Ratio to be maintained.

ANSWER:

Objectives of Capital Adequacy Norms	**The fundamental objectives are:** (a) to strengthen the soundness and stability of the banking system, (b) to achieve a high degree of consistency in its application to banks in different countries.
Minimum Capital Adequacy Ratio	All India Scheduled commercial Banks (excluding Regional Rural Banks) as well as foreign banks operating in India are required to achieve such % of Capital Adequacy Ratio (i.e., Ratio of Capital Fund to Risk Weighted Assets and off Balance Sheet Items) as may be prescribed by RBI.

QUESTION 2: What are Non-Banking Assets? Also state the provision relating to the disclosure and disposition of these assets.

ANSWER:

Meaning:	Non-banking Assets are the immovable properties *or* tangible assets which are acquired in satisfaction of claims.
Disclosure:	NBA are to be disclosed under the head 'Other Assets' on the Assets Side of Balance Sheet.
Disposition:	NBA must be disposed off within 7 years from the date of acquisition *or* period extended by RBP [Sec 9]

QUESTION 3: Mention the condition when a cash credit overdraft account is treated as 'out of order'.

ANSWER: A cash credit overdraft account is treated as NPA if it remains out of order for a period of more than 90 days. An account is treated as 'out of order' if any of the following conditions is satisfied:

(a) The outstanding balance remains continuously in excess of the sanctioned limit/drawing power.

(b) Though the outstanding balance is less than the sanctioned limit/drawing power –

  (i) there are no credits continuously for more than 90 days as on the date of balance sheet; *or*

  (ii) credits during the aforesaid period are not enough to cover the interest debited during the same period.

(c) Further any amount due to the bank under any credit facility is 'overdue' if it is not paid on the due date fixed by the bank.

QUESTION 4: What is the percentage of NPA provision to be made by banks in respect of fully secured doubtful advances of more than 3 years old?

ANSWER: In case of Banking Companies, 100% NPA provision is made in respect of fully secured doubtful advances of more than 3 years. This provision is made irrespective of whether the advance is fully/partly secured *or* unsecured. However, in the case of government guaranteed advances this rate of provision does not apply.

QUESTION 5: What are the restrictions imposed by the Banking Regulations Act, 1949 on payment of dividend in case of banking companies?

ANSWER: As per the Banking Regulations Act 1949, a banking company cannot pay dividend on its shares until all its capitalized expenses including preliminary expenses, organization expenses, share selling commission, brokerage, amount of losses incurred by tangible assets and any other item of expenditure not represented by tangible assets are completely written off. However, as per the Act, it is permissible for a banking company to pay dividend on its shares without writing off:

(i) The depreciation in the value of its investments in approved securities where such depreciation has not actually been capitalized *or* otherwise accounted for as a loss.

(ii) The depreciation in the value of its investments in shares, debentures *or* bonds (other than approved securities) where adequate provision for such deprecation has been made to the satisfaction of its auditors; and

(iii) The bad debts where adequate provision for such bad debts has been made to the satisfaction of its auditors.

QUESTION 6: State the Minimum % of profits to be transferred to Reserve Fund by a Banking Company.

ANSWER: 25%

QUESTION 7: Interest on performing assets ₹ 100 lacs, out of which only ₹ 80 lacs received Interest on non-performing assets ₹ 100 lacs, out of which only ₹ 80 lacs received Calculate interest income to be recognised.

ANSWER:

Interest on performing assets (on accrual basis)	₹ 100 lacs
Interest on non-performing assets (on cash basis)	₹ 80 lacs
	₹ 180 lacs

QUESTION 8:

Performing Assets (realizable value of security ₹ 90 lacs) ₹ 100 lacs

Non-performing Assets for 12 months (secured) ₹ 200 lacs

Non-performing Assets for 12 months (unsecured) ₹ 300 lacs

Non-performing Assets for 24 months (unsecured) ₹ 400 lacs

Non-performing Assets for 24 months (secured) ₹ 500 lacs

Non-performing Assets for 36 months (secured) ₹ 600 lacs

Non-performing Assets for 37 months (secured) ₹ 700 lacs

Non-performing Assets for 50 months (secured) ₹ 800 lacs

Calculate the amount of provision to be made.

ANSWER:

Particulars	Amount	% Provision	Provision
Standard	100	0.40%	0.40
Sub-standard (Secured)	200	15%	30.00
Sub-standard (Unsecured)	300	25%	75.00
Doubtful upto 1 year (Unsecured)	400	100%	400.00
Doubtful upto 1 year (Secured)	500	25%	125.00

Doubtful (Exceeding 1 year but not exceeding			
3 year (Secured)	600	40%	240.00
Doubtful (Exceeding 1 year but not exceeding			
3 year (Secured)	700	40%	280.00
Doubtful (Exceeding 3 years)	800	100%	800.00
Total Provision required			1950.40

QUESTION 9: In X Bank Ltd., the doubtful assets (since Jan 2012) as on 31.3.2015 is ₹ 1,000 lakhs. The value of security (including DICGC 100% cover of ₹ 100 lakhs) is ascertained at ₹ 500 lakhs. How much provision must be made in the books of the Bank towards doubtful assets?

ANSWER:

Particulars	(₹ in lakhs)
Doubtful Assets (more than 3 years)	1,000
Less: Value of security (excluding DICGC cover)	(400)
Less: DICGC cover	(100)
Unsecured Portion	500
Provision for unsecured portion @100%	500
Provision for secured portion @100%	400
Total Provision to be made	900

QUESTION 10: State the journal entry passed by a Banking Co. on discounting bills. How are discounted bills disclosed in Balance Sheet?

ANSWER:

JOURNAL

Date	Particulars		Dr. (₹)	Cr.(₹)
	Discounted Bills A/c	Dr.	xxx	
	To Discount A/c			xxx
	To Customers A/c			xxx
	(Being bills discounted & purchased)			

Disclosure: Discounted Bills are assets which are shown under the head 'Advances' (Schedule 9) on the assets side of the Balance Sheet.

QUESTION 11: How will you calculate the Amount of Rebate on bills Discounted?

ANSWER: = Total Annual Discount × (No. of days after the of year/365)

QUESTION 12: State the journal entry passed by a banking co. to record Rebate on Bills Discounted. How is it disclosed in Profit and Loss Account and Balance Sheet?

ANSWER:

JOURNAL

Date	Particulars		Dr. (₹)	Cr.(₹)
	Discount on Bills A/c	Dr.	xxx	
	To Rebate on Bills Discounted A/c (Being unexpired discount carried over to Next Year)			xxx

Disclosure: Rebate on Bills Discounted A/c is a liability and is shown under the head 'Other Liabilities and 'Provisions (Schedule 5)' on the liabilities side of the Balance Sheet.

QUESTION 13: A 3 month's bill of ₹ 5,00,000 dated 9.3.2015 was discounted @16% p.a. Give journal entries on 9.3.2015 and 31.3.2015.

ANSWER:

JOURNAL

Date	Particulars		Dr. (₹)	Cr.(₹)
09.03.2015	Discounted Bills A/c	Dr.	5,00,000	
	To Discount A/c			20,000
	To Customer's A/c (Being bills discounted & purchased)			4,80,000
31.03.2015	Discount A/c	Dr.	16,000	
	To Rebate on bill discounted A/c (₹ 80,000 × 73/365)			16,000
	To Profit & Loss A/c (Being unexpired discount carried over to Next Year & Balance T/f to P & L A/c)			4,000

QUESTION 15: Fixed Deposits ₹ 50,000 lacs, Recurring Deposits ₹ 1,700 lacs, Saving Deposits ₹ 45,000 lacs, Current Accounts (Cr.) ₹ 52,012 lacs. Current Accounts (Dr) ₹ 1,000 lacs. Calculate Cash Reserve @ 4% and Liquidity Reserve @ 23 % to be maintained.

ANSWER:

Cash Reserve = 4% of Net Demand and Time Liabilities [i.e. FD + RD + SD + C A/c (Cr)]
= 4% [₹ 50,000 + ₹ 1,700 + ₹ 45,000 + ₹ 52,012] = ₹ 5948.48 lacs

Liquidity Reserve = 23% of Net Demand and Time Liabilities
= 23% [₹ 50,000 + ₹ 1,700 + ₹ 45,000 + ₹ 52,012] = ₹ 34,204

Note: Current A/c (Dr balance) is not adjusted.

QUESTION 16: In the trial balance of Tulsian Bank Ltd as at 31st March, 2015, Interest & Discount and Income from Investments appear at ₹ 8,880 and ₹ 30 respectively.

Additional Information:

(a) Rebate on bills discounted: on 31.3.2014	**₹ 15**
on 31.3.2015	**₹ 45**
(b) Interest accrued on Investments	**₹ 10**

How will you disclose the relevant items in the final accounts for the year ended 31st March, 2015? (The figures being in thousands)

ANSWER:

SCHEDULE 13—INTEREST EARNED

Particulars	₹ '000
I Interest & Discount [8,880 + 15 (Opening Rebate) – 45 (Closing Rebate)]	8,850
II Income on Investments [30 + 10 (accrued)]	40
	8,890

SCHEDULE 5—OTHER LIABILITIES AND PROVISIONS

Particulars	₹ '000
I Rebate on Bills Discounted	45

SCHEDULE 11—OTHER ASSETS

Particulars	₹ '000
Interest accrued on Investments	10

QUESTION 17: How will you disclose the following ledger balances in the final accounts of Tulsian Bank Ltd for the year ended 31st March 2015: (The figures being in thousands)

Interest and Discount	8,850
Income on Investments	40
Rebate on Bills Discounted as (at 31.3.2015)	45
Interest accrued on Investments as (at 31.3.2015)	10

ANSWER:

SCHEDULE 13—INTEREST EARNED

Particulars	₹ '000
I Interest & Discount	8,850
II Income on Investments	40
	8,890

SCHEDULE 5—OTHER LIABILITIES AND PROVISIONS

Particulars	₹ '000
I Rebate on Bills Discounted	45

SCHEDULE 11—OTHER ASSETS

Particulars	₹ '000
Interest accrued on Investments	10

Note: No further adjustment has been in respect of Rebate on Bills Discounted (45) and Interest accrued on Investments since (10) since these items have already been adjusted in figure of Interest & Discount and Income on Investments repectively.

QUESTION 18: Interest and discount ₹ 8,850 lacs, Other Income ₹ 220 lacs, Income from investment ₹ 40 lacs, interest expended ₹ 2,720 lacs, Operating Expenses ₹ 2,662 lacs. Additional Information: Provision for NPA ₹ 1,060.50 lacs, Total Investments ₹ 800 of which 25% are held to maturity. The market value of Investment, is 80%. Tax to be provided @35%. Calculate the amount of Provision and Contingences.

ANSWER:

CALCULATION OF THE AMOUNT OF PROVISION AND CONTINGENCES

A. Provision for Diminution in Value of Investments (other than Held to Maturity) = (₹ 800 – 25% of ₹ 800) – (80% of ₹ 600)	₹ 120
B. Provision for NPA	₹ 1,060.50
C. Provision & Contingencies (excluding tax) [₹ 1,060.50 + ₹ 120]	₹ 1,180.50
D. Tax = 35% of [Total Income – Total Expenditure (excluding tax)] = 35% of [(8,890 + 220) – (2,720 + 2,662 + 1180.50)]	₹ 891.625

FINANCIAL STATEMENTS OF ELECTRICITY COMPANIES

QUESTION 1: Tulsian Electricity Compamy which maintains accounts under the Double Account System laid down a main at a cost of ₹ 30 lacs. Some years later, the company laid down an auxillary main for one-fifth of the length of the old main at a cost of ₹ 15 lacs. It decides to replace the rest of the length of the old main at a cost of ₹ 60 lacs. It is ascertained that the proportion of Labour to materials in the main then and now is 3 : 5 and overheads constitute 20% of total expenditure. The cost of materials and labours have gone up by 40% and 80% respectively.

Old materials valued at ₹ 2,40,000 were used in renewal and those value at ₹ 50,000 were used in the construction of the auxiliary main. Some old materials were sold for ₹ 7,50,000.

Required: Find out the amount to be capitalised and also the amount to be charged to Revenue. Pass the necessary journal entries.

ANSWER:

COMPUTATION OF AMOUNT TO BE CHARGED TO REVENUE ACCOUNT

Particulars		₹
A Old Cost of 4/5th of Old Asset [₹ 30,00,000 × 4/5]		24,00,000
B Effect of Increases in various components of old cost		
(a) Increase in Materials Cost 40% of (₹ 24 lacs – 20%) × 5/8]	4,80,000	
(b) Increase in Labour Cost 80% of (₹ 24 lacs – 20%) × 3/8]	5,76,000	
(c) Increase in Overheads [25% of (₹ 4,80,000 + ₹ 5,76,000]	2,64,000	13,20,000
C Current Cost of Old Asset (A + B)		37,20,000
D *Less:* Recoveries from Old Asset		
(a) Sale Proceeds of Old Materials	7,50,000	
(b) Value of Old Materials Reuses	2,40,000	9,90,000
E Amount to be written off to Revenue A/c (C – D)		27,30,000

COMPUTATION OF AMOUNT TO BE CAPITALISED

Particulars	₹
ACash Cost of New Asset (Excluding the Value of Old Materials, if any, reused)	60,00,000
B*Less:* Current Cost of Old Asset	(37,20,000)
CCurrent Cash Cost to be Capitalised (A – B)	22,80,000
D*Add:* Value of Old Materials Reused	2,40,000
ECurrent Total Cost to be Capitalised (C + D)	25,20,000

JOURNAL

Date	Particulars		L.F.	Dr. (₹)	Cr. (₹)
	New Main A/c	Dr.		22,80,000	
	Replacement A/c	Dr.		37,20,000	
	To Bank A/c				60,00,000
	(Being the current cost of replacement of 4/5th of the old main charged to Replacement A/c)				
	New Main A/c	Dr.		2,40,000	
	To Replacement A/c				2,40,000
	(Being the cost of old materials used in the main)				
	New Auxilliary Main A/c	Dr.		15,50,000	
	To Bank A/c				15,00,000
	To Replacement A/c				50,000
	(Being the capitalisation of cost incurred on laying auxiliary main including old materials worth ₹ 50,000)				
	Bank A/c	Dr.		7,50,000	
	To Replacement A/c				7,50,000
	(Being the sale of old materials)				
	Revenue A/c	Dr.		26,80,000	
	To Replacement A/c				26,80,000
	(Being the transfer of balances in Replacement A/c to Revenue A/c)				

QUESTION 2: State any four alternative Accounting Treatment of the Fund received by an Electricity Company from consumer towards Capital Expenditure/Service Line Contribution.

ANSWER: Capital Service Line Contribution: Different SERCs prescribe Service Line cum Defvelopment (SLD) Charges Norms as per Sec. 47 of the Electricity Act. Accounting for and Reporting of this source of funds of Electricity Companies may be in any of the following ways:

1. Initial Recording as Liability, and subsequently recognized as Income over the life of the asset.
2. Recording as Reserves (as the amount is not refundable) and reported under the head Reserves and Surplus, without transferring any proportionate amount to the Income Statement over the life of asset,
3. Recording as Reserves (as the amount is not refundable) and subsequent transfer of proportionate amount to Income Statement during the expected life of the asset to match against Depreciation on total cost of such asset, or
4. Recording as reduction in the Cost of Non-Current Asset, and providing Depreciation on such reduced cost.

FINANCIAL STATEMENTS OF LIFE INSURANCE COMPANIES

QUESTION 1: Explain in Brief the following principles and term of insurance business:

(i) **Principle of Indemnity;**

(ii) **Insurable interest;**

(iii) **Principle of "UBERRIMAE FIDEI";**

(iv) **Catastrophic Loss**

ANSWER:

(i) Principle of Indemnity	Insurance is a contract of indemnity. The insurer is called idemnifier and the insured is the indemnified. In a contract of indemnity, only those who suffer loss are compensated to the extent of actual loss suffered by them. One cannot make profit by insuring his risks.
(ii) Insurable interest	All and sundry cannot enter into contracts of insurance. ***For Example***, A cannot insure the life of B who is a stranger. But if B, happens to be his wife *or* his debtor *or* business manager, A has insurable interest i.e. vested interest and therefore he can insure the life of B. For every type of policy insurable interest is insisted upon. In the absence of such interest the contract will amount to a wagering contract.
(iii) Principle of UBERRIMAE FIDEI	All contracts of insurance are contracts of uberrima fidei, i.e., contracts of utmost good faith. In a contract of insurance, however there is an implied condition that each party must disclose every material fact known to him. This is because the assessment of the risk and the determination of the premium by the insurer depend on the full and frank disclosure of all material facts is the proposal form.
(iv) Catastrophic Loss	A loss (or related losses) which is unbearable i.e. it causes severe consequences such as bankruptcy to a family, organization, *or* insurer.

QUESTION 2: What is Life Assurance Fund?

ANSWER: It refers to the fund which is retained to meet the aggregate liability on all outstanding policies. Until the liability on all outstanding policies is computed, the amount of profit of the life business cannot be ascertained. A life business is said to have earned profit only if its Life Assurance Fund exceeds its net liability on all outstanding policies.

The computation of the net liability on all outstanding policies is a complicated mathematical process which can be done only by experts in the field called 'Actuaries'. This Computation is carried out by LIC, every two years. As such, the life Insurance business cannot ascertain its profits every year.

QUESTION 3: How is the Surplus of a Life Insurance Company distributed?

ANSWER: According to Section 28 of the Life Insurance Corporation Act 1956, 95% of the surplus disclosed on a valuation must be allocated/reserved for the policy holders and the remaining (i.e., 5%) must be utilised for such purposes as the Government may determine. The profit allocated to the policy-holders is distributed as bonus on with profit policies.

STATEMENT SHOWING THE DISTRIBUTION OF SURPLUS

Particulars	₹
A. Total Surplus after Taxation	xxx
B. *Less:* Surplus to be carried forward	(xxx)
C. Surplus Available for distribution (A – B)	xxx
D. Share of Shareholders @ 5%	xxx
E. Share of Policy holders @ 95%	xxx
F. *Less:* Interim Bonus already paid	(xxx)
G. Amount Due to Policy holders (E – F)	xxx

QUESTION 4: How is the Net Profit for the valuation period calculated?

ANSWER:

STATEMENT SHOWING THE NET PROFIT FOR VALUATION PERIOD

Particulars	₹
A. Surplus as per Valuation Balance Sheet	xxx
B. *Add:* Interim Bonus already paid	xxx
C. *Less:* Surplus in the Beginning	(xxx)
D. Net Profit for the valuation period	xxx

QUESTION 5: The company declared a reversionary bonus of ₹ 12 per ₹ 1,000 and gave the policyholders an option to get the bonus in cash for ₹ 5 per ₹ 1,000. Total business of the company is ₹ 15 crores, 40% of the policyholders decided to get bonus in cash. Give the necessary journal entries.

ANSWER:

JOURNAL

Date	Particulars		Dr. (₹)	Cr.(₹)
	Profit and Loss A/c	Dr.	3,00,000	
	To Bonus payable in cash A/c			3,00,000
	(Being the bonus payable in cash)			
	Profit and Loss A/c	Dr.	10,80,000	
	To Life insurance Fund A/c			10,80,000
	(Being transfer to Life Insurance Fund for liability)			

QUESTION 6: The Life Fund of Well-life Assurance Co. was ₹ 90,00,000 as on 31st March 2015. The interim bonus paid during the valuation period was ₹ 1,50,000. The periodical actuarial valuation determined the net liability at ₹ 75,00,000. Surplus brought forward from the previous valuation was ₹ 9,00,000. The directors of the company proposed to carry forward ₹ 10,00,000 and to divide the balance between the shareholders and the policy holders. You are required to show:

(i) The Valuation Balance Sheet.

(ii) The Net Profit for the valuation period.

(iii) The Distribution of the Surplus.

ANSWER:

WELL-LIFE ASSURANCE CO
VALUATION BALANCE SHEET AS AT 31ST MARCH, 2015

₹ in lakhs

Liabilities	₹	Assets	₹
To Net Liability as per actuarial valuation	75,00,000	By Life Insurance Fund	90,00,000
To Surplus (B/F)	15,00,000		
	90,00,000		90,00,000

STATEMENT SHOWING THE NET PROFIT FOR VALUATION PERIOD

Particulars	₹
A. Surplus as per Valuation Balance Sheet	16,50,000
B. *Add:* Interim Bonus already paid	1,50,000
C. *Less:* Surplus in the Beginning	(9,00,000)
D. Net Profit for the valuation period	7,50,000

STATEMENT SHOWING THE DISTRIBUTION OF SURPLUS

Particulars	₹
A. Total Surplus after Taxation	16,50,000
B. *Less:* Surplus to be carried forward	(10,00,000)
C. Surplus Available for distribution (A – B)	6,50,000
D. Share of Shareholders @ 5%	32,500
E. Share of Policy holders @ 95%	6,17,500
F. *Less:* Interim Bonus already paid	(1,50,000)
G. Amount Due to Policy holders (E – F)	4,67,500

FINANCIAL STATEMENTS OF GENERAL INSURANCE COMPANIES

QUESTION 1: What is Re-insurance?

ANSWER: Re-insurance is an arrangement under which one insurance Company (called Re-insurer *or* Re-insurance Co.) insures the whole *or* a part of the subject matters already insured by another insurance Company (called Re-insured *or* Ceding Company). Thus, Ceding Company agrees to pass on whole *or* a part of risk to reinsurance company which agrees to accept the transferred risk.

Re-insurer receives the premium from the Re-insured and pays the commission and claim to the Re-insurer.

QUESTION 2: What is Average Clause under Insurance?

ANSWER:

Why introduced?	To discourage under insurance.
Applicability	Average clause is applicable in case of under insurance (i.e., where the sum insured of policy is less than the value of the subject matter of the insurance).
Actual Claim in case of Under Insurance	$\text{Claim} = \text{Actual Loss} \times \frac{\text{Sum Insured}}{\text{Sum Insurable}}$

QUESTION 3: What is Double Insurance?

ANSWER: When more than one policy is taken to cover the same risk, it is called double insurance. Any person is free to insure her/his goods *or* property against fire *or* perils of the sea under more than one policy. But, in such cases, the insured cannot recover more than the insured value of peroperty from his insurers. All the insurers with whom she/he had insured will be liable to pay only a reteable proportion of the loss suffered by the insured.

QUESTION 4: What is Provision for Unexpired Risks?

ANSWER:

1. Meaning	Provision for Unexpired Risks is a provision created to meet the claims which may arise in respect of the policies which remain unexpired at the end of the year.
2. Minimum Reserve to be kept	*Types of General Insurance Business* — *% of Net Premium* I. Marine Hull Insurance — 100% II. Fire, Marine Cargo and Misc. Insurance — 40% However, the income tax authorities allow 100% of the net premium in case of marine insurance and 50% of the net premium in case of other insurance. Since there is no bar on creating such reserve at a percentage higher than those laid down by the Executive Committee, the Company may maintain such reserve at a higher percentage. The excess reserve over the minimum reserve is termed as 'Additional Reserve'.
3. Accounting Treatment	1. The difference between the aggregate amount of minimum provision and additional provision in the beginning and aggregate amount there of at the end is disclosed as 'Changes in Provision for Unexpired Risks' in Revenue Account. 2. Balance of Minimum provision and additional provision of unexpired risks is shown on the liabilities side of Balance Sheet.

QUESTION 5: From the following information of Tulsian Fire Insurance Company for the year ended 31st March 2015, Calculate the Net Premium earned and Reserve for Unexpired Risk which is to be maintained @ 40%. Additional Reserve is to be maintained @ 5%. The balance of Reserve for Unexpired Risk as on 01.04.2014 was ₹ 31,95,000 (including Additional Reserve ₹ 3,55,000)

Particulars	Direct Business (₹)	Reinsurance (₹)
Premium received	**75,25,000**	**8,25,000**

Premium Receivable as on 01.04.2014	**3,25,000**	**2,00,000**
Premium Receivable as on 31.03.2015	**5,00,000**	**3,75,000**
Premium Paid		**4,90,000**
Premium Payable as on 01.04.2014		**1,00,000**
Premium payable as on 31.03.2015		**4,50,000**

ANSWER:

SCHEDULE 1 – PREMUM EARNED (NET)

Particulars	This Yr
Premiums from Direct Business written (75,25,000 + 5,00,000 – 3,25,000)	77,00,000
Add: Premium on Re-Insurance accepted (8,25,000 + 3,75,000 – 2,00,000)	10,00,000
Less: Premium on Re-Insurance ceded (4,90,000 + 4,50,000 – 1,00,000)	(8,40,000)
Total Premium Earned (Net)	78,60,000
Less: Adjustment for change in Unexpired Risk Reserve (Note)	(3,42,000)
Total Premium Earned (Net)	75,18,000

Note: Adjustment for Changes in Reserve for Unexpired Risks is computed as under:

Particulars	Reserve
Closing balance required [(40% of 78,60,000) + (5% of 78,60,000)]	35,37,000
Less: Opening Balance available(28,40,000 + 3,55,000)	31,95,000
Amt to be transferred to Reserve for the year	3,42,000

QUESTION 6: From the following information of Tulsian Fire Insurance Company for the year ended 31st March 2015, calculate the Net Claims Incurred:

Particulars		Direct Business (₹)	Reinsurance (₹)
Claims Paid during the Year		**49,70,000**	**5,10,000**
Claims Payable:	**1st April 2014**	**6,85,000**	**95,000**
	31st March 2015	**7,38,000**	**70,000**
Claims Received		**–**	**3,95,000**
Claims Receivable:	**1st April 2014**	**–**	**75,000**
	31st March 2015	**–**	**1,25,000**
Commission:	**On Insurance Accepted**	**1,60,000**	**15,000**
	On Insurance Ceded	**–**	**18,000**

ANSWER:

SCHEDULE 2 – CLAIMS PAID (NET)

Particulars	This Yr
Claims Paid – Direct (49,70,000 + 7,38,000 – 6,85,000)	50,23,000
Add: Claims on Re-Insurance accepted (5,10,000 + 70,000 – 95,000)	4,85,000
Less: Claims on Re-Insurance Ceded (3,95,000 + 1,25,000 – 75,000)	(4,45,000)
Add: Surveyor's Fees	45,000

Add: Legal Expenses	55,000
Total claims Incurred	51,63,000

QUESTION 7: From the following information of Tulsian Fire Insurance Company for the year ended 31st March 2015, Calculate the Net Commission earned:

Particulars		Direct Business (₹)	Reinsurance (₹)
Commission:	On Insurance Accepted	1,60,000	15,000
	On Insurance Ceded	–	18,000

ANSWER:

SCHEDULE 3 – COMMISSION

Particulars	This Yr
Commision paid: Direct	1,60,000
Add: Commission on Re-Insurance accepted	15,000
Less: Commission on Re-Insurance ceded	(18,000)
Net Commission	1,57,000

QUESTION 8: Tulsian Fire Insurance Company submits the following information for the year ended 31st march 2015:

Particulars		Direct Business (₹)	Reinsurance (₹)
Premium received		77,00,000	10,00,000
Premium Paid			8,40,000
Claims Paid during the Year		50,23,000	4,85,000
Claims Received			4,45,000
Expenses of Management		2,90,000	–
Commission:	On Insurance Accepted	1,60,000	15,000
	On Insurance Ceded	–	18,000

The aollowing additional information are also available:

(i) **Expenses of Management include ₹ 45,000 Surveyor's Fees and ₹ 55,000. Legal Expenses for settlement of claims.**

(ii) **Reserve for Unexpired Risk is to be maintained @ 40%. Additional Reserve is to be maintained @ 5%. The balance of Reserve for Unexpired Risk as on 01.04.2014 was ₹ 31,95,000 (including Additional Reserve ₹ 3,55,000)**

(iii) **Interest, Dividend & Rent Received (after TDS @ 10%) ₹ 34,200**

You are required to make the Revenue Account for the year ended 31st March 2015.

ANSWER:

FROM–B–RA–REVENUE ACCOUNT OF TULSIAN FIRE INSURANCE CO. LTD

for the year ending 31st March 2015

Particulars	Sch.	Current Yr	Previous Yr
Premium Earned (Net)	1	75,18,000	

Interest, Dividend & Rent (Gross) (₹ 34,200 × 100/90)		38,000	
Total (A)		75,56,000	
1. Claims Incurred (Net)	2	51,63,000	
2. Commission	3	1,57,000	
3. Operating Expenses related to Insurance Business	4		
(2,90,000 – Legal Exps 55,000 – Surveyor Fees 45,000)		1,90,000	
Total (B)		55,10,000	
Operating Profit/(Loss) from Insurance Business (A – B)		20,46,000	
Appropriations		NIL	
Total (C)		20,46,000	

SCHEDULE 1 – PREMUM EARNED (NET)

Particulars	This Yr
Premiums from Direct Business written	77,00,000
Add: Premium on Re-Insurance accepted	10,00,000
Less: Premium on Re-Insurance ceded	(8,40,000)
Total Premium Earned (Net)	78,60,000
Less: Adjustment for change in Unexpired Risk Reserve (Note)	(3,42,000)
Total Premium Earned (Net)	75,18,000

Note: Adjustment for Changes in Reserve for Unexpired Risks is computed as under:

Particulars	Reserve
Closing balance required [(40% of 78,60,000) + (5% of 78,60,000)]	35,37,000
Less: Opening Balance available (28,40,000 + 3,55,000)	31,95,000
Amt to be transferred to Reserve for the year	3,42,000

SCHEDULE 2 – CLAIMS PAID (NET)

Particulars	This Yr
Claims Paid – Direct	50,23,000
Add: Claims on Re-Insurance accepted	4,85,000
Less: Claims on Re-Insurance Ceded	(4,45,000)
Add: Surveyor's Fees	45,000
Add: Legal Expenses	55,000
Total claims Incurred	51,63,000

SCHEDULE 3 – COMMISSION

Particulars	This Yr
Commision paid: Direct	1,60,000
Add: Commission on Re-Insurance accepted	15,000
Less: Commission on Re-Insurance ceded	(18,000)
Net Commission	1,57,000

SECTION A : GENERALLY ACCEPTED ACCOUNTING PRINCIPLES & ACCOUNTING SYSTEMS

1 ACCOUNTING PROCESS

ACCOUNTING EQUATION

PROBLEM 1

Show the Accounting Equation on the basis of the following transactions and prepare the Balance Sheet at last.

(a) Shri Ganesh commenced business with Cash ₹ 35,000, Goods ₹ 8,000, Furniture ₹ 7,000.
(b) Bought furniture from M/s Mohan Furnitures on credit for ₹ 3,000.
(c) Purchased goods from Sohan for cash ₹ 35,000.
(d) Sold goods to Shyam for cash ₹ 40,000 (costing ₹ 30,000).
(e) Bought goods from Ramesh for ₹ 30,000.
(f) Sold goods to Shyam costing ₹ 30,000 for ₹ 50,000.
(g) Received ₹ 49,500 from Shyam in full settlement.
(h) Paid ₹ 29,700 to Ramesh in full settlement.
(i) Paid half the amount owed to M/s Mohan.
(j) Withdrew ₹ 1,000 for personal use.
(k) Withdrew goods for personal use (Cost ₹ 500, Sale Price ₹ 600).
(l) Purchased household goods for ₹ 15,000 giving ₹ 5,000 in cash and the balance through a loan.
(m) Paid cash ₹ 500 for loan and ₹ 300 for Interest.
(n) Goods destroyed by fire (Cost ₹ 500, Sale Price ₹ 600).
(o) Paid salary ₹ 500 and salary outstanding ₹ 100.
(p) Paid rent in advance ₹ 2,000.
(q) Accrued Interest ₹ 500.
(r) Commission received in advance ₹ 1,000.
(s) Charged depreciation of ₹ 400 on furniture.

SOLUTION

(See Solution on page 1.2).

BALANCE SHEET OF SHRI GANESH AS AT....

Liabilities + Capital	₹	Assets	₹
Creditor for furniture	1,500	Cash	50,000
Creditor for household goods	9,500	Stock	12,000
Outstanding salary	100	Prepaid Rent	2,000
Commission received in advance	1,000	Accrued Interest	500
Capital	62,000	Furniture	9,600
	74,100		74,100

Solution to Problem 1:

ACCOUNTING EQUATION: ASSETS = LIABILITIES + CAPITAL

Trans.	Assets						Liabilities			+ Capital
	Cash	+ Stock	+ Debtors	+ Furniture	+ Prepaid Expenses	+ Accrued Income	Creditors	+ Lenders	+ Income Received in advance + O/s Exp.	+ Capital
(a)	35,000	+ 8,000	+ 0	+ 7,000	+ 0	+ 0	0	+ 0	+ 0 + 0	+ 50,000
New Equation	35,000	+ 8,000	+ 0	+ 7,000	+ 0	+ 0	0	+ 0	+ 0 + 0	+ 50,000
(b)	0	+ 0	+ 0	+ 3,000	+ 0	+ 0	3,000	+ 0	+ 0 + 0	+ 0
New Equation	35,000	+ 8,000	+ 0	+ 10,000	+ 0	+ 0	3,000	+ 0	+ 0 + 0	+ 50,000
(c)	–35,000	+ 35,000	+ 0	+ 0	+ 0	+ 0	0	+ 0	+ 0 + 0	+ 0
New Equation	0	+ 43,000	+ 0	+ 10,000	+ 0	+ 0	3,000	+ 0	+ 0 + 0	+ 50,000
(d)	40,000	– 30,000	+ 0	+ 0	+ 0	+ 0	0	+ 0	+ 0 + 0	+ 10,000
New Equation	40,000	+ 13,000	+ 0	+ 10,000	+ 0	+ 0	3,000	+ 0	+ 0 + 0	+ 60,000
(e)	0	+ 30,000	+ 0	+ 0	+ 0	+ 0	30,000	+ 0	+ 0 + 0	+ 0
New Equation	40,000	+ 43,000	+ 0	+ 10,000	+ 0	+ 0	33,000	+ 0	+ 0 + 0	+ 60,000
(f)	0	– 30,000	+ 50,000	+ 0	+ 0	+ 0	0	+ 0	+ 0 + 0	+ 20,000
New Equation	40,000	+ 13,000	+ 50,000	+ 10,000	+ 0	+ 0	33,000	+ 0	+ 0 + 0	+ 80,000
(g)	49,500	+ 0	– 50,000	+ 0	+ 0	+ 0	0	+ 0	+ 0 + 0	– 500
New Equation	89,500	+ 13,000	+ 0	+ 10,000	+ 0	+ 0	33,000	+ 0	+ 0 + 0	+ 79,500
(h)	– 29,700	+ 0	+ 0	+ 0	+ 0	+ 0	–30,000	+ 0	+ 0 + 0	+ 300
New Equation	59,800	+ 13,000	+ 0	+ 10,000	+ 0	+ 0	3,000	+ 0	+ 0 + 0	+ 79,800
(i)	–1,500	+ 0	+ 0	+ 0	+ 0	+ 0	–1,500	+ 0	+ 0 + 0	+ 0
New Equation	58,300	+ 13,000	+ 0	+ 10,000	+ 0	+ 0	1,500	+ 0	+ 0 + 0	+ 79,800
(j)	–1,000	+ 0	+ 0	+ 0	+ 0	+ 0	0	+ 0	+ 0 + 0	– 1,000

Contd... Solution to Problem 1

Trans.	Assets						Liabilities			+ Capital
	Cash	+ Stock	+ Debtors	+ Furniture	+ Prepaid Expenses	+ Accrued Income	Creditors	+ Lenders	+ Income Received in advance + O/s Exp.	+ Capital
New Equation	57,300	+ 13,000	+ 0	+ 10,000	+ 0	+ 0	1,500	+ 0	+ 0 + 0	+ 78,800
(k)	0	– 500	+ 0	+ 0	+ 0	+ 0	0	+ 0	+ 0 + 0	– 500
New Equation	57,300	+ 12,500	+ 0	+ 10,000	+ 0	+ 0	1,500	+ 0	+ 0 + 0	+ 78,300
(l)	–5,000	+ 0	+ 0	+ 0	+ 0	+ 0	0	+ 10,000	+ 0 + 0	– 15,000
New Equation	52,300	+ 12,500	+ 0	+ 10,000	+ 0	+ 0	1,500	+ 10,000	+ 0 + 0	+ 63,300
(m)	–800	+ 0	+ 0	+ 0	+ 0	+ 0	0	– 500	+ 0 + 0	– 300
New Equation	51,500	+ 12,500	+ 0	+ 10,000	+ 0	+ 0	1,500	+ 9,500	+ 0 + 0	+ 63,000
(n)	0	– 500	+ 0	+ 0	+ 0	+ 0	0	+ 0	+ 0 + 0	– 500
New Equation	51,500	+ 12,000	+ 0	+ 10,000	+ 0	+ 0	1,500	+ 9,500	+ 0 + 0	+ 62,500
(o)	–500	+ 0	+ 0	+ 0	+ 0	+ 0	0	+ 0	+ 100	+ 600
New Equation	51,000	+ 12,000	+ 0	+ 10,000	+ 0	+ 0	1,500	+ 9,500	+ 100	+ 61,900
(p)	–2,000	+ 0	+ 0	+ 0	+ 2,000	+ 0	0	+ 0	+ 0	+ 0
New Equation	49,000	+ 12,000	+ 0	+ 10,000	+ 2,000	+ 0	1,500	+ 9,500	+ 100	+ 61,900
(q)	0	+ 0	+ 0	+ 0	+ 0	+ 500	0	+ 0	+ 0 + 0	+ 500
New Equation	49,000	+ 12,000	+ 0	+ 10,000	+ 2,000	+ 500	1,500	+ 9,500	+ 100	+ 62,400
(r)	1,000	+ 0	+ 0	+ 0	+ 0	+ 0	0	+ 0	+ 1,000	+ 0
New Equation	50,000	+ 12,000	+ 0	+ 10,000	+ 2,000	+ 500	1,500	+ 9,500	+ 1,000+100	+ 62,400
(s)	0	+ 0	+ 0	– 400	+ 0	+ 0	0	+ 0	+ 0	– 400
New Equation	50,000	+ 12,000	+ 0	+ 9,600	+ 2,000	+ 500	1,500	+ 9,500	+ 1,000+100	+ 62,000

JOURNALISING

PROBLEM 2

Journalise the following transactions in the books of Shri Ganesh.

2015	Particulars	₹
April 1	Shri Ganesh started his business with Cash	50,000
2	Purchased goods	5,000
3	Purchased goods for Cash	10,000
4	Purchased goods from Mr Sun for Cash	15,000
5	Sold goods	6,000
6	Sold goods for Cash	12,000
8	Sold goods to Mr Sky for Cash	18,000
9	Purchased goods from Mr Moon	10,000
10	Purchased goods from Mr Star on Credit	20,000
11	Sold goods to Mr Sea	12,500
12	Sold goods to Mr Ocean on Credit	25,000
13	Mr Sea returned goods	2,500
15	Returned goods to Mr Moon	2,000
16	Received from Mr Sea	9,900
	Allowed him discount	100
17	Paid Mr Moon	7,880
	Discount allowed by him	120
29	Withdrew for personal use	1,000
30	Withdrew goods for private use (Cost ₹ 500, Selling Price ₹ 600)	
31	Paid Salary to Mr Sevakram, an employee	500
31	Paid Rent to Mr Estate, landlord	500

SOLUTION

JOURNAL OF SHRI GANESH

Date	Particulars	L.F.	Dr.(₹)	Cr.(₹)
2015	Cash A/c Dr.		50,000	
April 1	To Capital A/c			50,000
	(Being the capital brought in by Shri Ganesh)			
2	Purchases A/c Dr.		5,000	
	To Cash A/c			5,000
	(Being the goods purchased for cash)			
3	Purchases A/c Dr.		10,000	
	To Cash A/c			10,000
	(Being the goods purchased for cash)			

4	Purchases A/c To Cash A/c (Being the goods purchased for cash)	Dr.	15,000	 15,000
5	Cash A/c To Sales A/c (Being the goods sold for cash)	Dr.	6,000	 6,000
6	Cash A/c To Sales A/c (Being the goods sold for cash)	Dr.	12,000	 12,000
8	Cash A/c To Sales A/c (Being the goods sold for cash)	Dr.	18,000	 18,000
9	Purchases A/c To Mr Moon (Being the goods purchased on credit from Mr Moon)	Dr.	10,000	 10,000
10	Purchases A/c To Mr Star A/c (Being the goods purchased on credit from Mr Star)	Dr.	20,000	 20,000
11	Mr Sea A/c To Sales A/c (Being goods sold on credit to Mr Sea)	Dr.	12,500	 12,500
12	Mr Ocean A/c To Sales A/c (Being goods sold on credit to Mr Ocean)	Dr.	25,000	 25,000
13	Sales Returns A/c To Mr Sea A/c (Being the goods returned by Mr Sea)	Dr.	2,500	 2,500
15	Mr Moon A/c To Purchase Returns A/c (Being the goods returned to Mr Moon)	Dr.	2,000	 2,000
16	Cash A/c Discount Allowed A/c To Mr Sea (Being Cash received from Mr Sea & allowed him discount ₹ 100)	Dr. Dr.	9,900 100	 10,000
17	Mr Moon To Cash A/c To Discount Received A/c (Being Cash paid to Mr Moon & received discount of ₹ 120)	Dr.	8,000	 7,880 120

29	Drawings A/c To Cash A/c (Being the cash withdrawn for personal use)	Dr.	1,000	1,000
30	Drawings A/c To Purchases A/c (Being the goods costing ₹ 500 withdrawn for personal use)	Dr.	500	500
31	Salary A/c To Cash A/c (Being the salary paid to Sevakram)	Dr.	500	500
31	Rent A/c To Cash A/c (Being rent paid to landlord)	Dr.	500	500
	Total		2,08,500	2,08,500

PROBLEM 3

Journalise the following transactions in the Journal of Mr Tulsian:

01 Jan 2015	Started business with Cash ₹ 2,00,000, Goods ₹ 1,00,000, Furniture ₹ 50,000.
01 Jan 2015	Opened Current Account with ₹ 1,00,000.
02 Jan 2015	Placed an order with Ritik Roshan for the supply of goods of the list price of ₹1,00,000. In this connection, we paid 9% of the list price as an advance by cheque.
03 Jan 2015	Ritik Roshan supplied goods of the list price of ₹ 1,00,000 less 12% trade discount. Packing and Delivery charges ₹ 1,000.
04 Jan 2015	Purchased goods from Murli of the list price of ₹ 1,00,000 less 12% trade discount and paid him by cheque under a cash discount of 5%.
05 Jan 2015	Received an order from Shyam for supply of goods of the list price of ₹ 1,00,000 with an advance of 10% of list price.
06 Jan 2015	Supplied the above goods at 10% trade discount. Packing and delivery charges ₹ 1,000.
07 Jan 2015	Goods costing ₹ 80,000 sold to Mr X at a profit of 20% on sales less 10% trade discount and received a cheque under 2% Cash discount.
08 Jan 2015	Goods (Cost ₹ 3,000, Sale Price ₹ 4,000) taken away by the proprietor for his personal use.
09 Jan 2015	Shyam became insolvent and paid 80 paise in a rupee in full & final settlement.
10 Jan 2015	Paid Ritik 80% on account.
11 Jan 2015	Goods (Cost ₹ 3,000, Sale Price ₹ 4,000) stolen.
12 Jan 2015	Paid Life Insurance Premium ₹ 1,000.
13 Jan 2015	Cash embezzled by an employee ₹ 1,000.

SOLUTION

JOURNAL OF MR TULSIAN

Date	Particulars		L.F.	Dr.(₹)	Cr.(₹)
2015					
Jan 01	Cash A/c	Dr.		2,00,000	
	Purchases A/c	Dr.		1,00,000	
	Furniture A/c	Dr.		50,000	
	To Capital A/c				3,50,000
	(Being the cash, goods & furniture brought in as Capital)				
Jan 01	Bank A/c	Dr.		1,00,000	
	To Cash A/c				1,00,000
	(Being the current account opened with ₹ 1,00,000)				
Jan 02	Ritik Roshan	Dr.		9,000	
	To Bank A/c				9,000
	(Being advance paid to Ritik)				
Jan 03	Purchases A/c	Dr.		89,000	
	To Ritik Roshan				89,000
	(Being the goods purchased on credit)				
	List Price	₹ 1,00,000			
	Less: Trade Discount @ 12%	₹ 12,000			
		₹ 88,000			
	Add: Packing & Delivery Charges	₹ 1,000			
		₹ 89,000			
Jan 04	Purchases A/c	Dr.		88,000	
	To Bank A/c				83,600
	To Discount Received A/c				4,400
	(Being the goods purchased against cheque)				
	List Price	₹ 1,00,000			
	Less: Trade Discount 12%	₹ 12,000			
		₹ 88,000			
	Less: Cash Discount 5%	₹ 4,400			
		₹ 83,600			
Jan 05	Cash A/c	Dr.		10,000	
	To Shyam				10,000
	(Being an advance received from Shyam)				
Jan 06	Shyam	Dr.		91,000	
	To Sales A/c				91,000
	(Being the goods sold on credit)				

Date	Particulars		L.F.	Dr. (₹)	Cr. (₹)
	List Price	₹ 1,00,000			
	Less: Trade Discount @ 10%	₹ 10,000			
		₹ 90,000			
	Add: Packing & Delivery charges	₹ 1,000			
		₹ 91,000			
Jan 07	Bank A/c	Dr.		88,200	
	Discount Allowed A/c	Dr.		1,800	
	To Sales A/c				90,000
	(Being the goods sold against cheque)				
	Cost	₹ 80,000			
	Add: Profit @ 25%	₹ 20,000			
	List Price	₹ 1,00,000			
	Less: Trade Discount @ 10%	₹ 10,000			
		₹ 90,000			
	Less: Cash Discount @ 2%	₹ 1,800			
		₹ 88,200			
Jan 08	Drawings A/c	Dr.		3,000	
	To Purchases A/c				3,000
	(Being the goods taken away by the proprietor for personal use)				
Jan 09	Cash A/c	Dr.		64,800	
	Bad Debts A/c	Dr.		16,200	
	To Shyam				81,000
	(Being 80 paise in a rupee received from Shyam in full and final settlement)				
Jan 10	Ritik	Dr.		64,000	
	To Cash A/c				64,000
	(Being 80% of the balance i.e. (₹ 89,000 – ₹ 9,000) paid)				
Jan 11	Loss by Theft A/c	Dr.		3,000	
	To Purchases A/c				3,000
	(Being the goods stolen)				
Jan 12	Drawings A/c	Dr.		1,000	
	To Cash A/c				1,000
	(Being life insurance premium paid)				
Jan 13	Loss by Embezzlement A/c	Dr.		1,000	
	To Cash A/c				1,000
	(Being cash embezzled by an employee)				
		Total		9,80,000	9,80,000

PROBLEM 4

Journalise the following transactions in the books of Bharat Tulsian:

1. Received ₹ 9,000 from Hari Krishan in full settlement of his account for ₹ 10,000.
2. Received ₹ 9,000 from Shyam on his account for ₹ 10,000.
3. Received a first and final dividend of 90 paise in the rupee from the Official Receiver of Mr Rajan who owed us ₹ 10,000.
4. Paid ₹ 9,000 to Mohan in full settlement of his account for ₹ 10,000.
5. Paid ₹ 9,000 to Sohan on his account for ₹ 10,000.
6. Withdrawn for personal use: Goods (Sale Price ₹ 8,000, Cost ₹ 6,000), Cash ₹ 1,000
7. Goods costing ₹ 9,000 given as charity. (Sale Price ₹ 12,000)
8. Goods costing ₹ 3,000 distributed as free samples. (Sale Price ₹ 4,000)
9. Goods stolen in transit: (Sale Price ₹ 8,000, Cost ₹ 6,000)
10. Goods destroyed by fire (Sale Price ₹ 4,000, Cost ₹ 3,000)
11. Goods stolen by an employee (Sale Price ₹ 8,000, Cost ₹ 6,000), Cash embezzled by an employee ₹ 1,000.
12. Goods used in making of Furniture (Sale Price ₹ 12,000, Cost ₹ 9,000)
13. Paid Rent of building ₹ 50,000 half of the building is used by the proprietor for residential use.
14. Paid Fire Insurance of the above building in advance ₹ 20,000.
15. Paid Life Insurance Premium ₹ 20,000.
16. Paid Income tax ₹ 50,000.
17. Salary due to clerk ₹ 30,000.
18. Received commission ₹ 1,00,000 half of which is in advance.
19. Brokerage due to us ₹ 50,000.
20. Purchased Secondhand Machinery from Jawahar for ₹ 30,000 against a cheque.
21. Goods used in repairs of Machinery. (Sale Price ₹ 12,000, Cost ₹ 9,000)
22. Paid Installation Charges of Machinery ₹ 1,000.
23. Provide Depreciation for one month on above Machinery @ 15% p.a.

SOLUTION

JOURNAL

Date	Particulars		L.F.	Dr.(₹)	Cr.(₹)
1.	Cash A/c	Dr.		9,000	
	Discount allowed A/c	Dr.		1,000	
	To Hari Krishan				10,000
	(Being the cash received from Hari Krishan after allowing him discount of ₹ 1,000)				
2.	Cash A/c	Dr.		9,000	
	To Shyam				9,000
	(Being the Cash received from Shyam on account)				
3.	Cash A/c	Dr.		9,000	
	Bad Debts A/c	Dr.		1,000	
	To Rajan				10,000
	(Being the 90 paise in the rupee received from Rajan in full settlement)				

4.	Mohan To Cash A/c To Discount received A/c (Being the Cash paid to Mohan after receiving discount of ₹ 1,000)	Dr.		10,000	 9,000 1,000
5.	Sohan To Cash A/c (Being the Cash paid to Sohan on account)	Dr.		9,000	 9,000
6.	Drawings A/c To Purchases A/c To Cash A/c (Being the Goods & Cash withdrawn for personal use)	Dr.		7,000	 6,000 1,000
7.	Charity A/c To Purchases A/c (Being the Goods distributed as charity)	Dr.		9,000	 9,000
8.	Free Sample A/c/Sales Promotion A/c To Purchases A/c (Being the Goods distributed as free samples)	Dr.		3,000	 3,000
9.	Loss in Transit A/c To Purchases A/c (Being the Goods stolen in transit)	Dr.		6,000	 6,000
10.	Loss due to fire A/c To Purchases A/c (Being the Goods destroyed by fire)	Dr.		3,000	 3,000
11.	Loss by Embezzlement A/c To Purchases A/c To Cash A/c (Being the Goods & Cash stolen by an employee)	Dr.		7,000	 6,000 1,000
12.	Furniture A/c To Purchases A/c (Being the Goods used in making furniture)	Dr.		9,000	 9,000
13. (i)	Rent A/c To Cash A/c (Being the rent paid for building)	Dr.		50,000	 50,000
13. (ii)	Drawings A/c To Rent A/c (Being the rent for half building charged to proprietor)	Dr.		25,000	 25,000
14. (i)	Fire Insurance premium A/c To Cash A/c (Being the fire insurance premium paid for building)	Dr.		20,000	 20,000

14. (ii)	Drawing A/c Prepaid Insurance Premium A/c To Fire Insurance Premium A/c (Being the fire insurance premium for half building charged to proprietor and remaining paid in advance)	Dr. Dr.		10,000 10,000	20,000
15.	Drawings A/c To Cash Ac (Being the life insurance premium paid)	Dr.		20,000	20,000
16.	Drawings A/c To Cash A/c (Being the Income Tax paid)	Dr.		50,000	50,000
17.	Salary A/c To Outstanding Salary A/c (Being salary due to clerk)	Dr.		30,000	30,000
18. (i)	Cash A/c To Commission A/c (Being the commission received)	Dr.		1,00,000	1,00,000
18. (ii)	Commission A/c To Commission received in advance A/c (Being the commission received in advance adjusted)	Dr.		50,000	50,000
19.	Accrued Brokerage A/c To Brokerage A/c (Being the brokerage due to us adjusted)	Dr.		50,000	50,000
20.	Machinery A/c To Bank A/c (Being the machinery purchased and paid by cheque)	Dr.		30,000	30,000
21.	Machinery A/c To Purchases A/c (Being the Goods used in repairs of Machinery)	Dr.		9,000	9,000
22.	Machinery A/c To Cash A/c (Being the installation charges of machinery capitalised)	Dr.		1,000	1,000
23.	Depreciation A/c [₹ 40,000 × 15/100 × 1/12] To Machinery A/c (Being the depreciation on Machinery provided)	Dr.		500	500

PROBLEM 5

1st January 2015, the position of V. Mathur was as follows:

Stock-in-hand ₹ 2,400, Bills Payable ₹ 400, Cash at Bank ₹ 1,800, Plant & Machinery ₹ 1,000, Owing by debtors ₹ 500, Owing to creditors ₹ 800, Investments ₹ 2,000, Loan from S. Sethi ₹ 1,500.

Required: What was the amount of V. Mathur's Capital on this date? Show an opening journal entry.

SOLUTION

(a) Calculation of the Capital as at 1.4.2015

BALANCE SHEET AS AT 1.1.2015

Liabilities	₹	Assets	₹
Bills Payable	400	Cash at Bank	1,800
Owing to Creditors	800	Owing by debtors	500
Loan from S. Sethi	1,500	Stock-in-hand	2,400
Capital (Balancing figure)	5,000	Investments	2,000
		Plant & Machinery	1,000
	7,700		7,700

(b) Opening Entry

JOURNAL

Date	Particulars		L.F.	Dr.(₹)	Cr.(₹)
2015	Cash at Bank	Dr.		1,800	
Jan. 1	Owing by Debtors	Dr.		500	
	Stock-in-hand	Dr.		2,400	
	Investments	Dr.		2,000	
	Plant & Machinery	Dr.		1,000	
	To Bills Payable				400
	To Owing to creditors				800
	To Loans from S. Sethi				1,500
	To Capital A/c				5,000
	(Being the balances of various assets and liabilities brought forward from last year)				

SUBSIDIARY BOOKS I – CASH BOOK

PROBLEM 6

Prepare a Three Column Cash Book of M/s Tulsian & Co. from the following particulars.

2015	Particulars
Jan. 1	Cash in hand ₹ 50,000, Bank Overdraft ₹ 20,000.
2	Paid into bank ₹ 10,000.
3	Bought goods from Hari for ₹ 200 for cash.

4	Bought goods for ₹ 2,000 paid cheque for them, discount allowed 1%.
5	Sold goods to Mohan for cash ₹ 1,175.
6	Received a crossed cheque from Shyam to whom goods were sold for ₹ 800. Discount allowed 12.5%.
7	Shyam's cheque deposited into bank.
8	Purchased an old typewriter for ₹ 200. Spent ₹ 50 on its repairs.
9	Bank notified that Shyam's cheque has been returned dishonoured and debited the account in respect of charges ₹ 10.
10	Received a money order for ₹ 25 from Hari.
11	Shyam settled his account by means of a crossed cheque for ₹ 820, ₹ 20 being for interest charged.
12	Withdrew from bank ₹ 10,000.
18	Discounted a B/E for ₹ 1,000 at 1% through bank.
20	Honoured our own acceptance by cheque ₹ 5,000.
22	Withdrew for personal use ₹ 1,000.
24	Paid trade expenses ₹ 2,000.
25	Withdrew from bank for private expenses ₹ 1,500.
26	Purchased machinery from Rajiv for ₹ 5,000 and paid him by means of a bank draft purchased for ₹ 5,005.
27	Issued cheque to Ram Saran for cash purchase of furniture ₹ 1,575.
28	Received a crossed cheque for commission ₹ 500 from R. & Co. and deposited into bank.
29	Ramesh who owed us ₹ 500 became bankrupt and paid us 50 paise in the rupee.
30	Received payment of a loan of ₹ 5,000 and deposited ₹ 3,000 out of its into bank.
31	Paid rent to landlord 'Mohan' by a cheque of ₹ 220.
31	Interest allowed by bank ₹ 30.
31	Half yearly bank charges ₹ 50.

SOLUTION

[See Solution on page 1.14]

Solution to Problem 6:

Dr.
TULSIAN & CO.

THREE COLUMN CASH BOOK OF M/S

Cr.

Date	Particulars	L.F.	Discount	Cash ₹	Bank	Date	Particulars	L.F.	Discount	Cash ₹	Bank ₹
2015						2015					
						Jan. 1	By Balance b/d				20,000
Jan. 1	To Balance b/d			50,000		Jan. 2	By Bank A/c	C		10,000	
2	" Cash	C			10,000	3	" Purchases A/c			200	
5	" Sales			1,175		4	" Purchases A/c		20		1,980
7	" Cheque-on-hand				700	8	" Typewriter			200	
10	" Hari			25			" Typewriter			50	
11	" Shyam				820	9	" Shyam		100		700
							" Bank charges				10
12	" Bank	C		10,000		12	" Cash	C			10,000
18	" B/E		10		990	20	" B/P				5,000
28	" Commission				500	22	" Drawings			1,000	
29	" Ramesh			250		24	" Trade expenses			2,000	
30	" Loans			5,000		25	" Drawings				1,500
	" Cash	C			3,000	26	" Machinery				5,000
31	" Interest				30		" Draft Commission				5
31	" Balance c/d				30,000	27	" Furniture				1,575
	(Bank overdraft)					30	" Bank	C		3,000	
						31	" Rent				220
							" Bank charges				50
							" Balance c/d				50,000
			10	66,450	46,040				120	66,450	66,450
2015						2015					
Feb. 1	To Balance b/d			50,000		Feb. 1	By Balance b/d				30,000

SUBSIDIARY BOOKS I – BOOKS OTHER THAN CASH BOOK

PROBLEM 7

On Jan. 1, 2015 Moti's Assets were:

Cash ₹ 2,000; Due from Jeevan ₹ 1,000; Stores ₹ 3,000; Furniture ₹ 500 and he had to pay to Kishore ₹ 2,000.

The following transactions took place:

Jan. 2	Purchased furniture from Hanuman for ₹ 200.
5	Received payment from Jeevan, discount allowed being 2%.
8	Sold to Mahendra 10 watches. Sent invoice at ₹ 30 per watch; allowed 10% trade discount.
12	Sent to Mahendra a credit note because price per watch was ₹ 25 and not ₹ 30.
20	Settled Kishore's Account to the extent of ₹ 1,000 only, he allowed with 2½% discount.
25	Purchased from Kishore goods of the list price of ₹ 1,500. He allowed 20% trade discount.
28	Paid the amount due to Hanuman.
31	Paid salaries ₹ 200 and rent ₹ 100.

Required: Prepare Moti's Subsidiary Books.

SOLUTION

Dr. **CASH BOOK** Cr.

Date	Particulars	L.F	Dis. ₹	Cash ₹	Date	Particulars	L.F.	Dis. ₹	Cash
2015					2015				
Jan. 1	To Balance b/d			2,000	Jan. 20	By Kishore		25	975
5	To Jeevan		20	980	28	By Hanuman			200
					31	By Salaries			200
					31	By Rent			100
					31	By Balance c/d			1,505
			20	2,980				25	2,980
Feb. 1	To Balance b/d			1,505					

PURCHASES BOOK

Date	Purchase Invoice No.	Name of Supplier		L.F.	Details ₹	Amount ₹
2015						
Jan. 25		Kishore				1,200
		Purchases A/c	Dr.			1,200

SALES BOOK

Date	Sales Invoice No.	Name of Customer	L.F.	Details ₹	Amount ₹
2015					
Jan. 8		Mahendra 10 watches @ ₹ 30 per watch			270
		Sales A/c Cr.			270

SALES RETURNS BOOK

Date	Credit Note No.	Name of Customer	L.F.	Details ₹	Amount ₹
2015					
Jan. 12	101	Mahendra Sent a Credit Note because price per watch was ₹ 25 and not ₹ 30 Invoice date Jan. 8, 2015			45
		Sales Returns A/c Dr.			45

GENERAL JOURNAL OR JOURNAL PROPER

Date	Particulars		L.F.	Dr.(₹)	Cr.(₹)
2015					
Jan. 1	Cash A/c	Dr.		2,000	
	Jeevan A/c	Dr.		1,000	
	Store A/c	Dr.		3,000	
	Furniture A/c	Dr.		500	
	To Kishore				2,000
	To Capital A/c				4,500
	(Being the opening balances brought forward from previous year's books)				
2	Furniture A/c	Dr.		200	
	To Hanuman				200
	(Being the furniture purchased from Hanuman)				

PROBLEM 8

From the following transactions of the month of April 2015, prepare the Journal Proper of Jindal & Co., a saree dealer, who also maintains Purchases Book, Sales Book, Returns Books and Cash Book:

Date	Transaction
1	Purchased on credit from Goyal Mills, Surat 25 polyester sarees @ ₹ 100.
3	Purchased on credit from Bansal & Co., 2 typewriters @ ₹ 3,500.
5	Sold on credit to Goyal & Co., 5 polyester sarees @ ₹ 125.
6	Returned one typewriter (being defective) @ ₹ 3,500 to Bansal & Co.

8	Sold on credit two old typewriters to Murli @ ₹ 500.
10	Sold for cash to Garg & Co., 20 Kota sarees @ ₹ 50.
12	Returned to Goyal Mills, Surat 5 polyester sarees @ ₹ 100.
14	Murli returned one old typewriter @ ₹ 500.
16	Purchased for cash from Kansal & Co., 2 chairs @ ₹ 3,700.
18	Returned one chair (being defective) @ ₹ 3,700.
20	Sold two old chairs for cash to Manohar @ ₹ 500.
21	Manohar returned one old chair @ ₹ 500.
22	Goyal & Co. became insolvent and paid only 80 paise in a rupee in full & final settlement.
24	Mr B.K. Jindal (Proprietor of Jindal & Co.) took away 2 silk sarees (costing ₹ 350 each sale price ₹ 700 each) from the shop and presented to his wife on her 25th birthday.
25	A cheque of ₹ 3,500 received from Mittal & Co., a customer, endorsed in favour of Bansal & Co., a creditor. On 30.4.2015, the bank informed that this cheque was dishonoured.
30	Rent due to landlord, Ram ₹ 1,000.
30	Salaries due to employee Shyam ₹ 1,000.

SOLUTION

JOURNAL PROPER OF M/S JINDAL & CO.

Date	Particulars		L.F.	Dr.(₹)	Cr.(₹)
2015 April 3	Typewriters A/c To Bansal & Co. (Being 2 typewriters purchased on credit from Bansal & Co.)	Dr.		7,000	7,000
6	Bansal & Co. To Typewriters A/c (Being 1 typewriter returned to Bansal & Co.)	Dr.		3,500	3,500
8	Murli To Typewriters A/c (Being 2 typewriters sold on credit to Murli)	Dr.		1,000	1,000
14	Typewriters A/c To Murli (Being 1 typewriter returned by Murli)	Dr.		500	500
22	Bad Debts A/c To Goyal & Co. (Being 20% of the dues from Goyal & Co. written-off as bad on their insolvency)	Dr.		125	125
24	Drawings A/c To Purchases A/c (Being 2 silk sarees costing ₹ 350 each, taken away by the proprietor for personal use)	Dr.		700	700

25	Bansal & Co. Dr. To Mittal & Co. (Being a cheque received from Mittal & Co. endorsed in favour of Bansal & Co.)		3,500	3,500
30	Mittal & Co. Dr. To Bansal & Co. (Being a cheque (endorsed) dishonoured)		3,500	3,500
30	Rent A/c Dr. To Outstanding Rent A/c (Being rent due to landlord)		1,000	1,000
30	Salaries A/c Dr. To Outstanding Salaries A/c (Being Salaries due to employee)		1,000	1,000
	Total		21,825	21,825

Note: The other transactions have not been recorded in the Journal Proper due to reasons mentioned below:

Transaction	Reason
Purchases of polyester Sarees	To be recorded in Purchases Book
Sales of polyester sarees	To be recorded in Sales Book
Cash sale of Kota sarees	To be recorded in Cash Book
Return of polyester sarees	To be recorded in Purchases Returns Book
Purchases of chairs	To be recorded in Cash Book
Returns of chairs to Kansal & Co.	To be recorded in Cash Book
Sale of old chairs	To be recorded in Cash Book
Return of old chair	To be recorded in Cash Book
Receipts of Cash from Goyal & Co.	To be recorded in Cash Book

RECTIFICATION ERRORS

PROBLEM 9

Pass the necessary journal entries to rectify the following errors:

(a) Goods (Cost ₹ 10,000, Sale Price ₹ 12,000) taken away by the proprietor were not recorded anywhere.

(b) Goods (Cost ₹ 20,000, Sale Price ₹ 24,000) distributed as free samples among prospective customers were not recorded anywhere.

(c) Goods (Cost ₹ 30,000, Sale Price ₹ 36,000) were returned by Ram, a customer and were taken into stock on the same date but no entry was passed in the books.

(d) Materials from store of ₹ 10,000 and Wages ₹ 4,000 had been used in making tools and implements for use in own factory, but no adjustments were made in the books.

(e) A credit purchase of old machinery from Sohan for ₹ 17,000 was entered in the Purchases Book as purchase from Mohan for ₹ 71,000. ₹ 3,000 paid as repairing charges on the reconditioning of a newly purchased second hand Machinery debited to General Expenses Account.

(f) A cheque for ₹ 12,800 received from Farid was dishonoured and has been posted to the debit of Sales Returns Account.

(g) An amount of ₹ 5,720 due from Lalta Prasad, written off as bad in a previous year, was recovered and credited to the personal account of Lalta Prasad.

(h) A discounted Bill of Exchange receivable for ₹ 16,000 returned by the firm's bank had been credited to the Bank Account and debited to Bills Receivable Account. A cheque was received later from the Customer for ₹ 16,000 and duly paid.

SOLUTION

JOURNAL

Date	Particulars		L.F.	Dr. (₹)	Cr. (₹)
(a)	Drawings A/c	Dr.		10,000	
	To Purchases A/c				10,000
	(Being goods taken away by the proprietor omitted to berecorded, now recorded)				
(b)	Free Samples A/c	Dr.		20,000	
	To Purchases A/c				20,000
	(Being goods distributed as free samples omitted to be recorded, now recorded)				
(c)	Sales Returns A/c	Dr.		36,000	
	To Ram's A/c				36,000
	(Being sales returns omitted to be recorded, now recorded)				
(d)	Tools & Implements A/c	Dr.		14,000	
	To Purchases A/c				10,000
	To Wages A/c				4,000
	(Being materials and wages used in making tools, omitted to be adjusted, now adjusted)				
(e)	Mohan	Dr.		71,000	
	Machinery A/c	Dr.		20,000	
	To Sohan				17,000
	To Purchases A/c				71,000
	To General Expenses A/c				3,000
	(Being purchase of old machinery recorded the Purchases Book and repairing charges debited to General ExpensesA/c, now rectified)				
(f)	Farid	Dr.		12,800	
	To Sales Returns A/c				12,800
	(Being dishonour of a cheque wrongly debited to Sales Returns A/c now rectified)				
(g)	Lalta Prasad	Dr.		5,720	
	To Bad Debts Recovered A/c				5,720
	(Being Bad Debts Recovered wrongly debited to Lalta Prasad now rectified)				

(h)	Customer To Bills Receivable A/c (Being dishonour of a B/R wrongly debited to Bills Receivable A/c now rectified)	Dr.		16,000	16,000

PROBLEM 10

Pass the necessary journal entries to rectify the following errors:

(a) A cash sale of Goods to X ₹17,000 posted as ₹ 71,000

(b) A credit sale of Goods to Y ₹17,000 posted as ₹ 71,000.

(c) A credit sale of Furniture to Z for ₹17,000 posted as ₹ 71,000.

(d) Bills Receivable from Henry of ₹ 16,000 posted to the credit of Bills Payable Account and also credited to Henry.

(e) Discounts received of ₹ 14,200 had been debited to discount allowed.

(f) A credit sale of Goods of ₹ 4,230 to Krishan passed through the Purchase Book as ₹ 4,320 and posted therefrom to the credit of Kishan as ₹ 4,230.

(g) Goods (Cost ₹ 4,230, Sale Price ₹ 4,320) taken by Ganesh, the proprietor for his personal use recorded in the Sales Book.

(h) An amount of ₹ 8,000 owing by a customer had been omitted from the list of Sundry Debtors.

(i) A credit sale of old furniture to Rohan for ₹ 17,000 omitted to be posted.

(j) Bills payable worth ₹ 3,000 accepted in favour of Murari, was passed through bills receivable book with ₹ 300 and Murari's account was debited with ₹ 3,000. Pass the Rectifying Entry.

SOLUTION

JOURNAL

Date	Particulars		L.F.	Dr. (₹)	Cr. (₹)
(a)	Sales A/c To Suspense A/c (Being posting to Sales A/c, now rectified)	Dr.		5,400	5,400
(b)	Suspense A/c To X (Being the posting to X's A/c, now rectified)	Dr.		5,400	5,400
(c)	Furniture A/c To Z (Being error in posting, now rectified)	Dr.		5,400	5,400
(d)	Bills Payable A/c Bills Receivable A/c To Suspense A/c (Being a B/R received from Henry wrongly posted to the credit of B/P, now rectified)	Dr. Dr.		16,000 16,000	32,000
(e)	Suspense A/c To Discount Allowed A/c To Discount Received A/c (Being Discount Received wrongly posted to Discount Allowed A/c, now rectified)	Dr.		28,400	14,200 14,200

(f)	Krishan Kishan Suspense A/c To Sales A/c To Purchases A/c (Being sale recorded as purchase with wrong amount and wrong posting therefrom, now rectified)	Dr. Dr. Dr.	4,230 4,230 90	 4,230 4,320
(g)	Sales A/c Drawings A/c To Ganesh A/c To Purchases A/c (Being the goods taken by proprietor for his personal use reco. in sales book, now rectified)	Dr. Dr.	4,320 4,230	 4,320 4,230
(h)	Sundry Debtors To Suspense A/c (Being a debtor omitted from the list now included) [**Note:** Debtor's A/c need not be posted again in the ledger in this case since it is already correctly balanced].	Dr.	8,000	 8,000
(i)	No Journal Entry is to be passed as it has already been correctly passed in the Journal. Merely posting in both the accounts in the ledger is required.			
(j)	Suspense A/c To B/R A/c To B/P A/c (Being B/P recorded in B/R Book but Murari's A/c correctly posted, now rectified)	Dr.	3,300	 300 3000

PROBLEM 11

The Trial Balance of Mr X failed to agree and the difference was put into Suspense Account pending investigation which discovered the following:

(a) Discount received ₹ 1,320 had been debited to Discount allowed as ₹ 132.

(b) Goods of the value of ₹ 200 returned by Kishan were entered in the Sales Day Book and posted therefrom to the credit of Krishan as ₹ 20.

(c) A credit purchase of ₹ 500 from N. Kumar was recorded as sale to M. Kumar for ₹ 50.

(d) A credit sale of machine to P. Dass for ₹ 600 recorded through Sales Day Book as sale to C. Dass for ₹ 60.

Required: Pass Rectifying Entries and prepare the Suspense Account.

SOLUTION

JOURNAL

Date	Particulars		L.F.	Dr. (₹)	Cr. (₹)
(a)	Suspense A/c	Dr.		1,452	
	To Discount Allowed A/c				132
	To Discount Received A/c				1,320
	(Being Discount Received wrongly posted to Discount Allowed A/c, now rectified)				
(b)	Krishan	Dr.		20	
	Sales A/c	Dr.		200	
	Sales Returns A/c	Dr.		200	
	To Kishan				200
	To Suspense A/c				220
	(Being sale returns recorded as sale with wrong amount and wrong posting therefrom, now rectified)				
(c)	Sales A/c	Dr.		50	
	Purchases A/c	Dr.		500	
	To N. Kumar				500
	To M. Kumar				50
	(Being the credit purchase recorded as sale, now rectified)				
(d)	P. Dass	Dr.		600	
	Sales A/c	Dr.		60	
	To Machine A/c				600
	To C. Dass				60
	(Being the credit sale of machine recorded as sale, now rectified)				

PROBLEM 12

Pass the necessary journal entries to rectify the following errors:

(a) A builder's bill for ₹ 4,600 for erection of a small shed was debited to repairs account.

(b) Repairs to plant amounting to ₹ 900 had been charged to Plant and Machinery Account.

(c) Wages paid to the firm's workmen for making certain additions to machinery amounting to ₹ 340 were debited to Wages account.

(d) A cheque for ₹ 750 received from S. Desai was credited to the account of R Ram.

(e) Goods to the value of ₹ 700 returned by X were included in the closing stock but no entry was made in the books.

(f) Goods costing ₹ 2,000 were purchased for various members of the staff and the cost was included in "Purchases". A similar amount was deducted from the salaries of the staff members concerned and the net payments to them debited to Salaries account.

(g) A bill of exchange (received from Hari) for ₹ 3,000 had been returned by the Bank, with whom it had been discounted, as dishonoured and had been credited to Bank Account and debited to Bills receivable Account.

(h) Goods sold to Z for ₹ 475 have been wrongly entered in the Sales Book as ₹ 745.

SOLUTION

JOURNAL

Date	Particulars		L.F.	Dr. (₹)	Cr. (₹)
(a)	Building A/c	Dr.		4,600	
	To Repairs A/c				4,600
	(Being the erection charges wrongly shown as revenue expenditure, now rectified by capitalising the same)				
(b)	Repairs A/c	Dr.		900	
	To Plant & Machinery A/c				900
	(Being the repairs wrongly capitalised instead of being treated as revenue expenditure, now rectified)				
(c)	Plant & Machinery A/c	Dr.		340	
	To Wages A/c				340
	(Being the wages for additions to Machinery wrongly treated as Revenue expenditure, now rectified by capitalising the same)				
(d)	R. Ram A/c	Dr.		750	
	To S. Desai A/c				750
	(Being the wrong posting of cheque received rectified)				
(e)	Returns Inward A/c	Dr.		700	
	To X A/c				700
	(Being the returns inward not recorded by mistake, now rectified)				
(f)	Salaries A/c	Dr.		2,000	
	To Purchases A/c				2,000
	(Being the goods purchased for staff members wrongly recorded as purchases, now rectified)				
(g)	Hari A/c	Dr.		3,000	
	To Bills Receivable A/c				3,000
	(Being the dishonour of discounted Bill recorded in the books as Bills Receivable by mistake, now rectified)				
(h)	Sales A/c	Dr.		270	
	To Z A/c				270
	(Being the excess recording of Sales in Sales Day Book rectified)				

PROBLEM 13

Pass the necessary journal entries to rectify the following errors:

1. Debtors also include Shyam for dishonoured bill of ₹ 10,000. Half the amount of Shyam's bills is irrecoverable.
2. Remuneration of ₹ 2,000 paid to Sh. B. Barua, a temporary employee, stands debited to his personal account.
3. On 31st March, Goods for ₹ 50,000 were sent to a customer on 'Sale or Return' basis at a profit of 25% on cost and recorded as actual sales.
4. Goods costing ₹ 20,000 (Sale Price ₹ 25,000) were taken by the proprietor for his personal use but not recorded .
5. Goods costing ₹ 30,000 (Sale Price ₹ 37,500) were distributed as free samples but not recorded.
6. On 31st March Goods costing ₹ 10,000 (Sale Price ₹ 12,500) were destroyed by fire it was fully insured but the insurance company admitted the claim to the extent of 60% only.
7. Wages include a sum of ₹ 4,000 spent on the erection of a cycle shed for employees and customers.
8. A Machine costing ₹ 45,000 was purchased during the year but it was not recorded in the books as no payment was made of it. Wages ₹ 5,000 paid for its Installation have been debited to Wages Account.

SOLUTION

JOURNAL

Date	Particulars		L.F.	Dr. (₹)	Cr. (₹)
1.	Bad Debts A/c	Dr.		5,000	
	To Debtors A/c				5,000
	(Being Bad Debts recorded)				
2.	Salaries A/c	Dr.		2,000	
	To Debtors A/c				2,000
	(Being remmuneration debited to personal account, now rectified)				
3(i)	Sales A/c	Dr.		50,000	
	To Debtors A/c				50,000
	(Being sale on approval reversed)				
3(ii)	Stock with Customer A/c	Dr.		40,000	
	To Trading A/c				40,000
	(Being the cost of goods sold on approval taken into stock)				
4.	Drawings A/c	Dr.		20,000	
	To Purchases A/c				20,000
	(Being goods taken away by the proprietor omitted to be recorded, now recorded)				
5.	Free Samples A/c	Dr.		30,000	
	To Purchases A/c				30,000
	(Being goods distributed as free samples omitted to be recorded, now recorded)				

6.	Loss of Stock by fire A/c Dr. Insurance co. Dr. To Purchases A/c (Being Loss of Stock and claim now recorded)		4,000 6,000	10,000
7.	Building A/c Dr. To Wages A/c (Being erection exp. debited to Wages A/c, now rectified)		4,000	4,000
8(i)	Machinery A/c Dr. To Supplier's A/c (Being purchase of old machinery recorded the Purchases Book and repairing charges debited to General ExpensesA/c, now rectified)		45,000	45,000
8(ii)	Machinery A/c Dr. To Wages A/c (Being Installation exp. debited to Wages A/c, now rectified)		5,000	5,000

PROBLEM 14

Pass the necessary journal entries for the following:

1. Included amongst the Debtors is ₹ 3,000 due from Z and included among the Creditors ₹ 1,000 due to him.
2. Furniture (book value ₹ 2,000) was old and the same was disposed off for ₹ 760 in exchange of new furniture costing ₹ 1,680. The net invoice of ₹ 920 was passed through Purchase Register. (No Depreciation need be charged on old and new furniture).
3. Printing and Stationery expenses of ₹ 55,000 relating to previous year had not been provided in that year but was paid in current year by debiting Outstanding Liabilities for Expenses

SOLUTION

JOURNAL

Date	Particulars	L.F.	Dr. (₹)	Cr. (₹)
1.	Creditors A/c Dr. To Debtors A/c (Being Mutual owings cancelled)		1,000	1,000
2.(a)	New Furniture A/c Dr. Profit & Loss A/c Dr To Old Furniture A/c (Being the exchange of Old Furniture for New one for ₹ 760 recorded)		760 1,240	2,000
2.(b)	New Furniture A/c Dr. To Purchases A/c (Being the Purchase of New Furniture recorded in Purchases Book,now rectified)		920	920

3	Outstanding Liabilities for Expenses A/c Dr. To Capital A/c (Being the previous year 's Expenses debited to , Capital A/c)		55,000	55,000

PROBLEM 15

X Ltd. writes off depreciation @ 10% per annum on the diminishing balance. It was discovered in the year 2014-2015 that:

1. Heavy repairs of ₹ 30,000 effected to Plant and Machinery (completed on September 30, 2012) were debited to the Machinery Account.
2. A machine costing ₹ 12,000 was entered in the Purchases Book on 1st January, 2013. The expenses on installation, ₹ 800, were debited to General Expenses Account.

Required: Pass the necessary journal entries to rectify the errors on 1st April, 2014

SOLUTION

JOURNAL

Date	Particulars	L.F.	Dr. (₹)	Cr. (₹)
1.	Profit & Loss A/c Dr. To Plant & Machinery A/c (Being the repairs wrongly capitalised instead of being treated as revenue expenditure, now rectified)		25,650	25,650
2.	Plant & Machinery A/c Dr. To Profit & Loss A/c (Being the purchase of new machine and installation expenses wrongly treated as revenue expenditure, now rectified)		11,232	11,232

Working Note: *Calculation of Book Value of Repairs and New Machine*

	Particulars	Repairs ₹	New Machine ₹
A	Cost on 1.12.2012/1.1.2013	30,000	12,800
B	*Less:* Depreciation for 2012-2013	1,500	320
C	Book value as on 1.4.2013	28,500	12,480
D	*Less:* Depreciation for 2013-2014	2,850	1,248
E	Book Value as on 1.4.2014	25,650	11,232

2 APPLICABILITY OF ACCOUNTING STANDARDS

THEORETICAL BASE

QUESTION 1: What is the meaning of "small and medium sized company" as per the companies Accounting Standards) Rules, 2006?

ANSWER: As per the companies (Accounting Standards) Rules, 2006 "Small and Medium Sized Company" (SMC) means, a company which satisfies all the following 5 conditions at the end of relevant accounting period.

1. Non-Listed	Whose equity or debt securities are not listed or are not in the process of listing on any stock exchange, whether in India or outside India.
2. Non-Banking etc.	Which is not a bank, financial institution or an insurance company;
3. Turnover up to 50 Crores	Whose turnover (excluding other income) does not exceed ₹ 50
4. Borrowings up to 10 crore	crores crore in the immediately preceding accounting year; Whose total borrowings (including public deposits) does not exceed₹ 10 crore at any time during the immediately preceding accounting year; and
5. Neither Holding nor Subsidiary	Which is not a holding or subsidiary company of a company which is not small and medium-sized company.

QUESTION 2: XYZ, with a turnover of ₹ 35 lakhs and borrowing of ₹ 10 lakhs during any time in the previous year, wants to avail the exemptions available in adoption of Accounting Standard applicable to companies for the year ended 31.3.2015. Advise the management the exemptions that are available as per Companies (AS) Rules, 2006.

ANSWER:

(a) XYZ, is a small and medium sized enterprise (SME) company as per Companies (AS) Rules, 2006. Since its turnover does not exceed ₹ 50 crores and its borrowings do not exceed ₹ 10 crores. It is assumed that its shares are not listed and it is neither Banking Co. nor a financial institution nor an insurance Co. nor a holding Co. nor a subsidiary Co. of a company which is not SMC.

(b) The following relaxations and exemptions are available.

1. As 3 "Cash Flow Statements" is not mandatory.
2. As 17 "Segment Reporting" is not mandatory.
3. SMEs are exempt for some paragraphs of AS 19 "Leases".
4. SMEs are exempt for disclosures of diluted EPS (both including and excluding extraordinary items).
5. SMEs are allowed to measure the 'value in use' on the basis of reasonable estimate thereof instead of computing the value in use by present value technique under AS 28 "impairment of Assets".
6. SMEs are exempt from disclosure requirements of paragraphs 66 and 67of AS 29 "Provisions , Contingent Liabilities and Contingent Assets".
7. SMEs are exempt from certain requirements of AS 15 "Employee Benefits".

8. Accounting Standards 21, 23, 27 are not applicable to SMEs.

If XYZ is not a company, it will be treated as a level III enterprise instead of level II enterprise; XYZ Ltd. will be exempt from requirements of AS 18 "Related Party Disclosures" and AS 24 "Discontinuing Operations".

QUESTION 3: Is XYZ Ltd, on Indian company (having Turnover & Borrowing each of ₹ 60 crores listed on NASDAQ only and having 51% Equity in S Ltd., an Indian Unlisted company with negligible Turnover and Borrowings required to prepare consolidated financial statements?

ANSWER: XYZ Ltd. is not required to prepare Consolidated Financial Statements even though it is non-SMC enterprise becouse SEBI requires only those Indian companies whose shares are listed on Indian Stock exchange, to prepare CFS.

QUESTION 4: X Ltd. an US company (having Turnover of 51 crores and Borrowings of ₹ 1 crore) is listed on NASDAQ only, has acquired 51% equity in S Ltd. an Indian unlisted company (having Turnover & Borrowings of ₹ 40 lakhs each). Is X Ltd. required to prepare Consolidated Financial Statement (CFS)? Is S Ltd. required to prepare Cash Flow Statement?

ANSWER:

(a) X Ltd is not required to prepare. CFS even though it is non SMC since its equity is not listed in India.

(b) S Ltd is not required to prepare Cash Flow Statement since it is a subsidiary of non-Indian holding company.

QUESTION 5: Y Ltd avail Sales Tax deferral benefit under which it is required to pay the Tax collected after 5 years to the Govt. Such Tax collected of ₹ 11 crores is shown as Unsecured Loan. Is Y Ltd a SMC or Non-SMC enterprise?

ANSWER: Y Ltd is a SMC since Tax deferral would not be considered as 'Borrowing' for the purposes of determine SMC or Non-SMC enterprise since the amount has not been actually borrowed.

QUESTION 6: Is Z Ltd. engaged only in insurance broking business a SMC on Non-SMC enterprise?

ANSWER: Z Ltd. is a SMC enterprise since Insurance broking business would not be considered as "Insurance Business' for the purpose of determining SMC or Non-SMC enterprise.

QUESTION 7: W Ltd., an unlisted and a Not-for-profit company registered u/s 25 of The Companies Act. provides micro finance to backward classes and its interest income is ₹ 40 crores. Is W Ltd. a SMC or non-SMC enterprise?

ANSWER: W Ltd. is a Non-SMC enterprise since it is engaged in commercial activities (i.e. providing loans & earning Interest therefrom). The objective of formation of enterprise is not relevant for the purpose of determining SMC or Non-SMC enterprises.

QUESTION 8: An organization whose objects are charitable or religious, holds that the Accounting Standards are not applicable to it since only a very small proportion of its activities are business in nature. Comment.

ANSWER: Accounting Standards apply in respect of any enterprise (whether organised in corporate, co-operative or other forms) engaged in commercial, industrial or business activities, whether or not profit oriented and even if established for charitable or religious purposes. Exclusion of an enterprise from the applicability of the Accounting Standards would be permissible only if no part of the activity of such enterprise is commercial, industrial or business in nature. Even if a very small proportion of the activities of an enterprise were considered to be commercial, industrial or business in nature, the Accounting Standards would apply to all its activities including those, which are not commercial, industrial or business in nature.

QUESTION 9: Comment whether the following Companies can be classified as a Small and Medium Sized Company (SMC) as per the Companies (Accounting standards) Rules, 2006:

(i) A Pvt. Ltd., a subsidiary of a multinational company listed on London Stock Exchange. It has a turnover of ₹.12 crores and borrowings of ₹ 5 crores.

(ii) B Pvt. Ltd. has a turnover of ₹ 45 crores, other income of ₹ 7 crores and bank borrowings of ₹ 9 crores.

(iii) C Ltd. Has appointed Merchant bankers to prepare a Red-herring prospectus for the purpose of filing the same with Securities and Exchange Board of India.

ANSWER:

(a) As per the Companies (Accounting Standards) Rules 2006, "Small and Medium Sized Company" (SMC) means, a company:

(i) Whose equity or debt securities are not listed or are not in the process of listing on any stock exchange, whether in India or outside India;

(ii) Which is not a bank, financial institution or an insurance company;

(iii) Whose turnover (excluding other income) does not exceed rupee; fifty crore in the immediately preceding accounting year,

(iv) Which does not have borrowings (including public deposits) in excess of rupees ten crore at any time during the immediately preceding accounting year; and

(v) which is not a holding or subsidiary company of a company which is not a small and medium-sized company.

Explanation: For the purposes of clause (f) , a company shall qualify as a Small and Medium Sized Company, if the conditions mentioned. therein are satisfied as at the end of the relevant accounting period.

(a) As per the definition of SMC, point (v), a company will be a SMC if it is not a holding or subsidiary company of another company which is not a SMC. Since A Pvt. Ltd. is a subsidiary of another Company which is listed, on London Stock Exchange (and is therefore not a SMC), A Pvt. Ltd. cannot be a SMC. The turnover and borrowings are not relevant in this case.

(b) As per the definition of SMC, point (iii), a company will be a SMC if its turnover does not exceed ₹ 50 corers or borrowings do not exceed ₹ 10 crore. For calculating this turnover, other income is not to be included. Since B Pvt. Ltd. has a turnover of ₹ 45 corers and borrowing; of ₹ 9 corers, it will satisfy the definition and can be classified as SMC.

(c) As per the definition of SMC, point (i) a company will be a SMC if it is not listed or in the process of listing. Since C Pvt. Ltd. has appointed merchant bankers to prepare a Red Herring Prospectus for the purpose of filling the same with SEBI, it is in the process of listing on a Stock Exchange. Hence C Ltd. cannot be classified as a SMC.

3 AS 1—DISCLOSURE OF ACCOUNTING POLICIES

THEORETICAL BASE

QUESTION 1: What is meant by Accounting Policies?

ANSWER: Accounting Policies refer to-

(i) Specific Accounting Principles. For example, valuations of inventories at lower of Cost or Net Realizable Value or Systematic allocation of cost of fixed assets in different accounting years.

(ii) Methods of applying those Principles. For example, using First In First Out Method (FIFO) or Weighted Average Method for valuation of inventories or using Straight Line or Written Down Value method for providing depreciation.

QUESTION 2: Mention six areas in which different accounting policies are followed by companies.

ANSWER:

1. Valuation of Fixed Assets
2. Valuation of Investments
3. Valuation of Inventories
4. Methods of Depreciation, Depletion and Amortization.
5. Treatment of Goodwill.
6. Treatment of Expenditure during construction

QUESTION 3: State the Three Considerations in Selection of Accounting Policies.

ANSWER:

1. Prudence [Ignore Anticipated Profits but Make Provision for Known Liabilities]
2. Substance Over Form
3. Materiality

QUESTION 4: State the Disclosures Requirements as to Accounting Policies.

ANSWER: All significant Accounting Policies should be disclosed normally at one place & should form part of Financial Statements.

QUESTION 5: When is the Change in Accounting Policy recommended?

A change in the Accounting Policy should be made only if adoption of different Accounting Policy is required

- by Statute, or
- For compliance with an Accounting Standard, or
- If it is considered that the change would result in more appropriate presentation of financial statements.

QUESTION 6: State the Disclosures Requirements as to Change in Accounting Policies.

ANSWER:

Case	What is to be disclosed ?
(a) ***When the change has material effect in current Period*** the	(i) The nature of change. (ii) Financial effect of change on items to period extent ascertainable. (iii) Where the amount is not ascertainable in wholly or part then indicate this fact.
(b) ***When the change hasmaterial effect in later period(s).***	(i) The nature of change. (ii) The fact that change in accounting policies has an effect in later period.

For example, if depreciation method is changed from straight-line method to written-down value method, or if cost formula used for inventory valuation is changed from weighted average to FIFO, or if interest is capitalized which was earlier not in practice, or if proportionate amount of interest is changed to inventory which was earlier not the practice, all these may increase or decrease the net profit. Unless the effect of such change in accounting policy is quantified, the financial statements may not help the users of accounts. Therefore, it is necessary to quantify the effect of change on financial statement items like assets, liabilities, profit/loss.

QUESTION 7: State the Three Fundamental Accounting Assumptions. Also State the Disclosures Requirements as to Fundamental Accounting Assumptions.

ANSWER: Accounting Standard (AS) 1 recognizes three fundamental accounting assumptions. These are as follows:

1. **Going Concern:** The financial statements are normally prepared on the assumption that an enterprise will continue its operations in the foreseeable future and neither there is intention, nor there is need to materially curtail the scale of operations.
2. **Consistency:** The principle of consistency refers to the practice of using same accounting policies for similar transactions in all accounting periods unless the change is required (i) by a statute, (ii) by an accounting standard or (iii) for more appropriate presentation of financial statements.
3. **Accrual basis of accounting:** Under this basis of accounting, transactions are recognised as soon as they occur, whether or not cash or cash equivalent is actually received or paid.

Disclosure Requirements

Case	What is to be disclosed ?
(a) If All FAA are followed.	No specific disclosure is required.
(b) If any of FAA is not followed.	The fact that accounting assumption is notfollowed must be disclosed.

QUESTION 8: What are Financial indicators to be considered for evaluating the assumption of Going Concern.

ANSWER:

1. Negative Net Worth or Negative Working without realistic prospects.
2. Fixed-term borrowings approaching maturity without realistic prospects.
3. Adverse key financial ratios.
4. Substantial Operating Losses.
5. Substantial Negative Cash Flows from Operations.
6. Arrears of Discontinuance of Dividends.
7. Inability to pay Creditors on due dates.

8. Difficulty in complying with the terms of Loan Agreements.
9. Change from credit to Cash-on-delivery transactions with suppliers.
10. Inability to obtain financing for essential new product development or other essential investments.
11. Entering into a scheme of arrangement with creditors for reduction of liability.

QUESTION 9: X Ltd. sold its building to Mini Ltd. for Rs 60 lakhs on 30.09-2014 and gave possession of the property to Mini Ltd. However, documentation and legal formalities are pending. Due to this,the company has not recorded the sale and has shown the amount received as an advance.The book value of the building is Rs 25 lakhs as on 31st March, 2015. Do you agree with this treatment? If you do not agree, explain the reasons with reference to the accounting standard.

ANSWER:

PROVISION OF AS 1

Principles of prudence, substance over form and materiality should be looked into, to ensure true and fair consideration in a transaction.

ADVICE

The economic reality and substance of the transaction is that the rights and beneficial interest in the property has been transferred although legal title has not been transferred. Hence, X Ltd. should record the sale and recognize the profit of Rs 35 lakhs in its financial statements for the year ended 31st March, 2015; value of building should be removed balance sheet. Therefore the treatment given by the company is not correct.

QUESTION 10: XYZ Company is engaged in the business of financial services and is undergoing tight liquidity position, since most of the assets of the company are blocked in various claims/ petitions in a Special Court. XYZ has accepted Inter-Corporate Deposits (ICDs) and, it making its best efforts of settle the dues. There were claims at varied rates of interest, from lenders, from the due date of ICDs to the date of repayment. The company has provided interest, as per the terms of the contract till the due date and a note for non-provision of interest on the due date to date of repayment was effected in the financial statements. On account of uncertainties existing regarding the determination of the amount and in the absence of any specific legal obligation at present as per the terms of contracts, the company considers that these claims are in the nature of "claims against the company not acknowledged as debt", and the same has been disclosed by way of a note in the accounts instead of making a provision in the Profit & Loss Account. State whether the treatment done by the company is correct or not.

ANSWER:

PROVISION OF AS 1

Pare 17 of AS-1 'Disclosure of Accounting Policies' recognises 'prudence' as one of the major consideration governing the selection and application of accounting policies. In view of the uncertainty attached to future events, profits are not anticipated but recognised only when realised through not necessarily in cash. Provision is made for all known liabilities and losses even through the amount cannot be determined with certainty and represents only a best estimated in the light of available information.

Also as per para 10 of the AS 1, 'accrual' is one of the fundamental accounting assumptions. Irrespective of the terms of the contract, so long as the principal amount of a loan is not repaid, the lender cannot be replaced in a disadvantageous position of non-payment of interest in respect of overdue amount.

ADVICE

It is apparent that the company has an obligation on account of the overdue interest. In this situation, the company should provide for the liability (since it is not waived by the lenders) at an amount estimated or on reasonable basis based on facts and circumstances of each case. However, in respect of the overdue interest amounts, which are settled, the liability should be accrued to the extend of amounts settled. Non-provision of the overdue interest liability amounts to violation of accrual basis of accounting. Therefore, the treatment, done by the company, of not providing the interest amount from due date to the date of repayment is not correct.

4 AS 2—VALUATION OF INVENTORIES

THEORETICAL BASE

QUESTION 1: State the areas to which AS 2 is not applicable.

ANSWER:

1. Work - in - progress arising under construction contracts, including directly related service contracts (see AS-7: Accounting for Construction Contracts);
2. Work - in - progress arising in ordinarily course of business of service providers;
3. Shares, debentures and other financial instruments held as stock - in - trade; and
4. Producers' inventories of live stock, agriculture and forest product and mineral oils, ores and gases to the extent that they are measured at Net Realizable Value in accordance with well-established practices in those industries.

QUESTION 2: State the Meaning of Inventory.

ANSWER: Inventories are assets that are -

(a) held for sale in ordinary business;e.g.Finished Goods

(b) in the process of production for such sale; e.g. WIP or

(c) in the form of materials or supplies to be consumed in the production process or in the rendering of services. e.g.Raw Materials

INVENTORY = FINISHED GOODS+ WIP+ RAW MATERIALS

Note: Machinery spares which are specific to a particular item of fixed asset should be capitalized in accordance with AS - 10 and should not be treated as inventories for the purpose of AS - 2.

QUESTION 3: What are the items that are to be included in determination of the cost of inventories as per AS-2?

ANSWER:

1. **Cost of Purchase.**

   [**INCLUDES** Purchase Price+ Duties & Taxes (which are NOT subsequently recoverable) + other expenditure directly attributable to acquisition (Like Freight Inward) **BUT EXCLUDES** Trade Discount, Rebates, Duty Drawbacks Subsidies and Taxes (which are subsequently recoverable)]

2. **Cost of Conversion.**

   [**INCLUDES** Direct Labour, Direct Expenses, Sub Contracted Work and Production Overheads absorbed on the basis of Normal Capacity]

3. **Other Costs** incurred in bringing the inventories to their present location and condition. e.g. costs incurred in designing products for specific customers

QUESTION 4: What are the items that are to be excluded in determination of the cost of inventories as per AS-2?

ANSWER: Items that are to be excluded in determination of the cost of inventories as per para 13 of AS 2 on 'Valuation of Inventories' are:

(1) Abnormal Amounts of wasted materials, labour or other production costs.
(2) Storage Costs unless those costs are necessary in the production process prior to a further production stage.
(3) Administrative Overheads that do not contribute to bringing the inventories to their present location and condition; and
(4) Selling and Distribution Costs.

Question 5: State the Techniques for Allocating Production Cost.

ANSWER:

1. Standard Costing
2. Retail Cost Method

Question 6: State the Cost Formulae to be used As per AS 2.

Item of Inventory	Cost Formulae to be used
1. For items that are not ordinarily interchangeable and goods or services produced and segregated for specific projects	Specific Identification of Cost Method
2. For Other Items	First-In-First-Out Method (FIFO) or Weighted Average Method

Question 7: State the Rule of Lower of Cost or Net Realizable Value.

ANSWER: The inventories should be valued at the lower of cost and net realizable value at each Balance Sheet date.

Note: *Net Realizable Value = Estimated Selling Price – Estimated Costs of Completion – Estimated Costs necessary to make the sale.*

Question 8: State the Two Methods of Comparision of Cost with NRV

ANSWER:

1. Item by item Method
2. Group Method

Note: *The Comparison of Cost with NRV ON Aggregate basis is not permissible.*

Question 9: How are Materials and Other Supplies valued as per AS 2?

ANSWER:

Case	Valuation of Materials
1. If Finished Product are expected to be sold at or above the cost	Materials and other supplies should be valued at cost even if there is decline in the price of materials.
2. If Finished Product are expected to be sold below cost	Materials and other supplies should be valued at NRV if there is decline in the price of materials. In such circumstances, the replacement cost of the materials may be the best available measure of their net realizable value.

Question 10: State the Disclosure Requirements as per AS 2.

ANSWER:

1. Accounting Policies

2. Cost Formula Used
3. Total Carrying Amount of Inventories

PRACTICAL QUESTIONS FOR PRACTICE

APPLICABILITY OF AS 2

QUESTION 1: Following persons valued the year end inventory on Net Realizable Value on the ground that AS-2 dose not apply to their inventory:

(a) A whole seller in agriculture and forest product
(b) A Dealer in Shares, Debentures and other Financial Instruments
(c) A whole seller in live stock
(d) A whole seller in mineral oils, ores and gases

Comment on the practice adopted.

ANSWER

Case	Practice	Reason
(a)	**Incorrect**	AS-2 does not apply to producers of agriculture and forest product but applies to traders in agriculture and forest product. Hence the inventory should be valued at lower of cost or Net Realizable Value.
(b)	**Correct**	AS-2 does not apply to Shares, Debentures and other Financial Instruments held as stock - in – trade. Hence the inventory can be valued at Net Realizable Value.
(c)	**Incorrect**	AS-2 does not apply to producers of live stock but applies to traders in live stock. Hence the inventory should be valued at lower of cost or Net Realizable Value.
(d)	**Incorrect**	AS-2 does not apply to producers of mineral oils, ores and gases but applies to traders in mineral oils, ores and gases. Hence the inventory should be valued at lower of cost or Net Realizable Value.

QUESTION 2: BHARAT LTD. manufacturing cars has installed several machines, valued the year end inventory of all Machinery spares(of which some are specific to a particular Machine and some are common to all Machines) on Net Realizable Value on the ground that AS-2 dose not apply to their inventory. Comment on the practice adopted.

ANSWER

1. Machinery spares which are specific to a particular item of fixed asset should be capitalized in accordance with AS - 10 and should not be treated as inventories for the purpose of AS - 2.Hence the practice adopted is incorrect.
2. Machinery spares which are not specific to a particular item of fixed asset should be treated as inventories for the purpose of AS – 2 and the inventory should be valued at lower of cost or Net Realizable Value Hence the practice adopted is incorrect.

QUESTION 3: Night Ltd. sells beer to customers; some of the customers consume the beer in the bars run by Night Limited. While leaving the bars, the consumers leave the empty bottles in the bars and the company takes possession of these empty bottles. The company has laid down a detailed internal record procedure for accounting for these empty bottles which are sold by the company by calling for tenders. Keeping this in view.

(i) Decide whether the stock of empty bottles is an asset of the company;

(ii) If so, whether the stock of empty bottles existing as on the date of Balance Sheet is to be considered as inventories of the company and valued as per AS-2 or to be treated as scrap and show at realizable value with corresponding credit to 'Other Income"?

ANSWER:

(i) Tangible objects or intangible right carrying probable future benefits, owned by an enterprise are called assets. Night Ltd. sells these empty bottles by calling tenders. It means further benefits are accrued on its sale. Therefore, empty bottles are assets for the company.

(ii) As per AS 2 "Valuation of Inventories", inventories are assets held for sale in the ordinary course of business. Stock of empty bottles existing on the Balance Sheet date is the inventory and Night Ltd. has detailed controlled recording and accounting procedure which duly signify its materiality. Hence stock of empty bottles cannot be considered as scrap and should be valued as inventory in accordance with AS 2.

CALCULATION OF COST OF CLOSING STOCK WHEN THERE IS NO NORMAL/ABNORMAL LOSS

QUESTION 4:

Particulars		*Kg.*	*₹*
Opening Stock	**Finished goods**	**1,000**	**25,000**
	Raw materials	**1,100**	**11,000**
Purchases		**10,000**	**1,00,000**
Labour			**76,500**
Overheads (Fixed)			**75,000**
Sales		**10,000**	**2,80,000**
Closing Stock	**Raw Materials**	**900**	
	Finished goods	**1,200**	

The expected production for the year was15,000 kg. of the finished good product. Due to fall in market demand the sales price for the finished goods was ₹ 20 per kg. and the replacement cost for the raw material was ₹ 9.50 Kg. on the closing day.

Required: Calculate the Value of the Closing Stock

ANSWER:

CALCULATION OF COST PER UNIT

Particulars	*Amount (₹)*	*Quantity (units)*	*Per unit cost*
Purchases	1,00,000	10,000	10.00
Add: Opening Stock	11,000	1,100	10.00
Less: Closing stock of materials	9000	900	10.00
Cost of Purchases	1,02,000	10,200	10.00
Add: Direct labour	76,500		7.50
Add: Production Overhead (Fixed)	75,000		5.00
			(75,000/15,000)
Total Cost per unit			22.50

Hence closing stock should be valued at NRV (i.e. ₹ 20 per unit), since it is less than cost (i.e ₹. 22.50 per unit).

CALCULATION OF COST OF STOCK WHEN THERE IS NORMA AND ABNORMAL LOSS

QUESTION 5: In a production process, normal waste is 5% of input. 5,000 MT of input were put in process resulting in a wastage of 300 MT. Cost per MT of input is ₹ 1,900. The entire quantity of waste is on stock at the year end. State with reference to Accounting standard the treatment of normal loss and abnormal loss and also find out the amount of abnormal loss, if any and the value of closing inventories.

ANSWER:

1. Normal Loss Qty = 5% of 5,000 MT = 250 MT

   Treatment: No entry is passed for normal loss. However, normal loss increases the cost per good unit

2. Cost of Good units = Total Cost/(Total Qty – Normal Loss Qty) = (5000 × ₹1,900)/(5000 – 250) = ₹ 2,000

3. Abnormal Loss Qty = Total Loss – Normal Loss = 300 MT – 5% of 5,000 MT = 50 MT

   Cost of Abnormal Loss = 50MT × ₹ 2,000= ₹ 1,00,000

   Treatment: As per AS 2, abnormal amounts of waste materials, labour and other production costs are excluded from cost of inventories and such costs are recognized as expenses in the period in which they are incurred.. Hence, the Cost of Abnormal Loss of ₹ 1,00,000 should be charged to Profit & Loss A/c.

4. Closing Inventory Qty = 5,000 MT – 250 MT – 50 MT = 4,700 MT

   Cost of Closing Inventory =4,700 MT × ₹ 2,000= ₹ 94,00,000

QUESTION 6: Tulsian Limited took Bank Overdraft at an interest rate of 15% p.a. specifically for the purpose of purchasing 10,000 kg. of certain material at ₹ 100 per kg. The purchase price includes excise duty ₹ 10 per kg., in respect of which full CENVAT credit is admissible. Freight, loading and unloading charges incurred amounted to ₹ 40,800. Interest on such Bank Overdraft amounted to ₹ 25,000. Normal Transit Loss is 2%. The enterprise actually received 9,760 kg. and consumed 9,500 kg. Determine cost of inventory and allocation of material cost as per AS 2 "Valuation of Inventory".

ANSWER:

DETERMINATION OF NORMAL COST PER KG

Particulars	*Amount (₹)*
Purchase price (10,000 kg. × ₹ 100)	10,00,000
Less: CENVAT credit (10,000 kg. × 10)	(1,00,000)
Add: Freight, loading and unloading charges	40,800
Total Material Cost	9,40,800
Number of units after normal loss (i.e. 98% of 10,000 kg.)	9,800
Norma Cost per kg.	₹ 96

Note: Interest and other borrowing costs are usually considered as overheads that don't contribute to bringing the inventories to their present location and condition.Hence, Interest on bank overdraft will not form part of cost of production.

ALLOCATION OF MATERIAL COST

	Kg.	₹/Kg.	Amount (₹)
Material consumed	9,500	63	9,12,000
Closing inventory (9,760 – 9,500)	260	96	24,960
Abnormal Loss (9,800 – 9,760)	40	96	3,840
Total material cost	9,800	96	9,40,800

VALUATION OF CLOSING STOCK AS PER RETAIL METHOD

QUESTION 7: The retailer has large numbers of rapidly changing inventory items that have similar margins and for which it is impracticable to use other costing methods. He furnishes the following details:

Particulars	*Items*	*Cost*	*Retail Price*
Opening stock	10,000 units	50 per unit	80 per unit
Purchases	1,00,000 units	60 per unit	100 per unit
Sales ₹ 86,40,000			

Calculate the value of closing stock as per retail method.

ANSWER:

VALUATION OF CLOSING STOCK AS PER RETAIL METHOD

Particulars	*Cost*	*Retail Price*
A Opening stock	5,00,000	8,00,000
B Purchases	60,00,000	1,00,00,000
C Total [A + B]	65,00,000	1,08,00,000
D Sales		86,40,000
E Closing Stock at Retail Price		21,60,000
F Closing Stock at Cost [E × 65 / 108]	13,00,000	

COST FORMULAE: FIFO AND WEIGHTED AVERAGE METHOD

QUESTION 8: From the following data, find out value of inventory as on 30th April using (a) LIFO method, and (b) Weighted Average Method:

1. 1st April Purchased	10 units @₹.70 per unit
2. 6th April Sold	5 units @ ₹.90 per unit
3. 9th April Purchased	20 units @ ₹.75 per unit
4. 18th April Sold	14 units @₹.100 per unit

ANSWER:

(A) VALUATION OF CLOSING INVENTORY BY LIFO METHOD

Date	*Receipts*			*Issue*			*Balance*		
	Unit	*Cost/unit*	*Amount*	*Unit*	*Cost/unit*	*Amount*	*Unit*	*Cost/unit*	*Amount*
Apr. 1	10	70	700				10	70	700
Apr. 6				5	70	350	5	70	350
Apr. 9	20	75	1500				5	70	350
							20	75	1500
Apr. 18				14	75	1,050	5	70	350
							6	75	450

Value of Closing Inventory as per LIFO Method =(4 units × ₹ 70)+(6 units × ₹ 75)= ₹ 730

(B) VALUATION OF CLOSING INVENTORY BY WEIGHTED AVERAGE METHOD

Date	*Receipts*			*Issue*			*Balance*		
	Unit	*Cost/unit*	*Amount*	*Unit*	*Cost/unit*	*Amount*	*Unit*	*Cost/unit*	*Amount*
Apr. 1	10	70	700				10	70	700
Apr. 6				5	70	350	5	70	350
Apr. 9	20	75	1500				25	74	1850
Apr. 18				14	74	1,036	11	74	814

Value of Closing Inventory as per WEIGHTED AVERAGE Method: = ₹ 814

QUESTION 9: HP is a leading distributor of petrol. A detail inventory of petrol in hand is taken when the books are closed at the end of each month. At the end of month following information is available:

Sales:	₹ 47,25,000
General overheads cost	₹ 1,25,000
Inventory at beginning	1,00,000 litres @ ₹ 15 per litre

Purchases:

June 1 two lakh litres @ ₹ 14.25

June 30 one lakh litres @ ₹ 15.15

Closing inventory 1.30 lakh litres

Compute the following by the FIFO as per AS 2:

(i) Value of Inventory on June, 30.

(ii) Amount of cost of goods sold for June.

(iii) Profit/Loss for the month of June.

ANSWER:

(i) Cost of closing inventory for 1,30,000 litres as on 30th June

	₹
1,00,000 litres @ ₹ 15.15	15,15,000
30,000 litres @ ₹ 14.25	4,27,500
Total	19,42,500

(ii) Calculation of Cost of Goods Sold

	₹
Opening inventories (1,00,000 litres @ ₹ 15)	15,00,000
Purchases: June-1 (2,00,000 litres @ ₹ 14.25)	28,50,000

	June-30 (1,00,000 litres @ ₹ 15.15)	15,15,000
		58,65,000
Less:	Closing inventories	19,42,500
Cost of goods sold		39,22,000

(iii) Profit = ₹ 47,25,000 – (₹ 39,22,500 + ₹ 1,25,000) = ₹ 6,77,500

LOWER OF COST OR NRV RULE

QUESTION 10:

Unsold units with Agent	**1,000**
Cost per unit	**₹ 10**
Estimated Selling Price per unit as at Balance Sheet Date	**₹ 8**
Agent's Commission on Sales	**5 %**

What should be the Value of Closing Stock?

ANSWER:

I. Cost of Closing Stock (1,000 × ₹ 10)	₹ 10,000
II. Net Realizable Value	
A. Total Realizable Value (1,000 × ₹ 8)	₹ 8,000
B. *Less:* Realizable Expenses (here agent's commission is realizable expense) (₹ 8,000 × 5/100)	₹ 400
C. Net Realizable Value (A – B)	₹ 7,600
III. Valuation since out of cost (which is ₹ 10,000 as calculated above) and NRV (which is ₹ 7,600), NRV is lower, the said unsold stock should be valued at ₹ 7,600.	

QUESTION 11: On 31st March 2015 a business firm finds that cost of a partly finished unit on that date is ₹ 530. The unit can be finished in 2015-2016 by an additional expenditure of ₹ 310. The finished unit can be sold for ₹ 750 subject to payment of 4% brokerage on selling price. The firm seeks your advice regarding:

(i) the amount at which the unfinished unit should be valued as at 31st Mach, 2015 for preparation of final accounts and

(ii) the desirabilty or otherwise of producing the finished unit.

ANSWER:

VALUATION OF UNFINISHED UNIT

Particulars	₹
Net selling price	750
Less: Estimated cost of completion	(310)
	440
Less: Brokerage (4% of 750)	30
Net Realisable Value	410
Cost of inventory	530
Value of inventory (Lower of cost and net realisable value)	410

Incremental cost ₹ 310 (cost to complete) is less than incremental revenue ₹ 720 (₹ 750 – ₹ 30). The enterprise will therefore decide to finish the unit for sale at ₹ 750.

Note: The above answer is given on the assumption that partly finished unit cannot be sold in semi finished form and its NRV is zero without processing it further.

QUESTION 12: X Ltd. has 5,000 AC in stock on 31st March, 2010. The cost of each AC amount to ₹ 10,000. There is firm commitment of sale of 1,000 AC by the company in April, 2010 @ ₹ 15,000 per AC. However, the general price of this AC at year end amounts to ₹ 9,500 per AC. Calculate the Value of Stock.

ANSWER:

CALCULATION OF VALUE OF STOCK

	Particulars	*RS.*
A	Value of 1,000 AC covered under firm commitment at Cost	1,00,00,000
B	Value of 4,000 AC not covered under firm commitment at NRV since it is less than cost	3,80,00,000
C	Total Value of Stock [A + B]	4,80,00,000

QUESTION 13: As a Company Auditor how would you react of the following situations?

Inventories of a Car manufacturing company include the value of items, required for the manufacture of a model which was removed from the production line five years back, at cost price.

ANSWER:

PROVISION OF AS-2

As per AS-2 on "Valuation of Inventories" the cost of inventories may not be recoverable if those inventories are damaged, or have become wholly or partially obsolete, or if their selling prices have declined. Accordingly, the auditor should examine whether appropriate allowance has been made for the defective, damaged, obsolete and slow-moving inventories in determining the Net Realizable Value.

ADVICE

Items required for the manufacture of a model which has been withdrawn from the production line five years ago are included in the stock at cost price resulting in overstatement of inventory and profit.

It becomes necessary to write down the obsolete. Inventory to 'Net Realizable Value' if the cost is not recoverable. Under the circumstance, the auditor should qualify the Audit Report appropriately.

TWO METHODS OF COMPARISION OF COST WITH NRV

QUESTION 14: From the following data, calculate the value of stock, to be shown

(i) by the item-by-item method

(ii) by the group method.

Article	Group	No. of units	Cost (₹) per unit	Realizable value (₹) per unit.	Realization Expenses
1	A	100	100	120	8-1/3 %
2	B	200	200	200	10 %
3	C	300	150	156	8-1/3 %
4	D	400	250	290	10 %

ANSWER:

VALUATION OF STOCK ACCORDING TO ITEM BY ITEM METHOD

Article	*Cost (₹)*	*NRV (₹)*	*Lower of cost/ NRV ₹*
1	10,000	11,000	10,000
2	40,000	36,000	36,000
3	45,000	42,900	42,900
4	1,00,000	1,04,400	1,00,000
			1,88,900

VALUATION OF STOCK ACCORDING TO GROUP METHOD

GROUP 'A'

Article	*Cost (₹)*	*NRV (₹)*	*Lower of cost/ NRV ₹*
1	10,000	11,000	
3	45,000	42,900	
	55,000	53,900	53,900

GROUP 'B'

Article	*Cost (₹)*	*NRV (₹)*	*Lower of cost/ NRV ₹*
2	40,000	36,000	
4	1,00,000	1,04,400	
	1,40,000	1,40,400	1, 40,000

Value of Closing Stock = ₹ 53,900 + ₹ 1, 40, 000 = ₹ 1,93,900

QUESTION 15: Best Ltd. deals in five products, P, Q, R, S, and T which are neither similar nor interchangeable. At the time of closing of its accounts for the year ending 31st March 2013, the historical cost and net realizable value of the items of the dosing stock are determined as follows:

Items	*Historical Cost ₹*	*Net Realizable Value ₹*
P	5,70,000	4,75,000
Q	9,80,000	10,32,000
R	3,16,000	2,89,000
S	4,25,000	4,25,000
T	1,60,000	2,15,000

What will be the value of closing stock as at 31st March 2013 as per AS 2 "Valuation of Inventories"?

ANSWER: As per para 5 of AS 2 "Valuation of Inventories, inventories should be valued at the lower of cost and net relizable value. Inventories should be written down to net realizable value on an item-by-item basis.

VALUATION OF INVENTORY (ITEM WISE) AS AT 31ST MARCH 2013

Item	*Historical Cost ₹*	*Net realizable value ₹*	*Valuation of closing stock ₹*
P	5,70,000	4,75,000	4,75,000

Q	9,80,000	10,32,000	9,80,000
R	3,16,000	2,89,000	2,89,000
S	4,25,000	4,25,000	4,25,000
T	1,60,000	2,15,000	1,60,000
			23,29,000

The value of inventory as at 31st March 2013 = ₹ 23,29,000.

VALUATION OF MATERIALS AND OTHER SUPPLIES

QUESTION 16: Tulsian Ltd. which manufactures three products namely 'OM', 'NAMO' and 'SHIVAY' using raw materials M1. M2 and M3 respectively provides you the following information about the Closing Stock:

Items	***Historical Cost (₹ in Lakhs)***	***Net Realizable Value (₹ in Lakhs)***	***Replacement Value (₹ in Lakhs)***
OM	10	11	12
NAMO	20	18	19
SHIVAY	30	27	28
M1	5		3
M2	6		5
M3	7		8

Required: Calculate the value of Closing Stock.

ANSWER:

Items	***Historical Cost (₹ in Lakhs)***	***Net Realizable Value (₹ in Lakhs)***	***Valuation of Stock (₹ in Lakhs)***
OM	10	11	10
NAMO	20	18	18
SHIVAY	30	27	27
M1	5	3 (Replacement Cost)	5 (Since Finished Product is expected to be sold at above cost)
M2	6	5 (Replacement Cost)	5 (Since Finished Product is expected to be sold below cost)
M3	7	8 (Replacement Cost)	7
		Total	72

QUESTION 17: U.S.A Ltd. purchased raw material @ ₹ 400 per kg. Company does not sell raw material but uses in production of finished goods. The finished goods in which raw material is used are expected to sold at below cost. At the end of the accounting year, company is having 10,000 kg of raw material in stock. As the company never sells the raw material, it does not know the selling price of raw material and hence can not calculate the realizable value of the raw material for valuation of inventories at the end of the year. However replacement cost of raw material is ₹ 300 per kg. How will you value as inventory of raw material?

ANSWER:

PROVISION OF AS 2

As per Para 24 of AS 2 (Revised) " Valuation of Inventories", materials and other supplies held for use in the production of inventories are not written down below cost if the finished products in which they will be incorporated are expected to be sold at or above cost. However, when there has been a decline in the price of materials and it is estimated that the cost of the finished products will exceed net realizable value, the materials are written down to net realizable value. In such circumstances, the replacement cost of the materials may be the best available measure of their net realizable value.

ADVICE

USA Ltd. should value the stock of raw material at ₹ 30,00,000 (i.e. 10,000 Kg @₹ 300 per kg.).

QUESTION 18: Raw materials inventory of a company includes certain material purchased at ₹100 per kg The price of the material is on decline and replacement cost of the inventory at the year end is ₹ 75 per kg. It is possible to convert the material into finished product at conversion cost of ₹ 125.

Decide whether to make the product or not to make the product if selling price is (i) ₹ 175 and (ii) ₹ 225. Also find out the value of inventory in each case.

ANSWER: As per para 24 of AS 2 'Valuation of Inventories', materials and other supplies held for use in the production of inventories are not written down below cost if the finished products in which they will be incorporated are expected to be sold at or above cost. However, when there has been a decline in the price of materials and it is estimated that the cost of the finished products will exceed net realizable value, the materials are written down to net realisable value. In such circumstances, the replacement cost of the materials may be the best available measure of their net realisable value.

(i) When selling price is ₹ 175

Incremental Profit = ₹ 175 – ₹ 125 = ₹ 50

Current price of the material = ₹ 75

Therefore, it is better not to make the product. Raw material inventory would be valued at net realisable value i.e. ₹ 75 because the selling price of the finished product is less than ₹225 (100 + 125) per kg.

(ii) When selling price is ₹ 225

Incremental Profit = ₹ 225 – ₹ 125 = ₹ 100

Current price of the raw material = ₹ 75.

Therefore, it is better to make the product.

Raw material inventory would be valued at ₹ 100 per kg because the selling price of the finished product is not less than ₹ 225.

QUESTION 19: Calculate the value of raw materials and closing stock based on the following information:

Raw material X	
Closing Balance	500 units
	₹ per unit
Cost price including excise duty	200
Exercise duty (Cenvat credit is receivalbe on the excise duty paid)	10
Freight inward	20
Unloading charges	10
Replacement cost	150

Finished good Y	
Closing Balance	1200 units
	₹ per unit
Material consumed	220
Direct labour	60
Direct overhead	40

Total Fixed overhead for the year was ₹ 2,00,000 on normal capacity of 20,000 units.

Calculate the value of the closing stock, when

(i) Net Realizable Value of the Finished Goods Y is ₹ 400.

(ii) Net Realizable Value of the Finished Goods Y is ₹ 300.

ANSWER:

Situation (i)

When Net Realisable Value of the Finished Goods Y is ₹ 300

NRV is greater than the cost of Finished Goods Y i.e. ₹ 330

Hence, Raw Material and Finished Goods are to be valued at cost

VALUE OF CLOSING STOCK

	Qty	*Rate*	*Amount (₹)*
Raw Material X	500	220	1,10,000
Finished Goods Y	1,200	330	3,96,000
Total Cost of Closing Stock			5,06,000

Situation (ii)

When Net Realisable Value of the Finsihed Goods Y is ₹ 300

NRV is less than the cost of Finished Goods Y i.e. ₹ 330

Hence, Raw Material is to be valued at replacement cost and

Finished Goods are to be valued at NRV since NRV is less than the cost

VALUE OF CLOSING STOCK

	Qty	Rate	₹
Raw Material X	500	150	75,000
Finished Goods Y	1,200	330	3,60,000
Total Cost of Closing Stock			4,35,000

Note: It has been considered that Raw Material X is used for the production of Finished Goods Y.

WORKING NOTES:

Raw Materials X	₹
Cost Price	200
Less: Cenvat Credit	(10)
Add: Freight Inward	20
Unloading charges	10
Cost	220

Finished goods Y	*1*
Materials consumed	220
Direct Labour	60
Direct overhead	40
Fixed overhead (₹ 2,00,000/20,000 units)	10
Cost	330

MISCELLANEOUS

QUESTION 20: A private limited company manufacturing fancy terry towels had valued its closing stock of inventories of finished goods at the realizable value, inclusive of profit and the export cash incentives. Firm contracts had been received and goods were packed for export, but the ownership in these goods had not been transferred to the foreign buyers.

Comment on the valuation of the stocks by the company.

ANSWER:

PROVISION OF AS-2 AND AS 9

Revenue cannot be recognized on the goods since sale is not complete m accordance with AS-9. Such goods should be valued at Cost or Net Realizable Value which ever is lower as per AS 2.

ADVICE

The closing stock of the finished goods (fancy terry towel) should be valued at lower of cost, and Net Realizable Value and not at Net Realizable value, Further, export incentives are recorded only in the year the export sale takes place. Therefore, the policy adopted by the company for valuing its closing stock of inventory of finished goods is not correct as per AS 9 since the ownership has not been transferred.

QUESTION 21: Vintage Ltd. has been in the business of sale of Vintage Wines for the last 12 years and is an extremely cash rich company. In FY 2014-2015 the Board of the company decided to venture into new areas of business and identified the activity of acquiring Vintage Properties such as old Bungalows, Heritage buildings and the like at prime locations and after carrying out renovation and refurbishment of the same to let out these properties on lease to willing parties. The new business was commenced as a separate division of the company in FY 2014-2015 during which the company managed to identify 19 such properties of which 17 were acquired and 9 given on lease. Being the initial year of operations and also since some of the lease arrangements were entered into at the fag end of the year the income from leasing was only a paltry amount. After the acquisition of the properties as aforesaid very attractive offers for sale of 14 of the properties were received. Vintage Ltd. after negotiation accepted 12 of the offers and sold these 12 properties making large profits in the bargain. The accountant of Vintage Ltd. hasc accounted the acquisition and disposals of properties as ₹Purchases' and ₹Sales' in the Profit & Loss account of the Property Division and treated the lease incomes as part of the other income of the company. The contention of the accountant of Vintage Ltd., was that since a majority of the properties were disposed off within a short span of time, the properties are to be considered as stock in trade only. Further since the lease income was insignificant it does not become the main source of income and hence considered as part of other income. You are required to examine the correctness of the contentions of the accountant of Vintage Ltd. considering the relevant Accounting Standards and provisions of Schedule III of Companies Act, 2013.

ANSWER:

PROVISION OF AS 2

As per para 3 of AS 2 "Valuation of Inventories", inventories are assets that are (a) held for sale in the ordinary course of business; (b) in the process of production for such sale; or (c) in the form of materials or supplies to be consumed in the production process or in the rendering of services. The properties acquired by Vintage Ltd. Should not be construed as stock in trade in spite of the fact that they are being sold within a short span of time.

ADVICE

As per AS 10, a fixed asset is one which is held with the intention of being used for the purpose of producing goods or services and is not held for sale in the normal course of business. The acquisition of the heritage properties is done by the company with the intention to provide the service of leasing of such properties. Hence the intention of the company was to use such property for generating revenue for the company by leasing out such properties. The sale of 12 properties can't be considered as part of normal business operations of the company. Hence the treatment of the properties as 'Stock-in-Trade' is incorrect as the properties are to be considered only as Fixed Assets of the company. The purchase and sale in short span of time to make huge profit will require disclosure as per AS 5 'Net Profit or Loss for the Period, Prior Period Items and Changes in Accounting Policies'. The lease income from these properties will be considered as main business income and cannot be considered as part of other income. Such income will be disclosed under the head Revenue from operations.

Thus the contentions of the accountant regarding accounting the acquisition and sale of these properties as sale and purchase, treating them as stock in trade, considering lease income as other income are incorrect in line with provisions of relevant accounting standards.

QUESTION 22: T. Ltd. Commenced its manufacturing activities from 1st April, 2014. In the course of production the company generated certain by-products. As at 31st March 2015 the company did not value the by-products considering the value as insignificant. The auditor of the company is of the opinion that the by-products are inventory of the company and it should be valued and brought into books of account. Comment.

ANSWER:

PROVISION OF AS 2

As per AS-2 on "Valuation of Inventories", a production process may result in more than one product being produced simultaneously. This is the case when joint products are produced or when there is a main product & by-products. If the costs of conversion of each product are not separable, they are allocated on a rational & consistent basis.Most of the by-products as well as scrap or waste materials, by their nature, are immaterial. They are often measured at net realizable value & this value is deducted from the cost of the main product. In the given case, as the value of the by-products is insignificant, the realizable value of by products should be ascertained and it should be deducted from the cost of the main product. An asset is a resource controlled by an enterprise as a result of past events from which the future economic benefits are expected. As per AS 2- Inventories are assets (a) held for sale in the ordinary course of business (b) in the process of production for such sale (c) in the form of materials or supplies to be consumed in the production process or in the rendering of services.

ADVICE

As the stock of by-product is a resource controlled by T Ltd., it is an asset and it is inventory because it is held for sale in the ordinary course of business. T Ltd. should deduct the realizable value of its by products from the cost of production of main product.

5 AS 4—CONTINGENCIES AND EVENTS OCCURING AFTER THE BALANCE SHEET DATE

THEORETICAL BASE

QUESTION 1: What is meant by Events occurring after the balance sheet date?

ANSWER: Events occurring after the balance sheet date are those significant events, both favourable and unfavourable, that occur between the balance sheet date and the date on which the financial statements are approved by the Board of Directors in the case of a company, and, by the corresponding approving authority in the case of any other entity.

QUESTION 2: State the Accounting Treatment of Events occurring after the Balance Sheet Date.

ANSWER:

Nature of Events occurring after the Balance Sheet Date	Accounting Treatment
1. Events that provide additional evidence to assist the estimation of amounts relating to conditions existing at the balance sheet date.	Assets and Liabilities should be adjusted.
2. Events that indicate that the fundamental accounting assumption of going concern (i.e., the continuance of existence or substratum of the enterprise) is not appropriate.	Assets and Liabilities should be adjusted.
3. Dividend proposed or declared by the enterprise after the Balance Sheet Date	Dividend should be adjusted.
4. Other events occurring after the Balance Sheet Date that represent material changes and commitments affecting the financial position of the enterprise.	Disclosure should be made in the report of Approving Authority.

QUESTION 3: State the Disclosure Requirements as to Events occurring after the Balance Sheet Date.

ANSWER:

1. Nature of the Event
2. An Estimate of the financial effect, or a statement that such an estimate cannot be made.

PRACTICAL QUESTIONS FOR PRACTICE

QUESTION 1: Which of the following events should be taken into account while finalizing (on 30th September, 2015) the annual accounts for the year ending March 31, 2015

(a) The wages of the employees are revised retrospectively from January 1, 2015 vide agreement with the trade union signed on August 1, 2015.

(b) In the Finance Act passed in May 2015, the surcharge on income tax applicable for the assessment year 2015–2016 is increased by 5%.

(c) A debtor against whom insolvency proceedings were instituted prior to March 31, 2015 is declared insolvent on July 21, 2015.

(d) A theft of cash of ₹ 1 crore by the Cashier in Jan. 2015 was detected on 17th May 2015.

(e) A major production plant destroyed by fire on August 28, 2015.

(f) The factory of the entrepreneur is permanently sealed under Supreme Court order since it was polluting industry on September 20, 2015.

(g) The board of directors at their meeting on September 30, 2015 have recommended a dividend of 20% to be paid to shareholders after it is approved at the annual general meeting.

(h) A major debtor died along with his family in Gujarat earthquake on May 13,2015.

(i) A fire occurred in the godown on April 1, 2015, damaging a huge quantity of stocks.

(j) During Aug. 2015 it was estimated that the total cost of project shall be inflated by ₹ 50 crores which would not be recoverable from contractee.

(k) One of the several factories destroyed by fire on July 28, 2015.

ANSWER:

ACCOUNTING TREATMENT OF VARIOUS EVENTS

Event	Accounting Treatment
(a)	Liability on account of arrears of wages for 3 months from January 1, 2015 should be provided. **Reason:** As per AS 4 Assets and liabilities should be adjusted for events occurring after the balance sheet date that provide additional evidence to assist the estimation of amounts relating to conditions existing at the balance sheet date.
(b)	Liability on account of increase in surcharge should be provided. **Reason:** As per AS 4 Assets and liabilities should be adjusted for events occurring after the balance sheet date that provide additional evidence to assist the estimation of amounts relating to conditions existing at the balance sheet date.
(c)	Debtors should be reduced by the amount of bad debts. **Reason:** As per AS 4 Assets and liabilities should be adjusted for events occurring after the balance sheet date that provide additional evidence to assist the estimation of amounts relating to conditions existing at the balance sheet date.
(d)	Loss due to theft should recognised. Reason: As per AS 4 Assets and liabilities should be adjusted for events occurring after the balance sheet date that provide additional evidence to assist the estimation of amounts relating to conditions existing at the balance sheet date.
(e)	The financial statements should be prepared by not following the fundamental assumption of going concern. **Reason:** As per AS – 4, assets and liabilities should be adjusted for events occurring after the balance sheet date that indicate that the fundamental accounting assumption of going concern (i.e., the continuance of existence or substratum of the enterprise) is not appropriate.
(f)	The financial statements should be prepared by not following the fundamental assumption of going concern. **Reason:** As per AS – 4, assets and liabilities should be adjusted for events occurring after the balance sheet date that indicate that the fundamental accounting assumption of going concern (i.e., the continuance of existence or substratum of the enterprise) is not appropriate.
(g)	Dividend should be adjusted. **Reason:** As per para 14 of AS 4, dividends in respect of period covered by the financial statements, which are proposed or declared by the enterprise after the Balance Sheet Date but before the approval of the financial statements should be adjusted in the financial statements. The Schedule III, classifies 'Proposed Dividend' as commitments'.Accounting Standards now have overriding impact over Schedule III. Therefore, unless Para 14 of AS 4 is changed, Proposed Dividend shall be adjusted.

(h)	Disclosure should be made in the report of the approving authority since the amount of loss is material. Such loss should not be recognised in the financial statements for the year 2014-2015 since such event does not relate to the conditions existing at the Balance Sheet Date.
(i)	Disclosure should be made in the report of the approving authority since the amount of loss is material. Such loss should not be recognised in the financial statements for the year 2014-2015 since such event does not relate to the conditions existing at the Balance Sheet Date.
(j)	Liability on account of increase in cost should be provided. **Reason:** As per AS 4 Assets and liabilities should be adjusted for events occurring after the balance sheet date that provide additional evidence to assist the estimation of amounts relating to conditions existing at the balance sheet date.
(k)	Disclosure should be made in the report of the approving authority if the amount of loss is considered material. Such loss should not be recognised in the financial statements for the year 2014-2015 since such event does not relate to the conditions existing at the Balance Sheet Date.

QUESTION 2: State the disclose requirement of Proposed Dividend while preparing Financial Statements on company.

ANSWER:

Schedule III	The Schedule III, classifies 'Proposed Dividend' as commitments'.
AS 4	Para 14 of AS 4 requires that "Dividends stated to be in respect of the period covered by the financial statements, which are proposed or declared by the enterprise after the Balance Sheet Date but before approval of the financial statements, should be adjusted." Accounting Standards now have overriding impact over Schedule III. Therefore, unless Para 14 of AS 4 is changed, Proposed Dividend shall be adjusted.
ICAI Guidance Note	The ICAI Guidance Note on the Schedule III has clarified that the 'Proposed Dividend' is a provision.

QUESTION 3: A Ltd. Company closed its accounting year on 31.3.2015 and the accounts for that period were considered and approved by the board of directors on 20th August, 2015. The company was engaged in laying pipe line for an oil company, deep beneath the earth. While doing the boring work on 1.9.2015, it had met a rocky surface for which it was estimated that there would be an extra cost to tune of ₹ 80 lakhs. You are required to state with reasons, how the event would be dealt with the financial statements for the year ended 31.3.2015.

ANSWER:

PROVISION OF AS 4

As per AS 4'events occurring after the balance sheet date' are those significant events, both favourable and unfavourable, that occur between the balance sheet date and the date on which financial statements are approved by the Board of Directors in the case of a company'.

ADVICE

The incidence, which was expected to push up cost, became evident after the date of approval of the accounts. Hence it is not an 'event occurring after the balance sheet date'.

QUESTION 4: A company deals in petroleum products. The sale price of petrol is fixed by the Government. After the balance sheet date, but before the finalization of the company's accounts, the Government unexpectedly increased the price retrospectively. Can the company account for additional revenue at the close of the year? Discuss.

ANSWER: The unexpected increase in petroleum product prices retrospectively by the Government before the finalization of the company accounts can be considered as an event occurring after the balance sheet date which requires an adjustment on the balance sheet date as per AS - 4 assuming that there were no circumstances of price increase persisting on the date of balance sheet.

QUESTION 5: A major fire has damaged the assets in a factory of a Limited Company on 5th April – five days after the year end and closure of accounts. The loss is estimated at ₹.10 crores out of which ₹.7 crores will be recoverable from the insurers. Explain briefly how the loss should be treated in the final accounts for the previous year.

ANSWER: The loss due to break out of fire is an example of event occurring after the balance sheet date. The event does not relate to conditions existing at the balance sheet date. It has not affected the financial position as on the date of balance sheet and therefore requires no specific adjustments in the financial statements. However, paragraph 8.6 of AS 4 states that disclosure is generally made of events occurring after balance sheet date i.e.in subsequent periods that represent unusual changes affecting the existence or substratum of the enterprise after the balance sheet date. In the given case, the amount of loss of assets in a factory is material and may be considered as an event affecting the substratum of the enterprise. Hence, as recommended in paragraph 15 of AS 4, disclosure of the event should be made in the report of the approving authority.

QUESTION 6: In Raj Co. Ltd., theft of cash of ₹ 2 lakhs by the cashier in January, 2015 was detected in May, 2015. The accounts of the company were not yet approved by the Board of Directors of the company. Whether the theft of cash has to be adjusted in the accounts of the company for the year ended 31.3.2015. Decide.

ANSWER:

PROVISION OF AS 4

As per AS 4(revised), assets and liabilities should be adjusted for events occurring after the balance sheet date that provide additional evidence to assist the estimation of amounts relating to conditions existing at the balance sheet date.

ADVICE

Since the theft of cash is an additional information materially affecting the determination of the cash amount relating to conditions existing at the balance sheet date, it is necessary to adjust theft of cash in the financial statements of the company for the year ended 31st March, 2015.

QUESTION 7: A Company follows April to March as its financial year. The Company recognizes cheques dated 31st March or before, received from customers after balance sheet date, but before approval of financial statement by debiting 'Cheques in hand account' and crediting 'Debtors account'. The 'cheques in hand' is shown in the Balance Sheet as an item of cash and cash equivalents. All cheques in hand are presented to bank in the month of April and are also realised in the same month in normal course after deposit in the bank. State with reasons, whether the collection of cheques bearing date 31st March or before, but received after Balance Sheet date is an adjusting event and how this fact is to be disclosed by the company?

ANSWER:

PROVISION OF AS 4

Since the cheques bearing the date 31st March or before, and received after 31st March do not represent any **condition existing on the balance sheet** date i.e. 31st March. The collection of cheques after balance sheet date is not an adjusting event. Cheques that are received after the Balance Sheet Date should be accounted for in the period in which they are received.

ADVICE

Since the collection of cheques after balance sheet date does not represent any **material change affecting financial position of the enterprise,** no disclosure in the Director's Report is **necessary**.

QUESTION 8: An earthquake destroyed a major warehouse of ACO Ltd. on 20.5.2015. The accounting year of the company ended on 31.3.2015. The accounts were approved on 30.6.2015. The loss from earthquake is estimated at ₹ 30 lakhs. State with reasons, whether the loss due to earthquake is an adjusting or non-adjusting event and how the fact of loss is to be disclosed by the company?

ANSWER:

PROVISION OF AS 4

As per AS 4 adjustments to assets and liabilities are not appropriate for events occurring after the balance sheet date, if such events do not relate to conditions existing at the balance sheet date.

ADVICE

(i) The destruction of warehouse due to earthquake did not exist on the balance sheet date i.e. 31.3.2015. Therefore, loss occurred due to earthquake is not to be recognised in the financial year 2014-2015.

(ii) Since the earthquake has caused major destruction; fundamental accounting assumption of going concern is called upon. Hence, the fact of earthquake together with an estimated loss of ₹ 30 lakhs should be disclosed in the Report of the Directors for the financial year 2014-2015.

QUESTION 9: A company entered into an agreement to sell its immovable property to another company for 35 lakhs. The property was shown in the Balance Sheet at ₹ 7 lakhs. The agreement to sell was concluded on 15th February, 2015 and sale deed was registered on 30th April, 2015. The financial statements for the year 2014-2015 were approved by the Board on 12th May, 2015. You are required to state, how this transaction would be dealt with in the financial statements for the year ended 31st March, 2015.

ANSWER:

PROVISION OF AS-4

As per AS 4 assets and liabilities should be adjusted for events occurring after the balance sheet date that provide additional evidence to assist the estimation of amounts relating to conditions existing at the balance sheet date.

ADVICE

Since agreement to sell before the balance sheet date and Registration of the sale deed after the balance sheet date provides additional information relating to the conditions existing at the balance sheet date, adjustment to assets for sale of immovable property is necessary in the financial statements for the year ended 31st March, 2015.

QUESTION 10: While preparing its final accounts for the year ended 31st March 2015, a company made a provision for bad debts @4% of its total debtors (as per trend follows from the previous years). In the first week of March 2015, a debtor for ₹ 3,00,000 had suffered heavy loss due to an earthquake; the loss was not covered by any insurance policy. In April, 2015 the debtor became a bankrupt. Can the company provide for the full loss arising out of insolvency of the debtor in the final accounts for the year ended 31st March, 2015.

ANSWER:

PROVISION OF AS 4

As per AS 4 adjustment to assets and liabilities are required for events occuring after the balance sheet date that provide additional information materially affecting the determination of the amounts relating to conditions existing at the Balance Sheet date.

ADVICE

A debtor for ₹ 3,00,000 suffered heavy loss due to earthquake in the first week of March, 2015 and he became bankrupt in April, 2015 (after the balance sheet date). The loss was also not covered by any insurance policy. Accordingly, full provision for bad debts amounting ₹ 3,00,000 should be made, to cover the loss arising due to the insolvency of a debtor, in the final accounts for the year ended 31st March 2015.

QUESTION 11:

(i) The Company's sales tax assessment for assessment year 2012-2013 has been completed on 14th February, 2015 with a demand of ₹ 2.76 crore. The company paid the entire due under protest without prejudice to its right of appeal. The Company files its appeal before the appellate authority wherein the grounds of appeal cover tax on additions made in the assessment order for a sum of 2.10 crore. Advise.

(ii) The Company has entered into a wage agreement in May, 2015 whereby the labour union has accepted a revision in wage from June, 2011. The agreement provided that the hike till May, 2015 will not be paid to the employees but will be settled to them at the time of retirement. The company agrees to deposit the arrears in Government Bonds by September, 2015.

ANSWER:

(i) Since the company is not appealing against the addition of ₹ 0.66 crore, the same should be provided for, in its accounts for the year ended on 31st March, 2015. The amount paid under protest can be kept under the sub-heading 'Short-term Loans & Advances' and disclosed along with the contingent liability of ₹ 2.10 crore.

(ii) The arrears for the period from June, 2011 to March, 2015 are required to be provided for in the accounts of the company for the year ended on 31st March, 2015:

QUESTION 12: The Company invested ₹ 560 lakhs in April, 2015 in the acquisition of another company doing similar business, the negotiations for which had started during the current financial year.

ANSWER:

PROVISION OF AS 4

As per AS 4 no adjustment to assets and liabilities is required if the event does not affect the determination and the condition of the amounts stated in the financial statements for the year ended 31st March, 2015: Disclosure should be made in the report of the approving authority of those events occurring after the balance sheet date that represent material changes and commitments affecting the financial position of the enterprise.

ADVICE

The investment of ₹ 560 lakhs in April, 2015 in the acquisition of another company should be disclosed in the report of the Board of Directors to enable users of financial statements to make proper evaluations and decisions.

QUESTION 13: On 15th April, 2015, due to destruction of the factory by fire, X, one of the company's debtors, declared himself insolvent. He owed ₹ 3,00,000 to Z Ltd. Advice the Z Ltd. about the treatment of the above in the final statement of accounts for the year ended 31st March, 2015.

ANSWER:

PROVISION OF AS 4

As per AS 4 Assets and liabilities should be adjusted for events occurring after the balance sheet date that provide additional evidence to assist the estimation of amounts relating to conditions existing at the balance sheet date.

ADVICE

The debtor became insolvent on 15th April, 2015 I.e. after the balance sheet date because of destruction of his factory by fire. In this case this event does not provide any information about the condition existing at balance sheet date. However, a disclosure is required to be made in director's report.

QUESTION 14: Bottom Ltd. entered into a sale deed for its immovable property before the end of the year. But registration was done with registrar subsequent to balance sheet date. But before finalization, is it possible to recognize the sale and the gain at the balance sheet date? Give your view with reasons.

ANSWER:

PROVISION OF AS 4

As per AS 4 Assets and Liabilities should be adjusted for events occurring after the balance sheet date that provide additional evidence to assist the estimation of amounts relating to conditions existing at the balance sheet date.

ADVICE

Sale of immovable property was concluded before approval by the board. This is clearly an event occurring after the balance sheet date. Agreement to sell was entered into before the balance sheet date. Registration of the sale deed simply provides additional information relating to the conditions existing at the balance sheet date. So adjustments to assets are necessary as per AS - 4.

QUESTION 15: You are an accountant preparing accounts of A Ltd., as on 31.3.2015. After year end the following events have taken place in April, 2015:

(i) A fire broke out in the premises damaging, uninsured stock worth ₹ 10 lakhs (Salvage value ₹ 2 lakhs).

(ii) Dividend proposed @ 20% on share capital of ₹ 100 lakhs.

Describe, how above will be dealt with in the account of the company for the year ended on 31.3.2015.

ANSWER:

(i) Events occurring after the Balance Sheet date that represent material changes and commitments affecting the financial position of the enterprise must be disclosed as per AS-4 on Contingencies and Events occurring after the Balance Sheet date. Hence, fire accident and loss thereof must be disclosed by **way of Note in the Report of Directors.**

(iii) There are events which although take place after the balance sheet date, are sometimes reflected in the financial statements because of statutory requirements or because of their special nature. Such items include the amount of dividend proposed or declared by the enterprise after the balance sheet date in respect of the period covered by financial statements. Thus, dividends which are proposed or declared after the balance sheet date but before approval of the financial statements, **should be adjusted as per AS-4.**

QUESTION 16: One of the manufacturing unit of B Ltd. equal to 40% of the total assets was destroyed in a fire for which there was no insurance cover. The chief accountant of the company contends that the destruction of the unit took place only after the date of the Balance Sheet and therefore there was no need to make disclosure of loss in the annual accounts as at the Balance Sheet date. Comment.

ANSWER:

PROVISION OF AS 4

As per AS 4 Assets and liabilities should be adjusted for events occurring after the balance sheet date that provide additional evidence to assist the estimation of amounts relating to conditions existing at the balance sheet date or that indicate that the fundamental accounting assumption of going concern (i.e., the continuance of existence or substratum of the enterprise) is not appropriate.

ADVICE

Therefore, having regard to the quantum of loss, the auditor has to consider whether it is material enough to affect the very existence of the enterprise. In case destruction of 40% of total assets for which no insurance cover is available affects the existence of B Ltd. then annual accounts would have to be prepared by not following the fundamental accounting assumption of going concern despite the fact that the event has occurred after the balance sheet date. Alternatively, if due to loss the enterprise not ceased to be a going concern then the disclosure stating nature of event and estimate of the financial effect or a statement that such an estimate cannot be made will have to be made in the report of Board of Directors.

QUESTION 17: There was a government notification in June, 2015 increasing the limit of gratuity payment with effect from 24th September, 2015. The accounts were approved by the board of directors in July, 2015. The chief accountant is of the opinion that since the change took place after the balance sheet date, no effect should be given to it in the financial statements for the year ended 31st March, 2015. Comment.

ANSWER:

PROVISION OF AS 4

As per AS – 4, Assets and Liabilities should be adjusted for events occurring after the balance sheet date that provide additional evidence to assist the estimation of amounts relating to conditions existing at the balance sheet date.

ADVICE

In this instant case increasing the limit of gratuity by the government provide additional evidence in estimating the amount of gratuity payable by the company. Hence, the company must provide for increase in gratuity in the financial statements of the year 2014 – 2015.

QUESTION 18: Some companies are notified for air pollution in the vicinity of a historic building. It was certain that legislation will be brought shortly requiring close down of air pollution units. Court proceeding shows evidence that the Supreme Court will direct such units to close down. What is the treatment under AS – 4?

ANSWER:

PROVISION OF AS 4

As per AS 4 Assets and liabilities should be adjusted for events occurring after the balance sheet date that provide additional evidence to assist the estimation of amounts relating to conditions existing at the balance sheet date or that indicate that the fundamental accounting assumption of going concern (i.e., the continuance of existence or substratum of the enterprises) is not appropriate.

ADVICE

In this case, the fundamental accounting assumption of going concern (i.e., continuance of existence or substratum of the enterprise) is not appropriate and therefore assets and liabilities should be adjusted.

QUESTION 19: After the close of the accounting year 2014 – 2015 of ABC Co. Ltd., there was a severe earthquake. As a result of which, a portion of the building and the rolling mill was destroyed. The extent of the damage was beyond repair. The company's resources were inadequate to fund the replacement of the assets so destroyed, Comment.

ANSWER:

PROVISION OF AS 4

As per AS – 4, assets and liabilities should be adjusted for events occurring after the balance sheet date that indicate that the fundamental accounting assumption of going concern (i.e., the continuance of existence or substratum of the enterprise) is not appropriate

ADVICE

In this case it is evident that a company cannot continue further as a going concern hence, its assets and liabilities should be adjusted and financial statements for the year 2013 – 2014 should be prepared on liquidation basis

QUESTION 20: A company's financial year end on 31st March, 2015. Its accounts were considered and approved by the board of directors on 15th May, 2015. The company had taken a large - sized civil construction contract, for a public sector undertaking, valued at ₹ 10 crores. In the course of execution of the work on 29th May, 2015, the company found while raising the foundation work that it had met a rocky surface and costs of contract would go up by an extra ₹ 1 crore which would not be recoverable from the contractee. How this event would be dealt in the financial statements for the year ended 31st March, 2015.

ANSWER:

PROVISION OF AS 4

As per AS – 4, events occurring after the balance sheet date are those events, both favourable and unfavourable, that occur between the balance sheet date and the date on which financial statements are approved.

ADVICE

In this case the incidence, which was expected to push up cost, became evident after the date of approval of the balance sheet. So that was not any 'event occurring after the balance sheet date'. If the cost push up is believed to be material, this may be mentioned in the Director's report. (Even if the contract is profitable after taking into account the additional cost, it would be prudent to disclose the fact of increase in the cost of the contract in the director's report).

QUESTION 21: Pure Oil Ltd. closed the books of accounts on March 31, 2015 for which financial statements were finalized by the Board of Directors on September 04, 2015 During the month of December 2014, company under took the project of lying a pipeline across the country and during May 2015 engineers realized that due to unexpected heavy rain, the total cost of the project shall be inflated by ₹ 50 crores. How this should be provided for in the balance sheet of 2014 – 2015 in accordance with AS – 4.

ANSWER: The event occurred after March 31, 2015 but before September 04, 2015 hence it is event occurring after the balance sheet date. But this event is not affecting financial position on the date of balance sheet therefore it should be disclosed in the financial statement by the directors.

QUESTION 22: The Company invested ₹ 50 lakhs in April, 2015 in the acquisition of another company doing similar business, the negotiations for which had started during the current financial year. How will you deal with the financial statements for the year ended 31st March 2015?

ANSWER:

PROVISION OF AS 4

As per AS 4 no adjustment to assets and liabilities is required if the event does not affect the determination and the condition of the amounts stated in the financial statements for the year ended 31st March, 2015: Disclosure should be made in the report of the approving authority of those events occurring after the balance sheet date that represent material changes and commitments affecting the financial position of the enterprise.

ADVICE

The investment in April, 2015 in the acquisition of another company should be disclosed in the report of the Board of Directors to enable users of financial statements to make proper evaluations and decisions.

QUESTION 23: Cashier of A-One Limited embezzled cash amounting to ₹ 6,00,000 during March, 2015. However same comes to the notice of Company management during April, 2015 only. financial statements of the company are not approved by the Board of Directors of the company.

(a) With the help of provisions of AS 4 "contingencies and Event Occurring after the Balance Sheet Date" decide, whether the embezzlement of cash should be adjusted in the books of accounts for the ending March, 2015?

(b) What will be your replay, if embezzlement of cash comes to the notice of company management only after approval of financial statements by the Board Directors of the company?

ANSWER:

PROVISION OF AS 4

As per AS 4, Assets and Liabilities should be adjusted for events occurring after the balance sheet date that provide additional evidence to assist the estimation of amounts relating to conditions existing at the balance sheet date.

ADVICE

(a) Though the theft, by the cashier ₹ 6,00,000 was detected after the balance sheet date (before approval of financial statements) but it is an additional information materially affecting the determination of the cash amount relating to conditions existing at the balance sheet date. Therefore, it is necessary to make the necessary adjustments in the financial statements of the company for the ended 31st March, 2015 for recognition of the loss amounting ₹ 6,00,000.

(b) If embezzlement of cash comes to the notice of company management only after approval of financial statements by board of directors of the company, then the treatment will be done as per the provisions of AS 5. This being extra ordinary item should be disclosed in the Statement of Profit and Loss as a part of loss for the year ending March, 2015. The nature and the amount of prior period item should be separately disclosed on the Statement of Profit and Loss in a manner that its impact on current profit on loss can be perceived.

QUESTION 24: During the year 2014-2015, X Ltd. was used by a competitor for ₹ 50 lakhs for infringement of a trademark. Based on the advice of the company's legal counsel, the company provided for a sum of ₹ 30 lakhs in its financial statements for the year ended 31st March, 2015. On 20th May, 2015, the Court decided in favour of the party alleging infringement

of the trademark and ordered the company to pay the aggrieved party a sum of ₹ 45 lakhs. The financial statements were prepared by the company's management on 30th April, 2015, and approved by the Board on 31st May, 2015. Should the company adjust its financial statements for the year ended 31st March, 2015?

ANSWER:

PROVISION OF AS 4

As per para 8 of AS 4, "Adjustments" to Assets and Liabilities are required for events occurring after the Balance Sheet date that provide additional information materially affecting the determination of the amounts relating to conditions existing at the Balance Sheet date.

ADVICE

The decision of the Court for payment of the penalty will constitute as an adjusting event because it is an event occurred before approval of the financial statements. Therefore, the company should adjust the provision upward by ₹ 15 lakhs to reflect the amount decreed by the Court and to be paid by them to its competitor.

PROBLEM 25: During the course of audit of D Co. Ltd. you as an auditor have observed that inter Corporate deposit of ₹ 50 lakhs has been overdue. The D Co. Ltd. have disclosed this in the notes to Accounts Note No. 15 in schedule no. 21 stating that ₹ 50 lakhs is overdue from XYZ Co. Ltd. and the said company is the process of liquidation. The management is taking steps to appoint the liquidators. Comment

ANSWER:

PROVISION OF AS 4

As per AS-4 "Contingencies and Events occurring after the Balance Sheet Date", adjustments to assets and liabilities are required for events occurring after the balance sheet date that provide additional information materially affecting the determination of the amounts relating to conditions existing at the balance sheet date.

ADVICE

It appears from the note no 15 that the overdue to outstanding inter corporate deposit may not be realisable in full. The company is the process of liquidation, makes it clear that on the balance sheet date, the amount of deposit is not safe and is not likely to be realised.

Therefore as per AS 4 provision for the loss is required in the accounts. Hence the auditor should qualify the Audit Report.

QUESTION 26: AS-4 prescribes that adjustments to assets and liabilities are required for events occurring after the Balance Sheet date that provide additional information materially affecting the determination of the amount relating to conditions existing at the Balance sheet date-generally called adjusting events. "Proposed Dividend" is shown and adjusted in the Balance Sheet even if it is not an adjusting event as per AS-4 because it is proposed by the Board of Directors of the company after the Balance sheet date. Keeping this in view, is it not violation of AS-4 to show proposed dividends as current liabilities and provisions?

ANSWER:

PROVISION OF AS 4

As per para 8 of AS 4 "Contingencies arid Events occurring after the Balance sheet Date", adjustments to assets and liabilities are required for events occurring after the balance sheet date that provide additional information materially affecting the determination of the amounts relating to conditions existing at the balance sheet date. Accordingly, proposed dividend is not an adjusting event. However, para 14 of the Standard states that dividends stated to be in respect of the period covered by the financial statements, which are proposed or declared by the enterprise after the balance sheet date but before approval of the Financial statements, should be adjusted in the financial statements. Revised Schedule VI of the Companies Act 1956 prescribes that proposed dividend should be in the Notes to Accounts.

ADVICE

Proposed Dividends under the head **'Current Liabilities'** and Subhead, **'Short-term Provisions'** by adjusting it in the Balance Sheet is not in violation of AS 4.

QUESTION 27: Neel Limited has its corporate office in Mumbai and sells its products to stockists all over India. On 31st March, 2015, the company wants to recognize receipt of cheques bearing date 31st March, 2015 or before, as "Cheques in Hand" by reducing "Trade Receivables". The "Cheques in Hand" is shown in the Balance Sheet as an item of cash and cash equivalents. All cheques are presented to the bank in the month of April 2015 and are also realized in the same month in normal course after deposit in the bank. State with reasons, whether each of the following is an adjusting event and how this fact is to be disclosed by the company, with reference to the relevant accounting standard.

(i) Cheques collected by the marketing personnel of the company from the stockists on or before 31st March, 2015.

(ii) Cheques sent by the stockists through courier on or before 31st March, 2015.

ANSWER:

(i) 1. Collection of cheques by the marketing personnel is an adjusting event as per AS 4 'Contingencies and Events Occurring after the Balance Sheet Date'.

2. Reason: Handing over of cheques by the stockist to the marketing employees discharges the liability of the stockist. Therefore, cheques collected by the marketing personnel of the company on or before 31-3-2015 require adjustment from the Stockists' Accounts i.e. from 'Trade Receivables A/c' even though these cheques (dated on or before 31-3-2015) are presented in the bank in the month of April, 2015 in the normal course.

3. Disclosure: Such 'cheques in hand' will be shown in the Balance Sheet as 'Cash and Cash equivalents' with a disclosure in the Notes to accounts about the accounting policy followed by the company from such cheques.

(ii) **1.** The collection of cheques after balance sheet date is not an adjusting event since Collection of cheques after 31-3-2015 does not represent any condition existing on the Balance Sheet date i.e. 31st March.

2. Cheques that are received after the balance sheet date should be accounted for in the period in which they are received even though the same may be dated 31st March or before as per AS 4.

3. The collection of cheques after Balance Sheet date does not represent any material change affecting financial position of the enterprise, hence no disclosure in the Director's Report is necessary.

AS 5—NET PROFIT OR LOSS FOR THE PERIOD, PRIOR ITEMS & CHANGES IN ACCOUNTING POLICIES

THEORETICAL BASE

QUESTION 1: State the Meaning and Disclosure Requirements of Ordinary Activities.

ANSWER:

Meaning	Ordinary activities are any activities which are undertaken by an enterprise as part of its business and such related activities in which the enterprise engages in furtherance of, incidental to, or arising from, these activities.
Disclosure Requirements	The nature and the amount of such items should be disclosed separately when items of income and expense within profit or loss from ordinary activities are of such size, nature or incidence that their disclosure is relevant to explain the performance of the enterprise for the period.
Circumstances under which separate Disclosure required	Circumstances which may give rise to separate disclosure of items of income and expense includes: 1. the write-down of inventories to net realizable value as well as the reversal of such write-downs; 2. a restructuring of the activities of an enterprise and the reversal of any provisions for the costs of restructuring; 3. disposals of items of fixed assets; 4. disposals of long-term investments; 5. legislative changes having retrospective application; 6. litigation settlements; and 7. other reversals of provisions.

QUESTION 2: State the Meaning, Examples and Disclosure Requirements of Extraordinary Items.

ANSWER:

Meaning	Extraordinary items are incomes or expenses that arise from events or transactions that are clearly distinct from the ordinary activities of the enterprise and, therefore, are not expected to recur frequently or regularly. **Example:** Attachment of property of the enterprise; or an Earthquake.
Examples	1. Loss due to earthquakes/fire/strike 2. Attachment of property of the enterprise by government
Disclosure Requirements	1. Extraordinary items should be disclosed in the statement of profit and loss as part of net profit or loss for the period. 2. The nature and the amount of each extraordinary item should be separately disclosed in the statement of profit and loss in a manner that its impact on current profit or loss can be perceived.

QUESTION 3: State the Meaning, Examples and Disclosure Requirements of Prior Period Items.

ANSWER:

Meaning	(i) Prior period items are incomes or expenses which arise in the current period as a result of errors or omissions in the preparation of the financial statements of one or more prior periods.
	(ii) The term 'prior period items', as defined refers only to incomes or expenses which arise in the current period as a result of errors or omissions in the preparation of the financial statements of one or more prior periods.
	(iii) The term does not include other adjustments necessitated by circumstances, which though related to prior periods, are determined in the current period, e.g., arrears payable to workers as a result of revision of wages with retrospective effect during the current period.
Examples	1. Applying incorrect Rate of Depreciation in one or more prior periods.
	2. Omission to account for Income or Expenditure in one or more prior periods.
	3. Omission to include Stock Sheets containing inventory costing ₹ 20 lacs while valuing closing stock of previous year.
	4. Omission to pass an entry for receipt of insurance claim received during previous year.
	5. Theft of stock during previous year but detected during current year
Disclosure Requirements	1. The nature and amount of prior period Requirements items should be separately disclosed in the statement of profit and loss in a manner that their impact on the current profit or loss can be perceived.
	2. Prior period items are normally included in the determination of net profit or loss for the current period (above line).
	3. An alternative approach is to show such items in the statement of profit and loss after the determination of current net profit or loss (below line).

QUESTION 4: State the Meaning, Examples, Accounting Treatment and Disclosure Requirements of Accounting Estimate.

ANSWER:

Meaning	As a result of the uncertainties inherent in business activities, many financial statement items cannot be measured with precision but can only be estimated.
Examples	1. Estimates of likely bad debts 2. Estimates of Inventory Obsolescence 3. Estimates of useful lives of depreciable assets. 4. Provision for Warranties, Restructuring Costs, Gratuity 5. Contingencies 6. Estimates of Insurance Reserves by insurance companies.
Accounting Treatment	1. The effect of a change in an accounting estimate should be included in the determination of net profit or loss in (a) The period of the change, if the change affects the period only; or (b) The period of the change and future periods, if the change affects both. 2. The effect of a change in an accounting estimate should be classified using the same classification in the statement of profit and loss as was used previously for the estimate.

Disclosure Requirements	1. The nature and amount of a change in an accounting estimate which has a material effect in the current period, or which is expected to have a material effect in subsequent periods, should be disclosed. 2. If it is impracticable to quantify the amount, this fact should be disclosed.
Whether Restatement is required when there is Change in Accounting Estimate?	No

QUESTION 5: When is the Change in Accounting Policies recommended?

ANSWER: A change in the Accounting Policy should be made only if adoption of different Accounting Policy is required

1. by Statute or
2. For compliance with an Accounting Standard or
3. If it is considered that the change would result in more appropriate presentation of financial statements.

QUESTION 6: Give two examples of Change in Accounting Policy.

ANSWER:

1. Change of Depreciation method from WDV to SLM and vice-versa.
2. Change in Cost formula in measuring the cost of inventories.

QUESTION 7: State the Disclosure Requirements as to the Change in Accounting Policies .

ANSWER:

Case	***What is to be disclosed?***
(a) When the change has material effect in current period.	(i) The nature of change. (ii) Financial effect of change on Accounting Policies items to the extent ascertainable. (iii) Where the amount is not ascertainable in wholly or part then indicate this fact.
(b) When the change has material effect in later period(s).	(i) The nature of change. (ii) The fact that change in accounting policies has an effect in later period.

QUESTION 8: Whether Restatement is required when there is change in accounting policy?

ANSWER: Yes

PRACTICAL QUESTIONS FOR PRACTICE

QUESTION 1: Give two examples on each of the following items:

(i) Change in Accounting Policy
(ii) Change in Accounting Estimate
(iii) Extra Ordinary Items
(iv) Prior Period Items

ANSWER:

(i) Examples of Changes in Accounting Policy:

1. Change of Depreciation method from WDV to SLM and vice-versa.
2. Change in Cost formula in measuring the cost of inventories.

(ii) Examples of Changes in Accounting Estimates:

1. Change in estimate of provision for doubtful debts on sundry debtors.
2. Change in estimate of useful life of fixed assets.

(iii) Examples of Extraordinary items:

1. Loss due to earthquakes/fire/strike
2. Attachment of property of the enterprise by government

(iv) Examples of Prior period items:

1. Applying incorrect Rate of Depreciation in one or more prior periods.
2. Omission to account for Income or Expenditure in one or more prior periods.
3. Omission to include Stock Sheets containing inventory costing ₹ 20 lacs while valuing closing stock of previous year.
4. Omission to pass an entry for receipt of insurance claim received during previous year.
5. Theft of stock during previous year but detected during current year.

QUESTION 2: The surplus arising from a change in the basis of accounting was set off by X Ltd. against a non-recurring loss. Comment.

ANSWER:

PROVISION OF AS 5

As per AS-5 any change in any accounting policy which has a material effect should be disclosed. The impact of, and the adjustments resulting from such change, if material, should be shown in the financial statements of the period in which such changes is made, to reflect the effect of such change. Transactions which are of an abnormal or non-recurring nature may also be considered material, even though prima facie, they do not appear to be material. Materiality is an important and relevant consideration in determining whether or not such exclusion/non-disclosure will distort the true and fair view of the financial statements.

ADVICE

Thus, it would be important that users must know the quantum of non-recurring loss. **In off setting and aggregating items, care need to be taken to ensure that material items are not offset against each other.** Accordingly, it would not be prudent to set off the surplus emanating from a 'change in the basis of accounting' against a 'non-recurring loss'. Accordingly, it would be better to disclose the surplus on account of change in the basis of accounting and non-recurring loss separately.

QUESTION 3: A Limited Company finds that the stock sheets as on 31.3.2014 had included twice an item the cost of which was ₹ 20,000. You are asked to suggest, how the error would be dealt with in the accounts of the year ended 31.3.2015.

ANSWER:

PROVISION OF AS 5

As per AS-5 the nature and amount of prior period items should be separately disclosed in the statement of profit and loss in a manner that their impact on the current profit or loss can be perceived.

ADVICE

The error in the recording of closing stock of the year ended 31st March, 2014 must have also resulted in overstatement of profits of previous year, brought forward to the current year ended

31st March, 2015. Accordingly, ₹ 20,000 should be deducted from opening stock in the Profit and Loss Account and ₹ 20,000 should be charged as prior period adjustment in the Profit and Loss Account for the year ended 31st March 2015. The prior period item should be adjusted by passing the following entries.

Prior Period Expense A/c	Dr.	₹ 20,000	
To Opening Inventory			₹ 20,000
Profit and Loss A/c	Dr.	₹ 20,000	
To Prior Period Expense A/c			₹ 20,000

QUESTION 4: While finalizing the financial statements of the year ending 31/03/2015 the company finds that the stock sheets of 31/03/2014 did not include two pages containing details of inventory worth ₹ 25 lakhs. Comment.

ANSWER

PROVISION OF AS 5

As per AS-5 prior period items are incomes or expenses which arise in the current period as a result of errors or omissions in the preparation of the financial statements of one or more prior periods. The nature and amount of prior period items should be separately disclosed in the statement of profit and loss in a manner that their impact on the current profit or loss can be perceived.

ADVICE

In this case stock sheet of 31/03/2014 (prior year) did not include two pages containing details of inventory worth ₹ 25 lakhs which is the omission, and this omission was detected in current period i.e. 31/03/2015. Therefore, it is a prior item. It has resulted in under statement of profit of previous period. Entry to be passed is as under:

JOURNAL

₹ in Lakhs

Opening Inventory A/c	Dr.	25	
To Prior Period Income			25
Prior Period Income	Dr.	25	
To Profit and Loss A/c			25

QUESTION 5: Fuel surcharge is billed by the State Electricity Board at provisional rates. Final bill for fuel surcharge of ₹ 5.30 lakhs for the period October 2006 to September, 2013 has been received and paid in February, 2015. Comment.

ANSWER:

PROVISION OF AS 5

As per AS-5 the nature and amount of prior period items should be separately disclosed in the statement of profit and loss in a manner that their impact on the current profit or loss can be perceived.

ADVICE

The final bill having been paid in February, 2015 should have been accounted for in the annual accounts of the company for the years ending 31st March, 2007, 31st March, 2011, 31st March, 2012, 31st March, 2013 and 31st March, 2014. However it seems that as a result of error or omission in the preparation of the financial statements of prior period i.e., for the year 31st March, 2007, 31st March, 2011, 31st March, 2012, 31st March, 2013 and 31st March, 2014, this material charge has arisen in the current period i.e., year ends 31st March, 2015.

It may be mentioned that it is an expense arising from the **ordinary course of business**. Although abnormal in amount or infrequent in occurrence, such an expense **does not qualify as an extraordinary item as per AS-5.** For better understanding, the fact that power bill is accounted for at provisional rated billed by the State Electricity Board and final adjustment thereof is made as and when final bill is received may be mentioned as accounting policy.

QUESTION 6: During the course of the last three years, a company owning and operating Helicopters lost four Helicopters. The company directors felt that after the crash, the maintenance provision created in respect of the respective helicopters was no longer required, and proposed to write - back to the profit and loss account as prior period item. Is the company's proposed accounting treatment correct? Comment.

ANSWER: No, the company's accounting treatment is not correct. Because writing back the balance of the maintenance provision, no longer required due to crash of the helicopters, is not a prior period item as there is no error in the preparation of previous period financial statements. The amount so written - back (if material) should be disclosed separately as per AS - 5 in the profit and loss account.

QUESTION 7: A company created a provision of ₹ 75,000 for staff welfare while preparing the financial statements for the year 2014-2015. On 31st March, in a meeting with staff welfare association, it was decided to increase the amount of provision for staff welfare to ₹ 1,00,000. The accounts were approved by Board of Directors on 15th April, 2015. Explain the treatment of such revision in financial statements for the year ended 31st March, 2015.

ANSWER:

PROVISION OF AS 5

As per AS 5 normally, all items of income and expense which are recognised in a period are included in the determination of the net profit or loss for the period. This includes extraordinary items and the effects of changes in accounting estimates. However, the effect of such change in accounting estimate should be classified using the same classification in the statement of profit and loss, as was used previously, for the estimate.

ADVICE

As per AS 5 in the change in amount of staff welfare provision amounting ₹ 25,000 is neither a prior period item nor an extraordinary item. It is a change in estimate, which has occurred in the year 2014-2015.

QUESTION 8: Closing stock for the year ending on 31.3.2015 is ₹ 50,000 which includes stock damaged in a fire in 2013-2014. On 31.3.2014, the estimated net realisable value of the damaged stock was ₹ 12,000. The revised estimate of net realisable value of damaged goods amounting ₹ 4,000 has been included in closing stock of ₹ 50,000 as on 31.3.2015. Find the value of closing stock to be shown in Profit and Loss account for the year 2014-2015.

ANSWER:

PROVISION OF AS 5

As per AS 5 the effect of a change in accounting estimate should be classified using the same classification in the statement of profit and loss as was used previously for the estimate.

ADVICE

The fall in estimated net realisable value of damaged stock ₹ 8,000 is the effect of change in accounting estimate. Thus, the value of closing stock for the year 2014-2015 will be as follows:

Particualrs	₹
Closing Stock (including damaged goods)	50,000
Less: Revised value of damaged goods	(4,000)
Closing stock (excluding damaged goods)	46,000

QUESTION 9: Goods of ₹ 5,00,000 were destroyed due to flood in September, 2012. A claim was lodged with insurance company, but no entry was passed in the books for insurance claim. In March, 2015, the claim was passed and the company received a payment of ₹ 3,50,000 against the claim. Explain the treatment of such receipt in final accounts for the year ended 31st March, 2015.

ANSWER:

PROVISION OF AS 5

As per the provisions of AS 5 prior period items are income or expenses, which arise, in the current period as a result of error or omissions in the preparation of financial statements of one or more prior periods. Further, the nature and amount of prior period items should be separately disclosed in the statement of profit and loss in a manner that their impact on current profit or loss can be perceived.

ADVICE

It is clearly a case of error in preparation of financial statements for the year 2012-2013. Hence, claim received in the financial year 2013-2014 is a prior period item and should be separately disclosed in the Statement of Profit and Loss.

QUESTION 10: XY Ltd. was making provisions for non-moving stocks based on no issues for the last 12 months upto 31.03.2014. Based on technical evaluation the company wants to make provisions during the year 31.03.2015

Total value of stock — ₹ 150 lakhs.

Provisions required based on 12 months issue ₹ 4.0 lakhs.

Provisions required based on technical evaluation ₹ 3.20 lakhs.

Does this amount to change in accounting policy? Can the company change the method of provision?

ANSWER:

PROVISION OF AS 5

As per AS 5. The method of estimating the amount of provision may be changed, in case, a more prudent estimate can be made by adopting the changed method.

ADVICE

The decision of making provision for non-moving stocks on the basis of technical evaluation does not amount to change in accounting policy as per AS 5. In the given case, considering the total value of stocks, the change in the amount of required provision of non-moving stocks from ₹ 4.0 lakhs to ₹ 3.20 lakhs is also not material. The disclosure can be made for such change by way of notes to the accounts in the financial statements of XY Ltd. for the year ending on 31.03.2015, in the following manner:

"The company has provided for non-moving stocks on the basis of technical evaluation unlike preceding years. Had the same method been followed as in the previous year, the profit for the year and the corresponding effect on the year end, the net assets would have been higher by ₹ 0.80 lakhs".

QUESTION 11: There was a major theft of stores valued at ₹ 46 lakhs in the preceding year detected only during the current financial year.

ANSWER:

PROVISION OF AS 5

As per AS 5. The adjustments are required to be made in the current year as 'Prior Period Items'.

ADVICE

Due to major theft of stores in the preceding year which was detected only during the current financial year there was overstatement of closing stock of stores in the preceding year. This must have also resulted in the overstatement of profits of previous year, brought forward to the current year; Accordingly, the adjustments relating to both opening stock of the current year and profit brought forward from the previous year should be separately disclosed in the Statement of Profit and Loss together with their nature and amount in a manner that their impact on the current profit or loss can be perceived. The disclosure as to the theft and the resulting loss is required in the notes to the accounts for the current year.

QUESTION 12: M/s Dinesh & Company signed an agreement with workers tor increase in wages with retrospective effect. The out-flow on account of arrears was for 2011-2012—₹ 10.00 lakhs, for 2012–2013 ₹ 12.00 lakhs and for 2013-2014 ₹ 12.00 lakhs. This amount is payable in September, 2014. The accountant wants to charge ₹ 22.00 lakhs as prior period charges in financial statement for 2014-2015. Discuss.

ANSWER:

PROVISION OF AS 5

As per AS 5 the term prior period item refers only to income or expenses which arise in the current period as a result of errors or omission in the preparation of the financial statements of one or more prior periods. The term does not include other adjustments necessitated by circumstances, which though related to prior periods are determined in the current period.

ADVICE

The full amount of wage arrears paid to workers will be treated as an expense of current year and it will be charged to profit and loss account as current expenses and not as prior period expenses.

It may be mentioned that additional wages is an expense arising from the ordinary activities of the company. Although abnormal in amount, such an expense does not qualify as an extraordinary item. However, as per Para 12 of AS 5 (Revised), when items of income and expense within profit or loss from ordinary activities are of such size, nature or incidence that their disclosure is relevant to explain the performance of the enterprise for the period, the nature and amount of such items should be disclosed separately.

QUESTION 13: In the previous year "R" Ltd. has made a provision of 11% of the contract value on an ongoing project. The actual loss on completion of the contract in the subsequent year was 12%. The management adjusted the difference in the previous year's account. Comment.

ANSWER:

PROVISION OF AS 5

As per AS 5 on 'Net Profit of Loss for the Period, Prior Period Items and Changes in Accounting Policies', effect of a change in an accounting estimate should be included in determination of net profit or loss in the period of the change, if the change affects the period only.

ADVICE

The provision of loss of 11% of the contract value of R Ltd. in previous year is in the nature of accounting estimate since due to uncertainties inherent in any business activity; it is difficult to measure such item in a precise manner. Accordingly, adjusting the difference in the previous year's account is not correct. Thus, the management should adjust the difference in the current period only. If such treatment is not done the auditor should quality his report.

QUESTION 14: MRE Ltd. provided ₹ 25 lakhs for inventory obsolence in 2014-2015. In the subsequent years, it was determined the 50% of such stock was usable. The Board of Directors wants to adjust the same through prior period adjustment. Comment.

ANSWER:

PROVISION OF AS 5

As per AS 5 on "Net Profit or Loss for the Period, Prior Period Items and Changes in Accounting Policies", prior period items are income or expenses which arise in the current period as a result of errors or omissions in the preparation of the financial statements of one or more prior periods. The write-back of provision made in respect of inventories in the earlier year does not constitute prior period adjustment sine it *neither* constitutes error *nor* omission but it merely involves making estimates based on prevailing circumstance when financial statements were being prepared. It is a mere estimate process involving judgement based on the latest information available.

An estimate may have to be revised if changes occur regarding the circumstances on which the estimate was based, or as a result of new information, more experience or subsequent development. The revision of the estimate, by its nature, does not bring the adjustment with in the definitions of an extraordinary item or a prior period item.

ADVICE

MRE Ltd. provided ₹ 25 lakhs for inventory obsolescence in 2014-2015. In the subsequent year due to change in circumstances, it was determined at 50% of such stock was usable. Revision of such an estimate does not bring the resulting amount of ₹ 12.5 lakhs within the definition either of a prior period item or of an extraordinary item. The amount, however, involved is material and requires separate disclosure to understand the financial position and performance of an enterprise. Accordingly, adjustment in the value of the inventory through prior period item would not be proper.

QUESTION 15:

(i) The difference between actual expense or income and the estimated expense or income as accounted for in earlier year's accounts, does not necessarily constitute the item to be a "prior period" item. Comment.

(ii) When can an item qualify to be a prior period item ?

ANSWER:

(i) To statement given in the question is correct and is in accordance with the accounting standard AS-5.

The use of reasonable estimates is an essential party of the preparation of financial statements and does not undermine their reliability. An estimate may have to be revised if changes occur regarding the circumstances on which the estimate was based, or as a result of new information or subsequent developments. The revision of the estimate, by its nature, does not bring the adjustments within the definition of an extraordinary item or a prior period item.

(ii) Prior Period Item: When incomes or expenses arise in the current period as a result of errors or omissions in the preparation of the financial statements of one or more prior periods, the said incomes or expenses have to be classified as prior period items. The errors may occur as a result of mathematical mistakes, mistakes in applying accounting policies, misinterpretation of facts or oversight.

QUESTION 16: During the year 2014 - 2015, a company write down its inventories to net realizable value by ₹ 10,00,000. Is a disclosure in this behalf is necessary?

ANSWER:

PROVISION OF AS 5

As per AS-5 when item of income and expense within profit and loss from ordinary activities are of such size, nature or incidence that their disclosure is relevant to explain the performance of enterprise for the period, the nature and amount of such items should be disclosed separately.

ADVICE

Yes, it is necessary to make a separate disclosure in respect of writing down inventories to its net realizable value. Accordingly, the nature and amount of this item should be disclosed separately as per AS-5.

QUESTION 17: X Ltd. has been including interest in the valuation of closing stock. In 2014-2015, the management of the company decided to follow AS - 2 and accordingly interest has been excluded from the valuation of closing stock. This has resulted in a decrease in profits by ₹ 5,00,000. Is a disclosure necessary?

ANSWER:

PROVISION OF AS 5

As per AS-5, a change in accounting policy should be made only if adoption of different accounting policy is required by statute or for compliance with an accounting standard or if it is considered that the change would result in more appropriate presentation. As per AS - 5, whenever there is a change in accounting policy and the change have material effect in current period then the company must disclose the nature of change, financial affect of change on items to the extent ascertainable and where the amount is not ascertainable in wholly or part then indicate this fact.

ADVICE

Yes, disclosure is necessary since this is change in accounting policy. This change has been made for compliance with AS-2.

QUESTION 18: A suit for damages for ₹ 1 lakhs for breach of contract of sale (breach occurred in 2008) was decided in favour of May Ltd. in March 2015. The Company has included the amount in its turnover for the financial year 2014-2015.

ANSWER:

PROVISION OF AS 5

As per AS-5 The separate disclosure of such an item should be called for in case having regard to nature, size or incidence of the item concerned and that the separate disclosure is relevant to explain the performance of the enterprise for the period.

ADVICE

It is not a prior period item as the suit was decreed only during the current financial year. Securing damages for breach of contract cannot be treated as an extraordinary item also since it forms part of ordinary activities of the business. **Thus, having regard to the materially of the amount received it may be considered whether the same way be disclosed separately the profit and loss account. Alternatively, a separate disclosure may be made in the notes to financial statements.**

QUESTION 19: A Limited company estimated 1 % bad debt while preparing financial statements for the year ended 31.03.2014. Provision for doubtful debts was created accordingly. However, it appears in 2014-2015 that some receivables are still lying uncollected. The management

feels that an additional 40 % provision is necessary on such debts. Should such change in estimate be treated as extraordinary item? Is it prior period item? Discuss briefly.

ANSWER:

PROVISION OF AS 5

As per AS-5 a change in accounting estimate which has a material effect in the current period should be disclosed and quantified. Any change in an accounting estimate which is expected to have a material effect in later periods should also be disclosed.

ADVICE

The preparation of financial statements involve making estimates which are based on the circumstances existing at the time when the financial statements are prepared. It may be necessary to revise an estimate in a subsequent period if there is a change in the circumstances on which the estimate was based. As per AS - 5, revision of an estimate does not bring the resulting amount within the definition either of prior period item or of an extraordinary item.

In the given case, a limited company estimated 1 % debt at the end of the accounting year 2013-2014 and accordingly made a provision for doubtful debt. Subsequently in 2014-2015 they revised the estimates based on the changed circumstances and wants to create 40% provision. As per AS - 5, this change in estimate is neither a prior period item nor an extraordinary item.

QUESTION 20: A loss of ₹ 2 lakhs on account of embezzlement of cash was suffered by the company and it was debited to salary account. Comment.

ANSWER:

PROVISION OF AS 5

As per AS-5 when item of income and expense within profit and loss from ordinary activities are of such size, nature or incidence that their disclosure is relevant to explain the performance of enterprise for the period, the nature and amount of such items should be disclosed separately.

ADVICE

In this instant case the loss on account of embezzlement should be disclosed separately and not be merged with salary account

QUESTION 21: A company deals in petroleum products. The sale price of petrol is fixed by the Government. In the current year the Government unexpectedly increased the price of the petrol retrospectively. Can the revenue from unexpected increase relating to prior periods be treated as prior period item? Discuss.

ANSWER: The revenue relating to prior periods due to the unexpected increase in petroleum product prices retrospectively by the Government cannot be considered as prior period item as per AS - 5 because there was no error or omission in preparation of financial statements of previous year. Therefore, revenue due to unexpected increase in prices is to be recognized only in the year when the Government announced the price increase.

QUESTION 22: Some of the transport claims lodged in 2014-2015 has been settled by the carrier in February, 2015 by paying ₹ 2,00,000. These claims were not recorded in the books of the company so far. Comment.

ANSWER: As per AS - 9 where the ability to assess the ultimate collection with reasonable certainty is lacking at the time of raising any claim, revenue recognition is postponed the extent of uncertainty involved. As per AS - 9 when recognition of revenue is postponed due to the effect of uncertainties, it is also considered as revenue of the period in which it is reasonable certain that ultimate collection will be made. In this case, it may be assumed that collectability of claim was not certain in the earlier years. So this transaction cannot be taken as 'Prior - period item'. It will not be treated as extraordinary item as per AS-5. However, AS-5 states that when item of income and expense within profit and loss from ordinary activities are of such size, nature or incidence that their disclosure is relevant to explain the performance of enterprise for the period, the nature and amount of such items should be disclosed separately. Accordingly, the nature and amount of this item should be disclosed separately as per AS-5.

QUESTION 23: Finished Goods costing ₹ 10 Lakhs were damaged due to flood in July 2013. These goods were included in Closing Stock as on March 31, 2014 at an estimated realizable value of ₹ 4.00 Lakhs. These goods could be ultimately sold for ₹ 3 Lakhs only in August 2014. The difference of ₹ 1 Lakh was debited as Prior Period expenditure in financial year 2014-2015. As an auditor, please comment in the light of provisions of Accounting Standards.

ANSWER:

PROVISION OF AS 5

Prior Period Item: Write–back of provision made in respect of inventories in the earlier year does not constitute Prior Period Adjustment since it is not an error or omission relating to prior period Financial Statements. It merely involves making estimates based on prevailing circumstances when these Financial Statements were being prepared.

Revision of Estimate: An estimate may have to be revised – (a) if changes occur in the circumstances on which the estimate was based, (b) or as a result of new information, more experience or subsequent developments. The revision of the estimate, by its nature, does not bring the adjustment within the definitions of an Extra–Ordinary Item or a Prior Period Item.

ADVICE

There is no error or omission in the Prior Period. It is a case of change in accounting estimates as to the estimated NRV of damaged item, which have changed when the damaged goods have been finally sold.

The difference of ₹ 1 Lakh is not a Prior Period Item. Hence, debiting it to Prior Period Expenditure in the accounting year 2014–2015 is a **wrong accounting treatment.**

QUESTION 24: A Limited company created a provision for bad and doubtful debts at 5% on debtors in preparing the financial statements for the year 2014-2015. Subsequently on a review of the credit period allowed and financial capacity of the customers, the company decided to increase the provision to 10% on debtors as on 31-03-2015. The accounts are not approved by the Board of Directors till the date of decision. While applying the relevant accounting standard, can this revision be considered as an extraordinary item or prior period item?

ANSWER:

PROVISION OF AS 5

As per AS 5 'Net Profit or Loss for the Period, Prior Period Items and Changes in Accounting Policies', the preparation of financial statements involve making estimates which are based on the circumstances existing at the time when the financial statements are prepared. It may be necessary to revise an estimate in a subsequent period if there is a change in the circumstances on which the estimate was based. Revision of an estimate, by its nature, does not bring the adjustment within the definitions of a prior period item or an extra ordinary item.

ADVICE

The change in estimated provision for doubtful debts is neither a prior period item nor an extra ordinary item.

However, as per para 27 of the standard, a change in accounting estimate which has material effect in the current period should be disclosed and quantified. Any change in the accounting estimate which is expected to have a material effect in later periods should also be disclosed and quantified.

QUESTION 25: X Co. Ltd. signed an agreement with its employees union for revision of wages in June, 2015. The wage revision is with retrospective effect from 1.4.2011. The arrear wages upto 31.3.2015 amounts to ₹ 80 lakhs. Arrear wages for the period from 1.4.2015 to 30.6.2015 (being the date of agreement) amounts to ₹ 7 lakhs. Decide whether a separate disclosure of arrear wages is required.

ANSWER

PROVISION OF AS 5

As per AS 5, when items of income and expense within profit or loss from ordinary activities are of such size, nature or incidence that their disclosure is relevant to explain the performance of the enterprise for the period, the **nature and amount of such items should be disclosed separately.**

ADVICE

It is given that revision of wages took place in June, 2015 with retrospective effect from 1.4.2011. The arrear wages payable for the period from 1.4.2011 to 30.6.2015 cannot be taken as an error or omission in the preparation of financial statements and hence this expenditure **cannot be taken as a prior period item.**

Additional liability on account of wages amounting ₹ 87 lakhs (from 1.4.2011 to 30.6.2015) should be included in current year's wages.

It may be mentioned that additional wages is an expense arising from the ordinary activities of the company. Although abnormal in amount, such an expense does not qualify as an extraordinary item. However, wages payable for the current year (from 1.4.2015 to 30.6.2015) amounting ₹ 7 lakhs is not a prior period item hence need not be disclosed separately. This may be shown as current year wages.

7 AS 10—FIXED ASSETS

THEORETICAL BASE

QUESTION 1: What are the areas to which AS – 10 is not applicable?

ANSWER:

1. Accounting for Fixed Assets under Inflation Accounting
2. Accounting for Forests, Plantations and similar Regenerative Natural Resources;
3. Accounting for Wasting Assets including Mineral Rights, expenditure on the exploration for and extraction of Minerals, Oil and Natural Gas and similar Non - Regenerative Resources;
4. Accounting for Expenditure on Real Estate Development;
5. Accounting for Live stock.
6. Allocation of the Depreciable Amount of Fixed Assets to future periods which is dealt with AS 6
7. Treatment of Government Grants and subsidies which is dealt with AS 12
8. Assets under Leasing Rights.
9. Borrowing Cost which is dealt with AS 16
10. Assets acquired in an Amalgamation or Merger which is dealt with AS 14

QUESTION 2: What is meant by the term 'Fixed Asset'?

ANSWER: Fixed asset is an asset held with the intention of being used for the purpose of producing or providing goods or services and is not held for sale in the normal course of business

QUESTION 3: What is meant by the term 'Gross Book Value of a Fixed Asset'?

ANSWER:

Gross Book Value = Historical Cost or other amount substituted 'for historical cost in the books of account of financial statements.

Net Book Value = Gross Book Value – Accumulated Depreciation

QUESTION 4: What is meant by term 'Fair Market Value of a Fixed Asset?

ANSWER: FMV is the price that would be agreed to in an open and unrestricted market between knowledgeable and willing parties dealing at arm's length who are fully informed and are not under any compulsion to transact.

QUESTION 5: What are the various components of cost of Fixed Asset?

ANSWER:

1. Purchase Price (Less any Trade Discounts and Rebates)
2. Import Duties and other non Refundable Taxes or Levies;
3. Directly attributable cost of bringing the asset to its working condition for its intended use. (e.g. site preparation, initial delivery and handling costs installation cost, such as special foundations for plant, professional fees of architects and engineers)

4. Finance Cost as dealt in AS-16.
5. Expenditure incurred on start-up and commissioning of the project,(including the expenditure incurred on test runs and experimental production)

Note: Administration and other general overhead expenses not relating to a specific fixed asset are usually excluded from the cost of fixed assets.

QUESTION 6: What is the treatment of expenses incurred ?

(a) upto the date of commencement of commercial production

(b) between the date at which a project is ready to commence commercial production and the date at which commercial production actually begins

(c) after the date of commencement of commercial production

ANSWER:

TREATMENT OF EXPENDITURE

1. Expenditure incurred upto the date of commencement of commercial production	Should be capitalized
2. Expenditure incurred between the date at which the project becomes ready to commence commercial production and the date at which commercial production actually begins	Should be treated as Revenue/Deferred Revenue Expenditure.
3. Subsequent Expenditures	Should be capitalized only if they increase the future benefits from the existing asset beyond its previously assessed standard of performance

QUESTION 7: How is the Gross Book Value of Self Constructed Fixed Asset computed?

ANSWER: It should comprise those costs that—

(a) relate directly to the specific asset, and

(b) that are attributable to the construction activity in general and can be allocated to the specific asset.

Note: Any internal profits are eliminated in arriving at such costs.

QUESTION 8: How is the fixed asset acquired in exchange of another asset recorded?

ANSWER: The cost of such asset acquired should be recorded either—

(a) at FMV of the asset given up or the asset acquired, whichever is more clearly evident. or

(b) at the Net Book Value of the asset given up, (*plus/minus* other consideration, if any)

QUESTION 9: How is the fixed asset acquired in exchange of Securities recorded?

ANSWER: The cost of such asset acquired should be recorded either at FMV of Asset acquired or Securities issued whichever is more clearly evident.

QUESTION 10: How should first revaluation of asset be accounted for?

ANSWER:

1. Surplus should be credited to Revaluation Reserve.
2. Deficiency should be charged to Profit & Loss A/c.

QUESTION 11: How should the subsequent revaluation be accounted for?

ANSWER:

1. Surplus to the extent of decrease arising on revaluation previously charged to Profit & Loss A/c should be credited to Profit & Loss A/c and remaining surplus should be credited to Revaluation Reserve.
2. Deficiency to the extent of increase arising on revaluation previously credited to Revaluation Reserve should be reversed or utilized and remaining deficiency should be charged to Profit & Loss A/c

QUESTION 12: Should Accumulated Depreciation existing at the date of upward revaluation be credited to P&L A/c?

ANSWER: No

QUESTION 13: How should the Balance of Revaluation Reserve after Disposal be treated?

ANSWER: T/F to General Reserve. It is not mandatory.

QUESTION 14: Can Business losses be adjusted against Revaluation Reserve?

ANSWER: No

QUESTION 15: State the Accounting Treatment of Profit/Loss on Disposal of Fixed Asset.

ANSWER:

Case	Treatment
1. Profit on Retirement/Disposal	Credit to Profit & Loss A/c
2. Loss on Retirement/Disposal	
(i) Related to increase already credited to Revaluation Reserve	Credit to Revaluation Reserve
(ii) Other Loss	Debit to Profit & Loss A/c

QUESTION 16: How should the Fixed Assets retired from active use and held for disposal be stated in the financial statements?

ANSWER: These should be stated at the **lower** of their Net Book Value *or* Net Realizable Value and shown appropriately in the financial statements.

QUESTION 17: How are the Fixed Assets owned by the enterprise jointly with others disclosed?

ANSWER:

1. In the case of fixed assets owned by the enterprise jointly with others, the extent of the enterprise's share in such assets, and the proportion of the original cost, accumulated depreciation and written down value should be stated in the balance sheet.
2. Alternatively, the pro-rata cost of such jointly owned assets may be grouped together with similar fully owned assets with an appropriate disclosure thereof

QUESTION 18: How is the value apportioned to fixed assets when various fixed assets are purchased for a consolidated price?

ANSWER: Where several assets are purchased for a consolidated price, the consideration should be apportioned to the various assets on a fair basis as determined by competent valuers.

QUESTION 19: When should Goodwill be recorded ? How should Goodwill be amortized?

ANSWER:

1. Goodwill should be recorded in the books only when some consideration in money or money's worth has been paid for it.
2. It should be amortized as per AS 26.

QUESTION 20: State the Disclosure Requirements as per AS 10.

ANSWER:

1. Gross and net book values of fixed assets at the beginning and at the end of an accounting period showing additions, disposals, acquisitions and other movements;
2. Expenditure incurred on account of fixed assets in the course of construction or acquisition; and
3. Revalued amounts substituted for historical costs of fixed assets, the method adopted to compute the revalued amounts, the nature of indices used, the year of any appraisal made, and whether an external valuer was involved, in case where fixed assets are stated at revalued amounts.

PRACTICAL QUESTIONS FOR PRACTICE

COST OF NEW ASSET ACQUIRED AS PER AS 10

QUESTION 1: S Ltd. acquired a land for their factory site for ₹ 100 Lakhs. It demolished an old building constructed on land and sold the scrap for ₹ 1 lakhs. From the data given below compute the amount to be capitalized in Land A/c.

Particulars	₹ in Lakhs
Legal fees for registration of Sale deed.	**2**
Title Gurantee Insurance	**1**
Cost of demolition of old building	**3**

ANSWER:

CALCULATION OF COST OF LAND TO BE CAPITALIZED AS PER AS 10

Particulars	₹ in Lakhs	
A. Purchase Cost		100
B. Legal fees for registration of Sale deed.		2
C. Title Gurantee Insurance		1
D. Cost of demolition of old building	₹ 3 Lakhs	
Less: Sale proceeds from sale of the scrap	₹ 1 Lakhs	2
E. Cost of land to be capitalized		105

QUESTION 2: X Ltd. purchased machinery from Y Ltd. on 30th Sept. 2014. The price was 522.50 lakhs after charging 10 % Vat and giving a trade discount of 5% on the quoted price. Transport charges were 0.25 % on the quoted price and installation charges come to 1% on the quoted price.

A loan of ₹ 500 lakhs was taken from bank on which interest at 15 % per annum was to be paid.

Expenditure incurred on the trial run was: Material ₹ 50,000, wages ₹ 40,000 and overheads ₹ 30,000.

Machinery was ready for use on 1st Dec. 2014. However it was actually put to use only on 1st May, 2015. Find out the cost of the machine and suggest the accounting treatment for the expenses incurred in the interval between the dates 1st Dec. 2014 to 1st May 2015. The entire loan amount remained unpaid on 1st May 2015. X Ltd. does not intend to utilize the input tax paid on capital good.

ANSWER:

CALCULATION OF COST OF MACHINE TO BE CAPITALIZED AS PER AS 10

Particulars		₹ in lakhs
A. Quoted Price of machine		500.00
B. Trade discount @ 5 % on ₹ 500		25.00
C. Price after discount [A – B]		475.00
D. VAT @ 10 % on ₹ 475		47.50
E. Selling Price [C + D]		522.50
F. Transportation charges [0.25 % of ₹ 500]		1.25
G. Installation charges [1 % of ₹ 500]		5.00
H. Borrowing cost [₹ 500 lakhs × 15% × 2/12]		12.50
I. Expenditure on Trial Run		
Material:	0.50	
Wages:	0.40	
Overheads:	0.30	1.20
J. Total Cost of the machinery to be capitalized [E + F + G + H + I]		542.45

As per AS - 16, the capitalization of interest should cease when substantially all the activities necessary for intended use are completed. Therefore, interest for the period 01.12.2014 to 01.05.2015 should be expensed.

Working notes:

1. Selling Price before VAT = ₹ 522.50 lakh × 100/110 = ₹475 lakhs
2. Quoted Price before Trade Discount = ₹475 lakh × 100/95 = ₹500 lakhs
3. As per As 16 interest should be capitalized only for the period when substantially all the activities necessary for intended use are completed. In present case machinery was ready for use on 1st Dec. 2012. Hence in this case capitalization of interest should be done for only two months (i.e. from 30th Sept. 2014 to 1st Dec., 2014)

   Interest for the two months = 500 lakhs × 15 % × (2 months/12 months) = 12.50 lakhs.

QUESTION 3: Amna Ltd. contracted with a supplier to purchase a specific machinery to be installed in Department A in two months time. Special foundations were required for the plant, which were to be prepared within this supply lead time. The cost of site preparation and laying foundations were ₹ 47,290. These activities were supervised by a technician during the entire period, who is employed for this purpose of ₹ 15,000 per month. The technician's services were given to Department A by Department B, which billed the services at ₹ 16,500 per month after adding 10% profit margin.

The machine was purchased at ₹ 52,78,000. Sales Tax was changed at 4% on the invoice ₹ 18,590 transportation charges were incurred to bring the machine to the factory. An Architect

was engaged at a fee of ₹ 10,000 to supervise machinery installation at the factory premises. Also, payment under the invoice was due in 3 months. However, the Company made the payment in 2nd month. The company operates on Bank Overdraft@ 11%.

Ascertain the amount at which the asset should be capitalized under AS 10.

ANSWER:

CALCULATION OF COST OF FIXED ASSET (I.E. MACHINE)

Particulars	₹
Purchase Price (Given)	52,78,000
Add: Sales Tax at 4% (₹ 52,78,000 × 4%)	2,11,120
Site Preparation Cost (Given)	47,290
Technician's Salary (Specific/Attributable overheads for 2 months)	30,000
Initial Delivery Cost (Transportation)	18,590
Professional Fees for Installation (Architect's Fees)	10,000
Total Cost of Asset	55,95,000

Notes:

1. Interest on Bank Overdraft for earlier payment of invoice is not relevant under AS 10. It may be noted that overdraft facility is generally used for working capital purpose.
2. Internally booked profits should be eliminated in arriving at the cost of Fixed Assets.
3. In the absence of information about excise, CENVAT credit has been ignored.
4. It has been assumed that the purchase price of ₹ 52,78,000 excludes amount of sales tax.

QUESTION 4: W Ltd. purchased machinery for ₹ 80 lakhs from X Ltd. during 2014-2015 and installed the same immediately. Price includes excise duty of ₹ 8 lakhs. During the year 2014-2015, the company produced exciseable goods on which excise duty of ₹ 7.20 lakhs was charged.

Give necessary entries explaining the treatment of Cenvat Credit.

ANSWER:

JOURNAL — **₹ in lakhs**

Particulars		Dr.	Cr.
(a) Machinery A/c	Dr.	72	
Cenvat credit receivable on capital goods A/c	Dr.	8	
To Bank A/c or Creditors A/c			80
(Being capitalization of machinery)			
(b) Excise duty A/c	Dr.	7.2	
To Cenvat credit receivable on capital goods A/c			4.0
To Bank A/c			3.2
(Being excise duty set off to the extent of 50% of excise duty paid in the first year of acquisition of capital asset)			

QUESTION 5: Comptech Ltd. having office at Chennai, acquired a sophisticated three dimensional (3D) computer printer having all inclusive MRP (Maximum Retail Price) of ₹ 50 lakhs from a supplier located at New Delhi. The terms of the purchase were as under:

(i) The supplier would buy back the existing unit with Comptech that has carrying amount of ₹ 10.20 lakhs. Prevailing CST rate is 2%.

(ii) The supplier would give a special discount of 10% on MRP to Comptech considering their long standing relationship.

(iii) A cash payment of ₹ 38.25 lakhs would be made by Comptech Ltd. to the supplier.

(iv) Accessories required to operate the machine costing ₹ 7.60 lakhs (inclusive of all taxes) will be purchased by Comptech.

(v) The supplier will deliver free of cost certain heavy duty cables etc. having MRP of ₹ 5.75 lakhs, that are required to run the machine.

(vi) Transit insurance cost will be borne by Comptech @ 2% of MRP.

(vii) Freight and other incidentals amounting to ₹ 2.30 lakhs is borne by Comptech.

You are required to arrive at the cost of the new asset and show the profit/(loss) incurred by Comptech on the buy back arrangement and also draft the Journal Entries to record the above transaction.

ANSWER:

PROVISION OF AS 10

As per para 22 of AS 10 ₹ Accounting for Fixed Assets', when a fixed asset is acquired in part exchange for another asset, the cost of the asset acquired should be recorded either at fair market value or at the net book value of the asset given up, adjusted for any balancing payment. In the given question the FMV of the new machine is its MRP net of special concession given to the buyer.

CALCULATION OF COST OF NEW ASSET

Particulars	₹ in lakhs
MRP of Printer	50
Less: Special Discount 10% of MRP	5
Add: Accessories	7.6
Add: Transit Insurance Cost (2% of 50 lakh)	1
Add: Freight and other incidental amount	2.30
	55.9

PROFIT /LOSS INCURRED ON BUY-BACK ARRANGEMENT

Particulars	₹ in lakhs
Discounted price of new machine	45.00
Less: Cash portion thereof	38.25
FMV of old machine	6.75*
Less: Book Value thereof	10.20
Loss on Buy back	3.45
*This includes CST of 2%. Thus the CST will be 6.75 × 2/102 = 0.13 lakh	

JOURNAL

Particulars	Dr. (₹ in lakhs)	Cr. (₹ in lakhs)
1. 3D Computer Printer A/c Dr.	49.15	
To Cash A/c		49.15
(Being the expenses incurred for purchase of 3D computer – cash payment 38.25 + accessory 7.6 + insurance 1 and freight 2.3)		
2. 3D Computer Printer A/c Dr.	6.75	
Loss on buy back of old machine A/c Dr.	3.45	
To Old Machine A/c		10.20
(Being the transfer of FMV of ₹ 6.75 lakhs of old machine to new printer under buy-back scheme and recognition of loss on buy back)		

Note: It is assumed that the cash payment of ₹ 38.25 lakhs is the full and final payment to the supplier for the printer.

TREATMENT OF SUBSEQUENT EXPENDITURES

QUESTION 6: List 4 Examples of Subsequent Expenditures which are treated as (a) Capital Expenditure (b) Revenue Expenditure.

ANSWER:

Examples of Subsequent Expenditures to be treated as Capital Expenditure	Examples of Subsequent Expenditures to be treated as Revenue Expenditure
1. Cost of Improvements which will increase earning capacity.	1. Routine Repairs & overhauling of Machinery to maintain it in good condition
2. Cost of Improvements which will decrease cost.	2. Cost of Dismantling and re-erection.
3. Cost of Replacements which doubled the output.	3. Expenses on shifting existing machine on new site.
4. Compensation to existing tenants so as to lease the property at higher rates.	4. Cost of Building of a new foundation to shift an existing machine.
5. Cost of Trial Run sub-standard Production.	

QUESTION 7: From the following information state the amount to be capitalized as per AS 10 with reason. ₹ 5 lakhs as routine repairs and ₹ 1 lakh on partial replacement of a part of a machine. ₹ 10 lakhs on replacement of part of a machinery which will improve the efficiency of a machine.

ANSWER:

PROVISION OF AS 10

1. As per AS 10 "Accounting for Fixed Assets", expenditure on repairs and improvements to the asset should be capitalised if it increases the efficiency of the asset or the expected useful life of the asset or if it reduces the operating cost of the asset.
2. Expenditure in the nature of routine repairs which is incurred to maintain the asset is required to be expensed in the year in which it is incurred.

DECISION

1. ₹ 5 Lakhs incurred as routine repairs and ₹ 1 Lakhs on partial replacement of a part a machine should be expensed as these do not increase pre-assessed benefits from the assets.
2. ₹ 10 Lakhs spent on improvement of machinery will be capitalized as it improves the efficiency of the asset.

QUESTION 8: X Ltd. purchases a building that already has non moving tenants. Subsequently X Ltd. pays significant compensation to these tenants, so that the property could be leased to a third party at much higher rates. Advise X Ltd. on the treatment of the compensation.

ANSWER:

PROVISION OF AS 10

As per AS 10 Subsequent expenditures that increases the future benefits from the existing asset beyond its previously assessed standard of performance is capitalized.

ADVICE

In a present situation, compensation paid to the tenants increases the future benefits of the building beyond its previously assessed standard of performance. Hence, the compensation paid to the tenants should be capitalized as cost of the building.

QUESTION 9: A company undertook a repair and overhauling of its machinery at cost of ₹ 3 crores to maintain them in good condition and capitalized the amount as it is more than 30% of the original cost of the machinery. What should be your comment as a company auditor.

ANSWER:

PROVISION OF AS 10

As per AS 10 expenditure that increases the future benefits from the existing asset beyond its previously assessed standard of performance should be capitalized.

ADVICE

In present case *neither* the earning capacity has increased *nor* there is any reduction in the cost of production, hence there is no increase in future benefits beyond its originally assessed standard of performance. In the absence of these criteria, it is to be treated as revenue expenditure. The mere fact that expenditure on maintenance is more than 30 % of the original cost of the machinery would not change its nature. Consequently, the auditor would be required to qualify his report.

QUESTION 10: During the year, P Limited incurred the following expenses on machinery: ₹ 2.50 lacs as routine repairs and ₹75,000 on partial replacement of a part. ₹ 7 lacs on replacement of part of a machinery which will improve the efficiency of the machine. Which amount should be capitalized as per AS 10?

ANSWER:

PROVISION OF AS 10

As per only those expenditures that increase the future benefits from the existing assets, is to be included in the gross book value. Example: Increase in capacity.

ADVICE

₹3.25 lacs spent on repairs and partial replacement of a part of the machinery should be charged to Profit and Loss Account as they will help in maintaining the capacity but will not improve the efficiency of the machine. However, ₹ 7 lacs incurred on replacement of a part of the machinery, which will increase the efficiency, should be capitalized by inclusion in the gross book value of assets,

QUESTION 11: A company is in the process of setting up a production line for manufacturing a new product. Based on trial runs conducted by the company, it was noticed that the production lines output was not of the desired quality. However, company has taken a decision to manufacture and sell the sub-standard product over the next one year due to the huge investment involved. In the background of the relevant accounting standard, advice the company on the cut - off date for capitalization of the project cost.

ANSWER:

PROVISION OF AS 10

As per AS 10 the expenditure incurred after the plant has begun commercial production i.e., production intended for sale or captive consumption is not capitalized and is treated as revenue expenditure

ADVICE

In the present case, the company decided to sell the sub - standard production, and therefore, the expenditure incurred to this date will be capitalized as it will be deemed that commercial production intended for sale has begun and the cut - off date would be the date when the trial run of sub - standard product was completed.

QUESTION 12: A company has scrapped a semi - automatic part of a machine (not written off) and replaced with a more expensive fully automatic part, which has doubled the output of the machine. At the time to the machine was moved to a more suitable place in the factory, which involved the building of a new foundation in addition to the cost of dismantling and re-erection. The company wants to charge the whole expenditure to revenue. As an auditor give your comments for this situation.

ANSWER:

Subsequent Expenditure on fully automatic part	It should be capitalized as it has doubled the output of the machine, hence it has increased future benefits beyond the machines' pre - assessed standard of performance
Expenses for shifting the machine and building of a new foundation & the cost of dismantling	These costs should be charged to profit and loss statement. Since these do not contribute to any new future benefit from the existing asset. They only serve to maintain performance of the machine.

CALCULATION OF GROSS BOOK VALUE OF SELF CONSTRUCTED FIXED ASSET

QUESTION 13: PQR Ltd. constructed a fixed asset and incurred the following expenses on its construction:

Particulars	₹
Materials	**16,00,000**
Direct Expenses	**3,00,000**
Total Direct Labour	**6,00,000**
(1/15th of the total labour time was chargeable to the construction)	
Total Office & Administrative Expenses	**9,00,000**
(4% is chargeable to the construction)	
Depreciation on assets used for the construction of this asset	**15,000**

Calculate the Cost of the fixed asset.

ANSWER:

CALCULATION OF COST OF FIXED ASSETS

Particulars	₹
Materials	16,00,000
Direct expenses	3,00,000
Direct labour 1/15th of ₹ 6,00,000)	40,000
Office and administrative expenses (4% ₹ 9,00,000)	36,000
Depreciation on assets	15,000
Cost of fixed asset	19,91,000

Note: It is assumed that 4% of office and administrative expenses are specifically attributable to construction of a fixed asset. Alternatively, it may be assumed that 4% of office and administraive expenses are only allocated to construction project and is not specifically attributable to it. In such a case, the cost of fixed assets will be ₹19,55,000.

QUESTION 14: A company has made additions to its factory buildings by its own workmen, at cost of ₹8,00,000 for wages and materials. The lowest estimate from an outsider contractor to carry out the same work was for ₹10,00,000. The directors contend that as they were fully entitled to employ an outside contractor, it is reasonable to debit the factory building account with ₹10,00,000. As an auditor of the company, what shall be your advice in the above case.

ANSWER:

PROVISION OF AS 10

As per AS 10 cost of a self-constructed fixed asset should comprise those costs that relate directly to the specific asset and those that are attributable to the construction activity in general and can be allocated to the specific asset. Any internal profits are eliminated in arriving at such costs.

ADVICE

Hence the factory building should be capitalized with ₹8,00,000 and not ₹10,00,000 as contended by the Board.

RECORDING OF FIXED ASSET ACQUIRED IN EXCHANGE OF ANOTHER ASSET

QUESTION 15:

Book value of old assets exchanged	**₹ 8,000**
Additional cash given for exchange of asset	**₹ 5,000**

Determine the cost of new asset acquired and show the accounting treatment in this regard in the following cases:

(a) If no other information is given

(b) Fair market value of old asset exchanged is ₹18,000

(c) Fair market value of new asset acquired in exchange of old asset is ₹25,000

ANSWER:

Case (a) When the market value of asset given up/ acquired is not clearly evident

JOURNAL

New Asset A/c	...Dr.	₹ 13,000	
To Bank A/c			₹ 5,000
To Old Asset A/c			₹ 8,000
(Being the cost of asset acquired is recorded at the book value of asset given up and adjusted for payment.)			

Case (b) When the market value of asset given up is more clearly evident

JOURNAL

New Asset A/c	...Dr.	₹ 23,000	
To Bank A/c			₹ 5,000
To Old Asset			₹18,000
(Being the cost of asset acquire d is recorded at the fair market value of asset given up and adjusted for payment)			
Old Asset A/c	...Dr.	₹10,000	
To Profit & loss A/c			₹10,000
(Being the excess of fair market value over book value is transferred to P&L A/c)			

Case (c) When the market value of asset acquired is more clearly evident

JOURNAL

New Asset A/c	...Dr.	₹ 25,000	
To Bank A/c			₹ 5,000
To Old Asset A/c			₹ 20,000
(Being the cost of asset acquired is recorded at its fair market value)			
Old Asset A/c	...Dr.	₹ 12,000	
To Profit & Loss A/c			₹ 12,000
(Being credit balance in Old Asset A/c is transferred to P&L A/c)			

QUESTION 16: One customer from whom ₹5 lakhs are recoverable for credit sales gives a motorcar in full settlement of the dues. The directors estimate that the market value of the motorcar transferred is ₹5.25 lakhs. As on the date of balance sheet the car has not been registered in the name of the auditee.Comment.

ANSWER:

PROVISION OF AS 10

As per AS 10 the asset acquired in an exchange of assets should be valued at the fair market value of assets acquired or the asset given up, whichever is more clearly evident.

ADVICE

Here fair market value of the assets given up obviously more clearly evident. Hence, the motorcar should be valued at ₹5 lakhs. Also the motorcar should be recognized as an asset even though it is not yet registered in auditee's name. This is because legal title is not necessary for an asset to exist. What is necessary is control as per the framework for preparation and presentation of financial statements. Applying substance over form it is concluded that since price has been settled, the auditee has control, hence it should be reflected as an asset along with a note to the effect that the registration in auditee name is pending.

RECORDING OF FIXED ASSET ACQUIRED IN EXCHANGE OF SECURITIES

QUESTION 17: XYZ Ltd. issue 1,00,000 equity shares of ₹10 each (fully paid up) in consideration for supply of a machinery by PQR Ltd. The shares exchanged for machinery are quoted on National Stock Exchange (NSE) at ₹25 per share, at the time of transaction. In the absence of fair market value of the machinery acquired, how the value of machinery would be recorded in the books of company.

ANSWER:

PROVISION OF AS 10

As per AS 10, fixed asset acquired in exchange for shares or other securities in the enterprise should be recorded at the fair market value of the asset acquired or the fair market value of the securities issued, whichever is more clearly evident.

ADVICE

Since, the market value of the shares exchanged for the asset is more clearly evident, the company should record the value of machinery at ₹ 25,00,000 (i.e. 1,00,000 shares × ₹ 25 per share being the market price). Journal entry in respect of this transaction is as follows:

JOURNAL

Machinery A/c ...Dr.	25,00,000	
To Share Capital A/c		10,00,000
To Securities Premium A/c		15,00,000
(Being machinery recorded at the fair market value of the securities issued in consideration for machinery acquired)		

ACCOUNTING FOR FIRST AND SUBSEQUENT REVALUATION OF ASSET AND TREATMENT OF PROFIT/LOSS ON DISPOSAL OF FIXED ASSET

QUESTION 18: Tulsian Ltd. provides you the following information:

Particulars	Plot of Land 1	Plot of Land 2	Plot of Land 3	Plot of Land 4	Plot of Land 5
Book Value on 1st April, 2013	1,00,000	1,00,000	1,00,000	1,00,000	1,00,000
Revalued on 31st March, 2014	1,20,000	1,20,000	80,000	80,000	1,20,000
Revalued on 31st March, 2015	1,15,000	95,000	1,00,000	1,05,000	1,15,000
Sold on 1st April, 2015	1,20,000	90,000	90,000	90,000	1,10,000

Pass the Journal Entries on 31st March, 2014, on 31st March, 2015 and 1st April, 2015.

ANSWER:

JOURNAL

Date	Particulars		Dr. (₹)	Cr. (₹)
31.03.2014	Asset 1 A/c	...Dr.	20,000	
	To Revaluation Reserve A/c			20,000
	(Being whole of the surplus arising on revaluation transferred to Revaluation Reserve A/c.)			
31.03.2014	Asset 2 A/c	...Dr.	20,000	
	To Revaluation Reserve A/c			20,000
	(Being whole of the surplus arising on revaluation transferred to Revaluation Reserve A/c.)			
31.03.2014	Profit & Loss A/c	...Dr.	20,000	
	To Asset 3 A/c			20,000
	(Being whole of the deficiency arising on revaluation transferred to P & LA/c.)			
31.03.2014	Profit & Loss A/c	...Dr.	20,000	
	To Asset 4 A/c			20,000
	(Being whole of the deficiency arising on revaluation transferred to P & LA/c.)			
31.03.2014	Asset 5 A/c	...Dr.	20,000	
	To Revaluation Reserve A/c			20,000
	(Being whole of the surplus arising on revaluation transferred to Revaluation Reserve A/c.)			
31.03.2015	Revaluation Reserve A/c	...Dr.	5,000	
	To Asset 1 A/c			20,000
	(Being deficiency to the extent of increase arising on revaluation previously credited to Revaluation Reserve utilized)			
31.03.2015	Revaluation Reserve A/c	...Dr.	20,000	
	Profit & Loss A/c	...Dr.	5,000	
	To Asset 2 A/c			25,000
	(Being deficiency to the extent of increase arising on revaluation previously credited to Revaluation Reserve utilized and remaining deficiency charged to Profit & Loss A/c)			
31.03.2015	Asset 3 A/c	...Dr.	20,000	
	To Profit & Loss A/c			20,000
	(Being Surplus to the extent of decrease arising on revaluation previously charged to Profit & Loss A/c credited to P & L A/c)			

31.03.2015	Asset 4 A/c	...Dr.	25,000	
	To Profit & Loss A/c			20,000
	To Revaluation Reserve A/c			5,000
	(Being Surplus to the extent of decrease arising on revaluation previously charged to Profit & Loss A/c credited to P & L A/c and remaining surplus credited to Revaluation Reserve A/c)			
31.03.2015	Revaluation Reserve A/c	...Dr.	5,000	
	To Asset 5 A/c			20,000
	(Being deficiency to the extent of increase arising on revaluation previously credited to Revaluation Reserve utilized)			
01.04.2015	Bank A/c	...Dr.	1,20,000	
	To Asset 1 A/c			1,20,000
	(Being the Asset sold)			
01.04.2015	Asset 1 A/c	...Dr.	5,000	
	To Profit & Loss A/c			5,000
	(Being profit on sale of land transferred to P & L A/c)			
01.04.2015	Revaluation Reserve A/c	...Dr.	15,000	
	To General Reserve A/c			15,000
	(Being balance of Revaluation Reserve A/c transferred to General Reserve A/c.)			
01.04.2015	Bank A/c	...Dr.	90,000	
	To Asset 2 A/c			90,000
	(Being the Asset sold)			
01.04.2015	Profit & Loss A/c	...Dr.	5,000	
	To Asset 2 A/c			5,000
	(Being Loss on sale of land transferred to P & L A/c)			
01.04.2015	Bank A/c	...Dr.	90,000	
	To Asset 3 A/c			90,000
	(Being the Asset sold)			
01.04.2015	Profit & Loss A/c	...Dr.	10,000	
	To Asset 3 A/c			10,000
	(Being Loss on sale of land transferred to P & L A/c)			
01.04.2015	Bank A/c	...Dr.	90,000	
	To Asset 4 A/c			90,000
	(Being the Asset sold)			
01.04.2015	Revaluation Reserve A/c	...Dr.	5,000	
	Profit & Loss A/c	...Dr.	10,000	
	To Asset 4 A/c			15,000
	(Being loss to the extent it is related to an increase previously credited to Revaluation Reserve A/c utilized.)			

01.04.2015	Bank A/c ...Dr. To Asset 5 A/c (Being the Asset sold)	1,10,000	1,10,000
01.04.2015	Revaluation Reserve A/c ...Dr. To Asset 5 A/c (Being loss to the extent it is related to an increase previously credited to Revaluation Reserve A/c utilized.)	5,000	5,000
01.04.2015	Revaluation Reserve A/c ...Dr. To General Reserve A/c (Being balance of Revaluation Reserve A/c transferred to General Reserve A/c.)	10,000	10,000

QUESTION 19: The company has written up its fixed assets by ₹ 100 lakhs and transferred the accumulated depreciation of ₹25 lakhs to Profit & Loss A/c. Advice the company on changes to be affected in the draft financial statements. Give reasons in support of advice.

ANSWER:

PROVISION OF AS 10

As per AS 10 when fixed assets are revalued upwards, the accumulated depreciation existing on the date of revaluation should not be credited to profit and loss account. The increase on account of revaluation should be credited to Revaluation Reserve Account.

ADVICE

Hence, the transfer of accumulated depreciation of ₹25 lakhs to profit and loss account is contrary to principles laid down in AS 10.

QUESTION 20: At the beginning of the year, the company has a capital of ₹10 crores, free reserves of ₹2 crores and Revaluation Reserve of ₹8 crores. In the relevant year under audit, the company has incurred a loss of ₹7 crores. The company proposes to adjust the loss with the Revaluation Reserve. As a statutory auditor of a Public Limited Company, how would you deal with such situation?

ANSWER:

PROVISION OF AS 10

As per AS 10 Losses and accumulated losses cannot be adjusted against the revaluation reserves which were created on the revaluation of assets.

ADVICE

Hence, in a present case, the contentions of the company are not correct.

QUESTION 21: The Directors of ABC Ltd. are of the opinion that before declaration of dividends, it would be necessary to set off the carried forward amount of debit balance in the profit and loss account against current revenue profits but the same could be set off against existing revaluation reserve. As an auditor of the company do you agree with the contentions of directors?

ANSWER:

PROVISION OF AS 10

If the debit balance in the Profit and Loss Account is set off against revaluation reserve, and then dividend is declared from out of revenue profits, it should amount to payment of dividend out of capital without making good the lower of loss or depreciation.

ADVICE

Such a declaration shall be violation of the provisions of Section 123 of the Companies Act, 2013. Hence, the opinion of the directors of ABC Ltd. is not correct.

TREATMENT OF FIXED ASSETS RETIRED FROM ACTIVE USE AND HELD FOR DISPOSAL

QUESTION 22: Tulsian Ltd. provides you the following information:

Particulars	Plot of Land 1	Plot of Land 2	Plot of Land 3	Plot of Land 4	Plot of Land 5
Book Value on 1st April, 2013	1,00,000	1,00,000	1,00,000	1,00,000	1,00,000
Revalued on 31st March, 2014	1,20,000	1,20,000	80,000	80,000	1,20,000
Revalued on 31st March, 2015	1,15,000	95,000	1,00,000	1,05,000	1,15,000
Estimated Net Realizable Value on 1st April, 2015	1,20,000	90,000	90,000	90,000	1,10,000

How shall the retirement of land from active use on 1st April, 2015 be accounted for?

ANSWER:

JOURNAL

Date	Particulars	Dr. (₹)	Cr. (₹)
01.04.2015	Revaluation Reserve A/c (Asset 1) ...Dr.	15,000	
	To General Reserve A/c		15,000
	(Being balance of Revaluation Reserve A/c transferred to General Reserve A/c.)		
01.04.2015	Profit & Loss A/c ...Dr.	5,000	
	To Asset 2 A/c		5,000
	(Being Loss on sale of land transferred to P & L A/c)		
01.04.2015	Profit & Loss A/c ...Dr.	10,000	
	To Asset 3 A/c		10,000
	(Being Loss on sale of land transferred to P & L A/c)		
01.04.2015	Revaluation Reserve A/c ...Dr.	5,000	
	Profit & Loss A/c ...Dr.	10,000	
	To Asset 4 A/c		15,000
	(Being loss to the extent it is related to an increase previously credited to Revaluation Reserve A/c utilized.)		

01.04.2015	Revaluation Reserve A/c ...Dr. To Asset 5 A/c (Being loss to the extent it is related to an increase previously credited to Revaluation Reserve A/c utilized.)	5,000	5,000
01.04.2015	Revaluation Reserve A/c ...Dr. To General Reserve A/c (Being balance of Revaluation Reserve A/c transferred to General Reserve A/c.)	10,000	10,000

QUESTION 23: F Limited includes those items of Fixed assets which have not been in active use and held for disposal, as inventory item in the Schedule of Inventory.

ANSWER:

PROVISION OF AS 10

AS-10 "Accounting for Fixed Assets", requires that the item of fixed assets that have been retired form active used and are held for disposal be stated at the lower of their net book value and net realizable value and are shown separately in the financial statements. As per AS-2 "Valuation of Inventories", "inventories" are assets' held for sale in the ordinary course of business in the process of production for such sale; or in the form of materials or supplies to be consumed in the production process or in the rendering of services.", whereas, the sale of fixed assets cannot be treated as sale arising from the ordinary course of business.

ADVICE

Thus, F Ltd's inclusion of fixed assets not in active use and held for disposal, as inventory item in the schedule of inventory is not in line with the requirements of AS-10 and AS-2. Such fixed assets should be stated at lower of net book value and net realizable value and are shown separately in financial statements.

TREATMENT OF FIXED ASSETS OWNED BY THE ENTERPRISE JOINTLY WITH OTHERS

QUESTION 24: A computerized machinery was purchased by two companies jointly. The price shared equally. It was also agreed that they would use the machinery equally and show in their Balance Sheets, 50% of the value of machinery and charge 50% of the depreciation in their respective books of account.

ANSWER:

PROVISION OF AS 10

As per AS 10 in case of fixed assets owned jointly by enterprises, the extent of the entity's share in such assets, and the proportion in the original cost, accumulated depreciation and written down value should be stated in the Balance Sheet *Alternatively*, AS-10 also recommends that the pro-rata cost of such jointly owned assets may be grouped together with similar fully owned assets and appropriate disclosure of the same should be made.

ADVICE

Accordingly, the treatment followed by the companies reflecting 50% of the value of the machinery and charging 50% in their respective books of accounts is proper. However such jointly owned assets should be indicated, separately in the Fixed Asset Register maintained by the company.

MISCELLANEOUS QUESTIONS

QUESTION 25: On 1st April, 2011. BHARAT TUSHAR Ltd. purchased a Fixed Asset worth ₹ 125 lakhs. The Salvage Value at the end of useful life of 4 years was estimated at ₹ 51.20 lakhs. The Asset was revalued upward by 60% on 1.4.2012. The Asset was revalued downward by 25% on 1.4.2013. The asset was sold on 1.4.2014 at a Loss @5%. The company charged straight line depreciation. The company also charged the excess depreciation to Revaluation Reserve.

Required: Show Fixed Assets A/c, Depreciation A/c, Revaluation Reserve A/c.

ANSWER:

Dr. **FIXED ASSETS ACCOUNT** Cr.

Date	Particulars	₹ lakhs	Date	Particulars	₹ lakhs
1.4.2011	To Bank A/c	125.00	31.3.2012	By Depreciation A/c [(125 – 51.2)/4]	18.45
				By Balance c/d	106.55
		125.00			125.00
1.4.2012	To Balance b/d	106.55	31.3.2013	By Depreciation A/c [(106.55 + 63.93 – 51.2)/3]	39.76
1.4.2012	To Revaluation Reserve [106.55 × 60%]	63.93		By Balance c/d	130.72
		170.48			170.48
1.4.2013	To Balance b/d	130.72	1.4.2013	By Revaluation Reserve [(130.72 × 25%)]	32.68
			31.3.2014	By Depreciation A/c [(130.72 – 32.68 – 51.2)/2]	23.42
				By Balance c/d	74.62
		130.72			130.72
1.4.2014	To Balance b/d	74.62	1.4.2014	By Revaluation Reserve A/c [74.62 × 5%]	3.371
				By Bank A/c [74.62 × 95%]	70.889
		74.62			74.62

Dr. **DEPRECIATION ACCOUNT** Cr.

Date	Particulars	₹ lakhs	Date	Particulars	₹ lakhs
31.3.2012	To Fixed Assets A/c	18.45	31.3.2012	By P & L A/c	18.45
31.3.2013	To Fixed Assets A/c	39.76	31.3.2013	By P & L A/c	18.45
				By Revaluation Reserve	21.31
		39.76			39.76
31.3.2014	To Fixed Assets A/c	23.42	31.3.2014	By P & L A/c	18.45
				By Revaluation Reserve	4.97
		23.42			23.42

Dr. **REVALUATION RESERVE ACCOUNT** Cr.

Date	Particulars	₹ lakhs	Date	Particulars	₹ lakhs
31.3.2013	To Depreciation A/c [63.93/3]	21.31	1.4.2012	By Fixed Assets A/c	63.93
	To Balance c/d	42.62			
		63.93			63.93
31.3.2014	To Fixed Assets A/c	32.68	1.4.2013	By Balance b/d	42.62
	To Depreciation A/c [(42.62 – 32.68)/2]	4.97			
	To Balance c/d	4.97			
		42.62			42.62
1.4.2014	To Fixed Assets A/c	3.731	1.4.2014	By Balance b/d	4.97
	To General Reserve	1.239			
		4.97			4.97

QUESTION 26: ABC Ltd. purchased fixed assets worth ₹ 200 lakhs on 1st April, 2011. The life of the assets is 10 years and they are to be depreciated on straight - line basis. The assets were revalued on 1st April, 2013 when 50 % of the assets were assessed at 15 % less than the book value, and the remaining assets were at 20 % higher than book value. The assets were ultimately sold on 01.04.2015 for ₹ 120 lakhs. Excess depreciation on revaluation, if any should be charged to Revaluation Reserve.

Required: **Prepare Fixed Assets Account, Depreciation Account and Revaluation Reserve Account, supported by workings wherever necessary.**

ANSWER:

Dr. **FIXED ASSETS ACCOUNT** Cr.

Date	Particulars	₹ lakhs	Date	Particulars	₹ lakhs
1.4.2011	To Bank A/c	200	31.3.2012	By Depreciation A/c [200/10]	20
				By Balance c/d	180
		200			200
1.4.2012	To Balance b/d	180	31.3.2013	By Depreciation A/c	20
				By Balance c/d	160
		180			180
1.4.2013	To Balance b/d	160	31.3.2014	By Profit & Loss A/c (80 × 15%)	12.00
	To Revaluation Reserve A/c (80 × 20%)	16	31.3.2014	By Depreciation A/c (8.50 + 12)	20.50
				By Balance c/d	143.50
		176			176
1.4.2014	To Balance b/d	143.50	31.3.2015	By Depreciation A/c [74.62 × 5%]	20.50
				By Balance c/d	123.00
		143.50			143.50

1.4.2015	To Balance b/d	123	1.4.2015	By Revaluation Reserve A/c	3
				By Bank A/c	120
		123			123

Dr. **DEPRECIATION ACCOUNT** Cr.

Date	Particulars	₹ lakhs	Date	Particulars	₹ lakhs
31.3.2012	To Fixed Assets A/c	20	31.3.2012	By P & L A/c	20
31.3.2013	To Fixed Assets A/c	20	31.3.2013	By P & L A/c	20
31.3.2014	To Fixed Assets A/c	20.50	31.3.2014	By P & L A/c	18.50
				By Revaluation Reserve	2.00
		20.50			20.50
31.3.2015	To Fixed Assets A/c	20.50	31.3.2015	By P & L A/c	18.50
				By Revaluation Reserve	2.00
		20.50			20.50

Dr. **REVALUATION RESERVE ACCOUNT** Cr.

Date	Particulars	₹ lakhs	Date	Particulars	₹ lakhs
31.3.2014	To Depreciation A/c [16/8]	2	1.4.2013	By Fixed Assets A/c	16
	To Balance c/d	14			
		16			16
31.3.2015	To Depreciation A/c	2	1.4.2014	By Fixed Assets A/c	14
	To Balance c/d	12			
		14			14
1.4.2015	To Fixed Assets A/c	3	1.4.2015	By Balance b/d	12
	To General Reserve	9			
		12			12

QUESTION 27: BHARAT TUSHAR Ltd. purchased machinery from Y Ltd. on 30.09.2008. The price was 480.70 lakhs after charging 10 % Vat and giving a trade discount of 5 % on the quoted price. Transport charges were 0.25 % on the quoted price and installation charges come to 1% on the quoted price. A loan of ₹460 lakhs was taken from bank on which interest at 15 % per annum was to be paid. The entire loan amount remained unpaid on 01.04.2009.

Expenditure incurred on the trial run was: Material ₹ 1,00,000, Wages ₹ 60,000 and Overheads ₹ 45,000.Machinery was ready for use on 01.12.2008. However it was actually put to use only on 01.04.2009. X Ltd. does not intend to utilize the input tax paid on capital good.

On 1st April, 2009. it got Government grant of ₹ 250 lakhs. The Salvage Value at the end of useful life of 4 years was estimated at ₹ 102.40 lakhs. The company charged depreciation on Written Down Value basis. From 3rd year, company decided to change the method of depreciation from Written Down Value Method to Straight Line Method . On 1.4.2012, the Asset 's useful life was reassessed at 6 years instead of 4 years and it was revalued upward by 60%. On 1.4.2013 the Asset was revalued downward by 25%. On 31.3.2015 the asset was retired from active use but not disposed off. Estimated Realizable Value and Realizable Expenses were ₹ 52 lakhs and ₹ 80,000 respectively. The company also charged the excess depreciation to Revaluation Reserve.

Required: (a)Find out the cost of the machine (b) suggest the Accounting Treatment for the expenses incurred in the interval between the dates 01.12.2008 to 01.04.2009.(c)Prepare Fixed Assets A/c, Depreciation A/c, Revaluation Reserve A/c.

ANSWER:

(A) CALCULATION OF COST OF MACHINE AS PER AS 10

Particulars		₹ in lakhs
A. Quoted Price of machine		460.00
B. *Less:* Trade discount @ 5 % on ₹460		23.00
C. Price after discount [A – B]		437.00
D. *Add:* VAT @ 10 % on ₹437		43.70
E. Selling Price [C + D]		480.70
F. *Add:* Transportation charges [0.25 % of ₹460]		1.15
G. *Add:* Installation charges [1 % of ₹460]		4.60
H. *Add:* Borrowing cost upto 01.12.2008 [₹460 lakhs × 15% × 2/12]		11.50
I. *Add:* Expenditure on Trial Run:		
Material:	1.00	
Wages:	0.60	
Overheads:	0.45	2.05
J. Total Cost of the machinery to be capitalized [E + F + G + H + I]		500.00

Working Notes:

1. Selling Price before VAT = ₹ 480.7 lakh=100/110 = ₹ 437 lakhs
2. Quoted Price before Trade Discount = ₹ 437 lakh = 100/95 = ₹ 460 lakhs
3. As per As 16 interest should be capitalized only for the period when substantially all the activities necessary for intended use are completed. In present case machinery was ready for use on 01.12.2008. Hence in this case capitalization of interest should be done for only two months (i.e. from 30.09.2008 to 30.11.2008)

   Interest for the two months = 460 lakhs × 15 % × (2 months / 12 months) = 11.50 lakhs.

(b) Accounting Treatment for Interest for the period 01.12.2008 to 01.04.2009: It should be expensed since As per AS – 16, the capitalization of interest should cease when substantially all the activities necessary for intended use are completed

Dr. **FIXED ASSETS ACCOUNT** **Cr.**

Date	Particulars	₹ lakhs	Date	Particulars	₹ lakhs
1.4.2009	To Bank A/c	500.00	1.4.2009	By Govt. Grant A/c	250.00
			31.3.2010	By Depreciation A/c	50.00
				By Balance c/d	200.00
		500.00			500.00
1.4.2010	To Balance b/d	200.00	31.3.2011	By Depreciation A/c	40.00
				By Balance c/d	160.00
		200.00			200.00

1.4.2011	To Balance b/d To Profit & Loss A/c	160.00 16.20	31.3.2012	By Depreciation A/c By Balance c/d	36.90 139.30
		176.20			176.20
1.4.2012 1.4.2012	To Balance b/d To Revaluation Reserve [139.3 × 60%]	139.30 83.58	31.3.2013	By Depreciation A/c [(139.30 + 83.58 – 102.4)/3] By Balance c/d	40.16 182.72 182.72
		222.88			222.88
1.4.2013	To Balance b/d	180.72	1.4.2013 31.3.2014	By Revaluation Reserve [180.72 × 25%] By Depreciation A/c [(180.72 – 45.18 – 102.4)/2] By Balance c/d	45.18 16.57 118.97
		180.72			180.72
1.4.2014	To Balance b/d	118.97	31.3.2015	By Depreciation A/c By Profit & Loss A/c By Balance c/d	16.57 51.20 51.20
		118.97			118.97

Dr. **DEPRECIATION ACCOUNT** **Cr.**

Date	Particulars	₹ lakhs	Date	Particulars	₹ lakhs
31.3.2010	To Fixed Assets A/c	50.00	31.3.2010	By P & L A/c	50.00
31.3.2011	To Fixed Assets A/c	40.00	31.3.2011	By P & L A/c	40.00
31.3.2012	To Fixed Assets A/c	36.90	31.3.2012	By P & L A/c	36.90
31.3.2013	To Fixed Assets A/c	40.16	31.3.2013	By P & L A/c	12.30
				By Revaluation Reserve	27.86
		40.16			40.16
31.3.2014	To Fixed Assets A/c	16.57	31.3.2014	By P & L A/c	11.30
				By Revaluation Reserve	5.27
		16.57			16.57
31.3.2015	To Fixed Assets A/c	16.57	31.3.2015	By P & L A/c	11.30
				By Revaluation Reserve	5.27
		16.57			16.57

Dr. **REVALUATION RESERVE ACCOUNT** **Cr.**

Date	Particulars	₹ lakhs	Date	Particulars	₹ lakhs
31.3.2013	To Depreciation A/c [83.58/3]	27.86	1.4.2012	By Fixed Assets A/c	83.58
	To Balance c/d	55.72			
		83.58			83.58

31.3.2014	To Fixed Assets A/c	45.18	1.4.2013	By Balance b/d	55.72
	To Depreciation A/c [(55.72 – 45.18)/2]	5.27			
	To Balance c/d	5.27			
		55.72			55.72
31.3.2015	To Depreciation A/c	5.27	1.4.2014	By Balance b/d	5.27
		5.27			5.27

Working Notes:

1. WDV Depreciation Rate (on 1.4.2009) = $1 - \sqrt[4]{102.40/250}$
   = 1 – 0.8 = 0.2 or 20%
2. WDV Depreciation for 2 years = [250 – (250 × 80% × 80%)] = ₹ 90 lakhs
3. SLM Depreciation p.a. = [(250 – 102.4)/4] = ₹ 36.90 lakhs
4. SLM Depreciation for 2 years = ₹ 36.90 lakhs × 2 = ₹ 73.80 lakhs
5. Excess Depreciation provided = ₹ 90 lakhs – ₹ 73.80 lakhs = ₹ 16.20 lakhs

QUESTION 28: A company transferred land from 'fixed assets' to 'current assets' at market price and adjusted the excess value under capital reserve instead of Revaluation Reserve. In subsequent years, the value was written down gradually as 'decline in market value' - whether this would constitute unusual accounting?

ANSWER:

The treatments in different situations are as follows:

(1) In case where enterprise wants to deal in the assets

(a) Fixed assets reclassified as current assets should be valued at their carrying amount appearing in the balance sheet or at the net realizable value, whichever is lower. In this case, no appreciation would be recognized either in the capital reserve or in the revaluation reserve or

(b) It would be appropriate to value assets which were until now classified as fixed assets at their market price in order to determine the correct profit on sale of such assets in the ordinary course of business. The excess of market value over the carrying amount at the date of reclassification can be transferred to the revaluation reserve. It is noted that revaluation reserve arising in a situation where a fixed asset is revalued and continues to be a fixed asset then balance in such a revaluation reserve cannot be utilized. However in case of an asset which was previously classified as fixed asset and currently classified as current asset, the profit on revaluation can be transferred to capital reserve instead of revaluation reserve. It may be noted that under Companies Act, 1956 the capital reserve is not free for distribution.

(2) In case the intention of the enterprise is not to deal in the assets which were until now treated as fixed assets, but assets retired from active use and held for disposal, these should continue to be classified as fixed assets and treated as per AS 10 which requires that such items should be stated at the lower of their net book value and net realizable value and shown separately in the financial statements.

QUESTION 29: A Ltd. entered into a binding contract with C Ltd. to buy a machine for ₹ 1,00,000. The machine is to be delivered on 15th February, 2015. On 1st January, 2015, A Ltd. changed its process of production. The new process will not require the machine ordered and it shall have to be scrapped after delivery. The expected scrap value of the machine is nil. Explain how A Ltd. should recognise the entire transaction in the books of account for the year ended 31st March, 2015.

ANSWER: A Ltd. entered into a binding contract with C Ltd. and therefore, it should recognise a liability of ₹1,00,000. The entire amount of purchase price of the machine should be recognised in the year ended 31st March, 2013 as loss because future economic benefit from the machine to the enterprise is improbable.

JOURNAL ENTRY

Particulars	Dr. (₹)	Cr. (₹)
Profit & Loss A/c ...Dr.	1,00,000	
To C Ltd.		1,00,000
(Being value of machinery fully depreciated because of change in the process of production i.e. obsolescence)		

QUESTION 30: A company is engaged in the manufacture of electronic products and systems. As per Chief Accountant a prototype system was installed at one of the customer's locations in June 2014 for getting acceptance on the performance of the system. The Chief Accountant has stated that as the ownership of the system installed for field trials was vested with the company for accounting and control purposes, the prototype system installed at customer's location in 2014 was capitalized in the accounts for the year 2014-2015 at its bought-out cost. State whether the accounting treatment adopted by the company is correct or not?

ANSWER:

PROVISION OF AS 10

As per para 3 of AS-2 'Valuation of invemtories', inventories mean assets held for sale in the ordinary course of business, or in the process of production for which sale, or for consumption in the production of goods or services for sale, including maintenance supplies and consumables other than machinery spares.

And as per para 6.1 of 10 'Accounting for fixed Assets', fixed asset is an asset held with the intention of being used for the purpose of producing of providing goods or services and is not held for sale in the normal course of business.

ADVICE

Accordingly, the system installed by the company at customer's site for the acceptance, based on the field trials of the system, is an item of inventory, and is not a fixed asset. Installation of such prototype system at customers' sites for their acceptance is akin to sale of goods on approval basis. Therefore, the capitalisation of such prototype system is at its bought-out-cost is not correct.

At the time of installation of such systems at the customers' site, value of the same should be transferred to a separate account such as 'Goods sent for approval account'.

As it does not qualify the definition of fixed assets, therefore, no depreciation can be charged on it.

QUESTION 31: In the notes to accounts of C Co. Ltd. as on 31-03-2015 Note No. 11 states that 'Certain machinery items are lying at customer warehouses and company has paid ₹1000 lakhs up to 30-0-6-2014 as detention changes, out of which a sum of ₹ 600 lakhs is written back during the year 2014-2015 based on settlement with the concemed authorities in respect of a major spares of machinery. For the remaining machinery items negotiations are pending and a provision of ₹ 50 lakhs is made. As such total amount of ₹ 450 lakhs paid/provided on account of detention charges have been capitalized and included in the Fixed Assets/Capital work in progress. The management is of the view that these expenses are directly attributable to the acquisition of the related Fixed Asset. Comment.

ANSWER:

PROVISION OF AS 10

As per AS 10 "Accounting for Fixed Assets", the cost of an item of fixed asset comprise its purchase price, including import duties and other non-refundable taxes or levies and any directly attributable cost of bringing the asset to its working condition for its intended use.

ADVICE

Generally, detention charges represent an abnormal expenditure, as these expenditures are not directly attributable to the cost of asset.

The auditor will quality the report appropriately in the paragraph before stating that the balance sheet gives that and fair view and the Profit and Loss Account show true and fair profit to the year ending on 31-03-2015. The qualification will be as follows:

"Attention is invited to Note No. 11 regarding Capitalization of detention charges to ₹450 lakhs during the year and on account of delays in respect of clearing from custom werehouses for certain machinery items". In our opinion the detention charge are not directly attributable to the acquisition of related fixed assets. The said amount of ₹450 lakhs should have been written off in the Profit & Loss Account. Had these expenses been so written off the profit for the year would have been lower by ₹ 450 lakhs and Reserves & Surplus as well as Fixed Assets/Capital WIP would have been lower by ₹450 lakhs.

QUESTION 32: Tulsian Ltd. provides in the following information:

1. On 01.04.2014 Book Value of Plant and Machinery ₹ 10,00,000
2. On 01.04.2014, out of the above a Machine having book value ₹2,00,000 has been retired from use and held for disposal. The net realizable value of the same is ₹ 20,000.
3. On 01.04.2014 Book value of old Machine No. 1 exchanged for ₹ 1,00,000. Additional cash given for exchange of asset ₹ 10,000, Fair market value of new Machine No. 100 acquired in exchange of old Machine is ₹ 40,000
4. On 01.04.2014 Issued 1,00,000 equity shares of ₹ 10 each (fully paid up) in consideration for supply of a machinery by PQR Ltd. The shares exchanged for machinery are quoted on National Stock Exchange (NSE) at ₹ 25 per share, at the time of transaction
5. Rate of depreciation is 10% p.a. on WDV basis
6. Goodwill was valued at ₹1,20,000 by independent valuers and no consideration was paid. The Company has not yet recorded the same.

Required: Prepare the Journal for the year 2014-2015. How will you dislose the relevent items in the Financial Statements of the company.

ANSWER:

JOURNAL

Date	Particulars	Dr. (₹)	Cr. (₹)
01.04.2014	Profit & Loss A/c ...Dr.	1,80,000	
	To Plant and Machinery A/c		1,80,000
	(Being the Loss on retirement charged to P & L A/c)		

01.04.2014	New Asset A/c ...Dr. To Bank A/c To Old Asset A/c (Being the cost of asset acquired is recorded at its fair market value)	40,000	 10,000 30,000
01.04.2014	Old Asset A/c ...Dr. To Profit & Loss A/c (Being credit balance in Old Asset A/c is transferred to P&L A/c)	70,000	 70,000
01.04.2014	Machinery A/c ...Dr. To Share Capital A/c To Securities Premium A/c (Being machinery recorded at the fair market value of the securities issued in consideration for machinery acquired)	25,00,000	 10,00,000 15,00,000
31.03.2015	Depreciation A/c ...Dr. To Plant and Machinery A/c [Being the Depreciation provided @10% on ₹ 32,40,000(i.e. 10,00,000 – 2,00,000 – 1,00,000 + 40,000 + 25,00,000)]	3,24,000	 3,24,000
31.03.2015	Profit & Loss A/c ...Dr. To Depreciation A/c (Being the T/F of Depreciation A/c to P & L A/c)	3,24,000	 3,24,000

AN EXTRACT OF STATEMENT OF PROFIT & LOSS FOR THE YEAR ENDED 31.03.2015

Loss on retirement	₹ 1,80,000
Loss on Exchange of an Old Machine	₹ 70,000
Depreciation on Plant and Machinery	₹ 3,24,000

AN EXTRACT OF BALANCE SHEET AS AT 31.03.2015

Share Capital (Issued for Consideration other than Cash)	₹ 10,00,000
Reserves & Surplus (Securities Premium)	₹ 25,00,000
Plant and Machinery	₹ 32,40,000
Machine retired from use and held for disposal(at NRV)	₹ 20,000

Treatment of Goodwill: As per para 16 of AS 10 'Accounting for Fixed Assets' goodwill is to be recorded only when some consideration in money or money's worth has been paid for it.; Since the goodwill is self generated and no money or money's worth has been paid for the same, therefore, it is not to be recorded in the books.

Note: As per para 11 of the AS 10, the new machine has been recorded at the Fair Market Value of the securities issued as it is more clearly evident.

QUESTION 33: Ascertain the value at which various items of Fixed Assets are to be shown in the Financial Statements of Velvet Ltd. and amount to be debited to the Profit and Loss Account in the context of the relevant Acounting Standard.

Narrations for the adjustments made should form part of the answer:

(i) **Goodwill was valued at ₹1,20,000 by independent valuers and no consideration was paid. The Company has not yet recorded the same.**

(ii) **Balance of Office Equipment as on 01.04.2013 is ₹ 1,20,000. On 01.04.2013, out of the above office equipment having book value ₹20,000 has been retired from use and held for disposal. The net realizable value of the same is ₹ 2,000. Rate of depreciation is 15% p.a. on WDV basis.**

(iii) **Book Value of Plant and Machinery as on 01.04.2013 was ₹ 7,20,000. On 01.08.2013 an item of machinery was purchased in exchange for 500 equity shares of face value ₹10. The Fair Market value of the equity shares on 01.08.2013 was ₹120. Rate of depreciation is 10% p.a. on WDV basis.**

ANSWER:

TREATMENT AND VALUE OF VARIOUS ITEMS OF FIXED ASSETS

Item of Fixed Assets (₹)		Amount Debited to P & L in current year	Amount	Narration	Closing Balance to be shown in the Financial Statements
(i) Goodwill		0			
Opening Balance					
Closing Balance					0
(ii) Office Equipment	1,20,000				
Opening Balance	20,000				
Less: Retired from use	1,00,000				
Less: Depreciation @ 15%	15,000		15,000	Depreciation	
Closing Balance	85,000				
Office Equipment (Retired from use)					85,000
Opening balance		20,000			
Less: Closing Balance (At NRV)		2,000			2,000
Loss on retirement charged to P&L		18,000	18,000	Loss on retirement of asset	
(iii) Plant and Machinery	7,20,000				7,04,000
Opening Balance	60,000				
Add: Machine purchased					
	7,80,000				
Less: Depreciation					
on old machine	72,000				
On New machine	4,000	76,000	76,000	Depreciation	
Closing Balance		7,04,000			
		1,09,000			7,91,000

Notes:

1. As per para 16 of AS 10 'Accounting for Fixed Assets' goodwill is to be recorded only when some consideration in money or money's worth has been paid for it.; Since the goodwill is self generated and no money or money's worth has been paid for the same, therefore, it is not to be recorded in the books.
2. Office equipment having book value of ₹ 20,000 has been retired from use. As per Para II of AS 10 It has been recorded at Net Realisable Value (NRV) as the NRV is lower than the book value and shown separatley in the financial statements.
3. As per para 11 of the AS 10, the new machine has been recorded at the Fair Market Value of the securities issued as it is more clearly evident.

8 AS 11—THE EFFECTS OF CHANGES IN FOREIGN EXCHANGE RATES

THEORETICAL BASE

QUESTION 1: State the areas to which AS 11 is not applicable.

ANSWER:

1. Accounting for Foreign Currency Derivatives to which AS-30 applies,
2. Hedge Accounting for foreign currency items,
3. Hedging of a Net Investment in a Foreign Operation.

QUESTION 2: Define Foreign Currency Transaction as per AS 11.

ANSWER: A foreign currency transaction is a transaction which is denominated in or requires settlement in a foreign currency, including transactions arising when an enterprise *either*:

(a) buys or sells goods or services whose price is denominated in a foreign currency; *or*

(b) borrows or lends funds when the amounts payable or receivable are denominated in a foreign currency; *or*

(c) otherwise acquires or disposes of assets, or incurs or settles liabilities, denominated in a foreign currency

QUESTION 3: Define Exchange Rate, Average Rate, Closing Rate, Monetary Items and Non-Monetary Items as per AS 11.

ANSWER:

1. Exchange Rate	Exchange Rate is the ratio for exchange of two currencies.
2. Average Rate	Average Rate is the mean of the exchange rates in force during a period. **Note:** Average Rate should not be used if exchange rates fluctuate significantly.
3. Closing Rate	Closing rate is the Exchange rate at the Balance Sheet Date
4. Monetary Items	Monetary items are money held and assets and liabilities to be received or paid in fixed or determinable amounts of money, *e.g.*, Cash, Receivables, Payables,Loans.
5. Non-Monetary Items	Non-monetary items are assets and liabilities other than the monetary items *e.g.* Fixed Assets, Inventories, Investments in equity shares.

QUESTION 4: Define Exchange Difference as per AS 11. When does Exchange Difference arise?

ANSWER:

Meaning	Exchange difference is the difference resulting from reporting the same number of units of a foreign currency in the reporting currency at different exchange rates.
When arises	An exchange difference results when there is a change in the exchange rate between the transaction date and the settlement date/reporting date of any foreign currency monetary items.

QUESTION 5: State the indications that a Foreign Operation is a Non-Integral Foreign Operation as per AS 11.

ANSWER:

1. Degree of Autonomy
2. Proportion of the Foreign Operation's Activities;
3. Proportion of Finance from the reporting enterprise.
4. Settlement of Foreign Operation's Sales, Purchases, Other Transactions

QUESTION 6: Distinguish between Integral and Non Integral Foreign Operations as per AS 11.

ANSWER:

Basis of Comparison	Integral Foreign Operations [IFO]	Non-Integral Foreign Operations [NIFO]
1. Meaning	A foreign operation, the activities of which are an integral part of those of the reporting enterprise [*e.g.* Foreign Branch]	A foreign operation that is not an integral foreign operation [*e.g.*Foreign Subsidiary]
2. Treatment of Exchange Difference arising on translation	Recognised as Income or Expense in the period which they arise.	Accumulated in Foreign Currency Translation Reserve until the disposal of Net Investment
3. Exchange Rate To Be Used For Reporting		
(a) Opening Stock if carried at historical cost	Actual Exchange Rate as on the date of purchase	Opening Rate
(b) Closing Stock if carried at historical cost	Actual Exchange Rate as on the date of purchase	Closing Rate
(c) Non-Monetary Items (excluding Stocks) carried at Historical [*e.g.* Fixed Assets]	Actual Exchange Rate as on the date of purchase	Closing Rate
(d) Depreciation if asset is carried at historicalcost	Actual Exchange Rate as on the date of purchase	Closing Rate

QUESTION 7: State the Items for which the same translation rate is used for Integral and Non Integral Foreign Operations as per AS 11.

ANSWER:

Basis of Comparison	Integral Foreign Operations [IFO]	Non-Integral Foreign Operations [NIFO]
(a) Monetary Items [e.g. Cash, Debtors, Creditors, Prepaid Exp., O/s Exp.,	Closing Rate	Closing Rate
(b) Contingent Liability	Closing Rate	Closing Rate
(c) Other Revenue Items [e.g. Purchases, Sales, Interest, Expenses]	Actual Exchange Rate	Actual Exchange Rate

(d) Remittances	Actual Exchange Rate	Actual Exchange Rate
(e) Goods received from HO/ Sent to HO	Taken at amounts recorded in H.O.Books	Taken at amounts recorded in H.O.Books
(f) Balance in HO A/c in Branch Books	Taken at amounts recorded in H.O.Books	Taken at amounts recorded in H.O.Books

QUESTION 8: State the Option available to Companies for Treatment of Exchange Difference as per Para 46A of The Companies (Accounting Standards) Rules, 2012.

ANSWER:

1. Long-term Foreign Currency Loans relating to Depreciable Assets	Exchange Difference should be debited(in case of Exchange Loss) or credited (in case of Exchange Profit) to **Respective Asset A/c.**
2. Long-term Foreign Currency Loans relating to Non-Depreciable Assets like land	1. Exchange Difference should be debited(in case of Exchange Loss) or credited (in case of Exchange Profit) to **Foreign Currency Monetary Items Translation Difference A/c.** 2. Such Exchange Difference should be transferred to Profit & Loss A/c in equal proportion over reporting periods ending on March 31,2020. **Note:** The Dr. or Cr. Balance of FCMITD A/c should be shown on the Equity & Liabilities side of the Balance Sheet under the head **'Reserves & Surplus'.**
Note: Once Option as per Para 46A is exercised,it is irrevocable. If Option as per Para 46A is not exercised, the Exchange Difference is transferred to Profit & Loss A/c.	

QUESTION 9: state the accounting treatment of a foreign currency transaction at date of transaction as per as 11.

ANSWER: At date of transaction a foreign currency transaction will be recorded at an Amount =Foreign Currency Amount × Exchange Rate as on Date of Transaction

QUESTION 10: State the accounting treatment of a foreign currency transaction at Reporting Date as per as 11.

ANSWER:

1. At Reporting date a foreign currency transaction will be recorded at an Amount
   = Foreign Currency Amount × Exchange Rate as on Reporting Date
2. Exchange Difference will be recognised as Income/Expense in Profit and Loss A/c:
   = Foreign Currency Amount × (Exchange Rate as on Date of Transaction – Exchange Rate as on Date of Reporting)

QUESTION 11: State the accounting treatment of a foreign currency transaction at Settlement Date as per as 11.

ANSWER: At Settlement date Exchange Difference will be recognised as Income/Expense in Profit and Loss A/c for the period in which settlement takes place.

= Foreign Currency Amount × (Exchange Rate as on Date of Reporting – Exchange Rate as on Date of Settlement)

QUESTION 12: State the accounting treatment of Forward Exchange Contracts entered for trading or speculation purposes as per as 11.

ANSWER:

1. **Premium/Discount** on Forward Contract [i.e. the difference between the Spot Rate and the Forward Contract Rate] **will not be recorded in the books.**
2. Only **when** the Forward Contract is **sold** the **difference** between the Forward Contract rate and Sale Rate will be **recorded** in the Profit & Loss Account.

QUESTION 13: State the accounting treatment of Forward Exchange Contracts entered for hedging purposes.

ANSWER:

1. Premium/Discount on Forward Exchange contracts entered for hedging purposes.
   = Forward Contract Amount × (Forward Contract Rate – Spot Rate)
2. Premium/Discount pertaining to the period falling in current financial year will be recognised in the Profit and Loss A/c for the current financial year.
3. Premium/Discount pertaining to the period falling in next financial year will be recognised in the Profit and Loss A/c for the next financial year.

QUESTION 14: State the Disclosure Requirements as per AS 11.

ANSWER:

1. Exchange Differences transferred to Profit & Loss A/c.
2. Exchange Differences capitalized as per Para 46 of The Companies (Accounting Standards) Rules, 2012 alongwith benefits.
3. Net Exchange Differences accumulated in Foreign Currency Translation Reserve as a separate component of shareholders' funds, and a reconciliation of the amount of such exchange differences at the beginning and end of the period
4. Reason for & Impact of the Change in classification of Foreign Operation as IFO/NIFO on shareholders' funds; or on net profit or loss
5. Realistic Rate to be disclosed if Closing Rate is not used.

QUESTION 15: Explain "Monetary Item" as per Accounting Standard 11. How are foreign currency monetary items to be recognized at each Balance Sheet date? Classify the following as monetary or non-monetary item:

(i) Share Capital (ii) Trade Receivables (iii) Investments (iv) Fixed Assets

ANSWER:

1. As per AS 11 'The Effects of Changes in Foreign Exchange Rates', Monetary items are money held and assets and liabilities to be received or paid in fixed or determinable amounts of money.
2. Foreign currency monetary items should be reported **using the closing rate** at each balance sheet date. However, in certain circumstances, the closing rate may not reflect with reasonable accuracy the amount in reporting currency that is likely to be realised from, or required to disburse, a foreign currency monetary item at the balance sheet date. In such circumstances, the relevant monetary item should be reported in the reporting currency at the amount which is likely to be realised from or required to disburse, such item at the balance sheet date.

Share capital	Non-monetary
Trade receivables	Monetary
Investments	Non-monetary
Fixed assets	Non-monetary

PRACTICAL QUESTIONS FOR PRACTICE

QUESTION 1: On 31st March, 2015, the following ledger balances have been extracted from the books of Washington branch office:

Ledger Accounts	**$**
Building	**180**
Opening Stock	**26**
Cash and Bank Balances	**57**
Purchases	**96**
Sales	**110**
Commission receipts	**28**
Debtors	**46**
Creditors	**65**

You are required to convert above Ledger balances into Indian Rupees. Use the following rates of exchange:

	₹ per $
Opening rate	**46**
Closing rate	**50**
Average rate	**48**
For fixed assets	**42**

ANSWER:

CONVERSION OF LEDGER BALANCES (IN DOLLARS) INTO RUPEES

	$ Ruees	**Rate per $**	**Amount in**
Building	180	42	7,560
Opening Stock	26	46	1,196
Cash and bank balances	57	50	2,850
Purchases	96	48	4,608
Sales	110	48	5,280
Commission receipts	28	48	1,344
Debtors	46	50	2,300
Creditors	65	50	3,250

QUESTION 2: Goods purchased on 24.2.2015 of US $ 1,000 for which payment made on 05.06.2015. Exchange Rate on: 24.2.2015 ₹ 61.60 per US$, 31.3.2015 ₹ 62.00 per US $, 05.06.2015 ₹ 62.50 per US $. State the Accounting Treatment at the date of transaction,reporting date and settlement date as per AS 11.

ANSWER: Accounting Treatment at the Date of Transaction

As per para 9 of AS 11 on 'The Effects of Changes in Foreign Exchange Rates', a foreign currency transaction should be recorded, on initial recognition in the reporting currency, by applying to the foreign currency amount the exchange rate at the date of the transaction. Accordingly, Goods purchased and corresponding Creditors would be recorded at ₹ 61,600 [i.e. 1,000 × ₹ 61.60]

Accounting Treatment at the Reporting Date

As per para 11 of AS 11, at balance sheet date all monetary items should be reported using the Closing Rate.Accordingly,

1. Closing Creditors will be reported at ₹ 62,000 [i.e. 1,000 × ₹ 62.00]
2. Exchange Loss of ₹ 400 [i.e.₹ 62,000 – ₹ 61,600] should be debited in Profit and Loss Account for the year 2014-2015.

Accounting Treatment at the Settlement Date

Exchange Differences on settlement of monetary items should be transferred to Profit and Loss Account as gain or loss, Accordingly,Exchange Difference of ₹ 500 [i.e.₹ 62,500 – ₹ 62,000] should be debited in Profit and Loss Account for the year 2015-2016.

QUESTION 3: Sunshine Company Limited imported raw materials worth US Dollars 9,000 on 25th February, 2015, when the exchange rate was ₹ 44 per US Dollar. The transaction was recorded in the books at the above mentioned rate. The payment for the transaction was made on 10th April, 2015, when the exchange rate was ₹ 48 per US Dollar. At the year end 31st March, 2015, the rate of exchange was ₹ 49 per US Dollar.

The Chief Accountant of the company passed an entry on 31st March, 2015 adjusting the cost of raw material consumed for the difference between ₹ 48 and ₹ 44 per US Dollar. Discuss whether this treatment is justified as per the provisions of AS-11 (Revised).

ANSWER:

PROVISION OF AS-11

As per AS 11, 'The Effects of Changes in Foreign Exchange Rates', initial recognition of a foreign currency transaction is done in the reporting currency by applying the exchange rate at the date of the transaction.

ACCOUNTING TREATMENT

1. **At the Date of Transaction** the raw material purchased and its creditors will be recorded at US dollar 9,000 × ₹ 44 = ₹ 3,96,000.
2. **At Balance Sheet date** such transaction is reported at closing rate of exchange, hence it will be valued at the closing rate i.e. ₹ 49 per US dollar (USD 9,000 × ₹ 49 = ₹ 4,41,000)
3. The difference of ₹ 5 (i.e., 49 – 44) per US dollar i.e. ₹ 45,000 (USD 9,000 × ₹ 5) will be shown as an exchange loss in the profit and loss account for the year ended 31st March, 2015 and **will not be adjusted against the cost of raw materials.**
4. **At settlement date**, the company would recognize or provide in the Profit and Loss account an exchange gain of ₹ 1 per US dollar, i.e. the difference from balance sheet date to the date of settlement between ₹ 49 and ₹ 48 per US dollar i.e. ₹ 9,000.
5. Hence, the accounting treatment adopted by the Chief Accountant is not as per AS 11.

QUESTION 4: Mr. A bought a forward contract for three months of US $ 1,00,000 on 1st December at 1 US $ = ₹ 62.10 when exchange rate was US $ 1 = ₹ 62.02, On 31st December when he closed his books, exchange rate was US $ 1 = ₹ 62.15. On 31st January, he decided to sell the contract at ₹ 62.18 per dollar. Show how the profits from contract will be recognised in the books.

ANSWER:

PROVISION OF AS-11

As per AS 11 'Effect of Changes in Foreign Exchange Rates', in recording a forward exchange contract intended for trading or speculation purpose, the premium or discount on the contract is ignored and at each balance sheet date, the value of contract is marked to its current market value and the gain or loss on the contract is recognised.

TREATMENT OF PROFIT ON FORWARD CONTRACT FOR TRADING/SPECULATION PURPOSES

It is apparent from the facts given in the QUESTION that Mr. A entered into forward exchange contract for speculation purpose.Hence,

1. Premium on forward contract [i.e. the difference between the spot rate and the forward contract rate] will not be recorded in the books.
2. Only when the forward contract is sold the difference between the forward contract rate and sale rate will be recorded in the Profit & Loss Account.
   Profit on contract = Contract Amount × [Sale Rate – Contract Rate]
   = US$ 1,00,000 × (₹ 62.18 – ₹ 62.10)] = ₹ 8,000 will be recognized on 31st January.

DISCLOSURE

An enterprise should disclose the following:

(i) The amount of exchange differences included in the net profit or loss for the period.

(ii) Net exchange differences accumulated in foreign currency translation reserve as a separate component of shareholder's funds, and a reconciliation of the amount of such exchange differences at the beginning and end of the period.

Note: The answer has been given on the basis thai Mr. A is a small and mediumsized entity and AS 30 "Financial Instruments: Recognition and Measurement" is not applicable to him.

QUESTION 5: Sterling Ltd. purchased a plant for US $20,000 on 31st December, 2014 payable after 4 months. The company entered into a forward contract for 4 months @ ₹ 48.85 per dollar. On 31st December, 2014, the exchange rate was ₹ 47.50 per dollar.How will you recognize the profit or loss on forward contract in the books of Sterling Limited for the year ended 31st March, 2015.

ANSWER:

TREATMENT OF PROFIT ON FORWARD CONTRACT FOR HEDGING PURPOSES

Particulars	₹
Premium on entering into forward contract = [$20,000 × (₹ 48.85 - ₹ 47.50)]	₹ 27,000
Loss for 3 months falling in the year 2014-2015 will be (₹ 27,000 × 3/4)	20,250
Balance Loss of ₹ 6,750 (i.e. ₹ 27,000 × 1/4) for the month of April, 2015 will be recognised in the financial year 2015-2016.	

QUESTION 6: X Ltd. borrowed US $ 3,78,000 on 31-12-2014 when the exchange rate was ₹ 60 per US Dollar. X Ltd. prepares its financial statements ending on 31-03-2015 when the exchange rate was ₹ 62 per US Dollar. Discuss Accounting treatment as per AS-11 (Revised) in each of the following cases:

(a) If Option as per Para 46A is not exercised

(b) If Option as per Para 46A is exercised and such Loan relates to purchase of a Machine

(c) If Option as per Para 46A is exercised and such Loan relates to purchase of Land

(d) If Borrower is a Partnership Firm and not a Company

ANSWER: Exchange Loss = $ 3,78,000 × (₹ 60 – ₹ 62) = (₹ 7,56,000)

If Option as per Para 46A is not exercised	Exchange Loss (₹ 7,56,000) should be debited to Profit & Loss A/c.
If Option as per Para 46A is exercised and such Loan relates to purchase of a Machine	Exchange Loss (₹ 7,56,000) should be debited to Machine A/c. Depreciation on the revised book value will be provided prospectively over the residual useful life of the asset.

If Option as per Para 46A is exercised and such Loan relates to purchase of Land	1. Exchange Loss (₹ 7,56,000) should be debited to Foreign Currency Monetary Items Translation Difference A/c. 2. Such Exchange Loss should be transferred to Profit & Loss A/c in equal proportion over reporting periods ending on March 31,2020. Hence ₹ 1,26,000 (i.e.₹ 7,56,000 /8) should be transferred to Profit & Loss A/c on 31.03.2015. **Note:** The Dr. Balance of FCMITD A/c (i.e. ₹ 6,30,000) should be shown on the Equity & Liabilities side of the Balance Sheet under the head 'Reserves & Surplus'.
If Borrower is a Partnership Firm and not a Company	Exchange Loss(₹7,56,000) should be debited to Profit & Loss A/c since Option as per Para 46A is available only to a Company.

QUESTION 7: X Ltd. purchased Fixed Assets costing ₹ 6,000 lakhs on 1.4.2014. This was financed by foreign currency loan (U.S. Dollars) payable in three annual equal instalments. Exchange rates were 1 Dollar = ₹ 57 and ₹ 62 as on 1.4.2014 and 31.3.2015 respectively. First instalment was paid on 31.3.2015. X Ltd. provides depreciation on Fixed Assets @20% on WDV basis.State, how these transactions would be accounted for?

ANSWER:

PROVISION OF AS-11

As per AS 11 (Revised) exchange differences arising on the settlement of monetary items or on reporting an enterprise's monetary items at rates different from those at which they were initially recorded during the period, or reported in previous financial statements, should be recognized as income or as an expense in the period in which they arise. Thus, exchange differences arising on repayment of liabilities incurred for the purpose of acquiring fixed assets are recognized as income or expenses.

Exchange Difference

Foreign Exchange Loan = ₹ 6000 lakhs/140 = US $150 lakhs

Exchange Difference = US $150 lakhs × (₹ 62 – ₹ 57) = ₹ 750 lakhs.

ACCOUNTING TREATMENT

1. Initially Fixed Assets should be recognised at ₹ 6,000 lakhs.
2. Exchange Loss of ₹ 750 lakhs should be charged to Profit and Loss Account for the year ended 31st March 2015,.
3. Depreciation of ₹ 1200 lakhs (i.e. 20% of ₹ 6,000 lakhs) should be provided in the Financial Statements for the year ended 31st March 2015.
4. Closing Balance of Fixed Assets will be ₹ 4,800 lakhs.

QUESTION 8: X Ltd. purchased Fixed Assets costing ₹ 6,000 lakhs on 1.4.2014. This was financed by foreign currency loan (U.S. Dollars) payable in three annual equal instalments. Exchange rates were 1 Dollar = ₹ 57 and ₹ 62 as on 1.4.2014 and 31.3.2015 respectively. First instalment was paid on 31.3.2015. X Ltd. provides depreciation on Fixed Assets @20% on WDV basis. The company excercises the Option as per Para 46A . State, how these transactions would be accounted for?

ANSWER:

PROVISION OF PARA 46A OF THE COMPANIES (ACCOUNTING STANDARDS) RULES, 2012.

As per Para 46A, in case of **Long-term Foreign Currency Loans relating to Depreciable Assets,** Exchange Difference should be debited(in case of Exchange Loss) or credited (in case of Exchange

Profit) to the Respective Asset A/c.

Exchange Difference

Foreign Exchange Loan = ₹ 6000 lakhs/140 = US $150 lakhs

Exchange Difference = US $150 lakhs × (₹ 62 – ₹ 57) = ₹ 750 lakhs.

ACCOUNTING TREATMENT

1. Initially Fixed Assets should be recognised at ₹ 6,000 lakhs.
2. Exchange Loss of ₹ 750 lakhs should be debited to **Fixed Assets** Account.
3. Depreciation of ₹ 1350 lakhs (i.e. 20% of ₹ 6,750 lakhs) should be provided in the Financial Statements for the year ended 31st March 2015.
4. Closing Balance of Fixed Assets will be ₹ 5,400 lakhs.

QUESTION 9: X Ltd. purchased Land costing ₹ 6,000 lakhs on 1.4.2014. This was financed by foreign currency loan (U.S. Dollars) payable in three annual equal instalments. Exchange rates were 1 Dollar = ₹ 57 and ₹ 62 as on 1.4.2014 and 31.3.2015 respectively. First instalment was paid on 31.3.2015. The company excercises the Option as per Para 46A . State, how these transactions would be accounted for?

ANSWER:

PROVISION OF PARA 46A OF THE COMPANIES (ACCOUNTING STANDARDS) RULES, 2012.

1. In case of **Long-term Foreign Currency Loans relating to Non-Depreciable Assets** Exchange Difference should be debited(in case of Exchange Loss) or credited (in case of Exchange Profit) to Foreign Currency Monetary Items Translation Difference A/c.
2. Such Exchange Difference should be transferred to Profit & Loss A/c in equal proportion over reporting periods ending on March 31,2020.
3. The Dr. or Cr. Balance of FCMITD A/c should be shown on the Equity & Liabilities side of the Balance Sheet under the head 'Reserves & Surplus'.

Exchange Difference

Foreign Exchange Loan = ₹ 6000 lakhs/140 = US $150 lakhs

Exchange Difference = US $150 lakhs × (₹ 62 – ₹ 57) = ₹ 750 lakhs

ACCOUNTING TREATMENT

1. Exchange Loss (₹ 750 lakhs) should be debited to Foreign Currency Monetary Items Translation Difference A/c.
2. Such Exchange Loss should be transferred to Profit & Loss A/c in equal proportion over reporting periods ending on March 31,2020. Hence ₹ 125 lakhs (i.e. ₹ 750 lakhs /6) should be transferred to Profit & Loss A/c on 31.03.2015.
3. The Dr. Balance of FCMITD A/c (i.e. ₹ 625 lakhs) should be shown on the Equity & Liabilities side of the Balance Sheet under the head 'Reserves & Surplus'.
4. Initially Land should be recognised at ₹ 6,000 lakhs.

QUESTION 10: X Limited, a newly incorporated company in India commenced its business from April 1, 2012. The Company purchased fixed assets costing ₹ 4,000 lakhs on 01-04-2012 and the same was fully financed by foreign currency loan (U.S. Dollars) payable in three annual equal installments. Exchange rates were 1 Dollar = ₹ 40.00 and ₹42.50 as on 01- 04-2012 and 31-03-2013 respectively. The company worked out foreign exchange loss as per AS 11 at ₹250 Lakhs and expensed the entire amount in the profit and loss account. The Managing Director of the company was worried about this heavy revenue loss and asked the accountant not to follow AS 11 issued by the ICAI for this particular transaction. The Accountant of the company, followed the instruction of the Managing Director and removed exchange loss from

the profit and loss account but then he added the entire exchange loss to the value of fixed asset and computed the depreciation thereon. As an Auditor of X Limited how you would deal with this particular transaction?

ANSWER:

PROVISION OF AS 11

As per new para 46A(1) of AS 11 "The Effects of Changes in Foreign Exchange Rates" inserted by Ministry of Corporate Affairs by way of notification, the exchange differences arising on reporting of long- term foreign currency monetary items in so far as they relate to the acquisition of a depreciable capital asset in respect of accounting periods commencing on or after the 1st April, 2011. Such exchange differences can be added to or deducted from the cost of the asset and shall be depreciated over the balance life of the asset, and in other cases, it can be accumulated in a "Foreign Currency Monetary Item Translation Difference Account" in the enterprise's financial statements and amortized over the balance period of such long term asset or liability, by recognition as income or expense in each of such periods.

ADVISE

X Ltd. has the choice to avail this option. However, the company should disclose the fact of such option and of the amount remaining to be amortized in the financial statements of the period in which such option is exercised and in every subsequent period so long as any exchange difference remains unamortized.

QUESTION 11: Explain briefly the Accounting Treatment needed in the following cases as per AS 11:

1. **Sundry Debtors include amount receivable from Ted of U.S., ₹ 5,00,000 recorded at the prevailing exchange rate on the date of sales, transaction recorded at $1 = 50.**
2. **Long term loan taken from a U.S. Company, amounting to ₹ 49,00,000. It was recorded at $1 = ₹49, taking exchange rate prevailing at the date of transactions.**

   Exchange rates at the end of the year were as under:

   $1 Receivable = ₹ 60

   $ 1 Payable = ₹ 61.

ANSWER:

PROVISION OF AS-11

AS 11 'The Effects of Changes in Foreign Exchange Rates' provides that exchange differences attributable to monetary items should be taken to Statement of Profit and Loss. In case the option under para 46A is exercised, the exchange differences arising on long-term foreign currency monetary items can be adjusted in the cost of the depreciable capital asset or in other cases transferred in Foreign Currency Monetary Item Translation Difference Account (FCMITD) and amortised.

ACCOUNTING TREATMENT

1. Exchange Gain = US $ 10,000 × (₹50 – ₹ 60) = ₹ 1,00,000 should be credited to Profit and Loss Account.
2. Exchange Loss = US $1,00,000 × (₹49 – ₹ 61) = ₹ 12,00,000 should be debited to Profit and Loss Account or transfer to FCMITD A/c and amortise.

QUESTION 12: X Ltd. borrowed US $5,00,000 on 31-12-2014 which will be repaid (settled) as on 30-6-2015. X Ltd. prepares its financial statements ending on 31-03-2015. Rate of exchange between reporting currency (Rupee) and foreign currency (US $) on different dates are as under:

31-12-2014	**1 US $ = ₹ 44.00**
31-03-2015	**1 US $ = ₹ 44.50**
30-06-2015	**1 US $ = ₹ 44.75**

(i) Calculate Borrowings in reporting currency to be recognised in the books on above mentioned dates and also show journal entries for the same.

(ii) If Borrowings were repaid (settled) on 28-2-2015 on which date exchange rate was 1 US $ = ₹ 44.20 than what entry should be passed?

ANSWER:

PROVISION OF AS-11

As per para 9 of As 11 "Changes in Foreign Exchange Rates", a foreign currency transaction should be recorded, on initial recognition in the reporting currency, by applying to the foreign currency amount the exchange rate between the reporting currency and the foreign currency at the date of the transaction.

As per para 11(a) of the standard, at each balance sheet date, foreign currency monetary items should be reported using the closing rate.

ACCOUNTING TREATMENT

Accordingly, on 31.12.2014 borrowings will be recorded at ₹ 2,20,00,000 (i.e., ₹ 5,00,000 × ₹ 44.00). Accordingly, on 31.12.2015, borrowings (monetary items) will be recorded at ₹ 2,22,50,000 (i.e., $ 5,00,000 × ₹ 44.50).

(I) JOURNAL OF X LTD.

Date	Particulars		Dr. (₹)	Cr. (₹)
31-12-2014	Bank A/c	Dr.	2,20,00,000	
	To Borrowings			2,20,00,000
31-03-2015	Profit & Loss A/c	Dr.	2,50,000	
	To Borrowings			2,50,000
30.06.2015	Borrowings A/c	Dr.	2,22,50,000	
	Profit & Loss A/c	Dr.	1,25,000	
	To Bank A/c			2,23,75,000

(ii) In case Borrowings were repaid before balance sheet date then the entry would be as follows:

(II) JOURNAL OF X LTD.

Date	Particulars		Dr. (₹)	Cr. (₹)
28-02-2015	Borrowings A/c	Dr.	2,20,00,000	
	Profit & Loss A/c	Dr.	1,00,000	
	To Bank A/c			2,21,00,000

Working Notes:

1. The exchange difference of ₹ 2,50,000 is arising because the transaction has been reported at different rate (₹ 44.50 = 1 US $) from the rate initially recorded (i.e., ₹ 44 = 1 US $) from the rate initially recorded (i.e., ₹ 44 = 1 US $).
2. The exchange difference of ₹ 12,500 is arising because the transaction has been settled at an exchange rate (₹ 44.75 = 1 US $) different from the rate at which reported in the last financial statement (₹ 44.50 = 1 US $).

(iii) The exchange difference of ₹ 1,00,000 is arising because the transaction has been settled at a different rate (i.e., ₹ 44.20 = 1 US $) than the rate at which initially recorded (1 US $ = ₹ 44.00).

QUESTION 13: X Ltd. of India purchased a machinery from U.S.A. at $ 1.5 million on 01/10/2014 by borrowing U.S $ 1 million from a foreign bank @10% p.a. when the exchange rate was ₹ 42 per dollar. If the loan was taken in India on the same conditions and term then the rate of interest would have been 15% p.a. The machinery is ready to put to use when purchased. This machinery is to be depreciated @ 10% on SLM basis. X Ltd. paid U.S. $ 1,00,000. to foreign bank towards principal and interest on 31/03/2015 when the exchange rate was ₹ 43.50 per dollar.. How these transactions are shown in the financial statements of X Ltd. for the year 2014 - 2015.

ANSWER

CALCULATION OF AMOUNT TO BE RECOGNIZED IN MACHINERY A/C, DEPRECIATION FOR THE YEAR AND CLOSING BALANCE OF THE MACHINERY ACCOUNT

Particulars	Amount
A. Cost of machinery	$ 15,00,000
B. Exchange rate per dollar existing on date of transaction	₹ 42.00
C. Cost of machinery to be recognized (A × B)	₹ 6,30,00,000
D. Depreciation for the Year (C × 10% × 0.5)	₹ 31,50,000
E. Closing balance of the machinery (C – D)	₹ 5,98,50,000

CALCULATION OF AMOUNT TO BE RECOGNIZED IN LOAN A/C, INTEREST FOR THE YEAR AND CLOSING BALANCE OF THE LOAN ACCOUNT.

Particulars		Amount
A. Loan borrowed from a foreign bank		$ 10,00,000
B. Loan to be recognized in the books of X Ltd. (₹ 42 × A)		₹ 4,20,00,000
C. Borrowing Cost as per AS – 16		
Amount borrowed	$ 10,00,000	
Add: Interest @ 10% p.a. for 6 months	$ 50,000	
Total:	$ 10,50,000	
Less: Payment received	$ 1,00,000	
Balance	$ 9,50,000	
Liability towards loan at year end due to interest and change in exchange rate		
Principal paid ($ 50,000 × 1.50)	₹ 75,000	
Interest paid ($ 50,000 × 43.50)	₹ 21,75,000	
Increase in closing liability ($ 9,50,000 × 1.50)	₹ 14,25,000	
Total (A)	₹ 36,75,000	
Interest that would have been payable if loan is taken in India (₹ 4.2 crores × 15% × 6/12) (B)		₹ 31,50,000
Borrowing cost (A) or (B) whichever is lower		₹ 31,50,000
D. Exchange difference (₹ 36,75,000 – ₹ 31,50,000)		₹ 5,25,000
E. Payment made ($ 1,00,000 × 43.50)		₹.43,50,000
F. Closing Balance (B + C + D – E)		₹ 4,13,25,000

9 AS 15—EMPLOYEE BENEFITS

THEORETICAL BASE

QUESTION 1: What is the objective of Introduction of AS 15?

ANSWER: The objective of AS 15 is to prescribe the accounting and disclosure for employee benefits.The statement requires an enterprise to recognise:

(a) a liability when an employee has provided service in exchange for employee benefits to be paid in the future; and

(b) an expense when the enterprise consumes the economic benefit arising from service provided by an employee in exchange for employee benefits.

QUESTION 2: What are the types of Employees Benefits as per AS 15?

ANSWER:

There are four types of employee benefits according to AS 15 (Revised 2005). They are:

1. Short-Term Employee Benefits	1. Short-Term Employee Benefits (other than termination benefits) are those Employee Benefits which are payable within 12 months after the the end of the period in which the service is rendered., such as wages, salaries and social security contributions (e.g., contribution to an insurance company by an employer to pay for medical care of its employees), paid annual leave, profit-sharing and bonuses (if payable within twelve months of the end of the period) and non-monetary benefits (such as medical care, housing, cars and free or subsidised goods or services) for current employees;
2. Post-Employment Benefits	2. Post-Employment Benefits such as gratuity, pension, other retirement benefits, post-employment life insurance and post-employment medical care;
3. Other Long-Term Employee Benefits	3. Other Long-Term Employee Benefits, including long-service leave or sabbatical leave, jubilee or other long-service benefits, long-term disability benefits and, if they are not payable wholly within twelve months after the end of the period, profit-sharing, bonuses and deferred compensation;
4. Termination Benefits	4. Termination Benefits are employee benefits payable as a result of either an enterprise's decision to terminate an employee's employment before the normal retirement date or an employee's decision to accept voluntary redundancy in exchange for those benefits (e.g., payments under VRS).

QUESTION 3: State the provisions relating to Short-term Employee Benefits as per AS 15.

ANSWER:

1. Meaning	Short-term Employee Benefits (other than termination benefits) are those Employee Benefits which are payable within 12 months after the the end of the period in which the service is rendered.

2. Classification	These are broadly classified into four categories: 1. Regular Period Benefits (e.g., wages, salaries); 2. Short-term Compensated Absences (e.g., paid annual leave, maternity leave, sick leave etc.); 3. Profit Sharing and Bonuses payable within twelve months after the end of the period in which employee render the related services and 4. Non-Monetary Benefits (e.g., medical care, housing, cars etc.)
3. No Actuarial Assumptions	Accounting for these benefits is generally straightforward because no Actuarial Assumptions are required to measure the obligation or cost.
4. General Recognition Criteria	1. Recognize the undiscounted amount of all short-term employee benefits attributable to services that been already rendered in the period as an Expense; and 2. Recognize any difference between the amount of Expenses so recognized and cash payments made during the period as a liability or prepayment (asset) as appropriate.
5. Additional Requirements in respect of Short-Term Compensated Absences	1. An enterprise should measure the expected cost of accumulating compensated absences as the additional amount that the enterprise expects to pay as a result of the unused entitlement that has accumulated at the balance sheet date'. 2. No distinction should be made between vesting and non-vesting entitlements. However, in measuring non-vesting entitlements, the possibility of employees leaving the enterprise before receiving them should be taken into account. 3. Cost of non-accumulating absences should be recognized as and when they arise. Therefore, an enterprise recognizes no liability or expense until the time of the absence.
6. Additional Requirements in respect of Profit Sharing and Bonus Plans	1. The enterprise should recognize the expected cost of profit sharing and bonus payments in the financial statements. 2. Recognition of expenses for Profit Sharing And Bonus Plans would depend on fulfillment of following conditions : (a) Enterprise has a present obligation to make such payments as a result of past events; and (b) Reliable estimate of the obligation can be made. The second condition can be satisfied only when the profit sharing and bonus plans contained a formula for determining the amount of benefit.

QUESTION 4: State the provisions relating to Post Employment Benefits as per AS 15.

ANSWER: The accounting treatment and disclosures required for a post-employment benefit plan depend upon whether it is a Defined Contribution or A Defined Benefit Plan.

Basis of Comparision	Defined Contribution Plans	Defined Benefit Plans
1. Meaning	Defined Contribution Plans are post-employment benefit plans under which an enterprise pays fixed contributions into a separate fund and will have no obligation to pay further contributions.	Defined Benefit Plans are post-employment benefit plans other than defined contribution plans.

2. Actuarial & Investment Risk	Actuarial Risk (that benefits will be less than expected) and Investment Risk (that assets invested will be insufficient to meet expected benefits) fall on the employee.	Actuarial and Investment Risk fall on the employer.
3. Charge	Contribution is charged to income statement.	Detailed actuarial calculation is performed to determine the charge.

QUESTION 5: Is the gratuity scheme a defined contribution or defined benefit scheme?

ANSWER: An enterprise may pay insurance premiums to fund a post-employment benefit plan. The enterprise should treat such a plan as a defined contribution plan unless the enterprise will have an obligation to either:

(a) pay the employee benefits directly when they fall due;

(b) pay further amounts if the insurer does not pay all future employee benefits relating to employee service in the current and prior periods.

On the asset side, a question arises as to whether the funds under the scheme as certified by LIC would be treated as plan assets or reimbursement rights. The distinction is important (though both are measured on fair valuation basis) because plan assets are reduced from the defined benefit obligation and the net amount is disclosed in the balance sheet, whereas, in the case of reimbursement rights, the defined benefit obligation and the reimbursement rights are shown separately as liability and asset on the balance sheet. This would have the impact of making the balance sheet heavy both on the asset side as well as the liabilities side.

QUESTION 6: Define Termination Benefits. State the conditions for their recognition. How will you deal with the following situations?

(a) Where the termination benefits fall due within 12 months after the balance sheet date

(b) Where the termination benefits fall due more than 12 months after the balance sheet date

(c) Where an offer has been made to encourage voluntary redundancy

(d) Where there is uncertainty with regard to the number of employees who will accept an offer of voluntary redundancy

ANSWER:

MEANING OF TERMINATION BENEFITS

Termination Benefits are employee benefits payable as a result of either an enterprise's decision to terminate an employee's employment before the normal retirement date or an employee's decision to accept voluntary redundancy in exchange for those benefits (e.g., payments under VRS).

CONDITIONS FOR RECOGNITION

Termination benefits are recognized by an enterprise as a liability and an expense only when the enterprise has

(i) a detailed formal plan for the termination which is duly approved, and

(ii) a reliable estimate can be made of the amount of the obligation.

Situation	**Treatment**
1. Where the termination benefits fall due within 12 months after the balance sheet date,	An undiscounted amount of such benefits should be recognized as liability in the balance sheet with a corresponding charge to Profit & Loss Account

2. Where the termination benefits fall due more than 12 months after the balance sheet date	Such benefits should be discounted using an appropriate discount rate.
3. Where an offer has been made to encourage voluntary redundancy	The Termination Benefits should be measured by reference to the number of employees expected to accept the offer.
4. Where there is uncertainty with regard to the number of employees who will accept an offer of voluntary redundancy	A Contingent Liability exists and should be so disclosed as per AS 29 'Provisions, Contingent Liabilities and Contingent Assets'

QUESTION 7: State the Seven Components of Defined Employee Benefit Costs:

ANSWER:

1. Current Service Cost;
2. Interest Cost;
3. The Expected Return on any Plan Assets (and any Reimbursement Rights);
4. Actuarial Gains and Losses (To the extent they are Recognized);
5. Past Service Cost (To the extent they are Recognized);
6. The Effect of any Curtailments or Settlements; And
7. The Extent To Which The Negative Net Amount of Defined Benefit Liability exceeds the amount mentioned in Para 59(ii) of the Standard.

QUESTION 8: When should the gains or losses on settlement or curtailment of a defined benefit plan be recognized?

ANSWER:

1. A settlement occurs when an employer enters into a transaction that eliminates all further legal or constructive obligations for part or whole of the benefits provided under a defined benefit plan. For example, the commuted portion of pension.
2. A curtailment occurs when an employer either commits to reduce the number of employees covered by a plan or reduces the benefits under a plan.
3. The gains or losses on the settlement or curtailment of a defined benefit plan should be recognized when the settlement or curtailment occurs.

QUESTION 9: What are the Disclosures requirements of AS 15 Where there is uncertainty about the number of employees who will accept an offer of termination benefits?

ANSWER:

1. As required by AS 29, "Provisions, Contingent Liabilities and Contingent Assets" an enterprise discloses information about the contingent liability unless the possibility of an outflow in settlement is remote.
2. As required by AS 5, "Net Profit or Loss for the Period, Prior Period items and Changes in Accounting Policies" an enterprise discloses the nature and amount of an expense if it is of such size, nature or incidence that its disclosure is relevant to explain the performance of the enterprise for the period.Termination benefits may result in an expense needing disclosure in order to comply with this requirement.
3. Where required by AS 18, "Related Party Disclosures", an enterprise discloses information about termination benefits for key management personnel.

QUESTION 10: How will you deal with Actuarial gains and losses?

ANSWER:

1. Actuarial gains and losses should be recognized immediately in the Statement of profit and loss as income or expense.

2. While this is the general principle, as per AS 15, in case an enterprise adopts the option to defer the recognition of any subsequent actuarial gains is limited to excess of cumulative (unrecognized gains) over the unrecognized portion of increase in transitional liability.

QUESTION 11: How will you calculate:

(a) Actual Returns on Plan Assets

(b) Expected Rate of Return

(c) Expected Returns on Plan Assets,

(d) Acturial Gains/losses on Plan Assets

(e) Net Acturial Gains/losses on Plan Assets?

ANSWER:

(a) Actual Returns on Plan Assets	
A. Closing Balance of Fair Value of Plan Assets	XXX
B. *Add:* Benefits Paid	XXX
C. *Less:* Contributions Received	(XXX)
D. *Less:* Opening Balance of Fair Value Of Plan Assets	(XXX)
E. Actual Return on Plan Assets	**XXX**
(b) Expected Rate of Return = Interest & Dividend Income after tax payable by the Fund + Realized and Unrealized Gains on plan assets (after tax) – Fund Administrative Costs.	
(c) Expected Return on Plan Assets	
A. Return on Opening Balance of Fair Value of Plan Assets	XXX
B. Return on Net Contributions Received [(Contributions – Benefits Paid) × Equivalent Half Yearly Compounding Interest Rate]	XXX
C. Expected Return on Plan Assets [A+ B]	**XXX**
Note: Equivalent Half Yearly Compounding Interest Rate = $\sqrt{(1+ \text{Expected Rate of Return})} - 1$	
(d) Acturial Gains on Plan Assets = Actual Return on Plan Assets – Expected Return on Plan Assets	
(e) Net Acturial Gains on Plan Assets = Acturial Gains on Plan Assets – Acturial Losses on the obligations	

QUESTION 12: How will you Calculate Acturial Gains/losses on Present Value of Defined Benefit Obligations?

ANSWER:

CALCULATION OF ACTURIAL GAINS/LOSSES ON PV OF DBO

Particulars	₹
A. Present Value of Defined Benefit obligation in the beginning of the year	XXX
B. *Add:* Current Service Cost	XXX
C. *Add:* Interest cost	XXX
D. *Add:* Past Service Cost (Vested)	XXX
E. *Add:* Unrecognised Past Service Cost (Unvested)	XXX
F. *Less:* Benefits Paid	(XXX)
G. *Less:* Curtailment	(XXX)

H. Present Value of Defined Benefit Obligation at the end of the year	XXX
I. Acturial Losses [H – (A + B + C + D + E – F – G)]	XXX

QUESTION 13: State the Calculation of Defined Benefit Liability/ASSET as per AS 15.

ANSWER:

CALCULATION OF DEFINED BENEFIT LIABILITY/ASSET

Particulars	₹
A. Present Value of the Defined Benefit Obligation	XXX
B. *Less:*Unrecognized Past Service Cost	XXX
C. *Less:*Fair Value of Plan Assets	XXX
D. Defined Benefit Liability [A–B–C]	XXX

Note: If Defined Benefit Liability turns negative ,the resulting asset should be recognized at the lower of:-

1. the amount so determined; and
2. the Present Value of any Economic Benefits available in the form of refunds from the plan or reductions in future contributions to the plan.

PRACTICAL QUESTIONS FOR PRACTICE

QUESTION 1: As on 1st April, 2014 the Fair Value of Plan Assets was ₹ 2,00,000 in respect of a pension plan of Bharat & Tushar Ltd. The plan paid out benefits of ₹ 25,000 and received inward contributions of ₹ 55,000. On 31st March, 2015 the Fair Value of Plan Assets was ₹ 3,00,000 and Acturial losses on the Defined Benefit Obligations for the year 2014-2015 were ₹ 30,000.On 1st April, 2014 the company made the following estimates, based on its market studies, understanding and prevailing prices:

Interest & Dividend Income, after tax payable by the fund 11.25% ,Realized and Unrealized Gains on plan assets (after tax) 3%, Fund Administrative Costs 4%.

Required: Calculate(a) Actual Returns on Plan Assets, (b) Expected Rate of Return ,(c) Expected Returns on Plan Assets,(d) Acturial Gains/losses on Plan Assets(e) Net Acturial Gains/losses for the year 2014-2015.

ANSWER:

(a)	**Actual Returns on Plan Assets**	
	A. Closing Balance of Fair Value of Plan Assets	₹ 3,00,000
	B. *Add:* Benefits Paid	₹ 25,000
	C. *Less:* Contributions Received	(₹ 55,000)
	D. *Less:* Opening Balance of Fair Value Of Plan Assets	(₹ 2,00,000)
	E. Actual Return on Plan Assets	₹ 70,000
(b)	**Expected Rate of Return = 11.25% + 3% – 4% = 10.25%**	
(c)	**Expected Returns on Plan Assets**	
	A. Return on Opening Balance of Fair Value of Plan Assets [₹ 2,00,000 × 10.25% × 12/12]	₹ 20,500
	B. Return on Net Contributions Received [Contributions – Benefits Paid] [(₹ 55,000 – ₹ 25,000) × 5%]	₹ 1,500
	C. Expected Return on Plan Assets [A+B]	₹ 22,000

	Note: Equivalent Half Yearly Compounding Interest Rate = √(1+ Expected Rate of Return) –1 = √(1 + 0.1025) – 1 = 0.05 or 5%
(d)	**Acturial Gains on Plan Assets =** Actual Return on Plan Assets – Expected Return on Plan Assets = ₹ 70,000 – ₹ 22,000 = ₹ 48,000
(e)	**Net Acturial Gains =** Acturial Gains on Plan Assets – Acturial losses on the obligations = ₹ 48,000 – ₹.30,000 = ₹ 18,000
	Assumptions:
	1. All Contributions are received and Benefits are paid in middle of the year.
	2. Expected Rate of Return is compounded half yearly.

QUESTION 2: Calculate Acturial Gains/Losses on Present Value of Defined Benefit Obligations from the following:

Present Value of Defined Benefit obligation as at 01.04.2014	**₹ 5,00,000**
Interest cost	**19,500**
Current Service Cost	**50,000**
Benefits Paid	**1,10,000**
Past Service Cost (Vested)	**40,000**
Unrecognised Past Service Cost (Unvested)	**70,000**
Curtailment	**1,00,000**
Present Value of Defined Benefit Obligation as at 31.03.2015	**4,99,500**

ANSWER:

CALCUALTION OF ACTURIAL GAINS/LOSSES ON PV OF DBO

Particulars	₹
A. Present Value of Defined Benefit obligation as at 01.04.2014	5,00,000
B. *Add:* Interest cost	19,500
C. *Add:* Current Service Cost	50,000
D. *Less:* Benefits Paid	(1,10,000)
E. *Add:* Past Service Cost (Vested)	40,000
F. *Add:* Unrecognised Past Service Cost (Unvested)	70,000
G. *Less:* Curtailment	(1,00,000)
H. Present Value of Defined Benefit Obligation as at 31.03..2015	4,99,500
I. Acturial Losses [H – (A + B + C – D + E + F – G)]	30,000

QUESTION 3: A lump-sum benefits of 25% of last drawn salary would be payable for each completed year of service if employee retires after completing minimum five years of service in an enterprise. Current Salary is ₹ 1,49,021 which is expected to grow at 10% p.a. An employee joins the service in the beginning of year and it is probable that he will retire after completing five years of service.

Required: Calculate the Present Value of Defined Benefit Obligation, Current Service Cost and Interest Cost if discount rate is 8 % and Pass Journal Entries for the five years.

ANSWER:

Step 1: Expected Last Drawn Salary = ₹ 1,49,021 × 110% × 110% × 110% × 110% × 110%
= ₹ 2,40,000

Step 2: Defined Benefit Obligation = ₹ 2,40,000 × 25% × 5 = ₹ 3,00,000

Step 3: Calculation of Current Service Cost

Year	Equal apportioned amount of DBO [i.e ₹ 3 ,00,000/ 5 years]	PV Factor @ 8 %	Current Service Cost
A	B	C	D = B × C
1	60,000	0.735 (4 yrs.)	44,100
2	60,000	0.794 (3 yrs.)	47,640
3	60,000	0.857 (2 yrs.)	51,420
4	60,000	0.926 (1 yr.)	55,560
5	60,000	1 (0 yr.)	60,000

Step 4: Calculation of Present Value of Defined Benefit Obligation, Current Service Cost and Interest Cost

Year	Opening balance of Present value of Benefit Obligation	Interest Cost	Current Service Cost	Closing balance of Present value of benefit obligations
A	B	C = B × 8%	D	E = B + C + D
1	0	0	44,100	44,100
2	44,100	3,528	47,640	95,268
3	95,268	7,621	51,420	1,54,309
4	1,54,309	12,345	55,560	2,22,214
5	2,22,214	17,786*	60,000	3,00,000

*Due to approximations used in calculation, this figure is adjusted accordingly.

Step 5:

JOURNAL

Date	Particulars		Dr. (₹)	Cr. (₹)
Year 1	Interest Cost A/c	Dr.	0	
	Current Service Cost A/c	Dr.	44,100	
	To PV of Defined Benefit Obligation A/c			44,100
	(Being Expenses recorded)			
Year 2	Interest Cost A/c	Dr.	3,528	
	Current Service Cost A/c	Dr.	47,640	
	To PV of Defined Benefit Obligation A/c			51,168
	(Being Expenses recorded)			
Year 3	Interest Cost A/c	Dr.	7,621	
	Current Service Cost A/c	Dr.	51,420	
	To PV of Defined Benefit Obligation A/c			59,041
	(Being Expenses recorded)			
Year 4	Interest Cost A/c	Dr.	12,345	
	Current Service Cost A/c	Dr.	55,560	
	To PV of Defined Benefit Obligation A/c			67,905
	(Being Expenses recorded)			

Year 5	Interest Cost A/c	Dr.	17,786	
	Current Service Cost A/c	Dr.	60,000	
	To PV of Defined Benefit Obligation A/c			77,786
	(Being Expenses recorded)			
	PV of Defined Benefit Obligation A/c	Dr.	3,00,000	
	To Bank A/c			3,00,000
	(Being the Retirement benefits paid)			

QUESTION 4: Tulsian (C) Ltd. operates a pension plan that provides a pension of 2% of final salary for each year of service. The benefits become vested after five years of service. On 31st Dec. 2014 the enterprise improves the pension to 2.5% of final salary for each year of service starting from 1 January, 2008. At the date of the improvement, the present value of the additional benefits for service from 1 January, 2008 to 31st Dec. 2014 is as follows:

Employees with more than five years' service at 31.12.2014	**₹ 200 lacs**
(Benefit already vested)	
Employees with less than five years' service at 31.12.2014	
(Average period unit vesting: three years)	**₹ 150 lacs**
	₹ 350 lacs

Discuss the treatment of Employee benefit as per AS-15 and Pass the Journal Entries.

ANSWER: The enterprise recognizes 200 lacs immediately because the benefits are already vested. Enterprise should recognize 150 lacs on straight line basis over three years i.e. ₹ 50 lacs each year.

JOURNAL

Date	Particulars		Dr. (₹)	Cr. (₹)
31.12.2014	Past Service Cost (Vested) A/c	Dr.	200	
	Unrecognised Past Service Cost (Unvested) A/c	Dr.	150	
	To PV of Defined Benefit Obligation A/c			350
	(Being the additional liability recorded)			
	Profit & Loss A/c	Dr.	200	
	To Past Service Cost (Vested) A/c			200
	(Being Past Service Cost (Vested) recorded immediately)			
31.12.2015	Profit & Loss A/c	Dr.	50	
	To Unrecognised Past Service Cost (Unvested) A/c			50
	(Being Unrecognised Past Service Cost (Unvested) w/o over 3 years i.e.150/3)			
31.12.2016	Profit & Loss A/c	Dr.	50	
	To Unrecognised Past Service Cost (Unvested) A/c			50
	(Being Unrecognised Past Service Cost (Unvested) w/o over 3 years i.e.150/3)			
31.12.2017	Profit & Loss A/c	Dr.	50	
	To Unrecognised Past Service Cost (Unvested) A/c			50
	(Being Unrecognised Past Service Cost (Unvested) w/o over 3 years i.e.150/3)			

QUESTION 5: BHARAT (C) Ltd. discontinues a business segment and employees of the discontinued segment will earn no further benefits. This is a curtailment without a settlement. Using current actuarial assumptions (including current market interest rates and other current market prices) immediately before the curtailment, the enterprise has defined obligation with a fair value of ₹ 20,000 and unrecognized past service cost of ₹ 500. The fair value of plan Assets on the date was estimated at ₹ 16,000. After curtailment the Net Present Value of the defined obligation is ₹ 19,000. Of the previously unrecognized past service cost, 10% relates to the part of the obligation that was eliminated through the curtailment.

Required: Pass the necessary Journal Entry to record the Gain form curtailment and calculate the amount to be recognized as Asset/Liability after curtailment in the Balance Sheet.

ANSWER:

(A) GAIN FROM CURTAILMENT

Particulars	₹
Reduction in gross obligation [₹ 20,000 – ₹ 19,000]	1,000
Less: Proportion on unamortised past service cost [10% of ₹ 500]	(50)
Gain from Curtailment	950

(B) JOURNAL

Date	Particulars	Dr. (₹)	Cr. (₹)
	PV of Defined Benefit Obligation A/c Dr. [₹ 20,000 – ₹ 19,000]	1,000	
	To Unrecognised Past Service Cost (Unvested) A/c [500 × 10%]		50
	To Profit & Loss A/c (Being the Gain for curtailment recorded)		950

(C) CALCULATION OF LIABILITY TO BE RECOGNISED AFTER CURTAILMENT IN THE BALANCE SHEET

Particulars	₹
Reduced gross obligation	19,000
Less: Fair value of plan assets	(16,000)
Less: Unamortised past service cost [500 – 50]	(450)
Liability to be recognised in the balance sheet	2,550

QUESTION 6: A defined benefit plan has the following characteristics.

Present value of the Defined Benefit Obligation	**₹ 1,100 lacs**
Fair Value of Plan Assets	**₹ 1,190 lacs**
Unrecognized Past Service Cost	**₹ (70) lacs**

Required: Calculate the amount to be recognized as asset/liability in the Balance Sheet.

ANSWER:

CALCULATION OF AMOUNT TO BE RECOGNIZED AS ASSETS

P.V. of obligation	₹ 1,100 lacs
Less: Fair Value of Plan Assets	₹ 1,190 lacs
Less: Unrecognized Past Service Cost	₹ (70) lacs
Since it is negative amount hence, the assets to be recognized at ₹ 20 lacs.	₹ (20) lacs

QUESTION 7: DAG Ltd. make an amendment to its pension plan on 31.3.2015. The following information is provided to you by the Chief Accountant.

	31.3.2015 Before Amendment	31.3.2015 After Amendment
Total Provision	**₹ 10 lacs**	**₹ 12.50 lacs**
Projected Obligation	**₹ 2 lacs**	**₹ 15.00 lacs**

Required: What should be the amount to be charged to Profit & Loss Account? What will be the amount to be amortized over future periods as a result of amendment if the obligation has already vested on the employee.

ANSWER:

1. Amount to be charged to Profit and Loss A/c is ₹ 2 lacs (i.e., ₹ 12 lacs – ₹ 10 lacs)
2. The additional obligation of ₹ 3 lacs (i.e., 15 lacs – 12 lacs) should also be recognized immediately in Profit & Loss if the obligation has already vested on the employee.

QUESTION 8: Kumar Ltd., is in engineering industry. The company received an actuarial valuation for the first time for its pension scheme which revealed a surplus of ₹ 6 lakhs. It wants to spread the same over the next 2 years by reducing the annual contribution to ₹ 2 lakhs instead of ₹ 5 lakhs. The average remaining life of the employee is estimated to be 6 years. You are required to advise the company.

ANSWER: AS 15As per AS 15, "Employee Benefits", actuarial gains and losses should be recognized immediately in the statement of profit and loss as income or expense.

ADVICE

1. Surplus of ₹ 6 lakhs in the pension scheme on its actuarial valuation is required to be credited to the Profit and Loss Statement of the current year.
2. Hence, Kumar Ltd. cannot spread the actuarial gain of ₹ 6 lakhs over the next 2 years by reducing the annual contributions to ₹ 2 lakhs instead of ₹ 5 lakhs. It has to contribute ₹ 5 lakhs annually for its pension schemes.

QUESTION 9: A company has a scheme for payment of settlement allowance to retiring employees. Under the scheme, retiring employees are entitled to reimbursement of certain travel expenses for class they are entitled to as per company rule and to a lump-sum payment to cover expenses on food and stay during the travel. Alternatively employees can claim a lump sum amount equal to one month pay last drawn.

The company's contentions in this matter are:

(i) Settlement allowance does not depend upon the length of service of employee. It is restricted to employee's eligibility under the Travel rule of the company or where option for lump-sum payment is exercised, equal to the last pay drawn.

(ii) Since it is not related to the length of service of the employees, it is accounted for on claim basis.

State whether the contentions of the company are correct as per relevant Accounting Standard. Give reasons in support of your answer.

ANSWER:

PROVISION OF AS 15

As per AS 15, "Employee Benefits", Para 49 covers cases where payment promised to be made to an employee at or near retirement presents significant difficulties in the determination of periodic charge to the statement of profit and loss.

ADVICE

The contention of the Company that the settlement allowance will be accounted for on claim basis is not correct even if company's obligation under the scheme is uncertain and requires estimation. In estimating the obligation, assumptions may need to be made regarding future conditions and events, which are largely outside the company's contr ol. Thus,

1. Settlement allowance payable by the company is a defined retirement benefit, covered by AS I5 (Revised).
2. A provision should be made every year in the accounts for the accruing liability on account of settlement allowance. The amount of provision should be calculated according to actuarial valuation.
3. Where, however, the amount of provision so determined is not material, the company can follow some other method of accounting for settlement allowances.

QUESTION 10: TULSIAN Ltd has 500 employees on its payroll. Each employee is entitled to 30 working days of leave per annum. Financial year followed is calendar year. At 31st December, 2014 the average unused leave was 5 per employee. Unused leave is carried forward only for one calendar year. Utilisation of leave taken during the year is done on LIFO basis i.e. leave is first taken out of current year entitlement and then out of any balance brought forward from the previous year. TULSIAN Ltd from its past experience expects that 400 of its employees will take less than 30 days working leave in calendar year 2015 and the remaining employees will take an average of 4 days leave over 30 days leave. Average pay for each employee per day for TULSIAN Ltd. works out to be ₹ 500.

Required: Pass necessary journal entries in the books of TULSIAN Ltd for the year 2014 regarding accumulating compensated absences.

ANSWER:

JOURNAL OF TULSIAN LTD.

Particulars		Dr (₹)	Cr (₹)
Expense for Accumulating Compensated Absences A/c	Dr	2,00,000	
To Liability for Accumulating Compensated Absences A/c			2,00,000
(Being liability created for compensating unused leave taken during the year and expected to be utilized during next year i.e ₹ 500 × (500 – 400) employees × 4 day leave.)			
Profit & Loss A/c	Dr	2,00,000	
To Expense for Accumulating Compensated Absences A/c			2,00,000
(Being expense recognized in respect of expected accumulating compensated absences.)			

QUESTION 11: Suppose in QUESTION 11 each employee is entitled to 10 additional working day paternity leave and this additional paternity leave are not carried forward to next calendar year. At December 2015 the average used paternity leave comes out to be 0.5 days per employee.

Required: Pass necessary journal entries in this regard.

ANSWER:

JOURNAL OF TULSIAN LTD.

Particulars		Dr. (₹)	Cr. (₹)
Profit & Loss A/c	Dr	1,25,000	
To Expense on Paternity Leave* A/c			1, 25,000

(Being compensation made on account of paternity leave recognized as an expense (i.e 500 × 0.5 × ₹ 500)		

*It is not necessary to pass this separate entry. A situation may exist where it is already included in an amount already recognized as an expense for short – term employee benefits. For example if employee had taken paternity leave, but no amount is deducted from his pay on account of such paternity leave as such paternity leave is allowed, then in such a case expense on account of paternity leave shall already be included in his pay since no amount is deducted for said paternity leave and as such there is no need to recognise separate expense regarding paternity leave.

QUESTION 12: P Ltd. has three business segments which are FMCG, Batteries and Sports Equipment. The Battery segment has been consistently underperforming and P Ltd. after several discussions with Labour unions have finally decided on closure of this segment. Under the agreement with the Labour Union the employees of the Battery Segment will earn no further benefit as the arrangement is a curtailment without settlement wherein the employees of the discontinued segment will continue to receive benefits for services rendered when the segment was functioning. As a result of the curtailment, the company's obligations that were arrived on the basis of actuarial valuations before the curtailment have come down. The following information is also furnished:

(i) The value of gross obligations before the curtailment calculated on actuarial basis was ₹ 4,000 lakhs.

(ii) The value of Unamortized past service costs is ₹ 100 lakhs.

(iii) The Curtailment will bring down gross obligations by ₹ 500 lakbs and P Ltd. anticipates a proportional decline in the value of unamortized past service costs also.

(iv) The Fair Value of plan assets on date is estimated at ₹ 3,250 lakhs.

You are required to calculate the gain from curtailment and also show the liability to be recognized in the Balance Sheet of P Ltd. after the curtailment.

ANSWER:

GAIN FROM CURTAILMENT

Particulars	(₹) in lakhs
Reduction in gross obligation (12.5% of 4,000)	500.00
Less: Proportion of unamortised past service cost (12.5% of ₹ 100)	(12.50)
Gain from curtailment	487.50
The liability to be recognised after curtailment in the balance sheet of P Ltd. is estimated as under:	
Reduced gross obligation (₹ 4,000 *less* ₹ 500)	3,500.00
Less: Fair value of plan assets	(3,250.00)
	250.00
Less: Unamortised past service cost (87.5% of ₹ 100)	(87.50)
Liability to be recognised in the balance sheet	162.50

QUESTION 13: An employee Roshan has joined a company XYZ Ltd. in the year 2015. The annual emoluments of Roshan as decided is ₹ 14,90,210. The company also has a policy of giving a lump sum payment of 25% of the last drawn salary of the employee for each completed year of service if the employee retires after completing minimum 5 years of service. The salary of the Roshan is expected to grow @ 10% per annum. The company has inducted Roshan in the beginning of the year and it is expected that he will complete the minimum five year term before retiring. What is the amount the company should charge in its Profit and

Loss account every year as cost for the Defined Benefit obligation? Also calculate the current service cost and the interest cost to be charged per year assuming a discount rate of 8%. (P.V factor for 8% - 0.735, 0.794, 0.857, 0.926, 1)

ANSWER:

CALCULATION OF DEFINED BENEFIT OBLIGATION

Expected last drawn salary = ₹ 14,90,210 × 110% × 110% × 110% × 110% × 110%
= ₹ 24,00,000

Defined Benefit Obligation (DBO) = ₹ 24,00,000 × 25% × 5 = ₹ 30,00,000

Amount of ₹ 6,00,000 will be charged to Profit and Loss Account of the company every year as cost for Defined Benefit Obligation.

CALCULATION OF CURRENT SERVICE COST

Year	Equal apportioned amount of DBO [i.e. ₹ 30,00,000/5 years]	PV factor@ 8%	Present Value
A	B	C	D = B × C
1	6,00,000	0.735 (4 Years)	4,41,000
2	6,00,000	0.794 (3 Years)	4,76,400
3	6,00,000	0.857 (2 Years)	5,14,200
4	6,00,000	0.926 (1 Year)	5,55,600
5	6,00,000	1 (0 Year)	6,00,000

CALCULATION OF INTEREST COST TO BE CHARGED PER YEAR

Year	Opening balance	Interest cost	Current service cost	Closing balance
A	B	C = B × 8%	D	E = B + C + D
1	0	0	4,41,000	4,41,000
2	4,41,000	35,280	4,76,400	9,52,680
3	9,52,680	76,214	5,14,200	15,43,094
4	15,43,094	1,23,447	5,55,600	22,22,141
5	22,22,141	1,77,859*	6,00,000	30,00,000

*Due to approximations used in calculation, this figure is adjusted accordingly.

QUESTION 14: Z Ltd changed its employee remuneration policy from 1st of April 2012 t o S provide for 12% contribution to provident fund on leave encashment also. As per the leave encashment policy the employees can either utilize or encash it. As at 31st March 2015 the company obtained an actuarial valuation for leave encashment liability. However it did not provide for 12% PF contribution on it. The auditor of the company wants it to be provided but the management replied that as and when the employees availed leave encashment, the provident fund contribution was made. The company further contends that this is the correct treatment as it is not sure whether the employees will avail leave encashment or utilize it Comment.

ANSWER:

PROVISION OF AS 15

As per para 11 of AS-15 on "Employee Benefits", issued by The Institute of Chartered Accountants of India, an enterprise should recognize the expected cost of short-term employee benefits in the form of compensated absences in the case of accumulating compensated absences, when the employees render service that increases their entitlement to future compensated absences

ADVICE

Since the company obtained actuarial valuation for leave encashment, it is obvious that the compensated absences are accumulating in nature. An enterprise should measure the expected cost of accumulating compensated absences as the additional amount that the enterprise expects to pay as a result of the unused entitlement that has accumulated at the balance sheet date.Here, Z Ltd will accumulate the amount of leave encashment benefits as it is the liability of the company to provide 12% PF on amount of leave encashment. The contention of the auditor is correct that full provision should be provided by the company.

10 AS 16—BORROWING COSTS

THEORETICAL BASE

QUESTION 1: State the meaning and components of Borrowing Costs.

ANSWER:

Meaning	Borrowing costs are interest and other costs incurred by an enterprise in connection with the borrowing.
Components	(a) Interest and commitment charges on bank borrowings and other short-term and long-term borrowings; (b) amortization of discounts or premiums relating to borrowings; (c) amortization of ancillary costs incurred in connection with the arrangement of borrowings; (d) finance charges in respect of assets acquired under finance leases or under other similar arrangements; and (e) exchange differences arising from foreign currency borrowings to the extent that they are regarded as an adjustment to interest costs.

QUESTION 2: State the meaning of Qualifying Asset. Name the Assets that are not considered as qualifying assets.

ANSWER:

Meaning	A qualifying asset is an asset that necessarily takes a substantial period of time (**ordinarily, a period of 12 months**) to get ready for its intended use or sale. Examples of qualifying assets are manufacturing plants, power generation facilities, inventories that require a substantial period of time to bring them to a saleable condition and investment properties.
Assets that are not considered as qualifying assets	1. Other investments and those inventories that are routinely manufactured or otherwise produced in large quantities on a repetitive basis over a short period of time. 2. Assets that are ready for their intended use or sale when acquired,

QUESTION 3: State the treatment of Borrowing Costs in case of Specifically borrowed funds.

ANSWER: The amount of borrowing costs eligible for capitalization on that asset should be determined as the actual borrowing costs incurred on that borrowing during the period *less* any income on the temporary investment of those borrowings.

QUESTION 4: State the treatment of Borrowing Costs in case of General borrowed funds.

ANSWER: The amount of borrowing costs eligible for capitalization should be determined by applying a capitalization rate to the expenditure on that asset. The capitalization rate should be the weighted average of the borrowing costs applicable to the borrowings of the enterprise that are outstanding during the period, other than borrowings made specifically for the purpose of obtaining a qualifying asset.

Note: *The amount of borrowing costs capitalized during a period should not exceed the amount of borrowing costs incurred during that period.*

QUESTION 5: State the Relevant Period for Capitalization of Borrowing Costs.

ANSWER:

Case	Relevant Period
1. When all the activities necessary to prepare the qualifying asset for its intended use or sale are in progress	Capitalization of borrowing costs should continue during the period in which active development is in progress.
2. When all the activities necessary to prepare the qualifying asset for its intended use or sale are interrupted.	Capitalization of borrowing costs should be suspended during extended periods in which active development is interrupted.
3. When all the activities necessary to prepare the qualifying asset for its intended use or sale are complete	Capitalization of borrowing costs should cease completion of active development.

QUESTION 6: How will deal with the Foreign Currency Borrowings.

ANSWER:

Case	Borrowing Costs as per AS 16	Exchange Difference to be treated as per AS 11
(a) If the difference between the interest on local currency borrowings and the interest on foreign currency borrowings is less than the exchange difference on the amount of principal of the foreign currency borrowings	= Interest on Local Currency Borrowings	= Increase in liability towards principal amount of the foreign currency borrowings – (Interest on Local Currency Borrowings and Interest on Foreign Currency Borrowings)
(b) If the difference between the interest on local currency borrowings and the interest on foreign currency borrowings is equal to or more than the exchange difference on the amount of principal of the foreign currency borrowings	= Interest on Foreign Currency Borrowings + Increase in liability towards principal amount of the foreign currency borrowings	NIL

QUESTION 7: State the Disclosure Requirements as per AS 16.

ANSWER:

1. The accounting policy adopted for borrowing costs; and
2. The amount of borrowing costs capitalized during the period.

PRACTICAL QUESTIONS FOR PRACTICE

QUESTION 1: BHARAT LTD. obtained a 14% loan from a bank for ₹ 120 lakhs on 1st June, 2014 to be utilized as follows:

Particulars	Amount (₹ in lakhs)
Construction of a Building (work was held up totally for 1 month during the year due to heavy rains)	50
Purchase of a Machinery	40
Working Capital	20
Advance for Purchase of Truck	10

Construction of Building was completed on 31.12.2014 but was put to use only on 01.04.2015 The machinery was installed on the same date. Delivery of truck was not received. During the year 2014-2015, the company had invested idle fund out of loan raised in banks' fixed deposit and had earned an interest of ₹ 2,00,000.

Required: **Show the treatment of Interest as per AS 16 and pass the Journal Entries relating to Interest on Loan.**

ANSWER:

PROVISSION OF AS 16

1. According to para 6 of AS 16 "Borrowing Costs", borrowing costs that are directly attributable to the acquisition, construction or proiduction of a qualifying asset should be capitalised as part of the cost of that asset. Other borrowing costs should be recognised as an expense in the period in which they are incurred.
2. A qualifying asset is an asset that necessarily takes a substantial period of time (usually 12 months or more) to get ready for its intended use or sale. If an asset is ready for its intended use or sale at time of its acquisition then it is not treated as a qualifying asset for that purposes of AS 16.
3. The amount of borrowing costs eligible for capitalization on that asset should be determined as the actual borrowing costs incurred on that borrowing during the period *less* any income on the temporary investment of those borrowings.

Particulars	Nature	Treatment of Interest
1. Construction of a Building	Qualifying Asset	Interest to be capitalized As per
2. Purchase of Machinery	Not a Qualifying Asset*	Interest to be charged to P&L A/c
* On the basis that Plant & Machinery is ready for its intended use at the time of its acquisition/ purchase.		
3. Working capital	Not a Qualifying Asset	Interest to be charged to P&L A/c
4. Advance for Purchase of Truck	Not a Qualifying Asset	Interest to be charged to P&L A/c

Total Borrowing Cost = ₹ 120 lakhs × 14% × 10/12 = ₹ 14 lakhs

Eligible Borrowing Cost = ₹ 14,00,000 – ₹ 2,00,000 = ₹ 12,00,000

Qualifying Asset as per AS-16 = ₹ 50 lakhs (construction of a Building)

Borrowing Cost to be capitalized = 12 × 50/120 = ₹ 5 lakhs

Interest to be debited to Profit or Loss Account during 2014-2015 = ₹ (12 – 5) lakhs

= ₹ 7 lakhs

JOURNAL

Date	Particulars		Dr. (₹)	Cr. (₹)
31.03.2015	Interest on Loan A/c	...Dr.	14,00,000	
	To Loan A/c			14,00,000
	(Being the Interest on Loan accrued)			
	Land & Building A/c	...Dr.	5,00,000	
	To Interest on Loan A/c			5,00,000
	(Being the Interest on Loan capitalized)			
31.03.2015	P & L A/c	...Dr.	7,00,000	
	To Interest on Loan A/c			7,00,000
	(Being Interest on Loan charged to P&L Account)			

QUESTION 2: An industry borrowed ₹40,00,000 for construction of machinery on 1.6.2014. Interest on loan is 9% per annum. The machinery was put to use from 1.1.2015. Pass journal entries for the year ended 31.3.2015 to record the borrowing cost of loan as per AS 16.

ANSWER:

Particulars	₹
A. Interest upto 31.3.2015 (40,00,000 × 9% × 10/12 months)	3,00,000
B. *Less:*Interest relating to pre-operative period to be capitalized [3,00,000 × 7/10]	2,10,000
C. Amount to be charged to P & L A/c [3,00,000 × 3/10]	90,000

JOURNAL

Date	Particulars		Dr. (₹)	Cr. (₹)
31.03.2015	Interest on Loan A/c	...Dr.	3,00,000	
	To Loan A/c			3,00,000
	(Being the Interest on Loan accrued)			
	Machinery A/c	...Dr.	2,10,000	
	To Interest on Loan A/c			2,10,000
	(Being the Interest on Loan capitalized)			
31.03.2015	P & L A/c	...Dr.	90,000	
	To Interest on Loan A/c			90,000
	(Being Interest on Loan charged to P&L Account)			

QUESTION 3: X Ltd. purchased machinery from Y Ltd. on 30/09/2014. The price was 522.50 lakhs after charging 10 % VAT and giving a trade discount of 5 % on the quoted price. Transport charges were 0.25 % on the quoted price and installation charges come to 1% on the quoted price.

A loan of ₹500 lakhs was taken from bank on which interest at 15 % per annum was to be paid.

Expenditure incurred on the trial run was: Material ₹50,000, wages ₹40,000 and overheads ₹30,000.

Machinery was ready for use on 01/12/2014. However, it was actually put to use only on 01/05/2015. Find out the cost of the machine and suggest the accounting treatment for the expenses incurred in the interval between the dates 01/12/2014 to 01/05/2015. The entire loan amount remained unpaid on 01/05/2015. X Ltd. does not intend to utilize the input tax paid on capital good.

ANSWER:

CALCULATION OF COST OF MACHINE AS PER AS 10

	Particulars		₹ in lakhs
A	Quoted Price of machine		500.00
B	Trade Discount @ 5 % on ₹ 500		(25.00)
C	Price after discount [A – B]		475.00
D	VAT @ 10 % on ₹ 475		47.50
E	Selling Price [C + D]		522.50
F	Transportation charges [0.25 % of ₹ 500]		1.25
G	Installation charges [1 % of ₹ 500]		5.00
H	Borrowing cost [₹ 500 lakhs × 15% × 2/12]		12.50
I	Expenditure on Trial Run		
	Material:	0.50	
	Wages:	0.40	
	Overheads:	0.30	1.20
J	Total Cost of the Machinery to be capitalized [E + F + G + H + I]		542.45

As per AS - 16, the capitalization of interest should cease when substantially all the activities necessary for intended use are completed. Therefore, interest for the period 01/12/2014 to 01/05/2015 should be expensed.

QUESTION 4: Southern Tower Ltd. purchased a plant from M/s. Tatamaco Ltd. on 30.09.2014 with a quoted price ₹ 180 lakhs. Tatamaco offer 3 months credit with a condition that discount of 1.25% will be allowed if the payment were made within one month. VAT is 12.5% on the quoted price. Company incurred 2% on transportation costs and 3% on erection costs of the quoted price, Preoperative cost amount ₹ 1.50 lakhs. To Finance the purchase of the machinery, company took a term bank loan of ₹ 125 lakhs at an interest rate of 14.50% per annum. The machine was ready for use on 31.12.2014; however, it was put to use only on 01-04-2015:

(i) Find out the original cost.

(ii) Suggest the accounting treatment for the cost incurred during the period between the date the machine was ready for use and the actual date the machine was put to use.

ANSWER:

(I) ORIGINAL COST OF THE MACHINE

Particulars	In lakhs	In lakhs
Quoted price	180.00	
Less: Discount @1.25%	2.25	177.75
Add: VAT@12.5%		22.50
Transportation @ 2%		3.60
Erection Cost @ 3%		5.40
Pre-operative Cost		1.50

Finance Cost (14.5% on ₹ 125 lakhs for the period 01.10.2014 to 31.12.2015)		4.53
Total		215.28

(ii) Cost incurred during the period between the date the machine was ready for use and the actual date the machine was put to use

Finance cost amounting to ₹ 4.53 lakhs (14.50% on ₹ 125 lakhs for the period 01.01.2015 to 31.03.2015) will be charged to Profit and Loss Account as per AS 16 "Borrowing Costs".

QUESTION 5: Suhana Ltd. issued 12% secured debentures of ₹ 100 Lakhs on 01.05.2014, to be utilized as under:

Particulars	Amount (₹ in lakhs)
Construction of factory building	**40**
Purchase of Machinery	**35**
Working Capital	**25**

In March 2015, construction of the factory building was completed and machinery was installed and ready for it's intended use. During the year 2014-2015, the company had invested idle fund out of money raised from debentures in banks' fixed deposit and had earned an interest of ₹ 2,00,000.

Show the treatment of interest under Accounting Standard 16 and also explain nature of assets.

ANSWER:

PROVISSION OF AS 16

According to para 6 of AS 16 "Borrowing Costs", borrowing costs that are directly attributable to the acquisition, construction or proiduction of a qualifying asset should be capitalised as part of the cost of that asset. The amount of borrowing costs eligible for capitalisation should be determined in accordance with this Standard. Other borrowing costs should be recognised as an expense in the period in which they are incurred.

Also para 10 of AS 16 "Borrowing Costs" states that to the extent that funds are borrowed specifically for the purpose of obtaining a qualifying asset, the amoubnt of borrowing costs eligible for capiotalisation on that asset should be determined as the actual borrowing costs incurred on that borrowing during the period *less* any income on the temporary investment of those borrowings.

Decision: Eligible borrowing cost = ₹ 11,00,000 – ₹ 2,00,000 = ₹ 9,00,000

Sr. No.	Particulars	Nature of assets	Interest to be Capitalized (₹)	Interest to be charged to Profit & Loss Account (₹)
i.	Construction of factory building	Qualifying Asset	9,00,000 × 40/100 = ₹ 3,60,000	NIL
ii.	Purchase of Machinery	Not a Qualitfying Asset	NIL	9,00,000 × 35/100 = ₹ 3,15,000
iii.	Working Capital	Not a Qualifying Asset	NIL	9,00,000 × 25/100 = ₹ 2,25,000
	Total		₹ 3,60,000	₹ 5,40,000

QUESTION 6: Rainbow Limited borrowed an amount of ₹ 150 crores on 1.4.2014 for construction of boiler plant @ 11% p.a. The plant is expected to be completed in 4 years. The weighted average cost of capital is 13% p.a. The accountant of Rainbow Ltd. capitalised interest of ₹19.50 crores for the accounting period ending on 31.3.2015. Due to surplus fund out of ₹ 150 crores, an income of ₹ 3.5 crores was earned and credited to profit and loss account. Comment on the above treatment of accountant with reference to relevant accounting standard.

ANSWER:

PROVISSION AS-16

As per AS 16 'Borrowing Cost' states, To the extent that funds are borrowed specifically for the purpose of obtaining a qualifying asset, the amount of borrowing costs eligible for capitalisation on that asset should be determined as the actual borrowing costs incurred on that borrowing during the period *less* any income on the temporary investment of those borrowings". The capitalisation rate should be the weighted average of the borrowing costs applicable to the borrowings of the enterpnse that are outstanding during the period, other than borrowings made specifically for the purpose of obtaining a qualifying asset.

ADVICE

The amount of ₹ 150 crores was specifically borrowed for construction of boiler plant. Therefore, treatment of accountant of Rainbow Ltd. is not correct and the amount of borrowing costs to be capitalised for the financial year 2014-2015 should be calculated as follows:

Particulars	₹ (in crores)
Interest paid for 2014-2015 (11% on ₹ 150 crores)	16.50
Less: Income on temporary investment from specific borrowings	3.50
Borrowing costs to be capitalised during 2014-2015	13.00

QUESTION 7: Bharat Tushar Ltd. borrowed funds for modernization and development of its factory as follows:

Date on which Funds borrowed	Funds Borrowed	Rate of Interest
1/4/2015	12,00,000	13 %
1/7/2015	40,00,000	14 %
1/10/2015	16,00,000	15.5 %

Expenditure incurred on Construction of a Building	Date on which it is incurred
6,00,000	01/04/2014
2,00,000	01/05/2014
3,00,000	01/7/2014
8,00,000	01/12/2014

The Construction of a Building completed on 31.12.2014.However,it was put to use only on 01.04.2015.A sum of ₹ 20 lakhs has been advanced for purchase of Plant & machinery which was installed by 31st March, 2015. ₹ 29 lakhs has been utilized for working capital requirements.

***Required:* Show the treatment of Interest as per AS 16 and pass the Journal Entries relating to Interest.**

ANSWER: As per AS 16, borrowing costs that are directly attributable to the acquisition, construction or production of a qualifying asset should be capitalized. A qualifying asset is an asset that necessarily takes a substantial period of time (usually 12 months or more) to get ready for its intended use or sale. If an asset is ready for its intended use or sale at time of its acquisition then it is not treated as a qualifying asset for that purposes of AS 16.

Particulars	Nature	Treatment of Interest
1. Construction of a Building = ₹ 1.12 lakhs	Qualifying Asset	Interest to be capitalized As per W.N.(iii)
2. Advance for Purchase of Plant & machinery	Not a Qualifying Asset*	Interest to be charged to P&L A/c
* On the basis that Plant & Machinery is ready for its intended use at the time of its acquisition/ purchase.		
3. Working Capital	Not a Qualifying Asset	Interest to be charged to P&L A/c

Interest Costs to be charged to Profit & Loss Account
= Total Interest – Interest to be capitalized = ₹ 7,00,000 – ₹ 1,12,000 = ₹ 5,88,000

JOURNAL

Date	Particulars		Dr. (₹)	Cr. (₹)
31.03.2015	Interest on Loan A/c	...Dr.	7,00,000	
	To Loan A/c			7,00,000
	(Being the Interest on Loan accrued)			
	Land & Building A/c	...Dr.	1,12,000	
	To Interest on Loan A/c			1,12,000
	(Being the Interest on Loan capitalized)			
31.03.2015	P & L A/c	...Dr.	5,88,000	
	To Interest on Loan A/c			5,88,000
	(Being Interest on Loan charged to P&L Account)			

Working Notes:

(I) CALCULATION OF CAPITALIZED RATE

Date of Loan	O/S Loan	Interest Rate	Months for Loan is O/S	Product	Total Interest
A	B	C	D	E = B × D	F= B × C × D/12
1/4/2014	12,00,000	13%	12	1,44,00,000	1,56,000
1/7/2014	40,00,000	14 %	9	3,60,00,000	4,20,000
1/10/2014	16,00,000	15.5 %	6	96,00,000	1,24,000
			Total	6,00,00,000	7,00,000

Average Amount Outstanding = 600,00,000/12 = 50,00,000

Capitalization Rate = (7,00,000/50,00,000)*100 = 14 %

(II) CALCULATION OF AVERAGE CARRYING AMOUNT OF THE BUILDING DURING A PERIOD

Expenditure incurred is incurred	Date on which it	Months	Products
A	B	C	D = A × C
6,00,000	01/04/2014	9	54,00,000
2,00,000	01/05/2014	8	16,00,000

3,00,000	01/7/2014	6	18,00,000
8,00,000	01/12/2014	1	8,00,000
		Total	96,00,000

Average carrying amount of Building during a period = 96,00,000/12 = 8,00,000

(iii) Interest to be capitalized = Average carrying amount of Building × Capitalization Rate
= ₹ 8,00,000 × 0.14 = ₹ 1,12,000

QUESTION 8: Axe Limited began construction of a new plant on 1st April, 2014 and obtained a special loan of ₹ 4,00,000 to finance the construction of the plant. The rate of interest on loan was 10%.

The expenditure that were made on the project of plant were as follows:

Particulars	₹
1st April, 2014	**5,00,000**
1st August, 2014	**12,00,000**
1st January, 2015	**2,00,000**

The company's other outstanding non-specific loan was ₹ 23,00,000 at an interest rate of 12%.

The construction of the plant completed on 31st March, 2015. You are required to:

(a) Calculate the amount of interest to be capitalized as per the provisions of AS 16 "Borrowing Cost".

(b) Pass a journal entry for capitalizing the cost and the borrowing cost in respect of the plant.

ANSWER:

TOTAL EXPENSES TO BE CAPITALIZED FOR BORROWINGS AS PER AS 16 "BORROWING COSTS".

Particulars	₹
Cost of Plant (5,00,000 + 12,00,000 + 2,00,000)	19,00,000
Add: Amount of interest to be capitalised	1,54,000
	20,54,000

JOURNAL

Date	Particulars		Dr. (₹)	Cr. (₹)
31.03.2015	Plant A/c	Dr.	20,54,000	
	To Bank A/c			19,00,000
	To Interest on Loan A/c			54,000
	[Being amount of cost of plant and borrowing cost thereon capitalized]			

Working Notes:

(i) *Computation of average Accumulated Expenses*

Particulars		₹
1st April, 2014	(₹5,00,000 × 12/12)	5,00,000
1st August, 2014	(₹12,00,000 × 8/12)	8,00,000
1st January, 2015	(₹2,00,000 × 3/12)	50,000
		13,50,000

(ii) *Amount of interest capitalised*

Particulars	₹
On specific borrowing (₹ 4,00,000 × 10%)	40,000
On non-specific borrowings (₹ 13,50,000 – ₹ 4,00,000) × 12%	1,14,000
Amount of interest to be capitalised	1,54,000

QUESTION 9: X Ltd. began construction of a new building on 1st January, 2015. It obtained ₹1 lakh special loan to finance the construction of the building on 1st January, 2015 at an interest rate of 10%. The company's other outstanding two non-specific loans were:

Amount	*Rate of Interest*
₹ 5,00,000	**11%**
₹ 9,00,000	**13%**

The expenditure that were made on the building project were as follows:

		₹
January	**2015**	**2,00,000**
April	**2015**	**2,50,000**
July	**2015**	**4,50,000**
December	**2015**	**1,20,000**

Building was completed by 31st December, 2015. Following the principles prescribed in AS-16 'Borrowing Cost,' calculate the amount of interest to be capitalized and pass one Journal Entry for capitalizing the cost and borrowing cost in respect of the building.

ANSWER:

1. COMPUTATION OF AVERAGE ACCUMULATED EXPENSES

Particulars	₹
₹ 2,00,000 × 12 / 12	= 2,00,000
₹ 2,50,000 × 9 / 12	= 1,87,500
₹ 4,50,000 × 6 / 12	= 2,25,000
₹ 1,20,000 × 1 / 12	= 10,000
	6,22,500

2. CALCULATION OF AVERAGE INTEREST RATE OTHER THAN FOR SPECIFIC BORROWINGS

Amount of Loan (in ₹) A	Rate of interest B	Interest (in ₹) C = A × B/100
5,00,000	11%	55,000
9,00,000	13%	1,17,000
		1,72,000

Weighted Average Rate of Interest = 12.285% (approx)

3. INTEREST ON AVERAGE ACCUMULATED EXPENSES

Specific borrowings (₹ 1,00,000 × 10%)	= 10,000
Non-specific borrowings (₹ 5,22,500* × 12.285%)	= 64,189
Amount of interest to be capitalized	= 74,189

4. TOTAL EXPENSES TO BE CAPITALIZED FOR BUILDING

Cost of building ₹ (2,00,000 + 2,50,000 + 4,50,000 + 1,20,000)	10,20,000
Add: Amount of interest to be capitalised	74,189
	10,94,189

5. JOURNAL ENTRY

Date	Particulars		Dr. (₹)	Cr. (₹)
31.12.2015	Building A/c	Dr.	10,94,189	
	To Bank A/c			10,20,000
	To Interest on Loan A/c			74,189
	(Being amount of cost of building and borrowing cost thereon capitalized)			

QUESTION 10: The borrowings profile of Santra Pharmaceutical Ltd. set up for the manufacture of antibiotics at Navi Mumbai is as under:

Date	Nature of borrowings	Amount borrowed ₹	Purpose of borrowings	Incidental expenses
1.1.2014	**15% Demand loan**	**60 lakhs**	**Acquisition of Fixed Assets**	**8.33%**
1.7.2014	**14.5% Term Loan**	**40 lakhs**	**Acquisition of plant and Machinery**	**5%**
1.10.2014	**14% Bonds**	**50 lakhs**	**Acquisition of Fixed Assets**	**8%**

The incidental expenses consist of commission and service charges for arranging the loans and are paid after founding off to the nearest lakh.

Fixed assets considered as qualifying assets are as under:	**₹**
Sterile Manufacturing shed	**10,00,000**
Plant and machinery (total)	**90,00,000**
Other fixed assets	**10,00,000**

The Project is completed on 1st January, 2015 and is ready for commercial production. Show the capitalization of the borrowing costs.

ANSWER:

(a) Specific Borrowings	
14.5% Term Loan for acquisition of Plant & Machinery	₹
Interest from 1.7.2014 to 31.12.2014 [₹ 40,00,000 × 14.5% × 6/12]	2,90,000
Incidental Expenses	2,00,000
Total	4,90,000
General Borrowings	

A. 15% Demand Loan	
Interest from 1.1.2014 to 31.12.2014 [₹ 60,00,000 × 15%]	9,00,000
Incidental Expenses	5,00,000
Total (A)	14,00,000
B. 14% Bonds	
Interest from 1.10.2014 to 31.12.2014 [₹ 50,00,000 × 14% × 3/12]	1,75,000
Incidental Expenses	4,00,000
Total (B)	5,75,000
C. Total General Borrowing Cost (A + B)	19,75,000
D. Total Average Outstanding Borrowings = [(60,00,000 × 12 + 50,00,000 × 3)/12]	72,50,000
E. Weighted Average Borrowing Cost =	

ALLOCATION OF GENERAL BORROWING FUND

Item	Cost	Specific Borrowing	Net of specific borrowing
Sterile Manufacturing Shed	10,00,000	Nil	10,00,000
Plant & Machinery	90,00,000	40,00,000	50,00,000
Other Fixed Assets	10,00,000	Nil	10,00,000

Item	Expenditure on qualifying asset out of general	Capitalization Rate	Cost eligible for capitalization borrowing fund
Sterile Manufacturing Shed	10,00,000	27.24	2,72,400
Plant & Machinery	50,00,000	27.24	13,62,000
Other Fixed Assets	10,00,000	27.24	2,72,400

BORROWING COSTS TO BE CAPITALIZED

Asset	*Specific Borrowing Cost*	*General Borrowing Cost*	*Total*
Sterile Manufacturing shed	Nil	2,72,400	2,72,400
Plant & Machinery	4,90,000	13,62,000	18,52,000
Other Fixed Assets	Nil	2,72,400	2,72,400
Total	4,90,000	19,06,800*	23,96,800

QUESTION 11: RTP Ltd. has undertaken a significant expansion programme for its manufacturing facilities. The details are as follows:

1. **Details of Capital Expenditure:**

Facility	**Amount (₹)**	**Remarks**
Plant A	**68 crores**	**Specific borrowing to the extent of ₹48 crores**
Plant B	**40 crores**	**Specific borrowing to the extent of ₹ 12 crores**
Power generation facility at:		
Plant C	**8 crores**	**No specific borrowings**

Plant D	8 crores	No specific borrowings
Corporate Offices	16 crores	No specific borrowings
	140 crores	

2. **Facility expansion commenced on June 1, 2014 on all facilities. As of March 31, 2015, the status of completion of these facilities was as follows:**
   - **Plant A was completed as of December 31,2014**
   - **Plant B was competed as of November 30, 2014**
   - **Power generation facility at Plant C is still under construction as of March 31, 2015.**
   - **Plant D was completed as of February 28, 2015.**
   - **Corporate offices were still under construction as of March 31, 2015**
3. **Detail of Debts**
   - **₹40 crores 11% Secured Debentures raised on July 1, 2012 redeemable in four equal annual installments commencing from July 1, 2014.**
   - **₹ 30 crores Secured Working Capital 14% loan obtained on April, 1, 2014. This was partially repaid on December 31, 2014 in the amount ₹ 10 crores.**
   - **14% Loan from financial institutions amounting to ₹60 crores obtained for construction of Plant A and B, on May 1, 2014.**
   - **Foreign currency loans from financial institutions amounting to $ 12 million bearing interest at LIBOR Plus 2% obtained on June 1, 2014. The contracted LIBOR rate was 6% p.a. The exchange rate as of that date was US $ 1 = ₹43.00. The exchange rate as of March 31, 2015 was US $ 1 = ₹46.50. The average exchange rate during 2014-2015 was ₹45.00.**

None of the loans were repaid as of March 31, 2015.

Required: **Calculate the amount of borrowing cost to be capitalized.**

ANSWER:

Step 1: Calculation of Average Unspecified Borrowings Outstanding during the year

	Particulars	₹ (in crores)
(i)	11% Secured Debentures (40 × 3/12) + (30 crores × 9/12)	32.50
(ii)	14% Secured Working Capital Loan [(30 × 9/12) + (20 × 3/12)]	27.50
(iii)	Foreign Current Loan [120 × 10/12 × ₹ 43]	43.00
		103.00

Step 2: Calculation of Average Interest on Unspecified Borrowings for the year.

	Particulars	₹ *(in crores)*
(i)	On 11% Secured debentures [(40 × 11% × 3/12) + (30 ×11% × 9/12)	3.575
(ii)	On 14% Secured working capital Loan [(30 × 14% × 9/12) + (20 × 14% × 3/12)]	3.85
(ii)	On Foreign Currency Loan (120 × 8% × 10/12 × ₹ 45)	3.60
		11.025

Step 3: Average Interest Rate for the year =

Step 4: Calculation of Average Interest on Unspecified Borrowing for the year.

	Particulars	₹ *(in crores)*
(i)	Plant A	
	On Specific Borrowing: (48 crores × 14% × 7/12)	3.9200

On Non-specific Borrowing (20 crores × 10.7% × 7/12)	1.2483
	5.1683
(ii) Plant B	
On Specific Borrowing: (12 crores × 14% × 6/12 crores)	0.8400
On Unspecific Borrowing (28 crores × 10.7% × 6/12)	1.4980
	2.3380
(iii) Power generation facility at Place C	
On unspecific borrowing: (8 crores × 10.7% × 10/12]	0.7133
(iv) Plant D	
On unspecific borrowing: [8 crores × 10.7% × 9/12]	0.6420
(v) Corporate office	
On unspecific borrowing (16 crores × 10.7% × 10/12]	1.4266
	10.2882

Note: *Treatment of currency exchange differences on borrowing costs has been ignored.*

Assumptions:

(a) Interest in payable at half yearly rests

(b) Interest payment during the year paid at the average exchange rate for the year.

QUESTION 12: X Ltd. began construction of a new building on 1st April, 2014. It obtained Rs1 lakh special loan to finance the construction of the building on 1st 1st April, 2014 at an interest rate of 10%. The company's other outstanding two non-specific loans were:

Loans	Rate of Interest
₹ 5,00,000	11%
₹ 9,00,000	13%

The expenditure that were made on the building project were as follows:

Particulars	₹
1st April 2014	2,00,000
1st July 2014	2,50,000
1st Oct 2014	4,50,000
1st March 2014	1,20,000

Building was completed by 31st March, 2015 Following the principles prescribed in AS-16'Borrowing Cost,' calculate the amount of interest to be capitalized and pass one Journal Entry for capitalizing the cost and borrowing cost in respect of the building.

ANSWER:

1. COMPUTATION OF AVERAGE ACCUMULATED EXPENSES

Particulars	₹
₹ 2,00,000 × 12/12	2,00,000
₹ 2,50,000 × 9/12	1,87,500
₹ 4,50,000 × 6/12	2,25,000

₹ 1,20,000 × 1/12	10,000
	6,22,500

2. CALCULATION OF AVERAGE INTEREST RATE OTHER THAN FOR SPECIFIC BORROWINGS

Amount of loan (in ₹)	Rate of interest	Ampount of interest (in ₹)
5,00,000	11%	55,000
9,00,000	13%	1,17,000
14,00,000		1,72,000
Weighted average rate of interest		12.285% (approx)

3. INTEREST ON AVERAGE ACCUMULATED EXPENSES

Particulars	₹
Specific borrowings (₹ 1,00,000 × 10%)	= 10,000
Non-specific borrowings (₹ 5,22,500 × 12.285%)	= 64,189
Amount of interest to be capitalized	= 74,189

4. TOTAL EXPENSES TO BE CAPITALIZED FOR BUILDING

Particulars	₹
Cost of building ₹(2,00,000 + 2,50,000 + 4,50,000 + 1,20,000)	10,20,000
Add: Amount of interest to be capitalised	74,189
	10,94,189

5. JOURNAL ENTRY

Date	Particulars	Dr. (₹)	Cr. (₹)
31.03.2015	Building account Dr.	10,94,189	
	To Bank account		10,94,189
	(Being amount of cost of building and borrowing cost thereon capitalized)		

QUESTION 13: XYZ Ltd. has taken a loan of US$ 20,000 on April 1, 2014, for a specific project at an interest rate of 5% p.a., payable annually. On April 1, 2014, the exchange rate between the currencies was ₹40 per US$. The exchange rate, as at March 31, 2015, is ₹43 per US$.

Required: Calculate the amount of exchange difference arising from foreign currency borrowings to the extent that they are regarded as an adjustment to interest costs, if the corresponding amount could have been borrowed by XYZ Ltd. in local currency at an interest rate of (a)11% p.a. and (b) 13% p.a. as on April 1, 2014.

ANSWER:

CALCULATION OF THE AMOUNT OF EXCHANGE DIFFERENCE ARISING FROM FOREIGN CURRENCY BORROWINGS TO THE EXTENT THAT THEY ARE REGARDED AS AN ADJUSTMENT TO INTEREST COSTS

	Particulars	11%	13%
A	Increase in liability towards principal amount [USD 20,000 × (₹ 43 – ₹ 40)]	60,000	60,000
B	Interest on foreign currency borrowing (USD 20,000 × ₹ 43 × 5%)	43,000	43,000
C	Exchange differences on the amount of principal of the foreign currency borrowingsm (A + B)	1,03,000	1,03,000
D	Interest on local currency borrowings		
	(US$ 20,000 × ₹ 40 × 11%)	88,000	
	(US$ 20,000 × ₹ 40 × 13%)		1,04,000
E	Total borrowing costs as per AS 16 (C or D whichever is *less*)	88,000	1,03,000
F	Exchange difference to be treated as per AS 11 (C – D)	15,000	0

QUESTION 14: Sun Co-operative society Ltd has borrowed a sum of US $12.50 million at the commencement of the financial year 2014-2015 for its solar energy project at LIBOR (London Interbank offered rate of 1%) + 4%. The interest is payable at the end of the respective financial year. The loan was availed at the then rate of ₹45 to US dollar while the rate as on 31st March, 2015 is ₹48 to the US dollar. Had Sun Co-operative Society Ltd. Borrowed the Rupee equivalent in India, the interest would have been 11%. You are required to compute 'Borrowing Cost' also showing the amount of exchange difference as per prevailing Accounting Standards.

ANSWER:

CALCULATION OF THE AMOUNT OF EXCHANGE DIFFERENCE ARISING FROM FOREIGN CURRENCY BORROWINGS TO THE EXTENT THAT THEY ARE REGARDED AS AN ADJUSTMENT TO INTEREST COSTS

	Particulars	(₹ in lacs)
A	Increase in liability towards principal amount [USD 12.50 × (₹ 48 – ₹ 45)]	37.50
B	Interest on foreign currency borrowing [USD 12.50 × ₹ 48 × 5%]	30.00
C	Exchange differences on the amount of principal of the foreign currency borrowings (A + B)	67.50
D	Interest on local currency borrowings [USD 12.50 × ₹ 45 × 11%]	61.875
E	Total borrowing costs as per AS 16 (C or D whichever is *less*)	61.875
F	Exchange difference to be treated as per AS 11 (C – D)	5.625

11 RECONCILIATION STATEMENTS

BANK RECONCILIATION STATEMENT

PROBLEM 1

On comparing the Cash Book of Mr Tulsian with the Bank Pass Book, the following discrepancies were noted:

(a) Out of ₹ 20,500 paid in cash and by cheques into the bank on 27th March, cheque amounting to ₹ 7,500 were collected on 7th April.

(b) Cheque and cash amounting to ₹ 4,800 were deposited in bank on 26th March but credit was given for ₹ 3,800 only.

(c) Out of cheques amounting to ₹ 7,800 drawn on 26th March a cheque for ₹ 2,500 was encashed on 3rd April.

(d) Cheques issued to creditor amounting to ₹ 20,000 on 25th March of which cheques worth ₹ 3,000 were presented to bank up to 31st March.

(e) A cheque for ₹ 1,000 entered in Cash Book but omitted to be banked on 31st March.

(f) A cheque for ₹ 600 deposited into bank but omitted to be recorded in Cash Book and was collected by the bank on 30th March.

(g) A bill receivable for ₹ 520 previously discounted (Discount ₹ 20) with the bank had been dishonoured but advice was received on 1st April.

(h) A bill for ₹ 10,000 was retired/paid by the bank under a rebate of ₹ 150 but the full amount of the bill was credited in the bank column of the Cash Book.

(i) A cheque of ₹ 1,080 credited in the Pass Book on March 28 being dishonoured is debited again in the Pass Book on 1st April. There was no entry in the Cash Book about the dishonour of the cheque until 15th April.

(j) A cheque of ₹ 200 drawn on his Saving Deposit Account has been shown as drawn on Current Account in Cash Book.

Required: Prepare a Bank Reconciliation Statement as at 31st March if the Balance as per Cash Book on 31st March was ₹ 39,570.

SOLUTION

BANK RECONCILIATION STATEMENT AS AT 31ST MARCH ...

Particulars	*Plus Items ₹*	*Minus Items ₹*
Debit Balance as per Cash Book	39,570	
(a) Cheque deposited on 27th March but not yet collected till 31st March		7,500
(b) Cheques deposited on 26th March but not yet collected till 31st March		1,000
(c) Cheques issued on 26th March but not yet presented for payment till 31st March	2,500	
(d) Cheque issued on 25th March but not yet presented for payment till 31st March	17,000	
(e) A Cheque entered in Cash Book but not yet banked		1,000
(f) A Cheque deposited into bank but not yet entered in Cash Book	600	

(g) Discounted B/R dishonoured, not yet entered in Cash Book		520
(h) Rebate on bill not entered in Cash book	150	
(i) Cheque drawn on Saving Bank A/c but recorded in Current A/c	200	
	60,020	10,020
Credit Balance as per Pass Book	50,000	

Note: A cheque of ₹ 1,080 credited in Pass book on March 28, later debited in Pass Book on 1st April has no effect on Bank Reconciliation Statement as at 31st March.

PROBLEM 2

From the following particulars, prepare a Bank Reconciliation Statement as on 31st March.

(a) Bank Balance as per Cash Book is ₹ 10,000

(b) A Cheque for ₹ 1,000 deposited but not recorded in the Cash Book. (Note: Bank has collected and credited this cheque.)

(c) A Cash deposit of ₹ 200 was recorded in the Cash Book as if there is no Bank Column therein.

(d) A Cheque issued for ₹ 250 was recorded as ₹ 205 in the Cash Column. (Note: Bank has made the payment of this cheque.)

(e) The debit balance of ₹ 1,500 as on the previous day was brought forward as a credit balance.

(f) The payment side of the Cash Book (Bank column) was under cast by ₹ 100.

(g) A cash discount allowed of ₹ 112 was recorded as ₹ 121 in the Bank Column.

(h) A cheque of ₹ 500 received from a debtor was recorded in the Cash Book but not deposited in the Bank for collection.

(i) One outgoing cheque of ₹ 300 was recorded twice in the Cash Book.

SOLUTION

BANK RECONCILIATION STATEMENT AS AT 31ST MARCH ...

Particulars	*Plus Items ₹*	*Minus Items ₹*
A. Debit Balance as per Cash Book	10,000	
B. *Add:* (a) Error in carrying forward	3,000	
(b) Cheque recorded twice in Cash Book	300	
(c) Cash deposit but not recorded in Bank Column	200	
(d) Cheque deposited but not recorded	1,000	
C. *Less:* (a) Under Casting of Payment Side		100
(b) Cheque issued but not entered		250
(c) A cash discount wrongly recorded in Bank Column		121
(d) Cheque recorded but not deposited		500
	14,500	971
D. Credit Balance as per Pass Book	13,529	

PROBLEM 3

The Cash book of Mr Avinash shows ₹ 8,364 as the balance at bank as on 31st March, but you find that this does not agree with the balance as per the Bank Pass Book. On scrutiny, you find the following discrepancies.

(a) On 15th March, the payments side of the Cash Book was undercast by ₹ 100.

(b) A cheque for ₹ 131 issued on 25th March, was recorded in the Cash column.

(c) One deposit of ₹ 150 was recorded in the Cash Book as if there is not Bank Column therein.

(d) On 18th March, the debit balance of ₹ 1,526 as on the previous day, was brought forward as a credit balance.

(e) Of the total cheques amounting to ₹ 11,514 drawn in the last week of March, cheques aggregating ₹ 7,815 were encashed in March.

(f) Dividends of ₹ 250 collected by the Bank and subscription of ₹ 100 paid by it, were not recorded in the Cash Book.

(g) One outgoing cheque of ₹ 350 was recorded twice in the Cash Book.

Required: Prepare a Bank Reconciliation Statement as on 31st March.

SOLUTION

BANK RECONCILIATION STATEMENT AS AT 31ST MARCH ...

		Particulars	*Plus Items ₹*	*Minus Items ₹*
A.	Debit Balance as per Cash book		8,364	
B.	*Add:*	Error in bringing forward ₹ 1,526 debit balance as a credit balance on 18th December,	3,052	
C.	*Add:*	Cheques issued but not presented (₹ 11,514 – ₹ 7,815)	3,699	
D.	*Add:*	Dividends directly credited by the bank but not entered in the Cash Book	250	
E.	*Add:*	Outgoing cheque recorded twice in Cash Book	350	
F.	*Add:*	Deposit not recorded in the Bank Column	150	
G.	*Less:*	Payment side undercast		100
H.	*Less:*	Cheques issued but not entered in Bank Column		131
	Less:	Subscription paid by the bank directly not yet recorded in the Cash Book		100
			15,865	331
I.	Credit Balance as per Pass Book		15,534	

PROBLEM 4

From the following particulars, prepare the Bank Reconciliation Statement of Shri Krishan as on 31st March.

(a) Balance as per Pass Book is ₹ 10,000.

(b) Bank collected a cheque of ₹ 500 on behalf of Shri Krishan but wrongly credited it to Shri Kishan's A/c (another customer).

(c) Bank recorded a Cash deposit of ₹ 1,589 as ₹ 1,598.

(d) Withdrawal column of the Pass Book undercast by ₹ 100.

(e) The credit balance of ₹ 1,500 as on page 5 of the Pass Book was recorded on page 6 as the debit balance.

(f) The payment of a cheque of ₹ 350 was recorded twice in the Pass Book.

(g) The Pass Book showed a credit for a cheque of ₹ 1,000 deposited by Shri Kishan (another customer of the Bank).

SOLUTION

BANK RECONCILIATION STATEMENT AS AT 31ST MARCH ...

		Particulars	Plus Items ₹	Minus Items ₹
A.	Credit Balance as per Pass Book		10,000	
B.	*Add:*	(a) Cheque wrongly credited to another customers A/c	500	
		(b) Error in carrying forward	3,000	
		(c) Cheque recorded twice	350	
C.	*Less:*	(a) Excess credit for Cash Deposit		9
		(b) Undercasting of withdrawal column		100
		(c) Wrong credit		1,000
			13,850	1,109
D.	Debit Balance as per Cash Book		12,741	

PROBLEM 5

From the following particulars, prepare Bank Reconciliation Statement as on 31st March, (a) without amended Cash Book (b) with amended Cash Book.

	Particulars	₹
1.	Balance as per Cash Book	400
2.	Cheques received and recorded in Bank Column but not yet sent to Bank for collection	1,000
3.	Cheques deposited into the bank but not recorded in the Cash Book	2,000
4.	Cheques deposited but not yet collected by the Bank	1,500
5.	Cheques issued but not yet presented for payment	2,500
6.	Bank Charges debited in Pass Book only	200
7.	Interest allowed in Pass Book only	100
8.	Insurance Premium paid directly by Bank under standing advice	500
9.	Bills receivables directly collected by the Bank	2,000
10.	Cheques deposited for collection, returned dishonoured and recorded in Pass Book only	1,000
11.	'Cheques Issued' returned on technical grounds	300
12.	A wrong debit given by bank in pass book	800
13.	A wrong credit given by bank in pass book	400
14.	Bills discounted dishonoured but not recorded in Cash Book	4,000
15.	Direct payment by a customer into the bank but not recorded in Cash Book	700

16.	A Cash receipt recorded in Bank Column	1,000
17.	A Cash payment recorded in Bank Column	600

SOLUTION

(a) Without Amended Cash Book

BANK RECONCILIATION STATEMENT AS AT 31ST MARCH ...

	Particulars	*Plus Items ₹*	*Minus Items ₹*
A.	Debit Balance as per Cash Book	400	
B.	*Add:* Cheques deposited into the bank but not recorded in Cash Book	2,000	
	Cheques issued but not yet presented for payment	2,500	
	Interest allowed in pass book only	100	
	Bills receivables directly collected by Bank	2,000	
	'Cheques Issued' returned on technical grounds	300	
	A wrong credit given by bank in Pass Book	400	
	Direct payment by a customer into the bank but not recorded in Cash Book	700	
	A Cash payment wrongly recorded in Bank Column	600	
C.	*Less:* Cheques received and recorded in Bank column but not yet sent to Bank for collection		1,000
	Cheques deposited but not yet collected by the Bank		1,500
	Bank Charges debited in pass book only		200
	Insurance a premium paid directly by bank under standing advice		500
	Cheques deposited for collection, returned dishonoured and recorded in Pass Book only		1,000
	A wrong debit given by Bank in Pass Book		800
	Bills dis. dishonoured but not recorded in Cash Book		4,000
	A Cash receipt wrongly recorded in Bank Column		1,000
		9,000	10,000
D.	Overdraft as per Pass Book		1,000

(b) With Amended Cash Book

Dr. **CASH BOOK (AMENDED BANK COLUMN)** Cr.

Particulars	₹	*Particulars*	₹
To Balance b/d	400	By Bank charges	200
To Cheque deposited but not recor.	2,000	By Insurance premium	500
To Bills Receivables	2,000	By Cheques dishonoured	1,000
To Interest allowed	100	By Bill discounted	4,000
To Cheques issued returned	300	By Cash receipt wrongly recor.	1,000
To Direct Payment by Customers	700		

To Cash Payment wrongly recor.	600		
To Balance c/d	600		
	6,700		6,700

BANK RECONCILIATION STATEMENT AS AT 31ST MARCH ...

	Particulars	*Plus Items ₹*	*Minus Items ₹*
A.	Adjusted Bank Overdraft as per Amended Cash Book		600
B.	*Add:* Cheques issued but not yet presented for payment	2,500	
	A wrong credit given by bank in Pass Book	400	
C.	*Less:* Cheques received and recorded in Bank column but not yet sent to Bank for collection		1,000
	Cheques deposited but not yet collected by the Bank		1,500
	A wrong debit given by Bank in Pass Book		800
		2,900	3,900
D.	Overdraft as per Pass Book		1,000

STOCK RECONCILIATION STATEMENT

PROBLEM 6

Determine the value of stock to be taken to the Balance Sheet of Tushar Tulsian Ltd. as at March 31, from the following information:

The stock was physically verified on 24th March and was valued at ₹ 4,00,000. After stock taking, the following transactions had taken place till 31st March.

(a) Purchases ₹ 2,00,000 out of which 20% of goods were returned.

(b) Sale of good units ₹ 2,00,000 out of which 20% goods were returned by the customer.

(c) Sale of defective units ₹ 1,80,000 at 10% less than the normal selling price.

(d) On 21st March goods of the sale value of ₹ 2,00,000 were sent on sale or return basis to a customer, the period of approval being two weeks. He returned 20% of the goods and approved 80% of the remaining on 31st March.

(e) On 23rd March goods of the sale value of ₹ 2,00,000 were sent on consignment basis. 80% of these goods had been sold on 31st March.

(f) On 23rd March goods costing ₹ 2,00,000 were received for sale on consignment basis. 80% of these goods had been sold on 31st March.

Notes:

(i) Goods are sold by the trader at a profit of 25% on cost.

(ii) The sales referred to in (d), (e) and (f) are not included in (b) above.

SOLUTION

STATEMENT SHOWING THE VALUATION OF STOCK AS ON 31ST MARCH

	Particulars	₹
A	Stock as per physical verification as at 24th March	4,00,000

B	*Add:*	Cost of Net Goods purchased after stock taking till 31st March [₹ 2,00,000 – 20% of ₹ 2,00,000]	1,60,000
C	*Less:*	Cost of Net Goods sold after stock taking till 31st March Good Units: [80% of (₹ 2,00,000 – 20% of ₹ 2,00,000)]	(1,28,000)
	Defective Units: [80% of (₹ 1,80,000 + 1/9th of ₹ 1,80,000)]		(1,60,000)
D	*Add:*	Cost of goods returned by Customer to whom goods were sent on approval [80% of (20% of ₹ 2,00,000)]	32,000
E	*Add:*	Cost of unsold goods lying with other on our behalf:	
		Goods sent on approval	
		{80% of [20% of (₹ 2,00,000 – 20% of ₹ 2,00,000)]	25,600
		Goods sent on Consignment [80% of (20% of ₹ 2,00,000)]	32,000
F	*Less:*	Cost of goods received for sale on Consignment basis included in stock given as on 24th March	(2,00,000)
G	Stock as per books as at 31st March		1,61,600

PROBLEM 7

Determine the value of stock to be taken to the Balance Sheet of PCT Ltd. as at 31st March from the following information:

The stock was physically verified on 7th April and was valued at ₹ 4,00,000. After 31st March the following transactions had taken place till the date of stock taking.

(a) Purchases ₹ 2,00,0000 out of which 20% goods were returned.

(b) Sales of good units ₹ 2,00,000 out of which 20% goods were returned by the customers

(c) Sales of defective units ₹ 1,80,000 at 10% less than the normal selling price.

(d) On 26th March goods of the sale value of ₹ 2,00,000 were sent on sale or return basis to a customer, the period of approval being two weeks. He returned 20% of the goods and approved 80% of the remaining on 6th April.

(e) On 27th March goods of the sales value of ₹ 2,00,000 were sent on consignment basis. 80% of these goods had been sold on 6th April.

(f) On 28th March goods costing ₹ 2,00,000 were received for sale on consignment basis. 80% of these goods had been sold on 6th April.

Notes:

(i) Goods are sold by the trader at a profit of 25% on cost.

(ii) The sales referred to in (d), (e) & (f) are not included in (b) above.

SOLUTION

STATEMENT SHOWING THE VALUATION OF STOCK AS ON 31ST MARCH

	Particulars	₹
A	Stock as per physical verification as at 7th April	4,00,000
B	*Less:* Cost of Net goods purchased after 31st March till stock taking [₹ 2,00,000 – 20% of ₹ 2,00,000]	(1,60,000)
C	*Add:* Cost of Net goods sold after 31st March till Stock taking	
	Good Units: [80% of (₹ 2,00,000 – 20% of ₹ 2,00,000)]	1,28,000
	Defective units: [80% of (₹ 1,80,000 + 1/9th of ₹ 1,80,000)]	1,60,000

D	*Add:* Cost of goods lying with others on our behalf as on 31st March	
	Goods sent as approval [80% of (₹ 2,00,000 – 20% of ₹ 2,00,000)]	1,28,000
	Goods sent on consignment [80% of ₹ 2,00,000]	1,60,000
E	*Less:* Cost of goods lying with as on behalf of others	
	Goods received for sale on consignment basis [20% of ₹ 2,00,000]	(40,000)
F	Stock as per books as at 31st March	7,76,000

Notes:

(i) No adjustment has been made in respect of goods returned by customers to whom goods were sent on approval basis since there goods are already included in the stock given as on 7th April.

(ii) No adjustment has been made in respect of goods sold out of those received for sale on consignment basis since these goods are not included in the stock given as on 7th April.

PROBLEM 8

Determine the value of stock to be taken to the Balance Sheet of BT Ltd. as at March 31, from the following information:

The stock was physically verified on 7th April and was valued at ₹ 4,00,000. After 31st March the following transactions had taken place till the date of stock-taking:

(a) Purchases ₹ 2,00,000 out of which 20% goods were returned.

(b) Sales of good units ₹ 2,00,000 out of which 20% goods were returned by the customers.

(c) Sales of defective limits ₹ 1,80,000 at 10% less than the normal selling price.

(d) On 1st April, goods of the sale value of ₹ 2,00,000 were sent a sale or return basis to a customer, the period of approval being two weeks. He returned 20% of the goods and approved 80% of the remaining on 6th April.

(e) On 2nd April, goods of the sale value of ₹ 2,00,000 were sent on consignment basis. 80% of these goods had been sold by 6th April.

(f) On 3rd April, goods costing ₹ 2,00,000 were received for sale on consignment basis. 80% of there goods had been sold by 6th April.

Notes:

(i) Goods are sold by the trader at a profit of 25% or Cost.

(ii) The sales referred to in (d), (e) & (f) are not included in (b) above.

SOLUTION

STATEMENT SHOWING THE VALUATION OF STOCK AS ON 31ST MARCH

	Particulars	₹
A	Stock as per physical verification as at 7th April	4,00,000
B	*Less:* Cost of Net goods purchased after 31st March till stock taking [₹ 2,00,000 – 20% of ₹ 2,00,000]	(1,60,000)
C	*Add:* Cost of Net goods sold after 31st March till stock taking	
	Goods Units: [80% of (₹ 2,00,000 – 20% of ₹ 2,00,000)]	1,28,000
	Defective Units: [80% of (₹ 1,80,000 + 1/9th of ₹ 1,80,000)]	1,60,000
D	*Add:* Cost of Net goods sent to others after 31st March till stock taking:	
	Goods sent on approval:	

	[80% of (₹ 2,00,000 – 20% of ₹ 2,00,000)]	1,28,000
	Goods sent on Consignment	
	[80% of ₹ 2,00,000]	1,60,000
E	*Less:* Goods received for sale on Consignment basis & still remaining unsold [20% of ₹ 2,00,000]	(40,000)
F	Stock as per books as at 31st March	7,76,000

Notes:

(i) No adjustment has been made in respect of goods returned by customers to whom goods were sent on approval basis since these goods are already included in the stock given as on 7th April.

(ii) No adjustment has been made in respect of goods sold out of those received for sale on consignment basis since there goods are not included in the stock given as on 7th April.

PROBLEM 9

The draft Profit & Loss Account of Bharat Tulsian showed a net profit of ₹ 1,02,800 after considering the closing stock of ₹ 67,500 on 31st March. Subsequently the following information was obtained from the scrutiny of the books.

(a) The proprietor has taken goods costing ₹ 1,000 for his personal use without making entry in the books.

(b) The proprietor has given away goods costing ₹ 1,000 as free samples for which no entry was made in the books of accounts.

(c) Purchases for the year included a purchase of furniture costing ₹ 200 on 31st March.

(d) Sales included a sale of furniture having a book value of ₹ 900 for ₹ 850 on 31st March.

(e) Invoices for goods costing ₹ 1,700 have been entered on 26th March but the goods have not yet been received till 31st March.

(f) Goods costing ₹ 4,000 have been purchased and received on 27th March but the invoices have not yet been recorded till 31st March.

(g) Invoices of goods of ₹ 1,000 (Cost ₹ 800) were entered on 28th March but the goods were not delivered till 31st March.

(h) Goods of ₹ 4,000 (Cost ₹ 3,200) sold and delivered on 29th March but the invoices were not entered till 31st March.

(i) Goods (Cost ₹ 2,880, selling price ₹ 3,600) were returned by Ram, a customer on 30th March and were taken into stock on the same date but no entry was passed in the books.

(j) Stock at the end does not include the goods (cost ₹ 6,000, Selling Price ₹ 7,500) returned by Shayam a customer for which the entry has already been passed.

(k) On 26th March goods of the sale value of ₹ 2,00,000 were sent on sale or return basis to Gopal, a customer, the period of approval being two weeks. He returned 20% of the goods and approved 80% of the remaining on 31st March. These goods were sent at a profit of 25% on cost.

Required: Calculate the value of stock on 31st March and the adjusted net profit for the year ended on that date.

SOLUTION

STATEMENT SHOWING THE VALUATION OF STOCK AS AT 31ST MARCH

	Particulars	₹
A	Stock as already stated	67,500

B *Add:* Cost of Goods purchased but not yet received	1,700
C *Less:* Cost of Goods sold but not yet delivered	(800)
D *Add:* Cost of Goods returned by a customer now included	6,000
E *Add:* Cost of Goods sent on approval (neither returned nor retained)	25,600
F Stock as on 31st March	1,00,000

Dr. **PROFIT & LOSS ADJUSTMENT ACCOUNT** Cr.

Particulars	₹	*Particulars*	₹
To Furniture A/c (Sale of Furniture)	850	By Profit as per P & L A/c	1,02,800
To Furniture A/c (Loss on Sale of Furniture) of Furniture)	50	By Drawings (Goods for Personal Use)	1,000
To Creditors for Goods A/c (Omitted purchases)	4,000	By Furniture A/c (Purchase of furniture)	200
To Closing Stock A/c	800	By Closing Stock (in transit) A/c	1700
To Ram (Omitted Sales Return)	3,600	By Debtors A/c (Omitted Sales)	4,000
To Gopal (Cancellation of Sales)	32,000	By Closing Stock A/c	
(Goods sold but not delivered)		(Good returned, included)	6,000
To Adjusted Net Profit for the year	1,00,000	By Closing Stock A/c	25,600
		(Cost of Goods neither returned nor retained)	
	1,41,300		1,41,300

PROBLEM 10

Determine the value of stock as per books of BT Ltd at 31st March from the following information:

(a) The cost of stock as per physical verification as on 24th March amounted to ₹ 2,00,000.

(b) Purchases as per Purchase Book after stock taking till 31st March amounted to ₹ 2,00,000 and included the following:
  (i) ₹ 10,000 for goods received till 23rd March
  (ii) ₹ 20,000 for goods received on 1st April.

(c) Sales as per Sales Book after stock taking, till 31st March amounted to ₹ 2,00,000 and included the following:
  (i) ₹ 10,000 for goods delivered till 23rd March
  (ii) ₹ 20,000 for goods delivered on 1st April.

(d) Goods are sold by the trader at a profit of 25% on Cost.

SOLUTION

STATEMENT SHOWING THE VALUATION OF STOCK AS AT 31ST MARCH

Particulars		₹
A. Stock as per physical verification as at 24th March		2,00,000
B. *Add:*	Cost of goods purchased after stock taking till 31st March (whether or not received)	1,90,000
	[₹ 2,00,000 – ₹ 10,000 (being already received)]	

C. *Less:* Cost of goods sold after stock taking till 31st March (whether or not delivered) [80% of (₹ 2,00,000 – ₹ 10,000) (being already delivered)]	(1,52,000)
D. Stock as per Books as at 31st March	2,38,000

PROBLEM 11

Determine the cost of physical stock as at 31st March in Problem 10.

SOLUTION

STATEMENT SHOWING THE COST OF PHYSICAL STOCK AS AT 31ST MARCH

Particulars	₹
A. Stock as per physical verification as at 24th March	2,00,000
B. *Add:* Cost of Goods purchased and received after stock taking till 31st March [₹ 2,00,000 – ₹ 10,000 (being already received) – ₹ 20,000 (being not yet received)]	1,70,000
C. *Less:* Cost of goods sold and delivered after stock taking till 31st March [80% of ₹ 2,00,000 – ₹ 10,000 being already delivered – ₹ 20,000 (being not yet delivered)]	(1,36,000)
D. Cost of Physical Stock in hand as at 31st March	2,34,000

RECEIVABLES PAYABLES RECONCILIATION STATEMENT

PROBLEM 12

Tulsian & Co. sold goods on credit to various customers. Details related to one of the customer, Shiv for the Quarter ending on 31st March, 2015, are given below:

Particulars	₹	*Particulars*	₹
Trade Debtors as on 1.1.2015	1,00,000	Cash received from Debtors	1,00,000
Bills Receivable drawn of which Bills of ₹ 1,00,000 were dishonoured	4,00,000	Cheques received from Debtors of which cheques of ₹ 1,00,000 were dishonoured	3,00,000
Discount Allowed	5,000	Credit Sales	6,10,000
Bad Debts W/O (after deducting bad debts recovered ₹ 1,000)	4,000	Return Inwards	10,000

SOLUTION

RECEIVABLE FROM SHIV - RECONCILIATION STATEMENT

Particulars	*Amount* (₹)
Opening Balance as on 1.1.2015	1,00,000
Credit Sales	6,10,000
Less: Goods returned by the Customer	10,000
Less: Cash received from Debtors	1,00,000
Less: Cheques received from Debtors	3,00,000

Less: Bills Receivable drawn	4,00,000
Less: Discount Allowed	5,000
Less: Bad Debts W/O (₹ 4,000 + ₹ 1,000)	5,000
Add: Cheques dishonoured	1,00,000
Add: Bills Receivable dishonoured	1,00,000
Net Receivable from Customer	90,000

PROBLEM 13

Tulsian & Co. sold goods on credit to various customers. Details related to one of the customer, Shanker for the Quarter ending on 31st March, 2015, are given below:

(a) Trade Debtors as on 1.1.2015 ₹ 2,00,000

(b) Gross Sales (including Cash Sales of ₹ 4,00,000) ₹ 16,20,000

(c) Return Inwards ₹ 20,000

(d) Discount Allowed ₹ 11,000 (of which later on ₹ 1,000 disallowed)

(e) Cash received from Debtors ₹ 2,20,000 (including ₹ 20,000 from a person to whom an old fixed asset was sold)

(f) Cheques received from Debtors ₹ 4,40,000 of which cheques amounting to ₹ 40,000 were dishonoured. Out of these dishonoured cheques a cheque for ₹ 10,000 was dishonoured for non-payment as the customer became insolvent and his estate realised nothing.

(g) Bills Receivables drawn during the year totalled ₹ 6,60,000 of which bills amounting to ₹ 60,000 were endorsed in favour of suppliers. Bills dishonoured ₹ 30,000 (including Bills of ₹ 10,000 endorsed to suppliers).

(h) Interest on Overdue Accounts ₹ 45,000

(i) Bad Debts written off in earlier years recovered ₹ 20,000

(j) Provision for Doubtful Debts on Debtors ₹ 25,000.

(k) Transfer to Bought Ledger ₹ 15,000.

SOLUTION

RECEIVABLE FROM SHIV - RECONCILIATION STATEMENT

Particulars	*Amount* (₹)
Opening Balance as on 1.1.2015	2,00,000
Credit Sales	12,20,000
Less: Goods returned by the Customer	20,000
Less: Cash received from Debtors	2,00,000
Less: Cheques received from Debtors of which cheques of ₹ 1,00,000 were dishonoured	4,40,000
Less: Bills Receivable drawn of which Bills of ₹ 1,00,000 were dishonoured	6,60,000
Less: Discount Allowed	11,000
Less: Bad Debts W/O	10,000
Add: Cheques dishonoured	40,000
Add: Bills Receivable dishonoured	20,000
Add: Endorsed Bills Receivable dishonoured	10,000

Add: **Interest on Overdue Accounts**	45,000
Add: Discount Disallowed	1,000
Less: **Transfer to Bought Ledger**	15,000
Net Receivable from Customer	1,80,000

Note: Cash Sales, Bad Debts Recovered and Provision for Doubtful Debts do not appear in the Total Debtors Account.

PROBLEM 14

CWA Ltd. sold goods on credit to various customers. Details related to one of the customer, Mr. X, is as under:

(i) Goods sold on credit ₹ 3,00,000

(ii) Goods returned by the customer ₹ 18,000 due to defective quality, credit note raised but not recorded.

(iii) Payment received from customer in cash ₹ 60,000 and by cheques ₹ 1,38,000. Out of cheques received, a cheque of ₹ 22,800 was dishonoured by bank.

(iv) Customer accepted two Bills of ₹ 11,400 and ₹ 31,800 for 2 months and 3 months respectively.

(v) Credit note raised against the customer ₹ 2,040 for excess payment charged against one of the consignment.

Mr.X, the customer is in need to ascertain the actual balance due to CWA Ltd. Prepare a Reconciliation Statement.

SOLUTION

RECEIVABLE FROM MR. X - RECONCILIATION STATEMENT

Particulars	*Amount (₹)*
Credit Sales during the period	3,00,000
Less: Goods returned by the Customer, adjustment of credit note	18,000
Less: Payment received in cash	60,000
Less: Payment received by cheque less dishonored cheque (1,38,000 – 22,800)	1,15,200
Less: Bills Receivable accepted by Customer, yet to be matured (11,400 + 31,800)	43,200
Less : Adjustment of Credit Note raised	2,040
Net Receivable from Customer	61,560

PAYABLES RECONCILIATION STATEMENT

PROBLEM 15

Tulsian & Co. purchased goods on credit from various suppliers. Details related to one of the supplier, Vishnu for the Quarter ending on 31st March, 2015, are given below:

Particulars	₹	*Particulars*	₹
Creditors as on 1.1.2015	2,00,000	Cash paid to Creditors	2,00,000

Bills Payables accepted of which Bills of ₹ 1,00,000 were dishonoured	7,00,000	Cheque issued to Creditors of which cheques of ₹ 1,00,000 were dishonoured	5,00,000
Returns Outward	20,000	Discount Received	10,000
Credit Purchases	12,20,000		

SOLUTION

PAYABLE TO VISHNU- RECONCILIATION STATEMENT

Particulars	*Amount* (₹)
Opening Balance as on 1.1.2015	2,00,000
Credit Sales	12,20,000
Less: Goods returned to the supplier	20,000
Less: Cash paid to Creditors	2,00,000
Less: Cheque issued to Creditors	5,00,000
Less: Bills Payables accepted	7,00,000
Less: Discount Received	10,000
Add: Cheques dishonoured	1,00,000
Add: Bills Payables dishonoured	1,00,000
Net Payables to Supplier	1,90,000

PROBLEM 16

Tulsian & Co. purchased goods on credit from various suppliers. Details related to one of the supplier, Vishnu for the Quarter ending on 31st March, 2015, are given below:

(a) Trade Creditors as on 1.1.2015 ₹ 4,00,000.

(b) Gross Purchases (including Cash Purchases of ₹ 8,00,000) ₹ 32,40,000.

(c) Returns Outward ₹ 40,000.

(d) Discount Received ₹ 22,000 (of which later on ₹ 2,000 returned)

(e) Cash paid to Creditors ₹ 4,40,000 (including ₹ 40,000 to a supplier of a fixed asset)

(f) Cheques issued to Creditors ₹ 8,80,000 of which cheque amounting to ₹ 80,000 were dishonoured due to technical reasons.

(g) Bills Payable accepted (including renewals) during the year totalled ₹ 13,20,000. Bills payable withdrawn upon renewals amounted to ₹ 20,000.

(h) Bills amounting to ₹ 1,20,000 were endorsed in favour of suppliers. Out of these endorsed B/R, B/R for ₹ 20,000 was dishonoured.

(i) Interest on Overdue Accounts ₹ 90,000.

(j) Transfer from Sales Ledger ₹ 30,000.

(k) Reserve for Discount on Creditors ₹ 50,000.

SOLUTION

PAYABLE TO VISHNU- RECONCILIATION STATEMENT

Particulars	*Amount* (₹)
Opening Balance as on 1.1.2015	4,00,000

Credit Sales	24,40,000
Less: Goods returned to the supplier	40,000
Less: Cash paid to Creditors	4,00,000
Less: Cheque issued to Creditors	8,80,000
Less: Bills Payables accepted	13,20,000
Less: Bills Receivable Endorsed	1,20,000
Less: Discount Received	22,000
Add: Cheques dishonoured	80,000
Add: Bills Payables dishonoured	20,000
Add: Endorsed Bills Receivable dishonoured	20,000
Add: **Interest on Overdue Accounts**	90,000
Add: Discount Disallowed	2,000
Less: **Transfer from Sales Ledger**	30,000
Net Payables to Supplier	2,40,000

Note: Cash Purchases and Reserve for Discount on Creditors do not appear in the Total Creditors' Account.

PROBLEM 17

Bhola purchases goods on credit from various suppliers. However, there is a difference of opinion which has arised with one of its suppliers. While the Supplier claims that the amount receivable from Bhola is ₹ 1,51,800, on the other hand, Bhola claims that the amount payable is ₹ 1,41,000. On evaluation of records the following were identified:

(i) A purchase of ₹ 42,600 was recorded by the supplier as ₹ 46,800.

(ii) Goods returned by Bhola amounting to ₹ 3,000, but the stock is in transit and has not reached the supplier/vendor.

(iii) Cheques issued to vendor for ₹ 16,800, in transit.

(iv) Bills raised for goods purchased from the supplier, amounting ₹ 13,200, but goods are yet to reach the warehouse/godown of Bhola

Prepare a suitable Reconciliation statement.

SOLUTION

AMOUNT DUE TO SUPPLIER – PAYABLE RECONCILIATION STATEMENT

Particulars	*Amount* (₹)
Amount due to supplier (as per books of the Supplier)	1,51,800
Less: Overstatement of sales figure in the books of supplier (i.e. goods sold by supplier to Bhola for ₹ 42,600 but recorded as ₹ 46,800)	4,900
Less: Goods returned to supplier, now in transit	3,000
Less: Cheques issued to vendor, now in transit	16,800
Add: Bills raised against goods purchased, not stock-in-transit, i.e. not yet reached the warehouse of the supplier	13,200
Amount due to supplier (as per books of Bhola)	1,41,000

This Page has been intentionally left blank

SECTION B : PREPARATION OF ACCOUNTS

12 ACCOUNTING FOR DEPRECIATION

PROBLEM 1

On July 1, 2012 Vijay Ltd purchased second-hand machinery for ₹ 20,000 and spent ₹ 3,000 on reconditioning and installing it. On January 1, 2013 the firm purchased new machinery worth ₹ 12,000. On June 30, 2014 the machinery purchased on January 1,2013 was sold for ₹ 8,000. On July 1,2014 fresh machnery was purchased on instalment basis, payment for this machinery was to be made as follows:

July 1, 2014	₹ 5,000
June 30, 2015	₹ 6,000
June 30, 2016	₹ 5,500

Payments in 2015 and 2016 include interest ₹ 1,000 and ₹ 500 respectively.

The Company writes off depreciation @ 10% p.a. on original cost. The accounts are closed every year on 31st March. Show the Machinery Account for three years ending on March 31, 2015.

SOLUTION

Dr. **MACHINERY ACCOUNT** **Cr.**

Date	Particulars	₹	Date	Particulars	₹
01.07.2012	To Bank A/c: Machine I	20,000	31.03.2013	By Depreciation A/c:	
	To Bank A/c (Expenses)	3,000		Machine I	1,725
				Machine	300
01.01.2013	To Bank A/c (Machine II)	12,000		By Balance c/d:	
				Machine I	21,275
				Machine II	11,700
		35,000			35,000
01.04.2013	To Balance b/d:		31.03.2014	By Depreciation A/c:	
	Machine I	21,275		Machine I	2,300
	Machine II	11,700		Machine II	1,200
				By Balance c/d	
				Machine I	18,975
				Machine II	10,500
		32,975			32,975
01.04.2014	To Balance b/d:		30.06.2014	By Depreciation A/c	300
	Machine I	18,975		By Bank A/c (Machine II)	8,000
	Machine II	10,500			
01.07.2014	To Hire vendor's A/c			By P & L A/c (Loss)	2,200
	(Cash price)	15,000	31.03.2015	By Depreciation A/c:	
	Machine III			Machine I	2,300
				Machine III	1,125
				By Balance c/d:	
				Machine I	16,675
				Machine III	13,875
		44,475			44,475

Working Notes:

1. Book value of Machine II as on date of sale = ₹ 10,500 – ₹ 300 = ₹ 10,200
2. Loss on Sale = ₹ 10,200 – ₹ 8,000 = ₹ 2,200
3. Cash price of Machine III = ₹ 5,000 + ₹ 6,000 + ₹ 5,500 – (₹ 1000 + ₹ 500) = ₹ 15,000
4. Depreciation on Machine III = ₹ 15000 × 10/100 × 9/12 = ₹ 1,125

PROBLEM 2

Tulsian Ltd. Provides you the following information:

Date	Particulars
01.04.2012	Purchased 10 second hand Machines for ₹ 9,00,000. incurred ₹ 70,000 towards freight & insurance, ₹ 20,000 towards carriage inward, Residual Value ₹ 4,09,600, Useful life 4 years.
01.01.2013	Incurred ₹ 7,000 towards Repairs and ₹ 3,000 on installation of machines and ₹ 12,000 towards Annual Insurance Premium and commenced the commercial production.
01.10.2013	Sold one machine at a profit of 10%
01.01.2014	Incurred Rs.10,000 on repairs of Machines
01.01.2015	Sold one machine at a loss of 10% and purchased a new machine for Rs.90,000 and spent Rs.10,000 on its installation

Required: Prepare the Machinery Account for the years 2012 – 2015.

SOLUTION

Dr. **MACHINE ACCOUNT** **Cr.**

Date	Particulars	₹	Date	Particulars	₹
1.04.2012	To Bank A/c	9,00,000	31.03.2013	By Depreciation A/c [10,00,000 × 20% × 3/12]	50,000
01.04.2012	To Bank A/c	90,000		By Balance c/d	9,50,000
01.01.2013	To Bank A/c	10,000			
		10,00,000			10,00,000
1.04.2013	To Balance b/d	9,50,000	01.10.2013	By Depreciation A/c [95,000 × 20% × 6/12]	9,500
	To P & L A/c [Profit] [(95,000 – 9,500) × 10%]	8,550		By Bank A/c [(95,000 – 9,500) + 10%]	94,050
			31.03.2014	By Depreciation A/c [(9,50,000 – 95,000) × 20% × 12/12]	1,71,000
				By Balance c/d	6,84,000
		9,58,550			9,58,550
01.04.2014	To Balance b/d	6,84,000	01.01.2015	By Depreciation A/c [76,000 × 20% × 9/12]	11,400
01.01.2015	To Bank A/c	90,000		By Bank A/c [(76,000 – 11,400) – 10%)]	58,140

	To Bank A/c	10,000		By P & L A/c [Loss] [(76,000 – 11,400) × 10%)]	6,460
			31.03.2015	By Depreciation A/c:	
				Old [(6,84,000 – 76,000) × 20%)]	1,21,600
				New [1,00,000 × 20% × 3/12]	5,000
				By Balance c/d:	
				Old 4,86,400	
				New 95,000	5,81,400
		7,84,000			7,84,000

Note: WDV rate of Depreciation = $1 - \sqrt[4]{\frac{₹4,09,600}{₹10,00,000}} = 20\%$

WHEN PROVISION FOR DEPRECIATION ACCOUNT IS MAINTAINED

PROBLEM 3

On April 1, 2012, a firm purchased a machinery for ₹ 2,00,000. On 1st October in the same accounting year, additional machinery costing ₹ 1,00,000 was purchased. On 1st October, 2013, the machinery purchased on 1st April, 2012, having become obsolete, was sold off for ₹ 90,000. On October 1, 2014, new machinery was purchased for ₹ 2,50,000 while the machinery purchased on 1st October, 2012 was sold for ₹ 85,000 on the same day. The firm provides depreciation on its machinery @ 10% per annum on original cost on 31st March every year. Show Machinery Account, Provision for Depreciation Account and Depreciation Account for the period of three accounting years ending March 31, 2015.

SOLUTION

Dr. **MACHINERY ACCOUNT** **Cr.**

Date	Particulars	₹	Date	Particulars	₹
01.04.2012	To Bank A/c	2,00,000	31.03.2013	By Balance c/d	3,00,000
01.12.2012	To Bank A/c	1,00,000			
		3,00,000			3,00,000
01.04.2013	To Balance b/d	3,00,000	01.12.2013	By Bank A/c	90,000
				By Provision for Depreciation A/c	30,000
				By Profit and Loss A/c	80,000
			31.03.2014	By Balance c/d	1,00,000
		3,00,000			3,00,000
01.04.2014	To Balance b/d	1,00,000	01.12.2014	By Bank A/c	85,000

01.12.2014	To Bank A/c	2,50,000		By Provision for Depreciation A/c	20,000
	To Profit and Loss A/c	5,000	31.03.2015	By Balance c/d	2,50,000
		3,55,000			3,55,000

Dr. **DEPRECIATION ACCOUNT** **Cr.**

Date	Particulars	₹	Date	Particulars	₹
31.03.2013	To Provision for Depreciation A/c	25,000	31.03.2013	By Profit and Loss A/c	25,000
		25,000			25,000
01.12.2013	To Provision for Depreciation A/c	10,000	31.03.2014	By Profit and Loss A/c	20,000
31.03.2014	To Provision for Depreciation A/c	10,000			
		20,000			20,000
01.12.2014	To Provision for Depreciation A/c	5,000	31.03.2015	By Profit and Loss A/c	17,500
31.03.2015	To Provision for Depreciation A/c	12,500			
		17,500			17,500

Dr. **PROVISION FOR DEPRECIATION ACCOUNT** **Cr.**

Date	Particulars	₹	Date	Particulars	₹
31.03.2013	To Balance c/d	25,000	31.03.2013	By Depreciation A/c (₹ 20,000 + ₹ 5,000)	25,000
		25,000			25,000
01.12.2013	To Machinery A/c (₹ 20,000 + ₹ 10,000)	30,000	01.04.2013	By Balance b/d	25,000
			01.12.2013	By Depreciation A/c	10,000
31.03.2014	To Balance c/d	15,000	31.03.2014	By Depreciation A/c	10,000
		45,000			45,000
01.12.2014	To Machinery A/c (₹ 5,000 + ₹ 10,000 + ₹ 5,000)	20,000	01.04.2014	By Balance b/d	15,000
			01.12.2014	By Depreciation A/c	5,000
31.03.2015	To Balance c/d	12,500	31.03.2015	By Depreciation A/c	12,500
		32,500			32,500

PROBLEM 4

Shippers Ltd. which depreciates the machines @ 25% p.a. on the reducing balance method, provides you the following particulars:

Cost on 31.12.2013 ₹ 2,46,000. Provision for Depreciation (on 31.12.2013) ₹ 1,24,000. No amounts being charged in the year of sale but full charge is being made for the years during which addition is made. On 1.7.2015, one new machine was purchased for ₹ 24,000 and old machinery purchased on 1.7.2012 for ₹ 20,000 was discarded but could not be sold immediately. However, it was expected to realise ₹ 5,000 for the same. Prepare

(a) Machinery Account, (b) Provision for Depreciation Account, and (c) Machinery Disposal Account for the years 2014 and 2015.

SOLUTION

Dr. **MACHINERY ACCOUNT** **Cr.**

Date	Particulars	₹	Date	Particulars	₹
01.01.2014	To Balance b/d	2,46,000	31.12.2014	By Balance c/d	2,46,000
01.01.2015	To Balance b/d	2,46,000	01.07.2015	By Machinery Disposal A/c	20,000
01.07.2015	To Bank A/c	24,000	31.12.2015	By Balance c/d	2,50,000
		2,70,000			2,70,000

Dr. **PROVISION FOR DEPRECIATION ACCOUNT** **Cr.**

Date	Particulars	₹	Date	Particulars	₹
31.12.2014	To Balance c/d	1,54,500	01.01.2014	By Balance b/d	1,24,000
			31.12.2014	By Depreciation A/c [25% of (₹ 2,46,000 – ₹ 1,24,000]	30,500
		1,54,500			1,54,500
01.07.2015	To Machinery Disposal A/c	11,563	01.01.2015	By Balance b/d	1,54,500
31.12.2015	To Balance c/d	1,69,703	31.12.2015	By Depreciation A/c [25% of (₹ 2,50,000 – ₹ 1,54,500 + ₹ 11,563)]	26,766
		1,81,266			1,81,266

Dr. **MACHINERY DISPOSAL ACCOUNT** **Cr.**

Date	Particulars	₹	Date	Particulars	₹
01.07.2015	To Machinery A/c	20,000	01.07.2015	By Provision for Depreciation A/c	11,563
				By P and L A/c (Loss) (Prudence concept)	3,437
				By Balance c/d	5,000
		20,000			20,000

Working Note: *Calculation of Depreciation provided on Machine discarded*

	Particulars	Book Value ₹	Accumulated Depreciation ₹
A	Original Cost	20,000	–
B	*Less:* Depreciation for 2012	5,000	5,000
C	Book value on 1.1.2013	15,000	
D	*Less:* Depreciation for 2013	3,750	3,750
E	Book Value on 1.1.2014	11,250	

F *Less:* Depreciation for 2014	2,813	2,813
	8,437	11,563

PROBLEM 5

Metropol Ltd acquired a machine for ₹ 5,40,000 on April 1, 2012. Depreciation was to be charged at 20% p.a. on straight line method. During 2014-2015, a modification was made to improve its technical reliability at a cost of ₹ 50,000 which it was considered would extend the useful life of the machine for two years At the same time an important component of the machine was replaced at a cost of ₹ 10,000 because of excessive wear and tear. Routine maintenance during the said accounting period cost ₹ 7,500. Show the Machinery Account, Provision for Depreciation on Machinery Account and the charge to Profit and Loss Account for the year ending March 31, 2015 only assuming that the company follows a policy of charging full year's depreciation on additions.

SOLUTION

Dr. **MACHINERY ACCOUNT** **Cr.**

Date	Particulars	₹	Date	Particulars	₹
01.04.2014	To Balance b/d	5,40,000	31.03.2015	By Balance c/d	6,00,000
2014-2015	To Bank A/c	50,000			
	To Bank A/c	10,000			
		6,00,000			6,00,000

Dr. **AN EXTRACT OF PROFIT AND LOSS ACCOUNT** **Cr.**

Date	Particulars	₹	Date	Particulars	₹
	To Repair & Maintanence	7,500			
	To Depreciation on Machinery	76,800			

Dr. **PROVISION FOR DEPRECIATION ACCOUNT** **Cr.**

Date	Particulars	₹	Date	Particulars	₹
31.03.2015	To Balance c/d	2,92,800	01.04.2014	By Balance b/d [₹ 5,40,000 × 20/100 × 2]	2,16,000
			31.03.2015	By Depreciation A/c [20% of (₹ 6,00,000 – ₹ 2,16,000]	76,800
		2,92,800			2,92,800

Working Notes:

1 *The amount spent on routine maintenance is of revenue nature and not of capital nature and hence not debited to Machinery Account.*

2. *The unamortised depreciable amount (i.e. ₹ 5,40,000 – ₹ 2,16,000 + ₹ 50,000 + ₹ 10,000) has been charged over the revised remaining useful life (i.e. 5 years).*

MACHINERY ACCOUNT INVOLVING RECTIFICATION OF ERRORS

PROBLEM 6

X Ltd. writes off depreciation @ 10% per annum on the diminishing balance. On April 1, 2014, the Machinery Account showed a balance of ₹ 2,98,000. It was discovered in the year 2014-2015 that:

(a) Heavy repairs effected to Plant and Machinery (completed on September 30, 2012) were debited to the Machinery Account. The amount was ₹ 30,000; and

(b) A machine costing ₹ 12,000 was entered in the Purchases Book on 1st January, 2013. The expenses on installation, ₹ 800, were debited to General Expenses Account.

Necessary corrections were made in the year 2014-2015. On September 30, 2014 a machine which had cost ₹ 40,000 on April 1, 2012 was disposed of for ₹ 29,000 and a new machine costing ₹ 58,000 was installed on the same date, the expenses on installing the machine being ₹ 3,000.

Required: Show the Machinery Account for the year ended March 31, 2015.

SOLUTION

Dr. **MACHINERY ACCOUNT** **Cr.**

Date	Particulars	₹	Date	Particulars	₹
01.04.2014	To Balance b/f	2,98,000	01.04.2014	By Profit & Loss A/c (Repairs)	25,650
	To Profit & Loss A/c (for Machine Purchased on 1.1.96)	11,232		By Bank A/c	29,000
30.09.2014	To Bank A/c [₹ 58,000 + ₹ 3,000]	61,000	30.09.2014	By Depreciation— For 6 months on the machine sold (3)	1,620
				By Profit & Loss A/c (Loss)	1,780
			31.03.2015	By Depreciation A/c	28,168
			31.03.2015	By Balance c/d	2,84,014
		3,70,232			3,70,232

Working Notes:

1. CALCULATION OF BOOK VALUE OF REPAIRS AND NEW MACHINE

Particulars	Repairs ₹	New Machine ₹
A Cost on 1.12.2012/1.1.2013	30,000	12,800
B *Less:* Depreciation for 2012-2013	1,500	320
C Book value as on 1.4.2013	28,500	12,480
D *Less:* Depreciation for 2013-2014	2,850	1,248
E Book Value as on 1.4.2014	25,650	11,232

2. CALCULATION OF PROFIT/LOSS ON SALE OF MACHINE

Particulars	₹
A Cost as on 1.4.2012	40,000
B *Less:* Depreciation for 2012-2013	4,000
C Book value as on 1.4.2013	36,000
D *Less:* Depreciation for 2013-2014	3,600
E Book value as on 1.4.2014	32,400
F *Less:* Depreciation for 2014-2015 for 6 month	1,620
G Book value as on 1.10.2014	30,780
H *Less:* Sale Proceeds	29,000
I Loss on Sale (G – H)	1,780

3. CALCULATION OF BOOK VALUE OF MACHINERY (OTHER THAN SCRAPPED) (AFTER RECTIFICATION OF MISTAKES) AS ON 1.4.2014

Particulars	₹
A Undjusted Book Value as on 1.4.2014	2,98,000
B *Add:* Book Value of Machine purchased on 1.1.2013	11,232
C *Less:* Book Value of repairs wrongly debited	25,650
D *Less:* Book Value of Machine sold	32,400
	2,51,182

4. CALCULATION OF DEPRECIATION FOR 2014-2015

Particulars	₹
A On old Machine [10% on ₹ 2,51,182]	25,118
B On New Machine [₹ 61,000 × 10/100 × 6/12]	3,050
	28,168

CHANGE IN METHOD OF DEPRECIATION

PROBLEM 7

Messrs Mill and Wright commenced business on January 1, 2011, when they purchased plant and equipment for ₹ 7,00,000. They adopted a policy of (i) charging depreciation at 15% p.a. on diminishing balance basis and (ii) charging full year's depreciation on additions. Over the years, their purchases of plant have been: 1.8.2012 ₹ 1,50,000, 30.9.2015 ₹ 2,00,000.

On 1.1.2015, it was decided to change the method and rate of depreciation to 10% p.a. on straight line basis with retrospective effective from 1.1.2011, the adjustment being made in the accounts for the year ending December 31, 2015.

Required: Calculate the difference in depreciation to be adjusted in the Plant and Equipment Account on 1.1.2015 and show the ledger account for the year 2015.

SOLUTION

CALCULATION OF SHORT/EXCESS DEPRECIATION

Year A	Cost B	WDV as on 1.1.2014 C	Dep. under WDV D = B – C	Dep. under SLM E
2011	7,00,000	(7,00,000 × .85 × .85 × .85 × .85) = ₹ 3,65,404	3,34,596	(7,00,000 × 10% × 4) = 2,80,000
2012	1,50,000	(1,50,000 × .85 × .85 × .85) = ₹ 92,119	57,881	(1,50,000 × 10% × 3) = 45,000
	8,50,000	4,57,523	3,92,477	3,25,000

Excess Depreciation charged = ₹ 3,92,477 – ₹ 3,25,000 = ₹ 67,477

Current year's profit would be increased by ₹ 67,477 due to change in the method of depreciation.

Dr. **PLANT AND EQUIPMENT ACCOUNT** **Cr.**

Date	Particulars	₹	Date	Particulars	₹
31.12.2015	To Profit and Loss A/c (depreciation written back)	67,477	31.12.2015	By Depreciation A/c (10% of original cost)	1,05,000
30.09.2015	To Bank A/c	2,00,000	31.12.2015	By Balance c/d	6,20,000
01.01.2015	To Balance b/d (8,50,000 – 3,92,477)	4,57,523			
		7,25,000			7,25,000

PROBLEM 8

The Plant and Machinery Account of a Company had a debit balance of ₹ 1,47,390 on 1st January, 2015. The company was incorporated in 2012 and has been following the practice of charging full year's depreciation every year on Diminishing Balance System @ 15% p.a. In 2015, it was, however, decided to change the method from Reducing System to Straight Line with retrospective effect from 2012 and to give effect of the change while preparing the Final Accounts for the year ended 31st December, 2015, the rate of depreciation remaining same as before. In 2015, new machine was purchased at a cost of ₹ 50,000. All the other machines were acquired in 2012.

Required: Show the Plant and Machinery Account from 2012 to 2015.

SOLUTION

Dr. **PLANT AND MACHINERY ACCOUNT** **Cr.**

Date	Particulars	₹	Date	Particulars	₹
01.01.2012	To Bank A/c	2,40,000	31.12.2012	By Depreciation A/c (15% on ₹ 2,40,000)	36,000
				By Balance c/d	2,04,000
		2,40,000			2,40,000
01.01.2013	To Balance b/d	2,04,000	31.12.2013	By Depreciation A/c (15% of ₹ 2,04,000)	30,600
				By Balance c/d	1,73,400
		2,04,000			2,04,000

01.01.2014	To Balance b/d	1,73,400	31.12.2014	By Depreciation A/c (15% of ₹ 1,73,400)	26,010
				By Balance c/d	1,47,390
		1,73,400			1,73,400
01.01.2015	To Balance b/d	1,47,390	31.12.2015	By Depreciation A/c [15% of (₹ 2,40,000 + ₹ 50,000)]	43,500
	To Bank A/c (purchases)	50,000		By Profit and Loss A/c (Short provision due to change in method)	15,390
				By Balance c/d	1,38,500
		1,97,390			1,97,390

Working Notes:

1. Cost as on 1.1.2012 = ₹ 1,47,390 × 100/85 × 100/85 × 100/85 = ₹ 2,40,000
2. *Short Provision of Depreciation*

A.	Depreciation to be charged under SLM = [(15% on ₹ 2,40,000) × 3]	1,08,000
B.	Depreciation already charged under WDV = [(₹ 36,000 + ₹ 30,600 + ₹ 26,010]	92,610
C.	Short depreciation to be charged due to change in method (A – B)	15,390

PROBLEM 9

Ram Ltd which depreciates its machinery at 10% p.a. on Diminishing Balance Method, had on January 1, 2014 ₹ 9,72,000 on the debit side of Machinery Account. During the year 2014, machinery purchased on January 1, 2012 for ₹ 80,000 was sold for ₹ 45,000 on July 1, 2014 and a new machinery at a cost of ₹ 1,50,000 was purchased and installed on the same date, installation charges being ₹ 8,000. The company wanted to change the method of depreciation from Diminishing Balance Method to Straight Line Method with effect from January 1, 2012. Difference of depreciation upto December 31, 2014 to be adjusted. The rate of depreciation remains the same as before.
Required: Show Machinery Account.

SOLUTION

Dr. MACHINERY ACCOUNT FOR THE YEAR 2014 Cr.

Date	Particulars	₹	Date	Particulars	₹
01.01.2014	To Balance b/d	9,72,000	01.07.2014	By Bank A/c (Sale)	45,000
01.07.2014	To Bank A/c	1,50,000	01.07.2014	By Depreciation A/c	4,000
	To Bank A/c	8,000	31.12.2014	By P & L A/c (Loss on sale)	15,000
			31.12.2014	By P & L A/c (Additional Depreciation)	12,000
			31.12.2014	By Depreciation A/c	1,19,900
				By Balance c/d	9,34,100
		11,30,000			11,30,000

Working Notes:

1. CALCULATION OF W.D.V. AS ON 01.01.2012

Particulars	₹
A. W.D.V. as on 1.1.2014	9,72,000
B. *Add:* Depreciation during 2013 (₹ 9,72,000 × 1/9)	1,08,000
C. W.D.V. as on 1.1.2013	10,80,000
D. *Add:* Depreciation during 2012 (₹ 10,80,000 × 1/9)	1,20,000
E. W.D.V. as on 1.1.2012	12,00,000

2. CALCULATION OF LOSS ON SALE OF MACHINERY

Particulars	₹
A. Original Cost as on 1.1.2012	80,000
B. *Less:* Depreciation @ 10% for 2½ years	20,000
C. Book Value as on 1.7.2014	60,000
D. Sale Proceeds	45,000
E. Loss on sale	15,000

3. CALCULATION OF DEPRECIATION FOR 2014

(a) On Machines (Other than sold one) existing as on 1.1.2014 @ 10% on (₹ 12,00,000 – ₹ 80,000)	₹ 1,12,000
(b) On Machine Purchased on 1.7.2014 (10% on ₹ 1,58,000 for 6 months)	₹ 7,900
	₹ 1,19,900

4. CALCULATION OF DIFFERENCE IN THE AMOUNT OF DEPRECIATION UNDER OLD METHOD AND NEW METHOD ON THE MACHINERIES

A. Depreciation on SLM basis for 2 years [₹ 12,00,000 × 10% × 2]			₹ 2,40,000
B. Depreciation on W.D.V. basis for 2 years			
for 2012 on	₹ 12,00,000	₹ 1,20,000	
for 2013 on	₹ 10,80,000	₹ 1,08,000	₹ 2,28,000
C. Difference still to be adjusted (A – B)			₹ 12,000

PROBLEM 10

ABC Ltd. purchased on 1st October, 2011, a machinery for ₹ 4,50,000 and spent ₹ 10,000 on freight and transit insurance. On 25th December, 2011, it further spent ₹ 40,000 on its erection. The machinery was put to use on 1-1-2012. On 1st July 2012, it purchased another machinery for ₹ 1,00,000. During the year 2013, it spent 10,000 for repairs on 1-4-2013.

However, on 1-4-2014, a part of the machinery, purchased on 1-10-2011, costing ₹ 2,00,000 was sold for ₹ 1,50,000. On 1-10-2014 it purchased another machinery for ₹ 3,00,000.

On 1st July, 2015, however, machinery purchased on 1st July, 2012 was sold for ₹ 65,000. Depreciation was charged by the firm @ 10% per annum by written down value method. During the year 2015, ABC Ltd. decided to change the method of providing depreciation and adopted the Straight Line Method of charging depreciation @10% per annum.

Required: Prepare Machinery Account us per the provisions of AS-6 upto the year ending 31-12-2015.

SOLUTION

Dr. **MACHINERY ACCOUNT** **Cr.**

Date	Particulars	₹	Date	Particulars	₹
01.12.2011	To Bank A/c	4,50,000	31.12.2011	By Balance c/d	5,00,000
01.12.2011	To Bank A/c (Freight)	10,000			
25.12.2011	To Bank A/c (Erection)	40,000			
		5,00,000			5,00,000
01.01.2012	To Balance b/d	5,00,000	31.12.2012	By Depreciation A/c:	
01.07.2012	To Bank A/c (II)	1,00,000		Math I 50,000	
				Math II 5,000	55,000
			31.12.2012	By Balance c/d:	
				I 4,50,000	
				II 95,000	5,45,000
		6,00,000			6,00,000
01.01.2013	To Balance b/d	5,45,000	31.12.2013	By Depreciation A/c:	
				I 45,000	
				II 9,500	54,500
			31.12.2013	By Balance c/d:	
				I 4,05,000	
				II 85,500	4,90,000
		5,45,000			5,45,000
01.01.2014	To Balance b/d	4,90,500	01.04.2014	By Bank A/c	1,50,000
01.12.2014	To Bank A/c	3,00,000	01.04.2014	By Depreciation A/c	4,050
			01.04.2014	By Profit & Loss A/c-Loss	7,950
			31.12.2014	By Depreciation	40,350
				By Balance c/d	5,88,150
		7,90,500			7,90,500
01.01.2015	To Balance c/d	5,88,150	01.07.2015	By Depreciation A/c	5,000
			01.07.2015	By Bank A/c	65,000
				By Profit & Less A/c (loss)	5,000
			31.12.2015	By Profit & Loss A/c – Additional dep.	10,650
				By Depreciation A/c	60,000
				By Balance c/d	4,42,500
		5,88,150			5,88,150

Working Notes:

1. Loss on sale of Machine = Sale Proceeds – WDV as on date of Sale
   = ₹ 1,50,000 – (₹ 2,00,000 × 90% × 90% × 97.5%) = ₹ 7,950

2. DEPRECIATION FOR 2014

Particulars	₹
W.D.V. of Total Machine on 1.1.2014	4,90,500
Less: W.D.V. of Machine sold of on 1.1.2014	1,62,000
W.D.V. of Machine used during 2014	3,28,500
Depreciation for 2012 for full year	32,850
Depreciation on Machine Purchased on 01.10.2014 for months	7,500
	40,350

3. Loss on sale of Machine = Sale Proceeds – Book Value as on date of Sale
= ₹ 65,000 – [₹ 1,00,000 – (₹ 1,00,000 × 10% × 3 years) = ₹ 5,000

4. EFFECT OF CHANGE OF DEPRECIATION

Particulars	W.D.V.	S.L.M.
Cost of Machine on 01.01.2012 (₹. 3,00,000)		
Depreciation for 2012	30,000	30,000
Depreciation for 2013	27,000	30,000
Depreciation for 2014	24,300	30,000
Cost of Machine II ₹ 3,00,000		
Depreciation for 2014	7,500	7,500
A. Total Depreciation	88,800	97,500
Cost of Machine on 1.7.2012 (₹ 1,00,000)		
Depreciation for 2012	5,000	5,000
Depreciation for 2013	9,500	10,000
Depreciation for 2014	8,550	10,000
B. Total Depreciation	23,050	25,000
C. Total Depreciation (A + B)	1,11,850	1,22,500

Additional Depreciation to be charged = ₹ 1,22,500 – ₹ 1,11,850 = ₹ 10,650

Note: Depreciation is charged from the date the machine is put to use. Since machine is put to use on 1.01.2012 so depreciation will be charged from 1.01.2012 onward and not for 2011.

PROBLEM 11

Tulsian Ltd. provides you the following information:

Date	Particulars
01.04.2012	Purchased 10 second hand Machines for ₹ 9,00,000. incurred ₹ 70,000 towards freight & insurance, ₹ 20,000 towards carriage inward, Residual Value ₹ 4,09,600, Useful life 4 years.
01.01.2013	Incurred ₹ 7,000 towards Repairs and ₹ 3,000 on installation of machines and ₹ 12,000 towards Annual Insurance Premium and commenced the commercial production.
01.10.2013	Sold one machine at a profit of 10%
01.01.2014	Incurred Rs.10,000 on repairs of Machines

01.01.2015	Sold one machine at a loss of 10% and purchased a new machine for Rs.90,000 and spent Rs.10,000 on its installation

Depreciation was annually provided on 31st March on the written down value. On 31st March, 2015, it was decided to adopt the method of providing depreciation @ 20% p.a. on original cost.

Required: Prepare the Machinery Account for the years 2012 – 2015.

SOLUTION

Dr. **MACHINE ACCOUNT** **Cr.**

Date	Particulars	₹	Date	Particulars	₹
01.04.2012	To Bank A/c	9,00,000	31.03.2013	By Depreciation A/c [10,00,000 × 20% × 3/12]	50,000
01.04.2012	To Bank A/c	90,000		By Balance c/d	9,50,000
01.01.2013	To Bank A/c	10,000			
		10,00,000			10,00,000
1.04.2013	To Balance b/d	9,50,000	01.10.2013	By Depreciation A/c [95,000 × 20% × 6/12]	9,500
	To P & L A/c [Profit] [(95,000 – 9,500) × 10%]	8,550		By Bank A/c [(95,000 – 9,500) + 10%]	94,050
			31.03.2014	By Depreciation A/c [(9,50,000 – 95,000) × 20% × 12/12]	1,71,000
				By Balance c/d	6,84,000
		9,58,550			9,58,550
01.04.2014	To Balance b/d	6,84,000	01.01.2015	By Depreciation A/c [76,000 × 20% × 9/12]	11,400
01.01.2015	To Bank A/c	90,000		By Bank A/c [(76,000 – 11,400) – 10%)]	58,140
	To Bank A/c	10,000		By P & L A/c [Loss] [(76,000 – 11,400) × 10%)]	6,460
			31.03.2015	By P & L A/c (Short Depreciation)	8,000
				By Depreciation A/c:	
				Old [8,00,000 × 20%)]	1,60,000
				New [1,00,000 × 20% × 3/12]	5,000
				By Balance c/d:	
				Old 4,40,000	
				New 95,000	5,35,000
		7,84,000			7,84,000

Working Notes:

1. WDV rate of Depreciation $= 1 - \sqrt[4]{\frac{₹4,09,600}{₹10,00,000}} = 20\%$

2. Calculation of Excess/Short Depreciation on 8 Machines

(A) Depreciation already provided on WDV basis @ 20% p.a.
= [8,00,000] – [8,00,000 × .95 × .80] = ₹ 1,92,000

(B) Depreciation which should have been provided on SLM basis @ 20% p.a.
= [8,00,000 × 20% × 15/12] =₹ 2,00,000

(C) Short Depreciation still to be written off (A – B) = ₹ 8,000

PROBLEM 12

Tulsian Ltd. provides you the following information:

Date	Particulars
	The Machinery Account of Tulsian Ltd had a debit balance of ₹ 6,84,000 on 1st April, 2014
01.04.2012	Purchased 10 second hand Machines of the same type and incurred ₹ 70,000 towards freight & insurance, ₹ 20,000 towards carriage inward
01.01.2013	Incurred ₹ 7,000 towards Repairs and ₹ 3,000 on Installation of machines and ₹ 12,000 towards Annual Insurance Premium and commenced the commercial production.
01.10.2013	Sold one machine at a profit of 10%
01.01.2014	Incurred Rs.10,000 on repairs of Machines
01.01.2015	Sold one machine at a loss of 10% and purchased a new machine for Rs.90,000 and spent Rs.10,000 on its installation

Depreciation was annually provided on 31st March @ 20% p.a on the written down value. On 31st March, 2015, it was decided to adopt the method of providing depreciation @ 20% p.a. on original cost.

Required: Prepare the Machinery Account for the years 2012 – 2015.

SOLUTION

CALCULATION OF PURCHASE PRICE OF 10 MACHINES AS ON 01.04.2012

Particulars	₹
A. W.D.V. of 9 Machines as on 1.4.2014	8,64,000
B. *Add:* Depreciation during 2013-2014 (₹8,64,000 × 20/80)	1,71,000
C. W.D.V. of 9 Machines as on 1.4.2013	8,55,000
D. Book Value of 1 Machine (8,55,000 × 1/9)	95,000
E. W.D.V. of 10 Machines as on 1.4.2013	9,50,000
F. *Add:* Depreciation during 2012-2013 (₹ 9,50,000 × 5/95)	50,000
G. Total Cost of 10 Machines as on 1.1.2013	10,00,000
H. *Less:* Repairs and on Installation Incurred on 1.1.2013	10,000
I. *Less:* freight & insurance, and carriage inward Incurred on 1.4.2012	90,000
J. Purchase Price of 10 Machines as on 1.4.2012	9,00,000

Remaining solution same as given in the previous Problem.

PROBLEM 13

X Ltd. purchased a second-hand machinery on January 1, 2012 for ₹ 37,000 and immediately spent ₹ 2,000 on its repairs and ₹ 1,000 on its erection. On July 1, 2013, it purchased another machine for ₹ 10,000 and on July 1, 2014 sold off the first machine purchased in 2012 for ₹ 28,000; on the same date it purchased a machinery for ₹ 25,000. On 1st July, 2015 the second machinery purchased for ₹ 10,000 was also sold off for ₹ 2,000. Depreciation was provided on the Machinery at a rate of 10% p.a. on the original cost annually on 31st December. In 2015, however, the company changed the method of providing depreciation and adopted the written down value method, the rate of depreciation being 15% p.a. with effect from January 1, 2012.

Required: Prepare the Machinery Account for four calender years commencing from January 1, 2012. Calculations are to be made to the nearest rupee.

SOLUTION

Dr. **MACHINERY ACCOUNT** **Cr.**

Date	Particulars	₹	Date	Particulars	₹
01.01.2012	To Bank A/c: Machine I	37,000	31.12.2012	By Depreciation A/c	4,000
	To Bank A/c			By Balance c/d	36,000
				(erection and repairs)	3,000
		40,000			40,000
01.01.2013	To Balance b/d	36,000	31.12.2013	By Depreciation A/c:	
01.07.2013	To Bank A/c (Machine II)	10,000		Machine I 4,000	
				Machine II 500	4,500
				By Balance c/d:	
				Machine I 32,000	
				Machine II 9,500	41,500
		46,000			46,000
01.01.2014	To Balance b/d:		01.07.2014	By Depreciation A/c [₹ 40,000 × 10/100 × 6/12]	2,000
	Machine I 32,000				
	Machine II 9,500	41,500			
01.07.2014	To Bank A/c Machine III	25,000		By Profit & Loss A/c (Loss) [(₹ 32,000 – ₹ 2,000) – ₹ 28,000]	2,000
				By Bank A/c	28,000
			31.12.2014	By Depreciation A/c:	
				Machine II 1,000	
				Machine III 1,250	2,250
				By Balance c/d:	
				Machine II 8,500	
				Machine III 23,750	32,250
		66,500			66,500
01.01.2015	To Balance b/d:		01.07.2015	By Depreciation A/c	590
	Machine II 8,500		01.07.2015	By Bank A/c	2,000
	Mahcine III 23,750	32,250	31.12.2015	By Profit & Loss A/c (Loss) [₹ 7,272 – ₹ 2,000]	5,272

			31.12.2015	By Profit & Loss A/c [Short Depreciation]	1,263
			31.12.2015	By Depreciation A/c [15% on (₹ 25,000 – 15% of ₹ 25,000 for 6 months)]	3,469
				By Balance c/d	19,656
		32,250			32,250

Working Notes:

1. CALCULATION OF LOSS ON SALE OF MACHINE II

A.	Cost of Machine II	₹ 10,000	
B.	*Less:* Depreciation @15% for 1/2 year	₹ 750	
C.	Book Value as on 31.12.2013	₹ 9,250	
D.	*Less:* Depreciation @15%	₹ 1,388	
E.	Book Value as on 31.12.2014	₹ 7,862	
F.	*Less:* Depreciation @15% for 1/2 year	₹ 590	
G.	Book Value as on Date of Sale	₹ 7,272	
H.	Sale Proceeds Loss on Sale	₹ 2,000	₹ 5,272

2. CALCULATION OF EXCESS/SHORT DEPRECIATION ON MACHINE II & III

A.	Depreciation already provided on SLM basis @ 10% p.a	
	Machine II (₹ 500 + ₹ 1,000)	₹ 1,500
	Machine III	₹ 1,250
		₹ 2,750
B.	Depreciation which should have been provided on WDV basis @ 15% p.a.	
	Machine II [10,000 – (10,000 × .925 × .85)]	2,138
	Machine III [25,000 – (25,000 × .925)]	1,875
		4,013
C.	Short Depreciation still to be adjusted (A – B) = ₹ 4,013 – ₹ 2750 = ₹ 1,263	

PROBLEM 14

Green Channel Co. purchased a second-hand machine on 1st January, 2012 for ₹ 1,60,000. Overhauling and erection charges amounted to ₹ 40,000. Another machine was purchased for ₹ 80,000 on 1st July, 2012.

On 1st July, 2014, the machine installed on 1st January, 2012 was sold for ₹ 1,00,000. On the same date another machine was purchased for ₹ 30,000 and was installed on 30th September, 2014.

Under the existing practice the company provides depreciation @ 10% p.a. on original cost. However, from the year 2015 it decided to adopt WDV method and to charge depreciation @ 15% p.a. This change was to be made with retrospective effect.

Prepare Machinery Account in the book of Green Channel Co. for the year 2012 to 2015.

SOLUTION

Dr. **MACHINERY ACCOUNT** **Cr.**

Date	Particulars	₹	Date	Particulars	₹
01.01.2012	To Bank A/c	1,60,000	31.12.2012	By Depreciation A/c (₹ 20,000 + ₹ 4,000)	24,000
01.01.2012	To Bank A/c (Erection charges)	40,000			
01.07.2012	To Bank A/c	80,000	31.12.2012	By Balance c/d (₹. 1,80,000 + ₹ 76,000)	2,56,000
		2,80,000			2,80,000
01.01.2013	To Balance b/d	2,56,000	31.12.2013	By Depreciation A/c (₹ 20,000 + ₹ 8,000)	28,000
			31.12.2013	By Balance c/d (₹ 1,60,000 + ₹ 68,000)	2,28,000
		2,56,000			2,56,000
01.01.2014	To Balance b/d	2,28,000	01.07.2014	By Bank A/c	1,00,000
30.9.2014	To Bank A/c	30,000		By Profit and Loss A/c (Loss on Sale)	50,000
			31.12.2014	By Depreciation A/c (₹ 10,000 + ₹ 8,000 + ₹ 750)	18,750
				By Balance c/d (₹ 60,000 + ₹ 29,250)	89,250
		2,58,000			2,58,000
01.01.2015	To Balance b/d	89,250	31.12.2015	By Profit and Loss A/c	6,910
				By Depreciation A/c (₹ 8,019.75 + ₹ 4,331.25)	12,351
				By Balance c/d (₹ 45,445.25 + ₹ 24,543.75)	69,989
		89,250			89,250

Working Notes:

1. CALCULATION OF SLM DEPRECIATION AND LOSS ON SALE OF MACHINE

Particulars	Machine I ₹	Machine II ₹	Machine III ₹
A. Cost	2,00,000	80,000	30,000
B. Depreciation for 2012	20,000	4,000	
C. Written down value as on 31.12.2012	1,80,000	76,000	
D. Depreciation for 2013	20,000	8,000	
E. Written down value as on 31.12.2013	1,60,000	68,000	
F. Depreciation for 2014	10,000	8,000	750
G. Written down value as on 31.12.2014	1,50,000	60,000	29,250

H. Sale Proceeds	1,00,000		
I. Loss on sale	50,000		

2. CALCULATION OF DEPRECIATION OF MACHINES UNDER WDV METHOD

Particulars	Machine II ₹	Machine III ₹
Cost	80,000	30,000
Depreciation		
2012	6,000	
2013	11,100	
2014	9,435	1,125
Total depreciation	26,535	1,125

3. RETROSPECITVE EFFECT OF CHANGE IN DEPRECIATION METHOD FOR MACHINES II AND III

Particulars	₹
A. Depreciation under WDV (₹ 26,535 + ₹ 1,125)	27,660
B. Depreciation under SLM (₹ 20,000 + ₹ 750)	20,750
C. Short depreciation to be charged to Profit & Loss A/c	6,910

PROBLEM 15

X Ltd. purchased on 1st January, 2012 certain machinery for ₹ 1,94,000 and spent ₹ 6,000 on its erection. On 1st July, 2012 additional machinery costing ₹ 1,00,000 was purchased. On 1st July, 2014 the machinery purchased on 1st January, 2012 having become obsolete was auctioned for ₹ 1,00,000 and on the same date, new machinery was purchased at a cost of ₹ 1,50,000. Depreciation was provided for annually on 31st December at the rate of 10% per annum on the original cost of the machinery. No depreciation need be provided when a machinery is sold or auctioned, for that part of the year in which sale or auction took place. In 2015 however, X Ltd. changed this method of providing depreciation and adopted the method of writing off 15% p.a. on the written down value on the balance as appeared in machinery account on 1-1-2015.

Required: Show the machinery account for the calender years 2012 to 2015.

SOLUTION

Dr. **MACHINERY ACCOUNT** **Cr.**

Date	Particulars	₹	Date	Particulars	₹
01.01.2012	To Bank A/c: Machine I	1,94,000	31.12.2012	By Depreciation A/c:	
01.01.2012	To Bank A/c (expenses)	6,000		on Machine I 20,000 on Machine II 5,000	25,000
01.07.2012	To Bank A/c: Machine II	1,00,000	31.12.2012	By Balance c/d: Machine I 1,80,000 Machine II 95,000	2,75,000
		3,00,000			3,00,000

01.01.2013	To Balance b/d: Machine I 1,80,000 Machine II 95,000	2,75,000	31.12.2013	By Depreciation A/c: on Machine I 20,000 on Machine II 10,000	30,000
			31.12.2013	By Balance c/d: Machine I 1,60,000 Machine II 85,000	2,45,000
		2,75,000			2,75,000
01.01.2014	To Balance b/d: Machine I 1,60,000 Machine II 85,000	2,45,000	01.07.2014	By Bank A/c	1,00,000
			01.07.2014	By Profit & Loss A/c [1,60,000 – 1,00,000]	60,000
01.07.2014	To Bank A/c (Machine III)	1,50,000	31.12.2014	By Depreciation A/c: on Machine II 10,000 on Machine III 7,500	17,500
				By Balance c/d: Machine II 75,000 Machine III 1,42,500	2,17,500
		3,95,000			3,95,000
01.01.2015	To Balance b/d: Machine II 75,000 Machine III 1,42,500	2,17,500	31.12.2015	By Profit & Loss A/c	11,919
			31.12.2015	By Depreciation A/c on Machine II10,024 on Machine III20,812	30,836
			31.12.2015	By Balance c/d: Machine II 56,807 Machine III 1,17,938	1,74,745
		2,17,500			2,17,500

Working Note:

CALCULATION OF EXCESS/SHORT DEPRECIATION ON MACHINE II & III

Particulars	Machine II	Machine III	Total
A. Depreciation on SLM Basis @ 10%			
1,00,000 × 10/100 × 2.5	25,000		25,000
1,50,000 × 10/100 × 0.5		7,500	7,500
	25,000	7,500	32,500
B. Depreciation on WDV basis @15%			
for 2012	7,500	–	7,500
for 2013	13,875	–	13,875
for 2014	11,794	11,250	23,044
	33,169	11,250	44,419
C. Short Depreciation still to be adjusted [A – B]			11,919

PROBLEM 16

X Ltd. purchased on January 1, 2011 a second hand plant for ₹ 60,000 and immediately spent ₹ 40,000 in putting the same in working condition. On July 1, 2011 additional machinery costing ₹ 40,000 was purchased. On January 1, 2013 the plant purchased on January 1, 2011 became obsolete and was sold for ₹ 50,000. On July 1, 2013 new machinery was purchased at a cost of ₹ 1,20,000. The firm provided depreciation on straight line method at 10% per annum on the original cost of the asset. In 2015, the company decided to provide depreciation on written down value basis at 15% p.a. Show Machinery Account for the calendar years 2011 to 2015.

SOLUTION

Dr. **PLANT AND MACHINERY ACCOUNT** **Cr.**

Date	Particulars	₹	Date	Particulars	₹
01.01.2011	To Bank A/c (Cost)	60,000	31.12.2011	By Depreciation A/c:	
01.01.2011	To Bank A/c (Overhaul)	40,000		Machine I 10,000 Machine II 2,000	12,000
01.07.2011	To Bank A/c (Machine II)	40,000		By Balance c/d: Machine I 90,000 Machine II 38,000	1,28,000
		1,40,000			1,40,000
01.01.2012	To Balance b/d: Machine I 90,000 Machine II 38,000	1,28,000	31.12.2012	By Depreciation A/c: Machine I 10,000 Machine II 4,000	14,000
				By Balance c/d: Machine I 80,000 Machine II 34,000	1,14,000
		1,28,000			1,28,000
01.01.2013	To Balance b/d: Machine I 80,000 Machine II 34,000	1,14,000	01.01.2013	By Bank A/c (Sale Proceeds)	50,000
01.07.2013	To Bank A/c (Machine III)	1,20,000		By P & L A/c (Loss on Sale) [₹ 80,000 – ₹ 50,000]	30,000
			31.12.2013	By Depreciation A/c: Machine II 4,000 Machine III 6,000	10,000
				By Balance c/d Machine II 30,000 Machine III 1,14,000	1,44,000
		2,34,000			2,34,000
01.01.2014	To Balance b/d: Machine II 30,000 Machine III 1,14,000	1,44,000	31.12.2014	By Depreciation A/c: Machine II 4,000 Machine III 12,000	16,000
				By Balance c/d: Machine II 26,000 Machine III 1,02,000	1,28,000
		1,44,000			1,44,000
01.01.2015	To Balance b/d: Machine II 26,000 Machine III 1,02,000	1,28,000	31.12.2015	By Profit & Loss A/c [Short Depreciation]	10,928

			31.12.2015	By Depreciation A/c: Machine II 3,408 Machine III 14,153	17,561
				By Balance c/d: Machine II 19,314 Machine III 80,197	99,511
		1,28,000			1,28,000

Working Notes:

1. CALCULATION OF EXCESS/SHORT DEPRECIATION ON MACHINE II AND III

Particulars	Machine II	Machine III	Total
A Depreciation on SLM basis @ 10% p.a			
40,000 × 10/100 × 3.5	14,000	—	14,000
1,20,000 × 10/100 × 1.5		18,000	18,000
	14,000	18,000	32,000
B Depreciation on WDV basis @ 15% p.a.			
for 2011	3,000	—	3,000
for 2012	5,550	—	5,550
for 2013	4,718	9,000	13,718
for 2014	4,010	16,650	20,660
	17,278	25,650	42,928
C Short Depreciation still to be adjusted (A – B)			10,928

2. CALCULATION OF DEPRECIATION ON MACHINE II AND III FOR CURRENT YEAR

Particulars	Machine II	Machine III
A Cost	40,000	1,20,000
B *Less:* Depreciation [as per WN (i)]	17,278	25,650
C WDV on 1.1.2015	22,722	94,350
D *Less:* Depreciation for 2015 @ 15% p.a.	3,408	14,153
E WDV as on 31.12.2015	19,314	80,197

PROBLEM 17

Hanuman Enterprises purchased on 1.4.2012 certain machinery for ₹ 72,800 and paid ₹ 2,200 on its installation. On 1.10.2012 another machinery for ₹ 25,000 was acquired. On 1.4.2013, the first machinery was sold at ₹ 50,000 and on the same date a fresh machinery was purchased at a cost of ₹ 45,000. Depreciation was annually provided on 31st March at 10% p.a. on written down value. On 1.4.2014, however, the firm decided to change the method of providing depreciation and adopted the method of providing depreciation @ 10% p.a. on the original cost, with retrospective effect.

Required: Ascertain the value of machinery as on 31.3.2015.

SOLUTION

Dr. **MACHINERY ACCOUNT** **Cr.**

Date	Particulars	₹	Date	Particulars	₹
01.04.2012	To Bank A/c: Machine I	72,800	31.03.2013	By Depreciation A/c:	
	To Bank A/c (Installation Charges)	2,200		Machine I 7,500 Machine II 1,250	8,750
01.12.2012	To Bank A/c (Machine II)	25,000		By Balance c/d: Machine I 67,500 Machine II 23,750	91,250
		1,00,000			1,00,000
01.04.2013	To Balance b/d: Machine I 67,500 Machine II 23,750	91,250	01.04.2013	By Bank A/c	50,000
				By P & L A/c (loss on sale)	17,500
	To Bank A/c (Machine III)	45,000	31.03.2014	By Depreciation A/c: Machine II 2,375 Machine III 4,500	6,875
				By Balance c/d: Machine II 21,375 Machine III 40,500	61,875
		1,36,250			1,36,250
01.04.2014	To Balance b/d: Machine II 21,375 Machine III 40,500	61,875	01.04.2014	By P & L A/c [Short Depreciation provided in earlier years written-off]	125
			31.03.2015	By Depreciation A/c Machine II [10% on 25,000] 2,500 Machine III [10% on 45,000] 4,500	7,000
				By Balance c/d: Machine II 18,750 Machine III 36,000	54,750
		61,875			61,875

Working Note:

CALCULATION OF EXCESS/SHORT DEPRECIATION ON MACHINE II & III

Particulars	Machine II	Machine III	Total
A Depreciation on WDV basis @10%			
for 2012—2013	1,250	—	1,250
for 2013—2014	2,375	4,500	6,875
	3,625	4,500	8,125
B Depreciation on SLM basis @ 10%			
25,000 × 10/100 × 1.5 years	3,750	—	3,750

45,000 × 10 × 100 × 1 year	—	4,500	4,500
	3,750	4,500	8,250
C Short Depreciation to be written off [A – B]			125

PROBLEM 18

A firm purchased, on 1st January, 2011, certain machinery for ₹ 19,40,000 and spent ₹ 60,000 on its erection. On 1st July in the same year additional machinery costing ₹ 10,00,000 was acquired. On 1st July, 2013 the machinery purchased on 1st January, 2011 having become obsolete was auctioned for ₹ 8,00,000 and on the same date fresh machine was purchased at a cost of ₹ 15,00,000.

Depreciation was provided for annually 2014 on 31st December at the rate of 10% per annum on the original cost of the asset. In 2014 however, the firm changed this method of providing depreciation and adopted the method of writing off 20% on the written down value.

Required: Give the Machinery Account as it would stand at the end of each year from 2011 to 2015.

SOLUTION

Dr. **MACHINERY ACCOUNT** **Cr.**

Date	Particulars	₹	Date	Particulars	₹
01.01.2011	To Bank A/c (Cost of new machinery)	19,40,000	31.12.2011	By Depreciation A/c (₹2,00,000 + ₹50,000)	2,50,000
	To Bank A/c (Erection charges)	60,000	31.12.2011	By Balance c/d (₹18,00,000 + ₹9,50,000)	27,50,000
01.07.2011	To Bank A/c (Cost of new machinery)	10,00,000			
		30,00,000			30,00,000
1.1.2012	To Balance b/d	27,50,000	31.12.2012	By Depreciation A/c (₹2,00,000 + ₹1,00,000)	3,00,000
				By Balance c/d	24,50,000
		27,50,000			27,50,000
1.1.2013	To Balance b/d	24,50,000	1.7.2013	By Bank A/c	8,00,000
1.7.2013	To Bank A/c	15,00,000	31.12.2013	By Profit and Loss A/c (Loss on sale)	7,00,000
				By Depreciation (₹ 1,00,000 + ₹ 1,00,000 + ₹ 75,000)	2,75,000
				By Balance c/d (₹ 7,50,000 + 14,25,000)	21,75,000
		39,50,000			39,50,000
1.1.2014	To Balance b/d	21,75,000	31.12.2014	By Depreciation A/c (₹ 1,50,000 + ₹ 2,85,000)	4,35,000

				By Balance c/d (₹ 6,00,000 + ₹ 11,40,000)	17,40,000
		21,75,000			21,75,000
1.1.2015	To Balance b/d	17,40,000	31.12.2015	By Depreciation A/c (₹ 1,20,000 + ₹ 2,28,000)	3,48,000
				By Balance c/d (₹ 4,80,000 + ₹ 9,12,000)	13,92,000
		17,40,000			17,40,000

Working Note: Loss on sale = (₹ 20,00,000 – ₹ 5,00,000) – ₹ 8,00,000 = ₹ 7,00,000

CHANGE IN METHOD OF DEPRECIATION WHEN PROVISION FOR DEPRECIATION ACCOUNT IS MAINTAINED

PROBLEM 19

ABC Ltd. purchased on 1st Jan., 2012 second hand plant for ₹ 30,000 and immediately spent ₹ 20,000 in overhauling it. On Ist July, 2012 additional machinery of a cost of Its. 25,000 was purchased. On 1st July 2014, the plant purchased on 1st Jan., 2012 became obsolete and was sold for ₹ 10,000. On that date new machinery was purchased at cost of ₹ 60,000.

Depreciation was provided at 10% per annum on the original cost of the asset. In 2015 the company changed this method of providing depreciation to 15% per annum W. D. V. with retrospective effect.

Required: Show Plant and Machinery A/c, Provision for Depreciation A/c and Machine Disposal Account for the years 2012-2015.

SOLUTION

Dr. **MACHINERY ACCOUNT** **Cr.**

Date	Particulars	₹	Date	Particulars	₹
1.1.2012	To Bank A/c-I	30,000	31.12.2012	By Balance c/d	75,000
1.1.2012	To Bank A/c	20,000			
1.7.2012	To Bank A/c-II	25,000			
		75,000			75,000
1.1.2013	To Balance b/d	75,000	31.12.2013	By Balance c/d	75,000
1.1.2014	To Balance b/d	75,000	01.07.2014	By Machine Disposal A/c	50,000
1.6.2014	To Bank A/c-III	60,000	31.12.2014	By Balance c/d	85,000
		1,35,000			1,35,000
1.1.2015	By Balance b/d	85,000	31.12.2015	By Balance c/d	85,000

Dr. **PROVISION FOR DEPRECIATION ACCOUNT** Cr.

Date	Particulars	₹	Date	Particulars		₹
31.12.2012	To Balance c/d	6,250	31.12.2012	By Depreciation A/c: I II (6 months)	 5,000 1,250	6,250
		6,250				6,250
31.12.2013	To Balance c/d	13,750	01.01.2013	By Balance b/d: I II	 5,000 2,500	7,500
		13,750				13,750
01.07.2014	To Machine Disposal A/c	10,000	01.01.2014	By Balance b/d		13,750
	To Balance c/d	9,250	31.12.2014	By Depreciation II (for 6 months) III	 2,500 3,000	5,500
		19,250				19,250
31.12.2015	To Balance c/d	23,623	01.01.2015	By Balance b/d		
			31.12.2015	By Profit & Loss A/c (Additional Depreciation)		
			31.12.2015	By Depreciation A/c: Machine II Machine II	 2,506 8,325	10,831
		23,623				23,623

Dr. **MACHINE DISPOSAL ACCOUNT** Cr.

Date	Particulars	₹	Date	Particulars	₹
01.07.2014	To Machine A/c	50,000	01.07.2014	By Provision for Depreciation	10,000
				By Depreciation (for 6 months)	2,500
				By Bank A/c	10,000
				By Profit and Loss A/c Loss (Balancing figure)	27,500
		50,000			50,000

Working Notes:

1. CALCULATION OF EFFECT DUE TO CHANGE OF METHOD

Old Method	New 10% SLM	Method 15% WDV
Depreciation for 2012		
Machine II	1,250	1,875

Depreciation for 2013		
Machine II	2.500	3,469
Depreciation for 2014		
Machine II	2,500	2,498
Machine III	3,000	4,500
	9,250	12,792

Depreciation to bo provided = 3,542

2. *Depreciation for current year as per New Method*

Machine II (25,000 – 1,875 – 3,469 – 2948) × 15/100 = 2,506

Machine III (60,000 – 4,500) × = 8,325

PROBLEM 20

M/s. S.S. Traders commenced business on 1st January, 2012, when they purchased machinery of ₹ 7,00,000. They adopted a policy of (i) charging depreciation at 15% per annum on diminishing balance basis, and (ii) charging full year's depreciation on additions made during the year. Over the years, the purchases of Machinery have been:

Date	₹
1-8-2013	1,50,000
30-9-2015	2,00,000

On 1st January, 2015, it was decided to change the method of depreciation and rate of depreciation to 10% on straight line basis with retrospective effect from 1-1-2012, the adjustment being made in the accounts for the year ending 31st December, 2015.

Required: Prepare Machinery Account and Provision for Depreciation Account for the year 2015.

SOLUTION

Dr. **PLANT AND MACHINERY ACCOUNT** **Cr.**

Date	Particulars	₹	Date	Particulars	₹
1.1.2015	To Balance b/d	8,50,000	31.12.2015	By Balance c/d	10,50,000
30.9.2015	To Bank A/c	2,00,000			
		10,50,000			10,50,000

Dr. **PROVISION FOR DEPRECIATION ACCOUNT** **Cr.**

Date	Particulars	₹	Date	Particulars	₹
1.1.2015	To Profit and Loss A/c (Additional Depreciation written back)	71,738	01.01.2015	By Balance b/d	3,11,738
			31.12.2015	By Deprecation A/c	1,05,000
	To Balance c/d	3,45,000			
		4,16,738			4,16,738

Working Notes:

Dr. **(I) PLANT AND MACHINERY ACCOUNT** Cr.

Date	Particulars	₹	Date	Particulars	₹
1.1.2012	To Bank A/c	7,00,000	31.12.2012	By Balance c/d	7,00,000
1.1.2013	To Balance b/d	7,00,000	31.12.2013	By Balance c/d	8,50,000
1.8.2013	To Bank A/c	1,50,000			
		8,50,000			8,50,000
1.1.2014	To Balance b/d	8,50,000	31.12.2014	By Balance c/d	8,50,000

Dr. **(II) PROVISION FOR DEPRECIATION ACCOUNT** Cr.

Date	Particulars	₹	Date	Particulars	₹
31.12.2012	To Balance c/d	1,05,000	31.12.2012	By Depreciation A/c	1,05,000
31.12.2013	To Balance c/d	2,16,750	01.01.2013	By Balance b/d	1,05,000
				By Depreciation A/c	1,11,750
		2,16,750			2,16,750
31.12.2014	To Balance c/d	3,11,738	1.1.2014	By Balance b/d	2,16,750
				By Depreciation A/c	94,988
		3,11,738			3,11,738

(III) CALCULATION OF SHORT/EXCESS DEPRECIATION

Particulars	15%WDV Old Method	10%SLM New Method
On Machine I ₹. 7,00,000		
for 2012	1,05,000	70,000
for 2013	89,250	70,000
for 2014	75,863	70,000
	2,70,113	2,10,000
On Machine- II ₹. 1.50,000		
for 2013	22,500	15,000
for 2014	19,125	15,000
	41,625	30,000
Total Depreciation:	3,11,738	2,40,000

Difference = ₹ 3,11,738 – ₹ 2,40,000 = ₹ 71,738

SINKING FUND METHOD

PROBLEM 21

Tulsian Ltd. purchased a machinery for ₹ 9,00,000 on 1 April 2011 and incurred ₹ 1,00,000 towards freight, insurance, carriage inwards and installation charges. It was estimated that the machinery will have a scrap value of ₹ 71,800 at the end of its useful life which is 4 years. It was decided to institute a sinking fund for the purpose of accumulating sufficient funds to replace the machinery at the end of its useful life and to invest in some readily convertible securities yielding 10% interest p.a. Reference to the table shows that ₹ 1 p.a. at 10% compound interest amounts to ₹ 4.641 in 4 years. Investments are to be made in the bonds of ₹ 100 each available at par. On 31 March 2015, the investments realised ₹ 6,80,000 and scrap value of machinery realised ₹ 73,800 only. A new machine costing ₹ 10,00,000 was purchased on 31.3.2015.

Required: Prepare the journal and the necessary ledger accounts in the books of Tulsian Ltd. for 4 years.

SOLUTION

JOURNAL OF TULSIAN LTD.

Date	Particulars	L.F.	Dr. (₹)	Cr. (₹)
01.04.2011	Machinery Dr. To Bank A/c (Being the Machinery purchased)		9,00,000	9,00,000
01.04.2011	Machinery Dr. To Bank A/c (Being the expenses incurred towards freight, insurance, carriage inwards and installation charges)		1,00,000	1,00,000
31.03.2012	Depreciation A/c Dr. To Depreciation Fund A/c (Being the depreciation provided)		2,00,000	2,00,000
	Profit and Loss A/c Dr. To Depreciation A/c (Being the closure of Depreciation A/c)		2,00,000	2,00,000
	Depreciation Fund Investment A/c Dr. To Bank A/c (Being the investments made in the multiples of ₹ 100)		2,00,000	2,00,000
31.03.2013	Bank A/c Dr. To Interest on DFI A/c (Being the receipt of interest on DFI)		20,000	20,000
	Interest on DFI A/c Dr. To Depreciation Fund A/c (Being the transfer of Interest on DFI to DF A/c)		20,000	20,000
	Depreciation A/c Dr. To Depreciation Fund A/c (Being the depreciation provided)		2,00,000	2,00,000
	Depreciation Fund Investments A/c Dr. To Bank A/c (Being the Investment made in the multiples of ₹ 100)		2,20,000	2,20,000
	Profit and Loss A/c Dr. To Depreciation A/c (Being the closure of Depreciation A/c)		2,00,000	2,00,000

31.03.2014	Bank A/c Dr. To Interest on DFI A/c (Being the receipt of interest on DFI)		42,000	42,000
	Interest on DFI A/c Dr. To Depreciation Fund A/c (Being the transfer of Interest on DFI to DF A/c)		42,000	42,000
	Depreciation A/c Dr. To Depreciation Fund A/c (Being the depreciation provided)		2,00,000	2,00,000
	Profit and Loss A/c Dr. To Depreciation A/c (Being the closure of Depreciation A/c)		2,00,000	2,00,000
	Depreciation Fund Investment A/c Dr. To Bank A/c (Being the investments made in the multiples of ₹ 100)		2,42,000	2,42,000
31.03.2015	Bank A/c Dr. To Interest on DFI A/c (Being the receipt of interest on DFI)		66,200	66,200
	Interest on DFI A/c Dr. To Depreciation Fund A/c (Being the transfer of Interest on DFI to DF A/c)		66,200	66,200
	Depreciation A/c Dr. To Depreciation Fund A/c (Being the depreciation provided)		2,00,000	2,00,000
	Profit and Loss A/c Dr. To Deprecation A/c (Being the closure of Depreciation A/c)		2,00,000	2,00,000
	Bank A/c Dr. To Depreciation Fund Investment A/c (Being the realisation of Investments)		6,80,000	6,80,000
	Depreciation Fund Investment A/c Dr. To Depreciation Fund A/c (Being the transfer of profit on sale of Investments)		18,000	18,000
	Debenture Redemption Fund A/c Dr. To Machinery A/c (Being the transfer of the balance in DF A/c to Asset Account)		9,46,200	9,46,200
	Bank A/c Dr. To Machinery A/c (Being the machinery sold)		73,800	73,800
	Machinery A/c Dr. To Profit and Loss A/c (Being the transfer of Profit on sale of machinery)		20,000	20,000

LEDGER ACCOUNTS

MACHINERY ACCOUNT

Dr. Cr.

Date	Particulars	₹	Date	Particulars	₹
01.04.2011	To Bank A/c	9,00,000	31.03.2012	By Balance c/d	10,00,000
01.04.2011	To Bank A/c (freight etc.)	1,00,000			
		10,00,000			10,00,000
01.04.2012	To Balance b/d	10,00,000	31.03.2012	By Balance c/d	10,00,000
01.04.2013	To Balance b/d	10,00,000	31.03.2014	By Balance c/d	10,00,000
01.04.2014	To Balance c/d	10,00,000	31.03.2015	By Depreciation Fund A/c	9,46,200
31.03.2015	To Profit and Loss A/c (Profit)	20,000		By Bank A/c (scrap realised)	73,800
		10,20,000			10,20,000

DEPRECIATION FUND ACCOUNT

Dr. Cr.

Date	Particulars	₹	Date	Particulars	₹
31.03.2012	To Balance c/d	2,00,000	31.03.2012	By Depreciation A/c	2,00,000
31.03.2013	To Balance c/d	4,20,000	01.04.2012	By Balance b/d	2,00,000
			31.03.2013	By Interest on DFI A/c	20,000
				By Depreciation A/c	2,00,000
		4,20,000			4,20,000
31.03.2014	To Balance c/d	6,62,000	01.04.2013	By Balance c/d	4,20,000
			31.03.2014	By Interest on DFI A/c	42,000
				By Depreciation A/c	1,00,000
		6,62,000			6,62,000
31.03.2015	To Machinery A/c (transfer)	9,46,200	01.04.2014	By Balance b/d	6,62,000
			31.03.2015	By Interest on DFI A/c	66,200
				By Depreciation A/c	2,00,000
				By Depreciation Fund Investment A/c (Profit)	18,000
		9,46,200			9,46,200

DEPRECIATION FUND INVESTMENT (DFI) ACCOUNT

Dr. Cr.

Date	Particulars	₹	Date	Particulars	₹
31.03.2012	To Bank A/c	2,00,000	31.03.2012	By Balance c/d	2,00,000
01.04.2012	To Balance b/d	2,00,000	31.03.2013	By Balance c/d	4,20,000
31.03.2013	To Bank A/c	2,20,000			
		4,20,000			4,20,000
01.04.2013	To Balance b/d	4,20,000	31.03.2014	By Balance c/d	6,62,000
31.03.2014	To Bank A/c	2,42,000			
		6,62,000			6,62,000

01.04.2014	To Balance b/d	6,62,000	31.03.2015	By Bank A/c (Sales)	6,80,000
31.03.2015	To Depreciation Fund A/c (Profit)	18,000			
		6,80,000			6,80,000

Dr. **NEW MACHINERY ACCOUNT** **Cr.**

Date	Particulars	₹	Date	Particulars	₹
31.03.2015	To Bank A/c	10,00,000	31.03.2015	By Balance c/d	10,00,000

Working Notes:

1. CALCULATION OF THE AMOUNT TO BE CHARGED TO PROFIT AND LOSS ACCOUNT

Particulars	₹
A. Original Cost	9,00,000
B. *Add:* Capital Expenditure	1,00,000
C. *Less:* Estimated scrap value	71,800
D. Depreciate Cost (A + B – C)	9,28,200
E. Value of annuity per ₹ 1	4,641
F. Annual amount to be charged (D/E)	2,00,000

2. CALCULATION OF THE AMOUNT OF INVESTMENTS AND INTEREST

Year	Opening Balance B	Interest C = B × 10/100	Savings D	Investments E	Closing Balance F = B + E
2011-2012	—	—	2,00,000	2,00,000	2,00,000
2012-2013	2,00,000	20,000	2,00,000	2,20,000	4,20,000
2013-2014	4,20,000	42,000	2,00,000	2,42,000	6,62,000
2014-2015	6,61,000	66,200	2,00,000	—	—

ANNUITY METHOD

PROBLEM 22

A lease is purchased on 1st April, 2011 for 4 years at a cost of ₹ 40,000. It is proposed to depreciate the lease by the annuity method charging interest @ 5% p.a. A reference to the annuity table shows that to depreciate ₹ 1 by annuity method over 4 years charging interest at 5% p.a. one must write off a sum of ₹ 0.2820. Show the Lease Account for four years and also the relevant entries in the Profit and Loss Account.

SOLUTION

Dr. **LEASE ACCOUNT** **Cr.**

Date	Particulars	₹	Date	Particulars	₹
01.04.2011	To Bank A/c	40,000	31.03.2012	By Balance c/d	30,720

31.03.2012	To Interest A/c (5% on ₹ 40,000)	2,000		By Depreciation A/c (₹ 40,000 × .2820)	11,280
		42,000			21,000
01.01.2012	To Balance b/d	30,720	31.03.2013	By Depreciation A/c	11,280
31.03.2013	To Interest A/c (5% on ₹ 30,720)	1,536		By Balance b/d	20,976
		32,256			32,256
01.01.2013	To Balance b/d	20,976	31.03.2014	By Depreciation A/c	11,280
31.03.2014	To Interest A/c (5% on ₹ 10,488)	1,048		By Balance c/d	10,744
		22,024			22,024
01.01.2014	To Balance b/d	10,744	31.03.2015	By Depreciation A/c	11,280
31.03.2015	To Interest A/c (5% on ₹ 10,744)	536			
		11,280			11,280

Dr. **AN EXTRACT OF PROFIT AND LOSS ACCOUNT** **Cr.**

Date	Particulars	₹	Date	Particulars	₹
31.03.2012	To Depreciation A/c	11,280	31.03.2012	By Interest A/c	2,000
31.03.2013	To Depreciation A/c	11,280	31.03.2013	By Interest A/c	1,536
31.03.2014	To Depreciation A/c	11,280	31.03.2014	By Interest A/c	1,048
31.03.2015	To Depreciation A/c	11,280	31.03.2015	By Interest A/c	536

PROBLEM 23

Taking the same information as given in previous problem along with the fact that ₹ 4,000 would also be refunded after 4 years, show the Lease Account.

SOLUTION

CALCULATION OF ANNUAL DEPRECIATION CHARGE

A Cost of Lease paid	₹	40,000
B *Less:* Refundable amount	₹	4,000
C Depreciable amount (A – B)	₹	36,000
D Annuity Factor @ 5% interest for 4 years	₹	0.2820
E Fixed Depreciation Charge (C × D)	₹	10,142
F Interest on Salvage @ 5% on ₹ 2,000 for a year	₹	200
G Annual Depreciation Charge (E + F)	₹	10,352

Dr. **LEASE ACCOUNT** **Cr.**

Date	Particulars	₹	Date	Particulars	₹
01.04.2011	To Bank A/c	40,000	31.03.2012	By Depreciation A/c	10,352
31.03.2012	To Interest A/c (5% on ₹ 40,000)	2,000		By Balance c/d	31,648
		42,000			42,000
01.04.2012	To Balance b/d	31,648	31.03.2013	By Depreciation A/c	10,352
31.03.2013	By Interest A/c (5% on ₹ 31,648)	1,582		By Balance c/d	22,878
		33,230			33,230
01.01.2013	To Balance b/d	22,878	31.03.2014	By Depreciation A/c	10,352
31.03.2014	To Interest A/c (5% on ₹ 22,878)	1,144		By Balance c/d	13,670
		24,022			24,022
01.01.2014	To Balance b/d	13,670	31.03.2015	By Depreciation A/c	10,354
31.03.2015	To Interest A/c (5% on ₹ 6,835)	684		By Bank A/c	4,000
		14,354			14,354

PROBLEM 24

A lease was purchased on 1.4.2011 for five years at a cost of ₹ 1,00,000. It is proposed to depreciate the lease by annuity method charging interest at 5% p.a. The reference to the annuity table shows that to depreciate ₹ 1 by annuity method over 5 years by charging interest @ 5% p.a. one must write off a sum of ₹ 0.230975 every year. Show the Lease Account for 5 financial years and also the relevant entries in the Profit and Loss Account.

SOLUTION

Dr. **LEASE ACCOUNT** **Cr.**

Date	Particulars	₹	Date	Particulars	₹
01.04.2011	To Bank A/c	1,00,000.00	31.03.2012	By Depreciation A/c	23,097.50
31.03.2012	To Interest A/c (5% on ₹ 1,00,000)	5,000.00	31.03.2012	By Balance c/d	81,902.50
		1,05,000.00			1,05,000.00
01.04.2012	To Balance b/d	81,902.50	31.03.2013	By Depreciation A/c	23,097.50
31.03.2013	To Interest A/c	4,095.12	31.03.2013	By Balance c/d	62,900.12
		85,997.62			85,997.62
01.04.2013	To Balance b/d	62,900.12	31.03.2014	By Depreciation A/c	23,097.50
31.03.2014	To Interest A/c	3,145.00	31.03.2014	By Balance c/d	42,947.62
		66,045.12			66,045.12
01.04.2014	To Balance b/d	42,947.62	31.03.2015	By Depreciation A/c	23,097.50
31.03.2015	To Interest A/c	2,147.38	31.03.2015	By Balance c/d	21,997.50
		45,095.00			45,095.00

01.04.2015 31.03.2016	To Balance b/d To Interest A/c	21,997.50 1,100.00	31.03.2016	By Depreciation A/c	23,097.50
		23,097.50			23,097.50

Dr. **AN EXTRACT OF PROFIT AND LOSS ACCOUNT** **Cr.**

Date	Particulars	₹	Date	Particulars	₹
31.03.2012	To Depreciation A/c	23,097.50	31.03.2012	By Interest A/c	5,000.00
31.03.2013	To Depreciation A/c	23,097.50	31.03.2013	By Interest A/c	4,095.12
31.03.2014	To Depreciation A/c	23,097.50	31.03.2014	By Interest A/c	3,145.00
31.03.2015	To Depreciation A/c	23,097.50	31.03.2015	By Interest A/c	2,147.38
31.03.2016	To Depreciation A/c	23,097.50	31.03.2016	By Interest A/c	1,100.00

Working Note: Annual Depreciation = ₹ 0.230975 × ₹ 1,00,000 = ₹ 23,097.50

DEPLETION METHOD

PROBLEM 25

Tulsian Ltd. acquired a lease right for 10 years of a mine on 1.1.2011 on a lumpsum payment of ₹ 9,00,000 to the landlord. It was estimated by the expert that the coal deposit of the mine was 40,00,000 tonnes, 75% of which could be raised within time period allowed. Tulsian Ltd. decided to depreciate the lease on Depletion Method. The sales and stocks (in tonnes) were as under:

Year	2011	2012	2013	2014	2015	2016
Sales	30,000	62,000	1,96,000	4,02,000	4,02,000	3,98,000
Closing Stock	10,000	8,000	12,000	10,000	8,000	10,000

Required: Show the Lease Account from 1st Jan. 2011 to 31st Dec. 2016.

SOLUTION

Dr. **LEASE ACCOUNT** **Cr.**

Date	Particulars	₹	Date	Particulars	₹
01.01.2011	To Bank A/c	9,00,000	31.12.2011	By Depreciation A/c By Balance c/d	12,000 8,88,000
		9,00,000			9,00,000
01.01.2012	To Balance b/d	8,88,000	31.12.2012	By Depreciation A/c By Balance c/d	18,000 8,70,000
		8,88,000			8,88,000
01.01.2013	To Balance b/d	8,70,000	31.12.2013	By Depreciation A/c By Balance c/d	60,000 8,10,000
		8,70,000			8,70,000
01.01.2014	To Balance b/d	8,10,000	31.12.2014	By Depreciation A/c By Balance c/d	1,20,000 6,90,000
		8,10,000			8,10,000

01.01.2015	To Balance b/d	6,90,000	31.12.2015	By Depreciation A/c By Balance c/d	1,20,000 5,70,000
		6,90,000			6,90,000
01.01.2016	To Balance b/d	5,70,000	31.12.2016	By Depreciation A/c By Balance c/d	1,20,000 4,50,000
		5,70,000			5,70,000

Working Notes:

1. Depreciation per tonne = Total Cost/Total Expected Outputwithin Lease Period
   = ₹ 9,00,000/75% of 40,00,000 = ₹ 9,00,000/30,00,00
   = ₹ 0.30 per tonne
2. Annual raisings = Sales + Closing Stock – Opening Stock

MACHINE HOUR RATE METHOD

PROBLEM 26

Tulsian Ltd. purchased a machine for ₹ 2,20,000 on 1st January, 2011 and incurred ₹ 40,000 towards freight, insurance, carriage inwards and installation charges. It was estimated that the machinery will have a scrap value of ₹ 20,000 at the end of its useful life which is 10 years of 12,000 hours each. Tulsian Ltd. decided to depreciate the machines on 'Machine Hour Rate Method'. The machine hours during first six years were as under:

Year	2011	2012	2013	2014	2015	2016
Machine Hours	6,000	8,000	10,000	14,000	14,000	12,000

Show the Machinery Account from 1st January, 2011 to 31st December, 2016.

SOLUTION

Dr. **MACHINERY ACCOUNT** **Cr.**

Date	Particulars	₹	Date	Particulars	₹
01.01.2011	To Bank A/c To Bank A/c	2,20,000 40,000	31.12.2011	By Depreciation A/c By Balance c/d	12,000 2,48,000
		2,60,000			2,60,000
01.01.2012	To Balance b/d	2,48,000	31.12.2012	By Depreciation A/c By Balance c/d	16,000 2,32,000
		2,48,000			2,48,000
01.01.2013	To Balance b/d	2,32,000	31.12.2013	By Depreciation A/c By Balance c/d	20,000 2,12,000
		2,32,000			2,32,000
01.01.2014	To Balance b/d	2,12,000	31.12.2014	By Depreciation A/c By Balance c/d	28,000 1,84,000
		2,12,000			2,12,000

01.01.2015	To Balance b/d	1,84,000	31.12.2015	By Depreciation A/c By Balance c/d	28,000 1,56,000
		1,84,000			1,84,000
01.01.2016	To Balance b/d	1,56,000	31.12.2016	By Depreciation A/c By Balance c/d	24,000 1,32,000
		1,56,000			1,56,000

Working Note: *Calculation of Rate of depreciation per Machine Hour*

Machine Hour Rate = (Cost of Acquisition – Scrap Value)/Life of the asset (in Hours)

= ₹ 2,00,000 – ₹ 20,000/10 × 12,000 = ₹ 2 per hour

DOUBLE DECLINING METHOD

PROBLEM 27

On 1st April 2011, Tulsian Ltd. purchased a machinery for ₹ 2,00,000 and incurred ₹ 14,000 towards freight and insurance, ₹ 2,000 towards carriage inwards and ₹ 4,000 towards installation charges. It was established that the machinery will have a scrap value of ₹ 20,000 at the end of its useful life which is 4 years. On 1st April, 2014, ₹ 4,000 were incurred on repairs and renewals of machine.

Required: Determine (a) Rate of Depreciation, (b) Show the Machinery Account for the first four financial years ending on 31st March each year according to the Double Declining Method.

SOLUTION

(a) Rate of Depreciation 200%/n = 200%/4 = 50%

Dr. **MACHINERY ACCOUNT** **Cr.**

Date	Particulars	₹	Date	Particulars	₹
01.04.2011	To Bank A/c To Bank A/c To Bank A/c To Bank A/c	2,00,000 14,000 2,000 4,000	31.03.2012	By Depreciation A/c By Balance c/d	1,10,000 1,10,000
		2,20,000			2,20,000
01.04.2012	To Balance b/d	1,10,000	31.03.2013	By Depreciation A/c By Balance c/d	55,000 55,000
		1,10,000			1,10,000
01.04.2013	To Balance b/d	55,000	31.03.2014	By Depreciation A/c By Balance c/d	27,500 27,500
		55,000			55,000
01.04.2014	To Balance b/d	27,500	31.03.2015	By Depreciation A/c By Balance c/d	7,500 20,000
		27,500			27,500

Note: *Though apparently, the amount of depreciation @ 50% p.a. on ₹ 27,500 comes to ₹ 13,750 but only a sum of ₹ 7,500 has been provided for as depreciation since the value of the asset is not to be reduced below the scrap value of the asset (i.e. ₹ 20,000)*

SUM OF YEARS' DIGITS METHOD

PROBLEM 28

On 1st April 2011, Tulsian Ltd. purchased a machinery for ₹ 2,00,000 and incurred ₹ 14,000 towards freight and insurance, ₹ 2,000 towards carriage inwards and ₹ 4,000 towards instalation charges. It was established that the machinery will have a scrap value of ₹ 20,000 at the end of its useful life which is 4 years. On 1st April, 2014, ₹ 4,000 were incurred on repairs and renewals of machine.

Required: Determine (a) Rate of Depreciation, (b) Amount of Depreciation, (c) Show the Machinery Account for the first four financial years ending on 31st March each year according to the Sum of Years' Digits Method.

SOLUTION

(a) Rate of Depreciation = Number of Years Life Remaining/Sum of Years Digits × 100

Sum of Years' Digits = n (n + 1)/2 = 4 (4 + 1)/2 = 20/2 = 10

1st Year = 4/10 × 100 = 40%, 2nd Year = 3/10 × 100 = 30%

3rd Year = 2/10 × 100 = 20%, 4th Year = 1/10 × 100 = 10%

(b) Calculation of the Amount of Depreciation p.a.

= Number of Years Life Remaining/Sum of Years Digits × (Original Cost – Scrap Value)

Year	Rate	Original Cost less Scrap Value [₹1,00,000 + ₹ 7,000 + ₹ 1,000 + ₹ 2,000 – ₹ 10,000]	Amount of Depreciation ₹
2011	40%	2,00,000	40% of 2,00,000 = 80,000
2012	30%	2,00,000	30% of 2,00,000 = 60,000
2013	20%	2,00,000	20% of 2,00,000 = 40,000
2014	10%	2,00,000	10% of 2,00,000 = 20,000

Dr. **(C) MACHINERY ACCOUNT** **Cr.**

Date	Particulars	₹	Date	Particulars	₹
01.04.2011	To Bank A/c	2,00,000	31.03.2012	By Depreciation A/c	80,000
	To Bank A/c	14,000		By Balance c/d	1,40,000
	To Bank A/c	2,000			
	To Bank A/c	4,000			
		2,20,000			2,20,000
01.04.2012	To Balance b/d	1,40,000	31.03.2013	By Depreciation A/c	60,000
				By Balance c/d	80,000
		1,40,000			1,40,000
01.04.2013	To Balance b/d	80,000	31.03.2014	By Depreciation A/c	40,000
				By Balance c/d	40,000
		80,000			80,000
01.04.2014	To Balance b/d	40,000	31.03.2015	By Depreciation A/c	20,000
				By Balance c/d	20,000
		40,000			40,000

REVALUATION METHOD

PROBLEM 29

On 1st April, 2014, the value of loose tools was ₹ 20,000 and during the year ₹ 10,000 worth of tools were purchased and ₹ 2,000 realised by way of sale of scrapped loose tools. At the end of the year, the loose tools are considered to be worth only ₹ 12,000. Required: Calculate the amount to be charged to Profit & Loss Account.

SOLUTION

STATEMENT SHOWING THE AMOUNT TO BE CHARGED TO PROFIT AND LOSS ACCOUNT

	Particulars			₹
A	Opening Balance of Loose tools			20,000
B	*Add:* Purchased during the year			10,000
C	*Less:*	(a) Sale of scrapped Loose tools	2,000	
		(b) Closing Balance of Loose tools (at revalued figure)	12,000	14,000
D	Depreciation to be charged to Profit & Loss Account (A + B – C)			16,000

REPAIRS PROVISION METHOD

PROBLEM 30

Tulsian Ltd. purchased a machine for ₹ 1,20,000 on 1st April, 2011 and incurred ₹ 40,000 towards freight, insurance, carriage inward and installation charges. It was estimated that its life is 4 years during which period a sum of ₹ 60,000 is likely to be spent on its repairs and maintenance and at the end of useful life, the scrap value will be ₹ 20,000. Actual repairs were as under:

2011-2012—₹ Nil, 2012-2013—₹ 10,000, 2013-2014—₹ 20,000, 2014-2015—₹ 30,000

At the end of useful life, the scrap value of the machine realised ₹ 16,000 only.

Prepare Machinery Account, and Provision for Depreciation and Repairs Account.

SOLUTION

Dr. MACHINERY ACCOUNT Cr.

Date	Particulars	₹	Date	Particulars	₹
01.04.2011	To Bank A/c	1,20,000	31.03.2012	By Balance c/d	1,60,000
	To Bank A/c	40,000			
		1,60,000			1,60,000
01.04.2012	To Balance b/d	1,60,000	31.03.2013	By Balance c/d	1,60,000
01.04.2013	To Balance b/d	1,60,000	31.03.2014	By Balance c/d	1,60,000
01.04.2014	To Balance b/d	1,60,000	31.03.2015	By Provision for Depreciation and Repairs A/c	1,40,000
				By Bank A/c	16,000

				By P & L A/c (Loss)	4,000
		1,60,000			1,60,000

Dr. **PROVISION FOR DEPRECIATION AND REPAIRS ACCOUNT** Cr.

Date	Particulars	₹	Date	Particulars	₹
31.03.2012	To Balance c/d	50,000	31.03.2012	By P & L A/c	50,000
31.03.2013	To Repairs A/c	10,000	01.04.2012	By Balance b/d	50,000
	To Balance c/d	90,000	31.03.2013	By P & L A/c	50,000
		1,00,000			1,00,000
31.03.2014	To Repairs A/c	20,000	01.04.2013	By Balance b/d	90,000
	To Balance c/d	1,20,000	31.03.2014	By P & L A/c	50,000
		1,40,000			1,40,000
31.03.2015	To Repairs A/c	30,000	01.04.2014	By Balance b/d	1,20,000
	To Machinery A/c	1,40,000	31.03.2015	By P & L A/c	50,000
		1,70,000			1,70,000

Working Note: *Calculation of the annual amount to be provided for*

Annual Amount to be provided for

= (Original Cost – Residual Value) + Estimated Total Cost of Repairs/Expected Useful Life of the Asset

= ₹ 1,60,000 – ₹ 20,000) + ₹ 60,000/4 = ₹ 2,00,000/4 = ₹ 50,000

PROBLEM 31

The following particulars are available from the books of X Ltd. Provision for Repairs and Renewals as on 1.4.2013 ₹ 1,00,000. Actual repair charges incurred during 2013-2014—₹ 60,000, during 2014-2015—₹ 90,000.

X Ltd. transfers annually a sum of ₹ 80,000 to the Provision for Repairs and Renewals Account.

Required: Prepare the Provision for Repairs and Renewals Account for the year 2013-2014 and 2014-2015.

SOLUTION

Dr. **PROVISION FOR REPAIRS AND RENEWALS ACCOUNT** Cr.

Date	Particulars	₹	Date	Particulars	₹
31.03.2014	To Bank A/c	60,000	01.04.2013	By Balance c/d	1,00,000
	To Balance c/d	1,20,000	31.03.2014	By Profit and Loss A/c	80,000
		1,80,000			1,80,000
31.03.2015	To Bank A/c	90,000	01.04.2014	By Balance b/d	1,20,000
	To Balance c/d	1,10,000	31.03.2015	By Profit and Loss A/c	80,000
		2,00,000			2,00,000

AS 6 – DEPRECIATION ACCOUNTING

THEORETICAL BASE

QUESTION 1: What are the areas in which AS – 6 is not applicable? Does AS – 6 apply to land?

ANSWER:

1. Forests, Plantations and Similar Regenerative Natural Resources;
2. Wasting Assets including expenditure on the exploration for and extraction of Minerals, Oils, Natural Gas and similar Non-Regenerative Resources;
3. Expenditure on Research and Development;
4. Goodwill;
5. Livestock.

AS - 6 does not apply to land unless it has a limited useful life for the enterprise.

QUESTION 2: What is the meaning of term 'Depreciation'?

ANSWER:

1. Depreciation is a measure of the wearing out, consumption or other loss of value of a depreciable asset arising from use, effluxion of time or obsolescence through technology and market changes.
2. Depreciation is allocated so as to charge a fair proportion of the depreciable amount in each accounting period during the expected useful life of the asset.
3. Depreciation includes amortization of assets whose useful life is predetermined.

QUESTION 3: What are Depreciable Assets?

ANSWER:

Depreciable assets are assets which-

(i) are expected to used during more than one accounting period; and

(ii) have a limited useful life; and

(iii) are held by an enterprise for use in the production or supply of goods and services, for rental to others, or for administrative purposes and not for the purpose of sale in the ordinary course of business.

QUESTION 4: What are the factors which determine the amount of depreciation?

ANSWER:

1. **Historical Cost:** It represents its money outlay or its equivalent in connection with its acquisition, installation and commissioning as well as for additions to or improvement to thereof. The historical cost of a depreciable asset may undergo subsequent changes arising as a result of price adjustments, changes in duties or similar factors.
2. **Expected Useful Life:** It is the period over which a depreciable asset is expected to be used by the enterprise; or the number of production or similar units expected to be obtained from the use of the asset by the enterprise.

3. **Estimated Residual Value:** It is value expected to be realized on its sale or exchange on the expiry of its useful life.

QUESTION 5: What is the meaning of term 'Depreciable Amount'? How should depreciable amount be allocated?

ANSWER:

1. Depreciable amount of a depreciable asset is its historical cost, or other amount substituted for historical cost in the financial statements, *less* the estimated residual value.
2. The depreciable amount of a depreciable asset should be allocated on a systematic basis to each accounting period during the useful life of the asset.

QUESTION 6: At which rate depreciation should be provided Management's Rate Vs. Statute Rate?

ANSWER: The statute governing an enterprise may provide the basis for computation of the depreciation. *For example*, the Companies Act, 2013 lays down the rates of depreciation in respect of various assets.

Case	Rate
(i) ***Where the management's estimate of the useful life of an asset is shorter than that envisaged under the statute.***	The depreciation provision should appropriately be computed by applying a higher rate of management.
(ii) ***Where the management's estimate of the useful life of an asset is longer than that envisaged under the statute.***	The depreciation provision should appropriately be computed by applying a higher rate of statute.

QUESTION 7: When should the change in the method of depreciation be made? How should the change in the method of depreciation be accounted for? What are the disclosure requirements regarding change in accounting method?

ANSWER:

When	A change in the method of depreciation should be made only if - - Adoption of different accounting policy is required by statute or - For compliance with an accounting standard or - If it is considered that the change would result in more appropriate presentation.
How	**Step 1:** *Recalculate depreciation as per new method from the date of the asset coming into use.* **Step 2:** *Calculate Deficiency or Surplus* **Step 3:** *Charge Deficiency OR Credit Surplus in the Statement of Profit and Loss for the year in which the method of depreciation is changed.*
Disclosure Requirements	Such a change should be treated as a change in accounting policy and its effect should be quantified and disclosed.

QUESTION 8: How should Depreciation be provided in the following cases?

(a) **after review of useful life**

(b) **after the change in historical cost due to change in long-term liability**

(c) **after revaluation of assets**

(d) **after addition or extension**

ANSWER:

Case	How to provide Depreciation
After Review of Useful Life	The unamortized depreciable amount should be charged over the revised remaining useful life.
After the Change in Historical Cost due to Change in Long-term Liability	The depreciation on the revised unamortized depreciable amount should be provided prospectively over the residual useful life of the asset.
After Revaluation of Assets	1. The Provision for depreciation should be based on the revalued amount and on the estimate of the remaining useful lives of such assets. 2. In case the revaluation has a material effect on the amount of depreciation, the same should be disclosed separately in the year in which revaluation is carried out.
After addition or extension ***(i) Where any addition or extension becomes an integral part of the existing asset.***	1. Such addition or extension should be depreciated over the remaining useful life of that existing asset of which any addition or extension becomes an integral part of existing asset, or 2. The depreciation on such addition or extension may also be provided at the rate applied to the existing asset.
(ii) Where an addition or extension retains a separate identity and is capable of being used after the existing asset is disposed of	Depreciation should be provided independently on the basis of an estimate of its own useful life.

QUESTION 9: What are the disclosure regarding (a)each class of depreciable assets(b) depreciation policy?

ANSWER:

For each class of Depreciable Assets	1. the Historical Cost or other amount substituted for historical cost of each class of depreciable assets; 2. Total Depreciation for the period for each class of assets; and 3. the related Accumulated Depreciation.
For Depreciation Policy	1. Depreciation Methods used; and 2. Depreciation Rates or the Useful Lives of the assets, if they are different from the principal rates specified in the statute governing the enterprise.

PRACTICAL QUESTIONS FOR PRACTICE

CALCULATION OF DEPRECIABLE AMOUNT

QUESTION 1: X Ltd. set up a new factory in the backward area and purchased plant for ₹ 500 Lakhs for the purpose. Purchases were entitled for the Cenvat credit of 2% and along with this Government agreed to extend 30% subsidy for backward area development. Estimated residual value at the end of Useful life ₹ 43 Lakhs Compute depreciable amount for the Asset.

ANSWER:

CALCULATION OF DEPRECIABLE AMOUNT

Particulars	₹ In Lakhs
A. Purchase price of the plant	500
B. *Less:* Cenvat Credit @ 2%	10
C. Balance (A – B)	490
D. *Less:* Government Subsidy @ 30%	147
E. *Less:* Estimated Residual Value	43
F. Depreciable Amount	300

CALCULATION OF DEPRECIATION AFTER REVIEW OF USEFUL LIFE

QUESTION 2: A computer costing ₹ 60,000 is depreciated on straight line basis, assuming 10 years working life and Nil residual value, for three years. The estimate of remaining useful life after third year was reassessed at 5 years. Calculate Depreciation as per the provisions of AS - 6 "Depreciation Accounting".

ANSWER: Present Book Value (i.e. after three years) [₹ 60,000 – (₹ 6,000 × 3 yrs) = ₹ 42,000

Depreciation for the current year and onwords [₹ 42,000/5 years] = ₹ 8,400 p.a.

QUESTION 3:

Machinery purchased	**₹ 1,00,000**
Estimated residual value at the end of the 10th year	**₹ 10,000**
Method of providing depreciation in use	**Straight line method.**

At the end of the 4th year due to change in technology the total useful life of an asset is reduced to 8 years and residual value at the end of 8th year is ₹3000.

ANSWER:

CALCULATION OF UNAMORTIZED AMOUNT TO BE DEPRECIATED

Particulars	₹
Cost	1,00,000
Less: Depreciation for Year 1	9,000
Balance	91,000
Less: Depreciation for Year 2	9,000
Balance	82,000
Less: Depreciation for Year 3	9,000
Balance	73,000
Depreciation for the Year 4 and onwards = (₹ 73,000 – ₹ 3,000) / 5 = ₹14,000	

CALCULATION OF DEPRECIATION AFTER THE CHANGE IN HISTORICAL COST DUE TO CHANGE IN LONG-TERM LIABILITY

QUESTION 4: A machinery was purchased on 1st April, 2011 for ₹ 1,50,000 and the useful life of the machine is estimated to be 10 years. The net book value of the machinery on 1st April, 2014 was ₹ 1,05,000. The liability for acquiring this machine was increased by ₹ 14,000 due to

price adjustments on 31st March, 2015. What will be the depreciation for the year 2014-2015 and onwards? (Assume depreciation has been provided on SLM)

ANSWER:

COMPUTATION OF DEPRECIATION

Net Book Value on 1st April, 2014	₹ 1,05,000
Add: Increase in liability on 31st March, 2015	14,000
Total unamortized amount	1,19,000

Depreciation for year 2014 - 2015 and onwards (₹ 1,19,000/7) = ₹ 17,000

CALCULATION OF DEPRECIATION AFTER REVALUATION OF ASSETS

QUESTION 5:

Cost of machine **₹ 1, 30, 000**

Residual value **NIL**

Useful life **10 years**

Method of Depreciation in use **Straight line method**

After 8 years, the machine was revalued to ₹ 80,000

ANSWER:

COMPUTATION OF DEPRECIATION

	Particulars	₹
A	Original cost	1,30,000
B	*Less:* Aggregate Depreciation up to 8 years [(₹1,30,000 – NIL) × 8/10]	1,04,000
C	Existing Unamortized Depreciable Amount (A – B)	26,000
D	*Add:* Profit on revaluation (80,000 – 26,000)	54,000
E	Revised unamortized depreciable amount (C + D)	80,000
F	Depreciation for 9th year (₹ 80,000 / 2)	40,000

Note: Remaining useful life is 2 years.

QUESTION 6: A building costing ₹ 12,00,000 is depreciated for three years on straight line basis, assuming 10 years working life and ₹ 2,00,000 residual value. At the beginning of fourth year, the building was revalued upwards by ₹ 3,00,000. Residual value also revalued upwards by ₹ 1,00,000. The remaining useful life was reassessed as 10 years. Find depreciation to be charged for the fourth year onwards.

ANSWER:

A.	Original Cost	12,00,000
B.	*Less:* Depreciation till Revaluation [₹ (12,000,000 – ₹ 2,00,000) × 3 years]	(3,00,000)
C.	Book value [A – B]	9,00,000
D.	*Add:* Upward Revaluation	3,00,000
E.	Revised Value	12,00,000
F.	Depreciation from the fourth year onwards = (₹ 12,00,000 – ₹ 3,00,000)/10 years = ₹ 90,000 per year.	

QUESTION 7: On 01.04.2012 a machine was acquired at ₹ 4,00,000. The machine was expected to have a useful life of 10 years. The residual value was estimated at 10% of the original cost. At the end of the 3rd year, an attachment was made to the machine at a cost of ₹ 1,80,000 to enhance its capacity. The attachment was expected to have a useful life of 10 years and zero terminal value. During the same time the original machine was revalued upwards by ₹ 90,000 and remaining useful life was reassessed at 9 years and residual value was reassessed at NIL.

Calculate depreciation for the year, if

(i) attachment retains its separate identity.

(ii) attachment becomes integral part of the machine

ANSWER:

1. DEPRECIATION ON ORIGINAL MACHINE

Particulars	₹
A. Depreciation for 3 Years [(₹ 4,00,000 – ₹ 40,000) × 10 × 3]	1,08,000
B. Written down value at the end of 3rd year (4,00,000 – 1,08,000)	2,92,000
C. *Add:* Revaluation	90,000
D. Total Book Value after revaluation	3,82,000
E. Ressessed remaining useful life	9 Years
F. Depreciation per year from 2015-2016 [D/E]	42,444

2. Depreciation on Attachment = ₹ 1,80,000/10 = ₹ 18,000

(i) Total Depreciation for the year if Arttachment retains its separate identity
= ₹ 42,444 + ₹ 18,000 = ₹ 60,444

(ii) Total Depreciation for the year if Attachment becomes integral part of the Machine
= (₹ 3,82,000 + ₹ 1,80,000)/9 = ₹ 62,444

Note: Since, upward revaluation of the machine and ressesment of remaining useful life had been made at the end of the 3rd year, it is implied that depreciation for the 3rd year has been charged on the basis of old calculation & remaining useful life of 9 years is to be calculated from the beginning of the 4th year onwards.

QUESTION 8: Tulsian Ltd. provides you the following information:

Machinery purchased on 1st April, 2011	**₹ 1,00,000**
Estimated residual value at the end of 5th year	**₹ 5,000**
Method of Depreciation	**Written down value method**
Rate of Depreciation	**55 %**
Addition to machinery on 1st April, 2012	**₹ 50,000**
Estimated Residual Value at the end of 4th year	**₹ 2,000**

This addition becomes an integral part of the existing asset.

Calculate depreciation for the year, if

1. **Addition retains its separate identity.**
2. **Addition becomes integral part of the machine**

ANSWER:

	Case 1			Case 2
Particulars	Existing	New Asset	Total	
Cost as on 1.4.2011	1,00,000	0	1,00,000	1,00,000
Less: Depreciation for 2011-2012	55,000	0	1,00,000	55,000

Balance/Addition as on 1.4.2012	45,000	50,000	95,000	95,000
Less: Depreciation for 2012-2013	24,750	25,000	49,750	52,250
Balance as on 1.4.2013	20,250	25,000	45,250	42,750
Less: Depreciation for 2013-2014	11,138	12,500	23,638	23,513
Balance as on 1.04.2014	9,112	12,500	21,612	19,237
Less: Depreciation for 2014-2015	5,012	6,250	11,262	10,580
Balance as on 1.4.2015	4,100	6,250	10,350	8,657

*Rate of depreciation is calculated by the formula $= 1 - \sqrt[n]{s/c} = 1 - \sqrt[4]{5,000/50,000} = 50\%$

CHANGE IN THE METHOD OF DEPRECIATION

QUESTION 9: M/s. Son Ltd. charged depreciation on its assets on SLM basis. In the year ended 31st March, 2015 it changed to WDV basis. The impact of the change when computed from the date of the assets putting into use amounts to ₹ 18 lakhs being additional depreciation. Discuss, when should an enterprise change method of charging depreciation and how it should be dealt with in Profit and Loss A/c.

ANSWER:

PROVISION OF AS 6

As per AS 6 'Depreciation Accounting', an enterprise can change one method of charging depreciation to another method only if the adoption of the new method is required by statute or for compliance with an accounting standard or if it is considered that the change would result in a more appropriate preparation or presentation of the financial statements of the enterprise.

When such a change in the method of depreciation is made, depreciation should be recalculated in accordance with the new method from the date of the asset coming into use. The deficiency or surplus arising from retrospective recomputation of depreciation in accordance with the new method should be adjusted in the accounts through statement of profit and loss in the year in which the method of depreciation is changed. In case the change in the method results in deficiency in depreciation in respect of past years, the deficiency should be charged in the statement of profit and loss.

ADVICE

Additional Depreciation of ₹ 18 lakhs should be provided for as under:

Date	Particulars	Dr. (₹)	Cr.(₹)
	Profit & Loss A/c Dr.	₹ 18 lakhs	
	To Assets A/c		₹ 18 lakhs
	(Being the additional depreciation due to change in the method of depreciation w/o to Profit & Loss A/c)		

QUESTION 10:

Machinery purchased **₹ 1,00,000**

Estimated residual value at the end of the 10th year **₹ 10,000**

Method of providing depreciation in use **Straight line method.**

From 5th year, company decided to change the method of depreciation from Straight Line Method to Written Down Value Method @ 20%.

ANSWER:

COMPUTATION OF DEFICIENCY / SURPLUS

Particulars	Straight Line Method	Written Down Value Method
Cost	1,00,000	1,00,000
Less: Dep. for Year 1	9,000	20,000
Balance	91,000	80,000
Less: Dep. for Year 2	9,000	16,000
Balance	82,000	64,000
Less: Dep. for Year 3	9,000	12,800
Balance	73,000	51,200
Less: Dep. for Year 4	9,000	10,240
Balance	64,000	40,960
Total Depreciation provided	36,000	59,040
Deficiency = ₹ 59,040 – ₹ 36,000 = ₹ 23, 040		

JOURNAL ENTRY TO ADJUST DEFICIENCY

Date	Particulars		Dr. (₹)	Cr.(₹)
	Profit & Loss A/c	Dr.	₹ 23,040	
	To Machinery A/c			₹ 23,040
	(Being the backlog depreciation relating to past years now adjusted)			

QUESTION 11: A company acquired a machine on 1.4.2011 for ₹ 5,00,000. The company charged depreciation upto 2013-2014 on straight line basis with estimated working life of 10 years and scrap value of ₹ 50,000. From 2014-2015, the company decided to change depreciation method at 20% on reducing balance method. Compute the amount of depreciation to be debited to Profit and Loss Account for the year 2014-2015.

ANSWER:

Annual depreciation charged by the company up to 2013-2014

= (Cost – Scrap Value)/Useful Life

= (5,00,000 – 50,0000)/10 = 45,000

WDV of machine at the end of 2013-2014 by Straight Line Method (SLM)

= ₹ 5,00,000 – {₹ 45,000 × 3} = ₹ 3,65,000

DEPRECIATION BY REDUCING BALANCE METHOD (RBM)

Year	Cost / WDV at the beginning of the year ₹	Depreciation ₹	WDV at the end of the year ₹	
2011-2012	5,00,000	5,00,000 × 20%	1,00,000	4,00,000
2012-2013	4,00,000	4,00,000 × 20%	80,000	3,20,000
2013-2014	3,20,000	3,20,000 × 20%	64,000	2,56,000
				2,44,000
2014-2015	2,56,000	2,56,000 × 20%	51,200	2,04,800

DEPRECIATION TO BE CHARGED IN 2014-2015

Particulars	₹
Book value of the machine as per SLM as on 1.4.2014	3,65,000
Less: Book value of the machine as per RBM as on 1.4.2014	(2,56,000)
Add: Depreciation for the year 2014-2015 as per RBM	51,200
Total Depreciation to be debited to Profit and Loss Account in the year 2014-2015	1,60,200

Such a change should be treated as a change in accounting policy and its effect should be quantified and disclosed as per AS 5. "Net Profit loss for the period, prior period items and changes in Accounting Policies).

QUESTION 12: An item of machinery was purchased on 1-04-2013 for ₹ 2,00,000. The WDV depreciation rate applicable to the machinery was 15%. The written down value of the machinery as on 31-03-2015 was ₹ 1,44,500. On 1-04-2015, the enterprise decided to change the method from written down value (WDV) to straight line method (SLM). The enterprise decided to write off the book value of ₹ 1,44,500, over the remaining useful life or machinery i.e., 5 years. Out of the total useful life 7 years, 2 years have already elapsed.

Required: Comment whether the accounting treatment is correct. If not, given the correct accounting treatment with reasons.

ANSWER:

PROVISION OF AS 6

As per para 15 of Accounting Standard 6, 'Depreciation Accounting', when the method of depreciation is changed, depreciation is recalculated in accordance with the new method form the date of the assets coming into use. The deficiency or surplus arising from retrospective re-computation of depreciation in accordance with the new method is adjusted in the statement of profit & loss in the year in which the method of depreciation is changed.

ADVICE

CALCULATION OF SURPLUS/DEFICIENCY DUE TO CHANGE IN METHOD OF DEPRECIATION

Particulars	₹
Purchase Price of Plant as on 01-04-2013	2,00,000
Less: Depreciation as per SLM, for the years 2013-2014 & 2014-2015 (Rs 2,00,000 × 2/7)	57,143
Balance as on 31-3-2015	1,42,857
Book Value as per WDV method [Given]	1,44,500
Book Value as per SLM	1,42,857
Excess Depreciation already provided	1,643

1. Such Excess Depreciation should be written back in the year of change by passing the following Journal Entry:

Machinery A/c	Dr.	₹1,643	
To Profit and Loss A/c			₹1,643

2. As a result of above entry, the balance of Machinery Account will be Rs 1,44,500 as on 1.4.2015
3. Depreciation should be charged @ 15% on WDV basis from the year 2015-16 onwards.

QUESTION 13: In the Trial Balance of M/s Sun Ltd. as on 31-3-2015, balance of machinery appears at ₹ 5,60,000. The company follows rate of depreciation on machinery @ 10% p.a. on WDV basis. On scrutiny it was found that a machine appearing in the books on 1-4-2014 at ₹ 1,60,000 was disposed of on 30-9-2014 at ₹ 1,35,000 in part exchange of a new machine costing ₹ 1,50,000.

You are required to calculate:

(i) Total depreciation to be charged in the Profit and Loss Account.

(ii) Loss on exchange of machine.

(iii) Book value of machinery in the Balance Sheet as on 31-3-2015.

ANSWER:

(I) TOTAL DEPRECIATION TO BE CHARGED IN THE PROFIT AND LOSS ACCOUNT

Particulars	₹
Depreciation on old machinery in use [10% of (5,60,000 – 1,60,000)]	40,000
Add: Depreciation on new machine [(1,50,000 × 10%) × 6/12]	7,500
Add: Depreciation on machine disposed of [(1,60,000 × 10%)6/12]	8,000
Total Depreciation to be charged in Profit and Loss A/c	55,500

(II) LOSS ON EXCHANGE OF MACHINE

Particulars	₹
Book value of machine as on 1.4.2012	1,60,000
Less: Depreciation for 6 months @ 10%	(8,000)
Written Down Value as on 30.9.2012	1,52,000
Less: Exchange value	(1,35,000)
Loss on exchange of machine	17,000

(III) BOOK VALUE OF MACHINERY IN THE BALANCE SHEET AS ON 31.03.2015

Particulars	₹
Balance as per trial balance	5,60,000
Less: Book value of machine sold	(1,60,000)
Add: Purchase of new machine	1,50,000
Less: Depreciation on machinery in use [40,000 + 7,500]	(47,500)

QUESTION 14: In the books of Optic Fiber Ltd., plant and machinery stood at ₹ 6,32,000 on 1.4.2014. However on scrutiny it was found that machinery worth ₹ 1,20,000 was included in the purchases on 1.6.2013. On 30.6.2014 the company disposed a machine having book value of ₹ 1,89,000 on 1.4.2014 at ₹ 1,75,000 in part exchange of a new machine costing ₹ 2,56,000. The company charges depreciation @ 20% WDV on plant and machinery.

You are required to calculate:

(i) Depreciation to be charged to P/L

(ii) Book value of Plant and Machinery A/c as on 31.3. 2015

(iii) Loss on exchange of machinery.

ANSWER:

RECTIFYING ENTRY

Machinery A/c	Dr.	₹ 1,20,000	
To Purchases A/c			₹ 1,20,000

1. DEPRECIATION TO BE CHARGED TO P/L ACCOUNT

(6,32,000 – 189,000) × 20%	₹ 88,600
1,89,000 × 20% × 3/12	₹ 9,450
2,56,000 × 20% × 9/12	₹ 38,400
1,20,000 × 20% × 10/12	₹ 20,000
	₹ 1,56,450

2. BOOK VALUE OF PLANT AND MACHINERY AS ON 31.3.2015

Book value of Plant and machinery before depreciation	₹ 8,19,000
(4,43,000 + 1,20,000 + 2,56,000)	
Less: Depreciation on existing assets (88,600 + 38,400 + 20,000)	₹ 1,47,000
	₹ 6,72,000

3. LOSS ON EXCHANGE OF MACHINERY

WDV of machinery disposed in part exchange	₹ 1,89,000
Less: Depreciation for 3 months	₹ 9,450
Book value of machinery on date of Exchange	₹ 1,79,550
Exchange Value	₹ 1,75,000
Loss on Exchange	₹ 4,550

MANAGEMENT'S RATE VS. STATUTE RATE

QUESTION 15: Narmada Ltd. purchased an existing bottling unit from Kaveri Ltd. Kaveri Ltd. followed straight line method of charging depreciation on machinery of the sold unit whereas Narmada Ltd. followed written down value method in its other units. The directors of Narmada Ltd. want to continue to charge depreciation for the acquired unit in Straight Line Method which is not consistent with the WDV method followed in other units.

Discuss the contention of the directors with reference to the Accounting Standard. Further during the year, Narmada Ltd. set up a new plant on coastal land. In view of the corrosive climate, the Company felt that its machine life is reducing faster. Can the Company charge a higher rate of depreciation?

ANSWER:

PROVISION OF AS 6

According to para 12 of AS 6 'Depreciation Accounting', there are several methods of allocating depreciation over the useful life of the assets. The management of a business selects the most appropriate method(s) based on various important factors e.g., (i) type of asset, (ii) the nature of the use of such asset and (iii) circumstances prevailing in the business. A combination of more than one method is sometimes used. A company may adopt different methods of depreciation for different types of assets, provided the same methods are followed consistently.

The statute governing an enterprise may provide the basis for computation of the depreciation. For example, the Companies Act lays down the rates of depreciation in respect of various assets. Where the management's estimate of the useful life of an asset of the enterprise is shorter than that envisaged under the provisions of the relevant statute, the depreciation provision is appropriately computed by applying a higher rate.

ADVICE

The Company can charge higher rates of depreciation based on its estimate of the useful life of machinery, provided that such estimate is not less than the rate prescribed by the Companies Act, for that class of assets. However, such higher depreciation rates and/or the reduced useful lives of the assets should be disclosed by way of notes to the accounts in the Financial Statements. Thus Narmada Ltd. can continue to charge depreciation for the acquired unit as per straight line method.

QUESTION 16: Progressive Company Limited has not charged depreciation for the year ended on 31st March 2015, in respect of a Spare Bus purchased during the Financial Year 2014-2015 and kept ready by the Company for use as a stand-by, on the ground that, it was not actually used during the year. State your views with reference to AS - 6 "Depreciation Accounting".

ANSWER:

PROVISION OF AS 6

Depreciation is to be charged if asset is "ready for use", whether put to use or not.

AS – 28 IMPAIRMENT OF ASSETS

THEORETICAL BASE

APPLICABILITY OF AS 28

QUESTION 1: State the Assets to which AS 28 does not apply.

ANSWER:

1. Inventories.
2. Assets arising from construction contracts.
3. Financial assets
4. Deferred tax assets.

QUESTION 2: What is Financial Asset?

ANSWER: A financial asset is any asset that is:

(a) Cash;

(b) an Equity Instrument of another entity;

(c) a Contractual Right:

(i) to receive cash *or* another financial asset from another entity; *or*

(ii) to exchange financial assets *or* financial liabilities with another entity under conditions that are potentially favourable to the entity; *or*

(d) a Contract that will *or* may be settled in the entity's own equity instruments and is:

(i) a Non-Derivative for which the entity is *or* may be obliged to receive a variable number of the entity's own equity instruments; *or*

(ii) a Derivative that will *or* may be settled other than by the exchange of a fixed amount of cash *or* another financial asset for a fixed number of the entity's own equity instruments. For this purpose the entity's own equity instruments do not include instruments that are themselves contracts for the future receipt *or* delivery of the entity's own equity instruments.

NET SELLING PRICE

QUESTION 3: What is Net Selling Price?

ANSWER: Net Selling Price = Amount receivable from the sale of an asset in an arm's length transaction between knowledgeable and willing parties – Disposal Costs.

QUESTION 4: What are Costs of Disposal?

ANSWER: Disposal Costs are incremental costs, directly attributable to the disposal of an asset excluding financing cost, income tax expenses and liabilities which have already been recognized in the financial statements of the enterprise.

QUESTION 5: How shall the Net Selling Price be determined?

ANSWER: Net Selling Price shall be determined in the following 3 ways given below in the order of their preference i.e., Method given later shall only be used if it is not possible to use method given earlier.

1. If Price is determinable under Binding Sale Agreement	Price determinable under **Binding Sale Agreement** – Disposal Costs
2. If Net Selling Price cannot be determined under Binding Sale Agreement	Net Selling Price = Current Market Price *or* Most Recent Price (if Current Market Price is not available) of similar conditioned asset in active market – Disposal Cost
3. If Net Selling Price cannot be determined under any of the above two methods	Net Selling Price = Estimated Selling Price – Disposal Cost

QUESTION 6: Determine the Net Selling Price of an Asset in the following cases:

Case 1: When the agreed price under a sale agreement is ₹ 10,000, sale price of similar conditioned asset is ₹ 10,500 in an active market and estimated sale proceeds of such an asset is ₹ 11,000. Disposal cost is ₹ 1,000.

Case 2: When the Selling Price of asset under a sale agreement is not available, sale price of similar conditioned asset is ₹ 10,500 in an active market and estimated sale proceeds of such an asset is ₹ 11,000. Disposal cost is ₹ 1,000.

Case 3: When the Selling Price of asset under a sale agreement and sale price of similar conditioned asset are not available and estimated sale proceeds of such an asset is ₹ 11,000. Disposal cost is ₹ 1,000.

ANSWER:

Case (1) Net Selling Price shall be ₹ 9,000 (i.e., Selling Price under sale agreement *less* disposal cost). The Selling Price of an asset in an active market and estimated sale proceeds are irrelevant in this case since Selling Price under sale agreement shall outshine later two amounts.

Case (2) Net Selling Price shall be ₹ 9,500 (i.e., sale price of an asset in active market less disposal cost). The estimated sale proceeds are irrelevant in this case since Selling Price under sale agreement is not available and in such a case sale price in an active market shall be preferred over estimated sale proceeds.

Case (3) Net Selling Price shall be ₹ 10,000 (i.e., estimated sale proceeds *less* disposal cost). In this case Selling Price under sale agreement and sale price in an active market are not available, then in such circumstances estimated sale proceeds become relevant and considered for determining net Selling Price.

VALUE IN USE

QUESTION 7: What is meant by the term 'Value in use'?

ANSWER: Value in use = Present Value of Estimated Future Cash Flows expected to arise from the continuing use of an asset and from its disposal at the end of its useful life.

Notes:

1. Estimated Future Cash Inflows shall not include inflows in relation to:
   (a) any other asset whose inflows are basically independent of cash inflows of the asset under assessment.
   (b) any future economic benefits which have already been recognized as assets.
2. Estimated Future Cash Outflows shall not include outflows in relation to any obligations which have been recognized as liabilities.
3. Estimated capital expenditure to be incurred in future for maintaining the asset at its original assessed standard shall be included in estimated cash outflows.
4. Estimated cash flows shall not include cash flows arising from:

(a) Financing Activities. This implies that cash flows shall be arrived at present value without taking into consideration any financing cost.

(b) Income Tax. This implies that cash flows shall be estimated without taking income tax in to consideration.

5. Inflation should not be taken in to consideration while estimating cash flows, since discount rate is adjusted for the inflation and as such cash flows should be taken in nominal terms. However if discount rate is not adjusted for the inflation then cash flows should be taken in real terms. (i.e., cash flows needs to be adjusted for inflation).

6. If cash flows are in foreign currency then value in use should be measured at that foreign currency. However after determining value in use in foreign currency, it should be translated in home currency using the exchange rate at the balance.

QUESTION 8: Whether the following items shall form part of the estimated cash flows of the Asset under review?

(i) Heavy capital expenditure of ₹ 100 crores incurred on the asset which shall increase its production capacity up to five times annually.

(ii) Sundry debtors of ₹ 10 lacs arising from sale of goods produced by the asset.

(iii) There was cash sale of ₹ 10 crores arising from sale of goods produced by the asset.

(iv) The enterprise is planning for future restructuring of an asset. This future restructuring shall be estimated at ₹ 10 crores. This reconstruction shall double the production capacity of the asset. However, no provision is made in the financial statements of the enterprise for future restructuring.

(v) The enterprise is planning for future restructuring of an asset. This future reconstruction shall be estimated at ₹ 10 crores. This restructuring shall double the production capacity of the asset. The provision is made in the financial statements of the enterprise for future restructuring by increasing the carrying amount of the asset.

(vi) The estimated cash outflows necessary for generating cash inflows from the continuing use of the asset comes at ₹ 5 Lacs. However, it also includes amount of ₹ 50,000 for which a liability has been created in financial statements.

ANSWER:

Item	ANSWER
(i)	Capital expenditure incurred on the asset shall be included in the carrying amount of the asset. As a result cash flows shall be estimated at revised capacity (i.e., at increased capacity) and after determining revised cash flows at revised capacity, revised value in use shall be determined.
(ii)	Sundry debtors is already included in the financial statements, hence it shall not be included in the estimated cash flows.
(iii)	Cash sale has already been realized, hence there is no question of including it in estimated cash flows.
(iv)	Since enterprise is yet not committed to future restructuring, there is no necessity to estimate cash flows at revised capacity.
(v)	As enterprise is committed to future reconstruction, the cash flows shall be estimated at revised capacity (i.e., at double capacity).
(vi)	Estimated cash outflows shall form part of estimated flows while determining value in use. However it shall only be included in the estimated flows to the extent of ₹ 4.5 lacs (i.e., ₹ 5,00,000 – ₹ 50,000) since liability of ₹ 50,000 has been recognized.

QUESTION 9: Determine value in use of the asset under review from the data given below:

Year	1	2	3	4	5	6	7	8	9	10
Cash Inflows	25000	26000	30000	32000	30000	28000	24000	20000	16000	10000
Cash Outflows	—	—	—	2000	3000	4000	5000	6000	7000	8000

Estimated useful life of the asset is 10 years and estimated net proceeds from the disposal of the asset at the end of its useful life is ₹ 1,000. Appropriate discount rate is 12 % (pre – tax rate). Income tax rate is 40 % and asset is purchased for ₹1,20,000 by borrowing from a bank at a rate of 15 % p.a.

ANSWER:

CALCULATION OF VALUE IN USE OF THE ASSET

Years	Cash Inflows	Cash Outflows	Net Proceeds at disposal of asset	Net Cash Flows	P.V. F @ 12 %	P.V of net cash flows
A	B	C	D	E = B – C + D	F	G = E × F
1	25000	0	0	25000	0.893	22325
2	26000	0	0	26000	0.797	20722
3	30000	0	0	30000	0.712	21360
4	32000	2000	0	30000	0.636	19080
5	30000	3000	0	27000	0.567	15309
6	28000	4000	0	24000	0.507	12168
7	24000	5000	0	19000	0.452	8588
8	20000	6000	0	14000	0.404	5656
9	16000	7000	0	9000	0.361	3249
10	10000	8000	1000	3000	0.322	966
			Asset's Value in use			129423

Notes:

(i) While calculating value in use, no impact of income tax should be taken into consideration.

(ii) Similarly no consideration should be given to financing cost arising from the loan taken from bank to purchase the asset under review.

QUESTION 10: Determine the Value in use from the data given below:

Year	1	2	3	4	5	6	7	8	9	10
Net Cash Inflows	30000	32000	34000	35000	32000	28000	24000	20000	16000	10000

Inflation rate is 8 % p.a and discount rate without adjusting for inflation is 12 % p.a.

ANSWER:

CALCULATION OF VALUE IN USE OF THE ASSET
[ALTERNATIVE 1: DISCOUNT RATE IS ADJUSTED FOR INFLATION]

Years	Net cash flows (nominal terms)	P.V.F @ 21 % (adjusted discount rate)	Present Value
A	B	C	D = B × C
1	30000	0.826	24780

2	32000	0.683	21856
3	34000	0.564	19176
4	35000	0.467	16345
5	32000	0.386	12352
6	28000	0.319	8932
7	24000	0.263	6312
8	20000	0.218	4360
9	16000	0.180	2880
10	10000	0.149	1490
	TOTAL		118483

Hence value in use is ₹ 1,18,483

Note:

Adjusted discount rate = [(1 + discount rate) × (1 + inflation rate)] – 1 = (1.12 × 1.08) – 1 = 0.21 (appx.)

CALCULATION OF VALUE IN USE OF THE ASSET
[ALTERNATIVE 2: CASH FLOWS ARE ADJUSTED IN REAL TERMS]

Years	Net Cash flows	P.V. F @ 8 % (adjusted factor for inflation)	Real terms (i.e. cash flows are adjusted for inflation)	P.V.F @ 12 %	Present Value
A	B	C	D = B × C	E	F = D × E
1	30000	0.926	27780	0.893	24807.54
2	32000	0.857	27424	0.797	21856.93
3	34000	0.794	26996	0.712	19221.15
4	35000	0.735	25725	0.636	16361.10
5	32000	0.681	21792	0.567	12356.06
6	28000	0.630	17640	0.507	8943.48
7	24000	0.583	13992	0.452	6324.38
8	20000	0.540	10800	0.404	4363.20
9	16000	0.500	8000	0.361	2888.00
10	10000	0.463	4630	0.322	1490.86
		TOTAL			118612.70

Hence value in use is ₹ 1,18,613 (appx)

From above it is evident that difference between two approaches is immaterial. Hence both of the alternative approaches may be used, depending upon the facts of the circumstances.

ESTIMATED CASH FLOWS WHEN GROWTH IS GIVEN

QUESTION 11: What is the maximum Period of estimation of cash flows?

ANSWER: Estimation of cash flows may be made up to maximum of 5 years, except in circumstances where a longer period can be justified.

QUESTION 12: How should cash flows be projected beyond the maximum period?

ANSWER: Cash flows beyond the maximum period should be projected by using a constant *or* a declining growth rate. However, this rate shall not exceed the long-term average growth rate for the products, industries country *or* countries in which the enterprise operates *or* for the market in which the asset is used.

QUESTION 12: Can increasing growth rate be used instead of constant *or* declining growth rate?

ANSWER: Increasing growth rate may be used instead of constant *or* declining growth rate, if it is justifiable in the relevant circumstances.

QUESTION 13: Can growth rate used may be more than long – term average growth rate?

ANSWER: Growth rate used may be more than long – term average growth rate, if circumstances warrant such growth rate.

QUESTION 14: Determine the estimated cash flows on the data given below in each of the cases:

Years	1	2	3	4	5
Budget's Forecast	25000	30000	35000	40000	43000

Asset's useful estimated life is 10 years.

Case 1: If growth rate is 5 % p.a.

Case 2: If growth rate is 5 % p.a which shall decrease by 40 % p.a.

Case 3: If growth rate is 5 % p.a which shall increase by 10 % p.a.

Case 4: If growth rate is (-) 20 % p.a.

ANSWER: Case (1)

ESTIMATED CASH FLOWS DURING THE ESTIMATED USEFUL LIFE OF THE ASSET

Years	Amount	Basis	Rate	Amount
1		As per Budget	N.A.	25000
2		As per Budget	N.A.	30000
3		As per Budget	N.A.	35000
4		As per Budget	N.A.	40000
5		As per Budget	N.A.	43000
6	43000	Steady growth rate	5 %	45150
7	45150	Steady growth rate	5 %	47408
8	47408	Steady growth rate	5 %	49778
9	49778	Steady growth rate	5 %	52267
10	52267	Steady growth rate	5 %	54880

Case (2)

ESTIMATED CASH FLOWS DURING THE ESTIMATED USEFUL LIFE OF THE ASSET

Years	Amount	Basis	Rate	Amount
1		As per Budget	N.A.	25000
2		As per Budget	N.A.	30000
3		As per Budget	N.A.	35000

4		As per Budget	N.A.	40000
5		As per Budget	N.A.	43000
6	43000	Declining growth rate	5	45150
7	45150	Declining growth rate	3 % (5 × 0.60)	46505
8	46505	Declining growth rate	1.8 % (3 × 0.60)	47342
9	47342	Declining growth rate	1.08 %(1.8 × 0.60)	47853
10	47853	Declining growth rate	0.648 % (1.08 × 0.60)	48163

Case (3)

ESTIMATED CASH FLOWS DURING THE ESTIMATED USEFUL LIFE OF THE ASSET

Years	Amount	Basis	Rate	Amount
1		As per Budget	N.A.	25000
2		As per Budget	N.A.	30000
3		As per Budget	N.A.	35000
4		As per Budget	N.A.	40000
5		As per Budget	N.A.	43000
6	43000	Increasing growth rate	5	45150
7	45150	Increasing growth rate	5.5 % (5 × 1.10)	47633
8	47633	Increasing growth rate	6.05 % (5.5 × 1.10)	50515
9	50515	Increasing growth rate	6.655 % (6.05 × 1.10)	53877
10	53877	Increasing growth rate	7.3205 % (6.655 × 1.10)	57821

Note: Increasing growth rate can only be used if circumstances warrant such growth rate.

Case (4)

ESTIMATED CASH FLOWS DURING THE ESTIMATED USEFUL LIFE OF THE ASSET

Years	Amount	Basis	Rate	Amount
1		As per Budget	N.A.	25000
2		As per Budget	N.A.	30000
3		As per Budget	N.A.	35000
4		As per Budget	N.A.	40000
5		As per Budget	N.A.	43000
6	43000	Negative growth rate	– 20 %	34400
7	34400	Negative growth rate	– 20 %	27520
8	27520	Negative growth rate	– 20 %	22016
9	22016	Negative growth rate	– 20 %	17613
10	17613	Negative growth rate	– 20 %	14090

DISCOUNT RATE AS PER AS – 28

QUESTION 15: What is the Discount Rate as per AS – 28?

ANSWER: As per AS – 28, discount rate should be a pre – tax rate(s) that reflect(s) current market assessments of the time value of money and the risks specific to the asset. The discount rate(s) should not reflect risks for which future cash flows estimates have been adjusted.

QUESTION 16: What are the factors influencing the determination of discount rate?

ANSWER:

1. Current market assessments of the time value of the money for the periods until the end of asset's useful life.
2. Risk specific to the asset (Beta).
3. Rate must be pre – tax rate i.e., returns before income – tax.

QUESTION 17: What are the various methods for determining Discount Rate?

ANSWER:

1. **Rate directly specific to the asset under review:** This rate is most reliable and must be used to the exclusion of others methods if available.
2. **Rate determined under Capital Asset Pricing Model (CAPM):** Rate determined under Capital Asset Pricing Model would be adjusted for the current market assessment of the time value of money and Beta (specific to the asset).
3. **Enterprise's incremental borrowing rate.**
4. **Other market borrowing rate.**

   Note: Rate determined under (iii) and (iv) bases should be adjusted for the following:

(i) Risks associated with cash flows of the asset under review; and

(ii) risks those are not relevant for cash flows of the asset under review.

QUESTION 18: What should be discount rate if cash flows itself are adjusted for uncertainties and risks?

ANSWER: In such a case, discount rate should only represent current market assessments of the time value of money over the periods until the useful life of an asset under review. It should not be adjusted for risks associated with cash flows of the asset, since cash flows are itself adjusted for risks and if in such a case discount rate is adjusted then it shall lead to double counting and under estimation of value in use.

QUESTION 19: Calculate Value in use from the data given below:

Years	1	2	3	4	5	6	7	8	9	10
Net Cash flows	25000	30000	35000	40000	43000	34000	28000	22000	18000	14000

These estimated cash flows are not adjusted for risks associated with it. The risk free rate is 7 % and the current market rate is 15 %. The risks coefficient (i.e., Beta) attached to estimated cash flows of the asset under review is 1.4.

ANSWER:

CALCULATION OF VALUE IN USE (WHERE DISCOUNT RATE IS ADJUSTED FOR RISKS)

Years	Net Cash flows	P.V.F @ 18.2 %	Present Value
A	B	C	D = B × C
1	25000	0.846	21150
2	30000	0.716	21480
3	35000	0.606	21210
4	40000	0.512	20480
5	43000	0.433	18619
6	34000	0.367	12478

7	28000	0.31	8680
8	22000	0.262	5764
9	18000	0.222	3996
10	14000	0.188	2632
TOTAL			1,36,489

Hence value in use is ₹ 1,36,489

Note:

Discount rate is calculated by using CAPM method.

Discount rate = Risk free rate + (Market rate – Risk free rate) × Beta co-efficient

= 7 + (15 – 7) × 1.4 = 7 + 8 × 1.4 = 7 + 11.2 = 18.2

IMPAIRMENT LOSS, CARRYING AMOUNT AND RECOVERABLE AMOUNT

QUESTION 20: What is an Impairment Loss?

ANSWER: Impairment Loss = Carrying Amount of an asset – its Recoverable Amount.

QUESTION 21: What is meant by Carrying Amount?

ANSWER: Carrying Amount is the amount at which an asset is recognized in the balance sheet after deducting any accumulated depreciation (amortization) and accumulated impairment losses thereon.

QUESTION 22: What is Recoverable Amount?

ANSWER: Recoverable amount is the higher of the followings:

1. An asset's Net Selling Price; *or*
2. An asset's Value in use

QUESTION 23: Determine the recoverable amount of the asset in each of the following cases from the data given below:

Years	1	2	3	4	5	6	7	8	9	10
Expected Cash Inflows	25000	26000	30000	32000	30000	28000	24000	20000	16000	14000
Expected Cash Outflows				2000	3000	4000	5000	6000	7000	8000

Estimated useful life of the asset is 10 years and estimated net proceeds from the disposal of the asset at the end of its useful life is ₹ 1,000. Appropriate discount rate is 12 %.

Case 1: Net Selling Price of an asset is ₹ 1,20,000

Case 2: Net Selling Price of an asset is ₹ 1,40,000

ANSWER: Case (1)

Recoverable amount of an asset shall be the higher of the following two amounts:

(i) Net Selling Price of an asset i.e., ₹ 1,20,000 *or*

(ii) Asset's value in use i.e.,1,29,423

Hence, recoverable amount of an asset shall be ₹ 1,29,423

Case (2)

Recoverable amount of an asset shall be the higher of the following two amounts:

(i) Net Selling Price of an asset i.e., ₹ 1,40,000 *or*

(ii) Asset's value in use i.e.,1,29,360

Hence, recoverable amount of an asset shall be ₹ 1,40,000

QUESTION 24: What shall be the recoverable amount when the asset's value in use materially exceeds its net Selling Price?

ANSWER: Net Selling Price of the asset.

QUESTION 25: What shall be the recoverable amount of the asset held for disposal?

ANSWER: Net Selling Price since value in use of the assets shall be close to the net Selling Price of the asset.

QUESTION 26: What shall be recoverable amount when asset is revalued at market price?

ANSWER: Since recoverable cost is higher of net Selling Price *or* value in use, in this case recoverable amount shall be nearer to the revalued amount of the asset as it is valued at market price *or* higher than revalued amount if value in use is greater than net Selling Price. However if disposal costs are not negligible then the net Selling Price shall be less than revalued amount and in such circumstances, if value in use is less than revalued amount then the asset is impaired and impairment loss shall be recognized accordingly.

QUESTION 27: What shall be recoverable amount if asset is valued on the basis other than its market value?

ANSWER: Recoverable amount shall be determined normally i.e. higher of net Selling Price *or* value in use and asset is tested for impairment accordingly.

RECOGNITION OF IMPAIRMENT LOSS

QUESTION 28: At what intervals does the company assess its asset for the Impairment Loss?

ANSWER: At each Balance Sheet Date

QUESTION 29: How shall impairment loss be recognized?

ANSWER:

Case	Treatment
(a) If asset is carried at revalued amount	Revaluation Reserve A/c Dr. Profit & Loss A/c Dr. To Provision for Impairment Loss A/c
(b) In other cases	Profit & Loss A/c Dr. To Provision for Impairment Loss A/c Impairment Loss shall be charged to Statement of Profit and Loss.

QUESTION 30: What shall be the treatment of an impairment loss if recoverable amount is in negative?

ANSWER: Impairment loss is limited to carrying amount of the asset. However impairment loss may increase and a simultaneous liability may be recognized only and only if it is permitted by another accounting standard.

QUESTION 31: Determine the amount of impairment loss to be charged to profit and loss statement in the following cases:

Case 1: Carrying amount of the asset is ₹ 1,00,000 and recoverable amount is ₹ 1,40,000

Case 2: Carrying amount of the asset is ₹ 1,00,000 and recoverable amount is ₹ 80,000

Case 3: Carrying amount of the asset is ₹ 1,00,000, revaluation surplus of the asset is ₹ 40,000 and the recoverable amount of the asset is ₹ 80,000

Case 4: Carrying amount of the asset is ₹ 1,00,000, revaluation surplus of the asset is ₹ 40,000 and the recoverable amount of the asset is ₹ 50,000

Case 5: Carrying amount of the asset is ₹ 1,00,000 and the recoverable amount of the asset is ₹ (20,000)

Case 6: Carrying amount of the asset is ₹ 1,00,000 and the recoverable amount of the asset is ₹ (20,000) and another accounting standard permits to recognize a liability against negative recoverable amount to the extent of ₹ 10,000

ANSWER:

Cases	Treatment
Case (1)	In this case there is no impairment loss, since recoverable amount is more than the carrying amount.
Case (2)	In this case impairment loss is ₹ 20,000 (i.e., carrying amount – recoverable amount) and such impairment loss shall be charged to profit and loss statement in full.
Case (3)	In this case impairment loss is ₹ 20,000 (i.e., carrying amount – recoverable amount) and such impairment loss shall be charged to revenue surplus of the asset.
Case (4)	In this case impairment loss is ₹50,000 (i.e., carrying amount – recoverable amount) and such impairment loss shall first be charged to revenue surplus of the asset to the extent of ₹ 40,000 (i.e., amount available in revenue surplus) and remaining balance of impairment loss of ₹ 10,000 (i.e., ₹ 50,000 – ₹ 40,000) shall be charged to profit and loss statement.
Case (5)	Impairment loss is ₹ 1,20,000 (i.e., ₹ 1,00,000 – (– 20000). However impairment loss to be recognized in this case shall be limited to carrying amount i.e., ₹ 1,00,000 and this amount shall be charged to profit and loss statement.
Case (6)	Impairment loss is ₹ 1,20,000 (i.e., ₹ 1,00,000 – (– 20000). However impairment loss to be recognized in this case shall be limited to carrying amount i.e., ₹ 1,00,000 and the amount allowed to be recognized as liability as per other Accounting Standard. Hence, in this case ₹ 1,10,000 shall be charged to profit and loss statement.

DEPRECIATION CHARGE AFTER ADJUSTING FOR IMPAIRMENT LOSS

QUESTION 32: How shall revised depreciation charge be determined after adjusting for Impairment Loss?

ANSWER: Depreciation charge = [Revised Carrying Amount of the asset – Residual Value]/ Remaining Useful Life of the asset

QUESTION 33: Calculate the revised depreciation charge of the asset in the following cases:

Case 1: Carrying amount of the asset as on 31.03.2015 is ₹ 1,00,000. Impairment loss is ₹ 40,000. Estimated residual value of the asset at the end of its estimated useful life is ₹ 10,000. Estimated remaining useful life of the asset is 5 years. Depreciation to be charged on straight line basis method over the estimated remaining useful life of the asset.

Case 2: Carrying amount of the asset as on 31.03.2015 is ₹ 1,00,000. Impairment loss is ₹ 40,000. Estimated residual value of the asset at the end of its estimated useful life is ₹ 10,000. Estimated remaining useful life of the asset is 5 years. Depreciation to be charged on written down value basis method over the estimated remaining useful life of the asset.

ANSWER:

Case (1) Revised carrying amount = Carrying Amount – Impairment Loss

= ₹ 1,00,000 – ₹ 40,000 = ₹ 60,000

Residual value = ₹ 10,000

Depreciation charge = (Revised carrying amount – residual value) / estimated remaining useful life of the asset = (₹ 60,000 – ₹10,000) / 5 = ₹ 10,000

Case (2) Revised carrying amount = carrying amount – impairment loss

= ₹ 1,00,000 – ₹ 40,000 = ₹ 60,000

Residual value = ₹ 10,000

Depreciation rate = $1 - \sqrt[n]{\text{Residual Value / Carrying Amount}} = \sqrt[5]{10{,}000 / 60{,}000}$

$= 1 - 0.70 = 0.30$

Hence, depreciation rate is 30 %.

CALCULATION AND TREATMENT OF IMPAIRMENT LOSS

Step 1: Calculate Value in use applying Pre - tax Discount Rate and ignoring financing cost arising from the loan taken from bank to purchase the asset.
Value in use = Present Value of Estimated Future Cash Flows expected to arise from the continuing use of an asset and from its disposal at the end of its useful life.
Step 2: Calculate Net Selling Price
Net Selling Price = Amount receivable from the sale of an asset in an arm's length transaction between knowledgeable and willing parties – Disposal Costs.
Note: Amount receivable from the sale of an asset in an arm's length transaction between knowledgeable and willing parties must be detemined strictly using **Binding Sale Agreement** *or* Current Market Price *or* Estimated Selling Price in the given order.
Step 3: Calculate Carrying Amount i.e. the amount at which an asset is recognized in the balance sheet after deducting any accumulated depreciation (amortization) and accumulated impairment losses thereon.
Step 4: Calculate Recoverable Amount [being Net Selling Price *or* Value in use **whichever is higher**]
Step 5: Calculate Impairment Loss = Carrying Amount of an asset – its Recoverable Amount.
Step 6: First Charge Impairment Loss to Revaluation Reserve to the extent of Revaluation Amount. Then, Charge Remaining Impairment Loss to Profit & Loss Account.
Step 7: Calculate Revised Carrying Amount after Impairment Loss. (Carrying Amount – Impairment Loss)
Step 8: Calculate Revised Depreciation [(Revised Carrying Amount – Estimated Residual Value)/ Remaining useful Life]

TREATMENT OF DEFERRED TAX ASSET *OR* LIABILITY UNDER IMPAIRMENT LOSS

QUESTION 34: How should Deferred Tax Asset *or* Liability be treated under Impairment Loss?

ANSWER: If impairment loss results in deferred tax asset *or* liability, it shall treated as per AS – 22.

QUESTION 34: X Ltd has an asset with carrying amount of ₹ 1 lacs at 31.03.2015 (i.e., Balance Sheet date). On balance sheet date company ascertain the recoverable amount of asset and find that asset has been impaired by ₹ 40,000. Determine the deferred tax asset *or* a liability that shall arise on impairment of asset if tax rate is 40 %.

ANSWER: Impairment loss = ₹ 40,000

Timing difference due to impairment loss = Impairment loss × Tax rate = ₹ 40,000 × 40 % = 16,000

Hence, impairment loss shall result in deferred tax asset to the extent of ₹ 16,000

QUESTION 36: X Ltd has an asset with carrying amount of ₹ 1 lacs at 31.03.2015 (i.e., Balance Sheet date). Asset's written down value as per income tax law is ₹ 90,000. On balance sheet date company ascertain the recoverable amount of asset and find that asset has been impaired by ₹ 40,000. Determine the deferred tax asset *or* liability that shall arise on impairment of asset if tax rate is 40 %.

ANSWER:

	Particulars	₹
A	Deferred tax asset arising on impairment loss (₹ 40,000 × 40%)	16,000
B	Deferred tax liability due to excess depreciation provided as per income – tax law [(₹ 1,00,000 – ₹ 90,000) × 40 %]	4,000
C	Balance in Deferred Tax Asset A/c (A – B)	12,000

QUESTION 37: X Ltd has an asset with carrying amount of ₹ 1 lacs at 31.03.2015 (i.e., Balance Sheet date). Asset's written down value as per income tax law is ₹ 1,15,000. On balance sheet date company ascertain the recoverable amount of asset and find that asset has been impaired by ₹ 40,000. Determine the deferred tax asset *or* liability that shall arise on impairment of asset if tax rate is 40 %.

ANSWER:

	Particulars	₹
A	Deferred tax asset arising on impairment loss (₹ 40,000 × 40 %)	16,000
B	Deferred tax asset due to less depreciation charged as per income – tax law [(₹ 1,15,000 – ₹ 1,00,000) × 40 %]	6,000
C	Balance in Deferred Tax Asset A/c (A + B)	22,000

CASH GENERATING UNIT

QUESTION 38: What is a Cash Generating Unit?

ANSWER: A Cash Generating Unit is the smallest identifiable group of assets that generates cash inflows from continuing use that are largely independent of the cash inflows from other assets *or* groups of assets. In other words cash generating unit is the smallest and identifiable peck of the individual assets that generates cash flows that are independent from the cash flows of the other assets not included in the peck.

QUESTION 39: What shall be the estimated future cash flows of the asset whose output is used internally whether partly *or* wholly?

ANSWER: Management's best estimate of future market prices for the output used internally

QUESTION 40: X Ltd has two plants, plant A and plant B. Plant A's total output is used internally by plant B. Plant B's output is sold out in the market. There exists active market for the output produced by plant A. From the following data determine the value in use for plant A and plant B.

Years	Plant A's output in units	Market Price per unit for plant A's output	Plant B's output in units	Market Price per unit for plant B's output
1	25000	100	10000	300
2	30000	110	12000	320
3	35000	125	14000	360
4	40000	140	16000	400

5	40000	160	16000	450
6	36000	180	14000	500
7	32000	200	13000	570
8	29000	230	12000	650
9	26000	260	10000	750
10	22000	300	9000	850

Above prices are in nominal terms (i.e., without adjusting for inflation). Discount rate after adjusting for inflation is 20 %.

ANSWER:

CALCULATION OF VALUE IN USE OF PLANT A

Years	Output in units of Plant A	Market Price of output of Plant A	Estimated Cash Inflows	P.V.F @ 20 %	Present Value
A	B	C	D = B × C	E	F = D × E
1	25000	100	2500000	0.833	2082500
2	30000	110	3300000	0.694	2290200
3	35000	125	4375000	0.579	2533125
4	40000	140	5600000	0.482	2699200
5	40000	160	6400000	0.402	2572800
6	36000	180	6480000	0.335	2170800
7	32000	200	6400000	0.279	1785600
8	29000	230	6670000	0.233	1554110
9	26000	260	6760000	0.194	1311440
10	22000	300	6600000	0.162	1069200
VALUE IN USE OF PLANT A					20068975

CALCULATION OF VALUE IN USE OF PLANT B

Years	Output in units of Plant B	Market Price of output of Plant B	Estimated Cash Inflows	Estimated Cash Outflows (i.e. estimated cash inflows of plant A)	Net Cash Flows	P.V.F @ 20 %	Present Value
A	B	C	D = B × C	E	F = D – E	G	H = F × G
1	10000	300	3000000	2500000	500000	0.833	416500
2	12000	320	3840000	3300000	540000	0.694	374760
3	14000	360	5040000	4375000	665000	0.579	385035
4	16000	400	6400000	5600000	800000	0.482	385600
5	16000	450	7200000	6400000	800000	0.402	321600
6	14000	500	7000000	6480000	520000	0.335	174200
7	13000	570	7410000	6400000	1010000	0.279	281790
8	12000	650	7800000	6670000	1130000	0.233	263290
9	10000	750	7500000	6760000	740000	0.194	143560

10	9000	850	7650000	6600000	1050000	0.162	170100
VALUE IN USE OF PLANT B							2916435

QUESTION 41: What shall be the estimated future cash flows of the asset whose output is used internally whether partly *or* wholly and no active market exists for its output?

ANSWER: Asset should be merged in to that smallest group of assets (i.e. cash generating unit) that generate cash flows that are grossly independent from the cash flows of other assets *or* cash generating units.

QUESTION 42: Determine the value in use in previous to previous question, if no active market exists for the output of plant A.

ANSWER: Plant A shall be grouped with Plant B and Plant A and Plant B shall form a cash generating unit whose cash flows are independent from cash flows of the other assets *or* units.

VALUE IN USE OF CASH GENERATING UNIT CONSISTING OF PLANT A AND PLANT B.

Years	Output in units of Plant B	Market Price of output of Plant B	Estimated Cash Inflows	P.V.F @ 20 %	Present Value
A	B	C	D = B × C	E	F = D × E
1	10000	300	3000000	0.833	2499000
2	12000	320	3840000	0.694	2664960
3	14000	360	5040000	0.579	2918160
4	16000	400	6400000	0.482	3084800
5	16000	450	7200000	0.402	2894400
6	14000	500	7000000	0.335	2345000
7	13000	570	7410000	0.279	2067390
8	12000	650	7800000	0.233	1817400
9	10000	750	7500000	0.194	1455000
10	9000	850	7650000	0.162	1239300
VALUE IN USE OF PLANT A AND PLANT B					22985410

QUESTION 43: How should the policy of identifying cash generating unit be applied?

ANSWER: Once cash generating unit is identified then it shall remain identified as such from period to period for the same asset *or* type of assets, unless and until a deviation from identification becomes justifiable.

QUESTION 44: What shall be the carrying amount of a cash generating unit?

ANSWER: Carrying amount of a cash generating unit shall consists of the aggregate of carrying amount of the all those assets that are attributed directly *or* allocated on a reasonable and consistent basis to a cash generating unit and that will generate the future cash inflows estimated in determining the cash-generating unit's value in use.

Note: While determination of the carrying amount of the cash generating unit any recognized liabilities shall not be deducted unless and until the recoverable amount of a cash generating unit is not capable of determination without such recognized liabilities.

QUESTION 45: An enterprise enters in to an agreement with the farmer to construct four clamp kilns in his land for brick making. Clamp kilns shall be constructed by digging out the sand from the land. The land with clamp kilns constructed in it shall be used by the enterprise

for brick making for continuous 5 years and afterwards the land shall be returned to the farmer. Agreement stipulates that enterprise must restore the land to its original form after completion of contract. The cost of restoration shall amount to ₹ 15 lacs after 5 years. The charges for using land during the 5 years shall be ₹ 50 lacs. The costs of constructing clamp kilns are ₹ 50 lacs. The estimated cash inflows from sale of bricks in 5 years are as follows:

Years	1	2	3	4	5
Cash Inflows	30,00,000	40,00,000	50,00,000	60,00,000	70,00,000

Discount rate is 20 %. Depreciation is to be provided uniformly in five years. The enterprise has received an offer to buy this project at the end of first year for ₹ 90 lacs. In this offer buyer shall also take the obligation of restoration cost. Determine the impairment loss if any at the end of first year.

ANSWER: Recoverable amount of the cash generating unit shall be the higher of the followings:

(i) Net Selling Price (i.e. ₹ 90,00,000) *or*

(ii) Value in use (i.e. ₹ 1,29,27,000)

Hence the recoverable amount is ₹ 1,29,27,000

CARRYING AMOUNT OF THE CASH GENERATING UNIT

	Particulars	Amount
A	Carrying amount of the project (As per W. No. 1)	8482400
B	Provision for cost of restoration (As per W. No 1 & 2)	603000
C	Carrying amount of the cash generating unit (A – B)	7879400

Since recoverable amount is higher than the carrying amount of the cash generating unit, there is no impairment loss at the end of 1st year.

Working notes:

(1) CARRYING AMOUNT OF LAND WITH CLAMP KILNS CONSTRUCTED IN IT AT THE END OF 1ST YEAR

	Particulars	Amount
A	Cost of using land for 5 years	5000000
B	Cost of clamp kilns	5000000
C	Present value of cost of restoration*	603000
D	Total cost of Project (A + B + C)	10603000
E	Depreciation for the year (D / 5)	2120600
F	Carrying amount of the project (D – E)	8482400

* A provision for cost of restoration is made as soon as sand is dug out from the land for constructing clamp kilns. This amount (i.e. present value of ₹ 15,00,000) provided as provision was recognised as part of the cost of the project.

(2) CALCULATION OF PRESENT VALUE OF COST OF RESTORATION

	Particulars	Amount
A	Cost of restoration after 5 years	1500000
B	P.V.F @ 20% for 5th year	0.402
C	Present value of cost of restoration (A × B)	603000

(3) VALUE IN USE FOR THE FIRST YEAR

Year	Cash Inflows	Cash Outflows	Net Cash flows	P.V.F @ 20%	Present Value
A	B	C	D = B – C	E	F = D × E
1	40,00,000	0	40,00,000	0.833	3332000
2	50,00,000	0	50,00,000	0.694	3470000
3	60,00,000	0	60,00,000	0.579	3474000
4	70,00,000	1500000	55,00,000	0.482	2651000
		TOTAL			12927000

QUESTION 46: How should impairment loss of the cash generating unit be allocated to the individual asset comprised in that cash generating unit?

ANSWER: Impairment loss of cash generating unit should be allocated to each asset of that unit on the basis of their carrying amount. These allocations of impairment loss to each asset shall be considered as impairment loss for individual asset and recognized accordingly.

QUESTION 47: What shall be the limit of allocated impairment loss applicable to each asset in a cash generating unit?

ANSWER: The allocated impairment loss of each asset shall be limited to the lower of the followings:

(i) Carrying amount

(ii) Carrying amount – Net Selling Price (if determinable) but not less than zero

(iii) Carrying amount – Value in use (if determinable) but not less than zero

The allocated impairment loss of any asset if cannot be allocated due to these limits then unallocated amount shall be allocated to the remaining asset on a pro – rata basis and this process shall continue till all impairment loss is allocated.

QUESTION 48: Following are the data about the assets comprised in a cash generating unit:

Assets	Carrying Amount	Net Selling Price	Value In Use
A	100000	40000	-
B	150000	50000	-
C	200000	60000	-
D	500000	450000	-

Value in use of cash generating unit is ₹ 8,00,000

Determine the impairment loss and their allocation to each asset in cash generating unit.

ANSWER: Recoverable amount of the cash generating unit shall be the higher of the followings:

(i) Net Selling Price (i.e. ₹ 40,000 + ₹ 50,000 + ₹ 60,000 + ₹ 4,50,000 = 6,00,000) *or*

(ii) Value in use (i.e. ₹ 8,00,000)

Hence the recoverable amount is ₹ 8,00,000

Carrying amount of cash generating unit (₹ 1,00,000 + ₹ 1,50,000 + ₹ 2,00,000 + ₹ 5,00,000 = ₹ 9,50,000)

Impairment loss of cash generating unit = Carrying amount of cash generating unit – Recoverable amount = ₹9,50,000 – ₹ 8,00,000 = ₹ 1,50,000

ALLOCATION OF IMPAIRMENT LOSS OF CASH GENERATING UNIT TO EACH ASSET IN CASH GENERATING UNIT

	Particulars	A	B	C	D	Total
A	Carrying amount of each asset	100000	150000	200000	500000	950000
B	Allocated impairment loss [150000 × (A / 950000)]	15790	23685	31580	78945	150000
C	Limit of impairment loss	60000	100000	140000	50000	
	Lower of the following three					
	Carrying amount of each asset	100000	150000	200000	500000	
	Carrying amount – Net Selling Price	60000	100000	140000	50000	
	Carrying amount – Value in Use	N.A	N.A	N.A	N.A	
D	Impairment loss to be allocated subject to limit at C	15790	23685	31580	50000	121055
E	Carrying amount after impairment loss (A – D)	84210	126315	168420	450000	828945
F	Unallocated impairment loss (₹8,28,945 – ₹8,00,000)					28945
G	Carrying amount of A, B and C after impairment loss	84210	126315	168420		378945
H	Allocated Impairment Loss [28945 × (G / 378945)]	6432	9648	12865		28945
I	Total impairment loss (D + H) subject to limit in C	22222	33333	44445	50000	150000
J	Carrying amount after impairment loss (A – I)	77778	116667	155555	450000	800000

QUESTION 49: What shall be the treatment if any individual asset in cash generating unit suffers more damages than other assets comprised in that cash generating unit?

ANSWER: If individual asset's recoverable amount is not determinable then impairment loss of cash generating unit shall be computed on aggregated basis and allocated on pro – rata basis since all assets of the cash generating unit work simultaneously. Hence it is not relevant that whether particular asset of the cash generating unit sustains more damages than the other assets of the unit.

QUESTION 50: Is individual asset included in cash generating unit should further be individually assessed for impairment loss after the assessment of relating cash generating unit for impairment loss?

ANSWER: If an asset is included in cash generating unit then such an asset should further be assessed for impairment loss after the assessment of related cash generating unit for impairment loss as under:

(i) If cash generating unit to which asset belongs suffers an impairment loss and such loss is allocated to an individual asset then such individual asset together with its allocated loss shall be compared with net Selling Price of an asset. If asset's carrying amount net of its allocated loss is more than the net Selling Price of an asset then such net carrying amount of an asset shall be reduced to its net Selling Price. However the carrying amount net of allocated loss cannot be reduced below net Selling Price of an asset due to application of limits.

(ii) If cash generating unit to which asset belongs does not suffer any impairment loss then there is no requirement to assessed individual asset for any further impairment loss.

CORPORATE ASSETS

QUESTION 51: What are Corporate Assets?

ANSWER: Corporate Assets are assets other than goodwill that contribute to the future cash flows of both the cash generating unit under review and other cash generating units. The main characteristics of corporate assets are that they do not generate cash flows which are independent from other assets *or* group of assets and their carrying amount cannot be fully attributed to the cash generating unit under review. These assets include buildings, division of the enterprise, computers, research centre, etc.

QUESTION 52: How should Corporate Assets be tested for impairment loss?

ANSWER: If there is any indication that corporate asset is impaired then recoverable amount is determined for the cash generating unit to which corporate asset belongs and then that amount is compared with the carrying amount of the cash generating unit and corporate asset and if there is any impairment loss then it is allocated on the basis of carrying amount. This method of allocating is known as bottom – up test.

QUESTION 53: How should corporate asset be tested for impairment loss if it cannot be allocated to cash generating unit?

ANSWER: In such a case the enterprise should perform top – down test i.e. if corporate asset cannot be allocated to any smallest cash generating unit then enterprise shall determine that group of cash generating units to which corporate asset may be allocated reasonably. After allocation the recoverable amount shall be determined for that group of cash generating units and compared with the carrying amounts of group of cash generating units and corporate assets.

QUESTION 54: X Ltd has 3 cash generating units P, Q & R. The carrying amounts of P, Q & R are ₹ 20 lacs, ₹ 35 lacs & ₹ 50 lacs respectively. All the operations are carried by the enterprise under the same building. The carrying amount of building is ₹ 90 lacs. The carrying amount of building can reasonably be allocated to P, Q & R on the basis of their carrying amount. The enterprise has also some assets which cannot be allocated reasonably with carrying amount of ₹ 20 lacs. The recoverable amounts of P, Q & R are ₹ 30 lacs, ₹ 60 lacs & ₹ 100 lacs respectively. The recoverable amount of entire X ltd is ₹ 200 lacs. Determine the impairment loss to the assets if any.

ANSWER:

IMPAIRMENT LOSS AND CARRYING AMOUNTS AFTER IMPAIRMENT LOSS:

	Particulars	P	Q	R	Building	Other Assets	Total
A	Carrying Amount of the units	2000000	3500000	5000000	9000000	2000000	21500000
B	Carrying amount of the building allocated in the ratio of 1:2:3	1714286	3000000	4285714	(9000000)	0	0
C	Combined carrying amount of the units and building (A + B)	3714286	6500000	9285714	0	2000000	21500000
D	Recoverable amount of the units	3000000	6000000	10000000			
E	Impairment loss	714286	500000	0			

F	Impairment loss allocated to building [E × (B / C)]	(329670)	(230769)	0	560439		
G	Carrying amount after impairment loss (A – E – F)	1615384	3230769	5000000	8439561	2000000	20285714
H	Recoverable amount of entire X ltd						20000000
I	Impairment loss (G – H)						285714
J	Impairment loss is allocated only to other assets since all assets have been reduced to their limits accept other assets.					285714	285714
K	Carrying amount after allocating impairment loss (G – J)	1615384	3230769	5000000	8439561	1714286	20000000

QUESTION 55: What shall be treatment of individual asset comprised in cash generating unit that suffers impairment loss if Net Selling Price of the individual asset is less than carrying amount net of allocated loss of cash generating unit?

ANSWER: If carrying amount net of allocated loss of cash generating unit of individual asset is less than its Selling Price then such asset shall further be reduced to its net Selling Price.

TESTING OF GOODWILL FOR IMPAIRMENT

QUESTION 56: Why goodwill cannot be treated as individual asset for impairment test?

ANSWER: Goodwill does not generate cash flows that are independent from the cash flow of other assets *or* group of assets, hence the recoverable amount of goodwill as an individual asset is not determinable. If recoverable amount of any asset cannot be determinable then it cannot be assessed for impairment test individually.

QUESTION 57: How should goodwill be tested for impairment as its recoverable amount is not determinable?

ANSWER: Goodwill shall be tested for impairment loss by allocating its carrying amount to the relevant cash generating unit.

QUESTION 58: How shall goodwill be allocated to the cash generating unit and tested for impairment loss and allocation of impairment loss if any?

ANSWER: Goodwill shall be allocated to any cash generating unit by following steps:

(i) Perform bottom – up test and identify the smallest cash generating unit to which goodwill can be allocated on a reasonable and consistent basis.

(ii) Allocate the carrying amount of goodwill to the identified cash generating unit.

(iii) Check the identified cash generating unit along with allocated goodwill for the impairment loss.

(iv) If there is any impairment loss then it shall first be deducted from allocated goodwill and balance if any remaining shall be deducted from the carrying amount of the identified cash generating unit.

QUESTION 59: X Ltd purchase entire Y ltd for ₹ 50 lacs in the beginning of year 2013. Y ltd has two cash generating units L & M. Net fair value of L & M are ₹20 lacs and 25 lacs respectively. At the end of year 2015 the recoverable amount of L & M are ₹ 14 lacs and 20 lacs respectively. Depreciation rate followed by the company is 10 % on W.D.V basis on its entire assets. Determine the impairment loss if any for L & M if goodwill can be allocated between L & M on its net fair value basis.

ANSWER:

CARRYING AMOUNT OF ASSETS AFTER IMPAIRMENT LOSS

	Particulars	L	M	Goodwill	Total
A	Net Fair Value at the beginning of 2013	2000000	2500000	500000	5000000
B	Depreciation for the year 2013	200000	250000	50000	500000
C	Carrying Amount at the beginning of 2014	1800000	2250000	450000	4500000
D	Depreciation for the year 2014	180000	225000	45000	450000
E	Carrying Amount at the beginning of 2015	1620000	2025000	405000	4050000
F	Depreciation for the year 2015	162000	202500	40500	405000
G	Carrying Amount at the end of 2015	1458000	1822500	364500	3645000
H	Allocation of Goodwill [(carrying amount of goodwill) × A / (2000000 + 2500000)]	162000	202500		364500
I	Carrying amount along with allocated goodwill (G + H)	1620000	2025000		3645000
J	Recoverable amount	1400000	2000000		3400000
K	Impairment loss (I – J)	220000	25000		245000
L	Impairment loss first be deducted from allocated goodwill	160000	25000		185000
M	Balance to be deducted from carrying amount of cash generating unit (K – L)	60000	0		60000
N	Deduction in respect of impairment loss to the carrying amount	60000	0	185000	245000
O	Carrying Amount at the end of 2015 after impairment loss (G – N)	1398000	1822500	179500	3400000

QUESTION 60: How shall goodwill be tested for impairment if it cannot be allocated to cash generating unit by performing bottom – up test and tested for impairment loss and allocation of impairment loss if any?

ANSWER: If goodwill cannot be allocated to any cash generating unit by performing bottom – up test then it should be allocated in the following manner:

(i) Identify the smallest cash generating units and check them for impairment loss if any without allocation of goodwill.

(ii) Perform top – down test i.e. group up the smallest cash generating units in to a unit to which goodwill can be allocated on a reasonable and consistent basis.

(iii) Check the grouped cash generating unit along with allocated goodwill for the impairment loss.

(iv) If there is any impairment loss then it shall first be deducted from allocated goodwill and balance if any remaining shall be deducted from the carrying amount of the grouped cash generating unit.

QUESTION 61: Determine the impairment loss in previous to previous if goodwill cannot be reasonably allocated to L & M.

ANSWER:

CARRYING AMOUNT OF ASSETS AFTER IMPAIRMENT LOSS

	Particulars	L	M	Goodwill	Total
A	Net Fair Value at the beginning of 2013	2000000	2500000	500000	5000000
B	Depreciation for the year 2013	200000	250000	50000	500000
C	Carrying Amount at the beginning of 2014	1800000	2250000	450000	4500000
D	Depreciation for the year 2014	180000	225000	45000	450000
E	Carrying Amount at the beginning of 2015	1620000	2025000	405000	4050000
F	Depreciation for the year 2015	162000	202500	40500	405000
G	Carrying Amount at the end of 2015	1458000	1822500	364500	3645000
H	Recoverable amount	1400000	2000000		3400000
I	Impairment loss if any before allocation of goodwill (I – J)	58000	0	0	58000
J	Carrying amount after adjusting impairment loss (G – I)	1400000	1822500	364500	3587000
K	Recoverable amount				3400000
L	Impairment loss after considering goodwill				187000
M	Impairment loss to be deducted from goodwill				187000
N	Total Impairment loss	58000	0	187000	245000
O	Carrying amount after impairment loss (G – N)	1400000	1822500	177500	3400000

REVERSAL OF AN IMPAIRMENT LOSS

QUESTION 62: What is Reversal of an Impairment Loss?

ANSWER: If impairment loss is recognized for an asset in prior accounting periods and if such recognized impairment loss no longer exists *or* may have decreased in current accounting period then it is reversal of an impairment loss.

QUESTION 63: At what interval should enterprise assess an asset for reversal of an impairment loss?

ANSWER: At each Balance Sheet Date

QUESTION 64: How shall reversal of an impairment loss of an individual asset be recognized?

ANSWER:

Case	Treatment
(a) If asset is carried at revalued amount	1. First reversal of an impairment loss to the extent of Impairment Loss previously recognized as expense in Statement of Profit and Loss of prior accounting periods shall be recognized as income in the Statement of Profit and Loss. 2. Then, the balance of Reversal of an Impairment Loss shall be added to Revaluation Surplus of the asset. **JOURNAL ENTRY** Asset A/c Dr. To Profit & Loss A/c
(b) In other cases	Reversal of an Impairment Loss shall be added to the carrying amount of an asset and simultaneously recognized as income in the Statement of Profit and Loss. **JOURNAL ENTRY** Asset A/c Dr. To Profit & Loss A/c To Revaluation Reserve A/c

QUESTION 65: What shall be the limit of the carrying amount of the asset after adjusting for reversal of an impairment loss?

ANSWER: The increased carrying amount of an asset due to a reversal of an impairment loss should not exceed the carrying amount that would have been determined (net of amortization *or* depreciation) had no impairment loss been recognized for the asset in prior accounting periods.

QUESTION 66: X Ltd had an asset with carrying amount of ₹20 lacs at the end of the year 2012. In that year asset is tested for impairment loss and ₹ 2.5 lacs was charged as impairment loss. In the year 2015 market conditions improved and asset was checked for reversal of an impairment loss. Its Recoverable Amount is determined at ₹ 22 lacs. Determine the amount of impairment loss to be reversed during the period if depreciation charged is 10 % WDV.

ANSWER:

REVERSAL OF AN IMPAIRMENT LOSS ON ASSET

	Particulars	₹
A	Carrying amount as on 31.12.2012	2000000
B	Impairment loss	250000
C	Carrying amount after impairment loss (A – B)	1750000
D	Depreciation for the year 2013 (C × 10 %)	175000
E	Carrying amount as on 31.12.2013 (C – D)	1575000
F	Depreciation for the year 2014 (E × 10 %)	157500
G	Carrying amount as on 31.12.2014 (E – F)	1417500
H	Depreciation for the year 2015 (G × 10 %)	141750
I	Carrying amount as on 31.12.2015 (G – H)	1275750

J	Recoverable amount		2200000
K	Amount to be reversed (J – I)		924250
L	Carrying amount subject to limit (I + K)		2200000
M	Limit		1458000
	Carrying amount as on 31.12.2012	2000000	
	Less: Depreciation for the year 2013 @ 10 %	200000	
	Carrying amount as on 31.12.2013	1800000	
	Less: Depreciation for the year 2014 @ 10 %	180000	
	Carrying amount as on 31.12.2014	1620000	
	Less: Depreciation for the year 2015 @ 10 %	162000	
	Carrying amount as on 31.12.2015	1458000	
N	Reduction in reversal of an impairment loss due to limit (L – M)		742000
O	Amount of impairment loss to be reversed after applying limit (K – N)		182250

QUESTION 67: How shall revised depreciation charge be determined after adjusting for reversal of an impairment loss?

ANSWER: Depreciation charge should be calculated so as to allocate revised carrying amount of the asset less residual value over the remaining useful life of the asset on the systematic and rational basis.

QUESTION 68: How should reversal of an impairment loss of the cash generating unit be allocated to the individual asset comprised in that cash generating unit?

ANSWER: Reversal of an impairment loss of cash generating unit should be allocated to each asset of that unit on the basis of their carrying amount. These allocations of reversal of an impairment loss to each asset shall be considered as reversal of an impairment loss for individual asset and recognized accordingly.

QUESTION 69: What shall be the limit of allocated reversal of an impairment loss applicable to each asset in a cash generating unit?

ANSWER: The allocated reversal of an impairment loss of each asset shall be limited to the lower of the followings:

(i) Carrying amount of the asset that would have been determinable (net of depreciation) if no impairment loss had been recognized in prior accounting periods – carrying amount of the asset

(ii) Recoverable amount of the asset (if determinable) – Carrying amount of the asset

The allocated reversal of an impairment loss of any asset if cannot be allocated due to these limits then unallocated amount shall be allocated to the remaining asset on a pro – rata basis and this process shall continue till all reversal of an impairment loss is allocated.

QUESTION 70: X Ltd had a cash generating unit that comprised three assets A, B & C. The carrying amounts of A, B & C as on 31.12.2013 were ₹ 20 lacs,30 lacs & 40 lacs respectively. On the same date this cash generating unit was tested for impairment loss and ₹ 15 lacs was charged as impairment loss and allocated among the assets in the ratio of 4:5:6. In year 2015 conditions of the market improved and asset is tested for reversal of an impairment loss. The recoverable amount of the cash generating unit is determined at ₹ 75 lacs. Determine the amount of impairment losses to be reversed on each asset if depreciation charged on A, B & C are 15 % (WDV),10 % (WDV) & 5 % (WDV) respectively.

ANSWER:

ALLOCATION OF THE REVERSAL OF IMPAIRMENT LOSS

	Particulars	A ₹	B ₹	C ₹	TOTAL ₹
A	Carrying amount of the assets as on 31.12.2013	2000000	3000000	4000000	9000000
B	Impairment loss on 31.12.2013 to be allocated in the ratio of 4: 5: 6	400000	500000	600000	1500000
C	Carrying amount of the assets as on 31.12.2013 after impairment loss (A – B)	1600000	2500000	3400000	7500000
D	Depreciation for the year 2014	240000	250000	170000	660000
E	Carrying amount of the assets as on 31.12.2014	1360000	2250000	3230000	6840000
F	Depreciation for the year 2015	204000	225000	161500	590500
G	Carrying amount of the assets as on 31.12.2015	1156000	2025000	3068500	6249500
H	Recoverable amount				7500000
I	Reversal of an impairment loss (H – G)				1250500
J	Allocation on the basis of ratio 4 : 5: 6	333467	416833	500200	1250500
K	Limits (as per working note)	289000	405000	541500	
L	Excess reversal in case of assets A & B (J – K)	44467	11833		
M	Adjustment of excess reversal	-44467	-11833	56300	
N	impairment loss to be reversed after applying limits on assets A & B (J + M)	289000	405000	556500	
O	Again applying limits on asset C (N – K)	0	0	15000	
P	Impairment loss to be reversed after applying limits on all assets (N – O)	289000	405000	541500	
Q	Carrying amount after adjustment of reversal of impairment loss (G + P)	1445000	2430000	3610000	7485000

Working Note:

CALCULATION OF LIMIT

	Particulars	A ₹	B ₹	C ₹	TOTAL ₹
A	Carrying amount of the assets as on 31.12.2013	2000000	3000000	4000000	9000000
B	Depreciation for the year 2014	300000	300000	200000	800000
C	Carrying amount of the assets as on 31.12.2014	1700000	2700000	3800000	8200000
D	Depreciation for the year 2015	255000	270000	190000	715000
E	Carrying amount of the assets as on 31.12.2015 if no impairment loss had been recognized in year 2013	1445000	2430000	3610000	7485000
F	Actual carrying amount as on 31.12.2015 before adjustment for reversal of impairment loss	1156000	2025000	3068500	7500000
G	Limits (E – F)	289000	405000	541500	

QUESTION 71: When reversal of an impairment loss on goodwill should be recognized?

ANSWER: Impairment loss is first allocated to goodwill hence reversal of an impairment loss should be allocated to goodwill at last only and only if

(a) the impairment loss was caused by a specific external event of an exceptional nature that is not expected to recur; and

(b) subsequent external events have occurred that reverse the effect of that event

Therefore, Impairment loss cannot be reversed for goodwill on account of change in estimates.

QUESTION 72: What are the requirements of this standard if enterprise approved a plan for discontinuance of operation?

ANSWER: If there is approval of discontinuance plan then the enterprise shall estimate a recoverable amount of each asset *or* cash generating unit of the discontinuance operation as per this standard.

DISCLOSURE REQUIREMENTS

QUESTION 73: What are the Disclosure Requirements regarding impairment losses and reversal of an impairment losses for each class of assets?

ANSWER: The enterprise should disclose for each class of assets the following information:

(a) the amount of impairment losses recognized in the statement of profit and loss during the period and the line item(s) of the statement of profit and loss in which those impairment losses are included;

(b) the amount of reversals of impairment losses recognized in the statement of profit and loss during the period and the line item(s) of the statement of profit and loss in which those impairment losses are reversed;

(c) the amount of impairment losses recognized directly against revaluation surplus during the period; and

(d) the amount of reversals of impairment losses recognized directly in revaluation surplus during the period.

Note: A class of asset is a group of assets of similar nature.

QUESTION 74: What are the disclosure requirements regarding each reportable segment as per AS – 17?

ANSWER: An enterprise that applies AS 17, Segment Reporting, should disclose the following for each reportable segment based on an enterprise's primary format (as defined in AS 17):

(a) the amount of impairment losses recognized in the statement of profit and loss and directly against revaluation surplus during the period; and

(b) the amount of reversals of impairment losses recognized in the statement of profit and loss and directly in revaluation surplus during the period.

QUESTION 75: What are the disclosure requirements regarding impairment loss *or* reversal of an impairment loss on individual asset *or* cash generating unit?

ANSWER: If impairment loss *or* reversal of an impairment loss on individual asset *or* cash generating unit is material then an enterprise should disclose the following information:

(a) The events and circumstances that led to the recognition *or* reversal of the impairment loss;

(b) the amount of the impairment loss recognized *or* reversed;

(c) for an individual asset:

   (i) the nature of the asset; and

   (ii) the reportable segment to which the asset belongs, based on the enterprise's primary format (as defined in AS 17, Segment Reporting);

(d) for a cash-generating unit:

(i) a description of the cash-generating unit (such as whether it is a product line, a plant, a business operation, a geographical area, a reportable segment as defined in AS 17 *or* other);

(ii) the amount of the impairment loss recognized *or* reversed by class of assets and by reportable segment based on the enterprise's primary format (as defined in AS 17); and

(iii) if the aggregation of assets for identifying the cash generating unit has changed since the previous estimate of the cash-generating unit's recoverable amount (if any), the enterprise should describe the current and former way of aggregating assets and the reasons for changing the way the cash-generating unit is identified;

(e) whether the recoverable amount of the asset (cash-generating unit) is its net Selling Price *or* its value in use;

(f) if recoverable amount is net Selling Price, the basis used to determine net Selling Price (such as whether Selling Price was determined by reference to an active market *or* in some other way); and

(g) If recoverable amount is value in use, the discount rate(s) used in the current estimate and previous estimate (if any) of value in use.

QUESTION 76: What are the Disclosure Requirements if aggregate of impairment losses (or reversals) during the period are material?

ANSWER: If impairment losses recognized (reversed) during the period are material in aggregate to the financial statements of the reporting enterprise as a whole, an enterprise should disclose a brief description of the following:

(a) the main classes of assets affected by impairment losses (reversals of impairment losses) for which no information is disclosed under above requirements; and

(b) the main events and circumstances that led to the recognition (reversal) of these impairment losses for which no information is disclosed under above requirements.

PRACTICAL QUESTIONS FOR PRACTICE

QUESTION 1: Y LTD. gives the following estimates of cash flows relating to fixed asset on 31.03.2015. The discount is 15%.

Year ended 31st March	2016	2017	2018	2019	2020
Cash Flow (₹ In lakhs)	4000	6000	6000	8000	4000

Residual value at the end of 2020 = ₹ 1000 lakhs
Fixed Asset purchased on 1-4-2012 = ₹ 40,000 lakhs
Useful life = 8 years
Selling Price on 31.03.2015 = ₹ 20,100 lakhs
Disposal Cost on 31.03.2015 = ₹ 100 lakhs

Year	1	2	3	4	5
PVF@15%	0.870	0.756	0.658	0.572	0.497

Required: Calculate (a) Value in use on 31.03.2015, (b) Carrying amount on 31.03.2015, (c) Impairment loss to be recognized for the year ended 31.03.2015 and Pass Journal Entry to record it, (d) Revised carrying amount, (e) Depreciation charge for the year ended 31.03.2016.

ANSWER:

	Particulars	₹ (in lakhs)
A	Cost of Fixed Asset	40,000
B	*Less:* Depreciation for 1st year [(40,000 – 1000) × 1/8]	4,875
C	Carrying Amount at the end of 1st year (A – B)	35,125
D	*Less:* Depreciation for 2nd year [(40,000 – 1000) × 1/8]	4,875
E	Carrying Amount at the end of 2nd year (C – D)	30,250
F	*Less:* Depreciation for 3rd year [(40,000 – 1000) × 1/8]	4,875
G	Carrying Amount before Impairment Loss (E – F)	25,375
H	*Less:* Recoverable Amount [being Net Selling Price (20,100 – 100) *or* Value in use (19,025) **whichever is higher**]	20,000
I	Impairment Loss to be charged to P&L A/c [Carrying Amount – Recoverable Amount]	5,375
J	Carrying Amount after Impairment Loss (Recoverable Amount – Impairment Loss)	20,000
K	*Less:* Depreciation for 4th year [(20,000 – 1,000)/5]	3,800
L	Carrying Amount at end of 4th year	16,200

TREATMENT OF IMPAIRMENT LOSS
JOURNAL ENTRY

Profit & Loss A/c	Dr.	₹ 5,375 lakhs	
To Provision for Impairment Loss A/c			₹ 5,375 lakhs

Working Note:

CALCULATION OF VALUE IN USE

Year	Cash Flow	Discount as per 15%	Discounted cash flow
2016	4000	0.870	3480
2017	6000	0.756	4536
2018	6000	0.658	3948
2019	8000	0.572	4576
2020	4000	0.497	1988
2020	1000	0.497	497
			19025

QUESTION 2: State the Treatment of Impairment Loss in the previous question if Upward Revaluation was done in last year by 50%.

ANSWER:

Carrying Amount in the beg. of 3rd year 40,000 – [(40,000 – 1000) × 2/8]	30,250
Add: Upward Revaluation (30,250 × 10%)	3,025
Carrying Amount at the end of 3rd year before Depreciation	33,275
Less: Depreciation [(33,275 – 1,000)/6]	5,379
Carrying Amount in the beg. of 4th year (including revaluation amount of 3,025 lakhs)	27,896

Less: Recoverable Amount [being Net Selling Price (20,100 – 100) *or* Value in use (19,025) **whichever is higher**]	20,000
Impairment Loss	7,896
Less: Impairment Loss to be charged to Revaluation Reserve	(3,025)
Impairment Loss to be charged to Profit and Loss Account	4,871

TREATMENT OF IMPAIRMENT LOSS
JOURNAL ENTRY

Profit & Loss A/c	Dr.	₹ 4,871 lakhs	
Revaluation Reserve A/c	Dr.	₹ 3,025 lakhs	
To Provision for Impairment Loss A/c			₹ 7,896 lakhs

QUESTION 3: From the following details of an asset, (i) Find out Impairment Loss, (ii) Treatment of Impairment Loss (iii) Find out Current Year Depreciation (iv) Pass Journal Entry Cost of asset ₹ 60 lakhs, Useful life period 10 years, Salvage value ₹ 4 lakhs, Useful life remaining 3 years, Upward Revaluation done in last year by 50%. Current Value in use = ₹ 12 lakhs, Current Selling Price ₹ 11 lakhs, Current Disposal Cost ₹ 1 lakh.

ANSWER:

PROVISION OF AS 28

1. As per AS 28, "Impairment of Assets", an impairment loss on a revalued asset is recognised as an expense in the statement of profit and loss. However, an impairment loss on a revalued asset is recognised directly against any revaluation surplus for the asset to the extent that the impairment loss does not exceed the amount held in the revaluation surplus for that same asset.
2. As per AS 28, "after the recognition of an impairment loss, the depreciation (amortization) charge for the asset should be adjusted in future periods to allocate the asset's revised carrying amount, less its residual value (if any), on a systematic basis over its remaining useful life."

ADVICE

Particulars	₹ lakhs
Carrying Amount in the beg. of 7th year 60 – (60 – 4)] × 6/10]	26.4
Add: Upward Revaluation (26.4 × 50%)	13.2
Carrying Amount at the end of 7th year before Dep.	39.6
Less: Depreciation [(39.6 – 4)/4]	8.9
Carrying Amount in the beg. of 8th year (including revaluation amount of ₹ 13.2 lakhs)	30.7
Less: Current Recoverable Amount (being Net Selling Price *or* Value in use whichever is higher)	(12)
Impairment Loss	18.7
Less: Impairment Loss Charged To Revaluation Reserve	(13.2)
Impairment Loss charged to Profit and Loss Account	5.5
Revised Carrying Amount after Impairment Loss	12
Depreciation for the Current Year [Carrying Amount/ Remaining Useful Life] [₹ 12,00,000/3]	4
Revised Carrying Amount	8

TREATMENT OF IMPAIRMENT LOSS
(I) JOURNAL ENTRY

Profit & Loss A/c	Dr.	₹ 5.5 lakhs	
Revaluation Reserve A/c	Dr.	₹ 13.2 lakhs	
To Provision for Impairment Loss A/c			₹ 18.7 lakhs

QUESTION 4: An asset does not meet the requirements of environment laws which have been recently enacted. The asset has to be destroyed as per the law. The asset is carried in the Balance Sheet at the year end at ₹ 6,00,000. The estimated cost of destroying the asset is ₹ 70,000. How is the asset to be accounted for?

ANSWER:

PROVISION OF AS 28

As per AS 28, "Impairment of Assets", impairment loss is the amount by which the carrying amount of an asset exceeds its recoverable amount, where, recoverable amount is the higher of an asset's net Selling Price * and its value in use.

ADVICE

Recoverable Amount will be nil [higher of value in use (nil) and net Selling Price (Rs 70,000)]. Thus impairment loss will be calculated as ₹ 6,00,000 [carrying amount (Rs 6,00,000) – recoverable amount (nil)]. Therefore, asset is to be fully impaired and impairment loss of ₹ 6,00,000 has to be recognized as an expense immediately in the statement of Profit and Loss as per para 58 of AS 28.

QUESTION 5: A plant was acquired 15 years ago at a cost of ₹ 5 crores. Its accumulated depreciation as at 31st March,2014 was ₹ 4,15 crores. Depreciation estimated for the Financial year 2014-2015 is ₹ 25 lakhs. Estimated Net Selling Price as on 31st March,2014 was ₹ 30 lakhs, which is expected to decline by 20 per cent by the end of the next financial year.

Its value in use has been computed at ₹,35 lakhs as on 1st April,2014, which is expected to decrease by 30 per cent by the end of the Financial year.

(i) Assuming that other conditions for applicability of the impairment Accounting Standard are satisfied, what should be the carrying amount of this plant as at 31st March,2015?

(ii) How much will be the amount of write off for the financial year ended 31st March,2015?

(iii) If the plant had been revalued ten years ago and the current revaluation reserves against this plant were to be ₹ 12 lakhs, how would you answer to questions (i) and (ii) above?

(iv) If the value in use was zero and the enterprise was required to incur a cost of ₹ 2 lakhs to dispose off the Plant, what would be your response to questions (i) and (ii) above?

ANSWER:

PROVISION OF AS 28

As per AS 28 "impairment of Assets", if the recoverable amount of an asset is less than its carrying amount, the carrying amount of the asset should be reduced to its recoverable amount and that reduction is an impairment loss. An impairment loss on a revalued asset is recognised as an expense in the Statement of Profit and Loss. However, an impairment loss on a revalued asset is recognised directly against any revaluation surplus for the asset to the extent that the impairment loss does not exceed the amount held in the revaluation surplus for that same asset.

ANSWER TO VARIOUS PARTS:

	Particulars	(₹ in lakhs)
(i)	Carrying amount of plant (after impairment) as on 31st March,2015 [Higher for ₹ 24 lakhs *or* ₹ 24.5 lakhs]	24.50
(ii)	Impairment Loss to be w/o [₹ 60 lakhs – ₹ 24.5 lakhs]	35.50
(iii)	If the Plant had been revalued ten years ago and Current Revaluation Reserve ₹ 12 lakh Debit to Revaluation Reserve	12.00
	Amount charged to Profit and Loss Account (₹ 35.50 lakhs – ₹ 12 lakhs)	23.50
(iv)	If Value in use is zero	
	Value in use (a)	Nil
	Net Selling Price (b)	(2.00)
	Recoverable amount [higher of (a) and (b)]	Nil
	Carrying amount (closing book value)	Nil
	Impairment Loss (₹ 60 lakhs – Nil)	60.00

Entire Book Value of plant will be written off and charged to Profit and Loss Account.

Working Note:

CALCULATION OF CLOSING BOOK VALUE, ESTIMATED NET SELLING VALUE, ESTIMATED VALUE IN USE OF PLANT

Particulars	(₹ in lakhs)
Opening book value as on 1.4.2014 (₹ 500 lakhs – ₹ 415 lakhs)	85
Less: Depreciation for financial year 2014-2015	(25)
Closing book value as on 31.3.2015	60
Estimated Net Selling Price as on 1.4.2014	30
Less: Estimated decrease during the year (20% of ₹ 30 lakhs)	(6)
Estimated net Selling Price as on 31.3.2015	24
Estimated value in use as on 1.4.2014	35.0
Less: Estimated decrease during the year (30% of ₹ 35 lakhs)	(10.5)
Estimated value in use as on 313.2015	24.5

QUESTION 6: G Ltd. acquired a machine on 1st April,2009 for ₹ 7 crore that had an estimated useful life of 7 years. The machine is depreciated on straight line basis and does not carry any residual value. On 1st April, 2013, the carrying value of the machine was reassessed at ₹ 5.10 crore and the surplus arising out of the revaluation being credited to revaluation reserve. For the year ended March 2015, conditions indicating an impairment of the machine existed and the amount recoverable ascertained to be only ₹ 79 lakhs. You are required to calculate the loss on impairment of the machine and show how this loss is to be treated in the books of G Ltd., G Ltd., had followed the policy of writing down the revaluation surplus by the increase charge of depreciation resulting from the revaluation.

ANSWER:

CALCULATION & TREATMENT OF IMPAIRMENT LOSS

Particulars		₹ in crores)
Carrying amount of the machine as on 1st April 2009		7.00
Depreciation for 4 years i.e.,2009-2010 to 2012-2013		(4.00)
Carrying amount as on 31.03.2013		3.00
Add: Upward Revaluation (credited to Revaluation Reserve account)		2.10
Carrying amount of the machine as on 1st April 2013 (revalued)		5.10
Less: Depreciation for 2 years i.e.,2013-2014 & 2014-2015		(3.40)
Carrying amount as on 31.03.2015		1.70
Less: Recoverable amount		(0.79)
Impairment loss		0.91
Less: Balance in revaluation reserve as on 31.03.2015:		
Balance in revaluation reserve as on 31.03.2013	2.10	
Less: Enhance depreciation met from revaluation reserve		
2013-2014 & 2014-2015 = [(1.70 – 1.00) × 2 years]	(1.40)	(0.70)
Impairment loss set of against revaluation reserve balance as per para 58 of AS 28 "Impairment of Assets"		
Impairment Loss to be debited to Profit and Loss Account		0.21

QUESTION 7: X Ltd. purchased a fixed asset four years ago for ₹ 150 lakhs and depreciates it at 10% p.a. on straight line method. At the end of the fourth year, it has revalued the asset at ₹ 75 lakhs and has written off the loss on revaluation to the profit and loss account. However, on the date of revaluation, the market price is ₹ 67.50 lakhs and expected disposal costs are ₹ 3 lakhs. What will be the treatment in respect of impairment loss on the basis that fair value for revaluation purpose is determined by market value and the value in use is estimated at ₹ 60 lakhs?

ANSWER:

TREATMENT OF IMPAIRMENT LOSS

PROVISION OF AS 28

As per para 57 of AS 28 "Impairment of assets", if the recoverable amount (higher of net Selling Price and its value in use) of an asset is less than its carrying amount, the carrying amount of the asset should be reduced to its recoverable amount.

ADVISE

CALCULATION OF CARRYING AMOUNT OF THE FIXED ASSET AT THE END OF THE FOURTH YEAR

	(₹ in lakhs)
Purchase price of a fixed asset	150.00
Less: Depreciation for four years [(150 lakhs / 10 years) × 4 years]	(60.00)
Carrying value at the end of fourth year	90.00

Less: Downward revaluation charged to Profit & Loss Account	(15.00)
Revalued carrying amount	75.00

Net Selling Price = ₹ 67.5 lacs – ₹ 3 lacs = ₹ 64.5 lacs

Impairment Loss = ₹ 75 lacs – ₹ 64.50 lacs = ₹ 10.50 lacs

Thus Impairment loss of 10.50 lakhs should be recognised as an expense in the Statement of Profit and Loss immediately since there was downward revaluation of asset which was already charged to Statement of Profit and Loss.

QUESTION 8: BHARAT TUSHAR LTD. provides the following information:

Fixed Asset purchased on 01.04.2012 ₹ 11 lakhs,Residual value at the end of Useful life ₹ 1 lakh, Useful Life 5 years, Recoverable Amount on 31.03.2013 = ₹ 7 lakhs, Recoverable Amount on 31.03.2015 = ₹ 7 lakhs, Determine the Carrying Amount at the end of each accounting year.

ANSWER:

CARRYING AMOUNT, SLM DEPRECIATION CHARGED AND AMOUNT OF IMPAIRMENT LOSS TO BE REVERSED

	Particulars	₹ (in lakhs)
A	Net Cost of Fixed Asset	11
B	*Less:* Depreciation [(11 – 1)/5]	2
C	Carrying Amount before Impairment Loss (A – B)	9
D	*Less:* Impairment Loss [9 – 7]	2
E	Carrying Amount as on 31st March,2013	7
F	*Less:* Depreciation [(7 – 1)/4]	1.5
G	Carrying Amount as on 31st March,2014	5.5
H	*Less:* Depreciation [(7 – 1)/4]	1.5
I	Carrying Amount before Reversal of Impairment Loss	4
J	*Add:* Reversal of Impairment Loss[Refer to Working Note]	1
K	Revised Carrying Amount as on 31st March,2014	5
L	*Less:* Depreciation [(5 – 1)/2]	2
M	Carrying Amount as on 31st March,2015	3
N	*Less:* Depreciation	2
O	Carrying Amount as on 31st March,2016	1

Working Note:

1. *Calculation of Amount of Impairment Loss to be reversed [Least of the following three]*

   A. Recoverable Amount – Current Carrying Amount = 7 – 4 = 3

   B. Current Carrying Amount (had no Impairment Loss been recognized) – Current Carrying Amount

   = {11 – [(11 – 1) × 3/5]} – 4 = 1

   C. Impairment Loss already recognized = 2

   Least of the above three = 1

QUESTION 9: X Ltd purchased entire Y Ltd for ₹ 55 lacs on 1.4.2011. Y Ltd has two cash generating units L & M. Net Fair Value of L & M are ₹.20 lacs and 30 lacs respectively. On 31.03.2014 the recoverable amount of L & M are ₹ 14.20 lacs and 20.30 lacs respectively.

On 31.03.2015 the recoverable amount of L & M are ₹ 13.20 lacs and 19.30 lacs respectively. Useful Life 10 years, Depreciation is provided on SLM basis on its entire assets. Determine the Carrying Amount as on 31st March,2015 (a) if any for L & M if Goodwill can be allocated between L & M on its Net Fair Value basis (ii) if Goodwill cannot be reasonably allocated to L & M and recoverable amount of Y Ltd is ₹ 35 lacs on 31.03.2014 and ₹ 33 lacs on 31.03.2015.

ANSWER:

(I) CARRYING AMOUNT OF ASSETS IF GOODWILL CAN BE ALLOCATED

	Particulars	L	M	Goodwill	Total
A	Net Fair Value on 1.4.2011	20	30	5	55
B	Depreciation for 3 years @10% for L & M, @20% for Goodwill as per AS14	6	9	3	18
C	Carrying Amount before Impairment Loss on 31.3.2014	14	21	2	37
D	Allocation of Goodwill [(carrying amount of goodwill) × A / (20,00,000 + 30,00,000)]	0.80	1.20		2
E	Carrying amount along with allocated goodwill	14.80	22.20		37.00
F	Recoverable amount	14.20	20.30		34.50
G	Impairment loss	0.60	1.90		2.50
H	Impairment loss first be deducted from allocated goodwill	0.60	1.20		1.80
I	Balance to be deducted from carrying amount of cash generating unit	0	0.70		0.70
J	Deduction in respect of impairment loss to the carrying amount	0	0.70	1.80	2.50
K	Carrying Amount after impairment loss on assets other than Goodwill	14	20.30	0.20	34.50
	Less: Depreciation [for L & M: Carrying Amount/7],[Goodwill Carrying Amount/2]	2	2.90	0.10	5
	Carrying Amount before Reversal of Impairment Loss	12	17.40	0.10	29.50
	Add: Reversal of Impairment Loss[Refer to WN]	0	0.60	0	0.60
	Revised Carrying Amount on 31.03.2015	12.00	18.00	0.10	30.10

Working Notes:

1. *Calculation of Impairment Loss to be reversed for M [Least of the following three]*
   A. Recoverable Amount – Current Carrying Amount = 19.30 – 17.40 = 1.90
   B. Current Carrying Amount (had no Impairment Loss been recognized) – Current Carrying Amount = {30 – [(30 – 0) × 4/10]} – 17.40 = 0.60
   C. Impairment Loss already recognized = 0.70
   Least of the above three = 0.60
2. *Impairment Loss of Goodwill is not to be reversed.*

(II) CARRYING AMOUNT OF ASSETS IF GOODWILL CANNOT BE ALLOCATED

Particulars	L	M	Goodwill	Total
A. Net Fair Value on 1.4.2011	20	30	5	55
B. Depreciation for 3 years @10% for L & M, @20% for Goodwill as per AS14	6	9	3	18
C. Carrying Amount before Impairment Loss on 31.3.2014	14	21	2	37
D. Recoverable Amount	14.20	20.30		34.50
E. Impairment Loss	0	0.70		0.70
Carrying Amount after impairment loss	14.00	20.30	2	36.30
Total Recoverable Amount of Y Ltd.				35.00
Impairment Loss				1.30
Impairment loss first allocated to Goodwill			1.30	1.30
Carrying Amount after impairment loss on 31.03.2014	14.00	20.30	0.70	35.00
Less: Depreciation [for L & M : Carrying Amount/7], [Goodwill Carrying Amount/2]	2	2.90	0.35	5.25
Carrying Amount before Reversal of Impairment Loss	12	17.40	0.35	29.75
Total Recoverable Amount of Y Ltd.				33.00
Add: Reversal of Impairment Loss [Refer to Working Note]		0	0.60	0
Revised Carrying Amount 31.03.2015		12.00	18.00	0.35

Working Notes:

1. *Calculation of Impairment Loss to be reversed for M [Least of the following three]*

   A. Recoverable Amount – Current Carrying Amount = 19.30 – 17.40 = 1.90

   B. Current Carrying Amount (had no Impairment Loss been recognized) – Current Carrying Amount = {30 – [(30 – 0) × 4/10]} – 7.40 = 0.60

   C. Impairment Loss already recognized = 0.70
   Least of the above three = 0.60

2. *Impairment Loss of Goodwill is not to be reversed.*

QUESTION 10: Good Drugs and Pharmaceuticals Ltd. acquired a sachet filling machine on 1st April,2015 for ₹ 60 lakhs. The machine was expected to have a productive life of 6 years. At the end of financial year 2015-2016 the carrying amount was ₹ 41 lakhs. A short circuit occurred in this financial year but luckily the machine did not get badly damaged and was still in working order at the close of the financial year. The machine was expected to fetch ₹ 36 lakhs, if sold in the market. The machine by itself is not capable of generating cash flows. However, the smallest group of assets comprising of this machine also, is capable of generating cash flows of ₹ 54 crore per annum and has a carrying amount of ₹ 3.46 crore. All such machines put together could fetch a sum of ₹ 4.44 crore if disposed. Discuss the applicability of Impairment loss.

ANSWER:

PROVISION OF AS 28

As per AS 28, "Impairment of Assets", impairment loss is not to be recognized for a given asset if the related cash generating unit (CGU) is not impaired.

ADVICE

In the given question, the related cash generating unit, which is group of asset to which the damaged machine belongs, is not impaired; as the recoverable amount is more than the carrying amount of group of assets. Hence there is no need to provide for impairment loss on the damaged sachet filling machine.

QUESTION 11: X Ltd.. is a multi-product manufacturing company, having its corporate office in a big building. As the area of building is large, X Ltd. has let out 1/4 area of the building at a monthly rent of ₹ 50 lakhs, the lease agreement with tenant is for next 10 years. Is the building cash-generating unit? It not what is the cash-generating unit of the building?

ANSWER:

PROVISION OF AS 28

As per para 66 of As 28 'Impairment of Assets, the cash-generating unit is smallest group of asset that includes the asset and that generates cash inflows from continuing use the are largely independent of the cash inflows from other assets.

ADVICE

In the instant case the primary purpose of the building is to serve as a corporate office of X Ltd. which is engaged in multi product manufacturing activities. Therefore, the building as a whole cannot be considered to generate cash inflows which are largely independent of the cash flow for the company as a whole. The building is not held as an investment; therefore, it would be inappropriate to determine 'value in use' of the building based on the future market rent.

Hence, building is not cash generating unit; the cash-generating unit for the building is X Ltd., the company a whole.

QUESTION 12: Acute Ltd is the owner of a CGU (Cash Generaung Unit) block of assets whose current carrying cost is ₹ 999 lakhs. The company after a detailed study by its technical team, has assessed the present recoverable amount of this CGU block of assets at ₹ 555 lakhs. The value of the block of assets as per the Income tax Records is ₹ 777 lakhs. The Board of Directors of the company have issued a signed statement confirming that the impairment in the value of CGU is only a temporary phenomenon which is reversible in subsequent periods and also assuring virtual certainty of taxable incomes in the foreseeable future. You are required to show Deferred Tax working as per Accounting standards in force, given the tax rate of 30% plus 10% aircharge thereon. The depreciation rate for tax purposes is 15% and that per books is 13.91%.

ANSWER: Assumption: "the given value of Fixed Assets (Cash Generating Unit) are as the Balance Sheet date after charging depreciation for the corresponding time period ending on that date."

1. DEFERRED TAXES PRIOR TO IMPAIRMENT LOSS

(a)	Excess Depreciation Claimed under Income Tax Law [999 – 777]	₹ 222 Lakhs
(b)	Deferred Taxes Liability (₹ 222 Lakhs × 33%)	₹73.26 Lakhs

2. DEFERRED TAXES AFTER IMPAIRMENT LOSS

(a)	Excess Depreciation Claimed under Income Tax Law [555 lacs – ₹ 777 lacs]	₹ 222 lakhs
(b)	Impairment Loss as per Books, not deductible under Income Tax Income	₹ 444 lakhs
(c)	Excess Deduction as per Books will result in Creation of DTA [A – B]	₹ 222 lakhs
(d)	Deferred Tax Asset (₹ 222 lakhs × 33%)	₹ 73.26 lakhs

3. EFFECTIVE JOURNAL ENTRY:

Date	Particulars		Dr. (₹)	Cr. (₹)
	Deferred Tax Liability A/c	Dr.	73.76	
	Deferred Tax Asset A/c	Dr.	73.26	
	To Profit & Loss A/c			146.52
	(Being creation of DTA and reversal of DTL)			

13 PREPARATION OF FINANCIAL STATEMENTS OF PROFIT MAKING ORGANISATIONS

SOLVED PROBLEMS I

PROBLEM 1

The following trial balance is extracted from the books of Mr Goyal, a merchant on 31st March 2015:

Particulars	*Dr. (₹)*	*Cr. (₹)*
Furniture and Fittings	1,280	
Motor Vehicles	12,500	
Buildings		15,000
Capital Accounts	—	25,000
Bad Debts	250	
Provision for Doubtful debts	—	400
Sundry Debtors and Creditors	7,600	5,000
Opening Stock	6,920	
Purchases and Sales	10,950	30,900
Bank Overdraft	—	5,700
Sales and Purchases Returns	400	250
Advertising	900	—
Interest Account	236	—
Commission	—	750
Cash	1,300	—
Taxes and Insurance	2,500	—
General expenses	1,564	—
Salaries		6,600
	68,000	68,000

The following adjustments are to be made:

(a) Closing Stock was ₹ 6,500.

(b) Depreciate Building @ 5%, Furniture and Fittings @ 10% and Motor Vehicles @ 20%.

(c) ₹ 170 is due for interest on Bank Overdraft.

(d) Salaries ₹ 600 and Taxes ₹ 240 are outstanding.

(e) Insurance amounting to ₹ 200 is prepaid.

(f) One-third of the commission received is in respect of work to be done next year.

(g) Write off further ₹ 200 as bad Debts and Provision for Doubtful Debts is to be made equal to 10% on Sundry Debtors

Required: Prepare Trading and Profit and Loss Account for the year ending 31st March, 2015 and a Balance Sheet as on that date.

SOLUTION

TRADING AND PROFIT & LOSS ACCOUNT

Dr. *for the year ending on 31st March, 2015* Cr.

Particulars		₹	*Particulars*		₹
To Opening Stock		6,920	By Sales	30,900	
To Purchases	10,950		*Less:* Sales Returns	400	30,500
Less: Returns	250	10,700	By Closing Stock		6,500
To Gross Profit c/d		19,380			
(Transferred to Profit & Loss A/c)					
		37,000			37,000
To Bad Debts	250		By Gross Profit b/d		
Add: Further Bad Debts	200		(Transferred from Trading A/c)		19,380
Add: New Provision	740		By Commission	750	
(10% of 7,400)			*Less:* Received in advance	250	500
Less: Old Provision	400	790			
To Advertising		900			
To Interest on Bank Overdraft	236				
Add: Outstanding	170	406			
To General Expenses		1,564			
To Salaries	6,600				
Add: Outstanding	600	7,200			
To Taxes & Insurance					
Premium	2,500				
Add: Outstanding Taxes	240				
	2,740				
Less: Prepaid insurance					
Premium	200	2,540			
To Depreciation:					
Buildings @ 5%	750				
Furniture @ 10%	128				
Motor Vehicles @ 20%	2,500	3,378			
To Net Profit t/f to capital A/c		3,102			
		19,880			19,880

BALANCE SHEET

as at 31st March, 2015

Liabilities		₹	*Assets*		₹
Capital:			**Fixed Assets:**		
Opening Balance	25,000		Furniture & Fittings	1,280	
Add: Net Profit	3,102	28,102	*Less:* Depreciation	128	1,152
Current Liabilities:			Motor Vehicles	12,500	
Sundry Creditors		5,000	*Less:* Depreciation	2,500	10,000
Bank Overdraft		5,700	Buildings	15,000	
Outstanding expenses:			*Less:* Depreciation	750	14,250
Salaries		600	**Current Assets:**		
Taxes		240	Sundry Debtors	7,600	
Interest on Bank overdraft		170	*Less:* Written off	200	
Commission received in Advance		250		7,400	
			Less: Provision @ 10%		
			for Doubtful Debts	740	6,660

		Cash	1,300
		Closing Stock	6,500
		Pre-paid Insurance Premium	200
	40,062		40,062

PROBLEM 2

The Trial Balance of Mr. Sun as on 31st March, 2015, was as follows:

Particulars	*Dr. (₹)*	*Cr. (₹)*
Purchases/Sales	16,25,050	25,24,000
Provision for Doubtful debts	—	52,000
Sundry Debtors/Sundry Creditors	5,02,000	3,05,260
Bills Payable	—	39,500
Opening Stock	2,67,250	
Wages		2,31,370
Salaries		55,750
Furniture		72,500
Postage		42,260
Power and fuel	13,500	
Trade expenses	58,310	
Bad debts	5,250	
Loan to Ram @ 10% (Dec. 1, 2014)	30,000	
Cash in hand and at bank	1,00,000	
Trade Expenses accrued but not paid	—	7,000
Drawing A/c/Capital A/c	44,520	1,00,000
Outstanding Wages	—	20,000
	30,47,760	30,47,760

Required: Prepare Trading and Profit and Loss Account for the year March 31, 2015 and the Balance Sheet as on that date after taking into consideration the following information:

(a) Depreciation on furniture is to be charged @ 10%.

(b) Sundry debtors include an item of ₹ 5,000 due from a customer who has become insolvent.

(c) Provision for Doubtful debts is to be maintained @ 5% on sundry debtors.

(d) Goods of the value of ₹ 15,000 have been destroyed by fire and insurance company admitted a claim for ₹ 10,000.

(e) Closing Stock was ₹ 1,25,500.

SOLUTION

TRADING AND PROFIT & LOSS ACCOUNT

for the year ending on 31st March, 2015

Dr. *Cr.*

Particulars		₹	*Particulars*	₹
To Opening Stock		2,67,250	By Sales	25,24,000
To Purchases	16,25,050		By Closing Stock	1,25,500
Less: Loss	(15,000)	16,10,050		

To Wages		2,31,370		
To Power & Fuel		13,500		
To Gross Profit t/f to P&L A/c		5,27,330		
		26,49,000		26,49,000
To Irrecoverable loss of stock		5,000	By G/P b/d	5,27,330
To Salary		55,750	By Prov. for doubtful debt 52,000	
To Postage		42,260	*Less:* 5% Provision 24,850	27,150
To Trade Expenses		58,310	By Interest on Loan	1,000
To Bad Debts	5,250			
Add: Further Bad Debts	5,000	10,250		
To Depreciation		7,250		
To Net Profit t/f to capital A/c		3,76,660		
		3,55,480		3,55,480

BALANCE SHEET
as at 31st March, 2015

Liabilities		₹	*Assets*		₹
Current Liabilities:			**Current Assets:**		
Creditors		3,05,260	Insurance Co.		10,000
B/P		39,500	Cash in Hand		1,00,000
O/s Wages		20,000	Closing Stock		1,25,500
Trade Expenses Accrued		7,000	Debtors	5,02,000	
Capital:			*Less:* Bad Debts	5,000	
Opening Balance	1,00,000			4,97,000	
Less: Drawings	45,520		*Less:* Provision	24,850	4,72,150
Add: Net Profit	3,76,660	4,32,140	Loan to Ram	30,000	
			Add: Interest on Loan	1,000	31,000
			Fixed Assets:		
			Furniture	72,500	
			Less: Depreciation	7,250	65,250
		8,03,900			8,03,900

PROBLEM 3

On 31st March, 2015, the following Trial Balance was extracted from the books of Mr. Ghayal.

	₹		₹
Dr. Balances:		Rates, Taxes and Insurance	28,910
Drawings	30,000	Advertising	32,640
Sundry Debtors	2,01,000	General Expenses	34,890
Interest on Loan	2,850	Bill Receivable	68,820
Cash in hand	20,500	*Cr. Balances:*	
Opening Stock	68,390	Capital	2,80,000
Motor Vehicles	1,00,000	Sundry Creditors	1,04,010
Cash at Bank	35,550	Loan on Mortgage	95,000
Land and Buildings	1,20,000	Provision of doubtful debts	7,100
Bad Debts	5,250	Sales	11,02,430
Purchases	6,64,580	Purchases returns	13,460
Sales Returns	78,210	Discounts	5,400
Carriage Outward	24,190	Bills Payable	26,140
Carriage Inward	29,290	Rent Received	2,500
Salaries	90,970		

Required: Prepare Trading and Profit and Loss Account for the year ended 31st March, 2015 and Balance Sheet as on that date, after making adjustments for the following matters:

(a) Depreciate Land and Buildings at 2½ per cent and Motor Vehicles at 20 per cent.
(b) Interest on Loan at 6 per cent per annum is unpaid for six months.
(c) Goods costing ₹ 5,000 were sent to a customer on sale or return for ₹ 6,000 on 30th March, 2015 and had been recorded in the books as actual sales.
(d) Salaries amounting to ₹ 7,500 and rates amounting to ₹ 3,500 are outstanding.
(e) Prepaid Insurance amounted to ₹ 1,500.
(f) The provision for Doubtful Debts is to be maintained at 5 per cent Sundry Debtors.
(g) Provide for Manager's Commission at 10% on net profits after charging such commission.
(h) Closing Stock was valued at ₹ 62,500.

SOLUTION

TRADING AND PROFIT & LOSS ACCOUNT
for the year ending on 31st March, 2015

Dr. *Cr.*

Particulars		₹	*Particulars*		₹
To Opening Stock		68,390	By Sales	11,02,430	
To Purchases	6,64,580		*Less:* Sale Price of		
Less: Returns	13,460	6,51,120	Goods on approval	6,000	
To Carriage Inwards		29,290	*Less:* Returns	78,210	10,18,220
To Gross Profit t/f to P & L Account		3,36,920	By Stock in hand	62,500	
			Add: Cost of Goods		
			Sent on Approval	5,000	67,500
		10,85,720			10,85,720
To Interest on Loan	2,850		By Gross Profit b/d		3,36,970
Add: Outstanding	2,850	5,700	By Discount		5,400
To Bad Debts	5,250		By Rent Received		2,500
Add: New Provision	9,750				
Less: Old Provision	7,100	7,900			
To Carriage Outwards		24,190			
To Salaries (₹ 90,970 + 7,500)		98,470			
To Rates, Taxes, & Ins.	28,910				
Add: Rates due	3,500				
Less: Insurance Prepaid	1,500	30,910			
To Advertising		32,640			
To General Expenses		34,890			
To depreciation:					
Land & Building @ 2½%		3,000			
Motor vehicles @ 20%		20,000			
To Manager's Commission		7,920			
To Net Profit transferred to Capital A/c		79,200			
		3,44,820			3,44,820

BALANCE SHEET
as at 31st March, 2015

Liabilities		₹	*Assets*		₹
Current Liabilities:			**Current Assets:**		
Billy Payable		26,140	Cash in hand		20,500
Sundry Creditors		1,04,010	Cash at bank		35,550
Outstanding Expenses:			Bills Receivable		68,820
Salaries		7,500	Sundry Debtors	2,01,000	
Manager's Commission		7,920	*Less:* Goods sent on app.	8,000	
Rates		3,500	*Less:* Provision	9,750	1,85,250
Loans on Mortgage	95,000		Stock (₹ 62,500 + ₹ 5,000)		67,500
Add: Interest	2,850	97,850	Land and Buildings	1,20,000	
Capital:			*Less:* Depreciation	3,000	1,17,000
Opening Balance	2,80,000		Motor Vehicles	10,000	
Less: Drawings			*Less:* Depreciation	20,000	80,000
(₹ 30,000)	30,000		Prepaid Insurance		1,500
Add: Profit	79,200	3,29,200			
		5,76,120			5,76,120

PROBLEM 4

From the following Trial Balance of Mr *X*, prepare Trading and Profit and Loss Account for the ended 31st March 2015 and a Balance Sheet as on that date, after giving effect to the adjustments:

Debit Balances	₹	*Credit Balances*	₹
Drawings	32,500	Capital	1,80,000
Opening Stock	1,74,450	Rent Outstanding	1,300
Return Inwards	5,540	Returns Outward	8,400
Carriage Inwards	12,400	Creditors	30,000
Deposits with Mr. *Y* (Inte.. Free)	13,750	Provision for Doubtful debts	12,000
Carriage Outwards	7,250	Sales	12,79,140
5% Loan to Mr. *Z*	10,000	Interest on Loan	250
Rent	8,200		
Purchases	11,29,700		
Debtors	40,000		
Goodwill	17,300		
Advertisement Expenses	9,540		
Bad Debts	4,000		
Patents and Trade Marks	5,000		
Cash in hand	620		
Discount Allowed	3,300		
Wages	7,540		
Plant and Machinery (Purchased on 1.4.2014)	30,000		
	15,11,090		15,11,090

Adjustments:

(a) Increase Bad Debts by ₹ 6,000. Make Provision for Doubtful Debts @ 10% and Provision for Discount on Debtors @ 5%. (b) The value of the Closing Stock is ₹ 1,87,920. (c) Wages include ₹ 2,000 paid for erection of Machinery on 1.4.2014. (d) Provide depreciation on Machinery @ 10% p.a.

SOLUTION

TRADING AND PROFIT & LOSS ACCOUNT

for the year ending on 31st March, 2015

Dr. Cr.

Particulars		₹	*Particulars*		₹
To Opening Stock		1,74,450	By Sales	12,79,140	
To Purchases	11,29,700		*Less:* Returns	5,540	12,73,600
Less: Returns	8,400	11,21,300	By Closing Stock		1,87,920
To Carriage inward		12,400			
To Wages and Salaries	7,540				
Less: erection of machine	2,000	5,540			
		1,47,830			
		14,61,520			14,61,520
To Carriage outward		7,250	BY Gross Profit b/d		1,47830
To Rent		8,200	By Interest	250	
To Discount		3,300	*Add:* Accrued interest	250	500
To Advertisement		8,540			
To Bad debts					
Add: Provisional for debt	1,400				
Add: Provisional for discount	1,530	2,930			
To Depreciation on Plant and Machinery		3,200			
To Net Profit t/f to Capital A/c		1,13,910			
		1,48,330			1,48,330

BALANCE SHEET

as at 31st March, 2015

Liabilities		₹	*Assets*		₹
Current Liabilities:			**Fixed Assets:**		
Creditors		30,000	Goodwill		17,300
Outstanding rent		1,300	Plant and Machinery	30,000	
Capital:			*Add:* Erection of machinery	2,000	
Opening Balance	1,80,000		*Less:* Depreciation	3,200	28,800
Add: Net Profit	1,13,910		Trade Marks		5,000
Less: Drawings	32,500	2,61,410	**Investments:**		
			12% Investments	10,000	
			Add: Interest on investment	250	10,250
			Deposit with Mr Z		13,750
			Current Assets:		
			Debtors	40,000	
			Less: Further Bad debts	6,000	
			Less: Provision for doubtful	3,400	
			Less: Provision for Discount	1,530	29,070
			Cash in hand		620
			Closing Stock		1,87,920
		2,92,710			2,92,710

PROBLEM 5

From the following balances taken from the Ledger of Shri Krishna on 31st March 2015, prepare the Trading and Profit and Loss A/c for the year ended 31st March, 2015 and the Balance Sheet as at 31st March, 2015, Shri Krishna:—

	₹		₹
Sundry Creditors	19,000	Bad Debts	100
Building	15,000	Loan from Ram	2,500
Income Tax	1,025	Sundry Debtors	9,500
Loose Tools	1,000	Investment	6,500
Cash at Bank	16,200	Provision for Doubtful Debts	1,600
Sundry Expenses	1,990	Rent & Rates	850
Bank Interest (Cr.)	75	Furniture	3,000
Purchases	1,57,000	Opening Stock	27,350
Wages	10,000	Capital	47,390
Carriage Inwards	1,120	Discount allowed	630
Sales	1,85,000	Dividends received	535
Motor Van	12,500	Drawings	2,000
Cash in Hand	335	Bills payable	10,000

Adjustments:

Write off further ₹ 300 as bad out of Sundry Debtors and create a provision for Doubtful Debts @ 20% on Debtors. (b) Dividends accrued and due on investments is ₹ 135, Rates paid in advance ₹ 100 wages owing ₹ 450. (c) Closing Stock was valued at ₹ 15,000 and Loose Tools were valued at ₹ 800. (d) Write off 5 percent for depreciation on Buildings and 40 percent on Motor Van. (e) Provide for interest at 12 per cent per annum due on Loan taken on 1-6-2014. (f) Income tax paid has to be treated as Drawings.

SOLUTION

TRADING AND PROFIT & LOSS ACCOUNT

Dr. *for the year ending on 31st March, 2015* *Cr.*

Particulars		₹	*Particulars*		₹
To Opening Stock		27,350	By Sales		1,85,000
To Purchases		1,57,000	By Closing Stock		15,000
To Wages	10,000				
Add: Outstanding	450	10,450			
To Carriage Inwards		1,120			
To Gross Profit c/d		4,080			
		2,00,000			2,00,000
To Rent & Rates	850		By Gross Profit b/d		4,080
Less: Prepaid	100	750	By Bank Interest		75
To Sundry Expenses		1,990	By Dividends	535	
To Interest on loan		250	*Add:* Accrued and due	135	670
(12/100 × 10/12 × 2,500)			By Net Loss		5,385
To Depreciation:			(Bal. fig. Transferred to Capital)		
Building		750			
Motor Van		5,000			
Loose Tools		200			
To Discount allowed		630			
To Provision for Doubtful					
Debts Closing	1,840				
Add: Bad Debts (100 + 300)	400				
Less: Opening	1,600	640			
		10,210			10,210

BALANCE SHEET
as at 31st March, 2015

Liabilities		₹	*Assets*		₹
Capital Account:			Building	15,000	
Opening Balance	47,390		*Less:* Depreciation		
Less: Drawings	2,000		(15/100 × 15,000)	750	14,250
			Motor Van	12,500	
Less: Net Loss	5,385		*Less:* Depreciation		
	40,005		(40/100 × 12,500)	5,000	7,500
Less: Income tax	1,025	38,980	Loose Tools	1,000	
Loan from Ram		2,500	*Less:* Depreciation		
Sundry Creditors		19,000	(10/100 × 1,000)	200	800
Interest outstanding on			Furniture		3,000
loan from Ram		250	Investments	6,500	
Bills Payable		10,000	*Add:* Dividend		
Outstanding wages		450	accrued & due	135	6,635
			Closing Stock		15,000
			Sundry Debtors	9,500	
			Less: Bad Debts (adj.)	300	
			Less: Reserve for Bad	9,200	
			Debts (20/100 × 9200)	1,840	7,360
			Cash at Bank		16,200
			Cash in Hand		335
			Prepaid Rates		100
		71,180			71,180

PROBLEM 6

From the following figures extracted from the books of Shri Govind, you are required to prepare a Trading and Profit and Loss Account for the year ended 31st March, 2015 and a Balance Sheet as on that date after making the necessary adjustments:

	₹		₹
Shri Govind's Capital	2,28,800	Bills payable	5,500
Shri Govind's drawings	13,200	Opening Stock	38,500
Plant and Machinery	99,000	Wages	35,200
Freehold property	66,000	Sundry Creditors	44,000
Purchases	1,10,000	Postage and Telegrams	1,540
Returns outwards	1,100	Insurance	1,760
Salaries	13,200	Gas and Fuel	2,970
Office expenses	2,750	Bad Debts	660
Office furniture	5,500	Office Rent	2,860
Discount A/c (Dr.)	1,320	Freight	9,900
Sundry Debtors	29,260	Loose Tools	2,200
10% Loan to Shri Krishna	44,000	Factory Lighting	1,100
Cash at Bank	29,260	Provision for Doubtful Debts	880
Sales	2,31,440	Interest on loan to Shri Krishna	1,100
		Cash in hand	2,640

Adjustments:

(a) Closing Stock was valued at ₹ 72,600. (b) A new machine was installed during the year costing ₹ 15,400 but it was not recorded in the books as no payment was made for it. Wages ₹ 1,100 paid for its erection have been debited to wages account. (c) Depreciate plant and machinery by 33–1/3%, Furniture by 10%, Freehold property by 5% (d) Loose tools were valued at ₹ 1,760 (e) Of the Sundry debtors ₹ 660 are bad and should be written off. (f) Maintain a provision of 5% on Sunday Debtors for doubtful debts. (g) The manager is entitled to a commission of 10% of the net profits after charging such commission.

SOLUTION

TRADING AND PROFIT & LOSS ACCOUNT

for the year ending on 31st March, 2015

Dr. Cr.

Particulars		₹	*Particulars*		₹
To Opening Stock		38,500	By Sales		2,31,440
To Purchases	1,10,000		By Closing Stock		72,600
Less: Returns Outward	1,100	1,08,900			
To Wages	35,200				
Less: for erection of new machinery	1,100	34,100			
To Gas & Fuel		2,970			
To Freight		9,900			
To Factory Lighting		1,100			
To Gross Profit c/d		1,08,570			
		3,04,000			3,04,000
To Salaries		13,200	By Gross Profit b/d		1,08,570
To Office expenses		2,750	By Interest	1,100	
To Postage & Telegram		1,540	*Add:* Accrued but not		
To Insurance		1,760	yet received	3,300	4,400
To Office Rent		2,860	(10/100 × 44,000)		
To Discount Allowed		1,320			
To Provision for Doubtful Debts Closing	1,430				
Add: Bad Debts (660 + 660)	1,320				
	2,750				
Less: Opening	880	1,870			
To Depreciation:					
Machinery	38,500				
Furniture	550				
Freehold property	3,300				
Loose Tools	440	42,790			
To Commission to Manager (10/100 × 44,880)		4,080			
To Net Profit (transferred to capital)		40,800			
		1,12,970			1,12,970

BALANCE SHEET
as at 31st March, 2015

Liabilities		₹	*Assets*		₹
Capital:			Plant & Machinery	99,000	
Opening Balance	2,28,800		*Add:* New Machinery	16,500	
Less: Drawings	13,200			1,15,500	
Add: Net Profit	40,800	2,56,400	*Less:* Depreciation	38,500	77,000
Bills Payable		5,500	[1/3 × 1,15,500]		
Sundry Creditors		59,400	Freehold Property	66,000	
Commission to Manager			*Less:* Depreciation	3,300	62,700
(yet to be paid)		4,080	(20/100 × 66,000)		
			Office Furniture	5,500	
			Less: Depreciation	550	4,950
			(10/100 × 5,500)		
			Loose Tools	2,200	
			Less: Depreciation	440	1,760
			(2,200 – 1,760)		
			Closing Stock		72,600
			Sundry Debtors	28,600	
			Less: Provision for		
			Doubtful Debts	1,430	27,170
			(5/100 × 28,600)		
			Loan to Shri Krishna	44,000	
			Add: Interest accrued		
			but not yet received	3,300	47,300
			Cash at Bank		29,260
			Cash in Hand		2,640
		3,25,280			3,25,380

PROBLEM 7

The following Trial Balance was extracted from the Books of Mr. Selfish as on 31st March, 2015:

Particulars	*Dr.* (₹)	*Particulars*	*Cr.* (₹)
Plant and Machinery	2,00,000	Capital Account	8,00,000
Manufacturing wages	3,45,000	Sundry Creditors	4,45,600
Salaries	1,58,500	Bank loan	1,50,000
Furniture	1,00,000	Purchase returns	17,400
Freight on purchase	18,600	Sales	25,08,500
Freight on sales	21,400	Provision for Doubtful debts	
Buildings	2,40,000		
Manufacturing expenses	95,000		
Insurance and tax	42,000		
Goodwill	2,50,000		
General expenses	82,000		
Factory fuel and power	12,800		
Sundry debtors	7,82,000		
Factory lighting	9,500		
Opening Stock	3,42,000		

Motor car	1,20,000		
Purchases	10,20,000		
Sales returns	31,000		
Bad Debts	14,000		
Interests and Bank Charges	4,000		
Cash at bank	42,000		
Cash in hand	11,200		
	39,41,500		39,41,500

Required: Prepare the Trading Profit and Loss Accounts for the year ended 31st March, 2015, and the Balance Sheet as on that date taking into consideration the following information:

(a) Closing Stock was valued at ₹ 3,05,000.

(b) Deprecate Plant and Machinery by 10% p.a., Furniture by 5% p.a. and Motor car by ₹ 10,000.

(c) Create provision for doubtful debts at 5% on Sundry Debtors.

(d) A commission of 1% on the gross profit is to be provided to Works Manager.

(e) General Manager is to be allowed a commission @ 2% on net profit after charging works Manager's and before charging General Manager's Commission.

SOLUTION

TRADING AND PROFIT & LOSS ACCOUNT

for the year ending on 31st March, 2015

Dr. *Cr.*

Particulars		₹	*Particulars*		₹
To Opening Stock		3,42,000	By Sales	25,08,500	
To Purchases	10,20,000		*Less:* Returns	31,000	24,77,500
Less: Returns	17,400	10,02,600	By Closing Stock		3,05,000
To Manufacturing wages		3,45,000			
To Freight on purchase		18,600			
To Manufacturing Expenses		95,000			
To Factory Fuel and Power		12,800			
To Factory lighting		9,500			
To Gross Profit c/d		9,57,000			
		27,82,500			27,82,500
To Works Manager's Commission		9,570	By Gross Profit b/d		9,57,000
To Salaries		1,58,500			
To Freight on Sales		21,400			
To Prov. for doubtful Debt	39,100				
Less: Existing provision	20,000	19,100			
To Insurance		42,500			
To General Expenses		82,000			
To Bad Debts		14,000			
To Interest & Rent		4,000			
To Depreciation on:					
Plant & Machinery	20,000				
Furniture	5,000				
Motor Car	10,000	35,000			
To Net Profit t/f to capital A/c		5,59,510			
		9,57,000			9,57,000

BALANCE SHEET
as at 31st March, 2015

Liabilities		₹	*Assets*		₹
Current Liabilities:			**Current Assets:**		
Creditors		4,45,600	Cash in Hand		11,200
Outstanding Commission (Works)		9,570	Cash at Bank		42,000
Outstanding Commission (General)		11,420	Debtors	7,82,000	
Loans:		1,50,000	*Less:* Provision	39,100	7,52,900
Capital:			Closing Stock		3,05,000
Opening Balance	8,00,000		**Fixed Assets:**		
Add: Net Profit	5,59,510	13,59510	Furniture	1,00,000	
			Less: Depreciation	5,000	95,000
			Plant & Machinery	2,00,000	
			Less: Depreciation	20,000	1,80,000
			Motor Car	1,20,000	
			Less: Depreciation	10,000	1,10,000
			Goodwill		2,50,000
			Building		2,40,000
		19,76,100			19,76,100

PROBLEM 8

The following is the Trial Balance of Mr *X* as at 31st March 2015:

Debit Balances	₹	*Credit Balances*	₹
Opening Stock	46,800	*X*'s Capital A/c	86,690
Returns Inwards	8,600	Sales	3,89,600
Purchases	3,21,700	Returns Outward	5,800
Freight & Carriage	18,600	Sundry Creditors	14,800
Rent & Taxes	5,700	Bank Loan @ 6% p.a.	20,000
Salaries & Wages	9,300	Miscellaneous Income	250
Sundry Debtors	24,000	Discount Earned	4,190
Bank Interest	900		
Printing and Advertising	14,600		
Cash at Bank	8,000		
Furniture & Fittings	5,000		
Discount Allowed	1,800		
General Expenses	11,450		
Insurance	1,300		
Postage & Telegrams	2,330		
Cash in hand	380		
Travelling Expenses	870		
Drawings	40,000		
	5,21,330		5,21,330

The following adjustments should be made:

(a) Included amongst the Debtors is ₹ 3,000 due from *Z* and included among the creditors ₹ 1,000 due to him. (b) Provision for Doubtful Debts be created @ 5% and

Reserve for Discount @ 2% on Sundry Debtors. (c) Depreciation on furniture & Fittings @ 10% shall be written off. (d) Personal Purchases amounting to ₹ 600 had been included in the Purchases Day Book. (e) Interest on Bank Loan shall be provided for the whole year. (f) A quarter of the amount of Printing and Advertising is to be carried forward to the next year. (g) Credit Purchase Invoice amounting to ₹ 400 had been omitted from the Books. (h) Closing Stock was ₹ 78,600.

Required: Prepare Trading and Profit & Loss Account for the year ended 31.3.2015 and Balance Sheet as on that date.

SOLUTION

TRADING AND PROFIT & LOSS ACCOUNT

for the year ending on 31st March, 2015

Dr. *Cr.*

Particulars		₹	*Particulars*		₹
To Opening Stock		46,800	By Sales	3,89,000	
To Purchases	3,21,700		*Less:* Returns Inward	8,000	3,81,000
Add: Invoices Omitted	400		By Closing Stock		78,000
Less: Returns Outward	5,800				
Less: Drawing of Goods	600	3,15,700			
To Freight & Carriage		18,600			
To Gross Profit c/d		78,500			
		4,59,600			4,59,600
To Rent and Taxes		7,700	By Gross Profit b/d		78,500
To Salaries & Wages		9,300	By Miscellaneous Income		250
To Interest on Bank Loan	900		By Discount Earned		4,190
Add: Outstanding	300	1,200			
To Printing & Advertisement	14,600				
Less: Prepaid (1/4 × 14,600)	3,650	10,950			
To Discount allowed		1,800			
To General expenses		11,450			
To Insurance		1,300			
To Postage & Telegram		2,330			
To Travelling expenses		870			
To Provision for Doubtful Debts		1,150			
To Provision for Disc.. on Debtors		437			
To Depreciation on Furniture		500			
To Net Profit (transferred to capital)		35,953			
		82,940			82,940

BALANCE SHEET
as at 31st March, 2015

Liabilities		₹	*Assets*		₹
Capital:			Furniture & Fitting	5,000	
Opening balance	86.690		*Less:* Depreciation	500	4,500
Less: Drawing of Cash	40,000		Sundry Debtors	24,000	
Less: Drawings of Goods	600		*Less:* Mutual Debt set off		
Add: Net Profit	35,953	82,043	(Mr. Abraham)	1,000	
			Less: Provision for		
Bank Loan		20,000	Doubtful Debts	1,150	
Outstanding Expenses:			(23,000 × 5/100)		
Interest on Bank Loan		300		21,850	
Sundry Creditors	14,800		*Less:* Provisions for		
Add: Purchase Invoice			Discount of Debtors	437	21,413
Omitted	400		(21,850 × 2/100)		
			Closing Stock		78,600
Less: Mutual debt set off			Prepaid Expenses:		
(Mr. Abraham)	1,000	14,200	Printing & Advertisement		3,650
			Cash at bank		8,000
			Cash in Hand		380
		1,16,543			1,16,543

PROBLEM 9

The following Trial Balance was extracted from the books of Mr "A" as on 31st March 2015:

Debit Balances	₹	*Credit Balances*	₹
Plant & Machinery	78,000	Capital Account	1,00,000
Furniture	2,000	Sales	1,27,000
Purchases	60,000	Returns of Goods	750
Returns of Goods	1,000	Discount	800
Opening Stock	30,000	Sundry Creditors	25,000
Discount	425	Provision for Doubtful debts	525
Sundry Debtors	45,000		
Salaries	7,550		
Manufacturing wages	10,000		
Carriage Outwards	1,200		
Rent, Rates and Taxes	10,000		
Advertisement	2,000		
Cash	6,9030		
	2,54,075		2,54,075

Prepare Trading and Profit and Loss Account for the year ended March 31, 2015, and a Balance Sheet as on that date after taking into account the following adjustments:—

(i) Closing Stock was valued at ₹ 34,220

(ii) Provision for Doubtful Debts is to be kept at ₹ 500.

(iii) Allow Interest on Capital at 10% p.a.

(iv) Furniture was old and the same was disposed off for ₹ 760 in exchange of new furniture costing ₹ 1,680. The net invoice of ₹ 920 was passed through Purchase Register. (No Depreciation need be charged on old and new furniture).

(v) Depreciate Plant and Machinery by 10% p.a.

(vi) The proprietor Mr A has taken goods worth ₹ 5,000 for personal use, and distributed goods worth ₹ 1,000 as samples.

SOLUTION

TRADING AND PROFIT & LOSS ACCOUNT
for the year ending on 31st March, 2015

Dr. | | Cr.

Particulars		₹	*Particulars*		₹
To Opening Stock		30,000	By Sales	1,27,000	
To Purchases	60,000		*Less:* Return Inward	1,000	1,26,000
Less: Drawings of goods	5,000		By Closing stock		34,220
Less: Distribution of free samples	1,000				
Less: Returns Outwards	750				
Less: Furniture wrongly debited	920	52,330			
To Manufactured Wages		10,000			
To Gross Profit c/d		67,890			
		1,60,220			1,60,220
To Salaries		7,550	By Gross Profit b/d		67,890
To Rent, Rates & Taxes		10,000	By Provision for Doubtful Debts		
To Carriage Outwards		1,200	Debts: Opening	525	
To Distribution of Free Samples		1,000	*Less:* Closing	500	25
To Advertisement		2,000	By Discount Received		800
To Discount Allowed		425			
To Loss on sale of furniture (₹ 2,000 – ₹ 760)		1,240			
To Depreciation on Plant & Machinery		7,800			
To Interest on capital		10,000			
To Net Profit (transferred to capital)		27,500			
		68,715			68,715

BALANCE SHEET
as at 31st March, 2015

Liabilities		₹	*Assets*		₹
Capital	1,00,000		Plant & Machinery	78,000	
Less: Drawings of Goods	5,000		*Less:* Depreciation (10/100 × 18,000)	7,800	70,200
Add: Interest on Capital	10,000		Furniture	2,000	
Add: Net Profit	27,500	1,32,500	*Add:* Purchases	920	
Sundry Creditors		25,000	*Less:* Loss on sale (₹ 2,000 – ₹ 760)	1,240	1,680
			Closing Stock		34,220
			Sundry Debtors	45,000	
			Less: Provision for Doubtful Debts	500	44,500
			Cash in Hand		6,900
		1,57,500			1,57,500

PROBLEM 10

The following Trial Balance of Shri Om, as on 31st March, 2015. You are requested to prepare the Trading and Profit and Loss Account for the year ended 31st March, 2015 and a Balance Sheet as on that date after making the necessary adjustments:—

Particulars	*Dr.* (₹)	*Cr.* (₹)
Sundry Debtors/Creditors	5,00,000	2,00,000
Outstanding liability for Expenses	55,000	—
Wages	1,00,000	—
Carriage Outwards	1,10,000	—
Carriage Inwards	50,000	—
General Expenses	70,000	—
Cash Discounts	20,000	—
Bad Debts	10,000	—
Motor Car	2,40,000	—
Printing and Stationery	15,000	—
Furniture and Fittings	1,10,000	—
Advertisement	85,000	—
Insurance	45,000	—
Salesman's commission	87,500	—
Postage and Telephone	57,500	—
Salaries	1,60,000	—
Rates and Taxes	25,000	—
Capital Account/Drawings	20,000	14,43,000
Purchases/Sales	15,50,000	19,87,500
Opening Stock	2,50,000	—
Cash at Bank	60,000	—
Cash in Hand	10,500	—
	36,30,500	36,30,500

The following adjustments are to be made:

(a) Closing Stock was valued at ₹ 7,25,000.

(b) A Provision for Doubtful Debts are to be created to the extent of 5 percent on Sundry Debtors.

(c) Depreciate—Furniture and Fittings by 10%, Motor Car by 20%.

(d) Shri Om had withdrawn goods worth ₹ 25,000 during the year.

(e) Sales include goods worth ₹ 75,000 sent out to Shanti and Company on approval and remaining unsold till 31st March. The cost of the goods was ₹ 50,000.

(f) The Salesman was entitled to a Commission of 5% on total sales.

(g) Debtors include ₹ 25,000 bad debts.

(h) Printing and Stationery expenses of ₹ 55,000 relating to previous year had not been provided in that year but was paid in this year by debiting outstanding liabilities.

(i) Purchases include purchases of Furniture worth ₹ 50,000.

SOLUTION

TRADING AND PROFIT & LOSS ACCOUNT

Dr. *for the year ending on 31st March, 2015* *Cr.*

Particulars		₹	*Particulars*		₹
To Opening Stock		2,50,000	By Sales	19,87,500	
To Purchases	15,50,000		*Less:* Goods sent out for approval	75,000	19,12,500
Less: Drawings	25,000		By Closing Stock	7,25,000	
Less: Furniture	50,000	14,75,000	*Add:* Cost of Stock out on approval	50,000	7,75,000
To Wages		1,00,000			
To Capital Inwards		50,000			
To gross Profit c/d		8,12,500			
		26,87,500			26,87,500
To Salaries		1,60,000	By Gross Profit b/d		8,12,500
To Rates & Taxes		25,000			
To Postage & Telephone		57,500			
To Insurance		45,000			
To Printing & Stationery		15,000			
To General Expenses		70,000			
To Depreciation:					
Furniture (10/100 × 1,60,000)		16,000			
Motor Car (20/100 × 2,40,000)		48,000			
To Salesman's Commission	87,500				
Add: Outstanding (5/100 × 19,12,500)	8,125	95,625			
To Advertisement		85,000			
To Carriage Outwards		1,10,000			
To Provision for Doubtful Debts (5/10 × ₹ 4,00,000)		20,000			
To Cash Discount		20,000			
To Bad Debts (₹ 10,000 + ₹ 25,000)		35,000			
To Net Profit t/f to Capital A/c)		10,375			
		8,12,500			8,12,500

BALANCE SHEET
as at 31st March, 2015

Liabilities		₹	*Assets*		₹
Capital	14,43,000		Furniture & Fittings	1,10,000	
Less: Drawings of Cash	20,000		*Add:* Purchased during year	50,000	
Less: Drawings of Goods	25,000		*Less:* Depreciation	16,000	1,44,000
Less: Printing & Stationery			Motor Car	2,40,000	
(expenses of previous year)	55,000		*Less:* Depreciation	48,000	1,92,000
Add: Net profit	10,375	15,53,375	Stock	7,25,000	
Sundry Creditors		2,00,000	*Add:* Stock on approval	50,000	7,75,000
Outstanding Commission to Salesmen		8,125	Sundry Debtors	5,00,000	
			Less: Goods sent on Approval	75,000	
			Less: Add: Bad Debts	25,000	
				4,00,000	
			Less: Provision for (5/100 × 4,00,000)	20,000	3,80,000
			Cash at bank		60,000
			Cash in Hand		10,500
		15,61,500			15,61,500

14 FINANCIAL STATEMENTS OF NOT-FOR-PROFIT PROFIT-MAKING ORGANISATIONS

SHORT ANSWER PRACTICAL PROBLEMS

PROBLEM 1

Omshanti Club has 500 members with annual fee of ₹ 1,000 per member. At the end of the accounting year, accountant noticed that 40 members have not paid annual fee and 70 members had paid fee in advance. Help the accountant to compute cash receipts of annual fee for the year.

Solution

COMPUTATION OF CASH RECEIPTS OF ANNUAL FEE FOR THE YEAR

Particulars	₹
Total Fee receivable during the year (500 members × ₹ 1,000)	5,00,000
Less: Fee not received (40 members × ₹ 1,000)	(40,000)
Add: Fee received in advance (70 members × ₹, 1,000)	70,000
Cash received during the year towards annual fee	5,30,000

PROBLEM 2

During the year ended 31st March 2015, Sachin Cricket Club received sbscriptions as follows:

	(₹)
For year ending 31st March, 2014	12,000
For year ending 31st March, 2015	6,15,000
For year ending 31st March, 2016	18,000
Total	6,45,000

There are 500 members and annual subscription is ₹ 1,500 per member.

On 31st March, 2015, a sum of ₹ 15,000 was still in arrears for subscriptions for the year ended 31st March, 2014.

Ascertain the amount of subscriptions that will appear on the credit side of Income and Expenditure Account for the year ended 31st March, 2015. Also show how the items would appear in the Balance Sheet as on 31st March, 2014 and the Balance Sheet as on 31st March, 2015.

Solution

AN EXTRACT OF INCOME AND EXPENDITURE ACCOUNT

Dr. ***for the year ended 31st March 2015*** **Cr.**

Expenditure	₹	*Income*	₹
		By Subscription (500 × ₹ 1500)	7,50,000

AN EXTRACT OF BALANCE SHEET AS AT 31ST MARCH, 2015

Liabilities	₹	*Assets*		₹
Subscription received in advance	18,000	Subscription Outstanding		
		for 2013-2014	15,000	
		for 2014-2015	1,35,000	1,50,000

AN EXTRACT OF BALANCE SHEET AS AT 31ST MARCH, 2014

Liabilities	₹	*Assets*	₹
		Subscription Outstanding	27,000

PROBLEM 3

From the following extract of Receipts and Payments Account and the additional information, you are required to calculate the Income from Subscription for the year ending March 31, 2015 and show them in the Income & Expenditure Account, and the Balance Sheet of a Club.

AN EXTRACT OF RECEIPTS AND PAYMENTS ACCOUNT FOR THE YEAR ENDED 31ST MARCH, 2015

Receipts		₹	*Payments*	₹
To Subscription				
2013-2014	4,000			
2014-2015	20,000			
2015-2016	5,000	29,000		

Information:

(i) Subscription outstanding on 31.03.2014 ₹ 5,000

(ii) Subscription outstanding on 31.03.2015 ₹ 4,000

(ii) Subscription received in advance on 31.03.2014 for 2014-2015 ₹ 5,000

Solution

INCOME AND EXPENDITURE ACCOUNT FOR THE YEAR ENDING 31ST MARCH, 2015

Income	₹
Subscription: Received	20,000
Add: Outstanding at end (4,000 – 1,000)	3,000
Add: Received in advance last year for current year	5,000
	28,000

AN EXTRACT OF BALANCE SHEET AS AT ON 31ST MARCH, 2015

Liabilities	
Subscription received in advance for next year	5,000
Assets	
Subscription o/s: [₹ 1,000 (P.Yr) + 3,000 (C.Yr)	4,000

LONG ANSWER PRACTICAL PROBLEMS

INCOME AND EXPENDITURE ACCOUNT

PROBLEM 3

Following is the Receipts and Payments Account of Mayur Club for the year ended 31st March, 2015:

Receipts	₹	*Payments*	₹
Opening Balances:		Sports materials	3,04,500
Cash on hand	39,100	Salaries	3,15,000
Cash at bank	50,000	Equipment purchased on 1st Oct.	60,000
Receipts:		Bank fixed deposits on 31st March	1,50,000
Subscriptions		Rent	1,48,500
For the year 2013-2014	18,000	Ground maintenance	22,120
For the year 2014-2015	9,63,000	Insurance	38,400
For the year 2015-2014	4,500	Stationery	3,450
Interest on bank		Sundry expenses	5,880
Fixed deposits @10%	45,000	Closing Balances:	
		Cash on hand	31,750
		Cash at bank	40,000
	11,19,600		11,19,600

Following additional information is provided to you:

(*i*) The club has 220 members. The annual subscription is ₹ 4,500 per member.

(*ii*) Depreciation to be provided on furniture at 10% p.a. and on sports equipment at 15% p.a.

(*iii*) On 31st March, 2015, stock of sports material in hand (after members use during the year) is valued at ₹.78,000 and stock of stationery at ₹.3,150. Rent for 1 month is outstanding. Unexpired insurance amounts to ₹.9,600.

(*iv*) On 31st March, 2014 the club had the following assets:

Furniture	₹ 2,70,000
Sports equipment	₹ 1,80,000
Bank fixed deposit	₹ 4,50,000
Stock of stationery	₹ 1,500
Stock of sports material	₹ 73,500
Unexpired insurance	₹ 8,400
Subscription in arrear	₹ 22,500

Note:There was no liability on 31.3.2014.

You are required to prepare:

(*i*) Income and Expenditure Account; and

(*ii*) Balance Sheet as at 31st March, 2015.

Solution

(i) INCOME AND EXPENDITURE ACCOUNT FOR THE YEAR ENDED 31.3.2015

Expenditure		₹	*Income*	₹
To Sports Material used			By Subscription	9,90,000
Opening stock	73,500		By Interest on Fixed Deposit	45,000
Add: Purchases	3,04,500			
Less: Closing stock	(78,000)	3,00,000		
To Salaries		3,15,000		
To Rent	1,48,500			
Add: Outstanding	13,500	1,62,000		
To Ground maintenance		22,120		
To Insurance	38,400			
Less: Unexpired at the end	(9,600)			
	28,800			
Add: Unexpired in the beg.	8,400	37,200		
To Stationery used				
Opening Stock	1,500			
Add: Purchases	3,450			
Less: Closing Stock	3,150	1,800		
To Sundry expenses		5,880		
To Depreciation on :				
Furniture	27,000			
Sports equipment	31,500	58,500		
To Surplus		1,32,500		
		10,35,000		10,35,000

BALANCE SHEET AS AT 31ST MARCH, 2015

Liabilities		₹	*Assets*		₹
Capital Fund:			Equipments:		
			Opening balance	1,80,000	
Opening Balance	10,95,000		*Add:* Addition	60,000	
Add: Surplus	1,32,500	12,27,500	*Less:* Depreciation	31,500	2,08,500
Rent outstanding		13,500	Furniture:	2,70,000	
Subscription received in advance			*Less:* Depreciation	27,000	2,43,000
		4,500	Sports material		78,000
			Stock of Stationery		3,150
			Fixed deposit in bank		
			(₹ 4,50,000 + ₹ 1,50,000)		6,00,000
			Subscription in arrears:		
			For 2013-2014	4,500	
			For 2014-2015	27,000	31,500
			Prepaid insurance (unexpired)		9,600
			Cash on hand		31,750
			Cash at bank		40,000
		12,45,500			12,45,500

Working Notes:

(*i*) **BALANCE SHEET AS AT 31ST 31.3.2014**

Liabilities	₹	*Assets*	₹
Capital Fund (Bal. fig.)	10,95,000	Sports equipment	1,80,000
		Furniture	2,70,000
		Sports materials	73,500
		Stock of stationery	1,500
		Fixed deposits in bank	4,50,000
		Subscription in arrears	22,500
		Prepaid insurance (unexpired)	8,400
		Cash on hand	39,100
		Cash at bank	50,000
	10,95,000		10,95,000

(*ii*) Subscription still in arrears of 2013-2014 = ₹ 22,500 – ₹ 18,000 = ₹ 4,500

(*iii*) Subscription in arrear on 31.3.2015 = ₹ 9,90,000 – ₹ 9,63,000 = ₹ 27,000

(*iv*) Depreciation on sports equipment

On ₹.1,80,000 @ 15% for full year	27,000
On ₹.60,000 @ 15% for 6 months	4,500
Total	31,500

(*v*) Outstanding Rent = ₹ 1,48,500 × 1/11 = ₹ 13,500

PROBLEM 4

The following is the Receipts and Payments Account of Sydney Club for the year ended on 31st March, 2015:

Receipts	₹	*Payments*	₹
Opening Balances:		Salaries	1,20,000
Cash	10,000	Creditors	15,20,000
Bank	3,850	Printing and Stationery	70,000
Subscription Received	2,02,750	Postage	40,000
Entrance Donation	1,00,000	Telephones and Telex	52,000
Interest Received	58,000	Repairs and Maintenance	48,000
Sale of Assets	8,000	Glass and Table Linen	12,000
Miscellaneous Income	9,000	Crockery and Cutlery	14,000
Receipts at:		Garden Upkeep	8,000
Coffee Room	10,70,000	Membership Fees	4,000
Wines and Spirits	5,10,000	Insurance	5,000
Swimming Pool	80,000	Electricity	28,000
Tennis Court	1,02,000	*Closing Balances:*	
		Cash	8,000
		Bank	2,24,600
	21,53,600		21,53,600

The Assets and Liabilities as on 1.4.2014 were as follows:

Fixed Assets (net): ₹ 5,00,000; Stock: ₹ 3,80,000; Investment in 12% Tax free Government Securities: ₹ 5,00,000; Outstanding Subscription: ₹ 12,000; Prepaid Insurance: ₹ 1,000; Sundry Creditors: ₹ 1,12,000; Subscription received in advance: ₹ 15,000, Entrance Donation Received pending membership: ₹ 1,00,000; Gratuity Fund: ₹ 1,50,000.

The following adjustments are to be made while drawing up the Accounts:

(a) Subscription received in advance as on 31st March, 2015 was ₹ 18,000.

(b) Outstanding Subscription as on 31st March, 2015 was ₹ 7,000.

(c) Outstanding Expenses are: Salaries: ₹ 8,000 and Electricity: ₹ 15,000.

(d) 50% of the Entrance Donation was to be capitalised. There was no pending membership as on 31st March, 2015.

(e) The cost of assets sold net as on 1.4.2014 was ₹ 10,000.

(f) Depreciation is to be provided at the rate of 10% on assets.

(g) A sum of ₹ 20,000 received in October 2014 as Entrance Donation from an applicant was to be refunded as he had not fulfilled the requisite membership qualifications. The refund was made on 3.6.2015.

(h) Purchases made during the year amounted to ₹ 15,00,000.

(i) The value of closing stock was ₹ 2,10,000.

(j) The club as a matter of policy charges off to Income and Expenditure Account all purchases made on Account of crockery, cutlery, glass and linen in the year of purchase.

You are required to prepare an Income and Expenditure Account for the year ended on 31st March, 2015 and the Balance Sheet as on 31st March, 2015 alongwith necessary workings.

Solution

INCOME AND EXPENDITURE ACCOUNT OF SYDNEY CLUB
for the year ending on 31st March, 2015

Dr. Cr.

Expenditure	₹	*Income*	₹
To Salaries	1,28,000	By Subscription	1,94,750
To Printing and Stationery	70,000	By Entrance Donation	90,000
To Postage	40,000	By Interest	60,000
To Telephone and Telex	52,000	By Miscellaneous Income	9,000
To Repairs and Maintenance	48,000	By Profit from Operations	92,000
To Glass and Table Linen	12,000	By Excess of Expenditure Over Income transferred to Capital Fund	30,250
To Crockery and Cutlery	14,000		
To Garden Upkeep	8,000		
To Membership Fees	4,000		
To Insurance	6,000		
To Electricity Charges	43,000		
To Loss on Sale of Assets	2,000		
To Depreciation	49,000		
	4,76,000		4,76,000

BALANCE SHEET OF SYDNEY CLUB AS AT 31ST MARCH, 2015

Liabilities		₹	*Assets*		₹
Capital Fund:			*Fixed Assets:*		
Opening Balance	10,29,850		Opening Balance	5,00,000	
Add: Donation	90,000		*Less:* Sale	10,000	
Less: Deficit	30,250	10,89,600	*Less:* Depreciation	49,000	4,41,000
Gratuity Fund		1,50,000	Stock		2,10,000
Sundry Creditors		92,000	Investments		5,00,000
Subscription Received in Advance		18,000	Outstanding Subscription		7,000
Entrance Donation refundable		20,000	Interest Accrued		2,000
Outstanding Salaries		8,000	Bank		2,24,600
Outstanding Electricity Charges		15,000	Cash		8,000
		13,92,600			13,92,600

Working Notes:

(i) BALANCE SHEET OF SYDNEY CLUB AS AT 1ST APRIL, 2014

Liabilities	₹	*Assets*	₹
Sundry Creditors	1,12,000	Fixed Assets	5,00,000
Subscription Received in Advance	15,000	Stock	3,80,000
Entrance Donation Received in Advance	1,00,000	Investments	5,00,000
Gratuity Fund	1,50,000	Outstanding Subscription	12,000
Capital Fund (*Balancing figure*)	10,29,850	Prepaid Expenses	1,000
		Cash	10,000
		Bank	3,850
	14,06,850		14,06,850

Dr. (ii) SUBSCRIPTION ACCOUNT Cr.

Particulars	₹	*Particulars*	₹
To Outstanding Subscription A/c (Beginning)	12,000	By Advance Subscription A/c (Beginning)	15,000
To Income and Expenditure A/c	1,94,750	By Bank A/c	2,02,750
To Advance Subscription A/c (End)	18,000	By Outstanding Subscription A/c (End)	7,000
	2,24,750		2,24,750

(iii) Entrance Donation

A. Entrance Donation received during the year	1,00,000	
B. *Add:* Received in Advance as on 1.4.2014	1,00,000	2,00,000
C. *Less:* Entrance Donation refundable in respect of In-eligible Member	20,000	1,80,000
D. *Less:* 50% Capitalised		90,000
E. Taken to Income and Expenditure Account		90,000

(iv) Loss on Sale of Assets = Cost – Sale Proceeds = ₹ 10,000 – ₹ 8,000 = ₹ 2,000.

(v) Depreciation= On unsold Fixed Assets = 10% of (₹ 5,00,000 – ₹ 10,000) = ₹ 49,000.

(vi) Interest Accrued = ₹ 60,000 – ₹ 58,000 = ₹ 2,000

Dr. (vii) TRADING ACCOUNT Cr.

Particulars	₹	*Particulars*	₹
To Opening Stock	3,80,000	By Receipts from Coffee Room	10,70,000
To Purchases	15,00,000	By Receipts from Wines and Spirits	5,10,000
To Profit from Operations	92,000	By Receipts from Swimming Pool	80,000
		By Receipts from Tennis Court	1,02,000
		By Closing Stock	2,10,000
	19,72,000		19,72,000

Dr. (viii) SUNDRY CREDITORS ACCOUNT Cr.

Particulars	₹	*Particulars*	₹
To Bank A/c	15,20,000	By Balance b/d	1,12,000
To Balance c/d	92,000	By Purchases	15,00,000
	16,12,000		16,12,000

PROBLEM 5

On the basis of the following information, prepare Income and Expenditure Account for the year ended 31st March, 2015:

RECEIPTS AND PAYMENTS ACCOUNT FOR THE YEAR ENDED 31ST MARCH, 2015.

Receipts	₹	*Payments*	₹
To Cash in hand (opening)	1,300	By Salaries	2,58,000
To Cash at bank (opening)	3,850	By Rent	71,500
To Subscriptions	4,94,700	By Printing & Stationery	3,870
To Interest on 8% Government bonds	4,000	By Conveyance	10,600
		By Scooter purchased	50,000
To Bank interest	160	By 8% Government bonds	1,00,000
		By Cash in hand (closing)	840
		By Cash at bank (closing)	9,200
	5,04,010		**5,04,010**

(*i*) Salaries paid includes ₹ 6,000 paid in advance for April, 2015. Monthly salaries paid were ₹ 21,000.
(*ii*) Outstanding rent on 31st March, 2014 and 31st March, 2015 amounted to ₹ 5,500 and ₹ 6,000 respectively.
(*iii*) Stock of printing and stationery material on 31st March, 2014 was ₹ 340; it was ₹ 365 on 31st March, 2015.
(*iv*) Scooter was purchased on 1st October, 2014. Depreciation @ 20% per annum is to be provided on it.
(*v*) Investments were made on 1st April, 2014.
(*vi*) Subscriptions due but not received on 31st March, 2014 and 31st March, 2015 totalled ₹ 14,000 and ₹ 12,800 respectively. On 31st March, 2015, subscriptions amounting to ₹ 700 had been received in advance for April, 2015.

Solution

Dr. **INCOME AND EXPENDITURE ACCOUNT FOR THE YEAR ENDED 31ST MARCH. 2015** *Cr.*

Expenditure	₹	*Income*	₹
To Salaries	2,52,000	By Subscription	4,92,800
To Rent	72,000	By Interest on 8% Government bonds	8,000
To Printing and stationery	3,845	By Bank interest	160
To Conveyance	10,600		
To Depreciation on Scooter	5,000		
To Surplus	1,57,515		
	5,00,960		**5,00,960**

Working Notes:

	₹
(i) Salaries paid	2,58,000
Less: Salary paid in advance at the end	6,000
Salaries for the year	**2,52,000**
(ii) Rent paid	71,500
Add: Outstanding rent at the end	6,000
	77,500
Less: Outstanding rent at the beg.	5,500

Rent for the current year		72,000
(iii) Printing and stationery		3,870
Add: Stock in the beg.		340
		4,210
Less: Stock at the end		365
Printing and stationery consumed during the current year		**3,845**

(iv) Depreciation on scooter = ₹ 50,000 × $\frac{20}{100}$? $\frac{6}{12}$? Rs. 5,000

(v) Interest on Government bonds received		4,000
Add: Interest due but not received at the end		4,000
Interest income for the current year		**8,000**
(vi) Subscription received		4,94,700
Add: Accrued subscription at the end		12,800
Less: Accrued subscription at the beg.	14,000	
Unearned subscription at the end	700	
		(14,700)
Income for the current year		**4,92,800**

PROBLEM 6

The following is the Receipt and Payment Account of Park View Club in respect of the year ended 31st March. 2015.

Receipt	₹	*Payments*	₹
To Balance b/d	1,02,500	By Salaries	2,08,000
To Subscriptions:		By Stationery	40,000
2013-2014	4,500	By Rent	60,000
2014-2015	2,11,000	By Telephone expenses	10,000
2015-2014	7,500	By Investment	1,25,000
To Profit on sports meet	1,55,000	By Sundry expenses	92,500
To Income from investments	1,00,000	By Balance c/d	45,000
	5,80,500		5,80,500

Additional information:

(1) There are 450 members each paying an annual subscnption of ₹ 500. On 1st April, 2014 outstanding subscription was ₹ 5,000.

(2) There was an outstanding telephone bill for ₹ 3,500 on 31st March. 2015.

(3) Outstanding sundry expenses as on 31st March, 2014 totalled ₹ 7,000

(4) Stock of stationery: On 31st March, 2014 ₹ 5,000, On 31st March, 2015 ₹ 9,000

(5) On 31st March, 2015 building stood in the books at ₹ 10,00,000 and it was subject to depreciation @ 5% per annum.

(6) Investment on 31st March, 2014 stood at ₹ 20,00,000.

(7) On 31st March, 2015. income accrued on the investments purchased during the year amounted to ₹ 3,750.

Required: Prepare an Income and Expenditure Account for the year ended 31st March, 2015 and the Balance Sheet as at that date.

Solution

PARK VIEW CLUB
INCOME AND EXPENDITURE ACCOUNT
for the year ending on 31st March 2015

Dr. | | | | Cr.

Expenditure		₹	*Income*		₹
To Salaries		2,08,000	By Subscriptions		2,25,000
To Stationery consumed		36,000	By Profit on sports meet		1,55,000
To Rent		60,000	By Income on investments	1,00,000	
To Telephone expenses	10,000		*Add.* Income accrued	3,750	1,03,750
Add: o/s at end	3,500	13,500			
To Sundry expenses at	92,500				
Less: o/s at beg	(7,000)	85,500			
To Depreciation on building		50,000			
To Surplus		30,750			
		4,83,750			4,83,750

BALANCE SHEET AS AT 31ST MARCH 2015

Liabilities		₹	*Assets*		₹
Capital fund	31,05,500		Outstanding subscriptions		14,500
Add: Surplus	30,750	31,36,250	Investments (20,00,000 + 1,25,000)		21,25,000
Subscriptions received in advance		7,500	*Add:* Interest accrued on investments		3,750
Outstanding telephone bills		3,500	Building	10,00,000	
			Less: Depreciation	(50,000)	9,50,000
			Stock of stationery		9,000
			Cash balance		45,000
		31,47,250			31,47,250

Working Notes:

(i) BALANCE SHEET AS AT 31ST MARCH 2014

Liabilities	₹	*Assets*	₹
Outstanding sundry expenses	7,000	Building	10,00,000
Capital Fund (Bal. fig.)	31,05,500	Investments	20,00,000
		Stock of Stationery	5,000
		Cash Balance	1,02,500
		Outstanding subscriptions	5,000
	31,12,500		31,12,500

(ii) SUBSCRIPTION ACCOUNT

Dr. | | | Cr.

Particulars	₹	*Particulars*	₹
To Outstanding Subscriptions A/c	5,000	By Cash A/c	2,23,000
To Income & Expenditure A/c	2,25,000	By Outstanding Subscriptions A/c (End) (Bal. fig.)	14,500
To Advance Subscriptions [₹ 500 × 450]	7,500		
	2,37,500		2,37,500

Dr. **(iii) STATIONERY ACCOUNT** Cr.

Particulars	₹	*Particulars*	₹
To Balance b/d	5,000	By Income & Expenditure A/c	
To Banks (Purchases)	40,000	(consumed) (b.f.)	36,000
		By Balance c/d	9,000
	45,000		45,000

PROBLEM 7

The Young Trust runs a Charitable Hospital and a Dispensary. The following information is available for the year ended 31st March, 2015 from the books of accounts:

	Dr. (₹)	*Cr. (₹)*
Capital/fund		9,00,000
Donations received during the year		6,00,000
Recovery of the rent		2,75,000
Fee received from patients		3,00,000
Recovery of food supplies		1,40,000
Surgical equipments	4,55,000	
Building & Operation theatres	3,20,000	
Consumption in the hospital of:		
Medicines	1,20,000	
Foodstuff	90,000	
Chemicals	30,000	
Closing stock of hospital		
Medicines	20,000	
Foodstuff	4,000	
Chemicals	1,000	
Sales of medicines (dispensary)		3,10,000
Opening stock of medicines (dispensary)	55,000	
Purchase of medicines (dispensary)	3,00,000	
Salaries:		
Administrative staff	30,000	
Doctors/Nurses	1,50,000	
Assistant at the dispensary	15,000	
Electricity & power charges:		
Hospital	1,05,000	
Dispensary	2,000	
Furniture & equipments	80,000	
Ambulance	30,000	
Postage & telephone expenses less recovery	26,000	
Subscription to medical journals	21,000	
Ambulance maintenance charges less recovery		800
Consumption of bed sheets	90,000	
Fixed deposits made on 01-04-2014 for three years at interest @11% p.a.	5,00,000	
Cash & bank balances	41,300	
Sundry debtors (dispensary)	60,500	
Sundry creditors (dispensary)		41,000
Remuneration to trustees, trust office expenses etc.	21,000	

Additional information:

(a) The dispensary supplied medicines to the hospital worth ₹ 60,000, for which no adjustment was made in the books.
(b) The closing stock of the medicines was ₹ 40,000 at the dispensary.
(c) The stock of medicines on 31st March, 2015 at the hospital included ₹ 4,000 worth of medicines belonging to the patients, which has not been considered while arriving at the figure of consumption of medicines.
(d) The donations were received towards Corpus of the Trust.
(e) On 15th August, 2014, surgical equipments were donated having market value of ₹ 40,000.
(f) The hospital is to receive the grant of 25% of the amount spent on treatment of the poor patients from the Red Cross Society. Such expenditure was ₹ 50,000.
(g) Out of the fee recovered from the patients, 10% is to be given to the Specialist retained by the Hospital.
(h) Depreciation on the assets on the closing balances: *Surgical Equipments @ 20%, Building @ 5%, Furniture & Equipments @ 10%, Ambulance @ 30%*

You are required to prepare:

(i) Income and Expenditure Account of the Hospital, Dispensary and Trust.
(ii) Statement of Affairs of the Trust for the year ended 31st March, 2015.

Solution

INCOME & EXPENDITURE ACCOUNT OF DISPENSARY
for the year ended 31st March, 2015

Dr. *Cr.*

Particulars	₹	*Particulars*	₹
To Opening stock of medicines	55,000	By Sales of medicine	3,10,000
To Purchase of medicines	3,00,000	By Supply of Medicines to hospital	60,000
To Salaries to assistants	15,000	By Closing stock of medicines	40,000
To Electricity & power charges	2,000		
To Surplus transferred to Trust Income & Expenditure account (Bal. Fig.)	38,000		
	4,10,000		**4,10,000**

INCOME & EXPENDITURE ACCOUNT OF HOSPITAL
for the year ended 31st March, 2015

Dr. *Cr.*

Particulars		₹	*Particulars*	₹
To Consumption of:			By Fees received from patients Medicines	3,00,000
[1,20,000 + 60,000 + 4,000]	1,84,000		By Recovery for rent	2,75,000
Foodstuff	90,000		By Recovery of food supplies	1,40,000
Chemicals	30,000	3,04,000	By Ambulance maintenance charges less recovery	800
To Salaries:			By Grant receivable from Red Cross Society (25% of ₹ 50,000)	12,500
Admn. staff	30,000		By Deficit Transferred to Trust Income & Expenditure A/c	1,33,700
Doctors & nurses	1,50,000	1,80,000		
To Electricity & power charges		1,05,000		
To Subscription to medical journals		21,000		
To Consumption of bed sheets		90,000		
To Retainership of specialists outstanding [10% of ₹ 3,00,000]		30,000		
To Depreciation on:				
Surgical equipments	99,000			

Building	16,000			
Furniture fixtures	8,000			
Ambulance	9,000	1,32,000		
		8,62,000		**8,62,000**

INCOME & EXPENDITURE ACCOUNT OF THE YOUNG TRUST

for the year ended 31st March, 2015

Dr. Cr.

Particulars	₹	*Particulars*	₹
To Deficit from hospital	1,33,700	By Surplus from dispensary	38,000
To Postage & telephone expenses *less:* recovery	26,000	By Interest accrued on fixed deposits	55,000
To Remuneration to trustees, trust office expenses etc.	21,000	By Deficit	87,700
	1,80,700		**1,80,700**

STATEMENT OF AFFAIRS OF YOUNG TRUST AS ON 31ST MARCH, 2015

Liabilities		₹	*Assets*		₹
Capital Fund:			Building	3,20,000	
Opening balance	9,00,000		*Less:* Depreciation	(16,000)	3,04,000
Add: Donations:			Surgical Equipment	4,55,000	
Cash	6,00,000		*Add:* Donations:	40,000	
Surgical equipment	40,000			**4,95,000**	
			Less: Depreciation	(99,000)	3,96,000
	15,40,000		Furniture	80,000	
Less: Deficit	87,700	14,52,300	*Less:* Depreciation	8,000	72,000
Sundry Creditors			Ambulance	30,000	
(dispensary)		41,000	*Less:* Depreciation	9,000	21,000
Outstanding retainership to			Stock:		
specialist		30,000	Medicines:		
[10% of ₹ 3,00,000]			Dispensary	40,000	
			Hospital	16,000	
			Foodstuff		
			Hospital (20,000 – 4,000)	4,000	
			Chemicals	1,000	61,000
			Sundry Debtors (Dispensary)		60,500
			Grant receivable from Red Cross Society		12,500
			Fixed deposits		5,00,000
			Interest accrued		55,000
			Cash & bank balance		41,300
		15,23,300			**15,23,300**

***Note:** It is presumed that surgical equipment donated on 15th August 2014 was not included in the closing balance of surgical equipments as on 31st March, 2015.*

RECEIPTS AND PAYMENTS ACCOUNT

PROBLEM 8

The Income and Expenditure A/c of City Sports Club for the year ended 31st March, 2015 was as follows:

Expenditure	₹	*Income*	₹
To Salaries	1,20,000	By Subscriptions	1,60,000
To Printing and Stationery	6,000	By Entrance Fees	10,000
To Rent	12,000	By Contribution for Annual dinner	20,000
To Repairs	10,000	By Profit on Annual Sports meet	20,000
To Sundry Expenses	8,000		
To Annual Dinner Expenses	30,000		
To Interest to Bank	6,000		
To Depreciation of Sports equipment	6,000		
To Surplurs	12,000		
	2,10,000		**2,10,000**

The above account had been prepared after the following adjustments:

	₹
Subscriptions outstanding in the beg.	12,000
Subscriptions received in advance in the beg.	9,000
Subscriptions received in advance at the end.	5,400
Subscriptions outstanding at the end.	15,000

Salaries outstanding at the beginning and at the end of the financial year were ₹ 8,000 and ₹ 10,000 respectively. Sundry expenses included prepaid insurance expenses of ₹ 1,200.

The Club owned a freehold ground valued ₹ 2,00,000. The Club has sports equipment on 01.04.2010 valued at ₹ 52,000. At the end of the year, after depreciation, the sports equipment amounted to ₹ 54,000. The Club raised a loan of ₹ 40,000 from a bank on 01.01.2014, which was unpaid till 31.03.2015. On 31.03. 2015, cash in hand was ₹ 32,000.

Required: Prepare Receipts and Payments account of the Club for the year ended 31st March, 2015 and Balance Sheet as on that date.

Solution

Dr. RECEIPT AND PAYMENTS ACCOUNT FOR THE YEAR ENDED 31ST MARCH, 2015 *Cr.*

Receipts	(₹)	*Payments*	(₹)
To Balance b/d (Bal. Fig.)	27,800	By Salaries:	
To Subscription:		for 2013-2014	8,000
for 2013-2014	12,000	for 2014-2015	1,10,000
for 2014-2015	1,36,000	By Printing & Stationery	6,000
for 2015-2014	5,400	By Rend	12,000
To Entrance Fees	10,000	By Repairs	10,000
To Contribution for Annual Dinner	20,000	By Sundry Expenses (8,000 + 1,200)	9,200
To Profit on Annual Sports Meet	20,000*	By Annual Dinner Expenses	30,000
		By Interest to Bank	6,000
		By Sports Equipment	8,000
		By Balance c/d	32,000
	2,31,200		**2,31,200**

BALANCE SHEET AS AT 31ST MARCH, 2015

Liabilities	(₹)	(₹)	*Assets*	(₹)	(₹)
Capital Fund	2,34,800		Freehold Ground		2,00,000
Add: Surplus	12,000	2,46,800	Sports Equipment	52,000	
Bank Loan		40,000	*Add*: Additions	8,000	
Outstanding Salaries		10,000		60,000	
Subscription in Advance		5,400	*Less:* Depreciation	(6,000)	54,000
			Subscription in Arrear		15,000
			Prepaid Insurance		1,200
			Cash in Hand		32,000
		3,02,200			**3,02,200**

Working Notes:

(i) BALANCE SHEET AS AT 31ST MARCH, 2014

Liabilities	₹	*Assets*	₹
Capital Fund (Bal. Fig.)	2,34,800	Freehold Ground	2,00,000
Bank Loan	40,000	Sports Equipment	52,000
Outstanding Salaries	8,000	Subscription in Arrear	12,000
Subscription in Advance	9,000	Cash in hand	27,800
	2,91,800		**2,91,800**

Dr. **(ii) SPORTS EQUIPMENT ACCOUNT** *Cr.*

Particulars	₹	*Particulars*	₹
To Balance b/d	52,000	By Depreciation A/c	6,000
To Bank A/c	8,000	By Balance c/d	54,000
	60,000		**60,000**

Dr. **(iii) SUBSCRIPTION ACCOUNT** *Cr.*

Particulars	₹	*Particulars*	₹
To Income & Exp. A/c	1,60,000	By Advance Subscription A/c	9,000
		By Bank A/c	1,36,000
		By O/s Subscription A/c	15,000
	1,60,000		**1,60,000**

PROBLEM 9

Income and Expenditure Account for the year ended 31[s1] March, 2015 of South Asia Club is given below:

Expenditure	₹	*Income*	₹
To Salaries & wages	47,500	By Subscription	75,000
To Miscellaneous expenses	5,000	By Entrance fee	2,500
To Audit fee	2,500	By Contribution for annual day (After deducting expenses (₹ 7,500)	7,500
To Executive's honorarium	10,000		
To Sports day expenses	5,000		
To Printing & stationary	4,500		
To Interest on bank loan	1,500		

To Depreciation on sports equipment	3,000		
To Excess of income over expenditure	6,000		
	85,000		**85,000**

Following additional information are also available:

	Opening	Closing
(1) Subscription received in advance	4,500	2,700
(2) Subscription outstanding	6,000	7,500
(3) Salaries outstanding	4,000	4,500
(4) Sports equipment (After deducting depreciation)	26,000	27,000
(5) Cash in hand	?	16,000

(6) The club took a 5% loan of ₹ 30,000 from a bank during 2013-2014 for which interest was not paid in the financial year 2014-2015.

Prepare Receipts and Payments account of South Asia Club for the year ending 31st March 2015.

Solution

Dr. RECEIPTS AND PAYMENTS ACCOUNT FOR THE ENDED 31ST MARCH, 2015 *Cr.*

Receipts	₹	*Payments*	₹
To Balance b/d (Bal.fig.)	12,300	By Salaries & Wages	47,000
To Subscription	71,700	By Miscellaneous Expenses	5,000
To Entrance fee	2,500	By Audit fee	2,500
To Contribution for annual day (7,500 + 7,500)	15,000	By Executive's honorarium	10,000
		By Sports Day Expenses	5,000
		By Printing & Stationary	4,500
		By Expenses of Annual Day	7,500
		By Sports Equipment	4,000
		By Balance c/d	16,000
	1,01,500		**1,01,500**

Working Notes:

(i) Subscription received during the year

Cash and cash equivalents consist of cash in hand and balances with banks and investments in money market instruments for short period.

		₹
Subscription credited to Income and Expenditure A/c		75,000
Add: Outstanding subscription at the beginning of the year		6,000
Advance subscription received at the end of the year		2,700
		83,700
Less: Outstanding subscription at the end of the year	7,500	
Advance subscription received at the beginning of the year	4,500	12,000
Subscription received during the year		**71,700**

(ii) Salaries & Wages paid during the year = ₹ 47,500 + ₹ 4,000 – ₹ 4,500 = ₹ 47,000

Dr. **(i) SPORTS EQUIPMENT** *Cr.*

Particulars	₹	*Particulars*	₹
To Balance b/d	26,000	By Depreciation A/c	3,000
To Cash (Bal. Fig.)	4,000	By Balance c/d	27,000
	30,000		**30,000**

PROBLEM 10

From the following Income & Expenditure A/c of Premium Club for the year ended 31st March 2015, you are required to prepare Receipts & Payments A/c for the year ended 31st March 2015, and Balance Sheet as on that date:

Expenditure	₹	*Income*	₹
To Salaries	1,18,800	By Subscriptions	4,20,000
To Rent	2,16,000	By Entrance Fee	1,20,000
To Printing & Telephone	28,000	By Profit on sale of Sports Material	5,500
To Postage & Telephone	41,600	By Interest on 8% Government Bonds	12,000
To Electricity Charges	38,500	By Sale of Old Newspaper	11,600
To Garden Upkeep	19,300		
To Sports Material Utilized	62,800		
To Repairs & Maintenance	18,700		
To Depreciation	13,000		
To Miscellaneous Expenses	5,700		
To Membership Fee	3,200		
To Surplus carried to Capital Fund	3,500		
	5,69,100		5,69,100

The following additional information is provided to you:

(a) Position at Year Beginning and End

	Opening (₹ in lakhs)	*Closing (₹ in lakhs)*
Fixed Assets	2,40,000	?
Bank Balance	8,300	?
Stock of Sports Material	43,450	35,670
Outstanding Subscription	10,200	5,700
Subscription received in advance	2,400	4,900
8% Government Bonds	1,50,000	1,50,000
Outstanding Salaries	16,000	14,300
Outstanding Rent	21,000	15,000
Advance for Stationery	1,350	1,550
Outstanding Repairs & Maintenance	1,200	Nil
Creditors for Purchase of Sports Material	3,400	4,200

(b) Some of Fixed Assets were purchased on 01.10.2014 and Depreciation is to be charged at 5% p.a.

(c) Sports Material worth ₹ 72,000 was purchased on credit during the year.

(d) The Club became a Member of State Table Tennis Association on 01.01.2015 when it paid fee up to 31.12.2015.

(e) 50% of Entrance Fee is to be capitalized.

(f) Interest on 8% Government Bonds was received for two quarters only.
(g) A Fixed Deposit of ₹ 80,000 was made on 31st March 2015.

Solution

Dr. **(i) RECEIPTS AND PAYMENTS ACCOUNT FOR THE YEAR ENDED 31.03.2015** Cr.

Receipts	₹	*Payments*	₹
To balance b/d	8,300	By Fixed Assets	40,000
To Sale of Sports Material	22,480	By Salary	1,20,500
To Entrance Fees (1,20,000/50%)	2,40,000	By Rent	2,22,000
To Interest on Government Bonds		By Repairs	19,900
received (1,50,000 × 8% × 2 / 4)	6,000	By Stationery	28,200
To Subscriptions A/c	4,27,000	By Creditors for Sports Materials	71,200
To Sale of Old Newspapers	11,600	By Membership Fees (3,200 × 12/3)	12,800
		By Fixed Deposit	80,000
		By Postage & Telephone	41,600
		By Electricity	38,500
		By Garden Upkeep	19,300
		By Miscellaneous Expenses	5,700
		By balance c/d (bal. fig.)	**15,680**
	7,15,380		7,15,380

(ii) BALANCE SHEET AS AT 31.03.2015

Liabilities		₹	*Assets*	₹
Capital Fund:			Fixed Assets	2,67,000
Opening Balance	4,09,300		8% Govt Bonds	1,50,000
Add: Surplus	3,500		Fixed Deposits	80,000
Add: Entrance Fee	1,20,000	5,32,800	Stock of Sports Materials	35,670
Creditors for Sports Materials		4,200	Subscriptions Receivable	5,700
Advance Subscriptions		4,900	Advance for Stationery	1,550
Salary Outstanding		14,300	Accrued Interest	
Rent Outstanding		15,000	(1,50,000 × 8% × 2/4)	6,000
			Prepaid Membership Fee	9,600
			(3,200 × 9/3)	
			Cash at Bank	15,680
		5,71,200		5,71,200

Working Notes:

Dr. **(i) SUBSCRIPTION ACCOUNT** Cr.

Particulars	₹	*Particulars*	₹
To balance b/d (o/s Sub. Beg.)	10,200	By Balance b/d (Adv. Sub beg)	2,400
To Income and Expenditure A/c		By Cash/Bank (Receivecr)	4,27,000
(Income)	4,20,000	By Balance c/d (o/s Subs. at end)	5,700
To Balance c/d (Adv. Sub at end)	4,900		
	4,35,100		4,35,100

Dr. **(ii) STATIONERY ACCOUNT** Cr.

Particulars	₹	Particulars	₹
To Balance b/d (Advance)	1,350	By Income & Expenditure A/c	28,000
To Bank (paid) (bal. fig.)	28,200	By Balance c/d (Adv. at end)	1,550
	29,550		29,550

Dr. **(iii) CREDITORS FOR SPORTS MATERIAL ACCOUNT** Cr.

Particulars	₹	Particulars	₹
To Bank (paid) (bal. fig.)	71,200	By Balance b/d	3,400
To balance c/d	4,200	By Purchases	72,000
	75,400		75,400

Dr. **(iv) FIXED ASSETS ACCOUNT** Cr.

Particulars	₹	Particulars	₹
To Balance b/d	2,40,000	By Depreciation A/c	13,000
To Bank (Purchases)	40,000	By balance c/d (balancing figure)	2,67,000
	2,80,000		2,80,000

Note: Depreciation on existing Fixed Asset = ₹ 2,40,000 × 5% = ₹ 12,000

Depreciation on New Fixed Asset = ₹ 13,000 – ₹ 12,000 = ₹ 1,000

Cost of New Asset = 1000 × 100/2.5 = ₹ 40,000

Dr. **(v) EXPENSES ACCOUNT** Cr.

Particulars	Salary	Rent	R & M	Particulars	Salary	Rent	R & M
To R&P A/c (Paid)	1,20,000	2,22,000	19,900	By Balance b/d	16,000	21,000	1,200
To balance c/d	14,300	15,000	—	By Income & Exp. A/c	1,18,800	2,16,000	18,700
	1,34,800	2,37,000	19,900		1,34,800	2,37,000	19,900

Dr. **(vi) SPORTS EQUIPMENT ACCOUNT** Cr.

Particulars	₹	Particulars	₹
To Balance b/d	43,450	By Income & Exp. A/c – Consumption	62,800
To Bank (Purchases)	72,000	By Bank (Sale Proceeds) (b.f.)	22,480
To Income & Expenditure A/c (Gain on Sale of Sports Material)	5,500	By Balance c/d	35,670
	1,20,950		1,20,950

(vii) BALANCE SHEET AS AT 01.04.2014

Liabilities	₹	Assets	₹
Capital Fund (*balancing figure*)	4,09,300	Fixed Assets	2,40,000
Creditors for Sports Material	3,400	8% Govt Bonds	1,50,000
Subscriptions Received in Advance	2,400	Stock of Sports Materials	43,450
Salary Expenses Outstanding	16,000	Subscriptions Receivable	10,200
Rent Expenses Outstanding	21,000	Advance for Stationery	1,350
Repairs Expenses Outstanding	1,200	Cash at Bank	8,300
	4,53,300		4,53,300

PROBLEM 11

The following information relates to Country Sports Club for the year ended 31.3.2015. You are required to prepare the Receipts and Payments Account for the year ended 31.3.2015 and Balanace Sheet as on that date.

Expenditure	₹	*Income*		₹
To salaries	3,36,000	By Subscriptions		8,40,000
To Repairs and maintenance	88,000	By Receipts for		
To Ground upkeep	1,66,500	Annual Sports	3,25,000	
To Electricity charges	82,600	*Less:* Sports expenses	2,75,000	50,000
To Sports material used	1,48,000	By Entrance fees		1,80,000
To Printing and stationery	42,200	By Interest on 10% govt. bond		12,000
To Groundsman wages	80,000	By Rent on hire of club ground		84,000
To Depreciation	1,36,000	By Profit on sale of sports material		10,500
To Prizes distributed		By Sale of old newspaper		3,500
(net of fund income)	4,000			
To Surplus carried to capital fund	96,700			
	11,80,000			11,80,000

Additional information:

(a)

	Balance as on 1.4.2014 (₹)	*Balance as on 31.3.2015 (₹)*
Fixed Assets (net block)	6,36,000	7,20,000
Stock of sports material	1,24,000	1,38,000
Investment in 10% government bond	1,20,000	1,20,000
Subscription received in advance	64,000	72,000
Outstanding subscriptions	1,24,000	88,000
Outstanding repairs expenses	13,500	24,500
Creditors for sports material	78,600	62,500
Salary paid in advance	32,000	28,000
Prize Fund	2,40,000	2,40,000
Prize Fund investments	2,36,000	2,36,000
Bank balance	54,500	?

(b) During the year the club purchased sports material of ₹ 1,80,000, out of which 75% was credit purchase.

(c) 25% of the entrance fees is to be capitalized.

(d) As per the Club's policy any excess of expense for prizes distributed over prize fund income is to be charged to Income and Expenditure A/c and vice versa:

Prize Fund Income earned during the year ₹ 36,000

Prizes distributed during the year ₹ 40,000

(e) Interest on Government bond is received half yearly on 30th June and 31st December each year.

Solution

RECEIPT AND PAYMENT ACCOUNT FOR THE YEAR ENDED 31.3.2015

Receipts		₹	Payments		₹
To Balance b/d		54,500	By Salaries	3,36,000	
To Subscription		8,84,000	*Less:* advance in beg.	(32,000)	
To Sale of Sports Materials		28,500	*Add:* advance at end	28,000	3,32,000
To rent on hire of club ground		84,000	By Repairs and Maint.	88,000	
To Entrance fees (1,80,000/75%)		2,40,000	*Less:* O/s at end	(24,500)	
To Receipts for annual sports		3,25,000	*Add:* O/s at beg.	13,500	77,000
To Interest on Govt			By Ground upkeep		1,66,500
Bonds	12,000		By Electricity charges		82,600
Receivable beg.	3,000		By Printing and stationery		42,200
Receivable end	(3,000)	12,000	By groundsman wages		80,000
To Sale of old news papers		3,500	By Exp. of annual sports		2,75,000
To Income from Prize fund		36,000	By Purchases (1,80,000 × 25%)		45,000
			By Prize Fund Expenses		40,000
			By Fixed Assets		2,20,000
			By Creditors for Sports Materials		1,51,000
			By Balance c/f		1,56,100
		16,67,500			16,67,500

BALANCE SHEET AS AT 31.3.2015

Liabilities		₹	Assets	₹
Capital Fund:			Fixed Assets	7,20,000
Opening Balance	9,33,400		Stock of sports material	1,38,000
Add: Entrance fees	60,000		Investment in 10% Govt bonds	1,20,000
(2,40,000 × 25%)			O/s Subscription	88,000
Add: Surplus	96,700	10,90,100	Prize fund investment	2,36,000
Prize Fund		2,40,000	Bank Balance	1,56,100
Outstanding Repairs Expenses		24,500	Interest receivable on	
Advance Subscription		72,000	Government bonds	3,000
Creditors for sports materials		62,500	(1,20,000 × 3/12)	
			Advance salary	28,000
		14,89,100		14,89,100

Working Notes:

Dr **1. FIXED ASSETS ACCOUNT** Cr

Particulars	₹	Particulars	₹
To Balance B/f	6,36,000	By depreciation A/c	1,36,000
To Bank A/c (B.F.)	2,20,000	By Balance C/f	7,20,000
	8,56,000		8,56,000

Dr **2. SUBSCRIPTION ACCOUNT** Cr

Particulars	₹	Particulars	₹
To Balance B/f	1,24,000	By Balance B/f	64,000
To Income and exp A/c	8,40,000	By Bank A/c (B.F.)	8,84,000
To Balance C/f	72,000	By Balance C/f	88,000
	9,92,000		9,92,000

Dr **3. CREDITORS FOR SPORTS MATERIAL ACCOUNT** Cr

Particulars	₹	Particulars	₹
To Bank A/c (B.f)	1,51,000	By Balance B/f	78,600
To Balance C/f	62,500	By Purchase (1,80,000 × 75%)	1,35,000
	2,13,600		2,13,600

Dr **4. SPORTS MATERIAL ACCOUNT** Cr

Particulars	₹	Particulars	₹
To Balance B/f	1,24,000	By Bank A/c (b.f.)	**28,500**
To purchases	1,80,000	By Income and Expenditure A/c	1,48,000
To profit on sale on materials	10,500	By Balance C/f	1,38,000
	3,14,500		3,14,500

5. BALANCE SHEET AS AT 1.4.2014

Liabilities	₹	Assets	₹
Capital Fund (b.f.)	**9,33,400**	Fixed Assets	6,36,000
Prize Fund	2,40,000	Stock of Sports Materials	1,24,000
O/S Repairs Expenses	13,500	Investment in 10% Govt bonds	1,20,000
Advance Subscription	64,000	O/s subscription	1,24,000
Crs for Sports Materials	78,600	Prize fund investment	2,36,000
		Bank Balance	54,500
		Interest receivable on Government bonds (1,20,000 × 3/12)	3,000
		Advance salary	32,000
	13,29,500		13,29,500

COMPREHENSIVE PROBLEMS

PROBLEM 12

The Income & Expenditure Account of Neo Sports Club for the year ending March 31, 2015 is as follows:

Expenditure	₹	*Income*	₹
To Salaries	7,20,000	By Subscription	9,00,000
To Depreciation	90,000		
To Bank interest	38,400		
ToAuditfee	20,000		
To Insurance	9,000		
To Surplus transferred to balance sheet	22,600		
	9,00,000		9,00,000

Following adjustments have been made while preparing Income & Expenditure A/c as above:

1. Subscription outstanding as on 31-03-2014 amounting to ₹ 72,000 and as on 31-03-2015 amounting to ₹ 90,000.
2. Subscription received in advance as on 31-03-2014 amounting to ₹ 54,000 and as on 31-03-2015 amounting to ₹ 32,400.
3. Salary outstanding as on 31-03-2014 amounting to ₹ 55,000 and as on 31-03-2015 amounting to ₹ 60,000.
4. Audit fee is same for financial year 2013-2014 and financial year 2014-2015. As a standard practice, audit fee of one financial year is paid during next financial year, after completion of audit.
5. A loan amounting to ₹ 3,20,000 has been taken from bank by Club on 01-10-2013. Interest on loan is payable @ 12% p.a. Interest of one financial year paid on April, 01 of next financial year. No amount of principal is repaid by the club till 31-03-2015.
6. Assets of club as on 31 -03-2014 were as under:

Land at Cost	₹ 10,00,000
Building at WDV (Original cost ₹ 7,00,000)	₹ 6,65,000
Sports Equipments WDV (Original cost ₹ 5,00,000,)	₹ 4,50,000

7. Depreciation on building to be provided @ 5% on straight line basis. There is no addition to building during financial year 2014-2015.
8. Depreciation on sports equipments to be provided @ 10% on straight line basis. Fresh sports equipments purchased during financial year 2014-2015 on 01-10-2014.
9. Insurance is paid on October 01, during each financial year which remains valid till September 30 of next financial year prepaid insurance as on 31-03-2014 was ₹ 4,200.
10. Cash & bank balance as on 31-03-2015 amounting to ₹ 1,56,000 and as on 31-03-2014 amounting to ₹ 7,59,400.

Required: Prepare Receipts and Payments A/c for the year ending on March 31, 2015.

Solution

Dr. **RECEIPTS AND PAYMENTS A/C FOR THE YEAR ENDING MARCH 31, 2015** *Cr.*

Receipts	₹	*Payments*		₹
To Balance b/d	1,59,400	By Salaries	7,20,000	
To Subscription	8,60,400	*Add:* Outstanding in beg.	55,000	
		Less: Outstanding at end	(60,000)	7,15,000
		By Sports equipments purchased		1,00,000
		By Bank interest		19,200

		By Auditfee(2013-2014)	20,000
		By Insurance	9,600
		By Balance c/d	1,56,000
	10,19,800		10,19,800

Working Notes:

(i) SUBSCRIPTION RECEIVED DURING THE YEAR 2014-2015

	₹
Subscription as per Income and Expenditure A/c	9,00,000
Add: Outstanding at the beg.	72,000
Add: Advance at the end	32,400
Less: Outstanding at the beg.	(90,000)
Advance at the end	(54,000)
Subscription received during the year	8,60,400

(ii) INTEREST ON LOAN FROM BANK

	₹
Interest for the financial year 2013-2014, paid on 01.04.2014, for six months from (i.e. 01.10.2013 to 31.03.2014) (₹ 3,20,000 x 12% p.a. × 6/12)	19,200

(iii) SPORTS EQUIPMENTS PURCHASED DURING THE YEAR

	₹
Depreciation as per Income & Expenditure A/c	90,000
Less: Depreciation on Building @ 5% on ₹ 7,00,000	(35,000)
Less: Depreciation on opening sports equipments @ 1 0% on ₹ 5,00,000	(50,000)
Depreciation on sports equipments purchased on 1.10.2014	5,000

Value of sports equipments purchased on 01.10.2014 will be (Amount of Depreciation/Rate of Depreciation) × (12/Period for which sports equipments held during the year)

[₹ 5,000 x (100/10)] x (12/6) ₹ 1,00,000

(iv) INSURANCE PAID DURING THE YEAR

Particulars	₹
Insurance as per Income & Expenditure A/c	9,000
Less: Prepaid as on 31.03.2014 i.e. paid during financial year 2013- 2014 for the period 01.04.2014 to 30.09.2014	(4,200)
Insurance paid during the financial year, for the period 01.10.2014 to 31.03.2015	4,800
Therefore, insurance paid during the financial year 2012-11, for the period 01.10.2014 to 30.09.2015 therefore will be [(4,800/6) x 12]	9,600

PROBLEM 13

Bear Bar Club was registered in a city and the accountant prepared the following Receipts and Payments Account for the year ended March 31, 2015 and showed a deficit of ₹ 14,520.

Receipts	*Amount*	*Payments*	*Amount*
Subscriptions	62,130	Premises	30,000
Fair receipts	7,200	Honorarium to Secretary	12,000
Variety show receipts (net)	12,810	Rent	2,400
Interest	690	Rate & Taxes	3,780
Bar Collection	22,350	Printing & Stationary	1,410
Excess Cash spent	1,000	Sundry Expenses	5,350
Deficit	14,520	Wages	2,520
		Fair Expenses	7,170
		Bar purchases payments	17,310
		Repair	960
		New car (*less* proceeds of old car ₹ 9,000)	37,800
	1,20,700		1,20,700

The following additional information are:

	01-04-2014	*31-03-2015*
Cash in hand	450	–
Bank balances as per pass book	24,690	10,440
Cheque issued not presented for sundry expenses	270	90
Subscriptions due	3,600	2,940
Premises at cost	87,000	1,17,000
Accumulated depreciation on premises	56,400	—
Car at cost	36,570	46,800
Accumulated depreciation on car	30,870	—
Bar stock	2,130	2,610
Creditors for the bar purchases	1,770	1,290

Cash excess spent represent honorarium to secretary not withdrawn due to cash deficit. His annual honorarium is ₹ 12,000.

Depreciation on premises and car is to be provided at 5% and 20% on written down value method.

Required: Prepare the correct Receipts and Payments Account, Income and Expenditure Account and Balance Sheet on March 31,2015.

Solution

Dr. **RECEIPTS & PAYMENTS ACCOUNT FOR THE YEAR ENDED 31.03.2015** *Cr.*

Receipts		₹	*Payments*	₹
To Balance b/d:			By Honorarium to Secretary (12,000 – 1,000)	11,000
Cash in hand	450			
Bank	24,420	24,870	By Rent	2,400
To Subscriptions		62,130	By Rates & taxes	3,780
To Fair receipts		7,200	By Printing & stationery	1,410
To Variety show receipts		12,810	By Sundry expenses	5,350
To Interest		690	By Wages	2,520
To Bar collection		22,350	By Fair expenses	7,170
To Car sold (old)		9,000	By Bar purchases	17,310

		By Repairs	960
		By Premises	30,000
		By Car (37,800 + 9,000)	46,800
		By Balance c/d Bank	10,350
	1,39,050		1,39,050

INCOME & EXPENDITURE ACCOUNT
for the year ended 31.03.2015

Dr. *Cr.*

Expenditure	₹	*Income*		₹
To Honorarium to secretary	12,000	By Subscription	62,130	
To Rent	2,400	*Less:* Outstanding		
To Rates & taxes	3,780	in the beg.	(3,600)	
To Printing & stationery	1,410	*Add:* Outstanding		
To Sundry expenses	5,350	at the end.	2,940	61,470
To Wages	2,520	By Fair receipts	7,200	
To Repairs	960	*Less:* Fair expenses	(7,170)	30
To Depreciation on:		By Variety show	12,810	
Premises (1,530 + 1,500)	3,030	By Interest		690
Car	9,360	By Profit from bar		6,000
To Surplus	43,490	By Profit on sale of car		3,300
	84,300			84,300

BALANCE SHEET AS AT 31.03.2015

Liabilities		₹	*Assets*		₹
Capital Fund			Premises	87,000	
Opening balance	65,130		*Add:* Addition in the year	30,000	
Add: Surplus	43,490	1,08,620		1,17,000	
Sundry creditors		1,290	Less: Accumulated		
Outstanding Honorarium		1,000	Depredation	(59,430)	57,570
			Car	36,570	
			Add: Addition	46,800	
			Less: Book Sold	(36,570)	
			Less: Depreciation	(9,360)	37,440
			Bar Stock		2,610
			Subscription due		2,940
			Cash at bank		10,350
		1,10,910			1,10,910

Working Notes:

(i) BALANCE SHEET AS AT 31.03.2014

Liabilities		₹	*Assets*	₹
Capital Fund (bal. fig.)		65,130	Premises	87,000
Sundry Creditors for bar		1,770	Car	
36,570				
Accumulated depreciation on			Bar stock	2,130
Premises	56,400		Subscription due	3,600
Car	30,870	87,270	Cash at bank	24,420
			Cash in hand	450
		1,54,170		1,54,170

Dr. **(ii) CREDITORS FOR BAR PURCHASES** Cr.

Particulars	₹	*Particulars*	₹
To Bank	17,310	By Balance b/d	1,770
To Balance c/d	1,290	By Purchases (Bal. fig.)	**16,830**
	18,600		18,600

Dr. **(iii) TRADING ACCOUNT (OF BAR)** Cr.

Particulars	₹	*Particulars*	₹
To Opening stock	2,130	By Bar collections (Cash)	22,350
To Purchases	16,830	By Closing stock	2,610
To Profit (Bal. fig.)	**6,000**		
	24,960		24,960

Dr. **(iv) ACCUMULATED DEPRECIATION ON PREMISES** Cr.

Particulars	*₹ in '000*
Opening Balance	56,400
Add: Depreciation on old premises [(87,000 – 56,400) × 5%]	1,530
Depreciation on new premises (30,000 × 5%)	1,500
	59,430

Dr. **(v) PROFIT ON SALE OF CAR** Cr.

Particulars	₹	₹
Sales price of a car		9,000
Less: Book value of old car sold	36,570	
Less: Accumulated depreciation	(30,870)	(5,700)
Profit on sale		3,300

Dr. **(vi) BANK BALANCE AS PER CASH BOOK** Cr.

Particulars	*1.4.2014* ₹	*31.3.2015* ₹
Bank balance as per Pass book	24,690	10,440
Less: Cheque issued but not presented for payment	(270)	(90)
Bank balance as per cash book	24,420	10,350

PROBLEM 14

The following particulars relate to Hanuman Sports Club:

INCOME & EXPENDITURE ACCOUNT

for the year ending on 31st March, 2015

Dr. *Cr.*

Expenditure	₹	*Income*	₹
To Secretary's Salary	15,000	By Entrance Fees	1,05,000
To Printing & Stationery	22,000	By Subscriptions	1,56,000
To Advertising	16,000	By rent	28,000
To Audit Fees	5,000	By Interest on Investments	12,000
To Fire Insurance	10,000		
To Depreciation:			
—Sports Equipments	90,000		
—Furniture	5,000		
To Surplus	1,38,000		
	3,01,000		3,01,000

RECEIPTS & PAYMENTS ACCOUNT

for the year ending on 31st March, 2015

Dr. *Cr.*

Receipts	₹	*Payments*	₹
To Balance b/d	4,2000	By Secretary's Salary	10,000
To Entrance Fee 2013-2014	1,0000	By Printing & stationery	26,000
To Entrance Fee 2014-2015	1,00,000	By Advertising	16,000
To Subscriptions 2013-2014	6000	By Fire Insurance	12,000
To Subscription 2014-2015	15,0000	By 12% Investments	
To Subscription 2015-2014	4000	(purchased on 1.10.2014)	2,00,000
To Rent received	2,4000	By Furniture	20,000
To Interest received	6000	By Balance c/d	58,000
	3,42,000		3,42,000

The assets on 1st April, 2014 included Club Grounds & Pavilion ₹ 4,40,000, Sports Equipments ₹ 2,50,000 and Furniture and Fixtures ₹ 40,000. Subscriptions in arrear on that date were ₹ 8,000. Subscriptions received in advance on that date were ₹ 2,000. Creditors for Printing & Stationery on that date were ₹ 5,000. Prepare the Closing Balance Sheet of the Club.

Solution

BALANCE SHEET AS ON 31ST MARCH, 2015

Liabilities	₹	₹	*Assets*	₹	₹
			Fixed Assets:		
Capital Fund:			Club, Grounds & Pavilion		4,40,000
Opening Balance	7,83,000		Furniture & Fixitures	40,000	
Add: Surplus	1,38,000	9,21,000	*Add*: Additions	20,000	
Current Liabilities:				60,000	
Outstanding Salary		5,000	*Less*: Depreciation	(5,000)	55,000
(15,000 – 10,000)					
Outstanding Audit Fees		5,000	Sports Equipments	2,50,000	
Creditors for Printing &			*Less*: Depreciation	(90,000)	1,60,000

Stationery {22,000 – (26,000 – 5,000)}	1,000		
Subscription received in advance	4,000	Investments:	
		Investment (at cost)	2,00,000
		Accrued Interest [₹ 12,000 – ₹ 6,000]	6,000
		Current Assets:	
		Accrued rent (28,000 – 24,000)	4,000
		Subscription receivable	
		For 2013–12 (8,000 – 6,000)	2,000
		For 2014–13 {(1,56,000 – 1,50,000 + 2,000)}	4,000
		Entrance Fees receivables (1,05,000 – 1,00,000)	5,000
		Prepaid Insurance (12,000 – 10,000)	2,000
		Cash and bank	58,000
	9,36,000		9,36,000

Working Notes:

Calculation of Capital Fund as on 1st April, 2014

BALANCE SHEET OF SPORTS CLUB
As at 31st March 2014

Liabilities	₹	*Assets*	₹
Capital Fund (Balance Fig.)	7,83,000	Fixed Assets :	
Current Liabilities:		Club, Grounds & Pavilion	4,40,000
Subscription received in advance	2,000	Furniture & Fixtures	40,000
Creditors for Printing and Stationery	5,000	Sports Equipments	2,50,000
		Current Assets:	
		Entrance Fees receivables	10,000
		Subscription receivables	8,000
		Cash and Bank	42,000
	7,90,000		7,90,000

PROBLEM 15

Highend Club appointed a new accountant for maintaining books of account. He prepared following Receipts and Payments A/c for the year ended as on 31st March, 2015.

RECEIPTS AND PAYMENTS ACCOUNT

Receipts		₹	*Payments*	₹
To Balance b/d		9,000	By Printing & Stationery	21,000
To Annual subscription for current year	9,18,000		By Telephone Expenses	45,000
Add: Outstanding of last year received this year	36,000		By Repair & Maintenance Expenses (including payment for sports material ₹ 54,000)	1,26,000
	9,54,000			

Less Subscription recd. in Advance as on 31-03-2014	18,000	9,36,000	By Garden Upkeep	55,000
To Sale of Old Newspaper		36,000	By Electricity Charged	36,000
To 5% Interest on Investments		27,000	By Loss on sale of furniture (Cost as per books ₹ 90,000)	36,000
			By Balance c/d	25,57,000
To Entrance Fees		68,000		
To Donation for building		18,00,000		
		28,76,000		28,76,000

Additional information:

	01.4.2014 ₹	*01.4.2015* ₹
Furniture	3,60,000	
Stock of Sports material	1,33,200	36,000
Subscription receivable		54,000
Subscription received in advance		18,000
Outstanding Printing & Stationery Exp.	1,500	2,500
Outstanding Electricity Charges		3,200

50% Entrance Fees is to be capitalized.

Do you agree with above Receipts and Payments Account? If not, prepare correct Receipts and Payments Account and Income and Expenditure Account for the year ended 31st March, 2015 and Balance Sheet as on that date.

Solution

CORRECT RECEIPTS AND PAYMENTS ACCOUNT OF HIGHEND CLUB
for the year ended 31st March, 2015

Receipts		*Amount* ₹	*Payments*	*Amount* ₹
To bal. b/d		9,000	By Printing & Stationery	21,000
To annual subscription	9,18,000		By Telephone expenses	45,000
Less: Receivable on 31.3.2015	(54,000)		By Garden upkeep	55,000
Add: Advance received for year			By Electricity charges	36,000
2015–14	18,000		By Repairs & maintenance	72,000
Add: Receivable as on 31.3.2014	36,000		(1,26,000 – 54,000)	
Less: Advance received on 31.3.2014	(18,000)	9,00,000		
To Sale of furniture (90,000 – 36,000)		54,000	By Sports material	54,000
To Sale of old newspaper		36,000	By bal. c/d	26,11,000
To Entrance fee		68,000		
To Donation for building		18,00,000		
To Interest on investments		27,000		
		28,94,000		28,94,000

INCOME & EXPENDITURE ACCOUNT OF HIGHEND CLUB
for the year ended 31st March, 2015

Expenditure	Amount ₹	Income	Amount ₹
To Printing and Stationery expenses (W.N.1)	22,000	By subscription	9,18,000
To Repairs and Maintenance (1,26,000 – 54,000)	72,000	By Entrance fee (50% of 68,000)	34,000
To Telephone expenses	45,000	By Sale of old newspapers	36,000
To Sports material (W.N.2)	1,51,200	By Interest on investments	27,000
To Garden upkeep	55,000		
To Electricity charges (W.N.3)	39,200		
To Loss on sale of furniture	36,000		
To Excess of surplus over expenditure	5,94,600		
	10,15,000		10,15,000

BALANCE SHEET OF HIGHED CLUB
as on 31st March, 2015

Expenditure		Amount ₹	Income		Amount ₹
Capital Fund (W.N.4)	10,58,700		Furniture	3,60,000	
Add: Entrance fee capitalized	34,000		*Less*: sale	90,000	2,70,000
Add: Surplus	5,94,600	16,87,300	Sports material		36,000
Building fund		18,00,000	5% investments		5,40,000
Outstanding Electricity charges		3,200	Cash in hand		26,11,000
Outstanding printing and stationery exp.		2,500	Subscription receivable		54,000
Subscription received in advance		18,000			
		35,11,000			35,11,000

Working Notes:

1. **Printing and Stationery expenses for the year = ₹ 21,000 + ₹ 2,500 – ₹ 1,500 = ₹ 22,000**
2. **Depreciation on Sports material = ₹ 1,33,200 + ₹ 54,000 – ₹ 36,000 = ₹ 1,51,200**
3. **Electricity charges for the year = ₹ 36,000 + ₹ 3,200 = ₹ 39,200**
4. **Value of Investment = ₹ 27,000 × 100/5 = ₹ 5,40,000**

5.

BALANCE SHEET
as at 1st April, 2014

Liabilities	₹	Assets	₹
Capital fund (balancing fig.)	10,58,700	Furniture	3,60,000
Subscription received in advance	18,000	Sports material	1,33,200
Outstanding printing and stationery charges	1,500	Subscription receivables	36,000
		Investments	5,40,000
		Cash in hand	9,000
	10,78,200		10,78,200

Note: The above solution is prepared on the basis of the assumption that club is not registered under the Companies Act, 1956.

15 SINGLE ENTRY SYSTEM

SHORT ANSWER PRACTICAL PROBLEMS

CALCULATION OF PROFIT OR LOSS

PROBLEM 1

On 1st April Chhotu started business with an initial Capital of ₹ 70,000. On 1st October he introduced additional capital of ₹40,000. On 7th of every month, he withdraws ₹ 5,000 for household expenses. On 31st March his Assets and Liabilities were ₹2,00,000 and ₹ 70,000 respectively. *Ascertain the profit earned by Chhotu during the year ended 31st March.*

Solution

STATEMENT SHOWING THE PROFIT OR LOSS

	Particulars	₹
A	Closing Capital (₹ 2,00,000 – ₹ 70,000)	1,30,000
B	*Add:* Drawings (₹ 5,000 × 12 months)	60,000
C	*Less:* Additional capital introduced	(40,000)
D	Adjusted Closing Capital	1,50,000
E	*Less:* Opening Capital	(70,000)
F	Profit for the year ended	80,000

PROBLEM 10.4

Find out the profit of Mr. A from the following information:

Particulars	₹
Capital at the beginning of the year	20,00,000
Drawings made by Mr. A	2,00,000
Capital at the end of the year	25,00,000
Additional capital introduced during the year	1,00,000

Solution

STATEMENT SHOWING PROFIT EARNED DURING THE YEAR

	Particulars	₹
A	Capital at the end of the year	25,00,000
B	*Add:* Drawings	2,00,000
C	*Less:* Additional capital introduced during the year	(1,00,000)
D	Adjusted Closing Capital	26,00,000
E	*Less:* Capital at the beginning of the year	(20,00,000)
F	Profit earned during the year	6,00,000

PROBLEM 2

The closing capital of Mr. *A* was ₹ 1,50,000. Opening capital was ₹ 60,000. During the year he had drawn ₹ 40,000 for domestic expenses. He introduced ₹ 25,000 as additional capital. Find out his net profit for the year

Solution

Statement showing calculation of Profit for the year ended ....

	Particulars	₹
A	Closing Capital	1,50,000
B	Add: Drawings during the year	40,000
C	*Less:* Additional capital introduced	(25,000)
D	Adjusted Closing Capital	1,65,000
E	*Less:* Opening Capital	(60,000)
F	Net Profit for the year	1,05,000

CALCULATION OF DRAWINGS

PROBLEM 3

The closing capital of Mr. B was ₹ 4,00,000. Opening capital was ₹ 3,50,000. His net profit for the year was ₹ 1,00,000. He introduced ₹ 30,000 as additional capital. Find out the amount drawn by Mr. B for his domestic expenses.

Solution

COMPUTATION OF DRAWINGS DURING THE YEAR

	Particulars	₹
A	Opening Capital	3,50,000
B	*Add:* Net profit	1,00,000
C	*Add:* Additional capital introduced	30,000
D	Adjusted Closing Capital	4,80,000
E	*Less*: Closing Capital	(4,00,000)
F	Drawings by Mr. 'B'	80,000

STATEMENT OF AFFAIRS METHOD

PROBLEM 4

A, B and *C* run a business sharing profits and losses in proportion of 2:2:1. On 1st January their respective capitals were ₹ 96,000, ₹ 90,000 and ₹ 84,000.

On 30th June the following was the position:

	₹
Creditors	30,000
Furniture	9,000
Book debts	1,80,000
Stock	90,000
Cash in hand and at bank	36,000

The drawings of the partners respectively were ₹12,000, ₹ 9,000 and ₹ 6,000 during the half-year. Each partner is entitled to an interest at the rate of 5% p.a. on capital. Interest on drawings was calculated as ₹ 600 for A, ₹ 450 in case of B and ₹ 300 in case of C.

You are required to prepare:

(i) A statement of affairs as on 30th June.

(ii) Calculate the profits for the half-year ending on 30th June and allocate the same amongst the partners. Also calculate capital of each partner as on 30th June.

Solution

STATEMENT OF AFFAIRS OF A, B & C AS AT 30TH JUNE

Liabilities	₹	*Assets*	₹
Capital (Bal. Fig.)	2,85,000	Furniture	9,000
Creditors	30,000	Stock	90,000
		Book debts	1,80,000
		Cash in hand and at bank	36,000
	3,15,000		3,15,000

(ii) STATEMENT SHOWING PROFIT OR LOSS OF PARTNERS A, B AND C

for six months ending on 30th June

	Particulars	₹
A	Closing Capital	2,85,000
B	*Add:* Drawings of A, B and C (₹ 12,000 + ₹ 9,000 + ₹ 6,000)	27,000
C	*Add:* Interest on drawings of A, B and C (₹ 600 + ₹ 450 + ₹ 300)	1,350
D	*Less:* Interest on capital of A, B and C (₹ 2,400 + ₹ 2,250 + ₹ 2,100)	(6,750)
E	*Adjusted Closing Capital*	3,06,000
F	*Less:* Opening Capital (₹ 96,000 + ₹ 90,000 + ₹ 84,000)	(2,70,000)
G	Net Profit	**36,600**

STATEMENT SHOWING ALLOCATION OF PROFITS AND OTHER ADJUSTMENTS IN THE CAPITAL ACCOUNTS OF A, B AND C

Particulars	*A (₹)*	*B(₹)*	*C(₹)*
Opening Capital	96,000	90,000	84,000
Add: Net Profit in the ratio of 2:2:1	14,640	14,640	7,320
Add: Interest on Capital @ 5% p.a. for 6 months	2,400	2,250	2,100
Less: Drawings	(12,000)	(9,000)	(6,000)
Less: Interest on drawings	(600)	(450)	(300)
Closing Capital	**1,00,440**	**97,440**	**87,120**

CALCULATION OF CLOSING DEBTORS

PROBLEM 5

From the following information, calculate the amount of closing sundry debtors:

Opening Debtors ₹ 50,000.

Bad debts are 2% and discount to the customers is given @ 1% of the opening balance of sundry debtors.

Returns from the customers are ₹ 3,000.

Cash received from debtors is ₹ 2,30,000.

Cash received from debtors in transit is ₹ 14,000.

Cash sales are ₹ 5,00,000.

Credit sales are ₹ 2,50,000.

Solution

Dr. **SUNDAY DEBTORS ACCOUNT** *Cr.*

Particulars	*₹*	*Particulars*	*₹*
To Balance b/d	50,000	By Cash A/c	2,30,000
To Credit Sales	2,50,000	By Cash-in-transit	14,000
		By Saler Returns A/c	3,000
		By Bad Debts	1,000
		By Discount Allowed	500
		By Balance c/d (b/f)	**51,500**
	3,00,000		3,00,000

CALCULATION OF PROVISION FOR DOUBTFUL DEBTS

PROBLEM 6

In a concern, the opening provision for doubtful debts is ₹ 51,000. During the year a sum of ₹10,000 was written off as bad debt. The closing balance of sundry debtors amounts to ₹ 6,30,000. It was decided that 10% of the debtors is to be maintained as provision. Calculate the closing balance towards provision for doubtful debts and pass journal entry for giving effect to the provision maintained.

Solution

Closing provision for doubtful debts to be maintained @ 10% =	₹ 63,000
Less: Opening Provision for doubtful debts	₹ 51,000
Additional provision to be maintained	₹ 12,000

JOURNAL ENTRY

Profit and Loss A/c	Dr.	₹ 12,000	
To Provision for doubtful debts			₹ 12,000
(Being additional provision on doubtful debts maintained @ 10%)			

CALCULATION OF CLOSING STOCK

PROBLEM 7

A trader purchased goods for ₹ 1, 70,000, The opening stock of inventory prior to the said purchase was ₹ 30,000. His sales was ₹ 2,10,000. Find out the closing stock of inventory if the Gross profit margin is 25% on cost.

Solution

Calculation of Closing Stock

Cost of Goods Sold = Sales – Gross Profit
= ₹ 2,10,000 – (₹ 2,10,000 × 25/125) = ₹ 1,68,000
Closing Stock = Opening Stock + Purchases – Cost of goods sold
= ₹ 30,000 + ₹ 1,70,000 – ₹ 1,68,000 = ₹,32,000

CALCULATION OF SALES

PROBLEM 8

A company sold 25% of the goods on cash basis and the balance on credit basis. Debtors are allowed 2 months credit and their balance as on 31st March is ₹1,40,000. Assume that the sale is uniform through out the year. Calculate the total sales of the company for the year ended 31st March.

Solution

Credit sales per month = ₹ 1,40,000/2 = ₹ 70,000

Credit sales for the year = ₹ 70,000 × 12 = ₹ 8,40,000

Add: Cash sales $[8{,}40{,}000 \times 25/75]$ = ₹ 2,80,000

Total Sales of the company = ₹ 11,20,000

CALCULATION OF TOTAL SALES AND TOTAL PURCHASES

PROBLEM 9

Ice Limited gives you the following information to find out Total Sales and Total Purchases:

Particulars	₹	Particulars	₹
Opening Debtors	70,000	Discount allowed by Suppliers	7,000
Opening Creditors	81,000	Discount allowed to Customers	9,000
Bills Receivable received during the year	47,000	Endorsed Bills Receivable dishonoured	3,000
Bills Payable issued during the year	53,000	Sales Returns	11,000
Cash received from Customers	1,56,000	Bills Receivable Discounted	8,000
Cash paid to Suppliers	1,72,000	Discounted Bills Receivable dishonoured	2,000
Bad Debts Recovered	16,000	Cash Sales	1,68,500
Bills Receivables endorsed to Creditors	27,000	Cash Purchases	1,97,800
Bills Receivables dishonoured by Customers	5,000	Closing Debtors	82,000
		Closing Creditors	95,000

Solution

Dr. **(i) TOTAL DEBTORS ACCOUNT** *Cr.*

Particulars	₹	Particulars	₹
To Balance b/d (given)	70,000	By Cash/ Bank A/c	1,56,000
To Bills Receivable A/c	5,000	By Discount Allowed A/c	9,000
To Creditors A/c	3,000	By Bills Receivable A/c	47,000
To Bank A/c	2,000	By Sales Returns A/c	11,000
To Sales A/c	**2,25,000**	By Balance c/d	82,000
	3,05,000		3,05,000

Dr. **(ii) TOTAL CREDITORS ACCOUNT** *Cr.*

Particulars	₹	Particulars	₹
To Cash/ Bank A/c	1,72,000	By Balance b/d	81,000
To Discount Received A/c	7,000	By Debtors A/c	3,000
To Bills Payable A/c	53,000	By Purchases A/c (bal. fig) (Credit)	**2,70,000**
To Bills Receivable	27,000		
To Balance c/d	95,000		
	3,54,000		3,54,000

1. **Total Sales** = ₹ 2,25,000 + ₹ 1,68,500 = **₹ 3,93,500**
2. **Total Purchases** = ₹ 2,70,000 + ₹ 1,97,800 = **₹ 4,67,800**

LONG ANSWER PRACTICAL PROBLEMS

SIMPLE PROBLEMS

PROBLEM 10

Lucky does not maintain proper books of accounts. However, he maintains a record of his bank transactions and also is able to give the following information from which you are requested to prepare his final accounts for the year 2014–2015:

	Opening ₹	*Closing* ₹
Debtors	1,02,500	?
Creditors	?	46,000
Stock	50,000	62,500
Bank Balance	?	50,000
Fixed Assets	7,500	9,000

Details of his bank transactions were as follows:

	₹
Received from debtors	3,40,000
Additional capital brought in	5,000
Sale of fixed assets (book value ₹ 2,500)	1,750
Paid to creditors	2,80,000
Expenses paid	49,250
Personal drawings	25,000
Purchase of fixed assets	5,000

No cash transactions took place during the year. Goods are sold at cost plus 25%. Cost of goods sold was ₹ 2,60,000.

Solution

TRADING AND PROFIT AND LOSS ACCOUNT
for the year ended 31st March, 2015

Dr. *Cr.*

Particulars	₹	*Particulars*	₹
To Opening stock	50,000	By Sales (₹ 2,60,000 × 125/100)	3,25,000
To Purchases (balancing figure)	2,72,500	By Closing Stock	62,500
To Gross profit c/d (₹ 2,60,000 × 25/100)	65,000		
	3,87,500		3,87,500
To Expenses	49,250	By Gross Profit b/d	65,000
To Loss on sale of fixed assets	750		
To Depreciation on fixed asset (W.N,1)	1,000		
To Net profit	14,000		
	65,000		65,000

BALANCE SHEET AS AT 31ST MARCH, 2015

Liabilities		₹	*Assets*	₹
Capital	169,000		Fixed assets	9,000
Add: Additional capital	5,000		Debtors	87,500
New profit	14,000		Stock	62,500
	1,88,000		Bank Balance	50,000
Less: Drawings	25,000	1,63,000		
Creditors		46,000		
		2,09,000		2,09,000

Working Notes:

Dr. **(i) FIXED ASSETS ACCOUNT** Cr.

Particulars	₹	*Particulars*	₹
To Balance b/d	7,500	By Bank (sale)	1,750
To Bank	5,000	By Loss on sale of fixed asset	750
		By Depreciation (balancing figure)	1,000
		By Balance c/d	9,000
	12,500		12,500

Dr. **(ii) BANK ACCOUNT** Cr.

Particulars	₹	*Particulars*	₹
To Balance b/d *(balancing figure)*	62,500	By Creditors	2,80,000
To Debtors	3,40,000	By Expenses	49,250
To Capital	5,000	By Drawings	25,000
To Sale of fixed assets	1,750	By Fixed Assets	5,000
		By Balance c/d	50,000
	4,09,250		4,09,250

Dr. **(iii) DEBTORS' ACCOUNT** Cr.

Particulars	₹	*Particulars*	₹
To Balance b/d	1,02,500	By Bank	3,40,000
To Sales [₹ 2,60,000 × 125/100]	3,25,000	By Balance c/d (b.f.)	87,500
	4,27,500		4,27,500

Dr. **(iv) CREDITORS ACCOUNT** Cr.

Particulars	₹	*Particulars*	₹
To Bank	2,80,000	By Balance b/d (balancing figure)	53,500
To Balance c/d	46,000	By Purchases (from trading account)	2,72,500
	3,26,000		3,26,000

(v) BALANCE SHEET AS ON 1ST APRIL, 2014

Liabilities	₹	*Assets*	₹
Creditors	53,500	Fixed assets	7,500
Capital *(balancing figure)*	1,69,000	Debtors	1,02,500
		Stock	50,000
		Bank balance	62,500
	2,22,500		2,22,500

PROBLEM 11

From the following particulars furnished by Shri Ramji, prepare Trading and Profit and Loss account for the year ended 31.3.2015. Also draft his Balance Sheet as at 31.03.2015.

	Opening ₹	*Closing* ₹
Creditors	3,15,400	2,48,000
Expenses outstanding	12,000	6,600
Fixed Assets (includes machinery)	2,32,200	2,40,800
Stock in hand	1,60,800	2,22,400
Cash in hand	59,200	24,000
Cash at Bank	80,000	1,37,600
Sundry Debtors	3,30,600	?

Details of the year's transactions are as follows:

	₹		₹
Cash and discount credited to debtors	12,80,000	Returns from debtors	29,000
		Bad debts	8,400
Sales (Both cash and credit)	14,36,200	Discount allowed by creditors	14,000
Returns to creditors	8,000	Capital introduced by cheque	1,70,000
Cash purchases	20,600	Expenses paid by cash	1,91,400
Drawings by cheque	8,600	Machinery acquired by cheque	63,600
Cash deposited into bank	1,00,000	Cash withdrawn from Bank	1,84,800
Cash sales	92,000	Payment to creditors by cheque	12,05,400
Collection from debtors (Deposited into bank after receiving cash)	12,50,000		

Note: Ramji has not sold any Fixed Asset during the year.

Solution

TRADING AND PROFIT AND LOSS ACCOUNT

for the year ended 31st March, 2015

Dr. Cr.

Particulars		₹	*Particulars*		₹
To Opening Stock		1,60,800	By Sales:		
To Purchases:			Cash	92,000	
Cash	20,600		Credit	13,44,200	
Credit	11,60,000			14,36,200	
	11,80,600		*Less:* Returns	29,000	14,07,200
Less: Returns	8,000	11,72,600	By Closing Stock		2,22,400
To Gross Profit c/d		2,96,200			
		16,29,600			16,29,600
To Discount allowed		30,000	By Gross Profit b/d		2,96,200
To Bad Debts		8,400	By Discount (received)		14,000
To Expenses		1,86,000			
To Depreciation		55,000			
To Net Profit		30,800			
		3,10,200			3,10,200

BALANCE SHEET AS AT 31ST MARCH, 2015

Liabilities		₹	*Assets*		₹
Capital			Sundry Assets	2,32,200	
Opening Balance	5,35,400		*Add:* New Machinery	63,600	
Add: Additional Capital	1,70,000			2,95,800	
Net Profit	30,800		*Less:* Depreciation	55,000	2,40,800
	7,36,200		Stock in trade		2,22,400
*Less:*Drawings	8,600	7,27,600	Sundry debtors		3,57,400
Sundry Creditors		2,48,000	Cash in hand		24,000
Outstanding expenses		6,600	Cash at Bank		1,37,600
		9,82,200			9,82,200

Working Notes:

(i) STATEMENT OF AFFAIRS AS AT 31ST MARCH, 2014

Liabilities	₹	*Assets*	₹
Sundry Creditors	3,15,400	Sundry Assets	2,32,200
Outstanding expenses	12,000	Stock	1,60,800
Ramji's Capital (b.f.)	5,35,400	Debtors	3,30,600
		Cash in hand	59,200
		Cash at bank	80,000
	8,62,800		8,62,800

Dr. **(ii) SUNDRY DEBTORS ACCOUNT** Cr.

Particulars	₹	Particulars	₹
To Balance b/d	3,30,600	By Cash	12,50,000
To Sales (14,36,200 – 92,000)	13,44,200	By Discount Allowed	30,000
		By Returns (sales)	29,000
		By Bad debts	8,400
		By Balance (b.f.)	3,57,400
	16,74,800		16,74,800

Dr. **(iii) SUNDRY CREDITORS ACCOUNT** Cr.

Particulars	₹	Particulars	₹
To Bank Payments	12,05,400	By Balance b/d	3,15,400
To Discount	14,000	By Purchases (b.f.)	11,60,000
To Returns	8,000		
To Balance c/d	2,48,000		
	14,75,400		14,75,400

Dr. **(iv) FIXED ASSETS ACCOUNT** Cr.

Particulars	₹	Particulars	₹
To Balance b/d	2,32,200	By Depreciation A/c (b.f.)	55,000
To Bank A/c (Purchases)	63,600	By Balance c/d	2,40,800
	2,95,800		2,95,800

Dr. **(v) EXPENSES ACCOUNT** Cr.

Particulars	₹	Particulars	₹
To Cash A/c	1,91,400	By Outstanding Exp. A/c (o/s in the beginning)	12,000
To Outstanding Exp. A/c (o/s at the end)	6,600	By Profit & Loss A/c (b.f.)	1,86,000
	1,98,000		1,98,000

Dr. **(vi) CASH AND BANK ACCOUNT** Cr.

Particulars	Cash ₹	Bank ₹	Particulars	Cash ₹	Bank ₹
To Balance b/d	59,200	80,000	By Purchases	20,600	–
To Capital	–	1,70,000	By Expenses	1,91,400	–
To Debtors	–	12,50,000	By Plant and Machinery	–	63,600
To Bank	1,84,800	–	By Drawings	–	8,600
To Cash	–	1,00,000	By Creditors	–	12,05,400
To Sales	92,000	–	By Cash	–	1,84,800
			By Bank	1,00,000	–
			By Balance c/d	24,000	1,37,600
	3,36,000	16,00,000		3,36,000	16,00,000

PROBLEM 12

Mr. X runs a retail business. Suddenly he finds on 31.03.2015 that his Cash and Bank balances have reduced considerably. He provided you the following information.

(i) *Balances*

	Opening ₹	Closing ₹
Sundry Debtors	35,400	58,800
Sundry Creditors	84,400	22,400

Cash at Bank	1,08,400	2,500
Cash in Hand	10,400	500
Rent (Outstanding for one month)	2,400	3,000
Stock	11,400	20,000
Electricity and Telephone bills-outstanding		6,400

(ii) Bank Pass-book reveals the following:

	₹
Total Deposits	10,34,000
Withdrawals:	
Creditors	8,90,000
Professional charges	34,000
Furnitures and Fixtures (acquired on 1st Oct.)	54,000
Proprietor's drawings	1,61,900

(iii) Rent has been increased from January, 2015.

(iv) Mr. X deposited all cash sales and collections from debtors after meeting wages, shop expenses, rent, electricity and telephone charges.

(v) Mr. X made all purchases on credit.

(vi) His credit sales during the year amounts to ₹.9,00,000.

(vii) He incurred ₹.6,500 per month towards wages.

(viii) He incurred following expenses:

(a) Electricity and telephone charges ₹.24,000 (paid)

(b) Shop expenses ₹.18,000 (paid).

(ix) Charge depreciation on furniture and fixtures @ 10% p.a.

Required: Finalise the accounts of Mr. X and compute his profit for the year ended 31.03.2015. Prepare his statement of affairs and reconcile the profit and capital balance.

Solution

TRADING AND PROFIT AND LOSS ACCOUNT

for the year ended 31st March, 2015

Dr. Cr.

Particulars		₹	*Particulars*		₹
To Opening Stock		11,400	By Sales:		
To Purchases		8,28,000	Cash	2,97,500	
To Gross Profit c/d		3,78,100	Credit	9,00,000	11,97,500
			By Closing Stock		20,000
		12,17,500			12,17,500
To Wages		78,000	By Gross Profit b/d		3,78,100
To Rent Paid	30,000				
Less: o/s in the beg.	(2,400)				
	27,600				
Add: o/s at the end	3,000	30,600			
To Electricity & Telephone					
Paid	24,000				
o/s at the end	6,400	30,400			
To Professional Charges		34,000			
To Shop Expenses		18,000			
To Depreciation		2,700			
$\left[(\therefore 54{,}000 \times \frac{10}{100} \times \frac{1}{2}\right]$					
To Net Profit		1,84,400			
		3,78,100			3,78,100

STATEMENT OF AFFAIRS OF MR. X AS ON 31.03.2014 & 31.03.2015

Liabilities	*31.3.2014* ₹	*31.3.2015* ₹	*Assets*	*31.3.2014* ₹	*31.3.2015* ₹
Capital A/c (b.f.)	78,800	1,01,300	Furniture		51,300
Sundry Creditors	84,400	22,400	Stock	11,400	20,000
Outstanding Rent	2,400	3,000	Sundry Debtors	35,400	58,800
Outstanding Electricity & Telephone		6,400	Bank	1,08,400	2,500
			Cash	10,400	500
	1,65,600	1,33,100		1,65,600	1,33,100

RECONCILIATION OF PROFIT

Particulars	₹
Closing Capital	1,01,300
Add: Drawings	1,61,900
Less: Opening Capital	(78,800)
Profit for the year	1,84,400

Working Notes:

Dr. **(i) TOTAL DEBTORS ACCOUNT** *Cr.*

Liabilities	₹	*Assets*	₹
To Balance b/d	35,400	By Cash A/c (b.f.)	8,76,600
To Credit Sales	9,00,000	By Balance c/d	58,800
	9,35,400		9,35,400

Dr. **(ii) TOTAL CREDITORS ACCOUNT** *Cr.*

Particulars	₹	*Particulars*	₹
To Bank A/c	8,90,000	By Bank b/d	84,400
To Balance c/d	22,400	By Credit Purchases	8,28,000
	9,12,400		9,12,400

Dr. **(iii) CASH ACCOUNT** *Cr.*

Particulars	*Cash* ₹	*Bank* ₹	*Particulars*	*Cash* ₹	*Bank* ₹
To Balance b/d	10,400	1,08,400	By Bank	10,34,000	–
To Sundry Debtors	8,76,600	–	By Wages	78,000	–
To Cash Sales (b.f.)	2,97,500	–	By Rent	30,000	–
To Cash A/c (Contra)		10,34,000	By Electricity & Tel.	24,000	
			By Shop Expenses	18,000	
			By Professional Charges	–	34,000
			By Sundry Creditors A/c	–	8,90,000
			By Furniture	–	54,000
			By Drawings A/c	–	1,61,900
			By Balance c/d	500	2,500
	11,84,500	11,42,400		11,84,500	11,42,400

PROBLEM 13

Mr. Ashok keeps his books in Single Entry System. From the following information, prepare Trading and Profit & Loss Account for the year ended 31st March, 2015 and the Balance Sheet as on that date:

Assets and Liabilities	*Opening* ₹	*Closing* ₹
Sundry Creditors	30,000	25,000
Outstanding Expenses	1,000	500
Fixed Assets	23,000	22,000
Stock	16,000	22,500
Cash in Hand and at Bank	14,000	16,000
Sundry Debtors	?	36,000

Following further details are available for the Current Year:

	₹		₹
Total receipts from debtors	1,30,000	Cash Purchases	2,000
Returns inward	3,000	Fixed Assets purchased and paid by cheque	1,000
Bad Debts	1,000	Drawings by cheques	6,500
Total Sales	1,50,000	Deposited into the bank	10,000
Discount received	1,500	Withdrawn from bank	18,500
Return outwards	1,000	Cash in hand at the end	2,500
Capital introduced (paid to Bank)	15,000	Paid to creditor by cheques	1,20,000
Cheques received from Debtors	1,25,000	Expenses paid	20,000

Solution

TRADING AND PROFIT AND LOSS ACCOUNT
for the year ended on 31st March, 2015

Dr. Cr.

Particulars		₹	*Particulars*		₹
To Opening Stock		16,000	By Sales:		
To Purchases:			Cash	6,500	
Cash	2,000		Credit	1,43,500	
Credit	1,17,500			1,50,000	
	1,19,500		*Less:* Returns	3,000	1,47,000
Less: Returns	1,000	1,18,500	By Stock		22,500
To Gross Profit c/d		35,000			
		1,69,500			1,69,500
To Expenses	20,000		By Gross profit b/d		35,000
Add: O/s at the end	500		By Discount received		1,500
	20,500				
Less: O/s at the beg.	1,000	19,500			
To Bad Debts		1,000			
To Depreciation		2,000			
To Net Profit		14,000			
		36,500			36,500

BALANCE SHEET AS AT 31ST MARCH, 2015

Liabilities		₹	*Assets*		₹
Capital:			Fixed Assets	23,000	
Opening Balance	48,500		*Add:* Additions	1,000	
Add: Additional Capital	15,000		*Less:* Depreciation	2,000	22,000
Add: Net Profit	14,000		Stock		22,500
Less: Drawings	6,500	71,000	Cash		2,500
Creditors		25,000	Bank		13,500
Outstanding Exp.		500	Debtors		36,000
		96,500			96,500

Working Notes:

Dr. **(i) CASH ACCOUNT** *Cr.*

Particulars	₹	*Particulars*	₹
To Balance b/d	4,500	By Purchases	2,000
To Sales (b.f.)	6,500	By Bank (contra)	10,000
To Debtors	5,000	By Expenses	20,000
To Bank (contra)	18,500	By Balance c/d	2,500
	34,500		34,500

Dr. **(ii) BANK ACCOUNT** *Cr.*

Particulars	₹	*Particulars*	₹
To Balance b/d (b.f.)	9,500	By Fixed Assets	1,000
To Capital	15,000	By Drawings	6,500
To Cash (contra)	10,000	By Cash (contra)	18,500
To Debtors	1,25,000	By Creditors	1,20,000
		By Balance c/d	13,500
	1,59,500		1,59,500

Dr. **(iii) CREDITORS ACCOUNT** *Cr.*

Particulars	₹	*Particulars*	₹
To Bank	1,20,000	By Balance b/d	30,000
To Returns	1,000	By Purchase (b.f.)	1,17,500
To Discount received	1,500		
To Balance c/d	25,000		
	1,47,500		1,47,500

Dr. **(iv) DEBTORS ACCOUNT** *Cr.*

Particulars	₹	*Particulars*	₹
To Balance b/d (b.f.)	26,500	By Cash	5,000
To Sales	1,43,500	By Bank	1,25,000
		By Bad Debts	1,000
		By Returns	3,000
		By Balance c/d	36,000
	1,70,000		1,70,000

(v) OPENING BALANCE SHEET AS AT 31.03.2014

Liabilities	₹	*Assets*	₹
Creditors	30,000	Fixed Assets	23,000
O/s Expenses	1,000	Stock	16,000
Capital (b.f.)	48,500	Cash	4,500
		Bank	9,500
		Debtors	26,500
	79,500		79,500

PROBLEM 14

Mr. Y keeps his books under single entry system. On 31st March, 2014 his Balance Sheet was as follows:

Liabilities	₹	*Assets*	₹
Capital of Mr Y	4,50,000	Fixed Assets	2,25,000
Creditors	8,70,000	Stock	9,15,000
Bills payable	1,87,500	Debtors	2,22,000
Expenses outstanding	67,500	Bill Receivable	90,000
		Prepaid insurance	3,000
		Cash/Bank balance	1,20,000
	15,75,000		15,75,000

(i) *Following are the summary of cash and bank transactions for the year ended 31st March, 2015.*

	₹
Cash sales	1,10,70,000
Collection from debtors	22,65,000
Payments to creditors	1,12,60,500
Paid for bills payable	12,22,500
Sundry expenses paid	9,31,050
Drawings for domestic expenses by Mr. Y	3,60,000
Cash and bank balance as on 31.3.2015	1,90,950

(ii) *Following further details are furnished:*

	₹
Gross profit on sales @ 10%	
Bills receivable from debtors during the year	6,52,500
Discount allowed to debtors	54,000
Discount received from creditors	42,000
Bills receivable endorsed to creditors	22,500
Annual fire Insurance is paid on 1st August every year	
Depreciate fixed assets @ 10%	9,000

(iii) *Balances as on 31.3.2015 are given below:*

	₹
Stock in hand	9,75,000
Debtors	2,28,000
Bills receivable	2,10,000
Bills payable	2,10,000
Outstanding expenses	7,500

Required: Prepare Trading, Profit and Loss Account for the year ended 31st March, 2015 and Balance Sheet on that date.

Solution

Dr. **TRADING AND PROFIT AND LOSS ACCOUNT FOR THE YEAR 31.3.2015** Cr.

Particulars	₹	*Particulars*		₹
To Opening Stock	9,15,000	By Sales: Cash	1,10,70,000	
To Purchases	1,27,02,750	Credit	29,77,500	1,40,47,500
To Gross Profit c/d	14,04,750	By Closing Stock		9,75,000
	1,50,22,500			1,50,22,500
To Expenses	8,71,050	By Gross Profit b/d		14,04,750
To Discount allowed	54,000	By Discount received		42,000
To Depreciation	22,500			
To Net Profit	4,99,200			
	14,46,750			14,46,750

BALANCE SHEET OF MR Y AS AT 31ST MARCH, 2015

Liabilities		₹	*Assets*		₹
Capital	4,50,000		Fixed Assets	2,25,000	
Add: Net profit	4,99,200		*Less:* Depreciation	22,500	2,02,500
	9,49,200		Stock		9,75,000
Less: Drawings	3,60,000	5,89,200	Debtors		2,28,000
Bills payable		2,10,000	Bills receivable		2,10,000
Creditors		10,02,750	Prepaid insurance		3,000
Outstanding expenses		7,500	Cash on hand/bank		1,90,950
		18,09,450			18,09,450

Working Notes:

Dr. **(i) BILLS RECEIVABLE ACCOUNT** Cr.

Particulars	₹	*Particulars*	₹
To Balance b/f	90,000	By Bank A/c (*Balancing figure*)	5,10,000
To Debtors	6,52,500	By Creditors (Bills endorsed)	22,500
		By Balance c/f	2,10,000
	7,42,500		7,42,500

Dr. **(ii) TOTAL DEBTORS ACCOUNT** Cr.

Particulars	₹	*Particulars*	₹
To Balance b/f	2,22,000	By Cash/Bank	22,65,000
To Credit Sales (b.f.)	29,77,500	By Discount allowed	54,000
		By Bills receivable	6,52,500
		By Balance off	2,28,000
	31,99,500		31,99,500

Dr. **(iii) BILLS PAYABLE ACCOUNT** Cr.

Particulars	₹	*Particulars*	₹
To Bank A/c	12,22,500	By Balance b/f	1,87,500
To Balance c/f	2,10,000	By Creditors (b.f.)	12,45,000
	14,32,500		14,32,500

Dr. **(iv) TOTAL CREDITORS ACCOUNT** Cr.

Particulars	₹	*Particulars*	₹
To Cash/Bank	1,12,60,500	By Balance b/d	8,70,000
To Discount	42,000	By Purchases	1,27,02,750
To B/R endorsed	22,500		
To B/P	12,45,000		
To Balance (b.p.)	10,02,750		
	1,35,72,750		1,35,72,750

Dr. **(v) STOCK ACCOUNT** Cr.

Particulars	₹	Particulars	₹
To Balance b/f	9,15,000	By Cost of goods sold (₹ 1,40,47,500 × 90%)	1,26,42,750
To Purchases (*Balancing figure*)	1,27,02,750	By Balance c/d	9,75,000
	1,36,17,750		1,36,17,750

Dr. **(vi) EXPENSES ACCOUNT** Cr.

Particulars	₹	Particulars	₹
To Prepaid Expenses in the beg.	3,000	By O/s Expense in the beg.	67,500
To Bank A/c	9,31,050	By P&L A/c	8,71,050
To O/s Exp. at the end	7,500	By Prepaid Exp. at end	3,000
	9,41,550		9,41,550

PROBLEM 15

The books of Mr. Z showed the following information:

	Opening	*Closing*
Bank balance	–	50,000
Debtors	–	87,500
Creditors	–	46,000
Stock	50,000	62,500
Fixed assets	7,500	9,000

The following are the details of the bank transactions:

	₹
Receipt from customers	3,40,000
Payments to creditors	2,80,000
Capital brought in	5,000
Sale of fixed assets	1,750
Expenses paid	49,250
Drawings	25,000
Purchase of fixed assets	5,000

Other information:

(*i*) Cost of goods sold ₹.2,60,000

(*ii*) Gross profit 25% on cost of goods sold

(*iii*) Book value of assets sold ₹.2,500

Prepare Trading, Profit and Loss account for the year ended 31st March 2015 and Balance Sheet as at 31st March 2015.

Solution

TRADING AND PROFIT & LOSS ACCOUNT
for the year ended 31st March, 2015

Dr. *Cr*

Particulars	₹	Particulars	₹
To Opening Stock	50,000	By Sales	3,25,000
To Purchases	2,72,500	By Closing stock	62,500
To Gross Profit	65,000		
	3,87,500		3,87,500
To Expenses	49,250	By Gross profit	65,000
To Loss on sale of fixed asset	750		
To Depreciation on fixed assets	1,000		
To Net Profit	14,000		
	65,000		65,000

BALANCE SHEET AS AT 31ST MARCH 2015

Laibilities		₹	*Assets*	₹
Capital Opening Balance	1,69,000		Fixed Assets	9,000
Add: Net Profit	14,000		Debtors	87,500
Additional Capital	5,000		Stock	62,500
Less: Drawings	(25,000)	1,63,000	Bank	50,000
Creditors		46,000		
		2,09,000		2,09,000

Working Notes:

(*i*) **BALANCE SHEET AS AT 31ST MARCH 2014**

Liabilities	₹	*Assets*	₹
Capital (Bal. Fig.)	1,69,000	Fixed Assets	7,500
Creditors	53,500	Debtors	1,02,500
		Stock	50,000
		Bank Balance	62,500
	2,22,500		2,22,500

(*ii*)

Dr. **BANK ACCOUNT** *Cr*

Particulars	₹	*Particulars*	₹
To Balance b/d (Bal. Fig.)	62,500	By Creditors	2,80,000
To Debtors	3,40,000	By Expenses	49,250
To Capital	5,000	By Drawings	25,000
To Fixed Assets	1,750	By Fixed Assets (purchased)	5,000
		By Balance c/d	50,000
	4,09,250		4,09,250

(*iii*) *Dr.* **DEBTORS ACCOUNT** *Cr.*

Particulars	₹	*Particulars*	₹
To Balance b/d (Bal. Fig.)	1,02,500	By Bank	3,40,000
To Sales	3,25,000	By Balance c/d	87,500
	4,27,500		4,27,500

(*iv*) *Dr.* **CREDITORS ACCOUNT** *Cr*

Particulars	₹	*Particulars*	₹
To Bank	2,80,000	By Balance b/d (Bal. Fig.)	53,500
To Balance c/d	46,000	By Purchases	2,72,500
	3,26,000		3,26,000

(*v*) *Dr.* **FIXED ASSETS ACCOUNT** *Cr.*

Particulars	₹	*Particulars*	₹
To Balance b/d	7,500	By Bank (Sale)	1,750
To Bank	5,000	By Profit and Loss A/c (loss on sale)	750
		By Depreciation (Bal. Fig.)	1,000
		By Balance c/d	9,000
	12,500		12,500

(*vi*) Gross Profit = ₹ 2,60,000 × 25% = ₹ 65,000.

(*vii*) **Cost of goods sold** = Opening stock + Purchases – Closing stock

₹.2,60,000 = ₹.50,000 + Purchases – ₹.62,500

Purchase = ₹ 2,72,500.

(*viii*) Sales = Cost of goods sold + gross profit = ₹.2,60,000 + ₹.65,000 = ₹.3,25,000.

PROBLEM 16

The books of account of Ruk Ruk Maan of Mumbai showed the following figures:

Particulars	*Opening* ₹	*Closing* ₹
Furniture & fixtures	2,60,000	2,34,000
Stock	2,45,000	3,20,000
Debtors	1,25,000	?
Cash in hand & bank	1,10,000	?
Creditors	1,35,000	1,90,000
Bills Payable	70,000	80,000
Outstanding Salaries	19,000	20,000

An analysis of the cash book revealed the following:

Particulars	₹
Cash sales	16,20,000
Collection from debtors	10,58,000
Discount allowed to debtors	20,000
Cash purchases	6,15,000
Payment to creditors	9,73,000
Discount received from creditors	32,000
Payment for bills payable	4,30,000
Drawings for domestic expenses	1,20,000
Salaries paid	2,36,000
Rent paid	1,32,000
Sundry trade expenses	81,000

Depreciation is provided on furniture & fixtures @10% p.a. on diminishing balance method. Ruk Ruk Maan maintains a steady gross profit rate of 25% on sales.

You are required to prepare Trading and Profit and Loss account for the year ended 31st March, 2014 and Balance Sheet as on that date.

Solution

Dr. **TRADING & PROFIT & LOSS ACCOUNT FOR THE YEAR ENDED 31ST MARCH, 2015** *Cr.*

Particulars	₹	*Particulars*	₹
To Opening Stock	2,45,000	By Sales:	
To Purchases:		Cash	16,20,000
Cash	6,15,000	Credit	11,00,000
Credit	15,00,000	By Closing Stock	3,20,000
To Gross profit c/d	6,80,000		
	30,40,000		**30,40,000**

	₹		₹
To Salaries	2,37,000	By Gross Profit b/d	6,80,000
To Rent	1,32,000	By Discount received	32,000
To Sundry Trade Expenses	81,000		
To Discount allowed	20,000		
To Depreciation on Furniture & Fixtures	26,000		
To Net Profit	2,16,000		
	7,12,000		**7,12,000**

BALANCE SHEET AS AT 31ST MARCH, 2015

Liabilities		₹	*Assets*	₹
Capital:			Fixed Assets	
Opening balance	5,16,000		Furniture & fixtures	2,34,000
Add: Net profit	2,16,000		*Current Assets:*	
			Stock	3,20,000
Less: Drawings	1,20,000	6,12,000	Debtors	1,47,000
Current Liabilities & Provisions:			Cash & Bank	2,01,000
Creditors		1,90,000		
Bills Payable		80,000		
Outstanding Salaries		20,000		
		9,02,000		**9,02,000**

Working Notes:

Dr. **(i) BILLS PAYABLE ACCOUNT** Cr.

Particulars	₹	*Particulars*	₹
To Cash/Bank	4,30,000	By Balance b/d	70,000
To Balance c/d	80,000	By Trade Creditors (Bal. fig.)	4,40,000
	5,10,000		**5,10,000**

Dr. **(ii) CREDITORS ACCOUNT** Cr.

Particulars	₹	*Particulars*	₹
To Cash/Bank	9,73,000	By Balance b/d	1,35,000
To Bills Payable A/c	4,40,000	By Credit purchases (Bal. fig.)	15,00,000
To Discount received	32,000		
To Balance c/d	1,90,000		
	16.35,000		**16.35,000**

Dr. **(iii) CALCULATION OF CREDIT SALES** Cr.

	₹
Opening Stock	2,45,000
Add: Purchases (6,15,000 + 15,00,000)	21,15,000
Less: Closing Stock	3,20,000
Cost of Goods Sold	20,40,000
Total Sales [₹ 20,40,000 × 100/75]	27,20,000
Less: Cash Sales	16,20,000
Credit Sales	**11,00,000**

Dr. **(iv) DEBTORS ACCOUNT** Cr.

Particulars	₹	Particulars	₹
To Balance b/d	1,25,000	By Cash/Bank	10,58,000
To Credit sales	11,00,000	By Discount allowed	20,000
		By Balance c/d (Bal. fig.)	1,47,000
	12,25,000		**12,25,000**

Dr. **(v) SALARIES** Cr.

Particulars	₹
Salaries paid during the year	2,36,000
Add: Outstanding salaries at the end	20,000
	2,56,000
Less: Outstanding salaries at the beg.	19,000
	2,37,000

(vi) CASH/BANK ACCOUNT

Particulars	₹	Particulars	₹
To Balance b/d	1,10,000	By Cash purchases	6,15,000
To Cash Sales	16,20,000	By Creditors	9,73,000
To Debtors	10,58,000	By Bills payable	4,30,000
		By Drawings	1,20,000
		By Salaries	2,36,000
		By Rent	1,32,000
		By Sundry trade expenses	81,000
		By Balance c/d	2,01,000
	27,88,000		**27,88,000**

BALANCE SHEET AS AT 31ST MARCH, 2014

Liabilities	₹	Assets	₹
Creditors	1,35,000	Furniture & fixtures	2,36,000
Bills payable	70,000	Stock	2,45,000
Outstanding Salaries	19,000	Debtors	1,25,000
Capital (Bal. fig.)	5,16,000	Cash & bank	1,10,000
	7,40,000		**7,40,000**

PROBLEM 17

The following is the balance sheet of CANJA on 31st March, 2014:

Liabilities	₹	*Assets*	₹
Capital	10,00,000	Fixed Assets	4,00,000
Creditors (Trade)	1,40,000	Stock	3,00,000
Profit & Loss A/c	60,000	Debtors	1,50,000
		Cash & Bank	3,50,000
	12,00,000		12,00,000

The management estimates the purchases and sales for the year ended 31st March, 2015 as under.

	upto 28.2.2015	*31.3.2015*
Purchases	₹ 14,10,000	1,10,000
Sales	19,20,000	2,00,000

It was decided to invest ₹ 1,00,000 in purchases of fixed assets, which are depreciated @ 10% on cost.

The time lag for payment to Trade Creditors for purchase and receipt from Sales is one month. The business earns a gross profit of 30% on turnover. The expenses against gross profit amount to 10% of the turnover. The amount of depreciation is not included in these expenses.

Required: Draft a balance sheet as at 31st March, 2015 assuming that creditors are all Trade Creditors for purchases and debtors for sales and there is no other item of current assets and liabilities apart from stock and cash and bank balances. *[Nov. 2001]*

Solution

DRAFT BALANCE SHEET AS AT 31ST MARCH 2015

Liabilities		₹	*Assets*		₹
Capital		10,00,000	Fixed Assets	4,00,000	
Profit & Loss Account			Additions	1,00,000	
as on 1-4-2000	60,000			5,00,000	
Add: Net Profit for			*Less:* Depreciation	50,000	4,50,000
the year	3,74,000	4,34,000	Stock in Trade		3,36,000
Creditors (Trade)		1,10,000	Sundry Debtors		2,00,000
			Cash & Balances		5,58,000
		15,44,0000			15,44,000

Working Notes:

(i)

PROJECTED TRADING & PROFIT & LOSS ACCOUNT

for the year ending 31st March, 2015

Dr. *Cr.*

Particulars	₹	*Particulars*	₹
To Opening stock	3,00,000	By Sales	21,20,000
To Purchases	15,20,000	By Closing Stock	
To Gross Profit (30% on Sales)	6,36,000	(Balancing Figure)	3,36,000
	24,56,000		24,56,000
To Sundry Expenses (10% of the Sales)	2,12,000	By Gross Profit b/d	6,36,000
To Depreciation	50,000		
To Net Profit	3,74,000		
	6,36,000		6,36,000

Dr. **(ii) CASH AND BANK ACCOUNT** *Cr.*

Particulars	₹	*Particulars*	₹
To Balance b/d	3,50,000	By Sundry Creditors	15,50,000
To Sundry Debtors (₹ 1,50,000 + 19,20,000)	20,70,000	(₹ 1,40,000 + 14,10,000)	
		By Expenses	2,12,000
		By Fixed Assets	1,00,000
		By Balance c/d	5,58,000
	24,20,000		24,20,000

(iii) It has been assumed that entire sales and purchases are on credit basis.

PROBLEM 18

A trader keeps his books of account under single entry system. On 31st March, 2014 his statement of affairs stood as follows:

Liabilities	₹	*Assets*	₹
Trade Creditors	5,80,000	Furniture, Fixtures and Fittings	1,00,000
Bills Payable	1,25,000	Stock	6,10,000
Outstanding Expenses	45,000	Trade Debtors	1,48,000
Capital Account	2,50,000	Bills receivable	60,000
		Unexpired Insurance	2,000
		Cash in Hand and at Bank	80,000
	10,00,000		10,00,000

The following was the summary of Cash-book for the year ended 31st March, 2015:

Receipts	₹	*Payments*	₹
Cash in Hand and at Bank on 1st April, 2015	80,000	Payments to Trade Creditors	75,07,000
Cash Sales	73,80,000	Payments for Bills payable	8,15,000
Receipts from Trade Debtors	15,10,000	Sundry Expenses paid	6,20,700
Receipts for Bills Receivable	3,40,000	Drawings	2,40,000
		Cash in Hand and at Bank on 31st March, 2015	1,27,300
	93,10,000		93,10,000

Discount allowed to trade debtors and received from trade creditors amounted to ₹ 36,000 and ₹ 28,000 respectively. Bills endorsed amounted to ₹ 15,000. Annual Fire Insurance premium of ₹ 6,000 was paid every year on 1st August for the renewal of the policy. Furniture, fixtures and fittings were subject to depreciation @ 15% per annum on diminishing balances method.

You are also informed about the following balances as on 31st March, 2015

Stock	₹ 6,50,000
Trade Debtors	₹ 1,52,000
Bills Receivable	₹ 75,000
Bills Payable	₹ 1,40,000
Outstanding Expenses	₹ 5,000

The trader maintains a steady gross profit of 10% on sales.

Required: Prepare Trading and Profit and Loss Account for the year ended 31st March, 2015 and Balance Sheet as at that date.

Solution

TRADING AND PROFIT AND LOSS ACCOUNT
for the year ended 31st March, 2015

Dr. *Cr.*

Particulars	₹	*Particulars*		₹
To Opening Stock	6,10,000	By Sales		
To Purchases	84,10,000	Cash	73,80,000	
To Gross profit c/d (10% of 93,00,000)	9,30,000	Credit	19,20,000	93,00,000
		By Closing stock		6,50,000
	99,50,000			99,50,000

	₹		₹
To Sundry expenses	5,80,700	By Gross profit b/d	9,30,000
To Discount allowed	36,000	By Discount received	28,000
To Depreciation (15% of ₹ 1,00,000)	15,000		
To Net Profit	3,26,300		
	9,58,000		9,58,000

BALANCE SHEET AS AT 31ST MARCH, 2015

Liabilities		₹	*Assets*		₹
Capital			Furniture & Fittings	1,00,000	
Opening balance	2,50,000		*Less:* Depreciation	15,000	85,000
Less: Drawing	2,40,000		Stock		6,50,000
Add: Net profit for the year	3,26,300	3,36,300	Trade debtors		1,52,000
Bills payable		1,40,000	Bills receivable		75,000
Trade creditors		6,10,000	Unexpired insurance		2,000
Outstanding expenses		5,000	Cash in hand & at bank		1,27,300
		10,91,300			10,91,300

Working Notes:

Dr. **(i) BILLS RECEIVABLE ACCOUNT** *Cr.*

Particulars	₹	*Particulars*	₹
To Balance b/d	60,000	By Cash	3,40,000
To Trade debtors	3,70,000	By Trade creditors (Bills endorsed)	15,000
		By Balance c/d	75,000
	4,30,000		4,30,000

Dr. **(ii) TRADE DEBTORS ACCOUNT** *Cr.*

Particulars	₹	*Particulars*	₹
To Balance b/d	1,48,000	By Cash/Bank	15,10,000
To Credit sales (Balancing figure)	19,20,000	By Discount allowed	36,000
		By Bills receivable	3,70,000
		By Balance c/d	1,52,000
	20,68,000		20,68,000

Dr. **(iii) MEMORANDUM TRADING ACCOUNT** *Cr.*

Particulars	₹	*Particulars*	₹
To Opening stock	6,10,000	By Sales	93,00,000
To Purchase (Balancing figure)	84,10,000	By Closing stock	6,50,000
To Gross Profit (10% on sales)	9,30,000		
	99,50,000		99,50,000

Dr. **(iv) BILLS PAYABLE ACCOUNT** *Cr.*

Particulars	₹	*Particulars*	₹
To Cash/Bank	8,15,000	By Balance b/d	1,25,000
To Balance c/d	1,40,000	By Creditors (balancing figure)	8,30,000
	9,55,000		9,55,000

Dr. **(v) TRADE CREDITORS ACCOUNT** Cr.

Particulars	₹	Particulars	₹
To Cash/Bank	75,07,000	By Balance b/d	5,80,000
To Discount received	28,000	By Purchases (as calculated in W. N. 3)	84,10,000
To Bills Receivable	15,000		
To Bills Payable	8,30,000		
To Balance c/d (balancing figure)	6,10,000		
	89,90,000		89,90,000

Dr. **(vi) SUNDRY EXPENSES ACCOUNT** Cr.

Particulars	₹	Particulars	₹
To Prepaid Expenses (In the beginning)	2,000	By Outstanding Expenses (in the beginning)	45,000
To Bank A/c	6,20,700	By Profit & Loss A/c	5,80,700
To Outstanding Expenses (at the end)	5,000	By Prepaid Expenses (at the end)	2,000
	6,27,700		6,27,700

PROBLEM 19

The following is the Balance Sheet of the retail business of Sri CAMII as at 31st March 2014

Liabilities	₹	Assets	₹
Sri Srinivas's capital	1,00,000	Furniture	10,000
Liabilities for goods	20,500	Stock	70,000
Rent	1,000	Debtors	25,000
		Cash at bank	14,500
		Cash in hand	2,000
	1,21,500		1,21,500

You are furnished with the following information:

(i) Sri CAMII sells his goods at a profit of 20% on sales.

(ii) Goods are sold for cash and credit. Credit customers pay by cheques only.

(iii) Payments for purchases are always made by cheques.

(iv) It is the practice of Sri CAMII to send to the bank every weekend the collections of the week after paying every week, salary of ₹ 300 to the clerk, Sundry expenses of ₹ 50 and personal expenses ₹ 100.

Analysis of the Bank Pass-book for the 13 week period ending on 30 th June, 2015 disclosed the following:

	₹
Payments to creditors	75,000
Payments of rent upto 30th June 2015	4,000
Amounts deposited into the bank (include ₹ 30,000 received from debtors by cheques)	1,25,000
The following are the balances on 30th June 2015:	
Stock	40,000
Debtors	30,000
Creditors for goods	36,500

On the evening of 30th June 2015 the Cashier absconded with the available cash in the cash box. There was no cash deposit in the week ended on that date.

Required: Prepare a Account showing the amount of cash defalcated by the Cashier and also a Trading & Profit and Loss Account for the period ended 30th June, 2015 and a Balance Sheet as on that date.

Solution

ACCOUNT SHOWING DEFALCATION OF CASH
as at 30th March, 2015

Dr. Cr.

Receipts	₹	*Payments*	₹
To Balance b/d	2,000	By Salary to Clerk (₹ 300 × 13)	3,900
To Cash Sales	1,16,250	By Sundry Expenses (₹ 50 × 13)	650
		By Drawing (₹ 100 × 13)	1,300
		By Bank (₹ 1,25,000 - ₹ 30,000)	95,000
		By Defalcation (*balancing figure*)	17,400
	1,18,250		1,18,250

TRADING AND PROFIT & LOSS ACCOUNT
for the Period ended 30th June 2015

Dr. Cr.

Particulars		₹	*Particulars*	₹
To Opening Stock		70,000	By Sales (116250 + 35000)	1,51,250
To Purchases		91,000	By Closing Stock	40,000
To Gross Profit c/d		30,250		
		1,91,250		1,91,250
To Salary to Clerk		3,900	By Gross Profit b/d	30,250
To Sundry Expenses		650		
To Rent	4,000			
Less: Outstanding at beginning	1,000	3,000		
To Defalcation		17,400		
To Net Profit t/f to Capital A/c		5,300		
		30,250		30,250

BALANCE SHEET OF SHRI CAMMI AT 30TH JUNE, 2015

Liabilities		₹	*Assets*	₹
Capital	1,00,000		Furniture	10,000
Add: Net Profit	5,300		Stock	40,000
	1,05,300		Debtors	30,000
Less: drawing	1,300	1,04,000	Cash at bank	60,500
Creditors		36,500		
		1,40,500		1,40,500

Working Notes:

(i) Purchases = Payment to Creditors + Closing balance of Creditors – Opening balance of Creditors

Purchases = ₹ 75,000 + ₹ 36,500 – ₹ 20,500 = ₹ 91,000

(ii) Cost of Good Sold = Purchases + Opening Stock – Closing Stock
= ₹ 91,000 + ₹ 70,000 – ₹ 40,000 = ₹ 1,21,000

(iii) Sales = Cost of Goods sold + Gross Profit
= 1,21,000 + 25% on cost = ₹ 1,51,250

(iv) Credit Sales = Cash Received from debtors + Closing balance – Opening balance = ₹ 30,000 + ₹ 30,000 – ₹ 25,000 = ₹ 35,000

(v) Cash Sales = Total Sales – Credit Sales = ₹ 1,51,250 – ₹ 35,000 = ₹ 1,16,250

(vi) Dr. **BANK ACCOUNT** Cr.

Particulars	₹	*Particulars*	₹
To Balance b/d	14,500	By Creditors A/c	75,000
To Debtors A/c	30,000	By Rent A/c	4,000
To Cash A/c	95,000	By Balance c/d (*balancing fig.*)	60,500
	1,39,500		1,39,500

PROBLEM 20

Shri Rashid furnishes you with the following information relating to his business:

(a) *Assets and liabilities as on*

	01.04.2014	*31.03.2015*
	₹	₹
Furniture (*w.d.v.*)	6,000	6,350
Stock at cost	8,000	7,000
Sundry debtors	16,000	?
Sundry creditors	11,000	15,000
Prepaid expenses	600	700
Unpaid expenses	2,000	1,800
Cash in hand and at bank	1,200	625

(b) *Receipts and payments during the year:*

Collections from debtors, after allowing discount of ₹ 1,500 amounted to ₹ 58,500.

Collections on discounting of bills of exchange, after deduction of discount of ₹ 125 by the bank, totalled to ₹ 6,125.

Creditors of ₹ 40,000 were paid ₹ 39,200 in full settlement of their dues.

Payment for freight inwards ₹ 3,000

Amounts withdrawn for personal use ₹ 7,000.

Payment for office furniture ₹ 1,000.

Investment carrying annual interest of 4% were purchased at ₹ 96 on 1st Oct. and payment made therefor.

Expenses including salaries paid ₹ 14,500.

Miscellaneous receipts ₹ 500.

(c) Bills of exchange drawn on and accepted by customers during the year amounted to ₹ 10,000. Of these, bills of exchange of ₹ 2,000 were endorsed in favour of creditors. An endorsed bill of exchange of ₹ 400 was dishonoured.

(d) Goods costing ₹ 900 were used as advertising materials.

(e) Goods are invariably sold to show a gross profit of 33.1/3% on sales.

(f) Difference in cash book, if any, is to be treated as further drawing or introduction by Shri Rashid.

(g) Provide at 2.5% for doubtful debts on closing debtors.

Required: Prepare Trading and Profit and Loss Account for the year ended 31st March 2015 and the Balance Sheet as on that date.

Solution

TRADING AND PROFIT AND LOSS ACCOUNT OF SHRI RASHID

for the year ended 31st March, 2015

Dr. Cr.

Particulars	₹	₹	*Particulars*	₹
To Opening Stock		8,000	By Sales	73,050
To Purchases	45,600		By Closing Stock	7,000
Less: For advertising	900	44,700		
To Freight inwards		3,000		
To Gross profit c/d		24,350		
		80,050		80,050
To Sundry expenses:		14,200	By Gross Profit b/d	24,350
To Advertisement		900	By Interest on Investments $\left(\text{Rs. }100 \times \frac{4}{100} \times \frac{1}{2}\right)$	2
To Discount allowed				
Debtors	1,500		By Discount received	800
Bills receivable	125	1,625	By Miscellaneous income	500
To Depreciation on furniture		650		
To Provision for doubtful debts		486		
To Net Profit		7,791		
		25,652		25,652

BALANCE SHEET AS AT 31ST MARCH 2015

Liabilities	₹	₹	*Assets*	₹	₹
Capital:			Furniture (w.d.v.)	6,000	
Opening Balance	18,800		Additions during the year	1,000	
Less: Drawings	7,904		*Less:* Depreciation	650	6,350
Add: Net Profit	7,791	18,687	Investment		96
Sundry creditors		15,000	Interest accrued		2
Outstanding expenses		1,800	Closing stock		7,000
			Sundry debtors	19,450	
			Less: Provision for doubtful debts	486	18,964
			Bills receivable		1,750
			Cash in hand and at bank		625
			Prepaid expenses		700
		35,487			35,487

Working Notes:

(i) *Calculation of Opening Capital*

BALANCE SHEET AS AT 1ST APRIL 2014

Liabilities	₹	*Assets*	₹
Capital (*Balancing figure*)	18,800	Furniture (w.d.v.)	6,000
Creditors	11,000	Stock at cost	8,000
Outstanding expenses	2,000	Sundry debtors	16,000
		Cash in hand and at bank	1,200
		Prepaid expenses	600
	31,800		31,800

(ii) *Calculation of Purchases made during the year*

Dr. **SUNDRY CREDITORS ACCOUNT** Cr.

Particulars	₹	Particulars	₹
To Cash and bank A/c	39,200	By Balance b/d	11,000
To Discount received A/c	800	By Sundry debtors A/c	400
To Bills receivable A/c	2,000	By Purchases A/c	45,600
To Balance c/d	15,000	(*Balancing figure*)	
	57,000		57,000

(iii) *Calculation of Sales made during the year*

		₹
Opening Stock		8,000
Purchases	45,600	
Less: For advertising	900	44,700
Freight inwards		3,000
		55,700
Less: Closing Stock		7,000
Cost of goods sold		48,700
Add: Gross profit (@ 50% on cost)		24,350
Sales		73,050

(iv) *Calculation of Closing Debtors*

Dr. **SUNDRY DEBTORS ACCOUNT** Cr.

Particulars	₹	Particulars	₹
To Balance b/d	16,000	By Cash and bank A/c	58,500
To Sales A/c	73,050	By Discount allowed A/c	1,500
To Sundry creditors A/c		By Bills receivable A/c	10,000
(bill dishonoured)	400	By Balance c/d (*Balancing figure*)	19,450
	89,450		89,450

(v) Dr. **CASH AND BANK ACCOUNT** Cr.

Particulars	₹	Particulars	₹
To Balance b/d	1,200	By Freight inwards A/c	3,000
To Sundry debtors A/c	58,500	By Furniture A/c	1,000
To Bills receivable A/c	6,125	By Investment A/c	96
To Miscellaneous income A/c	500	By Expenses A/c	14,500
		By Creditors A/c	39,200
		By Drawings A/c	7,904
		[₹ 7,000 +	
		₹ 904 (Additional drawings)]	
		By Balance c/d	625
	66,325		66,325

(vi) Dr. **EXPENSES ACCOUNT** Cr.

Particulars	₹	Particulars	₹
To Prepaid expenses A/c (beg.)	600	By Outstanding expenses A/c (beg.)	2,000
To Bank A/c	14,500	By Profit and loss A/c (b.f.)	14,200
To Outstanding expenses A/c (end)	1,800	By Prepaid expenses A/c (end)	700
	16,900		16,900

(vii) Dr. **BILLS RECEIVABLE ACCOUNT** Cr.

Particulars	₹	*Particulars*	₹
To Debtors A/c	10,000	By Creditors A/c	2,000
		By Bank A/c	6,125
		By Discount on bills receivable A/c	125
		By Balance c/d (*Balancing figure*)	1,750
	10,000		10,000

Note: *As regards investment, it has been assumed that investment purchased for ₹ 96 was of the face value ₹ 100.*

PROBLEM 21

From the following information in respect of a Trader, prepare Trading and Profit and Loss Account for the year ended 31st March 2015, and a Balance Sheet as at that date:

(in ₹)

Assets and Liabilities as on	*Opening*	*Closing*
Stock-in-Trade	1,60,000	1,40,000
Debtors for Sales	3,20,000	?
Bills Receivable	–	?
Creditors for Purchases	2,20,000	3,00,000
Furniture at Written Down Value	1,20,000	1,27,000
Expenses Outstanding	40,000	36,000
Prepaid Expenses	12,000	14,000
Cash on Hand	4,000	3,000
Bank Balance	20,000	9,500

Receipts and Payments during the year:

Particulars	₹
Collections from Debtors (after allowing 21/2% discount)	11,70,000
Payment to Creditors (after receiving 2% discount)	7,74,000
Proceeds of Bills Receivable discounted at 2%	1,22,500
Proprietor's Drawings	1,40,000
Purchase of Furniture midway through the year	20,000
4% Government Securities purchased at 96% on 1st Oct.	1,92,000
Expenses	3,50,000
Miscellaneous Income	10,000

Other information:

1. Sales are effected so as to realize a Gross Profit of 33-1/3 % on the Sale Proceeds.
2. Goods, costing ₹ 18,000, were issued as Advertisement Articles.
3. During the year, Bills Receivable of ₹ 2,00,000 were drawn on Debtors. Of these, Bills amounting to ₹ 40,000 were endorsed in favour of Creditors. Out of this latter amount, a Bill for ₹ 8,000 was dishonoured by the Debtor.
4. Capital introduced during the year by the Proprietor by cheques was omitted to be recorded in the Cash Book, though the Closing Bank Balance was ₹ 9,500 (as shown above) is after taking the same into account.
5. Purchases and Sales are made only on credit.

Solution

Dr. **TRADING AND PROFIT AND LOSS ACCOUNT FOR THE YEAR ENDED 31.03.2015** Cr.

Particulars		₹	*Particulars*	₹
To Opening Stock		1,60,000	By Sales	13,71,000
To Purchases (9,12,000 – 18,000]		8,94,000	By Closing Stock	1,40,000
To Gross Profit (l/3rd on Sales)		4,57,000		
		15,11,000		15,11,000
To Expenses for the year		3,44,000	By Gross Profit b/d	4,57,000
To Discount Allowed:			By Miscellaneous Income	10,000
Debtors	30,000		By Discount Received	16,000
Bills Receivable	2,500	32,500	By Interest on 4% Government	4,000
To Advertisement Expenses		18,000	Securities	
To Depreciation on Furniture		13,000	[2,00,000 × 4% × 6/12]	
To Net Profit		79,500		
		4,87,000		4,87,000

BALANCE SHEET AS AT 31.03.2015

Liabilities	₹	*Assets*	₹
Capital	4,87,500	Furniture	1,27,000
Sundry Creditors	3,00,000	4% Govt. Securities at Cost	1,92,000
Outstanding Expenses	36,000	(NV ₹ 2,00,000)	
		Accused Interest on Govt. Securities	4,000
		Stock in Trade	1,40,000
		Sundry Debtors	2,99,000
		Bills Receivable	35,000
		Cash on Hand	3,000
		Bank Balance	9,500
		Prepaid Expenses	14,000
	8,23,500		8,23,500

Working Notes:

(i) BALANCE SHEET AS AT 31.03.2014

Liabilities	₹	*Assets*	₹
Capital (*balancing figure*)	3,76,000	Furniture	1,20,000
Creditors	2,20,000	Stock	1,60,000
Outstanding Expenses	40,000	Debtors	3,20,000
		Cash on Hand	4,000
		Bank Balance	20,000
		Prepaid Expenses	12,000
	6,36,000		6,36,000

Dr. **(ii) CREDITORS ACCOUNT** Cr.

Particulars	₹	*Particulars*	₹
To Bills Receivable (endorsed)	40,000	By Balance B/d	2,20,000
To Bank (payment)	7,84,000	By Debtors (endorsed bills	
To Discount Received		dishonoured)	8,000
[7,84,000 × 2%/98%)	16,000	By Purchases (*balancing figure*)	**9,12,000**
To Balance c/d	3,00,000		
	11,40,000		11,40,000

(iii) Computation of Sales

A. Cost of Goods Sold = 1,60,000 + 8,94,000 – 1,40,000 = ₹ 9,14,000

B. P = l/3rd on Sales = 1/2 on COGS = 1/2 × ₹ 9,14,000 = ₹ 4,57,000

C. Sales = COGS + GP = [A + B] = ₹ 13,71,000

Dr. **(iv) DEBTORS ACCOUNT** Cr.

Particulars	₹	*Particulars*	₹
To Balance b/d	3,20,000	By Bills Receivable	2,00,000
To Sales	13,71,000	By Bank (Collections)	11,70,000
To Creditors (endorsed bills dishonoured)	8,000	By Discount Allowed (11,70,000 × 2.5%/97.5%)	30,000
		By Balance c/d (*balancing figure*)	**2,99,000**
	16,99,000		16,99,000

Dr. **(v) BILLS RECEIVABLE ACCOUNT** Cr.

Particulars	₹	*Particulars*	₹
To Sundry Debtors [B/R received]	2,00,000	By Creditors [B/R endorsed]	40,000
		By Bank [B/R discounted]	1,22,500
		By Discount on Bills Receivable [1,22,500 × 2%/98%]	2,500
		By Balance c/d (*balancing figure*)	**35,000**
	2,00,000		2,00,000

Dr. **(vi) EXPENSES ACCOUNT** Cr.

Particulars	₹	*Particulars*	₹
To Balance b/d	12,000	By Balance b/d	40,000
To Bank A/c	3,50,000	By P&L (b/f)	**3,44,000**
To Balance c/d	36,000	By Balance c/d	14,000
	3,98,000		3,98,000

Dr. **(vii) FURNITURE ACCOUNT** Cr.

Particulars	₹	*Particulars*	₹
To Balance b/d	1,20,000	By Depreciation (*balancing figure*)	**13,000**
To Bank A/c (Purchases)	20,000	By Balance c/d	1,27,000
	1,40,000		1,40,000

Dr. **(viii) CASH AND BANK ACCOUNT** Cr.

Particulars	*Cash*	*Bank*	*Particulars*	*Cash*	*Bank*
To balance b/d	4,000	20,000	By Creditors		7,84,000
To Debtors		11,70,000	By Drawings		1,40,000
To Bills Discounted		1,22,500	By Expenses		3,50,000
To Misc. Income (assumed cash)	10,000		By 4% Govt. Securities		1,92,000
			By Fixed Asset (Purchase)		20,000
To Cash (Contra)		11,000	By Bank (Contra) (bal. fig.)	**11,000**	
To Capital A/c (Additional Cap. (*balancing figure*)		**1,72,000**	By Balance c/d	3,000	9,500
	14,000	**14,95,500**		**14,000**	**14,95,500**

Dr. (xi) CAPITAL ACCOUNT Cr.

Particulars	₹	Particulars	₹
To Drawings	1,40,000	By Balance b/d	3,76,000
To Balance c/d (*balancing figure*)	**4,87,500**	By Bank A/c (Additional Capital	1,72,000
		By Net Profit for the year (from P&L)	79,500
	6,27,500		**6,27,500**

PROBLEM 22

'A' and 'B' are in partnership sharing profits and losses equally. They keep their books by single entry system. The following balances are available from their books as on 31.3.2014 and 31.3.2015.

	Opening ₹	*Closing* ₹
Building	1,50,000	1,50,000
Equipments	2,40,000	2,72,000
Furniture	25,000	25,000
Debtors	?	1,00,000
Creditors	65,000	?
Stock	?	70,000
Bank loan	45,000	35,000
Cash	60,000	?
Outstanding Expenses	—	3,000

The transactions during the year ended 31.3.2015 were the following:

	₹
Collection from debtors	3,80,000
Payment to creditors	2,50,000
Cash purchases	65,000
Expenses paid	40,000
Drawings by 'A'	30,000

Discount allowed ₹ 5,500 during the year.
Discount earned ₹ 4,800 during the year.

On 1.4.2014 an equipment of book value ₹ 20,000 was sold for ₹ 15,000. On 1.10.2014, some equipments were purchased.

Cash sales amounted to 10% of Sales.
Credit sales amount to ₹ 4,50,000.
Credit sales amounted to ₹ 4,50,000
Credit purchases were 80% of total purchases.
The firm sells goods at cost *plus* 25%.

Capital of 'A' as on 31.3.2014 was ₹ 15,000 more than the capital of 'B', equipments and furniture to be depreciated at 10% p.a. and building @ 2% p.a.

You are required to prepare:

(i) Trading and Profit and Loss account for the year ended 31.3.2015 and
(ii) The Balance Sheet as on that date.

Solution

Dr. **TRADING AND PROFIT AND LOSS A/C FOR THE YEAR ENDED 31.3.2015** Cr.

Particulars		₹	*Particulars*		₹
To Opening Stock		1,45,000	By Sales: Cash	50,000	
To Purchases: Cash	65,000		Credit	4,50,000	5,00,000
Credit	2,60,000	3,25,000	By Closing Stock		70,000
To Gross Profit c/d		1,00,000			
		5,70,000			5,70,000
To Loss on sale of equipment (20,000 – 15,000)		5,000	By Gross Profit b/d		1,00,000
			By Discount received		4,800
To Depreciation					
Building	3,000				
Furniture	2,500				
Equipment	24,600	30,100			
To Expenses paid	40,000				
Add: Outstanding expenses	3,000	43,000			
To Discount allowed		5,500			
To Net Profit Transferred to:					
A's Capital A/c	10,600				
B's Capital A/c	10,600	21,200			
		1,04,800			1,04,800

BALANCE SHEET AS AT 31.3.2015

Liabilities		₹	*Assets*		₹
A's Capital	2,80,250		Building	1,50,000	
Less: Drawings	30,000		*Less:* Depreciation	3,000	1,47,000
	2,50,250		Equipments	2,72,000	
Add: Net Profit	10,600	2,60,850	*Less:* Depreciation	24,600	2,47,400
B's Capital	2,65,250		Furniture	25,000	
Add: Net Profit	10,600	2,75,850	*Less:* Depreciation	2,500	22,500
Sundry Creditors		70,200	Debtors		1,00,000
Bank Loan		35,000	Stock		70,000
Outstanding expenses		3,000	Cash balance		58,000
		6,44,900			6,44,900

Working Notes:

(i) Calculation of Cash Sales

Let Total Sales be X

Total Sales = Cash Sales + Credit Sales

X = .10 X + ₹ 4,50,000

X = ₹ 4,50,000/.9 = ₹ 5,00,000

Cash sales = 10% of 5,00,000 = ₹ 50,000

(ii) Calculation of Credit Purchases

Let Total Purchases be Y

Total Purchases = Cash Purchases + Credit Purchases

Y = ₹ 65,000 + .80 Y

Y = ₹ 65,000/.2 = ₹ 3,25,000

Credit purchases = ₹ 3,25,000 – ₹ 65,000 = ₹ 2,60,000

Dr. **(iii) STOCK ACCOUNT** Cr.

Particulars	₹	*Particulars*	₹
To Balance b/d *(Balancing Figure)*	1,45,000	By Cost of goods sold	
To Total purchases	3,25,000	[5,00,000 × 100/125]	4,00,000
		By Balance c/d	70,000
	4,70,000		4,70,000

Dr. **(iv) EQUIPMENT ACCOUNT** Cr.

Particulars	₹	*Particulars*	₹
To Balance b/f	2,40,000	By Cash A/c (Sale)	15,000
To Cash A/c (Purchases)	52,000	By Profit and Loss A/c	
(Balancing Figure)		(Loss on Sale)	5,000
		By Balance c/d	2,72,000
	2,92,000		2,92,000

Depreciation on equipment:

@ 10% p.a. on ₹ 2,20,000 (i.e. ₹ 2,40,000 – ₹ 20,000) =	22,000
@ 10% p.a. on ₹ 52,000 for 6 months (i.e. during the year) =	2,600
	24,600

Dr. **(v) CREDITORS ACCOUNT** Cr.

Particulars	₹	*Particulars*	₹
To Cash A/c	2,50,000	By Balance b/d	65,000
To Discount received	4,800	By Credit Purchases	2,60,000
To Balance c/d *(Balance Figure)*	70,200		
	3,25,000		3,25,000

Dr. **(vi) DEBTORS ACCOUNT** Cr.

Particulars	₹	*Particulars*	₹
To Balance b/d (Balancing Figure)	35,500	By Cash	3,80,000
To Sales (Credit)	4,50,000	By Discount allowed	5,500
		By Balance c/d	1,00,000
	4,85,500		4,85,500

Dr. **(vii) BALANCE SHEET AS AT 31.3.2014** Cr.

Liabilities	₹	*Assets*	₹
Combined Capital Accounts of A&B	5,45,500	Building	1,50,000
(Balancing Figure)		Equipments	2,40,000
Creditors	65,000	Furniture	25,000
Bank Loan	45,000	Debtors	35,500
		Stock	1,45,000
		Cash balance	60,000
	6,55,500		6,55,500

	₹
Combined Capitals of A & B	5,45,500
Less: Difference in Capitals of A and B	15,000
	5,30,500

A's Capital = 5,30,500/2 = 2,65,250 + 15,000 = ₹ 2,80,250

B's Capital = 5,30,500/2 = ₹ 2,65,250

Dr. **(viii) CASH ACCOUNT** Cr.

Particulars	₹	*Particulars*	₹
To Balance b/d	60,000	By Creditors	2,50,000
To Debtors	3,80,000	By Purchases	65,000
To Equipment (Sales)	15,000	By Expenses	40,000
To Cash Sales	50,000	By A's drawings	30,000
		By Bank loan paid (45,000 – 35,000)	10,000
		By Equipment purchased	52,000
		By Balance c/d Bal. Fig.	58,000
	5,05,000		5,05,000

ADVANCED PROBLEMS

PROBLEM 23

Mr. A runs a business ofreadymade garments. He closes the books of accounts on 31st March, 2012. The Balance Sheet as on 31st March, 2014 was as follows:

Liabilities	₹	*Assets*	₹
A's Capital A/c	4,04,000	Furniture	40,000
Creditors	82,000	Stock	2,80,000
		Debtors	1,00,000
		Cash in hand	28,000
		Cash at bank	38,000
	4,86,000		4,86,000

You are furnished with the following information:

(a) His sales, for the year ended 31st March, 2015 were 20% higher than the sales of previous year, out of which 20% sales was cash sales. Total sales during the year 2009-10 were ₹ 5,00,000.

(b) Payments for all the purchases were made by cheques only.

(c) Goods were sold for cash and credit both. Credit customers pay be cheques only.

(d) Deprecition on furniture is to be charged 10% p.a.

(e) Mr A sent to the bank the collection of the month at the last date of the each month after paving salary of ₹ 2,000 to the clerk, office expenses ₹ 1,200 and persona! expenses ₹ 500.

Analysis of bank pass book for the year ending 31st March 2015 disclosed the following:

Particulars	₹
Payment to creditors	3,00,000
Payment of rent up to 31st March, 2015	16,000
Cash deposited into the bank during the year	80,000

The following are the balances on 31st March, 2015:

Particulars	₹
Stock	1,60,000
Debtors	1,20,000
Creditors for goods	1,46,000

On the evening of 31st March 2015, the cashier absconded with the available cash in the cash book.

Required: Prepare Trading and Profit and Loss A/c for the year ended 31st March, 2015 and Balance Sheet as on that date. All the workings should form part of the answer.

Solution

TRADING AND PROFIT AND LOSS ACCOUNT

Dr. *for the year ending 31st March 2015* Cr.

Particulars	₹	Particulars		₹
To Opening Stock	2,80,000	By Sales		
To Purchases	3,64,000	Credit	4,80,000	
To Gross Profit c/d	1,16,000	Cash	1,20,000	6,00,000
		By Closing stock		1,60,000
	7,60,000			7,60,000
To Salary	24,000	By Gross Profit b/d		1,16,000
To Rent	16,000			
To Office expenses	14,400			
To Loss of cash	23,600			
To Depreciation on furniture	4,000			
To Net Profit	34,000			
	1,16,000			1,16,000

BALANCE SHEET AS AT 31ST MARCH, 2015

Liabilities		₹	Assets		₹
A's Capital	4,04,000		Furniture	40,000	
Add: Net Profit	34,000		*Less*: Depreciation	(4,000)	36,000
Less: Drawings	(6,000)	4,32,000	Stock		1,60,000
Creditors		1,46,000	Debtors		1,20,000
			Cash at bank		2,62,000
		5,78,000			5,78,000

Working Notes:

Dr. **(i) CREDITORS ACCOUNT** Cr.

Particulars	₹	Particulars	₹
To Bank A/c	3,00,000	By Baance b/d	82,000
To Balance c/d	1,46,000	By Purchases (Bal.fig.)	3,64,000
	4,46,000		4,46,000

(ii) **Total Sales** = ₹ 5,00,000 + 20% = ₹ 6,00,000
(iii) **Credit Sales** = 80% of ₹ 6,00,000 = ₹ 4,80,000

Dr. **(iv) DEBTORS ACCOUNT** Cr.

Particulars	₹	Particulars	₹
To Balance b/d	1,00,000	By Bank A/c (Bal. fig.)	**4,60,000**
To Sales A/c	4,80,000	By Balance c/d	1,20,000
	5,80,000		5,80,000

Dr. **(v) BANK ACCOUNT** Cr.

Particulars	₹	Particulars	₹
To Balance b/d	38,000	By Creditors A/c	3,00,000
To Debtors A/c	4,60,000	By Rent A/c	16,000
To Cash A/c	80,000	By Balance c/d (b.f.)	**2,62,000**
	5,78,000		5,78,000

(vi) CALCULATION OF THE AMOUNT OF CASH DEFALCATED BY THE CASHIER

Particulars		₹
A. Cash balance in the beg. of the year		28,000
B. *Add:* Cash sales during the year		1,20,000
C. *Less:* Salary (₹ 2,000 × 12)	24,000	
Office expenses (₹ 1,200 × 12)	14,400	
Drawings of A (₹ 500 × 12)	6,000	
Cash deposited into bank during the year	80,000	1,24,400
D. Cash balance at the end of the year (defalcated by the cashier)		23,600

PROBLEM 24

The following is the Balance Sheet of M/s Neel and Company as on 31st March, 2014:

Liabilities	₹	Assets	₹
Capital	1,92,000	Building	1,30,000
Loan	60,000	Furniture	20,000
Creditors	1,24,000	Motor car (for business)	36,000
		Stock	80,000
		Debtors	68,000
		Cash in hand	8,000
		Cashatbank	34,000
	3,76,000		3,76,000

A riot occurred on the night of 31st March, 2015 in which ail books and records were lost The cashier had absconded with the available cash. The following information is available:

(i) The sales for the year ended 31st March, 2015 were 20% higher than the previous year's sales. Firm always sells the goods at cost plus 25%; 20% of the total sales for the year ended 31st March, 2015 were for cash. There were no cash purchases.

(ii) On 1st April, 2014, the stock level was raised to ₹ 1,20,000 and stock was maintained at this new level all throughout the year.

(iii) Collections from Debtors amounted to ₹ 5,60,000 of which ₹ 1,40,000 was received in cash. Business expenses amounted to ₹ 80,000 of which ₹ 20,000 was outstanding on 31st March, 2015 and ₹ 24,000 was paid by cheque.

(iv) Analysis of the pass book revealed the following for the year ended 31-3-2015:

	₹
Payment to creditors	5,50,000
Personal Drawings	30,000
Cash deposited into bank	2,86,000
Cash withdrawn from bank	48,000

(v) Gross profit as per last year's audited accounts was ₹ 1,20,000.

(vi) Provide depreciation on Building and Furniture @ 5% and Motor Car @ 20%.

(vii) The amount defalcated by the cashier may be treated as recoverable from him.

Required: Prepare the Trading and Profit and Loss Account for the year ended 31st March, 2015 and the Balance Sheet as on date.

Solution

TRADING AND PROFIT & LOSS ACCOUNT

for the year ended 31st March, 2015

Dr. *Cr.*

Particulars		₹	*Particulars*	₹
To Opening Stock A/c		80,000	By Sales A/c	7,20,000
To Purchases A/c		6,16,000	By Closing stock	1,20,000
To Gross Profit c/d		1,44,000		
		8,40,000		8,40,000
To Business Expenses A/c		80,000	By Gross Profit b/d	1,44,000
To Depreciation on:				
Building	6,500			
Furniture	1,000			
Motorcar	7,200	14,700		
To Net Profit		49,300		
		1,44,000		1,44,000

BALANCE SHEET AS AT 31ST MARCH, 2015

Liabilities		₹	*Assets*		₹
Capital Account			Building	1,30,000	
Opening Balance	1,92,000		*Less:* Depreciation	6,500	1,23,500
Add: Net Profit	49,300		Furniture	20,000	
	2,41,300		*Less:* Depreciation	1,000	19,000
Less: Drawings	(30,000)	2,11,300	Motor Car	36,000	
Loan		60,000	*Less:* Depreciation	7,200	28,800
Sundry Creditors		1,90,000	Stock in trade		1,20,000
Outstanding business expenses		20,000	Sundry Debtors		84,000
			Cash at Bank		88,000
			Sundry Advance (Amount recoverable from cashier)		18,000
		4,81,300			4,81,300

Working Notes:

(i) Last years Total Sales $= \frac{\text{Gross Profit}}{25} \times (100 + 25)$
= ₹ 1, 20,000 x 125/25 = ₹ 6,00,000

(ii) Current year's Total Sales = ₹ 6,00,000 + (100 + 20) %
= ₹ 7,20,000

(iii) Current year's – Credit Sales = ₹ 7,20,000 x 80% = ₹ 5,76,000
– Cash Sales = ₹ 7,20,000 x 20%= ₹ 1,44,000

(iv) Gross Profit for the current year = ₹ 7,20,000 x 25/125 = ₹ 1,44,000

(v) Cost of Goods Sold = Sales – Gross Profit
= ₹ 7,20,000 – ₹ 1,44,000 = ₹ 5,76,000

(vi) Purchases = Cost of goods sold + Closing stock – Opening stock
= ₹ 5,76,000 + ₹ 1,20,000 – ₹ 80,000 = ₹ 6,16,000.

Dr. **(vii) DEBTORS ACCOUNT** Cr.

Particulars	₹	*Particulars*	₹
To Balance b/d	68,000	By Bank A/c (₹ 5,60,000 – ₹ 1,40,000)	4,20,000
To Credit Sales	5,76,000	By Cash A/c	1,40,000
		By Balance c/d (bal.fig.)	**84,000**
	6,44,000		6,44,000

Dr. **(viii) CREDITORS ACCOUNT** Cr.

Particulars	₹	*Particulars*	₹
To Bank A/c	5,50,000	By Balance b/d	1,24,000
To Balance c/d (bal.fig.)	**1,90,000**	By Purchases A/c	6,16,000
	7,40,000		7,40,000

Dr. **(ix) CASH AND BANK BALANCE** Cr.

Particulars	*Cash* ₹	*Bank* ₹	*Particulars*	*Cash* ₹	*Bank* ₹
To Balance b/d	8,000	34,000	By Business Expense A/c	36,000	24,000
To Sales A/c	1,44,000	—	By Drawings A/c	—	30,000
To Sundry Debtors	1,40,000	4,20,000	By Sundry Creditors A/c	—	5,50,000
To Cash A/c (Contra)	—	2,86,000	By Bank A/c (Contra)	2,86,000	
To Bank A/c (Contra)	48,000	—	By Cash A/c (Contra)	—	48,000
			By Sundry Advance (Defalcation of cash balance) (bal.fig.)	18,000	
			By Balance c/d (bal.fig.)	—	88,000
	3,40,000	7,40,000		3,40,000	7,40,000

PROBLEM 25

K. Azad, who is in business as a wholesaler in sunflower oil, is a client of your accounting firm. You are required to draw up his final accounts for the year ended 31.3.2015. From the files, you pick up his Balance Sheet as at 31.3.2014 reading as below:

BALANCE SHEET AS AT 31.3.2014

Liabilities	₹	*Assets*		₹
K. Azad's Capital	1,50,000	Cash and Bank Balances		75,000
Creditors for Oil Purchases	2,00,000	Debtors		1,60,000
12% Security Deposit from Customers	50,000	Stock of Oil (125 tins)		1,25,000
Creditors for Expenses:		Furniture	30,000	
Rent	6,000	*Less:* Depreciation	3,000	27,000
Salaries	4,000	Rent Advance		12,000
Commission	20,000	Electricity Deposit		1,000
		3-Wheeler Tempo Van	40,000	
		Less: Depreciation	10,000	30,000
	4,30,000			4,30,000

A Summary of the rough Cash Book K. Azad for the year ended 31.3.2015 is as below:

CASH AND BANK SUMMARY

	₹
Receipts	
Cash Sales	5,26,500
Collections from Debtors	26,73,500
Payments	
To Landlord	79,000
Salaries	48,000
Miscellaneous Office Expenses	12,000
Commission	20,000
Personal Income-tax	50,000
Transfer on 1.10.2014 to 12% Fixed Deposit	6,00,000
To Creditors for Oil Supplies	24,00,000

A scrutiny of the other records gives you the following information:

(i) During the year oil was purchased at 250 tins per month basis at a unit cost of ₹ 1,000. 5 tins were damaged in transit in respect of which insurance claim has been preferred. The surveyors have since approved the claim at 80%. The damaged ones were sold for ₹ 1,500 which is included in the cash sales. One tin has been used up for personal consumption. Total number of tins sold during the year was 3,000 at a unit price of ₹ 1,750.

(ii) Rent until 30.9.2014 was ₹ 6,000 per month and was increased thereafter by ₹ 1,000 per month. Additional advance rent of ₹ 2,000 was paid and this is included in the figure of payments to landlord.

(iii) Provide depreciation at 10% and 25% of WDV on furniture and tempo van respectively.

(iv) It is further noticed that a customer has paid ₹ 10,000 on 31.3.2015 as security deposit by cash. One of the staff has defaulted. The claim against the Insurance Company is pending.

Required: Prepare final accounts for the year ended 31.3.2015.

Solution

TRADING AND PROFIT AND LOSS ACCOUNT
for the year ended 31st March, 2015

Dr. | Cr.

Particulars		₹	*Particulars*	₹
To Opening Stock		1,25,000	By Sales	52,50,000
To Purchases	30,00,000		By Damaged Stock A/c	5,000
Less: Transferred to			By Closing Stock	1,19,000
drawings A/c	1,000	29,99,000		
To Gross Profit c/d		22,50,000		
		53,74,000		53,74,000
To Salaries		44,000	By Gross Profit b/d	22,50,000
To Rent		78,000	By Interest accrued	
To Miscellaneous Office Expenses		12,000	on Fixed Deposit	36,000
To Loss of Deposit		10,000	By Profit on Damaged Stock	500
To Interest on Security Deposits		6,000		
To Depreciation:				
Furniture	2,700			
Tempo Van	7,500	10,200		
To Capital A/c		21,26,300		
(Net Profit Transferred)				
		22,86,500		22,86,500

BALANCE SHEET AS AT 31ST MARCH, 2015

Liabilities		₹	*Assets*		₹
K. Azad's Capital			Furniture	27,000	
Balance	1,50,000		*Less:* Depreciation	2,700	24,300
Add: Net Profit	21,26,300		3-Wheeler Tempo Van	30,000	
Less: Drawings	51,000	22,25,300	*Less:* Depreciation	7,500	22,500
12% Security Deposit from Customers		60,000	Closing Stock		1,19,000
Interest Payable on Security Deposit		6,000	Debtors		22,11,500
Creditors for Oil Purchases		8,00,000	Cash and Bank Balances		66,000
Outstanding Rent		7,000	Fixed Deposit		6,00,000
			Interest Accrued on Fixed Deposit		36,000
			Rent Advance		14,000
			Electricity Deposit		1,000
			Insurance Claim Receivable		4,000
		30,98,300			30,98,300

Working Notes:

(i) MEMORANDUM STOCK ACCOUNT

Dr. | Cr.

Particulars	*Tins*	₹	*Particulars*	*Tins*	₹
To Opening Stock	125	1,25,000	By Damages	5	5,000
To Purchases	3,000	30,00,000	By Drawings	1	1,000
			By Sales	3,000	3,0,00,000
			By Closing Stock	119	1,19,000
	3,125	31,25,000		3,125	31,25,000

Dr. **(ii) DAMAGED STOCK ACCOUNT** Cr.

Particulars	₹	Particulars	₹
To Trading Account	5,000	By Insurance Claim Receivable A/c	4,000
To Profit and Loss Account (Balance Transferred)	500	By Cash and Bank A/c (Sales)	1,500
	5,500		5,500

Dr. **(iii) DEBTORS ACCOUNT** Cr.

Particulars	₹	Particulars	₹
To Balance b/d	1,60,000	By Cash and Bank A/c	26,73,500
To Sales A/c (Credit Sales*)	47,25,000	By Balance c/d	22,11,500
	48,85,000		48,85,000

*Credit Sales in respect of (normal) sales of 3,000 tins

Total Sales (3,000 × ₹ 1,750)	=	52,50,000
Less: Cash Sales (5,26,500 – 1,500)	=	5,25,000
		47,25,000

Dr. **(iv) CREDITORS ACCOUNT** Cr.

Particulars	₹	Particulars	₹
To Cash and Bank A/c	24,00,000	By Balance b/d	2,00,000
To Balance c/d	8,00,000	By Purchases A/c	30,00,000
	32,00,000		32,00,000

Dr. **(v) CASH AND BANK ACCOUNT** Cr.

Particulars	₹	Particulars	₹
To Balance b/d	75,000	By Rent A/c	79,000
To Sales A/c	5,25,000	By Salaries A/c	48,000
To Damaged Stock A/c	1,500	By Miscellaneous Office Expenses	12,000
To Debtors A/c	26,73,500	By Commission	20,000
To Security Deposit A/c	10,000	By Drawings A/c (Personal Income-tax)	50,000
		By Fixed Deposit A/c	6,00,000
		By Creditors A/c	24,00,000
		By Loss of deposit A/c (Defalcation of security deposit)	10,000
		By Balance c/d	66,000
	32,85,000		32,85,000

(vi) 12% interest on Fixed Deposit is assumed to be per annum. Similar assumption applies to 12% Security Deposit from customers.

(vii) The treatment of claim pending against the Insurance Company in respect of defalcation of security deposit by one of the staff has been considered on the basis of Prudence Principle. Prudence Principle suggests non-consideration of claim as an asset in anticipation. Where the ability to assess the ultimate collection with reasonable certainly is lacking at the time of raising any claim, revenue recognition is postponed to the extent of uncertainty involved (AS-9). In this case, it may be reasonably assumed that collectability of claim is not certain.

PROBLEM 26

The following information relates to the business of Mr. Shiv Kumar, who requests you to prepare a Trading and Profit & Loss Account for the year ended 31st March, 2015 and a Balance Sheet as on that date:

(a)

	Opening	Closing
Building	₹ 3,20,000	₹ 3,60,000
Furniture	60,000	68,000
Motorcar	80,000	80,000
Stocks	?	40,000
Bills payable	28,000	16,000
Cash and Bank balances	1,80,000	1,04,000
Sundry Debtors	1,60,000	?
Bills receivable	32,000	28,000
Sundry Creditors	1,20,000	?

(b) Cash transactions during the year included the following certain other items:

	₹		₹
Sale of old papers and miscellaneous income	20,000	Cash Purchases	48,000
Miscellaneous Trade expenses (including salaries etc.)	80,000	Payment to Creditors	1,84,000
Collection from debtors	2,00,000	Cash Sales	80,000

(c) Other information:

(i) Bills receivable drawn during the year amount to ₹ 20,000 and Bills payable accepted Rs16,000.

(ii) Some items of old furniture whose written down value on 31st March, 2014 was ₹ 20,000 was sold on 30th September, 2014 for ₹ 8,000. Depreciation is to be provided on Building and Furniture @ 10% p.a. and on Motorcar @ 20% p.a. Depreciation on sale of furniture to be provided for 6 months and for additions to Building for whole year.

(iii) Of the Debtors, a sum of ₹ 8,000 should be written off as Bad Debt and a reserve for doubtful debts is to be provided @ 2%.

(iv) Mr. Shivkumar has been maintaining a steady gross profit rate of 30% on turnover.

(v) Outstanding salary on 31st March, 2014 was ₹ 8,000 and on 31st march, 2015 was ₹ 10,000. Profit and Loss Account had a credit balance of ₹ 40,000.

(vi) 20% of total sales and total purchases are to be treated as for cash.

(vii) Additions in Furniture Account took place in the beginning of the year and there was no opening provision for doubtful debts.

Solution

TRADING AND PROFIT AND LOSS ACCOUNT OF MR. SHIV KUMAR

for the year ended 31st March, 2015

Dr. *Cr.*

Particulars	₹	Particulars	₹
To Opening Stock (b.f.)	80,000	By Sales	4,00,000
To Purchases	2,40,000	By Closing stock	40,000
To Gross profit c/d (@ 30% on sales)	1,20,000		
	4,40,000		4,40,000
To Miscellaneous Expenses (₹ 80,000 – ₹ 8,000 + ₹ 10,000)	82,000	By Gross profit b/d	1,20,000
To Depreciation:		By Miscellaneous receipts	20,000
		By Net loss transferred to Capital A/c	25,840

Building ₹ 36,000 Furniture ₹ 7,800 (₹ 6,800 + ₹ 1,000) Motor Car ₹ 16,000	59,800		
To Loss on sale of furniture	11,000		
To Bad debts	8,000		
To Provision for doubtful debts	5,040		
	1,65,840		1,65,840

BALANCE SHEET OF MR. SHIV KUMAR AS ON 31ST MARCH, 2015

Liabilities		₹	*Assets*		₹
Opening Capital		7,16,000	Building: Op. Balance	3,20,000	
Profit and Loss A/c			*Add:* Addition	40,000	
Opening balance	40,000			3,60,000	
Less: Net Loss	25,840	14,160	*Less:* Provision for		
Sundry creditors		1,12,000	depreciation	36,000	3,24,000
Bills payable		16,000	Furniture	60,000	
Outstanding salary		10,000	*Less:* Sold during the year	20,000	
			Add: Addition	40,000	
				28,000	
				68,000	
			Less: Depreciation	6,800	61,200
			Motor car (at cost)	80,000	
			Less: Depreciation	16,000	64,000
			Stock in trade		40,000
			Sundry debtors	2,52,000	
			Less: Provision @ 2%	5,040	2,46,960
			Bills receivable		28,000
			Cash in hand and at bank		1,04,000
		8,68,160			8,68,160

Working Notes:

Dr. **(i) SUNDRY DEBTORS' ACCOUNT** *Cr.*

Particulars	₹	*Particulars*	₹
To Balance b/d	1,60,000	By Cash/Bank A/c	2,00,000
To Sales A/c	3,20,000	By Bills receivable A/c	20,000
		By Bad debts A/c	8,000
		By Balance c/d (balancing fig)	2,52,000
	4,80,000		4,80,000

Dr. **(ii) SUNDRY CREDITORS ACCOUNT** *Cr.*

Particulars	₹	*Particulars*	₹
To Cash/Bank A/c	1.84,000	By Balance b/d	1,20,000
To Bills payable A/c	16,000	By Purchases A/c	1,92,000
To Balance c/d (balancing figure)	1,12,000		
	3,12,000		3,12,000

Dr. **(iii) BILLS RECEIVABLE ACCOUNT** *Cr.*

Particulars	₹	*Particulars*	₹
To Balance b/d	32,000	By Cash/Bank A/c (balancing figure)	24,000
To Sundry debtors A/c	20,000	By Balance c/d	28,000
	52,000		52,000

Dr. **(iv) BILLS PAYABLE ACCOUNT** Cr.

Particulars	₹	Particulars	₹
To Cash/Bank A/c (balancing figure)	28,000	By Balance b/d	28,000
To Balance c/d	16,000	By Sundry creditors A/c	16,000
	44,000		44,000

Dr. **(v) FURNITURE ACCOUNT** Cr.

Particulars	₹	Particulars	₹
To Balance b/d	60,000	By Bank/Cash A/c	8,000
To Bank A/c	28,000	By Depreciation A/c	1,000
		By Profit and loss A/c (loss on sale)	11,000
		By Depreciation A/c	6,800
		By Balance c/d	61,200
	88,000		88,000

Dr. **(vi) CASH/BANK ACCOUNT** Cr.

Particulars	₹	Particulars	₹
To Balance b/d	1,80,000	By Misc. trade expenses A/c	80,000
To Miscellaneous receipts A/c	20,000	By Purchase A/c	48,000
To Sundry debtors A/c	2,00,000	By Furniture A/c (balancing figure)	28,000
To Sales A/c	80,000	By Sundry Creditors A/c	1,84,000
To Furniture A/c (sale)	8,000	By Bills payable A/c	28,000
To Bills receivable A/c	24,000	By Building A/c	40,000
		By Balance c/d	1,04,000
	5,12,000		5,12,000

(vii) OPENING BALANCE SHEET AS ON 31ST MARCH, 2014

Liabilities	₹	Assets	₹
Capital (balancing figure)	7,16,000	Building	3,20,000
Profit and loss A/c	40,000	Furniture	60,000
Sundry creditors	1,20,000	Motor car	80,000
Bills Payable	28,000	Stock in trade	80,000
Outstanding	8,000	Sundry debtors	1,60,000
		Bills receivable	32,000
		Cash in hand and at bank	1,80,000
	9,12,000		9,12,000

PROBLEM 27

The following is the Balance Sheet of Sri Agni Dev as on 31st March, 2014:

Liabilities	₹	*Assets*	₹
Capital Account	2,52,500	Machinery	1,20,000
Sundry Creditors for purchases	45,000	Furniture	20,000
		Stock	33,000
		Debtors	1,00,000
		Cash in hand	8,000
		Cash at Bank	16,500
	2,97,500		2,97,500

Roits occurred and fire broke out on the evening of 31st March, 2015, destroying the books of accounts and Furniture. The cashier was grievously hurt and the cash available in the cash box was stolen.

The trader gives you the following information:

(i) Sales are effected as 25% for cash and the balance on credit. His total sales for the year ended 31st March, 2015 were 20% higher than the previous year. All the sales and purchases of goods were evenly spread throughout the year (as also in the last year).

(ii) Terms of Credit

Debtors	2 months
Creditors	1 month

(iii) Stock level was maintained at ₹ 33,000 all through the year.

(iv) A steady Gross Profit rate of 25% on the turnover was maintained throughout. Creditors are paid by cheque only, except for cash purchase of ₹.50,000.

(v) His private records and the Bank Pass-book disclosed the following transactions for the year:

(i) Miscellaneous Business Expenses	₹.1,57,500 (including ₹ 5,000 paid by cheque and ₹.7,500 was outstanding as on 31st March, 2015)
(ii) Repairs	₹ 3,500 (paid by cash)
(iii) Addition to Machinery	₹.60,000 (paid by cheque)
(iv) Private drawings	₹.30,000 (paid by cash)
(v) Travelling expenses	₹.18,000 (paid by cash)
(vi) Introduction of additional capital by depositing into the Bank	₹.5,000

(vi) Collection from debtors were all through cheques.

(vii) Depreciation on Machinery is to be provided @ 15% on the Closing Book Value.

(viii) The Cash stolen is to be charged to the Profit and Loss Account.

(ix) Loss of furniture is to be adjusted from the Capital Account.

Required: Prepare Trading, Profit and Loss Account for the year ended 31st March, 2015 and a Balance Sheet as on that date. Make appropriate assumptions whenever necessary. All workings should form part of your answer.

Solution

TRADING AND PROFIT AND LOSS ACCOUNT
for the year ended 31st March, 2015

Dr. Cr,

Particulars	₹	*Particulars*	₹
To Opening Stock	33,000	By Sales	9,60,000
To Purchases	7,20,000	By Closing Stock	33,000
To Gross Profit c/d	2,40,000		
	9,93,000		9,93,000

	₹		₹
To Business Expenses	1,57,500	By Gross Profit b/d	2,40,000
To Repairs	3,500		
To Depreciation	27,000		
To Travelling Expenses	18,000		
To Loss by theft	1,500		
To Net Profit	32,500		
	2,40,000		2,40,000

BALANCE SHEET AS AT 31ST MARCH, 2015

Liabilities		₹	*Assets*		₹
Capital: Op. Balance	2,52,500		Machinery	1,80,000	
Add: Additional Capital	5,000		*Less:* Depreciation	27,000	1,53,000
Net Profit	32,500				
	2,90,000		Stock in Trade		33,000
Less: Loss of Furniture	20,000		Sundry Debtors		1,20,000
Drawings	30,000	2,40,000			
Bank Overdraft		2,667			
Sundry Creditors		55,833			
Outstanding Expenses		7,500			
		3,06,000			3,06,000

Working Notes:

		₹
(i)	*Sales during the current year*	
	Total Credit Sales during the previous year (₹ 1,00,000 × 6)	6,00,000
	Cash Sales (₹ 6,00,000 × 1/3)	2,00,000
	Total Sales during the previous year	8,00,000
	Increase @ 20% during current year	1,60,000
	Total sales during current year	9,60,000
	Cash Sales: 1/4th	2,40,000
	Credit Sales: 3/4th	7,20,000
(ii)	Debtors equal to two months' credit sales (₹ 7,20,000 × 2/12)	1,20,000
(iii)	Purchases	
	Sales during the current year	9,60,000
	Gross Profit @ 25%	2,40,000
	Cost of goods sold being purchases	7,20,000
	(Since there is no change in stock level)	
(iv)	Sundry Creditors for goods	
	(₹ 7,20,000 – ₹ 50,000)/12 = ₹ 6,70,000/12	55,833

(v) DEBTORS ACCOUNT

Dr.			Cr.
To Balance b/d	1,00,000	By Bank A/c (b.f.)	7,00,000
To Credit Sales	7,20,000	By Balance c/d	1,20,000
	8,20,000		8,20,000

(vi) CREDITORS ACCOUNT

Dr.			Cr.
To Bank A/c	6,59,167	By Balance b/d	45,000
To Balance c/d	55,833	By Credit Purchases (₹.7,20,000 – ₹.50,000)	6,70,000
	7,15,000		7,15,000

Dr. **(vii) CASH AND BANK ACCOUNT** Cr.

Particulars	Cash ₹	Bank ₹	Particulars	Cash ₹	Bank ₹
To Balance b/d	8,000	16,500	By Payment to Creditors	50,000	6,59,167
To Collection from Debtors	–	7,00,000	By Misc. Expenses	1,45,000	5,000
To Sales	2,40,000	–	By Repairs	3,500	–
To Additional Capital	–	5,000	By Addition to Machinery	–	60,000
To Balance c/d (Bank overdraft)	–	2,667	By Travelling Expenses	18,000	–
			By Private Drawings	30,000	–
			By Balance c/d (Loss by theft)	1,500	–
	2,48,000	7,24,167		2,48,000	7,24,167

PROBLEM 28

Following is the Balance Sheet of Mr. Ram, a small trader as on 31.3.2014.

Liabilities	₹	Assets	₹
Capital	4,00,000	Fixed Assets	2,90,000
Creditors	1,00,000	Stock	80,000
		Debtors	1,00,000
		Cash on Hand	10,000
		Cash at Bank	20,000
	5,00,000		5,00,000

A fire destroyed the accounting records as well as the closing cash of the trader on 31.3.2015. However, the following information was available.

(a) Debtors and Creditors on 31.3.2015 showed an increase of 20% as compared to 31.3.2014.

(b) Credit Period:

Debtors—1 month: Creditors—2 months

(c) Stock was maintained at the same level throughout the year.

(d) Cash sales constituted 20% of total sales.

(e) All purchases were for credit only.

(f) Current ratio as on 31.3.2015 was exactly 2.

(g) Total expenses excluding depreciation for the year amounted to ₹ 5,00,000.

(h) Depreciation was provided at 10% on the closing value of fixed assets.

(i) Bank and cash transactions:

(1) Payments to creditors included ₹ 1,00,000 by cash.

(2) Receipts from debtors included ₹ 11,80,000 by way of cheques.

(3) Cash deposited into the bank ₹ 2,40,000.

(4) Personal drawings from bank ₹ 1,00,000.

(5) Fixed assets purchased and paid by cheques ₹ 4,50,000.

You are required to prepare:

(a) The Trading and Profit & Loss Account of Shri Ram for the year ended 31.3.2015 and

(b) A Balance Sheet on that date.

Solution

TRADING AND PROFIT & LOSS ACCOUNT
for the year ending on 31st March, 2015

Dr. *Cr.*

Particulars	₹	*Particulars*		₹
To Opening Stock	80,000	By Sales:		
To Purchases	7,20,000	Cash	3,60,000	
To Gross Profit c/d	10,80,000	Credit	14,40,000	18,00,000
		By Closing Stock		80,000
	18,80,000			18,80,000
To Expenses	5,00,000	By Gross Profit b/d		10,80,000
To Depreciation	74,000			
To Cash destroyed	20,000			
To Net Profit	4,86,000			
	10,80,000			10,80,000

BALANCE SHEET AS AT 31ST MARCH, 2015

Liabilities		₹	*Assets*		₹
Capital	4,00,000		Fixed Assets	2,90.000	
Add: Net Profit	4,86,000		*Add:* Purchases	4,50,000	
	8,86,000		*Less:* Depreciation	(74,000)	6,66,000
Less: Drawings	1,00,000	7,86,000	Stock		80,000
Creditors		1,20,000	Debtors		1,20,000
			Cash at Bank		40,000
		9,06,000			9,06,000

Working Notes:

(i) *Calculation of Cash received from Debtors*

		₹
A.	Debtors Opening balance	1,00,000
B.	Closing Balance (₹ 1,00,000 + 20%)	1,20,000
C.	Credit Sales (₹ 1,20,000 × 12)	14,40,000
D.	Total Sales (₹ 14,40,000/80%)	18,00,000
E.	Cash Sales (₹ 18,00,000 × 20%)	3,60,000
F.	Receipt of cash from debtors (₹ 1,00,000 + ₹ 14,40,000 – ₹ 1,20,000 – ₹ 11,80,000)	2,40,000

(ii) *Calculation of Payment to Creditors by Cheque*

A.	Creditors Opening balance	1,00,000
B.	Closing Balance (₹ 1,00,000 + 20%)	1,20,000
C.	Credit purchases (₹ 1,20,000 × 6)	7,20,000
D.	Payment by cheque (₹ 1,00,000 + ₹ 7,20,000 – ₹ 1,20,000 – ₹ 1,00,000)	6,00,000

(iii) *Calculation of Closing Bank Balance*

Closing Bank Balance:

Creditors i.e. current liability	1,20,000
Current assets (₹ 1,20,000 × 2)	2,40,000

Bank Balance = Current assets – Stocks – Debtors
= ₹ 2,40,000 – ₹ 80,000 – ₹ 1,20,000 = ₹ 40,000

(iv) CASH & BANK ACCOUNT

Dr. Cr.

Particulars	Cash ₹	Bank ₹	Particulars	Cash ₹	Bank ₹
To Balance b/d	5,000	20,000	By Creditors	1,00,000	6,00,000
To Debtors	2,40,000	11,80,000	By Drawings		1,00,000
To Cash Sales	3,60,000		By Bank (c)	2,40,000	
To Cash (c)		2,40,000	By Expenses (b.f)	2,50,000	2,50,000
			By Assets		4,50,000
			By Cash Destroyed (b.f.)	20,000	
			By Balance c/d		40,000
	6,10,000	14,40,000		6,10,000	14,40,000

RATIO BASED PROBLEMS

PROBLEM 29

Following incomplete information of X Ltd. are given below:

TRADING AND PROFIT & LOSS ACCOUNT FOR THE YEAR ENDED 31ST MARCH, 2015

Particulars	₹ '000	Particulars	₹ '000
To Opening stock	700	By Sales	?
To Purchases	?	By Closing Stock	?
To Direct Expenses	175		
To Gross Profit c/d	?		
	....		....
To Establishment expenses	740	By Gross Profit b/d	?
To Interest on Loan	60	By Commission	100
To Provision for taxation	?		
To Net Profit c/d	?		
	....		....
To Proposed dividends	?	By Balance b/f	140
To Transfer to general reserve	?	By Net Profit b/d:	
To Balance t/f to B/S	?		
	....		....

BALANCE SHEET AS AT 31ST MARCH, 2015

Liabilities	₹ '000	Assets	₹ '000
Paid-up Capital	1,000	**Fixed Assets:**	
General Reserve:		Plant & Machinery	1,400
Balance at the beginning of the year		Other Fixed Assets	?
Proposed addition	?	**Current Assets:**	?
Profit and Loss Account	?	Stock	?
10% Loan Account	?	Sundry Debtors	?
Current Liabilities	?	Cash at Bank	125
Provision for Tax	?		
Proposed Dividend	?		
	....		....

Other Informations:

(i) Current Ratio is 2:1.
(ii) Closing stock is 25% of sales.
(iii) Proposed dividend to paid-up Capital ratio is 2:3
(iv) Gross Profit ratio is 60% of turnover.
(v) Loan is half of Current Liabilities (other than Provisions).
(vi) Transfer to general reserves to proposed dividends ratio is 1:1.
(vii) Profit carried forward is 10% of proposed dividends.
(viii) Provision for taxation is equal to the amount of net profit of the year.
(ix) Balance to credit of general reserve at the beginning of the year is twice the amount transferred to that account from the current year's profits.

All working notes should be part of your answer. You are required to complete:

(i) Trading and Profit and Loss Account for the year ended 31st March, 2015 and
(ii) The Balance Sheet as on that date.

Solution

Dr. **TRADING PROFIT & LOSS A/C FOR THE YEAR ENDED 31ST MARCH, 2015** Cr.

Particulars	*₹ 000*	*Particulars*	*₹ 000*
To Opening Stock (*Given*)	700	By Sales	5,366.66
To Purchases (*Balancing Figure*)	2613.33	By Closing Stock	1341.67
To Direct Expenses (*Given*)	175		
To Gross Profit c/d	3,220		—
	6,708.33		6,708,33
To Established Expenses (*Given*)	740	By Gross Profit b/d (Bal. Fig.)	3,220
To Interest on Loan (Given)	60	By Commission (Given)	100
To Provision for Tax	1,260		
To Net profit c/d	1,260		
	3,320		3,320
To Proposed Dividends	666.67	By Balance b/f	140
To Transfer to General Reserve	666.67	By Net Profit (Balancing Figure)	1,260
To Balance Transferred to B/S	66.66		
	1,400		1,400

BALANCE SHEET AS AT 31ST MARCH, 2015

Liabilities		*₹ 000*	*Assets*	*₹ 000*
Paid-up Capital		1,000	**Fixed Assets:**	
General Reserve			Plant & Machinery	1,400
Opening Balance:	1333.34		Other Fixed Assets (B.F.)	2,993.34
Add: Addition	666.67	2,000.01	**Current Assets:**	
P&L Account		66.66	Stock	1,341.66
10% Loan A/c		600	Sundry Debtors	933.34
Current Liabilities		1,200	Cash at Bank (Given)	125
Provision for Tax		1,260		
Proposed Dividend		666.67		
		6,793.33		6,793.33

Working Notes:

(i) Proposed Dividend = $\frac{2}{3}$ of Paid up capital = $1,000 \times \frac{2}{3}$ = 666.67

(ii) Transfer to General Reserve = Proposed dividends = 666.67

(iii) Profit carried forward to Balance Sheet = 10% of Proposed Dividend = 666.67 × 10%
= 66.66

(iv) 10% Loan = $60 \times \frac{100}{10} = 600$

(v) Loan = Current Liabilities × 2 = 600 × 2 = 1,200

(vi) Current Ratio i.e., $\frac{\text{Current Assets}}{\text{Current Liabilities}} = \frac{2}{1}$

i.e. Current Assets = 2 × Current Liabilities or 2 × 1,200 = 2,400

(vii) Current Net Profit (666.67 + 666.67 + 66.66 – 140) = 1,260

(viii) Provision for Taxation is equal to Current N.P. i.e. = 1,260

(ix) G.P. being balancing figure of P/L A/c = 3,220

(x) G.P. = 60% of sales

3,220 = 60% × Sales *Or,* sales = 3,220/60% = 5,366.67

(xi) Closing stock = 25% of sales = 25% of ₹ 5,366.67 = 1,341.67

(xii) Purchases being balancing figure of Trading A/c = 2,613.33

(xiii) Debtors = Current Assets – Closing Stock – Cash at Bank

= 2,400 – 1,341.67 – 125 = 933.33

(xiv) Balance of General Reserves at the beginning of the year = 2 × the amount transferred to general reserve during the year = 2 × 666.67 = 1,333.34

(xv) Other Fixed Assets = Total of Balance Sheet – Current Assets – Plant and Machinery

= 6,793.33 – 2,400 – 1,400 = 2,993.33

PROBLEM 30

Follwoing information of the Final Accounts of Kumaran Ltd. are missing as shown below:

TRADING AND PROFIT & LOSS ACCOUNT FOR THE YEAR ENDED 31ST MARCH, 2015

Particulars	*₹ 000*	*Particulars*	*₹ 000*
To Opening stock	7000	By Sales	?
To Purchases	?	By Closing Stock	?
To Direct Expenses	1750		
To Gross Profit c/d	?		
	....		....
To Office & Adm. expenses	7,400	By Gross Profit b/d	?
To Interest on Loan	600	By Commission	1000
To Provision for taxation	?		
To Net Profit c/d	?		
	....		....
To Proposed Dividends	?	By Balance b/f	1400
To Transfer to General Reserve	?	By Net Profit b/d:	
To Balance t/f to B/S	?		
	....		....

BALANCE SHEET AS AT 31ST MARCH, 2015

Liabilities	*₹ 000*	*Assets*	*₹ 000*
Paid-up Capital	10,000	**Fixed Assets:**	
General Reserve:		Plant & Machinery	14,000
Balance at the beginning of the year		Other Fixed Assets	?
Proposed addition	?	**Current Assets:**	?
Profit and Loss Account	?	Stock	?
10% Debentures	?	Sundry Debtors	?
Current Liabilities	?	Cash at Bank	1,250
	....		....

You are required to provide the missing figures with the help of following information:

(i) Curent ratio 2 : 1.

(ii) Closing stock is 25% of sales.

(iii) Proposed dividends are 40% of the paid up capital.

(iv) Gross profit ratio is 60%

(v) Ratio of Current Liabilities to Debentures is 2 : 1.

(vi) Transfer to General Reserves is equal to proposed dividends.

(vii) Profit carried forward are 10% of the proposed dividends.

(viii) Provision for taxation is 50% of profits.

(ix) Balance to the credit of General Reserves at the beginning of the year is twice the amount transferred to that account from the current profits.

Solution

Dr. **TRADING PROFIT & LOSS A/C FOR THE YEAR ENDED 31ST MARCH, 2015** Cr.

Particulars	*₹ 000*	*Particulars*	*₹ 000*
To Opening Stock (*Given*)	7000	By Sales	35,000
To Purchases (*Balancing Figure*)	14,000	By Closing Stock	8,750
To Direct Expenses (*Given*)	1750		
To Gross Profit c/d	21,000		—
	43,750		43,750
To Office & Adm. Expenses (*Given*)	7400	By Gross Profit b/d (Bal. Fig.)	21,000
To Interest on Loan (Given)	600	By Commission (Given)	1,000
To Provision for Tax	7,000		
To Net profit c/d	7,000		
			22,000
To Proposed Dividends	4,000	By Balance b/f	1,400
To Transfer to General Reserve	4,000	By Net Profit (Balancing Figure)	7,000
To Balance Transferred to B/S	400		
	8,400		8,400

BALANCE SHEET AS AT 31ST MARCH, 2015

Liabilities		₹ 000	Assets	₹ 000
Paid-up Capital		10,000	**Fixed Assets:**	
General Reserve			Plant & Machinery	14,000
Opening Balance:	8,000		Other Fixed Assets (B.F.)	2,400
Add: Addition	4,000	12,000	**Current Assets:**	
P&L Account		400	Stock	8,750
10% Debentures		6,000	Sundry Debtors	14,000
Current Liabilities		12,000	Cash at Bank (Given)	1,250
		40,400		40,400

Working Notes:

1. Proposed Dividend = 40% of Paid up capital = 10,000 × 40% = 4,000
2. Transfer to General Reserve = Proposed Dividends = 4,000
3. Profit carried forward to Balance Sheet = 10% of Proposed Dividend
   = 4,000 × 10% = 400
4. 10% Debentures = 600× (100 /10) = 600
5. Debentures = Current Liabilities = Debentures × 2 = 6000 × 2 = 12,000
6. Current Assets = 2 × Current Liabilities = 2 × 12,000 = 24,000
7. Current Net Profit = (4,000 + 4,000 + 400) – 1,400 = 7,000
8. Provision for Taxation = Current N.P.= 7,000
9. G.P. = Net Profit + All Exp. – Comm. Received = (7,000 + 7,000 + 600 + 7,400) – 1000 = 21,000
10. Sales = 21,000 / 60% = 35,000
11. Closing Stock = 25% of Sales = 25% of 35,000 = 8,750
12. Purchases being balancing figure of Trading A/c = 14,000
13. Debtors = Current Assets – Closing Stock – Cash at Bank = 24,000 – 8,750 – 1,250 = 14,000
14. Balance of General Reserves at the beginning of the year = 2 × T/F to General Reserve
    = 2 × 4,000 = 8,000
15. Total of Balance Sheet = 10,000 + 12,000 + 400 + 6,000 + 12,000 = 40,400
16. Other Fixed Assets = Total of Balance Sheet – Current Assets – Plant and Machinery
    = 40,400 – 24,000 – 14,000 = 2,400

PROBLEM 31

A sole trader requests you to prepare his Trading and Profit & Loss Account for the year ended 31st March, 2015 and Balance Sheet as at that date. He provides you the following information:

STATEMENT OF AFFAIRS AS AT 31ST MARCH, 2014

Liabilities	₹	Assets	₹
Bank Overdraft	4,270	Furniture	96,000
Outstanding Expenses		Computer	24,300
Salaries 8,000		Mobile Phone	8,000
Rent 6,000	14,000	Stock	89,500
Bills Payable	22,500	Trade Debtros	55,000
Trade Creditors	52,500	Bills Receivable	15,000
Capital		Unexpired Insurance	
2,400			
(balancing figure)	1,97,430	Stock of Stationery	200
		Cash in Hand	300
	2,90,700		2,90,700

He informs you that there has been no addition to or sale of Furniture, Computer and Mobile Phone during the accounting year 2014–2015. The other assets and liabilities on 31st March, 2015 are as follows:

	₹
Stock	95,400
Trade Debtors	65,000
Bills Receivable	20,000
Unexpired Insurance	2,500
Stock of Stationery	250
Cash at Bank	18,000
Cash at Hand	7,230
Salaries Outstanding	8,300
Rent Outstanding	6,000
Bills Payable	26,500
Trade Creditors	76,000

He also provides to you the following summary of his cash transactions:

Receipts	₹	*Payments*	₹
Cash Sales	5,09,800	Trade Creditors	3,06,000
Trade Debtors	1,51,900	Bills Payable	80,000
Bills Receivable	65,000	Salaries	99,000
		Rent	72,000
		Insurance Premium	10,000
		Stationery	1,500
		Mobile Phone Expenses	9,000
		Drawings	1,20,000

It is found prudent to depreciate Furniture @ 5%, Computer @ 10% and Mobile Phone @ 25%. A provision for doubtful debts @ 5% on Trade Debtors is also considerded desirable.

Solution

TRADING AND PROFIT AND LOSS ACCOUNT

Dr. **for the year ending 31st March, 2015** *Cr.*

Particulars		₹	*Particulars*	₹	₹
To Opening Stock		89,500	By Sales:		
To Purchases		4,13,500	Credit	2,31,900	
To Gross profit c/d (Bal. Fig.)		3,34,100	Cash	5,09,800	7,41,700
			By Closing stock		95,400
		8,37,100			8,37,100
To Insurance		9,900	By Gross profit b/d		3,34,100
To Salaries		99,300			
To Rent		72,000			
To Stationery		1,450			
To Mobile Phone expenses		9,000			
To Provision for doubtful debts (5% of 65,000)		3,250			
To Depreciation:					
Furniture	4,800				
Computer	2,430				
Mobile Phone	2,000	9,230			
To Net Profit		1,29,970			
		3,34,100			3,34,100

BALANCE SHEET AS ON 31ST MARCH, 2015

Liabilities	₹	₹	Assets	₹	₹
Capital A/c:			Furniture	96,000	
Opening Balance	1,97,430		*Less*: Depreciation	(4,800)	91,200
Less: Drawings	(1,20,000)		Computer	24,300	
	77,430		*Less*: Depreciation	(2,430)	21,870
Add: Net Profit	1,29,970	2,07,400	Mobile Phone	8,000	
Bills Payable		26,500	*Less*: Depreciation	(2,000)	6,000
Trade Creditors		76,000	Trade Debtors	65,000	
Outstanding expenses:			*Less*: Provision for	(3,250)	61,750
Salaries		8,300	doubtful debts		
Rent		6,000	Bills Receivable		20,000
			Closing Stock		95,400
			Unexpired Insurance		2,500
			Stock of Stationery		250
			Cash at bank		18,000
			Cash in hand		7,230
		3,24,200			3,24,200

Working Notes:

1. **TRADE DEBTORS ACCOUNT**

	₹		₹
To Balance b/d	55,000	By Cash/Bank	1,51,900
To Credit Sales (Bal. Fig.)	2,31,900	By Bills Receivable A/c	70,000
		By Balance c/d (given)	65,000
	2,86,900		2,86,900

2. **BILLS RECEIVABLE ACCOUNT**

	₹		₹
To Balance b/d	15,000	By Cash/Bank	65,000
To Sundry Debtors (Bal. Fig.)	70,000	By Bal. c/d (given)	20,000
	85,000		85,000

3. **TRADE CREDITORS ACCOUNT**

	₹		₹
To Bank/Cash	3,06,000	By Bal. b/d	52,500
To Bills payable A/c	84,000	By Credit Purchases (Bal. Fig.)	4,13,500
To Balance c/d (given)	76,000		
	4,66,000		4,66,000

4. **BILLS PAYABLE ACCOUNT**

	₹		₹
To Cash/Bank A/c	80,000	By Balance b/d	22,500
To Balance c/d (given)	26,500	By Sundry Creditors (Bal. Fig.)	84,000
	1,06,500		1,06,500

5. **INSURANCE EXPENSES FOR THE YEAR**

	₹
Insurance paid during the year	10,000
Add: Unexpired Insurance in the beginning	2,400
Less: Unexpired Insurance at the end	(2,500)
	9,900

6. **SALARIES FOR THE YEAR**

	₹
Salaries paid during the year	99,000
Add: Salaries outstanding at the end	8,300
Less: Salaries outstanding at the beginning	(8,000)
	99,300

7. **RENT EXPENSES FOR THE YEAR**

	₹
Rent paid during the year	72,000
Add: Rent outstanding at the end	6,000
	78,000
Less: Rent outstanding at the beginning	(6,000)
	72,000

8. **STATIONERY EXPENSES FOR THE YEAR**

	₹
Opening Stock of Stationery	200
Add: Stationery purchased during the year	1,500
	1,700
Less: Closing Stock of Stationery	(250)
	1,450

PROBLEM 32

The details of Assets and Liabilities of Mr. 'A' as on 31-3-2014 and 31-3-2015 are as follows:

	31.3.2014 ₹	*31.3.2015* ₹
Assets:		
Furniture	50,000	
Building	1,00,000	
Stock	1,00,000	2,50,000
Sundry Debtors	60,000	1,10,000
Cash in hand	11,200	13,200
Cash at Bank	60,000	75,000
Liabilities:		
Loans	90,000	70,000
Sundry Creditors	50,000	80,000

Mr. 'A' decided to provide depreciation on building by 2.5% and furniture by 10% for the period ended on 31-3-2015. Mr. 'A' purchased jewellery for ₹ 24,000 for his daughter in December 2014. He sold his car on 30-3-2015 and the amount of ₹ 40,000 is retained in the business.

You are required to :

(i) Prepare statement of affairs as on 31-3-2014 and 31-3-2015.

(ii) Calculate the profit received by 'A' during the year ended 31-3-2015.

Solution

(i) STATEMENT OF AFFAIRS

Liabilities	*31.3.12* ₹	*31.3.13* ₹	*Assets*	*31.3.12* ₹	*31.3.13* ₹
Loans	90,000	70,000	Furniture	50,000	45,000
Creditors	50,000	80,000	Building	1,00,000	97,500
Capital A/c	2,41,200	4,40,700	Stock	1,00,000	2,50,000
			Debtors	60,000	1,10,000
			Cash in hand	11,200	13,200
			Cash at Bank	60,000	75,000
	3,81,200	5,90,700		3,81,200	5,90,700

Working Notes:

Dep. on Building	₹ 2,500	(2.5% of ₹ 1,00,000)
Dep. on Furniture	₹ 5,000	(10% of ₹ 50,000)

(ii) Calculation of Profit earned by A during the year ended 31st March, 2015.

CAPITAL ACCOUNT

	₹		₹
		By balance b/d	2,41,200
To Drawings	24,000	By Additional Capital	
To balance c/d	4,40,700	(Car sale proceeds)	40,000
		By P&L A/c (Balancing Figure)	1,83,500
	4,64,700		4,64,700

Note: Interest on drawings and capital has been ignored in the absence of information.

PROBLEM 33

Following are the incomplete information of Moonlight Traders:

The following balances are available as on 31.03.2014 and 31.03.2015.

Balances	*31.03.2014 ₹*	*31.03.2015 ₹*
Land and building	5,00,000	5,00,000
Plant and Machinery	2,20,000	3,30,000
Office equipment	1,05,000	85,000
Debetors	?	2,25,000
Creditors for purchases	95,000	?

Creditors for office expenses	20,000	15,000
Stock	?	65,000
Long term loan from SBI @ 12%.	1,25,000	1,00,000
Bank	25,000	?
Provision for tax (rate 30%)	35,000	30,000

Other Information	₹
Collection from debetors	9,25,000
Payment to creditors for purchases	5,25,000
Payment of office expenses	42,000
Salary paid	32,000
Selling expenses	15,000
Cash sales	2,50,000
Credit sales (80% of total sales)	
Credit purchases	5,40,000
Cash purchases (40% of total purchases)	
GP Margin at cost plus 25%	
Discount Allowed	5,500
Discount Received	4,500
Bad debts (2% of closing debtors)	
Depreciation to be provided as follows	
Land and Building	5%
Plant and Machinery	10%
Office Equipment	15%

Other adjustments:

(i) On 01.10.2014 they sold machine having Book Value ₹ 40,000 (as on 31.03.2014) at a loss of ₹ 15,000. New machine was purchased on 01.01.2015.

(ii) Office equipment was sold at its book value on 01.04.2014.

(iii) Loan was partly repaid on 31.03.2015 together with interest for the year.

Prepare Trading P & L A/c and Blanace Sheet as on 31.03.2015.

Solution

Dr. **Trading Account for the year ended 31.03.2015** Cr.

Particulars	₹	*Particulars*	₹
To Opening Stock A/c (Bal. fig.)	1,65,000	By Sales	12,50,000
To Purchases	9,00,000	By Closing Stock	65,000
To Gross profit (12,50,000 × 25/125)	2,50,000		
	13,15,000		13,15,000

PROFIT AND LOSS ACCOUNT FO THE YEAR ENDED 31.03.2015

Particulars		₹	Particulars	₹
To Discount		5,500	By Gross profit	2,50,000
To Salaries Expenses		32,000	By Discount	4,500
To Office expenses		37,000		
To Selling expenses		15,000		
To Interest on loan (12% on ₹ 1,25,000)		15,000		
To Bad debts (2% of ₹ 2,25,000)		4,500		
To Loss on sale of Machinery		15,000		
To Depreciation:				
Land & Building	25,000			
Plant & Machinery	23,750			
Office Equipment	12,750	61,500		
To Tax Provision* (69,000 × 30%)		20,700		
To Net profit after tax		48,300		
		2,54,500		2,54,500

BALANCE SHEET AS AT 31.3.2015

Liabilities	₹	₹	Assets	₹
Capital	8,95,500		Land and Building (5,00,000 – 25,000)	4,75,000
Add: Net Profit	48,300	9,43,800	Plant and Machinery (3,30,000 – 21,750)	3,08,250
Creditors for Purchase		1,05,500	Office Equipment (85,000 – 12,750)	72,250
Outstanding expenses		15,000	Debtors less Bad debts	2,20,500
Loan from SBI		1,00,000	Stock	65,000
Tax Provision		30,000	Bank balance	53,300
		11,94,300		11,94,300

Working Notes:

1. Total Sales = (₹ 2,50,000 × 100/20) = ₹ 12,50,000
2. Total Purchases = ₹ 5,40,000 × 100/60 = ₹ 9,00,000
3. DR. **OFFICE EXPENSES ACCOUNT** CR.

Particulars	₹	Particulars	₹
To Bank A/c	42,000	By Balance b/d	20,000
To Balance c/d	15,000	By Profit & loss A/c	37,000
	57,000		57,000

4.(a) **Plant and Machinery Account**

Particulars	₹	Particulars	₹
To Balance b/d	2,20,000	By Bank (Sale)	40,000
To bank (Purchases)	1,50,000	By c/d	3,30,000
	3,70,000		3,70,000

(B) CALCULATION OF DEPRECIATION ON PLANT & MACHINERY

Particulars	₹
1,80,000 × 10% (for full year)	18,000
[3,30,000 – (2,20,000 – 40,000] × 10% × 3/12 (for 3 months)	3,750
40,000 × 10% × 6/12 (for 6 months)	2,000
	23,750

(c) Dr. **Machinery Account** Cr.

Particulars	₹	Particulars	₹
To Plant & Machinery	40,000	By Depreciation	2,000
		By Profit and Loss A/c	15,000
		By Bank (bal. fig.) (Sale)	**23,000**
	40,000		40,000

5. DEPRECIATION ON OFFICE EQUIPMENTS

	₹
Opening balance	1,05,000
Less: Closing Balance	85,000
Sale of Office Equipments	20,000
Balance of Office Equipments after sale	85,000
Depreciation @15%	12,750

6. OPENING BALANCE SHEET AS AT 31.03.2014

Liabilities	₹	Assets	₹
Creditors	95,000	Land & Building	5,00,000
Creditor for Exp.	20,000	Plant & Machinery	2,20,000
Loan	1,25,000	Office Equipment	1,05,000
Provision for Tax	35,000	Debtors	1,55,500
Capital (Bal. fig.)	**8,95,500**	Stock	1,65,000
		Bank	25,000
	11,70,500		11,70,500

7. Dr. **Sundry Debtors Account** Cr.

Particulars	₹	Particulars	₹
To Balance b/d (bal. fig.)	1,55,500	By Bank	9,25,000
To Sales [₹ 12,50,000 × 80%]	10,00,000	By Discount	5,500
		By Bad debts	4,500
		By Bal. c/d	2,20,500
	11,55,500		11,55,500

8. DR. **SUNDRY CREDITORS ACCOUNT** CR.

Particulars	₹	Particulars	₹
To Bank A/c	5,25,000	By Balance b/d	95,00
To Discount	4,500	By Purchases	5,40,000
To Balance c/d (bal. fig.)	1,05,500	[₹ 9,00,000 × 60%]	
	6,35,000		6,35,000

9. Dr. **Bank Account** Cr.

Particulars	₹	Particulars	₹
To Balance b/d	25,000	By Creditors	5,25,000
To Debtors	9,25,000	By Office Expenses	42,000
To cash Sales	2,50,000	By Salary Expense	32,000
To Sale of Machinery	23,000	By Selling Expenses	15,000
To Sale of equipment	20,000	By Purchases (cash)	3,60,000
		By Purchase of Machinery	1,50,000
		By Bank Loan & Interest	40,000
		By Tax	25,700
		By Balance c/d (bal. fig.)	53,300
	12,43,000		12,43,000

10. Dr. **PROVISION FOR TAX ACCOUNT** Cr.

Particulars	₹	Particulars	₹
To Bank (bal. fig.)	25,700	By Balance b/d	35,000
To Balance c/d	30,000	By Profit and Loss A/c	20,700
	55,700		55,700

11. Repayment of Bank Loan and interest

Particulars	₹
Interest [1,25,000 × 12%]	15,000
Loan (1,25,000 – 1,00,000)	25,000
	40,000

1. Tax profit are the same as accounting profits.
2. The figure of ₹ 2,25,000, being the closing balance of Sundry Debtors as given in the question is before providing for bad debts. Accordingly, the closing balance has been reduced by the amount of bad debts.

16 ACCOUNTING FOR PARTNERSHIP FIRMS—FUNDAMENTALS

SHORT ANSWER PRACTICAL PROBLEMS

PROBLEM 1

On 1st April, *X*, *Y* and *Z* enter into partnership introducing capital of ₹ 80,000, ₹ 50,000 and ₹ 50,000 respectively. They agree to share Profits and Losses equally. At the end of the accounting year on 31st March, *X* claims that he be paid interest on his additional Capital of ₹ 30,000 @ 10% per annum, while *Z* demands salary of ₹ 600 per month for the extra hours devoted by him daily at the shop. The partnership deed is silent on these matters. Decide the matters with reasons.

Solution

When the partnership deed is silent on the matter of interest on capitals and salary to partners, then no partner is entitled to claim interest on capital and salary. Therefore, claim of *X* and *Z* is not tenable. However, inclusion of specific provision regarding the said issues in partnership deed can make them entitled for interest on capital and salary.

PROBLEM 2

A concern made a net profit of ₹ 2,00,000 for the year. The normal rate of return in that type of business is 20%. What is the value of business under "Profit Capitalisation method"?

Solution

$$\text{Value of business as per profit capitalisation method} = \frac{\text{Net Profit}}{\text{Normal Rate of Return}} \times 100$$

$$= \frac{₹\,2{,}00{,}000}{20} \times 100 = ₹\,10{,}00{,}000$$

PROBLEM 3

Shiv and Mohan are partners in a firm sharing profits and losses equally. On 31st March, 2013 the balances of their capital accounts were ₹ 3.00,000 and ₹ 2,00,000 respectively. The average profits of the firm are ₹ 1,36,000 and the rate of normal profit ts 20%.

On 1st April, 2013 they agreed to admit Hari as a partner for one fourth share. Hari will bring ₹ 1,00,000 as capital.

You are required to compute the value of the goodwill of the firm on admission of Hari, if goodwill is to be calculated on the basis of:

(1) 5 years' purchase of Super Profit
(2) Capitalization Method
(3) 3 years' purchase of Average Profit.

Solution

VALUATION OF GOODWILL

(1) 5 years' Purchase of Super Profit

Value of Goodwill = 5 × Super Profit

= 5 × [₹ 1,36,000 – (20% of ₹ 5,00,000)] = ₹ 1,80,000

(2) Capitalisation Method

Value of Goodwill = Normal Value of business – Actual capital employed = 6,80,000

= [₹ 1,36,000/20%] – [₹ 3,00,000 + ₹ 2,00,000] = ₹ 1,80,000

(3) 3 years' Purchase of Average Profits

Goodwill = 3 × Average Profit = 3 × ₹ 1,36,000 = ₹ 4,08,000

LONG ANSWER PRACTICAL PROBLEMS

PROBLEM 4

Good, Better and Best are in Partnership sharing profits and losses in the ratio 3:2:4. Their Capital Account balances as on 31st March 2015 are as follows: Good ₹ 1,70,000 (Cr), Better ₹ 1,10,000 (Cr), Best ₹ 1,22,000 (Cr)

Following further information provided:

1. ₹ 22,240 is to be transferred to General Reserve.
2. Good, Better and Best are paid monthly salary in cash amounting to ₹ 2,400, ₹ 1,600 and ₹ 1,800 rspectively.
3. Partners are allowed interest on their Closing Capital Balance at 6% p.a. and are charged interest on drawings at 8% p.a.
4. Good and Best are entitled to Commission at 8% and 10% respectively of the Net Profit before making any appropriation.
5. Better is entitled to Commission at 15% of the Net Profit before charging Interest on Drawings but after making all other appropriations.
6. During the year, Good withdrew ₹ 2,000 at the beginning of every month, Better ₹ 1,750 at the end of every month and Best ₹ 1,250 at the middle of every month.
7. The Firm's Accountant is entitled to a Salary of ₹ 2,000 per month and a Commission of 12% of Net Profit after charging such Commission.

The Net Profit of the Firm for the year ended 31st March 2015, before providing for any of the above adjustments was ₹ 2,76,000. You are required to prepare Profit and Loss Appropriation Account for the year ended on 31st March 2015.

Solution

Dr. **PROFIT AND LOSS ACCOUNT** *Cr.*

Particulars	₹	*Particulars*	₹
To Accountant's Salary (2,000 × 12)	24,000	By Net Profit b/d	2,76,000
To Accountant's Commission [(2,76,000 – 24,000) × 12/112]	27,000		
To Net Profit c/d (bal. fig.)	2,25,000		
	2,76,000		2,76,000

Dr. **PROFIT AND LOSS APPROPRIATION ACCOUNT** *Cr.*

Particulars		₹	*Particulars*		₹
To General Reserve		22,240	By Net Profit b/d		2,25,000
To Salary:			By Interest on Drawings:		
Good (2,400 × 12)	28,800		Good (24,000 × 8% × 6.5 / 12)	1,040	
Better (1,600 × 12)	19,200		Better (21,000 × 8% × 5.5 / 12)	770	
Best (1,800 × 12)	21,600	69,600	Best (15,000 × 8% × 5.5 / 12)	600	2,410
To Interest on Capital:					
Good (1,70,000 × 6%)	10,200				
Better (1,10,000 × 6%)	6,600				
Best (1,22,000 × 6%)	7,320	24,120			

Particulars		₹	*Particulars*	₹
To Commission:				
Good (2,25,000 × 8%)	18,000			
Best (2,25,000 × 10%)	22,500			
Better (68,540 × 15%)	10,281	50,781		
To Net Profit tfrd to Capital A/c:				
Good (60,669 × 3/9)	20,223			
Better (60,669 × 2/9)	13,482			
Best (60,669 × 4/9)	26,964	60,669		
		2,27,410		2,27,410

Notes:

1. Salary and Commission to Firm's Accountant are in the nature of charges against Firm's Profits, and not an appropriation out of Profit to Partners. Hence, this amounts have been debited to Profit & Loss Account.
2. Better's Commission = [2,25,000 – 22,240 – 69,600 – 24,120 – 40,500] × 15% = ₹ 10,281

17 RECONSTITUTION OF PARTNERSHIP—CHANGE IN PROFIT SHARING RATIO

SHORT ANSWER PRACTICAL PROBLEMS

PROBLEM 1

'*A*' and '*B*' are partners sharing Profits and Losses in the ratio of 3:1. Their capitals were ₹ 3,00,000 and ₹ 2,00,000 respectively. As from 1st April, 2015, it was agreed to change the profit sharing ratio to 3:2. According to the partnership deed, goodwill should be valued at two years' purchase of the average of three years' profits. The profits of the previous three years ending 31st March were: 2013, ₹ 7,50,000; 2014 ₹ 2,00,000 and 2015 ₹ 2,50,000. Pass the necessary journal entry to give effect to the above arrangement in the capital accounts of the partners.

Solution

JOURNAL

Date	*Particulars*	*Dr (₹)*	*Cr (₹)*
	B's Capital A/c Dr.	60,000	
	To A's Capital A/c		60,000
	(Being the adjusting entry for goodwill, passed due to change in profit and loss sharing ratio, through capital accounts of partners)		

Working Notes:

(i) *Calculation of Goodwill*

Average Profit = (₹ 1,50,000 + ₹ 2,00,000 + ₹ 2,50,000)/3 = ₹ 2,00,000

Goodwill = ₹ 2,00,000 × 2 = ₹ 4,00,000

(ii) *Effect of change in Profit Sharing Ratio*

Gaining Ratio = New Ratio – Old Ratio

For $A = \frac{3}{5} - \frac{3}{4} = \frac{12-15}{20} = \frac{3}{20}$ i.e. *A* loses by $\frac{3}{20}$

For $B = \frac{2}{5} - \frac{1}{4} = \frac{8-5}{20} = \frac{3}{20}$ i.e. *B* loses by $\frac{3}{20}$

(iii) *Compensation payable by B to A* = ₹ 4,00,000 × 3/20 = ₹ 60,000

18 RECONSTITUION OF PARTNERSHIP—ADMISSION OF A PARTNER

SHORT ANSWER PRACTICAL PROBLEMS

PROBLEM 1

A and *B* are equal partners. They admit *C* and *D* as partners with 1/5 and 1/6 share respectively. What is the profit sharing ratio of all the partners?

Solution

Let total profits or losses of the firm be 1

Shares of *C* and *D* is $\frac{1}{5}$ and $\frac{1}{6}$ respectively.

Balance remaining: $1-\frac{1}{5}+\frac{1}{6}=1-\frac{11}{30}=\frac{19}{30}$

$\frac{19}{30}$ to be shared equally by *A* and *B* as $\frac{9.5}{30}:\frac{9.5}{30}$

New profit sharing ratio will be *A* : *B* : *C* : *D*

$$\left[\frac{9.5}{30}\times\frac{2}{2}\right]:\left[\frac{9.5}{30}\times\frac{2}{2}\right]:\left[\frac{1}{5}\times\frac{12}{12}\right]:\left[\frac{1}{6}\times\frac{10}{10}\right]$$

Thus, new profit sharing Ratio will be 19 : 19 : 12 : 10.

PROBLEM 2

A, *B*, and *C* are partners sharing profits and losses in the ratio of 3 : 2 : 1. *B* retired from firm. Partners *A* and *C* decided to take his share in 3:1 ratio. What is the new ratio the partners *A* and *C*?

Solution

Calculation of new profit and loss sharing ratio of partners *A* and *C*

1/3rd share of *B* taken by partners *A* & *C* in 3:1 i.e.

A will receive from $B=\frac{1}{3}\times\frac{3}{4}=\frac{1}{4}$

C will receive from $B=\frac{1}{3}\times\frac{1}{4}=\frac{1}{12}$

Total share of *A* and *C* will be:

$$A=\frac{3}{6}+\frac{1}{4}=\frac{12+6}{24}=\frac{18}{24}\text{ or }\frac{3}{4}$$

$$C=\frac{1}{6}+\frac{1}{12}=\frac{2+1}{12}=\frac{3}{12}\text{ or }\frac{1}{4}$$

Therefore, new profit and loss sharing ratio of A and C will be 3 : 1.

PROBLEM 3

P, *Q* and *R* share profit and losses in the ratio of 4:3:2 respectively. *Q* retires and *P* and *R* decide to share future profits and losses in the ratio of 5:3. Then immediately *H* is admitted for 3/10 share of profits half of which was gifted by *P* and the remaining share was taken by *H* equally from *P* and *R*. Calculate the new profit sharing ratio after H's admission and gaining ratio of *P* and *R* after Q's retirement.

Solution

(*a*) Calculation of new profit sharing ratio after H's admission

$$P = \frac{5}{8}-\left[\frac{3}{10}\times\frac{1}{2}\right]-\left[\frac{3}{10}\times\frac{1}{4}\right] = \frac{5}{8}-\frac{3}{20}-\frac{3}{40} = \frac{25-6-3}{40}=\frac{16}{40}$$

$$R = \frac{3}{8}-\left[\frac{3}{10}\times\frac{1}{4}\right] = \frac{3}{8}-\frac{3}{40}=\frac{15-3}{40}=\frac{12}{40}$$

$$H = \frac{3}{8} \text{ or } \frac{3}{10}\times\frac{4}{4}=\frac{12}{40}$$

Hence, New Ratio of P : R : H = 16:12:12 Or 4 : 3 : 3

(*b*) Calculation of gaining ratio of *P* and *R* after *Q*'s retirement

$$P = \frac{5}{8}-\frac{4}{9}=\frac{45-32}{72}=\frac{13}{72}$$

$$R = \frac{3}{8}-\frac{2}{9}=\frac{27-16}{72}=\frac{11}{72}$$

PROBLEM 4

A and *M* are partners, sharing profits and losses in the ratio of 3:2. *G* is admitted for 1/4th share. Thereafter, N enters the partnership for 20 Paise in a Rupee. Compute new profit sharing ratio.

Solution

Let the total share be	= 1
Share of new partner G	= 1 / 4
Remaining share of profit	= 1 – (1 / 4) = 3 / 4
New ratio of (A)	= (3 / 4) × (3 / 5) = 9 / 20
New ratio of (M)	= (3 / 4) × (2 / 5) = 6 / 20
New ration of A:M:G	= 9:6:5
Again, let the total share at the time of admission of N	= 1
Share of new partner N is 20% i.e 1 / 5	
Remaining share	= 1 – (1 / 5) = 4 / 5
New ratio of A	= (4 / 5) × (9 / 20) = 9 / 25
New ratio of M	(4 / 5) × (6 / 20) = 6 / 25
New ratio of G	= (4 / 5) × (5 / 20) = 5 / 25
New ratio of A:M:G:N	= 9:6:5:5

PROBLEM 5

A and *B* are partners in a firm sharing profits and losses in the ratio of 3 : 2. Their capitals are ₹ 60,000 and ₹ 40, 000 respectively. They admit *C* as a new partner who will get 1/6th share in the profit of the firm. *C* brings in ₹ 25,000 as his capital. Find out the amount of goodwill on the basis of the above information.

Solution

Calculation of Goodwill

Total capital of new firm= ₹ 25,000 x 6 = ₹ 1 ,50,000

Capital of old partners should be= ₹ 1, 50,000 – ₹ 25,000 = ₹ 1,25,000

Actual combined capital of old partners= ₹ 60,000 + ₹ 40,000 = ₹ 1 ,00,000

So, the goodwill of the firm= ₹ 1, 25,000 – ₹ 1,00,000 = ₹ 25,000

PROBLEM 6

(i) Anil and Mukesh an partners sharing profit and losses in the ratio of 3: 2. Govind is admitted for ¼th share of firm. Thereafter Madan enters for 20 paise in a rupee. Compute new profit sharing ratios under both the admission of partners.

(ii) The following Goodwill Account was opened by the partners R and S, on the admission of H as a new partner into firm Om and Sons. Calculate the share of profit agreed to be given to "H".

Dr. **GOODWILL ACCOUNT** *Cr.*

Date	*Particulars*	₹	*Date*	*Particulars*	₹
1-4-2010	To R's Capital A/c	24,800	1-4-2010	By R's Capital A/c	12,400
1-4-2010	To S's Capital A/c	18,600	1-4-2010	By S's Capital A/c	12,400
			1-4-2010	By H's Capital A/c	18,600
		43,400			**43,400**

Solution

(i) At the time of admission of Govind

Let the total share of profit at the time of admission of Govind = 1

Share of New Partner – Govind = ¼

Remaining share of profit = 1 – ¼ = ¾

Now,

New share of Anil = $\frac{3}{4} \times \frac{3}{5} = \frac{9}{20}$

New share of Mukesh = $\frac{3}{4} \times \frac{2}{5} = \frac{6}{20}$

New ratio of Anil, Mukesh and Govind

$\frac{9}{20} : \frac{6}{20} : \frac{1}{4}$ i.e = 9 : 6 : 5

(ii) At the time of admission of Madan

Let total share at the time of admission of Madan = 1

Share of new partner – Madan = 1/5 = 4/5

Remaining share = 1 – 1/5 = 4/5

Now, New share of Anil = $\frac{4}{5} \times \frac{9}{20} = \frac{9}{25}$

New share of Mukesh = 4/5 x 6/20 = 6/25

New share of Govind = 4/5 x 5/20 = 5/25

New ratio of Anil, Mukesh, Govind and Madan

$\frac{9}{25}:\frac{6}{25}:\frac{5}{25}:\frac{1}{5}$ i.e. 9 : 6 : 5 : 5

(ii) $\text{H's share} = \frac{\text{Share of H in Goodwill}}{\text{Total Goodwill}} = \frac{18{,}600}{43{,}400} = \frac{3}{7}$

PROBLEM 7

Arul and Varun were partners sharing profits in the ratio of 13 : 11 respectively. On 1st April they admitted Tarun as a new partner on the following conditions:

(i) All partners would share profits equally in the new firm.

(ii) Tarun would bring in ₹ 52,000 as his capital and ₹ 36,000 as his share of goodwill. No goodwill account appeared in the books of the firm at the time of Tarun's admission and it was decided not to open any goodwill account. Adjustment for Tarun's goodwill being made through capital accounts.

Pass journal entries to record all the transactions on Tarun's admission.

Clearly show the calculation of ratio of sacrifice.

Solution

JOURNAL ENTRIES ON TARUN'S ADMISSION

Date	Particulars		Dr (₹)	Cr (₹)
1st Apr	Bank A/c	Dr	88,000	
	To Tarun's Captital A/c (52,000 + 36,000)			88,000
	(Being the capital and share of goodwill brought in)			
	Tarun's Capital A/c	Dr.	36,000	
	To Arun's Capital A/c			25,000
	To Varun's Capital A/c			13,000

(Being Tarun's share of goodwill credited to the old partners in the sacrificing ratio 5 : 3)

CALCULATIONS OF SACRIFICING RATIO

Arun = 13/24 – 1/3 = 5/24, Varun = 11/24 – 1/3 = 3/24

Therefore, Sacrificing Ratio of Arun and Varun is 5 : 3

PROBLEM 8

A and B are in partnership sharing profits and losses in the ratio of 3 : 2. The capitals of A and B are ₹ 80,000 and ₹ 60,000 respectively. They admit C as a partner who contributes ₹ 35,000 as capital for $1/5^{th}$ share of profits-to be acquired equally from both A & B. The capital accounts of old partners are to be adjusted on the basis of the proportion of C's capital to his share in the business. Calculate the amount of actual cash to be paid off or brought in by the old partners for the purpose and pass the necessary Journal Entries.

Solution

SHARE OF PROFIT TAKEN FROM A AND B EACH= 1/5 × 1/2 = 1/10 EACH
CALCULATION OF NEW PROFIT SHARING RATIO

Particulars	*A*	*B*
Existing Share	3/5	2/5
Less: Share of profit transferred to C	(1/10)	(1/10)
New Share	5/10	3/10
New Profit Sharing Ratio of A : B : C = 5/10 : 3/10 : 2/10		
Total Capital = ₹ 35,000 × (5/1) = ₹ 1,75,000		

CALCULATION OF ACTUAL CASH TO BE PAID OR BROUGHT IN BY OLD PARTNERS

Particulars	*A* ₹	*B* ₹	*C* ₹
New capital of ₹ 1,75,000 distributed in the ratio 5 : 3 : 2	87,500	52,500	35,000
Less: Adjusted Old Capitals of A & B	(80,000)	(60,000)	–
Cash brought in	7,500		35,000
Cash to be paid		(7,500)	

JOURNAL

Date	*Particulars*		*L.F.*	*Dr.* (₹)	*Cr.* (₹)
	Cash A/c	Dr.		7,500	
	To A's Capital A/c				7,500
	(Being the shortage of capital brought in cash by A)				
	B's Capital A/c	Dr.		7,500	
	To Cash A/c				7,500
	(Being the excess capital withdrawn by B)				

LONG ANSWER PRACTICAL PROBLEMS

SIMPLE PROBLEMS

PROBLEM 9

Amit and Sumit are partners sharing profits and losses in the ratio of 3:2. Their Balance Sheet as on 31st March 2015 is given below:

Liabilities	₹	*Assets*		₹
Capital Accounts:		Land & building		3,20,000
Amit	1,76,000	Investments		
Sumit	2,54,000	(Market value ₹ 55,000)		50,000
Loan from Puneet	3,00,000	Debtors	3,00,000	
General Resetve	30,000	*Less:* Provision	10,000	2,90,000
Employer's provident fund	10,000	Stock		1,10,000
Creditors	50,000	Cash at bank		50,000
	8,20,000			8,20,000

They decided to admit Puneet as a new partner from 1st April, 2015 on the following terms:

(1) Amit will give 1/3rd of his share and Sumit will give 1/4th of his share to Puneet.
(2) Puneet's loan account will be converted into his capital.
(3) The Goodwill of the firm is valued at ₹ 3,00,000. Puneet will bring his share of goodwill in cash and the same was immediately withdrawn by the partners.
(4) Land and building was found undervalued by ₹ 1,00,000.
(5) Stock was found overvalued by ₹ 60,000.
(6) Provision for doubtful debts will be made equal to 5% of debtors.
(7) Investments are to be valued at their market price.

It was decided that the total capital of the firm after admission of new partner would be ₹ 10,00,000. Capital accounts of partners will be readjusted on the basis of their profit sharing ratio and excess or deficiency will be adjusted in cash.

Required: Prepare (a) Revaluation A/c (b) Partners'capital A/cs (c) Balance Sheet of the firm after admission of a new partner

Solution

Dr. **REVALUATION ACCOUNT** *Cr,*

Particulars	₹	*Particulars*	₹
To Stock	60,000	By Land & building	1,00,000
To Provision for doubtful debts	5,000	By Investments	5,000
To Profit transferred to:			
Amit's capital A/c	24,000		
Sumit's capital A/c	16,000		
	1,05,000		1,05,000

Dr. **PARTNERS' CAPITAL ACCOUNTS** Cr.

Particulars	Amit ₹	Sumit ₹	Puneet ₹	Particulars	Amit ₹	Sumit ₹	Puneet ₹
To Amit's Capital A/c	—	—	60,000	By Balance b/d	1,76,000	2,54,000	—
To Puneet's Capital A/c	—	—	30,000	By Puneets' Loan A/'c	—	—	3,00,000
To Bank A/c	60,000	30,000	—	By Puneet's capital A/c	60,000	30,000	—
To Balance c/d	4,00,000	3,00,000	3,00,000	By Bank A/c	—	—	90,000
				By Revaluation A/c	24,000	16,000	
				By General reserve	18,000	12,000	—
				By Bank	1,82,000	18,000	—
	4,60,000	3,30,000	3,90,000		4,60.000	3,30,000	3.90,000

BALANCE SHEET AS AT 1ST APRIL, 2015
(AFTER ADMISSION OF A NEW PARTNER)

Liabilities	₹	Assets		₹
Capital accounts:		Land & Building		
Amit	4,00,000	(3,20,000 + 1,00,000)		4,20,000
Sumit	3,00,000	Investments		55,000
Puneet	3,00,000	Debtors	3,00,000	
Creditors	50,000	*Less:* Provision for		
Employers' Provident Fund	10,000	doubtful debts	(15,000)	2,85,000
		Stock (1,10,000 – 60,000)		50,000
		Cash at bank		2,50,000
	10,60,000			10,60,000

Working Notes:

(i) Calculation of incoming partner's share, new profit sharing ratio and sacrificing ratio

Particulars	Amit	Sumit
Old profit sharing ratio	3/5	2/5
Surrendered by old partners	3/5 × 1 /3 = 1/5	2/5 × 1/4 = 1/10
Remaining share	3/5 – 1/5 = 2/5	2/5 – 1/10 = 3/10

Puneet's total share in profits = 1/5 + 1/10 = 3/10

New profit sharing ratio of Amit: Sumit: Puneet = 2/5 : 3/10 : 3/10 = 4:3:3

Sacrificing ratio of Amit: Sumit is 1/5 :1/10 : or 2:1

(ii) Share of Puneet in goodwill = ₹ 3,00,000 × 3/10 = ₹ 90,000

Goodwill will be distributed among the old partners in their sacrificing ratio of 2:1 i.e. ₹ 60,000 by Amit and ₹ 30,000 by Sumit.

Dr. **(iii) BANK ACCOUNT** Cr,

Particulars	₹	Particulars	₹
To Balance b/d	50,000	By Amit's Capital A/c	60,000
To Puneefs Capital A/c	90,000	By Sumit's Capital A/c	30,000
To Sumit's Capital A/c	18,000	By Balance c/d	2,50,000
To Amit's Capita] A/c	1,82,000		
	3,40,000		3,40,000

ADVANCED PROBLEMS

PROBLEM 10

Laurel and Hardy are partners of the firm LH & Co., from 1.4.2009 Initially both of them contributed ₹ 1,00,000 each as capital. They did not contribute any capital thereafter. They maintain accounts of the firm on mercantile basis. They were sharing profits and losses in the ratio of 5:4. After the accounts for the year ended 31.3.2003 were finalized, the partners decided to share profits and losses equally with effect from 1. 4. 2009.

It was also discovered that in ascertaining the results in the earlier years certain adjustments, details of which are given below, had not been noted.

Year ended 31st March	*2010* ₹	*2011* ₹	*2014* ₹	*2015* ₹
Profit as per accounts prepaid and finalized	1,40,000	2,60,000	3,20,000	3,60,000
Expenses not provided for (as at 31st March)	30,000	20,000	36,000	24,000
Incomes not taken into account (as at 31st March)	18,000	15,000	12,000	21,000

The partners decided to admit Chaplin as a partner with effect from 1.4.2015. It was decided that Chaplin would be allotted 20% share in the firm and he must bring 20% of the combined capital of Laurel and Hordy.

Following is the Balance sheet of the firm as on 31.3.2015 before admission of Chaplin and before adjustment of revised profits between Laurel and Hardy.

BALANCE SHEET OF LH & CO. AS AT 31.3.2015

Liabilities	₹	*Assets*	₹
Capital Accounts:		Plant and Machinery	60,000
Laurel	2,11,500	Cash on hand	10,000
Hardy	1,51,500	Cash at bank	5,000
Sundry Creditors	2,27,000	Stock in trade	3,10,000
		Sundry Debtors	2,05,000
	5,90,000		**5,90,000**

You are required to prepare:

(i) Profit and Loss Adjustment account;
(ii) Capital accounts of the partners; and
(iii) Balance Sheet of the firm after the admission of Chaplin.

Solution

Dr. **PROFIT & LOSS ADJUSTMENT ACCOUNT** *Cr.*

Particulars	₹	*Particulars*	₹
To Expenses not provided for (years 2004-2007)	1,10,000	By Income not considered (for years 2004-2007)	66,000
		By Partners' Capital A/c (loss)	
		Laurel	22,000
		Hardy	22,000
	1,10,000		**1,10,000**

Dr. **(ii) PARTNER'S CAPITAL ACCOUNTS** *Cr.*

Particulars	Laurel ₹	Hardy ₹	Dhaplin ₹	Particular	Laurelq ₹	Hardy ₹	Chaplin ₹
To P & L Adjustment A/c	22,000	22,000	—	By Balance b/d	2,11,500	1,51,500	—
To Hardy	60,000			By Laurel	—	60,000	—
To Balance c/d	1,29,500	1,89,500	63,800	By Cash	—	—	63,800
	2,11,500	2,11,500	63,800		2,11,500	2,11,500	63,800

(iii) BALANCE SHEET AS AT 1.4.2015 (AFTER ADMISSION OF CHAPLIN)

Liabilities	₹	*Assets*	₹
Capital Accounts:		Plant and machinery	60,000
Laurel	1,29,500	Sundry debtors	2,05,000
Hardy	1,89,500	Stock in trade	3,10,000
Chaplin	63,800	Accrued income	66,000
Sundry Creditors	2,27,000	Cash on hand (10,000 + 63,800)	73,800
Outstanding Expenses	1,10,000	Cash at bank	5,000
	7,19,800		7,19,800

Working Notes:

(i) Computation of Profit and Loss distributed among partners

Total Profit = ₹ 1,40,000 + ₹ 2,60,000, ₹ 3,20,000 + ₹ 3,60,000
= ₹ 10,80,000

	Laurel ₹	*Hardy* ₹	*Total* ₹
Profit shared in old ratio i.e. 5:4	6,00,000	4,80,000	10,80,000
Profit to be shared as per new ratio i.e. 1:1	5,40,000	5,40,000	10,80,000
Excess share	60,000		
Deficit share		(60,000)	

Laurel to be debited by ₹ 60,000 and Hardy to be credited by ₹ 60,000.

(ii) Capital brought in by Chaplin

Capital to be brought in by Chaplin must be equal to 20% of the combine capital of Laurel and Hardy

	₹
Capital of Laurel (2,11,500 – 22,000 – 60,000)	1,29,500
Capital of Hardy (1,1,500 – 22,000 + 60,000)	1,89,500
Combined Capital	3,19,000
20% of the combined capital brought in by Chaplin (20% of ₹ 3,19,000)	63,800

PROBLEM 11

P, Q, R are three doctors who are running a Polyclinic. Their capital on 31st March, 2014 was ₹ 1,00,000 each. They agreed to admit X, Y and Z as partners w.e.f. 1st April 2014. The terms for sharing profits & losses were as follows:

(a) 70% of the visiting fee is to go to the specialist concerned.
(b) 50% of the chamber fee will be payable to the individual specialist.
(c) 40% of operation fee and fee for pathological reports, X-rays and ECG will accrue in favour of the doctor concerned.
(d) Balance of profit or loss is shared equally.
(e) All the partners are entitled for 6% interest on capital employed.

They further agreed that:

(i) X, Y and I brought in ₹ 20,000 each as goodwill. Goodwill is shared by the existing partners equally.
(ii) X, Y and Z brought in ₹ 50,000 each as capital. Each of the original partners also contributed ₹ 50,000 by way of capital.

THE RECEIPTS FOR THE YEAR AFTER ADMISSION OF NEW PARTNERS WERE:

Name of doctors	*Particulars*	*Visiting Fees* ₹	*Chambers Fees* ₹	*Fees for reports, operation etc.* ₹
P	General Physician	1,50,000	2,00,000	—
Q	Gynecologist	25,000	1,75,000	1,00,000
R	Cardiologist		1,00,000	75,000
X	Child Specialist	1,00,000	1,50,000	—
Y	Pathologist			1,00,000
I	Radiologist		40,000	2,00,000
	Total	**2,75,000**	**6,65,000**	**4,75,000**

EXPENSES FOR THE YEAR WERE AS FOLLOWS:

Particulars	(₹)
Medicines, injections and other consumables	1,00,000
Printing and stationery	5,000
Telephone expenses	5,000
Rent	42,000
Power and light	10,000
Nurses salary	20,000
Attendants wages	20,000
Total	**2,02,000**
Depreciation:	15,000
X-Ray machines	5,000
ECG equipments	5,000
Furniture	5,000
Surgical Equipments	5,000
Total	**30,000**

You are requested to:

(i) Pass necessary journal entries on admission of partners.
(ii) Prepare the Profit and Loss Account of the polyclinic for the year ended 31st March, 2015.
(iii) Prepare capital accounts of all the partners at the end of the financial year 2014-2015. Also show the distribution of profit among partners.

Solution

(i) JOURNAL ENTRIES (ON ADMISSION OF PARTNERS)

Date	*Particulars*		*Dr.* (₹)	*Cr.* (₹)
01.04.12	X's Capital A/c	Dr.	20,000	
	Y's Capital A/c	Dr.	20,000	
	Z's Capital A/c	Dr.	20,000	

To P's Capital A/c		20,000
To Q's Capital A/c		20,000
To R's Capital A/c		20,000
(Being goodwill adjusted through capital accounts)		
Bank A/c Dr.	2,10,000	
To X's capital A/c (20,000 + 50,000)		70,000
To Y's capital A/c (20,000 + 50,000)		70,000
To Z's capital A/c (20,000 + 50,000)		70,000
(Being goodwill and capital brought in by new partners)		
Bank A/c Dr.	1,50,00	
To P's capital A/c		50,000
To Q's capital A/c		50,000
To R's capital A/c		50,000
(Being capital brought in by existing partners)		

(ii) PROFIT & LOSS A/C FOR THE YEAR ENDED 31ST MARCH, 2015

Particulars		₹	*Particulars*	₹
To Medicines, injections and other consumables		1,00,000	By Visiting fee	2,75,000
To Printing and stationery		5,000	By Chamber fee	6,65,000
To Telephone expenses		5,000	By Fee for report, operation etc.	4,75,000
To Rent		42,000		
To Power and light		10,000		
To Nurses salary		20,000		
To Attendants wages		20,000		
To Depreciation				
X-ray machine	15,000			
ECG equipment	5,000			
Furniture	5,000			
Surgical equipment	5,000	30,000		
To Interest on capital		39,600		
To Net Profit		11,43,400		
		14,15,000		**14,15,000**

(ii) PARTNERS' CAPITAL ACCOUNT FOR THE YEAR ENDED 31ST MARCH, 2015

Debit side

Particulars	*P* ₹	*Q* ₹	*R* ₹	*X* ₹	*Y* ₹	*Z* ₹
To P, Q, & R A/cs (Goodwill)	–	–	–	20,000	20,000	20,000
To Balance c/d	4,56,600	3,96,600	3,31,600	2,69,400	1,64,400	2,24.400
	4,56,600	**3,96,600**	**3,31,600**	**2,89,400**	**1,84,400**	**2,44,400**

Credit side

Particulars	P ₹	Q ₹	R ₹	X ₹	Y ₹	Z ₹
By Balance b/d	1,00,000	1,00,000	1,00,000	–	–	–
By X, Y & Z /cs (Goodwill)	20,000	20,000	20,000	–	–	–
By Bank A/c	50,000	50,000	50,000	70,000	70,000	70,000
By Interest on Capital	10,200	10,200	10,200	3,000	3,000	3,000
By Fee (share)	2,05,000	1,45,000	80,000	1,45,000	40,000	1,00,000
By Profit (share)	71,400	71,400	71,400	71,400	71,400	71,400
	4,56,600	**3,96,600**	**3,31,600**	**2,89,400**	**1,84,400**	**2,44,400**

Working Notes:

(i) STATEMENT SHOWING DISTRIBUTION OF FEE AMONG PARTNERS

Partner Name	*Visiting Fees (70%) ₹*	*Chambers Fees (50%) ₹*	*Operations Fees (40%) ₹*	*Total ₹*
P	1,05,000	1,00,000	—	2,05,000
Q	17,500	87,500	40,000	1,45,000
R	—	50,000	30,000	80,000
X	70,000	75,000	—	1,45,000
Y	—	—	40,000	40,000
Z	—	20,000	80,000	1,00,000
	1,92,500	**3,32,500**	**1,90,000**	**7,15,000**

(ii) STATEMENT SHOWING DISTRIBUTION OF FEE AMONG PARTNERS

	₹
Profits as per profit and loss account	11,43,400
Less: Fee payable to partners	7,15,000
Profit to be divided equally among partners	**4,28,400**
Share of each partner in remaining profit = 4,28,400/6 = 71,400.	

(iii) INTEREST ON CAPITAL EMPLOYED

Particulars	*P* ₹	*Q* ₹	*R* ₹	*X* ₹	*Y* ₹	*Z* ₹
Opening balance	1,00,000	1,00,000	1,00,000	—	—	—
Add: Goodwill	20,000	20,000	20,000	—	—	—
Add: Capital brought in cash	50,000	50,000	50,000	50,000	50,000	50,000
	1,70,000	1,70,000	1,70,000	50,000	50,000	50,000
Interest @ 6%	10,200	10,200	10,200	3,000	3,000	3,000

Total Interest = ₹ 39,600.

(*iv*) It is assumed that amount of premium for goodwill brought in by new partners X, Y and Z has not been withdrawn by old partners P, Q and R and it is still kept in the business.

PROBLEM 11

The Balance Sheet of Amit, Bhushan and Charan, who share profits and losses as 3 : 2 : 1 respectively, as on 01.04.2015 is as follows:

Liabilities	*Amount (₹)*	*Assets*		*Amount (₹)*
Capital Accounts: Amit	1,80,000	Machinery		1,50,000
Bhushan	1,60,000	Furniture		1,50,000
Charan	1,40,000	Debtors	80,000	
Current Accounts: Bhushan	16,000	*Less:* Provision	4,000	76,000
Creditors	1,20,000	Stock		2,10,000
		Cash		20,000
		Current Account: charan		10,000
	6,16,000			6,16,000

Dev is admitted as a partner on the above date for 1/5th share in the profit and loss. Following are agreed upon:

(1) The profit and loss sharing ratio among the old partners will be equal.

(2) Dev brings in ₹ 1,50,000 as capital but is unable to bring the required amount of premium for goodwill.

(3) The goodwill of the firm is valued at ₹ 60,000.

(4) Assets and liabilities are to be valued as follows:

Machinery ₹ 2,06,000 : Furniture ₹ 1,28,000 : Provision for doubtful debts @ 10% on debtors.

(5) Necessary adjustments regarding goodwill and Profit/loss on revaluation are to made through the Partner's Current Accounts.

(6) It is decided that the revalued figures of assets and liabilities will not appear in the Balance Sheet of the new firm.

(7) Capital Accounts of the oild partners in the new firm should be proportionate to the new profit and loss sharing ratio, taking Dev's Capital as base. The existing partners will not bring cash for further capital. The necessary adjustments are to be made through the partner's Current Account.

Prepare Partner's Capital & Current Account, and the Balance Sheet of the new firm after admission.

Solution

Dr. **PARNTER'S CAPITAL ACCOUNTS** Cr.

Particular	*Amit*	*Bhushan*	*Charan*	*Dev*	*Particulars*	*Amit*	*Bhushan*	*Charan*	*Dev*
To Balance c/d	2,00,000	2,00,000	2,00,000	1,50,000	By Balance b/d	1,80,000	1,60,000	1,40,000	
					By Bank A/c	–	–	–	1,50,000
					By Partner'ps Current A/cs (bal. fig)	**20,000**	**40,000**	**60,000**	–
	2,00,000	2,00,000	2,00,000	1,50,000		2,00,000	2,00,000	2,00,000	1,50,000

Dr. **PARNTER'S CAPITAL ACCOUNTS** Cr.

Particular	Amit	Bhushan	Charan	Dev	Particulars	Amit	Bhushan	Charan	Dev
To Balance b/d	–	–	10,000	–	By Balance b/d	–	16,000	–	–
To Amit & Bhushan (Profit)			3,000	6,000	By Dev & Charan	7,000	2,000		–
To Amit and Bhushan (Goodwill adjustment)	–	–	6,000	12,000	By Dev and Charan (Goodwill adjustment)	14,000	4,000	–	
To Partners Capital A/cs	20,000	40,000	60,000	–	By Balance c/d	–	18,000	79,000	18,000
To Balance c/d	1,000	–	–						
	21,000	40,000	79,000	18,000		21,000	40,000	79,000	18,000

BALANCE SHEET OF NEW FIRM AFTER DEV'S ADMISSION

Liabilities	₹	*Assets*		₹
Amit	2,00,000	Machinery		1,50,000
Bhushan	2,00,000	Furniture		1,50,000
Charan	2,00,000	Stock		2,10,000
Dev	1,50,000	Debtors	80,000	
Current Account: Amit	1,000	*Less:* Provision	4,000	76,000
Creditors	1,20,000	Cash		1,70,000
		Current Accounts:		
		Bhushan	18,000	
		Charan	79,000	
		Dev	18,000	1,15,000
	8,71,000			8,71,000

Working Notes:

1. Dev. joins the business for 1/5th share and brings ₹ 1,50,000 as capital. Thus, total capital of new firm will be ₹ 7,50,000 (1,50,000 × 5). Total capital of Amit, Bhushan 7 Charan will be ₹ 6,00,000 (7,50,000 – 1,50,000) which will be shared by them equally i.e. 2,00,000 each.

2. **New Profit Sharing Ratio**

Amit	*Bhushan*	*Charan*	*Dev*
4/5 × 1/3	4/5 × 1/3	4/5 × 1/3	1/5
4/15	4/15	4/15	3/15

NR = 4:4:4:3

3. **Adjustment of Goodwill**

Sacrifice/Gain of Partners

Amit	*Bhushan*	*Charan*	*Dev*
4/15 – 3/6 = 21/90 (Sacrifice)	4/15 – 2/6 = 6/90 (Sacrifice)	4/15 – 1/6 = 9/90 (gain)	1/5 (Gain)

JOURNAL ENTRY TO ADJUST GOODWILL

Charan [₹ 60,000 × 9/90]	Dr.	₹ 6,000	
Dev [₹ 60,000 × 1/5]	Dr.	₹ 12,000	
To Amit [₹ 60,000 × 21/90]			₹ 14,000
To Bhushan [₹ 60,000 × 6/90]			₹ 4,000

4. **Net Effect of Revaluation of Assets and liabilities**

Increase in value of Machinery			₹ 56,000
Decrease in value of Furniture			(₹ 22,000)
Increase in Provision for Doubtful Debts			(₹ 4,000)
Journal Entry to Adjust Profit on Revolution			₹ 30,000
Charan [₹ 30,000 × 9/90]	Dr.	₹ 3,000	
Dev [₹ 30,000 × 1/5]	Dr.	₹ 6,000	
T Amit [30,000 × 21/90]			₹ 7,000
To Bhusan [30,000 × 6/90]			₹ 2,000

19 RECONSTITUION OF PARTNERSHIP—RETIREMENT/DEATH OF A PARTNER

SHORT ANSWER PRACTICAL PROBLEMS

PROBLEM 1

X, Y and Z are partners sharing profits an losses in the ratio of 4:3:2 respectively. On 31st March Y retires and X and Z decide to share profits and losses in the ratio of 5:3. Then immediately, W is admitted for 3/10th shares in profits, 2/3rd of which was given by X and rest was taken by W from Z. Goodwill of the firm is valued at ₹ 2,16,000 W brings required amount of goodwill.

Pass Journal Entries to adjust goodwill on retirement of Y and admission of W.

Solution

JOURNAL ENTRIES

Date	*Particulars*		*L.F.*	*Dr. (₹)*	*Cr. (₹)*
31st Mar	X's Capital A/c	Dr.		39,000	
	Z's Capital A/c	Dr.		33,000	
	To Y's Capital A/c (3/9 × ₹ 2,16,000)				72,000
	(Being Y's share of goodwill adjusted in the capital accounts of gaining partners in their gaining ratio 13:11)				
	Cash A/c	Dr.		64,800	
	To W's Capital A/c (3/10 × ₹ 2,16,000)				64,800
	(Being the amount of goodwill brought in by W)				
	W's Capital A/c	Dr.		64,800	
	To X's Capital A/c				43,200
	To Z's Capital A/c				21,600
	(Being the goodwill credited to sacrificing partners in their sacrificing ratio 2:1)				

Working Note: **Calculation of Gaining Ratio of X and Z**

Gaining Ratio = New Ratio – Old Ratio

X = 5/8 – 4/9 = 13/72, Z = 3/8 – 2/9 = 11/72

Hence, Gaining Ratio = 13:11

PROBLEM 2

X, Y and Z are Partners, sharing profits and losses equally. On 1st December 2014, Z retired from the Partnership Firm. The Capitals of the Partners, after all necessary adjustments stood at ₹ 45,000, ₹ 75,000 and ₹ 50,000 respectively. X and Y continued to carry on the business without settling the accounts of Z. Final Payment to Z made on 1st March 2015. The Partnership Firm made profit amounting to ₹ 30,000 during the period from 1st December 2014 to 29th February 2015.

What are the rights of Z to share subsequent profit as per the provisions of Sec.37 of the Indian Partnership Act?

Solution

Capital Ratio of X, Y, Z = 45 : 75 : 50, i.e. 9 : 15: 10

(i) Profit 30,000 × 10/34 = ₹ 8,824, *or*

(ii) Interest at 6% p.a. = 50,000 x 6% × 3/12 = ₹ 750

whichever is **beneficial.** Hence Z eligible to opt for Share in the Profit = **₹ 8,824.**

LONG ANSWER PRACTICAL PROBLEMS

RETIREMENT OF A PARTNER

PROBLEM 3

Atul, Balbir and Chatur were carrying on a business in partnership sharing profits in the ratio of 5 : 3: 2 respectively. On 31st March, 2015 their Balance Sheet stood as follows:

Liabilities	₹	*Assets*		₹
Atul's Capital	6,25,000	Goodwill		80,000
Balbir's Capital	3,75,000	Land & Buildings		7,00,000
Chatur's Capital	2,50,000	Furniture		1,65,000
General Reserve	1,00,000	Stock		2,86,000
Trade Creditors	2,10,000	Trade Debtors	1,80,000	
		Less: Provision	3,600	1,76,400
		Cash at Bank		1,52,600
	15,60,000			15,60,000

Atul retired on the above mentioned date and partners agreed that:

(i) The current value of goodwill be taken to be equal to the book value of the asset.

(ii) Land and Buildings be considered worth ₹ 9,00,000.

(iii) The provision for bad debts on trade debtors be raised to 5%.

(iv) Provision be made for compensation of ₹ 5,000 to an ex-employee.

(v) Half of the amount due to Atul be paid immediately in cash and tghe balance be treated as 10% loan, repayable within 3 years.

In order to facilitate cash payment to Atul, Balbir and Chatur brought in ₹ 3,00,000 in the ratio of 3 : 2 respectively.

Prepare Revaluation Account, the Capital of all tghe partners and Bank Account. Also draw the initial Balance Sheet of Balbir and Chatur, immediately after Atul's retirement.

Solution

Dr. **REVALUATION ACCOUNT** *Cr.*

Particulars	₹	*Particulars*	₹
To Provision for Doubtful Debts	5,400	By Building	2,00,000
To Provision for compensation	5,000		
To Profit on Revaluation t/f to:			
Atul	94,800		
Balbir	56,880		
Chatur	37,920		
	2,00,000		2,00,000

Dr. **PARTNERS' CAPITAL ACCOUNTS** *Cr.*

Particulars	*Atul* ₹	*Balbir* ₹	*Chatur* ₹	*Particulars*	*Atul* ₹	*Balbir* ₹	*Chatur* ₹
To Goodwill A/c	40,000	24,000	16,000	By Balance b/d	6,25,000	3,75,000	2,50,000
To Cash A/c	3,84,900			By General Reserve	50,000	30,000	20,000
To 10% Loan	3,84,900			By Revaluation A/c	94,800	56,880	37,920
To Atul Capital A/c	—	24,000	16,000	By Balbir & Chatur's A/c	40,000		
To Balance c/d		5,93,880	3,95,920	By Cash A/c		1,80,000	1,20,000
	8,09,800	6,41,880	4,27,920		8,09,800	6,41,880	4,27,920

BANK ACCOUNT

Particulars	₹	*Particulars*	₹
To Balance b/s	1,52,600	By Atul's Capital A/c	3,84,900
To Balbir's capital A/c	1,80,000	By Balance c/d	67,700
To Chatur's capital A/c	1,20,000		
	4,52,000		4,52,600

BALANCE SHEET OF as at 31.03.2015 (Atul's retirement)

Liabilities	₹	*Assets*		₹
Balbir's Capital	5,93,880	Land and Building		9,00,000
Chatur's Capital	3,95,920	Furniture		1,65,000
10% Loan from Atul	3,84,900	Stock		2,86,000
Trade Creditors	2,10,000	Trade Debtors	1,80,000	
Provision for Compensation	5,000	*Less:* Provision	9,000	1,71,000
		Cash at Bank		67,700
	15,89,700			15,89,700

DEATH OF A PARTNER

PROBLEM 4

The Balance Sheet of Amitabh, Abhishek and Amrish as at 31.12.2014 stood as follows: X

Liabilities	₹	*Assets*		₹
Capitals:		Land & Buildings		74,000
Amitabh	60,000	Investments		10,000
Abhishek	40,000	Goodwill		37,800
Amrish	40,000	Life Policy (at surrender value):		
Creditors	25,800	Amitabh		2,500
General Reserve	8,000	Abhishek		2,500
Investment Fluctuation Reserve	2,400	Amrish		1,000
		Stock		20,000
		Debtors	20,000	
		Less: Provision	1,600	18,400
		Cash & bank balance		10,000
	1,76,200			1,76,200

Amrish died on 31 March, 2015, due to this reason the following adjustments were agreed upon:

(i) Land and Buildings be appreciated by 50%.
(ii) Investment be valued at 6% less than the cost.
(iii) All debtors (except 20% which are considered as doubtful) were good.
(iv) Stock to be reduced to 94%.
(v) Goodwill to be valued at 1 year's purchase of the average profits of the past five years.
(vi) Amrish's share of profit to the date of death be calculated on the basis of average profits of the three completed years immediately preceeding the year of death.

The profits of the last five years are as follows:

Year	₹
2010	23,000
2011	28,000
2012	18,000
2013	16,000
2014	20,000

The life policies have been shown at their surrender values representing 10% of the sum assured in each case. The annual premium of ₹.1,000 is payable every year on 1st August.

Give the necessary Journal Entries in the books of account and prepare the Balance Sheet of the reconstituted firm.

Solution

JOURNAL

Date	*Particulars*		*Dr. (₹)*	*Cr. (₹)*
1.	Insurance Company's A/c	Dr.	10,000	
	To Life Policy A/c			10,000
	(Being the policy on the life of Amrish matured on his death)			
2.	Life Policy A/c	Dr.	9,000	
	To Amitabh's Capital A/c			3,000
	To Abhishek's Capital A/c			3,000
	To Amrish's Capital A/c			3,000
	(Being the transfer of balance in life policy account to all partners' capital accounts)			
3.	Amitabh's Capital A/c	Dr.	12,600	
	Abhishek's Capital A/c	Dr.	12,600	
	Amrish's Capital A/c	Dr.	12,600	
	To Goodwill A/c			37,800
	(Being goodwill standing in the books written off fully)			
4.	Land & Buildings A/c	Dr.	37,000	
	To Revaluation A/c			37,000
	(Being an increase in the value of assets recorded)			
5.	Investment Fluctuation Reserve A/c	Dr.	600	
	To Investment A/c			600
	(Being reduction in the cost of investment adjusted through Investment Fluctuation Reserve)			

6.	Revaluation A/c	Dr.	3,600	
	To Stock A/c			1,200
	To Provision for Doubtful Debts A/c			2,400
	(Being the fall in value of assets recorded)			
7.	Amitabh's Capital A/c	Dr.	3,500	
	Abhishek's Capital A/c	Dr.	3,500	
	To Amrish's Capital A/c			7,000
	(Being the share of Amrish's revalued goodwill adjusted through capital accounts of the remaining partners)			
8.	Profit & Loss Suspense Account	Dr.	1,500	
	To Amrish's Capital A/c			1,500
	(Being Amrish's Share of profit to date of death credited to his account)			
9.	Revaluation A/c	Dr.	33,400	
	To Amitabh's Capital A/c			11,133
	To Abhishek's Capital A/c			11,133
	To Amrish's Capital A/c			11,134
	(Being the transfer of profit on revaluation)			
10.	General Reserve A/c	Dr.	8,000	
	Investment Fluctuation Reserve A/c (₹ 2,400 - ₹ 600)	Dr.	1,800	
	To Amitabh's Capital A/c			3,267
	To Abhishek's Capital A/c			3,267
	To Amrish's Capital A/c			3,266
	(Being the transfer of accumulated profits to capital accounts)			
11.	Amrish's Capital A/c	Dr.	53,300	
	To Amrish's Executor's A/c			53,300
	(Being the transfer of Amrish's Capital A/c to his Executor's A/c)			

BALANCE SHEET AS AT 31ST MARCH, 2015

Liabilities	₹	*Assets*		₹
Amithabh's Capital Account	61,300	Land & Building		1,11,000
Abhishek's Capital Account	41,300	Life Policy: Amitabh	2,500	
Amrish's Executor's Account	53,300	Abhishek	2,500	5,000
Sundry Creditors	25,800	Investments		9,400
		Stock		18,800
		Debtors	20,000	
		Less: Provisions	4,000	16,000
		Insurance Company		10,000
		Cash & Bank Balance		10,000
		Profit and loss Suspense A/c		1,500
	1,81,700			1,81,700

Working Notes:

(*i*) *Calculation of Amrish's Share of Profit*

Average Profit (₹ 18,000+16,000+20,000) = ₹.18,000

Profit for 3 months = 18,000 x 3/12 = 4,500

Amrish's share of Profit = 4,500 x 1/3 = 1,500

(*ii*) *Calculation of Goodwill*

Total profits for last five years = Rs1,05,000

Average Profit = 1,05,000/5 = ₹ 21,000

Goodwill at one year's purchase = ₹ 21,000 x 1 =₹ 21,000

PROBLEM 5

Ramu, Shamu and Raju were partners sharing profits and tosses in the ratio of 3 : 2 : 2. Their Balance Sheet as on 01-01-2015 was as follows:

Liabilities	₹	*Assets*	₹
Capital Accounts:		Fixed assets	80,000
Ramu	30,000	Stock	15,000
Shamu	20,000	Debtors	12,000
Raju	20,000	Cash & bank	1,951
Reserves	14,000		
Creditors	24,951		
	1,08,951		**1,08,951**

On 1st October, 2015, Ramu died. His heirs agreed that:

(i) Goodwill of the firm be valued at 2 years' purchase of average profit of past three years. Profits for the year 2012, 2013 and 2014 were ₹ 30,000, ₹ 40,000 and ₹ 47,600 respectively.

(ii) Fixed assets be revalued at ₹ 1,01,000

(iii) Profit to be shared, earned in subsequent period after death of Ramu till settlement of his executors' claim.

Ramu's heirs account was settled on 31-12-2015 by bringing in required cash by remaining partners in equal proportion leaving cash balance of ₹ 1,234. Each partner had drawn @ ₹ 1,000 per month for personal use.

Profit for the current year after charging depreciation of ₹ 9,000 (₹ 6,000 for first three quarters and ₹ 3,000 for last quarter) was ₹ 46,600 earned evenly through-out the year.

You are requested to prepare Profit & Loss Appropriation A/c, Cash & Bank A/c, Ramu's's Executor's A/c and Partners' Capital Accounts for the year ended on 31-12-2015 assuming remaining partners' decided not to retain goodwill in the books.

Solution

Dr. **(i) PROFIT & LOSS ACCOUNT** *Cr.*

Particulars	₹(for 9 months)	₹ (for 3 months)	*Particulars*	₹ (for 9 months)	₹,(for 3 months)
To Depreciation A/c	6,000	3,000	By Profit	041,700	13,900
To Net Profit	35,700	10,900			
	41,700	**13,900**		**41,700**	**13,900**

Dr. **PROFIT & LOSS APPROPRIATION ACCOUNT** *Cr.*

Particulars	₹(for 9 months)	₹ (for 3 3 months)	*Particulars*	₹ (for 9 months)	₹,(for 3 months)
To Partners' capital A/cs			By Net Profit	35,700	10,900
Ramu	15,300				
Shamu	10,200	3,043			
Raju	10,200	3,044			

To Ramu's Elxecutor A/c		4,813			
	35,700	10,900		35,700	10,900

Dr. **(ii) PARTNER'S CAPITAL ACCOUNTS AS ON 1ST OCTOBER, 2015** Cr.

Particulars	*Ramu* ₹	*Shamu* ₹	*Raju* ₹	*Particulars*	*Ramu* ₹	*Shamu* ₹	*Raju* ₹
To Drawings	9,000	9,000	9,000	By Balance b/d	30,000	20,000	20,000
To Ramu's Executors A/c	87,414	–	–	By Reserves	6,000	4,000	4,000
To Balance c/d	–	55,276	55,276	By Goodwill*	36,114	24,076	24,076
				By Fixed Assets**	9,000	6,000	6,000
				By Profit & Loss Appropriation A/c	15,300	10,200	10,200
	96,414	64,276	64,276		96,414	64,276	64,276

Dr. **(iii) PARTNERS' CAPITAL ACCOUNTS AS ON 31.12.2015** Cr.

Particulars	*Shamu* ₹	*Raju* ₹	*Particulars*	*Shamu* ₹	*Raju* ₹
To Drawings	3,000	3,000	By Balance b/d	55,276	55,276
To Goodwill	42,133	42,133	By Cash A/c	62,255	62,255
To Balance c/d	5,441	75.442	By Profit & Loss Appropriation A/c	3,043	3,044
	1,20,574	1,20,575		1,20,574	1,20.575

Dr. **RAMU'S EXECUTORS' A/C AQS ON 31.12.2015** Cr.

Particulars	₹	*Particulars*	₹
To BankA/c	92,227	By Balance b/d	87,414
		By P & L Appropriation A/c	4,813
	92,227		92,227

Dr. **CASH & BANK ACCOUNT** Cr.

Particulars	₹	*Particulars*	₹
To Balance b/d	1,951	By Ramu's executors A/c	92,227
To Shamu's capital A/c	62,255	By Partners' Capital A/cs	
To Raju's capital A/c	62,255	*(Drawings):*	
		Ramu	9,000
		Shamu	12,000
		Raju	12,000
		By Balance c/d	1,234
	1,26,461		1,26,461

(iv) As per para 36 of AS 10, 'Accounting for fixed Assets, 'goodwill should be recorded in the books only when some consideration in money or money's worth has been paid for it. However,in the above solution, goodwill has been raised in the books at the time of death of a partner and written off by the remaining partners, as per the information given in the question.

(v) Appreciation of fixed assets may also be recorded through "Revaluation Account".

Working Notes:

(i) **Profit for the year before depreciation = ₹ 46,600 + ₹ 9,000 = ₹ 55,600**

(ii) **As per section 37 of Partnership Act, in case of settlement of deceased partner's account on the date other then the date of death, the executor of deceased partner has a choice to take**

Either-

(A) Profit earned on un-settled capital = $\text{Profix} \times \dfrac{\text{Unsettled capital as on1st Oct.}}{\text{Total capital as on 1st Oct.}}$

$$= 10{,}900 \times \frac{87{,}414}{(87{,}414 + 55{,}276 + 55{,}276)}$$

$$= 10{,}900 \times \frac{87{,}414}{1{,}97{,}966} = \text{Rs. } 4{,}813$$

Or

(B) Interest on capital @ 6% i.e. 87,414 × 6% × 3/12 = 1,311

Option A is beneficial, therefore heirs of Ramu will opt for proportionate share of profit i.e. 4,813.

(iii) **Valuation of Goodwill:**

	₹	*Weight*	*Product*
Profit for 2012	30,000	1	30,000
2013	40,000	2	80,000
2014	47,600	3	1,42,800
	1,17,600	6	**2.52.800**

Weighted Average Profit = $\dfrac{2{,}52{,}000}{6}$ = Rs. 42, 133

Goodwill = 2 year's purchase of average profit = ₹ 42,133 × 2 = ₹ 84,266.

PROBLEM 6

A, *B* and *C* were partners of a firm sharing profits and losses in the ratio of 3 : 4 : 3. The Balance sheet of the firm, as at 31st March, 2014 was as under:

Liabilities	₹	*Assets*	₹
Capital Accounts:		Fixed Assets	1,00,000
A	48,000	*Current Assets*	
B	64,000	Stock	30,000
C	48,000	Debtors	60,000
Reserve	20,000	Cash and Bank	30,000
Creditors	40,000		
	2,20,000		2,20,000

The firm had taken a Joint Life Policy for ₹ 1,00,000; the premium periodically paid was charged to Profit and Loss Account. Partner *C* died on 30th September, 2014. It was agreed between the surviving partners and the legal representatives of *C* that:

(i) Goodwill of the firm will be taken at ₹ 60,000.

(ii) Fixed Assets will be written down by ₹ 20,000.

(iii) In lieu of profits, *C* should be paid at the rate of 25% per annum on his capital as on 31st March, 1998.

Policy money was received and the legal hairs were paid off. The profits for the year ended 31st March, 2015, after charging depreciation of ₹ 10,000 (Depreciation upto 30th September was agreed to be ₹ 6,000) were ₹ 48,000. Partner's Drawings Accounts showed balances as under:

A ₹ 18,000 (drawn evenly over the year)
B ₹ 24,000 (drawn evenly over the year)
C (up-to-date of death) ₹ 20,000

On the basis of the above figures, please indicate the entitlement of the legal heirs of *C*, assuming that they had not been paid anything other then the share in the Joint Life Policy.

Solution

COMPUTATION OF ENTITLEMENT OF LEGAL HEIRS OF C
(i) PROFITS FOR THE 1ST AND 2ND HALF YEAR

Particulars	₹
Profits for the year ended 31st March, 1999 (after depreciation)	48,000
Add: Depreciation	10,000
Profit before depreciation	58,000
Profits for the first half (assumed: evenly spread)	29,000
Less: Depreciation for the first half	6,000
Profit for the first half year (after depreciation)	23,000
Profits for the second half (i.e., 1st October, 1998 to 31st March, 1999)	29,000
Less: Depreciation for the second half	4,000
Profits for the second half year (after depreciation)	25,000

Dr. **(ii) CAPITAL ACCOUNTS OF PARTNERS AS ON 30TH SEPTEMBER, 2014** *Cr.*

Particulars	*A* ₹	*B* ₹	*C* ₹	*Particulars*	*A* ₹	*B* ₹	*C* ₹
To Fixed Assets (loss on revaluation)	6,000	8,000	6,000	By Balance b/d	48,000	64,000	48,000
To Drawings	9,000	12,000	20,000	By Reserve	6,000	8,000	6,000
To C Executor's A/c	—	—	52,000	By Goodwill	18,000	24,000	18,000
To Balance c/d	57,000	76,000	—	By P & L Appropriation A/c (Interest on ₹ 48,000 @ 25% for 6 months)	—	—	6,000
	72,000	96,000	78,000		72,000	96,000	78,000

(iii) Application of Section 37 of the Partnership Act

Legal heirs of C have not been paid anything other than the share in joint life policy. The amount due to the deceased partner carries interest at the mutually agreed upon rate. In the absence of any agreement, the representatives of the deceased partner can receive at their option interest at the rate of 6% per annum or the share of profit earned for the amount due to the deceased partner.

Thus, the representatives of C can opt for

Either,

(i) Interest on ₹ 52,000 for 6 months @ 6% p.a. = ₹ 1,560 or

(ii) Profit earned out of unsettled capital (in the second half year ended 31st March, 2015)

$$₹\ 25{,}000 \times \frac{52{,}000}{57{,}000)\ 76{,}000)\ 52{,}000} = \text{Rs. } 7{,}027 \text{ (approx.)}$$

In the above case, it would be rational to assume that the legal heirs would opt for ₹ 7,027.

(iv) Amount due to legal heirs of C

	₹
Balance in C's Executor's account	52,000
Amount of profit earned out of unsettled capital [calculated in (3)]	7,027
Amount due	59,027

RETIREMENT CUM ADDMISSION

PROBLEM 7

A, B and C are partners of the firm ABC & Co., sharing profits and losses in the ratio of 5:3:2. Following is the Balance Sheet of the firm as at 31.3.2015:

Liabilities	₹	*Assets*	₹
Partners' capital accounts:		Goodwill	1,00,000
A	4,50,000	Building	10,50,000
B	1,30,000	Machinery	6,50,000
C	1,70,000	Furniture	2,15,000
Investment fluctuation reserve	1,00,000	Investments (market)	
Contingency reserve	75,000	value ₹.75,000	60,000
Long-term loan	15,00,000	Stock	6,50,000
Bank overdraft	2,20,000	Sundry debtors	6,95,000
Sundry creditors	8,00,000	Advertisement suspense	25,000
	34,45,000		34,45,000

It was decided that B would retire from the partnership on 1.4.2015 and D would be admitted as a partner on the same date. Following adjustments are agreed amongst the partners for the retirement/admission:

(*i*) Goodwill is to be valued at ₹.5,00,000, but the same will not appear as an asset in the books of the firm.

(*ii*) Building and machinery are to be revalued at ₹.10,00,000 and ₹.5,20,000 respectively.

(*iii*) Investments are to be taken over by B at the market value.

(*iv*) Provision for doubtful debts is to be maintained at 20% on sundry debtors.

(*v*) The capital of the reconstituted firm will be ₹.10,00,000 to be contributed by the partners A, C and D in their new profit sharing ratio of 2 :2 : 1.

(*vi*) Surplus funds, if any will be used to pay the bank overdraft.

(*vii*) Amount due to retiring partner B will be transferred to his loan account.

Prepare:

(*i*) Revaluation Account;

(*ii*) Capital Accounts of the partners; and

(*iii*) Balance Sheet of the firm after reconstitution.

Solution

Dr. **(i) REVALUATION ACCOUNT** *Cr.*

Particulars	₹	*Particulars*		₹
To Building	50,000	By Investments		15,000
To Machinery	1,30,000	By Partners' capital A/cs		
(Loss on revaluation)				
To Provision for doubtful debts	1,39,000	*A*	1,52,000	
		B	91,200	
		C	60,800	3,04,000
	3,19,000			3,19,000

Dr. **(ii) PARTNERS' CAPITAL ACCOUNTS** Cr.

Particulars	A ₹	B ₹	C ₹	D ₹	Particulars	A ₹	B ₹	C ₹	D ₹
To Revaluation A/c	1,52,000	91,200	60,800	–	By Balance b/d	4,50,000	1,30,000	1,70,000	–
To Goodwill	50,000	30,000	20,000	–	By Contingency Reserve	37,500	22,500	15,000	–
To A and B	–	–	1,00,000	1,00,000	By Investment Fluctuation Reserve	50,000	30,000	20,000	–
To Investments	–	75,000	–	–					
To Advertisement suspense	12,500	7,500	5,000	–	By C and D	50,000	1,50,000	–	–
To *B*'s Loan A/c (Bal. fig.)	–	1,28,800	–	–	By Bank (Bal.fig.)	27,000	–	3,80,800	3,00,000
To Balance c/d	4,00,000	–	4,00,000	2,00,000					
	6,14,500	3,32,500	5,85,800	3,00,000		6,14,500	3,32,500	5,85,800	3,00,000

(iii) BALANCE SHEET AS AT 01.04.2015
(After retirement of B and admission of D)

Liabilities	₹	Assets		₹
Partners' Capital Accounts :		Building		10,00,000
A	4,00,000	Machinery		5,20,000
C	4,00,000	Furniture		2,15,000
D	2,00,000	Stock		6,50,000
Long term loan	15,00,000	Debtors	6,95,000	
B's loan	1,28,800	*Less:* Provision for		
Sundry creditors	8,00,000	doubtful debts	1,39,000	5,56,000
		Cash at bank		4,87,800
	34,28,800			34,28,800

Working Notes:

Dr. **(i) BANK ACCOUNT** Cr.

Particulars	₹	Particulars	₹
To A's capital A/c	27,000	By Balance b/d (Overdraft)	2,20,000
To C's capital A/c	3,80,800	By Balance c/d (Bal. fig.)	4,87,800
To D's capital A/c	3,00,000		
	7,07,800		7,07,800

(*ii*) Goodwill, already shown in the Balance Sheet of ₹ 1,00,000, is firstly written off and then an adjusting entry is passed for revalued goodwill of ₹ 5,00,000 in sacrificing and gaining ratio of partners. This treatment is given based on the para 36 of AS 10, which states that goodwill should be recorded in the books only when some consideration in money or money's worth has been paid for it.

(*iii*) *Calculation of sacrificing and gaining ratio*

Partners	New share	Old share	Share Sacrificed	Share Gained
A	$\frac{2}{5}$	$\frac{5}{10}$	$\frac{2}{5}-\frac{5}{10}=\frac{1}{10}$	
B		$\frac{3}{10}$		$\frac{3}{10}$

C	$\frac{2}{5}$	$\frac{2}{10}$	$\frac{2}{5} - \frac{2}{10} = \frac{1}{5}$
D	$\frac{1}{5}$		$\frac{1}{5}$

Adjusting Entry to adjust Goodwill :

C's Capital A/c (₹ 5,00,000 × 1/5)	Dr.	₹ 1,00,000	
D's Capital A/c (₹ 5,00,000 × 1/5)	Dr.	₹ 1,00,000	
To A's Capital A/c (₹ 5,00,000 × 1/10)			₹ 50,000
To B's Capital A/c (₹ 5,00,000 × 3/10)			₹ 1,50,000

(*iv*) Capitals of A, C and D as per new ratio ₹

Total Capital of the firm after admission 10,00,000

A's share = $10,00,000 \times 2/5 = 4,00,000$

C's share = $10,00,000 \times 2/5 = 4,00,000$

D's share = $10,00,000 \times 1/5 = 2,00,000$

PROBLEM 8

Ram, Rahim and Robert are partners, sharing Profits and Losses in the ratio of 5 : 3 : 2. It was decided that Robert would retire on 31.3.2015 and in his place Richard would be admitted as a partner with new profit sharing between Ram, Rahim and Richard at 3 : 2 : 1.

BALANCE SHEET OF RAM, RAHIM AND ROBERT AS AT 31.3.2015

Liabilities	₹	*Assets*	₹
Capital Accounts:		Cash in Hand	20,000
Ram	1,00,000	Cash at Bank	1,00,000
Rahim	1,50,000	Sundry Debtors	5,00,000
Robert	2,00,000	Stock in Trade	2,00,000
General Reserve	2,00,000	Plant & Machinery	3,00,000
Sundry Creditors	8,00,000	Land & Building	5,30,000
Loan from Richard	2,00,000		
	16,50,000		16,50,000

Retirement of Robert and admission of Richard is on the following terms:

(a) Plant & Machinery to be depreciated by ₹ 30,000.

(b) Land and Building to be valued at ₹ 6,00,000.

(c) Stock to be valued at 95% of book value.

(d) Provision for doubtful debts @ 10% to be provided on debtors.

(e) General Reserve to be apportioned amongst Ram, Rahim and Robert.

(f) The firm's goodwill to be valued at 2 years' purchase of the average profits of the last 3 years. The relevant figures are:
Year ended 31.3.2012 – Profit ₹ 50,000
Year ended 31.3.2013 – Profit ₹ 60,000
Year ended 31.3.2014 – Profit ₹ 55,000

(g) Out of the amount due to Robert ₹ 2,00,000 would be retained as loan by the firm and the balance will be settled immediately.

(h) Richard's capital should be equal to 50% of the combined capital of Ram and Rahim.

Required: Prepare

(i) Capital accounts of the partners; and

(ii) Balance Sheet of the reconstituted firm.

Solution

Dr. **Partners' Capital Accounts** Cr.

Particulars	Ram ₹	Rahim ₹	Robert ₹	Richard ₹	Particulars	Ram ₹	Rahim ₹	Robert ₹	Richard ₹
To Revaluation A/c	10,000	6,000	4,000	—	By Balance b/d	1,00,000	1,50,000	2,00,000	—
To Loan from Robert A/c	—	—	2,00,000	—	By General Reserve	1,00,000	60,000	40,000	—
To Bank	—	—	58,000	—	By Goodwill	55,000	33,000	22,000	—
To Balance c/d	2,45,000	2,37,000	—	—		—	—	—	—
	2,55,000	2,43,000	2,62,000	—		2,55,000	2,43,000	2,62,000	—
To Goodwill*	55,000	36,667	—	18,333	By Balance b/d	2,45,000	2,37,000	—	—
To Balance c/d	1,90,000	2,00,333	—	1,95,167	By Loan A/c-transfer	—	—	—	2,00,000
					By Bank	—	—	—	13,500
	2,45,000	2,37,000	—	2,13,500		2,45,000	2,37,000	—	2,13,500

BALANCE SHEET OF THE RECONSTITUTED FIRM (AFTER ADMISSION OF RICHARD)

Liabilities	₹	Assets	₹
Capital Accounts:		Land and Building	6,00,000
Ram	1,90,000	Plant and machinery	2,70,000
Rahim	2,00,333	Stock	1,90,000
Richard	1,95,167	Debtors	4,50,000
Sundry Creditors	8,00,000	Cash at bank	55,500
Loan from Robert	2,00,000	Cash in hand	20,000
	15,85,500		15,85,500

Working Notes:

(i) Calculation of Goodwill:

Average Profit = (₹ 50,000 + ₹ 60,000 + ₹ 55,000)/3 = ₹ 55,000

Goodwill = ₹ 55,000 × 2 years = ₹ 1,10,000.

As per para AS-26, goodwill should be recorded in the books only when some consideration in money or money's worth has been paid for it. Therefore, the goodwill raised at the time of retirement of Robert is to be written off in new raio among remaining partners including new partner—Richard.

Dr. **(ii) BANK ACCOUNT** Cr.

Particulars	₹	Particulars	₹
To Balance b/d	1,00,000	By Robert's Capital A/c	58,000
To Richard's Capital A/c	13,500	By Balance c/d	55,500
	1,13,500		1,13,500

(iii) REVALUATION ACCOUNT

Particulars	₹	Particulars	₹
To Plant and Machinery	30,000	By Land and building	70,000
To Stock	10,000	By Partners' Capital Accounts.	
To Debtors	50,000	Ram	10,000
		Rahim	6,000
		Robert	4,000
	90,000		90,000

PROBLEM 9

E, F and G were partners sharing Profits and Losses in the ratio of 5:3:2 respectively. On 31st March, 2015 Balance Sheet of the firm stood as follows:

Liabilities	₹	*Assets*	₹
Capital A/cs :		Buildings	55,000
E	50,000	Furniture	25,000
F	40,000	Stock	42,000
G	28,000	Debtors	20,000
Creditors	33,500	Cash at Bank	11,200
Outstanding Expenses	1,700		
	1,53,200		1,53,200

On 31st March, 2015, *E* decided to retire and *F* and *G* decided to continue as equal partners. Other terms of retirement were as follows:

(i) Building be appreciated by 20%. (ii) Furniture be depreciated by 10%.

(iii) A provision of 5% be created for bad debts on debtors.

(iv) Goodwill be valued at two years' purchase of profit for the latest accounting year. The firm's profit for the year ended 31st March, 2015 was ₹ 25,000. No goodwill account is to be raised in the books of accounts.

(v) Fresh capital be introduced by *F* and *G* to the extent of ₹ 10,000 and ₹ 35,000 respectively.

(vi) Out of sum payable to retiring partner *E*, a sum of ₹ 45,000 be paid immediately and the balance be transferred to his loan account bearing interest @ 12% per annum. The loan is to be paid off by 31st March, 2011.

One month after *E*'s retirement, *F* and *G* agreed to admit *E*'s son *H* as a partner with one-forth share in Profits/Losses. *E* agreed that the balance in his loan account be converted into *H*'s Capital. *E* also agreed to forgo one month's interest on his loan.

It was also agreed that *H* will bring in, his share of goodwill through book adjustment, valued at the price on the date of *E*'s retirement. No goodwill account is to be raised in the books.

You are requested to pass necessary Journal Entries to give effect to the above transactions and prepare Partner's Capital Accounts.

Solution

JOURNAL

Date.	*Particulars*		*Dr. (₹)*	*Cr. (₹)*
1.	Building A/c	Dr.	11,000	
	To Revaluation A/c			11,000
	(Being building appreciated)			
2.	Revaluation A/c	Dr.	3,500	
	To Furniture A/c			2,500
	To Provision for Doubtful Debts A/c			1,000
	(Being furniture depreciated by 10% and Provision for doubtful debts created @ 5% on Debtors)			
3.	Revaluation A/c	Dr.	7,500	
	To E's Capital A/c			3,750
	To F's Capital A/c			2,250
	To G's Capital A/c			1,500
	(Being profit on revaluation transferred to capital accounts of partners)			

	Particulars		Dr.	Cr.
4.	F's Capital A/c	Dr.	10,000	
	G's Capital A/c	Dr.	15,000	
	To E's Capital A/c			25,000
	(Being adjustment for E's share of goodwill)			
5.	Bank A/c	Dr.	45,000	
	To F's Capital A/c			10,000
	To G's Capital A/c			35,000
	(Being fresh capital introduced by F and G)			
6.	E's Capital A/c	Dr.	78,750	
	To Bank A/c			45,000
	To E's Loan A/c			33,750
	(Being settlement of E's capital on his retirement)			
7.	E's Loan A/c	Dr.	33,750	
	To H's Capital A/c			33,750
	(Transfer of E's Loan Account to H's Capital Account)			
8.	H's Capital A/c	Dr.	12,500	
	To F's Capital A/c			6,250
	To G's Capital A/c			6,250
	(Being adjustment entry passed for H's share of goodwill)			

Dr. **PARTNER'S CAPITAL ACCOUNTS** Cr.

Particulars	E ₹	F ₹	G ₹	H ₹	Particulars	E ₹	F ₹	G ₹	H ₹
To E (Goodwill)	—	10,000	15,000	—	By Balance b/d	50,000	40,000	28,000	—
To Bank	45,000	—	—	—	By Revaluation A/c	3,750	2,250	1,500	—
To E's Loan A/c	33,750	—	—	—	By F (Goodwill)	10,000	—	—	—
To Balance c/d	—	42,250	49,500	—	By G (Goodwill)	15,000	—	—	
					By Bank (fresh capital)	—	10,000	35,000	—
	78,750	52,250	64,500	—		78,750	52,250	65,500	—
To F (Goodwill)	—	—	—	6,250	By Balance b/d		42,250	49,500	—
To G (Goodwill)	—	—	—	6,250	By E's Loan A/c	—	—	—	33.750
To Balance c/d	—	48,500	55,750	21,250	By H (goodwill)		6,250	6,250	—
	—	48,500	55,750	33,750		—	48,500	55,750	33,750

Working Notes:

(i) CALCULATION OF GAINING RATIO

Partners	New ratio	Old ratio	Gain	Sacrifice
E		$\frac{5}{10}$		$\frac{5}{10}$
F	$\frac{1}{2}$	$\frac{3}{10}$	$\frac{1}{2}+\frac{3}{10}$; $\frac{2}{10}$	
G	$\frac{1}{2}$	$\frac{2}{10}$	$\frac{1}{2}+\frac{2}{10}$; $\frac{3}{10}$	

Hence, ratio of gain between F and G = 2:3

(ii) Value of Total Goodwill of the firm = ₹.25,000 × 2 = ₹ 50,000

E's Share = ₹ 50,000 × 5/10 = ₹ 25,000

F will bear = ₹ 25,000 × 2/5 = ₹.10,000

G will bear = ₹ 25,000 × 3/5 = ₹ 15,000

(iii) H's share of goodwill = ₹ 50,000 × 1/4 = ₹ 12,500

F and G share equal profits. Therefore, their sacrificing ratio will also be equal Hence, each of them will be credited with ₹ 6,250.

PROBLEM 10

P, Q and R were partners sharing profits and losses in the ratio of 2 : 2 : 1. R wants to retire from partnership on 31-3-2015 and S wants to join the partnership on the same date, to which both P & Q agreed. The Balance Sheet of the partnership firm as on 31-03-2015 and other information were as detailed below:

BALANCE SHEET AS AT 31-03-2015

Liabilities	₹	*Assets*	₹
Partners' Capital A/cs:		Fixed assets	6,00,000
P	4,80,000	Stockinhand	2,00,000
Q	3,20,000	Sundry debtors	2,80,000
R	2,40,000	Cash at bank	1,60,000
General reserve	40,000	Cash in hand	40,000
Sundry creditors	2,00,000		
	12,80,000		12,80,000

P, Q and S agree to share profits and losses in equal ratio in future. Value of goodwill is taken to be ₹ 1,80,000.Fixed assets are revalued upwards by ₹ 1,20,000 and stock by ₹ 40,000. A debtor from whom ₹ 20,000 was due, become insolvent. No amount will be received from him in future and same is not recorded in the books and balance sheet as above. Claim of R will be settled in full. P, Q and S agree to make their capital proportionate to their new profits sharing ratio. Balance amount receivable from/payable to partners will be brought in by partners/paid to partners immediately. Ail these transactions viz., claim of R and amount receivable/payable to partners will be routed through bank only. New partners also want to maintain ₹ 3,20,000 bank balance for working capital requirement. However, they don't want to show goodwill in the books of accounts.

(i) Revaluation account

(ii) Capital accounts of partners and

(iii) Balance Sheet of the firm as newly constituted.

Solution

Dr. **REVALUATION ACCOUNT** *Cr.*

Particulars	₹	*Particulars*	₹
To Sundry Debtors	20,000	By Fixed assets	1,20,000
To Profit on Revaluation t/f to:		By Stock in hand	40,000
P's Capital A/c	56,000		
Q's Capital A/c	56,000		
R's Capital A/c	28,000		
	1,60,000		1,60,000

Dr. **PARTNERS' CAPITAL ACCOUNTS** *Cr.*

Particulars	P ₹	Q ₹	R ₹	S ₹	*Particulars*	P ₹	Q ₹	R ₹	S ₹
To P, Q, and R	—	—	—	60,000	By Balance b/d	4,80,000	3,20,000	2,40,000	—
To Bank (Bal. fig.)	1,04,000	—	3,12,000	—	By General reserve	16,000	16,000	8,000	—
To Balance c/d	4,60,000	4,60,000	—	4,60,000	By Revaluation profit	56,000	56,000	28,000	—
					By S	12,000	12,000	36,000	—
					By Bank (Bal. fig)	—	56,000	—	5,20,000
	5,64,000	4,60,000	3,12,000	5,20,000		5,64,000	4,60,000	3,12,000	5,20,000

BALANCE SHEET AS AT 31.03.2015 (AFTER RETIREMENT OF R AND ADMISSION OF S)

Liabilities		₹	*Assets*	₹
Partners' capital A/cs (Bal. fig.)			Fixed assets	7,20,000
P	4,60,000		Stock in hand	2,40,000
Q	4,60,000		Sundry debtors	2,60,000
S	4,60,000	13,80,000	Cash at bank	3,20,000
Sundry Creditors		2,00,000	Cash in hand	40,000
		15,80,000		15,80,000

Working Notes:

(i) ADJUSTMENT OF GOODWILL

Particulars	*P* ₹	*Q* ₹	*R* ₹	*S* ₹	*Total* ₹
Credited to old partners in 2:2:1	72,000	72,000	36,000	—	1,80,000
Written off among remaining partners including Sin 1:1:1	60,000	60,000	—	60,000	1,80,000
Cr.	12,000	12,000	36,000		
Dr.				60,000	

(ii) As per balance sheet as on 31.03.2013 (after retirement of R and admission of S), balancing figure of total partners' capital is ₹ 13,80,000 (i.e. Total assets ₹ 15,80,000 – Sundry creditors ₹ 2,00,000). Since partners agree to make their capital proportionate to their new profit sharing ratio i.e. 1:1:1, capital of each partner will be ₹ 4,60,000 (i.e. ₹ 13,80,000/3).

Dr. **(iii) BANK ACCOUNT** *Cr.*

Particulars	₹	*Particulars*	₹
To Balance b/d	1,60,000	By P's Capital A/c	1,04,000
To Q's Capital A/c	56,000	By R's Capital A/c	3,12,000
To S's Capital A/c	5,20,000	By Balance c/d	3,20,000
	7,36,000		7,36,000

PROBLEM 11

P, Q and R were carrying on a business in partnership, sharing profits and losses in the ratio of 5 : 3 : 2 respectively. The firm earned a profit of ₹ 3,60,000 for the accounting year ended 31st March, 2014 on which date the firm's Balance Sheet stood as follows:

Liabilities	₹	*Assets*	₹
P's Capital	7,00,000	Freehold Land and Building	8,00,000
Q's Capital	5,70,000	Machinery	3,50,000
R's Capital	4,30,000	Furniture & Fixtures	1,02,000
Creditors	79,400	Stock	2,98,800
Outstanding Expenses	4,900	Debtors	1,60,000
		Cash at Bank	73,500
	17,84,300		17,84,300

P died on 31st August, 2014. According to firm's partnership deed, in case of death of a partner:

(i) Assets and Liabilities have to be revalued by an independent valuer.
(ii) Goodwill is to be calculated at two years' purchase of average profits for the last three completed accounting years and the deceased partner's capital account is to be credited with his share of goodwill.
(iii) The share of the deceased partner in the profits for the period between end of the pevious accounting year and the date of death is to be calculated on the basis of the previous accounting year's profits. Post death of P, Q & R will share profit in the ratio of 3 : 2.

Profits for the accounting yeas 2011-2012 and 2012-2013 were as follows:

	₹
For the year ended 31st March, 2012	2,90,000
For the year ended 31st March, 2013	3,40,000

Drawings by P from 1st April, 2014 to the date of his death totalled ₹ 46,000.

On revaluation, Freehold Land and Building was appreciated by ₹ 1,00,000:

Machinery was depreciated by ₹ 10,000 and a Provision for Doubtful Debts was created @ 5% on Debtors as on 31st March, 2014, P's sole heir was given ₹ 5,00,00 immediately and the balance along with interest @ 12% per annum was paid to him on 31st March, 2015.

Prepare Revaluation Account, P's Capital Account and P's Heir Account, giving important working notes.

Solution

Dr. **REVALUATION ACCOUNT** *Cr.*

Particulars	₹	₹	*Particulars*	₹
To Machinery		10,000	By Freehold Land & Building	1,00,000
To Provision for doubtful debts (5% of 1,60,000)		8,000		
To Capital accounts:				
P	41,000			
Q	24,600			
R (Profit transferred)	16,400	82,000		
		1,00,000		1,00,000

P'S CAPITAL ACCOUNT

Particulars	₹	*Particulars*	₹
To Drawings	46,000	By Balance b/d	7,00,000
To P's heir (B.f.)	**11,00,000**	By Q's capital A/c	1,98,000
		By R's capital A/c	1,32,000
		By Profit and Loss Suspense A/c	75,000
		By Revaluation A/c	41,000
	11,46,000		11,46,000

P'S HEIR ACCOUNT

Date	Particulars	₹	Date	Particulars	₹
31.8.12	To Bank A/c	5,00,000	31.8.12	By P's Capital A/c	11,00,000
31.3.13	To Bank A/c	6,42,000	31.3.13	By Interest A/c	
				$\left(6,00,000 \times 12\% \times \frac{7}{12}\right)$	42,000
		11,42,000			11,42,000

Working Notes:

1. Calculation of Gaining ratio of Partners Q and R

	New share	Old share	Gaining share	Sacrificing share
P		5/10		5/10
Q	3/5	3/10	$\frac{3}{5}-\frac{3}{10}=\frac{6-3}{10}=\frac{3}{10}$	
R	2/5	2/10	$\frac{2}{5}-\frac{2}{10}=\frac{4-2}{10}=\frac{2}{10}$	

2. Calculation of Goodwill

	₹
2011–10	2,90,000
2012–11	3,40,000
2013–12	3,60,000
	9,90,000

Average Profit = 9,90,000/3 = ₹ 3,30,000

Goodwill = 3,30,000 × 2 = ₹ 6,60,000

Share of P in goodwill =6,60,000 × 5/10 = ₹ 3,30,000

Adjustment for P's share of goodwill through Q's and R's capital accounts (in their gaining ratio 3 : 2) :

Q's capital A/c (3,30,000 × 3/5) ₹ 1,98,000

R's capital A/c (3,30,000 × 2/5) ₹ 1,32,000

3. Share of P in Profits for the period between 1.4.2014 to 31.8.2014 i.e. till the date of death

1st April, 2014 to 31st August, 2014 = 5 months

Profit for year 2013–2014 = ₹ 3,60,000

Estimated profit for 5 months = 3,60,000 × 5/12 = ₹ 150,000

Share of P = 1,50,000 × 5/10 = ₹ 75,000

PROBLEM 12

Pathak, Quereshi and Ranjeet were partners sharing profits in the ratio of 7 : 5 : 3 respectively. On 31st March, 2015 Quereshi retired when the firm's Balance Sheet was as follows:

Liabilities	₹	*Assets*		₹
Capital Accounts:		Land and Building		10,00,000
Pathak	8,50,000	Plant and Machinery		4,65,000
Quereshi	6,20,000	Furniture, Fixture and Fittings		2,30,100
Ranjeet	3,70,000	Stock		1,82,200
General Reserve	2,25,000	Trade Debtors	2,00,000	
Trade Creditors	1,13,000	*Less*: Provision for Bad Debts	6,000	1,94,000
		Cash at Bank		1,06,700
	21,78,000			21,78,000

It was agreed that:

(i) Land & Building be appreciated by 20%,

(ii) Plant & Machinery be depreciated by 10%,

(iii) Provision for Doubtful Debts be made equal to 4% of Trade Debtors.

(iv) Outstanding repairs bill amounting to ₹ 1500 be recorded in the books of account.

(v) Goodwill of the firm be valued at ₹ 3,00,000 and Quereshi's capital account be credited with his share of goodwill without raising goodwill account.

(vi) Half of the amount due to Quereshi be immediately paid to him by means of a cheque and the balance be treated as a loan bearing interest @ 12% per annum.

After Quereshi's retirement, Pathak and Ranjeet admitted Swamy as a new partner with effect from 1st April, 2015. Pathak, Ranjeet and Swamy agreed to share profits in the ratio of 2 : 1 : 1 respectively. Swamy brought patents valued at ₹ 20,000 and ₹ 3,80,000 in cash including payment for his share of goodwill as valued by the old firm. The entire amount of ₹ 4,00,000 was credited to Swamy's Capital Account. Adjustments were made in capital account for Swamy's share of goodwill.

You are required to :

(a) Pass journal entries for all the above transactions without any narration, and

(b) Prepare the capital account of all the partners. *[Nov. 2015]*

Solution

(a) **JOURNAL**

Particulars		₹	₹
1. Land and Building	Dr.	2,00,000	
To Revaluation A/c			2,00,000
2. Revaluation A/c	Dr.	46,500	
To Plants and Machinery			46,500

	Particulars		Dr. (₹)	Cr. (₹)
3.	Revaluation A/c	Dr.	3,500	
	To Provision for bad debts [(₹ 2,00,000 × 4%) – ₹ 6000]			2,000
	To Provision for Outstanding repair bills			1,500
4.	Pathak's Capital A/c	Dr.	70,000	
	Ranjeet's Capital A/c	Dr.	30,000	
	To Quereshi's Capital A/c			1,00,000
5.	Revaluation A/c	Dr.	1,50,000	
	To Pathak's Capital A/c			70,000
	To Quereshi's Capital A/c			50,000
	To Ranjeet's Capital A/c			30,000
6.	General reserve A/c	Dr.	2,25,000	
	To Pathak's Capital A/c			1,05,000
	To Quereshi's Capital A/c			75,000
	To Ranjeet's Capital A/c			45,000
7.	Quereshi's Capital A/c	Dr.	8,45,000	
	To Bank A/c			4,22,500
	To Quereshi's Loan A/c			4,22,500
8.	Patents	Dr.	20,000	
	Cash A/c	Dr.	3,80,000	
	To Swamy's Capital A/c			4,00,000
9.	Swamy's Capital A/c (₹ 3,00,000/4)	Dr.	75,000	
	To Pathak's Capital A/c			60,000
	To Ranjeet's Capital A/c			15,000

(b)

CAPITAL ACCOUNTS OF PARTNERS

	Amount					Amount			
	Pathak	Quereshi	Ranjeet	Swamy		Pathak	Quereshi	Ranjeet	Swamy
31.3.13					31.3.13				
To Quereshi	70,000		30,000		By Bal. b/d	8,50,000	6,20,000	3,70,000	
					By general reserve	1,05,000	75,000	45,000	
To Bank A/c		4,22,500			By Pathak & Ranjeet		1,00,000		
To Loan A/c		4,22,500			By Revaluation A/c	70,000	50,000	30,000	
To Bal. c/d	9,55,000		4,15,000						
	10,25,000	8,45,000	4,45,000			10,25,000	8,45,000	4,45,000	
1.4.13					1.4.13				
To Pathak				60,000	By Bal. b/d	9,55,000	4,15,000		
To Ranjeet				15,000	By Patents				20,000
To Bal/ c/d	10,15,000		4,30,000	3,25,000	By Cash				3,80,000
					By Swamy	60,000		15,000	
	10,15,000		4,30,000	4,00,000		10,15,000		4,30,000	4,00,000

Working Notes:

1. Calculation of Gaining ratio after retirement of Quereshi

Gain of Pathak New Ratio – Old Ratio = 7/10 – 7/15 = 35/150
Gain of Ranjeet 3/10 – 3/15 = 15/150
Gaining Ratio = 35 : 15 = 7 : 3

2. Calculation of Sacrificing ratio of Pathak and Ranjeet at time of admission of Swamy

New ratio 2 : 1 : 1

$$\frac{2}{4}-\frac{7}{10} \qquad \frac{1}{4}-\frac{3}{10}$$

$$\frac{10-14}{20} \qquad \frac{5-6}{20}$$

$$=\frac{4}{20} \qquad \frac{1}{20}$$

Sacrificing ratio 4 : 1

PROBLEM 13

Anuj, Ayush and Piyush are in partnership sharing profits and losses in the ratio 2 : 2 : 1. Their Balance Sheet as on 31.3.2014 is as follows:

Liabilities	₹	*Assets*	₹
Anuj's Capital	3,75,000	Fixed Assets: Plant	7,87,000
Ayush's Capital	2,80,000	Stock	1,03,000
Piyush's Capital	2,25,000	Debtors	1,56,000
General Reserve	1,88,000	Bank FD	2,25,000
Creditors	2,16,000	Bank balance	13,000
	12,84,000		12,84,000

Anuj decided to retire with effect from 1.4.2014.

The remaining partners agreed to share profits and losses equally in future.

The following adjustments were agreed to be made upon retirement of Anuj:

(i) Goodwill was to be valued at 1 year purchase of the average profits of the preceding 3 years on the date of retirement.

The average profits of the past 3 years were as follows:

Year ended	₹
31.3.2014	3,30,000 (as per draft accounts)
31.3.2015	2,32,000
31.3.2014	2,20,000

The partners decided not to raise goodwill account in the books.

(ii) Plant to be depreciated by 10%; Creditors amounting to ₹ 10,000 were omitted to be recorded; ₹ 6,000 is to be written off from stock; Provision for doubtful debts to be created @ 5% of the debtors; Interest accrued on FD amounting to ₹ 9,000 was omitted to be recorded.

The above adjustments were to be made from the profit for the year ended 31.3.2014 before calculation of goodwill.

(iii) Anuj agreed to make over the bank FD including interest accrued thereon in part payment of his dues and the balance would remain as a loand carrying interest of 8% p.a.

(iv) Ayush and Piyush agree to bring in sufficient cash to make their capital proportiionate and maintain a bank balance of ₹ 1,50,000.

You are required to prepare

(1) Capital accounts of parnters as on 1.4.2014 giving effect to the above adjustments.

(2) Balance Sheet as on 1.4.2014 after Anuj's retirement.

Solution

Dr **Capital Accounts of Partners** Cr

Particulars	Anuj ₹	Ayush ₹	Piyush ₹	Particulars	Anuj ₹	Ayush ₹	Piyush ₹
To Anuj's Capital A/c		22,950	68,850	By Balance b/d	3,75,000	2,80,000	2,25,000
To Bank FD A/c	2,25,000			By General Reserve A/c	75,200	75,200	37,600
To Accrued interest on FD	9,000			By Ayush's			
To Revaluation A/c	37,400	37,400	18,700	Capital A/c	22,950	–	–
To Anuj's Loan A/c	2,70,600			Capital A/c	68,850		
To Balance C/f	–	3,03,450	3,03,450	By Bank A/c	–	8,600	1,28,400
	5,42,000	3,63,800	3,91,000		5,42,000	3,63,800	3,91,000

BALANCE SHEET AS ON 31.3.2014 (AFTER ANUJ'S RETIREMENT)

Liabilities		₹	Assets		₹
Capital A/cs:			Plant	7,87,000	
Ayush (8,77,500/2)	3,03,450		*Less:* Depreciation	(78,700)	7,08,300
Pyish (8,77,500/2)	3,03,450	6,06,900	Stock	1,03,000	
Creditrors [2,16,000 – 10,000]		2,26,000	*Less:* Written off	(6,000)	97,000
Anuj's Loan		2,70,600	Debtors	1,56,000	
			Less: Provisions	(7,800)	1,48,200
			Interest Accrued on FD	9,000	—
			Less: Taken over by Anuj	(9,000)	—
			Bank FD	2,25,000	
			Less: Taken over by Anuj	(2,25,000)	—
			Bank Balance (13,000 + 8,600 + 1,28,400)		1,50,000
		11,03,500			11,03,500

Working Notes:

Dr **Revaluation Account** Cr

Particulars	₹	Particulars		₹
To Plant A/c	78,700	By interest accrued on FD		9,000
To Creditors A/c	10,000	By Capital A/c:		
To Stock A/c	6,000	Anuj	37,400	

To RDD A/c	7,800	Ayush	37,400	
		Piyush	18,700	93,500
	1,02,500			1,02,500

(2) Goodwill adjustment:

(a) Goodwill valuation:

Profit for the year ended 31.3.2014		₹ 2,20,000
Profit for the year ended 31.3.2015		₹ 2,32,000
Profit for the year ended 31.3.2014:		
Profit as per draft accounts	3,30,000	
Less: Depreciation on plant	(78,700)	
Less: Unrecorded creditors/purchases	(10,000)	
Less: Amount written off from stock	(6,000)	
Less: Provision	(7,800)	
Add: Interest accrued on FD	9,000	₹ 2,36,500
Total Profit for 3 years		₹ 6,88,500

Average Profit = 6,88,500/3 year = 2,29,500

Goodwill = 2,29,500 × 1 years' purchase = ₹ 2,29,500

(b) Goodwill adjustment:

	Anuj ₹	*Ayush ₹*	*Piyush ₹*
Goodwill raised (2:2:1)	91,800 Cr	91,800 Cr	45,900 Cr
Goodwill written off (1:1)	—	1,14,750 Dr	1,14,750 Dr
Net effect	91,800 Cr	22,950 Dr	68,850 Dr

20 DISSOLUTION OF PARTNERSHIP FIRMS

PROBLEM 1

P, Q and *R* are partners sharing profits and losses as to 2:2:1. Their Balance Sheet as on 31st March, 2015 is as follows:

Liabilities	₹	*Assets*	₹
Capital Accounts:		Plant and Machinery	1,08,000
P	1,20,000	Fixtures	24,000
Q	48,000	Stock	60,000
R	24,000	Sundry Debtors	48,000
Reserve Fund	60,000	Cash	60,000
Creditors	48,000		
	3,00,000		3,00,000

They decided to dissolve the business. The following are the amounts realized:

	₹
Plant and Machinery	₹ 1,02,000
Fixtures	₹ 18,000
Stock	₹ 84,000
Sundry Debtors	₹ 44,400

Creditors allowed a discount of 5% and realization expenses amounted to ₹ 1,500. There was an unrecorded asset of ₹ 6,000 which was taken over by Q at ₹ 4,800. A bill for ₹ 4,200 due for sales tax was received during the course of realization and this was also paid.

You are required to prepare:

(i) Realisation Account. (ii) Partners'Capital Accounts. (iii) Cash Account.

Solution

Dr. **REALISATION ACCOUNT** *Cr.*

Particulars		₹	*Particulars*		₹
To Debtors		48,000	By Creditors		48,000
To stock		60,000	By Cash A/c (Assets realized):		
To Fixtures		24,000	Plant and Machinery	1,02,000	
To Plant and Machinery		1,08,000	Fixtures	18,000	
To Cash A/c (Creditors)		45,600	Stock	84,000	
To Cash A/c (Sales tax)		4,200	Sundry Debtors	44,400	2,48,400
To Cash A/c (Realisation Expenses)		1,500	By Q (Unrecorded Asset)*		4,800
To Profit on Realisation t/f to:					
P	3,960				
Q	3,960				
R	1,980	9,900			
		3,01,200			3,01,200

Dr. **PARTNERS' CAPITAL ACCOUNTS** Cr.

Particulars	P ₹	Q ₹	R ₹	Particulars	P ₹	Q ₹	R ₹
To Realisation A/c (unrecorded asset)	—	4,800	—	By Balance b/d	1,20,000	48,000	24,000
To Cash (Bal. Fig.)	1,47,960	71,160	37,980	By Fund	24,000	24,000	12,000
				By Realisation A/c (Profit)	3,960	3,960	1,980
	1,47,960	75,960	37,980		1,47,960	75,960	37,980

Dr. **CASH ACCOUNT** Cr.

Particulars	₹	Particulars	₹
To Balance b/d	60,000	By Realisation A/c (Creditors)	45,600
To Realisation A/c (Assets)	2,48,400	By Realisation A/c (Expenses)	1,500
		By Realisation A/c (Sales Tax)	4,200
		By P's Capital A/c	1,47,960
		By Q's Capital A/c	71,160
		By R's Capital A/c	37,980
	3,08,400		3,08,400

Note: *An unrecorded asset is in the nature of gain hence realization account is credited. Since this asset has been taken over by Q, therefore, his account has been debited.*

PROBLEM 2

Read, Write and add give you the following Balance Sheet as on 31st March, 2015:

Liabilities		₹	Assets		₹
Read's Loan		15,000	Plant and Machinery		30,000
Capital Accounts:			Fixture and Fittings		2,000
Read	30,000		Stock		10,400
Write	10,000		Debtors	18,400	
Add	2,000	42,000	*Less:* Provision	400	18,000
Sundry Creditors		17,800	Joint Life Policy		15,000
Loan on Hypothecation of Stock		6,200	Patents and Trademarks		10,000
Joint Life Policy Reserve		12,400	Cash at Bank		8,000
		93,400			93,400

The partners shared profits and losses in the ratio of read 4/9, Write 2/9 and Add 1/3. The Firm was dissolved on the same date and you are given the following information:

(a) Add had taken a loan from insurers for ₹ 5,000 on the security of Joint Life Policy. The policy was surrendered and Insurers paid a sum of ₹ 10,200 after deducting ₹ 5,000 for Add's loan and ₹ 300 as interest thereon.

(b) One of the creditors took some of the patents whose book value was ₹ 6,000 at a valuation of ₹ 4,500. The balance to that creditors was paid in cash.

(c) The firm had previously purchased some shares in a joint stock company and had written them off on finding them useless. The shares were now found to be worth ₹ 3,000 and the loan creditors agreed to accept the shares at this value.

(d) The remaining assets realized the following amount;

Plant and Machinery	17,000
Fixtures and Fittings	1,000
Stock	9,000
Debtors	16,500

Patents 50% of their book value.

(e) The liabilities were paid and a total discount of ₹ 500 was allowed by the creditors.

(f) The expenses of realization amounted to ₹ 2,300.

Required: Prepare the Realisation Account, Bank Account and Partners Capital Accounts in Columnar from.

Solution

Dr. **REALISATION ACCOUNT** *Cr.*

Particulars	₹	*Particulars*		₹
To Plant and machinery	30,000	By Provision for doubtful debts		400
To Fixtures and fittings	2,000	By Loan on hypothecation of stock		
6,200				
To Stock	10,400	By Creditors		17,800
To Debtors	18,400	By Joint Life Policy Reserve A/c		12,400
To Patents and Trademarks	10,000	By Bank A/c		
To Bank A/c (Expenses)	2,300	Plant and machinery	17,000	
To Joint Life Policy A/c	15,000	Fixtures and fittings	1,000	
To Bank A/c (Creditors)	12,800	Stock	9,000	
(17,800 – 4,500 – 500)		Debtors	16,500	
To Bank A/c (Loan)	3,200	Patents and Trademarks	2,000	45,500
[6,200 – 3,000 (Shares)]		By Bank A/c (JLP)		10,200
		By Add's Capital A/c		5,300
		By Loss on Realisation t/f to:		
		Read's Capital Account	2,800	
		Write's Capital Account	1,400	
		Add's Capital Account	2,100	6,300
	1,04,100			1,04,100

Dr. **BANK ACCOUNT** *Cr.*

Particulars	₹	*Particulars*	₹
To Balance c/d	8,000	By Realisation A/c (Loan)	3,200
To Realisation A/c (JLP)	10,200	By Realisation A/c (Creditors)	12,800
To Realisation A/c (Assets)	45,500	By Creditors	12,800
To Add's Capital A/c	5,400	By Realisation A/c (expenses)	2,300
		By Read's Loan A/c	15,000
		By Read's Capital A/c	27,200
		By Write's Capital A/c	8,600
	69,100		69,100

Dr. **PARTNERS' CAPITAL ACCOUNTS** Cr.

Particulars	*Read* ₹	*Write* ₹	*Add* ₹	*Particulars*	*Read* ₹	*Write* ₹	*Add* ₹
To Realisation A/c			5,300	By Balance b/d	30,000	10,000	2,000
To Realisation A/c	2,800	1,400	2,100	By Bank A/c (b.f.)			**5,400**
To Bank (Bal. Fig.)	27,200	8,600					
	30,000	10,000	7,400		30,000	10,000	7,400

Working Notes:

Dr. **(I) READ'S LOAN ACCOUNT** Cr

Particulars	₹	*Particulars*	₹
To Bank A/c	15,000	By Balance b/d	15,000
	15,000		15,000

21 PARTNERSHIP—INSOLVENCY, PIECEMEAL DISTRIBUTION, SALE, AMALGAMATION AND CONVERSION

INSOLVENCY OF A PARTNER

PROBLEM 1

The firm of Kapil and Dev has four partners and as on 31st March, 2015, its Balance Sheet stood as follows:

Liabilities	₹	*Assets*	₹
Capital Accounts:		Land	50,000
F. Kapil	2,00,000	Building	2,50,000
S. Kapil	2,00,000	Office Equipment	1,25,000
R. Dev	1,00,000	Computers	70,000
Current Accounts:		Debtors	4,00,000
F. Kapil	50,000	Stock	3,00,000
S. Kapil	1,50,000	Cash at Bank	75,000
R. Dev	1,10,000	Other Current Assets	22,600
Loan from NBFC	5,00,000	*Current A/c:*	
Current Liabilities	70,000	B. Dev	87,400
	13,80,000		13,80,000

The partners have been sharing profits and losses in the ratio of 4 : 4 : 1 : 1. It has been agreed to dissolve the firm on the basis of the following understanding:

(a) The following assets are to be adjusted to the extent indicated with respect to the book values: Land 200%, Building 120%, Computers 70%, Debtors 95%, Stocks, 90%.

(b) In the case of the loan, the lenders are to be paid at their insistence a prepayment premium of 1%.

(c) B. Dev is insolvent and no amount is recoverable from him. His father, R. Dev, however, agrees to bear 50% of his deficiency. The balance of the deficiency is agreed to be apportioned according to law

Required: Prepare Bank Account, Realisation Account and the Partners' Capital Accounts.

Solution

Dr. **BANK ACCOUNT** *Cr.*

Particulars	₹	*Particulars*	₹
To Balance b/d	75,000	By Realisation A/c—	
To Realisation A/c		(payment of sundry liabilities)	5,75,000
(Realisation of Sundry assets)	12,46,600	By F. Kapil's Capital A/c	2,42,600
		By S. Kapil's Capital A/c	3,42,600
		By R. Dev's Capital A/c	1,61,400
	13,21,600		13,21,600

Dr. **REALISATION ACCOUNT** *Cr.*

Particulars		₹	*Particulars*		₹
To Land		50,000	By Current Liabilities		70,000
To Building		2,50,000	By Loan from NBFC		5,00,000
To Office Equipments		1,25,000	By Bank A/c:		
To Computers		70,000	Land	1,00,000	
To Debtors		4,00,000	Building	3,00,000	
To Stock		3,00,000	Office Equipment	1,25,000	
To Other Current Assets		22,600	Computers	49,000	
To Bank A/c:			Debtors	3,80,000	
Current liabilities	70,000		Stock	2,70,000	
Loan from NBFC	5,05,000	5,75,000	Current Assets	22,600	12,46,600
To Profit on Realisation					
t/f to Partner's Current A/cs:					
F. Kapil	9,600				
S. Kapil	9,600				
R. Dev	2,400				
B. Dev	2,400	24,000			
		18,16,600			18,16,600

Dr. **PARTNERS' CAPITAL ACCOUNTS** *Cr.*

Particulars	*F. Kapil* ₹	*S. Kapil* ₹	*R. Dev* ₹	*B. Dev* ₹	*Particulars*	*F. Kapil* ₹	*S. Kapil* ₹	*R. Dev* ₹	*B. Dev* ₹
To Partners's Current A/cs	—	—	—	85,000	By Balance b/d	2,00,000	2,00,000	1,00,000	—
To B. Dev A/c	—	—	42,500	—	By Partners' Current A/c	59,600	1,59,600	1,12,400	—
To B. Dev A/c	17,000	17,000	8,500	—	By R. Dev A/c	—	—	—	42,500
To Bank A/c	2,42,600	3,42,600	1,61,400	—	By F. Kapil A/c	—	—	—	17,000
					By S. Kapil A/c	—	—	—	17,000
					By R. Dev A/c (as per contra)	—	—	—	8,500
	2,59,600	3,59,600	2,12,400	85,000		2,59,600	3,59,600	2,12,400	85,000

Dr. **PARTNERS' CURRENT ACCOUNTS** *Cr.*

Particulars	*F. Kapil* ₹	*S. Kapil* ₹	*R. Dev* ₹	*B. Dev* ₹	*Particulars*	*F. Kapil* ₹	*S. Kapil* ₹	*R. Dev* ₹	*B. Dev* ₹
To Bal. b/d	—	—	—	87,400	By Bal. b/d	50,000	1,50,000	1,10,000	—
To Partners's Capital A/c (transfer)	59,600	1,59,600	1,12,400	—	By Real. A/c	9,600	9,600	2,400	2,400
					By Partners's Capital A/c (transfer)	—	—	—	85,000
	59,600	1,59,600	1,12,400	87,400		59,600	1,59,600	1,12,400	87,400

Note: *In the absence of specific information, it is assumed that the assets are realised at the agreed values.*

PROBLEM 2

Ajay, Vijay, Ram and Shyam are partners in a firm sharing profits and losses in the ratio of 4 : 1. 2 : 3. The following is their Balance Sheet as at 31st March, 2015:

Liabilities	₹	Assets		₹
Sundry Creditors	3,00,000	Sundry Debtors	3,50,000	
Capital Accounts:		*Less:* Doubtful Debts	50,000	3,00,000
Ajay	7,00,000	Cash in hand		1,40,000
Shyam	3,00,000	Stock		2,00,000
		Other Assets		3,10,000
		Capital Accounts:		
		Vijay		2,00,000
		Ram		1,50,000
	13,00,000			13,00,000

On the same date, the firm is dissolved and the following points are agreed upon:

—Ajay is to take over sundry debtors at 80% of book value
—Shyam is to take over the stocks at 95% of the value and
—Ram is to discharge sundry creditors.

Others assets realise ₹ 3,00,000 and the expenses of realisation come to ₹ 30,000.
Vijay is found insolvent and ₹ 21,900 is relaised from his estate.

Required: Prepare Realisation Account, Capiital Accounts of the Partners and Cash A/c. The loss arising out of capital deficiency may be distributed following the decision in Garner *vs* Murray.

Solution

Dr. **REALISATION ACCOUNT** *Cr.*

Particulars	₹	Particulars	₹
To Sundry Debtors	3,50,000	By Sundry Creditors	3,00,000
To Stock	2,00,000	By Provision for Doubtful Debts	50,000
To Other assets	3,10,000	By Ajay's Capital A/c (Debtors)	2,80,000
To Ram's Capital A/c (Creditors)	3,00,000	By Shayam's Capital A/c (Stock	1,90,000
To Cash A/c (Expenses on realisation)	30,000	By Cash A/c (Other assets)	3,00,000
		By Loss of Realisation t/f to:	
		Ajay's Capital A/c	28,000
		Vijay's Capital A/c	7,000
		Ram's Capital A/c	14,000
		Shyam's Capital A/c	21,000
	11,90,000		11,90,000

Dr. **CAPITAL ACCOUNTS OF PARTNERS** *Cr.*

Particulars	Ajay ₹	Vijay ₹	Ram ₹	Shyam ₹	Particulars	Ajay ₹	Vijay ₹	Ram ₹	Shyam ₹
To Balance b/f	—	2,00,000	1,50,000	—	By Balance b/f	7,00,000	—	—	3,00,000
To Realisation (Debtors)	2,80,000	—	—	—	By Realisation (Creditors	—	—	3,00,000	—
To Realisation (Stock)	—	—	—	1,90,000	By Cash	28,000	—	14,000	21,000
To Realisation(loss)	28,000	7,000	14,000	21,000	By Balance c/d	—	2,07,000	—	—
To Balance c/d	4,20,000	—	1,50,000	1,10,000					
	7,28,000	2,07,000	3,14,000	3,21,000		7,28,000	2,07,000	3,14,000	3,21,000

Particulars	Ajay ₹	Vijay ₹	Ram ₹	Shyam ₹	Particulars	Ajay ₹	Vijay ₹	Ram ₹	Shyam ₹
To Balance b/d	—	2,07,000	—	—	By Balance b/d	4,20,000	—	1,50,000	1,10,000
To Vijay's A/c	1,29,570	—	—	55,530	By Cash	—	21,900	—	—
To Cash	2,90,430	—	1,50,000	54,470	By Ajay	—	1,29,570	—	—
					By Shyam	—	55,530	—	—
	4,20,000	2,07,000	1,50,000	1,10,000		4,20,000	2,07,000	1,50,000	1,10,000

Dr. **CASH ACCOUNT** *Cr.*

Particulars	₹	Particulars	₹
To Balance b/f	1,40,000	By Realisation A/c (expenses)	30,000
To Realisation A/c	3,00,000	By Ajay's Capital A/c	2,90,430
To Vijay's Capital A/c	21,900	By Ram's Capital A/c	1,50,000
To Ajay's Capital A/c	28,000	By Shyam's Capital A/c	54,470
To Ram's Capital A/c	14,000		
To Shyam's Capital A/c	21,000		
	5,24,900		5,24,900

Notes: *(i) Since creditors are taken over by Ram as per Balance Sheet figures, a direct entry for the same in Ram's Capital A/c is also correct.*

(ii) Ajay takes over Debtors at 80% of ₹ 3,50,000 i.e. ₹ 2,80,000.

(iii) Vijay's deficiency will be borne by Ajay and Shyam in the ratio of 7 : 3 i.e. on opening Capitals of ₹ 7,00,000 and ₹ 3,00,000. Ram will not bear any portion of the loss since at the time of dissolution he had a debit balance in his capital account.

PROBLEM 3

Neptune, Jupiter, Venus and Pluto had been carrying on business in partnership sharing profits and losses in the ratio of 3 : 2 : 1 :1. They decide to dissolve the partnership on the basis of the following Balance Sheet as on 31st March, 2015:

Liabilities		₹	Assets		₹
Capital Accounts:			Premises		1,20,000
Neptune	1,00,000		Furniture		40,000
Jupiter	60,000	1,60,000	Stock		1,00,000
General Reserve		56,000	Debtors		40,000
Capital Reserve		14,000	Cash		8,000
Sundry Creditors		20,000	Capital Overdrawn:		
Mortgage Loan		80,000	Venus	10,000	
			Pluto	12,000	22,000
		3,30,000			3,30,000

(i) The assets were realised as under:
Debtors ₹ 24,000, Stock ₹ 60,000, Furniture ₹ 16,000, Premises ₹ 90,000

(ii) Expenses of dissolution amounted to ₹ 4,000.

(iii) Further Creditors of ₹ 12,000 had to be met.

(iv) General Reserve unlike Capital Reserve was built up by appropriation of profits.

Required: Prepare the Realisation Account, Partners' Capital Accounts and the Cash Account assuming that Venus becomes insolvent and nothing was realised from his private estate. Apply the principles laid down in Garner vs Murray.

Solution

Dr. **REALISATION ACCOUNT** *Cr.*

Particulars		₹	*Particulars*		₹
To Sundry Assets A/c (transfer):			By Sundry creditors A/c		20,000
Premises		1,20,000	By Mortgage Loan A/c		80,000
Furniture		40,000	By Cash A/c (assets realised):		
Stock		1,00,000	Premises	90,000	
Sundry Debtors		40,000	Furniture	16,000	
To Cash A/c (Mortgage Loan)		80,000	Stock	60,000	
To Cash A/c (creditors paid)		32,000	Debtors	24,000	1,90,000
To Cash A/c (expenses)		4,000	By Loss transferred to Capital Accounts:		
			Neptune	54,000	
			Jupiter	36,000	
			Venus	18,000	
			Pluto	18,000	1,26,000
		4,16,000			4,16,000

Dr. **CASH ACCOUNT** *Cr.*

Particulars		₹	*Particulars*	₹
To Balance b/d		8,000	By Realisation A/c (creditors)	32,000
To Realisation A/c (assets realised)		1,90,000	By Realisation A/c (expenses)	4,000
To Capital A/c (realisation loss made good):			By Realisation A/c (Mortgage Loan)	80,000
Neptune	54,000		By Neptune's Capital A/c	1,18,857
Jupiter	36,000		By Jupiter's Capital A/c	73,143
Pluto	18,000	1,08,000		
To Pluto's Capital A/c		2,000		
		3,08,000		3,08,000

Dr. **PARTNERS' CAPITAL ACCOUNTS** *Cr.*

Particulars	*Neptune* ₹	*Jupiter* ₹	*Venus* ₹	*Pluto* ₹	*Particulars*	*Neptune* ₹	*Jupiter* ₹	*Venus* ₹	*Pluto* ₹
To Balance b/d	—	—	10,000	12,000	By Balance b/d	1,00,000	60,000	—	—
To Realisation A/c (loss)	54,000	36,000	18,000	18,000	By General Reserve A/c (3 : 2 : 1 : 1)	24,000	16,000	8,000	8,000
To Venus's Capital A/c (loss)	11,143	6,857	—	—	By Capital Reserve A/c (3 : 2 : 1 : 1)	6,000	4,000	2,000	2,000
To Cash A/c	1,18,857	73,143	—	—	By Cash A/c (loss on realization)	54,000	36,000	—	18,000
					By Neptune's Capital A/c	—	—	11,143	—
					By Jupiter's Capital A/c	—	—	6,857	—
					By Cash A/c				2,000
	1,84,000	1,16,000	28,000	30,000		1,84,000	1,16,000	28,000	30,000

Note: *Venus's deficiency has been borne by Neptune and Jupiter in the proportion of 130 : 80 or 13 : 8, i.e. in the ratio of capital before dissolution but after transfer of all reserves.*

PROBLEM 4

Ram, Rahim and Robert are partners of the firm 'RR Traders' for the past 5 years. The partners decided to dissolve the firm consequent to insolvency of partner Robert in March 2015. The Balance Sheet of the firm as on 31st March 2015 is furnished below: They share profits and losses equally:

Liabilities	₹	*Assets*	₹
Capital Accounts:		Land and Building	5,00,000
Ram	4,50,000	Plant and Machinery	2,00,000
Rahim	4,50,000	Furniture and Fittings	50,000
Robert	2,00,000	Stock in Trade	3,00,000
General Reserve	2,10,000	Debtors	5,00,000
Creditors	2,90,000	Cash at Hand/Bank	50,000
	16,00,000		16,00,000

The partners Ram and Rahim decided to form a new firm 'RR Enterprises' and takeover all the assets and liabilities of the firm at values given below:

Land and Building	₹ 3,50,000
Plant and Machinery	₹ 1,50,000
Furniture and Fittings	₹ 20,000
Stock in trade	₹ 2,00,000

Debtors include ₹ 3,00,000 due from SK & Co. owned by Robert. (Nothing is recoverable from the said concern). Other debtors can be recovered fully.

Required: Prepare Realisation account, Partners' Capital accounts and the Balance Sheet of RR Enterprises (immediately after commencement).

Solution

Dr. **(I) REALISATION ACCOUNT** *Cr.*

Particulars	₹	*Particulars*		₹
To Sundry assets:		By Creditors		2,90,000
Land and Building	5,00,000	By RR Enterprises		9,70,000
Plant and Machinery	2,00,000	By Loss Transferred to		
Furniture and Fitting	50,000	Partners' Capital Accounts:		
Stock	3,00,000	Ram	1,10,000	
Debtors	2,00,000	Rahim	1,10,000	
Cash at Hand/Bank	50,000	Robert	1,10,000	3,30,000
To RR Enterprises (liability taken over)	2,90,000			
	15,90,000			15,90,000

Dr. **PARTNERS' CAPITAL ACCOUNTS** *Cr.*

Particulars	*Ram* ₹	*Rahim* ₹	*Robert* ₹	*Particulars*	*Ram* ₹	*Rahim* ₹	*Robert* ₹
To Sundry Debtors			3,00,000	By Balance b/d	4,50,000	4,50,000	2,00,000
To Realisation A/c	1,10,000	1,10,000	1,10,000	By General Reserve	70,000	70,000	70,000
To Robert's A/c (deficiency borne by Solvent Partners)	70,000	70,000	—	By Cash A/c	1,10,000	1,10,000	
				By Ram and Rahim (deficiency borne by Solvent Partners)	—	—	1,40,000
To Balance c/d Solvent	4,50,000	4,50,000	—				
	6,30,000	6,30,000	4,10,000		6,30,000	6,30,000	4,10,000

(II) BALANCE SHEET OF RR ENTERPRISES AS AT 31.03.2015 (IMMEDIATELY AFTER COMMENCEMENT)

Liabilities	₹	*Assets*	₹
Capital Accounts:		Land and building	3,50,000
Ram	4,50,000	Plant and machinery	1,50,000
Rahim	4,50,000	Furnite and fittings	20,000
Creditors	2,90,000	Stock in trade	2,00,000
		Debtors	2,00,000
		Cash at hand/bank	2,70,000
	11,90,000		11,90,000

Working Notes:

(i) *Agreed value of assets taken over by RR Enterprises*

	₹
Land and building	3,50,000
Plant and machinery	1,50,000
Furniture and fittings	20,000
Stock in trade	2,00,000
Debtors (5,00,000 – 3,00,000)	2,00,000
Cash at hand/bank	50,000
	9,70,000

(ii) *Cash in hand/bank balance of RR Enterprises*

	₹
Opening Balance	50,000
Add: Ram's and Rahim's contribution (₹ 1,10,000 + ₹ 1,00,000)	2,20,000
	2,70,000

PROBLEM 5

A, B, C and D are sharing profits and losses in the ratio 5 : 5 : 4 : 2. Frauds committed by C during the year were found out and it was decided to dissolve the partnership on 31[si] March, 2015 when their Balance Sheet was as under:

Liabilities	₹	*Assets*	₹
Capitals:		Building	1,20,000
A	90,000	Stock	85,500
B	90,000	Investments	29,000
C	—	Debtors	42,000
D	35,000	Cash	14,500
General reserve	24,000	C's Current A/c	15,000
Trade creditors	47,000		
Bills payable	20,000		
	3,06,000		**3,06,000**

Following information is given to you:

(a) A cheque for ₹ 4,300 received from debtor was not recorded in the books and was misappropriated by C.

(b) Investments costing ₹ 5,400 were sold by C at ₹ 7,900 and the funds transferred to his personal account. This sale was omitted from the firm's books.

(c) A creditor agreed to take overinvestments of the book value of ₹ 5,400 at ₹ 8,400. The rest of the creditors were paid off at a discount of 2%.

(d) The other assets realized as follows:

Building	*105% of book value*
Stock	*₹ 78,000*
Investments	*The rest of investments were sold at a profit of ₹ 4,800*
Debtors	*The rest of the debtors were realized at a discount of 12%*

(e) The bills payable were settled at a discount of ₹ 400.

(f) The expenses of dissolution amounted to ₹ 4,900

(g) It was found out that realization from C's private assets would only be ₹ 4,000.

Prepare the necessary Ledger Accounts.

Solution

Dr. **REALISATION ACCOUNT** *Cr.*

Particulars	₹	*Particulars*	₹
To Building	1,20,000	By Trade Creditors	47,000
To Stock	85,500	By Bills Payable	20,000
To Investment	29,000	By Cash:	
To Debtors	42,000	Building 1,26,000	
To Cash (creditors paid) [98% (47,000 – 8,400)]	37,828	Stock 78,000	
		Investments 23,000	
To Cash (expenses)	4,900	Debtors 33,176	2,60,176
To Cash (bills payable) (20,000 – 400)	19,600	[88% (42,000 – 4,300)]	
		By C's Capital A/c	
To Profit on Realisation t/f to		[Debtors (unrecorded)]	4,300
Partners' Capital A/cs:		By C's Capital A/c	
A	171	[Investments (unrecorded)]	7,900
B	171		
C	137		
D	69		
	3,39,376		**3,39,376**

Dr. **CASH ACCOUNT** *Cr.*

Particulars	₹	*Particulars*	₹
To Balance b/d	14,500	By Realisation (creditors paid)	37,828
To Realisation (assets) realised		By Realisation (Bills Payable)	19,600
Building 1,26,000		By Realisation (expenses)	4,900
Stock 78,000		By A's Capital A/c	90,528
Investments 23,000		By B's Capital A/c	90,528
Debtors 33,176	2,60,176	By D's Capital A/c	35,292
To C's capital A/c.	4,000		
	2,78,676		**2,78,676**

Dr. **PARTNERS' CAPITAL ACCOUNTS** Cr.

Particulars	A ₹	B ₹	C ₹	D ₹	Particulars	A ₹	B ₹	C ₹	D ₹
To Balance b/d	—	—	15,000	—	By Balance b/d	90,000	90,000	-	35,000
To Realisation A/c (Debtors)	—	—	4,300	—	By General Reserve	7,500	7,500	6,000	3,000
To Realisation A/c (Investment)	—	—	7,900	—	By Realisation A/c (Profit)	171	171	137	69
To C's capital A/c	7,143	7,143	—	2,777	By Cash A/c	—	—	4,000	—
To Cash A/c	90,528	90,528	—	35,292	By A's capital A/c	—	—	7,143	—
					By B's capital A/c	—	—	7,143	—
					By D's capital A/c	—	—	2,777	—
	97,671	**97,671**	**27,200**	**38,069**		**97,671**	**97,671**	**27,200**	**38,069**

Working Notes:

(i) *Amount received from sale of investments*

Book value	29,000
Less: Misappropriated by C	(5,400)
	23,600
Less: Taken over by a creditor	(5,400)
	18,200
Add: Profit on sale of investments	4,800
	23,000

(ii) *Deficiency of C*

Balance of Capital	15,000
Debtors-misappropriation	4,300
Investment-misappropriation	7,900
	27,200
Less: Realisation Profit	(137)
General Reserve	(6,000)
Contribution from private assets	(4.000)
Net Deficiency of Capital	17,063

This deficiency of ₹ 17,063 in C's capital account will be shared by other partners A, B and D in their capital ratio of 90: 90 : 35

Accordingly,

A's Share of Deficiency = [17,063 x (90/215)] = ₹ 7,143

B's Share of Deficiency = [17,063 × (90/215)] = ₹ 7,143

D's Share of Deficiency = [17,063 x (35/215)] = ₹ 2,777

PROBLEM 6

P, Q, R and S had been carrying on business in partnership sharing profits & losses in the ratio of 4 : 3 : 2 : 1.They decided to dissolve the partnership on the basis of following Balance Sheet as on 30th April, 2015:

Liabilities	₹	*Assets*	₹
Capital Accounts:		Land & building	2,46,000
P	1,68,000	Furniture & fixtures	65,000
Q	1,08,000	Stock	1,00,000
General reserve	95,000	Debtors	72,500
Capital reserve	25,000	Cash in hand	15,500
Sundry creditors	36,000	Capital overdrawn:	
Mortgage loan	1,10,000	R	25,000
		S	18,000
	5,42,000		5,42,000

(a) The assets were realized: Land & Building ₹ 2,30,000, Furniture & Fixtures ₹ 42, 000, Stock ₹ 72,000, Debtors ₹ 65,000

(b) Expenses of dissolution amounted to ₹ 7,800.

(c) Further creditors of ₹ 18,000 had to be met.

(d) R became insolvent and nothing was realized from his private estate.

Required: Applying the principles laid down in Garner Vs. Murray, prepare the Realisation Account, Partners' Capital Accounts and Cash Account.

Solution

Dr. **REALISATION ACCOUNT** *Cr.*

Particulars	₹	*Particulars*	₹
To Land and building	2,46,000	By Sundry Creditors	36,000
To Furniture and fixtures	65,000	By Mortgage Loan	1,10,000
To Stock	1,00,000	By Cash A/c:	
To Debtors	72,500	Land and building	2,30,000
To Cash A/c (Expenses)	7,800	Furniture & fixtures	42,000
To Cash A/c (Creditors)	54,000	Stock	72,000
(₹ 36,000 + ₹ 18,000)		Debtors	65,000
To Cash A/c (Mortgage loan)	1,10,000	By Loss on Realisation t/f to:	
		P's Capital A/c	40,120
		Q's Capital A/c	30,090
		R's Capital A/c	20,060
		S's Capital A/c	10,030
	6,55,300		6,55,300

Dr. **PARTNERS' CAPITAL ACCOUNTS** *Cr.*

Particulars	*P* ₹	*Q* ₹	*R* ₹	*S* ₹	*Particulars*	*P* ₹	*Q* ₹	*R* ₹	*S* ₹
To Balance b/d	—	—	25,000	18,000	By Balance b/d	1,68,000	1,06,000		
To Realization A/c (Loss)	40,120	30,090	20,060	10,030	By General Reserve	38,000	28,500	19,000	9,500
To ₹ Capital A/c (Deficiency)	12,636	8,424	—	—	By Capital Reserve	10,000	7,500	5,000	2,500
To Cash A/c	2,03,364	1,35,576	—	—	By Cash A/c (realization loss)	40,120	30,090	—	10,030
					By P's Capital A/c			12,636	
					By Q's Capital A/c			8,424	
					By Cash A/c				6,000
	2,56,120	1,74,090	45,060	28,030		2,56,120	1,74,090	45,060	28,030

Note: P, Q and S brought cash to make good, their share of the loss on realization. However, in actual practice they will not be bringing any cash, only a notional entry will be made as per Rule in *Garner vs. Murray*.

Dr. **CASH ACCOUNT** *Cr.*

Particulars	₹	*Particulars*	₹
To Balance b/d	15,500	By Realization A/c:	
To Realization A/c:		Expenses on dissolution	7,800
Land and building	2,30,000	Creditors (36,000 + 18,000)	54,000
Furnitures fixtures	42,000	Mortgage loan	1,10,000
Stock	72,000	By P's capital A/c	2,03,364
Debtors	65,000	By Q's capital A/c	1,35,576
To P, Q, S's capital A/cs (40,120 + 30,090 + 10,030)	80,240		
To S's capital A/c	6,000		
	5,10,740		5,10,740

Working Note:

CALCULATION OF CAPITAL RATIO OF SOLVENT PARTNERS

Particulars	*P* ₹	*Q* ₹	*S* ₹
Opening Capital	1,68,000	1,08,000	(18,000)
Add: General reserve	38,000	28,500	9,500
Capital reserve	10,000	7,500	2,500
	2,16,000	1,44,000	(6.000)

Though S is a solvent partner yet he cannot be called upon to bear loss on account of insolvency of R because his capital account has a debit balance.

Therefore, capital ratio of P & Q = 216 : 144 = 3 : 2

Deficiency of R = ₹ {(25,000 + 20,060) – (19,000 + 5,000)} = ₹ 45,060 – ₹ 24,000
= ₹ 21,060.

Deficiency of R will be shared by P & Q in the capital ratio of 3 : 2 i.e.

P = ₹ 21,060 × 3/5 = ₹ 12,636

Q = ₹ 21,060 × 2/5 = ₹ 8,424

PIECEMEAL DISTRIBUTION

PROBLEM 7

The firm of CANJE was dissolved on 31.3.2015, at which date its Balance Sheet stood as follows:

Liabilities	₹	*Assets*	₹
Creditors	2,00,000	Fixed Assets	45,00,000
Bank Loan	5,00,000	Cash and Bank	2,00,000
L's Loan	10,00,000		
Capitals:			
L	15,00,000		
M	10,00,000		
S	5,00,000		
	47,00,000		47,00,000

Partners share profits equally. A firm of Chartered Accounts is retained to realise the assets and distribute the cash after discharge of liabilities. Their fees which are to include all expenses is fixed at ₹ 1,00,000. No loss is expected on realisation since fixed assets include valuable land and building.

Realisations are: 1st ₹ 5,00,000, 2nd ₹ 15,00,000, 3rd ₹ 15,00,000, 4th ₹ 30,00,000, 5th ₹ 30,00,000.

The Chartered Accountant firm decided to pay off the partners in 'Higher Relative Capital Method'.

Required: Prepare a statement showing distribution of cash.

Solution

STATEMENT SHOWING THE DISTRIBUTION TOWARDS FIRM'S OUTSIDE DEBTS' AND PARTNER'S LOAN

Particulars	*Ratio* ₹	*Total* ₹	*Creditors* ₹	*Bank Loan* ₹	*L's Loan*
A Balance Due		17,00,000	2,00,000	5,00,000	10,00,000
B *Less:* Amount paid out of its instalment	2 : 5	6,00,000	1,71,429	4,28,571	—
C Balance Due (A – B)		11,000,000	28,571	71,429	10,00,000
D *Less:* Amount paid out of 2nd installment					
First ₹ 1,00,000	2 : 5	1,00,000	28,571	71,429	—
Next ₹ 10,00,000	0 : 0 : 1	10,00,000	—	—	10,00,000
E Balance Due (C – D)		Nil	Nil	Nil	Nil

STATEMENT SHOWING THE DISTRIBUTION OF CASH AMONG PARTNERS (ACCORDING TO PROPORTIONATE CAPITAL METHOD)

Particulars	*Ratio*	*Total* ₹	*L* ₹	*M* ₹	*S* ₹
A Balance Due		30,00,000	15,00,000	10,00,000	5,00,000
B *Less:* Amount paid out of 2nd instalment	1 : 0 : 0	4,00,000	4,00,000	—	—
C Balance Due (A – B)		26,00,000	11,00,000	10,00,000	5,00,000
D *Less:* Amount paid out of 3rd					

Instalment					
First ₹ 1,00,000		1,00,000	1,00,000	—	—
Next ₹ 10,00,000	1 : 1 : 0	10,00,000	5,00,000	5,00,000	—
Balance ₹ 4,00,000	1 : 1 : 1	4,00,000	1,33,334	1,33,333	1,33,333
		15,00,000	7,33,334	6,33,333	1,33,333
E Balance Due (C – D)		11,00,000	3,66,666	3,66,667	3,66,667
F *Add:* Realisation Profit credited (₹ 30,000,000 – ₹ 11,00,000)	1 : 1 : 1	19,00,000	6,33,334	6,33,333	6,33,333
G Balance Due (after taking into Realisation Profit (E + F)		30,00,000	10,00,000	10,00,000	10,00,000
H *Less:* Amount paid out of 4th Instalment	1 : 1 : 1	30,00,000	10,00,000	10,00,000	10,00,000
I Balance Due (G – H)		Nil	Nil	Nil	Nil
J *Add:* Realisation Profit credited	1 : 1 : 1	30,00,000	10,00,000	10,00,000	10,00,000
K Balance due (after taking into Realisation profit) (I + J)		30,00,000	10,00,000	10,00,000	10,00,000
L *Less:* Amount paid out of 5th Instalment	1 : 1 : 1	30,00,000	10,00,000	10,00,000	10,00,000
M Balance Due (K – L)		Nil	Nil	Nil	Nil

Working Notes:

(I) STATEMENT SHOWING THE COMPUTATION OF HIGHEST RELATIVE CAPITAL

Particulars	*L*	*M*	*S*
A Actual Capitals	15,00,000	10,00,000	5,00,000
B Profit Sharing Ratio	1	1	1
C Actual Capitals × Profit Sharing Ratio	15,00,000	10,00,000	5,00,000
D Proportionate Capital taking *S*'s Capital as Base Capital	5,00,000	5,00,000	5,00,000
E Surplus Capital (A – D)	10,00,000	5,00,000	—
F Profit Sharing Ratio	1	1	—
G Surplus Capital × Profit Sharing Ratio	10,00,000	5,00,000	—
H Revised Proportional Capital taking *M*'s Capital as Base Capital	5,00,000	5,00,000	—
I Revised Surplus Capital (E – G)	5,00,000	—	—

(ii) *Scheme of Distribution:* First ₹ 5,00,000 will be paid to *L*, next ₹ 10,00,000 will be distributed between *L* and *M* in their profit sharing ratio (i.e. 1 : 1) and the balance will be distributed among *L*, *M* and *S* in their profit sharing ratio (i.e. 1 : 1 : 1).

(iii) It has been assumed that the amounts of realisation given in the question pertain to realisation of fixed assets.

(iv) *Calculation of amount available for distribution at the time of first realisation of fixed asset*
= Cash & Bank Balance + 1st Realisation – Liquidator's remuneration
= ₹ 2,00,000 + ₹ 5,00,000 – ₹ 1,00,000 = ₹ 6,00,000.

PROBLEM 8

A, B and C are partners sharing profits and losses in the ratio of 5:3:2. Their capitals were ₹ 9,600, ₹ 6,000 and ₹ 8,400 respectively. After paying creditors, the liabilities and assets of the firm were:

Liabilities	₹	*Assets*	₹
Liability for interest on loans from:		Investments	1,000
Spouses of partners	2,000	Furniture	2,000
Partners	1,000	Machinery	1,200
		Stock	4,000

The assets realised in full in the order in which they are listed above. B is insolvent.

Required: Prepare a statement showing the distribution of cash as and when available, applying maximum possible loss procedure.

Solution

STATEMENT OF DISTRIBUTION OF CASH

Particulars	*Realisation*	*Interest on loans from partners' spouses*	*Interest on loans from partners*	*Partners' Capitals*			
				A	*B*	*C*	*Total*
	₹	₹	₹	₹	₹	₹	₹
Balances due		2,000	1,000	9,600	6,000	8,400	24,000
(i) Sale of investments	1,000	(1,000)					
		1,000					
(ii) Sale of furniture	2,000	(1,000)	(1,000)				
		—	—				
(iii) Sale of Machinery	1,200						
Maximum possible loss ₹ 22,800 (total of capitals ₹.24,000 less cash available ₹.1,200) allocated to partners in the profit sharing ratio i.e. 5 : 3 : 2				(11,400)	(6,840)	(4,560)	(22,800)
Amounts at credit				(1,800)	(840)	3,840	1,200
Deficiency of A and B written off against C				1,800	840	(2,640)	—
Amount paid				—	—	1,200	1,200
Balances in capital accounts				9,600	6,000	7,200	22,800
(iv) Sale of stock	4,000						
Maximum possible loss ₹.18,800 (₹.22,800 – ₹.4,000) Allocated to partners in the ratio 5 : 3 : 2				(9,400)	(5,640)	(3,760)	(18,800)
Amounts at credit and cash paid				200	360	3,400	(4,000)
Balances in capital accounts left unpaid–Loss				9,400	5,640	3,760	18,800

PROBLEM 9

Amar, Akbar and Antony are in partnership. The following is their Balance Sheet as at March 31, 2015 on which date they dissolved their partnership. They shared profit in the ratio of 5:3:2.

Liabilities	₹	*Assets*	₹
Creditors	80,000	Plant and Machinery	60,000
Loan A/c: Amar	20,000	Premises	80,000
Capital A/cs: Amar	1,00,000	Stock	60,000
Akbar	30,000	Debtors	1,20,000
Antony	90,000		
	3,20,000		3,20,000

It was agreed to repay the amounts due to the partners as and when the assets were realised, viz. April 15, ₹.60,000, May 1, ₹ 1,46,000, May 31, ₹ 94,000,

Required: Prepare a statement showing how the distribution should be made under maximum loss method and write up the cash account and partners' capital accounts.

Solution

STATEMENT SHOWING DISTRIBUTION OF CASH BY 'MAXIMUM LOSS METHOD'

Particulars	*Creditors* ₹	*Amar's loan* ₹	*Amar* ₹	*Akbar* ₹	*Antony* ₹
Balance due	80,000	20,000	1,00,000	30,000	90,000
On 15* April realised ₹.60,000					
Paid to creditors	(60.000)	—	—	—	—
Balance due	20,000	20,000	1,00,000	30,000	90,000
On 1st May, realised ₹.1 ,46,000					
Paid to Creditors (₹.20,000)	(20,000)	—	—	—	—
Paid Amar's ioan (₹.20,000)		(20,000)	—	—	—
Balance due (1)	Nil	Nil	1,00,000	30,000	90,000
Balance ₹ 1,06,000 Maximum loss (1,00,000 + 30,000 + 90,000 – 1,06,000) = ₹.1,14,000 shared in Profit & Loss ratio 5:3:2			(57,000)	(34,200)	(22,800)
			43,000	(4,200)	67,200
Akbar's deficiency shared by Amar & Antony in capital ratio 100:90			(2,210)	4,200	(1,990)
Cash paid			40,790	—	65,210
Balance due (3) [1 – 2]			59,210	30,000	65,210
On 31s1 May, realised ₹ 94,000 Maximum Loss [59, 210 + 30,000 + 24,790 – 94,000]= ₹ 20,000 shared in 5 : 3 : 2			(10,000)	(6,000)	(4,000)
Cash paid (4)			49,210	24,000	20,790
Loss on realisation* (3 – 4)			10,000	6,000	4,000

* It is assumed that realisation from assets on 31st May, is the final realisation and no further cash expected to be received.

Dr. **CASH ACCOUNT** Cr.

Particulars	₹	Particulars	₹
To Realization A/c	60,000	By Creditors A/c	60,000
To Realization A/c	1,46,000	By Creditors A/c	20,000
To Realization A/c	94,000	By Amar's Loan A/c	20,000
		By Amar's Capital A/c	40,790
		By Antony's Capital A/c	65,210
		By Amar's Capital A/c	49,210
		By Akbar's Capital A/c	24,000
		By Antony's Capital A/c	20,790
	3,00,000		3,00,000

Dr. **PARTNERS' CAPITAL ACCOUNTS** Cr.

Particulars	Amar ₹	Akber ₹	Antony ₹	Particulars	Amar ₹	Akber ₹	Antony ₹
To Cash	40,790	—	65,210	By Balance b/d	1,00,000	30,000	90,000
To Cash	49,210	24,000	20,790				
To Realization A/c (loss)	10,000	6,000	4,000		—	—	—
	1,00,000	30,000	90,000		1.00.000	30.000	90.000

PROBLEM 10

Ajay Enterprises, a Partnership firm in which A, B and C are three partners sharing profits and losses in the ratio of 4 : 3 : 3, the balance sheet of the firm as on 31st March, 2015 is as below:

Liabilities	₹	Assets	₹
A's Capital	15,000	Factory Building	24,160
B's Capital	7,500	Plant & Machinery	16,275
C's Capital	15,000	Debtors	5,400
B's Loan A/c	4,500	Stock	12,390
Sundry creditors	16,500	Cash at Bank	275
	58,500		58,500

On balance sheet data all the three partners have decided to dissolve their partnership. Since the realization of assets was protracted, they decide to distribute amounts as and when feasible and for this purpose they appoint C who was to get as his remunerations 1% of the value of the assets realized other than cash at Bank and 10% of the amount distributed to the partners.

Assets were realized price-meal as under:

Particulars	₹
First instalment	18,650
Second instalment	17,320
Third instalment	10,000
Last instalment	7,000
Dissolution expenses were provided for estimated amount of	3,000
The creditors were settled finally for	15,900

Required: Prepare a statement showing distribution of cash amongst the partners by 'Highest Relative capital method'.

Solution

STATEMENT SHOWING DISTRIBUTION OF CASH AMONGST THE PARTNERS BY HIGHEST RELATIVE CAPITAL METHOD (HRCM)

Particulars		*Creditors*	*B's Loan*	*Capitals*		
	(₹)	*(₹)*	*(₹)*	*A(₹)*	*B(₹)*	*C(₹)*
Balance due		16,500	4,500	15,000	7,500	15,000
On receipt of 1st instalment amount	18,650					
Add: Cash at bank	275					
	18,925					
Less: Dissolution expenses provided for	(3,000)					
	15,925					
Less: C's remuneration of 1% on assets realized (₹ 18,650 × 1%)	(187)					
	15,738					
Less: Payment made to creditors	(15,738)	(15,738)				
Balance due	Nil	762				
On realization of 2nd instalment	17,320					
Less: C's remuneration of 1% on assets realized (₹ 17,320 × 1%)	(173)					
	17,147					
Less: Payment made to creditors (settled for the total ₹ 15,900)	(162)	(162)				
Transferred to P&L A/c		600				
	16,985	Nil				
Less: Payment for B's loan A/c	(4,500)		(4,500)			
Amount available for distribution to partners	12,485		nil			
Less: C's remuneration of 10% of the amount distributed to partners (₹ 12,485 × 10/110)	(1,135)					
Balance distributed to partners on the basis of HRCM	11,350					
Less: Paid to C(See W.N.)	(3,750)					(3,750)
	7,600					11,250
Less: Paid to A and C in 4 : 3 in (See W.N.)	(7,600)			(4,343)	—	(3,257)
Balance due	nil			10,657	7,500	7,993
On C's remuneration of 1% on assets realized (₹ 10,000 × 1%)	(100)					
	9,900					
Less: C's remuneration realized (₹ 10,000 × 1%)	(100)					
	9,900					
Less: C's remuneration of 10% of the amount distributed to partners (₹ 9,900 × 10/110)	(900)					
	9,000					

Particulars		Creditors	B's Loan	Capitals		
	(₹)	(₹)	(₹)	A(₹)	B(₹)	C(₹)
Less: Paid to A and C in 4 : 3 upto ₹ 8,750 (i.e. ₹ 7,600 paid on receipt of second instalment and balance of ₹ 1,150 to be paid now) (See W.N.)	(1,150)			(657)		(493)
	7,850			10,000	7,500	7,500
Less: Now, Paid to A, B and C in 4 : 3 : 3	(7,850)			(3,140)	(2,355)	(2,355)
Balance due	nil			6,800	5,145	5,145
On realization of 4th and last instalment	7,000					
Less: C's remuneration of 1% on assets realized (₹ 7,000 × 1%)	(70)					
	6,930					
Less: C's remuneration of 10% of the amount distributed to partners (₹ 6,930 × 10/110)	(630)					
	6,300					
Less: Paid to A, B and C in 4 : 3 : 3	(6,300)			(2,250)	(1,890)	(1,890)
Loss suffered by partners				4,340	3,255	3,255

Working Note:

CALCULATION OF AMOUNT PAID TO PARTNERS ON THE BASIS OF HIGHEST RELATIVE CAPITAL METHOD

Particulars	A ₹	B ₹	C ₹
Balance of Capital Accounts (A)	15,000	7,500	15,000
Profit Sharing ratio	4	3	3
Capital/Profit sharing ratio	3,750	2,500	5,000
Proportionate Capitals taking B's Capital as base	10,000	7,500	7,500
Surplus Capitals	5,000	nil	7,500
Profit Sharing Ratio	4		3
Surplus Capitals/Profit Sharing Ratio	1,250		2,500
Revised Proportionate Capitals taking A's Capital as base	5,000		3,750
Revised Surplus Capital to be paid first	nil		3,750

Scheme of Distribution: First ₹ 3,750 will be paid to C. Then A and C will receive in proportion of 4 : 3 upto ₹ 8,750 to bring the capital of all partners A, B and C in proportion to their profit sharing ratio. Thereafter, balance available will be paid to all partners viz A, B and C in their profit sharing ratio of 4 : 3 : 3.

PROBLEM 10A

The partners P, Q & R have called you to assist them in winding up the affairs of their partnership on 31.12.2015. Their balance sheet as on that date is given below:

Liabilities	₹	*Assets*	₹
Capital Accounts:		Land & Building	50,000
P	65,000	Plant & Machinery	46,000
Q	50,500	Furniture & Fixture	10,000
R	32,000	Stock	14,500
Sundry Creditors	16,000	Debtors	14,000
		Cash at Bank	9,000
		Loan P	13,000
		Loan Q	7,000
	1,63,500		1,63,500

(a) The partners share profit and losses in the ratio of 4:3:2.

(b) Cash is distributed to the partners at the end of each month.

(c) A summary of liquidatioin transactions are as follows:

January 2014

- ₹ 9,000 - collected from debtors; balance is uncollectable.
- ₹ 8,000 - received from the sale of entire furniture
- ₹ 1,000 - Liquidation expenses paid.
- ₹ 6,000 - Cash retained in the business at the end of montjh

February 2014

- ₹ 1,000 - Liquidation expenses paid.
- As part payment of his capital, R accepted a machinery for ₹ 9,000 (book value ₹ 3,500)
- ₹ 2,000 - Cash retained in the business at the end of month

March 2014

- ₹ 38,000 - received on the sale of remaining plant and machinery.
- ₹ 10,000 - received from the sale of entire stock.
- ₹ 1,700 - Liquidation expenses paid.
- ₹ 41,000 - Received on sale of land & building.
- No Cash is retained in the business.

You are required to prepare a schedule of cash payments amongst the partners by "Higher Relative Capital Method".

Solution

Particulars	*Cash* ₹	*Creditors* ₹	*P (₹)*	*Capitals* *Q (₹)*	*R (₹)*
Balance due after loan		16,000	52,000	43,500	32,000
January					
Balance available	9,000				
Realization less expenses and cash retained	10,000				
Amount available and paid	19,000	(16,000)	–	–	3,000

Balance due	–	–	52,000	43,500	29,000
February					
Opening Balance	6,000				
Expenses paid and cash carried forward	3,000				
Available for distribution	3,000				
Cash paid to Q and Machinery given to R			–	3,000	9,000
Balance due	–		52,000	40,500	20,000
March					
Opening Balance	2,000				
Amount realized less expenses	87,300				
Amount paid to partners	89,300		41,689	32,767	14,844
Loss			10,311	7,733	5,156

Working Note:

(i) Highest Relative Capital Basis

Particulars	*P (₹)*	*Q (₹)*	*R (₹)*
Scheme of payment for January			
Balance of Capital Accounts	65,000	50,500	32,000
Less: Loans	(13,000)	(7,000)	
A. Net Actual Capital	52,000	43,5000	32,000
B. Profit Sharing Ratio	4	3	2
C. Capital/Profit sharing Ratio [A/B]	13,000	14,500	16,000
D. Capital in profit sharing ratio, taking P's capital as base capital	52,000	39,000	26,000
E. Surplus Capital [A – D]		4,500	6,000
F. Profit Sharing Ratio		3	2
G. Surplus Capital/Profit sharing Ratio [E/F]		1,500	3,000
H. Capital in profit sharing ratio, taking Q's capital as base capital		4,500	3,000
I. Revised Surplus Capital [E – G]			3,000

(ii) Scheme of distributiion of available cash for March:

Particulars	*P (₹)*	*Q (₹)*	*R (₹)*
A. Balance of Capital Accounts end of February	52,000	40,5000	20,000
B. Profit Sharing Ratio	4	3	2
C. Capital/Profit sharing Ratio [A/B]	13,000	13,500	10,000
D. Capital in profit sharing ratio, taking R's capital as base capital	40,000	30,000	20,000
E. Surplus Capital [A – D]	12,000	10,500	
F. Profit Sharing Ratio	4	3	
G. Surplus Capital/Profit sharing Ratio [E/F]	3,000	3,500	
H. Capital in profit sharing ratio taking P's capital as base	12,000	9,000	
I. Surplus Capital [E – H]	-	1,500	
J. Payment ₹ 1500		(1,500)	
K. Balance of Surplus Capital [H – J]	12,000	9,000	
L. Payment ₹ 21000	(12,000)	(9,000)	
M. Balance due [A – J – L]	40,000	30,000	20,000
N. Balance Cash Payment [₹ 89,300 – ₹ 22,500]	(29,689)	(22,267)	(14,844)
O. Total Cash Payment (₹ 89,000)	41,689	32,767	14,844
P. Loss [A – O]	10,311	7,733	5,156

SALE TO A COMPANY

PROBLEM 11

Riu, Inu and Sinu were running Partnership business sharing Profits and Losses in 2 : 2: 1 ratio. Their Balance Sheet as on 31st March, 2015 stood as follows:

(Figure in ₹ '000)

Liabilities		₹	*Assets*		₹
Fixed Capitals:			Fixed Assets		400.00
Riu	300.00		Investments		50.00
Inu	200.00		Current Assets:		
Sinu	100.00	600.00	Stock	100.00	
Current Accounts:			Debtors	275.00	
Riu	60.00		Cash at Bank	125.00	500.00
Sinu	40.00	100.00			
Unsecured Loans		100.00			
Current Liabilities		150.00			
		950.00			950.00

On 01.04.2015, they agreed to form a new company RIS (P) Ltd. with Inu and Sinu each taking up 200 shares of ₹ 10 each, which shall take over the firm as a going concern including Goodwill, but excluding Cash and Bank Balances. The following are also agreed upon:

(a) Goodwill will be valued at 3 year's purchase of share profits.
(b) The actual profit for the purpose of Goodwill valuation will be ₹ 2,00,000.
(c) The normal rate of return will be 18% per annum on Fixed Capital.
(d) All other Assets and Liabilities will be taken over at Book values.
(e) The Purchase consideration will be payment partly in shares of ₹ 10 each and partly in cash. Payment in cash being to meet the requirement to discharge Riu, who has agreed to retire.
(f) Inu and Sinu are to acquire interest in the new company at the ratio 3 : 2.
(g) Realisation expenses amounted to ₹ 51,000

Required: Prepare Realisation Account, Cash and Bank Account, RIS (P) Limited Account and Capital Account of Partners.

Solution

Dr. **REALISATION ACCOUNT** *Cr.*

Particulars		₹	*Particulars*	₹
To Sundry Assets:			By Unsecured Loans	1,00,000
Fixed Assets	4,00,000		By Current Liabilities	1,50,000
Investments	50,000		By RIS(P) Ltd.	8,51,000
Stock	1,00,000			
Debtors	2,75,000	8,25,000		
To Bank A/c (Realisation Expenses)		51,000		
To Profit on Realisation t/f to:				
Riu's Capital A/c		90,000		
Inu's Capital A/c		90,000		
Sinu's Capital A/c		45,000		
		11,01,000		11,01,000

Dr. **CASH AND BANK ACCOUNT** Cr.

Particulars	₹	Particulars	₹
To Balance b/d	1,25,000	By Realisation A/c (Expenses)	51,000
To RIS (P) Ltd. (b.f.)	3,76,000	By Riu's Capital A/c	4,50,000
	5,01,000		5,01,000

Dr. **RIS(P) LTD.** Cr.

Particulars	₹	Particulars	₹
To Realisation A/c	8,51,000	By Cash A/c	3,76,000
		By Equity Shares in RIS (P) Ltd. A/c (b.f.)	4,75,000
	8,51,000		8,51,000

Dr. **PARTNERS' CAPITAL ACCOUNTS** Cr.

Particulars	Riu ₹	Inu ₹	Sinu ₹	Particulars	Riu ₹	Inu ₹	Sinu ₹
To Cash A/c	4,50,000	—	—	By Balance b/d	3,00,000	2,00,000	1,00,000
To Sinu's A/c (Capital Adjustment)	—	5,000	—	By Current A/c	60,000	—	40,000
To Equity Shares in RIS(P) Ltd.	—	2,85,000	1,90,000	By Realisation A/c	90,000	90,000	45,000
				By Inu's A/c (Capital Adjustment)	—	—	5,000
	4,50,000	2,90,000	1,90,000		4,50,000	2,90,000	1,90,000

Working Notes:

(i) *Calculation of Goodwill*

		₹
A.	Actual profits	2,00,000
B.	*Less:* Normal Rate of Return @ 18% on ₹ 6,00,000	1,08,000
C.	Super Profits [A – B]	92,000
D.	Goodwill valued at 3 years' purchase [₹ 92,000 × 3]	2,76,000

(ii) *Calculation of Purchase Consideration*

		₹
A.	Total value of assets as per Balance Sheet	9,50,000
B.	*Less:* Cash and Bank Balance	1,25,000
C.	*Add:* Goodwill	2,76,000
D.	Total Assets taken over	11,01,000
E.	*Less:* Liabilities taken over [₹ 1,00,000 + ₹ 1,50,000]	2,50,000
F.	Purchase Consideration	8,51,000

(iii) *Shares in New Company received as Purchase Consideration have been divided between Inu and Sinu in the ratio 3 : 2.*

PROBLEM 12

X and Y carrying on business in partnership sharing Profit and Losses equally, wished to dissolve the firm and sell the business to 'X' Limited Company on 31.3.2015, when the firm's position was as follows:

Liabilities	₹	*Assets*	₹
X's Capital	1,50,000	Land and Building	1,00,000
Y's Capital	1,00,000	Furniture	40,0n00
Sundry Creditors	60,000	Stock	1,00,000
		Debtors	66,000
		Cash	4,000
	3,10,000		3,10,000

The arrangement with X Limited Company was as follows:

(a) Land and Building was purchased at 20% more than the book value.

(b) Fumiture and stock were purchased at book values *less* 15%,

(c) The goodwill of the firm was valued at ₹ 40,000.

(d) The firm's debtors, cash and creditors were not to be taken over, but the company agreed to collect the book debts of the firm and discharge the creditors of the firm as an agent, for which services, the company was to be paid 5% on all collections from the firm's debtors and 3% on cash paid to firm's creditors.

(e) The purchase price was to be discharged by the company in fully paid equity shares of ₹ 10 each at a premium of ₹ 2 per share.

The company collected all the amounts from debtors. The creditors were paid off less by ₹.1,000 allowed by them as discount. The company paid the balance due to the vendors in cash.

Required: Prepare the Realisation Account, the Capital Accounts of the Partners and the Cash account in the books of partnership firm.

Solution

Dr. **REALISATION ACCOUNT** *Cr.*

Particulars	₹	*Particulars*		₹
To Land & Building	1,00,000	By Sundry Creditors		60,000
To Furniture	40,000	By X Ltd. Co. (Purchase Consideration)		2,79,000
To Stock	1,00,000	By X Ltd. Company		
To Debtors	66,000	Sundry Debtors	66,000	
To X Ltd. Co. (Sundry Creditors)	59,000	*Less:* Commission @ 5% on	3,300	62,700
To X Ltd. Co. (Comm. @ 3% on ₹ 59,000)	1,770			
To Profits transferred to:				
A's Capital A/c	17,465			
B's Capital A/c	17,465			
	4,01,700			4,01,700

Dr. **CAPITAL ACCOUNTS OF PARTNERS** *Cr.*

Particulars	₹	₹	*Particulars*	₹	₹
To Shares in X Ltd. Co.	1,63,980	1,15,020	By Balance b/d	1,50,000	1,00,000
To Cash (Final Payment)	3,485	2,445	By Realisation A/c (Profit)	17,465	17,465
	1,67,465	1,17,465		1,67,465	1,17,465

Dr. **CASH ACCOUNT** Cr.

Particulars	₹	*Particulars*	₹
To Balance b/d	4,000	By A's Capital A/c (Final Payment)	3,485
To X Ltd. Co. (Amount realized from Debtors less amount paid to creditors)	1,930	By B's Capital A/c (Final Payment)	2,445
	5,930		5,930

Working Notes:

(i) *Calculation of Purchase consideration:*

	₹
Land & Building	1,20,000
Furniture	34,000
Stock	85,000
Goodwill	40,000
	2,79,000

(ii) *The shares received from the company have been distributed between the two partners A & B in the ratio of their final claims i.e., 1,67,465: 1,17,465*.*

No. of shares received from the company = 2,79,000/12 = 23,250

A gets $\frac{23,250 \text{ " } 1,67,465}{2,84,930}$ = 13,665 shares valued at 13,665 x 12 = ₹.1,63,980.

B gets the 2,84,930 remaining 9,585 shares, valued at ₹.1,15,020 (9,585 x 12)

(iii) *Calculation of net amount received from X Ltd on account of amount realized from debtors less amount paid to creditors.*

		₹
A.	Amount realized from Debtors	66,000
B.	*Less:* Commission for realization from debtors (5% on 66,000)	3,300
C.	*Less:* Amount paid to creditors	59,000
D.	*Less:* Commission for cash paid to creditors (3% on 59,000)	1,770
E.	Net amount received	1,930

(iv) In the above situation, shares received from X Ltd. Company have been distributed between two partners A and B in the ratio of their final claims. Alternatively, shares received from X Ltd, can be distributed among the partners in their profit sharing ratio i.e. ₹ 2,79,000 x 1/2 = ₹ 1,39,500 each. In that case, firm will pay cash amounting ₹ 27,965 to A and will receive cash ₹.22,035 from B.

PROBLEM 13

S and T were carrying on business as equal partners. Their Balance Sheet as at 31st March, 2015 stood as follows:

Liabilities	₹	*Assets*	₹
Capital Accounts:		Stock	2,70,000
S	6,40,000	Debtors	3,65,000
T	6,60,000	Furniture	75,000
Creditors	3,27,500	Joint life policy	47,500
Bank Overdraft	1,50,000	Plant	1,72,500
Bills Payable	62,500	Building	9,10,000
	18,40,000		18,40,000

The operations of the business were carried on till 30th September, 2015. S and T both withdrew in, equal amounts half the amount of profits made during the current period of 6 months after 10% p.a.. had been written off on Building and Plant and 5% p.a. written off on furniture. During the current period of 6 months, creditors were reduced by ₹ 50,000, Bills payables by ₹ 11,500 and Bank Overdraft by ₹ 75,000. The Joint life policy was surrendered for ₹ 47,500 on 30th September, 2015. Stock was valued at ₹ 3,17,000 and debtors at ₹ 3,25,000 on 30th September, 2015. The other items remained the same as they were on 31st March, 2015.

On 30th September, 2015 the firm sold its business to ST Ltd. The goodwill was estimated at ₹ 5,40,000 and the remaining assets were valued on the basis of the Balance Sheet as on 30th September, 2015. The ST Ltd. paid the purchase consideration in equity shares of ₹ 10 each.

Required: Prepare Realisation account and Capital accounts of the partners.

Solution

Dr. **(I) REALISATION ACCOUNT** *Cr.*

Particulars	₹	*Particulars*	₹
To Sundry Assets:		By Creditors	2,77,500
Stock	3,17,000	By Bills Payables	51,000
Debtors	3,25,000	By Bank Overdraft	75,000
Plant	1,63,875	By Shares in ST Ltd.	18,80,000
Building	8,64,500		
Furniture	73,125		
To Profit on Realisation t/f to:			
S's Capital A/c	2,70,000		
T's Capital A/c	2,70,000		
	22,83,500		22,83,500

Dr. **(I) PARTNERS' CAPITAL ACCOUNTS** *Cr.*

Particulars	*S* ₹	*T* ₹	*Particulars*	*S* ₹	*T* ₹
To Cash	20,000	20,000	By Balance b/d	6,40,000	6,60,000
To Shares in ST Ltd.	9,30,000	9,50,000	By Profit	40,000	40,000
			By Realisation A/c (Profit)	2,70,000	2,70,000
	9,50,000	9,70,000		9,50,000	9,70,000

Working Notes:

(I) BALANCE SHEET AS AT 30.9.2015

Liabilities	₹	*Assets*		₹
Sundry Creditors	2,77,500	Stock		3,17,000
Bills Payable	51,000	Debtors		3,25,000
Bank Overdraft	75,000	Plant	1,72,500	
Total Capital (bal. fig.)	13,40,000	*Less*: Depreciation	8,625	1,63,875
		Furniture	75,000	
		Less: Depreciation	1,875	73,125
		Building	9,10,000	
		Less: Depreciation	45,500	8,64,500
	17,43,500			17,43,500

(ii) *Profit earned during six months to 30.9.2015*

	₹
Total Capital on 30th Sept.	13,40,000
Total Capital on 1st April (₹ 6,40,000 + ₹ 6,60,000)	13,00,000
Net Increases (after drawings)	40,000

Since drawings are half of profits therefore, profit earned = ₹ 40,000 × 2 = ₹ 80,000

(ii) *Purchase Consideration:*

Total Assets excluding Goodwill	17,43,500
Add: Goodwill	5,40,000
Less: Liabilities	4,03,500
Purchase Consideration	18,80,000

(iv) *Alternatively, it may be assumed that the figure of bank overdraft is given before taking into consideration the realisation of Joint Life Policy.*

PROBLEM 14

XYZ & Co. is a partnership firm consisting of Mr. *X*, Mr. *Y* and Mr. *Z* who share profits and losses in the ratio of 2:2:1 and *ABC* Ltd. is a company doing similar business.

Following is the Balance Sheet of the firm and that of the company as at 31.3.2015:

Liabilities	*XYZ & Co.* ₹	*ABC Ltd.* ₹	*Assets*	*XYZ & Co.* ₹	*ABC Ltd.* ₹
Equity Shares of ₹ 10 each		20,00,000	Plant & Machinery	5,00,000	16,00,000
Partners Capitals:			Furniture & Fixture	50,000	2,25,000
			Stock in trade	2,00,000	8,50,000
X	2,00,000		Sundry Debtors	2,00,000	8,25,000
			Cash at bank	10,000	4,00,000
Y	3,00,000		Cash in hand	40,000	1,00,000
Z	1,00,000				
General Reserve	1,00,000	7,00,000			
Sundry Creditors	3,00,000	13,00,000			
	10,00,000	40,00,000		10,00,000	40,00,000

It was decided that the firm *XYZ* & Co. be dissolved and all the assets (except cash in hand and cash at bank) and all the liabilities of the firm be taken over by *ABC* Ltd. by issuing 50,000 shares of ₹ 10 each at a premium of ₹ 2 per share.

Partners of *XYZ* & Co. agreed to divide the shares issued by *ABC* Ltd. in the profit sharing ratio and bring necessary cash for settlement of their capital.

The creditors of *XYZ* & Co. includes ₹ 1,00,000 payable to *ABC* Ltd. An unrecorded liability of ₹ 25,000 of *XYZ* & Co. must also be taken over by *ABC* Ltd.

Required: Prepare

(i) Realisation Account, Partners' Capital Accounts and Cash in hand/Bank account in the books of *XYZ* & Co and

(ii) Pass Journal Entries in the books of *ABC* Ltd. for acquisition of *XYZ* & Co. and draw the Balance Sheet after the takeover.

Solution

REALISATION ACCOUNT OF XYZ & CO.

Dr. | Cr.

Particulars	₹	Particulars	₹
To Plant & Machinery	5,00,000	By Sundry Creditors	3,00,000
To Furniture & Fixture	50,000	By ABC Ltd.	6,00,000
To Stock in trade	2,00,000	By Partners' Capital Accounts (loss):	
To Sundry Debtors	2,00,000	X's Capital A/c	20,000
		Y's Capital A/c	20,000
		Z's Capital A/c	10,000
	9,50,000		9,50,000

PARTNERS' CAPITAL ACCOUNTS

Dr. | Cr.

Particulars	X ₹	Y ₹	Z ₹	Particulars	X ₹	Y ₹	Z ₹
To Realisation A/c	20,000	20,000	10,000	By Balance b/d	2,00,000	3,00,000	1,00,000
To Shares in *ABC* Ltd.	2,40,000	2,40,000	1,20,000	By General Reserve	40,000	40,000	20,000
To Cash A/c	—	80,000	—	By Cash A/c	20,000	—	10,000
	2,60,000	3,40,000	1,30,000		2,60,000	3,40,000	1,30,000

CASH AND BANK ACCOUNT

Dr. | Cr.

Particulars	₹	₹	Particulars	₹	₹
To Balance b/d	40,000	10,000	By Cash A/c (Contra)*	—	10,000
To Bank A/c (Contra)*	10,000		By Y	80,000	—
To X	20,000				
To Z	10,000				
	80,000	10,000		80,000	10,000

JOURNAL OF ABC LTD.

Date	Particulars		L.F.	Dr. (₹)	Cr. (₹)
1.	Business Purchase A/c	Dr.		6,00,000	
	To *XYZ* & Co.				6,00,000
	(Being business of *XYZ* & Co. purchased and payment due)				
2.	Plant and Machinery A/c	Dr.		5,00,000	
	Furniture and Fixture A/c	Dr.		50,000	
	Stock in Trade A/c	Dr.		2,00,000	
	Sundry Debtors A/c	Dr.		2,00,000	
	To Sundry Creditors A/c				3,00,000
	To Unrecorded Liability A/c				25,000
	To Business Purchase A/c				6,00,000
	To Capital Reserve A/c (*Bal. Fig.*)				25,000
	(Being take over of all assets and liabilities)				
3.	XYZ & Co.	Dr.		6,00,000	
	To Equity Share Capital A/c				5,00,000
	To Securities Premium A/c				1,00,000
	(Being purchase consideration discharged in the form of shares of ₹, 10 each issued at a premium of ₹, 2 each)				

Date	Particulars		L.F.	Dr. (₹)	Cr. (₹)
4.	Sundry Creditors A/c	Dr.		1,00,000	
	To Sundry Debtors A/c				1,00,000
	(Being mutual owings eliminated)				

BALANCE SHEET OF ABC LTD. AS AT 31.3.2015

Particulars	Note No	₹
I. Equity and Liabilities		
(1) Shareholders' Funds		
(a) Share Capital	1	25,00,000
(b) Reserves and Surplus	2	8,25,000
(2) Non-Current Liabilities		
(3) Current Liabilities		
(a) Trade Payables [Creditors] [3,00,000 + 13,00,000 – 1,00,000]		15,00,000
(b) Short-term Provisions [Unrecorded Liability]		25,000
Total		48,50,000
II. Assets		
(1) Non-Current Assets		
(a) Fixed Assets		
Tangible Assets	3	23,75,000
(2) Current Assets		
(a) Inventories [2,00,000 + 8,50,000]		10,50,000
(b) Trade Receivables [2,00,000 + 8,25,000 – 1,00,000]		9,25,000
(b) Cash and Cash Equivalents [4,00,000 + 1,00,000]		5,00,000
Total		48,50,000

Notes To Accounts:

Particulars	₹
1. Share Capital	
2,50,000 Equity Shares of ₹ 10 each	25,00,000
(Of the above 50,000 Shares were issued for consideration otherwise than cash)	
2. Reserves and Surplus	
General Reserve	7,00,000
Capital Reserve	25,000
Securities Premium	1,00,000
Total	8,25,000
3. Tangible Assets	
Plant & Machinery [5,00,000 + 16,00,000]	21,00,000
Furniture & Fixtures [50,000 + 2,25,000]	2,75,000
Total	23,75,000

Working Note:

(i) **Purchase Consideration** = 5000 × ₹ 12 = ₹ 6,00,000
Equity shares distributed among partners:

Partner *X*	=	20,000 shares @ ₹ 12	= ₹ 2,40,000
Partner *Y*	=	20,000 shares @ ₹ 12	= ₹ 2,40,000
Partner *Z*	=	10,000 shares @ ₹ 12	= ₹ 1,20,000
			₹ 6,00,000

(ii) It is assumed that cash at bank has been withdrawn to pay ₹.80,000 to partner *Y*. However payment to *Y* of ₹ 80,000 can also be made by cash ₹ 70,000 & by cheque ₹ 10,000.

PROBLEM 15

XYZ Limited was incorporated for taking over the business of Y from 1st April, 2010. The following is the Balance Sheet of Y on 31st March, 2015:

Liabilities	₹	*Assets*	₹
Capital	10,08,000	Land and Building	16,00,000
Loans	12,00,000	Plant and Machinery	2,80,000
Creditors	7,12,000	Furniture	2,00,000
		Sundry Debtors	8,40,000
	29,20,000		29,20,000

The company takes over the business with fixed assets and loans on the following terms:

(a) The fixed assets should be depreciated @10%.
(b) The value of Goodwill is estimated at ₹ 8,00,000.

The company realized ₹ 8,00,000 from Sundry debtors as the agent of the vendor in full settlement and discharged all the trade creditors by paying ₹ 6,80,000 for a commission of 3% on the amount collected and 2% on the amount paid.

(Commission is treated as pre-incorporation profit)

The lenders accepted 10% preference shares of ₹ 100 each in discharge of their loan. After realization of debts and discharge of the liabilities, the total amount due to the vendor was settled by payment of ₹ 54,400 in cash and the balance in shares of fully paid equity shares of ₹ 10 each.

You are required to:

(i) Compute Purchase Consideration.
(ii) Pass Journal Entries in the books of XYZ Limited after taking over the business of Y.
(iii) Prepare the Balance Sheet of the company as on 1st April, 2015.

Solution

(I) COMPUTATION OF PURCHASE CONSIDERATION

Particulars	(₹)
Assets taken over by Y	
Land and Building	16,00,000
Plant and Machinery	2,80,000
Furniture	2,00,000
	20,80,000
Less: Depreciation @ 10%	(2,08,000)
	18,72,000
Add: Goodwill	8,00,000
	26,72,000
Less: Loan	(12,00,000)
Purchase consideration	14,72,000

(II) JOURNAL OF XYZ LIMITED

Date	Particulars		Dr. (₹)	Cr. (₹)
1.4.13	Business Purchase A/c	Dr.	14,72,000	
	To Y			14,72,000
	(Being purchase consideration due for taking over the business of Y)			
	Land and Building A/c (16,00,000 – 1,60,000)	Dr.	14,40,000	
	Plant and Machinery A/c (2,80,000 – 28,000)	Dr.	2,52,000	
	Furniture A/c (2,00,000 – 20,000)	Dr.	1,80,000	
	Goodwill A/c	Dr.	8,00,000	
	To Loans A/c			12,00,000
	To Business Purchase A/c			14,72,000
	(Being assets and liabilities taken over)			
	Vendor's Debtors	Dr.	8,40,000	
	To Vendor's Suspense A/c			8,40,000
	(Being Vendor's debtors to be collected on behalf of Y)			
	Vendor's Suspense A/c	Dr.	7,12,000	
	To Vendor's Creditors			7,12,000
	(Being Vendor's creditors to be paid off on behalf of Y)			
	Bank A/c	Dr.	8,00,000	
	Vendor's Suspense A/c	Dr.	40,000	
	To Vendor's Debtors A/c			8,40,000
	(Being Vendor's debtors collected at loss)			
	Vendor's Creditors A/c	Dr.	7,12,000	
	To Bank A/c			6,80,000
	To Vendor's Suspense A/c			32,000
	(Being profit on payment to Vendor's creditors)			
	Vendor's Suspense A/c	Dr.	37,600	
	To Commission A/c			37,600
	(Being the commission @ 3% on Vendor's Debtors collected and 2% on payment to Vendor's Creditors)			
	Vendor's Suspense A/c	Dr.	82,400	
	To Y			82,400
	(Being transfer of the net balance of vendor's suspense account after realization of debtors and payment to creditors, to Y)			
	Y	Dr.	15,54,400	
	To Equity share capital A/c			15,00,000
	To Bank A/c			54,400
	(Being allotment of 1,50,000 equity shares of ₹ 10 each as fully paid up and payment of cash as agreed in discharge of total amount due to Y)			
	Loan A/c	Dr.	12,00,000	
	To 10% Preference share capital A/c			12,00,000
	(Being issue of 12,000 10% preference shares for discharge of loan)			

Date	Particulars	Dr. (₹)	Cr. (₹)
	Commission A/c Dr.	37,600	
	To Capital Reserve A/c		37,600
	(Being commission earned on settlement of vendor's debtors and creditors is treated as pre-incorporation profit which is transferred to capital reserve account)		

(III) BALANCE SHEET OF XYZ LIMITED AS AT 1ST APRIL, 2015

Particulars	Note No	₹
I. Equity and Liabilities		
(1) Shareholders' Funds		
(a) Share Capital	1	27,00,000
(c) Reserves and Surplus [Capital Reserve]		37,600
(2) Non-Current Liabilities		
(a) Long-term Borrowings		
(3) Current Liabilities		
Total		27,37,600
II. Assets		
(1) Non-Current Assets		
(a) Fixed Assets		
Tangible Assets		18,72,000
Intangible Assets [Goodwill]	2	8,00,000
(2) Current Assets		
(a) Cash and Cash Equivalents		65,600
Total		27,37,600

Notes To Accounts:

Particulars	₹
1. Share Capital	
1,50,000 Equity Shares of ₹ 10 each	15,00,000
12,000, 10% Pref. Shares of ₹ 100 each	12,00,000
(Of the above all Shares were issued for consideration otherwise than cash)	27,00,000
2. Tangible Assets	
Land & Building	14,40,000
Plant & Machinery	2,52,000
Furniture	1,80,000
	18,72,000

Working Note: *Calculation of Cash balance of XYZ Ltd.*

	₹
Cash collected from vendor's debtors	8,00,000
Less: Cash paid to vendor's creditors	(6,80,000)
Less: Cash paid to Y	(54,400)
	65,600

CONVERSION OF FIRM INTO A COMPANY

PROBLEM 1

Avinash, Rohit and Madwesh were carrying on business in partnership sharing Profit and Losses in the ratio of 5:4:3 respectively. The Trial Balance of the firm as on 31st March, 2015 was the following:

Particulars	*Dr. (₹)*	*Cr. (₹)*
Plant and Machinery at cost	1,05,000	—
Stock	60,200	—
Sundry Debtors	85,000	—
Sundry Creditors	—	1,05,200
Capital A/cs:		
Avinash	—	70,000
Rohit	—	50,000
Madwesh	—	30,000
Drawings A/cs:		
Avinash	30,000	—
Rohit	25,000	—
Madwesh	20,000	—
Depreciation on Plant and Machinery	—	35,000
Trading Profit for the year	—	1,29,800
Cash at Bank	94,800	—
	4,20,000	4,20,000

Additional Information:

(a) Interest on Capital Accounts at 10% on the amount standing to the credit of partners capital accounts at the beginning of the year was not provided before preparing the above Trial Balance.

(b) On 31st March, 2015 they formed a Private Ltd. Company Anagha (P) Ltd, to take over the partnership business.

(c) You are further informed as under:

(i) Plant and Machinery is to be transferred at ₹. 80,000.

(ii) Equity Shares of ₹. 10 each of the company are to be issued to the partners at par in such numbers to ensure that by reason of their share holdings alone, they will have the same rights of sharing Profits and Losses as they had in the partnership. Balance, if any in their Capital Accounts, will be settled by giving 7½% Preference Shares of ₹ 100 each at par.

(iii) Before transferring the business, the partners withdrew by cash from partnership the following amounts over and above the drawings as shown in the Trial Balance:

(a) Avinash ₹. 20,000, (b) Rohit ₹. 10,600, (c) Madwesh ₹. 14,200

(iv) All Assets and Liabilities except Plant and Machinery and the Bank Balance are to be transferred at their value in the books of the partnership as at 31st March, 2015.

Required: Prepare:

(a) Profit and Loss Adjustment Account for the year ending 31st March, 2015.

(b) Capital Accounts showing all the adjustments required to dissolve the partnership

(c) A statement showing the number of shares of each class to be issued by the company to each of the partners to settle their accounts.

(d) Prepare Balance Sheet of the company Anagha (P) Ltd. as on 31.03.2015 after take over of the business.

Solution

Dr. **PROFIT AND LOSS ADJUSTMENT ACCOUNT FOR THE YEAR ENDING 31ST MARCH, 2015** *Cr.*

Particulars		*₹.*	*Particulars*	*₹.*
To Interest on Capital Avinash:		7,000	By Balance b/d	1,29,800
	Rohit	5,000	By Plant and Machinery	10,000
	Madwesh	3,000		
To Profit t/f to Capital Accounts:				
	Avinash	52,000		
	Rohit	41,600		
	Madwesh	31,200		
		1,39,800		1,39,800

Dr. **(B) PARTNERS' CAPITAL ACCOUNTS** *Cr.*

Particulars	*Avinash* ₹	*Rohit* ₹	*Madwesh* ₹	*Particulars*	*Avinash* ₹	*Rohit* ₹	*Madwesh* ₹
To Drawings as per Trial Balance	30,000	25,000	20,000	By Balance b/d	70,000	50,000	30,000
To Additional Drawings	20,000	10,600	14,200	By Profit and Loss Adjustment A/c	52,000	41,600	31,200
To Balance c/d	79,000	61,000	30,000	By Interest on Capital	7,000	5,000	3,000
	1,29,000	96,600	64,200		1,29,000	96,600	64,200
To Equity Shares	50,000	40,000	30,000	By Balance b/d	79,000	61,000	30,000
To Preference Shares	29,000	21,000	—				
	79,000	61,000	30,060		79,000	61,000	30,000

(C) STATEMENT SHOWING THE NUMBER AND CLASSES OF SHARES ISSUED TO THE PARTNERS

Particulars	*Avinash*	*Rohit*	*Madwesh*
Closing Capital Balance (After Adjustments)	79,000	61,000	30,000
Taking Madwesh's Capital as base for ensuring same rights of share holding-Equity Shares of ₹ 10 each to be issued	50,000	40,000	30,000
Balance to be settled by issue of 7%% Preference Shares for Surplus Capital	29,000	21,000	—

BALANCE SHEET ANAGHA OF LTD. AS AT 31.3.2015

Particulars	*Note No*	*₹*
I. Equity and Liabilities		
(1) Shareholders'Funds		
(a) Share Capital	1	1,70,000
(c) Reserves and Surplus		—
(2) Non-Current Liabilities		—
(3) Current Liabilities		
(a) Trade Payables [Creditors]		1,05,200
Total		2,75,200

II. Assets		
(1) Non-Current Assets		
(a) Fixed Assets		
Tangible Assets (Plant and Machinery)		80,000
(2) Current Assets		
(a) Inventories		60,200
(b) Trade Receivables [Debtors]		85,000
(b) Cash and Cash Equivalents		50,000
Total		2,75,000

Notes To Accounts:

Particulars	₹
1. Share Capital	
12,000, Equity Shares of ₹. 10 each	1,20,000
500, 7.5% Pref. Shares of ₹. 10 each	50,000
(Of the above all Shares were issued for consideration otherwise than cash)	1,70,000

PROBLEM 2

P, Q and R are partners hsaring profits and losses in the ratio 3 : 2 : 1 after allowing interest on capital @ 9% p.a. Their balance Sheet as at 31st March, 2014 is as follows:

Liabilities	*(₹)*	*Assets*	*(₹)*
Capital Accounts:		Plant & Machinery	1,08,000
P	50,000	Fixtures	20,000
Q	30,000	Stock	50,000
R	20,000	Sundry Debtors	30,000
Reserve Fund	60,000		
Creditors	48,000		
	2,08,000		2,08,000

The applied for conversion of the firm into a Private Limited Company named PQR Pvt. Ltd. and the certificate was received on 01-04-2014. They decided to maintain same profit sharing ratio and the preserve the priority in regard to repayment of capital as far as possible. For that purpose they decided to insert a clause of issuance of Preference shares in Memorandum of Association in addition to issuance of Equity Shares of ₹ 10 each.

On 01.04.2014, the value of goodwill is to be determined on the basis of 2 years' purchase of the average profit from the business of the last 5 years. The particulars of profits are as under:

		₹
Year ended 31.03.2010	Profit	10,000
Year ended 31.03.2011	Loss	5,000
Year ended 31.03.2012	Profit	18,000
Year ended 31.03.2013	Profit	27,000
Year ended 31.03.2014	Profit	30,000

The loss for the year ended 31-03-2011 was on account of loss by strike to the extent of ₹ 10,000.

It was agreed that rest of the assets are valued on the basis of the Balance Sheet as at 31-03-2014 except Plant & machinery which is valued at ₹ 1,02,000.

You are required to prepare (a) the Balance Sheet of the Company as at 01.04.2014, (b) Partners' Capital Accounts and (c) Statement showing the final settlement between the partners taking Q's capital as basis.

Solution

(a) **BALANCE SHEET OF THE PQR PVT LTD. AS AT 1.4.2014**

Particulars	*Note No.*	*(₹)*
I. EQUITY AND LIABILITIES		
(1) Shareholders' Funds		
(a) Share Capital	1	1,90,000
(2) Non-Current Liabilities		
(3) Current Liabilities		
(a) Trade Payables		48,000
Total		2,38,000
II. ASSETS		
(1) Non-Current Assets		
(a) Fixed Assets		
(i) Tangible Assets	2	1,22,000
(ii) Intangible Assets	3	36,000
(2) Current Assets		
(a) Inventories		50,000
(b) Trade Receivables		30,000
Total		2,38,000

Notes **To Accounts:**

1. Share Capital

	(₹)
Authorised Capital	
18,000 Equity Shares of ₹ 10 each	1,80,000
9% Pref. Shares of ₹ 100 each	10,000
	1,90,000
Issued & Subscribed Capital	
18,000 Equity Shares of ₹ 10 each	1,80,000
9% Pref. Shares of ₹ 100 each	10,000
(All the shares have been issued for consideration other than cash)	1,90,000
2. Tangible Assets	
Plant and Machinery	1,02,000
Fixtures	20,000
	1,22,000
3. Intangible Assets	
Goodwill	36,000

(b) *Dr.* **CAPITAL ACCOUNTS OF PARTNERS** *Cr.*

Particulars	*P* ₹	*Q* ₹	*R* ₹	*Particulars*	*P* ₹	*Q* ₹	*R* ₹
To P & M A/c	3,000	2,000	1,000	By Balance b/d	50,000	30,000	20,000
To 9% Preference Shares	5,000	–	5,000	By Reserve fund	30,000	20,000	10,000
To Equity Shares	90,000	60,000	30,000	By Realization A/c (Profit on Sale of Business)	18,000	12,000	6,000
	98,000	62,000	36,000		98,000	62,000	36,000

The question of preference and equity shares to be issued to *P*, *Q* and *R* can be dealt with in the following manner:

Particulars	*P* ₹	*Q* ₹	*R* ₹
A. Total amount due as capital	95,000	60,000	35,000
B. Proportionate Capitals taking *Q*'s Capital as the Base Capital (for which Equity Shares should be issued)	90,000	60,000	30,000
C. Surplus Capital (A – B) (for which 9% Non-Cum Pref. Shares should be issued)	5,000	–	5,000

The above treatment is based on the principle that the function of interest in case of partnership is to compensate those partners who contribute capital in excess of what is required as per profit sharing ratio.

Working Notes: 1. Calculation of goodwill

year ended 31st March	*2010* ₹	*2011* ₹	*2012* ₹	*2013* ₹	*2014* ₹
Profits	10,000	(5,000)	18,000	27,000	30,000
Adjustment for abnormal loss in 2010-2011	–	10,000	–	–	–
	10,000	5,000	18,000	27,000	30,000
					₹
Total Profit from 2009-2011 to 2013-2014					90,000
Average Profit (90,000/5)					18,000
Goodwill equal to 2 years' Purchase					36,000

2. Computation of Purchase consideration

Assets	₹	₹
Goodwill	36,000	
Plant and Machinery	1,02,000	
Fixtures	20,000	
Stock	50,000	
Sundry Debtors	30,000	2,38,000
Less: Liabilities (Creditors)		(48,000)
Purchase Consideration		1,90,000

PROBLEM 3

The following is the Balance Sheet of M/s *P* and *Q* as on 31st March, 2014:

Liabilities	₹	*Assets*	₹
P's Capital	50,000	Machinery	54,000
Q's Capital	30,000	Furniture	5,000
Q's Loan	15,000	Investments	50,000
General Reserve	20,000	Stock	20,000
Creditors	40,000	Debtors	21,000
		Cash	5,000
	1,55,000		1,55,000

It was agreed that Mr. *R* is to be admitted for a fourth share in the future profits from 1st April, 2014. He is required to contribute cash towards goodwill and ₹ 15,000 towards capital. The following further information is furnished:

(a) *P* and *Q* share the profits in the ratio of 3 : 2.

(b) Mr *P* was receiving a salary of ₹ 750 p.m from the very inception of the firm in 2005 in addition to share of profit.

(c) The future profit sharing ratio between *P*, *Q* and *R* will be 2 : 1 : 1. Mr *P* will not get any salary after the admission of Mr *R*.

(d) The goodwill of the firm shall be determined on the basis of 3 years' purchase of the average profits from business of the last 5 years. The particulars of the profits are as under:

2009-2010 Profit ₹ 25,000, 2010-2011 Profit ₹ 12,500, 2011-2012 Loss ₹ 2,500, 2012-2013 Profit ₹ 35,000, 2013-2014 Profit ₹ 30,000.

The above profits and losses are after charging the salary of Mr *P*. The profit for the year ended. 31st March 2010 included an extraneous profits of ₹ 40,000 and the loss of the year ended 31st March 2012 was on account of loss by strike to the extent of ₹ 20,000. It was agreed that the value of the goodwill of the firm shall appear in the book of the firm.

(e) The cash trading profit for the year ended 31st March, 2015 was ₹ 50,000 before depreciation.

(f) Each partner withdrew ₹ 1,000 p.m. as drawings.

(g) The value of the other assets and liabilities as on 31st March, 2015 were Machinery (before depreciation) ₹ 60,000, Furniture (before depreciation) ₹ 10,000, Investments ₹ 50,000, Stock ₹ 15,000, Debtors ₹ 30,000, Creditors ₹ 20,000.

(h) Provide depreciation @ 10% on Machinery and @ 5% on furnitures on the closing balance and interest @ 6% on *Q*'s loan. The loan along with interest would be repaid within next 12 months.

(i) Investments are held from inception of the firm and interest is received @ 10% p.a.

(j) The partners applied for conversion of the firm into a Private Limited Company. Certificate was received on 1st April, 2015. They decided to convert Capital A/cs of the partners into share capital in the ratio of 2 : 1 : 1 on the basis of total Capital as on 31st March, 2015. If necessary, partners have to subscribe to fresh capital or withdraw.

Required: Prepare the Profit and Loss Account for the year ended 31st March, 2015 and the Balance Sheet as at 1st April 2015.

Solution

PROFIT AND LOSS ACCOUNT

Dr. *for the year ending on 31st March, 2015* *Cr.*

Particulars		₹	Particulars	₹
To Depreciation on Machinery		6,000	By Trading Profit	50,000
To Depreciation on furniture		500	By Interest on Investment	5,000
To Interest on Q's loan		900		
To Net Profit to:				
P's Capital A/c	23,800			
Q's Capital A/c	11,900			
R's Capital A/c	11,900	47,600		
		55,000		55,000

BALANCE SHEET OF THE PQR PVT LTD. AS AT 1.4.2015

Particulars	Note No.	(₹)
I. EQUITY AND LIABILITIES		
(1) Shareholders' Funds		
(a) Share Capital		1,41,600
(2) Current Liabilities		
(a) Short Term borrowings	1	15,900
(b) Trade Payables		20,000
Total		1,77,500
II. ASSETS		
(1) Non-Current Assets		
(a) Fixed Assets		
(i) Tangible Assets	2	63,500
(ii) Non-current investments		50,000
(2) Current Assets		
(a) Inventories		15,000
(b) Trade Receivables		30,000
(c) Cash and cash equivalents		19,000
Total		2,38,000

Notes To Accounts:

		₹
1. Short term borrowings		
Loan from Q		15,900
2. Tangible assets		
Machinery	54,000	
Furniture	9,500	63,500

Working Notes: 1. Calculation of goodwill

year ended 31st March	*2010* ₹	*2011* ₹	*2012* ₹	*2013* ₹	*2014* ₹
Profits/(Loss)	25,000	12,500	(2,500)	35,000	30,000
Adjustment for Abnormal Profit & Loss	(40,000)	—	20,000	—	—
Add: Salary of partner (750 × 12)	9,000	9,000	9,000	9,000	9,000
Less: Interest on Non-Trading Investments	(5,000)	(5,000)	(5,000)	(5,000)	(5,000)
	(11,000)	16,500	21,500	39,000	34,000
					₹
Total Profit for five years					1,00,000
Average Profit (` 1,00,000/5)					20,000
Goodwill equal to 3 years' Purchase					60,000
New partner's share of goodwill for 1/4 share					15,000

2. Sacrificing Ratio: P's sacrifice = 3/5 – 1/2 = 1/10, Q's sacrifice = 2/5 – 1/4 = 3/20
3. As per AS 26 "Intangible Assets", only purchased goodwill should appear in the books. Therefore, goodwill though required to be shown in the books as per the requirement of the question, has been adjusted through capital accounts of the partenrs in line with the provisions of AS 26.

4. *Dr.* **CAPITAL ACCOUNTS OF PARTNERS** *Cr.*

Particulars	*P* ₹	*Q* ₹	*R* ₹	*Particulars*	*P* ₹	*Q* ₹	*R* ₹
To Drawings A/c	12,000	12,000	12,000	By Balance b/d	50,000	30,000	—
To P	—	—	6,000	By General Reserve	12,000	8,000	—
To Q	—	—	9,000	By R	6,000	9,000	—
To Balance c/d	79,800	46,900	14,900	By Bank A/c	—	—	30,000
				By P & L A/c	23,800	11,900	11,900
	91,800	58,900	41,900		91,800	58,900	41,900

5. **BALANCE SHEET OF M/S XYZ & CO. AS AT 31ST MARCH, 2015**

Liabilities		₹	*Assets*		₹
P's Capital	79,800		Machinery	60,000	
Q's Capital	46,900		*Less*: Depreciation	(6,000)	54,000
R's Capital	14,900	1,41,600	Furniture	10,000	
			Less: Depreciation	(500)	9,500
Q's Loan	15,000		Investments		50,000
Add: Interest due	900	15,900	Stock-in-trade		15,000
Creditors		20,000	Debtors		30,000
			Cash		19,000
		1,77,500			1,77,500

6. **CALCULATION OF CLOSING CASH BALANCE**

Particulars	₹
Opening cash balance	5,000
Add: Cash brought in by R	30,000
Less: Drawings (12,000 + 12,000 + 12,000)	36,000
Less: Additions to Machine (60,000 – 54,000)	6,000
Less: Addition to Furniture (10,000 – 5,000)	5,000

Cash Trading Profit	50,000
Add: Investment Interest	5,000
Add: Decrease in Stock Balance	5,000
Less: Increase in Debtors	9,000
Less: Decrease in Creditors	20,000
Closing Cash Balance	19,000

7. **ADJUSTMENT OF CAPITALS**

Particulars	*P*	*Q*	*R*
A. Adjusted Capitals	79,800	46,900	14,900
B. Distribution of Shares in the ratio of 2:1:1	70,800	35,400	35,400
C. Surplus to be withdrawn (Shortage to be brought in)	9,000	11,500	(20,500)

AMALGAMATION

PROBLEM 3

Firm X & Co. conlsists of partners A and B sharing Profits and Losses in the rato of 3:2. The firm Y & Co. consists of partners B and C sharing Profits and Losses in the ratio of 5:3.

On 31st March, 2015 it was decided to amalgamate both the firms and form a new firm XY & Co., wherein A, B and C would be partners sharing Profits and Losses in the ratio of 4:5:1.

BALANCE SHEET AS AT 31.3.2015

Liabilities	*X & Co.* ₹	*Y & Co.* ₹	*Assets*	*X & Co.* ₹	*Y& CO.* ₹
Capital: A	1,50,000		Cash in hand & bank	40,000	30,000
B	1,00,000	75,000	Debtors	60,000	80,000
C	—	50,000	Stock	50,000	20,000
Reserve	50,000	40,000	Vehicles	—	90,000
Creditors	1,20,000	55,000	Machinery	1,20,000	—
			Building	1,50,000	—
	4,20,000	2,20,000		4,20,000	2,20,000

The following were the terms of amalgamation:

(i) Goodwill of X & Co., was valued at ₹. 75,000. Goodwill of Y & Co. was valued at ₹. 40,000. Goodwill account not to be opened in the books of the new firm but adjusted through the Capital accounts of the partners.

(ii) Building, Machinery and Vehicles are to be taken over at ₹. 2,00,000, ₹. 1,00,000 and ₹, 74,000 respectively.

(iii) Provision for doubfful debts at ₹, 5,000 in respect of X & Co. and ₹. 4,000 in respect of Y & Co, are to be provided.

You are required to:

(i) Show, how the Goodwill value is adjusted amongst the partners.

(ii) Propare the Balance Sheet of XY & Co. as at 31.3.2015 by keeping partners' capitals in their profit sharing ratio by taking capital of B as the basis. The excess or deficiency to be kept in the respective Partners' Current accounts.

Solution

ADJUSTMENT FOR RAISING AND WRITING OFF OF GOODWILL

Raised in Old Profit Sharing Ratio X & Co. (3 : 2) ₹.	Y & Co. (5 : 3) ₹.	₹.	*Total Written off in new ratio 4 : 5 : 1* ₹.	*Difference* ₹.
45,000	—	45,000 Cr.	46,000 Dr.	1,000 Dr.
30,000	25,000	55,000 Cr.	57,500 Dr.	2,500 Dr.
—	15,000	15,000 Cr.	11,500 Dr.	3,500 Cr
75,000	40,000	1,15,000	1,15,000	Nil

BALANCE SHEET OF X Y & CO. (NEW FIRM) AS AT 31.3.2015

Liabilities	₹.	*Assets*	₹
Capital Accounts:		Vehicle	74,000
A	1,72,000	Machinery	1,00,000
B	2,15,000	Building	2,00,000
C	43,000	Stock	70,000
Current Accounts:		Debtors	1,31,000
A	22,000	Cash & Bank	70,000
C	18,000		
Creditors	1,75,000		
	6,45,000		6,45,000

Working Notes:

(i) *Balance of Capital Accounts at the time of amalgamation of firms*

Particulars	*X & Co. (3:2)*		*Y & Co. (5:3)*	
	A's Capital ₹	*B's Capital* ₹	*B's Capital* ₹	*A's Capital* ₹
Balance as per Balance Sheet	1,50,000	1,00,000	75,000	50,000
Add: Reserves	30,000	20,000	25,000	15,000
Revaluation profit (Building)	30,000	20,000	—	—
Less: Revaluation loss (Machinery)	(12,000)	(8,000)	(10,000)	(6,000)
Provision for doubtful debt.	(3,000)	(2,000)	(2,500)	(1,500)
	1,95,000	1,30,000	87,500	57,500

(ii) *Balance of Capital Accounts in the Balance Sheet of the new firm as at 31.3.2015*

Particulars	*A* ₹	*B* ₹	*C* ₹
Balance b/d: X & Co.	1,95,000	1,30,000	
Y & Co.	—	87,500	57,500
	1,95,000	2,17,500	57,500
Adjustment for goodwill	(1,000)	(2,500)	3,500
	1,94,000	2,15,000	61,000
Total Capital ₹ 4,30,000 (B's Capital i.e. ₹ 2,15,000 × 2) to be contributed in 4:5:1 ratio.	1,72,000	2,15,000	43,000
Transfer to Current Account	22,000	—	18,000

PROBLEM 4

P and Q have been carrying on same business independently. Due to competition in the market, they decided to amalgamate and form a new company called PQ Ltd.

Following is the Balance Sheet of P and Q as at 31.3.2015:

Liabilities	P ₹	Q ₹	*Assets*	P ₹	Q ₹
Capital	7,75,000	8,55,000	Plant & machinery	4,85,000	6,14,000
Current liabilities	6,23,500	5,57,600	Building	7,50,000	6,40,000
			Current Assets	1,63,500	1,58,600
	13,98,500	14,12,600		13,98,500	14,12,600

Following are the additional information:

(a) The authorised capital of the new company will be ₹.25,00,000 divided into 1,00,000 equity shares of ₹. 25 each.

(b) Liabilities of P includes ₹ 50 000 due to Q for the purchases made. Q made a profit of 20% on sale to P

(c) P has goods purchased from Q, cost to him ₹. 10, 000. This is included in the Current asset of P as at 31st March, 2015.

(d) The assets of P and Q are to be revalued as under:

	P	Q
Plant and Machinery	₹ 5,25,000	₹ 6,75,000
Building	₹ 7,75,000	₹ 6,48,000

(e) The purchase consideration is to be discharged as under:

(i) Issue 24,000 equity shares of ₹. 25 each fully paid up in the proportion of their profitability in the preceding 2 years. Profits for the preceding 2 years are given below:

	P	Q
	₹	₹
Ist year	2,62,800	2,75,125
IInd Year	2,12,200	2,49,875
	4,75,000	5,25,000

(ii) Issue 12% preference shares of ₹. 10 each fully paid up at par to provide income equivalent to 8% return on capital employed in the business as on 31.3.2015 after revaluation of assets of P and Q respectively.

Required:

(i) Compute the amount of equity and preference shares issued to P and Q.

(ii) Prepare the Balance Sheet of P & 0 Ltd. immediately after amalgamation.

Solution

(i) Calculation of amount of equity shares issued to P and Q

Profit	P	Q
	₹	₹
Ist year	2,62,800	2,75,125
IInd year	2,12,200	2,49,875
Total	4,75,000	5,25,000

No. of shares to be issued = 24,000 equity shares in the proportion of the preceding 2 years profitability

	P	Q
24000 × 475/1000	11,400 equity shares	
24000 × 525/1000		12,600 equity shares

Calculation of amount of 12% Preference shares issued to P and Q

	P	Q
Capital Employed	₹ 8,40,000	₹ 9,24,000
8% Return on Capital Employed	₹ 67,200	₹ 73,920
12% Preference shares to be issued $\left[67{,}200 \times \frac{100}{12}\right]$	₹. 5,60,000	
$\left[73{,}920 \times \frac{100}{12}\right]$		₹ 6,16,000

Total Purchase Consideration

	P	Q
Equity Shares	₹ 2,85,000	₹ 3,15,000
12% Preference Shares	₹ 5,60,000	₹ 6,16,000
Total	₹ 8,45,000	₹ 9,31,000

(II) BALANCE SHEET OF PQ LTD. AS AT 31.3.2015

Particulars	*Note No*	*₹ (lacs)*
I. Equity and Liabilities		
(1) Shareholders' Funds		
(a) Share Capital	1	17,76,000
(b) Reserves and Surplus		—
(2) Non-Current Liabilities		—
(3) Current Liabilities		11,31,100
Total		29,07,100
II. Assets		
(1) Non-Current Assets		
(a) Fixed Assets		
Tangible Assets	2	26,23,000
Intangible Assets [Goodwill]		14,000
(2) Current Assets		2,70,100
Total		29,07,100

Notes To Accounts:

Particulars	*₹ (lacs)*
1. Share Capital	
24,000 Equity Shares of ₹. 25 each	6,00,000
1,17,600, 12% Pref. Shares of ₹. 10 each	11,76,000
(Of the above all Shares were issued for consideration otherwise than cash)	
	17,76,000
2. Tangible Assets	
Land & Building	14,23,000
Plant & Machinery	26,23,000
Total	26,23,000

Working Notes:

(i) **Goodwill**

	P ₹	*Q* ₹
Plant and machinery	5,25,000	6,75,000
Building	7,75,000	6,48,000
Current assets	1,63,500	1,58,600
	14,63,500	14,81,600
Less: Current Liabilities	6,23,500	5,57,600
Net assets taken (capital employed)	8,40,000	9,24,000
Less: Purchase consideration	8,45,000	9,31,000
Goodwill	5,000	7,000
Total purchased goodwill		12,000
Add: Unrealised profitof ₹.10,000 @ 20% ₹. 2,000 is adjusted from current assets and from goodwill (since P & L A/c is not given)		2,000
Total Goodwill		14,000

(ii) Current Assets

	P ₹	Q ₹
Balances before amalgamation	1,63,500	1,58,600
Less: Liabilities of P due to Q	—	50,000
Less: Unrealised Profit on Stock (i.e. ₹ 10,000 × 20%)	2,000	—
Total	1,61,500	1,08,600
Grand Total		2,70,100

(iii) Current Liabilities

	P ₹	Q ₹
Balances before amalgamation	6,23,500	5,57,600
Less: Liabilities of P due to Q	50,000	—
Total	5,73,500	5,57,600
Grand Total		11,31,100

PROBLEM 5

P and *Q* are partners of *P & Co.* sharing Profit and losses in the ratio of 3 : 1 and *Q* and *R* are partners of *R & Co.*, sharing profits and losses in the ratio of 2 : 1. On 31st March, 2015, they decide to amalgamate and form a new firm *M/s PQR & Co.*, wherein *P, Q* and *R* would be partners sharing profits and losses in the ratio of 3 : 2 : 1. The Balance Sheets of two firms on the above date are as under:

Liabilities	*P & Co.* ₹	*R & Co.* ₹	*Assets*	*P & Co.* ₹	*R & Co.* ₹
Capitals:			*Fixed Assets:*		
P	2,40,000	----	Building	50,000	60,000
Q	1,60,000	2,00,000	Plant & machinery	1,50,000	1,60,000
R	—	1,00,000	Office Equipment	20,000	6,000
Reserves	50,000	1,50,000	*Current Assets:*		
Sundry Creditors	1,20,000	1,16,000	Stock-in-trade	1,20,000	140,000
Due to *P & Co.*	....	1,00,000	Sundry Debtors	1,60,000	2,00,000
Bank overdraft	80,000	----	Bank Balance	30,000	90,000
			Cash in hand	20,000	10,000
	—	—	Due from *R & Co.*	1,00,000	—
	6,50,000	6,66,000		6,50,000	6,66,000

The amalgamated firm took over the business on the following terms:

(a) Building of *P & Co.* was valued at ₹. 1, 00, 000.

(b) Plant and machinery of *P & Co.* was valued at ₹. 2,50,000 and that of *R & Co.* at ₹. 2,00,000.

(c) All stock in trade is to be appreciated by 20%.

(d) Goodwill valued of *P & Co.* at ₹. 1,20,000 and *R & Co.* at ₹. 60,000, but the same will not appear in the books of *PQR & Co.*

(e) Partners of new firm wiil bring the necessary cash to pay other partners to adjust their capitals according to the profit sharing ratio.

(f) Provisions for doubtful debts has to be carried forward at ₹. 12,000 in respect of debtors of *P & Co.* and ₹. 26,000 in respect of debtors of *R & Co.*

Required: Prepare the Balance Sheet of new firm and Capital Accounts of the partners in the books of old firms.

Solution

BALANCE SHEET OF M/S PQR & CO. AS AT 31ST MARCH, 2015

Liabilities	₹	*Assets*		₹
Capitals:		Building		
P	5,52,000	(₹.1, 00,000 + ₹.60,000)		1,60,000
Q	3,68,000	Plant & Machinery		
R	1,84,000	(₹. 2,50,000 + ₹. 2,00,000)		4,50,000
Sundry Creditors		Office Equipment		
(₹. 1,20,000 + 1,16,000)	2,36,000	(₹. 20,000 + ₹. 6,000)		26,000
Bank overdraft	80,000	Stock-in-trade		
		(₹.1, 44 ,000 + ₹.1, 68,000)		3,12,000
		Sundry Debtors	3,60,000	
		(₹. 1, 60,000 + ₹ .2,00,000)		
		Less: Provision	(38,000)	
		(₹. 12,000 + ₹. 26,000)		3,22,000
		Bank Balance		
		(₹. 30,000 + ₹. 90,000)		1,20,000
	—	Cash in hand		30,000*
	14,20,000			14,20,000

Dr. **PARTNERS' CAPITAL ACCOUNTS IN THE BOOKS OF P & CO.** *Cr.*

Particulars	*P* ₹	*Q* ₹	*Particulars*	*P* ₹	*Q* ₹
To Capital A/cs – M/s PQR & Co.	4,89,000	2,43,000	By Balance b/d	2,40,000	1,60,000
			By Reserve (3 : 1)	37,500	12,500
			By Profit on Realisation A/'c	2,11,500	70,500
	4,89,000	2,43,000		4,89,000	2,43,000

Dr. **PARTNERS' CAPITAL ACCOUNTS IN THE BOOKS OF R & CO.** *Cr.*

Particulars	*P* ₹	*Q* ₹	*Particulars*	*P* ₹	*Q* ₹
To Capital A/cs -M/s PQR & Co	3,68,000	1,84,000	By Balance b/d	2,00,000	1,00,000
			By Reserve (2 : 1)	1,00,000	50,000
			By Profit on Realisation	68,000	34,000
	3,68,000	1,84,000		3,68,000	1,84,000

Working Notes:

(i) Computation of Purchase Consideration

Particulars	*P & Co.* ₹.	*R & Co.* ₹.
Assets:		
Goodwill	1,20,000	60,000
Building	1,00,000	60,000
Plant & machinery	2,50,000	2,00,000
Office equipment	20,000	6,000
Stock-in-trade	1,44,000	1,68,000
Sundry Debtors	1,60,000	2,00,000

Bank balance		30,000	90,000
Cash in hand		20,000	10,000
Due from R & Co.		1,00,000	—
	(A)	9,44,000	7,94,000
Less: Liabilities:			
Creditors		1,20,000	1,16,000
Provision for doubtful debts		12,000	26,000
Due to P & Co.		—	1,00,000
Bank overdraft		80,000	—
	(B)	2,12,000	2,42,000
Purchase Consideration (A – B)		7,32,000	5,52,000

(ii) Computation of Proportionate Capital

M/s *PQR* & Co. (Purchase Consideration) (₹. 7,32,000 + ₹. 5,52,000)	12,84,000
Less: Goodwill Adjustment	(1,80,000)
Total Capital of new firm (Distributed in ratio 3 : 2 : 1)	11,04,000
P's Proportionate Capital	5,52,000
Q's Proportionate Capital	3,68,000
R's proportionate capital	1,84,000

(iii) Computation of Capital Adjustments

Particulars	*P* ₹.	*Q* ₹.	*R* ₹.	*Total* ₹.
Balance transferred from P & Co.	4,89,000	2,43,000		7,32,000
Balance transferred from R & Co.	—	3,68,000	1,84,000	5,52,000
	4,89,000	6,11,000	1,84,000	12,84,000
Less: Goodwill written off in the ratio of 3 : 2 : 1	(90,000)	(60,000)	(30,000)	(1,80,000)
Existing capital	3,99,000	5,51,000	1,54,000	11,04,000
Proportionate capital	5,52,000	3,68,000	1,84,000	11,04,000
Amount to be brought in (paid off)	1,53,000	(1,83,000)	30,000	

Dr. **REALISATION ACCOUNT IN THE BOOKS OF P & CO.** *Cr.*

Particulars		₹	*Particulars*	₹
To Building		50,000	By Creditors	1,20,000
To Plant & Machinery		1,50,000	By Bank overdraft	80,000
To Office Equipment		20,000	By M/s PQR & Co. (purchase consideration)	7,32,000
To Stock-in-trade		1,20,000		
To Sundry debtors		1,60,000		
To Bank balance		30,000		
To Cash in hand		20,000		
To Due from R & Co.		1,00,000		
To Partners' Capital A/cs				
P	2,11,500			
Q	70,500	2,82,000		
		9,32,000		9,32,000

Dr. **REALISATION ACCOUNT IN THE BOOKS OF R & CO.** Cr.

Particulars		₹	Particulars	₹
To Building		60,000	By Creditors	1,16,000
To Plant & machinery		1,60,000	By Due to P & Co.	1,00,000
To Office equipment		6,000	By M/s PQR & Co.	5,52,000
To Stock-in-trade		1,40,000	(purchase consideration)	
To Sundry debtors		2,00,000		
To Bank balance		90,000		
To Cash in hand		10,000		
To Partners' Capital A/c:				
Q	68,000			
R	34,000	1,02,000		
		7,68,000		7,68,000

PROBLEM 6

A and B are partners of AB & Co. sharing profits and losses in the ratio of 2: 1 and C and D are partners of CD & Co. sharing profits and losses in the ratio of 3:2. On 1st April 2015, they decided to amalgamate and form a new firm M/S. AD & Co. wherein all the partners of both the firm would be partners sharing profits and losses in the ratio of 2:1:3:2 respectively to A, B, C and D.

Their balance sheets on that date were as under:

Liabilities	AB & Co. ₹	CD & Co. ₹	Assets	AB & Co. ₹	CD & Co. ₹
Capitals					
A	1,50,000		Building	75,000	90,000
B	1,00,000		Machinery	1,20,000	1,00,000
C		1,20,000	Furniture	15,000	12,000
D		80,000	Stock	24,000	36,000
Reserve	66,000	54,000	Debtors	65,000	78,000
Creditors	52,000	35,000	Due from CD		
Due to AB & Co.		47,000	& Co.	47,000	
			Cash at Bank	18,000	15,000
			Cash in hand	4,000	5,000
	3,68,000	3,36,000		3,68,000	3,36,000

The amalgamated firm took over the business on the following terms:

(a) Building was taken over at ₹ 1,00,000 and ₹ 1,25,000 of AB & Co. and CD & Co. respectively. And machinery was taken over at ₹ 1,25,000 and ₹ 1,10,000 of AB & Co. and CD & Co. respectively.

(b) Goodwill of AB & Co. was worth ₹ 75,000 and that of CD & Co. was worth ₹ 50,000. Goodwill account was not to be opened in the books of the new firm, the adjustments being recorded through capital accounts of the partners.

(c) Provision for doubtful debts has to be carried forward at ₹ 5,000 in respect of debtors of AB & Co. and ₹ 8,000 in respect of CD & Co.

You are required:

(i) Compute the adjustments necessary for goodwill.

(ii) Pass the Journal Entries in the books of AD & Co. assuming that excess/deficit capital (taking D's capital as base) with reference to share in profits are to be transferred to current accounts.

Solution

(I) ADJUSTMENT FOR RAISING & WRITING OFF OF GOODWILL

	Goodwill raised in old profit sharing ratio			*Goodwill written off in new ratio*	*Difference*
	AB&Co.	*CD&Co.*	*Total*	*AD&Co.*	
	₹	₹	₹	₹	₹
A	50,000		50,000 Cr.	31,250 Dr.	18,750 Cr.
B	25,000		25,000 Cr.	15,625 Dr.	9,375 Cr.
C		30,000	30,000 Cr.	46,875 Dr.	16,875 Dr.
D		20,000	20,000 Cr.	31,250 Dr.	11, 250 Dr.
	75,000	50,000	1,25,000	1,25,000	

(ii) In the books of AD&Co.

JOURNAL

Date	*Particulars*		*Dr. (₹)*	*Cr. (₹)*
01 April	Building A/c	Dr.	1,00,000	
	Machinery A/c	Dr.	1,25,000	
	Furniture A/c	Dr.	15,000	
	Stock A/c	Dr.	24,000	
	Debtors A/c	Dr.	65,000	
	CD & Co. A/c	Dr.	47,000	
	Cash at bank A/c	Dr.	18,000	
	Cash in hand A/c	Dr.	4,000	
	To Provision for doubtful debts A/c			5,000
	To Creditors A/c			52,000
	To A's capital A/c			2,10,667
	To B's capital A/c			1,30,333
	(Being the sundry assets and liabilities of AB & Co. taken over at the values stated as per the agreement)			
	Building A/c	Dr.	1,25,000	
	Machinery A/c	Dr.	1,10,000	
	Furniture A/c	Dr.	12,000	
	Stock A/c	Dr.	36,000	
	Debtors A/c	Dr.	78,000	
	Cash at bank A/c	Dr.	15,000	
	Cash in hand A/c	Dr.	5,000	
	To Provision for doubtful debts A/c			8,000
	To Creditors A/c			35,000
	To AB & Co. A/c			47,000
	To C's capital A/c			1,74,600
	To D's capital A/c			1,16,400
	(Being the sundry assets and liabilities of CD & Co. taken over at the values stated as per the agreement)			
	C's capital A/c	Dr.	16,875	
	D's capital A/c	Dr.	11,250	
	To A's capital A/c			18,750
	To B's capital A/c			9,375
	(Being adjustment in capital accounts of the partners on account of goodwill)			

Date	Particulars	Dr. (₹)	Cr. (₹)
	AB & Co. A/c Dr. To CD & Co. A/c (Being mutual indebtedness of AB & Co. and CD&Co. cancelled)	47,000	 47,000
	A's Capital A/c Dr. To A's Current A/c (Being excess amount in A's capital A/c transferred to A's current A/c)	1,24,267	 1,24,267
	B's Capital A/c Dr. To B's Current A/c (Being excess amount in B's capital A/c transferred to B's current A/c)	87,133	 87,133

Working Notes:

(i) Profit on Revaluation

	AB & Co. ₹	CD & Co. ₹
Building (1,00,000 – 75,000)	25,000	
(1,25,000 – 90,000)		35,000
Machinery (1,25,000 – 1,20,000)	5,000	
(1,10,000 – 1,00,000)		10,000
	30,000	45,000
Less: Provision for doubtful debts	(5,000)	(8,000)
	25,000	37,000

(ii) Balance of Capital Accounts of Partners

	A's Capital ₹	B's Capital ₹	C's Capital ₹	D's Capital ₹
Balance as per the B/S	1,50,000	1,00,000	1,20,000	80,000
Reserves	44,000	22,000	32,400	21,600
Profit on revaluation	16,667	8,333	22,200	14,800
	2,10,667	1,30,333	1,74,600	1,16,400

(iii) Calculation of Capital of each partner in the new firm

Particulars	*A* ₹	*B* ₹	*C* ₹	*D* ₹
Balance	2,10,667	1,30,333	1,74,600	1,16,400
Adjustment for goodwill	18,750	9,375	(16,875)	(11,250)
	2,29,417	1,39,708	1,57,725	1,05,150
Total Capital ₹ 4,20,600* in the new ratio of 2 : 1 : 3 : 2	(1,05,150)	(52,575)	(1,57,725)	(1,05,150)
Transfer to Current Account	1,24,267	87,133		

* Taking D's capital as the base which is 2/8th of total capital; total capital will be 1,05,150 × 8/2 i.e ₹ 4,20,600.

ACCOUNTING FOR ROYALTY

PROBLEM 1

Tulsian Ltd. leased a mine for 20 years to Jalan Ltd. for a minimum rent of ₹ 94,000 forr the first year with an annual increase of ₹2,000 till it reaches ₹ 1,00,000 merging into a royalty @ ₹ 100 per unit produced. Output (in units) were as under.

Year	2011	2012	2013	2014	2015
Outputs (in units)	500	900	1,140	1,260	200

Required: Prepare the Analysis of Royalty Payable and Short Workings in each of the following alternative cases:

Case (a) Shortworking is not recoupable.

Case (b) Shortworking is recoupable.

Case (c) Shortworking is recoupable within first 3 years only.

Case (d) Shortworking is recoupable within 3 years following the year in which the shortworking arose.

Case (e) In the event of strike or riot or flooding, the minimum rent would be reduced proportionately having regard to the length of the stoppage. During the year 2015 there was strike lasting 3 months. Shortworking is recoupable within 3 year following the year in which shortworking arose.

Case (f) In the event of strike or riot or flooding, that the minimum rent not being reached. The minimum rent would be reduced 1/3rd. During the year 2015 there was strike lasting 3 months. Shortworking is recoupable within 3 year following the year in which shortworking arose.

Case (g) In the event of strike or riot or flooding, that the minimum rent not being reached, the actual royalty earned during the year would be full royalty obligation for the year. During the year, 2015, there was strike lasting 3 months.

Case (h) In the event of strike, the minimum rent would be taken pro-rata on the basis of actual numbers of working days but in the event of lockout, the lessee would be enjoy a concession in respect of minimum rent of 50% of the period of lockout. There was strike for 73 days and lockout for 4 months during the year 2015. Recoumpent of short working of each year is allowed during the next 3 years subject to maximum of ₹ 5,000 p.a.

SOLUTION

(A) ANALYSIS OF ROYALTY PAYABLE AND SHORT WORKINGS

A Year	B Output (Units)	C = B × Rate Actual Royalty	D Minimum Rent	E = D – C Short Working	F Short Working Recouped	G = C + E – F Actual Payment	H Short Working W/O	$I_n = I_{n-1} + E - F - H$ Short Working C/F
2011	500	50,000	94,000	44,000	—	94,000	44,000	—
2012	900	90,000	96,000	6,000	—	96,000	6,000	—
2013	1,140	1,14,000	98,000	—	—	1,14,000	—	—
2014	1,260	1,26,000	1,00,000	—	—	1,26,000	—	—
2015	200	20,000	1,00,000	80,000	—	1,00,000	80,000	—

(B) ANALYSIS OF ROYALTY PAYABLE AND SHORT WORKINGS

A Year	B Output (Units)	C = B × Rate Actual Royalty	D Minimum Rent	E = D – C Short Working	F Short Working Recouped	G = C + E – F Actual Payment	H Short Working W/O	$I_n = I_{n-1} + E - F - H$ Short Working C/F
2011	500	50,000	94,000	44,000	—	94,000	—	44,000
2012	900	90,000	96,000	6,000	—	96,000	—	50,000
2013	1,140	1,14,000	98,000	—	16,000	98,000	—	34,000
2014	1,260	1,26,000	1,00,000	—	26,000	1,00,000	—	8,000
2015	200	20,000	1,00,000	80,000	—	1,00,000	—	88,000

(C) ANALYSIS OF ROYALTY PAYABLE AND SHORT WORKINGS

A Year	B Output (Units)	C = B × Rate Actual Royalty	D Minimum Rent	E = D – C Short Working	F Short Working Recouped	G = C + E – F Actual Payment	H Short Working W/O	$I_n = I_{n-1} + E - F - H$ Short Working C/F
2011	500	50,000	94,000	44,000	—	94,000	—	44,000
2012	900	90,000	96,000	6,000	—	96,000	—	50,000
2013	1,140	1,14,000	98,000	—	16,000	98,000	34,000	—
2014	1,260	1,26,000	1,00,000	—	—	1,00,000	—	—
2015	200	20,000	1,00,000	80,000	—	1,00,000	80,000	—

(D) ANALYSIS OF ROYALTY PAYABLE AND SHORT WORKINGS

A Year	B Output (Units)	C = B × Rate Actual Royalty	D Minimum Rent	E = D – C Short Working	F Short Working Recouped	G = C + E – F Actual Payment	H Short Working W/O	$I_n = I_{n-1} + E - F - H$ Short Working C/F
2011	500	50,000	94,000	44,000	—	94,000	—	44,000
2012	900	90,000	96,000	6,000	—	96,000	—	50,000
2013	1,140	1,14,000	98,000	—	16,000	98,000	—	34,000
2014	1,260	1,26,000	1,00,000	—	26,000	1,00,000	2,000	6,000
2015	200	20,000	1,00,000	80,000	—	1,00,000	6,000	80,000

(E) ANALYSIS OF ROYALTY PAYABLE AND SHORT WORKINGS

A Year	B Output (Units)	C = B × Rate Actual Royalty	D Minimum Rent	E = D – C Short Working	F Short Working Recouped	G = C + E – F Actual Payment	H Short Working W/O	$I_n = I_{n-1} + E - F - H$ Short Working C/F
2011	500	50,000	94,000	44,000	—	94,000	—	44,000
2012	900	90,000	96,000	6,000	—	96,000	—	50,000
2013	1,140	1,14,000	98,000	—	16,000	98,000	—	34,000
2014	1,260	1,26,000	1,00,000	—	26,000	1,00,000	—	6,000
2015	200	20,000	1,00,000	55,000	—	1,00,000	6,000	55,000

(F) ANALYSIS OF ROYALTY PAYABLE AND SHORT WORKINGS

A Year	B Output (Units)	C = B x Rate Actual Royalty	D Minimum Rent	E = D – C Short Working	F Short Working Recouped	G = C + E – F Actual Payment	H Short Working W/O	$I_n = I_{n-1} + E - F - H$ Short Working C/F
2011	500	50,000	94,000	44,000	—	94,000	—	44,000
2012	900	90,000	96,000	6,000	—	96,000	—	50,000
2013	1,140	1,14,000	98,000	—	16,000	98,000	—	34,000
2014	1,260	1,26,000	1,00,000	—	26,000	1,00,000	2,000	6,000
2015	200	20,000	66,667	46,667	—	66,667	6,000	46,667

(G) ANALYSIS OF ROYALTY PAYABLE AND SHORT WORKINGS

A Year	B Output (Units)	C = B x Rate Actual Royalty	D Minimum Rent	E = D – C Short Working	F Short Working Recouped	G = C + E – F Actual Payment	H Short Working W/O	$I_n = I_{n-1} + E - F - H$ Short Working C/F
2011	500	50,000	94,000	44,000	—	94,000	—	44,000
2012	900	90,000	96,000	6,000	—	96,000	—	50,000
2013	1,140	1,14,000	98,000	—	16,000	98,000	—	34,000
2014	1,260	1,26,000	1,00,000	—	26,000	1,00,000	2,000	6,000
2015	200	20,000	1,00,000	—	—	20,000	6,000	—

(H) ANALYSIS OF ROYALTY PAYABLE AND SHORT WORKINGS

A Year	B Output (Units)	C = B x Rate Actual Royalty	D Minimum Rent	E = D – C Short Working	F Short Working Recouped	G = C + E – F Actual Payment	H Short Working W/O	$I_n = I_{n-1} + E - F - H$ Short Working C/F
2011	500	50,000	94,000	44,000	—	94,000	—	44,000
2012	900	90,000	96,000	6,000	—	96,000	—	50,000
2013	1,140	1,14,000	98,000	—	5,000	1,09,000	—	45,000
2014	1,260	1,26,000	1,00,000	—	5,000	1,21,000	34,000	6,000
2015	200	20,000	63,333	43,333	—	63,333	6,000	43,333

PROBLEM 2

Tulsian Ltd. leased a mine for 20 years to Jalan Ltd. for a minimum rent of ₹ 94,000 for the first year with an annual increase of ₹ 20,000 till it reaches ₹ 1,00,000 merging into a royalty @ ₹ 100 per unit produced. Sales and closing stocks were an under.

Year	2011	2012	2013	2014	2015
Sale	400	800	1,200	1,100	450
Closing Stock	100	200	140	300	50

In the event of strike, the minimum rent would be taken pro-rata on the basis of actual numbers of working days but in the event of lockout, the lesseewould be enjoy a concession in respect of minimum rent for 50% of the period of lockout. There was strike for 73 days and lockout for 4 months during the year 2015.

Recoupment of shortworking of each year is allowed during the next 5 years following the year in which the shortworking arose.

Required: Pass the necessary journal entries and prepare the necessary Ledger accounts in the books of Tulsian Ltd. and Jalan Ltd.

SOLUTION

ANALYSIS OF ROYALTY PAYABLE AND SHORT WORKINGS

A Year	B Output (Units) Qty.	C = B × Rate Actual Royalty ₹	D Minimum Rent ₹	E = D − C Short Working ₹	F Short Working Recouped ₹	G = C + E − F Actual Payment ₹	H Short Working W/O ₹	$I_n = I_{n-1} + E - F - H$ Short Working C/F ₹
2011	500	50,000	94,000	44,000	—	94,000	—	44,000
2012	900	90,000	96,000	6,000	—	96,000	—	50,000
2013	1,140	1,14,000	98,000	—	5,000	1,09,000	—	45,000
2014	1,260	1,26,000	1,00,000	—	5,000	1,21,000	34,000	6,000
2015	200	20,000	63,333	43,333	—	63,333	6,000	43,333

JOURNAL OF JALAN LTD.

Date	Particulars		L.F.	Dr. (₹)	Cr. (₹)
2011	Royalty Payable A/c	Dr.		50,000	
	Shortworking Recoupment A/c	Dr.		44,000	
	To Tulsian Ltd. A/c				94,000
	(Being minimum royalty short working and provided for)				
	Tulsian Ltd. A/c	Dr.		94,000	
	To Bank A/c				94,000
	(Being payment made to landlord)				
	Profit & Loss A/c	Dr.		50,000	
	To Royalty Payable A/c				50,000
	(Being Royalty debited to Profit & Loss A/c)				
2012	Royalty Payable A/c	Dr.		90,000	
	Shortworking Recoupment A/c	Dr.		6,000	
	To Tulsian Ltd. A/c				96,000
	(Being minimum royalty short working and provided for)				
	Tulsian Ltd. A/c	Dr.		96,000	
	To Bank A/c				96,000
	(Being payment made to landlord)				
	Profit & Loss A/c	Dr.		90,000	
	To Royalty Payable A/c				90,000
	(Being royalty charged to Profit & Loss A/c)				
2013	Royalty Payable A/c	Dr.		1,14,000	
	To Tulsian Ltd. A/c				1,14,000
	(Being royalty payable provided full)				

	Tulsian Ltd. A/c To Bank A/c To Shortworking Recoupment A/c (Being payment made after ducting maximum shortworking)	Dr.		1,14,000	 1,09,000 5,000
	Royalty Payable A/c To Profit & Loss A/c (Being royalty charged to Profit & Loss A/c)	Dr.		1,14,000	 1,14,000
2014	Royalty Payable A/c To Tulsian Ltd. A/c (Being royalty payble provided for)	Dr.		1,26,000	 1,26,000
	Tulsian Ltd. A/c To Bank A/c To Shortworking Recoupment A/c (Being payment made after ducting maximum shortworking)	Dr.		1,26,000	 1,21,000 5,000
	Royalty Payable A/c To Profit & Loss A/c (Being royalty charged to Profit & Loss A/c)	Dr.		1,26,000	 1,26,000
	Shortworking Recoupment A/c To Profit & Loss A/c (Being irrecoverable shortworking written off)	Dr.		34,000	 34,000
2015	Royalty Payable A/c Shortworking Recoupment A/c To Tulsian Ltd. A/c (Being minimum royalty shortworking provided for)	Dr. Dr.		20,000 43,333	 63,333
	Tulsian Ltd. A/c To Bank A/c (Being payment made to landlord)	Dr.		63,333	 63,333
	Royalty Payable A/c To Profit & Loss A/c (Being royalty charged to Profit & Loss A/c)	Dr.		20,000	 20,000
	Shortworking irrecoverable account To Profit & Loss A/c (Being irrecoverable shortworking provided for)	Dr.		6,000	 6,000

Dr. **ROYALTY PAYABLE ACCOUNT** Cr.

Date	Particulars	₹	Date	Particulars	₹
2011	To Tulsian Ltd. A/c	50,000	2011	By P & L A/c	50,000
2012	To Tulsian Ltd. A/c	90,000	2012	By P & L A/c	90,000
2013	To Tulsian Ltd. A/c	1,14,000	2013	By P & L A/c	1,14,000
2014	To Tulsian Ltd. A/c	1,26,000	2014	By P & L A/c	1,26,000
2015	To Tulsian Ltd. A/c	20,000	2015	By P & L A/c	20,000

Dr. **TULSIAN LTD ACCOUNT** Cr.

Date	Particulars	₹	Date	Particulars	₹
2011	To Bank A/c	94,000	2011	By Royalty Payable A/c	50,000
			2011	By Short Working A/c	44,000
		94,000			94,000
2012	To Bank A/c	96,000	2012	By Royalty Payable A/c	90,000
			2012	By Short Working A/c	6,000
		96,000			96,000
2013	To Bank A/c	1,09,000	2013	By Royalty Payable A/c	1,14,000
2013	To Short Working (Recoupable)	5,000			
		1,14,000			1,14,000
2014	To Bank A/c	1,21,000	2014	By Royalty Payable A/c	1,20,000
2014	To Short Working (Recoupable)	5,000			
		1,26,000			1,26,000
2015	To Bank A/c	63,333	2015	By Royalty Payable A/c	20,000
			2015	By Short Working A/c	43,333
		63,333			63,333

Dr. **SHORT WORKING ACCOUNT** Cr.

Date	Particulars	₹	Date	Particulars	₹
2011	To Tulsian Ltd. A/c	44,000	2011	By Balance c/d	44,000
2012	To Balance c/d	44,000	2012	By Balance c/d	50,000
2012	To Tulsian Ltd. A/c	6,000			
		50,000			50,000
2013	To Balance c/d	50,000	2013	By Tulsian Ltd. A/c	5,000
			2013	By Balance c/d	45,000
		50,000			50,000
2014	To Balance c/d	45,000	2014	By Tulsian Ltd. A/c	5,000
			2014	By P & L A/c	34,000
			2014	By Balance c/d	6,000
		45,000			45,000
2015	To Balance c/d	6,000	2015	By P & L A/c	6,000
2015	To Tulsian Ltd. A/c	43,333	2015	By Balance c/d	43,333
		49,333			49,333

JOURNAL OF TULSIAN LTD.

Date	Particulars		L.F.	Dr. (₹)	Cr. (₹)
2011	Jalan Ltd. A/c	Dr.		94,000	
	To Royalty Receivable A/c				50,000
	To Shortworking Allowable A/c				44,000
	(Being royalty receivable short working provided for)				
	Bank A/c	Dr.		94,000	
	To Jalan Ltd. A/c				94,000
	(Being payment received from lessee)				
	Royalty Receivable A/c	Dr.		50,000	
	To Profit & Loss A/c				50,000
	(Being royalty received credited to Profit & Loss A/c)				
2012	Jalan Ltd. A/c	Dr.		96,000	
	To Royalty Recoupment A/c				90,000
	To Shortworking Allowable A/c				6,000
	(Being royalty and shortworking provided for)				
	Bank A/c	Dr.		96,000	
	To Jalan Ltd. A/c				96,000
	(Being royalty received from the lessee)				
	Royalty Receivable A/c	Dr.		90,000	
	To Profit & Loss A/c				90,000
	(Being royalty received credited to Profit & Loss A/c)				
2013	Jalan Ltd. A/c	Dr.		1,14,000	
	To Royalty Receivable A/c				1,14,000
	(Being royalty provided for)				
	Bank A/c	Dr.		1,09,000	
	Shortworking Allowable A/c	Dr.		5,000	
	To Jalan A/c				1,14,000
	(Being payment received net off shortworking recoupable)				
	Royalty Receivable A/c	Dr.		1,14,000	
	To Profit & Loss A/c				1,14,000
	(Being royalty received credited to Profit & Loss A/c)				
2014	Jalan Ltd. A/c	Dr.		1,26,000	
	To Royalty receivable A/c				1,26,000
	(Being royalty provided for)				
	Bank A/c	Dr.		1,21,000	
	Shortworking Allowable A/c	Dr.		5,000	
	To Jalan A/c				1,26,000
	(Being payment received net off shortworking recoupable)				

	Royalty Payable A/c	Dr.	1,26,000	
	To Profit & Loss A/c (Being royalty charged to Profit & Loss A/c)			1,26,000
	Shortworking Allowable A/c	Dr.	34,000	
	To Profit & Loss A/c (Being irrecoverable shortworking transferred to Profit & Loss A/c)			34,000
2015	Jalan Ltd. A/c	Dr.	63,333	
	To Royalty Receivable			20,000
	To Shortworking allowable A/c (Being royalty & shortworking provided for)			43,333
	Bank A/c	Dr.	63,333	
	To Jalan Ltd. A/c (Being payment received from lessee)			63,333
	Royalty Receivable A/c	Dr.	20,000	
	To Profit & Loss A/c (Being royalty receivable credited to Profit & Loss A/c)			20,000
	Shortworking Allowable A/c	Dr.	6,000	
	To Profit & Loss A/c (Being irrecoverable shortworking written off)			6,000

ROYALTY RECEIVABLE ACCOUNT

Date	Particulars	₹	Date	Particulars	₹
2011	To P & L A/c	50,000	2011	By Jalan A/c	50,000
2012	To P & L A/c	90,000	2012	By Jalan A/c	90,000
2013	To P & L A/c	1,14,000	2011	By Jalan A/c	1,14,000
2014	To P & L A/c	1,26,000	2011	By Jalan A/c	1,26,000
2015	To P & L A/c	20,000	2011	By Jalan A/c	20,000

JALAN LTD ACCOUNT

Date	Particulars	₹	Date	Particulars	₹
2011	To Royalty Receivable A/c	50,000	2011	By Bank A/c	94,000
2011	To Short working Allowable A/c	44,000			
		94,000			94,000
2012	To Royalty Receivable A/c	90,000	2012	By Bank A/c	96,000
2012	To Short working Allowable A/c	6,000			
		96,000			96,000

2013	To Royalty Receivable A/c	1,14,000	2013	By Bank A/c	1,09,000
			2013	By Short working Allowable A/c	5,000
		1,14,000			1,14,000
2014	To Royalty Receivable A/c	1,26,000	2014	By Bank A/c	1,21,000
			2014	By Short working Allowable A/c	5,000
		1,26,000			1,26,000
2015	To Royalty Receivable A/c	20,000	2015	To Bank A/c	63,333
2015	To Short working Allowable A/c	43,333			
		63,333			63,333

Dr. **SHORT ALLOWABLE ACCOUNT** Cr.

Date	Particulars	₹	Date	Particulars	₹
2011	To Balance c/d	44,000	2011	By Jalan Ltd. A/c	44,000
2012	To Balance c/d	50,000	2012	By Balance c/d	44,000
			2012	By Jalan Ltd. A/c	6,000
		50,000			50,000
2013	To Jalan Ltd. A/c	5,000	2013	By Balance c/d	50,000
	To Balance c/d	45,000			
		50,000			50,000
2014	To Jalan Ltd. A/c	5,000	2014	By Balance c/d	45,000
2014	To P & L A/c	34,000			
2014	To Balance c/d	6,000			
		45,000			45,000
2015	To Jalan Ltd. A/c	6,000	2015	By Balance c/d	6,000
			2015	By Jalan Ltd. A/c	43,333
		43,333			43,333

SUB-LEASING

PROBLEM 3

SN took on lease mining rights in an area of 100 square miles for a period of 33 years from 1st January 2014. Under the terms of the lease, a royalty of ₹ 1 per tonne is payable merging in a minimum rent of ₹ 40,000 per annum payable half-yearly on the 1st January and 1st July every year.

SN granted a sub-lease for 20 years on a portion of the above area measuring 50 square miles to KS from 1st June, 2014 in terms of which a royalty of ₹ 1.50 per tonne merging in a minimum rent of ₹ 39,000 per annum was payable—again in equal instalments on every 1st January and 1st July.

SN can recoup short working throughtout the period of lease whereas the sub-lease provides that any short workings could be recouped only out of excess workings in any of the three half years immediately following that in which the workings occured. Details for minerals obtained were:

Particulars	*Minerals raised by (in tonnes)*	
	SN	*KS*
For half year ending on:		
30th June, 2014	12,000	—
31st December, 2014	10,000	8,000
30th June, 2015	28,000	10,000
31st December, 2015	18,000	12,000
30th June, 2016	24,000	15,000
31st December, 2016	30,000	20,000

Required: Show the necessary accounts in the books of SN who close their books on a calendar year basis.

SOLUTION

Dr. **BOOKS OF SN LTD ROYALTY PAYABLE ACCOUNT** Cr.

Date	Particulars	₹	Date	Particulars	₹
30.06.2014 31.12.2014	To Landlors's A/c To Landlors's A/c	12,000 18,000	31.12.2014 31.12.2014	By Royalty Receivable A/c By Profit & Loss A/c	8,000 22,000
		30,000			30,000
30.06.2015 31.12.2015	To Landlors's A/c To Landlors's A/c	38,000 30,000	31.12.2015 31.12.2015	By Royalty Receivable A/c By Royalty Receivable A/c	10,000 12,000
				By Profit & Loss A/c	46,000
		68,000			68,000
30.06.2016 31.12.2016	To Landlors's A/c To Landlors's A/c	39,000 50,000	31.12.2016 31.12.2016	By Royalty Receivable A/c By Royalty Receivable A/c	15,000 20,000
				By Profit & Loss A/c	54,000
		89,000			89,000

Dr. **SHORT WORKING (RECOVERABLE) ACCOUNT** Cr.

Date	Particulars	₹	Date	Particulars	₹
30.06.2014	To Landlors's A/c	8,000	31.12.2014	By Balance c/d	10,000
31.12.2014	To Landlors's A/c	2,000			
		10,000			10,000
01.01.2015	To Balance c/d	10,000	30.06.2015	By Landlord's A/c	10,000

Dr. **LANDLORD'S ACCOUNT** Cr.

Date	Particulars	₹	Date	Particulars	₹
01.07.2014	To Bank A/c	20,000	30.06.2014	By Royalty Payable A/c	12,000
31.12.2014	To Balance c/d	20,000	30.06.2014	By Short Workings (Recoupable) A/c	8,000
			31.12.2014	By Royalty Payable A/c	18,000
			31.12.2014	By Short Workings (Recoupable) A/c	2,000
		40,000			40,000
01.01.2015	To Bank A/c	20,000	01.01.2015	By Balance b/d	20,000
30.06.2015	To Short Workings (Recoupable) A/c	10,000	30.06.2015	By Royalty Payable A/c	38,000
01.07.2015	To Bank A/c	28,000	31.12.2015	By Royalty Payable A/c	30,000
31.12.2015	To Balance c/d	30,000			
		88,000			88,000
01.01.2016	To Bank A/c	30,000	01.01.2016	By Balance b/d	30,000
01.07.2016	To Bank A/c	39,000	30.06.2016	By Royalty Payable A/c	39,000
31.12.2016	To Balance c/d	50,000	31.12.2016	By Royalty Payable A/c	50,000
		1,19,000			1,19,000

Dr. **ROYALTY RECEIVABLE ACCOUNT** Cr.

Date	Particulars	₹	Date	Particulars	₹
31.12.2014	To Royalty Payable A/c	8,000	31.12.2014	By M/s KS	12,000
	To Profit & Loss A/c	4,000			
		12,000			12,000
30.06.2015	To Royalty Payable A/c	10,000	30.06.2015	By M/s KS	15,000
			31.12.2015	By M/s KS	18,000
31.12.2015	To Royalty Payable A/c	12,000			
31.12.2015	To Profit & Loss A/c	11,000			
		33,000			33,000
30.06.2016	To Royalty Payable A/c	15,000	30.06.2016	By M/s KS	22,000
			31.12.2016	By M/s KS	30,000
31.12.2016	To Royalty Payable A/c	20,000			
31.12.2016	To Profit & Loss A/c	17,500			
		52,500			52,500

Dr. **SHORT WORKING (ALLOWABLE) ACCOUNT** Cr.

Date	Particulars	₹	Date	Particulars	₹
31.12.2014	To Balance c/d	7,500	31.12.2014	By M/s KS	7,500
31.12.2015	To Balance c/d	13,500	01.01.2015	By Balance b/d	7,500
			30.06.2015	By M/s KS	4,500
			31.12.2015	By M/s KS	1,500
		13,500			13,500
30.06.2016	To M/s KS	3,000	01.01.2016	By Balance b/d	13,500
30.06.2016	To Profit & Loss A/c	4,500			
31.12.2016	To M/s KS	6,000			
		13,500			13,500

Dr. **M/S KS'S ACCOUNT** Cr.

Date	Particulars	₹	Date	Particulars	₹
31.12.2014	To Royalty Receivable A/c	12,000	31.12.2014	By Balance c/d	19,500
31.12.2014	To Short Workings (Allowable) A/c	7,500			
		19,500			19,500
01.01.2015	To Balance b/d	19,500	01.01.2015	By Bank A/c	19,500
30.06.2015	To Royalty Receivable A/c	15,000	01.07.2015	By Bank A/c	19,500
			31.12.2015	By Balance c/d	19,500
30.06.2015	To Short Workings (Allowable) A/c	4,500			
31.12.2015	To Royalty Receivable A/c	18,000			
31.12.2015	To Short Workings (Allowable) A/c	1,500			
		58,500			58,500
01.01.2016	To Balance b/d	19,500	01.01.2016	By Bank A/c	19,500
30.06.2016	To Royalty Receivable A/c	22,000	30.06.2016	To Short Workings (Allowable) A/c	3,000
31.12.2016	To Royalty Receivable A/c	30,000	01.07.2016	By Bank A/c	19,500
			31.12.2016	To Short Workings (Allowable) A/c	6,000
				By Balance c/d	24,000
		72,000			72,000

WHEN PAYMENTS MADE TO LANDLORD ARE GIVEN

PROBLEM 4

The following balances appeared in the books of a lessee as on January 1, 2014:

Landlord's Account (Cr) ₹ 28,000 Short Working Account (Dr) ₹ 6,000 (out of which ₹ 3,000 arose in 2013, ₹ 2,000 in 2012 and the rest in 2011).

The Agreement of Royalty provided the following:

(a) Minimum rent ₹ 56,000 p.a.

(b) The power to recoup short working within 3 years immediately following the year in which it arise.

(c) Payments to the landlord to be made as under:

50% of the amount is payable in the year in which it becomes due and the balance of 50% in the next year.

You are given the following particulars from 2014 to 2017:

Year	Payments to Landlord ₹	Short Working ₹	Short Working Recouped ₹
2014	56,000	—	800
2015	58,000	—	5,000
2016	58,000	2,000	—
2017	60,000	—	2,000

Show the Royalty Account and Short Working Account from 2014 to 2017.

SOLUTION

Dr. **ROYALTY PAYABLE ACCOUNT** Cr.

Date	Particulars	₹	Date	Particulars	₹
31.12.2014	To Short Workings Recoupable A/c	800	31.12.2014	By Manufacturing A/c (Transfer)	56,800
31.12.2014	To Landlord A/c	56,000			
		56,800			56,800
31.12.2015	To Short Workings Recoupable A/c	5,000	31.12.2015	By Manufacturing A/c (Transfer)	65,000
31.12.2015	To Landlord A/c	60,000			
		65,000			65,000
31.12.2016	To Landlord A/c	54,000	31.12.2016	By Manufacturing A/c (Transfer)	54,000
		54,000			54,000
31.12.2017	To Short Workings Recoupable A/c	2,000	31.12.2017	By Manufacturing A/c (Transfer)	66,000
31.12.2017	To Landlord A/c	64,000			
		66,000			66,000

Dr. **SHORT WORKING RECOUPABLE ACCOUNT** Cr.

Date	Particulars	₹	Date	Particulars	₹
01.01.2014	To Balance b/d	6,000	31.12.2014	By Royalty Payable A/c	800
			31.12.2014	By Profit & Loss A/c (w/o)	200
			31.12.2014	By Balance c/d	5,000
		6,000			6,000
01.01.2015	To Balance b/d	5,000	31.12.2015	By Royalty Payable A/c	5,000
31.12.2016	To Landlord's A/c	2,000	31.12.2016	By Balance c/d	2,000
01.01.2017	To Balance b/d	2,000	31.12.2017	By Royalty Payable A/c	2,000

Working Note

STATEMENT SHOWING THE CALCULATION OF ACTUAL ROYALTY

A Year	B Total Payment made	C Payment for Previous year	D = B – C Payment for Current year	E = D × 2 Total Payment for due for Current year	F = E + S/W Recouped – S/W Actual Royalty
2014	56,000	28,000	28,000	56,000	56,000 + 800 = 56,800
2015	58,000	28,000	30,000	60,000	60,000 + 5,000 = 65,000
2016	58,000	30,000	28,000	56,000	56,000 – 2,000 = 54,000
2017	60,000	28,000	32,000	64,000	64,000 + 2,000 = 62,000

PROBLEM 5

Birla Coal Co. Ltd. holds a lease of coal mines for a period of twelve years, commencing from 1st April 2009. According to the lease, the company is to pay ₹ 7.50 as royalty per ton with a minimum rent of ₹ 1,50,000 per year. Short workings can, however, be recovered out of the royalty in excess of the minimum rent of the next two years only. For the year of a strike the minimum rent is to be reduced to 60%. The output in tons for the 6 years ending 31st March, 2015 is as under : 2009-2010 :10,000; 2010-2011: 12,000; 2011-2012:25,000; 2012-2013: 20,000; 2013-2014: 50,000; and 2014-2015: 15,000 (strike). Write up the necessary Ledger Accounts in the books of Birla Coal Co. Ltd and in the books of Landlord.

SOLUTION

ANALYSIS OF ROYALTY PAYABLE AND SHORT WORKINGS

Fig in (₹)

Year	Output (Tons)	Actual Royalties	Min. Rent	Excess Short Workings	Short workings				Amount
					Occurred	Recouped	Written off	C/F	Payable
2009-2010	10,000	75,000	150,000	—	75,000	—	—	75,000	150,000
2010-2011	12,000	90,000	150,000	—	60,000	—	—	135,000	150,000
2011-2012	25,000	187,500	150,000	37,500	—	37,500	37,500	60,000	150,000
2012-2013	20,000	150,000	150,000	—	—	—	60,000	—	150,000

2013-2014	50,000	375,000	150,000	225,000	—	—	—	—	375,000
2014-2015	15,000	112,500	90,000	22,500	—	—	—	—	112,500

BOOKS OF BIRLA COAL CO. LTD.

Dr. **ROYALTIES ACCOUNT** **Cr.**

Date	Particulars	₹	Date	Particulars	₹
31.03.2010	To Landlord's A/c	75,000	31.03.2010	By Profit & Loss A/c	75,000
31.03.2011	To Landlord's A/c	90,000	31.03.2011	By Profit & Loss A/c	90,000
31.03.2012	To Landlord's A/c	187,500	31.03.2012	By Profit & Loss A/c	187,500
31.03.2013	To Landlord's A/c	150,000	31.03.2013	By Profit & Loss A/c	150,000
31.03.2014	To Landlord's A/c	375,000	31.03.2014	By Profit & Loss A/c	375,000
31.03.2015	To Landlord's A/c	112,500	31.03.2015	By Profit & Loss A/c	112,500

Dr. **LANDLORD'S ACCOUNT** **Cr.**

Date	Particulars	₹	Date	Particulars	₹
31.03.2010	To Bank A/c	150,000	31.03.2010	By Royalties A/c	75,000
				By Short workings A/c	75,000
		150,000			150,000
31.03.2011	To Bank A/c	150,000	31.03.2011	By Royalties A/c	90,000
				By Short workings A/c	60,000
		150,000			
31.03.2012	To Bank A/c	150,000	31.03.2012	By Royalties A/c	187,500
	To Short workings A/c	37,500			
		187,500			187,500
31.03.2013	To Bank A/c	150,000	31.03.2013	By Royalties A/c	150,000
		150,000			150,000
31.03.2014	To Bank A/c	375,000	31.03.2014	By Royalties A/c	375,000
		375,000			375,000
31.03.2015	To Bank A/c	112,500	31.03.2015	By Royalties A/c	112,500
		112,500			112,500

Dr. **SHORT WORKINGS ACCOUNT** **Cr.**

Date	Particulars	₹	Date	Particulars	₹
31.03.2010	To Landlord A/c	150,000	31.03.2010	By Balance c/d	75,000
					75,000
1.4.2010	To Balance b/d	75,000	31.03.2011	By Balance c/d	135,000
31.03.2011	To Landlord A/c	60,000			
		135,000			135,000

1.4.2011	To Balance b/d	135,000	31.03.2012	By Landlord A/c	37,500
				By Profit & Loss A/c	37,500
				By Balance c/d	60,000
		135,000			135,000
1.4.2012	To Balance b/d	60,000	31.03.2013	By Profit & Loss A/c	60,000
		60,000			60,000

BOOKS OF LANDLORD

Dr. ROYALTY RECEIVABLE ACCOUNT Cr.

Date	Particulars	₹	Date	Particulars	₹
31.03.2010	To Profit & Loss A/c	75,000	31.03.2010	By Birla Coal Co.Ltd	75,000
31.03.2011	To Profit & Loss A/c	90,000	31.03.2011	By Birla Coal Co. Ltd	90,000
31.03.2012	To Profit & Loss A/c	1,87,500	31.03.2012	By Birla Coal Co. Ltd	1,87,500
31.03.2013	To Profit & Loss A/c	1,50,000	31.03.2013	By Birla Coal Co. Ltd	1,50,000
31.03.2014	To Profit & Loss A/c	3,75,000	31.03.2014	By Birla Coal Co. Ltd	3,75,000
31.03.2015	To Profit & Loss A/c	1,12,500	31.03.2015	By Birla Coal Co. Ltd	1,12,500

Dr. BIRLA COAL CO. LTD. (LESSEE) ACCOUNT Cr.

Date	Particulars	₹	Date	Particulars	₹
31.03.2010	To Royalties Receivable A/c	75,000	31.03.2010	By Bank A/c	150,000
	To Shortworkings Allowable A/c	75,000			
		150,000			150,000
31.03.2011	To Royalties Receivable A/c	90,000	31.03.2011	By Bank A/c	150,000
	To Shortworkings Allowable A/c	60,000			
		150,000			150,000
31.03.2012	To Royalties Receivable A/c	187,500	31.03.2012	By Bank A/c	150,000
				By Shortworkings Allowable A/c	37,500
		187,500			187,500
31.03.2013	To Royalties Receivable A/c	150,000	31.03.2013	By Bank A/c	150,000
		150,000			150,000

31.03.2014	To Royalties Receivable A/c	375,000	31.03.2014	By Bank A/c	375,000
		375,000			375,000
31.03.2015	To Royalties Receivable A/c	112,500	31.03.2015	By Bank A/c	112,500
		112,500			112,500

Dr. **SHORTWORKINGS ALLOWABLE ACCOUNT** **Cr.**

Date	Particulars	₹	Date	Particulars	₹
31.03.2010	To Balance c/d	75,000	31.03.2010	By Birla Coal Co. Ltd	75,000
			1.4.2010	By Balance b/d	75,000
31.03.2011	To Balance c/d	1,35,000	31.03.2011	By Birla Coal Co. Ltd	60,000
		1,35,000			1,35,000
31.03.2012	To Birla Coal Co. Ltd	37,000	1.4.2011	By Balance b/d	1,35,000
	To Profit & Loss A/c	37,500	31.03.2012	By Birla Coal Co. Ltd	37,000
	To Balance c/d	60,000			
		1,72,500			1,72,500
31.03.2013	To Profit & Loss A/c	60,000	1.04.2012	By Balance b/d	60,000
		60,000			60,000

PROBLEM 6

X Ltd. obtain from Y Ltd. a lease of some coal-bearing land, the terms being a royalty of ₹ 15 per ton of coal raised subject to a minimum rent of ₹ 75,000 p.a. with a right of recoupment of short-working over the first four years of the lease. From the following details, show (i) Short-working Account, (ii) Royalty Account and (iii) Y Ltd. Account in the books of X Ltd.

Year	Sales (Tons) ₹	Closing Stock (Tons) ₹
2011	2,000	300
2012	3,500	400
2013	4,800	600
2014	5,600	500
2015	8,000	800

SOLUTION

[Coal raised i.e., Production = Sales + Closing Stock – Opening Stock.]

Year	Sales	Closing Stock	Opening Stock	Net Production
2011	2,000	300	Nil	2,300
2012	3,500	400	300	3,600
2013	4,800	600	400	5,000

2014	5,600	500	600	5,500
2015	8,000	800	500	8,300

ANALYSIS OF ROYALTY PAYABLE AND SHORT WORKINGS

Year	Quantity	Rate ₹	Royalty ₹	Minimum Rent ₹	Short working ₹	Recoupment ₹	Short working carried forward ₹	Transferred to P&L A/c ₹	Payment to Landlord ₹
2011	2,300	15	34,500	75,000	40,500	---	40,500	---	75,000
2012	3,600	15	54,000	75,000	21,000	---	61,500	---	75,000
2013	5,000	15	75,000	75,000	---	---	61,500	---	75,000
2014	5,500	15	82,000	75,000	---	7,500	---	54,000	75,000
2015	8,300	15	1,24,500	75,000	---	---	---	---	1,24,500

IN THE BOOKS OF X LTD.

Dr. **Y LTD. (LANDLORD) ACCOUNT** Cr.

Date	Particulars	₹	Date	Particulars	₹
2011	To Bank A/c	75,000	2011	By Royalty A/c	34,500
				By Short Working A/c	40,500
		75,000			75,000
2012	To Bank A/c	75,000	2012	By Royalty A/c	54,000
				By Short Working A/c	21,000
		75,000			75,000
2013	To Bank A/c	75,000	2013	By Royalty A/c	75,000
		75,000			75,000
2014	To Bank A/c	75,000	2014	By Royalty A/c	75,000
		75,000			75,000
2015	To Bank A/c	1,24,500	2015	By Royalty A/c	1,24,500
		1,24,500			1,24,500

Dr. **SHORT-WORKING ACCOUNT** Cr.

Date	Particulars	₹	Date	Particulars	₹
2011	To Y Ltd.	40,500	2011	By Balance c/d	40,500
		40,500			40,500
2012	To Balance b/d	40,500	2012	By Balance c/d	61,500
	To Y Ltd.	21,000			
		61,500			61,500
2013	To Balance b/d	61,500	2013	By Balance c/d	61,500
		61,500			61,500

2014	To Balance b/d	61,500	2014	By Royalty A/c	7,500
				By Profit and Loss A/c	54,000
		61,500			61,500

Dr. **ROYALTY ACCOUNT** **Cr.**

Date	Particulars	₹	Date	Particulars	₹
2011	To Y Ltd.	34,500	2011	By Profit & Loss A/c	34,500
2012	To Y Ltd.	54,000	2012	By Profit & Loss A/c	54,000
2013	To Y Ltd.	75,000	2013	By Profit & Loss A/c	75,000
2014	To Short-working A/c	7,500	2014	By Profit & Loss A/c	82,500
	To Y Ltd.	75,000			
		82,500			82,500
2015	To Y Ltd.	1,24,500	2015	By Profit & Loss A/c	1,24,500

PROBLEM 7

The following information has been obtained from the books of a lesee relating to the years 2011-2012 to 2014-2015 :

Payments to Landlord (after tax deducted @ 20% at Source):	2011-2012	₹ 12,000
	2012-2013	₹ 12,000
	2013-2014	₹ 12,000
	2014-2015	₹ 19,200
Short-working recovered :	2012-2013	₹ 2,500
	2013-2014	₹ 1,000
Short-working written-off :	2013-2014	₹ 500

Balance of Short-working Account forward on April 1, 2011 ₹ 800 (which are in 2011-2012). According to the terms of agreement short-working is recoverable within the next two years following the year in which short-working arises.

You are required to show the necessary accounts in the books of the lessee for the four years ended 31st March 2015.

SOLUTION

Before preparing the ledger accounts we are to find out some missing information :

1. The recoupment which was made is 2012-2013 for ₹ 2,500 is inclusive of ₹ 800 of 2010-2011 and the balance ₹ 1,700 for 2011-2012.

   Again, the short-working which was recovered and written-off ₹ 1,000 and ₹ 500 (i.e., ₹ 1,500), respectively, in 2012-2013 are also for the year 2011-2012. So, the total short-working for 2011-2012 amounted to ₹ 3,200 (i.e., ₹ 1,700 + ₹ 1,500).
2. Rate of taxes @ 20% on gross i.e., 25% (i.e., 20/80 = 1/4) on net amount paid.
3. Actual Payment = Annual Royalty + Short-working – Recoupment.

Thus, actual royalty is calculated as under :

Particulars	2011-2012 ₹	2012-2013 ₹	2013-2014 ₹	2014-2015 ₹
Payment to landlord (after tax)	12,000	12,000	12,000	19,200
Add: Back Tax Deducted at Source @ ¼ th	3,000	3,000	3,000	4,800
Payment to landlord (before Tax)	15,000	15,000	15,000	24,000
Less: Short-working	3,200	—	—	—
Add: Recoupment	—	2,500	1,000	—
	11,800	17,500	16,000	24,000

IN THE BOOKS OF LESSEE

Dr. **ROYALTY ACCOUNT** **Cr.**

Date	Particulars	₹	Date	Particulars	₹
31.03.2012	To Landlord A/c	11,800	31.03.2012	By Profit and Loss A/c	11,800
		11,800			11,800
31.03.2013	To Short-working A/c	2,500	31.03.2013	By Profit and Loss A/c	17,500
	To Landlord A/c	15,000			
		17,500			17,500
31.03.2014	To Short-working A/c	1,000	31.03.2014	By Profit and Loss A/c	16,000
	To Landlord A/c	15,000			
		16,000			16,000
31.03.2015	To Landlord A/c	24,000	31.03.2015	By Profit and Loss A/c	24,000
		24,000			24,000

Dr. **SHORT-WORKING ACCOUNT** **Cr.**

Date	Particulars	₹	Date	Particulars	₹
01.04.2012	To Balance b/d	800	31.03.2012	By Balance c/d	4,000
	To Landlord A/c	3,200			
		4,000			4,000
01.04.2013	To Balance b/d	4,000	31.03.2013	By Royalty A/c	2,500
				By Balance c/d	1,500
		4,000			4,000
01.04.2014	To Balance b/d	1,500	31.03.2014	By Royalty A/c	1,000
				By Balance c/d	500
		1,500			1,500

Dr. **LANDLORD ACCOUNT** Cr.

Date	Particulars	Amount ₹	Date	Particulars	Amount ₹
31.03.2012	To Income-Tax Payable A/c	3,000	31.03.2012	By Royalty A/c	11,800
	To Bank A/c	12,000		By Short Working A/c	3,200
		15,000			15,000
31.03.2013	To Income-Tax Payable A/c	3,000	31.03.2013	By Royalty A/c	15,500
	To Bank A/c	12,000			
		15,000			15,000
31.03.2014	To Income-Tax Payable A/c	3,000	31.03.2014	By Royalty A/c	15,500
	To Bank A/c	12,000			
		15,000			15,000
31.03.2015	To Income-Tax Payable A/c	4,800	31.03.2015	By Royalty A/c	24,000
	To Bank A/c	19,200			
		24,000			24,000

PROBLEM 8

A fire occurred in the office premises of lessee in the evening of 31.3.2015 destroying most of the books and records. From the documents saved, the following information is gathered :

Short-working recovered :

2012-2013 ₹ 2,000 (towards short-workings which arose in 2009-2010)

2013-2014 ₹ 4,000 (including ₹ 1,000 for short-working 2010-2011)

2014-2015 ₹ 1,000

Short-working lapsed :

2011-2012 ₹ 1,500

2012-2013 ₹ 1,800

2014-2015 ₹ 1,000

A sum of ₹ 25,000 was paid to the landlord in 2011-2012. The agreement of Royalty contains a clause of Minimum Rent payable for fixed amount and recoupment of short-workings within 3 years following the year in which Short-workings arise.

Information as regards payments to landlord subsequent to the year 2011-2012 is not four years ended 31.3.2015.

SOLUTION

Year	Royalty ₹	Short working ₹	Short Working recovered ₹	Short Working Lapsed ₹	Payment to Landlord ₹
2011-2012	—	—	—	1,500	25,000
2012-2013	—	—	₹ 2,000 (for 2009-2010)	1,800	—

2013-2014	—	—	₹ 4,000 (including ₹ 1,000 for 2010-2011)	—	—
2014-2015	—	—	1,000	1,000	—

From the above statement it is quite clear that :

(i) Short-working lapsed in 2014-2015 ₹ 1,000 which relates to 2011-2012 as per terms, short-working should be recouped within three years i.e., 2014-2015 is the last year for recoupment.

(ii) Short-working recovered in 2013-2014 ₹ 4,000, out of which ₹ 1,000 for 2010-2011 and the balance ₹ 3,000 for the year 2008-2009.

(iii) Short-working recovered in 2014-2015 ₹ 1,000 which is also related to 2011-2012 in which year actually is arose.

Thus, the total short-working balance in 2011-2012 amounted to ₹ 5,000 (i.e., ₹ 1,000 + ₹ 3,000 + ₹ 1,000). Now, we can prepare our usual statement as under :

Hence, Actual Royalty = Payment to Landlord + Recoupment – Short-working

For, 2011-2012 = ₹ 25,000 + Nil – ₹ 5,000 = ₹ 20,000.

For, 2012-2013 = ₹ 25,000 + ₹ 2,000 – Nil = ₹ 27,000

For, 2013-2014 = ₹ 25,000 + ₹ 4,000 – Nil = ₹ 29,000

For, 2014-2015 = ₹ 25,000 + ₹ 1,000 – Nil = ₹ 26,000

Year	Royalty ₹	Short-working ₹	Recoupment ₹	Tr. to P&L A/c ₹	Payment to Landlord ₹
2011-2012	20,000	5,000	—	1,500	25,000
2012-2013	27,000	—	2,000	1,800	25,000
2013-2014	29,000	—	4,000	—	25,000
2014-2015	26,000	—	1,000	1,000	25,000

IN THE BOOKS OF LESSEE

ROYALTY ACCOUNT

Dr. Cr.

Date	Particulars	₹	Date	Particulars	₹
31.3.2012	To Landlord A/c	20,000	31.3.2012	By P & L A/c	20,000
		20,000			20,000
31.3.2013	To Short Working A/c	2,000	31.3.2013	By P & L A/c	27,000
	To Landlord A/c	25,000			
		27,000			27,000
31.3.2014	To Short Working A/c	4,000	31.3.2014	By P & L A/c	29,000
	To Landlord A/c	25,000			
		29,000			29,000
31.3.2015	To Short Working A/c	1,000	31.3.2015	By P & L A/c	29,000
	To Landlord A/c	25,000			
		26,000			26,000

Dr. **SHORT-WORKING ACCOUNT** **Cr.**

Date	Particulars	₹	Date	Particulars	₹
31.3.2012	To Balance b/d	6,300	31.3.2012	By P & L A/c	1,500
	To Landlord A/c	5,000		By Balance c/d	9,800
		11,300			11,300
31.3.2013	To Balance b/d	9,800	31.3.2013	By Royalty A/c	2,000
				By P & L A/c	1,800
				By Balance c/d	6,000
		9,800			9,800
31.3.2014	To Balance b/d	1,000	31.3.2014	By Royalty A/c	4,000
	To Landlord A/c	5,000		By Balance c/d	2,000
		6,000			6,000
31.3.2015	To Balance b/d	2,000	31.3.2015	By Royalty A/c	1,000
				By P & L A/c	1,000
		2,000			2,000

This is includes the following :

		₹
Lapsed :	in 2011-2012	1,500
	in 2012-2013	1,800
Recoupment :	in 2012-2013	2,000
	in 2013-2014	1,000
		6,300

PROBLEM 9

On 1.4.2010 X Ltd. got a mining lease and from that date a part of the mine was sub-leased to Y Ltd. The terms of payment and the production of 5 years are as below.

Particulars	Lessee	Sub-Lessee
Royalty (₹/Tonne)	2.00	3.00
Dead Rent per anum (₹)	15,000	10,000
Short working recoverable (Years)	3	2
Production (Year ended....31.3.)		
2011	1,000	1,000
2012	3,000	2,000
2013	12,000	5,000
2014	9,000	2,000 (strike)
2015	5,000	12,000

In case of strike, royalty earned will discharge all liabilities for the year only.

Show ledger accounts in the books of X Ltd.

SOLUTION

IN THE BOOKS OF X LTD.
ANALYSIS OF ROYALTY PAYABLE AND SHORT WORKINGS

Fig in (₹)

Year	Output (Tons)	Actual Royalties	Min. Rent	Excess Short Workings	Short Workings				Amount Payable
					Occurred	Recouped	Written off	C/F	
2011	2,000	4,000	15,000	—	11,000 0	—	—	11,000	15,000
2012	5,000	10,000	15,000	—	5,000	—	—	16,000	15,000
2013	17,000	34,000	15,000	19,000	—	16,000	—	—	18,000
2014	11,000	22,000	15,000	7,000	—	—	—	—	22,000
2015	17,000	34,000	15,000	19,000	—	—	—	—	34,000

ANALYSIS OF ROYALTY RECEIVABLE AND SHORT WORKINGS

Fig in (₹)

Year	Output (Tons)	Actual Royalties	Min. Rent	Excess Short Workings	Short Workings				Amount Payable
					Occurred	Recouped	Written off	C/F	
2011	1,000	3,000	10,000	—	7,000	—	—	7,000	10,000
2012	2,000	6,000	10,000	—	4,000	—	—	11,000	10,000
2013	5,000	15,000	10,000	5,000	—	5,000	2,000	4,000	10,000
2014	2,000	6,000	6,000	—	—	—	4,000	—	6,000
2015	12,000	36,000	10,000	26,000	—	—	—	—	36,000

Dr. **SHORTWORKINGS ACCOUNT** **Cr.**

Date	Particulars	₹	Date	Particulars	₹
31.03.2011	To Landlord's A/c	11,000	31.03.2011	By Balance c/d	11,000
		11,000			11,000
01.04.2011	To Balance b/d	11,000	31.03.2012	By Balance c/d	16,000
31.03.2012	To Landlord's A/c	5,000			
		16,000			16,000
01.04.2012	To Balance b/d	16,000	31.03.2013	By Royalty Payable A/c (recouped)	16,000
		16,000			16,000

Dr. **SHORTWORKINGS ALLOWABLE ACCOUNT** **Cr.**

Date	Particulars	₹	Date	Particulars	₹
31.03.2011	To Balance c/d	7,000	31.03.2011	By Y Ltd. A/c	7,000
		7,000			7,000
31.03.2012	To Balance b/d	11,000	01.04.2011	By Balance b/d	7,000
			31.03.2012	By Y Ltd. A/c	4,000
		11,000			11,000
31.3.2013	To Royalty Receivable A/c	5,000	01.04.2012	By Balance b/d	11,000

	To P& L A/c	2,000			
	To Balance c/d	4,000			
		11,000			11,000
31.03.2014	To P &L A/c	4,000	01.04.2013	By Balance b/d	4,000
		4,000			4,000

Dr. **ROYALTY RECEIVABLE ACCOUNT** **Cr.**

Date	Particulars	₹	Date	Particulars	₹
31.03.2011	To Royalties Payable A/c (1,000 × 2)	2000	31.03.2011	By Pathan A/c (1,000 × 3)	3,000
	To Profit & Loss A/c	1,000			
		3,000			3,000
31.03.2012	To Royalties Payable A/c (2,000 × 2)	4000	31.03.2012	By Y Ltd. A/c (2,000 × 3)	6,000
	To Profit & Loss A/c	2,000			
		6,000			6,000
31.03.2013	To Royalties Payable A/c (5,000 × 2)	10000	31.03.2013	By Short Workings Allowable A/c	5,000
	To Profit & Loss A/c	5,000		By Y Ltd. A/c (5,000 × 2)	10,000
		15,000			15,000
31.03.2014	To Royalties Payable A/c (2,000 × 2)	4000	31.03.2014	By Y Ltd. A/c (2,000 × 3)	6,000
	To Profit & Loss A/c	2,000			
		6,000			6,000
31.03.2015	To Royalties Payable A/c (12,000 × 2)	24000	31.03.2015	By Y Ltd. A/c (12,000 × 3)	36,000
	To Profit & Loss A/c	12,000			
		36,000			36,000

Dr. **ROYALTY PAYABLE ACCOUNT** **Cr.**

Date	Particulars	₹	Date	Particulars	₹
31.03.2011	To Landlord A/c (2000 × 2)	4000	31.03.2011	By Royalty Receivable A/c (1000 × 2)	2,000
				By Profit & Loss A/c	2,000
		4,000			4,000

31.03.2012	To Landlord A/c (5000 × 2)	10000	31.03.2012	By Royalty Receivable A/c (2000 × 2)	4,000
				By Profit & Loss A/c	6,000
		10000			10,000
31.03.2013	To Shortworkings A/c	16,000	31.03.2013	By Royalty Receivable A/c (5000 × 2)	10,000
	To Landlord A/c (17000 × 2)	18,000		By Profit & Loss A/c	24,000
		34,000			34,000
31.03.2014	To Landlord A/c(11000 × 2)	22000	31.03.2014	By Royalty Receivable A/c (2000 × 2)	4,000
				By Profit & Loss A/c	18,000
		22000			22,000
31.03.2015	To Landlord A/c (17000 × 2)		31.03.2015	By Royalty Receivable A/c (12000 × 2)	24,000
				By Profit & Loss A/c	10,000
					34,000

Notes:

1. Royalty to be paid to Landlord on total production including the production from sub-lessee.
2. Royalties receivable from sub lease to be adjusted against the payable amount to the extent of royalty payable to Landlord.

Dr. **Y LTD.'S ACCOUNT** **Cr.**

Date	Particulars	₹	Date	Particulars	₹
31.03.2011	To Royalties Receivable A/c	3,000	31.03.2011	By Bank A/c	10,000
	To Short Workings Allowable A/c	7,000			
		10,000			10,000
31.03.2012	To Royalties Receivable A/c	6,000	31.03.2012	By Bank A/c	10,000
	To Short Workings Allowable A/c	4,000			
		10,000			10,000
31.03.2013	To Royalties Receivable A/c	10,000	31.03.2013	By Bank A/c	6,000
		10,000			6,000
31.03.2014	To Royalties Receivable A/c	6,000	31.03.2014	By Bank A/c	6,000

		6,000			6,000
31.03.2015	To Royalties Receivable A/c	36,000	31.03.2015	By Bank A/c	36,000
		36,000			36,000

Dr. **LANDLORD'S ACCOUNT** **Cr.**

Date	Particulars	₹	Date	Particulars	₹
31.03.2011	To Bank A/c	15,000	31.03.2011	By Royalties A/c	4,000
				By Short Workings A/c	11,000
		15,000			15,000
31.03.2012	To Bank A/c	15,000	31.03.2012	By Royalties A/c	10,000
				By Short Workings A/c	5,000
		15,000			15,000
31.03.2013	To Bank A/c	18,000	31.03.2013	By Royalties A/c	34,000
	To Short Workings A/c	16,000			
		34,000			34,000
31.03.2014	To Bank A/c	22,000	31.03.2014	By Royalties A/c	22,000
		22,000			22,000
31.03.2015	To Bank A/c	34,000	31.03.2015	By Royalties A/c	34,000
		34,000			34,000

23 ACCOUNTING FOR HIRE PURCHASE

SHORT ANSWER PRACTICAL PROBLEMS

CALCULATION OF CASH PRICE

PROBLEM 1

A acquired on 1st January a machine under a Hire-Purchase agreement which provides for 5 half-yearly instalments of ₹ 6,000 each, the first instalment being due on 1st July. Assuming that the applicable rate of interest is 10 per cent per annum, calculate the cash value of the machine. All working should form part of the answer.

Solution

Installment A	*Closing Balance after Installment* B	*Installment* C	*Cl.Bal.before Installment* D = B + C	*Interest* E	*Op. Bal.* F = D– E
5th	—	6,000	6,000	286	5,714
4th	5,714	6,000	11,714	558	11,156
3rd	11,156	6,000	17,156	817	16,339
2nd	16,339	6,000	22,339	1,063	21,276
1st	21,276	6,000	27,276	1,299	25,977

Thus, Cash Price = ₹ 25,977.

PROBLEM 2

Ram & Co. acquired a motor lorry on hire-purchase basis. It has to make cash down payment of ₹1,00,000 at the beginning. The payments to be made subsequently are ₹2,63,000; ₹ 1,85,000 and ₹ 1,14,000 at the end of first year, second year and third year respectively. Interest charged is @ 14% per annum. Calculate the cash price of motor lorry and interest paid in each instalment.

Solution

CALCULATION OF CASH PRICE AND INTEREST

A *No. of instalment*	*B* *Closing Balance*	*C* *Amount of instalment*	*D = B + C* *Amount Due before Payment of Instalment*	*E = Dx14/114* *Interest*	*F = D – E* *Opening Balance*
III	0	1,14,000	1,14,000	14,000	1,00,000
II	1,00,000	1,85,000	2,85,000	35,000	2,50,000
I	2,50,000	2,63,000	5,13,000	63,000	4,50,000
				1,12,000	

Cash Price = ₹ 1,00,000 + ₹ 4,50,000 = ₹ 5,50,000

PROBLEM 3

From the following, calculate the Cash Price of the asset:

	₹
Hire Purchase Price of the asset	50,000
Down payment	10,000
Four annual instalments at the end of each year	10,000
Rate of interest	5% p.a

Solution

CALCULATION OF CASH PRICE

Number of Instalments	*Closing Balance*	*Amount of Instalment*	*Total*	*Interest 5/105*	*Opening balance*
4	0	10,000	10,000	476	9,524
3	9,524	10,000	19,524	930	18,594
2	18,594	10,000	28,594	1,362	27,232
1	27,232	10,000	37,232	1,773	35,459

Cash Price of the Asset = ₹ 1,000 (Down Payment) + ₹ 35,459 = ₹ 45,459

PROBLEM 4

On 1st April, 2015, Fastrack Motors Co. sells a truck on hire purchase basis to Teja Transport Co. for a total hire purchase price of ₹ 9,00,000 payable as to ₹ 2,40,000 as down payment and the balance in three equal annual instalments of ₹ 2,20,000 each payable on 31st March 2016, 2017 and 2018.

The hire vendor charges interest @ 10% per annum.

You are required to ascertain the Cash Price of the truck the Teja Transport Co. Calculations may be made to the nearest rupee.

Solution

CALCULATION OF CASH PRICE AND INTEREST

A No. of instalment	*B* Closing Balance	*C* Amount of instalment	*D = B + C* Amount Due before Payment of Instalment	*E = Dx10/110* Interest	*F = D – E* Opening Balance
III	0	2,20,000	2,20,000	20,000	2,00,000
II	2,00,000	2,20,000	4,20,000	38,182	3,81,818
I	3,81,818	2,20,000	6,01,818	54,711	5,47,107

Cash Price = ₹ 5,47,107 + ₹ 2,40,000 (down payment) = ₹ 7,87,107

CALCULATION OF INTEREST

PROBLEM 5

Mr. X purchased a machine on hire-purchase system, ₹30,000 being paid on delivery and the balance in five instalments of ₹60,000 each, payable annually on 31st December.The cash price of the machine was ₹3,00,000. Compute the amount of interest for each year.

Solution

			₹
1st year	=	Amount outstanding for interest after down payment	3,00,000
2nd year	=	Amount outstanding for interest after 1st Instalment	2,40,000
3rd year	=	Amount outstanding for interest after 2nd instalment	1,80,000
4th year	=	Amount outstanding for interest after 3rd instalment	1,20,000
5th year	=	Amount outstanding for interest after 4th instalment	60,000
Total interest	=	Hire Purchase Price – Cash Price	
	=	₹ 3,30,000 – ₹ 3,00,000 = ₹ 30,000	

Instalment outstanding ratio = 3,00,000 : 2,40,000 : 1,80,000 : 1,20,000 : 60,000

= 5:4:3:2:1

				₹
Interest for 1st year	=	5/15 × 30,000	=	10,000
Interest for 2nd year	=	4/15 × 30,000	=	8,000
Interest for 3rd year	=	3/15 × 30,000	=	6,000
Interest for 4th year	=	2/15 × 30,000	=	4,000
Interest for 5th year	=	1/15 x 30,000	=	2,000

PROBLEM 6

Mr. *X* purchased a machine on hire purchase system. He made cash payment of ₹ 30,000 and the balance was payable in 5 annual instalments of ₹ 60,000 each. The cash price of the machine is ₹ 3,00,000. Assume that the purchase was made on 1st April and the annual instalments are payable on 31st March of every year. Calculate the amount of interest for each year.

Solution

Hire Purchase Price = Total of all instalments + Down Payment

= (5 x 60,000) + 30,000 = ₹ 3,30,000

Total interest = H. P. Price – Cash Price

= ₹ 3,30,000 – ₹3,00,000 = ₹ 30,000

STATEMENT SHOWING CALCULATION OF INTEREST

Year	*Interest (₹)*
I	₹ 30,000 × $\frac{5}{15}$ = 10,000
II	₹ 30,000 × $\frac{4}{15}$ = 8,000
III	₹ 30,000 × $\frac{3}{15}$ = 6,000
IV	₹ 30,000 × $\frac{2}{15}$ = 4,000
V	₹ 30,000 × $\frac{1}{15}$ = 2,000
	30,000

PROBLEM 7

On 1st April a car company sold to Arya Bros., a motor car on hire-puchase basis. The total hire-puchase price was ₹ 4,60,000 with down payment of ₹ 1,60,000. Balance amount was to be paid in three annual instalments of ₹ 1,00,000 each. The first instalment payable on 31st March. The cash price of the car was ₹ 4,00,000.

How will Arya Bros, account for interest over three accounting years assuming books of accounts are closed on 31st March every year.

Solution

Total interest on hire purchase transactions = ₹ 4,60,000 – ₹ 4,00,000 = ₹ 60,000

As balance payment is made in three equal instalments, so interest is to be allocated in the ratio of 3:2:1

Therefore, interest for 1st year = ₹ 60,000 × 3/16 = ₹ 30,000
2nd year = ₹ 60,000 × 2/16 = ₹ 20,000
3rd year = ₹ 60,000 × 1/16 = ₹ 10,000

PREPARATION OF HIRE PURCHASER'S ACCOUNT

PROBLEM 8

On April 01, ABC & Associates acquired a Motor Car on hire purchase from MC & Co. The terms of the contract were as follows:

(i) Cash price of Motor Car was ₹ 2,70,000
(ii) ₹ 70,000 were to be paid on signing of the contract and balance in two equal annual installments plus interest, to be paid at the beginning of the onward financial years.
(iii) Interest chargeable on the outstanding balance was @ 12% p.a.
(iv) Depreciation @ 10% p.a. to be written-off using written down value method.

Required: You are required to prepare Motor Car A/c in the books of ABC & Associates.

Solution

Dr. **In the books of ABC & Associates Motor Car Account** Cr.

Date	Particulars	₹	Date	Particulars	₹
Year 1	To MC & Co.	2,10,000	Year 1	By Depreciation A/c	21,000
				By Balance c/d	1,89,000
		2,10,000			2,10,000
Year 2	To Balance b/d	1,89,000	Year 2	By Depreciation A/c	18,900
				By Balance c/d	1,70,100
		1,89,000			1,89,000
Year 3	To Balance b/d	1,70,100	Year 3	By Depreciation A/c	17,010
				By Balance c/d	1,53,090
		1,70,100			1,70,100

Note: Value of car will be taken at cash price while preparing Motor Car A/c. No adjustment required for down payment, installment and interest paid, in the Motor Car A/c.

VALUATION OF REPOSSESSED GOODS

PROBLEM 9

Computer Point sells computers on Hire Purchase basis at cost *plus* 25%. Terms of sale are ₹ 10,000 down payment and eight monthly instalments of ₹ 5,000 for each computer. Two computers were repossessed for non-payment of instalments and to be valued at 50% of cost price. Compute the value of repossessed computers.

Solution

Total HP Price per Computer [10,000 + (8 × 5,000)]	₹ 50,000
Cost Price per Computer [50,000/125]	₹ 40,000
Cost Price of 2 Repossessed Computers [₹ 40,000 × 2]	₹ 80,000
Value of Repossessed Computers = [50% of ₹ 80,000]	**₹ 40,000**

PROBLEM 10

On 1st April, 2014, M/s. Power Motors sold on hire purchase basis a truck whose cash price was ₹ 9,00,000 to M/s. Singh and Singh, a firm of transporters. The terms of the contract were that the transporters were to pay ₹ 3,00,000 down and six four-monthly instalments of ₹ 1,00,000 *plus* interest on outstanding amount of cash price for the intervening four months. The instalments were payable on 31st July, 30th November and 31st March in each one of the two accounting years. Interest was calculated @ 12% per annum.

M/s. Singh & Singh duly paid the instalment on 31st July, 2014 but failed to pay the instalment on 30th November, 2014. M/s. Power Motors, after legal formalities, repossessed the truck valuing it at ₹ 7,00,000.

M/s. Power Motors spent ₹ 80,000 on repairs and repainting of the truck and on 7th January, 2015 sold it for ₹ 7,50,000 cash.

You are required to prepare the account of M/s. Singh and Singh and Goods Repossessed Account in the books of M/s. Power Motors.

Solution

IN THE BOOKS OF M/S. POWER MOTORS
M/s. Singh & Singh's Account

Date	Particulars	₹	Date	Particulars	₹
1.4.2014	To Hire purchase sales A/c (Cash Price)	9,00,000	1.4.2014	By Bank (Down payment)	3,00,000
31.7.2014	To Interest A/c $\left(6,00,000 \times 12 \times \frac{4}{12}\right)$	24,000	31.7.2014	By Bank (1,00,000 + 24,000)	1,24,000
30.11.2014	To Interest A/c $\left(5,00,000 \times 12 \times \frac{4}{12}\right)$	20,000	30.11.2014	By Goods Repossessed A/c	7,00,000
30.11.2014	To Profit & Loss Account (Balance Fig.)	1,80,000			
		11,24,000			11,24,000

GOODS REPOSSESSED ACCOUNT

Date	Particulars	₹	Date	Particulars	₹
30.11.2012	To Singh & Singh's A/c	7,00,000	7.1.2015	By Bank A/c	7,50,000
7.1.2015	To Bank A/c (Repairs)	80,000	7.1.2015	By Profit & Loss A/c-loss	30,000
		7,80,000			7,80,000

PROBLEM 11

Happy Valley Florists Ltd. acquired a delivery van on hire purchase on 01.04.2012 from ganesh Enterprises. The items were as follows:

Particulars	Amount (₹)
Hire Purchase Price	1,80,000
Down Payment	30,000
1st installment payable after 1 year	50,000
2nd installment after 2 years	50,000
3rd installment after 3 years	30,000
4th installment after 4 years	20,000

Cash price of van ₹ 1,50,000 and depreciation is charged at 10% WDV.

You are required to:

(i) Calculate Total Interest and Interst included in each installment

(ii) Prepare Van A/c., Ganesh Enterprises A/c. in the books of Happy Valley Florists Ltd. up to 31.03.2016.

Solution

(a) Calculation of total Interest and Interest included in each installment

(i) Hire Purchase Price (HPP) = 30,000 + 50,000 + 50,000 + 30,000 + 20,000 = 1,80,000

(ii) Total Interest = 1,80,000 – 1,50,000 = 30,000

CALCUATION OF RATIO OF HPP IN BEGINNING OF EACH YEAR

Year	Outstanding HPP at beginning	Installment Paid	Outstanding balance at end
1	1,50,000	50,000	1,00,000
2	1,00,000	50,000	50,000
3	50,000	30,000	20,000
4	20,000	20,000	

1. Ratio of outstanding HPP at beginning for each year = 15:10:5:2
   Total Interest is of ₹ 1,30,000

Ist Year	= 30,000 × 15/32 = 14,062
IInd Year	= 30,000 × 10/32 = 9,375
IIIrd Year	= 30,000 × 5/32 = 4,688
IVth year	= 30,000 × 2/32 = 1,875

Dr. **Van Account** Cr.

Date	Particulars	₹	Date	Particulars	₹
1.4.2012	To Ganesh Enterprises	1,50,000	31.03.2013	By Depreciation A/c	15,000
				By balance c/d	1,35,000
		1,50,000			1,50,000
1.4.2013	To Balance b/d	1,35,000	31.03.2014	By Depreciation A/c	13,500
				By balance c/d	1,21,500
		1,35,000			1,35,000
1.4.2014	To Balance b/d	1,21,500	31.03.2015	By Depreciation A/.c	12,150
				By balance c/d	1,09,350
		1,21,500			1,21,500
1.4.2015	To Balance b/d	1,09,350	31.03.2016	By Depreciation A/c	10,935
				By Balance c/d	98,415
		1,09,350			1,9,350

Dr. **Ganesh Enterprises Account** Cr.

Date	Particulars	₹	Date	Particulars	₹
1.4.2012	To Bank A/c	30,000	1.4.2012	By Van A/c	1,50,000
31.3.2013	To Bank A/c	50,000	31.03.2013	By Interest A/c	14,062
	To Balance c/d	84,062			
		1,64,062			1,64,062
31.3.2014	To Bank A/c	50,000	1.4.2013	By Balance b/d	84,062
	To Balance c/d	43,437	31.03.2014	By Interest A/c	9,375
		93,437			93,437
31.3.2015	To Bank A/c	30,000	1.4.2014	By Balance b/d	43,437
	To Balance c/d	18,125	31.3.2015	By Interest A/c	4,688
		48,125			48,125
31.3.2016	To Bank A/c	20,000	1.4.2015	By Balance b/d	18,125
			31.3.2016	By Interest A/c	1,875
		20,000			20,000

Hire Purchase Trading Account

PROBLEM 12

Delhi Traders commenced business in 20X1, selling goods on hire purchase basis on the following terms:

Cost	Selling price	Deposit payable	Monthly instalment payable
₹ 2,000	3,000	20%	12

Monthly instalments are payable on the last date of the month in which the sale takes place. Other details are:

	20X1	20X2
Sales	300 Nos.	600 Nos.
Instalment received	₹ 3,75,000	10,70,000

Sales take place evenly throughout the year. In 20X2, 40 items sold in 20X1 on which a total of 300 instalments had been received were repossessed.

Required: Show ledger accounts for both the years in the books of Delhi Traders.

Solution

Dr. **(i) Hire Purchase Stock Account** Cr.

Date	Particulars	₹	Date	Particulars	₹
20X1	To Goods sold on Hire Purchase A/c	9,00,000	20X1	By Hire Purchase Debtors A/c (DP + Interest)	5,70,000
				By Balance c/d	3,30,000
		9,00,000			9,00,000
20X2	To Balance b/d	3,30,000	20X2	By Hire Purchase Debtors A/c	14,70,000
	To Goods sold on Hire Purchase A/c	18,00,000		By Balance c/d	6,60,000
		21,30,000			21,30,000

Dr. **(ii) Hire Purchase Debtors Account** Cr.

Date	Particulars	₹	Date	Particulars	₹
20X1	To Hire Purchase Stock A/c	5,70,000	20X1	By Cash A/c (Down Payment)	1,80,000
				By Cash (Instalment)	3,75,000
				By Balance c/d	15,000
		5,70,000			5,70,000
20X2	To Balance b/d	15,000	20X2	By Cash A/c (Down Payment)	3,60,000
	To Hire Purchase Stock A/c	14,70,000		By Cash (Instalments)	10,70,000
				By Goods Repossessed A/c	36,000
				By Balance c/d	19,000
		14,85,000			14,85,000

Dr. **(iii) Hire Purchase Adjustment Account (For 20X1)** Cr.

Particulars	₹	Particulars	₹
To Stock Reserve A/c (Load on Closing Stock)	1,10,000	By Goods Sold on Hire Purchase A/c (Load on Goods sold)	3,00,000
To Gross Profit t/f to P&L A/c	1,90,000		
	3,00,000		3,00,000

Dr. **(iv) Hire Purchase Adjustment Account (For 20X2)** Cr.

Particulars	₹	Particulars	₹
To Stock Reserve A/c (Load on Closing Stock)	2,20,000	By Goods Sold on Hire Purchase A/c (Load on Goods sold on H.P.)	6,00,000
To Goods Repossessed A/c	12,000	By Stock Reserve A/c (Load on Opening Stock)	1,10,000
To Gross Profit t/f P & L A/c	4,78,000		
	7,10,000		7,10,000

Dr. **(v) Goods Repossessed Account** Cr.

Particulars	₹	Particulars	₹
To Hire Purchase Debtors	36,000	By Hire Purchase Adjustment A/c (Loading)	12,000
		By Balance c/d	24,000
	36,000		36,000

Working Notes:

(i) *Calculation of H.P. Price, Cost Price and Loading an goods sold on H.P.*

	20X1	*20X2*
H.P. Price	₹ 9,00,000	₹ 18,00,000
Cost Price	₹ 6,00,000	₹ 12,00,000
Loading	₹ 3,00,000	₹ 6,00,000

(ii) *No. of Instalments due and No. of Instalments not yet due in respect of Sales during 20X1*

Month	*Units sold*	*Instalment Due per unit during*		*Total Instalments Due during*	
		20X1	*20X2*	*20X1*	*20X2*
January	25	12	0	300	—
February	25	11	1	275	25
March	25	10	2	250	50
April	25	9	3	225	75
May	25	8	4	200	100
June	25	7	5	175	125
July	25	6	6	150	150
August	25	5	7	125	175
September	25	4	8	100	200
October	25	3	9	75	225
November	25	2	10	50	250
December	25	1	11	25	275
				1,950	1,650

(iii) *No. of Instalments due in 20X2 and in 20X3 in respect of sales during 20X2*
Since the sale during 20X2 are 200% of the sales during 20X1, the no. of instalments due in 20X2 and 20X3 will be as under: Due in 20X2—3,900, Due in 20X3—3,300

PROBLEM 13

Krishna Agencies started business on 1st April, 20X1. During the year ended 31st March, 20X2, they sold undermentioned durables under two schemes—Cash Price Scheme (CPs) and Hire-purchase Scheme (HPS). Under the CPS, they priced the goods at cost *plus* 25% and collected it on delivery. Under the HPS, the buyers were required to sign a Hire-purchase Agreement undertaking to pay for the value of the goods including finance charges in 30 instalments, the value being calculated at Cash Price *plus* 50%. The following are the details available at the end of 31st March, 20X2 with regard to the products:

Product	*Nos. Purchased*	*Nos. sold under CPs*	*Nos. sold Under HPS*	*Cost/unit ₹*	*No. of instalments due during the year*	*No. of instalments received during the year*
TV sets	90	20	60	16,000	1,080	1,000
Washing Machine	70	20	40	12,000	840	800

The following were the expenses during the year: Rent ₹ 1,20,000, Salaries ₹ 1,44,000, Commission to Salesmen ₹ 12,000, Office Expenses ₹ 1,20,000.

From the above information, you are required to prepare: (a) Hire Purchase Trading Account, and (b) Trading and Profit & Loss Account.

Solution

Hire Purchase Trading Account

Dr. *for the year ending on 31st March, 20X2 (Rs in Lakhs)* Cr.

Particulars	*T. Sets ₹*	*W. Machine ₹*	*Total ₹*	*Particulars*	*T.Sets ₹*	*W. Machine ₹*	*Total ₹*
To Goods sold on Purchase	18.00	9.00	27.00	By Bank/Cash A/c	10.00	6.00	16.00
To Stock Reserve (on instalments not yet due)	3.36	1.26	4.62	By Instalment Due A/c	.80	.30	1.10
To Profit & Loss A/c	5.04	2.94	7.98	By Hire Purchase Stock A/c	7.20	2.70	9.90
				By Goods sold on Hire Purchase (Loading)	8.40	4.20	12.60
	26.40	13.20	39.60		26.40	13.20	39.60

Trading and Profit & Loss Account

Dr. *for the year ending on 31st March, 20X2 (₹ in Lakhs)* Cr.

Particulars	₹	₹	₹	*Particulars*	₹	₹	₹
To Purchases	14.40	8.40	22.80	By Sales	4.00	3.00	7.00
To Gross Profit c/d	.80	.60	1.40	By Closing Stock (b.f.)	1.60	1.20	2.80
				By Goods sold on H.P. A/c	9.60	4.80	14.40
	15.20	9.00	24.20		15.20	9.00	24.20
To Salaries			1.44	By Gross profit b/d			1.40
To Rent			1.20	By H.P. Trading A/c			7.98
To Commission			0.12				
To Office Expenses			1.20				
To Net Profit			5.42				
			9.38				9.38

Working Notes:

		T. Sets	W. Machine	Total
A	Units Sold	60	40	—
B	H.P. Price/Unit (Rs)	30,000	22,500	—
C	Cost Price/Unit (Rs	16,000	12,000	—
D	Loading/Unit (Rs)	14,000	10,500	—
E	Total H.P. Price (A × B)	18,00,000	9,00,000	27,00,000
F	Total Cost (A × C)	9,60,000	4,80,000	14,40,000
G	Total Loading (A × D)	8,40,000	4,20,000	12,60,000
H	Amount of each Instalment (H.P. Price/Nos. of Instalments)	1,000	750	
I	Nos. of Instalments per unit (H.P. Price/ Amount of each Instalment)	30	30	
J	Total Nos. of Instalments (Nos. of Instalments per unit × Nos. of units sold)	1,800	1,200	
K	Nos. of Instalments fallen due during the year	1,080	840	
L	Nos. of Instalments due and collected	1,000	800	
M	Nos. of Instalments due but not collected (K – L)	80	40	
N	Nos. of Instalments not yet due (J – K)	720	360	
O	Amount of Instalments fallen due (K × H)	10,80,000	6,30,000	
P	Amount of Instalments due and collected (L × H)		10,00,000	6,00,000
Q	Amount of Instalment due but not collected (M × H)		80,000	30,000
R	Amount of Instalments not yet due (N × H)		7,20,000	2,70,000
S	Stock Reserve = $\frac{\text{H.P. Price} - \text{Cost Price}}{\text{H.P. Price}}$ × Amount. of Instalments not yet due		3,36,000	1,26,000

PROBLEM 14

CANJA (Pvt.) Ltd. sells washing machines for outright cash as well as on hire-purchase basis. The cost of a washing machine to the company is ₹ 10,500. The company has fixed cash price of the machine at ₹ 12,300 and hire-purchase price at Rs 13,500 payable as to ₹ 1,500 down and the balance in 24 equal monthly instalments of ₹ 500 each.

On 1st April, 20X1 the company had 26 washing machines lying in its showroom. On that date 3 instalments had fallen due, but not yet received and 675 instalments were yet to fall due in respect of machines lying with the hire-purchase customers.

During the year ended 31st March, 20X2 the company sold 130 machines on cash basis and 80 machines on hire-purchase basis. After paying five monthly instalments, one customer failed to pay subsequent instalments and the company had to repossess the washing machine. After spending ₹ 1,000 on it, the company resold it for ₹ 11,500.

On 31st March, 20X2 there were 21 washing machines in stock, 810 instalments were yet to fall due and 5 instalments had fallen due, but not yet received in respect of washing machines lying with the hire-purchase customers. Total selling expenses and office expenses including depreciation on fixed assets totalled ₹ 1,60,000 for the year.

You are required to prepare for the Accounting Year ended 31st March, 20X2:

(i) Hire-purchase Trading Account, and

(ii) Trading and Profit & Loss Account showing net profit earned by the compay after making provision for Income-tax @ 35%.

Solution

Hire Purchase Trading Account

Dr. Particulars	₹	Particulars	Cr. ₹
To Hire Purchase Stock (₹ 500 × 675)	3,37,500	By Hire Purchase Stock Reserve (₹ 3,37,500 × 3000/13,500)	75,000
To Installments Due (₹ 500 × 3)	1,500	By Installments Collected— Bank (Working Note 1)	10,02,000
To Goods sold on Hire Purchases A/c (₹ 13,500 × 80)	10,80,000	By Repossessed Goods (₹ 13,500 – 1,500 – 2,500)	9,500
To Hire Purchase Stock Reserve (₹ 4,05,000 × 3,000/13,500)	90,000	By Goods sold on Hire Purchases A/c (Loading) (₹ 10,80,000 × 3,000/13,500)	2,40,000
To Profit and Loss Account: Transfer of Profit	2,25,000	By Hire Purchase Stock (₹ 500 × 810)	4,05,000
		By nstallment Due (₹ 500 × 5)	2,500
	17,34,000		17,34,000

Trading & Profit & Loss Account
for the year ended 31st March 2001

Dr. Particulars	₹	Particulars	Cr. ₹
To Opening Stock (₹10,500 × 26)	2,73,000	By Sales (₹ 12,300 × 130)	15,99,000
To Purchases (₹ 10,500 × 205) Working Note 2	21,52,500	By Goods sold on Hire-Purchase (₹ 10,80,000 – ₹ 2,40,000)	8,40,000
To Gross Profit c/d	2,34,000	By Closing Stock (₹ 10,500 × 21)	2,20,500
	26,59,500		26,59,500
To Sundry Expenses	1,60,000	By Gross b/d	2,34,000
To Provision for Income Tax @ 35% of ₹ 3,00,000	1,05,000	By Profit of Hire Purchase Trading	2,25,000
To Net Profit for the year	1,95,000	By Repossessed Goods (₹11,500 – ₹ 1,000 – ₹ 9,500)	1,000
	4,60,000		4,60,000

Working Notes:

(i) Memorandum Hire Purchase Stock Account

Dr. Particulars	₹	Particulars	Cr. ₹
To Balance b/d [₹ 500 × 675]	3,37,500	By Hire Purchase Debtors A/c (b.f.)	10,12,500
To Goods Sold on Hire Purchase A/c [₹ 13,500 × 80]	10,80,000	By Balance c/d (₹ 500 × 810)	4,05,000
	14,17,500		14,17,500

(ii) Memorandum Hire Purchase Debtors Account

Dr. Particulars	₹	Particulars	Cr. ₹
To Balance b/d [₹ 500 × 3]	1,500	By Cash/Bank A/c (b.f.)	10,02,000
To Hire Purchase Stock A/c	10,12,500	By Goods Repossessed A/c [₹ 13,500 – (₹ 1,500 + ₹ 2,500)]	9,500
		By Balance c/d (₹ 500 × 5)	2,500
	10,14,000		10,14,000

(iii) Washing Machines Purchases:

Closing Balance	21 Nos.
Add: Cash Sales	130 Nos.
Sales on Hire Purchase basis	80 Nos.
Less: Opening stock	(26 Nos.)
Purchase during the year	**205 Nos.**

Amount of Purchases = 205 Nos. × ₹ 10,500 = ₹ 21,52,500

PROBLEM 15

ABC Associates entered into a financial lease agreement on 1.4.20X1 with Flexible Leasing Ltd. for lease of a car. The price of the car was ₹ 2,00,000 and the quarterly lease rentals were agreed at Rs 90 per thousand payable at the beginning of every quarter. ABC Associates kept up their payments but by 25.3.20X2 they approached and obtained the consent of the leasing company for treating the arrangement as one of Instalment-purchase from the beginning, on the following terms:

Period: 3 years

Quarterly hire: ₹ 30,000 payable at the beginning of the quarter.

It was agreed that the lease rentals paid will be treated as hire monies and that the balance due upto 31.3.20X2 will be settled by ABC Associates on that date with interest at 18% p.a. on various instalments due during the year. The rate of depreciation on the car is 25%.

Required: Show the following accounts in the books of ABC Associates for the year 20X1-20X2: Flexible Leasing Ltd.'s A/c, Interest Suspense A/c.

Calculations are to be rounded off to the nearest rupee.

Solution

Dr. **Flexible Leasing Limited Account** *Cr.*

Date	*Particulars*	₹	*Date*	*Particulars*	₹
20X2			20X2		
March 25	To Lease Rental A/c	72,000	March 25	By Car on Hire Purchase A/c	2,00,000
March 31	To Bank A/c	53,400	March 25	By Interest Suspense A/c	1,60,000
March 31	To Balance c/d	2,40,000	March 31	By Interest A/c	5,400
		3,65,400			3,65,400

Dr. **Interest Suspense Account** *Cr.*

Date	*Particulars*	₹	*Date*	*Particulars*	₹
20X2			20X2		
March 25	To Flexible Leasing Ltd. A/c	1,60,000	March 31	By Interest on Hire Purchase A/c	72,727
			March 31	By Balance c/d	87,273
		1,60,000			1,60,000

Working Notes:

(i) *Calculation of Balance Payable on 31st March, 20X2 and the Amount of Interest*

Calculation of Difference Payable on 31.3.20X2 and Interest

Date Charges	*Quarterly Rentals* ₹	*Hire Lease Paid* ₹	*Quarterly Payable* ₹	*Difference From*	*Interest To*	*Amount of @18% p.a. Interest* ₹
01.04.20X1	30,000	18,000	12,000	01.04.20X1	31.03.20X2	2,160
01.07.20X1	30,000	18,000	12,000	01.07.20X1	31.03.20X2	1,620
01.10.20X1	30,000	18,000	12,000	01.10.20X1	31.03.20X2	1,080
01.01.20X2	30,000	18,000	12,000	01.01.20X2	31.03.20X2	540
		72,000	48,000			5,400

Amount Payable on 31st March, 20X2	₹
Balance due	48,000
Interest due	5,400
	53,400

(ii) *Ascertainment of Total Amount of Interest on Hire Purchase*

	₹
Hire Purchase Price of the car (₹ 30,000 × 12 instalments	3,60,000
Less: Cash Price	(2,00,000)
Total Amount of Interest	1,60,000

(iii) *Calculation of Interest on Hire Purchase Attributable to the Year 20X1-20X2*

Date	*Month for which O/s*	*Interest Calculation*	*Interest* ₹
01.04.20X1	–	– –	
01.07.20X1	33	1,60,000 × 33/198	26,667
01.10.20X1	30	1,60,000 × 30/198	24,242
01.01.20X1	27	1,60,000 × 27/198	21,818
			72,727

Note: Sum of 33, 30, 27 .... 3 = 198

PROBLEM 16

Omega Corporation sells computers on hire purchase basis at cost *plus* 25%. Terms of sales are ₹ 10,000 as down payment and 8 monthly instalments of ₹ 5,000 for each computer. From the following particulars prepare Hire Purchase Trading Account for the year 2008.

As on 1st January, 2008 last instalment on 30 computers was outstanding as these were not due up to the end of the previous year.

During 2008 the firm sold 240 computers. As on 31st December, 2008 the position of instalments outstanding were as under:

Instalments due but not collected:

2 instalments of 2 computers and last instalment on 6 computers.

Instalments not yet due:

8 instalments on 50 computers, 6 instalments on 30 and last instalment on 20 computers.

Two computers on which 6 instalments were due and one instalment not yet due on 31.12.2008 had to be repossessed. Repossessed stock is valued at 50% of cost. All other instalments have been received.

Solution

Hire Purchase Trading Account for the year ended on 31st December, 2008

Particulars	₹	Particulars	₹
To Hire Purchase stock (30 × ₹ 5,000)	1,50,000	By Cash A/c	90,30,000
		By Stock Reserve (₹ 1,50,000×20%)	30,000
To Goods Sold on Hire Purchase (240 × ₹ 50,000)	1,20,00,000	By Goods sold on Hire Purchase (₹ 1,20,00,000 × 20%)	24,00,000
To Stock Reserve (₹ 30,00,000 × 20%)	6,00,000	By Goods Repossessed (2 × ₹ 40,000 × 50%)	40,000
To Profit & Loss A/c (Transfer of Profit)	18,00,000	By Instalments Due [(2×2+1×6) × ₹ 5,000]	50,000
		Hy Hire Purchase Stock [8×50+6×30+1×20)× ₹ 5,000]	30,00,000
	1,45,50,000		1,45,50,000

Working Notes:

Dr. **(i) Memorandum Hire Purchase Stock Account** *Cr.*

Particulars	₹	Particulars	₹
To Balance b/d (30 × ₹ 5,000)	1,50,000	By Hire Purchase Debtors A/c (b.f.)	91,40,000
To Goods Sold on Hire Purchase A/c (240 × Rs 5,000)	120,00,000	By Goods Repossessed A/c (2 × 1 × Rs 5,000)	10,000
		By Balance c/d [(8 × 50) + (6 × 30) + (1 × 20)] × ₹ 5,000	30,00,000
	121,50,000		121,50,000

Dr. **(ii) Memorandum Hire Purchase Debtors Account** *Cr.*

Particulars	₹	Particulars	₹
To Balance b/d	—	By Cash/Bank A/c (b.f.)	90,30,000
To Hire Purchase Stock A/c	91,40,000	By Goods Repossessed A/c (6 × 2 × ₹ 5,000)	60,000
		By Balance c/d [(2 × 2 × 5,000) + (1 × 6 × 5,000)]	50,000
	91,40,000		91,40,000

PROBLEM 17

Sameera Corporation sells Computers on Hire-purchase basis at cost plus 25%. Terms of sales are ₹ 5,000 as Down payment and 10 monthly installment of ₹ 2,500 for each Computer. From the following particulars, prepare Hire-purchase Trading A/c for the year 2002-2003 :

As on 1st April, 2002, last instalment on 20 Computers were outstanding as these were not due upto the end of the previous year. During 2002-03, the firm sold 120 computers. As on 31st March, 2003 the position of instalments outstanding were as under:

Installments due but not collected	4 Installments on 4 Computers and Last installment on 9 Computers
Installments not yet due	6 Installments on 50 Computers, 4 Installments on 20 and Last Installment on 40 Computers

Two Computers on which 8 Installments were due and one Installment not yet due on 31.03.2003, had to be repossessed. Repossessed stock is valued at 50% of cost. All other Installments have been received.

Solution

Dr. **Hire Purchase Trading Account for the year ended 31st March, 2003** *Cr.*

Particulars	₹	*Particulars*	₹
To Hire Purchase Stock (20 × ₹ 2,500)	50,000	By Cash A/c	24,92,500
To Goods sold on Hire Purchase (120 × ₹ 30,000)	36,00,000	By Stock Reserve (₹ 50,00,000 × 20%)	10,000
To Stock Reserve (₹ 10,50,000 × 20%)	2,10,000	By Goods sold on Hire Purchase (₹ 36,00,000 × 20%)	7,20,000
To Profit and Loss A/c (Profit)	4,99,000	By Goods Repossessed (2 × ₹ 24,000 × 50%)	24,000
		By Installments due [(4 X 4 + 1× 9) × ₹ 2,500]	62,500
		By Hire Purchase Stock [(6×50 + 4 X 20 + 1×40) ₹ 2,500]	10,50,000
	43,59,000		43,59,000

Working Notes:

Dr. **(i) Memorandum Hire Purchase Stock Account** *Cr.*

Particulars	₹	*Particulars*	₹
To Balance b/d (20 × ₹ 2,500)	50,000	By Hire Purchase Debtors A/c (b.f.)	25,95,000
To Goods Sold on Hire Purchase A/c (120 × ₹ 30,000)	36,00,000	By Goods Repossessed A/c (2 × 1 × ₹ 2,500)	5,000
		By Balance c/d [(6 × 50) + (4 × 20) + (1 × 40)] × ₹ 2,500	10,50,000
	36,50,000		36,50,000

Dr. **(ii) Memorandum Hire Purchase Debtors Account** *Cr.*

Particulars	₹	*Particulars*	₹
To Balance b/d	—	By Cash/Bank A/c (b.f.)	24,92,500
To Hire Purchase Stock A/c	25,95,000	By Goods Repossessed A/c (2 × 8 × ₹ 2,500)	40,000
		By Balance c/d [(4 × 4 × 2,500) + (1 × 9 × 2,500)]	62,500
	25,95,000		25,95,000

PROBLEM 18

ABC Ltd. sells goods on Hire-purchase by adding 50% above cost from the following particulars, prepare Hire-purchase Trading account to reveal the profit for the year ended 31.3.2008:

	Particulars	₹
01.04.2007	Instalments due but not collected	10,000
01.04.2007	Stock at shop (at cost)	36,000
01.04.2007	Instalment not yet due	18,000
31.03.2008	Stock at shop	40,000
31.03.2008	Instalment due but not collected	18,000
Others details:		
Total instalments became due		1,32,000
Goods purchased		1,20,000
Cash received from customers		1,21,000

Some of the Goods on which due instalments could not be collected were repossessed and valued at 30% below original cost. The vendor spent ₹ 500 on getting goods overhauled and then sold for ₹ 2,800.

Solution

Dr. **Hire Purchase Trading Account** Cr.

Particulars	₹	Particulars	₹
To Opening Balance:		By Cash (₹ 1,21,000 + ₹ 2,800)	1,23,800
Hire Purchase Stock	18,000	By Stock Reserve (Opening)	6,000
Hire Purchase Debtors	10,000	By Goods sold on Hire	
To Goods sold on hire Purchase	1,74,000	Purchase (Loading)	58,000
To Cash (Overhauling charges)	500	By Closing Balances:	
To Stock Reserve (Closing)	20,000	Hire Purchase Stock	60,000
To Profit transferred to Profit		Hire Purchase Debtors	18,000
and Loss Account	43,300		
	2,65,800		2,65,800

Working Notes:

Dr. **(i) Memorandum Shop Stock Account** Cr.

Particulars	₹	Particulars	₹
To Balance b/d	36,000	By Goods Sold on hire purchase (b.f.)	1,16,000
To Purchases	1,20,000	By Balance c/d	40,000
	1,56,000		1,56,000

Dr. **(ii) Memorandum Instalment not yet due (Hire Purchase Stock) Account** Cr.

Particulars	₹	Particulars	₹
To Balance b/d	18,000	By Hire Purchase sales	1,32,000
To Goods Sold on Hire Purchase	1,74,000	By Balance c/d (b.f.)	60,000
	1,92,000		1,92,000

Dr. **(iii) Memorandum Instalment due but not collected (Hire Purchase Debtors) Account** Cr.

Particulars	₹	Particulars	₹
To Balance b/d	10,000	By Cash	1,21,000
To Hire Purchase Sales	1,32,000	By Repossessed stock (b.f.)	3,000
		By Balance c/d	18,000
	1,42,000		1,42,000

(iv) Profit/Loss on Repossessed Goods

A. Original Cost ₹ 3,000 × 100 / 150 = ₹ 2,000

B. Valuation of repossessed goods = ₹ 2,000 × 70% = ₹ 1,400

C. Loss on repossession (₹ 3,000 – ₹ 1,400) = Rs.1,600

D. Profit on sale of repossessed goods = ₹ 2,800 – (₹ 1,400 + ₹ 500) = ₹ 900

Dr. **(v) Goods Repossessed Account** Cr.

Particulars	₹	Particulars	₹
To Hire Purchase Debotrs	3,000	By Hire Purchase Trading A/c	1,600
		By Balance c/d	1,400
	3,000		3,000
To Balance b/d	1,400	By Cash	2,800
To Cash A/c (expenses)	500		
To Profit on sale	900		
	2,800		2,800

PROBLEM 19

S Ltd. has a Hire-purchase department. Goods are on hire-purchase at cost *plus* 60%. From the following particulars draft Hire-Purchase Trading Account and compute profit or loss for the year ended 31st March, 2008.

	₹
Goods with customers on 1.4.2007 (instalments are not due)	3,20,000
Instalments due on 1.4.2007 (customers are paying)	20,000
Goods sold on hire-purchase during the year (i.e. from 1.4.2007 to 31.3.2008)	16,00,000
Cash received from customers	11,20,000
Goods repossessed from customers (valued at 40% of unpaid Instalments)	16,000
Goods with customers as on 31.3.2008 (at hire-purchase price)	7,20,000

Solution

Hire Purchase Trading Account
for the year ended on 31st March, 2008

Dr. Cr.

Particulars	₹	Particulars	₹
To Opening Balances:		By Hire Purchase Stock Reserve A/c	1,20,000
Hire Purchase Stock	3,20,000	[₹ 3,20,000 × 60/160]	
Instalment due	20,000	By Bank A/c (Cash received)	11,20,000
To Goods sold on Hire Purchase	16,00,000	By Goods Respossessed A/c	16,000
To Hire Purchase Stock Reserve A/c	2,70,000	By Goods sold on hire purchase	
[₹ 7,20,000 × 60/160]		(loading)	6,00,000
To Profit and Loss A/c	4,26,000	[₹ 16,00,000 × 60/160]	
		By Closing Balances:	
		Hire Purchase stock	7,20,000
		Instalment due	60,000
	26,36,000		26,36,000

Working Notes:

Dr. **(i) Memorandum H. P. Stock Account** Cr.

Particulars	₹	Particulars	₹
To Balance b/d	3,20,000	By HP Debtors A/c (b.f.)	12,00,000
To Goods Sold on HP	16,00,000	By Balance c/d	7,20,000
	19,20,000		19,20,000

Dr. **(ii) Memorandum H. P. Debtors Account** Cr.

Particulars	₹	Particulars	₹
To Balance b/d	20,000	By Cash/Bank A/c	11,20,000
To HP Stock A/c	12,00,000	By Goods Repossessed A/c (Rs 16,000/0.40)	40,000
		By Balance c/d	60,000
	12,20,000		12,20,000

PROBLEM 20

Computer point sells computers on Hire-purchase basis at cost *plus* 25%. Terms of sale are ₹ 5,000 down payment and eight monthly instalments of ₹ 2,500 for each computer. The following transactions took place during the financial year 2006-2007:

Number of instalments not yet due as on 1.4.2006 = 25

Number of instalments due but not collected as on 1.4.2006 = 5

During the financial year 240 computers were sold. Out of the above sold computers during the year the outstanding positions were as follows as on 31.3.2007:

Instalments not yet due:

(i) Eight installments on 50 computers.

(ii) Six instalments on 30 computers.

(iii) Two instalments on 10 computers.

Instalments due but not collected. Two instalments on 5 computers during the year.

Two computers on which five instalments were due and two instalments not yet due were repossessed out of sales effected during current year. Repossessed stock is valued at 50% of cost. All instalments have been received. You are asked to prepare Hire-Purchase Trading Account for the year ending on 31.3.2007 :

Solution

Hire Purchase Trading Account
for the year ended on 31.3.07

Dr. Cr.

Particulars	₹	Particulars	₹
To Opening HP Stock	62,500	By Opening Stock Reserve (62,500 × 25/100)	12,500
To Opening HP Debtors	12,500	By Goods sold on HP A/c (60,000 × 25/100)	12,00,000
To Goods sold on HP A/c (240 × 2,500)	60,00,000	By Cash down payment	12,00,000
To Closing Stock Reserve (Loading) (₹ 15,000 × 25/25)	3,00,000	Instalments	33,15,000
To Profit t/f to Profit and Loss A/c	8,97,500	By Goods Repossessed A/c	20,000
		By Closing HP Debtors	25,000
		By Closing HP Stock	15,00,000
	72,72,500		72,72,500

Working Noes:

Dr. **(i) Memorandum HP Stock Account** Cr.

Particulars	₹	*Particulars*	₹
To Balance b/d [25 × ₹ 2500]	62,500	By HP Debtors A/c [b.t]	**45,52,500**
To Goods sold on HP A/c [240 × Rs 25,000]	60,00,000	By Goods Repossessed A/c [2 × 2 × ₹ 2,500]	10,000
		By Balance c/d [600 × ₹ 2,500]	15,00,000
	60,62,500		60,62,500

Dr. **(ii) Memorandum HP Debtors Account** Cr.

Particulars	₹	*Particulars*	₹
To Balance b/d [5 × ₹ 2,500]	12,500	By Cash A/c (down payment) [240 × ₹ 5,000]	12,00,000
To HP Stock A/c	45,52,500	By Goods Repossessed A/c [5 × 2 × ₹ 2,500]	25,000
		By Cash A/c (*Balancing figure*)	**33,15,000**
		By Balance c/d [5 × 2 × ₹ 2,500]	25,000
	45,65,000		45,65,000

(iii) *Calculation of Value of Cash Repossessed*

Hire purchase price of two

Repossessed Computers = 2 × [5,000 + (8 × 2,500)] = ₹ 50,000

Cost Price of Repossessed Computers = (50,000 × 100/125) = ₹ 40,000

Value of Repossessed Computers = 40,000 × 50/100 = ₹ 20,000

PROBLEM 21

Wye sells goods on Hire-purchase at cost *plus* 50%. Prepare Hire Purchase Trading Account from the information given below:

	₹
Stock with customers on hire-purchase price (opening)	1,62,000
Stock in hand at shop (opening)	3,24,000
Instalments overdue (opening)	1,35,000
Purchases during the year	10,80,000
Goods repossessed (instalments not due ₹ 36,000) (valued at)	9,000
Stock at shop excluding repossessed goods (closing)	3,60,000
Cash received during the year	10,35,000
Installments overdue (closing)	1,62,000

The vendor spent ₹ 2,000 on goods repossessed and then sold it for ₹ 15,000.

Solution

Dr. **Hire Purchase Trading Account** Cr.

Particulars	₹	Particulars	₹
To Opening balances :		By Cash received (on Instalments)	10,35,000
Hire Purchase Debtors	1,35,000	By Stock reserve (Opening)	54,000
Hire Purchase Stock	1,62,000	[₹ 1,62,000 × 50/150]	
To Goods sold on hire purchase	15,66,000	By Goods sold on hire purchase (loading)	5,22,000
To Cash (Expenses)	2,000	[₹ 15,66,000 × 50/150]	
To Stock reserve (closing) [₹ 6,30,000 × 50/150]	2,10,000	By Cash received (on sale of re-possessed goods)	15,000
To Profit t/f to Profit and and Loss A/c	3,43,000	By Closing Balance :	
		Hire Purchase Stock (Inst. Overdue)	6,30,000
		Hire Purchase Debtors	1,62,000
	24,18,000		24,18,000

Working Notes:

Dr. **(i) Stock at Shop Account** Cr.

Particulars	₹	Particulars	₹
To Balance b/d	3,24,000	By Goods sold on hire Purchase A/c	10,44,000
To Purchases (at cost)	10,80,000	By Balance c/d	3,60,000
	14,04,000		14,04,000

Dr. **(ii) Memorandum Hire Purchase Stock Account** Cr.

Particulars	₹	Particulars	₹
To Balance b/d	1,62,000	By Hire Purchase Debtors A/c	10,62,000
To Goods sold on H.P. A/c [₹ 10,44,000 + 50%]	15,66,000	By Goods repossessed A/c (instalments not due)	36,000
		By Balance c/d (Bal. fig.)	6,30,000
	17,28,000		17,28,000

Dr. **(iii) Memorandum Hire Purchase Debtors Account** Cr.

Particulars	₹	Particulars	₹
To Balance b/d	1,35,000	By Cash received	10,35,000
To Hire Purchase Stock A/c (b.f.)	10,62,000	By Balance c/d	1,62,000
	11,97,000		11,97,000

PROBLEM 22

Easilife Ltd. has a hire-purchase department which fixes hire-purchase price by adding 40% to the cost of the goods. The following additional information is provided to you:

	₹
On 1st April, 2009:	
Goods out on hire-purchase (at hire-purchase price)	2,10,000
Instalments due	14,000
Transactions during the year:	
Hire-purchase price of goods sold	9,80,000
Instalments received	8,12,000
Value of goods repossessed due to defaults (hire-purchase instalments unpaid ₹ 5,600)	7,800
On 31st March, 2010:	
Goods out on hire-purchase (at hire-purchase price)	3,78,000

You are required to prepare Hire-purchase Trading Account, ascertaining the profit made by the department during the year ended 31st March, 2010.

Solution

Dr. **Hire Purchase Trading Account** *Cr.*

Particulars	₹	*Particulars*	₹
To Opening Balances:		By Stock Reserve A/c	60,000
Hire Purchase Stock	2,10,000	[₹ 2,10,000 × 40/140]	
Instalments due	14,000	By Bank A/c	
To Goods sold on Hire		(instalments received)	8,12,000
Purchase A/c	9,80,000	By Goods Repossessed A/c	7,800
To Stock Reserve A/c		By Goods sold in Hire Purchase	
[₹ 3,78,000 × 40/140]	1,08,000	A/c (Loading)	2,80,000
To Profit & Loss A/c	2,34,200	[₹ 9,80,000 × 40/140]	
(Transfer of Profit)		By Closing Balances:	
		Hire Purchase Stock	3,78,000
		Instalments due	8,400
	15,46,200		**15,46,200**

Working Notes:

Closing instalments due :

Opening hire purchase stock		2,10,000
Opening instalments due		14,000
Goods sent on hire purchase		9,80,000
Less: Instalments received	8,12,000	
Unpaid instalments on repossessed goods	5,600	
Closing hire purchase stock	3,78,000	(11,95,600)
		8,400

PROBLEM 23

From the following information of M/s Chennai Traders, you are required to prepare Hire Purchase Trading Account to ascertain the profit made during the financial year 2009-10.

Chennai Traders sell goods on hire purchase basis at cost plus 25%. The following details are available:

(1)	Instalment not due on 31st March, 2009	4,50,000
(2)	Instalment due and collected during the financial year 2009-10	12,00,000
(3)	Instalment due but not collected during the financial year 2009-10 which includes ₹ 15,000 for which goods were repossessed	75,000
(4)	Instalment not due on 31st March, 2010 including ₹ 30,000 for which goods were repossessed	5,55,000
(5)	Instalment collected on repossessed stock	22,500
(6)	M/s Chennai Traders valued repossessed stock at 60% of original cost.	

Solution

Dr. **Hire Purchase Trading Account (at invoice value)** Cr.

Particulars	₹	Particulars	₹
To Goods with customers (Begaining)	4,50,000	By Stock reserve (Opening)	90,000
To Goods sold on Hire Purchase	13,50,000	By Hire purchase sales	12,75,000
To Bad debts	3,000	By Goods sold on hire purchase (loading)	2,70,000
To Loss on repossession	3,600	By Goods with customer (End)	5,25,000
To Stock Reserve (Closing)	1,05,000		
To Profit & Loss A/c (H.P. profit)	2,48,400		
	21,60,000		**21,60,000**

Working Notes:

(i) Hire Purchase Sales

Installments due and collected	12,00,000
Add: Installments due but not collected	75,000
	12,75,000

(i) Loss on Repossessed Goods

Hire Purchase Price of Repossessed goods	
Installments collected	22,500
Installments due	15,000
Installments not due	30,000
	67,500
Cost of Repossessed Goods (₹ 67,500 × 100/125)	54,000
Valuation of Repossessed Goods (₹ 54,000 × 60/100)	32,400
Less: Cost of installments due + Installments not yet due (₹ 15,000 + ₹ 30,000) × 100/125	36,000
Loss on repossession	3,600

(iii) Goods taken from shop stock

Hire Purchase Sales (12,00,000 + 75,000)	12,75,000
Add: Stock with customers (5,55,000 – 30,000) at end	5,25,000
Less: Stock with Customer in the begining	(4,50,000)
	13,50,000

Loading on goods taken from shop stock
= ₹ 13,50,000 × (25/125) = ₹ 2,70,000

(iv) Bad Debt

	₹
Installment due but not collected	15,000
Add: Installment not yet due at cost	24,000
	39,000
Less: Cost of installments due and not yet due	(36,000)
	3,000

In other words ₹ 15,000 × (25/125) = ₹ 3,000

Note: It is presumed that all the figures given in the question is at invoice price

PROBLEM 24

Sonam Corporation sells goods on hire purchase basis. The hire purchase price is cost *plus* 50%. From the following particulars prepare Hire Purchase Trading Account for the year ended 31st March, 2010:

	₹
Instalments not yet due on 01-04-09	3,00,000
Instalments due on 01-04-09	1,50,000
Goods sold on hire purchase during the year	9,00,000
Instalments collected from HP debtors	6,80,000
Stock with customers at hire purchase price	4,50,000
Goods re-possessed during the year	60,000
On 31-03-2010 Goods repossessed were valued at	Cost *less* 40%

Solution

Hire Purchase Trading Account for the year ended 31 .03 .2010

Particulars	₹	*Particulars*	₹
To Opening balances:		By H.P. Stock Reserve (opening)	1,00,000
Hire Purchase Stock	3,00,000	By Bank (Installments)Collected)	6,80,000
Hire Purchase Debtors	1,50,000	By Goods repossessed	24,000
To Goods sold on hire purchase		By Goods sold on hire	
To H.P. Stock reserve (closing)	1,50,000	purchase (loading)	3,00,000
To Profits Loss A/c	2,14,000	By Closing Balances:	
		Hire Purchase Stock	4,50,000
		Hire Purchase Debtors	1,60,000
	17,14,000		17,14,000

Working Notes:

(i) Memorandum Hire Purchase Stock Account

Particulars	₹	*Particulars*	₹
To Balance b/d	3,00,000	By H. P. Debtors A/c (Bal.fig.)	7,50,000
To Goods sold on hire purchase	9,00,000	By Balance c/d	4,50,000
	12,00,000		12,00,000

(ii) Memorandum Hire Purchase Debtors Account

Particulars	₹	*Particulars*	₹
To Balance b/d	1,50,000	By Bank/Cash	6,80,000
To Hire Purchase Stock A/c	7,50,000	By Goods repossessed	60,000
		By Balance c/d (Bal.fig.)	1,60,000
	9,00,000		**9,00,000**

(iii) Value of goods repossessed : $\left(60{,}000 \times \frac{100}{150} \times \frac{60}{100}\right) = ₹\ 24{,}000$

***Note:** It is assumed that figures given in the question are at invoice price.*

24 ACCOUNTING FOR BRANCHES

DEPENDENT BRANCH—DEBTORS METHOD

PROBLEM 1

Widespread Ltd. invoices goods to its branch at cost *plus* 20%. The branch sells goods for cash as well as on credit. The branch meets its expenses out of cash collected from its debtors and cash sales and remits the balance of cash to head office after withholding ₹ 10,000 necessary for meeting immediate requirements of cash. On 31st March, 2014 the assets at the branch were as follows:

	₹('000)
Cash in Hand	10
Trade Debtors	384
Stock, at Invoice Price	1,080
Furniture and Fittings	500

During the accounting year ended 31st March, 2015 the invoice price of goods dispatched by the head office to the branch amounted to ₹ 1 crore 32 lakhs. Out of the goods received by it, the branch sent back to head office invoiced at ₹ 72,000. Other transactions at the branch during the year were as follows:

	₹('000)
Cash Sales	9,700
Credit Sales	3,140
Cash collected by Branch from Credit Customers	2,842
Cash Discount allowed to Debtors	58
Returns by Customers	102
Bad Debts written off	37
Expenses paid by Branch	842

On 1st January, 2015 the branch purchased new furniture for ₹ 1 lakh for which payment was made by head office through a cheque.

On 31st March, 2015 branch expenses amounting to ₹ 6,000 were outstanding and cash in hand was again ₹ 10,000. Furniture is subject to depreciation @ 16% per annum on diminishing balance method.

Prepare Branch Account in the books of head office for the year ended 31st March, 2015.

Solution

BRANCH ACCOUNT IN THE HEAD OFFICE BOOKS

Dr. *for the year ended 31st March, 2015* *Cr.*

Particulars	*₹'000*	*Particulars*	*₹'000*
To Balance b/d:		By Balance b/d	
Cash in Hand	10	Stock Reserve (₹ 1,080 × 20/120)	180
Trade Debtors	384	By Goods sent to branch A/c	72
Stock	1,080	(Returns to H.O.)	
Furniture and Fittings	500	By Goods sent to branch A/c	2,188
To Goods sent to branch A/c	13,200	(Loading on net goods sent	

To Bank A/c (Payment for Furniture)	100	(₹ 13,128 × 20/120)	
To Balance c/d		By Bank A/c	
Stock Reserve (₹.1,470 x 20/120)	245	(Remittance from branch to H.O.)	11,700
Outstanding Expenses	6	By Balance c/d:	
To Profit and Loss A/c (Net Profit)	1,096	Cash in hand	10
		Trade debtors	485
		Stock	1,470
		Furniture and fittings	516
	16,621		16,621

Working Notes:

Dr. **(I) BRANCH STOCK ACCOUNT** Cr.

Particulars	*₹ ('000)*	*Particulars*	*₹ ('000)*
To Balance b/d	1,080	By Goods sent to branch	72
To Goods sent to branch	13,200	By Branch Cash	9,700
To Branch debtors	102	By Branch Debtors	3,140
		By Balance c/d (b.f.)	1,470
	14,382		14,382

Dr. **(II) BRANCH DEBTORS ACCOUNT** Cr.

Particulars	*₹ ('000)*	*Particulars*	*₹ ('000)*
To Balance b/d	384	By Balance Branch	2,842
To Branch Stock	3,140	By Branch Expenses Discount	58
		By Branch Stock (Returns)	102
		By Branch Expenses (Bad Debts)	37
		By Balance c/d (b.f.)	485
	3,524		3,524

Dr. **(III) BRANCH FURNITURE AND FITTINGS ACCOUNT** Cr.

Particulars	*₹ ('000)*	*Particulars*	*₹ ('000)*
To Balance b/d	500	By Depreciation (80 + 4)	84
To Bank	100	By Balance c/d (b.f.)	516
	600		600

Dr. **(IV) BRANCH CASH ACCOUNT** Cr.

Particulars	*₹ ('000)*	*Particulars*	*₹ ('000)*
To Balance b/d	10	By Branch Expenses	842
To Branch Stock	9,700	By Remittances to H.O.	11,700
To Branch Debtors	2,842	By Balance c/d	10
	12,552		12,552

PROBLEM 2

Pawan & Co. of Delhi has a branch at Jaipur. Goods are invoiced to the branch at cost *plus* 25%. The branch is instructed to deposit the receipts everyday in the head office account with the bank. All the expenses are paid through cheque by the head office except petty cash expenses which are paid by the

Branch. From the following information, you are required to prepare Branch Account in the books of Head office for the year ending 31st March, 2015:

	₹
Opening Stock at invoice price	1,64,000
Closing Stock at invoice price	1,92,000
Opening Debtors	63,400
Closing Debtors	84,300
Opening Furniture & fixtures	46,800
Cash sales	8,02,600
Credit sales	7,44,200
Goods invoiced to branch by head office	12,56,000
Expenses paid by h ead office	2,64,000
Petty expenses paid by the branch	20,900
Furniture acquired by the branch on 1.10.12 (payment was made by the branch from cash sales and collection from debtors)	5,000

Depreciation to be provided on branch furniture & fixtures @ 10% p.a. on WDV basis.

Solution

Dr. **JAIPUR BRANCH ACCOUNT** *Cr.*

Particulars	₹	*Particulars*	₹
To Opening Balances:		By Branch stock reserve	32,800
Branch Stock A/c	1,64,000	By Bank A/c	15,00,000
Branch Debtors A/c	63,400	By Goods Sent to branch A/c	2,51,200
Branch Furniture A/c	46,800	(Loading)	
To Goods sent to branch	12,56,000	By Closing Balances:	
To Bank A/c (branch expenses)	2,64,000	Branch Stock A/c	1,92,000
To Branch Stock Reserve A/c	38,400	Branch Debtors A/c	84,000
To Profit and Loss A/c (Bal. Fig.)	2,74,570	Branch Furniture A/c	46,870
	21,07,170		21,07,170

Working Notes:

(i) Depreciation on Furniture = (₹ 46,800 × 10/100) + (5,000 × 10/100 × 6/12) = ₹ 4,930

Dr. **(ii) BRANCH FURNITURE ACCOUNT** *Cr.*

Particulars	₹	*Particulars*	₹
To Balance b/d	46,800	By Depreciation A/c	4,930
To Bank A/c (Purchases)	5,000	BY balance c/d	46,870
	51,800		51,800

Dr. **(iii) BRANCH BEBTORS ACCOUNT** *Cr.*

Particulars	₹	*Particulars*	₹
To Balance b/d	63,400	By Bank A/c (Bal. Fig.)	7,23,300
To Sales	7,44,200	By Balance c/d	84,300
	8,07,600		8,07,600

(iv) Cash remitted by the branch to head office

Cash sales + Collection from debtors – Petty expenses – Furniture acquired by branch
= ₹ 8,02,600 + ₹ 7,23,300 – ₹ 20,900 – ₹ 5,000 = ₹.15,00,000

PROBLEM 3

XYZ Company is having its Branch at Kolkata. Goods are invoiced to the branch at 20% profit on sale. Branch has been instructed to send all cash daily to head office. All expenses are paid by head office except petty expenses which are met by the Branch Manager. From the following particulars prepare Branch Account in the books of Head Office.

Liabilities	₹	*Assets*	₹
Opening Stock (invoice price)	30,000	Discount allowed to debtors	160
Opening Sundry Debtors	18,000	Expenses paid by head office:	
Opening Cash in hand	800	Rent	1,800
Opening Office Furniture	3,000	Salary	3,200
Goods invoiced from the head		Stationery & Printing	800
office (invoice price)	1,60,000	Petty expenses paid by the branch	600
Goods return to Head Office	2,000	Depreciation to be provided	
Goods return by debtors	960	on branch furniture at 10% p.a.	
Cash received from debtors	60,000	Closing Stock (at invoice price)	28,000
Cash Sales	1,00,000	Credit sales	60,000

Solution

Dr. **KOLKATA BRANCH ACCOUNT IN THE BOOKS OF HEAD OFFICE** *Cr.*

Particulars		₹	*Particulars*		₹
To Balance b/d:			By Stock Reserve (opening)		6,000
Stock		30,000	By Remittances:		
Debtors		18,000	Cash Sales	1,00,000	
Cash in hand		800	Cash from Debtors	60,000	1,60,000
Furniture		3,000	By Goods sent to branch (loading)		32,000
To Goods sent to branch A/c		1,60,000	By Goods returned by		
To Goods returned by branch (loading)		400	branch (Return to H.O.)		2,000
To Bank (expenses paid by H.O.)			By Balance c/d:		
Rent	1,800		Stock		28,000
Salary	3,200		Debtors		16,880
Stationary & Printing	800	5,800	Cash (800 – 600)		200
To Stock Reserve (closing)		5,600	Furniture (3,000 – 300)		2,700
To Profit transferred to					
General Profits Loss A/c		24,180			
		2,47,780			2,47,780

Working Note:

Dr. **DEBTORS ACCOUNT** *Cr.*

Particulars	₹	*Particulars*	₹
To Balance b/d	18,000	By Cash A/c	60,000
To Sales A/c (credit)	60,000	By Sales Return A/c	960
		By Discount allowed A/c	160
		By Balance c/d	16,880
	78,000		78,000

Note: It is assumed that goods returned by branch are at invoice price.

PROBLEM 4

CAMIB Ltd. had three branches at Coimbatore, Trivandrum and Bangalore. The Head Office at Madras purchases goods and sends them to branches, to be sold at a uniform percentage of profit on cost. The following particulars are made available to you to prepare a Combined Trading Account for the year ending on 31st March, 2015:

Particulars	*Madras (₹)*	*Coimbatore (₹)*	*Trivandrum (₹)*	*Banglore (₹)*
Opening Stock	54,000	16,000	12,500	10,000
Purchases in the year	2,74,000	—	—	—
Sales	—	1,80,000	1,20,000	1,00,000
Closing Stock	28,000	6,000	5,000	2,500
Branch Accounts on 1st April,				
Coimbatore	15,000			
Triovandrum	32,000			
Bangalore	4,000			
Remittances from Branches	3,20,000	1,50,000	1,00,000	70,000

Madras Office invoices goods to the branches at fixed sales prices but maintains branch accounts in its ledgers at cost price. Show Branch Accounts in Madras Head Office Books.

Solution **COMBINED TRADING ACCOUNT OF MADRAS OFFICE AND ITS BRANCHES**

Dr. *for the year ending on 31st March, 2015* *Cr.*

Particulars	*Madras H.O.* ₹	*Coimbatore* ₹	*Trivandrum* ₹	*Bangalore* ₹	*Total* ₹
To Opening Stock at cost [See Working Note (iv)]	54,000	12,800	10,000	8,000	84,800
To Purchases	2,74,000	—	—	—	2,74,000
To Goods received from H.O. at cost (balancing figure)	—	1,36,000	90,000	74,000	3,00,000
To Gross Profit @ 20% on sales [See Working Note (i), (ii), (iii)]	—	36,000	24,000	20,000	80,000
	3,28,000	1,84,800	1,24,000	1,02,000	7,38,800
By Sales	—	1,80,000	1,20,000	1,00,000	4,00,000
By Goods sent to branch at cost	3,00,000	—	—	—	3,00,000
By Closing stock-at cost [See Working Note (iv)]	28,000	4,800	4,000	2,000	38,800
	3,28,000	1,84,800	1,24,000	1,02,000	7,38,800

Dr. **BRANCH ACCOUNT** *Cr.*

Particulars	*Coimbatore* ₹	*Trivandrum* ₹	*Bangalore* ₹	*Particulars*	*Coimbatore* ₹	*Trivandrum* ₹	*Bangalore* ₹
To Balance b/d	15,000	32,000	4,000	By Bank A/c	1,50,000	1,00,000	70,000
To Goods sent to branches —at cost	1,36,000	90,000	74,000	By Balance c/d (b.f)	37,000	46,000	28,000
To Combined Trading A/c— Gross profit	36,000	24,000	20,000				
	1,87,000	1,46,000	98,000		1,87,000	1,46,000	98,000

Working Notes:

(i) *Dr.* **STOCK ACCOUNT** *Cr.*

Particulars	₹	Particulars	₹
To Balance b/d	54,000	By Goods sent to Branches- at cost (balancing figure)	3,00,000
To Purchases	2,74,000	By Balance c/d	28,000
	3,28,000		3,28,000

(ii) *Computation of the amount of goods sent to branches at invoice price.*

Dr. **CONSOLIDATED BRANCH TRADING ACCOUNT** *Cr.*

Particulars	₹	Particulars	₹
To Opening Stock at branches (at invoice price)	38,500	By Sales	4,00,000
To Goods from H.O. (at invoice price) (b.f.)	3,75,000	By Closing Stock (at invoice price)	13,500
	4,13,500		4,13,500

(iii) *Computation of rate of profit added to the cost of goods sent to the branches:*

	₹
Goods sent to branches at invoice price	3,75,000
Less: Goods sent to branches at cost	(3,00,000)
Profit	75,000

Rate of profit at invoice price = (₹ 75,000/₹ 3,75,000) × 100 = 20%

(iv) *Valuation of Stock at cost*

	Opening Stock	Closing Stock
Coimbatore	[16,000 × 80/100] = ₹ 12,800	[6,000 × 80/100] = ₹ 4,800
Trivandrum	[12,500 × 80/100] = ₹ 10,000	[5,000 × 80/100] = ₹ 4,000
Bangalore	[10,000 × 80/100] = ₹ 8,000	[2,500 × 80/100] = ₹ 2,000

PROBLEM 5

LMN is having branch at Mumbai. Goods are invoiced to the Branch at 25% Profit on Sale. Branch has been instructed to send all cash daily to Head Office. All expenses are paid by Head Office except Petty Expenses, which are met by the Branch. From the following particulars, prepare Branch Account in the Books of Head Office:

Particulars	₹	Particulars	₹
Opening Stock (Invoice Price)	40,000	Credit Sales	70,000
Opening Sundry Debtors	25,000	Discount Allowed to Debetors	300
Opening Cash in Hand	1,000	Expenses Paid by Head Office:	
Opening Office Furntirue	4,000	Salary	4,000
Goods Invoiced from Head Office (Invoice Price)	1,80,000	Staff Welfare	750
Goods Return to Head Office	6,000	Telephone Expense	1,200
Goods Return by Debtors	1,250	Other Misc. Expenses paid by Branch	700
Cash Received from Debtors	65,000	Closing Stock (at Invoice Price)	35,000
Cash Sales	1,20,000	Depreciation to be provided on Branch Furniture	10%

Solution

Dr. **BRANCH ACCOUNT IN THE BOOKS OF HEAD OFFICE** Cr.

Particulars		₹	*Particulars*		₹
To Balance b/d:			By Stock Reserve on Op Stock (₹ 40,000 × 25%)		10,000
– Stock	40,000		By Stock Reserve (₹ 1,80,000 × 25%)		45,000
– Debtors	25,000				
– Furniture	4,000		By Goods Sent to Branch A/c (Returns)		6,000
– Cash	1,000	70,000	By H.O Cash (65,000 + 1,20,000)		1,85,000
To Goods sent to Branch A/c		1,80,000			
To Stock Reserve (₹ 6,000 × 25%)		1,500	By balance c/d:		
To Bank A/c:			– Stock	35,000	
– Staff Welfare	750		– Debetors	28,450	
– Salary	4,000		– Cash (1,000 – 700)	300	
– Telephone	1,200	5,950	– Furniture (4,000 – 10%)	3,600	67,350
To Stock Reserve on Cl Stock (35,000 × 25%)		8,750			
To P & L A/c –		47,150			
		3,13,350			**3,13,350**

Working Notes:

1. **BRANCH DEBETORS ACCOUNT (TO ASCERTAIN CLOSING DEBTORS)**

Particulars	₹	*Particulars*	₹
To balance b/d	25,000	By Cash (Collections)	65,000
To Credit Sales	70,000	By Sales Returns	1,250
		By Discount Allowed	300
		By balance c/d **(balancing figure)**	**28,450**
	95,000		**95,000**

2. Depreciation on Furniture is not debited as a separate item in the Branch Account since the Furniture (Closing Balance) at the end is shown at the Depreciated Value.
3. Sales Returns and Discount are accounted for automatically since opening and Closing baliances of Debetors are state in the Branch Account.

DEPENDENT BRANCH—STOCK & DEBTORS METHOD

PROBLEM 6

Concept & Co., with its Head Office at Mumbai has a branch at Nagpur. Goods are invoiced to the Branch at cost *plus* 33-1/3%. The following information is given in respect of the branch for the year ended 31st March, 2015:

	₹
Goods sent to Branch (invoice price)	4,80,000
Opening Stock at Branch (invoice price)	24,000
Cash Sales	1,80,000
Return of goods by customers to the Branch	6,000
Branch expenses (paid in cash)	53,500
Opening Branch Debtors	30,000
Discount allowed	1,000
Bad debts	1,500
Collection from Debtors	2,70,000
Branch debtors cheques returned dishonoured	5,000
Closing Stock at Branch (invoice price)	48,000
Closing Branch Debtors	36,500

Prepare, under the Stock and Debtors system, the following Ledger Accounts in the books of the Head Office:

(i) Nagpur Branch Stock Account.

(ii) Nagpur Branch Debtors Account.

(iii) Nagpur Branch Adjustment Account.

Solution

Dr. **NAGPUR BRANCH STOCK ACCOUNT** *Cr.*

Particulars	₹	*Particulars*		₹
To Balance b/d	24,000	By Bank A/c (Cash Sales)		1,80,000
To Goods Sent to Branch A/c	4,80,000	By Branch Debtors (Credit Sales)		2,80,000
To Branch Debtors	6,000	By Stock Shortage:		
		Branch P&L A/c	1,500	
		Branch Adjustment A/c (Loading)	500	2,000
		By Balance c/d		48,000
	5,10,000			5,10,000

Dr. **NAGPUR BRANCH DEBTORS ACCOUNT** *Cr.*

Particulars	₹	*Particulars*	₹
To Balance b/d	30,000	By Bank A/c (Collection)	2,70,000
To Bank A/c (Dishonour of cheques)	5,000	By Branch Stock A/c	6,000
To Branch Stock A/c (b.f.)	2,80,000	By Bad Debts	1,500
		By Discount allowed	1,000
		By Balance c/d	36,500
	3,15,000		3,15,000

Dr. **NAGPUR BRANCH ADJUSTMENT ACCOUNT** Cr.

Particulars	₹	Particulars	₹
To Branch Stock A/c (Loading of Loss)	500	By Stock Reserve A/c [₹ 24,000 × 25%]	6,000
To Stock Reserve [₹ 48,000 × 25%]	12,000	By Goods Sent to Branch A/c [₹ 4,80,000 × 25%]	1,20,000
To Gross Profit c/d	1,13,500		
	1,26,000		1,26,000
To Branch Stock A/c (Cost of Loss)	1,500	By Gross Profit b/d	1,13,500
To Branch Expenses [₹.53,500 + ₹.1,500 + ₹.1,000]	56,000		
To Net Profit t/f to General P&L A/c	56,000		
	1,13,500		1,13,500

PROBLEM 7

Ram Limited of Chennai has a branch at Nagpur to which office, goods are invoiced at cost *plus* 25%. The branch makes sales both for cash and on credit. Branch expenses are paid direct from Head Office and the branch has to remit all cash received into the Head Office Bank Account at Nagpur.

From the following details, relating to the year 2014-2015, prepare the accounts in Head Office Ledger and ascertain Branch Profit as per stock and debtors method. Branch does not maintain any books of accounts, but sends weekly returns to head office:

	₹
Goods received from head office at invoice price	1,20,000
Returns to head office at invoice price	2,400
Opening Stock at Nagpur branch at invoice price	12,000
Sales during the year – Cash	40,000
Credit	72,000
Opening Debtors at Nagpur branch	14,400
Cash received from debtors	64,000
Discounts allowed to debtors	1,200
Bad debts during the year	800
Sales returns at Nagpur branch	1,600
Salaries and wages at branch	12,000
Rent, rates and faxes at branch	3,600
Office expenses at Nagpur branch	1,200
Closing Stock at branch at invoice price	24,000

Solution

Dr. **NAGPUR BRANCH STOCK ACCOUNT** Cr.

Particulars	₹	Particulars	₹
To Balance b/d	12,000	By Goods sent to branch A/c (Returns)	2,400
To Goods sent to Branch A/c	1,20,000	By Bank A/c (Cash sales)	40,000
To Branch Bebtors A/c (Returns)	1,600	By Branch debtors A/c	72,000

To Branch Adjustment A/c (Surplus over Invoice Price)	4,800	(credit sales) By Balance c/d	24,000
	1,38,400		1,38,400

Dr. **NAGPUR BRANCH ADJUSTMENT ACCOUNT** Cr.

Particulars	₹	Particulars	₹
To Stock Reserve [₹ 24,000 × 20/100]	4,800	By Stock Reserve [₹ 12,000 × 20/120]	2,400
To Branch Profit & Loss A/c (Gross profit)	25,920	By Goods sent to branch A/c [₹ 1,17,600 × 20.120]	23,520
		By Branch Stock A/c	4,800
	30,720		30,720

Dr. **BRANCH PROFIT & LOSS ACCOUNT** Cr.

Particulars	₹	Particulars	₹
To Branch Expenses A/c	16,800	By Branch Adjustment A/c (Gross Profit)	25,920
To Branch Debtors A/c (Discount)	1,200		
To Branch Debtors A/c (Bad Debts)	800		
To Net Profit (transferred to Profit & Loss A/c)	7,120		
	25,920		25,920

Dr. **BRANCH EXPENSES ACCOUNT** Cr.

Particulars	₹	Particulars	₹
To Bank A/c (Rent, rates & taxes)	3,600	By Branch Profit and Loss A/c (Transfer)	16,800
To Bank A/c (Salaries & Wages)	12,000		
To Bank A/c (Office Expenses)	1,200		
	16,800		16,800

Dr. **BRANCH DEBTORS ACCOUNT** Cr.

Particulars	₹	Particulars	₹
To Balance b/d	14,400	By Bank A/c	64,000
To Branch Stock A/c	72,000	By Branch Profit and Loss A/c (Bad debts and discount)	2,000
		By Branch Stock A/c (Sales Returns)	1,600
		By Balance c/d (bal.fig.)	18,800
	86,400		86,400

Dr. **GOODS SENT TO BRANCH ACCOUNT** Cr.

Particulars	₹	Particulars	₹
To Branch Stock A/c	2,400	By Branch stock A/c	1,20,000
To Branch Adjustment A/c	23,520		
To Purchases A/c	94,080		
	1,20,000		1,20,000

PROBLEM 8

Neo Ltd., with headquarters at Mumbai, maintains a branch at Goa . Goods are invoiced at cost *plus* 25%. In respect of Goa branch, the following information pertaining to the year 'ended 31st March, 2015 are made available to you:

	₹
Goods sent to Branch (at Invoice price)	6,75,000
Goods returned by branch during the year (at Invoice price)	24,000
Cash sales effected by branch	1,85,000
Discount allowed to customers	2,500
Amount received from branch debtors	3,25,000
Cheques of customers which got dishonoured	8,000
Branch expenses met in cash	72,500
Sales return at Goa branch	10,000
Bad debts	5,500

	Closing	Opening
Branch debtors	1,05,000	50,000
Stock at branch (at Invoice price)	2,36,000	1,50,000

Adopting the Stock and debtors system, you are required to prepare the following Ledger accounts, as appearing in the books of the Head Office:

(i) Goa Branch Debtors Account;

(ii) Goa Branch Adjustment Account;

(iii) Goa Branch Profit and Loss Account.

Solution

Dr. **GOA BRANCH DEBTORS ACCOUNT** Cr.

Particulars	₹	Particulars	₹
To Balance b/d	50,000	By Bank (Collection from debtors)	3,25,000
To Bank A/c (Dishonour of cheques)	8,000	By Branch Stock (Goods returned by customers)	10,000
To Branch Stock A/c (Credit sales)	3,90,000	By Bad debts	5,500
		By Discount allowed	2,500
		By Balance c/d	1,05,000
	4,48,000		4,48,000

Dr. **GOA BRANCH ADJUSTMENT ACCOUNT** Cr.

Particulars	₹	Particulars	₹
To Goods sent to Goa Branch A/c (goods returns to H.O.)	4,800	By Balance b/d (Opening stock reserve)	30,000
To Branch P & L A/c (Profit on sale at invoice price) (Bal. Fig.)	1,13,000	By Goods sent to Goa Branch A/c (Loading)	1,35,000
To Balance c/d (Closing Stock Reserve)	47,200		
	1,65,000		1,65,000

GOA BRANCH PROFIT AND LOSS ACCOUNT FOR THE YEAR ENDING 31ST MARCH, 2015

Dr. Cr.

Particulars	₹	Particulars	₹
To Branch Expenses A/c	72,500	By Branch Adjustment A/c	1,13,000
To Branch Debtors - Discount	2,500		
Bad debts	5,500		
To Net Profit (Transferred to General Profit & Loss A/c)	32,500		
	1,13,000		1,13,000

Working Note :

Dr. **GOA BRANCH STOCK ACCOUNT** Cr.

Date	Particulars	₹	Date	Particulars	₹
	To Balance b/d	1,50,000		By Bank (Cash sales)	1,85,000
	To Goods sent to Goa Branch	6,75,000		By Branch Debtors (Credit sales)	3,90,000
	To Branch Debtors (Goods Returned)	10,000		By Goods sent to Goa Branch (Goods returned to H.O.)	24,000
	By Balance c/d	2,36,000			
		8,35,000			8,35,000

DEPENDENT BRANCH—WHOESALE BRANCH METHOD

PROBLEM 9

Rahul Limited operates a number of retail outlets to which goods are invoiced at wholesale price which is cost *plus* 25%. These outlets sell the goods at the retail price which is wholesale price *plus* 20%.

Following is the information regarding one of the outlets for the year ended 31.3.2015:

	₹
Opening Stock at the outlet	30,000
Goods invoiced to the outlet during the year	3,24,000
Gross profit made by the outlet	60,000
Goods lost by fire	?
Expenses of the outlet for the year	20,000
Closing Stock at the outlet	36,000

Required: Prepare the following accounts in the books of Rahul Limited for the year ended 31.3.2015:

(a) Outlet Stock Account.
(b) Outlet Profit & Loss Account.
(c) Stock Reserve Account.

Solution

Dr. **Outlet Stock Account** *Cr.*

Particulars	₹	*Particulars*	₹
To Balance b/d	30,000	By Sales [₹ 60,000 × 150/25]	3,60,000
To Goods sent to outlet A/c	3,24,000	By Goods Lost by fire [b.f]	18,000
To Gross Profit c/d	60,000	By Balance c/d	36,000
	4,14,000		4,14,000

Dr. **Outlet Profit & Loss Account** *Cr.*

Particulars	₹	*Particulars*	₹
To Expenses	20,000	By Gross Profit b/d	60,000
To Goods lost by fire	18,000		
To Profit Transferred	22,000		
	60,000		60,000

Dr. **Stock Reserve Account** *Cr.*

Particulars	₹	*Particulars*	₹
To HO P&L A/c (Transfer)	6,000	By Balance b/d [₹ 30,000 × 25/125]	6,000
To Balance c/d	7,200	By HO P&L A/c [₹ 36,000 × 25/125]	7,200
	13,200		13,200

Working Note: Cost-Price Relationship

		₹
A.	Cost	100
B.	*Add:* Wholesale Profit	25
C.	Wholesale Price [A + B]	125
D.	*Add:* Retail Profit + [20% of 125]	25
E.	Retail Price	150

PROBLEM 10

Following is the information of the Jammu branch of Best Ltd., New Delhi for the year ending 31st March, 2015 from the following:

(1) Goods are invoiced to the branch at cost *plus* 20%

(2) The sale price is cost *plus* 50%.

(3) Other informations:

Opening Stock	₹ 2,20,000
Goods sent during the year	₹ 11,00,000
Sales during the year	₹ 2,00,000
Expenses incurred at the branch	₹ 45,000

Ascertain:

(i) the profit earned by the branch during the year

(ii) branch stock reserve in respect of unrealized profit.

Solution

(a) (i) Calculation of Profit earned by the branch

Dr. **Jammu Branch Trading Account** *Cr.*

Particulars	₹	*Particulars*	₹
To Opening Stock	2,20,000	By Sales	12,00,000
To Goods received by Head office	11,00,000	By Closing stock	3,60,000
To Expenses	45,000		
To Gross Profit	1,95,000		
	15,60,000		15,60,000

(ii) Stock reserve in respect of unrealised profit = ₹ 3,60,000 × (20/120) = 60,000

(iii) Calculation of Closing Stock at Invoice Price

Opening Stock at invoice price	2,20,000	
Goods received during the year at invoice price	11,00,000	
	13,20,000	
Less: Cost of goods sold at invoice price	(9,60,000)	[12,00,000 x (120/150)]
Closing Stock	3,60,000	

Note : It is assumed that all figures given in the questions is at invoice price.

PROBLEM 11

A Limited has retail branch at Noida. Goods are sold to customers at cost plus 100%. The wholesale price is cost plus 80%. Goods are invoiced to Noida at wholesale price. From the following particulars, find out the profit made by the Head Office and Noida Branch for the year ended 31st March, 2015 using invoice method.

	Head Office ₹	Noida ₹
Opening Stock	50,000	—
Purchases	3,00,000	—
Goods sent to branch (at invoice value)	1,08,000	—
Sales	3,06,000	1,00,000
Expenses	90,000	4,000

Sales at Head Office are made only on wholesale basis and sales at branch are made only to customers. Stock at branch is valued at invoice price.

Solution

Dr. **TRADING ACCOUNT FOR THE YEAR ENDED 31ST MARCH, 2015** Cr.

Particulars	HO ₹	Branch ₹	Particulars	HO ₹	Branch ₹
To Opening Stock	50,000	—	By Sales	3,06,000	1,00,000
To Purchases	3,00,000	—	By Goods sent to Branch	1,08,000	—
To Goods received from Head Office	—	1,08,000	By Closing Stock	1,20,000	18,000
To Gross Profit	1,84,000	10,000			
	5,34,000	1,18,000		5,34,000	1,18,000

Dr. **PROFIT AND LOSS A/C FOR THE YEAR ENDED 31ST MARCH, 2015** Cr.

Particulars	₹	₹	Particulars	₹	₹
To Expenses	90,000	4,000	By Gross Profit	1,84,000	10,000
To Stock Reserve against Branch $\left(18,000 \times \frac{80}{180}\right)$	8 000	—			
To Net Profit	86,000	6,000			
	184,000	10,000		184,000	10,000

Working Note: **Calculation of Closing Stock**

Particulars	Head Office ₹	Noida Branch ₹
Opening Stock	50,000	—
Goods purchased or Received from Head Office	3,00,000	1,08,000
Less: Cost of Goods sold or sent to Branch:		
Head Office [3,06,000 + 1,08,000) x 100/180]	(2,30,000)	
Branch 1,00,000 × 180/200]		(90,000)
Value of Closing Stock	1,20,000	18,000

PROBLEM 12

Beta Ltd. having head office at Mumbai has a branch at Nagpur. The head office does wholesale trade only at cost *plus* 80%. The goods are sent to branch at the wholesale price viz., cost *plus* 80%. The branch at Nagpur is wholly engaged in retail trade and the goods are sold at cost to H.O. *plus* 100%.

Following details are furnished for the year ended 31st March, 2015:

	Head Office ₹	Branch ₹
Opening Stock	2,25,000	—
Purchases	25,50,000	—
Goods sent to branch (Cost to H.O. plus 80%)	9,54,000	—
Sales	27,81,000	9,50,000
Office Expenses	90,000	8,500
Selling Expenses	72,000	6,300
Staff Salary	65,000	12,000

Required: Prepare Trading and Profit and Loss Account of the head office and branch for the year ended 31st March, 2015.

Solution

TRADING AND PROFIT AND LOSS A/C OF BETA LTD.

Dr. *for the year ended 31st March 2015* *Cr.*

Particulars	Head Office ₹	Branch ₹	Particulars	Head Office ₹	Branch ₹
To Opening Stock	2,25,000	—	By Sales	27,81,000	9,50,000
To Purchases	25,50,000	—	By Goods sent to branch	9,54,000	—
To Goods received from head office	—	9,54,000	By Closing Stock	7,00,000	99,000
To Gross Profit c/d	16,60,000	95,000			
	44,35,000	10,49,000		44,35,000	10,49,000
To Office Expenses	90,000	8,500	By Gross Profit b/d	16,60,000	95,000
To Selling Expenses	72,000	6,300			
To Staff Salaries	65,000	12,000			
To Branch Stock Reserve	44,000	—			
To Net Profit	13,89,000	68,200			
	16,60,000	95,000		16,60,000	95,000

Working Notes:

(i) Closing Stock of head office = ₹ 2,25,000 + ₹ 25,50,000 – (37,35,000 × 100/180) = ₹ 7,00,000

(ii) Closing stock of branch = ₹ 9,54,000 – (9,50,000 × 180/200) = ₹ 99,000

(iii) Unrealised Profit in branch stock = ₹ 99,000 × 80/180 = ₹ 44,000

INDEPENDENT BRANCH—SHORT ANSWER QUESTIONS

PROBLEM 13

Head Office passes adjustment entry at the end of each month to adjust the position arising out of inter-branch transactions during the month. From the following inter-branch transactions in January, 2015 make the entry in the books of Head Office:

(a) Bombay Branch
  (1) Received Goods: ₹ 6,000 from Calcutta Branch, ₹ 4,000 from Patna Branch.
  (2) Sent Goods to: ₹ 10,000 to Patna, ₹ 8,000 to Calcutta.
  (3) Received B/R: ₹ 6,000 from Patna.
  (4) Sent Acceptance: ₹ 4,000 to Calcutta, ₹ 2,000 to Patna.
(b) Madras Branch (*Apart from the above*)
  (5) Received Goods: ₹ 10,000 from Calcutta, ₹ 4,000 from Bombay.
  (6) Cash Sent: ₹ 2,000 to Calcutta, ₹ 6,000 to Bombay.
(c) Calcutta Branch (*Apart from the above*)
  (7) Sent Goods to Patna: ₹ 6,000.
  (8) Paid B/P: ₹ 4,000 to Patna, ₹ 4,000 cash to Patna.

Solution

In the Books of Head Office
Journal

Date	*Particulars*		*L.F.*	*Dr. (₹)*	*Cr. (₹)*
2015 Jan. 31	Madras Branch A/c	Dr.		6,000	
	Patna Branch A/c	Dr.		16,000	
	To Bombay Branch A/c				6,000
	To Calcutta Branch A/c				16,000
	(Being adjustment entry passed by head office in respect of inter-branch transactions during the month.)				

Working Note:

Particulars	*Inter-branch transactions*			
	Bombay ₹	*Madras* ₹	*Calcutta* ₹	*Patna* ₹
(a) *Bombay Branch*				
(1) Received Goods	10,000 (Dr.)		6,000 (Cr.)	4,000 (Cr.)
(2) Sent Goods	18,000 (Cr.)		8,000 (Dr.)	10,000 (Dr.)
(3) Received B/R	6,000 (Dr.)			6,000 (Cr.)
(4) Sent Acceptance	6,000 (Cr.)		4,000 (Dr.)	2,000 (Dr.)
(b) *Madras Branch*				
(5) Received Goods	4,000 (Cr.)	14,000 (Dr.)	10,000 (Cr.)	
(6) Cash Sent	6,000 (Dr.)	8,000 (Cr.)	2,000 (Dr.)	
(c) *Calcutta Branch*				
(7) Sent Goods			6,000 (Cr.)	6,000 (Dr.)
(8) Paid B/P and Cash			8,000 (Cr.)	8,000 (Dr.)
	6,000 (Cr.)	6,000 (Dr.)	16,000 (Cr.)	16,000 (Dr.)

PROBLEM 14

Show adjustment Journal entry in the books of Head Office at the end of April, 2015 for incorporation of inter-branch transactions assuming that only Head Office maintains different branch accounts in its books.

A. Delhi Branch:
   1. Received goods from Mumbai – ₹ 35,000 and 15,000 from Kolkata.
   2. Sent goods to Chennai – ₹ 25,000, Kolkata – ₹ 20,000.
   3. Bill Receivable received – ₹ 20,000 from Chennai.
   4. Acceptances sent to Mumbai – ₹ 25,000, Kolkata – ₹ 10,000.

B. Mumbai Branch (apart from the above):
   5. Received goods from Kolkata – ₹ 15,000 , Delhi – ₹ 20,000.
   6. Cash sent too Delhi – ₹ 15,000, Kolkata – ₹ 7,000.

C. Chennai Branch (apart from the above):
   7. Received goods from Kolkata – ₹ 30,000.
   8. Acceptances and cash sent to Kolkata – ₹ 20,000 and ₹ 10,000 respectively.

D. Kolkata Branch (apart from the above):
   9. Sent goods to Chennai – ₹ 35,000.
   10. Paid cash to Chennai – ₹ 15,000.
   11. Acceptances sent to Chennai – ₹ 15,000

   All working should form part of the answer.

Solution

Journal Entry in the Books of Head Office

Date	*Particulars*		*Dr.* (₹)	*Cr.* (₹)
30.4.13	Mumbai Branch A/c	Dr.	3,000	
	Chennai Branch A/c	Dr.	70,000	
	To Delhi Branch A/c			15,000
	To Kolkata Branch A/c			58,000
	(Being adjustment entry passed by head office in respect of inter-branch transactions for the month of April, 2003.			

Working Note: **INTER-BRANCH TRANSACTIONS**

Particulars	*Delhi* ₹	*Mumbai* ₹	*Chennai* ₹	*Kolkata* ₹
A. Delhi Branch				
1. Received goods	50,000 (Dr.)	35,000 (Cr.)		15,000 (Cr.)
2. Sent goods	45,000 (Cr.)		25,000 (Dr.)	20,000 (Dr.)
3. Received B/R	20,000 (Dr.)		20,000 (Cr.)	
4. Sent acceptance	35,000 (Cr.)	25,000 (Dr.)		10,000 (Dr.)
B. Mumbai Branch				
5. Received goods	20,000 (Cr.)	35,000 (Dr.)		15,000 (Cr.)
6. Sent cash	15,000 (Dr.)	22,000 (Cr.)		7,000 (Dr.)
C. Chennai Branch				
7. Received goods			30,000 (Dr.)	30,000 (Cr.)
8. Sent cash and acceptances			30,000 (Cr.)	30,000 (Dr.)
D. Kolkata Branch				
9. Sent goods			35,000 (Dr.)	35,000 (Cr.)
10. Sent cash			15,000 (Dr.)	15,000 (Cr.)
11. Sent acceptances			15,000 (Dr.)	15,000 (Cr.)
	15,000 (Cr.)	3,000 (Dr.)	70,000 (Dr.)	58,000 (Cr.)

PROBLEM 15

Alphs & Co., having head office in Mumbai has a branch in Nagpur. The branch at Nagpur is an independent branch maintinaing separate books of account. On 31.3.2015, it was found that the goods dispatched by head office for ₹ 2,00,000 was received by the branch only to the extent of ₹ 1,50,000. The balance goods are in transit. What is the accounting entery to be passed by the branch for recording the goods in transit, in its books?

Solution

Nagpur Branch must include the inventory in its books as goods in transit

Goods in transit A/c To Head office A/c (Being Goods sent by Heat office is still in transit on the closing date)	Dr.	₹ 50,000	₹ 50,000

PROBLEM 16

Give Journal Entries in the books of Branch A to rectify or adjust the following:

(i) Head Office exp. ₹ 1,35,000 allocated to the Branch, but not recorded in Branch Books.

(ii) Depreciation of branch assests, whose accounts are kept by the Head Office not provided earlier for ₹ 1,15,000.

(iii) Branch paid ₹ 1,40,000 as salary to a H.O. Inspector, but the amount paid has been debited by the Branch to Salaries account.

(iv) H.O. collected ₹ 1,30,000 directly from a customer on behalf of the Branch, but no intimation to this effect has been received by the Branch.

(v) A remittance of ₹ 1,50,000 sent by the Branch has not yet been received by Head Office.

(vi) Branch A incurred advertisement expenses of ₹ 30,000 on behalf of Branch of B.

Solution

Journal of Branch A

Particulars		*L.F.*	*Dr. (₹)*	*Cr. (₹)*
(i) H.O. Expenses A/c To Head Office A/c (Being the allocated expenditure by the head office recorded in branch books)	Dr.		1,35,000	1,35,000
(ii) Depreciation A/c To Head Office A/c (Being the depreciation provided)	Dr.		1,15,000	1,15,000
(iii) Head Office A/c To Salaries A/c (Being the rectification of salary paid on behalf of H.O.)	Dr.		1,40,000	1,40,000
(iv) Head Office A/c To Debtors A/c (Being the adjustment of collection from branch debtors)	Dr.		1,30,000	1,30,000
(v) No entry in branch books but Cash-in-transit will be shown in H.O. Books				
(vi) Head Office A/c To Cash A/c (Being the expenditure on account of Branch B, recorded in books)	Dr.		30,000	30,000

PROBLEM 17

Give Journal entires in the books of Head Office to rectify or adjust the following:

(i) Goods set to Branch ₹ 12,000 stolen during transit. Branch manager refused to accept any liability.

(ii) Branch paid ₹ 15,000 as salary to the office of Head Office on his visit to the branch.

(iii) On 28th March the H.O. dispatched goods to the Branch invoiced at ₹ 25,000 which was not received by Branch till 31st March.

(iv) A remittance of ₹ 10,000 sent by the branch on 30th March, 2014, received by the Head Office on 1st April.

(v) Head Office made payment of ₹ 25,000 for purchase of goods by Branch and wrongly debited its own purchase account.

Solution

Journal of Head Office

Date	*Particulars*		*L.F*	*Dr. (₹)*	*Cr. (₹)*
(i)	Loss in transit A/c	Dr.		12,000	
	To Purchases A/c				12,000
	(Being the Goods lost on account of theft during transit)				
(ii)	Salaries A/c	Dr.		15,000	
	To Branch A/c				15,000
	(Being salary paid by the branch for H.P. employee)				
(iii)	No entry in the books of head office for goods sent to branch not received by branch till 31st March				
(iv)	Cash in transit A/c	Dr.		10,000	
	To Branch A/c				10,000
	(Being remittance by branch not received by 31st March)				
(v)	Branch A/c	Dr.		25,000	
	To Purchases A/c				25,000
	(Being rectification of entry for payment for goods purchased by branch wrongly debited to Purchase A/c)				

Note: In entry (i), it is assumed that refusal of branch manager (to accept liability of stolen goods) is accepted by the Head Office. Alternatively, Branch account will be credited on the basis of assumption that refusal of branch manager is not accepted by the Head Office.

PROBLEM 18

Pass necessary Journal entries in the books of an independent Brach of a Company, wherever required, to rectify or adjust the following:

(i) Income of ₹ 2,800 allocated to the Branch by Head Office but not recorded in the Branch books.

(ii) Provision for doubtful debts, whose accounts are kept by the Head Office, not provided earlier for ₹ 1,000.

(iii) Branch paid ₹ 3,000 as salary to a Head Office Manager, but the amount paid has been debited by the Branch to Salaries Account.

(iv) Branch incurred travelling expenses of ₹ 5,000 on behalf of other Branches, but not recorded in the books of Branch.

(v) A remittance of ₹ 1,50,000 sent by the Branch has not received by Head Office on the date of reconcillation of Accounts.

(vi) Head Office allocates ₹ 75,000 to the Branch as Head Office expenses, which has not yet been recorded by the Branch.

(vii) Head Office collected ₹ 30,000 directly from a branch Customer. The intimation of the fact has been received by the Branch only now.

(viii) Goods dispatched by the Head office amounting to ₹ 10,000, but not received by the Branch till date of reconcillation. The Goods have been received subsequently.

Solution

Journal of Branch

Date	*Particulars*		*Dr. (₹)*	*Cr. (₹)*
(i)	Head Office A/c	Dr.	2,800	
	To Income A/c			2,800
	(Being the income allocated by the Head office not recorded earlier, now recorded)			
(ii)	Provision for Doubtful Debts A/c	Dr.	1,000	
	To Head Office A/c			1,000
	(Being the provision for doubtful debts not provided earlier, now provided for)			
(iii)	Head Office A/c	Dr.	3,000	
	To Salaries A/c			3,000
	(Being rectification of salary paid on behalf of Head Office)			
(iv)	Head Office A/c	Dr.	5,000	
	To Cash A/c			5,000
	(Being expenditure incurred on account of other branch, now recorded in books)			
(v)	No entry in Branch Books is required.			
(vi)	Expenses A/c	Dr.	75,000	
	To Head Office A/c			75,000
	(Being allocated expenses of Head Office recorded)			
(vii)	Head Office A/c	Dr.	30,000	
	To Debtors A/c			30,000
	(Being adjustment entry for collection from Branch Debtrors directly by Head Office)			
(viii)	Good-in-transit A/c	Dr.	10,000	
	To Head Office Account			10,000
	(Being goods sent by Head Office still in-transit)			

INDEPENDENT BRANCH—LONG ANSWER QUESTIONS

PROBLEM 19

The following Trial Balance is extracted from the Books of the Nagpur Branch of CANGE Ltd as on 31st March, 2015:

Particulars	*Dr. (₹)*	*Cr. (₹)*
Opening Stock at Invoice price	25,000	
Branch Debtors	10,000	
Cash in hand	500	
Branch Creditors		3,000
Goods received from Head Office	80,000	
Branch Expenses	9,000	
Branch Sales		1,80,000
Current Account with Head Office	58,500	
	1,83,000	1,83,000

As on that date, Closing Stock with branch at invoice price were valued at ₹ 30,000. There was an amount of ₹ 18,500 remitted by the branch on 31st March, which had not been received by the head office on that date. The head office had sent goods, costing ₹ 20,000, to the branch on 29th March. These had not been received by the branch till the closing date.

The head office enters in its books all goods sent to the branch at cost. The branch enters these, in its books, at invoice price but sells them at an even higher one. At the end of each year, the difference is adjusted by being debited to the Branch and credited to the Profit and Loss Account in the books of the Head Office. The proportional difference, between cost and invoice price, was the same at all relevant times. The credit balance as on 31st March, 2015 of the Branch Account in the Head Office books, was ₹ 60,000 before making any of the above adjustment (though the above mentioned despatch of goods of ₹ 20,000, on 29th March, had of course, been duly debited to the Branch account).

Required: Prepare the Branch Profit and Loss Account and Head Office Profit and Loss Account (relevant protions only) for the year ending on 31st March, 2015.

Solution

It will be first appropriate to reconcile balance in H.O. Current Account as per Branch Books and balance in Branch Current Account as per H.O. Books:

Dr. **ADJUSTED BRANCH CURRENT ACCOUNT (IN H.O. BOOKS)** *Cr.*

Particulars	₹	*Particulars*	₹
To Profit and Loss A/c **(balancing figure)** (Loading on goods invoiced to branch)	**40,000**	By Balance b/d	60,000
		By Cash-in-transit	18,500
To Balance c/d	58,500	By Goods sent to Branch A/c (Reversal of entry as goods were not received by the branch till 31st March)	20,000
	98,500		98,500

Dr. **(MEMORANDUM) BRANCH PROFIT AND LOSS ACCOUNT** *Cr.*

Particulars	₹	*Particulars*	₹
To Opening Stock	25,000	By Branch Sales	1,80,000
To Goods received from H.O.	80,000	By Closing Stock	30,000
To Branch Expenses	9,000		
To Net Profit c/d	96,000		
	2,10,000		2,10,000

AN EXTRACT OF H.O. PROFIT AND LOSS ACCOUNT
for the year ending on 31st March, 2015

Dr. *Cr.*

Particulars	₹	*Particulars*	₹
To Stock Reserve (on Closing Stock)	15,000	By Branch A/c (Profit)	96,000
To Net Profit c/d	1,33,500	By Profit on goods sent to Branch	40,000
		By Stock Reserve (on Opening Stock)	12,500
	1,48,500		1,48,500

Working Notes:

(i) The Stock Reserve for unrealised profit on opening and closing stock is @ 50% of the respective stock at invoice price. This can be made out from the fact that goods sent to branch of ₹ 80,000, includes a loading of ₹ 40,000, as can be seen from the Adjusted Branch Current Account.

(ii) The Branch Profit and Loss A/c has been prepared at invoice price.

PROBLEM 20

CANGH Ltd commenced business on 1.4.2014 with the head office at Calicut and branch at Tiruchur. All goods were purchased by head office and normally packed immediately, but on 31.03.2015, goods costing ₹ 5,000 remained unpacked. Only the packed goods were sent to the branch which was charged at selling price *less* 10%. The following information is furnished to you as on 31st March 2015, from the Head Office and Branch Office books:

Particulars	*H.O.* ₹	*Branch* ₹
Capital Account	40,000	—
Drawing by Proprietor	10,000	—
Purchases	4,00,000	—
Packing materials bought	6,000	—
Sales	3,20,000	1,00,000
Despatch of goods to Branch	1,13,400	—
Selling expenses	16,000	800
Clerk's salary, wages, etc.	20,000	3,000
Sundry Debtors	28,000	4,200
Sundry Creditors	26,600	5,000
Head Office Current A/c	—	12,000
Branch Office Current A/c	19,000	—
Bank Balances	2,000	—
Goods received from Head office	—	1,08,000

Information:

(a) Sales by head office were a uniform gross profit, after charging packing materials, of 20% on the fixed selling price;

(b) Sales at Branch were at fixed selling price;

(c) Goods invoiced and despatched by head office to branch in March for ₹ 5,400 were received in the Branch only on 10th April.

(d) Stock of packing materials on hand as on 31st March was valued at ₹ 1,000.

(e) Remittance of ₹ 1,600 from the branch to the Head Office was in transit on 31st March.

(f) ₹ 2,000 worth of stock at selling price was damaged at the branch. For valuing stock, this was reduced by ₹ 1,090 below the invoice cost to the branch. It was decided that the Head office and branch would share equally the loss occasioned by this and also the deficit in stock, ascertained on actual stock taking at the Branch of goods at selling price of ₹ 500.

Required: Prepare the Profit and Loss Account of the Tiruchur and Calicut Office and also a Balance Sheet as at 31.03.2015 of the business.

Solution

TRADING AND PROFIT AND LOSS ACCOUNT

for the year ending on 31st March, 2015

Dr. *Cr.*

Particulars	*H.O.* ₹	*Branch* ₹	*Particulars*	*H.O* ₹	*Branch* ₹
To Purchases (*less* unpacked goods)	3,95,000	—	By Sales	3,20,000	1,00,000
To Packing material consumed	5,000	—	By Goods sent to Branch A/c (in transit ₹ 5,400)	1,13,400	—
To Goods from H.O. (including in transit)	—	1,13,400	By Stock damaged and shortage	—	1,540
To Gross Profit c/d [Working Notes (i) & (ii)]	76,600	10,000	By Closing Stock (balancing figure)	43,200	21,860
	4,76,600	1,23,400		4,76,600	1,23,400
To Salaries and Wages	20,000	3,000	By Gross Profit b/d	76,600	10,000
To Selling Expenses	16,000	800			
To Stock Reserve (Unrealised Profit)	2,350	—			
To Stock damaged and shortage	770	770			
To Net Profit t/f to Captial A/c	37,480	5,430			
	76,600	10,000		76,600	10,000

BALANCE SHEET AS AT 31ST MARCH, 2015

Liabilities		₹	*Assets*		₹
Capital	40,000		Stock-in-trade:		
Add: Net Profit	42,910		H.O.: Packed	43,200	
	82,910		Unpacked	5,000	
Less: Drawings	10,000	72,910	Packing Material	1,000	49,200
Sundry Creditors:			Branch: In hand	16,460	
H.O.	26,600		In transit	5,400	
Branch	5,000	31,600		21,860	
			Less: Unrealised Profit	2,350	19,510
			Sundry Debtors: H.O	28,000	
			Branch	4,200	32,200
			Cash at Bank		2,000
			Cash-in-transit		1,600
		1,04,510			1,04,510

Working Notes:

	₹
(i) Gross Profit made by Head Office (20% of Sales of ₹ 3,20,000)	64,000
10/90 of Goods sent to Branch (Since Invoice Price is 90% of normal selling price) [₹ 1,13,400× 100/90 × 10%]	12,600
	76,600

(ii)	The Gross Profit made by branch is 10% of sales (10% of ₹ 1,00,000)		10,000
(iii)	The amount to be written off at invoice value at branch is:		
	Amount written off on damaged goods	1,090	
	Invoice price of deficit in stock (₹ 500 × 90/100)	450	1,540
(iv)	*Value of damaged goods included in Closing Stock*		
	A Selling Price of Goods Damaged		2,000
	B Invoice Price of Goods Damaged (₹ 2,000 × 90/100)		1,800
	C Amount already written off		1,090
	D Amount still included in Closing Stock (B – C)		710
(v)	*Calculation of Stock Reserve Required*		
	A Stock (including Goods-in-transit)		21,860
	B *Less*: Value of damaged goods included		(710)
	C Value of Total Goods (A – B)		21,150
	D Stock Reserve required (₹ 21,150 × 10/90)		2,350

PROBLEM 21

CAS Ltd manufactures a range of goods which it sells to wholesale customers only from its head office. In addition, the H.O. transfers goods to a newly opened branch at factory cost *plus* 15%. The branch then sells these goods to the general public on cash basis. The selling price to wholesale customers is designed to give the factory profit which amounts to 30% of the sale value. The selling price to the general public is designed to give a gross margin (i.e., selling price *less* cost of goods from H.O.) of 30% of the sales value. The company operates from rented premises and leases all other types of fixed assets. The rent and hire charges for these are included in the overhead costs shown in the trial balances.
From the information given below, you are required to prepare for the year ending on 31st March 2015 in columnar form.

(a) A Profit and Loss Account for (i) H.O. (ii) the branch (iii) the entire business.
(b) A Balance Sheet as on 31st March 2015 for the entire business.

Particulars	*H.O.*		*Branch*	
	Dr. (₹)	*Cr.* (₹)	*Dr.* (₹)	*Cr.* (₹)
Raw materials purchased	35,000			
Direct Wages	1,08,500			
Factory overheads	39,000			
Opening Stock:				
Raw materials	1,800			
Finished goods	13,000		9,200	
Debtors	37,000			
Cash	22,000		1,000	
Administrative Salaries	13,900		4,000	
Salesmen's Salaries	22,500		6,200	
Other Administrative & Selling overheads	12,500		2,300	
Inter unit accounts	5,000			2,000
Capital		50,000		
Sundry Creditors		13,000		
Provision for unrealised profit in stock		1,200		
Sales		2,00,000		65,200
Goods sent to Branch		46,000		
Goods received from H.O.			44,500	
	3,10,200	3,10,200	67,200	67,200

Information:

(i) On 28th March the branch remitted ₹ 1,500 to the H.O. and this has not yet been recorded in the H.O. books. Also on the same date, the H.O. despatched goods to the branch invoiced at ₹ 1,500 and these too have not yet been entered into branch books, it is the company's policy to adjust items in transit in the books of the receipient.

(ii) The stock of raw materials held at the H.O. on 31st March was valued at ₹ 2,300.

(iii) You are advised that:

(a) no stock losses were incurred at the H.O. or at the branch;

(b) it is the company's practice to value finished goods stock at the H.O. at factory cost.

(c) there were no opening or closing stock of work-in progress.

(iv) Branch employees are entitled to bonus of ₹ 156 under a bilateral agreement.

Solution

TRADING AND PROFIT AND LOSS ACCOUNT

for the year ending on 31st March, 2015

Dr. Cr.

Particulars	H.O ₹	Branch ₹	Total ₹	Particulars	H.O. ₹	Branch ₹	Total ₹
*To Material consumed	34,500			By Sales	2,00,000	65,200	2,65,200
To Wages	1,08,500			By Goods sent to Branch	46,000	—	—
To Factory Overheads	39,000			By Closing Stock	15,000	9,560	24,560
Factory cost	1,82,000		1,82,000				
Add: Opening Stock	13,000	9,200	22,200				
	1,95,000						
To Goods from H.O.	—	46,000	—				
To Gross Profit	66,000	19,560	85,560				
	2,61,000	74,760	2,89,760		2,61,000	74,760	2,89,760
To Adm. Salaries	13,900	4,000	17,900	By Gross Profit	66,000	19,560	85,560
To Salesman Salaries	22,500	6,200	28,700	By Stock Reserve	1,200	—	1,200
To Other Adm. and Overheads	12,500	2,300	14,800				
To Stock Reserve	1,247	—	1,247				
To Bonus to Staff	—	156	156				
To Net Profit	17,053	6,904	23,957				
	67,200	19,560	86,760		67,200	19,560	86,760

BALANCE SHEET AS AT 31ST MARCH, 2015

Liabilities	*H.O* ₹	*Branch* ₹	*Total* ₹	*Assets*	*H.O.* ₹	*Branch* ₹	*Total* ₹
Capital	50,000	—	50,000	Fixed Assets	Nil	Nil	Nil
Profit-H.O.	17,053			Current Assets			
-Branch	6,904		23,957	Raw material	2,300	—	2,300
Trade Creditors	13,000		13,000	Finished Goods	15,000	9,560	**23,313
Bonus Payable		156	156	(*Less* Stock			
H.O. Account		10,404		Reserve)			
Stock Reserve	1,247			Debtors	37,000		37,000
				Cash	23,500	1,000	24,500
				Branch A/c	10,404		
	88,204	10,560	87,113		88,204	10,560	87,113

* Material Consumed = ₹ 1,800 + ₹ 35,000 – ₹ 2,300 = ₹ 34,500

**Closing Stock = ₹ 15,000 + ₹ 9,560 – ₹ 1,247 = ₹ 23,313

PROBLEM 22

CAMHA Ltd. commenced business on 1st April, 2014 with a head office and a branch. Purchases were made exclusively by the head office where the goods were processed before sale. There was no loss or wastage. Only processed goods received from the head office were handled by the branch, and these were charged to the branch at processed cost *plus* 10 per cent. All sales, whether by head office or the branch, were at uniform gross profit of 25 per cent on their respective cost. The following Trial Balance as on 31st March, 2015 was extracted from the books.

Particulars	*H.O.*		*Branch*	
	Dr. (₹)	*Cr. (₹)*	*Dr. (₹)*	*Cr. (₹)*
Capital		2,20,000		
Drawings	25,000			
Purchases	19,93,350			
Cost of Processing	34,650			
Sales		14,20,000		6,40,000
Goods sent to Branch/Received by Branch		6,51,200	6,40,200	
Selling & General Expenses	2,24,000		27,000	
Debtors/Creditors	2,30,000	5,83,350	92,000	2,400
Branch/H.O. Current A/c	2,05,550			1,50,800
Balance at Bank	1,62,000		34,000	
Total	28,74,550	28,74,550	7,93,200	7,93,200

Information:

(i) Goods charged by head office to branch in March at ₹ 11,000, were not received by the branch until April. A remittance of Rs 43,750 from the branch to head office in March is still in transit.

(ii) Stock-taking at Branch disclosed shortage of ₹ 5,000 (at selling price).

(iii) Cost of unprocessed goods at head office as on 31st March, 2015 was ₹ 1,80,000.

Required: Prepare in columnar from Profit and Loss Account and Balance Sheet of the Head Office, branch and the business as a whole.

Solution

Dr. **PROFIT AND LOSS ACCOUNT FOR THE YEAR ENDING ON 31ST MARCH, 2015** Cr.

Particulars	H.O ₹	Branch ₹	Total ₹	Particulars	H.O. ₹	Branch ₹	Total ₹
Purchases	19,93,350	—	19,93,350	Sales	14,20,000	6,40,000	20,60,000
Cost of processing	34,650	—	34,650	Goods sent to Branch	6,51,200	—	—
				Shortage		4,000	4,000
Goods Received from H.O.	—	6,51,200	—	Closing Stock	—	—	11,000
				Unprocessed	1,80,000	—	1,80,000
Gross Profit c/d	3,43,200	1,28,000	4,71,200	Processed	1,20,000	1,24,200	2,44,200
	23,71,200	7,79,200	24,99,200		23,71,200	7,68,200	24,99,200
Selling Exp.	2,24,000	27,000	2,51,000	Gross Profit b/d	3,43,200	1,28,000	4,71,200
Provision for unrealised profit on:							
Branch Stock	11,291	—	11,291				
Goods in transit	1,000	—	1,000				
Shortage	—	4,000	4,000				
Net Profit	1,06,909	97,000	2,03,909				
	3,43,200	1,28,000	4,71,200		3,43,200	1,28,000	4,71,200

BALANCE SHEET AS AT 31ST MARCH, 2015

Liabilities	H.O ₹	Branch ₹	Total ₹	Assets	H.O. ₹	Branch ₹	Total ₹
Capital	2,20,000			Sundry Debtors	2,30,000	92,000	3,22,000
Add: Profit	2,03,909			Stocks:			
	4,23,909			Unprocessed	1,80,000	—	1,80,000
Less: Drawings	25,000			Processed	1,20,000	1,24,200	2,44,200
	3,98,909		3,98,909	(*Less*: Reserve)			(11,291)
				In transit	—	11,000	11,000
				(Less: Reserve)			(1,000)
Sundry Creditors	5,83,350	2,400	5,85,750	Balance at Bank	1,62,000	34,000	1,96,000
H.O. Current A/c		2,58,800		Remittance in transit	43,750	—	43,750
Provision for unrealised profit on Stock (₹ 11,291 + ₹ 1,000)	12,291	—	—	Branch Current A/c	2,58,800	—	—
	9,94,550	2,61,200	9,84,659		9,94,550	2,61,200	9,84,659

Working Notes:

(i) *Calculation of Head Office Stock*

		₹
A.	Purchases	19,93,350
B.	*Less*: Stock of unprocessed goods	1,80,000
C.	Cost of Goods consumed before processing (A – B)	18,13,350
D.	*Add*: Cost of Processing	34,650

E. Cost of Processed goods (C + D)		18,48,000
F. *Less*: (a) Cost of goods sent to Branch (₹ 6,51,200 × 100/110)	5,92,000	
(b) Cost of goods sold by H.O. (₹ 14,20,000 × 80/100)	11,36,000	17,28,000
G. Closing Stock at head office (E – F)		1,20,000

(ii) *Calculation of Branch Stock*

A. Received from the H.O.		6,40,200
B. *Less*: (a) Invoice Price of Goods Sold (₹ 6,40,000 × 80/100)	5,12,000	
(b) Invoice Price of Shortage (₹ 5,000 × 80/100)	4,000	5,16,000
C. Stock at Branch, at Invoice Price (A – B)		1,24,200
D. Unrealised Profit included (₹ 1,24,200 × 10/110)		11,291

(ii) Dr. **BRANCH CURRENT ACCOUNT** *Cr.*

Particulars	₹	*Particulars*	₹
To Balance b/d	2,05,550	By Cash in transit	43,750
To Net Profit	97,000	By Balance c/d	2,58,800
	3,02,550		3,02,550

(IV) DR. **CAPITAL ACCOUNT OF H.O.** *CR.*

Particulars	₹	*Particulars*	₹
To Drawings	25,000	By Balance b/d	2,20,000
To Balance c/d	3,98,909	By Profit and Loss A/c (Profit)	2,03,909
	4,23,909		4,23,909

PROBLEM 23

COJIH Ltd. operates a branch as well as a head office. The following Trial Balance has been extracted from the books of the concern as on 31st March, 2015:

Particulars	*H.O.*		*Branch*	
	Dr. (₹)	*Cr. (₹)*	*Dr. (₹)*	*Cr. (₹)*
Capital account	—	4,71,000	—	—
Drawings	84,000	—	—	—
Plant at cost	2,40,000	—	1,20,000	—
Accumulated depreciation on plant	—	1,20,000	—	60,000
Goods to branch/from head office	—	7,92,000	7,20,000	—
Head Office Current Account	—	—	—	1,56,000
Branch Current Account	2,58,000	—	—	—
Branch Stock Provisions (Opening)	—	6,000	—	—
Operating expenses	30,000	—	15,000	—
Purchases	22,92,000	—	—	—
Rent and rates	45,000	—	18,000	—
Sales	—	21,00,000	—	9,00,000
Opening Stock	1,80,000	—	36,000	—
Debtors	90,000	—	75,000	—
Creditors	—	1,35,000	—	—
Salaries and wages	3,60,000	—	1,20,000	—
Cash and bank	45,000	—	12,000	—
	36,24,000	36,24,000	11,16,000	11,16,000

Additional information:

(a) All goods are purchased by the head office. The goods required by the branch are invoiced by the head office to the branch at cost *plus* 20%. On 31st March, 2015, the head office held stocks which had cost it ₹ 2,40,000. On the same date the branch held stocks which had been invoiced to it at ₹ 54,000.

(b) Fixed assets are to be depreciated at the rate of 50% per annum based on the reducing balance method. There had been no purchase or sale of fixed assets during the year.

(c) At 31st March, 2015, cash ₹ 30,000 was in transit from the branch to the head office.

(d) The following expenses were outstanding on 31st March, 2015.

	Head Office	*Branch*
	₹	₹
Salaries	2,000	1,000
Rent	1,000	2,000

Required: Prepare, in columnar form, for (i) the head office, (ii) the branch, and (iii) the business as a whole, the Trading and Profit & Loss Accounts for the year ended 31st March, 2015. Also, prepare a combined Balance Sheet as on that date.

Solution

TRADING AND PROFIT AND LOSS ACCOUNT

Dr. *for the year ended 31st March, 2015* *Cr.*

Particulars	*H.O* ₹	*Branch* ₹	*Total* ₹	*Particulars*	*H.O.* ₹	*Branch* ₹	*Total* ₹
To Op. Stock	1,80,000	36,000	2,16,000	By Sales	21,00,000	9,00,000	30,00,000
To Purchases	22,92,000	—	22,92,000	By Branch transfer	7,92,000	—	—
To Head Office-transfer	—	7,92,000	—	By Clo. Stock	2,40,000	54,000	2,94,000
To Gross Profit c/d.	6,60,000	1,98,000	8,58,000	By Stock *less* Provisions	—	—	3,45,000
				By Goods-in-transit		72,000	72,000
	31,32,000	10,26,000	33,66,000		31,32,000	10,26,000	33,66,000
To Salaries & Wages	3,62,000	1,21,000	4,83,000	By Gross Profit b/d	6,60,000	1,98,000	8,58,000
To Rent & Rates	46,000	20,000	66,000	By Stock Reserve (36,000 × 20/120)	6,000		6,000
To Operating exp.	30,000	15,000	45,000				
To Depreciation	60,000	30,000	90,000				
To Stock Reserve	21,000		21,000				
To Net Profit c/d	1,47,000	12,000	1,59,000				
	6,66,000	1,98,000	8,64,000		6,66,000	1,98,000	8,64,000

BALANCE SHEET AS AT 31ST MARCH, 2015

Liabilities		₹	*Assets*		₹
Capital:			Plant at cost	3,60,000	
Opening balance	4,71,000		*Less:* Depreciation	2,70,000	90,000
Add: Profit	1,59,000		Stock		
	6,30,000		H.O.	2,40,000	
Less: Drawings	(84,000)	5,46,000	Branch	54,000	
Creditors		1,35,000	Goods-in-Transit	72,000	
Outstanding expenses		6,000		3,66,000	
			Less: Reserve	21,000	3,45,000
			Debtors		1,65,000
			Cash & Bank		57,000
			Cash in transit		30,000
		6,87,000			6,87,000

Working Note: *Adjustment for Cash in transit:*

Cash in transit A/c.	Dr.	₹ 30,000	
To Branch Current A/c			₹ 30,000

PROBLEM 24

On 31st March, 2015 Kanpur Branch submits the following Trial Balance to its Head Office at Lucknow:

Debit Balances:	*₹ in lacs*
Furniture and Equipment	18
Depreciation on Furniture	2
Salaries	25
Rent	10
Advertising	6
Telephone, Postage and Stationery	3
Sundry Office Expenses	1
Opening Stock	60
Goods Received from Head Office	288
Debtors	20
Cash at Bank and in hand	8
Carriage Inwards	7
	448
Credit Balances:	
Outstanding Expenses	3
Goods Returned to Head Office	5
Sales	360
Head Office	80
	448

Additional Information:

Closing Stock was valued at ₹ 62 lacs. On 29th March the Head Office despatched goods costing ₹ 10 lacs to its branch. Branch did not receive these goods before 1st April. Hence, the figure of goods received from Head Office does not include these goods. Also the head office has charged the branch ₹ 1 lac for centralised services for which the branch has not passed the entry.

You are required to:

(i) Pass Journal Entries in the books of the Branch to make the necessary adjustments

(ii) Prepare Final Accounts of the Branch including Balance Sheet, and

(iii) Pass Journal Entries in the books of the Head Office to incorporate the whole of the Branch Trial Balance.

Solution

JOURNAL OF BRANCH

[₹ in lacs]

Particulars		*L.F.*	*Dr. (₹)*	*Cr. (₹)*
Goods in Transit A/c	Dr.		10	
To Head Office A/c				10
(Being the goods despatched by head office but not received by branch before 1st April)				
Expenses A/c	Dr.		1	
To Head Office A/c				1
(Being the amount charged by head office for centralised services)				

(III) TRADING AND PROFIT & LOSS ACCOUNT OF THE BRANCH

for the year ended 31st March, 2015

Dr. *Cr.*

Particulars		*₹ (in lacs)*	*Particulars*	*₹ in (lacs)*
To Opening Stock		60	By Sales	360
To Goods received from			By Closing Stock	62
Head Office	288			
Less: Returns	5	283		
To Carriage Inwards		7		
To Gross Profit c/d		72		
		422		422
To Salaries		25	By Gross Profit b/d	72
To Depreciation on Furniture		2		
To Rent		10		
To Advertising		6		
To Telephone, Postage & Stationery		3		
To Sundry Office Expenses		1		
To Head Office Expenses		1		
To Net Profit Transferred to Head Office A/c		24		
		72		72

BALANCE SHEET AS AT 31ST MARCH, 2015

Liabilites		₹ *(in lacs)*	*Assets*		₹ *in (lacs)*
Head Office	80		Furniture & Equipment	20	
Add: Goods in transit	10		*Less:* Depreciation	2	18
Head Office Expenses	1		Stock in hand		62
Net Profit	24	115	Goods in Transit		10
Outstanding Expenses		3	Debtors		20
			Cash at bank and in hand		8
		118			118

JOURNAL OF HEAD OFFICE [₹]

Particulars		*L.F.*	*Dr.* (₹)	*Cr.* (₹)
Branch Trading A/c	Dr.		355	
To Branch A/c				355
(Being the Opening Stock, Goods received, Carriage Inwards debited to Branch Trading Account)				
Branch A/c	Dr.		427	
To Branch Trading A/c				427
((Being the Total sales, closing stock and goods returned to Head Office credited to Branch Trading Account)				
Branch Trading A/c	Dr.		72	
To Branch Profit and Loss A/c				72
(Being the gross profit earned by branch credited to Branch P& L A/c				
Branch Profit and Loss A/c	Dr.		48	
To Branch A/c				48
(Being the total of the Branch Expenses debited to Branch P& L A/c)				
Branch Profit & Loss A/c	Dr.		24	
To Profit and Loss A/c				24
(Net Profit at branch credited to (general) Profit & Loss A/c)				
Branch Furniture & Equipment	Dr.		18	
Branch Stock	Dr.		62	
Branch Debtors	Dr.		20	
Branch Cash at Bank and in Hand	Dr.		8	
Goods in Transit	Dr.		10	
To Branch A/c				118
(Being the incorporation of different assets at the branch in H.O. books)				
Branch A/c	Dr.		3	
To Branch Outstanding Expenses A/c				3
(Being the Incorporation of Branch Outstanding expenses in H.O. books)				

PROBLEM 25

M/s Shah & Co. commenced business on 01.04.2014 with Head Office at Mumbai and a Branch at Chennai. Purchases were made exclusively by the Head Office, where the goods were processed before sale. There was no loss or wastage in processing.

Only the processed goods received from Head Office were handled by the Branch. The goods were sent to branch at processed cost *plus* 10%.

All sales, whether by Head Office or by the Branch, were at uniform gross profit of 25% on their respective cost.

Following is the Trial Balance as on 31.03.2015:

Particulars	Head Office Dr. (₹)	Head Office Cr. (₹)	Branch Dr. (₹)	Branch Cr. (₹)
Capital	–	3,10,000	–	–
Drawings	55,000			
Purchases	19,69,500			
Cost of Processing	50,500			
Sales	–	12,80,000	–	8,20,000
Goods sent to Branch	–	9,24,000	–	–
Administrative expenses	1,39,000	–	15,000	–
Selling Expenses	50,000	–	6,200	–
Debtors	3,09,600	–	1,13,600	–
Branch Current Account	3,89,800	–	–	–
Creditors	–	6,01,400	–	10,800
Bank Balance	1,52,000	–	77,500	–
Head Office Current Account	–	–	–	2,61,500
Goods received from H.O.	–	–	8,80,000	–
	31,15,400	31,15,400	10,92,300	10,92,300

Following further information is provided:

(i) Goods sent by Head Office to the Branch in March of ₹.44,000 were not received by the Branch till 2nd April.

(ii) A remittance of ₹.84,300 sent by the Branch to Head Office was also similarly not received upto 31st March.

(iii) Stock taking at the Branch disclosed a shortage of ₹.20,000 (at selling price to the branch).

(iv) Cost of unprocessed goods at Head Office on 31.03.2015 was ₹.1,00,000.

Prepare Trading and Profit and Loss Account in columnar form and Balance Sheet of the business as a whole as at 31.03.2015.

Solution

Dr. **TRADING AND PROFIT AND LOSS ACCOUNT** Cr.

Particulars	H.O. ₹	Branch ₹	Total ₹	Particulars	H.O. ₹	Branch ₹	Total ₹
To Purchases	19,69,500	–	19,69,500	By Sales	12,80,000	8,20,000	21,00,000
To Cost of processing	50,500	–	50,500	By Goods sent to BR.	9,24,000	–	–
To Goods rec. from H.O. (Incl. GIT)	–	9,24,000	–	(incl. GIT)			
				By Stock Shortage	–	16,000	16,000
To Gross Profit c/d	3,40,000	1,64,000	5,04,000	By Goods in transit	–	44,000	44,000
				By Closing Stock:			
				Processed goods	56,000	2,08,000	2,64,000
				Unprocessed goods	1,00,000	–	1,00,000
	23,60,000	10,88,000	25,24,000		23,60,000	10,88,000	25,24,000
To Admn. expenses	1,39,000	15,000	1,54,000	By Gross profit b/d	3,40,000	1,64,000	5,04,000
To Selling expenses	50,000	6,200	56,200				
To Stock shortage	–	16,000	16,000				
To Stock reserve	22,909	–	22,909				
To Net Profit	1,28,091	1,26,800	2,54,891				
	3,40,000	1,64,000	5,04,000		3,40,000	1,64,000	5,04,000

BALANCE SHEET AS AT 31ST MARCH, 2015

Liabilities		₹	*Assets*		₹
Capital	3,10,000		Debtors		
Add: Net Profit	2,54,891		H.O.	3,09,600	
	5,64,891		Branch	1,13,600	4,23,200
Less: Drawings	55,000	5,09,891	Closing Stock:		
Creditors			Processed Goods		
H.O.	6,01,400		H.O.	56,000	
Branch	10,800	6,12,200	Branch	2,08,000	
				2,64,000	
			Less: Stock Reserve	18,909	2,45,091
			Unprocessed goods		1,00,000
			Bank Balance		
			H.O.	1,52,000	
			Branch	77,500	2,29,500
			Goods in transit	44,000	
			Less: Stock reserve	4,000	40,000
			Cash in transit		84,300
		11,22,091			11,22,091

Working Notes:

		₹
(i) Stock at Head Office:		
Cost of goods processed ₹(19,69,500 + 50,500 – 1,00,000)		19,20,000
Less: Cost of goods sent to Branch (₹.9,24,000 × 100/110)	8,40,000	
Cost of goods sold (₹.12,80,000 × 100/125)	10,24,000	18,64,000
Stock of processed goods with H.O.		56,000
(ii) Stock at Branch:		₹
Goods received from H.O. (at invoice price)		8,80,000
Less: Invoice value of goods sold ₹.8,20,000 × 100/125)	6,56,000	
Invoice value of stock shortage (₹.20,000 × 100/125)	16,000	6,72,000
Stock at Branch at invoice price		2,08,000
Less: Stock Reserve (2,08,000 × 10/110)		18,909
Stock of processed goods with Branch (at cost)		1,89,091
(iii) Stock Reserve		
Unrealised profit on Branch Stock (₹ 2,08,000 × 10/110)		18,909
Unrealised profit on goods in transit (₹ 44,000 × 10/110)		4,000
		22,909

FOREIGN BRANCH

PROBLEM 26

The Washington branch of XYZ Limited, Mumbai sent the following trial balance as on 31st December, 2015:

	$	$
Head Office A/c	—	22,800
Sales —	—	84,000
Debtors and Creditors	4,800	3,400
Machinery	24,000	—
Cash at Bank	1,200	—
Opening Stock	11,200	—
Goods from H.O.	64,000	—
Expenses	5,000	—
	1,10,200	1,10,200

In the books of head office, the Branch a/c stood as follows:

Dr. **WASHINGTON BRANCH ACCOUNT** *Cr.*

Particulars	₹	*Particulars*	₹
To Balance b/d	8,10,000	By Cash	28,76,000
To Goods sent to branch	29,26,000	By Balance c/d	8,60,000
	37,36,000		37,36,000

Goods are sent to the branch at cost *plus* 10% and the branch sells goods at Inovice price *plus* 25%. Machinery was acquired on 1st January, 2014, when $ 1.00 = ₹ 48.

Rates of Exchange were:

1st January, 2015	$ 1.00 = ₹ 46
31st December, 2015	$ 1.00 = ₹ 48
Average	$ 1.00 = ₹ 47

Machinery is depreciated @ 10% and the Branch Manager is entitled to a commission of 5% on the profit of the branch.

You are required to:

(i) Prepare the Branch Trading & Profit & Loss A/c in dollars.

(ii) Convert the Trial Balance of branch into Indian currency and prepare Branch Trading & Profit and Loss A/c and the Branch A/c in the books of head office.

Solution

Dr. **(i) TRADING AND PROFIT & LOSS A/C (IN DOLLARS)** Cr.

Particulars	₹	Particulars	₹
To Opening Stock	11,200	By Sales	84,000
To Goods from H.O.	64,000	By Closing Stock	8,000
To Gross Profit c/d	16,800		
	92,000		92,000
To Expenses	5,000	By Gross Profit b/d	16,800
To Depreciation	2,400		
To Manager's Commission	448		
To Net Profit c/d	8,952		
	16,800		16,800

(II) (A) CONVERTED TRIAL BALANCE

Particulars	Rate per Re.	Dr. (₹)	Cr. (₹)
Machinery	48	11,52,000	
Opening Stock	46	5,15,200	
Goods from H.O.	—	29,26,000	
Sales	47	—	39,48,000
Expenses	47	2,35,000	—
Debtors & Creditors	48	2,30,400	1,63,200
H.O. A/c	—	—	8,60,000
Cash at Bank	—	57,600	—
Difference of Exchange	—	—	1,45,000
	—	51,16,200	51,16,200
Closing Stock $ 8,000 (W.N.2)	48		₹ 3,84,000

Dr. **(B) TRADING AND PROFIT & LOSS ACCOUNT** Cr.

Particulars	₹	Particulars	₹
To Opening Stock	5,15,200	By Sales	39,48,000
To Goods from H.O.	29,26,000	By Closing Stock	3,84,000
To Gross Profit c/d	8,90,800		
	43,32,000		43,32,000
To Expenses	2,35,000	By Gross Profit b/d	8,90,000
To Depreciation @ 10% on ₹ 11,52,000	1,15,200	By Exchange difference	1,45,000
To Manager's Commisson (W.N.1)	21,504		
To Net Profit c/d	6,63,296		
	10,35,000		10,35,000

Working Notes:

(i) Manager's Commission = 5/105 of [16,800 – (5,000 + 2,400] = $ 448 (approx)

Manager's commission in Rupees = $ 448 × 48 = ₹ 21,504

(ii) *Calculation of Closing Stock*

Opening Stock	11,200
Add: Goods from H.O.	64,000
Less: Cost of Goods Sold (at invoice price) [100/125 × 84,000]	(67,200)
Closing Stock	8,000

(iii) Alternatively, Manager's Commission may be calculated on Profit before charging Commission.

PROBLEM 27

DM Ltd., Delhi has a branch in London. London branch is an integral foreign operation of *DM* Ltd. At the end of the year 31st March, 2015, the branch furnishes the following trial balance in U.K. Pound:

Particulars	£ *Dr.*	£ *Cr.*
Fixed Assets (acquired on 1st April, 2011)	24,000	
Opening Stock	11,200	
Goods from head office	64,000	
Expenses	4,800	
Debtors	4,800	
Creditors		3,200
Cash at bank	1,200	
Head office account		22,800
Purchases	12,000	
Sales		96,000
	1,22,000	1,22,000

In head office books, the branch account stood as shown below:

Dr. **LONDON BRANCH ACCOUNT** *Cr.*

Particulars	₹	*Particulars*	₹
To Balance b/d	20,10,000	By Bank A/c	52,16,000
To Goods sent to branch A/c	49,26,000	By Balance c/d	17,20,000
	69,36,000		69,36,000

The following further information are given:

(a) Fixed assets are to be depreciated @ 10% p.a on straight line basis.

(b) On 31s' March, 2015:

Expenses outstanding	-	£ 400
Prepaid expenses	-	£ 200
Closing stock	-	£ 8,000

(c) Rate of Exchange:

1st April, 2011	-	₹ 70 to £ 1
1st April, 2014	-	₹ 76 to £ 1

31st March, 2015	-	₹ 77 to £ 1
Average	-	₹ 75 to £ 1

You are required to prepare:

(i) Trial balance, incorporating adjustments of outstanding and prepaid expenses, converting U.K. pound into Indian rupees.

(ii) Trading and profit and loss account for the year ended 31st March, 2015 and the Balance Sheet as on that date of London branch as would appear in the books of Delhi head office of *DM* Ltd.

Solution

(I) TRIAL BALANCE OF LONDON BRANCH AS ON 31ST MARCH, 2015

Particulars	*U.K. Pound*	*Rate per U.K. Pound*	*Dr. (₹)*	*Cr. (₹)*
Fixed assets	24,000	70	16,80,000	
Opening Stock	11,200	76	8,51,200	
Goods from head office	64,000	–	49,26,000	–
Sales	96,000	75	–	72,00,000
Purchases	12,000	75	9,00,000	–
Expenses (4,800 + 400 – 200)	5,000	75	3,75,000	–
Debtors	4,800	77	3,69,600	–
Creditors	3,200	77	–	2,46,400
Outstanding expenses	400	77	–	30,800
Prepaid expenses	200	77	15,400	–
Cash at bank	1,200	77	92,400	–
Head office account		–		17,20,000
Difference in foreign exchange translation				– 12,400
			92,09,600	92,09,600

Closing Stock will be (£ 8,000 × ₹ 77) = ₹.6,16,000

(II) TRADING AND PROFIT & LOSS ACCOUNT FOR THE YEAR ENDED 31ST MARCH, 2015

Particulars	₹	*Particulars*	₹
To Opening stock	8,51,200	By Sales	72,00,000
To Purchases	9,00,000	By Closing stock	6,16,000
To Goods from head office	49,26,000		
To Gross Profit	11,38,800		
	78,16,000		78,16,000
To Expenses	3,75,000	By Gross Profit	11,38,000
To Depreciation	1,68,000	By Profit due to foreign exchange difference	1,20,400
To Net Profit	6,08,200		
	11,51,200		11,51,200

(III) BALANCE SHEET AS AT 31ST MARCH, 2015

Liabilities	₹	₹	*Assets*	₹	₹
Head Office			Fixed Assets	16,80,000	
Balance	17,20,000		*Less*: Depreciation	(1,68,000)	15,12,000
Add: Net Profit	6,08,200	23,28,200	Debtors		3,69,600
Outstanding expenses		30,800	Prepaid expenses		15,400
Creditors		2,46,400	Closing stock		6,16,000
			Cash at bank		92,400
		26,05,400			26,05,400

PROBLEM 28

An Indian company Moon Star Limited has a branch at Verginia (USA). The Branch is a non-integral foreign operation of the Indian Company. The trial balance of the Branch as at 31st March, 2015 is as follows:

Particulars	*US $*	
	Dr.	*Cr.*
Office equipments	48,000	
Furniture	32,00	
Opening Stock	22,400	
Purchases	96,000	
Sales	—	1,66,400
Goods Sent from HO	32,000	
Salaries	3,200	
Carriage inward	400	
Rent, Rate & Taxes	800	
Insurance	400	
Trade Expenses	400	
Head Office Account	—	45,600
Sundry Debtors	9,600	
Sundry Creditors	—	6,800
Cash at Bank	2,000	
Cash in Hand	400	
	2,18,800	2,18,800

The following further information's are given:

(1) Salaries outstanding $400.
(2) Depreciate Office Equipment and Furniture @ 10% p.a. at written down value.
(3) The Head Office sent goods to Branch for ₹ 15,80,000
(4) The head Office shown an amount of ₹ 20,50,000 due from Branch.
(5) Closing Stock $21,500.
(6) There were no transit items either at the start or at the end of the year.
(7) On April 1,2013 when the fixed assets were purchased the rate of exchange was ₹ 43 to one $. On April, 1, 2014, the rate was ₹ 47 per $. On March 31, 2015 the rate was ₹ 50 per $. Average Rate during the year was ₹ 45 to one $.

Prepare:

(a) Trial Balance incorporating adjustment given converting dollars into rupees.
(b) Trading Profit and Loss Account for the year ended 31st March, 2015 and Balance Sheet as

on date depicting the profitability and net position of the Branch as would appear in the books of Indian company for the purpose of incorporating in the main Balance Sheet.

Solution

(A) IN THE BOOKS OF MOON STAR LTD. – AN INDIAN COMPANY TRIAL BALANCE (IN RUPEES) OF VERGINIA (USA) BRANCH AS ON 31ST MARCH, 2015

Dr. *Cr.*

Particulars	*Dr. US $*	*Cr. US $*	*Conversion rate*	*Dr. US $*	*Cr. US $*
Office Equipment	43,200		50	21,60,000	
Depreciation on Office Equipment	4,800		50	2,40,000	
Furniture and Fixtures	2,880		50	1,44,000	
Depreciation of furniture and fixtures	320		50	16,000	
Opening Stock	22,400		47	10,52,800	
Purchase	96,000		45	43,20,000	
Sales		1,66,400	45		74,88,000
Goods sent from H.O.	32,000			15,80,000	
Carriage inward	400		45	18,000	
Salaries (3,200 + 400)	3,600		45	1,62,000	
Outstanding salaries		400	50		20,000
Rent, rates and taxes	800		45	36,000	
Insurance	400		45	18,000	
Trade expenses	400		45	18,000	
Head Office A/c		45,600			20,50,000
Trade debtors	9,600		50	4,80,000	
Trade creditors		6,800	50		3,40,000
Cash at bank	2,000		50	1,00,000	
Cash in hand	400		50	20,000	
Exchange gain (bal. fig.)					4,66,800
	2,19,200	2,19,200		1,03,64,800	1,03,64,800

TRADING AND PROFIT AND LOSS ACCOUNT OF VERGINIA BRANCH

for the year ended 31st March, 2015

Dr. *Cr.*

Particulars	₹	*Conversion*	₹
To Opening stock	10,52,800	By Sales	74,88,000
To Purchases	43,20,000	By Closing Stock	
To Goods from Head Office	15,80,000	(21,500 US $ × 50)	10,75,000
To Carriage inward	18,000		
To Gross profit c/d	15,92,200		
	85,63,000		85,63,000
To Salaries	1,62,000	By Gross profit b/d	15,92,200
To Rent, rates and taxes	36,000		
To Insurance	18,000		
To Trade expenses	18,000		
To Depreciation on office equipment	2,40,000		
To Depreciation on Furniture	16,000		
To Net Profit c/d	11,02,200		
	15,92,200		15,92,200

BALANCE SHEET OF VERGINIA BRANCH AS ON 31ST MARCH, 2015

Liabilities	₹	₹	*Particulars*	₹	₹
Head Office A/c	20,50,000		Office Equipment	24,00,000	
Add: Net Profit	11,02,200	31,52,000	*Less:* Depreciation	2,40,000	21,60,000
Foreign Currency			Furniture and fixtures	1,60,000	
Translation Reserve		4,66,800	*Less:* Depreciation	16,000	1,44,000
Trade creditors		3,40,000	Closing Stock		10,75,000
Outstanding salaries		20,000	Trade Debtors		4,80,000
			Cash in hand		20,000
			Cash at bank		1,00,000
		39,79,000			39,79,000

PROBLEM 29

ABCD Ltd., Delhi, has a branch in New York, USA which is an integral foreign operation of the Company. At the end of 31st March, 2015, the following ledger balances have been extracted from the books of the Delhi Office and the New York office.

Particulars	*Delhi (₹ thousands)*		*New York ($ thousands)*	
	Debit	*Credit*	*Debit*	*Credit*
Share Capital	—	1,250	—	—
Reserve & Surplus	—	940	—	—
Land	475	—	—	—
Buildings (Cost)	1,000	—	—	—
Buildings Depreciation Reserve	—	200	—	—
Plant & Machinery (Cost)	2,000	—	100	—
Plant & Machinery Depreciation Reserve	—	500	—	20
Trade Receivables/ Payables	500	270	60	20
Opening Stock	250	—	25	—
Branch Stock Reserve	—	65	—	—
Cash & Bank Balances	125	—	4	—
Purchases/Sales	275	600	25	125
Goods sent to Branch	—	1500	30	—
Managing Director's salary	50	—	—	—
Wages & Salaries	100	—	18	—
Rent	—	—	6	—
Office Expenses	25	—	12	—
Commission Receipts	—	275	—	100
Branch/H.O. Current A/c	800	—	—	15
	5,600	5,600	280	280

Additional Information

(i) Closing Stock: Delhi ₹ 2,00,000, New York $ 10 (ii) Head Office always sent goods to the Branch at cost *plus* 25%, (iii) Provision is to be made for doubtful debts at 5%, (iv) Depreciation is to be provided on buildings at 10% and on plant and machinery at 20% on written down values,

You are required:

(a) to convert the Branch Trial balance into rupees; (use the following rates of exchange) Opening rate 1 $ = ₹ 50, Closing rate 1 $ = ₹ 55, Average rate 1 $ = ₹ 52, For Fixed Assets 1 $ = ₹ 45

(b) to prepare the Trading and Profit & Loss Account for the year ending on 31st March, 2015, showing to the extent possible, H.O. results and Branch results separately.

Solution

ABCD LTD.
(a) NEW YORK BRANCH TRIAL BALANCE (IN RUPEES) AS ON 31ST MARCH, 2015

Particulars	*Conversion rate per A $*	*(₹ '000) Dr.*	*(₹ '000) Cr.*
Plant & Machinery (cost)	₹ 45	45,00	
Plant & Machinery Depreciation Reserve	₹ 45		9,00
Trade Receivables/Trade Payables	₹ 55	33,00	11,00
Opening Stock	₹ 50	12,50	
Cash & Bank Balances	₹ 55	2,20	
Purchases/Sales	₹ 52	13,00	65,00
Goods received from H.O.	Actual	15,00	
Wages & Salaries	₹ 52	9,36	
Rent	₹ 52	3,12	
Office expenses	₹ 52	6,24	
Commission Receipts	₹ 52		52,00
H.O. Current Account	Actual		8,00
		139,42	145,00
Exchange loss (*balancing figure*)		5,58	—
		145,00	145,00

(b) TRADING AND PROFIT & LOSS ACCOUNT
for the year ending on 31st March, 2015

Dr. *Cr.*
(₹ '000)

Particulars	*H.O.* ₹	*Branch* ₹	*Total* ₹	*Particulars* ₹	*H.O.* ₹	*Branch* ₹	*Total*
To Opening Stock	250	1250	1500	By Sales	600	6500	7100
To Purchases	275	1300	1575	By Goods sent to Branch	1500	—	1500
To Goods received	—	1500	1500				
To Wages & Salaries	100	936	1036				
To Gross Profit	1675	1514.55	3189.55	By Closing Stock	200	0.55	200.55
	2300	6500.55	8800.55		2300	6500.55	8800.55
				By Gross Profit b/d	1675	1514.55	3189.55
To Rent	—	312	312	By Commission receipts	275	5200	5475
To Office expenses	25	624	649				
To Provision for doubtful debts @ 5%	25	165	190				
To Depreciation	380	720	1100				
To Balance c/d	1520	4893.55	6413.55				
	1950	6714.55	8664.55		1950	6714.55	8664.55
To Exchange loss			558	By Balance b/d			6413.55
To MD Salary			50	By Branch Stock Reserve			64.89
To Balance c/d			5870.44				
			6478.44				6478.44

Working Notes:

(i) *Calculation of Depreciation* (₹ '000)

		H.O.	Branch
A	Building-Cost	1000	—
B	*Less* : Depreciation Reserve	200	—
C	Building at WDV	800	
D	Depreciation on Building @ 10%	80	
E	Plant & Machinery Cost	2000	4500
F	*Less*: Depreciation Reserve	(500)	(900)
G	Plant & Machinery at WDV	1500	3600
H	Depreciation on Plant & Machinery @ 20%	300	720
I	Total Depreciation (D + H)	380	720

(ii) *Calculation of Branch Stock Reserve* (₹ *'000*)

A	Reserve on closing stock (0.55 × 1/5)	0.11
B	*Less* : Opening Branch Stock Reserve	(65)
C	Reversal of Reserve required	(64.89)

25 ACCOUNTING FOR DEPARTMENTS

SHORT ANSWER PRACTICAL QUESTIONS

PROBLEM 1

Goods are transfered from Department *P* to Department *Q* at a price 50% above cost. If closing stock of Department *Q* is ₹ 27,000, compute the amount of Stock Reserve.

Solution

Stock Reserve = ₹ 27,000 × 50/150 = ₹ 9,000

PROBLEM 2

Z Ltd. has three departments and submits the following information for the year ending on 31st March, 2015:

	A	*B*	*C*	*Total (₹)*
Purchases (units)	6,000	12,000	14,400	
Purchases (Amount)				6,00,000
Sales (Units)	6,120	11,520	14,976	
Selling Price (per unit) ₹	40	45	50	
Closing Stock (Units)	600	960	36	

You are required to prepare departmental trading account of Z Ltd., assuming that the rate of profit on sales is uniform in each case.

Solution

Dr. **DEPARTMENTAL TRADING ACCOUNT** *Cr.*

Particulars	*A* ₹	*B* ₹	*C* ₹	*Particulars*	*A* ₹	*B* ₹	*C* ₹
To Opening Stock	11,520	8,640	12,240	By Sales	2,44,800	5,18,400	7,48,800
To Purchases	96,000	2,16,000	2,88,000	By Closing Stock	9,600	17,280	720
To Gross Profit	1,46,880	3,11,040	4,49,280				
	2,54,400	5,35,680	7,49,520		2,54,400	5,35,680	7,49,520

Working Notes:

(i) *Profit Margin Ratio*

Selling price of unit purchased:	₹
Department A (6,000 x 40)	2,40,000
Department B (12,000 x 45)	5,40,000
Department C (14,400 x 50)	7,20,000
Total Selling Price	15,00,000
Less Purchase (Cost) Value	6,00,000
Gross Profit	9,00,000

Profit Margin Ratio = (90,00,000/15,00,000) × 100 = 60%

(II) STATEMENT SHOWING DEPARTMENT-WISE PER UNIT COST AND PURCHASE COST

	A	B	C
Selling Price (Per unit) (₹)	40	45	50
Less : Profit Margin @ 60% (₹)	(24)	(27)	(30)
Purchase Price per unit (₹)	16	18	20
Number of units purchased	6,000	12,000	14,400
(Purchased cost per unit X Units purchased)	96,000	2,16,000	2,88,000

(III) STATEMENT SHOWING CALCULATION OF DEPARTMENT-WISE OPENING STOCK (IN UNITS)

	A	B	C
Selling (Units)	6,120	11,520	14,976
Add : Closing Stock (Units)	600	960	36
Less : Purchases (Units)	(6,000)	(12,000)	(14,400)
Opening Stock (Units)	720	480	612

(IV) STATEMENT SHOWING DEPARTMENT-WISE COST OF OPENING STOCK & CLOSING STOCK

	A	B	C
Cost of Opening Stock	₹ 11,520 (₹ 720 x 16)	₹ 8,640 (₹ 480 x 18)	₹ 12,240 (₹ 612 x 20)
Cost of Closing Stock	₹ 9,600 (₹ 600 x 16)	17,280 (₹ 960 x 18)	720 (₹ 36 x 20)

PROBLEM 3

Brahma Limited has three departments and submits the following information for the year ending on 31st March, 2015:

Particulars	A	B	C	*Total (₹)*
Purchases (units)	5,000	10,000	15,000	
Purchases (Amount)				8,40,000
Sales (units)	5,200	9,800	15,300	
Selling price (₹ per unit)	40	45	50	
Closing Stock (Units)	400	600	700	

Required: Prepare departmental trading account of Brahma Limited assuming that the rate of profit on sales is uniform in each case.

Solution

Dr. **DEPARTMENTAL TRADING ACCOUNT FOR THE YEAR ENDED 31ST MARCH, 2015** *Cr.*

Particulars	*A* ₹	*B* ₹	*C* ₹	*Particulars*	*A* ₹	*B* ₹	*C* ₹
To Opening Stock	14,400	10,800	30,000	By Sales	2,08,000	4,41,000	7,65,000
To Purchases	1,20,000	2,70,000	4,50,000	By Closing stock	9,600		21,000
To Gross profit	83,200	1,76,400	3,06,000				
	2,17,600	4,57,200	7,86,000		2,17,600	4,57,200	7,86,000

Working Notes:

(I) GROSS PROFIT RATIO

Selling price of units purchased:		₹
Department A	(5,000 units × ₹ 40)	2,00,000
Department B	(10,000 units × ₹ 45)	4,50,000
Department C	(15,000 units × ₹ 50)	7,50,000
Total selling price of purchased units		14,00,000
Less: Purchases		(8,40,000)
Gross profit		5,60,000

$$\text{Gross Profit Ratio} = \frac{\text{Gross profit}}{\text{Selling price}} \times 100 = \frac{5,60,000}{14,00,000} \times 100 = 40\%$$

(II) STATEMENT SHOWING DEPARTMENT-WISE PER UNIT COST & PURCHASE COST

Particulars	*A*	*B*	*C*
Selling price per unit (₹)	40	45	50
Less: Profit margin @ 40% (₹)	(16)	(18)	(20)
Purchase price per unit (₹)	24	27	30
No. of units purchased	5,000	10,000	15,000
Purchases (purchase cost per unit × units purchased)	1,20,000	2,70,000	4,50,000

(III) STATEMENT SHOWING CALCULATION OF DEPARTMENT-WISE OPENING STOCK (IN UNITS)

Particulars	*A*	*B*	*C*
Sales (Units)	5,200	9,800	15,300
Add: Closing Stock (Units)	400	600	700
	5,600	10,400	16,000
Less: Purchases (Units)	(5,000)	(10,000)	(15,000)
Opening Stock (Units)	600	400	1,000

(VI) STATEMENT SHOWING DEPARTMENT-WISE COST OF OPENING AND CLOSING STOCK

Particulars	*A*	*B*	*C*
Cost of Opening Stock (₹)	600 × 24	400 × 27	1,000×30
	14,400	10,800	30,000
Cost of Closing Stock (₹)	400 × 24	600 × 27	700 × 30
	9,600	16,200	21,000

PROBLEM 4

X Ltd. has three departments A, B and C. From the particulars given below compute:

(a) the values of stock as on 31st March 2015 and

(b) the departmental results

(i)

	A ₹	*B* ₹	*C* ₹
Opening Stock	24,000	36,000	12,000
Purchases	1,46,000	1,24,000	48,000
Actual Sales	1,72,500	1,59,400	74,600
Gross Profit on normal selling price	20%	25%	33.1/3%

(ii) During the year certain items were sold at discount and these discounts were reflected in the value of sales shown above. The items sold at discount were:

	A ₹	B ₹	C ₹
Sales at normal price	10,000	3,000	1,000
Sales at actual price	7,500	2,400	600

Solution

1. CALCULATION OF DEPARTMENTAL RESULTS (ACTUAL GROSS PROFIT)

Particulars	*A (₹)*	*B (₹)*	*C (₹)*
Actual Sales	1,72,500	1,59,400	74,600
Add back: Discount	2,500	600	400
Normal Sale	1,75,000	1,60,000	75,000
Gross Profit % on normal Sales	20%	25%	33.33%
Normal Gross Profit	35,000	40,000	25,000
Less: Discount	(2,500)	(600)	(400)
Actual Gross Profit	32,500	39,400	24,600

2. COMPUTATION OF VALUE OF STOCK AS ON 31ST MARCH, 2015

Particulars	*A (₹)*	*B (₹)*	*C (₹)*
Opening Stock	24,000	36,000	12,000
Add: Purchases	1,46,000	1,24,000	48,000
	1,70,000	1,60,000	60,000
Add: Actual Gross Profit	32,500	39,400	24,600
	2,02,500	1,99,400	84,600
Less: Actual Sales	(1,72,500)	(1,59,400)	(74,600)
Closing Stock as on 31.12.2011 (bal Fig.)	30,000	40,000	10,000

Working Note:

COMPUTATION OF DISCOUNT ON SALES

Particulars	*A (₹)*	*B (₹)*	*C (₹)*
Sales at normal price	10,000	3,000	1,000
Less: Sales at actual price	(7,500)	(2,400)	(600)
	2,500	600	400

LONG ANSWER PRACTICAL QUESTIONS

PROBLEM 5

Siva Ltd. has two departments *X* and *Y*. From the following particulars prepare departmental trading accounts and General Profit and Loss Account for the year ending 31st March. 2015:

	Department X ₹	*Department Y* ₹
Opening Stock (at cost)	80,000	48,000
Purchases	3,68,000	2,72,000
Carriage inward	8,000	8,000
Wages	48,000	32,000
Sales	5,60,000	4,48,000
Purchased good transferred		
By department *Y* to *X*	40,000	-
By department *X* to *Y*	–	32,000
Finished goods transferred		
By department *Y* to *X*	1,40,000	–
By department *X* to *Y*	–	1,60,000
Return of finished goods		
By department *Y* to *X*	40,000	–
By department *X* to *Y*	–	28,000
Closing stock		
Purchased goods	18,000	24,000
Finished goods	96,000	56,000

Purchased goods have been transferred mutually at their respective departmental purchase cost and finished goods at departmental market price and that 25% of the closing finished stock with each department represents finished goods received from the other department.

Solution

DEPARTMENTAL TRADING ACCOUNT OF SIVA LTD.
for the year ended 31st March 2015

Dr. *Cr.*

Particulars	*Department X* ₹	*Department Y* ₹	*Particulars*	*Department X* ₹	*Department Y* ₹
To Opening Stock	80,000	48,000	By Sales	5,60,000	4,48,000
To Purchases	3,68,000	2,72,000	By Transfers:		
To Carriage inward	8,000	8,000	Purchased goods	32,000	40,000
To Wages	48,000	32,000	Finished goods	1,20,000*	1,12,000*
To Transfers:			By Closing Stock:		
Purchased goods	40,000	32,000	Purchased goods	18,000	24,000
Finished goods	1,12,000	1,20,000	Finished goods	96,000	56,000
To Gross Profit c/d	1,70,000	1,68,000			
	8,26,000	6,80,000		8,26,000	6,80,000

*Net transfers of finished goods by

Department *X* to *Y* = ₹.1,60,000 – ₹ 40,000 = ₹ 1,20,000

Department *Y* to *X* = ₹ 1,40,000 – ₹ 28,000 = ₹ 1,12,000

PROFIT AND LOSS ACCOUNT

Dr. ***for the year ended 31st March, 2015*** *Cr.*

Particulars	₹	*Particulars*	₹
To Provision for unrealized profit included in Closing Stock:		By Gross Profit b/d:	
Department X	1,70,000	Department X	7,200
Department Y	1,68,000	Department Y	3,500
To Net Profit	3,27,300		
	3,38,000		3,38,000

Working Notes:

(i) ***Calculation of Rates of Gross Profit Margin on Sales***

	Department X ₹	*Department Y* ₹
Sales	5,60,000	4,48,000
Add: Transfer of finished goods	1,60,000	1,40,000
	7,20,000	5,88,000
Less: Return of finished goods	(40,000)	(28,000)
	6,80,000	5,60,000
Gross Profit	1,70,000	1,68,000
Gross Profit Margin =	$\frac{1,70,000}{6,80,000} \times 100 = 25\%$	$\frac{1,68,000}{5,60,000} \times 100 = 30\%$

(ii) ***Finished goods from other department included in the Closing Stock***

	Department X ₹	*Department Y* ₹
Stock of Finished goods	96,000	56,000
Stock related to other department (25% of finished goods)	24,000	14,000

(iii) Unrealized profit included in the closing stock

Department X = 30% of ₹ 24,000 = ₹ 7,200

Department Y = 25% of ₹ 14,000 = ₹ 3,500

PROBLEM 6

Mis. AM Enterprise had two departments, Cloth and Readymade Clothes. The readymade clothes were made by the firm itself out of the cloth supplied by the Cloth Department at its usual selling price. From the following figures, prepare Departmental Trading and Profit & Loss Account for the year ended 31st March, 2015:

	Cloth Department ₹	Readymade Clothes Department ₹
Opening Stock on 1st April, 2014	31,50,000	5,32,000
Purchases	2,10,00,000	1,68,000
Sales	2,31,00,000	47,25,000
Transfer to Readymade Clothes Department	31,50,000	—
Manufacturing expenses	—	6,30,000
Selling expenses	2, 10,000	73,500
Rent & warehousing	8,40,000	5,60,000
Stockon 31st March, 2015	21,00,000	6,72,000

In addition to the above, the following information is made available for necessary consideration:

The stock in the Readymade Clothes Department may be considered as consisting of 75% cloth and 25% other expenses.The Cloth Department earned a gross profit at the rate of 15% in 2011-12. General expenses of the business as a whole amount to ₹ 10,85,000.

Solution

(a) **DEPARTMENTAL TRADING AND PROFIT AND LOSS ACCOUNT**

for the year ended 31st March, 2015

Dr. **Cr.**

Particulars	Cloth (₹)	Ready-made Clothes (₹)	Total (₹)	Particulars	Cloth (₹)	Ready-made Clothes (₹)	Total (₹)
To Opening stock	31,50,000	5,32,000	36,82,000	By Sales	2,31,00,000	47,25,000	2,78,25,000
To Purchases	2,10,00,000	1,68,000	2,11,68,000	By Transferto Ready-made Clothes Deptt.	31,50,000	—	31,50,000
To Transfer from Cloth Department	—	31,50,000	31,50,000	By Closing from Cloth Stock	21,00,000	6,72,000	27,72,000
To Manufacturing expenses	—	6,30,000	6,30,000				
To Gross profit c/d	42,00,000	9,17,000	51,17,000				
	2,83,50,000	53,97,000	3,37,47,000		2.83.50.000	53.97.000	3.37.47.000
To Sellingexpenses	2,10,000	73,500	2,83,500	By Gross profit b/d	42,00,000	9,17,000	51,17,000
To Rent & warehousing	8,40,000	5,60,000	14,00,000				
To Net profit	31,50,000	2,83,500	34,33,500				
	42,00,000	9,17,000	51,17,000		42,00,000	9,17,000	51,17,000

Dr. **GENERAL PROFIT AND LOSS ACCOUNT** *Cr.*

Particulars	₹	Particulars	₹
To General Expenses	10,85,000	By Net Profit	34,33,500
To Stock Reserve on Closing Stock	80,640	By Stock Reserve on Opening Stock (No longer required)	59,850
To General Net Profit (Bal. fig.)	23,27,710		
	34,93,350		34,93,350

Working Note: **Calculation of Stock Reserve**

$$\text{Gross Profit Ratio of Cloth Department} = \frac{\text{Gross Proflt}}{\text{Total Sales}} \times 100$$

$$= \frac{\text{Rs } 42,00,000}{\text{Rs } (2,31,000 + 31,50,000)} \times 100 = 16\%$$

Stock Reserve on Closing Stock = ₹ 6,72,000 × 75% × 16% = ₹ 80,640

Stock reserve on opening stock = (₹ 5,32,000 × 75% × 15%) = ₹ 59,850

PROBLEM 7

Department R sells goods to Department S at a profit of 25% on cost and Department T at 10% profit on cost. Department S sells goods to R and T at a profit of 15% and 20% on sales respectively. Department T charges 20% and 25% profit on cost to Department R and S respectively.

Department managers are entitled to 10% commission on net profit subject to unrealized profit on departmental sales being eliminated. Departmental profits after charging manager's commission, but before adjustment of unrealized profit are as under.

		₹
Department	*R*	54,000
Department	*S*	40,500
Department	*T*	27,000

STOCK LYING AT DIFFERENT DEPARTMENTS AT THE END OF THE YEAR ARE AS UNDER:

	Deptt. R ₹	*Deptt. S* ₹	*Deptt. T* ₹
Transfer from Department R	–	22,500	16,500
Transfer from Department S	21,000	–	18,000
Transfer from Department T	9,000	7,500	–

Find out the correct departmental profits after charging manager's commission.

Solution

CALCULATION OF CORRECT DEPARTMENTAL PROFITS AFTER CHARGING DEPARTMENTAL MANAGER'S COMMISSION

Particulars	*Departments*		
	R ₹	S ₹	T ₹
Profit	54,000	40,500	27,000
Add: Managerial commission (1/9)	6,000	4,500	3,000
	60,000	**45,000**	**30,000**
Less: Unrealised profit on stock	(6,000)	(6,750)	(3,000)
	54,000	**38,250**	**27,000**
Less: Managers'Commission @ 10%	5,400	3,825	2,700
	48,600	**34,425**	**24,300**

Working Notes: **Amount of Unrealised Profit**

Transfer by Department R to

S department (22,500 × 25/125)	= 4,500
T department 16,500 × 10/110)	= 1,500
	6,000

Transfer by department S to

R department (21,000 x 15/100)	= 3,150
T department (18,000 x 20/100)	= 3,600
	6,750

Transfer by department T to

R department (9,000 x 20/120)	= 1,500
S department (7,500 × 25/125)	= 1,500
	3,000

PROBLEM 8

Department *X* sells goods to Department *Y* at a profit of 20% on cost and to Department *Z* at 15% profit on cost. Department *Y* sells goods to *X* and *Z* at a profit of 10% and 20% on sales, respectively. Department *Z* charges 15% and 10% profit on cost to Department *X* and *Y*, respectively.

Department Managers are entitled to 10% commission on net profit after eliminating unrealised profit on departmental sales being eliminated. Departmental profits after charging Managers' commission, but before adjustment of unrealised profit are as under:

	₹
Department *X*	36,000
Department *Y*	27,000
Department *Z*	18,000

Stocks lying at different departments at the end of the year are as under:

	Dept. X ₹	*Dept. Y* ₹	*Dept. Z* ₹
Transfer from Department *X*	—	7,200	5,750
Transfer from Department *Y*	19,000	—	15,000
Transfer from Department *Z*	4,600	3,300	—

Required: Find out the correct departmental Profits after charging Managers' commission.

Solution

CALCULATION OF CORRECT DEPARTMENTAL PROFITS AFTER CHARGING DEPARTMENTAL MANAGER'S COMMISSION

Particulars	*Deptt. X* (₹)	*Deptt. Y* (₹)	*Deptt. Z* (₹)
Profit after charging managers' commission	36,000	27,000	18,000
Add: Managers' commission (1/9)	4,000	3,000	2,000
Profit before commission & unrealised profit	40,000	30,000	20,000
Less: Unrealised profit on stock	(1,950)	(4,900)	(900)
Profit before Manager's Commission	38,050	25,100	19,100
Less: Commission of Departmental Managers @10%	(3,805)	(2,510)	(1,910)
Correct Departmental Profits	34,245	22,590	17,190

Working Note:

UNREALISED PROFIT ON STOCK

Particulars	*Department X* ₹	*Department Y* ₹	*Department Z* ₹	*Total* ₹
Unrealised Profit of Department *X*	—	1/6 of 7,200 = 1,200	15/115 of 5,750 = 750	1,950
Unrealised Profit of Department *Y*	10% of 19,000 = 1,900	—	20% of 15,000 = 3,000	4,900
Unrealised Profit of Department *Z*	15/115 of 4,600 = 600	1/11 of 3,300 = 300	—	900

SECTION C : CONTROL OF ACCOUNTING SYSTEMS

26 SELF BALANCING AND SECTIONAL BALANCING LEDGERS

SHORT ANSWER PRACTICAL PROBLEMS

SALES LEDGER CONTROL ACCOUNT

PROBLEM 1

From the following particulars, prepare Customers Control Account in General Ledger:

Opening Balance in Customers Ledger: (Dr)	2,35,000	Cash/Cheques Received	5,90,000
		Bills Received	1,10,000
Opening Balance in Customers Ledger: (Cr)	3,500	Discount Allowed	9,000
		Cheque Received Dishonoured	5,000
Goods Sold During the Year	7,65,000	Bills Received Dishonoured	7,000
Returns Inwards	15,000	Bad Debts	9,000

A debit of ₹ 1,500 is to be transferred from Customers Ledger to Suppliers Ledger. Similarly a credit entry of ₹ 1,600 is to be transferred from Suppliers Ledger to Customers Ledger. Closing credit balance in Customers Ledger is ₹ 3,000.

Solution

Dr. **CUSTOMERS' CONTROL ACCOUNT (IN GENERAL LEDGER)** *Cr.*

Particulars	₹	*Particulars*	₹
To Balance b/d	2,35,000	By Balance b/d	3,500
To General Ledger		By General Ledger Control A/c:	
Control A/c: Sales	7,65,000	Bank/Cash	5,90,000
Bills Receivable (Dishonoured)	7,000	Return Inwards	15,000
Bank (Cheques dishonoured)	5,000	Bills Receivable	1,10,000
To Balance c/d	3,000	Discount	9,000
		Bad Debts	9,000
		Transfer (₹ 1,500 + 1,600)	3,100
		By Balance c/d	2,75,400
	10,15,000		10,15,000

PROBLEM 2

The following transactions have been extracted from the books of Mr *X*. You are required to prepare the Sales Ledger Adjustment Account :

	₹		₹
Debtors balance on Mar 1	50,000	Returns from Debtors	6,000
Transactions during the period:		Bills receivable dishonoured	1,500
Sales (including cash sales		Bad Debts written off (after deducting	

of ₹ 20,000)	1,28,000	bad debts recovered ₹ 1,000)	4,000
Cash received from Debtors	90,000	Sundry charges debited to customers	600
Discount allowed to Debtors	500	Transfer to bought ledger	300
Acceptance received from Debtors	8,000		

Solution

Dr. **SALES LEDGER ADJUSTMENT ACCOUNT (IN GENERAL LEDGER)** Cr.

Date	*Particulars*	₹	*Date*	*Particulars*		₹
Mar 1	To Balance b/f	50,000	Mar 31	By General Ledger		
Mar 31	To General Ledger			Adjustment A/c:		
	Adjustment A/c:			Cash		90,000
	Credit Sales			Discount		500
	(1,28,000 –20,000)	1,08,000		Bills receivable		8,000
	Bills Receivable			Sales returns		6,000
	(Dishonoured)	1,500		Bad Debts	4,000	
	Sundry charges	600		*Add:* Recovery of		
				bad debts	1,000	5,000
				Transfer to bought ledger		300
			Mar 31	By Balance c/d		50,300
		1,60,100				1,60,100

PROBLEM 3

From the following information available from the books of a Trader from Jan1 to Mar 31, you are required to draw up the Debtors Ledger Adjustment Account in the General Ledger:

(a) Total sales amounted to ₹ 1,80,000 including the sale of old Zerox Machine for ₹ 4,800 (Book value ₹ 8,000). The total Cash sales were 80% less than the total Credit sales.

(b) Collections from debtors amounted to 70% of the aggregate of the opening debtors and Credit sales for the period. Debtors were allowed a cash discount of ₹ 20,000.

(c) Bills Receivable drawn during the three months totalled ₹ 30,000 of which bills amounting to ₹ 10,000 were endorsed in favour of suppliers. Out of the endorsed Bills, one bill for ₹ 6,000 was dishonored for non-payment as the party became insolvent, his estate realised nothing.

(d) Cheques received from customers ₹ 8,000 were dishonoured, a sum of ₹ 2,000 was irrecoverable, Bad Debt written off in the earlier years realised ₹ 11,000.

(e) Sundry Debtors as on Jan1 stood at ₹ 50,000.

Solution

Dr. **DEBTORS LEDGER ADJUSTMENT ACCOUNT (IN THE GENERAL LEDGER)** Cr.

Date	Particulars	₹	Date	Particulars	₹
Jan 1	To Balance b/d	50,000		By General ledger Adjustment A/c:	
	To General Ledger Adjustment A/c:			Cash & Bank [70% of (50,000 + 1,46,000)]	1,37,200
	Credit Sales	1,46,000		Discount allowed	20,000
	Dish. of Endorsed B/R	6,000		B/R drawn	30,000
	Dish. of Cheques	8,000		Bad Debts (Drawee of Endorsed B/R)	6,000
				Bad Debts (Drawer of Dist. Ch.)	2,000
			Mar 31	By Balance c/d	14,800
		2,10,000			2,10,000

PROBLEM 4

Prepare the Sales Ledger Control Account in General Ledger from the following particulars:

	₹
Debit balance as on Oct 1	3,75,000
Credit balance as on Oct 1	500
Credit Sales	10,00,000
Cheques received	11,25,000
Bills Receivable received	1,25,000
Discounts allowed	12,500
Sales returns	25,000
Transfer from Purchases to Sales Ledger	25,000
Bad Debts	5,000
Bad Debts previously written off now recovered	10,000
Reserve for Discounts	25,200
Bills Receivable dishonoured	12,500
Debit Balance as on Mar 31	75,000
Credit Balance as on Mar 31	?

Solution

Dr. **SALES LEDGER CONTROL ACCOUNT (IN GENERAL LEDGER)** Cr.

Date	Particulars	₹	Date	Particulars	₹
Oct 1	To Balance b/d	3,75,000	Oct 1	By Balance b/d	500
Oct 1	To General Ledger		Oct 1	By General Ledger	
to	Control A/c		to	Control A/c	
Mar 31	Sales	10,00,000	Mar 31	Bank	11,25,000
	Bills Receivable (dishonoured)	12,500		Bills receivable	1,25,000
				Discount	12,500
Mar 31	To Balance c/d	5,500		Sales return	25,000
	(Balancing figure)			Bad debts	5,000
				Transfer	25,000
			Mar 31	By Balance c/d (given)	75,000
		13,93,000			13,93,000

Note: Reserve for discounts and bad debts previously written off now recovered do not appear in debtors account and hence this will not figure in the sales ledger control account.

PROBLEM 5

Ujju Enterprise furnishes you the following information for the quarter Jan. to March. You are requested to draw up Debtors Ledger Adjustment account in the General Ledger:

(i) Total sales amounted to ₹ 2,20,000 including sale of old motor car for ₹ 10,000 (book value 5,000). Total credit sates were 80% higher than the cash sales.

(ii) Cash collection from debtors amounted to 60% of the aggregate of the opening debtors amounting to ₹ 40,000 and credit sales for the period. Debtors were allowed discount of ₹ 10,000.

(iii) Bills receivables drawn during the period totalled ₹ 20,000 of which one bill of ₹ 5,000 was dishonoured for non-payment as the party became insolvent and his estate realized 50 paise in a rupee.

(iv) A sum of ₹ 3,000 was written off as bad debts, ₹ 7,000 was realized against bad debts written off in earlier years and provision of ₹ 6,000 was made for doubtful debts.

Solution

Dr. **DEBTORS LEDGER ADJUSTMENT ACCOUNT IN THE GENERAL LEDGER** Cr.

Date	Particulars	₹	Date	Particulars	₹
Jan. 1	To Balance b/d	40,000	Jan – Mar	By General Ledger	
				Adj. A/c:	
Jan – Mar	To General.			Collection from	1,05,000
	Ledger Adj A/c:			Debtors-bank [60% of	
	Sales	1,35,000		(40,000 + 1,35,000)]	

	Bills Receivables dishonoured	5,000		Discount allowed Bills Receivables Bad debts (₹ 2,500 + 3,000)	10,000 20,000 5,500
			31st Mar	By Balance c/d	39,500
		1,80,000			1,80,000

Note: No entries are to be made:

(a) For 7,000 realised against bad debts written off in earlier years, and

(b) For provision of 6,000 made for doubtful debts.

Working Notes:

Credit Sales = (2,20,000 – 10,000) – (2,10,000 × 100/280) = ₹ 1,35,000

PROBLEM 6

On 1st October, the debit balances of debtors account is ₹ 77,500 in the books of M/s Zee Ltd. Transactions during the 6 months ended on 31st March were as follows:

Particulars	₹
Total sales (including cash sales ₹ 14,000)	84,000
Payment received from debtors in cash	38,000
Bills receivable received	26,000
Bills Receivable dishonored (noting charges ₹ 250)	8,500
Bills Receivable endorsed to suppliers	5,000
Discount allowed to customers for prompt payment	1,000
Goods rejected and returned back by the customer	2,550
Bad debts recovered (written off in previous year)	900
Interest debited for delay in payment	1,250

You are required to prepare a Debtors Account for the period ending 31st March in the General of M/s Zee Ltd.

Solution

Dr. **TOTAL DEBTORS ACCOUNT IN THE GENERAL LEDGER OF M/S ZEE LTD.** *Cr.*

Date	*Particulars*	₹	*Date*	*Particulars*	₹
1st Oct.	To Balance c/d	77,500	Oct – Mar	By General Ledger Adjustment A/c:	
Oct – Mar	To General Ledger Adjustment A/c			Cash collected	38,000
	Sales (84,000 – 14,000)	70,000		Bills Receivable A/c	26,000
	Bills receivable			Discount allowed	1,000
	(Bill dishonored)	8,500		Sales returns	2,550
	Bank (Noting charges)	250	31st Mar	By Balance c/d	89,950
	Interest	1,250			
		1,57,500			1,57,500

Working Notes:

(i) Bad debts recovered will not appear in the Total Debtors account since these will be credited to Profit & Loss Account.

(ii) Bills Receivables of ₹ 5,000 endorsed to the supplier will not be shown in the Total Debtors account because at the time of endorsement Supplier's account will be debited and Bills receivable account will be credited.

SALES LEDGER CONTROL ACCOUNT AND PURCHASE LEDGER CONTROL ACCOUNT

PROBLEM 7

Prepare the Sales Ledger Control Account and Purchase Ledger Control Account from the following particulars:

Particulars	*Sales Ledger* ₹	*Purchase Ledger* ₹
Debit balance as on Oct 1	1,50,000	1,000
Credit balance as on Oct 1	200	1,25,000
Credit sales and purchases	4,00,000	3,80,000
Cheque received and paid	4,50,000	3,50,000
Advance paid to creditors	—	20,000
B/R received and B/P accepted	50,000	50,000
Discount allowed and received	5,000	3,000
Returns	10,000	5,000
Transfer from Purchases Ledger to Sales Ledger	10,000	10,000
Bad Debts	2,000	
Reserve for discounts	10,000	5,000
B/R and B/P dishonoured	5,000	5,000
Debit Balances as on Mar 31	30,000	?
Credit Balances as on Mar 31	?	72,000

Solution

Dr. **SALES LEDGER CONTROL ACCOUNT (IN GENERAL LEDGER)** *Cr.*

Date	*Particulars*	₹	*Date*	*Particulars*	₹
Oct 1	To Balance b/d	1,50,000	Oct 1	By Balance b/d	200
	To General Ledger			By General Ledger	
	Adjustment A/c:			Adjustment A/c:	
	Sales	4,00,000		Bank	4,50,000
	B/R (dishonoured)	5,000		B/R received	50,000
Mar 31	To Balance c/d	2,200		Discount	5,000
				Returns	10,000
				Bad debts	2,000
				Transfer from	
				Purchases Ledger	10,000
			Mar 31	By Balance c/d	30,000
		5,57,200			5,57,200
Apr 1	To Balance b/d	30,000	Apr 1	By Balance b/d	2,200

Dr. **PURCHASES LEDGER CONTROL ACCOUNT (IN GENERAL LEDGER)** *Cr.*

Date	*Particulars*	₹	*Date*	*Particulars*	₹
Oct 1	To Balance b/d	1,000	Oct 1	By Balance b/d	1,25,000
	To General Ledger Adjustment A/c:			By General Ledger Adjustment A/c:	
	Bank (Cheque paid)	3,50,000		Purchases	3,80,000
	Bank (Advance paid)	20,000		B/P (dishonoured)	5,000
	Bills Payable (accepted)	50,000	Mar 31	By Balance c/d	1,000
	Discount	3,000			
	Returns	5,000			
	Transfer to Sales Ledger	10,000			
Mar 31	To Balance c/d	72,000			
		5,11,000			5,11,000
Apr 1	To Balance b/d	1,000	Apr 1	By Balance b/d	72,000

PROBLEM 8

From the following information, prepare Sales Ledger Adjustment Account and Bought Ledger Adjustment Account in the General Ledger:

On Apr 1, Balances in Bought Ledger: Debit ₹ 10,000, Credit ₹ 96,000, Balances in Sales Ledger: Debit ₹ 1,41,880, Credit ₹ 2,240:

	₹		₹
Purchases	5,40,000	Discount received	7,200
Purchases returns	20,000	Bills receivable received	40,000
Total sales	7,68,000	Bills payable issued	22,400
Cash sales	40,000	Provision for doubtful debts	9,160
Sales returns	10,000	Cash paid to customers	1,840
Cash received from customers	6,24,000	Bills receivable dishonoured	6,000
Discount allowed	11,200	Bought Ledger Balance (Dr.)	10,400
Cash Paid to suppliers	4,80,000	Sales ledger Balance (Dr.)	1,83,200
Transfer from Sales Ledger to Bought Ledger	20,800		

Solution

Dr. **SALES LEDGER ADJUSTMENT ACCOUNT (IN GENERAL LEDGER)** Cr.

Date	Particulars	₹	Date	Particulars	₹
Apr 1	To Balance b/d	1,41,880	Apr 1	By Balance b/d	2,240
	To General Ledger Adjustment A/c:			By General Ledger Adjustment A/c:	
	Sales	7,28,000		Cash	6,24,000
	B/R dishonoured	6,000		B/R Received	40,000
	Cash paid	1,840		Discount	11,200
Mar 31	To Balance c/d	13,720		Returns	10,000
				Transfer to Bought Ledger	20,800
			Mar 31	By Balance c/d	1,83,200
		8,91,440			8,91,440
Apr 1	To Balance b/d	1,83,200	Apr 1	By Balance b/d	13,720

Dr. **BOUGHT LEDGER ADJUSTMENT ACCOUNT (IN GENERAL LEDGER)** Cr.

Date	Particulars	₹	Date	Particulars	₹
Apr 1	To Balance b/d	10,000	Apr 1	By Balance b/d	96,000
	To General Ledger Adjustment A/c:			By General Ledger Adjustment A/c:	
	Cash paid	4,80,000		Purchases	5,40,000
	Bills Payable (accepted)	22,400	Mar 31	By Balance c/d	10,400
	Discount	7,200			
	Returns	20,000			
	Transfer from Sales Ledger	20,800			
Mar 31	To Balance c/d	86,000			
		6,46,400			6,46,400
Apr 1	To Balance b/d	10,400	Apr 1	By Balance b/d	86,000

Notes:

(i) Credit Sales = Total Sales – Cash Sales = ₹ 7,68,000 – ₹ 40,000 = ₹ 7,28,000.

(ii) Provision for doubtful debts and cash sales are not considered.

(iii) Assumed that sales returns are out of credit sales.

PROBLEM 9

The following information is extracted from a set of books for the half-year ended 30th June:

	₹		₹
Sales	5,63,000	Cash paid to Creditors	1,80,000
Purchases	3,22,000	Bills Receivable Received	1,60,000
Returns Outward	7,600	Discount Received	4,200
Cash Received from Debtors	1,84,200	Bad Debts written off	12,000
Bills Payable Accepted	1,20,000	Discount Allowed	10,800
Returns Inward	16,800	Transfer from Purchases Ledger	6,800

The total of the Sales Ledger balances on 1st Jan, was ₹ 3,20,800 and that of the Purchases Ledger balances on the same date was ₹ 1,86,400.

Prepare Sales Ledger and Purchases Ledger Adjustment Account from the foregoing information.

Solution

Dr. **SALES LEDGER ADJUSTMENT ACCOUNT (IN GENERAL LEDGER)** Cr.

Date	*Particulars*	₹	*Date*	*Particulars*	₹
Jan. 1	To Balance b/d	3,20,800	June 30	By General Ledger	
June 30	To General Ledger			Adjustment A/c:	
	Adjustment A/c:			Cash	1,84,200
	Sales	5,63,000		Returns Inward	16,800
				Bills Receivable	1,60,000
				Bad Debts	12,000
				Discounts Allowed	10,800
				Transfer	6,800
			June 30	By Balance c/d	4,93,200
		8,83,800			8,83,800

Dr. **PURCHASES LEDGER ADJUSTMENT ACCOUNT (IN GENERAL LEDGER)** *Cr.*

Date	*Particulars*	₹	*Date*	*Particulars*	₹
June 30	To General Ledger		Jan 1	By Balance b/d	1,86,400
	Adjustment A/c:		June 30	By General Ledger	
	Cash	1,80,000		Adjustment A/c:	
	Returns Outward	7,600		Purchases	3,22,000
	Bills Payable	1,20,000			
	Discount Received	4,200			
	Transfers	6,800			
June 30	To Balance c/d	1,89,800			
		5,08,400			5,08,400

PROBLEM 10

The following information is extracted from the books of Shri Hari for the year ended 31st March, :

	₹
Sales	3,80,800
Purchases	3,26,000
Return outward	14,000
Cash received from debtors	1,78,200
Bills payable accepted	1,22,000
Returns inward	17,600
Cash paid to creditors	1,86,000
Bills receivable received	1,36,000
Discount received	4,000
Bad debts written off	24,000
Reserve for discount to debtors	2,000
Discount allowed	1,800
Transfers from purchases ledger	26,600

The total of the Sales Ledger balances on 1st April, was ₹ 90,600 and that of the Purchases Ledger balances on the same date was ₹ 78,600.

Required: Prepare Sales Ledger and Purchases Ledger Adjustment Accounts from the above information.

Solution

Dr. **SALES LEDGER ADJUSTMENT ACCOUNT** *Cr.*

Date	*Particulars*	₹	*Date*	*Particulars*	₹
Apr 1	To Balance b/d	90,600	Apr 1	By General Ledger	
Apr 1	To General Ledger		to	Adjustment Account:	
to	Adjustment A/c:		Mar 31	Cash	1,78,200
Mar 31	Sales	3,80,800		Returns Inward	17,600
				Bills Receivable	1,36,000
				Bad debts written off	24,000
				Discount allowed	1,800
				Transfer from	
				Purchase Ledger	26,600
			Mar 31	By Balance c/d	87,200
		4,71,400			4,71,400

Dr. **PURCHASE LEDGER ADJUSTMENT ACCOUNT** *Cr.*

Date	Particulars	₹	Date	Particulars	₹
Apr 1	To General Ledger		Apr 1	By Balance b/d	78,600
to	Adjustment A/c:		Apr 1	By General Ledger	
Mar 31	Cash	1,86,000	to	Adjustment A/c:	
	Returns outward	14,000	Mar 31	Purchases	3,26,000
	Bills payable	1,22,000			
	Discount received	4,000			
	Transfer to Sales Ledger	26,600			
Mar 31	To Balance c/d	52,000			
		4,04,600			4,04,600

PROBLEM 11

From the following information prepare the necessary adjustment accounts as they would appear in the General Ledger of Vatika Ltd.

	₹
Closing debtors balance (as per General Ledger Adjustment A/c)	60,000 (Cr.)
Credit sales	40,000
Credit purchases	15,000
Paid to creditors	7,500
Discount allowed	1,500
Bills payable accepted	5,000
Discount received	500
Received from debtors	20,000
Bad debts	5,000
Closing creditors balance (as per General Ledger Adjustment A/c)	30,000 (Dr.)
Bill accepted by customers	3,000

Discount allowed to debtors ₹ 500 was recorded as discount received from creditors.

Solution

Dr. **DEBTORS' LEDGER ADJUSTMENT ACCOUNT IN GENERAL LEDGER** Cr.

Particulars	₹	*Particulars*	₹
To Balance b/d (*balancing figure*)	49,500	By General Ledger Adjustment A/c:	
To General Ledger Adjustment A/c:		Cash from debtors	20,000
Credit sales	40,000	Bills receivable	3,000
		Bad debts	5,000
		Discount allowed (1,500 + 500)	2,000
		By Balance c/d (60,000 – 500)	59,500
	89,500		89,500

Dr. **CREDITORS' LEDGER ADJUSTMENT ACCOUNT** Cr.

Particulars	₹	*Particulars*	₹
To General ledger		By Balance b/d (balancing figure)	28,000
Adjustment account:		By General ledger adjustment	
Cash paid to credir	7,500	account: credit purchases	15,000
Bills payable	5,000		
To Balance c/d (30,000 + 500)	30,500		
	43,000		43,000

PROBLEM 12

From the following particulars as provided by Mis. Thirumala & Co., prepare Debtors Ledger Adjustment Ale and Creditors Ledger Adjustment Ale in General Ledger for the year ending 31st March:

	₹
Opening balance as on 1st April of sundry debtors	2,40,000
Opening balance as on 1st April of sundry creditors	2,77,500
Cash purchases	3,66,300
Credit purchases	14,65,200
Cash sales	4,22,400
Credit Sales	16,89,600
Cash paid to creditors	11,18,100
Bills payable accepted	3,50,900
Discount allowed by creditors	4,800
Sundry charges debited by creditors	7,200
Cash received from debtors	12,17,300
Bills receivable received	4,17,700
Discount allowed to debtors	7,750
Bad debts	6,700
Bad debts recovered, written off during earlier financial year	12,800
Provision for doubtful debts	38,500
Returns inward	13,150
Returns outward	9,000

[Nov. 2011]

Solution

DEBTORS LEDGER ADJUSTMENT ACCOUNT IN THE GENERAL LEDGER

Dr. *for the year ending 31st March, ...* *Cr.*

Date	Particulars	₹	Date	Particulars	₹
1st April	To Balance b/d	2,40,000	Apr – Mar	By General ledger	
Apr – Mar	To General ledger			– Adjustment A/c	
	Adjustment A/c:			– Cash	12,17,300
	– Credit sales	16,89,600		– Bills Receivable	4,17,700
				– Discount	7,750
				– Returns inward	13,150
				– Bad debts	6,700
			31st Mar	By Balance c/d	2,67,000
		19,29,600			19,29,600

Dr. **CREDITORS' LEDGER ADJUSTMENT ACCOUNT** *Cr.*

Date	Particulars	₹	Date	Particulars	₹
Apr – Mar	To General ledger		1st April	By Balance b/d	2,77,500
	Adjustment A/c:		Apr – Mar	By General ledger	
	– Cash	11,18,100		Adjustment A/c:	
	– Bills payable	3,50,900		Credit purchases	14,65,200
	– Discount	4,800		Sundry charges	7,200
	– Returns outward	9,000			
31st Mar	To Balance c/d	2,67,100			
		17,49,900			17,49,900

Note: Following should not be entered either in the Debtors Ledger Adjustment account or Creditors Ledger Adjustment account:

1. Cash purchases
2. Cash sales
3. Bad debts recovered, written off during earlier financial year
4. Provision for doubtful debts.

GENERAL LEDGER ADJUSTMENT ACCOUNTS

PROBLEM 8.13

From the following information, prepare Sales Ledger Adjustment A/c in the General Ledger:

On Apr 1: Balance in Sales Ledger	(DR) ₹ 1,41,880
	(CR) ₹ 2,240
On Mar 31	₹
Total Sales	7,68,000
Cash Sales	40,000
Sales Return	10,000
Cash received from customers	6,24,000

Discount allowed	11,200
Cash paid to supplier	4,80,000
Transfer from sales to bought ledger	20,800
Discount received	7,200
B/R received	40,000
Reserve for doubtful debts	9,160
Cash paid to customer	1,840
Bill received dishonoured	6,000
Sales Ledger Balance (DR)	1,81,200
Sales Ledger Balance (CR)	13,720

Solution

Dr. **GENERAL LEDGER SALES LEDGER ADJUSTMENT ACCOUNT** Cr.

Date	*Particulars*	₹	*Date*	*Particulars*	₹
Apr 1	To Balance b/d	1,41,880	Apr 1	By Balance b/d	2,240
Mar31	To General Ledger Adjustment A/c in Sales Ledger:		Mar31	By General Ledger Adjustment A/c in Sales Ledger:	
	Credit sales	7,28,000		Cash	6,24,000
	Cash paid	1,840		Discount allowed	11,200
	Bills receivable (dishonoured)	6,000		Transfers	20,800
	To Balance c/d	13,720		Bills Receivable received	40,000
				Sales Return	10,000
				By Balance c/d	1,83,200
		8,91,440			8,91,440

Note: *In the question paper the Sales Ledger Balance (DR) was wrongly printed as ₹ 1,81,200. The question has been rectified and solved accordingly.*

PROBLEM 14

Gupta Traders keep their ledgers on the self balancing system. They provide you the following information for the year ended 31st March.

Opening Debtors balance on 1st April	1,37,250
Credit sales	68,100
Returns inward	1,200
Returns outward	1,800
Cash received from customers	76,800
Discount received	2,010
Acceptances received	25,500
Bills receivable dishonoured	3,600
Bad debts written off	7,500

You are required to prepare General Ledger Adjustment A/c in Sales Ledger of Gupta Traders.

Solution

IN THE BOOKS OF GUPTA TRADERS

Dr. **GENERAL LEDGER ADJUSTMENT A/C IN THE SALES LEDGER** Cr.

Date	Particulars	₹	Date	Particulars	₹
Apr – Mar	To Sales Ledger Adjustment A/c (in General Ledger):		1 April	By Balance b/d	1,37,250
	Returns inward	1,200	Apr – Mar	By Sales Ledger Adjustment Account (in General Ledger):	
	Cash (received from customers)	76,800		Sales	68,100
	Bills receivables	25,500		B/R dishonoured	3,600
	Bad debts	7,500			
31st March	To Balance c/d	97,950			
		2,08,950			2,08,950

Note: Returns outward and discount received would be shown in the General Ledger Adjustment Account of Purchases Ledger.

PROBLEM 15

A business concern maintains self-balancing ledgers. On the basis of following information prepare General Ledger Adjustment Account in Debtors Ledger for month of April.

	(₹)
Debit balances in Debtors Ledger on 1st April	3,58,200
Credit balances in Debtors Ledger on 1st April	9,400
Transactions during the month of April are:	
Total Sales (including Cash Sales, ₹ 1,00,000)	20,95,400
Sales Returns	33,100
Cash received from credit customers	17,25,700
Bills Receivable received from customers	95,000
Bill Receivable dishonoured	7,500
Cash paid to customers for returns	6,000
Transfers to Creditors Ledger	16,000
Credit balances in Debtors Ledger on 30th April	9,800

Solution

GENERAL LEDGER ADJUSTMENT ACCOUNT IN DEBTORS LEDGER

Date	Particulars	₹	Date	Particulars	₹
Ist Apr.	To Balance b/d	9,400	1st Apr	By balance b/d	3,58,200
April	To Debtors Ledger Adjustment A/c		April	By Debtors Adnjustment A/c	
	Cash received	17,25,700		Credit sales	19,95,400

	Sales Return	33,100		Sales returns	6,000
	Bill receivable received	95,000		Bills receivable dishonoured	7,500
	Transfer to Creditors Ledger	16,000	30th Apr	By Balance c/d	9,800
30th Apr	To Balanced c/d (bal. fig.	4,97,700			
		23,76,900			23,76,900

PROBLEM 16

Prepare the General Ledger Adjustment Accounts as will appear in the Debtors' and Creditors' Ledger, from the information given below:

Balance on Apr 1

	Dr. (₹)	*Cr. (₹)*
Debtors' Ledger	47,200	240
Creditors' Ledger	280	26,300
Transactions for the year ended Mar 31		

	₹		₹
Total Sales	1,20,100	Bills Accepted by Customers	20,100
Cash Sales	8,100	Bills Receivables Dishonoured	1,500
Total Purchases	89,500	Bills Receivables Discounted	5,000
Credit Purchases	67,000	Bills Receivables Endorsed to Creditors	4,000
Creditors paid off (in Full Settlement of ₹ 40,000)	39,500	Endorsed Bills Dishonoured	1,000
Received from Debtors (in Full Settlement of ₹ 59,000)	58,200	Bad-debts Written off (after Deducting Bad-debts Recovered ₹ 300)	2,200
Returns from Debtors	2,600	Provision for Doubtful Debts	550
Returns to Creditors	1,800	Transfer from Debtors' Ledger to Creditors' Ledger	1,100
Bills Accepted for Creditors	5,500	Transfer from Creditors' Ledger to Debtors' Ledger	1,900
Bills Payable Matured	8,000		

Balance on Mar 31

Debtors' Ledger (Cr.) ₹ 380

Creditors' Ledger (Dr.) ₹ 420

Solution

Dr. **GENERAL LEDGER ADJUSTMENT ACCOUNT (IN DEBTORS LEDGER)** *Cr.*

Date	*Particulars*	₹	*Date*	*Particulars*	₹
Apr 1	To Balance b/d (Advances from customers)	240	Apr 1	By Balance b/d (Dues from Customers)	47,200
Mar 31	To Debtors Ledger Adjustment A/c:		Mar 31	By Debtors Ledger Adjustment A/c:	
	Cash (Received)	58,200		Credit Sales	1,12,000
	B/R (Drawn)	20,100		B/R (Dishonoured)	1,500
	Returns inwards	2,600		Endrosed B/R	

Particulars	₹	Particulars	₹
Discount allowed	800	Dishonoured	1,000
Bad Debt w/o [₹ 2,200 + ₹ 300]	2,500	To Balance c/d (Advances from Customers at the End)	380
Transfer to Purchase Ledger	1,100		
Transfer from Purchase Ledger	1,900		
To Balance c/d (Dues from Customers at the End)	74,640		
	1,62,080		1,62,080

Note: *Provision for Doubtful Debts and Bad Debts recovered not affect the aforesaid account since these items directly relate to Profit & Loss Account.*

Dr. **GENERAL LEDGER ADJUSTMENT ACCOUNT (IN CREDITORS' LEDGER)** *Cr.*

Date	*Particulars*	*₹*	*Date*	*Particulars*	*₹*
Apr 1	To Balance b/d (Due to Suppliers)	26,300	Apr 1	By Balance b/d (Advances to Suppliers)	280
Mar 31	To Creditors Ledger Adjustment A/c:		Mar 31	By Creditors Ledger Adjustment A/c:	
	Credit Purchases	67,000		Cash (Paid)	39,500
	Endorsed B/R (Dishonoured)	1,000		B/P Accepted	5,500
	To Balance c/d	420		B/R (Endorsed)	4,000
				Returns outwards	1,800
				Discount received	500
				Transfer from Sales Ledger	1,100
				Transfer to Sales Ledger	1,900
				By Balance c/d	40,140
		94,720			94,720

DEBTORS' LEDGER ADJUSTMENT A/C IN THE GENERAL LEDGER AND GENERAL LEDGER ADJUSTMENT A/C IN THE CREDITORS LEDGER

PROBLEM 17

From the following balances extracted from the books of Mr. Laxman, prepare Debtors' Ledger Adjustment A/c in the General Ledger and General Ledger Adjustment A/c in the Creditors Ledger:

Particulars	₹	*Particulars*	₹
Opening Balances: 1st April:		Bills payable accepted	70,000
Debtors' Ledger (Dr.)	2,80,000	Cash sales	1,00,000
Creditors' Ledger (Cr.)	3,40,000	Sundry charges debited to customers	1,200
Transactors during the year:		Allowances from creditors	3,200
Credit purchases	1,25,000	Bills payable dishonoured	16,000
Cash received from customers	1,54,000	Discount received by debtors	2,600
Cash paid to suppliers	1,84,000	Cash purchases	60,000
Returns from customers	6,000	Bills receivable dishonoured	4,000
Returns to suppliers	2,000	Bad debts received	1,000
Discount received	3,600	Transfer from Bought Ledger to Sales Ledger	3,200
Bad debts written off	14,000	Bills receivable discounted	5,000
Acceptances received from customers	51,000		

Solution

Dr. **DEBTORS' LEDGER ADJUSTMENT A/C IN THE GENERAL LEDGER** *Cr.*

Date	*Particulars*	₹	*Date*	*Particulars*	₹
1st April	To Balance b/f	2,80,000		By General Ledger Adjustment A/c	
	To General Ledger Adjustment A/c			Cash received	1,54,000
	Sundry charges	1,200		Returns inward	6,000
	Bills Receivable dishonoured	4,000		Bad debts written off	14,000
				Bills Receivable received	51,000
				Discount allowed	2,600
				Transfer from bought ledger	3,200
			31st March	By Balance c/f	54,400
		2,85,200			2,85,200

Dr. **GENERAL LEDGER ADJUSTMENT A/C IN THE CREDITORS' LEDGER** Cr.

Date	Particulars	₹	Date	Particulars	₹
1st April	To Balance b/f	3,40,000		By General Ledger Adjustment A/c	
	To General Ledger Adjustment A/c			Cash paid	1,84,000
	Purchases (Credit)	1,25,000		Returns outward	2,000
	Bills Payable dishonoured	16,000		Discount allowed	3,600
				Bills Payable	70,000
				Allowances	3,200
				Transfer to sales ledger	3,200
			31st March	By Balance c/f	2,15,000
		4,81,000			4,81,000

Notes:

(i) Debtors and creditors balances will not be affected by cash sales or cash purchases respectively and hence they are ignored.

(ii) Bills receivable discounted will not affect debtors balance, hence ignored.

(iii) Bad debts recovered will not affect both the ledgers, hence ignored.

PROBLEM 18

From the following prepare General Ledger Adjustment account in Debtors Ledger and Debtors Ledger Adjustment in General Ledger:

	₹
Balance as on 1st April	
Debit balances in Debtors Ledger	2,46,200
Credit balances in Debtors Ledger	3,400
Transactions during the month of April,	
Credit Sales	9,74,900
Sales Returns	21,700
Cash received from debtors	8,62,100
Discount allowed to debtors	39,200
Bills receivable received from debtors	51,200
Bills receivable dishonoured	3,500
Bills payable given to suppliers	27,000
Credit balance in Debtors ledger on 30th April	5,200

Solution

Dr. **GENERAL LEDGER ADJUSTMENT ACCOUNT IN DEBTORS LEDGER** Cr.

Date	Particulars	₹	Date	Particulars	₹
1st April	To Balance b/d	3,400	1st April	By Balance b/d	2,46,200
	To Debtors Ledger Adjustment A/c:			By Debtors Ledger Adjustment A/c:	
	Sales Returns	21,700		Sales	9,74,900
	Cash received	8,62,100		B/R dishonoured	3,500
	Discount allowed	39,200			
	B/R received	51,200			
30th April	To Balance c/d (b.f.)	2,52,200	30th April	By Balance c/d	5,200
		12,29,800			12,29,800

Dr. **DEBTORS LEDGER ADJUSTMENT ACCOUNT IN GENERAL LEDGER** Cr.

Date	Particulars	₹	Date	Particulars	₹
1st April	To Balance b/d	2,46,200	1st April	By Balance b/d	3,400
	To General Ledger Adjustment A/c:			By General Ledger Adjustment A/c:	
	Sales	9,74,900		Sales return	21,700
	B/R dishonoured	3,500		Cash received	8,62,100
30th April	To Balance c/d	5,200		Discount allowed	39,200
				B/R received	51,200
			30th April	By Balance c/d (b.f.)	2,52,200
		12,29,800			12,29,800

TOTAL DEBTORS ACCOUNT

PROBLEM 19

From the following information furnished by X & Co., prepare Total Debtors Account.

Transactions for the month of March	₹
(i) Sales (includes cash sales of ₹ 7,000)	68,000
(ii) Collections from debtors (cash)	57,000
(iii) Discount allowed	2,000
(iv) Bad debts written off	1,500
(v) Cheques received	10,000
(vi) Cheques dishonoured	2,000
(vii) Return inward	700

(viii) Bad debts written off- now recovered	500
(ix) Provision for doubtful debts	1,200
(x) Balance outstanding on 1st March (Receivables)	20,000

Solution

Dr. **TOTAL DEBTORS ACCOUNT** *Cr.*

Particulars	₹	*Particulars*	₹
To Balance b/d	20,000	By Discount allowed	2,000
To Sales	61,000	By Bank A/c	10,000
To Bank A/c (Cheques dishonoured)	2,000	By Cash A/c	57,000
		By Bad Debts A/c	1,500
		By Sales Returns A/c	700
		By Balance c/d	11,800
	83,000		83,000

PROBLEM 20

M/s. Big Systematic Ltd. maintains self-balancing ledgers preparing control accounts at the end of each calendar month.

On 3rd January, 2015 the accountant of the company located the following errors in the books of account:

(i) An amount of ₹ 8,700 received from customer Mehra was credited to Mehtra, another customer.

(ii) The sales book for December, 2014 was undercast by ₹ 1,000.

(iii) Goods invoiced at ₹ 15,600 were returned to supplier, M/s Mega Ltd., but no entry was made in the books for this return made on 28th December, 2014.

Pass the necessary Journal entries to rectify the above mentioned errors.

Solution

Date	*Particulars*		*L.F.*	*(₹)*	*(₹)*
(i)	Mehta (In Sales/Debtors Ledger)	Dr.		8,700	
	To Mehra (In Sales/Debtors Ledger)				8,700
	(Being amount received from Mehra was wrongly credited to Mehta, now rectified)				
(ii)	(a) Suspense A/c (In Sales/Debtors Ledger)	Dr.		1,000	
	To Sales A/c (In General Ledger)				1,000
	(b) Sales/Debtors Ledger Adjustment A/c (In General Ledger)	Dr.		1,000	
	To General Ledger Adjustment A/c (In Sales/Debtors Ledger)				1,000
	(Being rectification of the error resulting from under casting of the Sales Book)				

(iii) (a) M/s. Mega Ltd. A/c (In Creditors/Bought Ledger) Dr.		15,600	
To Purchase Returns A/c (In General Ledger)			15,600
(b) Creditors/Bought Ledger Adjustment A/c Dr. (In General Ledger)		15,600	
To General Ledger Adjustment A/c (In Creditors/Bought Ledger)			15,600
(Being goods returned to supplier not recorded earlier, now recorded)			

PROBLEM 20

From the following particulars, prepare the Creditors' Ledger Adjustment Account as would appear in the General Ledger of Mr. Sathish for the month of March .

Date	*Particulars*
1.	Purchased from Mr. Akash ₹ 7,500.
3	Paid ₹ 3,000 after adjusting the initial advance in full to Mr. Akash.
10	Paid ₹ 2,500 to Mr. dev towards the purchases made in February in full.
12	Paid advance to Mr. Giridhar ₹ 6,000.
14	Purchased goods from Mr. Akash ₹ 6,200
20	Returned goods worth ₹ 1,000 to Mr. Akash
24	Settled the balance due to Mr. Akash at a discount of 5%.
26	Goods purchased from Mr. Giridhar against the advance paid already.
29	Purchased from Mr. Nathan ₹ 3,500
30	Goods returned to Mr. Prem ₹ 1,200. The goods were originally purchased for cash in the month of February .

Solution

Dr. **CREDITORS LEDGER ADJUSTMENT ACCOUNT IN GENERAL LEDGER** Cr.

Date	*Particulars*	₹	*Date*	*Particulars*	₹
Apr 1	To Balance b/d	4,500	Apr 1	By Balance b/d	2,500
Mar 31	To General Ledger Adjustment A/c:		Mar 31	By General Ledger Adjustment A/c:	
	Cash paid	16,440		Purchases	23,200
	{3,000 + 2,500 + 6,000 + 4,940 (5,200 – 5%)}			(7,500 + 6,200 + 6,000 + 3,500)	
	Returns	1,000			
	Discount (5,200 × 5%)	260			
Mar 31	To Balance c/d	3,500	Mar 31	By Balance c/d	—
		25,700			25,700

SECTION D : ACCOUNTING IN SERVICE SECTOR

27 AS 9 – REVENUE RECOGNITION

THEORETICAL BASE

QUESTION 1: State the Revenues with which AS – 9 deals.

ANSWER:

AS 9 deals with the basis for recognition of revenue arising in the course of the ordinary activities of the enterprise from:

1. the sale of goods,
2. the rendering of services, and
3. the use by others of enterprise resources yielding interest, royalties and dividends

QUESTION 2: State the Revenues with which AS – 9 does not deal.

ANSWER:

1. Revenue arising from construction contracts;
2. Revenue arising from hire-purchase, lease agreements;
3. Revenue arising from government grants and other similar subsidies;
4. Revenue of insurance companies arising from insurance contracts.

QUESTION 3: Define the term ' Revenue'as per AS – 9.

ANSWER:

Revenue is the gross inflow of cash, receivables or other consideration arising in the course of the ordinary activities of an enterprise from:

1. the sale of goods,
2. the rendering of services, and
3. the use by others of enterprise resources yielding interest, royalties and dividends

Note: *In an agency relationship, the revenue is the amount of commission and the not the gross inflow of cash, receivables or other consideration.*

QUESTION 4: State the Items not included in the term 'Revenue'.

ANSWER:

1. Realized gains resulting from the disposal of, and unrealized gains resulting from the holding of, non-current assets e.g. appreciation in the value of fixed assets;
2. Unrealized holding gains resulting from the change in value of current assets, and the natural increases in herds and agricultural and forest products;
3. Realized or unrealized gains resulting from changes in foreign exchange rates and adjustments arising on the translation of foreign currency financial statements;
4. Realized gains resulting from the discharge of an obligation at less than its carrying amount;
5. Unrealized gains resulting from the restatement of the carrying amount of an obligation.

QUESTION 5: State the Meaning of Revenue Recognition.

ANSWER:

Revenue recognition means identifying the revenues for a particular accounting period. Revenue recognition is mainly concerned with the timing of recognition of revenue in the Statement of Profit and Loss of an enterprise.

QUESTION 6: When should revenue from sale of goods be recognized?

ANSWER:

Revenue from sale of goods should be recognized when:

1. The seller of goods has transferred to the buyer the property in the goods for a price or all significant risks and rewards of ownership have been transferred to the buyer and the seller retains no effective control of the goods transferred to a degree usually associated with ownership;
2. No significant uncertainty exists regarding the amount of the consideration that will be derived from the sale of goods.
3. At the time of performance it is reasonable to expect ultimate collection (i.e. there is a reasonable certainty of ultimate collection).

QUESTION 7: When should revenue from service transactions be recognized?

ANSWER:

Revenue from service transactions should be recognized when

1. No significant uncertainty exists regarding the amount of the consideration that will be derived from the rendering the service.
2. At the time of performance it is reasonable to expect ultimate collection.

QUESTION 8: When and on what basis should revenue from from Interest, Royalties and Dividends be recognized?

ANSWER:

WHEN SHOULD REVENUE BE RECOGNIZED?

Revenue arising from the use by others of enterprise resources yielding interest, royalties and dividends should only be recognized **when no significant uncertainty as to measurability or collectability exists.**

BASIS OF REVENUE RECOGNISION

Cases	Basis of Revenue Recognision
(i) Interest	**On a time proportion basis** taking into account the amount outstanding and the rate applicable.
(ii) Royalties	**On an accrual basis** in accordance with the terms of the relevant agreement.
(iii) Dividends from	When the owner's **right to receive** investment in payment is **established** (i.e. the Date of declaration of Final Dividend & ate of Payment of Interim Dividend)

Notes:

(i) Revenue arising from the use by others of enterprise resources yielding interest, royalties and dividends should only be recognized when no significant uncertainty as to measurability or collectability exists.

(ii) When interest, royalties and dividends from foreign countries require exchange permission and uncertainty in remittance is anticipated, revenue recognition may need to be postponed.

QUESTION 9: How should uncertainties about revenue recognition be treated?

ANSWER:

(i) ***Where the ability to assess the ultimate collection with reasonable certainty is lacking at the time of raising any claim, e.g., for escalation of price, export incentives, interest etc.***	Revenue recognition is **postponed** to the extent of uncertainty involved. In such cases, it may be appropriate to recognize revenue only when it is reasonably certain that the ultimate collection will be made. However, where there is no uncertainty as to ultimate collection, revenue is recognized at the time of sale or rendering of service even though payments are made by installments.
(ii) ***When the uncertainty relating to collectability arises subsequent to the time of sale or the rendering of the service***	A separate provision to reflect the uncertainty rather than to adjust the amount of revenue originally recorded.
(iii) ***Where consideration receivable for the sale of goods, the rendering of services or from the use by others of enterprise resources is not reasonably determinable.***	Recognition of revenue is postponed till it is reasonably determinable.

QUESTION 10: State the Disclosure Requirements AS PER AS 9.

ANSWER: In addition to the disclosures required by Accounting Standard 1 on 'Disclosure Of Accounting Policies' (AS 1), an enterprise should also disclose the circumstances in which revenue recognition has been postponed pending the reANSWERof significant uncertainties.

QUESTION 11: How is excise duty disclosed in presentation of revenue from sales transaction?

ANSWER: As per ASI 14, the amount of turnover should be disclosed in the following manner on the face of the statement of profit and loss:

Turnover (Gross)	XXX
Less: Excise Duty	XXX
Turnover (Net)	XXX

PRACTICAL QUESTIONS FOR PRACTICE

QUESTION 1: M/s. SEA Ltd. recognized ₹ 5.00 lakhs on accrual basis income from dividend during the year 2014-2015, on shares of the face value of ₹ 25.00 lakhs held by it in Rock Ltd. as at 31st March, 2015. Rock Ltd. proposed dividend @ 20% on 10th April, 2015. However, dividend was declared on 30th June, 2015. Please state with reference to relevant Accounting Standard, whether the treatment accorded by SEA Ltd. is in order.

ANSWER:

PROVISION OF AS 9

As per AS 9 "Revenue Recognition" states that dividend from investments in shares are not recognized in the statement of Profit and Loss until the right to receive dividend is established.

ADVICE

The dividend is proposed on 10th April, 2015, while it was declared on 30th June, 2015. Hence, the right to receive dividend is established on 30th June, 2015 only. Therefore, on applying the provisions stated in the standard, income from dividend on shares should be recognized by Sea Ltd. in the financial year 2015-2016 only.

Therefore, the recognition of income from dividend of ₹ 5 iakhs, on accrual basis, in the financial year 2014-2015 is not in accordance with AS 9.

QUESTION 2: Y Co. Ltd., used certain resources of X Co. Ltd. In return X Co. Ltd. received ₹ 10 lakhs and ₹ 15 lakhs as interest and royalties respectively from Y Co. Ltd. during the year 2014-2015. You are required to state whether and on what basis these revenue can be recognised by X Co. Ltd.

ANSWER: As per AS-9 on Revenue Recognition, revenue arising from the use by other of enterprise resources yielding interest and royalties should only be recognised when no significant uncertainty as to measurability or collectability exists. These revenues are recognised on the following bases:

(i) **Interest:** on a time proportion basis taking into amount outstanding and the rate applicable.

(ii) **Royalties:** on an accrual basis in accordance with the terms of the relevant agreement.

QUESTION 3: AQ Ltd., an investment company is finalizing its account for the Financial Year ending 2015 in the month of August 2015.

How will the following incomes be accounted for in the books of AQ Ltd.?

(1) X Ltd., has declared interim dividend which has not been received till 31-3-2015 but received on 25-4-2015.

(2) Y Ltd., has declared dividend on 8th May 2015 for the year ending 31-3-2015 which has been approved by the shareholders of the company on 30th June 2015.

(3) Z Ltd., a subsidiary of AQ Ltd., has declared dividend for the year ended 31-3-2015 on 25th May 2015 the AGM for which is to be held on September 2015.

ANSWER:

PROVISION OF AS-9

As per AS 9 "Revenue Recognition", dividends from investment in shares is recognized in the statement of Profit and Loss only when the owner's right to receive the payment is established.

ADVICE

(i) Since interim dividend was declared by X Ltd. before 31st March 2015 it means that the dividend had been vested (acrrued) to the shareholders of AQ Ltd. in the year 2014-2015. Therefore, though it is received on 25.4.2015 (before finalization of accounts) yet it should be recognized in the financial statements for the year ended 31st March, 2015.

(ii) Dividend declared by Y Ltd and approved by the shareholders of AQ Ltd. after balance sheet date but before finalization of accounts will be accounted for 2015-2016 as the right to receive dividend will arise when the AGM will approve the dividend i.e. on 30th June 2015. Since right to receive the dividend was not established on or before 31st March, 2015, it will not be accounted for in the books for the year ended 31st March, 2015.

(iii) Dividend declared by Z Ltd. will be approved in the AGM to be held on 30th September, 2015. Before that right to receive dividend cannot be established. Hence it will not be accounted for in the financial year ended on 31st March, 2015.

QUESTION 4: In the course of audit of T Ltd. you observed that export incentives are not accounted on accrual basis. The company's management contended that these would be accounted on cash basis citing the uncertainty about its receipts as they are not admitted as due by the customs authorities. Comment.

ANSWER:

PROVISION OF AS-9

As per AS 9 'Revenue Recognition", if at the time of raising the claim for incentive, it is unreasonable to expect ultimate collection, revenue recognition should be postponed. Therefore, as per accounting standard, if there is uncertainty is the receipt of the amounts, then the revenue in respect of such incentives ought not to be recognized in the books of accounts.

ADVICE

The exporters receive certain incentives (monetary or non-monetary) from the Government of India on export of goods. However due to various procedural delay sand laws involved which keep changing frequently, there is generally a delay in actual receipt of the export incentives. Further the receipt of the export incentives may not be assured in certain situations due to frequent changes in the policies of the Government. In such cases, ti may be reasonable to presume that the receipt of the incentives in uncertain till the time they are actually received.

The contention of management of T Ltd. to record the export incentive on cash basis is correct. There revenue is to be recognized only when there is reasonable certainty in the receipt of the same.

An Alternative view: Since the export incentives are due as and when the exports have been made from India, though customs authorities does not acknowledge them as due. This does not mean that an uncertainty arises about its receipt. If at all customs authorities have an objection it should be at the time of clearance of the goods for export. The only uncertainty is the timing of the receipt of such incentives, but not the incentive itself. Hence T Ltd. has to account the export incentives on Accrual basis.

QUESTION 5: X Ltd. entered into an agreement with Y Ltd. for sale of goods costing ₹ 2,00,000 at a profit of 20 % on sale. The sale transaction took place on 1st February, 2015. On the same day X Ltd. entered into another agreement with Y Ltd. for repurchasing the same goods at ₹ 2,80,000 on 1st August, 2015. State the treatment of above transaction in the financial statements of X Ltd. for the year 2014–2015. The predetermined repurchasing price covers, inter alia, the holding cost of Y Ltd.

ANSWER:

In this case X Ltd. concurrently agrees to repurchase the same goods from Y Ltd. at a later date. Also, the repurchase price is predetermined and covers Y Ltd. purchasing and holding costs. Hence, the transaction between X Ltd. and Y Ltd. on 1st February, 2015 should be accounted for as a financing transaction rather as a sale. The resulting cash inflow of ₹ 2,50,000 [i.e. ₹ 2,00,000 / (1.00 – 0.20)] is not revenue as per AS - 9.

Therefore the pattern of journal entries, required to be made in the books of X Ltd. during the year 2014-2015, are as follows:

JOURNAL

Date	Particulars	Dr. (₹)	Cr. (₹)
1.2.2015	Bank A/c ... Dr. To Advance from Y Ltd. A/c (Being amount received from Y Ltd. as per sale and repurchase agreement)	2,50,000	 2,50,000
31.3.2015	Financing charges A/c ... Dr. To Advance from Y Ltd. A/c [Being financing charges on ₹ 2,50,000 for 2 months (i.e. (₹.2,80,000 – ₹ 2,50,000) x (2 months / 6months)]	10,000	 10,000

31.3.2015	Profit and Loss A/c ...Dr. To Financing charges (Financing charges transferred)	10,000	10,000

Disclosures:

(I) AT EXTRACT OF BALANCE SHEET OF X LTD. AS AT 31ST MARCH 2015

Particulars	₹	₹
Current Liabilities:		
Advance money from Y Ltd.	2,50,000	
Add: Accrued finance charges	10,000	2,60,000
Current Assets:		
Goods lying with Y Ltd.		2,00,000

(ii) By way of notes:

(a) Goods lying with Y Ltd. costing ₹ 2,00,000 to be purchased after 6 months at ₹ 2,80,000

(b) Goods sold to Y Ltd. for ₹ 2,50,000 (cost ₹ 2,00,000) on repurchase agreement. The difference between sales price and repurchase price is treated as financing charge and located proportionately in the current accounting period.

QUESTION 6: B Ltd. entered into an agreement on 1st March, 2015 to buy computer spares from S Ltd. at prevailing market price for ₹ 1200 lakhs on which S Ltd. made a profit of 20% and received full advance payment. The transaction was concluded on 15th March, 2015. On the same day S Ltd. agrees to buy on 15th Sept., 2015 the same goods from B Ltd. at 20% over cost. The 20% mark up compensates B Ltd. for its inventory holding costs till sale date. You are required to show how both the buyer and seller account for the above transaction in the year 2015-2016 explaining in brief the justification for your treatment and also draft the Notes on Account on disclosure if any required in the annual accounts of year ended 31st March, 2015.

ANSWER: The transaction between S Limited and B Limited should be accounted for as financing transaction rather than as sale since S Ltd. concurrently agrees to repurchase the same goods from B Ltd. at a later date. Also, the repurchase price is predetermined and covers B Limited's purchasing and holding costs. Hence, the resulting cash inflow of ₹ 1,200 lakhs is not revenue as per AS-9 'Revenue Recognition'.

JOURNAL OF S LIMITED

Date	Particulars	Dr. (₹)	Cr. (₹)
15.3.2015	Bank A/c Dr. To Advance from B Limited A/c (Being amount received from B Ltd. as per sale and repurchasing agreement)	1,200	1,200
31.3.2015	Financing Charges A/c Dr. To Advance from B Ltd. A/c (Being the Financing charges 20% of ₹ 1200 lakhs for 1/2 month i.e. 240 x 0.5/6)	20	20
31.3.2015	Profit and Loss A/c Dr. To Financing charges (Being amount transferred to profit and loss account)	20	20

Disclosure in the Balance Sheet

1. **An Extract of Balance Sheet of S Ltd. as at 31.3.2015**

Particulars	(₹) in lakhs
Assets (Under the head "Current Assets")	
Short-term loans and advances	
Goods lying with B Limited (under sale and repurchase agreement)	1,000*
Liabilities (under the head "Secured Loans')	
Advance from B Limited	1,200
Add: Accrued finance charges	20
	1,220

2. **Notes to accounts:**
   (a) Goods lying with B Limited costing ₹ 1,000 lakhs to be repurchased after 6 months at ₹ 1,440 lakhs.
   (b) Goods sold to B Limited for ₹ 1,200 lakhs (cost ₹ 1,000 lakhs) on repurchase agreement. The difference between sale price and repurchase price is treated as financing charges and allocated proportionately in the current accounting period.

JOURNAL OF B LTD. **₹ in lakhs**

Date	Particulars		Dr. (₹)	Cr. (₹)
15.3.2015	Advance from B Limited A/c	Dr.	1,200	
	To Bank A/c		1,200	
	(Being amount paid to S Ltd. as per sale and repurchase agreement)			
31.3.2015	Accrued Finance Income A/c	Dr.	20	
	To Finance income			20
	(Financing charges 20% of ₹ 1200 lakhs for 1/2 month i.e. 240 × 0 .5/6)			
31.3.2015	Financing Income A/c	Dr.	20	
	To Profit and Loss A/c			20
	(Being financing charges received transferred to profit and loss account)			

Disclosure in the Balance Sheet

1. **An extract of Balance sheet of B Ltd. as on 31.3.2015**

Assets (Under the head 'Current Assets)'

Short-term loans and advances

Advance to S Ltd. (Under sale and repurchase agreement) ₹ 1,200 lakhs

Accrued Finance income ₹ 20 lakhs

(This advance is fully secured by goods of S Ltd. Market value of ₹ 1,200 lakhs lying with company as security)

2. **Notes to Account**

₹ 1,200 lakhs paid to S Limited against the sale and repurchase agreement against the security of goods of S Limited whose market value is ₹ 1,200 Lakhs.

The transaction is in the nature of a financing arrangement and hence is not recognized as a sale and hence the excess of repurchase price over sale price amounting to ₹ 240 lakhs have been treated as Finance charges allocated proportionately between accounting periods

2015-2016 and 2015-2016. The value of the computer spares lying with B Ltd. on Balance Sheet date is considered as part of the company's inventory held as security for the Financing obligation.

QUESTION 7: On 25th September, 2015, Planet Advertising Limited obtained advertisement rights to World Cup Hockey Tournament to be held in Nov./Dec., 2015 for ₹ 520 lakhs.

They furnish the following information:

1. **The company obtained the advertisements for 70% of available time for ₹ 700 lakhs by 30th September, 2015.**
2. **For the balance time they got bookings in October, 2015 for ₹ 240 lakhs.**
3. **All the advertisers paid the full amount at the time of booking the advertisements.**
4. **40% of the advertisements appeared before the public in Nov. 2015 and balance 60% appeared in the month of December, 2015.**

You are required to calculate the amount of profit/loss to be recognized for the month November and December, 2015 as per Accounting Standard-9.

ANSWER:

PROVISION OF AS 9

As per AS 9 in a transaction involving the rendering of services, performance should be measured either under the completed service contract method or under the proportionate completion method, whichever relates the revenue to the work accomplished. Further, appendix to AS 9 states that revenue from advertising should be recognized when the service is completed. The service as regards advertisement is deemed to be completed when the related advertisement appears before the public.

ADVICE

In the given QUESTION, 40% of the advertisement appeared before the public in November, and balance 60% in December.

CALCULATION OF TOTAL PROFIT

Particulars	₹ in lakhs
Advertisement for 70% of available time obtained by 30th September, 2013	700
Advertisement for 30% of available time obtained in by October, 2013	240
Total	940
Less: Cost of advertisement rights	(520)
Profit	420

The profit amounting ₹ 420 lakhs should be apportioned in the ratio of 40:60 for the months of November and December, 2015. Thus, the company should recognise ₹ 168 lakhs (i.e. ₹ 420 lakhs × 40%) in November, 2015 and rest ₹ 252 lakhs (i.e. ₹ 420 lakhs × 60%) in December, 2015.

QUESTION 8: ABC Advertisers obtained advertisement rights for one day world cup cricket tournament to be held in May 2015 for ₹ 800 lakhs in February 2015.

By 31/3/2014, they had paid ₹ 500 lakhs to secure these advertisements rights. The balance ₹ 300 lakhs was paid in April 2015. By March 2015, they procured advertisement for 75% of the available time for ₹ 1000 lakhs. The advertisers paid 60 % of the amount by that date. The balance 40 % was received in April 2015. Advertisements for balance 25 % time were procured in April 2015 for ₹ 200 lakhs. The advertisers paid the full amount while booking the advertisement. 25 % of the advertisement time is expected to be available in May 2015 and balance in June 2015. Journalise.

ANSWER:

JOURNAL **₹ in Lakhs**

Date	Particulars	Dr. (₹)	Cr. (₹)
2014 Feb.	Advertisement rights ...Dr. To Creditors for advertisement rights (Being advertisement rights obtained in February)	800	 800
March	Creditors for advertisement rights ...Dr. To Bank A/c (Being payment made by 31st March)	500	 500
March	Debtors for advertisement rights ...Dr. To Advertisement rights (Being 75 % of advertisement rights are booked)	1,000	 1,000
March	Bank A/c ...Dr. To Debtors for advertisement rights (Being 60 % of the amount paid by the debtors)	600	 600
April	Creditors for advertisement rights ...Dr. To Bank A/c (Being balance payment made in April)	300	 300
April	Bank A/c ...Dr. To Debtors for advertisement rights (Being 40 % of the amount paid by the debtors who booked the time for advertisement in March)	400	 400
April	Bank A/c ...Dr. To Advertisement rights (Being 25 % of advertisement rights are booked and paid)	200	 200
May	Advertisement rights ...Dr. To Revenue from advertisement rights (Being 25 % of the advertisement rights (i.e. 25 % of ₹ 400 lakhs) availed in May)	100	 100
June	Advertisement rights ...Dr. To Revenue from advertisement rights (Being balance of the advertisement rights (i.e. 75 % of ₹ 400 lakhs) availed in June)	300	 300

Note: *As per AS - 9, in a transaction involving the rendering of services, performance should be measured either under the completed service contract method or under the proportionate completion method, whichever relates the revenue to the work accomplished. Such performance should be regarded as being achieved when no significant uncertainty exists regarding the amount of consideration that will be delivered from rendering the service. Further, the revenue from advertising should be recognized when the service is completed. In this case the service as regards advertisement is deemed to be completed when the related advertisement appears before the public.*

As the 25 % of the advertisement appeared in May, 2015 and 75 % in June, 2015, therefore the net revenue of ₹ 400 lakhs [i.e. (₹ 1000 lakhs + ₹ 200 lakhs) - (₹ 800 lakhs)], should be apportioned in the ratio of 25 % and 75 % in May, 2013 and in June, 2015 respectively.

QUESTION 9: XYZ Ltd. purchased goods on credit from ABC Ltd. for ₹ 250 crores for export. The export order was cancelled. XYZ Ltd. decided to sell the same goods in the local market with a price discount. ABC Ltd. was requested to offer a price discount of 15 %. The directors of ABC Ltd. want to adjust the sales figure to the extent of the discount requested by XYZ Ltd. Comment.

ANSWER:

PROVISION OF AS 9

As per AS 9 trade discounts and volume rebates are not encompassed within the definition of revenue. Trade discounts and volume rebates given should be deducted in determining the revenue.

ADVICE

However, the price discount of 15 % in the instant case, is not the discount given during the ordinary course of the trade. Hence, it cannot be treated in the nature of discount eligible for deduction from sales price, the better alternate is to treat the amount as bad debt, therefore the contentions of directors of XYZ Ltd. are not correct.

QUESTION 10: M Ltd. manufactures machinery used in steel plants. It quotes prices in various tenders issued by steel plants. As per terms of contract, full price of machinery is not released by the steel plants, but 10% thereof is retained and paid after one year if there is satisfactory performance of the machinery supplied. The company accounts for only 90% of the invoice value as sales income and the balance amount in the year of receipt to the extent of actual receipts only. Comment.

ANSWER:

PROVISION OF AS 9

As per AS 9 Revenue from sale of goods should be recognized if the seller has transferred to the buyer the property in the goods for a price or all significant risks and rewards of ownership have been transferred to the buyer and the seller retains no effective control of the goods transferred to a degree usually associated with ownership and no significant uncertainty exists regarding the amount of consideration.

ADVICE

In this case, the goods as well as risks and rewards of ownership have been transferred. The invoice raised is for the full price but 10 % of the invoice amount is withheld from recognition of revenue. This is incorrect treatment since revenue in this case shall be recognized at full invoice amount. However, depending on the past experience of recovering the balance of 10 %, the **company may make a provision for receivables whose collectability is not certain.**

QUESTION 11: M/s Prima Co. Ltd. sold goods worth ₹ 50,000 to M/s Y and Company. M/s Y and Co. asked for discount of ₹ 8,000 which was agreed by M/s Prima Co. Ltd. The sale was effected and goods were despatched. After receiving, goods worth ₹ 7,000 was found defected, which they returned immediately. They made the payment of ₹ 35,000 to M/s Prima Co. Ltd. Accountant booked the sales for ₹ 35,000. Please discuss.

ANSWER:

PROVISION OF AS 9

As per AS 9, revenue is the gross inflow of cash, receivable or other consideration arising in the course of the ordinary activities of an enterprise from the sale of goods, from the rendering of services, and from the use by others of enterprise resources yielding interest, royalties and dividends.

ADVICE

M/s Prima. Co. Ltd. should record the sales at gross value of ₹ 50,000. Discount of ₹ 8,000 in price and goods returned worth ₹ 7,000 are to be adjusted by suitable provisions. M/s Prime Co. Ltd. might have sent the credit note of ₹ 15,000 to M/s Y and Co. to account for these adjustments. The contention of the accountant to book the sales for ₹ 35,000 is not correct.

QUESTION 12: Golden Eagle Ltd., has been successful jewellers for the past 100 years and sales are against cash only. The company diversified into apparels. A young senior executive was put in charge of Apparels business and sales increased 5 times. One of the conditions for sales that dealers can return the unsold stocks within one month of the end of season. Sales return for the year was 25% of sales. Suggest a suitable Revenue Recognitions Policy with references to AS 9.

ANSWER:

PROVISION OF AS 9

As per AS 9, "Revenue Recognition", revenue recognition is mainly concerned with the timing of recognition of revenue in Statement of Profit and Loss of an enterprise. The amount of revenue arising on a transaction is usually determined by the agreement between the parties involved in the transaction. When uncertainties exist regarding the determination of the amount, or its associated costs, these uncertainties may influence the timing of revenue recognition.

ADVICE

In the case of the Jewellery Business the company is selling for cash and returns are negligible. Hence, revenue can be recognized on sales. One the other hand, in Apparels industry, the dealers have a right to return the unsold goods within one month of the end of the season. In this case, the company is bearing the risk of sales return and therefore, the company should not recognize the revenue to the extent of 25% of its sales. The company may disclose suitable revenue recognition policy in its financial statements separately for both Jewellery and Apparels business. Thus, in a present case revenue recognition should be postponed until the ultimate collection becomes certain.

QUESTION 13: When do you recognize revenue in the following cases?

1. **'Bill and hold' scales i.e., delivery is delayed at buyer's request but buyer takes title and accepts billing.**
2. **Shipped subject to cash on delivery.**
3. **Installation fee.**
4. **Advertising commission.**

ANSWER:

1. Although physical delivery has been delayed, revenue should be recognized so long as there is every expectation that delivery will be made. But goods sold must be in hand, identified and ready for delivery. This should not be simply the items to be manufactured or procured at the time of delivery.
2. Revenue should be recognized on receipt of the cash by seller or his agent.
3. If installation are other than incidental to the sale of products, they should be recognized as revenue after installation of the equipment and acceptance by the customer.
4. For advertising agencies media commission will be recognized normally when the related advertisement or commercial appears before the public.

QUESTION 14: The Board of Directors decided on 31.3.2015 to increase the sale price of certain items retrospectively from 1st January, 2015.

In view of this price revision with effect from 1st January, 2015, the company has to receive ₹ 15 lakhs from its customers in respect to sales made from 1st January, 2012 to 31st March,

2015 and Accountant cannot make up his mind whether to include ₹ 15 lakhs in the Sales for 2014-2015.

ANSWER: If the company is able to assess the ultimate collection with reasonable certainty, then additional revenue arising out of the said price revision may be recognised in 2014-2015.

QUESTION 15: Some of the Transport claims lodged in 2014-2015 has been settled by the carrier in February, 2015 by paying ₹ 1,15,000. These claims were not recorded in the books of the company so far Comment.

ANSWER:

PROVISION OF AS 9

As per AS 9 where the ability to assess the ultimate collection with reasonable certainty is lacking at the time of raising any claim, revenue recognition is postponed to the extent of uncertainty involved. It is also that when recognition of revenue is postponed due to the effect of uncertainties, it is considered as revenue of the period in which it is reasonable certain that ultimate collection will be made

ADVICE

In this case, it may be assumed that collectability of claim was not certain in the earlier years. So this transaction cannot be taken as 'Prior-period item'.

It will not be treated as extra ordinary item as per AS-5. However, AS-5 states that when item of income and expense within profit and loss for ordinary activities are of such size, nature or incidence that their disclosure is relevant to explain the performance of enterprise for the period, the nature and amount of such items should be disclosed separately. Accordingly, the nature and amount of this item should be disclosed separately as per AS-5.

QUESTION 16: XYZ Company has taken a Transit Insurance Policy. Suddenly in the year 2014-2015 the percentage of accident has gone upto 10 % and company wants to recognize insurance claim as revenue in year 2014-2015 in accordance with relevant Accounting Standards. Comment.

ANSWER:

PROVISION OF AS 9

As per AS 9 the revenue should be recognized if it can be measured reliably and there is not any significant uncertainty in its ultimate collection.

ADVICE

In the instant case it appears that these are uncertainties in measuring the claim and the settlement of the insurance claim. Hence, insurance claim can be recognized only if the amount can be measured reliably and ultimate collection is reasonably certain.

QUESTION 17: ABC Ltd. sells agriculture products to dealers. One of the condition of sale is that interest is payable at the rate of 2 % per month, for delayed payments. Percentage of intent recovery is only 10 % on such overdue outstanding due to various reasons. During the year 2014-2015 the company wants to recognize the entire interest receivable. Do you agree?

ANSWER:

PROVISION OF AS 9

As per AS 9 to recognize the revenue there should not be significant uncertainty in ultimate collection of the amount.

ADVICE

In the instant case it appears that there are uncertainties in the collection of interest. Therefore income can be recognized only if the amount can be measured reliably and ultimate collection is reasonably certain.

QUESTION 18: Sale of goods costing ₹ 60,000 with a profit margin of 25 % on selling price is included in the inventory as delivery of goods was postponed at buyer's request. Comment.

ANSWER:

PROVISION OF AS 9

As per AS 9 Revenue from sale of goods should be recognized if the seller has transferred to the buyer the property in the goods for a price or all significant risks and rewards of ownership have been transferred to the buyer and the seller retains no effective control of the goods transferred to a degree usually associated with ownership. The transfer of property in goods, in most cases, results in or coincides with the transfer of significant risks and rewards of ownership.

ADVICE

In this case, all significant risks and rewards of ownership have been transferred to the buyer and the seller retains no effective control of the goods transferred to a degree usually associated with ownership but delivery is postponed at the buyer's request. Hence this transaction should be recognized as revenue. Thus, ₹ 60,000 should be deducted from inventory, and the amount of ₹ 80,000 [i.e. ₹ 60,000 / (1.00 – 0.25)] should be included in sales with correspondence increase in Debtor's balances.

QUESTION 19: A suit for damages of ₹ 1 lakhs for breach of contract of sale (breach occurred in 2009) was decreed in favour of May Ltd. in March 2015. The Company has included the amount in its turnover for the financial year 2014-2015.

ANSWER: The expression "turnover" normally implies the amount for which the sales are affected or services rendered by an enterprise. Thus, apparently as per this definition, the amount received on account of breach of contract of sales would not form part of the turnover.

QUESTION 20: A company is engaged in the business of ship building and ship repair. On completion of the repair work, a work completion certificate is prepared and countersigned by ship owner (customer). Subsequently invoice is prepared based on the work completion certificate describing the nature of work done together with the rate and the amount.

Customer scrutinizes the invoice and any variation is informed to the company. Negotiations take place between the company and the customer. Negotiations may result in a deduction being allowed from the invoiced amount either as a lumpsum or as a percentage of the invoiced amount The accounting treatment followed by the company is as follows:

(i) When the invoice is raised, the customer's account is debited and Ship Repair Income Account is credited with the invoiced amount.

(ii) Deduction, if any arrived after negotiation is treated as trade discount by debiting the Ship Repair Income Account.

(iii) At the close of the year, negotiation in respect of certain invoices had not been completed. In such cases, based on past experience, a provision for anticipated loss is created by debiting the Profit and Loss account. The provision is disclosed in Balance Sheet.

Following two aspects are settled in the negotiations:

(i) Errors in billing arising on account of variation between the quantities as per work completion certificate and invoice and other clerical errors in preparing the invoice.

(ii) Disagreement between the company and customer about the rate/cost on which prior agreement has not been reached between them.

Comment:

(i) Whether the accounting treatment of deduction as trade discount is correct? If not state the correct accounting treatment.

(ii) Whether the disclosure of the provision for anticipated loss in Balance Sheet is correct, if not state the correct accounting treatment.

ANSWER:

(i) As per AS 9 "Revenue Recognition", revenue is recognized at the time when the invoice is raised to the customers; however the treatment of deduction as trade discount is not in accordance with AS 9. Considering the treatment prescribed by adjustment of the difference between the invoice amount and the amount finally settled against 'Ship Repair Income' Account is in order. Events occurring up to the date of approval of the accounts by the Board of Directors should be taken into consideration in determining the amount of adjustment to be made in the regard. The description of the difference as 'trade discount' is not appropriate,

(ii) In respect to ship repair jobs for which negotiations between the ship owners and the company are not over, the accounting treatment is not appropriate. Instead, the amount of difference between the invoiced amount and the amount likely to the finally settled (as estimated on the basis of past experience) should be adjusted in the "Ship Repair Income" by a corresponding credit to the accounts of the respective ship owners. Consequently, the figure of sundry debtors included in the balance sheet would be net of adjustment for such difference. In other words, the amount of the difference would be neither shown under the head Provision nor shown as a deduction from the sundry debtors in the Balance Sheet.

QUESTION 21: Excel Ltd. is a Manufacturing Company in durable consumer goods with an annual turnover of ₹ 1,000 lakhs. The Company receives orders from its commission agents all over the country, but goods are despatched directly to the customers. The documents including Transport bills are sent through the bank for collection.

At the end of 6th year, it is found that documents covering the despatch of goods worth ₹ 100 lakhs were still lying with the banks not cleared by the customers even though the normal collection period of 20 days from the date of despatch has expired. Should Revenue be recognised in the above case?

ANSWER:

PROVISION OF AS 9

As per AS 9 Revenue can be recognised if the seller of goods has transferred to the buyer the property in the goods for a price or all significant risks and rewards of ownership have been transferred to the buyer and the seller retains no effective control of the goods transferred to a degree usually associated with the ownership. It is subject to the fact that there should not be any significant uncertainty about the realisation of price. Both these conditions are required to be evaluated with reference to various others relevant factors pertaining to specific circumstances e.g., intention of the parties for retaining the shipping documents, any explicit term in the contract, etc.

ADVICE

Applying these tests to the facts of case, since the transport bills were sent through the bank for collection, it may be said that the seller has retained effective control over his ownership. Further since the documents were not cleared by the customer even after the expiry of the normal period of collection, there is an uncertainty in the realisation of sale proceeds. Apparently, the amount also appears to be quite material being 10% of total turnover. Hence, revenue should not be recognised in this case.

28 AS 7 – CONSTRUCTION CONTRACTS

THEORETICAL BASE

QUESTION 1: What Is Construction Contract?

ANSWER: A construction contract is a contract specifically negotiated for the construction of an asset or a combination of assets that are closely interrelated or interdependent in terms of their design, technology and function or their ultimate purpose or use.

It may also include:

(a) Contracts for the rendering of services which are directly related to the construction of the asset, ***For example***, those for the services of project managers and architects; and

(b) Contracts for destruction or restoration of assets, and the restoration of the environment following the demolition of assets. *For example* contract for demolition of unauthorized storey of a building.

QUESTION 2: What are the types of construction contracts?

ANSWER: Construction contracts may be formulated in a number of ways. Some general types of contracts are given below:–

(i)	**Fixed Price Contracts**	The contractor agrees to fixed contract price, or a fixed rate per unit of output, which in some cases is subject to cost escalation clauses;
(ii)	**Cost Plus Contracts**	The contractor is reimbursed for allowable or otherwise defined costs, and is also allowed a percentage of these costs or a fixed fee.
(iii)	**Mixed Types of Contracts**	These types of construction contracts may contain characteristics of both of fixed price contracts and cost plus contracts.
(iv)	**Real Estate Project**	Some real estate projects indicate significant characteristics of construction contracts. These real estate projects then are subject to this standard.

QUESTION 3: State the items which constitute Contract Revenue.

ANSWER:

1. Initial amount of revenue agreed in the contract;
2. Variations in contract work;
3. Claims;
4. Incentive payments.

QUESTION 4: How should Contract Revenue be measured?

ANSWER: Contract Revenue should be measured at the consideration received or receivable.

QUESTION 5: Can original estimated contract revenue be revised?

ANSWER: Contract revenue is affected by number of uncertainties that depend on outcome of future events. Estimates are often reconsidered when events occur in future and / or uncertainties are resolved. Hence contract revenue as determined originally may change from one reporting period to the next reporting period. **When contract revenue is revised it is treated as changed in estimates.**

QUESTION 6: State the items which constitute Contract Costs.

ANSWER:

1. **Costs that are directly related to the specific contract**; *For Example*:
   (a) Site Labour Costs, including site supervision;
   (b) Costs of materials used in construction;
   (c) Depreciation of plant and equipment used on the contract;
   (d) Costs of moving plant, equipment and materials to and from the contract site;
   (e) Costs of hiring plant and equipment;
   (f) Costs of design and technical assistance that is directly related to the contract;
   (g) the estimated costs of rectification and guarantee work, including expected warranty costs; and
   (h) Claims from third parties.
2. **Costs which are generally related to the contract activity and are allocable to the specific contract;** *For Example:*
   (a) insurance;
   (b) costs of design and technical assistance that is not directly related to a specific contract; and
   (c) construction overheads which may include cost such as the preparation and processing of construction personnel payroll.
3. **Borrowing Costs;**
4. **Costs which are specifically chargeable to the customer under contract terms;**(i.e. those costs for which reimbursement is specific provided as per contract terms and may include some general administration cost and development cost.)
5. **Pre-contract Costs** (i.e. those costs which are incurred in securing the contract.)

QUESTION 7: State the costs which are not included in contract cost?

ANSWER:

1. general administration costs for which reimbursement is not specified in the contract;
2. selling costs;
3. research and development costs for which reimbursement is not specified in the contract; and
4. depreciation of idle plant and equipment that is not used on a particular contract.

QUESTION 8: State the accounting treatment of miscellaneous incomes .

ANSWER: Any miscellaneous income i.e. Rental Income, Sale of Surplus material, disposal of plant and equipment shall be **reduced from contract cost**.

QUESTION 9: When should contract revenue and contract cost should be recognized as revenue and expenses respectively?

ANSWER:

1. Contract revenue and contract cost should be recognized as revenue and expenses respectively by reference to the **stage of completion of the contract activity at the reporting period.**
2. However, recognization should only be done when the outcome of a construction contract can be **estimated reliably.**

QUESTION 10: When can the outcome of a construction contract be estimated reliably?

ANSWER: This degree of reliability would be provided if the following conditions are satisfied:

In case of Fixed Price Contracts	In case of Cost Plus Contracts
1. It is probable that the economic benefits associated with the contract will flow to the enterprise;	1. It is probable that the economic benefits associated with the contract will flow to the enterprise; and
2. total Contract Revenue can be measured reliably;	2. the contract costs attributable to the contract, whether or not specifically reimbursable, can be clearly identified and measured reliably.
3. both the contract costs to complete the contract and the stage of contract completion at the reporting date can be measured reliably; and	
4. the contract costs attributable to the contract can be clearly identified and measured reliably so that actual contract costs incurred can be compared with prior estimates.	

QUESTION 11: What is meant by term 'Stage of Completion Method' (Percentage Completion Method)?

ANSWER:

1. The stage of completion of contract is determined at the reporting date.
2. Contract Revenue is recognized as a certain percentage of Total Contract Revenue.
3. This revenue is matched with the contract cost incurred in reaching the stage of completion.
4. It is applied on a specific contract from year to year on a cumulative basis

QUESTION 12: What should be the treatment of an amount already recognized as contract revenue when an uncertainty arises about its collectability?

ANSWER:

Such amount should be recognized as an expense in the period in which uncertainty arises about the amount collectability.

QUESTION 13: What should be the treatment of contract cost the recovery of which is not probable?

ANSWER: Contract cost, the recovery of which is not probable should be recognized as expense.

QUESTION 14: What should be the treatment when the outcome of a construction contract cannot be estimated reliably?

ANSWER:

Revenue:– It should be recognized to the extent of contract cost incurred of which recovery is probable.

Expense:– Contract cost should be recognized as an expense in the period in which they are incurred.

QUESTION 15: What is Expected Loss? What should be the treatment of Expected Loss?

ANSWER:

MEANING OF EXPECTED LOSS

Expected loss is the excess of total contract cost over total contract revenue.

TREATMENT OF EXPECTED LOSS

When it is probable that expected loss shall occur, it should be recognized as an expense immediately irrespective of

(i) Whether or not work has commenced on the contract;

(ii) Whether or not the outcome of contract can be estimated reliably;

(iii) The stage of completion of contract activity;

(iv) The amount of profit expected on other contracts not treated as single contracts (i.e. segmented from single contract).

QUESTION 16: What is Contract Work – in – progress?

ANSWER: Contract costs incurred up to reporting date may include certain costs which relates to future activity on the contract. Such costs should not be matched with contract revenue recognized. Instead such contract costs should be recognized as an asset if it is probable that it shall be recovered and are classified as contract work – in – progress.

QUESTION 17: How should Contract Work in progress be determined?

ANSWER: Contract work in progress should be determined in the following manner:

Dr. **CONTRACT WORK IN PROGRESS ACCOUNT** **Cr.**

Particulars	₹	Particulars	₹
To balance b/d*	xxx	By balance b/d*	xxx
To Contract Cost incurred during current accounting period	xxx	By contract expense to be recognized during current accounting period	xxx
To Contract Revenue to be recognized during current accounting period	xxx	By costs, the recovery of which is not possible recognized as an expense during current accounting period	xxx
To balance c/d**	xxx	By Expected loss recognized during current accounting period	xxx
		By Miscellaneous income not recognized as contract revenue during current accounting period	xxx
		By Progress Billings during current accounting period	xxx
		By balance c/d**	xxx

*Only one of the figures shall appear at a time.

**Only one of the figures shall appear at a time.

Disclosure of Debit Balance: If there is debit balance in an account, then it shall be shown as an asset under the head **Gross amount due from customer for contract work.**

Disclosure of Credit Balance: If there is credit balance in an account, then it shall be shown as liability under the head **Gross amount due to customer for contract work**

QUESTION 18: What are the Disclosure Requirements AS TO construction contracts AND contracts in progress?

ANSWER:

For Construction Contract	1. the amount of contract revenue recognized as revenue in the period; 2. the methods used to determine the contract revenue recognized in the period; and 3. the methods used to determine the stage of completion of contracts in progress.
For Contracts in progress	1. the aggregate amount of costs incurred and recognized profits (less recognized losses) up to the reporting date; 2. the amount of advances received; 3. the amount of retentions.

Statement showing the computation of various amounts as per requirements of AS – 7 for various accounting periods.

Particulars	Years			
	1	2	3	4
A Opening Balance				
B Additions during the year Cost Incurred during the year Cost Incurred during the year				
Total [B]				
C Deductions during the year Expenses recognized during the year Costs not recoverable Expected loss Miscellaneous income				
Total [C]				
D Balance [A + B – C] **[As per disclosure requirement of AS – 7]**				
E Progress Billings				
F Cumulative Progress billings				
G Amount due from customers for contract work /(Amount due to customers for contract work) [D – F]				

A. Work Certified	500
B. Work Not Certified	105
C. Cost incurred till date/ Contract Expense[A + B]	605
D. Estimated Additional Cost	495
E. Estimated Total Cost [C + D]	1100
F. Contract Price	1000

G. Total Estimated Profit [F – E] OR Total Expected Loss [E – F]	
H. % of Completion [(C/E) × 100]	55%
I. Contract Revenue to be recognised as Turnover [Contract Price × % of Completion]	550
J. Loss for the current year [I – C]	55
K. Expected Loss to be recognized immediately as per para 35 of AS 7 [G – J]	45
L. Progress Billings [Progress Payment Received + To be Received]	540
M. Retentions (billed but not received from contractee)	140
N. Gross amount due to customers [C – G – L]	35

PRACTICAL QUESTIONS FOR PRACTICE

QUESTION 1: On 31st October, 2014 , Bharat Construction Co. Ltd. undertook a contract to construct a Flyover for ₹ 215 crores. On 31st March, 2015, company found that its work certified is for ₹ 100 crores and work to be certified is for ₹ 35 crores. Prudent estimate of additional cost for completion was ₹ 90 crores. What amount should be charged to Revenue in the final accounts for the year ended 31st March, 2015 as per provisions of Accounting Standard 7 (revised).

ANSWER:

PROVISION OF AS 7

1. As per AS-7 when the outcome of a construction contract can be estimated reliably, contract revenue and contract costs associated with the construction contract should be recognised as revenue and expenses respectively by reference to stage of completion of the contract activity at the reporting date.
2. As per AS-7 an expected loss on the Construction contract should be recognized as an expense immediately irrespective of (i) whether or not the work has commenced on the contract; or (ii) the stage of completion of the contract: or (iii) the amount of profits expected to arise in other contracts.

ADVICE

Particulars	₹ (crores)
A.Work Certified	100
B. Work Not Certified	35
C. Cost incurred till date/ Contract Expense [A + B]	135
D. Estimated Additional Cost	90
E. Estimated Total Cost [C + D]	225
F. Contract Price	215
G. Total Expected Loss [E – F]	10
H. % of Completion [(C/E) × 100]	60%
I. Contract Revenue to be recognised as Turnover [Contract Price × % of Completion]	129
J. Loss for the current year [I – C]	6
K. Expected Loss to be recognized immediately as per para 35 of AS 7 [G – J]	4

DISCLOSURES AS PER AS – 7

Particulars	₹ (crores)
Contract Revenue	129
Contract Expenses Charged	(135)
Provision for Expected Loss	(4)

QUESTION 2: X Limited undertook a contract to construct a building for ₹ 3 Crores on 1st September, 2014. On 31st March 2015, the Company found that it had already spent ₹ 1 Crore 80 Lakhs on the construction of which 60% has been certified. Prudent estimate of additional cost of completion was ₹ 1 Crore 40 Lakhs. What amount should be charged, to revenue in the final accounts for the year ended on 31st March 2015, as per the provisions of AS -7?

ANSWER:

PROVISION OF AS 7

1. As per AS-7 when the outcome of a construction contract can be estimated reliably, contract revenue and contract costs associated with the construction contract should be recognised as revenue and expenses respectively by reference to stage of completion of the contract activity at the reporting date.
2. As per AS-7 an expected loss on the Construction contract should be recognized as an expense immediately irrespective of (i) whether or not the work has commenced on the contract; or (ii) the stage of completion of the contract: or (iii) the amount of profits expected to arise in other contracts.

ADVICE

Particulars	₹ (lakhs)
A.Work Certified	108
B. Work Not Certified	72
C. Cost incurred till date/ Contract Expense [A + B]	180
D. Estimated Additional Cost	140
E. Estimated Total Cost [C + D]	320
F. Contract Price	300
G. Total Expected Loss [E – F]	20
H. % of Completion [(C/E) × 100]	56.25%
I. Contract Revenue to be recognised as Turnover [Contract Price × % of Completion]	168.75
J. Loss for the current year [I – C]	11.25
K. Expected Loss to be recognized immediately as per para 35 of AS 7 [G – J]	8.75

DISCLOSURES AS PER AS – 7

Particulars	₹ Lakhs
Contract Revenue	168.75
Contract Expenses	(180.00)
Provision for Expected Loss	(8.75)

QUESTION 3: An amount of ₹ 9,90,000 was incurred on a contract work upto 31.03.2013. Certificates have been received to date to the value of ₹ 12,00,000 against which ₹ 10,80,000 has been received in cash. The cost of work done but not certified amounted to ₹ 22,500. It is estimated that by spending an additional amount of ₹ 60,000 (including provision for contingencies) the work can be completed in all respects in another two months. The agreed contract price of work is ₹ 12,50,000. Compute a conservative estimate of the profit to be taken to the Profit and Loss Account as per AS 7.

ANSWER:

PROVISION OF AS 7

As per AS-7 when the outcome of a construction contract can be estimated reliably, contract revenue and contract costs associated with the construction contract should be recognised as revenue and expenses respectively by reference to stage of completion of the contract activity at the reporting date.

ADVICE

A.Work Certified	9,67,500
B. Work Not Certified	30,000
C. Cost incurred till date/ Contract Expense [A + B]	9,97,500
D. Estimated Additional Cost	52,500
E. Estimated Total Cost [C + D]	10,50,000
F. Contract Price	12,50,000
G. Total Estimated Profit [F – E]	2,00,000
H. % of Completion [(C/E) × 100]	95%
I. Contract Revenue to be recognised as Turnover [Contract Price × % of Completion]	11,87,500
J. Profit for the current year [I – C]	1,90,000

QUESTION 4: PRARTHANA LTD, a firm of contractors provides the following details for the year ended 31st March, 2013:

Particulars	(₹ in lakhs)
Total Contract Price	₹ 1,000 lacs
Work Certified	500
Work not Certified	105
Estimated further Cost to Completion	495
Progress Payment Received	400
To be Received	140

Required: Show the relevant disclosures under AS 7.

ANSWER:

PROVISION OF AS 7

1. As per AS-7 when the outcome of a construction contract can be estimated reliably, contract revenue and contract costs associated with the construction contract should be recognised as revenue and expenses respectively by reference to stage of completion of the contract activity at the reporting date.

2. As per AS-7 an expected loss on the Construction contract should be recognized as an expense immediately irrespective of (i) whether or not the work has commenced on the contract; or (ii) the stage of completion of the contract: or (iii) the amount of profits expected to arise in other contracts.

ADVICE

A. Work Certified	500
B. Work Not Certified	105
C. Cost incurred till date/ Contract Expense [A + B]	605
D. Estimated Additional Cost	495
E. Estimated Total Cost [C + D]	1100
F. Contract Price	1000
G. Total Expected Loss [E – F]	100
H. % of Completion [(C/E) × 100]	55%
I. Contract Revenue to be recognised as Turnover [Contract Price × % of Completion]	550
J. Loss for the current year [I – C]	55
K. Expected Loss to be recognized immediately as per para 35 of AS 7 [G – J]	45

DISCLOSURES AS PER AS – 7

Particulars	₹ Lakhs
Contract Revenue	550
Contract Expenses	(605)
Provision for Expected Loss	(45)
Progress Billings [Progress Payment Received + To be Received]	540
Retentions (billed but not received from Contractee)	140
Gross amount due to customers [605 – 100 – 540]	35

QUESTION 5: A firm of contractors obtain a contract for construction of a bridge across river Hindan. The following details are available in the records kept for the year ended 31st March, 2015:

Particulars	₹ in lakhs
Total Contract Price	**2,000**
Work Certified	**1,400**
Work Not Certified	**400**
Estimated Further Cost to Completion	**700**
Progress Payment: Received	**1,000**
To be Received	**200**

The firm seeks your advice and assistance in the presentation of accounts keeping in view the requirements of AS – 7.

ANSWER:

AMOUNT TO BE DISCLOSED AS PER DISCLOSURE REQUIREMENTS OF AS – 7

	Particulars	₹ In Lakhs
A	Additions during the year	
	Cost Incurred during the year (1,400 + 400)	1,800
	Revenue recognized during the year (2,000 × 1,400)/2,500	1,120
	Total [A]	2,920
B	Deductions during the year	
	Expenses recognized during the year (Work certified)	1,400
	Expected loss [(₹ 1,400 lakhs + ₹ 400 lakhs + ₹ 700 lakhs)	
	₹ 2,000 lakhs] – [₹ 1,400 lakhs – ₹ 1,120]	220
	Total [B]	1,620
C	Balance [A – B] As per disclosure requirement of AS – 7]	1,300
D	Progress Billings	1,200
E	Amount due from customers for contract work [D – E]	100
F	Progress payment received	1,000
G	Retentions [D – F]	200

QUESTION 6: The following information is extracted from the books of X Ltd. for the year ending 31st March, 2015.

Particulars	Contract			
	A	B	C	D
Contract revenue recognized during the year	50,000	1,25,000	1,00,000	2,00,000
Contract expense recognized during the year	50,000	1,00,000	1,20,000	1,50,000
Contract cost incurred during period	70,000	1,00,000	150,000	1,40,000
Expected loss		20,000		30,000
Progress billings	50,000	12,00,000	1,00,000	2,10,000
Advance received during year	20,000			10,000
Opening balance of contract work in progress			10,000	10,000
(Progress billing was not taken into consideration while determining this account)				

Required: How should this information should be disclosed as per AS – 7?

ANSWER:

AMOUNT TO BE DISCLOSED AS PER DISCLOSURE REQUIREMENTS OF AS – 7

Particulars	₹
Contract revenue recognized as revenue in the period	4,75,000
Aggregate amount of costs incurred and recognized profits	4,85,000
(less recognized losses) upto the reporting date	
Amount of advances received	30,000

Gross amount due from customers for contract work as an asset	15,000
Gross amount due to customers for contract work as a liability	10,000

Working Note:

	Particulars	Contracts				
		A	B	C	D	Total
A	Opening Balance			10,000	10,000	20,000
B	Additions during the year					
	Cost Incurred during the year	70,000	1,00,000	1,50,000	1,40,000	4,60,000
	Revenue recognized during the year	50,000	1,25,000	1,00,000	2,00,000	4,75,000
	Total B	1,20,000	2,25,000	2,50,000	3,40,000	9,35,000
C	Deductions during the year					
	Expenses recognized during the year	50,000	1,00,000	1,20,000	1,50,000	4,20,000
	Expected loss	20,000		30,000		50,000
	Total C	70,000	1,00,000	1,50,000	1,50,000	4,70,000
D	Balance [A + B – C]	50,000	1,25,000	1,10,000	2,00,000	4,85,000
E	Progress billings	50,000	1,20,000	1,00,000	2,10,000	4,80,000
F	Amount due from customers	0	5,000	10,000	0	15,000
G	Amount due to customers	0	0	0	10,000	10,000

SECTION E : ACCOUNTING FOR SPECIAL TRANSACTIONS

29 ACCOUNTING FOR BILLS OF EXCHANGE

DISHONOUR OF A BILL

PROBLEM 1

A sold goods to B for ₹ 10,000 on 1st Jan. and drew upon him a three months bill for the amount. B accepted the bill and returned to A. At maturity, the bill was dishonoured. Pass the necessary journal entries in the books of A and B in each of the following alternative cases:

Case (a) When A retained the bill till the due date and paid noting charges of ₹ 100.

Case (b) When A got the bill discounted with his bankers @ 15% p.a. on 4th Feb. and the bank paid the noting charges of ₹ 100.

Case (c) When A endorsed the bill one month after the acceptance in favour of his creditor C in settlement of his debt for ₹ 10,200 and C paid the noting charges of ₹ 100.

Case (d) When A sent the bill to his bankers for collection and the bank paid the noting charges of ₹ 100.

SOLUTION

A'S JOURNAL

Date	Particulars		L.F.	Dr. (₹)	Cr. (₹)
	Entries in all cases:				
Jan.1	B	Dr.		10,000	
	To Sales A/c				10,000
	(Being the goods sold to B on credit)				
Jan. 1	Bills Receivable A/c	Dr.		10,000	
	To B				10,000
	(Being the acceptance of the bill received from B)				
	Additional Entry in Case (a):				
Apr.4	B	Dr.		10,100	
	To Bills Receivable A/c				10,000
	To Cash A/c				100
	(Being the amount of dishonoured bill and noting charges debited to the drawee)				
	Additional Entries in Case (b):				
Feb. 2	Bank A/c	Dr.		9,750	
	Discount A/c	Dr.		250	
	To Bills Receivable A/c				10,000
	(Being the bill discounted @ 15% p.a)				
Apr. 4	B	Dr.		10,100	
	To Bank A/c				10,100
	(Being the amount of dishonoured bill and noting charges debited to the drawee).				

	Additional Entries in Case (c):				
Feb. 1	C	Dr.		10,200	
	To Bill Receivable A/c				10,000
	To Discount Received A/c				200
	(Being the bill of ₹ 10,000 endorsed to C in settlement of ₹ 10,200)				
Apr. 4	B	Dr.		10,100	
	Discount Received A/c	Dr.		200	
	To C				10,300
	(Being the amount of dishonoured bill and noting charges debited to the drawee and the discount received written back)				
	Additional Entries in Case (d):				
Jan. 1	Bills sent for Collection A/c	Dr.		10,000	
	To Bills Receivable A/c				10,000
	(Being the bill sent for collection)				
Apr. 4	B	Dr.		10,100	
	To Bill sent for Collection A/c				10,000
	To Bank A/c				100
	(Being the amount of dishonoured bill and noting charges debited to the drawee)				

B'S JOURNAL

Date	Particulars		L.F.	Dr. (₹)	Cr. (₹)
Jan.1	Purchases A/c	Dr.		10,000	
	To A				10,000
	(Being the goods purchased on credit from A)				
Jan. 1	A	Dr.		10,000	
	To Bills Payable A/c				10,000
	(Being the acceptance of the bill given to A)				
April 4	Bills Payable A/c	Dr.		10,000	
	Noting Charges A/c	Dr.		100	
	To A				10,100
	(Being the amount of dishonoured bill and noting charges credited to the drawer)				

PROBLEM 2

A bill receivable for ₹ 10,000, which had been discounted at ₹ 9,500, is dishonoured and bank paid ₹ 200 as Noting Charges. Give Journal Entries to record the above in the books of: (i) the Drawer; (ii) the Drawee, and (iii) the Bank.

SOLUTION

JOURNAL OF DRAWER

Date	Particulars		L.F.	Dr. (₹)	Cr. (₹)
	Drawee's A/c	Dr.		10,200	
	To Bank A/c				10,200
	(Being the amount of dishonoured bill and Noting Charges debited to Drawee's A/c)				

JOURNAL OF DRAWEE

Date	Particulars		L.F.	Dr. (₹)	Cr. (₹)
	Bills Payable A/c	Dr.		10,000	
	Noting Charges A/c	Dr.		200	
	To Drawer's A/c				10,200
	(Being the amount of dishonoured bill and Noting Charges credited to Drawer)				

JOURNAL OF BANK

Date	Particulars		L.F.	Dr. (₹)	Cr. (₹)
	Drawer's A/c	Dr.		10,200	
	To Bills Receivable Discounted A/c				10,000
	To Cash A/c				200
	(Being the dishonour of the bill and payment of Noting Charges)				

PROBLEM 3

Rahim owed Ram ₹ 70,000 for which he accepted a bill drawn on him by Ram payable after 3 Months from 1st January.

On the 4th January the bill was discounted by the drawer with his bank for 95% value.

The bill was not met on the due date and the bank, therefore, debited the same to the drawer's account with ₹ 10 incidental charges and ₹ 40 over due interest, on the 10th April.

The drawee settled the bill value together with cost on 11th April.

Required: Pass Journal Entries in the books of Rahim and of Ram for the above transactions.

SOLUTION

JOURNAL OF RAM

Date	Particulars		L.F.	Dr. (₹)	Cr. (₹)
Jan.1	Bills Receivable A/c	Dr.		70,000	
	To Rahim A/c				70,000
	(Being bill drawn on Rahim for 3 months and acceptance received)				

Jan. 2	Bank A/c	Dr.		66,500	
	Discounting Charges A/c	Dr.		3,500	
	To Bills Receivable A/c				70,000
	(Being the bill discounted with bank for 95% value)				
Jan. 10	Rahim A/c	Dr.		70,050	
	To Bank A/c				70,050
	(At maturity the discounted bill being dishonoured, Bill Value plus incidental charges & interest debited by Bank)				
Jan. 11	Bank A/c	Dr.		70,050	
	To Rahim A/c				70,050
	(Being the amount received from Rahim in settlement of the dishonoured bill)				

JOURNAL OF RAHIM

Date	Particulars		L.F.	Dr. (₹)	Cr. (₹)
Jan. 1	Bills of A/c	Dr.		70,000	
	To Bills Payable A/c				70,000
	(Being acceptance given to Ram)				
Apr. 4	Bills Payable A/c	Dr.		70,000	
	Interest A/c	Dr.		40	
	Incidental Charges A/c	Dr.		10	
	To Ram A/c				70,050
	(Being the acceptance dishonoured at maturity)				
Apr. 11	Ram A/c	Dr.		70,050	
	To Bank A/c				70,050
	(Being payment made to Ram in settlement of the dishonoured bill inclu.. incidental charges and interest)				

INSOLVENCY OF ACCEPTOR OF A BILL

PROBLEM 4

Yashpal owed money to Srinivas and hence accepted two bills each of ₹ 4,850 of three months duration drawn on him by the latter, on July 1. Srinivas endorsed one of the bills in favour of Hariram on July 7. On the same date he discounted the other bill with his bank and received net proceeds of ₹ 4,675.

Yashpal failed to meet both the bills on the due date. On 4th Oct., the bank debited the account of Srinivas with value of second bill plus their charges of ₹ 20.

Yashpal is declared insolvent and his estate paid 60 paise in the rupee, on 1st Nov.

Required: Show Journal Entries in respect of the above in the books of Yashpal and Srinivas.

SOLUTION

JOURNAL OF YASHPAL

Date	Particulars		L.F.	Dr. (₹)	Cr. (₹)
July. 1	Srinivas A/c	Dr.		9,700	
	To Bills Payable A/c				9,700
	(Being the two bills each of ₹ 4,850 payable 3 months after date accepted)				
Oct. 4	Bills Payable A/c	Dr.		9,700	
	Bank Charges A/c	Dr.		20	
	To Srinivas				9,720
	(Being the acceptances to Mr Srinivas dishonoured, ₹ 20 due to him for bank charges)				
Nov. 1	Srinivas A/c	Dr.		9,720	
	To Bank A/c				5,832
	To Deficiency A/c				3,888
	(Being the first and final payment made @ 60 paise in a rupee of the net amount due)				

JOURNAL OF SRINIVAS

Date	Particulars		L.F.	Dr. (₹)	Cr. (₹)
July 1	Bills Receivable A/c	Dr.		9,700	
	To Yashpal A/c				9, 700
	(Being the received two bills each of ₹ 4,850 payable 3 months after date)				
July 7	Hari Ram A/c	Dr.		4,850	
	To Bills Receivable A/c				4,850
	(Being the bills endorsed to Hari Ram)				
July 7	Bank A/c	Dr.		4,675	
	Discounting Charges A/c	Dr.		175	
	To Bills Receivable A/c				4,850
	(Being the bill discounted for ₹ 4,675)				
Oct. 4	Yashpal A/c	Dr.		4,870	
	To Bank A/c				4,870
	(Being the dishonoured bill taken over from Bank on payment of Bill value plus Bank Charges)				
	Yashpal A/c	Dr.		4,850	
	To Hari Ram A/c				4,850
	(Being the endorsed bill dishonoured)				
Nov. 1	Bank A/c	Dr.		5,832	
	Bad Debts A/c	Dr.		3,888	
	To Yashpal A/c				9,720
	(Being the first and final dividend received @ 60 paise in a rupee of the net amount due)				

PROBLEM 5

Amarnath drew on Parker a bill of exchange for ₹ 1,00,000 on 1st January payable after 3 months from 1st January, which Parker accepted. On 4th January Amarnath discounted the bill with his bankers at 18% p.a. Parker failed to meet the bill on due date and the bill was returned to Amarnath with bank charges ₹ 200 debited to him by the bank. Amarnath claimed the bill value plus bank charges from Parker. However only 40% of the amount claimed could be recovered by Amarnath on 8th April as Parker was declared insolvent.

Required: Pass Journal Entries in the books of Amarnath and Parker for the above transactions.

SOLUTION

JOURNAL OF AMARNATH

Date	Particulars		L.F.	Dr. (₹)	Cr. (₹)
Jan. 1	Bills Receivable A/c	Dr.		1,00,000	
	To Parker A/c				1,00,000
	(Being the Acceptance received payable 3 months after date)				
Jan.1	Bank A/c	Dr.		95,500	
	Discounting Charges A/c	Dr.		4,500	
	To Bills Receivable A/c				1,00,000
	(Being the bill discounted @ 18% p.a.)				
Apr. 4	Parker A/c	Dr.		1,00,200	
	To Bank A/c				1,00,200
	(Being the acceptance dishonoured, Bank Charges being ₹ 200)				
Apr. 8	Bank A/c	Dr.		40,080	
	Bad Debts A/c	Dr.		60,120	
	To Parker A/c				1,00,200
	(Being the first and final dividend received @ 40% of the net amount due)				

JOURNAL OF PARKER

Date	Particulars		L.F.	Dr. (₹)	Cr. (₹)
Jan. 1	Amarnath A/c	Dr.		1,00,000	
	To Bills Payable A/c				1,00,000
	(Being the acceptance given for 3 months after date)				
Apr. 4	Bills Payable A/c	Dr.		1,00,000	
	Bank Charges A/c	Dr.		200	
	To Amarnath A/c				1,00,200
	(Being the B/P cancelled)				
Apr. 8	Amarnath A/c	Dr.		1,00,200	
	To Bank A/c				40,080
	To Deficiency A/c				60,120
	(Being the first and final payment made @ 40% of the net amount due)				

RENEWAL OF A BILL

PROBLEM 6

Before the due date of the bill for ₹ 3,000.

(a) X, the acceptor approached us and pays ₹ 1,000 in cash and asks us to draw on him another bill for 5 months for ₹ 2,000 plus interest @ 18% p.a.

(b) X pays us interest @ 18% p.a. and accepts another bill for 5 months.

(c) X pays us ₹ 1,000 plus interest @ 18% p.a. and accepts another bill for 5 months for ₹ 2,000.

(d) X pays us ₹ 1,000 in cash and endorses over to us a bill of his for ₹ 1,000 and accepts a fresh bill for 5 months for the balance plus interest @ 18% p.a.

Required: Pass the necessary journal entries in each of the above alternative cases.

SOLUTION

JOURNAL OF RAM

Date	Particulars		L.F.	Dr. (₹)	Cr. (₹)
(a)	Cash A/c	Dr.		1,000	
	To X				1,000
	(Being cash received from X)				
	X	Dr.		150	
	To Interest A/c				150
	(Being the interest due from X)				
	Bills Receivable A/c	Dr.		2,150	
	To X				2,150
	(Being acceptance of B/R received)				
(b)	X	Dr.		225	
	To Interest A/c				225
	(Being interest due from X)				
	Cash A/c	Dr.		225	
	To X				225
	(Being interest received)				
	Bills Receivable A/c	Dr.		3,000	
	To X				3,000
	(Being the acceptance of B/R rceived)				
(c)	X	Dr.		150	
	To Interest A/c				150
	(Being interest due from X)				
	Cash A/c	Dr.		1,150	
	To X				1,150
	(Being cash received from X)				
	Bills Receivable A/c	Dr.		2.000	
	To X				2,000
	(Being B/R drawn upon X)				

(d)	Cash A/c	Dr.		1,000	
	Bills Receivable A/c	Dr.		1,000	
	To X				2,000
	(Being cash & B/R received from X)				
	X	Dr.		75	
	To Interest A/c				75
	(Being interest due from X)				
	Bills Receivable A/c	Dr.		1,075	
	To X				1,075
	(Being acceptance of B/R received)				

PROBLEM 7

On 15th Jan. Sun sold goods to Sky for ₹ 1,800. Sky paid ₹ 360 in cash and for balance accepted three Bills, No. 1 for ₹ 420 at one month, No. 2 for ₹ 480 at two months, and No. 3, ₹ 540 at three months.

Sun endorsed 1st bill to Moon his creditor on 16 Jan. in full settlement of ₹ 426; discounted the 2nd bill at his bank for ₹ 475 and retained the third bill till maturity.

The first bill is met at maturity. The second bill is dishonoured and ₹ 6 being paid as noting charges, Sun charges ₹ 9 for interest and draws on Sky a fourth bill for the amount at three months. At maturity, the third bill was renewed with interest @ 5% p.a. for three months. The fifth bill was duly accepted by Sky. The fourth and fifth bills were met at maturity. Give journal entries in the books of Sun.

SOLUTION

JOURNAL OF SUN

Date	Particulars		L.F.	Dr. (₹)	Cr. (₹)
Jan. 15	Sky A/c	Dr.		1,800.00	
	To Sales A/c				1,800.00
	(Being the goods sold to Shashi)				
	Cash A/c	Dr.		360.00	
	Bills Receivable (No. 1) A/c	Dr.		420.00	
	Bills Receivable (No. 2) A/c	Dr.		480.00	
	Bills Receivable (No. 3) A/c	Dr.		540.00	
	To Sky				1,800.00
	(Being the cash and the acceptance of three bills for 420, II for 480, and III for 540 received from Sky)				
Jan. 16	Moon	Dr.		426.00	
	To Bills Receivable (No. 1) A/c				420.00
	To Discount Received A/c				6.00
	(Being the first bill endorsed to Nahar in full settlement)				
	Bank A/c	Dr.		475.00	
	Discount A/c	Dr.		5.00	

	To Bills Receivable (No. 2) A/c (Being the second bill discounted with bank)			480.00
Mar. 18	Sky Dr. To Bank A/c (Being the second bill dishonoured on maturity and noting charges incurred ₹ 6)		486.00	486.00
	Sky Dr. To Interest A/c (Being the interest charged)		9	9
	Bills Receivable (No. 4) A/c Dr. To Sky (Being the acceptance of the fourth bill payable after three months received from Shashi)		495.00	495.00
Apr. 18	Sky Dr. To Bills Receivable A/c (Being the third bill cancelled)		540.00	540.00
	Sky Dr. To Interest A/c (Being the interest on the amount of third bill @ 5% p.a. for three months)		6.75	6.75
	Bill Receivable A/c Dr. To Sky (Being the acceptance of the fifth bill received from Shashi)		546.75	546.75
June 21	Cash A/c Dr. To Bills Receivable (No. 4) A/c (Being the fourth bill met at maturity)		495.00	495.00
July 21	Cash A/c Dr. To Bills Receivable (No. 5) A/c (Being the fifth bill met at maturity)		546.75	546.75

PROBLEM 8

Ramratan sold goods to Ahmed for ₹ 10,000 on 30th June, 2014, for which the latter accepted 4 bills of ₹ 2,500 each drawn on him payable after 2, 4, 5 and 8 months respectively. Ramratan retained the first bill. The second bill was sent by him for collection. The third bill was endorsed by him to C in part payment of ₹ 4,000 owed to him. The fourth bill was discounted by him with his bankers at a discount of 15% p.a.

The first bill was met on the date. As regards the second bill, Ahmed met Ramratan two days before the maturity date of the bill and paid him ₹ 1,000 and accepted a fresh bill for 1 month for the balance with interest of 18% p.a. This bill as well as the third bill were met by the drawee.

Ahmed was declared as insolvent on 31st December, 2014 and on the fourth bill becoming due, the Bank debited Ramratan with the amount of the bill and noting charges of ₹ 250. It is ascertained by Ramratan that the estate of Ahmed will not be in a position to meet liabilities to an extent of more than 40%.

What will be the journal entries to be made in the books of Ramratan for the accounting years 2014 and 2015 assuming a dividend of 40 paise in a rupee was realised from Ahmed's estate on 15.3.2015. Show Journal Entries (without narrations) in the books of Ramratan.

SOLUTION **JOURNAL OF RAMRATAN**

Date	Particulars		L.F.	Dr. (₹)	Cr. (₹)
2014	Ahmed's A/c	Dr.		10,000.00	
Jun 30	To Sales A/c				10,000.00
	Bills Receivable (No. 1) A/c	Dr.		2,500.00	
	Bills Receivable (No. 2) A/c	Dr.		2,500.00	
	Bills Receivable (No. 3) A/c	Dr.		2,500.00	
	Bills Receivable (No. 4) A/c	Dr.		2,500.00	
	To Ahmed's A/c				10,000.00
	Bills sent for Collection A/c	Dr.		2,500.00	
	To Bills Receivable (No. 2) A/c				2,500.00
	C's A/c	Dr.		2,500.00	
	To Bills Receivable (No. 3) A/c				2,500.00
	Bank A/c	Dr.		2,250.00	
	Discount A/c	Dr.		250.00	
	To Bills Receivable (No. 4) A/c				2,500.00
Sep. 2	Bank A/c	Dr.		2,500.00	
	To Bills Receivable (No. 1) A/c				2,500.00
Nov. 1	Ahmed's A/c	Dr.		2,500.00	
	To Bills sent for Collection A/c				2,500.00
Nov. 1	Bank A/c	Dr.		1,000.00	
	Bills Receivable (No. 5) A/c	Dr.		1,522.50	
	To Ahmed's A/c				2,500.00
	To Interest A/c				22.50
Dec. 3	Bank A/c	Dr.		1,522.50	
	To Bills Receivable (No. 5) A/c				1,522.50
Dec. 31	Profit and Loss A/c	Dr.		1,500.00	
	To Provision for Doubtful Debts A/c				1,500.00
2015					
Mar. 3	Ahmed's A/c	Dr.		2,750.00	
	To Bank A/c				2,750.00
Mar. 15	Bank A/c	Dr.		1,100.00	
	Bad Debts A/c	Dr.		1,650.00	
	To Ahmed's A/c				2,750.00

Notes:

No Entry is necessary

(i) *when Ramratan retains the first bill; and*

(ii) *when Ahmed met the third bill which was earlier endorsed by Ramratan to MrC.*

RETIREMENT OF A BILL

PROBLEM 9

Mr David draws two bills of exchange on 1st Jan. for ₹ 6,000 and ₹ 10,000. The bills of exchange for ₹ 6,000 is for two months while the bill of exchange for ₹ 10,000 is for three months. These bills are accepted by Mr Thomas. On 4th March Mr Thomas requests Mr David to renew the first bill with interest at 18% p.a. for a period of two months. Mr David agrees to this proposal. On 20th March, Mr Thomas retires the acceptance for ₹ 10,000, the interest rebate i.e., discount being ₹ 100. Before the due date of the renewed bill, Mr Thomas becomes insolvent and only 50 paise in a rupee could be recovered from the estate. You are to required to give the journal entries in the books of Mr David.

SOLUTION

JOURNAL OF MR DAVID

Date	Particulars		L.F.	Dr. (₹)	Cr. (₹)
Jan. 1	Bills Receivable No. 1 A/c	Dr.		6,000	
	Bills Receivable No. 2 A/c	Dr.		10,000	
	To Mr Thomas				16,000
	(Beings bills due on 4th March and 4th April respectively accepted by Mr Thomas)				
Mar. 4	Mr Thomas	Dr.		6,000	
	To Bills Receivable No. 1 A/c				6,000
	(Being cancellation of B/R No. 1 upon renewal)				
Mar. 4	Mr Thomas	Dr.		180	
	To Interest A/c				180
	(Being the interest due on ₹ 6,000 @ 18% p.a. for 2 months on renewal of bill)				
Mar. 4	Bills Receivable No. 3 A/c	Dr.		6,180	
	To Mr Thomas				6,180
	(Being B/R No. 3 due on 7th May, accepted by Mr Thomas in lieu of bill already cancelled)				
Mar. 20	Cash A/c	Dr.		9,900	
	Rebate A/c	Dr.		100	
	To Bills Receivable No. 2 A/c				10,000
	(Being the amount received on retirement of B/R No. 2 before due date)				
May 7	Mr Thomas	Dr.		6,180	
	To Bills Receivable No. 3 A/c				6,180
	(Being the entry for dishonour of B/R No. 3 on maturity)				

	Cash A/c	Dr.		3,090	
	Bad Debts A/c	Dr.		3,090	
	To Mr Thomas				6,180
	(Being a dividend of 50 paise in a rupee received from official assignee of Mr Thomas and the irrecovered balance written off as bad debts)				

PROBLEM 10

Record the following in the Journal of Ram.

(a) Shyam's acceptance for ₹ 4,500, due this day, returned dishonoured, Noting charges ₹ 10.

(b) Murli's acceptance for ₹ 20,000 renewed for three months, plus interest at 5% p.a.

(c) Our acceptance for ₹ 20,000 retired one month before the due date at a discount of 12% p.a.

(d) Our acceptance in favour of X for ₹ 1,500 dishonoured for want of instructions. X claims ₹ 1,510 which is paid by a cheque.

(e) Our acceptance to P to for ₹ 900 renewed for 3 months on the condition that ₹ 300 is paid in cash immediately and the remaining balance to carry interest @ 12% p.a.

(f) K's Promissorty Note for ₹ 720 endorsed in favour of D returned dishonoured. D paid ₹ 18 as noting charges. Ram pays D by cheque and accepts from K another bill for the amount due along with interest ₹ 48.

SOLUTION

JOURNAL OF RAM

Date	Particulars		L.F.	Dr. (₹)	Cr. (₹)
(a)	Shyam	Dr.		4,510	
	To Bills Receivable A/c				4,500
	To Cash A/c				10
	(Being B/R dishonoured, noting changes being ₹ 10)				
(b)	(i) Murli	Dr.		20,000	
	To Bills Receivable A/c				20,000
	(Being the old bill cancelled)				
	(ii) Murli	Dr.		250	
	To Interest A/c				250
	(Being interest due for 3 months)				
	(iii) Bills Receivable A/c	Dr.		20,250	
	To Murli				20,250
	(Being B/R renewed)				
(c)	Bills Payable A/c	Dr.		20,000	
	To Rebate on Bill A/c				200
	To Cash A/c				19,800
	(Being B/P retired @ 12% p.a. one month ago)				

(d)	Bills Payable A/c Noting charges A/c To X (Being B/P dishonoured)	Dr. Dr.		1,500 10	 1,510
	X To Bank A/c (Being cheque issued to X)	Dr.		1,510	 1,510
(e)	Bills Payable A/c Interest A/c To P (Being the original Bills Payable cancelled and interest charged for renewal of the same)	Dr. Dr.		900 18	 918
	P A/c To Cash A/c To Bills Payable A/c (Being P was paid off partly in cash and partly through fresh acceptance)	Dr.		918	 300 618
(f)	K A/c To D A/c (Being the endorsed Bill dishonoured)	Dr.		738	 738
	D A/c To Bank A/c (Being D paid off)	Dr.		738	 738
	K A/c To Interest A/c (Being the acceptance received)	Dr.		48	 48
	Bill Receivable A/c To K (Being the fresh acceptance received from K for the net amount due)	Dr.		786	 786

ACCOMMODATION BILLS

PROBLEM 11

Inder drew upon Mohan a bill for ₹ 9,000 on 1 April for three months, for mutual accommodation. Mohan accepted the draft. On 4th April Inder got it discounted at 6% p.a. and remitted one-third of the proceeds to Mohan. At maturity, Inder was not able to send the required sums and asked Mohan to receive a two month Promissory Note for ₹ 6,090 which Mohan did. Mohan got the Note discounted for ₹ 6,000 and met his acceptance. Inder became insolvent just before his Promissory Note was due for payment. Only 50% was received from his estate. Give Journal entries in the book of both Inder and Mohan.

SOLUTION

JOURNAL OF INDER

Date	Particulars		L.F.	Dr. (₹)	Cr. (₹)
April 1	Bills Receivable A/c	Dr.		9,000	
	To Mohan				9,000
	(Being the receipt of Mohan's acceptance for mutual accommodation)				
April 4	Bank A/c	Dr.		8,865	
	Discount A/c	Dr.		135	
	To Bills Receivable A/c				9,000
	(Being the bill discounted @ 6% p.a.)				
"	Mohan	Dr.		3,000	
	To Cash A/c				2,955
	To Discount A/c				45
	(Being 1/3 of proceeds remitted to Mohan and 1/3 discount debited to him)				
July 4	Interest A/c	Dr.		90	
	To Mohan				90
	(The interest due to Mohan for agreeing to wait for 2 months (₹ 6,090, the amount of new bill, minus ₹ 6,000 due)				
July 4	Mohan	Dr.		6,090	
	To Bills Payable A/c				6,090
	(Being the amount of the pronote issued in favour of Mohan)				
Sept. 7	Bills Payable A/c	Dr.		6,090	
	To Mohan				6,090
	(Being the note given to Mohan dishonoured due to insolvency)				
"	Mohan	Dr.		6,090	
	To Cash A/c				3,045
	To Deficiency A/c				3,045
	(Being a dividend fo 50 paisa in a rupee paid to Mohan and the undischarged balace transferred to Deficiency A/c)				

JOURNAL OF MOHAN

Date	Particulars		L.F.	Dr. (₹)	Cr. (₹)
April	Inder	Dr.		9,000	
	To Bills Payable A/c				9,000
	(Being the acceptance issued in favour of Inder for mutual accommodation)				

"	Cash A/c Dr. Discount A/c Dr. To Inder (Being 1/3 of the proceeds received from Inder and one-third discount credited to him.)		2,955 45	 3,000
July 4	Inder Dr. To Interest A/c (Being Interest due from Inder for a 2-month extension of time)		90	 90
"	Bills Receivable A/c Dr. To Inder (Being the receipt of his promissory note for ₹ 6,090)		6,000	 6,000
"	Bank A/c Dr. Discount A/c Dr. To Bills Receivable A/c (Being the bill discounted for ₹ 6,000)		6,000 90	 6,090
"	Bills Payable A/c Dr. To Cash A/c (Being the bill issued in favour of Inder discharged)		9,000	 9,000
Sept. 7	Inder Dr. To Bank A/c (Being the dishonour of Inder's pronote due to insolvency)		6,090	 6,090
"	Cash A/c Dr. Bad Debts A/c Dr. To Inder (Being the receipt of 50% of a amount due from Inder and the balance written-off as bad debt)		3,045 3,045	 6,090

PROBLEM 12

A and B were both in need of temporary accommodation. On 1 April, A accepted B's draft for ₹ 2,000 for three months and B accepted A's draft for ₹ 1,000 for three months. The two bills were discounted at the respective banks for ₹ 1,971 and ₹ 980. At maturity, A met his acceptance but B could not arrange to send the required amount to A and accepted A's draft for ₹ 1,500 for two months. this was discounted for ₹ 1,460 and A remitted to B ₹ 230. On Sept. 6, B was declared insolvent and his estate paid only 30%. Give Journal entries in the Books of A and the ledger account of A in B's books.

SOLUTION

JOURNAL OF A

Date	Particulars	L.F.	Dr. (₹)	Cr. (₹)
April 1	B Dr. To Bills Payable A/c (Being the acceptance given in favour of B)		2,000	 2,000

"	Bills Receivable A/c	Dr.		1,000	
	To B				1,000
	(Being the acceptance received from B)				
"	Bank A/c	Dr.		980	
	Discount A/c	Dr.		20	
	To Bills Receivable A/c				1,000
	(Being the B/R discounted for ₹ 980)				
"	Bills Payable A/c	Dr.		2,000	
	To Cash A/c				2,000
	(Being own acceptance for ₹ 2,000 met)				
July 4	Bills Receivable A/c	Dr.		1,500	
	To B	Dr.			1,500
	(Being the acceptance received from B)				
"	Bank A/c	Dr.		1,460	
	Discount A/c	Dr.		40	
	To Bills Receivable A/c				1,500
	(Being B's acceptance discounted for ₹ 1,460)				
"	B	Dr.		263.70	
	To Cash A/c				230.00
	To Discount A/c				33.70
	(Being ₹ 230 remitted to B and proportionate discount ₹ 33.70 (i.e. ₹ 40 ´ ₹ 1,230/₹ 1,460 charged)				
Sept. 7	B	Dr.		1,500	
	To Bank A/c				1,500
	(Being B 's acceptance dishonoured due to insolvency)				
"	Cash A/c	Dr.		380.00	
	Bad Debts A/c	Dr.		883.70	
	To B				1,263.70
	(Being a dividend of 30 paisa in a rupee received from B's estate and the balance wirtten-off as bad debt)				

Dr. **A'S ACCOUNT IN THE BOOKS OF B** **Cr.**

Date	Particulars	L.F.	₹	Date	Particulars	L.F.	₹
April 1	To Bills PayableA/c		1,000.00	April 1	By Bills Receivable A/c		2,000.00
July 4	To Bills Payable A/c		1,500.00	July 4	By Cash A/c		230.00
Sept. 7	To Cash A/c		379.00		By Discount A/c		33.70
"	To Deficiency (amount unpaid)		884.70		By Bills Payable A/c		1,500.00
			3,763.70				3,763.70

PROBLEM 13

Arun and Anand were friends and in need of funds. On 1st Jan., Arun drew a bill for ₹ 2,00,000 for 3 months on Anand. On 4th Jan. Arun got the bill discounted at 10% p.a. and remitted half of the proceeds to Anand. At maturity, Anand could not meet the bill, instead, Arun accepted Anand's bill for ₹ 1,20,000 on 4th April for two months. This was discounted by Anand at 12% p.a. Out of this, ₹ 19,600 was paid to Arun after deducting ₹ 400 discounting charges. Due to financial crisis, Arun became insolvent and the bill drawn on him was dishonoured and his estate paid 50%. Days of grace for discount purposes may be ignored. Give journal entries in the books of Arun. Also prepare Anand's Account in Arun's books and Arun's Account in the books of Anand.

SOLUTION

JOURNAL OF ARUN

Date	Particulars		L.F.	Dr. (₹)	Cr. (₹)
Jan. 1	Bills Receivable A/c	Dr.		2,00,000	
	To Anand				2,00,000
	(Being the bill for ₹ 2,00,000 drawn on Anand)				
Jan. 4	Bank A/c	Dr.		1,95,000	
	Discount A/c	Dr.		5,000	
	To Bills Receivable A/c				2,00,000
	(Being the bill discounted @ 10% p.a.)				
Jan. 4	Anand	Dr.		1,00,000	
	To Bank A/c				97,500
	To Discount A/c				2,500
	(Being half the proceeds sent to Anand)				
April 4	Anand	Dr.		1,20,000	
	To Bills Payable A/c				1,20,000
	(Being the bill of Anand accepted)				
April 4	Bank A/c	Dr.		19,600	
	Discount A/c	Dr.		400	
	To Anand				20,000
	(Being proceeds received from Anand)				
July 7	Bills Payable A/c	Dr.		1,20,000	
	To Anand				1,20,000
	(Being the bill dishonoured)				
	Anand	Dr.		1,20,000	
	To Bank A/c				60,000
	To Deficiency A/c				60,000
	(Being 50% payments made to Anand and unpaid balance transferred to Deficiency A/c)				

Dr. **ANAND'S ACCOUNT IN THE BOOKS OF ARUN** **Cr.**

Particulars	₹	Particulars	₹
To Bank A/c	97,500	By Bills Receivable A/c	2,00,000
To Discount A/c	2,500	By Bank A/c	19,600
To Bills Payable A/c	1,20,000	By Discount A/c	400
To Bank A/c	60,000	By Bills Payable A/c	1,20,000
To Deficiency A/c	60,000		
	3,40,000		3,40,000

Dr. **ARUN'S ACCOUNT IN THE BOOKS OF ANAND** **Cr.**

Particulars	₹	Particulars	₹
To Bills Payable A/c	2,00,000	By Bank A/c	97,500
To Bank A/c	19,600	By Discount A/c	2,500
To Discount A/c	400	By Bills Receivable A/c	1,20,000
To Bank A/c	1,20,000	By Bank A/c	60,000
		By Bad Debts A/c	60,000
	3,40,000		3,40,000

PROBLEM 14

On 1st Jan, A drew and B accepted a bill at three months for ₹ 2,000. On 4th Jan, A discounted the bill at 15% p.a. and remitted half the proceeds to B. On 1st Feb., B drew and A accepted a bill at four months for ₹ 1,500. On 4th Feb. B discounted the bill at 15% p.a. and remitted half the proceeds to A. A and B agreed to share the discounts equally. At maturity, A met his acceptance but B failed to meet and recourse was had to A. A drew and B accepted a new bill at three months for the amounts of the original bill plus interest at 18% p.a. On July 1, B became a bankrupt and paid to his creditors only 50 paise in the rupee. Record these transactions in A's journal and prepare B's Account.

SOLUTION

A'S JOURNAL

Date	Particulars		L.F.	Dr. (₹)	Cr. (₹)
Jan. 1	Bills Receivable A/c	Dr.		2,000.00	
	To B				2,000.00
	(Being the acceptance of a bill received from B)				
Jan. 4	Bank A/c	Dr.		1,925.00	
	Discount A/c	Dr.		75.00	
	To Bills Receivable A/c				2,000.00
	(Being the bill discounted @ 15% p.a.)				
Jan. 4	B	Dr.		1,000.00	
	To Bank A/c				962.50
	To Discount A/c				37.50
	(Being half of the proceeds remitted to B)				

Feb. 1	B Dr. To Bills Payable A/c (Being the acceptance of a bill given to B)		1,500.00	1,500.00
Feb. 4	Bank A/c Dr. Discount A/c Dr. To B (Being half of the proceeds of the bill received from B)		712.50 37.50	750.00
April 4	B Dr. To Bank A/c (Being the bill dishonoured)		2,000.00	2,000.00
April 4	B Dr. To Interest A/c (Being the interest charged for 3 months on ₹ 2,000 @ 18% p.a.)		90.00	90.00
April 4	Bills Receivable A/c Dr. To B (Being the acceptance of a bill received from B)		2,090.00	2,090.00
June 4	Bills Payable A/c Dr. To Bank A/c (Being the bill discharged at maturity)		1,500.00	1,500.00
July 1	B Dr. To Bills Receivable A/c (Being the bill dishonoured)		2,090.00	2,090.00
July 1	Bank A/c Dr. Bad Debts A/c Dr. To B (Being a dividend of 50 paise in a rupee received from estate of B and the balance written off as bad debts)		920.00 920.00	1,840.00

Dr. **B'S ACCOUNT IN A'S LEDGER** Cr.

Date	Particulars	₹ P	Date	Particulars	₹ P
Jan. 4	To Bank A/c	962.50	Jan. 1	By Bills Receivable A/c	2,000.00
Jan. 4	To Discount A/c	37.50	Feb. 4	By Bank A/c	712.50
Feb. 1	To Bills Payable A/c	1,500.00	Feb. 4	By Discount A/c	37.50
Apr. 4	To Bank A/c (B/R dishonoured)	2,000.00	Apr. 4	By Bills Receivable A/c	2,090.00
Apr. 4	To Interest A/c	90.00	July 1	By Bank A/c	920.00
July 1	To Bills Receivable A/c (Dishonoured)	2,090.00	July 1	By Bad Debts A/c	920.00
		6,680.00			6,680.00

PROBLEM 15

Shubham draws on Rajendra a bill for ₹ 45,000 on 1st June for 3 months. Rajendra accepts the bill and sends it to Shubham who gets it discounted for ₹ 44,100. Shubham immediately remits ₹ 14,700 to Rajendra. On the due date Shubham, being unable to remit the amount due, accepts a bill for ₹ 63,000 for three months which is discounted by Rajendra for ₹ 61,650. Rajendra sends ₹ 11,100 to Shubham. On the due date Shubham becomes insolvent, his estate paying forty paise in the rupee. Give Journal Entries in the books of Shubham and Rajendra.

SOLUTION

JOURNAL OF SHUBHAM

Date	Particulars		L.F.	Dr. (₹)	Cr. (₹)
1st June	Bills Receivable A/c	Dr.		45,000	
	To Rajendra				45,000
	(Being acceptance received from Rajendra)				
4th June	Bank A/c	Dr.		44,100	
	Discount A/c	Dr.		900	
	To Bills Receivable A/c				45,000
	(Being bill discounted with Bank)				
4th June	Rajendra	Dr.		15,000	
	To Bank A/c				14,700
	To Discount A/c				300
	(Being 1/3rd proceeds of the discounted bill remitted to Rajendra)				
4th Sept	Rajendra	Dr.		63,000	
	To Bills Payable A/c				63,000
	(Being acceptance given to Rajendra)				
4th Sept	Bank A/c	Dr.		11,100	
	Discount A/c	Dr.		900	
	To Rajendra				12,000
	(Being amount received from Rajendra)				
7th Dec	Bills Payable A/c	Dr.		63,000	
	To Rajendra				63,000
	(Being bill dishonoured due to insolvency)				
	Rajendra	Dr.		42,000	
	To Bank A/c				16,800
	To Deficiency				25,200
	(Being 40% share paid to Rajendra from our estate)				

Working Note: *Calculation of discount to be borne by Shubham*

A	Amount due by Shubham but not remitted to Rajendra (₹ 45,000 – ₹ 15,000)	30,000
B	*Add:* Amount received by Shubham from Rajendra	11,100
C	Total amount due to Rajendra	41,100
D	Discount to be borne = ₹ 1,350 × (41,110/61,650) = ₹ 900	

JOURNAL OF RAJENDRA

Date	Particulars		L.F.	Dr. (₹)	Cr. (₹)
1st June	Shubham	Dr.		45,000	
	To Bills Payable A/c				45,000
	(Being the acceptance given to Shubham)				
4th June	Bank A/c	Dr.		14,700	
	Discount A/c			300	
	To Shubham				15,000
	(Being 1/3rd proceeds of disczounted bill received from Shubham)				
4th Sept	Bills Receivable A/c	Dr.		63,000	
	To Shubham				63,000
	(Being acceptance received from Shubham)				
	Bank A/c	Dr.		61,650	
	Discount A/c	Dr.		1,350	
	To Bills Receivable A/c				63,000
	(Being the bill discounted with the bank)				
	Bills Payable A/c	Dr.		45,000	
	To Bank A/c				45,000
	(Being the bill discharged)				
	Shubham	Dr.		12,000	
	To Bank A/c				11,100
	To Discount A/c				900
	(Being the amount paid to Shubham)				
7th Dec	Shubham	Dr.		63,000	
	To Bank A/c				63,000
	(Being bill dishonoured due to Shubham's insolvency)				
	Bank A/c	Dr.		16,800	
	Bad Debts A/c	Dr.		25,200	
	To Shubham				42,000
	(Being 40% share received from Shubham)				

PROBLEM 16

Anil draws a bill for ₹. 9,000 on Sanjay on 5th April for 3 months, which Sanjay returns it to Anil after accepting the same. Anil gets it discounted with the bank for ₹. 8,820 and remits one-third amount to Sanjay.

On the due date Anil fails to remit the amount due to Sanjay, but he accepts a bill for ₹.12,600 for three months, which Sanjay discount it for ₹. 12,330 and remits ₹. 2,220 to Anil. Before the maturity of the renewed bill Anil becomes insolvent and only 50% was realised from his estate on 15th October.

Required: Pass necessary Journal entries for the above transactions in the books of Anil.

SOLUTION

JOURNAL OF ANIL

Date	Particulars		L.F.	Dr. (₹)	Cr. (₹)
5th April	Bills Receivable A/c	Dr.		9,000	
	To Sanjay's A/c				9,000
	(Being acceptance received from Sanjay for mutual accommodation)				
	Bank A/c	Dr.		8,820	
	Discount A/c	Dr.		180	
	To Bills receivable A/c				9,000
	(Being Bill discounted with bank)				
	Sanjay's A/c	Dr.		3,000	
	To Bank A/c				2,940
	To Discount A/c				60
	(Being one-third proceeds of the bill sent to Sanjay)				
8th July	Sanjay's A/c	Dr.		12,600	
	To Bills payable A/c				12,600
	(Being acceptance given)				
	Bank A/c	Dr.		2,220	
	Discount A/c	Dr.		180	
	To Sanjay's A/c				2,400
	(Being proceeds of second bill received from Sanjay)				
11th Oct	Bills payable A/c	Dr.		12,600	
	To Sanjay's A/c				12,600
	(Being bill dishonoured due to insolvency)				
15th Oct	Sanjay's A/c (6,000 + 2,400)	Dr.		8,400	
	To Bank A/c				4,200
	To Deficiency A/c				4,200
	(Being insolvent, only 50% amount paid to Sanjay)				

PROBLEM 17

On 1st July G drew a bill for ₹ 80,000 for 3 months on H for mutual accommodation. H accepted the bill of exchange.

G had purchased goods worth ₹ 81,000 from J on the same date. G endorsed H's acceptance to J in full settlement.

On 1st September J purchased goods worth ₹ 90,000 from H.J. endorsed the bill of exchange received from G to H and paid ₹ 9,000 in full settlement of the amount due to H.

On 1st October H purchased goods worth ₹ 1,00,000 from G. He paid the amount due to G by cheque.

Pass the necessary Journal Entries in the books of H.

SOLUTION

JOURNAL OF H

Date	Particulars		L.F.	Dr. (₹)	Cr. (₹)
1st July	G	Dr.		80,000	
	To Bills Payable A/c				80,000
	(Being Bill accepted)				
1st Sept	J	Dr.		90,000	
	To Sales A/c				90,000
	(Being the goods sold to J)				
	Bill Receivable A/c	Dr.		80,000	
	Cash A/c	Dr.		9,000	
	Discount A/c	Dr.		1,000	
	To J 's Capital A/c				90,000
	(Being B/R of ₹ 80,000 & Cash ₹ 9,000 received from J and allowed him discount of ₹ 1,000.)				
	Bills Payable A/c	Dr.		80,000	
	To Bills Receivable A/c				80,000
	(Being own acceptance received from J 's endorsement, cancelled)				
1st Oct	Purchases A/c	Dr.		1,00,000	
	To G A/c				1,00,000
	(Being the goods purchased from G)				
	G	Dr.		20,000	
	To Bank A/c				20,000
	(Being the Balance paid by cheque)				

PROBLEM 18

The following bills were accepted on 1st January for four months:

(i) By B, ₹ 10,000 and by C, ₹ 15,000 in favour of A, (ii) By A, ₹ 20,000 and by C, ₹ 5,000 in favour of B, (iii) By A, ₹ 10,000 and by B ₹ 20,000 in favour of C.

All bills were discounted @ 18% p.a. and the proceeds were shared by the three parties equally. On the due date C becomes insolvent and later, a dividend of 30% was received from his estate. Give journal entries in the books of A.

SOLUTION

JOURNAL OF A

Date	Particulars		L.F.	Dr. (₹)	Cr. (₹)
Jan. 1	Bills Receivable A/c	Dr.		25,000	
	To B				10,000
	To C				15,000
	(Being Bills accepted by B and C)				

Jan. 1	B	Dr.		20,000	
	C	Dr.		10,000	
	To Bills Payable A/c				30,000
	(Being acceptances given to B and C)				
Jan. 1	C	Dr.		15,000	
	To B				15,000
	(Being net effect of acceptances between B and C)				
Jan. 1	Bank A/c	Dr.		23,500	
	Discount A/c	Dr.		1,500	
	To Bills Receivable A/c				25,000
	(Being Bills discounted with Bank)				
Jan.1	Cash A/c	Dr.		1,567	
	Discount A/c	Dr.		100	
	To C				1,667
	(Being cash received from C to make distribution of proceeds equal)				
	B	Dr.		1,667	
	To C				1,667
	(Being net effect of cash received by B from C)				
May 4	C	Dr.		15,000	
	To Bank A/c				15,000
	(Being bill accepted by C dishonoured)				
May 4	C	Dr.		5,000	
	To B				5,000
	(Being bill accepted by C in favour of B dishonoured)				
May 4	Bills Payable A/c	Dr.		30,000	
	To Cash A/c				30,000
	(Being Bills payable discharged)				
May 4	Cash A/c	Dr.		8,000	
	Bad Debts A/c	Dr.		18,666	
	To C				26,666
	(Being 30% proceeds received from C and balance written off as bad debts)				
May 4	B	Dr.		9,333	
	To Bad Debts A/c				9,333
	(Being 50% bad debts transferred to B)				
May 4	Cash A/c	Dr.		1,000	
	To B				1,000
	(Being Cash received from B in final settlement)				

Working Notes:

(i) Distribution of Proceeds

Total Value of the bills as ₹ 80,000 and net proceeds after discount is (₹ 80,000 – ₹ 4,800) ₹ 75,200. The proceeds have been distributed equally amount the three persons as under:

Particulars	Total	A	B	C
Gross Amount	80,000	26,667	26,667	26,666
Discount	4,800	1,600	1,600	1,600
Net Amt.	75,200	25,067	25,067	25,066
Less: Proceeds of own bills		23,500	23,500	28,200
		1,567	1,567	3,134

Hence C will pay ₹ 1,567 to A and ₹ 1,567 to B to make the distribution equal.

Similarly discount will also be shared equally. Total discount of ₹ 4,800 will be shared equally i.e. ₹ 1,600 by each party. Hence A and B bear additional discount of ₹ 100.

(ii) Bad Debts have been shared equally by A and B.

30 ACCOUNTING FOR CONSIGNMENT

PROBLEM 1

On 1st September goods of the cost of ₹ 2,64,000 were consigned by Shri Shyamlal of Bangalore to his agent Shri Mahesh of Cochin at proforma invoice price of 20% profit on cost price. Shri Shyamlal paid insurance and other forwarding charges on consignment amounting to ₹ 10,000. Shri Mahesh was allowed ₹ 2,000 being establishment cost. He was entitled to 5% commission on gross sales and an additional 3% Delcredere commission on credit sales only. Shri Mahesh made an expense of ₹ 2,040 as landing charges.

Three fourth of the goods were sold at 33% profit on cost, half of which were credit sales. One half of the balance of goods were destroyed by fire and a claim lodged for ₹ 28,000 was settled at a discount of 10%. The balance of goods were in stock. Show the Consignment Account and the Stock Loss on Consignment Account as on 31st Dec. in the books of Shri Shyamlal.

SOLUTION

Dr. **CONSIGNMENT ACCOUNT** **Cr.**

Particulars	₹	Particulars	₹
To Goods sent on Consignment (2,64,000 × 120/100)	3,16,800	By Mahesh A/c	
To Bank A/c (Insurance & Forwarding changes)	10,000	Cash Sales 1,32,000 Credit Sales 1,32,000	2,64,000
To Shri Mahesh A/c: Establishment Landing charges 2,040 Landing charges 2,040	2,000	By Stock Lost on Consignment A/c [1/2 × 1/4 × [2,64,000 + 10,000 + 2,040]	34,505
Del-credere Commission (3% on ₹ 1,32,000) 3,960	21,200	By Consignment Stock [1/2 × 1/4 × (3,16,800 + 10,000 + 2,040)]	41,105
To Profit on Consignment (transferred to P & L A/c)	37,810	By Goods sent on Consignment A/c (Total Load = (₹ 3,16,800 – ₹ 2,64,000)	52,800
To Stock Reserve A/c (Load = ₹ 52,800 × 1/8)	6,600		
	3,93,010		3,93,010

Dr. **STOCK LOST ON CONSIGNMENT ACCOUNT** **Cr.**

Particulars	₹	Particulars	₹
To Consignment A/c	34,505	By Insurance Company (claim) (90% of ₹ 28,000)	25,200
		By P&L A/c	9,305
	34,505		34,505

PROBLEM 2

On 1st Dec., goods which cost X ₹ 33,000 were consigned by him to his agent Y at a proforma price which was 20% over cost. X paid insurance and freight charges amounting to ₹ 1,250. Y was allowed ₹ 3,000 per annum towards establishment cost, 5% commission on gross sales and 3% del credere commission. He was also allowed 5% extra commission on the profit on such consignment sales after charging such commission. Y incurred an expense of ₹ 255 as landing charges.

3/4ths of goods were sold at 33(1/3)% profit on cost, half of which were on credit; half of the balance of goods was damaged and a claim on insurance company was made for ₹ 4,400 which was settled at a discount of 10%.

Required: Prepare a Consignment Account and an Abnormal Loss Account in the books of X for the year ended 31st March.

SOLUTION

Dr. **CONSIGNMENT ACCOUNT** Cr.

Particulars	₹	Particulars	₹
To Goods sent on Consignment (33,000 × 120/100)	39,600	By Mahesh A/c	
To Bank A/c (Insurance & Forwarding changes)	1,250	Cash Sales 16,500 Credit Sales 16,500	33,000
To Shri Mahesh A/c: Establishment 1,000 Commission (5% on ₹ 33,000) 1,650		By Stock Lost on Consignment A/c [1/2 × 1/4 × (33,000 + 1,250 + 255]	4,313
Del-credere Commission (3% on ₹ 33,000) 990	3,895	By Consignment Stock [1/2 × 1/4 × (33,600 + 1,250 + 255]	5,138
To Stock Reserve A/c (₹ 6,600 × 1/8) To Y's (Extra Consignment))	825 165	By Goods sent on Consignment A/c (Total Load = (₹ 39,600 – ₹ 33,000)	6,600
To Profit on Consignment (transferred to P & L A/c)	3,315		
	49,051		49,051

Dr. **STOCK LOST ON CONSIGNMENT ACCOUNT** Cr.

Particulars	₹	Particulars	₹
To Consignment A/c	4,313	By Insurance Company (claim) (90% of ₹ 4,400)	3,960
		By P&L A/c	353
	4,313		4,313

PROBLEM 3

On 1st January, 2014 goods cost price of which was ₹ 1,32,000, were consigned by Shri Ganesh of Madras to his agent Shri Hari at Amritsar at a proforma invoice price of 20% above cost. Shri Harish paid freight and other forwarding charges amounting to ₹ 4,000. He was allowed ₹ 2,000 p.a. towards establishment costs, 5% commission and 5% del-credere commission on gross sales. Shri Harish paid ₹ 1,000 as rent of godown for the 3 months ended 31.3.2014.

Three-fourth of the goods were sold at 33-1/3% profit on cost, half of which were credit sales. Half the balance goods were stolen, but the stock being insured a claim lodged for ₹ 14,000 was settled for ₹ 13,800. Balance stock was valued at proforma invoice price.

Required: Prepare the Consignment Account and Stock lost on Consignment Account giving effect to abnormal loss, for 3 months ending on 31st March, 2014 in the books of Shri Ganesh.

SOLUTION

Dr. **CONSIGNMENT ACCOUNT** Cr.

Particulars		₹	Particulars		₹
To Goods sent on Consignment (1,32,000 × 120/100)		1,58,400	By Mahesh A/c		1,32,000
To Bank A/c		4,000	Cash Sales	66,000	
(Insurance & Forwarding changes)			Credit Sales	66,000	
To Y A/c:			By Stock Lost on Consignment A/c		17,000
Establishment	500		By Consignment Stock		20,300
Rent	1,000		[1/2 × 1/4 × (1,58,400 + 4,000)]		
Commission (5% on ₹ 1,32,000)	6,600		By Goods sent on Consignment A/c (Total hand = (₹ 1,58,400 – ₹ 1,32,000)		26,400
Del-credere Commission (3% on ₹ 1,32,000)	3,960	12,060			
To Stock Reserve A/c (Load = ₹ 26,400 × 1/8)		3,300			
To Profit on Consignment (transferred to P&L A/c)		17,940			
		1,95,400			1,95,400

Dr. **STOCK LOST ON CONSIGNMENT ACCOUNT** Cr.

Particulars	₹	Particulars	₹
To Consignment A/c	17,000	By Insurance Company (claim)	13,800
		By P&L A/c	3,200
	17,000		17,000

PROBLEM 4

Vandana Traders of Delhi purchased 10,000 pieces of Sarees @ ₹ 100 per Saree. Out of these Sarees, 6,000 were sent on consignment to Vastralaya of Jabalpur at the selling price of ₹ 120 per Saree. The consignors paid ₹ 3,000 for packing and freight.

Vastralaya sold 5,000 Sarees at ₹ 125 per Saree and incurred ₹ 1,000 for selling expenses and remitted ₹ 5,00,000 to Delhi on account. They are entitled to a commission of 5% on total sales plus a further 20% commission on any surplus price realised over ₹ 120 per Saree. 3,000 Sarees were sold at Delhi at ₹ 110 per Saree. Owing to fall in market price, the value of the Stock of Sarees in hand is to be reduced by 10%.

Required: Prepare the Consignment Account and Trading Account in the books of Vandana Traders and their account in the books of the agents Messrs. Vastralaya of Jabalpur.

SOLUTION

Dr. CONSIGNMENT TO JABALPUR ACCOUNT Cr.

Particulars	₹	Particulars	₹
To Goods sent on Consignment A/c	7,20,000	By Vastralaya's A/c (Sales)	6,25,000
To Bank A/c (Expenses)	3,000	By Goods Sent on Consignment A/c (₹ 6,000 × ₹ 20)	1,20,000
To Vastralaya's A/c (Expenses)	1,000		
To Vastralaya's A/c (Commission)	36,250	By Consignment Stock A/c	1,08,450
To Consignment Stock Reserve A/c	18,000		
To Profit on Consignment t/f to Profit & Loss A/c	75,200		
	8,53,450		8,53,450

Dr. TRADING AND PROFIT AND LOSS ACCOUNT FOR THE PERIOD ENDING ON ... Cr.

Particulars	₹	Particulars	₹
To Purchases	10,00,000	By Sales (3,000 × ₹ 110)	3,30,000
To Gross Profit c/d	20,000	By Goods Sent on Consignment	6,00,000
		By Closing Stock [1,00,000 – 10%]	90,000
	10,20,000		10,20,000
To Net Profit	95,200	By Gross Profit b/d	20,000
		By Consignment to Jabalpur A/c (Profit on Consignment)	75,200
	95,200		95,200

TULSIAN TRADERS (DELHI)'S ACCCOUNT
Dr. IN THE BOOKS OF VASTRALAYA (JABALPUR) Cr.

Particulars	₹	Particulars	₹
To Cash A/c/Bank A/c (Expenses)	1,000	By Cash/Debtors (sales)	6,25,000
To Commission A/c	36,250		
To Bank A/c	5,00,000		
To Balance c/d	87,750		
	6,25,000		6,25,000

Working Notes:

1. Commission payable = 5% on ₹ 6,25,000 + 20% = 20% on ₹ 25,000
   = ₹ 31,250 + ₹ 5,000 = ₹ 36,250
2. Valuation of Closing Stock as if there is not depression

A. Invoice Price of 1,000 sarees @ ₹ 120 (1000 × ₹ 120)	1,20,000
B. *Add:* Proportionate expenses incurred by Consignor (1,000 × ₹ 3,000/6,000)	500
	1,20,500
C. *Less:* 10%	12,050
	1,08,450

PROBLEM 5

On 1st April 2014, Mr Doshi of Darjeeling consigned 2,000 Kg. of Tea costing ₹ 60 per Kg. to Mr Naik of Nagpur. Mr Doshi incurred the following expenses:

Freight ₹ 2,000, Insurance ₹ 300, Sundry Expenses ₹ 700.

During the year ended 31st March, 2015, Mr Naik incurred the following expenses:

Freight ₹ 600, Godown Rent ₹ 500, Carriage to godown ₹ 1,000.

On 1st December, 2014, Mr Naik sold 1,200 Kg. of tea for cash at a profit of 25% on sales. On 15th December, 2014, Mr Naik returned 150 Kg. of Tea, which were of poor quality, to Mr Doshi and paid return freight and carriage of ₹ . 250. Out of the remaining Tea, 200 Kg. being partially damaged were valued at 30% less than cost. Mr Naik charged his commission at 5% and the balance so far due from him to Mr Doshi on 31st March, 2015. Mr Doshi closes his books every year on 31st March.

Required: Prepare the following Accounts in the books of Mr Doshi:

(a) Consignment to Nagpur. (b) Goods sent on Consignment, and (c) Personal Account of Mr Naik.

SOLUTION

Dr. **CONSIGNMENT TO NAGPUR ACCOUNT** **Cr.**

Particulars	₹	Particulars	₹
To Goods Sent on Consignment A/c	1,20,000	By Naik (Sale Proceeds) (1,200 × 80)	96,000
To Bank A/c (Expenses)	3,000	By Consignment Stock A/c:	
To Naik (Expenses)	2,100	Goods	27,900
To Naik (Return Freight)	250	Damaged	7,980
To B (Commission @ 5% on ₹ 96,000)	4,800	By Profit & Loss A/c (Loss on Damaged) (12,400 – 7,980)	4,420
To Profit t/f to P&L A/c	15,150	By Goods Sent on Consignment A/c (Return) (150 × ₹ 60)	9,000
	1,45,300		1,45,300

Dr. **NAIK'S ACCOUNT** **Cr.**

Particulars	₹	Particulars	₹
To Consignment to Nagpur A/c (sales)	96,000	By Consignment to Nagpur A/c (Exp.)	2,100
		By Consignment to Nagpur A/c (Exp.)	250
		By Consignment to Nagpur A/c (Comm.)	4,800
		By Bank A/c	88,850
	96,000		96,000

Working Note:

CALCULATION OF ABNORMAL LOSS AND UNSOLD STOCK

Particulars	Units	₹
A. Cost of Goods Sent	2,000	1,20,000
B. Expenses incurred by Consignor	—	3,000

C. Total Cost of Goods Sent (A + B)	2,000	1,23,000
D. *Add:* Non-recurring expenses incurred by Consignee	—	1,000
E. Cost of Goods received by consignee	2,000	1,24,000
F. Cost of Unsold Stock (Goods units) (450 kg)	450	27,900
G. Cost of Damaged units (200 kg)	200	12,240
H. Gross Realizable Value of Damaged Units (Cost—30%) (12,000 – 3,000)		8,400
I. *Less:* Consignee's Commission @ 5%		420
J. Net Realizable Value		7,980

Since stock is to be values at cost or NRV w.e. lower, stock has been valued at ₹ 7,980.

PROBLEM 6

Mr Shetty is a consignee agent for Electra Engineers Ltd., Bombay, who manufacture transistors. Model P and Model T are the most popular models with fixed retail selling price of ₹ 200 and ₹ 250 respectively, on which the manufacturers have a profit of 20% calculated on the selling prices. The consignment arrangement with Mr Shetty provides for the following commission structure:

(i) Model P—2(1/2)% on the selling price, (ii) Model T—4% on the selling price,

On July 1 stock with Mr Shetty was 200 Nos. of Model T and 200 Nos. of Model P. During the half year ended 31st Dec. the transactions were:

Particulars	Model P	Model T
Goods sent to Mr Shetty	2000 Nos.	1000 Nos.
Sales by Mr Shetty	2100 Nos.	900 Nos.

The consignments sent to Mr Shetty cost ₹ 30,000 in terms of freight incurred at consignor's end, and were transferred at cost. FIFO Method has been used.

Required: Show the Consignment A/c in the books of Electra Engineers Ltd., showing separately the computation of commission due and the value of closing stock.

SOLUTION

Dr. **CONSIGNMENT TO SHETTY ACCOUNT** **Cr.**

Particulars		₹	Particulars		₹
To Consignment Stock A/c:			By Shetty A/c-Sale proceeds:		
P 200 @ ₹ 160	32,000		P 2,100 @ ₹ 200	4,20,000	
T 200 @ ₹ 200	40,000	72,000	T 900 @ ₹ 250	2,25,000	6,45,000
To Goods Sent on Consignment A/c:			By Consignment Stock A/c:		
P 2,000 @ ₹ 160	3,20,000		P	17,000	
T 1,000 @ ₹ 200	2,00,000	5,20,000	T	63,000	80,000
To Bank A/c (freight)		30,000			
To Shetty A/c-commission					
2.5% on ₹ 4,20,000	10,500				
4% on ₹ 2,25,000	9,000	19,500			
To Profit on Consignment transferred to P/L A/c		83,500			
		7,25,000			7,25,000

Working Notes:

(i) Cost price of each set: Model P = 80% of ₹ 200 = ₹ 160,
Model T = 80% of ₹ 250 = ₹ 200

(ii) Freight charged per set: ₹ 30,000/3,000 = ₹ 10

(iii) Valuation of closing stock:

	₹
P 100 @ ₹ 160	16,000
T 300 @ ₹ 200	60,000
	76,000
Add: Freight for 400 sets @ ₹ 10	4,000
	80,000

PROBLEM 7

Ram & Co., Calcutta, sent 50 cases of hair oil valued at ₹ 200 each, to Krishna of Kakinada, for sale on consignment basis. They paid freight and insurance ₹ 200. Each case contained 40 bottles. When Krishna received the consignment, he found two cases damaged and he salvaged 40 bottles out of them.

Krishna, whose terms of commission were 5% normal commission and 1% Del Credere, sold 1,300 bottles at ₹ 8 each partly on credit and partly for cash. One customer who had lifted 100 bottles paid only for 75 bottles and the balance has become a bad debt.

Ram & Co., have decided to treat the damage in transit as an abnormal loss to be separately written off in their Profit and Loss Account. Show in the books of Ram and Co.;

(a) Consignment a/c; (b) Krishna's a/c, showing the amount due from him; and (c) Notes on calculation of closing stock on Consignment a/c.

SOLUTION

Dr. CONSIGNMENT TO KAKINADA ACCOUNT Cr.

Particulars	₹	Particulars	₹
To B (Commission @ 6% on ₹ 10,400)	624	By Krishna (Sale Proceeds) (1,300 × ₹ 8)	10,400
To Bank A/c (Expenses)	200	By Loss-in-transit A/c	204
To Goods Sent on Consignment A/c	10,000	By Consignment Stock A/c	3,366
To Profit t/f to P & L A/c	3,146		
	13,970		13,970

Dr. KRISHNA'S ACCOUNT Cr.

Particulars	₹	Particulars	₹
To Consignment to Kakinada A/c (sales)	10,400	By Consignment to Kakinada A/c (Comm.)	624
		By Balance c/d	9,776
	10,400		10,400

Working Note:

CALCULATION OF ABNORMAL LOSS AND UNSOLD STOCK

Particulars	Units	₹
A. Cost of Goods Sent	2,000	1,000
B. Expenses incurred by Consignor	—	200
C. Total Cost of Goods Sent (A + B)	2,000	10,200
D. *Less:* Cost of Goods not reached the city of Consignee	40	204
(a) Cost of Goods lost-in-transit		
E. Cost of Goods reached the city of Consigned (C – D)	1,960	9,966
F. Cost of Unsold Stock	660	3,566

PROBLEM 8

Niresh consigns 1,000 bats costing ₹ 500 each to Swaroop for sales and incurs ₹ 4,000 towards freight and ₹ 1,000 for insurance. Swaroop was able to take delivery of 900 bats only and 100 bats were destroyed in transit. Insurance Co. admitted the claim and paid the same. Swaroop will be entitled to a commission of 5% on sales, 2% Del credere commission on credit sales only. He will be entitled for additional commission of 25% of the excess if the sale price exceeds the cost price by more than 20%. Swaroop has spent ₹ 2,000 towards sales expenses. The sale account is as under:—

500 bats at ₹ 600 per bat each, 200 bats at ₹ 700 per bat credit.

Consignment debtors paid their dues except one customer to whom 4 bats sold for ₹ 2,800 could pay ₹ 800. Show Consignment Account, Consignment Debtors A/c, Swaroop A/c and commission calculation.

SOLUTION

Dr. **CONSIGNMENT ACCOUNT** **Cr.**

Particulars		₹	Particulars	₹
To Goods sent on Consignment A/c (₹ 1,000 × ₹ 500)		5,00,000	By Swaroop A/c Cash Sales (500 × ₹ 600) 3,00,000	
To Bank A/c:			Credit Sales (200 × ₹ 700) 1,40,000	4,40,000
Freight Insurance	4,000 1,000	5,000	By Stock Destroyed in Transit A/c 10/1000 (₹ 5,000 + ₹ 5,000)	50,500
To Swaroop A/c (Exp. & Comm.) Sales Expenses	2,000		By Consignment Stock A/c 200/1000 (5,00,000 + 5,000)	1,01,000
Commission (5% on 40,000)	22,000			
Del-credere Commission (2% on 1,40,000)	2,800			
Special Commission 25/100 × [4,40,000 – (700 × 500 × 120/100)]	5,000	31,800		
To Profit on Consignment (transferred to P&L A/c)		54,700		
		5,91,500		5,91,500

Dr. **CONSIGNMENT DEBTORS ACCOUNT** Cr.

Particulars	₹	Particulars	₹
To Swaroop A/c	1,40,000	By Bank A/c [1,40,000 –) (2,800 – 800)]	1,38,000
		By Swaroop A/c (Bad debts)	2,000
	1,40,000		1,40,000

Dr. **SWAROOP'S ACCOUNT** Cr.

Particulars	₹	Particulars	₹
To Consignment A/c	4,40,000	By Consignment A/c	31,800
To Consignment Debtors A/c	2,000	By Consignment Debtors	1,40,000
		By Bank (Balancing figure being remittance)	2,70,200
	4,42,000		4,42,000

PROBLEM 9

Goods are invoiced by Shri Amar, Consignor, to his agent Shri Ashok at selling price. The agent reports sales made and collection of book-debts by him and by monthly advice. He received 5% commission on cash collected plus an allowance of expenses @ ₹ 400 per annum.

During the half year ended 30th Sept. goods were invoiced to the agent at a value of ₹ 80,600. Such goods cost Shri Amar ₹ 59,000 plus freight and packing charges thereon ₹ 3,740. During the same period, sales were made by the agent amounting to ₹ 68,400. Debts collected were ₹ 57,600 and discounts were allowed amounted to ₹ 400. The agent remitted to Shri Amar ₹ 56,000.

Some of the goods consigned to Shri Ashok were damaged in transit and a claim on the insurance company was settled for ₹ 1,240.

On 30th Sept., the stock in the hands of the agent and unsold represented a cost of Shri Amar ₹ 8,200.

Required: Prepare the consignment account and the account of Shri Ashok in the books of Shri Amar, for the half year ended 30th Sept.

SOLUTION

Dr. **CONSIGNMENT TO ASHOK ACCOUNT** Cr.

Particulars	₹	Particulars	₹
To Goods Sent on Consignment A/c	59,000	By Ashok A/c-sales	68,400
To Bank A/c (freight etc.)	3,740	By Loss in Transit A/c	776
To Ashok A/c:		By Consignment Stock A/c	8,720
Allowance for expenses for 6 months	6,200		
Discount allowed to customers	400		
Commission @ 5% on ₹ 57,600	2,880		
To Profit on Consignment transferred to P/L A/c	11,676		
	77,896		77,896

Dr. **LOSS IN TRANSIT ACCOUNT** **Cr.**

Particulars	₹	Particulars	₹
To Consignment to Ashok A/c	776	By Bank A/c (insurance claim recovered)	1,240
To Profit & Loss A/c (transfer)	464		
	1,240		1,240

Dr. **ASHOK'S ACCOUNT** **Cr.**

Particulars	₹	Particulars	₹
To Consignment to Ashok A/c	68,400	By Consignment to Ashok A/c:	
		Allowable for expenses	200
		Discount allowed to customers	400
		Commission	2,880
		By Bank A/c	56,000
		By Balance c/f	8,920
	68,400		68,400

Working Notes:

(i) Cost of goods damaged in transit:

A. Cost of good sent	59,000
B. *Less:* Cost of goods sold: ₹ 59,000 × ₹ 68,400/ ₹ 80,600]	50,069
C. *Less:* Cost of Stock in the hands of consignee	8,200
D. Cost of goods damaged	731

(ii) Value of Goods damaged and Unsold Stock

A. Cost of Goods sent	59,000
B. Consignor's Expenses	3,740
C. Total Cost of Goods sent	62,740
D. *Less:* Cost of Goods lost in transit [62,740 × 730/59,000]	776
E. Cost of Goods reached the city of consignee	61,964
F. *Add:* Non-recurring Expenses	—
G. Cost of Goods received by Consignee	61,964
H. Cost of Unsold Stock [62,740 × 8,200/59,000]	8,720

PROBLEM 10

2,000 shirts were consigned by Bhagwan & Company of Delhi to Shreyans to Tokyo at a cost of ₹ 150 each. Bhagwan & Company paid freight ₹ 20,000 and insurance ₹ 3,000.

During the transit 200 shirts were totally damaged by fire. Sheryans took delivery of the remaining shirts and paid ₹ 28,800 as customs duty.

Shreyans had sent a bank draft to Bhagwan & Company for ₹ 1,00,000 as advance payment, 1,600 shirts were sold by him at ₹ 200 each. Expenses incurred by Shreyans on godown rent and advertisements, etc. amounted to ₹ 4,000. He is entitled to a commission of 5%.

One of the customers to whom the goods sold on credit could not pay the cost of 10 shirts.

Required: Prepare the consignment account and the account of Mr Shrenyas in the books of Bhagwan & Co., Shreyans settled his account immediately. Nothing was recovered from the insurers for the damaged goods.

SOLUTION

Dr. **CONSIGNMENT ACCOUNT** Cr.

Particulars		₹	Particulars		₹
To Goods sent on Consignment A/c		3,00,000	By Consignment Debtors A/c (Credit Sale = 1600 × 200)		3,20,000
To Bank A/c: (Expenses)			By Stock lost in transit A/c		
Freight	20,000		[200{(3,00,000 + 23,000)}/2,000]		
Insurance	3,000	23,000			32,300
To Shreyans (Exp. & Comm.)			By Consignment Stock A/c		
Customs duty	2,800		Cost (200 × 150)	30,000	
Expenses	4,000		Foreign & Ins. (23,000 × 200/2,000)	2,300	
Commission (5% on × 32,000)	16,000	48,800	Custom Duty (28,800 × 200/1,800)	3,200	35,500
To Consignment Debtors A/c (Bad Debts)		2,000			
To Profit on Consignment t/f to P&L A/c		14,000			
		3,87,000			3,87,000

Dr. **SHREYAN'S ACCOUNT** Cr.

Particulars	₹	Particulars	₹
To Consignment Debtors A/c (Collected)	3,18,000	By Bank A/c	1,00,000
		By Consignment A/c:	
		Customs duty 28,800	
		Expenses 4,000	
		Commission 16,000	48,000
		By Bank A/c	1,69,200
		(Balancing figure being final remittance)	
	3,18,000		3,18,000

PROBLEM 11

On 1st January Lila & Co., of Calcutta consigned 100 cases of Milk Powder to Shila & Co., of Bombay. The goods were charged at a proforma invoice value of ₹ 10,000 including a profit of 25% on invoice price. On the same date the consignors paid ₹ 600 for Freight and Insurance. On 1st July, the consignees paid Import Duty ₹ 1,000, Dock Dues ₹ 200 and sent to consignors a Bank Draft for ₹ 4,000 as advance. On 1st August, they sold 80 cases for ₹ 10,500 and sent a remittance for the balance due to the consignor after deducting commission at the rate 5% on gross sale proceeds. Show the Consignment Account and Shila & Co's Account in Lila & Co's Books.

SOLUTION

Dr. **CONSIGNMENT ACCOUNT** Cr.

Particulars	₹	Particulars	₹
To Good sent on Consignment	10,000	By Shila & Co. (sales)	10,500
To Bank A/c (Freight & Insurance	600	By Goods sent on Consignment (Load = 25% on ₹ 10,000)	2,500

To Shila & Co. (Exp. & Comm.) Import 1,000 Dock Dues 200 Commission (5/100 × 10,500) 525	1,725	By Consignment Stock A/c (20% of [10,000 + 600 + 1,000 + 200]	2,360
To Consignment Stock Reserve (20/100 × 2,500)	500		
To Profit transferred to P&L A/c	2,535		
	15,360		15,360

Dr. **SHILA & CO.S ACCOUNT** **Cr.**

Particulars	₹	Particulars	₹
To Consignment A/c	10,500	By Consignment A/c Import Duty 1,000 Dock Dues 200 Commission 525	1,725
		By Bank A/c (Bal. figure)	8,775
	10,550		10,500

PROBLEM 12

On 1st Jan. Mr John of Bombay consigned to Mr Raj of Madras goods for sale at invoice price. Mr Raj is entitled to a commission of 5 per cent on sales at invoice price and 20 per cent of any surplus price realised. Goods costing ₹ 1,00,000 were consigned to Madras at the invoice price of ₹ 1,50,000. The direct expenses of the consignment amounted to ₹ 10,000. On 31st March an account sales was received by Mr John from Mr Raj showing that he had effected sales of ₹ 1,20,000 in respect of 4/5th of the quantity of goods consigned to him. His actual expenses were ₹ 3,000. Mr Raj accepted a bill drawn by Mr John for ₹ 1,00,000 and remitted the balance due in cash.

Show the Consignment Account and the account of Mr Raj in the books Mr John.

SOLUTION

Dr. **CONSIGNMENT TO MADRAS ACCOUNT** **Cr.**

Particulars	₹	Particulars	₹
To Goods sent on Consignment A/c	1,50,000	By Mr. Raj A/c (sales)	1,20,000
To Bank A/c (Expenses)	10,000	By Goods sent on Consignment	50,000
To Mr. Raj A/c (Exp. & Comm.)		[Total Load = (1,50,000 – 1,00,000]	
Expenses 3,000		By Consignment Stock A/c	
Commission 6,000	9,000	[1/5 (1,50,000 + 10,000)]	32,000
To Stock Reserve A/c [30,000 × 1/3]	10,000		
To Profit on Consignment (transferred)	23,000		
	2,02,000		2,02,000

Dr. **MR. RAJ'S ACCOUNT** **Cr.**

Particulars	₹	Particulars	₹
To Consignment A/c	1,20,000	By Consignment A/c: Expenses 3,000 Commission 6,000	9,000

		By Bills Receivable A/c	1,00,000
		By Cash A/c	11,000
	1,20,000		1,20,000

PROBLEM 13

Mr Y consigned 800 packets of toothpaste, each packet containing 100 toothpastes. Cost price of each packet was ₹ 900. Mr Y spent ₹ 100 per packet as cartage, freight, insurance and forwarding charges. One packet was lost on the way and Mr Y lodged claim with insurance company and could get ₹ 570 as claim on average basis. Consignee took delivery of the rest of the packets and spent ₹ 39,950 as other non-recurring expenses and ₹ 22,500 as recurring expenses. He sold 740 packets at the rate of ₹ 12 per toothpaste. He was entitled to 2% commission on sales plus 1% del-credere commission.

You are required to prepare Consignment Account. Calculate the cost of stock at the end abnormal loss and profit or loss on consignment.[CA (Foundation) Nov., 1998, May, 2004]

SOLUTION

Dr. **CONSIGNMENT ACCOUNT** **Cr.**

Particulars		₹	Particulars		₹
To Goods sent on consignment (800 × ₹ 900)		7,20,000	By Consignee's A/c (Sales) (740 × ₹ 1,200)		8,88,000
To Bank A/c (Freight charges insurance etc (800 × ₹ 100)		80,000	By Profit & Loss A/c (abnormal loss) [₹ 1,000 – ₹ 570]		430
To Consignee's A/c:			By Cash A/c (claim)		570
Non Recurring Expenses	39,950		By Consignment Stock A/c Cost of 59 packets		53,100
Recurring Expenses	22,500	62,450	*Add:* Consignee's Exp.		
To Consignees A/c (Commission) 2% on ₹ 8,88,000 1% on ₹ 8,88,000	 17,760 8,880	26,640	(₹ 80,000 × 59/800) *Add:* Consignee's Exp. (₹ 39,950 × 59/799)	5,900 2,950	61,950
To Profit & Loss A/c (Profit)		61,860			
		9,50,950			9,50,950

Working Note:

CALCULATION OF ABNORMAL LOSS

Particulars	₹
A Cost of 1 packet	900
B Consignor's Expenses	100
C Total Cost of 1 packet [A + B]	1,000
D *Less:* Claim accepted	570
E Abnormal loss [C – D]	430

PROBLEM 14

X of Delhi purchased 10,000 meters of cloth for ₹ 2,00,000 of which 5,000 meters were sent on consignment to Y of Agra at the selling price of ₹ 30 per meter. X paid ₹ 5,000 for freight and ₹ 500 for packing, etc. Y sold 4,000 meters at ₹ 40 per meter and incurred ₹ 2,000 for selling expenses. Y is entitled to a commission of 5% on total sale proceeds plus a further 20 per cent on any surplus price realised over ₹ 30 per meter. 3,000 meters were sold at Delhi @ ₹ 30 per meter less ₹ 3,000 for expenses and commission. Owing to fall in market price,the stock of cloth in hand is to be reduced by 10 per cent. Prepare the Consignment Account and Trading and Profit & Loss Account in Books of X and his account in the books of Y.

SOLUTION

Dr. **CONSIGNMENT TO AGRA ACCOUNT** **Cr.**

Particulars	₹	Particulars		₹
To Goods sent on Consignment A/c (5,000 × ₹ 30)	1,50,000	By Goods sent on Consignment A/c (5,000 × ₹ 10)		50,000
To Cash A/c (Expenses)	5,500	By Y's A/c (Sales)		1,60,000
To Y's A/c (Expenses)	2,000	By Consignment Stock (1,000 × ₹ 20)	20,000	
To Y's A/c (Commission)	16,000	*Add:* Expenses (1/5 of ₹ 5,500)	1,100	
To Profit on Consignment transferred to Profit & Loss A/c	55,490	Value of Stock *Less:* 10%	21,100 2,110	18,990
	2,28,990			2,28,990

Dr. **TRADING AND PROFIT AND LOSS ACCOUNT FOR THE YEAR ENDING ON...** **Cr.**

Particulars	₹	Particulars		₹
To Purchases	2,00,000	By Sales		90,000
To Gross Profit c/d	26,000	By Goods sent on Consignment		1,00,000
		By Closing Stock Cost (2,000 × ₹ 20) *Less:* 10%	 40,000 4,000	36,000
	2,26,000			2,26,000
To Expenses	3,000	By Gross Profit b/d		26,000
To Net Profit	78,490	By Consignment to Agra A/c (Profit)		55,490
	81,490			81,490

Dr. **X'S ACCOUNT IN THE BOOKS OF Y** **Cr.**

Particulars	₹	Particulars	₹
To Cash A/c (Selling Expenses)	2,000	By Cash A/c (Sales)	1,60,000
To Commission A/c	16,000		
To Balance c/d	1,42,000		
	1,60,000		1,60,000

PROBLEM 15

M/s Ram & Co. of Delhi purchased 20,000 pieces of sarees @ ₹ 200 per saree. Out of these, 12,000 sarees were sent on consignment to M/s Laxman Traders of Bombay at the selling price of ₹ 240 per saree. The consignors paid ₹ 6,000 for packing and freight.

M/s Laxman Traders sold 10,000 sarees @ ₹ 250 per saree and incurred ₹ 2,000 towards selling expenses and remitted ₹ 10,00,000 to Delhi on account. M/s Laxman Traders are entitled to a commission of 5 per cent on total sales plus a further 20 per cent commission on any surplus price realised over ₹ 240 per saree.

6,000 sarees were sold at ₹ 220 per saree by the consignor. Owing to fall in the market price, the value of stock of sarees in hand is to be reduced by 10 per cent.

Prepare the Consignment Account and the account of M/s Laxman Traders in the books of the consignor.

SOLUTION

IN THE BOOKS OF M/S RAM & CO., DELHI

Dr. **CONSIGNMENT TO BOMBAY ACCOUNT** **Cr.**

Particulars	₹	Particulars	₹
To Goods sent on Consignment A/c (12,000 × ₹ 240)	28,80,000	By Laxman Traders (sales) (10,000 × 250)	25,00,000
To Bank A/c (expenses)	6,000	By Goods sent on Consignment	
To Laxman Traders (expenses)	2,000	(loading: 12,000 × ₹ 40)	4,80,000
To Laxman Traders (Commission)	1,45,000	By Consignment Stock A/c	3,60,900
To Profit & Loss A/c (Profit)	3,07,900		
	33,40,900		33,40,900

Dr. **LAXMAN TRADERS ACCOUNT** **Cr.**

Particulars	₹	Particulars	₹
To Consignment A/c (sales)	25,00,000	By Consignment A/c (Expenses)	2,000
		By Consignment A/c (Commission)	1,45,000
		By Bank A/c	10,00,000
		By Balance c/d	13,53,000
	25,00,000		25,00,000

Working Notes:

1. *Consignee's Commission = 5% of ₹ 25,00,000 + 20% of ₹ 1,00,000 = ₹ 1,45,000*
2. *Valuation of Closing Stock on Consignment*

A	Cost of 2,000 Sarees [2,000 × ₹ 200]	4,00,000
B	*Add:* proportionate expenses [₹ 6,000 × 2,000/12,000]	1,000
		4,01,000
C	*Less:* 10%	40,100
D	Value of closing stock to be brought into accounts	3,60,900

PROBLEM 16

'X' of Delhi purchased 10,000 pieces of Sarees @ ₹ 100 per Saree. Out of these Sarees, 6,000 were sent on consignment to 'Y' of Agra at a selling price of ₹ 120 per Saree. The Consignor paid ₹ 3,000 for packing and freight. 'Y ' sold 5,000 Sarees at ₹ 125 per Saree and incurred ₹ 1,000 for selling expenses and remitted ₹ 5,00,000 to Delhi on account. They are entitled to a commission of 5% on total sales plus a further 20% commission on any surplus price realised over ₹ 120 per Saree.

3,000 Sarees were sold in Delhi at ₹ 110 per Saree. Owing to fall in market price, the value of stock of Sarees in hand is to be reduced by 10%.

Required: Prepare the Consignment Account in the books of 'X' and their account in the book of the agent 'Y' of Agra.

SOLUTION

Dr. **CONSIGNMENT ACCOUNT** **Cr.**

Particulars		₹	Particulars	₹
To Goods sent on Consignment A/c (6,000 × ₹ 120)		7,20,000	By Goods sent on Consignment A/c—Loading (6,000 × ₹ 20)	1,20,000
To Bank A/c—Expenses		3,000	By Y—Sales (5,000 × ₹ 125)	6,25,000
To Y—Selling Expenses	1,000		By Stock on Consignment	
Commission	36,250	37,250		1,08,450
To Stock Reserve		18,000		
To Net Profit		75,200		
			8,53,450	8,53,450

Dr. **X 'S ACCOUNT IN THE BOOKS OF 'Y ' OF AGRA** **Cr.**

Particulars	₹	Particulars	₹
To Bank A/c (Expenses)	1,000	By Bank A/c (Sales)	6,25,000
To Commission	36,250		
To Bank A/c (Remittance)	5,00,000		
To Balance c/d	87,750		
	6,25,000		6,25,000

Working Notes:

	₹
1. Commission Payable 5% on ₹ 6,25,000	31,250
20% on ₹ (6,25,000 – 6,00,000 = 25,000)	5,000
	36,250
2. Valuation of Closing Stock on Consignment 1,000 sarees × ₹ 120	1,20,000
Add: Proportionate expenses {₹ 3,000 × 1,000/6,000}	500
	1,20,500
Less: 10%	12,050
Value of Closing Stock	1,08,450
3. Loading on Closing Stock (Stock Reserve) 1,000 sarees × ₹ 20	20,000
Less: 10%	2,000
	18,000

PROBLEM 17

X of Calcutta on 15th January sent to Y of Bombay a consignment of 250 televisions costing ₹ 10,000 each. Expenses of ₹ 7,000 were met by the consignor. Y of Bombay spent ₹ 4,500 for clearance on 30th January and the selling expenses were ₹ 500 per television as and when the sale made by Y.

Y sold, on 4th March, 150 televisions @ ₹ 14,000 per television and again on 10th April, 75 televisions @ ₹ 14,400.

Mr Y was entitled to a commission of ₹ 500 per television sold plus one-fourth of the amount by which the gross sale proceeds less total commission there on exceeded a sum calculated at the rate of ₹ 12,500 per television sold. Y sent the account sale and the amount due to X on 30th April by bank demand draft.

You are required to show the Consignment Account and Y's account in the books of X.

SOLUTION

Dr. **CONSIGNMENT TO BOMBAY ACCOUNT** **Cr.**

Particulars		₹	Particulars		₹
To Y's A/c:			By Y's A/c (Sales):		
Clearance	4,500		150 @ ₹ 14,000	21,00,000	
Selling Expenses	1,12,500	1,17,000	75 @ ₹ 14,400	10,80,000	31,80,000
To Goods sent on Consignment A/c		25,00,000	By Consignment Stock A/c:		
To Bank A/c (Expenses)		7,000	Cost of 25 TV @ ₹ 10,000	2,50,000	
To Y's A/c (Commission)		1,63,500	*Add:* Consignor's Exp. (7,000 × 25/250)	700	
To Profit & Loss A/c (Profit on Consignment)		6,43,650	*Add:* Consignee's Exp. (4,500 × 25/250)	450	2,51,150
		34,31,150			34,31,150

Dr. **Y 'S ACCOUNT** **Cr.**

Particulars	₹	Particulars		₹
To Consignment to Bombay A/c (Sales)	31,80,000	By Consignment to Bombay A/c:		
		— Clearance	4,500	
		— Selling Expenses	1,12,500	1,17,000
		By Cosignment to Bombay A/c (Commission)		1,63,500
		By Bank A/c		28,99,500
	31,80,000			31,80,000

Working Notes: *Calculation of Consignee's Commission*

1. Fixed Commission @ ₹ 500 = 225 × ₹ 500 = ₹ 1,12,500
2. Let the total Commission be X

   Variable Commission = 1/4 [(₹ 31,80,000 – X) – (225 × ₹ 12,500)]

   X – ₹ 1,12,500 = 1/4 [₹ 31,80,000 – X – ₹ 28,12,500]

   X – ₹ 1,12,500 = 1/4 (₹ 3,67,500 – X)

   X – ₹ 1,12,500 = 91,875 – 1/4 X

   X – 1,12,500 = 91,875 – .25 X

   1.25 X = 2,04,375

   X = ₹ 2,04,375/1.25 = 1,63,500

PROBLEM 18

Ramesh consigned 2,000 MT of chemicals at a cost of ₹ 800 per MT to John, Ramesh paid freight and insurance charges of ₹ 20,000. Of the above 500 MT of chemicals were destroyed by fire during transit. John cleared the balance of 1,500 MT of chemicals and sold 1,000 MT at an average price of ₹ 1,000 per MT. John incurred the following expenses. Godown Rent ₹ 5,000, Insurance ₹ 3,000, Clearing Charges ₹ 4,500. Insurance claim received against fire ₹ 4,00,000 after admitting the salvage value of Stock destroyed by fire at ₹ 10,000. John was entitled to a commission of 10% on sale proceeds. John sends the balance to Ramesh after adjusting his commission and expenses out of the sales proceeds, Prepare a Consignment Account and John's Account in the books of Ramesh.

SOLUTION

Dr. **CONSIGNMENT TO JOHN ACCOUNT** **Cr.**

Particulars	₹	Particulars	₹
To Goods sent on Consignment A/c	16,00,000	By John's (Sales)	10,00,000
To Bank (Freight and Insurance)	20,000	By Abnormal Loss A/c (₹ 4,05,000 – ₹ 10,000)	3,95,000
To John's A/c (Commission)	1,00,000	By Consignment Stock A/c:	
To John's A/c (Godown Rent)	5,000	Normal Stock	4,06,500
To John's A/c (Insurance)	3,000	Salvaged Stock	10,000
To John's A/c (Clearing Charges)	4,500		
To Profit and Loss A/c (Profit)	79,000		
	18,11,500		18,11,500

Dr. **JOHN'S ACCOUNT** **Cr.**

Particulars	₹	Particulars	₹
To Consignment to John A/c (Sale Proceeds)	10,00,000	By Consignment to John A/c:	
		Godown Rent	5,000
		Insurance	3,000
		Clearing Charges	4,500
		Commission	1,00,000
		By Bank A/c (Balance remitted)	8,87,500
	10,00,000		10,00,000

Working Note: *Valuation of Goods Destroyed and Unsold Goods*

Particulars	Goods Destroyed (500 MT) ₹	Unsold Goods (500 MT) ₹
A Cost (500 × ₹ 800)	4,00,000	4,00,000
B Proportionate Freight and Insurance (₹ 20,000 × 500/2,000)	5,000	5,000
C Proportionate Clearing Charges (₹ 4,500 × 500/1500)	—	1,500
D Total	4,05,000	4,06,500

PROBLEM 19

Rahim of Bombay consigned to Raju of Madras, goods to be sold at invoice price which represents 125% of cost. Raju is entitled to a commission of 10% on sales at invoice price and 25% of any excess realised over invoice price. The expenses on freight and insurance incurred by Rahim were ₹ 10,000. The account sales received by Rahim shows that Raju effected sales aggregating to ₹ 1,00,000 in respect of 75% of the consignment. His selling expenses to be reimbursed were ₹ 8,000. 10% of the consignment goods of the value of ₹ 12,500 were destroyed in fire at the Madras godown and the Insurance Company paid ₹ 12,000 net of salvage. Raju remitted the balance in favour of Rahim. Prepare Consignment Account and the Account of Raju in the books of Rahim along with necessary workings.

SOLUTION

Dr. **CONSIGNMENT TO MADRAS ACCOUNT** **Cr.**

Particulars	₹	Particulars	₹
To Goods sent on Consignment A/c	1,25,000.00	By Raju's A/c (Sales)	1,00,000.00
To Bank A/c (Freight & Insurance)	10,000.00	By Loss due to Fire A/c	11,000.00
To Raju's A/c (Expanses Incurred)	8,000.00	By Consignment Stock A/c	20,250.00
To Raju's A/c (Commission)	10,937.50	By Goods sent on Consignment	
To Consignment Stock Reserve A/c	3,750.00	[₹ 1,25,000 × 20/100]	25,000.00
		By Profit & Loss A/c (Loss)	1,437.50
	1,57,687.50		1,57,687.50

Dr. **RAJU'S ACCOUNT** **Cr.**

Particulars	₹	Particulars	₹
To Consignment to Madras A/c (Sales)	1,00,000.00	By Consignment to Madras A/c (Expenses)	8,000.00
To Loss due to Fire A/c (Insurance Claim)	12,000.00	By Consignment to Madras A/c (Commission)	10,937.50
		By Bank A/c (Balance remitted)	93,062.50
	1,12,000.00		1,12,000.00

Working Notes:

1. Invoice Value of Total Goods sent on Consignment
   (Invoice Value of Goods destroyed × 10) — 1,25,000.00
2. Calculation of Consignee's Commission

A	Sale Proceeds received by Raju on 75% of Consignment	1,00,000.00
B	Invoice Value of 75% of Consignment (75%of 1,25,000)	93,750.00
C	Excess sale price realised by Raju (A – B)	6,250.00
D	Commission payable to Raju	
	@ 10% on Invoice value of ₹ 93,750	9,375.00
	@ 25% on Excess sale price realised	1,562.50
		10,937.50

3. Calculation of Unsold Stock (being 15%)

A	Invoice value of Stock (₹ 1,25,000 × 15/100)	18,750
B	*Add:* Proportionate Freight and Insurance (₹ 10,000 × 15/100)	1,500
C	Value of Stock on Consignment (A + B)	20,250

4. Stock Reserve at 25% on cost (₹ 18,750 × 25/125) — 3,750
5. Calculation of Abnormal Loss

A	Cost price of goods destroyed (₹ 12,500 × 80/100)	10,000
B	*Add:* Proportionate Freight and Insurance (₹ 10,000 × 10/100)	1,000
		11,000

PROBLEM 20

Mr A of Assam sent on 18th February, 2004 a consignment of 1000 DVD players to B of Bengal costing of ₹ 100 each. Expenses of ₹ 1,500 were met by the consignor. B spent ₹ 3,000 for clearance and selling expenses were ₹ 20 per DVD player.

B sold on 15th March, 2004, 600 DVD Players sold @ ₹ 160 per DVD Player and again on 20th may, 2004, 300 DVD Players @ ₹ 170.

B is entitled to a commission of ₹ 25 per DVD Player sold plus 1/4 pf the amount by which the gross sale proceeds less total commission thereon exceeded a sum calculated @ ₹ 125 per DVD Player sold. B sent the amount due to A on 30th June, 2004.

You are requested to show the consignment account and B's account in the books of A.

SOLUTION

Dr. **CONSIGNMENT ACCOUNT IN THE BOOKS OF A** Cr.

Date	Particulars	₹	Date	Particulars	₹
18.02.04	To Goods sent on Consignment A/c	1,00,000	15.03.04	By B's A/c (sales) (600 × ₹ 160)	96,000
	To Cash/Bank A/c (Expenses)	1,500	20.05.04	By B's A/c (Sales) (300 × ₹ 170)	51,000
	To B's A/c (Clearance charges)	3000	30.06.04	By Consignment Stock A/c	10,450
30.06.04	To B's A/c Selling expenses				
	(900 × ₹ 20)	18,000			
	Commission	24,900			
30.06.04	To Profit and Loss A/c	10,500			
		1,57,450			1,57,450

Dr. **B'S ACCOUNT** Cr.

Date	Particulars	₹	Date	Particulars	₹
15.03.04	To Consignment A/c (Sales)	96,000	18.02.04	By Consignment A/c (Clearance charges)	3,000
20.05.04	To Consignment A/c (Sales)	51,000	30.06.04	By Consignment A/c	
				Selling expenses	18,000
				Commission	24,900
			30.06.04	By Cash/Bank A/c	1,01,000
		1,47,000			1,47,000

Working Notes:

1. Calculation of total commission:

   Let total commission be x

   x = 900 × ₹ 25 + 1/4 [(₹ 96,000 + ₹ 51,000) – x – (900 × ₹ 125)]

   x = ₹ 22,500 + 1/4 [₹ 1,47,000 – x – ₹ 1,12,500]

   x = ₹ 22,500 + 1/4 [₹ 34,500 – x]

   4x + x = ₹ 90,000 + ₹ 34,500

   5x = ₹ 1,24,500

   x = ₹ 24,900

2. Valuation of consignment stock:

	₹
100 DVD players @ ₹ 100 each	10,000
Add: Proportionate expenses of A (₹ 1,500 × 100)/1,000	150
Proportionate expenses paid by B (₹ 3,000 × 100)/1,000	300
	10,450

PROBLEM 21

M of Mathura, consigned 5,000 kg of oil costing ₹ 20 per kg to S of Surat. M paid ₹ 25,000 as freight and insurance. 125 kg of oil was destroyed in transit. The insurance claim was settled at ₹ 2,250 and was paid directly to the consignors.

S took delivery of consignment and accepted a Bill drawn upon them by M for ₹ 50,000. S reported as follows:

(i) 3,750 kg. were sold at ₹ 30 per kg

(ii) His expenses were: Godown Rent ₹ 10,000, Wages ₹ 1,000, Printing & Stationery, ₹ 5,000

(iii) 125 kg were lost due to leakage which is quite normal.

S is entitled to a commission of 5% on the sales effected. S paid the amount due in respect of the consignment. Show the Consignment Account, the account of S and the Abnormal Loss Account in the books of M for the year ended 31st March, 2015.

SOLUTION

Dr. **CONSIGNMENT TO MADRAS ACCOUNT** **Cr.**

Particulars		₹	Particulars	₹
To Goods sent on Consignment A/c		1,00,000	By Loss in Transit A/c (cost of 125 kg.)	3,125
To Cash A/c (freight & insurance)		25,000	By S (Sales)	1,12,500
To S A/c			By Consignment Stock A/c	25,658
Commission	5,625		By P & L A/c (Loss)	5,342
Expenses incurred	16,000	21,625		
		1,46,625		1,46,625

Dr. **RAMESH & CO.'S ACCOUNT** **Cr.**

Particulars	₹	Particulars	₹
To Consignment to Madras A/c (Sales)	1,12,500	By Bills Receivable A/c	50,000
		By Consignment to Madras A/c:	
		Expenses	16,000
		Commission	5,625
		By Bank A/c (Balance remitted)	40,875
		1,12,500	1,12,500

Dr. **LOSS IN TRANSIT ACCOUNT** **Cr.**

Particulars	₹	Particulars	₹
To Consignment to Madras A/c	3,125	By Insurance Claim (recovered)	2,250
		By Profit & Loss A/c (irrecovered)	875
	3,125		3,125

Working Note:

CALCULATION OF COST OF CLOSING STOCK

Particulars	Units	₹
A Cost of 5,000 kg, @ ₹ 20	5,000	1,00,000
B *Add:* Consignor's Expenses (Freight & insurance)	—	25,000
C Total Cost of 5,000 kg. (A + B)	5,000	1,25,000
D *Less:* Cost of 125 kg lost in transit (₹ 1,25,000 × 125/5,000)	125	3,125
E Cost of 4,875 kg that have reached the city of Consignee (C – D)	4,875	1,21,875
F *Less:* Normal Loss	125	—
G Cost of 4,750 kg available for sale (since 125 kg is normal loss)	4,750	1,21,875
H Cost of 1,000 kg in hand (₹ 1,21,875 × 1,000/4,750)	1,000	25,658

PROBLEM 22

Mr Karamchand, whose accounting year ends on 31st March, 2015 consigned 100 bags of sugar, each bag costing ₹ 300 to Amarchand of Bombay on 1st Jan. He had paid ₹ 500 towards freight and insurance. 15 bags were damaged in transit and on 30th March, the consignor had received ₹ 1,000 on account of the damaged bags from the Insurance Company. Amarchand took delivery of the goods on 10th Jan. and immediately accepted a bill drawn on him for ₹ 20,000 for 60 days. On 31st March, the consignee reported that—

(i) 70 bags were sold @ ₹ 350 per bag. (ii) The damaged bags were sold @ ₹ 110 per bag and (iii) He had paid Godown rent ₹ 700 Clearing charges ₹ 1,000, Carriage outwards ₹ 300.

He is entitled to a commission at 10% on the sale proceeds of all goods excepting damaged goods.

Assuming that Amarchand remits the balance by bank draft on 31st March, show the journal entries in the books of Mr Karamchand (including the entries passed at the time of closing the books). Assuming that no portion of the expenses incurred by the consignee is attributable to the damaged bags, determine the loss on the damaged bags.

SOLUTION

JOURNAL OF MR KARAMCHAND

Date	Particulars		Dr. (₹)	Cr. (₹)
2015	Consignment to Bombay A/c	Dr.	30,000	
Jan. 1	To Goods sent on Consignment A/c			30,000
	(For 100 bags of sugar costing ₹ 300 per bag sent on consignment to Amarchand of Bombay)			
	Consignment to Bombay A/c	Dr.	500	
	To Bank A/c			500
	(For freight and insurance charges paid in respect of consignment to Bombay)			
Jan. 10	Bills Receivable A/c	Dr.	20,000	
	To Amarchand's A/c			20,000
	(For B/R received from Amarchand)			

Mar. 30	Bank A/c	Dr.	1,000	
	To Consignment to Bombay A/c			1,000
	(For amount of claim received from Insurance Co.)			
Mar. 31	Amarchand's A/c	Dr.	26,150	
	To Consignment to Bombay A/c			26,150
	(For sale of 70 bags @ ₹ 350 per bag & 15 @ ₹ 110 per bag)			
	Abnormal Loss A/c	Dr.	1,925	
	To Consignment to Bombay A/c			1,925
	(For loss suffered on account of damage done to 15 bags)			
	Consignment to Bombay A/c	Dr.	4,450	
	To Amarchand's A/c			4,450
	(For expenses incurred and commission charged by the consignee as follows: Godown rent ₹ 700, Clearing Charges ₹ 1,000, Carriage outwards ₹ 300 and Commission @ 10% on ₹ 24,500, i.e. ₹ 2,450)			
	Bank A/c	Dr.	1,700	
	To Amarchand's A/c			1,700
	(For the Bank Draft received for balance due from him)			
	Consignment Stock A/c	Dr.	4,751	
	To Consignment to Bombay A/c			4,751
	(For stock with the consignee valued at cost plus proportionate non-recurring expenses)			
	Profit & Loss A/c	Dr.	1,124	
	To Consignment to Bombay A/c			1,124
	(For loss transferred to Profit and Loss A/c)			

Working Notes:

1. VALUATION OF CLOSING STOCK WITH CONSIGNEE

	Particulars	Damaged goods (15)	Unsold goods (15)
A	Cost of bags @ ₹ 300	4,500	4,500
B	*Add:* Proportionate non-recurring expenses of Consignor @ ₹ 5	75	75
C	*Add:* Proportionate non-recurring expenses of Consignee @ ₹ 11.76	—	176
		4,575	4,751

2. Loss on damaged goods = Cost – Sale proceeds – Claim from Insurance Co.
   = ₹ 4,575 — ₹ 1,650 – ₹ 1,000 = ₹ 1,925
3. It has been assumed that carriage outwards ₹ 300 spent by the consignee relates to sales.
4. Figures have been rounded off to the nearest rupee.

PROBLEM 23

Auto Agencies have sold out the following goods on behalf of different parties for which they have incurred some expenses and are entitled to commission and reimbursement of expenses.

Particulars	Life Light	Sieac	Akriti
	₹	₹	₹
Stock in hand	8,000	12,000	12,000
Goods Received	20,000	30,000	36,000
Goods sold	24,000	26,000	44,000
Expenses	600	400	800
Remittance	20,000	22,000	40,000
Commission	10%	6%	5%

Prepare the Consignors' Account and Commission Account in the Books of Auto Agencies.

SOLUTION

Dr. **CONSIGNOR'S ACCOUNT** Cr.

Particulars	Life Light ₹	Sieac Light ₹	Akriti Light ₹	Particulars	Life Light ₹	Sieac Light ₹	Akriti Light ₹
To Bank A/c (Exp)	600	400	800	By Bank A/c (sales)	24,000	26,000	44,000
To Commission A/c	2,400	1,560	2,200				
To Bank A/c (Remittance)	20,000	22,000	40,000				
To Balance c/d	1,000	2,040	1,000				
	24,000	26,000	44,000		24,000	26,000	44,000
				By Business b/d	1,000	2,040	1,000

Dr. **COMMISSION ACCOUNT** Cr.

Particulars	₹	Particulars	₹
To Profit & Loss A/c (b/f)	6,160	By Life Light	2,400
		By Sieac	1,560
		By Akriti	2,200
	6,160		6,160

PROBLEM 24

Karnath sold goods on behalf of Vijay Sales Corporation on Consignment basis. On January1, 2014, he had with him a stock of ₹ 20,000 consignment.

Karnath had instruction to sell the goods at cost plus 25% and was entitled to a commission of 4% on sales in addition to 1% del-credere commission on total sales.

During the year ended 31st December, 2014, cash sales were ₹ 1,20,000, credit sales were ₹ 1,05,000 and Karnath's expenses relating to the consignment ₹ 3,000 being salaries and insurance. Bad debts were ₹ 3,000 and goods sent on consignment ₹ 2,00,000.

Required: Prepare Consignment Account in the books Vijay Sales Corp.

SOLUTION

Dr. **CONSIGNMENT ACCOUNT** Cr.

Particulars		₹	Particulars	₹
To Consignment Stock A/c (op. stock)		20,000	By Karnath's A/c (Sales)	2,25,000
To Goods sent on consignment		2,00,000	By Consignment Stock A/c	40,000
To Karnath's A/c (Exp. & Comm.)			(Closing Stock)	
Salaries & Insurance	3,000		[20,000 + 2,00,000 – (100/125 x 2,25,000)]	
Ordinary Commission (4% on 2,25,000)	9,000			
Del-credere Commission (1% on x 2,25,000)	2,250	14,250		
To Profit on consignment transferred to Profit & Loss A/c		30,750		
		2,65,000		2,65,000

PROBLEM 25

Punjab Cycle Co. of Ludhiana consigned 100 bicycles to Kanpur Cycle Co. of Kanpur costing ₹ 1,500 each, invoiced at ₹ 2,000 each. The consignor paid freight ₹ 10,000 and insurance in transit ₹ 1,500. During transit, 10 bicycles were totally damaged. Kanpur Cycle Co. took delivery of the remaining bicycles and paid ₹ 1,530 for octroi duty. Kanpur Cycle Co. sent a bank draft to Punjab Cycle Co. for ₹ 50,000 as advance and later on sent an account sales showing that 80 bicycles had been sold @ ₹ 2,200 each. Expenses incurred by Kanpur Cycle Co. on godown rent were ₹ 2,000. Kanpur Cycle Co. is entitled to a commission of 5% on invoice price and 25% on any surplus of sale price over invoice price. Insurance claim was settled at ₹ 14,000.

Required: Prepare consignment account, consignee's account and accidental loss account in the books of the consignor.

SOLUTION:

Dr. **CONSIGNMENT TO KANPUR ACCOUNT** CR.

Particulars	₹	Particulars	₹
To Goods Sent on Consignment A/c	2,00,000	By Kanpur Cycle Co. (Sale Proceeds) (80 x ₹ 2,200)	1,76,000
To Bank A/c (Expenses)	11,500	By Loss-in-transit	21,320
To Kanpur Cycle Co. (Expenses):		By Consignment Stock A/c	
Octroi	1,530	By Goods Sent on Consignment A/c (100 x ₹ 500)	50,000
Godown Rent	2,000		
To Kanpur Cycle Co. (Commission)	12,000		
To Consignment Stock Reserve A/c	5,000		
To Profit f/t to P & L A/c	31,440		
	2,63,470		2,63,470

Dr. **KANPUR CYCLE CO. ACCOUNT** CR.

Particulars	₹	Particulars	₹
To Consignment to Kanpur A/c (sales)	1,76,000	By Bank A/c (Advance)	50,000
		By Consignment to Kanpur A/c (Exp.)	3,530

		By Consignment to Kanpur A/c (Comm.)	12,000
		By Balance c/d	1,10,470
	1,76,000		1,76,000

Dr. **LOSS-IN-TRANSIT ACCOUNT** CR.

Particulars	₹	Particulars	₹
To Consignment to Kanpur A/c	16,150	By Insurance Co. (Recovered Loss)	14,000
		By Profit & Loss A/c (Irrecovered Loss)	2,150
	16,150		16,150

Working Notes:

1. CALCULATION OF ABNORMAL LOSS AND UNSOLD STOCK

Particulars	Units	₹
A. Cost of Goods Sent	100	1,50,000
B. Expenses incurred by Consignor	—	11,500
C. Total Cost of Goods Sent (A + B)	100	1,61,500
D. *Less:* Cost of Goods not reached the city of Consignee Cost of Goods lost-in-transit	10	16,150
E. Cost of Goods reached the city of Consignee C – D	90	1,45,350
F. *Add:* Non-recurring expenses incurred by Consignee	—	1,530
G. Cost of Goods received by consignee (E + F)	90	1,46,880
H. Cost of Unsold Stock	10	16,320

2. CALCULATION OF INVOICE VALUE OF GOODS-IN-TRANSIT AND UNSOLD STOCK

Particulars	Unsold Stock
A. Cost	16,320
B. *Add:* Loading @ ₹ 500 per unit	5,000
C. Invoice Value [A + B]	21,320

3. COMMISSION

5% on Invoice Price (80 × ₹ 2,000 × 5/100)	8,000
25% of Surplus (80 × ₹ 200 × 25/100)	4,000
	12,000

PROBLEM 26

Kay sent 500 articles to his agent Jay at an invoice price of ₹ 25 per article and paid freight and cartage ₹ 460. Jay sold 300 articles @ ₹ 30 per article and sent an account sales, deducting ₹ 200 for storage charges and ₹ 300 for selling expenses. He charged 10% commission on the gross sale proceeds and remitted the amount due to Kay. Jay also informed Kay that 50 articles had been damaged in transit and they could fetch 70% of their cost.

Required: Record the above mentioned transactions in Kay's ledger showing the profit earned by the consignor.

SOLUTION:

Dr. **CONSIGNMENT TO KANPUR ACCOUNT** Cr.

Particulars	₹	Particulars	₹
To Goods Sent on Consignment A/c	12,500	By Jay (Sale Proceeds) (300 × ₹ 30)	9,000
To Bank A/c (Expenses)	460	By Loss on Goods damaged-in-transit A/c	389
To Jay (Expenses):	500	By Loss t/f to P&L A/c (Damaged)	176
To Jay Commission @ 10% on 9,000	900	By Consignment Stock A/c:	
		Good	3,888
		Damaged	907
	14,360		14,360

Working Note:

CALCULATION OF ABNORMAL LOSS AND UNSOLD STOCK

Particulars	Units	₹
A. Cost of Goods Sent	500	12,500
B. Expenses incurred by Consignor	—	460
C. Total Cost of Goods Sent (A + B)	500	12,960
D. Cost of Unsold Stock (Good)	150	3,888
E. Cost of Damaged units	50	1,296
F. *Less:* 30% Loss on damaged units		388.8
G. Realizable Value of damaged goods		907.2

PROBLEM 27

Renco Ltd., consign on 1.11.2014, 1,000 tins of groundnut oil from Ulhasnagar to their agent Khem Singh at Dhanbad. Each tin costs ₹ 30 at the rate of ₹ 3 per kg. Renco Ltd., pay 5,000 by way of freight and other expenses. During transit 25 tins were accidentally destroyed. Khem Singh takes delivery on 15.11.2014 and accepts a bill for ₹ 2,000 drawn by Renco Ltd. At 3 months. On 31.3.2015 Khem Singh sold 800 tins @ ₹ 50 per tin and reports to Renco Ltd., a theft of 35 tins. Khem Singh had also paid ₹ 600 as clearng charges, ₹ 1,000 as godown rent and ₹ 2,000 by way of labour charges and fire insurance. Khem Singh is entitled to receive a commission of 5% plus 1% for del credere risk.

Required: Show important Ledger Accounts up to 31.3. 2015 in the books of Renco Ltd. Assuming that Khem Singh pays the dues by bank draft.

SOLUTION

Dr. **CONSIGNMENT TO DHANBAD ACCOUNT** Cr.

Particulars		₹	Particulars	₹
To Goods Sent on Consignment A/c		30,000	By Khem Singh A/c (sale proceeds)	40,000
To Bank A/c (freight and other expenses)		5,000	By Profit & Loss A/c (accidental loss)	875
To Khem Singh A/c—expenses:			By Profit & Loss A/c (loss due to theft)	1,247
Clearing charges	600		By Consignment Stock A/c	4,986
Godown rent	1,000			
Labour charges	2,000	3,600		

To Khem Singh A/c (commission)				
Ordinary	2,000			
Del credere	400	2,400		
To Profit on Consignment				
Transferred to P/L A/c		6,108		
		47,108		47,108

Dr. **KHEM SINGH (CONSIGNEE) ACCOUNT** Cr.

Particulars	₹	Particulars	₹
To Consignment to Dhanbad A/c (sale proceeds)	40,000	By Bills Receivable A/c	20,000
		By Consignment to Dhanbad A/c:	
		Expenses	3,600
		Commission	2,400
		By Bank A/c (balance received)	14,000
	40,000		40,000

Working Note:

Valuation of losses and unsold stock:	Units	₹
A. Cost of Goods Sent	1,000	30,000
B. Consignor in Expenses	—	5,000
C. Total Cost of of Goods Sent	1,000	35,000
D. *Less:* Cost of Loss in transit	25	875
E. Cost of Goods reached the city of consignee	975	34,125
F. *Add:* Non-recurring expenses	—	600
G. Cost of Goods received by consignee	975	34,725
H. Cost of Goods Stolen [34,725 × 35/975]		1,247
I. Cost of Unsold Stock [34,725 × 140/975]		4,986

PROBLEM 28

Shri Jayaram of Madras consigned 1,000 cases of tinned fruit (Cost ₹ 7,500) to Govind Lal of Bombay on the 1st January, 2015, charging them at a proforma invoice price to show a profit of 25 per cent on sales. Jayaram paid on the same date ₹ 600 in respect of freight etc. During the half year ending 30th June, 2015, Govind Lal Incurred expenses of ₹ 200 on godown rent and sold 800 cases of the consignment for ₹ 8,000. Govind Lal is entitled to 5% Commission on sales. Record the entries in the books of Shri Jayaram. Also give the solution by Memorandum Column Method.

SOLUTION

Dr. **CONSIGNMENT TO BOMBAY ACCOUNT** Cr.

Particulars	₹	Particulars	₹
To Goods sent on Consignment A/c [₹ 7,500 + (₹ 7,500 × 25/75)]	10,000	By Goods sent on Consignment A/c [₹ 10,000 × 25/100]	2,500
To Cash A/c (Freight and Insurance)	600	By Govind Lal (Sales)	8,000

To Govind Lal (Expenses)	200	By Consignment Stock A/c		
To Govind Lal (Commission)	400	Invoice Price	2,000	
To Consignment Stock Reserve A/c	500	*Add:* Prop. Freight	120	2,120
[₹ 2,000 × 25/100]				
To Profit & Loss A/c (Profit)	920			
	12,620			12,620

Dr. **GOVIND LAL'S ACCOUNT** **Cr.**

Particulars	₹	Particulars	₹
To Consignment to Bombay A/c (Sales)	8,000	By Consignment to Bombay A/c:	
		Expenses	200
		Commission	400
		By Balance c/d	7,400
	8,000		8,000

MEMORANDUM COLUMN METHOD

Dr. **CONSIGNMENT TO BOMBAY ACCOUNT** **Cr.**

Particulars	Invoice Price ₹	Cost ₹	Particulars	Invoice Price ₹	Cost ₹
To Goods sent on Consignment (1,000 cases)	10,000	7,500	By Stock (200 cases) (Cost ₹ 1,500 plus ₹ 120)	2,120	1,620
To Cash (Freight & Insurance)	600	600	By Loss	1,080	
To Govind Lal			By Govind Lal (800 cases)	8,000	8,000
Commission	400	400			
Expenses	200	200			
To P & L A/c		920			
	11,200	9,620		11,200	9,620

PROBLEM 29

The Calicut Consignment Stock Account in the books of Ranjit of Bombay showed a debit balance of ₹ 1,500 representing the cost of ten bicycles on 1st January, 2015. On 1st March, Ranjit sent a further consignment to Calicut of 40 bicycles costing ₹ 160 each. The freight and other charges amounted to ₹ 210. On first June, Calicut agent sent an account sale showing that 8 bicycles from the old stock realised ₹ 140 each and 25 bicycles from the second consignment realised ₹ 200 each. 15 bicycles remained in stock unsold. The Calicut agent remitted an acceptance for ₹ 4,000 which was discounted for ₹ 3,915. Two bicycles from the old stock were unsalable, which the Agent returned to Bombay, on which he incurred an expenditure of ₹ 30. The agent is entitled to 5% commission, which covers all out of pocket expenses to consignment. Prepare Consignment Stock, Consignment Trading, Consignment Expenses and Consignment Profit & Loss Account, supposing that Ranjit closes his accounts on 30th June.

SOLUTION

Dr. **CALICUT CONSIGNMENT STOCK ACCOUNT** Cr.

Particulars	No.	₹	Particulars	No.	₹
To Balance b/d	10	1,500	By Consignment Trading A/c	33	5,200
To Goods sent on Consignment A/c	40	6,400	By Goods sent on Consignment A/c (Return)	2	300
			By Balance c/d	15	2,400
	50	7,900		50	7,900

CALICUT CONSIGNMENT TRADING ACCOUNT

Dr. *for the period ending on June 30, 2015* Cr.

Particulars	₹	Particulars	₹
To Consignment Stock A/c (Cost of goods sold)	5,200	By Calicut Agent's A/c (Sales)	6,120
To Gross Profit t/f to P & L A/c	920		
	6,120		6,120

Dr. **CALICUT CONSIGNMENT EXPENSES ACCOUNT** Cr.

Particulars	₹	Particulars	₹
To Bank A/c (freight & other charges)	210	By Calicut Consignment P & L A/c	467
To Calicut Agent's A/c (Expenses & Commission)	336	By Balance c/d (freight etc, on 15 bicycles)	79
	546		546

Dr. **CALICUT CONSIGNMENT PROFIT AND LOSS ACCOUNT** Cr.

Particulars	₹	Particulars	₹
To Consignment Expenses A/c	467	By Calicut Consignment Trading A/c (Gross Profit)	920
To Profit & Loss A/c (Profit)	453		
	920		920

PROBLEM 30

Star Mills Ltd. Surat, sends regular consignments of yarn to X who is the selling agent of the Mill and is entitled to a commission of 10 paise per kg of yarn sold. This includes del credere commission. Following further information is furnished to you: On 1st April 2014, stock of yarn with the agent 20,000 kg, costing ₹ 50,000. During the year ended 31st March, 2015. Total quantity of yarn consigned—1,60,000 kg @ ₹ 3 per kg, Total quantity of yarn sold—1,50,000 kg @ ₹ 3.75 per kg (these included that opening stock of 20,000 kg). Total remittances by the Agent— ₹ 5,10,000, Railway freight paid by the agent— ₹ 40,000. Of the sales made, X could not collect ₹ 11,000 due to the insolvency of the customer. 5,000 kg of yarn were damaged in transit by Railway for which the agent recovered ₹ 6,000. The damaged goods were sold at the rate of ₹ 1.50 per kg. Show the following Ledger Accounts in the books of Star Mills Ltd. for the year ended 31st March, 2015.

(a) Consignment Account (b) Goods damaged-in-transit Account, and (c) X's Account.

SOLUTION

Dr. CONSIGNMENT ACCOUNT Cr.

Particulars	₹	Particulars	₹
To Consignment Stock A/c (20,000 kg)	50,000	By X's A/c (Sales) (1,50,000 kg sold @ ₹ 3.75 per kg)	5,62,500
To Goods sent on Consignment A/c (1,60,000 kg @ ₹ 3 per kg)	4,80,000	By Goods Damaged A/c (Value of 5,000 kg damaged)	16,250
To X's A/c (Railway freight)	40,000	By Consignment Stock A/c	81,250
To X's A/c (Commission @ 10 Paise)	15,000		
To Profit & Loss A/c (Profit)	75,000		
	6,60,000		6,60,000

Dr. GOODS DAMAGED (IN TRANSIT) ACCOUNT Cr.

Particulars	₹	Particulars	₹
To X's A/c (Commission) [@ 10 Paise per kg on 5,000 kg]	500	By X's A/c (Amount recovered from Railway)	6,000
To Consignment A/c (5,000 kg)	16,250	By Profit and Loss A/c	3,250
		By X's A/c (5,000 kg damaged goods sold @ ₹ 1.50 per kg)	7,500
	16,750		16,750

Dr. X'S ACCOUNT Cr.

Particulars	₹	Particulars	₹
To Consignment A/c (1,50,000 kg of goods sold)	5,62,500	By Consignment A/c (Railway freight)	40,000
To Goods Damaged A/c (Amount recovered from Railway)	6,000	By Consignment A/c (Commission)	15,000
To Goods Damaged A/c (5,000 kg of damaged goods sold)	7,500	By Goods Damaged A/c (Commission)	500
		By Bank A/c (Remittance)	5,10,000
		By Balance c/d	10,500
	5,76,000		5,76,000

Working Note: Valuation of Goods Damaged in Transit and Closing Stock

Particulars	Goods damaged in transit (5,000 kg) ₹	Unsold stock (25,000 kg) ₹
A Cost @ ₹ 3 per kg	15,000	75,000
B *Add:* Proportionate freight @ 25 Paise per kg	1,250	6,250
	16,250	81,250

PROBLEM 31

On 1st April, 2014 Mantu of Madras consigned goods of the value of ₹ 50,000 to Pandey of Patna. The proforma invoice was made by adding 25% to the cost. Mantu paid thereon ₹ 2,500 for freight and ₹ 1,500 for insurance. During transit one-tenth of the goods were totally destroyed by fire and a sum of ₹ 2,400 was realised from the insurance company. On arrival of the goods, Pandey paid ₹ 1,800 as Carriage Inward. During the year ended 31st March, 2015. Pandey paid ₹ 3,600 for godown rent and ₹ 1,900 for selling expenses. One-ninth of the remaining goods were again destroyed by fire in godown and nothing was recovered from the Insurance Company. On 1st March, 2015, Pandey sold half the original goods for ₹ 30,000 and charged a commission of 5% on sales. On 31st March, 2015 Pandey sent a Bank Draft to Mantu for the amount so far due from him. Prepare (a) Consignment to Patna Account, (b) Goods destroyed by Fire Account, and (c) Personal Account of Pandey.

SOLUTION

Dr. **CONSIGNMENT TO PATNA ACCOUNT** **Cr.**

Particulars		₹	Particulars	₹
To Goods sent on Consignment A/c		50,000	By Pandey's A/c (Sales)	30,000
To Cash A/c:			By Goods Destroyed by fire A/c	9,000
Freight	2,500		By Goods sent on Consignment A/c	10,000
Insurance	1,500	4,000	(₹ 50,000 × 20/100)	
To Panday's A/c:			By Consignment Stock A/c	16,800
Carriage Inwards	1,800			
Godown Rent	3,600			
Selling Expenses	1,900	7,300		
To Pandey's A/c (Commission) (5% on ₹ 30,000)		1,500		
To Consignment Stock Reserve A/c (12,000 × 25/100)		3,000		
		65,800		65,800

Note: *There is no normal profit or loss on Consignment.*

Dr. **GOODS DESTROYED BY FIRE ACCOUNT** **Cr.**

Particulars		₹	Particulars	₹
To Consignment to Patna A/c:			By Cash: (Insurance claim for goods lost in transit)	2,400
In transit:	4,400	9,000	By Profit and Loss A/c	6,600
In godown:	4,600		(Irrecovered Abnormal loss)	
		9,000		9,000

Dr. **PANDEY'S ACCOUNT** **Cr.**

Particulars	₹	Particulars	₹
To Consignment to Patna A/c (Sales)	30,000	By Consignment to Patna A/c:	
		Expenses	7,300
		Commission	1,500
		By Bank A/c (Bank Draft)	21,200
	30,000		30,000

Working Note:

VALUATION OF GOODS DESTROYED AND CLOSING STOCK

Particulars	Goods destroyed in-transit ₹	Goods destroyed in godown ₹	Unsold stock ₹
A Cost of goods	4,000 (40,000 × 1/10)	4,000 (36,000/1/9)	12,000 (40,000 – 4,000 – 4,000 – 20,000)
B Consignor's proportionate expenses	400 (4,000 × 4,000/40,000)	400 (4,000 × 4,000/40,000)	1,200 (4,000 × 12,000/40,000)
C Consignee's proportionate expenses	—	200 (1,800 × 4,000/36,000)	600 (1,800 × 12,000/36,000)
D Load			3,000
	4,400	4,600	16,800

PROBLEM 32

A Co. Ltd manufactures and deals in edible oil, consigned to their Bangalore agent, 1,000 crates of oil (each crate containing 12 one-kilo sachets) in March, 2015. The consignment was sent at 20% over the cost price of ₹ 30 per kilo. A bill was drawn on the agent for 80% of the value of the consignment which was met on presentation. Expenses incurred by the company by way of freight and insurance came to ₹ 12,000. The agent received the consignment by lorry and sold in March, 2015, 900 crates at a profit margin of 25% on his cost (excluding consignor's expenses). He found that 500 sachets had got damaged in transit—the manufacturer accepted this as abnormal loss—and these were sold to consumers at ₹ 20 per sachet. The insurance company settled the loss claim for ₹ 2,500. Agent incurred expenses of ₹ 5,000 on his own account (unconnected with the liability under the agreement) and ₹ 3,000 on consignor's account. He is entitled to a commission of 5% on sales effected. By 15th April, 2015 the agent remitted the balance due by him to the company. Draw the accounts in the books of A Co. Ltd., to record the above transactions.

SOLUTION

Dr. **CONSIGNMENT TO BANGALORE ACCOUNT** **Cr.**

Particulars		₹	Particulars	₹
To Goods sent on Consignment A/c		4,32,000	By Bangalore Agent's A/c (900 × 12 × 45)	4,86,000
To Bank A/c (expenses)		12,000	By Bangalore Agent's A/c (500 × ₹ 20)	10,000
To Consignment Stock Reserve A/c (700 × ₹ 6)		4,200	By Loss in Transit A/c (500 × ₹ 11)	5,500
To Profit & Loss A/c (Profit)		1,23,400	By Consigment Stock A/c (700 × ₹ 37)	25,900
To Bangalore Agent's A/c:			By Goods sent on Consignment A/c:	
Expenses	3,000		(1,000 × 12 × ₹ 6)	72,000
Commission @ 5% on ₹ 4,96,000	24,800	27,800		
		5,99,400		5,99,400

Dr. **LOSS-IN-TRANSIT ACCOUNT** Cr.

Particulars	₹	Particulars	₹
To Consignment to Banagalore A/c [500 × ₹ 11]	5,500	By Bank A/c (Insurance claim)	2,500
		By Profit and Loss A/c (Transfer)	3,000
	5,500		5,500

Dr. **GOODS SENT ON CONSIGNMENT ACCOUNT** Cr.

Particulars	₹	Particulars	₹
To Consignment to Bangalore A/c	72,000	By Consignment to Bangalore A/c	4,32,000
To Trading A/c (Transfer)	3,60,000		
	4,32,000		4,32,000

Dr. **BANGALORE AGENT'S ACCOUNT** Cr.

Particulars	₹	Particulars	₹
To Consignment to Bangalore A/c (900 × 12 × ₹ 45)	4,86,000	By B/R A/c (Remittance)	3,45,600
To Consignment to Bangalore A/c (500 × ₹ 20)	10,000	By Consignment to Bangalore A/c (Expenses & Commission)	27,800
		By Bank A/c (Remittance)	1,22,600
	4,96,000		4,96,000

Working Notes:

(i) Cost of goods sent on consignment = 1,000 crates × 12 one – kilo sachets × ₹ 30
= ₹ 3,60,000

(ii) Invoice value of Goods sent on Consignment = ₹ 3,60,000 + 20% of ₹ 3,60,000
= ₹ 4,32,000

PROBLEM 33

A consigned goods to B costing ₹ 1,00,000. The proforma invoice was made so as to show a profit of 25 per cent on cost A paid freight and Insurance ₹ 2,000. B sold part of consignment for ₹ 88,000 at uniform price of 10 per cent over invoice price and spent ₹ 3,000 as warehousing charges, ₹ 1,000 as selling expenses. B is entitled to a commission of 5 per cent on sales and 20 per cent of the net profit after charging such commission on sales. B paid the amount due by bank draft. Draw up the Consignment Account and B's Account in the books of A.

SOLUTION

Dr. **CONSIGNMENT ACCOUNT** Cr.

Particulars	₹	Particulars	₹
To Goods sent on Consignment A/c	1,25,000	By B 's A/c (Sales Proceeds)	88,000
To Consignment Stock Reserve A/c (45,000 × 25,000/1,25,000)	9,000	By Goods Sent on Consignment A/c (₹ 1,25,000 × 20/100)	25,000
To B 's A/c (Expenses):	4,000	By Consignment Stock A/c	45,720
Commission 4,400			

Share of Profit 2,864	7,264		
To Bank A/c (Freight and Insurance)	2,000		
To Profit & Loss A/c (Profit)	11,456		
	1,58,720		1,58,720

Working Notes:

(i) *Calculation of value of Unsold Stock* ₹

		₹
A	Invoice Value of Unsold Stock (₹ 1,25,000 – ₹ 80,000)	45,000
B	Proportionate freight & Insurance (₹ 2,000 × 45,000/1,25,000)	720
C	Unsold Stock (A + B)	45,720

(ii) Agent's share of profit = 20% of ₹ 14,320 = ₹ 2,864

PROBLEM 34

Krishnamurty requests you to prepare a Consignment Account for the year ended 31st March, 2015 and for the purpose gives you the following information to ascertain the profit earned on consignment.

(a) Agent's commission @ 5% on gross sales 20,000, (b) Cost of goods fully damaged in transit (Insurance claim recovered ₹ 18,000) 20,000, (c) Expenses incurred by the agent: Godown Rent ₹ 400, Landing & Clearing ₹ 1,000 Advertisements ₹ 200, Carriage Inward ₹ 900, Selling expenses ₹ 1,000, (d) Freight expenses incurred by Krishnamurty 2,000, (c) Cost of unsold stock lying with agent at the end of the year 60,000 (f) All sales were effected by the agent at a profit of 25% on cost.

SOLUTION

Dr. **CONSIGNMENT ACCOUNT** **Cr.**

Particulars	₹	Particulars	₹
To Bank A/c (Freight)	2,000	By Agent's A/c (20,000 × 100/5)	4,00,000
To Goods sent on Consignment A/c [See Working Note (i)]	4,00,000	By Goods damaged in Transit A/c [See Working Note (ii)]	20,100
To Agent's A/c (Commission) (5% on ₹ 4,00,000)	20,000	By Consignment Stock A/c [See Working Note (ii)]	60,600
To Agent's A/c (Expenses): Godown rent 400 Landing & clearing 1,000 Advertisements 200 Carriage Inward 900 Selling expenses 1,000	3,500		
To Profit & Loss A/c (Profit)	55,200		
	4,80,700		4,80,700

Working Notes:

1. CALCULATION OF COST OF GOODS SENT ON CONSIGNMENT

Particulars	₹
A Gross Sales	4,00,000
B *Less:* Gross Profit (₹ 4,00,000 × 20/100)	80,000
C Cost of goods sold (A – B)	3,20,000

D	*Add:* Cost of goods damaged	20,000
E	*Add:* Cost of unsold stock	60,000
F	Cost of goods sent on Consignment (C + D + E)	4,00,000

2. CALCULATION OF VALUE OF GOODS DAMAGED

	Particulars	Damaged Goods	Unsold Goods
A	Cost (given)	20,000	60,000
B	*Add:* Proportionate expenses of Consignor (freight) @ 5%	100	300
C	*Add:* Proportionate expenses of Agent (Landing and Clearing and Carriage Inward)	—	300
	[1,900 × 60,000/(4,00,000 – 20,000)]	20,100	60,600

PROBLEM 35

The account sales received from an agent disclosed that the total sales effected by him during 2014-2015 amounted to ₹ 4,50,000. This included ₹ 3,12,500 for sales made at invoice price which is cost plus 25% and the balance at 10% above the Invoice price. He incurred expenses to the tune of ₹ 5,000 out of which a sum of ₹ 1,800 is recurring in nature. Forwarding expenses of the Consignor totalled ₹ 2,400. The Agent had remitted the balance due from him through Bank Draft after deducting the expenses, 5% commission on gross sales, Bad debts ₹ 850 and Bills Payable accepted by him for ₹ 10,000. The value of unsold stock at original cost lying with the Agent as on 31st March, 2015 amounted to ₹ 50,000. Prepare the Consignment Account and the Agents' Account in the Books of the Consignor.

SOLUTION

Dr. **CONSIGNMENT ACCOUNT** **Cr.**

Particulars	₹	Particulars	₹
To Goods sent on Consignment A/c	5,00,000	By Agent's A/c (Gross Sales)	4,50,000
To Bank A/c (Forwarding Expenses)	2,400	By Goods sent on Consignment A/c (₹ 5,00,000 – ₹ 4,00,000)	1,00,000
To Agent's A/c (Expenses) Recurring 1,800 Non-Recurring 3,200	5,000	By Consignment Stock A/c [see Working Note (ii)]	63,200
To Agent's A/c (Commission)	22,500		
To Agent's A/c (Bad Debt)	850		
To Consignment Stock Reserve A/c [₹ 50,000 × 25/100]	12,500		
To Profit & Loss A/c (Profit)	69,950		
	6,13,200		6,13,200

Dr. **AGENT'S ACCOUNT** **Cr.**

Particulars	₹	Particulars	₹
To Consignment A/c (Gross Sales)	4,50,000	By Consignment A/c (Expenses)	5,000
		By Cosignment A/c (Commission)	22,500

		By Consignment A/c (Bad Debts)	850
		By Bills Receivable A/c	10,000
		By Bank A/c (Draft sent)	4,11,650
	4,50,000		4,50,000

Working Notes:

1. CALCULATION OF INVOICE VALUE OF GOODS CONSIGNED

	Particulars	₹
A	Invoice Price of Sale of ₹ 3,12,500	3,12,500
B	Invoice Price of remaining sales [₹ 4,50,000 – ₹ 3,12,500) × 100/110]	1,25,000
C	Total Invoice Price of goods sold (A + B)	4,37,500
D	Total Cost price of goods sold [₹ 4,37,500 × 100/125]	3,50,000
E	*Add:* Cost Price of unsold stock (given)	50,000
F	Total Cost Price of Goods consigned (D + E)	4,00,000
G	Total Invoice Price of goods consigned: [₹ 4,00,000 × 125/100]	5,00,000
H	Total Load [₹ 5,00,000 – ₹ 4,00,000]	1,00,000

2. VALUE OF UNSOLD STOCK

A	Invoice Price (₹ 50,000 × 125/100)	62,500
B	*Add:* Proportionate Consignor's expenses: [2,400 × 50,000/4,00,000]	300
C	*Add:* Proportionate Consignor's Non-Recurring expenses [3,200 × 50,000/4,00,000]	400
		63,200

PROBLEM 36

On 5th Aug. Zuben consigns 2,000 Casettes to Suzie costing ₹ 15 each. The following invoice is made out to him at a figure to show a gross profit of 20% on sales, below which the consignee is not allowed to sell. On 25th Aug., the consignee sells half the consignment at a profit of 25% on sales. The expenses are:

5th Aug. Freight and insurance ₹ 1,500 (paid by consignor); 28th Aug. Landing charge, import duty, etc. ₹ 1,000 (paid by consignee). The Consignee is entitled to a commission of 5% on sales and to 1/6th of profits after both commission and share of profits. On 31st Aug. Suzie remits a sight draft for the balance to settle his account. Show the necessary accounts in the books of Consignor.

SOLUTION

Dr. **CONSIGNMENT ACCOUNT** **Cr.**

Date	Particulars	₹	Date	Particulars	₹
Aug. 5	To Goods Sent on Consignment A/c (2,000 × ₹ 18.75)	37,500	Aug. 25	By Suzie's A/c (Sales) (1,000 × ₹ 20)	20,000
	To Bank A/c (Freight and Insurance)	1,500	Aug. 31	By Cosignment Stock A/c	20,000
Aug. 5	To Suzie's A/c (Landing Charges Import duty, etc.)	1,000	Aug. 31	By Goods sent on Consignment A/c (2,000 × ₹ 3.75)	7,500

Aug. 20	To Suzie's A/c Commission 1,000 Share of Profit 393	1,393			
Aug. 31	To Consignment Stock Reserve A/c (1,000 × ₹ 3.75)	3,750			
Aug. 31	To Profit & Loss A/c (Profit)	2,357			
		47,500			47,500

Dr. **GOODS SENT ON CONSIGNMENT ACCOUNT** Cr.

Date	Particulars	₹	Date	Particulars	₹
Aug. 31	To Consignment A/c (Load)	7,500	Aug. 5	By Consignment A/c	37,500
Aug. 31	To Trading A/c (Transfer)	30,000			
		37,500			37,500

Dr. **SUZIE'S ACCOUNT** Cr.

Date	Particulars	₹	Date	Particulars	₹
Aug. 25	To Consignment A/c (Sales)	20,000	Aug. 20	By Consignment A/c (Landing charges, Import duty, etc.)	1,000
			Aug. 31	By Consignment A/c: Commission 1,000 Share of profit 393	1,393
			Aug. 31	By Bank (Sight draft)	17,607
		20,000			20,000

Dr. **CONSIGNMENT STOCK ACCOUNT** Cr.

Date	Particulars	₹	Date	Particulars	₹
Aug. 31	To Consignment A/c	20,000	Aug. 31	By Balance c/d	20,000

Dr. **CONSIGNMENT STOCK RESERVE ACCOUNT** Cr.

Date	Particulars	₹	Date	Particulars	₹
Aug. 31	To Balance c/d	3,750	Aug. 31	By Cosignment A/c	3,750

Working Notes:

1. *Calculation of Invoice Price and Load per Cassette*

   Let invoice Price be X

   Invoice Price = Cost + Load; Invoice Price – Load = Cost, X — 1/5 X = ₹ 15

   X = 15 × 5/4 = ₹ 18.75; Load = ₹ 18,75 – ₹ 15 = ₹ 3.75

2. *Calculation of Sale Price per cassette*

   Let Sale Price be X

   X – 1/4 X = ₹ 15, X = 15 × 4/3 = ₹ 20

3. *Value of Closing Stock*

Invoice Price of 2,000 cassettes (2,000 × ₹ 18.75)		₹ 37,500
Add: Freight and Insurance	₹ 1,500	
Landing charges, Import duty, etc.	₹ 1,000	₹ 2,500
Value of 2,000 Cassettes		₹ 40,000
Value of Closing Stock (40,000 × 1,000/2,000)		₹ 20,000

4. *Amount of Consignee's Commission and Share of profit*

A	Total of Credit side of Consignment A/c	₹ 47,500
B	*Less:* Total of Debit side of Consignment A/c (excluding Commission and Share of Profit)	₹ 43,750
C	Surplus subject to Commission and Share of Profit (A – B)	₹ 3,750
D	*Less:* Commission @ 5% of ₹ 20,000	₹ 1,000
E	Profit after Commission but before Share of Profit (C – D)	₹ 2,750
F	*Less:* Share of Profit (1/7th of ₹ 2,750)	₹ 393
G	Profit after Commission and Share of Profit on Consignment (E – F)	₹ 2,357

PROBLEM 37

On 31st March, 2014 CAMII P. Ltd., a trading organisation owned inventory costing ₹ 3 lakhs of which inventory valued ₹ 1 lakh was with consignees. It also has in its possession inventory valued at ₹ 10 lakhs belonging to its own principals. During the year ended 31st March, 2015 CAMII P. Ltd.:

(a) purchased inventory worth ₹ 50 lakhs of which 80% was despatched to its consignees, the transportation cost being 5% of the value of goods sent;

(b) received from its principals inventory of ₹ 150 lakhs;

(c) sold 90% of own goods received and lying with itself at 20% margin on sales;

(d) sold on behalf of principals 95% of goods available at 120% of the value thereof. CAMII P. Ltd. is entitled to commission at 10% of such sales.

The consignees sold at 125% of their per unit landed cost (consignees spending nil) 95% of goods available with them and were entitled to commission at 10% of sales.

Required: Prepare Consignment Account and Profit & Loss Account in the books of CAMII Ltd. for the year ended 31st March, 2015.

SOLUTION

Dr. **CONSIGNMENT ACCOUNT** **Cr.**

Particulars	₹	Particulars	₹
To Opening Stock	1,00,000	By Sales [43,00,000 × 95% × 125%]	51,06,250
To Good sent on consignment	40,00,000	By Closing Stock [43,00,000 × 5%]	2,15,000
To Transportation cost	2,00,000		
To Commission [51,06,250 × 10%]	5,10,625		
To Profit	5,10,625		
	53,21,250		53,21,250

REVENUE STATEMENT OF CAMII (P.) LTD.,

Dr. *for the year ended 31st March, 2015* Cr.

Particulars	₹	Particulars	₹
To Opening Stock	2,00,000	By Sales [Refer to working note No. 1]	13,50,000
To Purchases	50,00,000	By Good sent on consignment [50,00,000 × 80%]	40,00,000
To Profit	26,04,625	By Closing Stock [12,00,000 × 10%]	1,20,000
		By Profit on consignment	5,10,625
		By Commission [60,00,000 × 95% 120% × 10%]	18,24,000
	78,04,625		78,04,625

Working Note:

CALCULATION OF SALES AND COMMISSION

	Particulars	Goods held as Trader ₹	Goods held by Consignee ₹	Goods held as Consignee ₹
A	Opening Stock	2,00,000	1,00,000	10,00,000
B	Goods Purchased/Received	50,00,000	40,00,000	150,00,000
C	*Less:* Goods Sent to consignee	(40,00,000)	—	—
D	*Add:* Transportation cost [5% of 40,00,000]	—	2,00,000	—
E	Cost of Goods available for sale [A + B – C + D]	12,00,000	43,00,000	160,00,000
F	*Less:* Closing Stock	1,20,000	2,15,000	8,00,000
		[10% of 12,00,000]	[5% of 4,30,000]	[5% of 160,00,000]
G	Cost of Goods sold [E – F]	10,80,000	40,85,000	152,00,000
H	Sales	13,50,000	51,06,250	182,40,000
		[10,80,000 × 100/80]	[125% of 40,85,000]	[120% of 152,00,000]
I	Commission @ 10% on Sales		5,10,625	18,24,000

PROBLEM 38

Messrs. Goswami Brothers were appointed Agents by Sunrise Limited in 2014. You are given the following particulars relating to the year 2014-2015.

		₹
(i)	Cost of Goods despatched by the Company on consignment	7,50,000
(ii)	Goods fully destroyed in Transit (original cost)	50,000
(iii)	Expenses incurred by the Company towards:	
	Freight	2,500
	Insurance	1,500
(iv)	Expenses incurred by Goswami Brothers:	
	Landing & Clearing	1,500
	Godown Rent	1,000
	Transport Charges upto Godown	1,000
	Advertisements	800
	Insurance	800
(v)	Advance remitted by the Agent	1,50,000
(vi)	Bills payable accepted	25,000
(vii)	Goods destroyed by fire (at original cost) in Agent's godown	35,000
(viii)	Bad Debts	3,000
(ix)	Unsold stock with Agent at the close of the year (at original cost)	50,000
(x)	Insurance claim recovered by the Consignor towards loss in transit	48,000
(xi)	Insurance claim recovered by the Agent towards loss by fire.	35,000

All sales were effected by the Agent at 25% on original cost.

The Agent is entitled to a Commission of 10% on gross sales.

Required: Show the Consignor's Account (Sunrise Ltd.) as would appear in the Books of Goswami Brothers.

SOLUTION

Dr. **CONSIGNOR'S ACCOUNT** **Cr.**

Particulars	₹	Particulars		₹
To Cash/Bank A/c (Advance)	1,50,000	By Cash/Bank A/c (Claim)		35,000
To Cash/Bank A/c (Expenses)	5,100	By Cash/Bank A/c (Sales)		
To Bills Payable A/c	25,000	Cost	7,50,000	
To Bad Debts	3,000	Lost in Transit	(50,000)	
To Commission A/c (10% on ₹ 7,68,750)	76,875	Lost-in-Godown	(35,000)	
To Balance c/d	5,43,775	Unsold Stocks	(50,000)	
			6,15,000	
		+ Profit	1,53,750	7,68,750
	8,03,750			8,03,750

PROBLEM 39

The Account Sales of 1,200 Transistor sets received from and sold on account of and at the risk of Sri M. Chopra, Calcutta.

Particulars	₹	₹	₹
1,200 Transistor Sets @ ₹ 1,200			14,40,000
Less: Expenses:			
Unloading expenses	3,000		
Selling expenses	4,000		
Transport charges upto godown	6,100		
Godown rent	6,000		
Advertisements	2,000	21,100	
Less: Commission:			
5% Ordinary Commission	72,000		
1% Del credere Commission	14,400	86,400	1,07,500
			13,32,500
Less: Advance sent on 10.1.2015			2,50,000
Balance Draft enclosed herewith			10,82,500
Stock in hand (31.3.2015)-100 Sets.			
Dated, Madras the 26th April, 2015			E & O.E S. Raman

On further information received you come to know that:

(i) Bad debts amounted to ₹ 2,400 against 2 Sets.

(ii) 20% above the invoice price is the sale price which is equal to cost plus 50%.

(iii) Chopra incurred forwarding expenses @ ₹ 10 per Set.

(iv) During transit 10 Sets became fully damaged and Chopra recovered from insurance the full amount of original cost.

Required: Prepare the Consignment Account, Goods sent on Consignment Account and Loss in Transit Account in the books of Mr Chopra.

SOLUTION

Dr. **CONSIGNOR'S ACCOUNT** **Cr.**

Particulars	₹	Particulars	₹
To Goods Sent on Consignment A/c	13,10,000	By B (Sale Proceeds)	14,40,000
To Bank A/c (Expenses)	13,100	By Loss-in-transit A/c	8,100
To B (Expenses): Unloading	3,000	By Consignment Stock A/c	1,01,700
Transport Godown Rent	6,100 6,000	By Goods Sent on Consignment A/c (1,310 × ₹ 200)	2,62,000
Adv. Exp	2,000		
Selling Expenses	4,000		
To B (Commission)	86,400		
To Consignment Stock reserve A/c	20,000		
To Profit t/f to P&L A/c	3,61,200		
	18,11,800		18,11,800

Dr. **B'S ACCOUNT** **Cr.**

Particulars	₹	Particulars	₹
To Consignment to A/c (sales)	14,40,000	By Bank A/c (Advance)	2,50,000
		By Consignment A/c (Exp.)	21,100
		By Consignment A/c (Comm.)	86,400
		By Bank A/c	10,82,500
	14,40,000		14,40,00

Working Notes:

1. STATEMENT SHOWING THE CALCULATION OF ABNORMAL LOSS AND UNSOLD STOCK

Particulars	Units	₹
A. Cost of Goods Sent	1,310	10,48,000
B. Expenses incurred by Consignor	—	13,100
C. Total Cost of Goods Sent (A + B)	1,310	10,61,100
D. *Less:* Cost of Goods not reached the city of Consignee		
(a) Cost of Goods damaged-in-transit	10	8,100
E. Cost of Goods reached the city of Consignee (C – D)	1,300	10,53,000
F. *Add:* Non-recurring expenses incurred by Consignee	—	9,100
G. Cost of Goods received by Consignee	1,300	10,62,100
H. Cost of Unsold Stock	100	81,700

2. CALCULATION OF INVOICE VALUE OF UNSOLD STOCK

Particulars	Unsold Stock ₹
A. Cost	81,700
B. *Add:* Loading @ ₹ 200 per unit	20,000
C. Incoice Value [A + B]	1,01,700

3. Calculation of Invoice value of Unsold Stock

Let Cost be X and Invoice Price be Y

Sale Price = Cost + 50%

₹ 1,200 = X + 50% of X

X = ₹ 1,200/1.5 = ₹ 800

Sale Price = Invoice Price + 20% of Invoice Price

₹ 1,200 = Y + 20% of Y

Y = ₹ 1,200/1.2 = ₹ 1,000

Thus, Invoice Price = ₹ 1,000

31 ACCOUNTING FOR JOINT VENTURE

SEPARATE SET OF BOOKS METHOD

PROBLEM 1

Mr S and Mr R carrying on a business separately as contractors, jointly take up the work of constructing a building at an agreed price of ₹ 3,50,000 payable in cash ₹ 2,40,000 and the balance in fully paid shares of a Company. A bank account is opened in which Mr S and Mr R paid ₹ 75,000 and ₹ 50,000 respectively. The following costs were incurred in completing the construction and the contract price was duly realised:

Wages paid ₹ 90,000, Materials purchased for cash ₹ 2,10,000, Materials supplied by Mr R from the stock ₹ 27,000, Consulting Engineer's fees paid by Mr S ₹ 6,000.

The Accounts were closed, Mr. S taking up all the shares of the company at an agreed valuation of ₹ 48,000, and Mr R taking the remaining stock of materials at ₹ 9,000.

Required: Prepare the Joint Venture Account and the Personal Accounts of Mr S and Mr R assuming that the net result of the venture is shared by Mr S and Mr R in the ratio of 2 : 1.

SOLUTION

Dr. **JOINT VENTURE ACCOUNT** **Cr.**

Particulars		₹	Particulars	₹
To Joint Bank A/c:			By Joint Bank A/c	2,40,000
Wages	90,000		By Equity Shares A/c	1,10,000
Material	2,10,000	3,00,000	By Mr R (Material)	9,000
To Mr R (Material)		27,000	By Loss t/f to:	
To Mr S (Fees)		6,000	Mr S	24,000
To Equity Shares		62,000	Mr R	12,000
		3,95,000		3,95,000

Dr. **JOINT BANK ACCOUNT** **Cr.**

Particulars	₹	Particulars	₹
To S	75,000	By Joint Venture A/c	3,00,000
To R	50,000	By Mr S	9,000
To Joint Venture A/c	2,40,000	By Mr R	56,000
	3,65,000		3,65,000

Dr. **CO-VENTURERS' ACCOUNT** **Cr.**

Particulars	S ₹	R ₹	Particulars	S ₹	R ₹
To equity Shares A/c	48,000	—	By Joint Bank A/c	75,000	50,000
To Joint Bank A/c	—	9,000	By Joint Venture A/c	6,000	27,000
To Joint Venture A/c	24,000	12,000			
To Joint Bank A/c	9,000	56,000			
	81,000	77,000		81,000	77,000

PROBLEM 2

Gopal and Govind entered into a joint venture agreement to undertake the subscriptions of 50,000 Equity Shares of ₹ 10 each issued by a newly formed Limited Company at a premium of ₹ 2 per share. The underwriting commission is 4% as provided in the Articles:

Public subscriptions were received for 38,000 shares and the underwriters duly discharged their obligations by taking up the remaining shares. Gopal and Govind contributed ₹ 80,000 each and deposited the same in a Joint Bank Account. Sundry expenses incurred out of the joint Bank amounted to ₹ 5,000. The underwriting commission was received by cheque.

Towards the end of the venture 10,000 shares were sold by them in the open market @ ₹ 14 per share and the rest of the shares were taken up by them equally @ ₹ 13 per share.

Profits of the venture were shared equally.

Required: Prepare the joint venture account, joint Bank account and the personal accounts of the co-venturers.

SOLUTION

Dr. **JOINT VENTURE ACCOUNT** **Cr.**

Particulars	₹	Particulars	₹
To Joint Bank (12,000 shares @ ₹ 12)	1,44,000	By Co. (Under Sum.) [4% on ₹ 6,00,000)	24,000
To Joint Bank A/c (Exp.)	40,000	By Joint Bank (10,000 @ ₹ 14)	1,40,000
To Profit t/f to:		By Gopal (1,000 @ 13)	13,000
Gopal	20,500	By Govind (1,000 @ 13)	13,000
Govind	20,500		
	1,86,000		1,86,000

Dr. **JOINT BANK ACCOUNT** **Cr.**

Particulars	₹	Particulars	₹
To Gopal	80,000	By Joint Venture A/c	5,000
To Govind	80,000	By Joint Venture A/c	1,44,000
To Joint Venture A/c	1,40,000	By Gopal	87,500
To Joint Bank A/c	24,000	By Govind	87,500
	3,24,000		3,24,000

Dr. **CO-VENTURERS' ACCOUNT** **Cr.**

Particulars	Gopal ₹	Govind ₹	Particulars	Gopal ₹	Govind ₹
To Joint Venture A/c	13,000	13,000	By Joint Bank A/c	80,000	80,000
To Joint Bank A/c	87,500	87,500	By Joint Venture A/c	20,500	20,500
	1,00,500	1,00,500		1,00,500	1,00,500

RECORDING OF ALL JOINT VENTURE TRANSACTION IN THE BOOKS OF ONE CO-VENTURER ONLY

PROBLEM 3

A of Agra and B of Barellie enter into a joint venture to consign 100 bales to C of Shahdra, to be sold on their joint risk, which is in proportion of 4/7 and 3/7 respectively. A sent 75 bales of ₹ 2,600 each, paying for freight & other charges ₹ 4,900. B sent 25 bales at 2,500 each, paying for freight and other charges ₹ 1,800. All the bales except 5 reached in time. A recovered ₹ 12,000 from the Insurance Company. C sold the remaining bales @ ₹ 3,000 each. C after deducting ₹ 400 for his expenses and his commission @ 4%, remitted a bank draft for ₹ 2,20,000 to A and bank draft for the balance to B. Prepare Joint Venture Account and B's Account in the books of A assuming the final settlement between A and B was made by cheque.

SOLUTION

Dr. **JOINT VENTURE ACCOUNT** **Cr.**

Particulars	₹	Particulars	₹
To Purchases A/c (Goods)	1,95,000	By Bank A/c (Claim)	12,000
To Bank A/c (Exp.)	4,900	By C (Sales)	2,85,000
To B (Goods)	62,500		
To Bank A/c (Exp.)	1,800		
To C (Exp.)	400		
To C (Commission) [4% of ₹ 2,85,000]	11,400		
To Profit t/f to:			
A	12,000		
B	9,000		
	2,97,000		2,97,000

Dr. **B'S ACCOUNT** **Cr.**

Particulars	₹	Particulars	₹
To C A/c	53,200	By Joint Venture A/c	62,500
To Bank A/c	20,100	By Joint Venture A/c	1,800
		By Joint Venture A/c	9,000
	73,300		73,300

PROBLEM 4

A and B enter into a Joint Venture agreeing to share profits and losses in the ratio of 3:1 respectively. A sends ₹ 1,00,000 to B who purchased and sent the following goods to A. 200 silk shirts @ ₹ 100, 750 tericot shirts @ ₹ 80, 400 cotton shirts @ ₹ 50. The expenses incurred by B amounted to ₹ 1,000. A sold the first two varieties at double the purchase price but in respect of last variety, he made a profit of 33-1/3% on sales only. His expenses amounted to ₹ 4,000.

Required: Prepare Joint Venture Account, B's Account in the books of A, assuming the final settlement is made by cheque.

SOLUTION:

Dr. **JOINT VENTURE ACCOUNT** **Cr.**

Particulars		₹	Particulars		₹
To B (Goods)			By Bank A/c:		
Sick Shirts	20,000		Silk Shirts	40,000	
Ter. Shirts	60,000		Ter. Shirts	1,20,000	
Cott. Shirts	20,000	1,00,000	Cotton Shirts	30,000	1,90,000
To B (Exp.)		1,000			
To Bank A/c (Exp.)		4,000			
To Profit t/f to:					
A		63,750			
B		21,250			
		1,90,000			1,90,000

Dr. **B'S ACCOUNT** **Cr.**

Particulars	₹	Particulars	₹
To Bank A/c	1,00,000	By Joint Venture A/c	1,00,000
To Bank A/c	22,250	By Joint Venture A/c	1,800
		By Joint Venture A/c	21,250
	1,22,250		1,22,250

PROBLEM 5

Maganbhai of Rajkot and Ramanan of Madras enter into a joint venture deciding to share profits and losses in the ratio of 3:2 Maganbhai purchases 3,000 kg of material A for ₹ 1,50,000 and sends it to Nana of Pune for processing. Maganbhai pays the transport cost amounting to ₹ 6,000. Ramanan purchases 2,000 kg of material B for ₹ 2,00,000 and sends it to Nana of Pune for processing. The transport cost amounting to ₹ 10,000 is paid by Ramanan. Nana does the processing work and manufactures 4,800 units of finished product C. Nana prepares a "conversion cost" bill on the joint venture at ₹ 20 per unit. Maganbhai pays this bill. The goods are sent to Bannerjee of Calcutta. The transport cost amounting to ₹ 18,000 being paid by Maganbhai. Bannerjee sells 90% of the goods @ ₹ 150 per unit. He takes over the balance goods at ₹ 120 per unit. After deducting his own commission @ 10% of sale proceeds, he remits the amount to Maganbhai. The co-venturers agree to settle the account, after retaining 30% of the profits for taxation on the income of association of persons.

Required: Show the ledger accounts in the books of Maganbhai.

SOLUTION

Dr. **JOINT VENTURE ACCOUNT** **Cr.**

Particulars		₹	Particulars	₹
To Bank A/c:			By Banerjee A/c (Sales)	6,48,000
Purchases	1,50,000		By Banerjee A/c (Goods taken)	57,600

Transport Cost 6,000			
Conversion Cost 96,000			
Transportation Cost (Calcutta) 18,000	2,70,000		
To Romanan A/c:			
Purchases 2,00,000			
Transportation Cost 10,000	2,10,000		
To Banerjee A/c (Commission)	64,800		
To Net Profit c/d	1,60,800		
	7,05,600		7,05,600
To Provision for Taxation A/c @ 30%	48,200	By Net Profit b/d	1,60,800
To Profit & Loss A/c (Share of profit)	67,536		
To Romanan A/c (Share of profit)	45,024		
	1,60,800		1,60,800

Dr. **RAMANAN ACCOUNT** **Cr.**

Particulars	₹	Particulars		₹
To Bank A/c (Balance sent)	2,55,024	By Joint Venture A/c		
		Purchases	2,00,000	
		Transport	10,000	
		Share of profit	45,024	2,55,024
	2,55,024			2,55,024

Dr. **BANERJEE ACCOUNT** **Cr.**

Particulars	₹	Particulars	₹
To Joint Venture Account (Sales)	6,48,000	By Joint Venture A/c (Commission)	64,800
To Joint Venture A/c (Goods taken)	57,600	By Bank A/c	6,40,800
	7,05,600		7,05,600

Note: It has been assumed that no commission is payable on the unsold stock taken over by Benerjee and the amount for the provison for taxation lies with Maganbhai.

PROBLEM 6

Brown and Turner agreed to enter into a joint venture to buy and sell second hand ice cream vehicles and to share profits and losses in the ratio of 5:3 respectively. It was agreed that Brown would record all details of the venture in his books of account. On 1st Januar 2015, Turner purchased two vehicles and paid cash of ₹ 20,000. On 2nd January 2015, he spent sums of ₹ 2,480 on repairs, ₹ 240 on driver's wages and ₹ 360 on temporary insurance cover. He sold the vehicles a week later for ₹ 28,000 subject to a 2% cash discount, if paid within 7 days. He paid the proceeds of sale into his bank account on 10th January 2015. On 31st January, 2015, Brown purchased five vehicles for ₹ 50,000 of which he managed to sell three for ₹ 36,000 for cash on the same day, without incurring any expenses. The fourth vehicle was sold for ₹ 13,500 and, on 7th February, 2015 he received a bill receivable to be presented for payment in three months time. On 31st March. 2015, the fifth vehicle was still unsold and it was agreed that Turner should take over this vehicle at a valuation of ₹ 7,500. On 31st March, the parties made a settlement between themselves, Brown agreeing to take the bill receivable at a value of ₹ 13,180.

Required: Prepare the Joint Venture Account, and Turner's Account as they would appear in the books of Brown.

SOLUTION

Dr. **JOINT VENTURE ACCOUNT** **Cr.**

Date	Particulars	₹	Date	Particulars	₹
01.01.2015	To Tumer A/—Pur.	20,000	09.01.2015	By Tumer A/c (Sales)	28,000
02.01.2015	To Tumer A/c:		31.01.2015	By Bank A/c	36,000
	Repairs 2,480		07.02.2015	By Bills Receivable A/c	13,500
	Driver's Wages 240 Insurance 360	3,080	31.03.2015	By Tumer A/c (taken over)	7,500
10.01.2015	To Tumer A/c: (Discount)	560			
31.01.2015	To Bank A/c	50,000			
	To Dis. Received A/c (Bill)	320			
	To Profit & Loss A/c (share of Profit)	6,900			
	To Tumer A/c (Share of profit)	4,140			
		85,000			85,000

Dr. **TUMER ACCOUNT** **Cr.**

Date	Particulars	₹	Date	Particulars	₹
01.01.2015	To Joint Venture A/c (Sales)	28,000	21.12.2015	By Joint Venture A/c (Purchases)	20,000
31.03.2015	To Joint Venture A/c (Taken over)	7,500	02.01.2015	By Joint Venture A/c (Expenses)	3,080
			10.01.2015	By Joint Venture A/c (Discount allowed)	560
				By Joint Venture A/c (Share of profit)	4,140
			31.03.2015	By Bank A/c	7,720
		35,500			35,500

PROBLEM 7

John and Ali entered into a Joint Venture agreeing to share profits and losses in the ratio of 3: 2.

On 4th Jan., Ali purchased goods costing ₹ 60,000 and spent 2,000 as expense. On the same date, he sent to John a part of these goods costing ₹ 40,000.

On 7th Feb., John sent ₹ 30,000 to Ali. On 10th Feb he purchased goods costing ₹ 50,000 and sent half of the goods to Ali. He paid ₹ 1,000 as carriage.

On 24th March, Ali sold most of the goods in his possession for ₹ 55,000 and the remaining goods costing ₹ 3,000 were taken over by him at an agreed valuation of ₹ 4,000.

On 18th April, John sold all the goods in his possession for ₹ 75,000 except some damaged goods costing ₹ 5,000 which it was agreed to be written off as unsaleable. His selling expenses amounted to ₹ 2,000.

On 30th April, the amount required to settle the accounts between John and Ali was paid by the appropriate party. Show the Joint Venture Account and John's Account in the books of Ali.

SOLUTION

Dr. **JOINT VENTURE ACCOUNT IN THE BOOKS OF ALI** **Cr.**

Date	Particulars		₹	Date	Particulars	₹
4th Jan	To Bank A/c:			24th Mar	By Bank (A/c) (Goods sold)	55,000
	Goods Purchased	60,000		18th Apr	By Goods A/c (Taken over)	4,000
	Expenses	2,000	62,000		By John's A/c (Goods sold)	75,000
10th Feb	To John's A/c:					
	Goods					
	Purchased	50,000				
	Carriage	1,000	51,000			
18th Apr	To John's A/c (Selling Expenses)		2,000			
30th Apr	To Profit transferred to:					
	P&L A/c	7,600				
	John's A/c	11,400	19,000			
			1,34,000			1,34,000

Dr. **JOINT'S ACCOUNT IN THE BOOKS OF ALI** **Cr.**

Date	Particulars	₹	Date	Particulars	₹
18th Apr	To Jt. Venture A/c (Sales)	75,000	7th Feb	By Bank A/c (Advance)	30,000
30th Apr	To Bank A/c (Balance paid to John)	19,400	10th Feb	By Joint Venture A/c (Purchases & exp.)	51,000
			18th Apr	By Joint Venture A/c (Selling expenses)	2,000
			30th Apr	By Joint Venture A/c (Profit)	11,400
		94,400			94,400

Notes:

1. There will be no entries in respect of goods sent by Ali to John and also by John to Ali,
2. There will be no entry for damaged goods for which nothing has been realised.

RECORDING OF ALL JOINT VENTURE TRANSACTIONS IN THE BOOKS OF BOTH CO-VENTURERS

PROBLEM 8

Singh Sons bought goods of the value of ₹ 7,500 and consigned them to Rahim Sons to be sold by them on a joint venture, profits being divided equally. Singh sons paid ₹ 550 for freight and insurance. Singh Sons drew on Rahim Sons bill for ₹ 3,000. The bill was discounted for ₹ 2,900 Rahim Sons paid ₹ 300 for warehousing, cartage etc. Goods were sold for ₹ 12,500 and sales expenses paid by Rahim Sons amounted to ₹ 250. Rahim Sons sent Demand Draft for balance amount after deducting 5% commission the gross sale proceeds.

Required: Prepare Journal and Ledger Accounts in the books of both the parties.

SOLUTION

Dr. **JOINT VENTURE ACCOUNT** **Cr.**

Particulars	₹	Particulars	₹
To Bank (Goods)	7,500	By Rahim (Sales)	12,500
To Bank A/c (Exp.)	550		
To B/R (Discount)	100		
To Rahim (Exp.)	300		
To Rahim (Sales Exp.)	250		
To Rahim (Commission)	625		
To Profit t/f to:			
P&L A/c	1,587		
Rahim & Sons	1,588		
	12,500		12,500

Dr. **RAHIM SONS' ACCOUNT** **Cr.**

Particulars	₹	Particulars	₹
To Joint Venture A/c	12,500	By Joint Venture A/c	3,000
		By Joint Venture A/c	300
		By Joint Venture A/c	250
		By Joint Venture A/c	625
		By Joint Venture A/c	1,588
		By Bank A/c	6,737
	12,500		12,500

Note: Students are required to prepare the necessary accounts in the books of other party on the above pattern.

PROBLEM 9

A and B entered into a joint venture for underwriting 1,00,000 equity shares of ₹ 10 each in C Ltd. They paid all expenses upto allotment stage. They would receive 5,000 equity shares of ₹ 10 each as consideration for this underwriting business. A and B share profits in the ratio of 3: 1.

A introduced cash into the business to meet the following expenses:

Particulars	₹
Advertisement	4,000
Postage	5,000
Printing and Stationery	1,000
B introduced cash to meet the expenses:	
Rent	2,000
Salaries	3,000

Applications fell short of 1,00,000 shares by 3,000 shares. B further brought cash on joint account to pay for 3,000 shares to the company.

C Ltd. handed over to A and B 5,000 shares. The partnership sold all the shares. B received the sale proceeds of 2,000 shares amounting to ₹ 18,000 and A of the remaining 6,000 shares amounting to ₹ 50,000.

Required: Give the necessary ledger accounts in the books of both the parties.

Solution:

Dr. **JOINT VENTURE ACCOUNT** **Cr.**

Particulars	₹	Particulars	₹
To Bank A/c (Exp.)	10,000	By Bank A/c (Sale)	50,000
To B (Exp.)	5,000	By B (Sales)	18,000
To B (Shares)	30,000		
To Profit t/f to:			
A	17,250		
B	5,750		
	68,000		68,000

Dr. **B'S ACCOUNT** **Cr.**

Particulars	₹	Particulars	₹
To Joint Venture A/c	18,000	By Joint Venture A/c	5,000
To Balance c/d	22,750	By Joint Venture A/c	30,000
		By Joint Venture A/c	5,750
	40,750		40,750

Note: Students are required to prepare the necessary accounts in the books of other party on the above pattern.

PROBLEM 10

Ram and Rahim enter into a Joint Venture to take a building contract for ₹ 24,00,000. They provide the following information regarding the expenditure incurred by them:

Particulars	Ram ₹	Rahim ₹
Materials	6,80,000	5,00,000
Cement	1,30,000	1,70,000
Wages	—	2,70,000
Architect's Fee	1,00,000	—
Licence Fees	—	50,000
Plant	—	2,00,000

Plant was valued at ₹ 1,00,000 at the end of the contract and Rahim agreed to take it at that value. Contract amount of ₹ 24,00,000 was received by Ram. Profits or losses to be shared equally. You are asked to show:

(i) Joint Venture Account and Rahim's account in the books of Ram: and

(ii) Joint Venture Account and Ram's Account in the books of Rahim.

SOLUTION

BOOKS OF RAM

Dr. *Joint Venture Account* Cr.

Particulars	₹	Particulars	₹
To Bank A/c:			
— Materials	6,80,000	By Rahim's A/c	1,00,000
— Cement	1,30,000	By Bank A/c	24,00,000
— Architect's fee	1,00,000		
To Rahim's A/c:			
— Materials	5,00,000		
— Cement	1,70,000		
— Wages	2,70,000		
— License fees	50,000		
— Plant	2,00,000		
To P&L A/c	2,00,000		
To Rahim's A/c	2,00,000		
	25,00,000		25,00,000

RAHIM'S ACCOUNT

Particulars	₹	Particulars	₹
To JV A/c (Plant)	1,00,000	By Joint Venture A/c:	
To Balance c/d	12,90,000	— Materials	5,00,000
		— Cement	1,70,000
		— Wages	2,70,000

		— License fees	50,000
		— Plant	2,00,000
		By Joint Venture A/c (Profit)	2,00,000
	13,90,000		13,90,000

BOOKS OF RAHIM

Dr. *Joint Venture Account* Cr.

Particulars	₹	Particulars	₹
To Bank A/c:		By Plant A/c	1,00,000
— Materials	5,00,000	By Ram's A/c	24,00,000
— Cement	1,70,000		
— Wages	2,70,000		
— License fees	50,000		
— Plant	2,00,000		
To Ram's A/c:			
— Materials	6,80,000		
— Cement	1,30,000		
— Architect's fee	1,00,000		
To P&L A/c	2,00,000		
To Ram's A/c	2,00,000		
	25,00,000		25,00,000

Dr. **RAM'S ACCOUNT** Cr.

Particulars	₹	Particulars	₹
To Joint Venture A/c	24,00,000	By Joint Venture A/c (6,80,000 + 1,30,000 + 1,00,000)	9,10,000
		By Joint Venture A/c	2,00,000
		By Balance c/d	12,90,000
	24,00,000		24,00,000

MEMORANDUM JOINT VENTURE METHOD

PROBLEM 11

M and N entered into a Joint venture for the purchase and sale of second-hand motor car and to share profits and losses in the ratio of 3: 2.

On January 15, M bought 5 cars for ₹ 43,000 and on January 20, he paid tax and insurance amounting to ₹ 1,600. On January 31, he sold these cars for ₹ 58,000 out of which he remitted ₹ 11,000 to N paying the balance into his own bank account.

On January 20, N bought 3 cars for ₹ 36,000 and on January 25, he paid tax and insurance ₹ 1,400 and repair charges amounting to ₹ 2,000. He sold one car on February 2, for ₹ 14,000 which he paid into his own bank account. M then took other cars at a valuation of ₹ 26,000 and the venture was closed on February 10. Prepare the Memorandum Joint Venture Account and the Account of the Joint Venture with N in the books of M.

SOLUTION

Dr. **MEMORANDUM JOINT VENTURE ACCOUNT** **Cr.**

Particulars		₹	Particulars	₹
To M:			By M (Sales)	58,000
Purchases	43,000		By N (Sales)	14,000
Tax etc.	1,600	44,600	By N (Taken away)	26,000
To N:				
Purchases	36,000			
Tax etc.	1,400			
Repairs	2,000	39,400		
To Profit t/f to:				
M		8,400		
N		5,600		
		98,000		98,000

Dr. **JOINT VENTURE WITH N ACCOUNT IN THE BOOKS OF M** **Cr.**

Particulars	₹	Particulars	₹
To Bank A/c	44,600	By Bank A/c	58,000
To Bank A/c	11,000	By Balance c/d	6,000
To P&L A/c	8,400		
	64,000		64,000

PROBLEM 12

Ram and Shyam entered onto Joint Venture of underwriting the subscription a per of the entire share capital of Bright Star Ltd. Consisting of 1,00,000 equity shares of ₹ 10 each and to pay all expenses up all allotment. The profits were to be shared by them in the ratio of 3:2. The consideration in return for this agreement was the allotment of 12,000 other shares of ₹ 10 each to be issued to them as fully paid. Ram provided the funds for registration trees ₹ 12,800, advertising expenses of ₹ 10,000, for expenses on printing and distributing the prospectus amounting to ₹ 8,500 and printing and stationary expenses for ₹ 3,000.

Shyam contributed towards payment of office rent ₹ 5,000. Legal charges ₹ 11,500. Salary to clerical staff of ₹ 9,500 and other petty disbursement of ₹ 1,800. The prospectus was issued and applications fell short of the issue by 15,000 shares. Ram took these over on Joint account and paid for the same in full. The ventures received the 12,000 fully paid shares as underwriting commissions. They sold their entire holding at ₹ 12.50 less 50 paise brokerage as share, the net proceeds were received by Ram for 15,000 shares and Shyam for 12,000 shares.

Required: Prepare Memorandum Joint Venture Account and Shyam's Account in the books of Ram and Ram's Account in the books of Shyam.

SOLUTION

Dr. **MEMORANDUM JOINT VENTURE ACCOUNT** **Cr.**

Particulars	₹	Particulars	₹
To Ram:		By Ram (Sale proceeds of 15,000 shares @ ₹ 12.50 each less 50 paisa brokerage per share)	1,80,000
Registration Fee	12,800		
Advertising Expenses	10,000		
Printing & Distribution of Prospectus	8,500	By Shyam (Sale proceeds of 12,000 shares @ ₹ 12.50 per share less 50 paisa brokerage per share)	1,44,000
Stationery Expenses	3,000		
To Shyam:			
Office rent	5,000		
Legal charges	11,500		
Clerical staff	9,500		
Petty payments	1,800		
To Ram (Cost of shares)	1,50,000		
To Profit transferred to:			
A	67,140		
B	44,760		
	3,24,000		3,24,000

Dr. **JOINT VENTURE WITH SHYAM'S ACCOUNT IN THE BOOKS OF RAM** **Cr.**

Particulars	₹	Particulars	₹
To Bank A/c: Registration Fee	12,800	By Bank A/c (Sale proceeds of 15,000 shares)	1,80,000
Printing and Distribution of prospectus	8,500	By Bank A/c (Balance received from Shyam)	71,440
Advertising Expenses	10,000		
Printing & Stationery	3,000		
To Bank A/c (Payment for 15,000 shares)	1,50,000		
To Profit & Loss A/c (Share of profit)	67,140		
	2,51,400		2,51,400

Dr. **JOINT VENTURE WITH RAM ACCOUNT IN THE BOOKS OF SHYAM** **Cr.**

Particulars	₹	Particulars	₹
To Bank A/c:		By Bank A/c (Sale Proceeds of 12,000 shares)	1,44,000
Office Rent	5,000		
Legal Charges	11,500		
Staff Salary	9,500		
Other Expenses	1,800		

To Profit & Loss A/c (Share of Profit)	44,760		
To Bank A/c (Balance paid to Ram)	71,440		
	1,44,000		1,44,000

PROBLEM 13

Thread of Tatanagar are Needle of Nagpur entered into a Joint Venture to trade together in the buying and reselling of cheap machinery. Profit or loss to be shared in the ratio 2:3. Thread undertook to make the purchases and Needle to effect sales. Needle remitted ₹ 75,000 to Thread towards the Joint Venture. Thread purchased machinery worth ₹ 60,000 and paid ₹ 28,500 for repairs of these, 2-1/2% as buying commission and ₹ 2,700 for other sundry expenses. He then sent all the machines purchased and repaired to Needle at Nagpur. While taking delivery of the machinery at Nagpur, Needle incurred ₹ 4,500 towards Railway Freight and 2,100 towards Octroi. He sold part of the machinery for ₹ 1,05,000 and kept the remaining for himself at an agreed value of ₹ 22,500. Other expenses of Needle were (i) Godown rent ₹ 1,350 (ii) Insurance ₹ 1,680 (iii) Brokerage ₹ 2,490 and (iv) Miscellaneous ₹ 1,920.

Both the parties decided to close the venture at this stage. You are required to prepare Accounts for the Joint Venture to show how matters stood in each party's ledger and prepare Memorandum Joint Venture Account.

SOLUTION

Dr. **MEMORANDUM JOINT VENTURE ACCOUNT** **Cr.**

Particulars	₹	Particulars	₹
To Thread:		By Needle (Sale Proceeds)	1,05,000
Purchases of Machinery	60,000	By Needle (Value of Machinery retained)	22,500
Repairs	28,500		
Buying Comission	1,500		
Sundry Expenses	2,700		
To Needle:			
Railway Freight	4,500		
Octroi	2,100		
Godown Rent	1,350		
Insurance	1,680		
Brokerage	2,490		
Miscellaneous Expenses	1,920		
To Profit transferred to:			
Thread:	8,304		
Needle:	12,456		
	1,27,500		1,27,500

Dr. **JOINT VENTURE WITH NEEDLE ACCOUNT IN THREADS' LEDGER** **Cr.**

Particulars	₹	Particulars	₹
To Bank A/c:		By Bank A/c:	
Purchases of Machinery	60,000	(Amount received from Needle)	75,000
Repairs	28,500	By Balance c/d	26,004
Buying Comission	1,500		
Sundry Expenses	2,700		
To Profit & Loss A/c (Share of profit)	8,304		
	1,01,004		1,01,004
To Balance b/d	26,004		

Dr. **JOINT VENTURE WITH THREAD ACCOUNT IN NEEDLE LEDGER** **Cr.**

Particulars	₹	Particulars	₹
To Bank A/c (Amount sent to Thread)	75,000	By Bank A/c (Sales proceeds)	1,05,000
To Bank A/c:		By Purchases A/c:	
Railway Freight	4,500	(Value of Machinery retained)	22,500
Octroi	2,100		
Godown Rent	1,350		
Insurance	1,680		
Brokerage	2,490		
Miscellaneous Expenses	1,920		
To Profit & Loss A/c (Share of profit)	12,456		
To Balance c/d	26,004		
	1,27,500		1,27,500
		By Balance b/d	26,004

PROBLEM 14

Bhim and Arjun entered into a Joint Venture for buying and selling plastic goods and agreed to share profit and losses in the ratio of 3:2.

On October 1, 2014, Bhim purchases goods at a cost of ₹ 60,000 and half of the goods were handed over to Arjun. On October 15, he again purchased goods worth ₹ 20,000. He incurred expenses of ₹ 2,000.

On October 15, Arjun also made a purchase of ₹ 37,500 and on the same day he sent to Bhim goods worth ₹, 15,000. He incurred expenses of ₹ 900. On October 20, Bhim in order to help Arjun sent ₹ 16,000 to him. Both the parties sold goods at a profit of 25% on sale.

On March 31, 2015 Bhim had unsold stock of goods of ₹ 12,500, of these goods costing ₹ 5,000 were taken away by him and the remainder sold for ₹ 8,000. Arjun was able to sell away complete goods excepting goods costing ₹ 2,500 which were badly damaged and were treated as unsaleable. ₹ 3,000 owing to Bhim was unrecoverable and treated as joint loss.

On March 31, 2015 parties decided to close the books.

You are required to prepare:

(a) The Joint Venture Account as it would appear in the books of Bhim recording his own transactions, and

(b) A memorandum Joint Venture Account, showing the profits of the business.

SOLUTION

Dr. JOINT VENTURE WITH ARJUN'S ACCOUNT IN THE BOOKS OF BHIM Cr.

Date	Particulars	₹	Date	Particulars	₹
2014			2015		
Oct. 1	To Bank A/c Purchases	60,000	Mar. 31	By Sales	70,000
Oct. 15	To Bank A/c (Purchases)	20,000	Mar. 31	By Bank A/c (remittances received)	33,760
Oct. 15	To Bank A/c (Expenses)	2,000	Mar. 31	By Sales A/c (Stock sold)	8,000
Oct. 20	To Bank (Adv. to Arjun)	16,000	Mar. 31	By Purchases (Stock Taken over)	5,000
2015					
Mar. 31	To Profit & Loss A/c (Share of Profit)	15,760			
	To Bad Debts	3,000			
		1,16,760			1,16,760

Dr. MEMORANDUM JOINT VENTURE ACCOUNT Cr.

Date	Particulars	₹	Date	Particulars	₹
2015	To Purchases:		2015	By Sales:	
Oct. 1	Bhim	60,000	Mar. 31	Bhim	70,000
Oct. 15	Bhim	20,000	Mar. 31	Arjun	66,667
Oct. 15	Arjun	37,500	Mar. 31	Bhim	8,000
	To Expenses		Mar. 31	By Stock	
Oct. 15	Bhim	2,000		(Taken over by Bhim)	5,000
Oct. 15	Arjun	900			
2015	To Bad Debts				
	(incurred by Bhim)	3,000			
Mar. 31	To Net Profit:				
	Bhim	15,760			
	Arjun	10,507			
		1,49,667			1,49,667

Working Note: *Calculation of Sales:*

	Particulars	Bhim ₹	Arjun ₹
A	Purchases	80,000	37,500
B	*Add:* Received from their party	15,000	30,000
C	*Less:* Sent to other party	30,000	15,000
D	*Less:* Stock	12,500	2,500
E	Cost of Goods Sold	52,500	50,000

F	*Add:* Profit at 25% on Sales i.e. 33-1/3% on cost	17,500	16,667
G	Sales (E + F)	70,000	66,667

PROBLEM 15

Hari, an architect and Ram, a real estate dealer enter into an agreement for the purpose of purchasing a large land and converting it into plots. The purchase price (₹ 1,60,000) and the legal expenses (₹ 11,100) are paid by Hari, who borrowed the money from the bank.

Ram provides the materials costing ₹ 58,000 for the levelling of land and the development of plots. 10 plots of 200 sq. mts. each and 5 plots of 400 sq. mts. each are sold respectively @ ₹ 75 per sq. mt. and ₹ 70 per sq. mt. The sale proceeds of 5 plots of 200 sq. mts. each are received by Ram. The balance is received by Hari, who paid ₹ 15,000 for sales expenses. Hari repaid the loan and interest there on amounting to ₹ 9,600.

The agreement provides that after crediting Hari with the interest charged on the borrowed money and allowing 15 per cent on the cost of the levelling to cover overhead expenses. Hari is to receive two-third of the profit and Ram one-third.

Each party's ledger contains records of his own receipts and payments on the Joint Account. You are required to prepare (a) Memorandum Joint Venture Account and (b) the account of the venture in each party's ledger as it will finally appear.

SOLUTION

Dr. **MEMORANDUM JOINT VENTURE ACCOUNT** **Cr.**

Particulars		₹	Particulars	₹
To Hari:			By Ram Sales (5 × 200 × 75)	75,000
Land Legal Expenses	1,60,000 11,100		By Hari Sales (5 × 20 × 75) + (5 × 500 × 70)	2,15,000
Sales Expenses	15,000			
Interest	9,600	1,95,700		
To Ram:				
Levelling & Development				
Expenses	58,000			
Overhead Expenses	8,700	66,700		
To Profit on Venture				
Hari (2/3)	18,400			
Ram (1/3)	9,200	27,600		
		2,90,000		2,90,000

Dr. **JOINT VENTURE WITH RAM ACCOUNT IN HARI'S LEDGER** **Cr.**

Particulars		₹	Particulars	₹
To Bank A/c:			By Bank A/c (sales)	
Land	1,60,000		200 Sq. mts plots (5 × 200 × 75) 75,000	
Legal Expenses	11,100		400 Sq. mts plots (5 × 400 × 70)1,40,000	2,15,000
Sales Expenses	15,000			

Interest 9,600	1,95,700		
To Profit & Loss A/c (Share of Profit)	18,400		
To Balance c/d (due to Ram)	900		
	2,15,000		2,15,000

Dr. **JOINT VENTURE WITH HARI ACCOUNT IN RAM'S LEDGER** **Cr.**

Particulars	₹	Particulars	₹
To Bank A/c:		By Bank A/c (Sales)	75,000
Levelling & Development 58,000		[200 sq. mts plots (5 × 200 × 75)]	
Expenses		By Balance c/d (due from Hari)	900
Overhead Expenses 8,700	66,700		
To Profit & Loss A/c (Spare of profit)	9,200		
	75,900		75,900

PROBLEM 16

Mr Peter and Mr Paul agree to share the ultimate profit or loss of a certain business venture in the proportion of 3: 2.

Mr Peter, accordingly purchases a freehold house for ₹ 57,000. For this purpose Mr Peter borrows ₹ 30,000 from his bank and arranges ₹ 20,000 himself. Mr Paul pays the remaining ₹ 7,000. The house is converted into three flats at a total expense of ₹ 11,000 which is contributed equally by Mr Peter and Mr Paul. Timber from the garden is sold for ₹ 3,500 which is used to reduce Mr Peter's bank loan. The flats are let at rentals which produce ₹ 9,000 in all (received equally by the parties) and finally the whole property is sold for ₹ 80,000 less agent's commission ₹ 1,750. The net proceeds are received by Mr Peter and he repays his bank loan plus interest ₹ 1,500 (agreed to be borne by the venture). As between the parties it is agreed that Mr Peter shall receive interest out of the venture ₹ 300 and Mr Paul ₹ 100. Finally the venture comes to an end and the accounts are settled among the parties.

Required: Prepare (a) Memorandum Joint Venture Account and (b) the account of the joint venture with Mr Peter in the books of Mr Paul.

SOLUTION

Dr. **MEMORANDUM JOINT VENTURE ACCOUNT** **Cr.**

Particulars		₹	Particulars		₹
To Mr. Peter:			By Mr. Peter		
Freehold House	50,000		Sale (Timber)	3,500	
Expenses	5,500		Rentals	4,500	
Bank Interest	1,500		Sale (flats)	80,000	
Interest	300	57,300	*Less:* Agents	1,750	
To Mr. Paul			Commission		86,250
Freehold House	7,000		By Mr. Paul (Rentals)		4,500
Expenses	5,500				
Interest	100	12,600			
To Net Profit					

Mr. Peter 12,510			
Mr. Paul 8,340	20,850		
	90,750		90,750

Dr. IN THE BOOKS OF MR. PAUL JOINT VENTURE WITH MR. PETER ACCOUNT Cr.

Particulars	₹	Particulars	₹
To Bank A/c (Freehold House)	7,000	By Bank A/c (Rentals)	4,500
To Bank A/c (Expenses)	5,500	By Bank (final remittance)	16,440
To Interest	100		
To Profit & Loss A/c (Share of Profit)	8,340		
	20,940		20,940

PROBLEM 17

Mr A and Mr B entered into a joint venture of purchase and sell crackers during Diwali season. Profit or losses were to be shared equally between Mr A and Mr B. Mr A was to purchase crackers from Sivakasi and send it to Mr B of Bombay who would sell it.

On 1st August, 2015 Mr A purchased crackers worth ₹ 1,00,000 and incurred the following expenses in sending it to Mr B.

(i) Forwarding charges ₹ 6,000, (ii) Insurance charges ₹ 2,000.

He immediately drew upon Mr B ₹ 1,00,000 for 3 months. The acceptance was discounted @ 18% p.a.

Mr B paid the following expenses:

(i) Cartage charges ₹ 3,000, (ii) Commission to agents ₹ 5,000 and (iii) Rental charges ₹ 4,000. The whole crackers were disposed off for ₹ 2,00,000. He forwarded a cheque to Mr A for the amount due on 31st October, 2015. You are required to prepare the following accounts:

(a) Memorandum Joint Venture Account, (b) Mr B in Joint Venture Account in the books of Mr A, (c) Mr A in Joint Venture Account in the books of Mr B.

SOLUTION

MEMORANDUM JOINT VENTURE ACCOUNT

Dr. *for the period from August 1 to October 31, 2015* Cr.

Particulars	₹	Particulars	₹
To A's A/c:		By B 's A/c (Sales)	2,00,000
Purchase of crackers	1,00,000		
Forwarding charges	6,000		
Insurance charges	2,000		
Discount charges	4,500		
To B's A/c:			
Cartage charges	3,000		
Rental charges	4,000		
Commission to Agents	5,000		

To Profit transferred to:				
A	37,750			
B	37,750	75,500		
		2,00,000		2,00,000

Dr. **B IN JOINT VENTURE ACCOUNT IN THE BOOKS OF A** Cr.

Particulars	₹	Particulars	₹
To Bank A/c		By Bills Receivable A/c	1,00,000
(Purchases of crackers)	1,00,000	By Bank A/c	50,250
To Bank A/c:			
Forwarding charges	6,000		
Insurance charges	2,000		
To Discount charges	4,500		
To Profit and Loss A/c (Profit)	37,750		
	1,50,250		1,50,250

Dr. **A IN JOINT VENTURE ACCOUNT IN THE BOOKS OF B** Cr.

Particulars	₹	Particulars	₹
To Bank A/c:		By Bank A/c (Sale proceeds)	2,00,000
Cartage charges	3,000		
Commission to agents	5,000		
Rental charges	4,000		
To Bills Payable A/c	1,00,000		
To Profit and Loss A/c (Profit)	37,750		
To Bank A/c	50,250		
	2,00,000		2,00,000

PROBLEM 18

A and B decided to work a Joint Venture for the sale of electric motors. On 21st May, 2014, A purchased 200 electric motors at ₹ 175 each and despatched 150 motors to B incurring ₹ 1,000 as freight and insurance charges. 10 electric motors were damaged in transit. On 1st February, 2015, ₹ 500 were received by A from the Insurance Co., in full settlement of his claim. On 15th March, 2015, A sold 50 electric motors at ₹ 225 each. He received ₹ 15,000 from B on 1st April, 2015.

On 25th May, 2014 B took delivery of electric motors and incurred the following expenses:

Clearing Charges ₹ 170

Repair charges for 10 Electric Motors damaged in transit ₹ 300

Godown Rent for 3 months ₹ 600

He sold the Electric Motors as below:

1.2.2015	10 damaged motors at ₹ 170 each, 40 motors at ₹ 200 each
15.3.2015	20 motors at ₹ 315 each
1.4.2015	80 motors at ₹ 250 each

It is agreed that they are entitled to commission @ 10% on the respective sale effected by them and that the profits and losses shall be shared between A and B in the ratio of 2: 1. B remits to A the balance of monies due on 30th April, 2015. Prepare: (i) Joint Venture Account in the books of A. (ii) Memorandum Joint Venture Account.

SOLUTION

Dr. **JOINT VENTURE WITH B ACCOUNT IN THE BOOKS OF A** **Cr.**

Date	Particulars	₹	Date	Particulars	₹
2014			2015		
May 21	To Bank A/c (Goods purchased)	35,000	Feb. 01	By Bank A/c (Claim from Insurance Co.)	500
May 21	To Bank A/c (Freight and Insurance charges)	1,000	Mar. 15	By Bank A/c (Sales)	11,250
2015			Apr. 01	By Bank A/c (from B)	15,000
Apr. 30	To Commission on Sales (10% of ₹ 11,250)	1,125	Apr. 30	By Bank A/c (remittance from B)	14,345
	To Profit & Loss A/c (Share of Profit)	3,970			
		41,095			41,095

Dr. **MEMORANDUM JOINT VENTURE ACCOUNT** **Cr.**

Date	Particulars	₹	Date	Particulars	₹
2014			2015		
May 21	To Purchases (A)	35,000	Feb. 1	By Bank A/c (Claim from Insurance)	500
	To Expenses		Mar. 15	By Sales (A) (50 × ₹ 225)	11,250
May 21	A	1,000	Feb. 1	By Sales (B) (10 × ₹ 170)	1,700
May 25	B (₹ 170 + ₹ 300 + ₹ 600)	1,070	Feb. 1	By Sales (B) (40 × ₹ 200)	8,000
2015			Mar. 15	By Sales (B) (20 × ₹ 315)	6,300
Apr. 30	To Commission		Apr. 1	By Sales (B) (80 × ₹ 250)	20,000
	A (10% on 11,250)	1,125			
	B (10% on 36,000)	3,600			
	To Profit transferred to:				
	A 2/3 ₹	3,970			
	B 1/3 ₹1,985	5,955			
		47,750			47,750

Notes:

1. It has been presumed that no more rent of godown is payable by B.
2. No entry will be made for sending goods to the other party.

PROBLEM 19

A and B decided to work a joint venture for the sale of electric motors. On 21st May, 2014, A purchased 200 electric motors at ₹ 1,750 each and despatched 150 motors to B incurring ₹ 10,000 as freight and insurance charges. Ten electric motors were damaged in transit. On 1st February, 2015, ₹ 5,000 was received by A from the insurance company in full settlement of his claim. On 15th March, 2015, A sold 50 electric motors at ₹ 2,250 each. He received ₹ 1,50,000 from B on 1st April, 2015.

On 25th May, 2014 B took delivery of electric motors and incurred the following expenses:

Clearing charges ₹ 1,700; Repair charges for motors damaged in transit ₹ 3,000, Godown rent ₹ 6,000. He sold the electric motors as below:

1.2.2015	10 damaged motors at ₹ 1,700 each
1.2.2015	40 motors at ₹ 2,000 each
15.3.2015	20 motors at ₹ 3,150 each
1.4.2015	80 motors at ₹ 2,500 each

It is agreed that they are entitled to commission @ 10% on the respective sales effected by them and that the profits and losses shall be shared by A and B in the ratio of 2: 1.

B remits to A the balance of money due on 30th April, 2015.

Prepare: (i) Joint Venture Account in the books of A and (ii) Memorandum Joint Venture Account.

SOLUTION

Dr. JOINT VENTURE ACCOUNT WITH B IN THE BOOKS OF A Cr.

Date	Particulars	₹	Date	Particulars	₹
2014			2015		
May 21	To Cash (Purchases)	3,50,000	Feb. 01	By Cash (Receipt from insurance company)	5,000
May 21	To Cash (Expenses)	10,000	Mar. 15	By Cash (Sale Proceeds of 50 Motors)	1,12,500
2015			Apr. 01	By Cash (Receipt from B)	1,50,000
Mar. 15	To Commission	11,250	Apr. 30	By Cash (Receipt from B)	1,43,450
Apr. 30	To P & L Account (Share of Profit)	39,700			
		4,10,950			4,10,950

Dr. MEMORANDUM JOINT VENTURE ACCOUNT Cr.

Particulars	₹	Particulars	₹
To Cost of 200 motors	3,50,000	By Amount received from insurance company	5,000
To Freight and Insurance	10,000	By Sale Proceeds (of A)	1,12,500
To Clearing Charges	1,700	By Sales Proceeds (of B)	3,60,000
To Repairs	3,000		
To Godown Rent	6,000		
To A's Commission	11,250		
To B's Commission	36,000		

To Profit: A	39,700			
B	19,850	59,550		
		4,77,500		4,77,500

Working Note: *Calculation of Sale Proceeds of B*

			₹
1.2.2015	= 10 × 1700	=	17,000
1.2.2015	= 40 × 2000	=	80,000
15.3.2015	= 20 × 3150	=	63,000
1.4.2015	= 80 × 2500	=	2,00,000
			3,60,000

PROBLEM 20

Arun & Balu entered into a Joint Venture to purchase, recondition and sell second hand cars. Arun purchased 100 cars during the period 1st Oct to 31st Mar at the following prices and paid for the same:

20 cars	@ ₹ 15,000 each
40 cars	@ ₹ 25,000 each
40 cars	@ ₹ 55,000 each

Balu during the same period reconditioned the cars by spending the following amounts:

Spare Parts used	₹ 1,80,000	Testing Charges	₹ 20,000
Painting	₹ 2,00,000	Insurance	₹ 60,000
Air-conditioning-10 Cars	₹ 3,00,000	Labour Charges	₹ 10,40,000

Arun and Balu sold the cars, the details of which are as under:

	Sold by	
	Arun	Balu
A.C. Cars	5	4
Non-A.C. Cars	35	46

A.C. cars were sold at ₹ 1,75,000 each. Non-A.C. cars were sold:

Arun	35 cars @ ₹ 1.25 lakhs each
Balu	35 cars @ ₹ 1.10 lakhs each
	11 cars @ ₹ 0.80 lakhs each

During testing, one non-A.C. car met with an accident and the Insurance Company paid the actual cost as claim amount. Prepare the Memorandum Joint-venture Account and Account of Balu in the books of Arun.

SOLUTION

Dr. **MEMORANDUM JOINT VENTURE ACCOUNT** **Cr.**

Particulars		₹	Particulars		₹
To Cost of purchase of cars (Arun)			By Sales Proceeds (Arun)		
20 @ 15000	3,00,000		A.C. Cars 5@ ₹ 1,75,000	8,75,000	
40 @ 25,000	10,00,000		Non-A.C. Cars 35 @ ₹ 1,25,000	43,75,000	52,50,000

40 @ 55,000	22,00,000	35,00,000	By Sales Proceeds (Balu)		
To Spare Parts used (Balu)		1,80,000	A.C. Cars 4@ 1,75,000	7,00,000	
To Painting (Balu)		2,00,000	Non-A.C. Cars 35 @ ₹ 1,10,000	38,50,000	
To Air-Conditioning (Balu)		3,00,000	11 @ ₹ 80,000	8,80,000	54,30,000
To Testing Charger		20,000	By Insurance Claim (Balu)		50,000
To Insurance		60,000	By Closing Stock		
To Labour Charges		10,40,000	1 A.C. Car @ 80,000	80,000	
To Profit on venture:			8 Non-A.C. Cars	4,00,000	4,80,000
Arun	29,55,000				
Balu	29,55,000	59,10,000			
		112,10,000			112,10,000

Dr. **JOINT VENTURE WITH BALU ACCOUNT IN THE BOOKS OF ARUN** **Cr.**

Particulars	₹	Particulars	₹
To Bank A/c		By Bank A/c	52,50,000
(Cost of cars purchased)	35,00,000	By Balance c/d	12,05,000
To Profit & Loss A/c	29,55,000		
	64,55,000		64,80,000

Working Note: *Calculation of Cost of AC and Non-AC Car*

Average Cost of Purchase		A.C. Car	Non-A.C. Car
[(20 × 15,000 + 40 × 25,000 + 40 × 55,000)/(20 + 40 + 40)]		35,000	35,000
Spare Parts used	[₹ 1,80,000/100]	1,800	1,800
Painting	[₹ 2,00,000/100]	2,000	2,000
Air-Conditioning	[₹ 3,00,000/10]	30,000	—
Testing Charges	[₹ 20,000/100]	200	200
Insurance	[₹ 60,000/100]	600	600
Labour Charges	[₹ 10,40,000/100]	10,400	10,400
		80,000	50,000

PROBLEM 21

'D' of Delhi and 'B' of Mumbai entered into Joint Venture to purchase and sell old machines. 'D' to make the purchases and 'B' to make the sales. It was decided to share profit and loss in proportion of 2: 3 respectively. 'B' remitted ₹ 40,000 to 'D' towards the Joint Venture. 'D' purchased old machines worth ₹ 45,000 and paid 2% purchase commission, ₹ 12,000 for its repairs and ₹ 600 for other Sundry expenses. He despatched the machines to Mumbai.

'B' took delivery of the machine paying ₹ 2,400 for freight and ₹ 600 for octroi. He sold some of machines for ₹ 85,000 and kept the remaining machines for himself at an agreed value of ₹ 7,200. His other expenses were Godown rent ₹ 500 and Advertisement ₹ 1,700. Final settlement was made on Joint Venture.

Prepare Memorandum Joint Venture Account and also Joint Venture with 'D''s Account in the book of 'B' and Joint Venture with 'B''s Account in the book of 'D'.

SOLUTION

Dr. **MEMORANDUM JOINT VENTURE ACCOUNT** Cr.

Particulars		₹	Particulars	₹
To Purchases—D		45,000	By Sales—B	85,000
To Expenses			By Stock—	7,200
D	13,500			
B	5,200	18,700		
To Profit				
D	11,400			
B	17,100	28,500		
		92,200		92,200

Dr. **IN THE BOOKS OF 'D' JOINT VENTURE WITH 'B' ACCOUNT** Cr.

Particulars	₹	Particulars	₹
To Bank A/c (Purchases)	45,000	By Bank A/c (Received from B)	40,000
To Bank A/c (Repair & others)	13,500	By Bank A/c (Final settlement)	29,900
To Profit & Loss A/c (Share of profit)	11,400		
	69,900		69,900

Dr. **IN THE BOOKS OF 'B' JOINT VENTURE WITH 'D' ACCOUNT** Cr.

Particulars	₹	Particulars	₹
To Bank (Remittance)	40,000	By Bank (Sales)	85,000
To Bank Expenses	3,000	By Purchases (Stock)	7,200
To Bank Expenses	2,200		
To Profit and Loss A/c (Share of profit)	17,100		
To Bank A/c (Final settlement)	29,900		
	92,200		92,200

PROBLEM 22

Aswin of Madras and Gupta of Delhi entered into a joint venture on 1st Apr.2014 for the purpose of buying second hand cars, reconditioning and selling them as Diesel airconditioned cars Aswin has agreed to buy second hand cars, recondition them and fit diesel engines. Gupta has agreed to fix air conditioners and sell them at Delhi. They have agreed to share the profits and losses equally and settle their accounts at the end of each year.

The following are the details of purchases, sale and expenses incurred by Aswin and Gupta during the year 1st Apr.2014 to 31st Mar.2015:

Particulars	Aswin ₹	Gupta ₹
Cost of 10 Cars purchased at average price	5,00,000	
Reconditioning expenditure	45,000	
Cost of 10 diesel engines	30,000	

Labour charges	18,000	32,000
8 Air conditioners purchased		4,00,000
Buying commission @ 5%	25,000	
Selling commission @ 5%		60,000
Sale value realised on sale of 8 cars		12,00,000
Expenses incurred:		
Freight—local	10,000	8,000
Delhi	30,000	
Rent—Office	10,000	10,000
Garage	12,000	20,000
Insurance	16,000	20,000
Miscellaneous expenses	6,000	10,000

Gupta sent a cheque for ₹ 6,00,000 to Aswin on 1.3.2015. Of the balance of two cars, one car met with accident on the way to garage before reconditioning and the insurance company settled that claim at ₹ 30,000 as a total loss. The old petrol engines were sold @ ₹ 500 per engine and one diesel engine was sold at ₹ 3,000 by Aswin. All of them were sold before 31.3.2015. Aswin retained the balance of one car as a non-airconditioned diesel car for his personal use which was priced at average cost. Aswin/Gupta settled the balance due to/by them on 31.3.2015 by sending a crossed cheque as the case may be. Prepare: (a) Memorandum Joint Venture Account. (b) Joint Venture Account with Gupta in the books of Aswin (c) Joint Venture Account with Aswin in the books of Gupta.

SOLUTION

Dr. **MEMORANDUM JOINT VENTURE ACCOUNT** **Cr.**

Particulars	₹	Particulars	₹
To Cost of purchase of cars (Aswin)	5,00,000	By Sales (Gupta)	12,00,000
To Reconditioning expenses (Aswin)	45,000	By Insurance claim (Aswin)	30,000
To Cost of Diesel engine (Aswin)	30,000	By Sale of Petrol Engine (9 × ₹ 500) (Aswin)	4,500
To Labour charges —Aswin	18,000	By Cost of car taken by Aswin	68,211
—Gupta	32,000	By Sale of Diesel Engine (Aswin)	3,000
To Cost of airconditioners purchased	4,00,000		
To Commission —Buying	25,000		
—Selling	60,000		
To Freight-Local —Aswin	10,000		
—Gupta	8,000		
To Freight—Delhi —Aswin	30,000		
To Rent —Aswin	10,000		
—Gupta	10,000		
To Garage —Aswin	12,000		
To Garage —Gupta	20,000		
To Insurance —Aswin	16,000		
—Gupta	20,000		

To Misc. expenses —Aswin	6,000		
—Gupta	10,000		
To Profit on venture —Aswin 21,856			
—Gupta 21,855	43,711		
	13,05,711		13,05,711

Dr. JOINT VENTURE WITH GUPTA ACCOUNT IN THE BOOKS OF ASWIN Cr.

Particulars	₹	Particulars	₹
To Bank A/c (cost of cars purchased)	5,00,000	By Bank A/c (insurance claim)	30,000
To Bank A/c (reconditioning expenses)	45,000	By Bank A/c (sale of petrol engine) (₹ 500 × 9)	4,500
To Bank A/c (cost of diesel engines)	30,000	By Bank A/c (sale of diesel engine)	3,000
To Bank A/c (labour charges)	18,000	By Drawings A/c (cost of car taken for personal use)	68,211
To Bank A/c (buying commission)	25,000	By Bank A/c (remittance by Gupta on 1st Mar.)	6,00,000
To Bank A/c (local freight)	10,000	By Bank A/c (remittance by Gupta on 31st Mar.)	18,145
To Bank A/c (Delhi freight)	30,000		
To Bank A/c (office rent)	10,000		
To Bank A/c (garage rent)	12,000		
To Bank A/c (insurance)	16,000		
To Bank A/c (misc. expenses)	6,000		
To Profit and Loss A/c (share of profit)	21,856		
	7,23,856		7,23,856

Dr. JOINT VENTURE WITH ASWIN ACCOUNT IN THE BOOKS OF GUPTA Cr.

Particulars	₹	Particulars	₹
To Bank A/c (labour charges)	32,000	By Bank A/c (sales)	12,00,000
To Bank A/c (purchase of airconditioners)	4,00,000		
To Bank A/c (selling commission)	60,000		
To Bank A/c (Freight)	8,000		
To Bank A/c (office rent)	10,000		
To Bank A/c (garage rent)	20,000		
To Bank A/c (insurance)	20,000		
To Bank A/c (misc. exp.)	10,000		
To Profit & Loss A/c (share of profit)	21,855		
To Bank A/c (on 1st Mar.)	6,00,000		
To Bank A/c (remittance to Aswin on 31st Mar.)	18,145		
	12,00,000		12,00,000

Working Note: *Calculation of Cost of Non-Airconditioned Diesel Car*

Particulars	₹	₹
Cost of Car		50,000
Reconditioning	(₹ 45,000/9)	5,000
Diesel engine	(₹ 30,000/10)	3,000
Labour charges	(₹ 18,000/9)	2,000
Buying commission	(₹ 25,000/10)	2,500
Local Freight incurred by Aswin	(₹ 10,000/10)	1,000
Local Insurance	(₹ 16,000/10)	1,600
Office Rent, Garage Rent and Misc. Expenses	(₹ 28,000/9)	3,111
		68,211

PROBLEM 23

Mr H and Mr S entered into a joint venture to buy and sell Computer monitors on 1st August, 2014.

On 1.8.2014 H sent a draft for ₹ 5,00,000 in favour of S and on 5.8.2014. S purchased 250 Monitors at a cost of ₹ 4,000 each. The monitors were sent to Mr H by Truck under 'freight to pay' for ₹ 8,000 and were cleared by him on 12.8.2014.

Hard effected sales in the following manner:

Date	Nos. of Units	Sale price per unit ₹	Discount on sales price
13.8.2014	50	4,700	400 per unit
30.9.2014	100	5,000	10%
30.10.2014	100	4,600	5%

On 15.11.2014, Mr H settled the account by sending a draft in favour of Mr S. Profits being shared equally. S does not maintain any books. Show in H's book.

(i) Joint venture with Mr S Account; and

(ii) Memorandum Joint Venture Account.

SOLUTION

Dr. **JOINT VENTURE WITH MR S ACCOUNT IN THE BOOKS OF H** **Cr.**

Date	Particulars	₹	Date	Particulars	₹
01.08.2014	To Bank A/c	5,00,000	13.08.2014	By Bank A/c (sale proceeds)	2,15,000
12.08.2014	To Bank A/c (Freight)	8,000	30.09.2014	By Bank A/c (sale proceeds)	4,50,000
15.11.2014	To Profit and loss A/c (share of profit)	47,000	30.10.2014	By Bank A/c (sale proceeds)	4,37,000
15.11.2014	To Bank account (draft sent in settlement)	5,47,000			
		11,02,000			11,02,000

Dr. **MEMORANDUM JOINT VENTURE ACCOUNT** Cr.

Particulars		₹	Particulars	₹
To S (250 × ₹ 4,000)		10,00,000	By H—Sales (net):	
To H (Freight)		8,000	50 monitors @ ₹ 4,300	2,15,000
To Profit:			100 monitors @ ₹ 4,500	4,50,000
H	47,000		100 monitors @ ₹ 4,370	4,37,000
S	47,000	94,000		
		11,02,000		11,02,000

PROBLEM 24

A of Agra and B of Kanpur entered into a joint venture for purchase and sale of C.D. players. The cost of each C.D. player was ₹ 3,600 and the fixed retail selling price ₹ 4,500. The following transactions were recorded between them:

2015	A purchased 100 C.D. players paying ₹ 72,000 in cash on account.
July 1	A raised a loan from Bank for ₹ 50,000 at 18% p.a. which is repayable with interest on 1.9.2015. A forwarded 80 C.D. players to B incurring ₹ 2,880 as forwarding and insurance charges.
July 7	A received the consignment and paid ₹ 720 as clearing charges.
Aug. 1	A sold 5 mopeds for cash. B sold 20 mopeds for cash. A raised a loan of ₹ 1,50,000 from Bank, repayable with interest at 18% p.a. on 1.9.2015. B remitted ₹ 1,50,000 to A, incurring charges of ₹ 50. A paid the balance due for the C.D. players.
Aug.26	A sold the balance C.D. players for cash and paid selling expenses ₹ 5,000, B sold the balance C.D. players for cash and paid selling expenses ₹ 20,000.
Sept. 1	Accounts settled between the ventures and loans repaid, they shared profit equally. You are required to show: (i) The memorandum Joint Venture Account; (ii) Joint Venture with B account in A books; and (iii) Joint Venture with A Account in B books;

SOLUTION

MEMORANDUM JOINT VENTURE ACCOUNT

Dr. *for the period from July 1 to Sept 1, 2015* Cr.

Particulars	₹	Particulars		₹
To A:		By Sales:		
Cost of Mopeds	3,60,000	(80 × 4,500)	3,60,000	
Forwarding & insurance	2,880	A (20 × 4,500)	90,000	4,50,000
Interest (for 2 months)	1,500			
Selling Expenses	5,000			
To B:				
Clearing Charges	720			

Interest (for the month)	2,250		
Sundry Expenses (Telegraphic transfer charges)	50		
Selling Expenses	20,000		
To Profit transferred to:			
A	28,800		
B	28,800		
	4,50,000		4,50,000

Dr. JOINT VENTURE WITH B ACCOUNT IN THE BOOKS OF A Cr.

Particulars	₹	Particulars	₹
To Bank A/c (part payment of cost)	72,000	By Bank A/c (sale proceeds)	22,500
To Bank A/c (balance cost of purchases)	2,88,000	By Bank A/c (remittance from Laxman)	1,50,000
To Bank A/c (forwarding charges)	2,880	By Bank A/c (sale proceeds)	67,500
To Bank A/c (selling expenses)	5,000	By Bank A/c (cash received	1,58,180
To Bank A/c (Interest)	1,500	in settlement)	
To Profit & Loss A/c (share of profit)	28,800		
	3,98,180		2,98,180

Dr. JOINT VENTURE WITH A ACCOUNT IN THE BOOKS OF B Cr.

Particulars	₹	Particulars	₹
To Bank A/c (clearing charges)	720	By Bank A/c (Sale proceeds of 20 mopeds)	90,000
To Bank A/c remittance excluding charges)	1,50,000	By Bank A/c (Sale proceeds of 60 mopeds)	2,70,000
To Bank A/c (selling expenses)	20,000		
To Bank A/c (interest)	2,250		
To Sundry Expenses	50		
To Profit & Loss A/c (share of profit)	28,800		
To Bank A/c (paid in settlement)	1,58,180		
	3,60,000		3,60,000

32 GOODS SENT ON APPROVAL OR ON SALE OR RETURN BASIS

ORDINARY SALES METHOD

PROBLEM 1

On 31-03-2015 goods sold at sales price of ₹ 3,000 were lying with customer Anu to whom they were sold on 'Sale or Return' basis and recorded as actual sales. Since no consent has been received from the customer, you are required to pass adjustment entires presuming goods were sent on approval at a profit of cost plus 20%. Present market price is 10% less than the cost price.

SOLUTION

JOURNAL OF ANU

Date	Particulars	L.F.	Dr. (₹)	Cr. (₹)
31.3.2015	Sales A/c Dr.		3,000	
	To Anu's A/c			3,000
	[Being cancellation of sale entry for goods not yet approved]			
	Stock with customers A/c Dr.		2,250	
	To Trading A/c			2,250
	[Being stock with customers recorded at Market price]			

Working Note: Calculation of Cost and Market Price of Stock with customer

A.	Sale price of goods sent on approval	₹ 3,000
B.	*Less:* Profit [3,000 × 20/120]	500
C.	Cost of goods	2,500
D.	Market price = 2,500 – (2,500 × 10%) = 2,250	

Note: Since the market price is less than the cost price, stock with customer is valued at market price.

PROBLEM 2

Ramu sells goods to his approved customers on 'Sale or Return' basis at a profit of 20% on sales, treating as actual sales. On 15th March, goods costing ₹ 1,000 were sent to Usha Traders. No confirmation has been received from Usha Traders until 31st March.

Give the necessary journal entries in the books of Ramu.

SOLUTION

JOURNAL

Date	Particulars	L.F.	Dr. (₹)	Cr. (₹)
15th	Usha traders A/c Dr.		1,250	
March	To Sales A/c			1,250
	[Being the sales made with sale value of ₹ 1,250 (cost = 1,000 + Profit 20% on sales (25% on cost – 1000 × 25/100))]			

31st March	Sales A/c To Usha traders (Being the cancellation of sale recorded earlier)	Dr		1,250	1,250
31st March	Stock with customers A/c To Trading A/c (Being stock at the end recorded with the customers at cost price)	Dr.		1,000	1,000

PROBLEM 3

Mr. A, a trader, dispatched goods costing ₹ 16,000 to his customer Mr B on sale or return basis after charging a gross profit of 25% on cost. Mr. A had treated the transaction as credit sale at the time of dispatch of the goods. Pass Journal entries in the books of Mr. A, if:

(i) the customer had approved the goods on 31st March.

(ii) the customer had rejected all the goods on 31st March:

(iii) the customer had retained half of the goods while rejecting the other half on 31st March.

SOLUTION

JOURNAL

Date	Particulars		L.F.	Dr. (₹)	Cr. (₹)
	When goods are sent on approval:				
	Mr B's A/c	Dr.		20,000	
	To Sales A/c (Being goods sent on approval treated as credit sale)				20,000
(i)	**When goods are approved by customer**				
	No Entry need to be passed				
(ii)	**When the customer rejects all the goods:**				
	Sales A/c	Dr.		20,000	
	To Mr B's A/c (Being entry for credit sale reversed on rejection of the goods by the customer)				20,000
	Stock with customers A/c	Dr.		16,000	
	To Trading A/c (Being stock at the end recorded with the customers at cost price)				16,000
(iii)	**When the customer retains half the goods while rejecting the other half:**				
	Sales A/c	Dr.		10,000	
	To Mr B's A/c (Being entry for credit sale reversed for the rejected portion i.e. half of the goods)				10,000
	Stock with customers A/c	Dr.		8,000	
	To Trading A/c (Being stock at the end recorded with the customers at cost price)				8,000

Working Note:

Selling Price = Cost of goods sent + Gross Profit = ₹ 16,000 + 25% of ₹ 16,000 = ₹ 20,000

SEPARATE SET OF BOOKS METHOD

PROBLEM 4

M/s Metha Bros. sends out goods on approval at a profit of cost plus 25% as follows:

March 10. A - ₹ 300 March 13. A returned ₹ 100 rest retained.

March 12. B - ₹ 200 March 22. B retained all the goods.

March 30. C - ₹ 1,500 March 31. No intimation.

Show how these transactions will appear when Sale on approval books are kept on double entry system. Give Journal entries and ledger accounts.

SOLUTION

JOURNAL OF M/S MEHTA BROS.

Date	Particulars		L.F.	Dr. (₹)	Cr. (₹)
Mar. 10	A's A/c	Dr.		300	
	To Sale or Return A/c				300
	[Being goods sent on approval to 'A' entered in sale or return ledger]				
Mar. 12	B 's A/c	Dr.		200	
	To Sale or Return A/c				200
	[Being goods sent to B on approval entered in Sale or Return ledger]				
Mar. 13	Sale or Return A/c	Dr.		100	
	To A's A/c				100
	[Being goods returned by A entered in Sale or Return Ledger]				
Mar. 13	A's A/c (in main ledger)	Dr.		200	
	To A (in Sale or Return Leger)				200
	[Being goods approved transferred to Personal A/c in the main ledger]				
Mar. 13	Sale or Return A/c	Dr.		200	
	To Sales A/c (in main ledger)				200
	[Being goods approved transferred from Sale or Return ledger to main ledger]				
Mar. 22	B 's A/c (in main ledger)	Dr.		200	
	To B (in Sale or Return ledger)				200
	[Being goods approved transferred to Personal A/c in the main ledger]				
Mar. 22	Sale or Return A/c (in Sale or Return ledger)	Dr.		200	

	To Sales A/c (in main ledger) [Being goods approved transferred from Sale or Return ledger to main ledger]				200
Mar. 30	C 's A/c To Sale or Return A/c [Being goods sent on approval to C entered in Sale or Return ledger]	Dr.		1,500	1,500

Step 1: Recording in the books

SALE OR RETURN DAY BOOK

Date	Customer's Name	Sale or Return (L.F)	Amount (₹)
Mar. 10	A		300
Mar. 12	B		200
Mar. 30	C		1,500
			2,000

SALES AND RETURNS BOOK

Goods Sold					Goods Returned			
Date	Customer's Name	Regular L.F	Sale or Return L.F	₹	Date	Customer's Name	Sale or Return L.F.	₹
Mar. 13	A			200	Mar. 13	A		100
Mar. 22	B			200				

Step 2: Posting to Sales or Returns Ledger.

A'S ACCOUNT

Date	Particulars	₹	Date	Particulars	₹
Mar. 10	To Sale or Return A/c	300	Mar. 13	By A's A/c (in main ledger)	200
				By Sale or Return A/c	100
		300			300

B'S ACCOUNT

Date	Particulars	₹	Date	Particulars	₹
Mar. 12	To Sale or Return A/c	200	Mar. 22	By B's A/c (in main ledger)	200
		200			200

C 'S ACCOUNT

Date	Particulars	₹	Date	Particulars	₹
Mar. 30	To Sale or Return A/c	1,500	Mar. 31	By Balance c/d	1,500
		1,500			1,500

SALE OR RETURN ACCOUNT

Date	Particulars	₹	Date	Particulars	₹
Mar. 13	To A's A/c (returns)	100	Mar. 10	By A's A/c	300
Mar. 13	To Sales A/c (in main ledger)	200	Mar. 12	By B's A/c	200
Mar. 22	To Sales A/c (in main ledger)	200			
Mar. 31	To Balance c/d	1,500	Mar. 30	By C's A/c	1,500
		2,000			2,000

Step 3: Posting to Main Ledger.

A'S ACCOUNT

Date	Particulars	₹	Date	Particulars	₹
Mar. 13	To A (in Sale or Return ledger)	200	Mar. 31	By Balance c/d	200
		200			200

B'S ACCOUNT

Date	Particulars	₹	Date	Particulars	₹
Mar. 22	To B (in Sale or Return ledger)	200	Mar. 31	Balance c/d	200
		200			200

SALES ACCOUNT

Date	Particulars	₹	Date	Particulars	₹
Jan 31	To Balance c/d	400	Jan 13	By Sale or Return A/c (in Sale or Return ledger)	200
			Jan 22	By Sale or Return A/c (in Sale or Return ledger)	200
		400			400

PROBLEM 5

'X' supplied goods on sale or return basis to customer, the particulars of which are as under:

Date of Despatch	Party's Name	Amount ₹	Remarks
10.12.2015	ABC Co.	10,000	No information till 31.12.2015
12.12.2015	DEF Co.	15,000	Returned on 16.12.2015
15.12.2015	GHI Co.	12,000	Goods worth ₹ 2,000
			Returned on 20.12.2015
20.12.2015	DEF Co.	16,000	Goods Retained on 24.12.2015
25.12.2015	ABC Co.	11,000	Goods Retained on 28.12.2015
30.12.2015	GHI Co.	13,000	No information till 31.12.2015

Goods are to be returned within 15 days from the date of despatch, failing which it will be treated as Sales. The Books of 'X' are closed on the 31st December, 2015.

Prepare the following account in the book of 'X':

(i) Goods on Sales or Return, Sold and Returned Day Books.
(ii) Goods on Sales or Return Total Account.

SOLUTION

GOODS ON SALES OR RETURN, SOLD AND RETURNED DAY BOOKS

Date	Party to whom goods sent	L.F.	₹	Date	Sold ₹	Returned ₹
10.12.2015	M/s ABC Co.		10,000	25.12.2015	10,000	
12.12.2015	M/s DEF Co.		15,000	16.12.2015	—	15,000
15.12.2015	M/s GHI Co.		12,000	20.12.2015	10,000	
20.12.2015	M/s DEF Co.		16,000	24.12.2015	16,000	2,000
25.12.2015	M/s ABC Co.		11,000	28.12.2015	11,000	
30.12.2015	M/s GHI Co.		13,000	—	—	
			77,000		47,000	17,000

GOODS ON SALES OR RETURN TOTAL ACCOUNT

Date	Particulars	₹	Date	Particulars	₹
31.12.2015	To Returns	17,000	31.12.2015	By Goods Sent on Sales or Return	77,000
	To Sales	47,000			
	To Balance c/d	13,000			
		77,000			77,000

33 AVERAGE DUE DATE AND ACCOUNT CURRENT

SHORT ANSWER PRACTICAL PROBLEMS

AVERAGE DUE DATE

PROBLEM 1

A promissory note executed by Mr. X is due on 12th Aug. What is the maturity date of the promissory note including grace days?

Solution

Where the promissory note is due (including grace days) on public holiday, the preceding day shall be the due date. Hence, the due date is 14th Aug.

PROBLEM 2

Calculate Average Due Date from the following information: (Assume non-leap year)

Date of the bill	*Term*	*Amount*
August 10	3 months	6,000
October 23	60 days	5,000
December 4	2 months	4,000
January 14	60 days	2,000
March 8	2 months	3,000

Solution

CALCULATION OF AVERAGE DUE DATE (BASE DATE: 13TH NOV.)

Date of the Maturity	*Amount*	*No. of days from Base Date to Date of Maturity*	*Product*
13th Nov.	6,000	0	0
25th Dec.	5,000	17 + 25 = 42	2,10,000
07th Feb.	4,000	17+31 +31 +7=86	3,44,000
18th March	2,000	17 + 31 + 31 + 28 + 18 = 125	2,50,000
11th May.	3,000	17 + 31+ 31 + 28 + 31+ 30 + 11 = 179	5,37,000
	20,000		13,41,000

$$\text{Average Due Date} = \text{Base Date} + \frac{\text{Total of Products}}{\text{Total Amount}} = \text{13th Nov.} + \frac{13{,}41{,}000}{20{,}000}\text{ days}$$

$$= \text{13th Nov.} + 67.05 \text{ days} = \text{19th Jan.}$$

PROBLEM 3

Calculate Average due date from the following information:

Date of Bill	*Term*	*Amount (₹)*
1st March	2 months	4,000
10th March	3 months	3,000
5th April	2 months	2,000
20th April	1 month	3,750
10th May	2 months	5,000

Solution

CALCULATION OF AVERAGE DUE DATE

(Taking 4th May as the base date)

Date of Bill	*Term*	*Due Date*	*Amount*	*No. of days from the base date i.e. May 4*	*Product*
1st March	2 months	4th May	4,000	0	0
10th March	3 months	13th June	3,000	40	1,20,000
5th April	2 months	8th June	2,000	35	70,000
20th April	1 month	23rd May	3,750	19	71,250
10th May	2 months	13th July	5,000	70	3,50,000
			17,750		6,11,250

$$\text{Average due date} = \text{Base date} + \text{Days equal to } \frac{\text{Sum of Products}}{\text{Sum of Amounts}}$$

$$= \text{4th May} + \frac{6{,}11{,}250}{17{,}750} \text{ i.e. 34 days (approx)} = \text{7th June}$$

PROBLEM 4

Calculate average due date from the following information:

Date of Bill	*Term*	*Amount (₹)*
16 August, 2014	3 months	3,000
20 October, 2014	60 days	2,500
14 December, 2014	2 months	2,000
24 January, 2015	60 days	1,000
06 March, 2015	2 months	1,500

Solution

CALCULATION OF AVERAGE DUE DATE
(Taking November 19, 2012 as the base date)

Date of Bill	*Term*	*Due Date (including 3 grace days)*	*Amount*	*No of days from the base date*	*Product (No. of days × Amount)*
August 16, 2014	3 months	Nov. 19, 2012	3,000	0	0
October 20, 2014	60 days	Dec. 22, 2012	2,500	33	82,500
December 14, 2014	2 months	Feb. 17, 2013	2,000	90	1,80,000
January 24, 2015	60 days	March 27, 2013	1,000	129	1,29,000
March 06, 2015	2 months	May 09, 2013	1,500	172	2,58,000
			10,000		6,49,500

$$\text{Average due date} = \text{Base date} + \text{Days equal to } \frac{\text{Sum of Products}}{\text{Sum of Amounts}}$$

$$= \text{November 19} + \frac{6{,}49{,}500}{10{,}000}$$

$$= \text{November 19} + 65 \text{ days (approx.)} = \text{January 23}$$

PROBLEM 5

A accepted following several bills falling due on different dates, now desires to have these bills cancelled and to accept a new bill for the whole amount payable on the average due date:

S. No.	*Date of Bill*	*Amount (₹)*	*Usance of Bill*
1.	1st February	4,00,000	1 month
2.	14th February	6,00,000	3 months
3.	2nd March	7,50,000	2 months
4.	$10^{!h}$ March	5,00,000	4 months
5.	$18^{!h}$ March	9,00,000	1 month

From above, find the average due date, on which A can pay the whole amount.

Solution

CALCULATION AVERAGE DUE DATE TAKING BASE DATE AS 4TH MARCH

S. No	*Date of bill*	*Usance of bill*	*Due date of bill (₹)*	*Amount from base date*	*No. of days*	*Product*
1.	1st February	1 month	4th March	4,00,000	0	0
2.	14th February	3 months	17^{h} May	6,00,000	74	4,44,00,000
3.	2nd March	2 months	05th May	7,50,000	62	4,65,00,000
4.	10th March	4 months	13th July	5,00,000	131	6,55,00,000
5.	18th March	1 month	21st April	9,00,000	48	4,32,00,000
			Total	31,50,000		19,96,00,000

$$\text{Average due date} = \text{Base date} + \frac{\text{Sum of Product}}{\text{Sum of Amount}}$$

$$= 4^{th} \text{ March} = \frac{19{,}96{,}00{,}000}{31{,}50{,}000}$$

= 4th March+ 63.37 or 63 days = 6th May

The new bill of ₹ 31, 50, 000 will be payable on 6th May.

PROBLEM 6

M/s Stairs & Co. draw upon Marble & Co. several Bills of Exchange due for payment on different dates as under-

Date of Bill	*Amount ₹*	*Tenure of Bill*
12th May	44,000	3 months
10th June	45,000	4 months
1st July	14,000	1 month
19st July	17,000	2 months

Find out the Average Due Date on which payment may be made in one single amount by Marble & Co. to Stairs & Co.

Note: 15th August, Independence Day, is a National Holiday and 22nd September is a declared Emergency Holiday, due to death of a National Leader.

Solution

COMPUTATION OF AVERAGE DUE DATE (NOTE: BASE DATE = 04TH AUGUST)

Bill Date	*Due Date*	*No. of Days from Base Date*	*Amt (₹)*	*Product (₹)*
A	*B*	*C*	*D*	*E = C × D*
12th May	14th Aug	10	44,000	4,40,000
10th Jun	13th Oct	27 + 30 + 13 = 70	45,000	31,50,000
1st Jul	4th Aug	0	14,000	–
19th Jul	23rd Sept	27 + 23 = 50	17,000	8,50,000
			1,20,000	44,40,000

$$\text{Average Due Date} = \text{Base Date} \pm \frac{\text{Total of Products}}{\text{Total of Amount}} = \text{4th August} + \frac{44,40,000}{1,20,000}$$

= 4th August + 37 days (approx.) = **10th September**

PROBLEM 7

From the following details find out the Average Due Date:

Date of Bill	*Amount (₹)*	*Usance of Bill*
29th January	5,000	1 month
20th March	4,000	2 months
12th July	7,000	1 month
10th August	6,000	2 months

Solution

CALCULATION OF AVERAGE DUE DATE (TAKING 3RD MARCH AS BASE DATE)

Date of bill	*Term*	*Due date*	*Amount* (₹)	*No. of days from the base date* (₹)	*Product* (₹)
29th January	1 month	3rd March[1]	5,000	0	0
20th March	2 months	23rd May	4,000	81	3,24,000
12th July	1 month	14th Aug.[2]	7,000	164	11,48,000
10th August	2 months	13th Oct.	6,000	224	13,44,000
			22,000		**28,16,000**

Average due date $= \text{Base date} + \text{Days equal to } \dfrac{\text{Sum of Product}}{\text{Sum of Amount}}$

$= 3^{rd}\text{ March} + \dfrac{28{,}16{,}000}{22{,}000} = \text{3rd March} + 128\text{ days}$

= 9th July

PROBLEM 8

E owes to *F* following amounts:

(i) ₹ 5,000 due on 10th March
(ii) ₹ 18,000 due on 2nd April
(iii) ₹ 60,000 due on 30th April
(iv) ₹ 2,000 due on 10th June

He desires to make full payment on 30th June with interest at 10% per annum from the average due date. Find out the average due date and the amount of interest.

Solution

CALCULATION OF AVERAGE DUE DATE [BASE DATE = 10TH MARCH

Due Date	*Amount (₹)*	*No. of days from Base Date to Due*	*Product (₹)*
March 10	5,000	0	0
April 2	18,000	21 + 2 = 23	4,14,000
April 30	60,000	21 + 30 = 51	30,60,000
June 10	2,000	21 + 30 + 31 + 10 = 92	1,84,000
Total	85,000	Total	36,58,000

Average Due Date $= \text{Base date} + \dfrac{\text{Total of Products}}{\text{Total Amount}} = \text{10th March} + \dfrac{36{,}58{,}000}{85{,}000}$

$= \text{March} + 43.04\text{ day}$

$$= \text{10th March} + 43 \text{ days (app.)}$$

Average due date = 22nd April

$$\text{Interest} = 85{,}000 \times \frac{10}{100} \times \frac{69}{365} = \text{Rs } 1606.85 \text{ or Rs } 1{,}607$$

PROBLEM 9

T owes to K the following Amounts:

₹ 7,000 due on 15th March, ₹ 12,000 due on 5th April, ₹ 30,000 due on 25th April, ₹ 20,000 due on 11th June

He desires to make the full payment on 30th June along with interest @ 10% per annum from the average due date. Find out the average due date and the amount of interest. Amount of interest may be rounded off to the nearest rupee.

Solution

CALCULATION OF AVERAGE DUE DATE [BASE DATE 15TH MARCH]

Due Date	*Amount (₹)*	*No. of days from Base Date to Due*	*Product (₹)*
March 15	7,000	0	0
April 5	12,000	21	2,52,000
April 25	30,000	41	12,30,000
June 11	20,000	88	17,60,000
	69,000		32,42,000

$$\text{Average Due Date} = \text{Base Date} + \text{Days equal to } \frac{\text{Total of Products}}{\text{Total Amount}} \text{ days}$$

Average Due Date = 15th March + (32,42,000/ 69,000) = 15th March + 47 days = 1st May,

Interest therefore has been calculated on ₹ 69,000 from 1st May to 30th June i.e., for 60 days @ 10% per annum.

$$\text{Interest} = 69{,}000 \times \frac{10}{100} \times \frac{60}{365} = \text{Rs } 1{,}131$$

PROBLEM 10

Harish has the following bills due on ditterent dates. It was agreed to settle the total amount due by a single cheque payment. Find the date of the cheque.

(i) ₹ 5,000 due on 5th March

(ii) ₹ 7,000 due on 7th April

(iii) ₹ 6,000 due on 17th July

(iv) ₹ 8,000 due on 14th Sept.

Solution

CALCULATION OF NUMBER OF DAYS FROM THE BASE DATE

Due Date	*Amount (₹)*	*No. of Days from 5.3.09*	*Product*
5th March	5,0000	0	0
7th April	7,000	33	2,31,000
17th July	6,000	134	8,04,000
14th Sept.	8,000	193	15,44,000
	26,000		25,79,000

$$\text{Average due date} = \text{Base Date} + \frac{\text{Sum of Product}}{\text{Sum of Amount}} = \text{5th March} + \frac{25{,}79{,}000}{26{,}000} = 99 \text{ days}$$

The date of the cheque will be 99 days from the base date i.e. 12th June. So on 12th June, all bills will be settled by a single cheque payment.

PROBLEM 11

Swaminathan owed to *Subramanium* the following sums:

₹ 5,000 on 20th January
₹ 8,000 on 3rd March
₹ 6,000 on 5th April
₹ 11,000 on 30th April

Ascertain the average due date.

Solution

CALCULATION OF AVERAGE DUE DATE TAKING 20TH JANUARY AS THE BASE DATE

Due Date	*Amount ₹*	*No. of days from 20th January*	*Product*
20th January	5,000	0	0
3rd March	8,000	42	3,36,000
5th April	6,000	75	4,50,000
30th April	11,000	100	11,00,000
	30,000		18,86,000

$$\text{Average due date} = 20^{th}\text{ January} = \frac{\text{Total Product}}{\text{Total Amount}} = 20^{th}\text{ January} + \frac{18{,}86{,}000}{30{,}000}$$

$$= 20^{th}\text{ January} + 63 \text{ days (approx)} = 24^{th}\text{ March}$$

PROBLEM 12

Mr Green and Mr Red had the following mutual dealings and desire to settle their account on the balance on the average due date:

Purchases by Green from Red:	₹
6th January	6,000
2nd February	2,800
31st March	2,000
Sales by Green to Red:	
6th January	6,600
9th March	2,400
20th March	500

You are asked to ascertain the average due date.

Solution

Let the base date be 6th Jan.

Purchases by Green

Due Date	*Amount (₹)*	*No. of days from Base Date to Due Date*	*Product (₹)*
6th January	6,000	0	0
2nd February	2,800	27	75,600
31st March	2,000	84	1,68,000
	10,800		2,43,600

Sales by Green

Due Date	*Amount (₹)*	*No. of days from Base Date to Due*	*Product (₹)*
6th January	6,600	0	0
9th March	2,400	62	1,48,800
20th March	500	73	36,500
	9,500		1,85,300

No. of days from the Base date $= \dfrac{2,43,600 - 1,85,300}{10,800 - 9,500} = \dfrac{58,300}{1,300} = 44.85$ i.e. 45 days after

6 January

Average Due Date = 20th Feb.

On 20 Feb. Green, has to pay ₹ 1,300 to clear the account.

PROBLEM 13

R had the following bills receivable and bills payable against S. Calculate average due date when the payment can be made or received without any loss or gain of interest to either party.

Date of the Bill	Bills Receivable		Bills Payable		
	Amount (₹)	Tenure in months	Date of bill	Amount (₹)	Tenure in months
1st June	9,000	3	29th May	6,000	2
5th June	7,500	3	3rd June	9,000	3
9th June	10,000	1	10th June	10,000	2
12th June	8,000	2	13th June	7,000	2
20th June	12,000	3	27th June	11,000	1

Holiday intervening in the period 15th August, 16th August and 6th September.

Solution

CALCULATION OF AVERAGE DUE DATE (TAKING BASE DATE AS 12TH JULY, 2013)

Date	*Due date including days of grace*	*Amount (₹*	*No. of Days from July 12*	*Products (₹)*	*Remarks*
1st June	4th Sept.	9,000	54	4,86,000	B/R
5th June	8th Sept.	7,500	58	4,35,000	
9th June	12th July	10,000	0	0	
12th June	14th Aug.	8,000	33	2,64,000	
20th June	23rd Sept.	12,000	73	8,76,000	
		46,500		20,61,000	
29th June	1st Aug.	6,000	20	1,20,000	B/P
3rd June	5th Sept.	9,000	55	4,95,000	
10th June	13th Aug.	10,000	32	3,20,000	
13th June	14th Aug.	7,000	33	2,31,000	
27th June	30th July.	11,000	18	1,98,000	
		43,000		13,64,000	

Difference of Products = ₹ 20,61,000 – ₹ 13,64,000 = ₹ 6,97,000

Difference of Amount = ₹ 46,500 – ₹ 43,000 = ₹ 3,500

$$\text{Average Due Date} = \text{BaseDate} + \frac{\text{Difference of Products}}{\text{Difference of Amount}}$$

$$= \text{July } 12 + \frac{6{,}97{,}000}{3{,}500}$$

= July 12 + 199.14 or 199 days

= 27th January

Note:

(*i*) B/R of 12th June — Due date changed due to holidays

(*ii*) B/P of 3rd June — Due date changed due to holidays

(*iii*) B/P of 13th June — Due date changed due to holidays

PROBLEM 14

Hari owes Ram ₹ 2,000 on 1st April. From 1st April to 30th June the following further transactions took place between Hari and Ram:

April 10	Hari buys goods from Ram for ₹ 5,000.
May 16	Hari receives cash loan of ₹ 10,000 from Ram.
June 9	Hari buys goods from Ram for ₹ 3,000.

Hari pays the whole amount, together with interest @ 15% per annum, to Ram on 30th June. Calculate the interest payable on 30th June by the average due date method.

Solution

CALCULATION OF AVERAGE DUE DATE [BASE DATE 1ST APRIL]

Due Date	*Amount (₹)*	*No. of days from Base Date to Due*	*Product (₹)*
April 1	2,000	0	0
April 10	5,000	9	45,000
May 16	10,000	45	4,50,000
June 9	3,000	69	2,07,000
	20,000		7,02,000

$$\text{Average Due Date} = \text{Base Date} + \text{Days equal to } \frac{\text{Total of Products}}{\text{Total Amount}} \text{ days}$$

Average Due Date = 1st April + (7,02,000 / 20,000) = 1st April + 35.1 days = 6th May,

Interest therefore has been calculated on ₹ 20,000 from 6th May to 30th June i.e., for 55 days @ 15% per annum.

$$\text{Interest} = 20{,}000 \times \frac{15}{100} \times \frac{55}{365} = \text{Rs } 452.05$$

PROBLEM 15

A trader allows his customers, credit for one week only beyond which he charges interest @ 12% per annum. Anil, a cusfomer buys goods as follows:

Dafe of Sale/Purcnase	*Amount (₹)*
January 2	6,000
January 28	*5,500*
February 17	*7,000*
March 3	4,700

Anil settles his account on 31st March. Calculate the amount of interest payable by Anil using average due date method.

Solution

Let us assume 9th January to be the base date:

Date of Transaction	*Due date of payment*	*Amount (₹)*	*No. of days from 9th January*	*Product*
Jan. 2	Jan. 9	6,000	0	0
Jan. 28	Feb. 4	5,500	26	1,43,00
Feb. 17	Feb. 24	7,000	46	3,22,000
March 3	March 10	4,700	60	2,82,000
		23,200		7,47,000

$$\text{Average Due date} = \text{Base date} + \frac{\text{Sum of Product}}{\text{Sum of amount}}$$

$$= 9^{th}\text{ January} + \frac{7,47,000}{23,200} = 9^{th}\text{ January} + 32\text{ days}$$

i.e. 32 days from 9th January = 10th February

Thus, average due date = 10th February

No. of days from 10th February to 31st March = 49 days.

Interest payable by Anil on ₹23,200 for 49 days @ 12% per annum

$$= ₹\ 23,200 \times \frac{49}{365} \times \frac{12}{100} = \text{Rs. } 373.74$$

PROBLEM 16

A and B are partners in a firm and share profits and losses equally. A has withdrawn the following sum during the half year ending 30th June:

Date	*Amount* ₹
January 15	5,000
February 10	4,000
April 5	8,000
May 20	10,000
June 18	9,000

Interest on drawings is charged @ 10% per annum. Find out the average due date and calculate the interest on drawings to be charged on 30th June.

Solution

CALCULATION OF AVERAGE DUE DATE (BASE DATE 15TH JAN)

Date	₹	*No. of Days*	₹
January 15	5,000	0	0
February 10	4,000	26	1,04,000
April 5	8,000	80	6,40,000
May 20	10,000	125	12,50,000
June 18	9,000	154	13,86,000
	36,000		33,80,000

$$\text{Average due date} = \text{Base date} + \frac{\text{Total product}}{\text{Total amount}} \text{ days}$$

$$= 15^{th} \text{ Jan} + \frac{33,80,000}{36,000} \text{ days}$$

$$= 15^{th} \text{ Jan} + 94 \text{ days (approx.)} = 19^{*} \text{ April}$$

Number of days from 19th April to 30th June = 72 days

Interest on drawings from 19th April to 30th June @10%:

$$= ₹\ 36,000 \times \frac{72}{365} \times \frac{10}{100} = 7710$$

PROBLEM 17

Mr. Black accepted the following bills drawn by Mr. White:

Date of Bill	*Period*	*Amount (₹)*
9th March	4 months	4,000
16th March	3 months	5,000
7th April	5 months	6,000
18th May	3 months	5,000

He wants to pay all the bills on a single date. Interest chargeable is @ 18% p.a. and Mr. Black wants to save ₹ 150 on account of interest payment. Find out the date on which he has to effect the payment to earn interest of ₹ 150. Base date to be taken shall be the earliest due date.

Solution

CALCULATION OF AVERAGE DUE DATE TAKING BASE DATE AS 19TH JUNE

Date of Bill	*Period*	*Maturity date*	*No. of days from the base date*	*Amount ₹*	*Products*
9th March	4 months	12.07.2010	23	4,000	92,000
16th March	3 months	19.06.2010	0	5,000	0
7th April	5 months	10.09.2010	83	6,000	4,98,000
18th May	3 months	21.08.2010	63	5,000	3,15,000
				20,000	9,05,000

$$\text{Average due date} = \text{Base date} + \frac{\text{Total of product}}{\text{Total of amount}}$$

$$= 19.06.210 + \frac{9,05,000}{20,000} = 45 \text{ days (approx.)} = 3\text{rd August}$$

Computation of Date of Payment to earn Interest of ₹ 150

Interest per day = (₹ 20,000 × (18/100)]/365 days

= ₹ 3,600/365 = ₹ 10 per day (approx.)

To earn interest of ₹ 150, the payment should be made 15 days (₹ 150 / ₹ 10 per day) earlier to the due date. Accordingly, the date of payment would be:

Date of payment to earn interest of ₹ 150 = 3rd August – 15 days = 19st July.

PROBLEM 18

Mr. A advanced ₹30,000 to Mr. B on 1.4.2015. The amount is repayable in 6 equal monthly instalments commencing from 1.5.2015. Compute the average due date for the loan.

Solution

$$\text{Average due date} = \frac{\text{Date of loan + Sum of months from the date of lending to repayment}}{\text{No. of instalments}}$$

$$= 1.4.2008 + \frac{(1+2+3+4+5+6)}{6}$$

= 1.4.2013 + 3.5 months

= 16th July 2015

PROBLEM 19

Mr A owed ₹ 4,000 on 1st January, 2015 to Mr X. The following transactions took place between them. It is agreed be been the parties that interest @ 10% p.a. is to be calculated on all transactions.

		₹
15 January	X sold goods to Mr A	2,230
29 January	X bought goods from Mr A	1,200
10 February	Mr A paid cash to Mr X	1,000
13 March	Mr A accepted a bill drawn by Mr X for one Month	2,000

They agree to settle their complete accounts by one single payment on 15th March. Prepare Mr A in Account Current with Mr X and ascertain the amount to be paid, Ignore days of grace.

Solution

MR. A IN ACCOUNT CURRENT WITH MR. X

Dr. *(Interest upto 15th March, 2015 @ 10% p.a.)* *Cr.*

Date	*Particulars*	₹	*Days*	*Product*	*Date*	*Particulars*	₹	*Days*	*Product*
2015					2015				
Jan. 01	To Balance b/d	4,000	75	3,00,000	Jan. 29	By Purchases A/c	1,200	46	55,200
Jan. 15	To Sales	2,230	60	1,33,800	Feb. 10	By Cash A/c	1,000	34	34,000
Mar. 13	To Redink product (₹ 2,000 x 29)			58,000	Mar. 13	By Bills Receivable A/c	2,000		
Mar. 15	To Interest A/c $\left(\frac{\text{Rs } 4,02,600 \times 10 \times 1}{100 \times 366}\right)$	110			Mar. 15	By Balance of product			4,02,600
						By Balance c/d (amount to be paid)	2,140		
		6,340		4,91,800			6,340		4,91,800

PROBLEM 20

From the following transactions, draw up an account current by means of product up to 31st December, 2015 to be rendered by X to Y and give the amount of interest charging @ 8% per annum.

Date 2015	*Particulars*	*Amounts (₹ thousands)*
July 01	Balance owing by Y	600
July 15	Goods sold to Y	900
Aug. 21	Goods bought from Y	700
Aug. 23	Cash received from Y	450
Oct. 23	Y accepted X's bill at 3 months	300
Nov. 01	Goods bought from Y	950
Dec.03	Accepted a bill drawn by Y at 3 months (due date of bill is on Sunday)	400

On 31st December, 2015, X and Y settled their account after considering the interest factor. Show the cash amount received or paid by X on that date.

Solution

Y IN ACCOUNT CURRENT WITH X FOR THE PERIOD FROM 1ST JULY, 2013 TO 31ST DECEMBER, 2013

Dr. *Cr.*

Date	*Due Date*	*Particulars*	*Days upto 31st Dec.*	*Amt (₹ in 000s)*	*Product*	*Date*	*Due date*	*Particulars*	*Days upto 31st Dec.*	*Amt₹ in 000s)*	*Product*
2015 July 01	July 01	To Balance b/d	184	600	1,10,400	2015 Aug. 21	Aug. 21	By Purchases A/c	132	700	92,400
July 15	July 15	To Sales	169	900	1,52,100	Aug. 23	Aug. 23	By Cash A/c	130	450	58,500
Dec. 03	Mar. 05	To Bills Payable	(64)	400	(25,600)	Oct. 23	Jan.25	By Bills Receivable	(25)	300	(7,500)
						Nov. 01	Nov.01	By Purchases A/c	60	950	57,000
Dec. 31	Dec.31	To Interest [36,500 × 8%/365]		8			Dec. 31	By Balance of Product			36,500
Dec. 31	Dec.31	To Cash A/c		492							
				2,400	2,36,900					2,400	2,36,900

PROBLEM 21

On 1st January 2015, X's Account in Y's Ledger showed a debit balance of ₹ 5,000. The following transactions took place between Y and X during the quarter ended 31st March 2015:

2015	*Particulars*	₹
Jan. 11	Y sold goods to X	6,000
Jan. 24	Y received a Promissory Note from X, 3 months date	5,000
Feb. 01	X sold goods to Y	10,000
Feb. 04	Y sold goods to X	8,200
Feb. 07	X returned goods to Y	1,000
March 01	X sold goods to Y	5,600
March 18	Y sold goods to X	9,200
March 23	X sold goods to Y	4,000

Accounts were settled on 31st March 2015, by means of a cheque. Prepare an Account Current to be submitted by Y to X as on 31st March 2015, taking interest into account at 10% per annum. Calculate Interest to the nearest multiple of a rupee.

Solution

IN THE BOOKS OF Y (LEDGER FROM 1ST JAN 2013 TO 31ST MAR 2013)

Dr. **X IN ACCOUNT CURRENT WITH Y (INTEREST UPTO 31ST MARCH 2013 AT 10% P.A.)** *Cr.*

Date	Particulars	₹	Days	Product	Date	Particular	₹	Days	Product
Jan 1	To Bal. b/d	5,000	90	4,50,000	Jan 24	By B/R	5,000	(27)	(1,35,000)
Jan 11	To Sales	6,000	79	4,74,00	Feb 1	By Purchases	10,000	58	5,80,00
Feb 4	To Sales	8,200	55	4,51,000	Feb 7	By Sales Returns	1,000	52	52,000
Mar 18	To Sales	9,200	13	1,19,600	Mar 1	By Purchases	5,600	30	1,68,000
Mar 31	To Interest $\left[\frac{7,97,600 \times 10\%}{365}\right]$	219			Mar 23	By Purchases	4,000	8	32,0000
					Mar 31	By Bal. of Products			7,97,600
						By bal. c/d	3,019		
		28,619		14,94,600			28,619		14,94,600

PROBLEM 22

Roshan has a current account with partnership firm. It has debit balance of ₹ 75,000 as on July 1. He has further deposited the following amounts:

Date	Amount (₹)
July 14	1,38,000
Aug 18	22,000

He withdrew the following amounts:

Date	Amount (₹)
July 29	97,000
Sept 9	11,000

Show Roshan's A/c in the ledger of the firm. Interest is to be calculated at 10% on debit balance and 8% on credit balance. You are required to prepare current account as on 30th September.

Solution

ROSHAN'S CURRENT ACCOUNT WITH PARTNERSHIP FIRM (as on 30.9.2012)

Date	Particulars	Dr. (₹)	Cr. (₹)	Balance (₹)	Dr. or Cr.	Days	Dr. Product (₹)	Cr. Product (₹)
July 1	To Bal. b/d	75,000		75,000	Dr.	13	9,75,000	
July 14	By Cash A/c		1,38,000	63,000	Cr.	15		9,45,000
July 29	To Self	97,000		34,000	Dr.	20	6,80,000	
Aug 18	By Cash A/c		22,000	12,000	Dr.	22	2,64,000	
Sept 9	To Self	11,00		23,000	Dr.	22	5,06,000	
Sept30	To Interest A/c	457		23,457	Dr.			
Sept30	By Bal. c/d		23,457					
		1,83,457	1,83,457				24,25,000	9,45,000

Interest Calculation:

On ₹ 24,25,000 × 10% × 1/365 = ₹ 664

On ₹ 9,45,000 × 8% × 1/365 = ₹ 207

Net Interest to be debited = ₹ 457

Note: The above Current Account has been prepared by means of product of balances method.

PROBLEM 23

The following transactions took place between Thick and Thin. They desire to settle their account on average due date.

Purchases by Thick from Thin	**(₹)**
9th July	7,200
14th August	12,200
Sales by Thick to Thin	**(₹)**
15th July	18,000
31st August	16,500

Calculate Average Due Date and the amount to be paid or received by Thick.

Solution

COMPUTATION OF PRODUCTS FOR THICK'S PAYMENTS (Base date = 9th July)

Due date	*Amount* ₹	*No. of days from base date to due date*	*Product* ₹
9th July	7,200	0	0
14th August	12,200	36	4,39,200
	19,400		4,39,200

COMPUTATION OF PRODUCTS FOR THIN'S PAYMENTS (Base date = 9th July)

Due date	*Amount* ₹	*No. of days from base date to due date*	*Product* ₹
15th July	18,000	6	1,08,000
31st August	16,500	53	8,74,500
	34,500		9,82,500

Excess of Thin's products over Thick [9,82,500 – 4,39,200]	5,43,300
Excess of Thin's amounts over Thick [34,500 – 19,400]	15,100

Number of days from base date to date of settlement is = $\frac{5,43,300}{15,100}$ = 36 days (approx.)

Hence, the date of settlement of the balance amount is 36 days after 9th July, i.e. 14th August.

Thus, on 14th August, , Thin has to pay ₹15,100 to Thick.

PROBLEM 24

From the following particulars prepare a current account, as sent by Mr. Ram to Mr. Siva as on 31st October by means of product method charging interest @ 5% p.a.

	Particulars	₹
1st July	Balance due from Siva	750
15th August	Sold goods to Siva	1,250
20th August	Goods returned by Siva	200
22nd Sep	Siva paid by Cheque	800
15th Oct	Received cash from Siva	500

Solution

MR SIVA IN ACCOUNT CURRENT WITH MR RAM IN THE BOOKS OF MR RAM (INTEREST TO OCT 31 @ 5% P.A.)

Date	Particulars	Due date	Amount	Days	Products	Date	Particulars	Due date	Amount	Days	Products
July 1	To Balance B/f	July 1	750	122	91,500	Aug 20	By Sales return A/c	20.8.14	200	72	14,400
Aug 15	To Sales A/c	Aug 15	1,250	77	96,250	Sept 22	By bank A/c	22.9.14	800	39	31,200
Oct 31	To Interest A/c (1,34,150 X 5%) 365		18.38			Oct 15	By Cash A/c	15.10.14	500	16	8,000
						Oct 31	By Balance product (B.F.)				1,34,150
						Oct 31	By Balance C/f (B.F.)		518.38		
			2,018.38		1,87,750				2,018.38		1,87,750
1.11.2014	To Balance B/f			518.38							

PROBLEM 25

Kishanlal has made the following sales to Babulal. He allows a credit period of 10 days beyond which he charges interest @ 12% per annum.

Date of Sales	*Amount (₹)*
May 26	12,000
July 18	18,000
Aug 2	16,500
Aug 28	9,500
Sept 9	15,500
Sept 17	13,500

Babulal wants to settle his accounts on Sept 30. Calculate the interest payable by him using Average Due date (ADD). If Babulal wants to save interest of ₹ 588, how many days before Sept 30 does he have to make payment? Also find the payment date in this case.

Solution

Average Due Date:

Let us assume 5th June, 2014 to be the Base Date.

Date of Sale	*Due date*	*Amount*	*No. of days from 5th June,*	*Product*
May 26	05.06.2014	12,000	0	0
July 18	28.07.2014	18,000	53	9,54,000
Aug 2	12.08.2014	16,500	68	11,22,000
Aug 28	07.09.2014	9,500	94	8,93,000
Sept 9	19.09.2014	15,500	106	16,43,000
Sept 17	27.09.2014	13,500	114	15,39,000
		85,000	Total	61,51,000

Average Due Date = Base Date + days equal to Total Product/Total amount

= 5th June + 61,51,000/85,000 days

= 5th June + 72 days (approx.)

= 16th August

Interest payable by Babulal if account is settled on Sept 30:

No. of days from Average due date to settlement date = 45 days

Therefore, Amount of interest = 85,000 × 5% × 45/365 = ₹ 524 (approx.)

No. of days before 30.9.2014 Babulal will have to make the payment to save interest of ₹ 588

₹ 524 is Interest for = 45 days

₹ 1 is Interest for = 45/524 days

₹ 588 is Interest for = (45/524) × 588 = 50 days (Approx.)

34 ACCOUNTING FOR INVESTMENTS

SHORT ANSWER PRACTICAL PROBLEMS

INVESTMENT IN EQUITY SHARES ACCOUNT

PROBLEM 1

MY Ltd. had acquired 200 equity shares of YZ Ltd. at ₹105 per share on 1st Jan and paid ₹ 200 towards brokerage, stamp duty and STT. On 31st March, shares of YZ Ltd. were traded at ₹110 per share. At what value investment is to be shown in the Balance Sheet of MY Ltd. as at 31st March.

Solution

	₹
Purchase Price of Equity shares of YZ Ltd. (200 shares x ₹105 per share)	21,000
Add: Brokerage, stamp duty and STT	200
Cost of investment	21,200

If the investment is a long term investment than it will be shown at cost. Therefore value of investment will be ₹ 21,200. However, if the investment is a current investment, then it will be shown at lower of cost (i.e. ₹ 21,200) or net realizable value (i.e. ₹ 200 x 110 = ₹ 22,000). Therefore value of investment will be ₹ 21,200.

PROBLEM 2

On 1st April, 2014, Mr. Neel purchased 5,000 equity shares of ₹100 each in X Ltd. @ ₹120 each from a Broker, who charged 2% brokerage. He incurred ½% as cost of shares transfer stamps. On 31st January, 2015, Bonus was declared in the ratio of 1:2. Before and after the record date of bonus shares, the shares were quoted at ₹175 per share and ₹90 per share respectively. On 31st March, 2015, Mr. Neel sold bonus shares to a broker, who charged 2% brokerage. Show the Investment Account in the books of Mr. Neel, who held the shares as current assets and closing value of investments shall be made at cost or Market value, whichever is lower.

Solution

INVESTMENT ACCOUNT IN THE BOOKS OF MR. NEEL
for the year ended 31st March, 2015
(Scrip: Equity Shares of X Ltd .)

Dr. *Cr.*

Date	Particulars	Nominal (₹)	Cost (₹) Value	Date	Particulars	Nominal Value (₹)	Cost (₹)
1.4.2014	To Bank A/c	5,00,000	6,15,000	31.3.2015	By Bank A/c	2,50,000	2,20,500
31.01.2015	To Bonus Shares	2,50,000	—	31.3.2015	By Balance c/d	5,00,000	4,10,000
31.03.2015	To P & LA/c	—	15,500				
		7,50,000	6,30,500			7,50,000	6,30,500

Working Notes:

(i) *Calculation of Cost of Equity Shares purchased*

$$= (5{,}000 \times ₹120) + (2\% \text{ of } ₹6{,}00{,}000) + (\frac{1}{2}\% \text{ of } ₹6{,}00{,}000) = ₹6{,}15{,}000$$

(ii) *Calculation of Sale Proceeds of Equity Shares sold*

$$= (2{,}500 \times ₹90) - (2\% \text{ of } ₹2{,}25{,}000) = ₹2{,}20{,}500$$

(iii) *Calculation of Profit on Sale of Bonus Shares*

= Sale proceeds – Average cost

$$= 2{,}20{,}500 - \left(6{,}15{,}000 \times \frac{2{,}50{,}000}{7{,}50{,}000}\right) = \text{Rs. } 15{,}500$$

(iv) *Valuation of equity shares at the end*

$$\text{Cost} = 6{,}15{,}000 \times \frac{5{,}00{,}000}{7{,}50{,}000} = \text{Rs. } 4{,}10{,}000$$

Market value = 5,000 shares × ₹90 = ₹4,50,000
Closing Balance has been valued at ₹4,10,000 i.e. at cost which is lower than the market value.

PROBLEM 3

On 01-04-2014, Mr. T. Shakharan purchased 5,000 equity shares of ₹ 100 each in V Ltd. @ ₹ 120 each from a broker, who charged 2% brokerage. he incurred 50 paisa per ₹ 100 as cost of shares transfer stamps. On 31-01-2015 bonus was declared in the ratio of 1 : 2. Before and after the record date of bonus shares, the shares were quoted at ₹ 175 per share and ₹ 90 per share respectively. On 31-02-2015, Mr. T. Shekharan sold bonus shares to a broker, who charged 2% brokerage.
Show the Investment Account in the books of T. Shekharan, who held the shares as Current Assets and closing value of investments shall be made at cost or market value whichever is lower.

Solution

INVESTMENT ACCOUNT
for the year ended 31st March, 2015
(Scrip: Equity Shares of V Ltd.)

Dr. *Cr.*

Date	*Particulars*	*Nominal Value (₹)*	*Cost (₹)*	*Date*	*Particulars*	*Nominal Value*	*Cost (₹)*
1.4.2014	To Bank A/c	5,00,000	6,15,000	31.3.2015	By Bank A/c	2,50,000	2,20,500
31.01.2015	To Bonus Shares	2,50,000	—	31.3.2015	By Balance c/d	5,00,000	4,10,000
31.03.2015	To P & LA/c	—	15,500				
		7,50,000	6,30,500			7,50,000	6,30,500

Working Notes:

(i) *Calculation of Cost of Equity Shares purchased*

$$= (5{,}000 \times ₹120) + (2\% \text{ of } ₹6{,}00{,}000) + (\tfrac{1}{2}\% \text{ of } ₹6{,}00{,}000) = ₹6{,}15{,}000$$

(ii) *Calculation of Sale Proceeds of Equity Shares sold*

$$= (2{,}500 \times ₹90) - (2\% \text{ of } ₹2{,}25{,}000) = ₹2{,}20{,}500$$

(iii) *Calculation of Profit on Sale of Bonus Shares*

= Sale proceeds – Average cost

$$= 2{,}20{,}500 - \left(6{,}15{,}000 \times \frac{2{,}50{,}000}{7{,}50{,}000}\right) = \text{Rs. } 15{,}500$$

(iv) *Valuation of equity shares at the end*

$$\text{Cost} = 6{,}15{,}000 \times \frac{5{,}00{,}000}{7{,}50{,}000} = \text{Rs. } 4{,}10{,}000$$

Market value = 5,000 shares × ₹90 = ₹4,50,000

Closing Balance has been valued at ₹4,10,000 i.e. at cost which is lower than the market value.

PROBLEM 4

H purchased 500 equity shares of ₹ 100 each in the ABC Company Limited for ₹ 62,500 inclusive of brokerage and stamp duty. Some years later the company decided to capitalise its profit and to issue to the holders of equity shares one equity shares one equity share as Bonus for every equity share held by them. Prior to capitalization, the shares of ABC Company Limited were quoted at ₹ 175 per share. After the capitalization, the shares were quoted at ₹ 92.50 per share. H sold the Bonus shares and received ₹ 90 per share. Show Investment A/c in H's books on average cost basis as per AS 13.

Solution

Dr. **INVESTMENT ACCOUNT (EQUITY SHARES OF ABC CO. LTD.)** *Cr.*

Particulars	*Nominal Value ₹*	*Cost ₹*	*Particulars*	*Nominal Value ₹*	*Cost ₹*
To Balance b/d*	50,000	62,500	By Bank A/c	50,000	45,000
To Bonus Shares A/c	50,000	–	By Balance c/d	50,000	31,250
To Profit & Loss A/c (Profit on sale)		13,750			
	1,00,000	**76,250**		**1,00,000**	**76,250**

Working Notes:

(i) Profit on sale of bonus shares = (₹ 45,000 – (₹ 62,500 × 50,000/1,00,000) = ₹ 13,750

(ii) Value of investment will be least of market value ₹ 46,250 (i.e. 92.5% of ₹ 50,000) or average cost price (i.e. ₹ 31,250).

PROBLEM 5

On 1st April, 2014 XY Ltd. has 15,000 equity shares of ABC Ltd. at a book value of 15 per share (face value ₹ 10 per share). On 1st June, 2014, XY Ltd. acquired 5,000 equity shares of ABC Ltd. ₹ 1,00,000 on cum right basis. ABC Ltd. announced a bonus and right issue.

(1) Bonus was declared, at the rate of one equity share for every five shares held, on 1st July 2014.

(2) Right shares are to be issued to the existing shareholders on 1st September 2014. The company will issue one right share for every 6 shares at 20% premium. No dividend was payable on these shares.

(3) Dividend for the year ended 31.3.2014 were declared by ABC Ltd. @ 20%, which was received by XY Ltd. on 31st October 2014.

XY Ltd.

(i) Took up half the right issue.

(ii) Sold the remaining rights for ₹ 8 per share.

(iii) Sold half of its share holdings on 1st January 2015 at ₹ 16.50 per share. Brokerage being 1%

You are required to prepare Investment account of XY Ltd. for the year ended 31st March 2015 assuming the shares are being valued at average cost.

Solution

INVESTMENT IN EQUITY SHARES OF ABC LTD.

Dr. *for the year ended 31st March, 2015* Cr.

Date	Particulars	No. ₹	income ₹	Amount	Date	Particulars	No. ₹	Income ₹	Amount
2014 April 1	To Balance b/d	15,000	–	2,25,000	2014 Sept. 1	By Bank A/c	–	–	16,000
June 1	To Bank A/c	5,000	–	1,00,000	2009 Oct. 31	By Bank A/c (W.N. 5)	–	30,000	10,000
July 1	To Bonus Issue	4,000	–	–	2015 Jan. 1	By Bank A/c	13,000	–	2,12,355
Sept. 1	To Bank A/c	2,000	–	24,000	March 31	By Balance c/d	13,000	–	1,61,500
2015 March 31	To P & L A/c	–	–	50,855					
	To P & L A/c	–	–	30,000					
		26,000	30,000	3,99,855			26,000	30,000	3,99,855

Working Notes:

(i) **Bonus Shares** = $\frac{15{,}000 \text{ shares} + 5{,}000 \text{ shares}}{5} \times 1 = 4{,}000$ shares

(ii) **Right Shares** = $\frac{15{,}000 \text{ shares} + 5{,}000 \text{ shares} + 4{,}000 \text{ shares}}{6} = 4{,}000$ shares

Shares subcribed by XY Ltd. = $\frac{4{,}000}{2} = 2{,}000$ shares

Value of Right Shares subscribed = 2,000 shares @ 12 per share = 24,000

(iii) **Sale of Right Entitlement** = 2,000 shares × ₹ 8 per share = ₹ 16,000

(Since shares are purchased cum right basis, therefore, amount received from sale of rights will be credited to Investment Account)

(iv) **Profit on Sale of Shares**

Total holdings =	15,000 shares	original
	5,000 shares	purchased
	4,000 shares	bonus
	2,000 shares	right shares
	26,000 shares	

50% of the holdings were sold i.e. 13,000 shares (26,000 x1/2) were sold.

Cost of total holdings of 26,000 shares (on average basis)

= ₹ 2,25,000 + ₹ 1,00,000 + 24,000 – ₹ 16,000 – ₹ 10,000

= ₹3,23,000

Average cost of 13,000 shares would be

$= \frac{3{,}23{,}000}{26{,}000} \times 13{,}000 = \text{Rs. } 1{,}61{,}500$

	₹
Sale Proceeds of 13,000 shares (13,000 × ₹ 16.50)	2,14,500
Less: 1% Brokerage	(2,145)
	2,12,355
Less: Cost of 13,000 shares	(1,61,500)
Profit on sale	**50,855**

(v) Dividend received on investment held as on 1st April

= 15,000 shares × ₹ 10 × 20% = 30,000 will be transferred to Profit and Loss A/c

Dividend received on shares purchased on 1st June

= 5,000 shares × ₹ 10 × 20% = ₹ 10,000 will be adjusted to Investment A/c

Note: *It is presumed that no dividend is received on bonus shares as bonus shares are declared on 1st July, 2009 and dividend pertains to the year ended 31st March*

(vi) Closing Value of shares (on average basis) $= 13{,}000 \times \frac{3{,}23{,}000}{26{,}000} = \text{Rs. } 1{,}61{,}500.$

PROBLEM 6

Smart Investments made the following investments in the year 2013-14:

12% State Government Bonds having face value ₹ 100

Date	Particulars
01.04.2013	Opening Balance (1200 bonds) book value of ₹ 126,000
02.05.2013	Purchased 2,000 bonds @ ₹ 100 cum interst
30.09.2013	Sold 1,500 bonds at ₹ 105 ex interest

Interest on the bonds is received on 30th June and 31st Dec. each year.

Equity Shares of X Ltd.	
15.04.2013	Purchased 5,000 equity shares @ ₹ 200 on cum right basis Brokerage of 1% was paid in addition (Face Value of shares ₹ 10)
03.06.2013	The Company announced a bonus issue of 2 shares for every 5 shares held.
16.08.2013	The company made a rights issue of 1 share for every 7 shares held at ₹ 250 per share. The entire money was payable by 31.08.2013.
22.8.2013	Rights to the extent of 20% was sold @ ₹ 60. The remaining erights were subscribed.
02.09.2013	Dividend @ 15% for the year ended 31.03.2013 was received on 16.09.2013.
15.12.2013	Sold 3,000 shares @ ₹ 300. Brokerage of 1% was incurred extra.
15.01.2014	Received interim dividend @ 10% for the year 2013-14.
31.03.2014	The shares were quoted in the stock exchange @ ₹ 220

Prepare investment Accounts in the books of Smart Investments. Assume that the average cost method is followed.

Solution

BOOKS OF SMART INVESTMENTS
INVESTMENT IN 12% GOVT. BONDS ACCOUNT
FOR THE YEAR ENDED 31ST MARCH, 2014

Date	Particulars	Nos.	Income	Amount	Date	Particulars	Nos.	Income	Amount
1.4.13	To Opening balance b/d	1,200	3,600	1,26,000	30.6.13	By Bank A/c (Interest) (3,200 × 100 × 12% × 6/12)	–	19,200	–
2.5.13	To Bank A/c	2,000	8,000	1,92,000	30.9.13	By Bank A/c	1,500	4,500	1,57,500
31.3.14	To P & I A/c (Interest)		27,400		31.12.13	By Bank A/c (Interest) (1,700 × 100 × 12% × 6/12)	–	10,200	–
	To P & L A/c (Profit)			8,437.50	31.3.14	By Bal. c/d	1,700	5,100	1,68,937.50
		3,200	39,000	3,26,437.50			3,200	39,000	3,26,437.50

INVESTMENTS IN EQUITY SHARES OF X LTD. FOR YEAR ENDED 31.3.2014

Date	Particulars	Nos.	Income	Amount	Date	Particulars	Nos.	Income	Amount
15.4.13	To Bank A/c	5,000		10,10,000	22.8.13	By Bank (Sale of Rights)	–	–	12,000
3.6.13	To Bonus Issue	2,000	–	–	16.9.13	By Bank (Dividend)	–	–	7,5000
31.8.13	To Bank A/c	800		2,00,000	15.12.13	By Bank (Sale)	3,000	–	8,91,000
31.3.14	To P & L A/c		4,800	4,33,115	15.1.14	By Bank (interim dividend)		4,800	
					31.3.14	By Bal. c/d	4,800		7,32,615
		7,800	4,800	16,43,115			7,800	4,800	16,43,115

Working Notes:

1. Profit on sale of bonds = Sales proceeds – Average cost
   = ₹ 1,57,500 – ₹ [(1,26,000 + 1,92,000) × 1,500/3,200] = ₹ 8,437.50
2. Valuation of bonds = ₹ 3,18,000/3,200 × 1,700 = ₹ 1,68,937.50
3. Cost of equity shares purchased on 15th Apr.
   = (5,000 × ₹ 200) + 1% of (5,000 × ₹ 200) = ₹ 10,00,000
4. Sale proceeds of equity shared on 15th Dec
   = (3,000 × ₹ 300) – 1% of (3,000 × ₹ 300) = ₹ 8,91,000.
5. Profit on sale of shares on 15th Dec
   = ₹ 8,91,000 – ₹[(10,10,000 + 2,00,000 – 12,000 – 7,500) × 3,000/7,800] = ₹ 4,33,115.
6. Valuation of equity shares on 31st March,
   Cost = ₹ [11,90,500 × 4,800/7,800] ₹ 7,32,615
   Market Value = 4,800 shars × ₹ 220 = ₹ 10,56,000
   Closing stock of equity shares has been valued at ₹ 7,32,615 i.e. cost being lower than the market value.

Notes:

1. It is presumed that no dividend is received on bonus shares as bonus shares have been issued on 3.6.2013 and dividend pertains to the year ended 31.03.2013.
2. The amount of dividend for the period, for which shares were not held by the investor, has been treated as capital receipt.

PROBLEM 7

On 1st April, 2013, Rajat has 50,000 equity shares of P Lid. at a book value of ₹ 15 per share (face value ₹ 10 each). He provides you the further information:

(1) On 20th June, 2013, he purchased another 10,000 shares of P Ltd. at ₹ 16 per share.

(2) On 1st August 2013, P Ltd. issued one equity bonus share for every six shares held by the shareholders.

(3) On 31st October, 2013, the directors of P Ltd. announced a right sssue which entitle the holders to subscribe three shares for every seven shares at ₹ 15 per share. Shareholders can transfer their rights in full or in part.

Rajat sold 1/3rd of entitlement to Umang for a consideration of ₹ 2 per share and subscribe the rest on 5th November, 2013.

You are required to prepare Investment A/c in the books of Rajat for the year ending 31st March, 2014.

Solution

INVESTMENT ACCOUNT IN THE BOOKS OF RAJAT (EQUITY SHARES IN P LTD.)

Dr. *Cr.*

Date	Particulars	No. of shares	₹	Date	Particulars	No. of shares	₹
1.4.13	To Balance b/d	50,000	7,50,000	5.11.13	By Bank A/c (sale of rights)	—	20,000
20.6.13	To Bank A/c	10,000	1,60,000	31.3.14	By Balance c/d (Bal.flg.)	90,000	11,90,000
1.8.13	To Bonus issue	10,000	—				
5.11.13	To Bank A/c (right shares)	20,000	3,00,000				
		90,000	12,10,000			90,000	12,10,000

Working Notes:

(i) Bonus Shares = (50,000 + 10,000)/6 = 10,000 shares

(ii) Right Shares = [(50,000 + 10,000 + 10,000)/7] × 3 = 30,000 shares

(iii) Sale of Rights = (30,000 shares × 1/3) × ₹ 2 = ₹ 20,000

(iv) Rights subscribed = (30,000 Shares × 2/3) × ₹ 15 = ₹ 3,00,000

INVESTMENT IN BONDS ACCOUNT

PROBLEM 8

On 1st April, 'X' purchased 12% debentures in 'M' Ltd. for ₹ 6,50,000. The face value of these debentures were ₹ 6,00,000. Interest on debentures falls due on 30th June and 31st December. Compute the cost of acquisition of debentures.

Solution

COMPUTATION OF COST OF ACQUISITION OF DEBENTURES

	₹
Cum- interest purchase price of debentures	6,50,000
Less: Interest from the last date of payment of interest to the date of purchase [₹ 6,00,000 × 3/12 × 12%]	18,000
Cost of debentures at the time of acquisition	6,32,000

PROBLEM 9

The following information is presented by Mr. Z, relating to his holding in 9% Central Government Bonds.

Opening balance (face value) ₹1,20,000, Cost ₹1,18,000 (Face value of each unit is ₹100).

1.3.2012	Purchased 200 units, ex-interest at ₹98.
1.7.2012	Sold 500 units, ex-interest out of original holding at ₹100.
1.10.2012	Purchased 150 units at ₹ 98, cum interest.
1.11.2012	Sold 300 units, ex-interest at ₹ 99 out of original holdings.

Interest dates are 30th September and 31st March. Mr. Z closes his books every 31st December. Show the investment account as it would appear in his books.

Solution

Dr. **9% Central Government Bonds (Investment) Account** *Cr.*

Date 2012	*Particulars*	*Face Value* ₹	*Interest* ₹	*Principal* ₹	*Date* 2012	*Particulars*	*Face Value* ₹	*Interest* ₹	*Principal* ₹
Jan.1	To Balance b/d	1,20,000	2,700	1,18,000	March 31	By Bank A/c	-	6,300	-
March 1	To Bank A/c	20,000	750	19,600	July 1	By Bank A/c	50,000	1,125	50,000
July 1	To P&L A/c	-	-	833	Sept. 30	By Bank A/c	-	4,050	-
Oct. 1	To Bank A/c	15,000	-	14,700	Nov. 1	By Bank A/c	30,000	225	29,700
Nov. 1	To P&L A/c	-	-	200	Dec. 31	By Balance c/d	75,000	1,688	73,633
Dec. 31	To P&L A/c (Transfer)		9,938						
		1,55,000	13,388	1,53,333			1,55,000	13,388	1,53,333

Working Note: *Calculation of Closing Balance:*

	Units	₹
From original holding (1,20,000 – 50,000 – 30,000)	40,000	
39,333 i.e., (1,18,000 / 1,20,000) × 40,000		
Purchased on 1st March	20,000	19,600
Purchased on 1st October	15,000	14,700
	75,000	73,633

LONG ANSWER PRACTICAL PROBLEMS

INVESTMENT IN EQUITY SHARES ACCOUNT AND INVESTMENT IN BONDS ACCOUNT

PROBLEM 10

Mr.Brown has made following transactions during the financial year 2012-13:

Date	Particulars
01.05.2012	Purchased 24,000 12% Bonds of ₹ 100 each at ₹ 84 cum interest. Interest is payable on 30th September and 31st March every year.
15.06.2012	Purchased 1,50,000 Equity Shares of ₹ 10 each in Alpha Limited for ₹ 25 each through a Broker, who charged Brokerage at 2%.
10.07.2012	Purchased 60,000 Equity Shares of ₹ 10 each in Beeta Limited for ₹ 44 each through a Broker, who charged Brokerage at 2%.
14.10.2012	Alpha Limited made a Bonus Issue of two Shares for every three Shares held.
31.10.2012	Sold 80,000 Shares in Alpha Limited for ₹ 22 each.
01.01.2012	Received 15% Interim Dividend on Equity Shares of Alpha Limited.
15.01.2013	Beeta Limited made a Rights Issue of one Equity Share for every four Shares held at ₹ 5 per Share. Mr.Brown exercised his option for 40% of his entitlements and sold the balance rights in the market at ₹ 2.25 per Share.
01.03.2013	Sold 15,00012% Bonds at ₹ ex-interest.
15.03.2013	Received 18% Interim Dividend on Equity Shares of Beeta Limited.
	Interest on 12% Bonds was duly received on due dates.

Prepare separate Investment Account for 12% Bonds, Equity Shares of Alpha Limited and Equity Shares of Beeta Limited in the books of Mr.Brown for the year ended on 31st March 2013.

Solution

Dr. **(i) INVESTMENT IN 8% BONDS ACCOUNT** *Cr.*

(₹ in '000)

Date	Item	FV	Int.	Cost	Date	Item	FV	Int.	Cost
1 May	To Bank A/c	2400	24	1992	30 Sept	By Bank A/c	–	144	–
1 Mar	To P&L A/c	–	–	105	1 Mar	By Bank A/c	1500	75	1350
31 Mar	To P&L A/c		249		31 Mar	By Bank A/c	–	54	
					31 Mar	By bal c/d	900		747
		2400	273	2,097			2400	273	2,097

Working Notes:

(i) Cost of Purchase = (24000 × ₹ 84) – (24,000 × ₹ 100 × 12% × 1/12) = 19,92,000

(ii) Profit / (Loss) on Sale of Investments = Sale Proceeds – Cost

$$= (15{,}000 \times \text{Rs } 90) - \text{Rs } 19{,}92{,}000 \times \frac{15{,}00{,}000}{24{,}00{,}000}$$

$$= 1{,}05{,}000$$

Dr. **(ii) INVESTMENT IN EQUITY SHARES OF ALPHA LTD.** Cr.

(₹ in '000)

Date	Particulars	Shares	Div.	Cost	Date	Particulars	FV	Div.	Cost
15 June	To Bank A/c	15,0	–	38,25	31 Oct.	By Bank (Sale)	80	–	17,60
14 Oct.	To Bonus Shares	10,0	–	–	1 Jan	By Bank (Dividend)	–	255	–
31 Mar	To P&L A/c Dividend	–	255	–	1 Jan	To P&L A/c (Loss)			2,80
						By bal c/d	1,70	–	17,85
		2,50	255	3,825			250	255	3,825

Note: Cost of Investments Sold = ₹ 38,25,000 × $\frac{80,000 \text{ Shares}}{1,50,000 \text{ Shares}}$ = ₹ 20,40,000.

Hence, Loss on Sale = 20,40,000 – 17,60,000 = 2,80,000

Dr. **(iii) INVESTMENT IN EQUITY SHARES OF BEETA LTD.** Cr.

Date	Particulars	Shares	Dvd.	Cost	Date	Particulars	FV	Dvd.	Cost
10 Jul	To Bank A/c	60,000	–	26,92,800	31 Mar	By bal c/d	66,000	–	27,22,800
14 Oct	To Bank (Rights)	6,000	–	30,000*					
		66,000	–	27,22,800			66,000	–	27,22,800

*[(60,000 × 1/4 × 40% × ₹ 5)]

Note: The balance Right for 9,000 Shares are renounced at ₹ 2.25 per Share for ₹ 20,250. which will be credited to P&L A/c.

PROBLEM 11

Gaama Investment Company holds 1,000, 15% Debentures of ₹ 100 each in Beta industries Ltd, as on April 1, 2012 at a cost of ₹ 1,05,000. Interest is payable on June, 30 and December, 31 each year.

On May 1, 500 debentures are purchased cum-interest at ₹ 53,500. On November 1, 600 debentures are sold ex-interest at ₹ 57,300. On November 30, 400 debentures are purchased ex-interest at ₹ 38,400. On December 31, 400 debentures are sold cum-interest for ₹ 55,000.

Require: Prepare the Investment Account showing value of holdings on March 31, 2013 at cost, using FIFO Method.

Solution

Dr. **INVESTMENT ACCOUNT (15% DEBENTURES IN BETA INDUSTRIES LTD.)** *Cr.*

Date	Particulars	Nominal Value ₹	Interest ₹	Cost ₹	Date	Particulars	Nominal Values ₹	Interest ₹	Cost ₹
1.04.12	To Balance b/d	1,00,000	3,750	1,05,000	30.06.12	By Bank A/c	—	11,250	—
1.05.12	To Bank A/c	50,000	2,500	51,000	1.11.12	By Bank A/c	60,000	3,000	57,300
30.11.12	To Bank A/c	40,000	2,500	38,400	1.11.12	By Profit & Loss A/c	—	—	5,700
31 12.12	To Profit & toss A/c	—	—	10,000	31.12.12	By Bank A/c	40,000	3,000	52,000
31.03.13	To Profit & Loss A/c	—	18,625	—		By Bank A/c	—	6,750	—
					31.12.12	By Bank A/c	90,000	3375	89,400
					31.03.13				
		1,90,000	27,375	2,04,400			1,90,000	27,375	2,04,400

Working Notes:

(i) Accrued Interest as on 1st April = ₹ 1,00,000 × $\frac{15}{100} \times \frac{3}{12}$ = ₹.3,750

(ii) Accrued Interest = ₹.50,000 × $\frac{15}{100} \times \frac{4}{12}$ = ₹ 2,500

(iii) Cost of Investment for purchase on 1st May = ₹ 53,500 – ₹.2,500 = ₹.51,000

(iv) Interest received = ₹.1,50,000 × $\frac{15}{100} \times \frac{6}{12}$ = ₹.11,250

(v) Accrued Interest = ₹.60,000 × $\frac{15}{100} \times \frac{4}{12}$ = ₹.3,000

(vi) Accrued Interest = ₹ 40,000 × $\frac{15}{100} \times \frac{5}{12}$ = ₹.2,500

(vii) Accrued Interest = ₹.40,000 × $\frac{15}{100} \times \frac{6}{12}$ = ₹.3,000

(viii) Sale Price of Investment on 31st Dec. = ₹.55,000 – ₹.3,000 = ₹.52,000

(ix) Accrued Interest = ₹.90,000 × $\frac{15}{100} \times \frac{6}{12}$ = ₹.6,750

(x) Accrued Interest = ₹.90,000 × $\frac{15}{100} \times \frac{3}{12}$ = ₹.3,375

(xi) Cost of investment as on 31st March = ₹ 51,000 + ₹ 38,400 = ₹ 89,400

(xii) Loss on debentures sold on 1st Nov. = ₹ 57,300 – (₹ 1,05,000 × 600/1000) = ₹ 5,200

(xiii) Profit on debentures sold on 31st Dec. = ₹ 52,000 – (₹ 1,05,00 × 400/1000) = ₹ 10,000

PROBLEM 12

In 2011, M/s. Wye Ltd. issued 12% fully paid debentures of ₹ 100 each interest being payable half yearly on 30th September and 31st March of every accounting year.

On 1st December, 2012, M/s Bull & Bear purchased 10,000 of these debentures at ₹ 101 cum-interest price, also paying brokerage @ 1% of cum-interest amojunt of the purchase. On 1st March, 2013 the firm sold all of these debentjures at `106 cum-interest price, again paying brokerage @1% of cum-interest amount.

Prepare Investment Account in he books of M/s Bull & Bear for the period 1st December, 2012 to 1st March, 2013.

Solution

INVESTMENT ACCOUNT IN THE BOOKS OF M/S BULL & BEAR
for the period from 1st December 2012 to 1st March, 2013
(Scrip: 12% Debentures of M/s.Wye Ltd.)

Date	*Particulars*	*Nominal Value (₹)*	*Interest*	*Cost (₹)*	*Date*	*Particulars*	*Nominal Value (₹)*	*Interest*	*Cost (₹)*
1.12.2012	To Bank A/c	10,00,000	20,000	10,00,100	1.03.2013	By Bank A/c	10,00,000	50,000	9,99,400
1.03.2013	To P&L A/c		30,000		1.03.2013	By P&L A/c			700
		10,00,000	50,000	10,00,100			10,00,000	50,000	10,00,100

Working Notes:

(i) Cost of 12% debentures purchased on 1st Dec. ₹

Cost Value (10,000 × ₹ 101)	=	10,10,000
Add: Brokerage (1% of ₹ 10,10,000)	=	10,100
Less: Cum Interest (10,000 × 100 × 12% × 2/12)	=	(20,000)
Total	=	10,00,100

(ii) Sale proceeds of 12% debentures sold on 31st March ₹

Sales Price (10,000 × ₹ 106)	=	10,60,000
Less: Brokerage (1% of ₹10,60,000)	=	(10,600)
Less: Cum Interest (10,000 × 100 × 12% × 5/12)	=	(50,000)
Total	=	9,99,400

PROBLEM 13

On 01-05-2012, Mr. Mishra purchased 800 equity shares of 10 each in Fillco Ltd. @ ₹ 50 each from a broker who charged 5%. He incurred 20 paisa per 100 as cost of shares transfer stamps. On 31-10-2012, bonus was declared in the ratio 1 : 4. The shares were quoted at ₹ 110 and ₹ 60 per share before and after the record date of bonus shares respectively. On 30-11-2012, Mr. Mishra sold the bonus shares to a broker who charged 5%. You are required to prepare Investment Account in the books of Mr. Mishra for the year ending 31-12-2012 and closing value of Investment shall be made at cost or market value whichever is lower.

Solution

INVESTMENT ACCOUNT FOR THE YEAR ENDED 31ST MARCH, 2013

(Scrip: Equity Shares of Fillco Ltd .)

Date	*Particulars*	*Nominal Value (₹)*	*Cost (₹)*	*Date*	*Particulars*	*Nominal Value (₹)*	*Cost (₹)*
1.5.2012	To Bank A/c	8,000	42,080	30.11.12	By Bank A/c	2,000	11,400
31.10.12	To Bonus share	2,000	–	31.12.12	By Bal. c/d	8,000	33,664
31.12.12	To Profit & Loss A/c	–	2,984				
		10,000	45,064			10,000	45,064

Working Notes:

(i) Cost of equity shares purchased on 1.5.2012
= 800 × ₹50 + 5% of ₹ 40,000 + .002 of ₹ 40,000 = ₹ 42,080.

(ii) Sale proceeds of equity shares sold on 30.11.2012
= 200 × ₹60 – 5% of ₹12,000 = ₹ 11,400

(iii) Profit on sale of bonus shares on 30.11.12
= Sales proceeds – Average cost

Sales proceeds = ₹ 11,400

$$\text{Average cost} = ₹\frac{42,080}{10,000} \times 2,000$$

= ₹ 8,416

Profit = ₹ 11,400 – ₹ 8,416 = ₹ 2,984

(iv) Valuation of equity shares on 31st Dec., 2012
Cost = (₹42,080/10,000 × 8,000) = ₹33,664
Market Value = 800 × ₹ 60 = 48,000
Closing balance has been valued at ₹33,664 being lower than the market value.

AS 13 – INVESTMENTS

THEORETICAL BASE

QUESTION 1: What are the areas in which AS – 13 is not applicable?

ANSWER:

1. The bases for recognition of interest, dividends and rentals earned on investments which are covered by Accounting Standard 9 on Revenue Recognition;
2. Operating or Finance Leases;
3. Investments of Retirement Benefit Plans and Life Insurance Enterprises; and
4. Mutual Funds and/or the related asset management companies, banks and public financial institutions formed under a Central or State Government Act or so declared under the Companies Act, 1956.

QUESTION 2: What is meant by term 'Investments'?

ANSWER: Investments are assets held by an enterprise for earning income by way of dividends, interest, and rentals, for capital appreciation, or for other benefits to the investing enterprise.

Note: *Assets held as stocks - in - trade are not 'Investments'.*

QUESTION 3: What is meant the term 'Market Value'?

ANSWER: Market value is the amount obtainable from the sale of an investment in an open market, net of expenses necessarily to be incurred on or before disposals.

QUESTION 4: What is meant by the term 'Fair value'?

ANSWER: Fair value is the amount for which an asset could be exchanged between a knowledgeable, willing buyer and a knowledgeable, wiling seller in an arm's length transaction. Under appropriate circumstances, market value net or net realizable value provides an evidence of fair value.

QUESTION 5: What are the components of Cost of Investments?

ANSWER: Cost of Investments includes:

1. Purchase Price;
2. Acquisition charges such as brokerage, fees and duties.

QUESTION 6: What shall be Cost of Investment if it is acquired wholly or partly by the issue of shares or other securities?

ANSWER:

Cost of Investments = Fair Value of the securities issued (which in appropriate cases may be indicated by the issue price as determined by statutory authorities).

Note: *The fair value may not necessarily be equal to the nominal or par value of the securities issued.*

QUESTION 7: What shall be the cost of investments if it is acquired in exchange or part exchange, for another asset?

ANSWER:

Cost of Investments = Either Fair Value of the asset given up or Fair Value of the investment acquired if it is more clearly evident.

QUESTION 8: What is the Accounting Treatment of Interest, Dividends and Rentals earned on Investments?

ANSWER:

For Pre-acquisition period	• Should be credited to Investments Account
For Post-acquisition period	• Should be credited to Profit & Loss Account

QUESTION 9: What is the Cost of Investments when rights are subscribed?

ANSWER:

Case	Treatment
1. When rights entitlement is received because of existing holding and right shares are subscribed.	The cost of the right shares is added to the carrying amount of the original holding.
2. When rights entitlement is purchased and right shares are subscribed.	Cost incurred in purchasing the rights entitlement plus the subscription price of the right shares shall constitute the cost of right share.
3. When rights entitlement is received because of cum-right purchase of investment and right shares are subscribed.	The cost of the right shares is added to the cum-right purchase price of investment.

QUESTION 10: What should be the Accounting Treatment when rights are sold in the market?

ANSWER:

Case	Treatment
1. When rights entitlement is received because of existing holding and rights entitlement is sold in the market.	The sale proceeds are taken to the Profit and Loss Statement.
2. When rights entitlement is purchased and sold in the market.	Difference between the Purchase Price and Sale Price of the rights sold should be sold in the market.
3. When rights entitlement is received because of cum-right purchase of investment and rights entitlement is sold in the market. (a) Where the market value of investments immediately after their becoming ex-right is lower than the cost for which they were acquired. (b) Where the market value of investments immediately after their becoming ex-right is equal to the cost for which they were acquired.	(a) Sale proceeds of rights up to the reduction in the value of investment should be credited to investment account and balance sale proceeds should be taken to Profit and Loss Statement. (b) Sale Proceeds should be taken to Profit and Loss Statement.

QUESTION 11: State the meaning and accounting treatment of Current Investments?

ANSWER:

Meaning	A current investment is an investment that is by its nature readily realizable and is intended to be held for not more than one year from the date on which such investment is made.
Carrying	These should be carried **at the lower of cost and fair value** determined amount *either* on an individual investment basis *or* by category of investment, but not an overall (or global) basis.
Reduction & Reversal	Any reduction to fair value and any reversals of such reductions should be debited or credited to the Profit and Loss Statement.

QUESTION 12: State the meaning and accounting treatment of Long-term Investments?

ANSWER:

Meaning	A long-term investment is an investment other than a current investment.
Carrying	These should be carried **at cost**. However, provision for diminution Amount shall be made to recognize a decline, other than temporary, in the value of the investments, such reduction being determined and made for each investment individually.
Reduction	Any reduction in the carrying amount and any reversals of & Reversal such reductions should be charged or credited to the Profit and Loss Statement.

QUESTION 13: State the meaning and accounting treatment of Investment Properties?

ANSWER:

Meaning	An investment property is an investment in land or buildings that are not intended to be occupied substantially for use by, or in the operations of, the investing enterprise.
Accounting	As long term investments.
Cost of any Shares in a co-operative Society/a Company	The cost of any shares in a co-operative society or a company, the holding of which is directly related to the right to hold the estment property, is added to the carrying amount of the investment property.

QUESTION 14: State the accounting treatment of Disposal of An Investment?

ANSWER: The difference between the carrying amount and net disposal proceeds should be **charged or credited to the Profit and Loss Statement.**

QUESTION 15: State the Disclosure Requirements as to Investments as per AS 13.

ANSWER:

1. The accounting policies for determination of carrying amount of investments;
2. Classification of investments
3. The amounts included in Profit and Loss Statement for:
   (i) Interest, Dividends (showing separately dividends from subsidiary companies), and rentals on Investments showing separately such income from long-term and current investments. Gross income should be stated, the amount of income tax deducted at a source being included under Advance Tax Paid;
   (ii) Profits and Losses on disposal of Current Investments and changes in the carrying amount of such investments; and

(iii) Profits and Losses on disposal of long-term investments and changes in the carrying amount of such investments.

4. Significant restrictions on the right of ownership, realisability of investments or the remittance of income and proceeds of disposals;
5. The aggregate amount of quoted and unquoted investments, giving the aggregate market value of quoted investments;
6. Other disclosures as specifically required by the relevant statute governing the enterprise.

PRACTICAL QUESTIONS FOR PRACTICE

QUESTION 1:

Par Value of Shares	**₹ 18,000**
Fair Market Value of Shares	**₹ 20,000**
Fair Market value of an Investment acquired	**₹ 25,000**
Additional Cash Given for acquisition of an Investment	**₹ 4,000**

Determine the Cost of Investment acquired and show the accounting treatment in this regard.

ANSWER:

JOURNAL

Date	Particulars		Dr. (₹)	Cr. (₹)
	Investment A/c	...Dr.	₹ 24,000	
	To Bank A/c			₹ 4,000
	To Equity Share Capital A/c			₹18,000
	To Securities Premium A/c			₹ 2,000
	(Being the Cost of Investment acquired recorded at the Fair Value of Shares issued)			

QUESTION 2:

Book Value of Old Asset given up	**₹ 18,000**
Fair Market Value of old asset exchanged	**₹ 20,000**
Fair Market Value of an investment acquired in exchange of old asset	**₹ 25,000**
Additional Cash given for acquisition of an investment	**₹ 4,000**

Determine the cost of investment acquired and show the accounting treatment in this regard.

ANSWER:

1st Alternative

JOURNAL

Date	Particulars		Dr. (₹)	Cr. (₹)
	Investment A/c	...Dr.	₹ 24,000	
	To Bank A/c			₹ 4,000
	To Old Asset A/c			₹ 20,000
	(Being the Cost of Investment acquired recorded at the Fair Market Value of Asset given up and adjusted for payment)			

	Old Asset A/c	...Dr.	₹ 2,000	
	To Profit & Loss A/c.			₹ 2,000
	(Being the Excess of Fair Market Value over Book Value transferred to P & L A/c)			

2nd Alternative

JOURNAL

Date	Particulars		Dr. (₹)	Cr. (₹)
	Investment A/c	...Dr.	₹ 25,000	
	To Bank A/c			₹ 4,000
	To Old Asset A/c			₹ 21,000
	(Being the Cost of Investment acquired recorded at its Fair Market Value)			
	Old Asset A/c	...Dr.	₹ 3,000	
	To Profit & Loss A/c.			₹ 3,000
	(Being the credit balance in Old Asset A/c transferred to P&L A/c)			

QUESTION 3:

Cum - right purchase price of 100 shares on 1st Feb. 2015	**₹ 15,000**
Rights sold on 1st March 2015	**₹ 4,000**

Show the treatment of sale proceeds of rights if:

Ex - right purchase price of 100 shares on 31st Mar. 2015.

(a) **₹ 11,000**

(b) **₹ 12,000**

(c) **₹ 15,000**

(d) **₹ 16,000**

ANSWER:

Case	Amount to be transferred to the credit of Investment Account	Amount to be transferred to the credit of Profit & Loss Account
(a)	₹ 4,000	NIL
(b)	₹ 3,000	₹ 1,000
(c)	NIL	₹ 4,000
(d)	NIL	₹ 4,000

QUESTION 4: Mention two categories of investments defined by AS 13 and also state their valuation principles.

ANSWER: As per para 7 and 8 of AS 13 'Accounting for Investments', there are two categories of investments, viz., Current Investments and Long Term Investments. According to para 14 of the standard, the carrying amount for current investments is the lower of cost and fair value whereas para 17 states that Long Term Investments are valued at cost less permanent diminutions in value of investment. For current investments, para 16 of the standard states that, any reduction to fair value and any reversals of such reductions are included in the profit and loss statement.

QUESTION 5: Rose Ltd. had made an investment ot ₹ 500 lakhs in the equity shares of Nose Ltd. on 10.01. 2015. The realisable value of such investment, on 31.03.2015 became ₹.200 lakhs as Nose Ltd. lost a case of patent rights. Rose Ltd. follows financial year as accounting year. How will you recognize this reduction in Financial statements for the year 2014-2015.

ANSWER: Recognition of reduction in value of investment would depend upon the nature of investment and nature of decline as per Accounting Standard 13 "Accounting for Investments". As per provisions of the standard, if the investments were acquired for long term and decline is temporary in nature, reduction in value will not be recognized and investments would be carried at cost. If the decline is of permanent nature, it will be charged to Profit and Loss Account. If the investments are current investments, then the reduction should be recognized and charged to Profit and Loss Account as the current investments are carried at cost or fair value, *whichever is less.*

QUESTION 6: Innovative Garments Manufacturing Company Limited invested in the Shares of another Company on 1st October 2014, at a cost of ₹ 2,50,000. It also earlier purchased Gold of ₹ 4,00,000 and Silver of ₹ 2,00,000 on 1st March 2012. Market Value as on 31st March 2015 of above Investments are: Shares ₹ 2,25,000, Gold ₹ 6,00,000 and Silver ₹ 3,50,000.

How will the above Investments be shown in the books of accounts of Innovative Garments Manufacturing Limited for the year ending 31st March 2015, as per the provisions of AS-13?

ANSWER:

TREATMENT AS PER AS 13

Type of Investment	Valuation Principle	Carrying Amount
Equity Shares	Lower of Cost *or* Market Value	₹ 2,25,000
Gold	Cost (Long Term Investment, since the asset is held for more than 3 years)	₹ 4,00,000
Silver	Cost (Long Term Investment, since the asset is held for more than 3 years)	₹ 2,00,000
	Total	₹ 15,50,000

QUESTION 7: A unquoted long term investment is carried in the books at its cost of ₹ 5 lakhs. The Published Accounts of the unlisted company received in May, 2015 showed that the company was incurring cash losses with declining market share and the long term investment may not fetch more than ₹ 80,000.

ANSWER:

PROVISION OF AS 13

Investments classified as long term investments should be carried in the financial statements at cost. However, provision for diminution shall be made to recognise a decline, other than temporary, in the value of the investments, such reduction being determined and made of each investment individually. Para 17 to AS 13 'Accounting for Investments' states that indicators of the value of an investment are obtained by reference to its market value, the investee's assets and results and the expected cash flows from the investments.

ADVICE

The facts of the given case clearly suggest that the provision for diminution should be made to reduce the carrying amount of long term investment to ₹ 80,000 in the financial statements for the year ended 31st March, 2015.

PROVISION OF AS 30

As per AS 30, An Impairment Loss should be recognised in the Statement of Profit and Loss if there is an objective evidence that an impairment loss has been incurred on an unquoted equity instrument that is not carried at fair value.

ADVICE

Hence, An Impairment Loss of ₹ 4,20,000 (i.e.₹ 5,00,000 –₹ 80,000) should be recognised in the Statement of Profit and Loss for the year ended 31st March, 2015.

QUESTION 8: Anischit Finance Ltd. is a non-banking finance company. It makes available to you the costs and market price of various investments held by it for Trading as on 31.3.2015.

Particulars		(Figures in ₹ Lakhs)
	Cost	Market Price
Scripts:		
A. Equity Shares		
A	60.00	61.20
B	31.50	24.00
C	60.00	36.00
D	60.00	120.00
E	90.00	105.00
F	75.00	90.00
G	30.00	6.00
B. Mutual funds		
MF-1	39.00	24.00
MF-2	30.00	21.00
MF-3	6.00	9.00
C. Government Securities-		
GV-1	60.00	66.00
GV-2	75.00	72.00

(i) Can the company adjust depreciation of a particular item of investments within a category?

(ii) What should be the value of investments as on 31.3.2015?

(iii) Is it possible of off-set depreciation investment in mutual funds against appreciation of the value of investment in equity shares and government securities?

ANSWER:

(i) Quoted current investments for each category shall be valued at cost of market value, whichever is lower. For this purpose, the investments in each category shall be considered scrip-wise and the cost and market value aggregated for all investments in each category. If the aggregate market value for the category is less than the aggregate cost for that category, the net depreciation shall be provided for or charged to the profit and loss account. If the aggregate market value for the category exceeds the aggregate cost for the category, the net appreciation shall be ignored. Therefore, depreciation of a particular item of investments can be adjusted within the same category in investments.

(ii) Value of investments as on 31.3.2015

Type of investment	Valuation Principle	Value ₹ in lakhs
Equity Shares (Aggregated)	Lower of cost or market Value	406.50
Mutual Funds	NAV (market value, assumed)	54.00
Government securities	Cost	135.00
		595.50

As per par 14 of AS 13 "Accounting for investments", the carrying amount for current investments is the lower of cost and market price. Sometimes, the concern of an enterprise may be with the value of a category of related current investments and not with each individual investments, and accordingly, the investments may be computed at the lower of cost and market value computed category wise.

(iii) Inter category adjustments of appreciation and depreciation in values of investments cannot be done. It is possible to offset depreciation in investment in mutual funds against appreciation of the value of investments in equity shares and Government securities.

PROVISION OF AS 30

As per AS 30 Financial Instrument should be measured at Fair Value on the Date of Acquisition and on Subsequent Measurement. Any Gain or Loss on Subsequent Measurement is to be recognised in the Statement of Profit and Loss.

ADVICE

A. Total Maket Value of Investments = 61.2 + 24 + 36 + 120 + 105 + 90 + 6 + 24 + 21 + 9 + 66 + 72 = ₹ 634.2 lakhs

B. Total Cost of Investments = 60 + 31.5 + 60 + 60 + 90 + 75 + 30 + 39 + 30 + 6 + 60 + 75 = ₹ 616.5 lakhs

C. Total Gain [A – B] = ₹ 17.7 lakhs

Total Gain of ₹ 17.7 lakhs) should be recognised in the Statement of Profit and Loss for the year ended 31st March, 2015.

QUESTION 9: Suram Ltd. wants to re-classify its investment in accordance with AS 13. Decide on the treatment to be given in each of the following cases.

(i) A portion of Current Investments purchased for ₹ 20 lakhs to be reclassified as long-term investments, as the company has decided to retain them. The market value as on the date of Balance Sheet was ₹ 25 lakhs.

(ii) Another portion of Current Investments purchased for ₹ 15 lakhs has to be reclassified as Long-term Investments. The market value of these Investments as on the date of Balance Sheet was ₹ 6.5 Lakhs.

(iii) Certain Long-term Investments no longer considered for holding purposes have to be re-classified as Current Investments. The original cost of these was ₹ 18 lakhs but they had been written down to ₹ 12 lakhs to recognize permanent decline as per AS 13.

ANSWER: As per Para 24 of AS 13 'Accounting for Investments', where investments are reclassified from current to long-term, transfers are made at the lower of cost and fair value at the date to transfer.

(i) The market value of the investments is ₹ 25 Lakhs, which is higher than its cost i.e., ₹ 20 lakhs. Therefore, the transfer to long term investments should be carried at cost i.e., ₹ 20 lakhs.

(ii) The market value of the investment is ₹ 6.5 lakhs, which is lower than its cost i.e., ₹ 15 lakhs. Therefore, the transfer to long term investments should be carried in the books at the market value i.e., ₹ 6.5 lakhs. The loss of ₹ 8.5 lakhs should be charged to Profit and Loss account.

(iii) As per para 23 of AS 13, where long-term investments are reclassified as current investments, transfer are made at the lower of cost and carrying amount at the date of transfer.

The book value for the investment is ₹ 12 lakhs, which is lower than its cost i.e., ₹ 18 lakhs. Here, the transfer should be at carrying amount and hence this reclassified current investments should be carried at ₹ 12 lakhs.

PROVISION OF AS 30

As per AS 30 Financial Instrument should be measured at Fair Value on the Date of Acquisition and on Subsequent Measurement. Any Gain or Loss on Subsequent Measurement is to be recognised in the Statement of Profit and Loss.

ADVICE

(i) Gain of ₹ 5 lakhs should be recognised in the Statement of Profit and Loss.
(ii) Loss of ₹ 8.5 lakhs should be recognised in the Statement of Profit and Loss.
(ii) Loss of ₹ 6 lakhs should be recognised in the Statement of Profit and Loss.

QUESTION 10: Albert Finance Ltd, has made the following investments.

(i) Purchased the following equity shares from stock exchange on 1st June, 2014.

Particulars	Cost
Scrip X	1,80,000
Scrip Y	50,000
Scrip Z	1,70,000
	4,00,000

(i) Purchased gold of ₹ 3,00,000 on 1st April, 2011.
(iii) Invested in mutual funds at a cost of ₹ 6,00,000 on 31st March, 2014.
(iv) Purchased government securities at a cost of ₹ 5,00,000 on 1st April, 2014.
How will you treat these investments as per applicable AS in the books of the company for the year ended on 31st March, 2015, if the values of these investments are as follows:

Shares		
Scrip X	1,90,000	
Scrip Y	40,000	
Scrip Z	70,000	3,00,000
Gold		5,00,000
Mutual Funds		4,50,000
Government securities		7,00,000

Also explain is it possible to off-set depreciation in investment in mutual funds against appreciation of the value of investment in government securities?

ANSWER:

PROVISION OF AS 13

As per As 13 'Accounting for Investment' current investments should be carried in the financial statements at lower of cost and fair value determined either on an individual investment basis or by category of investment but not on an overall (or global) basis and long-term investments are carried at cost except when there is a decline, other than temporary, in the value of a long term investment, the carrying amount is reduced to recognize the decline.

ADVICE

(i) If the investment in shares is intended to he held for not more than one year from the date on which such investment is made: Scrip X should be valued at cost, i.e., ₹ 1,80,000 (lower of cost and fair value); Scrip Y should be valued at fair value, i.e., ₹ 40,000 (lower of cost and fair value) and Scrip Z should be valued at fair value i.e., ₹ 70,000 (lower of cost and fair value). The total loss of ₹ 1,00,000 (₹ 4,00,000 – ₹ 3,00,000) on scrip purchased on 1st June, 2014, is to be charged to Profit and Loss Account for the year ended 31st March, 2015.

If investment is intended to be held for long term period: Investment will continue to be shown at cost in the Balance sheet of the company. However, provision for diminution shall be made to recognize a decline, other than temporary, in the value of investments, such reduction being determined and made for each investment individually.

(ii) Investment in gold (purchased in April, 2011) shall continue to be shown at cost of ₹ 3,00,000 in the balance sheet as on 31.3.2015.

(iii) If mutual funds are intended to be held for short term period it will be valued at ₹ 4,50,000 as on 31st March, 2015 and if its is intended to be held for long term, then it should be valued at its cost i.e., ₹ 6,00,000.

(iv) Value of government securities (Purchased on 1st April, 2014) is to shown at cost of ₹ 5,00,000 in the balance sheet as on 31.3.2015.

Inter category adjustments of appreciation and depreciation in value of investments cannot be done. It is not possible to offset depreciation in investment in mutual funds against appreciation in value of investment in government securities.

PROVISION OF AS 30

As per AS 30 Financial Instrument should be measured at Fair Value on the Date of Acquisition and on Subsequent Measurement. Any Gain or Loss on Subsequent Measurement is to be recognised in the Statement of Profit and Loss.

ADVICE

A. Total Maket Value of Investments(except Gold)=1.9+0.4+0.7+4.5+7=₹ 14.5 lakhs

B. Total Cost of Investments(except Gold)=15 lakhs

Total Loss of ₹ 0.5 lakh should be recognised in the Statement of Profit and Loss.

Gold (not being a Financial Instrument) shall continue to appear at cost of ₹ 3 lakhs.

QUESTION 11: ABC Ltd. has acquired 100% of the equity shares of Company 'X' during 2012. Company 'X' is a defunct company. The net worth of the Company 'X' is represented by land and building it owns. ABC Ltd acquired the shares of Company 'X' only for the land and building owned by it. ABC Ltd. had proposed to start a software development facility at this site at the time of share purchase. The software development facility has not yet been set up, as Company's existing facility itself is under utilized.

In the financials of the year 2013, the above investment was classified fixed assets under the head 'land and building' to reflect the substance of the transaction, as the intention to acquire the shares was to use the land and building owned by Company 'X'.

During the year 2015, the Company has decided to sell these shares and has passed a reANSWER authorizing the chairman to negotiate and settle the price. As of March 2015, this investment is reflected as fixed assets in the books. The property is prime one and is an ideal one for setting up new software units, ware houses etc.

(a) Should the above shares be classified under investments or is the current treatment of grouping it under fixed assets correct?

(b) If the current treatment of disclosing the shares as land and building is correct, should we disclose the same as assets held for disposal, with appropriate classification and disclosures?

ANSWER:

PROVISION OF AS 13

AS per AS 1 'Disclosure of Accounting, Policies 'The substance of the transaction is an investment in fixed assets, through the "form" is acquisition of shares.

ADVICE

(a) In the given case, the acquisition of shares in Company X was with the sole motive of using the land and buildings, and not for earning income by way of dividends.

In view of this, the accounting treatment so far accorded by the Company, in classifying the shares as fixed assets is correct.

(b) Since the original intention has undergone a change, therefore, on account of the changed intention, i.e., "to dispose of the shares", the accountant should reclassify the holding in the Company X as investments as available for sale and bring the same in the books at Fair Value if it is reliably determinable otherwise at carrying amount.

QUESTION 12: JVR Limited has made investment of ₹ 97.84 Crores in Equity Shares of QSR Limited in pursuance of Joint Venture agreement in 2015-2016. The investment has been made at par. QSR Limited has been in continuous losses for the last 2 years. JVR Limited is willing to re–assess the carrying amount of its investment in QSR Limited and wish to provide for diminution in value of investment. However, QSR Limited has futuristic and profitable business plans and projection for the coming years. Discuss whether the connection of JVR Limited to bring down the Carrying Amount of Investment in QSR Limited is in accordance with Accounting Standards

ANSWER:

PROVISION OF AS 13

(i) **Carrying Amount:** Long–Term Investments are usually carried at Cost.

(ii) **Basis:** Long–Term Investments are of individual importance to an enterprise. So, the Carrying Amount is determined on an individual basis.

(iii) **Decline in Value:**

(a) When there is a permanent decline in the value of a long–term investment, the Carrying Amount is reduced in order to recognise the decline. The reduction in value shall be determined and made for each investment individually.

(b) Temporary Fall in the value of long–term investments need not be provided for.

ADVICE

If QSR Ltd has demonstrative future maintainable profits, then the present losses can be considered as "Temporary" in nature. Hence as there is no permanent decline in the value, there is no need for creating any provision for loss on value of investments.

QUESTION 13: K Ltd. had 5 subsidiaries as at 31st March 2015 and the investments in-subsidiaries are considered as long term and valued at cost. Two of the subsidiaries net worth eroded as at 31st March 13 and the prospects of their recovery are very bleak and the other three subsidiaries are doing exceptionally well. The company did not provide for the decline in the value of investments in two subsidiaries because the overall investment portfolio in subsidiaries did not suffer any decline' as the other three subsidiaries are doing exceptionally well. Comment.

ANSWER:

PROVISION OF AS 13

As per AS 13, "Accounting for Investments" long-term investments are usually of individual importance to the investing enterprise. The carrying amount of long-term investments is therefore determined on an individual investment basis. Investments classified as long term investments should be carried in the financial statements at cost. However, provision for diminution shall be made to recognize a decline, other than temporary, in the value of the investments, such reduction being determined and made for each investment individually.

ADVISE

K Ltd should provide for the decline in the value of investments in two subsidiaries despite the fact that the overall investment portfolio in subsidiaries did not suffer any decline.

QUESTION 14: Blue-chip Equity Investments Ltd., wants to re-classify its investments in accordance with AS 13.

- **(i) Long term investments in Company A, costing ₹ 8.5 lakhs are to be re-classified as current. The comp0any had reduced the value of these investments to ₹ 6.5 lakhs to recognize a permanent decline in value. The fair value on date of transfer is ₹ 6.8 lakhs.**
- **(ii) Long term investments in Company B, costing ₹ 7 lakhs are to be re-classified as current. The fair value on date of transfer is ₹ 8 lakhs and book value is ₹ 7 lakhs.**
- **(iii) Current investment in Company C, costing ₹ 10 lakhs are to be re-classified as long term as the company wants to retain them. The market value on date of transfer is ₹ 12 lakhs.**
- **(iv) Current investment in Company D, costing ₹ 15 lakhs are to be re-classified as long term. The market value on date of transfer is ₹ 14 lakhs.**

ANSWER:

As per AS 13 "Accounting for Investments", in case of reclassification of investment from long-term to current, transfer is to be made at lower of cost or carrying amount at the date of transfer. If investment is reclassified from current to long term, transfer is to be made at lower of cost and fair value. Keeping in view this provision, the answer is given below:

- (i) Reclassification from Long term to Current: Cost is ₹ 8.5 Lakhs and carrying amount is ₹ 6.5 Lakhs. Hence transfer will be made at ₹ 6.5 Lakhs.
- (ii) Reclassification from Long term to current: Cost is ₹ 7 Lakhs and carrying amount is ₹ 7 Lakhs. Hence transfer will be made at ₹ 7 Lakhs.
- (iii) Reclassification from current to Long term: Cost is ₹ 10 Lakhs and Fair Value is ₹ 12 Lakhs. Hence transfer will be made at ₹ 10 Lakhs.

35 INSURANCE CLAIMS

SHORT ANSWER PRACTICAL PROBLEMS

INSURANCE CLAIM FOR LOSS OF STOCK

PROBLEM 1

A company lodged a claim to insurance company for ₹ 5,00,000 in September. The claim was settled in February for ₹ 3,50,000. How will you record the short fall in claim settlement in the books of the company.

Solution

JOURNAL ENTRY

Particulars		*(₹)*	*(₹)*
Profif and Loss A/c	Dr.	1,50,000	
To Insurance Company A/c			1,50,000
[Being the shortfall in insurance claim is ths loss, transferred to Profit and Loss A/c]			

PROBLEM 2

Calculate the amount of Insurance claim to be lodged, based on the following information:

Value of stock destroyed by fire	₹ 90,000
Insurance policy amount (subject to average clause)	₹ 65,000
Value of stock salvaged from fire	₹ 40,000

Solution

Total stock before fire = ₹ 90,000 + ₹40,000 = ₹1,30,000.

$$\text{Amount of insurance claim} = \frac{\text{Stock destoyed by fire}}{\text{Total stock before fire}} \times \text{Amount insured}$$

$$= \frac{₹\ 90,000}{₹\ 1,30,000} \times ₹\ 65,000 = ₹\ 45,000$$

PROBLEM 3

In January a firm took an insurance policy for ₹ 60 lakhs to insure goods in its godown against fire subject to average clause. On 7th March a fire broke out destroying goods costing ₹ 44 lakhs. Stock in the godwon was estimated at ₹80 lakhs. Compute the amount of insurance claim.

Solution

$$\text{Amount of insurance claim} = \text{Amount of loss due to fire} \times \frac{\text{Amount insurance policy}}{\text{Total in the godown}}$$

$$= ₹\ 44\ \text{lakhs} \times \frac{₹\ 60\ \text{lakhs}}{₹\ 80\ \text{lakhs}} = ₹\ 33\ \text{lakhs}$$

PROBLEM 4

On 2.6.2015 the stock of Mr Black was destroyed by fire. However, following particulars were furnished from the records saved:

	₹
Stock at cost on 1.4.2014	1,35,000
Stock at 90% of cost on 31.3.2015	1,62,000
Purchases for the year ended 31.3.2015	6,45,000
Sales or the year ended 31.3.2015	9,00,000
Purchases from 1.4.2015 to 2.6.2015	2,25,000
Sales from 1.4.2015 to 2.6.2015	4,80,000

Sales upto 2.6.2015 includes ₹ 75,000 being the goods not dispatched to the customers. The sales invoice price is ₹ 75,000.

Purchases upto 2.6.2015 includes a machinery acquired for ₹ 15,000.

Purchases upto 2.6.2015 does not include goods worth ₹ 30,000 received from suppliers, as invoice not received upto the date of fire. These goods have remained in the godown at the time of fire.

Value of stock salvaged from fire ₹ 22,500 and this has been handed over to the insurance company.

The insurance policy is for ₹ 1,20,000 and it is subject to average clause.

Required: Ascertain the amount of claim for loss of stock.

Solution

Dr. **TRADING ACCOUNT FOR THE YEAR ENDED 31.3.2015** *Cr*

Particulars	₹	*Particulars*	₹
To Opening Stock	1,35,000	By Sales	9,00,000
To Purchases	6,45,000	By Closing Stock at cost	1,80,000
To Gross Profit	3,00,000	[₹ 1,62,000 × 100/90]	
	10,80,000		10,80,000

$$\text{G. P. Ratio} = \frac{3,00,000}{9,00,000} \times 100 = 33\frac{1}{3}\%$$

Dr. **MEMORANDUM TRADING ACCOUNT** *Cr*

for the period from 1.4.2015 to 2.6.2015

Particulars		₹	*Particulars*		₹
To Opening Stock at cost		1,80,000	By Sales	4,80,000	
To Purchases	2,25,000		*Less:* Goods not dispatched	75,000	4,05,000
Add: Goods received but invoice not received	30,000		By Closing stock (b.f.)		1,50,000
	2,55,000				
Less: Machinery	15,000	2,40,000			
To Gross Profit [₹ 4,05,000 × 33-1/3%]		1,35,000			
		5,55,000			5,55,000

Calculation of Insurance Claim

$$\text{Claim subject to average clause} = \text{Actual loss of stock} \times \frac{\text{Amount of Policy}}{\text{Value stock on the date of fire}}$$

$$= 1,50,000 \times \left(\frac{1,20,000}{1,50,000}\right) = ₹\ 1,20,000$$

Note: Salvaged stock amounting ₹ 22,500 handed over to the insurance company is also a loss to Mr Black.

PROBLEM 5

On 11.11.2015 the premises of Rocky Ltd. was destroyed by fire. The following information is made available:

	₹
Stock as on 1.4.2014	3,75,000
Purchases from 1.4.2014 to 31.3.2015	5,20,000
Sales from 1.4.2014 to 31.3.2015	8,55,000
Stock as on 31.3.2015	2,00,000
Purchase from 1.4.2015 to 11.11.2015	3,41,000
Sales from 1.4.2015 to 11.11.2015	4,35,500

In valuing the stock on 31.3.2015, due to damage 50% of the value of the stock which originally cost ₹ 22,000 was written off.

In June, 2015 about 50% of this stock was sold for ₹ 5,500 and the balance of obsolete stock is expected to realise the same price (i.e. 50% of the original cost).

The gross profit ratio is to be assumed as uniform in respect of other sales. Stock salvaged from fire amounts to ₹ 11,500.

Required: Compute the value of stock lost in fire.

Solution

TRADING ACCOUNT FOR THE YEAR ENDED 31.3.2015

Particulars	₹	*Particulars*	₹
To Opening Stock	3,75,000	By Sales	8,55,000
To Purchases	5,20,000	By Closing Stock	
To Gross Profit *(Balancing Figure)*	1,71,000	Given ₹ 2,00,000	
		Add: w/o 11,000	2,11,000
	10,66,000		10,66,000

$$\text{Gross profit Ratio} = \frac{\text{Gross Profit}}{\text{Sales}} \times 100 = \frac{₹1,71,000}{₹8,55,000} \times 100 = 20\%$$

MEMORANDUM TRADING ACCOUNT
for the period 1.4.2015 to 11.11.2015

Particulars	*Normal* ₹	*Abnormal* ₹	*Particulars*	*Normal* ₹	*Abnormal* ₹
To Opening Stock	1,89,000	11,000	By Sales	4,30,000	5,500
To Purchases	3,41,000		By Closing Stock	1,86,000	5,500
To Gross Profit @ 20%	86,000				
	6,16,000	11,000		6,16,000	11,000

Computation of Stock lost in Fire:

Total Closing Stock	= Normal Stock + Abnormal Stock
	= 1,86,000 + 5,500
	= ₹ 1,91,500
Less: Stock Salvaged	₹ 11,500
Stock lost in Fire	₹ 1,80,000

PROBLEM 6

A fire broke out in the godown of a business house on 8th July, 2015. Goods costing ₹ 2,03,000 in a small sub-godown remain unaffected by fire. The goods retrieved in a damaged condition from the main godown were valued at ₹ 1,97,000.

The following particulars were available from the books of accounts:

Stock on the last Balance Sheet date at 31st March, 2015 was ₹ 15,72,000. Purchases for the period from 1st April, 2015 to 8th July, 2015 were ₹ 37,10,000 and sales during the same period amounted to ₹ 52,60,000. The average gross profit margin was 30% on sales.

The business house has a fire insurance policy for ₹ 10,00,000 in respect of its entire stock. Assist the Accountant of the business house in computing the amount of claim of by fire.

Solution

CALCULATION OF LOSS OF STOCK

Particulars	₹	₹
Value of stock as on 8th July (Refer W.N.)		16,00,000
Less: Value of stock remaining unaffected by fire	2,03,000	
Agreed value of damaged goods	1,97,000	4,00,000
Loss of stock		12,00,000

Applying Average Clause:

$$\text{Amount of claim} = \frac{\text{Amount of policy}}{\text{Stock on the date of fire}} \times \text{Loss of stock}$$

$$= \frac{₹\,10,00,000}{₹\,16,00,000} \times 12,00,000 = ₹\ 7,50,000$$

Working Note:

MEMORANDUM TRADING ACCOUNT
for the period from 1st April, 2015 to 8th July, 2015

Particulars	₹	*Particulars*	₹
To Opening Stock	15,72,000	By Sales	52,60,000
To Purchases	37,10,000	By Closing Stock (Bal.Fig.)	16,00,000
To Gross Profit (30% of sales)	15,78,000		
	68,60,000		68,60,000

PROBLEM 7

On 20th October, 2015, the godown and business premises of Aman Ltd. were affected by fire. From the salvaged accounting records, the following information is available.

	₹
Stock of goods @ 10% lower than cost as on 31st March, 2015	2,16,000
Purchases *less* returns (1.4.2015 to 20.10.2015)	2,80,000
Sales *less* returns (1.4.2015 to 20.10.2015)	6,20,000

Additional Information:

(1) Sales upto 20th October includes ₹ 80,000 for which goods had not been dispatched.

(2) Purchases upto 20th October did not include ₹ 40,000 for which purchase invoices had not been received from suppliers, though goods have been received in Godown.

(3) Past records show the gross profit rate of 25%

(4) The value of goods salvage d from fire ₹ 31,000.

(5) Am an Ltd. has insure d their stock for ₹ 1,00,000.

Compute the amount of claim to be lodged to the insurance company.

Solution

MEMORANDUM TRADING ACCOUNT

Particulars	₹	*Particulars*	₹
To Opening Stock	2,40,000	By Sales	5,40,000
To Purchases	3,20,000	(₹ 6,20,00 – ₹ 80,000)	
(₹ 2,80,000 + ₹ 40,000)		By Closing stock	1,55,000
To Gross Profit		*(balancing figure)*	
(₹ 5,40,000 × 25%)	1,35,000		
	6,95,000		**6,95,000**

Stock on the date of fire (i.e. on 20.10.2015)	1,55,000
Less: Stock salvaged	(31,000)
Stock destroyed by fire	**1,24,000**

$$\text{Insurance claim} = \frac{\text{Loss of Stock}}{\text{Value of stock on the date of fire}} \times \text{Amount of Policy}$$

$$= \frac{1,24,000}{1,55,000} \times 1,00,000 = \text{Rs. } 80,000$$

Working Notes:

Stock as on 1st April was valued at 10% lower than cost.

Hence, original cost of the stock as on 1st April would be

$$= \frac{2,16,000}{90} \times 100 = ₹\ 2,40,000$$

PROBLEM 8

On 30th March fire occurred in the premises of M/s Suraj Brothers. The concern had taken an insurance policy of ₹ 60,000 which was subject to the average clause. From the books of accounts, the following particulars are available relating to the period 1st January to 30ih March.

(1) Stock as per Balance Sheet at 31st December ₹ 95,600.

(2) Purchases (including purchase of machinery costing ₹ 30,000) ₹ 1,70,000

(3) Wages (including wages ₹ 3,000 for installation of machinery) ₹ 50,000.

(4) Sales (including goods sold on approval basis amounting to ₹ 49,500) ₹ 2,75,000. No approval has been received in respect of 2/3rd of the goods sold on approval.

(5) The average rate of gross profit is 20% of sales.
(6) The value of the salvaged goods was ₹ 12,300.

You are required to compute the amount of the claim to be lodged to the insurance company,

Solution

COMPUTATION OF CLAIM FOR LOSS OF STOCK

	₹
A. Stock on the date of fire i.e. on 30st March (W.N.1)	62,600
B. *Less:* Value of Salvaged Stock	(12,300)
C. Loss of Stock [A – B]	50,300
D. Amount of Claim $= \dfrac{\text{Insured Value}}{\text{Total Cost of Stock on the date of fire}} \times \text{Loss of stock}$ $= \left(\dfrac{60,000}{62,600} \times 50,300\right)$	48,211 (approx.)

A claim of ₹ 48,211 (approx.) should be lodged by M/s Suraj Brothers to the insurance company.

Working Note:

MEMORANDUM TRADING ACCOUNT FOR
(from 1st January to 30th March)

Dr. *Cr.*

Particulars	₹	*Particulars*	₹
To Opening Stock	95,600	By Sales (₹ 2,75,000 – 33,000)	2,42,000
To Purchases (1,70,000 – 30,000)	1,40,000	By Goods with customers (for approval) at cost [80% of (₹ 49,500 × 2/3)]	26,400
To Wages (50,000 – 3,000)	47,000	By Closing Stock (Bal. fig.)	62,600
To Gross Profit (20% on sales)	48,400		
	3,31,000		3,31,000

PROBLEM 9

A fire occurred in the premises of M/s. Fireproof Co. on 3lst August, 2015. From the following particulars relating to the period from 1st April, 2015 to 31st August, 2015 you are requested ascertain the amount of claim to be filed with the insurance company for the loss of stock. The concern had taken an * insurance policy for ₹ 60,000 which is subject to average clause.

		₹
(i)	Stock as per Balance Sheet at 31-03-2015	99,000
(ii)	Purchases	1,70,000
(iii)	Wages (including wages for the installation of a machine ₹ 3,000)	50,000
(iv)	Sales	2,42,000
(v)	Sale value of goods drawn by partners	15,000
(vi)	Cost of goods sent to consignees on 16th August, 2015, lying unsold with them	16,500
(vii)	Cost of goods distributed as free samples	1,500

While valuing the stock at 31st March, 2015, ₹ 1,000 were written off in respect of a slow moving item. The cost of which was ₹ 5,000. A portion of these goods were sold at a loss of ₹ 500 on the original cost of ₹ 2,500. The remainder of the stock is now estimated to *be worth the original cost.* The value of goods salvaged was estimated at ₹ 20,000. The average rate of gross profit was 20% throughout.

Solution

MEMORANDUM TRADING ACCOUNT FOR THE PERIOD 1ST APRIL TO 31ST AUGUST

Particulars	*Normal*	*Abnml*	*Total*	*Particulars*	*Normal*	*Abnml*	*Total*
To Opening stock	95,000	5,000	1,00,000	By Sales	2,40,000	2,000	2,42,000
To Purchases (Refer W.N.)	1,56,500	–	1,56,500	By Goods sent to consignee	16,500	–	16,500
To Wages	47,000	–	47,000	By Loss	–	500	500
To Gross profit @ 20%	48,000	–	48,000	By Closing stock (Bal.fig.)	90,000	2,500	92,500
	3,46,500	5,000	3,51,500		3,46,500	5,000	3,51,500

STATEMENT OF CLAIM FOR LOSS OF STOCK

Particulars	₹
Book value of stock as on 31st August	92,500
Less: Stock salvaged	(20,000)
Loss of stock	72,500

Amount of claim to be lodged with insurance company

$$= \text{Loss of stock} \times \frac{\text{Policy value}}{\text{Value of stock on the date of fire}}$$

$$= ₹\ 72,500 \times \frac{60,000}{92,500} = ₹\ 47,027$$

Working Note:

Adjusted Purchases = 1,70,000 – 12,000 – 1,500 = 1,56,500

PROBLEM 10

On 19th May 2015, the premises of Shri Garib Das were destroyed by fire, but sufficient records were saved, wherefrom the following particulars were ascertained:

	₹
Stock at Cost on 01.01.2014	36,750
Stock at Cost on 31.12.2014	39,800
Purchases less Returns during 2014	1,99,000
Sales less returned during 2014	2,43,500
Purchases less Returns during 01.01.2015 to 19.05.2015	81,000
Sales less Returns during 01.01.2015 to 19.05.2015	1,15,600

In valuing the Stock for the Balance Sheet as at 31st December 2014, ₹ 1,150 had been written off on certain stock which was a poor selling line having the cost ₹ 3,450. A portion of these goods were sold in March, 2015 at a loss of ₹ 125 on original cost of ₹ 1,725. The remainder of this Stock was now estimated to be worth the original cost. Subject to the above exceptions, Gross Profit has remained at a uniform rate throughout. The stock salvaged was ₹ 2,900.

Required: Show the amount of the claim of stock destroyed by fire. Memorandum Trading Account to be prepared for the period from 01.01.2015 to 19.05.2015 for normal and abnormal items.

Solution

(i) TRADING ACCOUNT FOR THE YEAR ENDED 31ST DEC 2014

Particulars	*Normal*	*Abnml*	*Total*	*Particulars*	*Normal*	*Abnml*	*Total*
To Opening Stk	36,750	–	36,750	By Sales	2,43,500	–	2,43,500
To Purchases (b/f)	1,95,550	3,450	1,99,000	By Closing Stock (b/f)	37,500	2,300	39,800
To GP (b/f)	48,700	–	48,700	By Abn Item w/off	–	1,150	1,150
	2,81,000	3,450	2,84,450		2,81,000	3,450	2,84,450

$$\text{Normal Gross Profit Ratio} = \frac{\text{Gross Profit}}{\text{Sales}} \times 100 = \frac{48,700}{2,43,500} \times 100 = \mathbf{20\%}$$

(ii) MEMORANDUM TRADING ACCOUNT (1ST JAN TO 19TH MAY 2015)

Particulars		₹	*Particulars*		₹
To Opening Stock	39,800		By Sales	1,15,600	
Less: Abnormal Item	(2,300)	37,500	*Less:* Abnormal Item	(1,600)	1,14,000
To Purchases		81,000	By Stock on the date of fire		**27,300**
To Gross Profit = 20% on Sales		22,800	(*balancing figure*)		
		1,41,300			**1,41,300**

(iii) STATEMENT OF INSURANCE CLAIM

Particulars	₹
(a) Value of Normal Stock Lost	27,300
(b) *Add:* Value of Abnormal Stock (at Original Cost as given) [3,450 – 1,725]	1,725
(c) Total Value of Stock Lost	29,025
(d) *Less:* Salvaged Stock	(2,900)
(e) Net Claim	26,125

PROBLEM 11

On 29th August, 2015, the godown of a trader caught fire and a large part of the stock of goods was destroyed. However, goods costing ₹ 1,08,000 could be salvaged incurring fire fighting expenses amounting to ₹ 4,700.

The trader provides you the following additional information:

	₹
Cost of Stock on 1st April, 2014	7,10,500
Cost of Stock on 31st March, 2015	7,90,100
Purchases during the year ended 31st March, 2015	56,79,600
Purchases from 1st April 2015 to the date of fire	33,10,700
Cost of goods distributed as samples for advertising from 1st April, 2015 to the date of fire	4,000
Sales for the year ended 31st March, 2015	80,00,000
Sales from 1st April, 2015 to the date of fire	45,36,000

The insurance company also admitted firefighting expenses. The trader had taken the fire insurance policy for ₹ 9,00,000 with an average clause.

Calculate the amount of the claim that will be admitted by the insurance company.

Solution

Dr. **TRADING ACCOUNT FOR THE YEAR ENDED 31.3.2015** Cr

Particulars	₹	Particulars	₹
To Opening Stock	7,10,500	By Sales	80,00,000
To Purchases	56,79,600	By Closing Stock at cost	7,90,100
To Gross Profit	24,00,000	[₹ 1,62,000 × 100/90]	
	87,90,100		87,90,100

$$\text{G. P. Ratio} = \frac{24,00,000}{80,00,000} \times 100 = 30\%$$

Dr. **MEMORANDUM TRADING ACCOUNT** Cr

for the period from 1.4.2015 to 29.8.2015

Particulars		₹	Particulars	₹
To Opening Stock		7,90,100	By Sales	45,36,000
To Purchases	33,10,700		By Closing stock (b.f.)	8,82,600
Less: Advertisement	(41,000)			
Less: Drawings	(2,000)	32,67,700		
To Gross Profit		13,60,800		
[₹ 45,36,000 × 30%]				
		54,18,600		54,18,600

2. STATEMENT OF INSURANCE CLAIM

Particulars	₹
Value of Stock Lost	8,82,600
Less: Salvaged Stock	(1,08,000)
Add: Fire Fighting Expenses	4,700
Net Claim	7,79,300

Note: Since policy amount is more than claim amount, average clauise will not apply. Therefore, claim amount of 7,79,300 will be admitted by the Insurance Company.

PROBLEM 12

From the following information, ascertain the value of stock as on 31st March, 2015:

	₹
Stock as on 01-04-2014	28,500
Purchases	1,52,500
Manufacturing Expenses	30,000
Selling Expenses	12,100
Administration Expenses	6,000
Financial Expenses	4,300
Sales	2,49,000

At the time of valuing stock as on 31st March, 2014, a sum of ₹ 3,500 was written off on a particular item, which was originally purchased for ₹ 10,000 and was sold during the year for ₹ 9,000. Barring the transaction relating to this item, the gross profit earned during the year was 20% on sales.

Solution

STATEMENT SHOWING VALUATIO OF STOCK AS ON 31.03.2015

Particulars		*₹ (lacs)*
Stock as on 01.04.2014	28,500	
Less: Book value of abnormal stock (₹10,000 – ₹ 3,500)	6,500	22,000
Add: Purchases		1,52,500
Manufacturing Expenses		30,000
		2,04,500
Less: Cost of Sales		
Sales as per Books	2,49,000	
Less: Sales of Abnormal item	(9,000)	
	2,40,000	
Less: Gross Profit @ 20%	(48,000)	(1,92,000)
Value of Stock as on 31st March, 2015		12,500

PROBLEM 13

A fire occurred in the premises of M/s Kailash & Co. on 31st September 2015. Form the following particulars relating to the period from 1st April 2015 to 30th September 2015, you are required to ascertain the amount of claim to be filed with the Insurance Company for the loss of stock. The company has taken as Insurance policy for ₹ 75,000 which is subject to average clause. The value of goods salvaged was estimated at ₹ 27,000. The average rate of Gross Profit was 20% throughout the period.

Particulars	*Amount in ₹*
i. Opening Stock	1,20,000
ii. Purchases made	2,40,000
iii. Wages paid (including wages for the installation of a machine ₹ 5,000)	75,000
iv. Sales	3,10,000
v. Goods taken by the Properietor (Sale Value)	25,000
vi. Cost of goods sent to Consignee on 20th September 2015, lying unsold with them	18,000
vii. Free Samples distributed – Cost	2,500

Solution

MEMORANDUM TRADING ACCOUNT FROM 1.4.2015 TO 30.9.2015

Particulars	₹	*Particulars*	₹
To Opening stock	1,20,000	By Sales	3,10,000
To Purchases	2,40,000	By Drawings(25,000–20% on sales)	20,000
To Wages 75,000		By Goods sent on consignment	18,000
Less: Installation wages (5,000) 2,500	70,000	By goods distributed as fee samples	
To Gross Profit (3,10,000 × 20%)	62,000	By Stock on date of fire (B.F.)	1,41,500
	4,92,000		4,92,000

Goods lost by fire:

Stock on date of fire	₹ 1,41,500
Less: Salvages	₹ (27,000)
	₹ 1,14,500

Amount of Claim: Goods lost by fire X insurance policy amount
Stock on date of fire
= (1,14,500 × 75,000)/1,41,500 = ₹ 60,689

INSURANCE CLAIM FOR LOSS OF PROFIT

PROBLEM 13

A trader intends to take a loss of profit policy with indemnity period of 6 months, however, he could not decide the policy amount. From the following details, suggest the policy amount:

Turnover in last financial year	₹ 4,50,000
Standing charges in last financial year	₹ 90,000

Net profit earned in last year was 10% of turnover and the same trend expected in subsequent year.

Increase in turnover expected 25%.

To achieve additional sales, trader has to incur additional expenditure of ₹ 31,250.

Solution

(a) Gross Profit = $\frac{\text{Net Profit + Standing Charges}}{\text{Turnover}} \times 100 = \frac{45,000 + 90,000}{4,50,000} \times 100 = 30\%$

(b) Calculation of Policy amount to cover loss of profit

Turnover in the last financial year	4,50,000
Add: 25% increase in turnover	1,12,500
	5,62,500
Gross profit on increased turnover (5,62,500 × 30%)	1,68,750
Add: Additional standing charges	31,250
Policy Amount	**2,00,000**

Therefore, the trader should go in for a loss of profit policy of 2,00,000.

PROBLEM 14

On account of a fire on 15 June, 2015 in the business house of a company, the working remained disturbed upto 15 Dec., 2015 as a result of which, it was not possible to affect any sales. The company had taken out an insurance policy with an average clause against consequential losses for ₹ 1,40,000 and a period of 7 months has been agreed upon as indemnity period. An increase of 25% was marked in the current year's sales as compared to last year. The company incurred an additional expenditure of ₹ 12,000 to make sales possible and made a saving of ₹ 2,000 in the insured standing charges.

Ascertain the claim under the consequential loss policy keeping the following additional information in view:

	₹
Actual sales from 15 June, 2015 to 15 Dec., 2015	70,000
Sales from 15 June, 2014 to 15 Dec., 2014	2,40,000
Net profit for last Financial year	80,000

Insured standing charges for the last Financial year	70,000
Total standing charges for the last Financial year	1,20,000
Turnover for the last Financial year	6,00,000
Turnover for one year: 16 June, 2014 to 15 June, 2015	5,60,000

Solution

Step 1: Calculation of Short Sales:

	₹
Sales for the period 15.6.2014 to 15.12.2014	2,40,000
Add: 25% increase in sales	60,000
Estimated sales in current period	3,00,000
Less: Actual sales from 15.6.2015 to 15.12.2015	70,000
Short Sales	2,30,000

Step 2: Calculation of Gross Profit:

$$\text{Gross Profit} = \frac{\text{Net Profit + Insured Standing Charges}}{\text{Turnover}} \times 100$$

$$= \frac{₹\ 80{,}000 + ₹\ 70{,}000}{₹\ 6{,}00{,}000} \times 100$$

$$= \frac{₹\ 1{,}50{,}000}{₹\ 6{,}00{,}000} \times 100 = 25\%$$

Step 3: Calculation of Loss of Profit: ₹ 2,30,000 × 25% = ₹ 57,500

Step 4: Calculation of Claim for Increased Cost of Working: Least of the following:

(i) Actual expense = ₹ 12,000

(ii) $\text{Expenditure} \times \frac{\text{Gross Profit on Adjusted Turnover}}{\text{Gross Profit as above + Uninsured standing charges}}$

$$= ₹\ 12{,}000 \times \frac{\frac{25}{100} \times ₹\ 7{,}00{,}000}{\frac{25}{100} \times ₹\ 7{,}00{,}000 + ₹\ 50{,}000} = ₹\ 9{,}333 \text{ approx.}$$

Where

Adjusted turnover	₹
Turnover from 16.06.2014 to 15.06.2015	5,60,000
Add: 25% increase	1,40,000
	7,00,000

(iii) Gross profit on sales generated due to Additional expenditure
= 25% × ₹ 70,000 = ₹ 17,500

₹ 9,333 being the least, shall be the increased cost of working.

Step 5: Calculation of Total Loss of Profit

	₹
Loss of profit	57,500
Add: Increased cost of working	9,333
	66,833
Less: Saving in insured standing charges	(2,000)
	64,833

Step 6: Calculation of Insurable Amount:

Adjusted Turnover × G.P. rate = ₹ 7,00,000 × 25% = ₹ 1,75,000

Step 7: Total Claim for Consequential Loss of Profit:

$$= \frac{\text{Insured Amount}}{\text{Insurable Amount}} \times \text{Total loss of profit}$$

$$= \frac{₹\ 1{,}40{,}000}{₹\ 1{,}75{,}000} \times ₹\ 64{,}833 = ₹\ 51{,}866.40$$

PROBLEM 15

From the following details, calculate consequential loss claim:

1. Date of fire: 1st September;;
2. Indemnity period: 6 months;
3. Period of disruption : 1st September to 1st February;
4. Sum insured: ₹ 1,08,900;
5. Sales were ₹ 6,00,000 for preceding financial year ended on 31st March;
6. Net profit for preceding financial year ₹ 36,000 plus insured standing charges ₹ 72,000;
7. Rate of Gross Profit 18%;
8. Uninsured standing charges ₹ 6,000;
9. Turnover during the disruption period ₹ 67,500;
10. Annual turnover for 12 months immediately preceding the date of fire ₹ 6,60,000;
11. Standard turnover i.e. for corresponding months (1st September to 1st February) in the year preceding the date of fire ₹ 2,25,000;
12. Increase in the cost of working capital ₹ 12,000 with a saving of insured standing charges ₹ 4,500 during the disruption period;
13. Reduced turnover avoided through increase in working capital ₹ 30,000;
14. Special clause stipulated:

    (*a*) Increase in rate of G.P. 2%.

    (*b*) Increase in turnover (standard and annual) 10%.

Solution

Computation of the amount of claim for consequential loss

(*i*) Calculation of short sales

	₹
Standard turnover for the period 1st September to 1st October (P. Year)	2,25,000
Add: Increase of 10% due to upward trend	22,500
Adjusted turnover	2,47,500
Less: Actual turnover during disruption period i.e. 1st September to 1st October (following year)	67,500
	1,80,000

(*ii*) Increased rate of G.P. = 18% + 2% = 20% on sales.

(*iii*) Loss of profit on short sales = 20% of ₹ 1,80,000 = ₹ 36,000.

(*iv*) Calculation of claim for increased cost of working capital

Increased cost of working will be lower of ₹

(i) Actual expenses ₹ 12,000

(ii) $\text{Additional expenses} \times \dfrac{\text{G.P. on Annual turmover}}{\text{G.P. on Annual turnover} + \text{Uninsured standing charges}}$

$12{,}000 \times \dfrac{1{,}45{,}200}{1{,}45{,}200 + 6{,}000}$ 11,523

(iii) G.P. on additional sales = 30,000 × 20% 6,000

₹ 6,000 is lower of above three, so additional expenses would be ₹ 6,000.

Net claim for increased cost of working capital = ₹ 6,000 *minus* savings in insured standing charges

= ₹ 6,000 – ₹ 4,500 = ₹ 1,500

(v) Calculation of adjusted annual sales

	₹
Sales for 12 months preceding the date of fire	6,60,000
Add: 10% of increase in trend	66,000
Adjusted Annual Sales	7,26,000

(*vi*) Insurable Amount i.e gross profit on adjusted annual sales

	₹
Adjusted annual sales	7,26,000
Rate of Gross Profit	20%
Insurable amount (₹7,26,000 × 20%)	1,45,200

(*vii*) Amount of Insurance Claim

$$= \frac{\text{Insured Amount}}{\text{Insurable Amount}} \times \text{Total Loss (Loss of profit + Claim for increased cost)}$$

$$= \frac{1,08,900}{1,45,200} \times (36,000\ 1,500) = ₹\ 28,125.$$

PROBLEM 16

The premise of Green Limited was partially destroyed by fire on March 01, 2015 and as a result, the business was practically disorganized up to August 31, 2015. The company is insured under a loss of profits policy for ₹ 6,60,000, having an indemnity period of 6 months.

From the information given below, find out claim under the policy:

	₹
Actual turnover from March 01, 2015 to August 31, 2015	3,20,000
Turnover from March 01, 2014 to August 31, 2014	9,60,000
Turnover from March 01, 2014 to February 28, 2015	24,00,000
Net profit for last financial year	3,60,000
Insured standing charges for last financial year	2,40,000
Uninsured standing charges for last financial year	20,000
Turnover for the last financial year	20,00,000

The company incurred additional expenses amount to ₹ 40,000 immediately after fire, which reduced the loss in turnover. Otherwise turnover during the period of dislocation would have been only amount to ₹ 2, 20,000. The saving in insured standing charges in consequences of the fire amounted to ₹ 10,800.

There had been a considerable increase in trade since the date of the last annual accounts and it has been agreed that an adjustment of 10% be made in respect of the upward trend in turnover. Assume that, trend adjustment is required on total amount of annual turnover.*[CA (PCC) Nov. 2013]*

Solution

Computation of Loss of Profit - Insurance Claim

Step 1: **Gross Profit Ratio** $= \frac{\text{Net Profit + Insured Standing Charges}}{\text{Turnover}} \times 100$

$$= \frac{₹\ 3,60,000 + ₹\ 2,40,000}{₹\ 20,00,000} \times 100 = 30\%$$

Step 2: **Short Sales** = ₹ 9,60,000 + ₹ 96,000 – ₹ 3,20,000 = ₹ 7,36,000

Step 3: **Annual (Adjusted) Turnover** = ₹ 24,00,000 + 10% = ₹ 26,40,000

Step 4: **Additional expenses**

	₹
(i) Actual expenses	40,000
(ii) Gross profit on sales generated by additional expenses (₹ 3,20,000 – ₹ 2,20,000) x 30/100	30,000
(iii) [Gross profit on annual (adjusted) turnover/ (Gross profit on annual (adjusted) turnover + Uninsured standing charges)] × Additional expenses [(₹ 26,40,000 × 30%)/{(₹ 26,40,000 × 30%) + ₹ 20,000}] × RS 40,000 i.e. [₹ 7,92,000/₹ 8,12,000] × 40,000	39,015
Least of the above three figures is allowable i.e.	30,000

Step 5: **Gross Claim:**

	₹
Loss of Profit on short sales (₹ 7, 36,000 × 30%)	2,20,800
Add: Allowable additional expenses	30,000
Less: Savinq in insured standing charges	(10,800)
Gross claim	2,40,000

Calculation of claim under the policy by applying average clause

= (Gross claim/Gross profit on adjusted turnover) × Policy amount

= [₹ 2,40,000/(₹ 26,40,000 × 30%)] × ₹ 6,60,000 = ₹ 2,00,000

INSURANCE CLAIM FOR LOSS OF STOCK AND LOSS OF PROFIT

PROBLEM 17

Ramda & Sons had taken out policies (without Average Clause) both against Loss of Stock and Loss of Profit, for ₹ 2,10,000 and ₹ 3,20,000 respectively. A fire occurred on 1st July 2015, and as a result of which sales were seriously affected for a period of 3 months.

TRADING AND PROFIT & LOSS A/C FOR THE YEAR ENDED ON 31ST MARCH 2015

Particulars	₹	*Particulars*	₹
To Opening Stock	96,000	By Sales	12,00,000
To Purchases	7,56,000	By Closing Stock	1,85,000
To Wages	1,58,000		
To Manufacturing Expenses	75,000		
To Gross Profit c/d	3,00,000		
	13,85,000		13,85,000
To Administrative Expenses	83,600	By Gross Profit b/d	3,00,000
To Selling Expenses (Fixed)	72,400		
To Commission on Sales	34,200		
To Carriage Outwards	49,800		
To Net Profit	60,000		
	3,00,000		3,00,000

Further detail provided is as below:

(a) Sales, Purchases, Wages and Manufacturing Expenses for the period 01.04.2015 to

30.06.2015 were ₹ 3,36,000, ₹ 2,14,000 ₹ 51,000 and ₹ 12,000 respectively.

(b) Other Sales figure were as follows:

From 01.04.2014 to 30.06.2014 ₹ 3,00,000
From 01.07.2014 to 30.09.2014 ₹ 3,20,000
From 01.07.2015 to 30.09.2015 ₹ 48,000

(c) Due to decrease in the Material Cost, Gross Profit during 2015-2014 was expected to increase by 5% on Sales.

(d) ₹ 1,98,000 were additionally incurred during the period after fire. The amount of policy included ₹ 1,56,000 for Expenses leaving ₹ 42,000 uncovered.

Required: Compute the Claim for Stock, Loss of Profit and Additional Expenses.

Solution

COMPUTATION OF CLAIM FOR LOSS OF STOCK

1. MEMORANDUM TRADING ACCOUNT (1ST APRIL TO 30TH JUN 2015)

Particulars	₹	*Particulars*	₹
To Opening Stock	1,85,000	By Sales	3,36,000
To Purchases	2,14,000	By Stock on the date of fire	2,26,800
To Wages	51,000	(balancing figure)	
To Manufacturing Expenses	12,000		
To Gross Profit @ 30%	1,00,800		
	5,62,800		5,62,800

Note: Normal GP Rate = $\frac{3,00,000}{12,00,0000}$ = 25%, Adjusted GP Rate = 25% + 5% = 30%

2. STATEMENT OF INSURANCE CLAIM

Particulars	₹
Value of Stock Lost on 30th June	2,26,800
Less: Salvaged Stock	Nil
Net Claim	2,26,800

COMPUTATION OF CLAIM FOR LOSS OF PROFIT

(i) Basic GP Rate = $\frac{\text{Net Profit} + \text{Insured Standing Charges}}{\text{Sales}} = \frac{60,000 + 1,56,000}{12,00,000} \times 100 = 18\%$

(ii) Adjusted GP Rate = 18% + 5% = 23%

(iii) Trend Precentage Increase in Sales = $\frac{3,36,000 - 3,00,000}{3,00,000} \times 100 = 12\%$

(vi) Insurable Amount = GP on Annual Adjusted Turnover

= 23% (₹ 12,00,000 + 12%) = ₹ 3,09,120

(V) COMPUTATION OF SHORT SALES

Particulars	₹
Turnover from 1st July to 30th Sept. (previous year corresponding to Indemnity Period)	3,20,000
Add: Adjustment for Increase (₹ 3,20,000 × 12%)	38,400
Adjusted/Expected Turnover during Indemnity Period 3,58,400	
Less: Actual Turnover during Indemnity Period, i.e. from 01.07.2015 to 30.09.2015	(48,000)
Short Sales	3,10,400

(vi) Computation of Turnover for 12 months preceding the date of Fire is as under-

A. Sales from 1st Apr to 30th June (i.e. 3 mths of Year) is trend adjusted at 112% = 3,36,000 (Given)

B. After Trend Adjustment, Normal Value of Sales for 3 months of Year = 3,36,000/112% = 3,00,000

C. Sales from 1st July to 31st March (i.e. 9 months of Year) = 12,00,000/112% = 9,00,000

D. Normal Value of Sales for 12 months preceding the date of Fire (B + C) = 12,00,000

(vii) COMPUTATION OF ALLOWABLE ADDITIONAL EXPENSES

Particulars	₹
Actual Additional Expenses	1,98,000
GP on Sales generated by Additional Expenses (₹ 48,000 × 23%)	11,040
Additional Expenses × $\frac{\text{GP on Adjusted Annual Turnover}}{\text{GP on Adjusted Annual Turnover + Uninsured Standing Charges}}$ $= ₹\ 1{,}98{,}000 \times \frac{23\% \times 13{,}44{,}000}{(23\% \times 13{,}44{,}000) + 42{,}000} = ₹\ 1{,}98{,}000 \times \frac{3{,}09{,}120}{3{,}51{,}120}$	
Allowable Additional Expenses = Least of the above	11,040

(viii) COMPUTATION OF CLAIM

	Particulars	₹
	Loss of Profit = Gross Profit on Short Sales = 23% on 3,10,400	71,392
Add:	Allowable Additional Expenses	11,040
Less:	Saving in Insured Standing Charges	Nil
	Net Claim for Loss of Profit	82,432

PROBLEM 18

On 15th December, 2014, a fire occurred in the premises of M/s. OM Exports. Most of the stocks were destroyed. Cost of stock salvaged being ₹ 1,40,000. From the books of account, the following particulars were available:

(i) Stock at the close of account on 31st March, 2014 was valued at ₹ 9,40,000.

(ii) Purchases from 01-04-2014 to 15-12-2014 amounted to ₹ 13,20,000 and the sales during that period amounted to ₹ 20,25,000.

On the basis of his accounts for the past three years, it appears that average gross profit ratio is 20% on sales.

Compute the amount of the claim, if the stock were insured for ₹ 4,00,000.

Solution

Memorandum Trading Account
For the period 01.04.2014 to 15.12.2014

Particulars	₹	*Particulars*	₹
To Opening stock	9,40,000	By Sales	20,25,000
To Purchases	13,20,000	By Closing Stock	6,40,000
To Gross Profit @20%	4,05,000	(Balancing figure)	
	26,65,000		26,65,000

STATEMENT OF CLAIM

	₹
Estimated value of Stock as at date of fire	6,40,000
Less: Value of Salvaged Stock	1,40,000
Estimated Value of Stock lost by fire	5,00,000

As the value of stock is more than insured value, amount of claim would be subject to average clause.

$$\text{Amount of Claim} = \frac{\text{Amount of Policy}}{\text{Value of Stock}} \times \text{Actual Loss of Stock}$$

$$\text{Amount of Claim} = \frac{4,00,000}{6,40,000} \times 5,00,000 = ₹\ 3,12,500$$

PROBLEM 19

Monalisa & Co. runs plastic goods shop. Following details are available from quarterly sales tax return filed.

Sales	*2011* ₹	*2012* ₹	*2013* ₹	*2014* ₹
From 1st January to 31st March	1,80,000	1,70,000	2,05,950	1,62,000
From 1st April to 30th June	1,28,000	1,86,000	1,93,000	2,21,000
From 1st July to 30th September	1,53,000	2,10,000	2,31,000	1,75,000
From 1st October to 31st December	1,59,000	1,47,000	1,90,000	1,48,000
Total	6,20,000	7,13,000	8,19,950	7,06,000

Period	₹
Sales from 16-09-2013 to 30-09-2013	34,000
Sales from 16-09-2014 to 30-09-2014	Nil
Sales from 16-12-2013 to 31-12-2013	60,000
Sales from 16-12-2014 to 31-12-2014	20,000

A loss of profit policy was taken for ₹1,00,000. Fire occurred on 15th September, 2014. Indemnity period was for 3 months. Net Profit was ₹1,20,000 and standing charges (all insured) amounted to ₹43,990 for year ending 2013.
Determine the Insurance Claim.

Solution

1. **Gross profit ratio**

	₹
Net profit in year 2013	1,20,000
Insured standing charges	43,990
Gross profit	1,63,990

$$\text{Ratio of gross profit} = \frac{1,63,990}{8,19,950} = 20\%$$

2. **Calculation of Short sales**

Indemnity period: 16.9.2014 to 15.12.2014

Standard sales to be calculated on basis of corresponding period of year 2013

	₹
Sales for period 16.9.2013 to 30.9.2013	34,000
Sales for period 1.10.2013 to 15.12.2013 (Note 1)	1,30,000
Sales for period 16.9.2013 to 15.12.2013	1,64,000
Add: upward trend in sales (15%) (Note 2)	24,600
Standard Sales (adjusted)	1,88,600
Actual sales of disorganized period	
Calculation of sales from 16.9.2014 to 15.12.2014	
Sales for period 16.9.2014 to 30.9.2014	Nil
Sales for 1.10.2014 to 15.12.2014 (₹1,48,000 – ₹20,000)	1,28,000
Actual Sales	1,28,000
Short Sales (₹ 1,88,600 – ₹ 1,28,000)	60,600

3. **Loss of gross profit**

Short sales × gross profit ratio = 60,600 × 20% 12,120

4. **Application of average clause**

$$\text{Net claim} = \text{Gross claim} \times \frac{\text{policy value}}{\text{gross profit on annual turnover}}$$

$$= 12{,}120 \times \frac{1{,}00{,}000}{1{,}79{,}860 \text{ (Note 3)}}$$

Amount of claim = 6,738.57 (approx) i.e. ₹ 6,739 (round off)

Working Notes:

1. **Sales for period** 1.10.2013 to 15.12.2013

Sales for 1.10.2013 to 31.12.2013 (given)	1,90,000
Sales for 16.12.2013 to 31.12.2013 (given)	60,000
Sales for period 1.10.2013 to 15.12.2013	1,30,000

2. **Calculation of upward trend in sales**

Total Sales in year 2011 = 6,20,000

Increase in sales in year 2012 as compared to 2011 = 93,000

$$\% \text{ increase} = \frac{93{,}000\ (7{,}13{,}000 - 6{,}20{,}000)}{6{,}20{,}000} = 15\%$$

Increase in sales in year 2013 as compared to year 2012

$$\% \text{ increase} = \frac{1{,}06{,}950\ (8{,}19{,}950 - 7{,}13{,}000)}{7{,}13{,}000} = 15\%$$

Thus annual percentage increase trend is of 15%.

3. Gross profit on annual turnover

Sales from 16.9.2013 to 30.9.2013	34,000
1.10.2013 to 31.12.2013	1,90,000
1.1.2014 to 31.3.2014	1,62,000
1.4.2014 to 30.6.2014	2,21,000
1.7.2014 to 15.9.2014 (1,75,000 – Nil)	1,75,000
Sales for 12 months just before date of fire	7,82,000
Add: 15% upward trend	1,17,300
Adjusted sales of 12 months just before the date of fire	8,99,300
Gross profit on adjusted annual sales @ 20%	1,79,860

SECTION F : ACCOUNTING FOR BANKING, INSURANCE AND ELECTRICITY COMPANIES

36 FINANCIAL STATEMENTS OF BANKING COMPANIES

SHORT ANSWER PRACTICAL QUESTIONS

CALCULATION OF INTEREST ON PERFORMING ASSETS AND NON-PERFORMING ASSETS

PROBLEM 1

Following are the statements of interest on advances in respect of performing and non-performing assets of YES Bank Ltd. Find out the income to be recognised for the year ended 31st March, 2015:

(₹ in lakhs)

Assets	*Interest earned*	*Interest received*
Performing Assets		
Cash Credit and Overdrafts	1,800	1,060
Term Loan	480	320
Bills Purchased and Discounted	700	550
Non-Performing Assets		
Cash Credit and Overdrafts	450	70
Term Loan	300	40
Bills Purchased and Discounted	350	36

Solution

Interest on Performing Assets should be recognised on accrual basis, but interest on Non Performing Assets should be recognised on cash basis.

CALCULATION OF INTEREST INCOME *(₹ in lakhs)*

Interest *A*	*On Performing Assets* *B*	*On Non-Performing Assets* *C*	*Total* *D = B + C*
Interest on Cash Credit and Overdraft	1,800	70	1,870
Interest on Term Loan	480	40	520
Interest on Bills Purchased & Discounted	700	36	736
	2,980	146	3,126

PROBLEM 2

Find out the income to be recognised in the case of YES Bank Ltd. for the year :

(₹ in lakhs)

	Performing Assets		*Non-performing Assets*	
	Interest accrued	*Interest received*	*Interest accrued*	*Interest received*
Term Loans	240	160	150	10
Cash Credits and Overdrafts	1,500	1,240	300	24

Solution

CALCULATION OF INTEREST INCOME OF YES BANK LTD.

		(₹ in lacs)
Term Loans		
Interest accrued on Performing Assets	240	
Interest received on Non - Performing Assets	10	250
Cash credit and overdraft		
Interest accrued on Performing Assets	1,500	
Interest received on Non - Performing Assets	24	1,524
Total Interest to be recognised		1,774

PROBLEM 2A

Find out the Income to be recognized by ABC Bank Ltd, for the year , in respect of Interest on Advance [₹ in Lakhs] as detailed below:

	Performing Assets		*Non-performing Assets*	
	Interest earned	*Interest received*	*Interest earned*	*Interest received*
Term Loans	280	180	170	20
Cash Credits and Overdrafts	1,700	1,630	310	48
Bills Purchased and Discounted	400	400	180	70

Solution

CALCULATION OF INTEREST INCOME

Particulars	*Performing Asset (On Accrual basis)*	*Non-Performing Asset (On Receipt Basis)*	*Total Interest (in ₹ Crores)*
Interest on Term Loan	280	20	300
Interest on Cash Credit and Overdrafts	1,700	48	1,748
Interest on Bills Purchased and Discounted	40	70	470
Total Income to be recognised	**2380**	**138**	**2,518**

CALCULATION OF PROVISION ON ADVANCES 10 BE MADE IN PROFIT AND LOSS ACCOUNT

PROBLEM 3

From the following information find out the amount of provisions to be shown in the Profit and Loss Account of a Commercial Bank:

Assets	₹ (in lakhs)
Standard	4,000
Sub-standard	2,000
Doubtful upto one year	900
Doubtful upto three years	400
Doubtful more than three years	300
Loss Assets	500

Solution

COMPUTATION OF PROVISION

Assets	*Amount*	*% of Provision (₹ in lakhs)*	*Provision (₹ in lakhs)*
Standard	4,000	0.40	16
Sub-standard	2,000	15	300
Doubtful upto one year*	900	25	225
Doubtful upto three years*	400	40	160
Doubtful more than three years*	300	100	300
Loss	500	100	500
			1501

* Dobutful assets are taken as fully secured.

PROBLEM 4

From the following information, compute the amount of provisions to be made in the Profit and Loss Account of a Commercial Bank:

Assets	*₹ in lakhs*
(i) Standard (Value of security ₹ 6,000 lakhs)	7,000
(ii) Sub-standard	3,000
(iii) Doubtful	
(a) Doubtful for less than one year (Realisable value of security ₹ 500 lakhs)	1,000
(b) Doubtful for more than one year, but less than 3 years (Realisable value of security ₹ 300 lakhs)	500
(c) Doubtful for more than 3 years (No security)	300

Solution

COMPUTATION OF PROVISION

(a) *Asset*	*Amount* ₹ in lakhs	*% of Provision*	*Provision* ₹ in lakhs
Standard	7,000	0.40	28
Sub-standard	3,000	15	450
Doubtful (less than one year)			
On Secured Portion	500	25	125
On Unsecured Portion	500	100	500
Doubtful (more than one year but less than			

three year)			
On Secured Portioin	300	40	120
On Unsecured Portion	200	100	200
Doubtful Unsecured (more than three years)	300	100	300
Total Provision			1,723

PROBLEM 5

From the following information of details of advances of X Bank Limited calculate the amount of provisions to be made in Profit and Loss Account:

Asset Classification	₹ in lakhs
Standard	6,000
Sub-standard	4,400
Doubtful:	
For one year	1,800
For two years	1,200
For three years	800
For more than three years	600
Loss Assets	1,600

Solution

CALCULATION OF PROVISIONS ON VARIOUS ASSETS

Asset Classification	*Amount ₹ in lakhs*	*Provision %*	*Amount of Provision ₹ in lakhs*
Standard	6,000	0.40	24
Sub-standard**	4,400	15	660
Doubtful**			
one year	1,800	25	450
2 years	1,200	40	480
3 years	800	40	320
More than 3 years	600	100	600
Loss assets	1,600	100	1,600
			4,134

Note: ** Sub standard and doubtful assets have been treated as fully secured.

PROBLEM 6

From the following information of Great Bank Limited, compute the provisions to be made in the Profit and Loss account:

	₹ in lakhs
Assets:	
Standard	20,000
Substandard	16,000
Doubtful	
For one year (secured)	6,000
For two years and three years (secured)	4,000
For more than three years (secured by mortgage of plant and machinery ₹.600 lakhs)	2,000
Non-recoverable Assets	1,500

Non-Recoverable Assets

Solution

CALCULATION OF AMOUNT OF PROVISION TO BE MADE IN THE P & L ACCOUNT

Classification of Assets	*Amount of advances (₹ in lakhs)*	*Amount of Provision*	*% age of Provision (₹ in lakhs)*
Standard assets	20,000	0.40	80
Sub-standard assets	16,000	15*	2,400
Doubtful assets:			
For one year (secured)	6,000	25	1,500
For two to three years (secured)	4,000	40	1,600
For more than three years (unsecured)	1,400	100	1,400
(secured)	600	100	600
Non-recoverable assets (Loss assets)	1,500	100	1,500
Total Provision required			9,080

*Sub-standards assets have been assumed as fully secured.

PROBLEM 7

From the followings information of details of advances of Zenith Bank Ltd., calculate the amount of provisions to be made in Profit and Loss Account:

	₹
Assets classification	10,000
Standard	6,400
Substandard	3,200
Doubtful:	
for one year	3,200
for two year	1,800
For three years	900
For more than three years	1,100
Loss assets	3,000

CALCULATION OF PROVISIONS ON VARIOUS ASSETS

Assets classification	*Amount (₹) in lakhs)*	*Provision (%)*	*Amount of provision in lakhs)*
Standard	10,000	0.40	40
Sub-standard	6,400	15	960
Doubtful:			
for one year	3,200	25	800
for two years	1,800	40	720
for three years	900	40	360
for more than 3 years	1,100	100	1,100
Loss assets	3,000	100	3,000
		Total	**6,980**

Note: It is assumed that substandard assets and all doubtful assets are fully secured.

PROBLEM 8

From the information given below, find out the amount of provision to be shown in the Profit and Loss Account of a Commercial Bank:

Assets	*(₹ in lakhs)*
Standard	4,500
Sub-standard	3,000
Doubtful for more than three years (Fully Secured)	250
Loss Assets	750

Solution

CALCULATION OF PROVISION ON ASSETS

Assets	*Amount (₹ in lakhs)*	*% of provision***	*Provision (₹ in lakhs)*
Standard	4,500	0.40	18
Sub-standard	3,000	15	450
Doubtful for more than three years (Fully secured)	250	100	250
Loss assets	750	100	750
Total	8,500		1468

*It is assumed that sub-standard assets are fully secured.

PROBLEM 9

From the following information, compute the amount of provisions to be made in the Profit and Loss Account of A commercial Bank:

Assets (Category of Advances)	*₹ in Lakhs*
Standard Advances	7,000
Sub-standard Advances	3,500
(include secured exposures ₹ 1,000 lakhs and balances unsecured exposures ₹ 2,500 Lakhs includes ₹ 1,500 Lakhs in respect of infrastructure loan accounts where escrow accounts are available)	
Doubtful advances-unsecured portion	1,500
Doubtful advances-secured portion	
For doubtful up to 1 year	500
For doubtful more than 1 year and up to 3 years	600
Four doubtful more than 3 years	300
Loss Advances	200

Solution

CALCULATION OF THE AMOUNT OF PROVISIONS ON ASSETS *[` in lakhs]*

Assets	*Amount*	*% of Provision*	*Provision*
Standard	7,000	0.40	28
Sub-standard:			
Secured portion	1,000	15	150
Unsecured infrastructure loan account where escrow account is available	1,500	20	300
Other unsecured	1,000	25	250
Doubtful-Secured portion:			
Upto one year	500	25	125
More than 1 year but upto 3 years	600	40	240
For more than three years	300	100	300
Doubtful-unsecured portion	1,500	100	1,500
Loss	200	100	200
Required provision			**3,093**

CALCULATION OF PROVISION ON ADVANCES GUARANTEED BY DICGC/ECGC

PROBLEM 10

Rajatapeeta Bank Ltd. had extended the following credit lines to a Small Scale Industry, which had not paid any Interest since 1st March, 2007:

	Term Loan	*Export Loan*
Balance Outstanding on 31.03.2015	₹ 35 lakhs	₹ 30 lakhs
DICGC/ECGC cover	40%	50%
Securities held	₹ 15 lakhs	₹ 10 lakhs
Realisable value of Securities	₹ 10 lakhs	₹ 8 lakhs

Required: Compute necessary provisions to be made for the year ended 31st March, 2015.

Solution

CALCULATION OF PROVISION

	Particulars	*Term Loan*	*Export Loan*
A.	Balance Outstanding	35.0	30.0
B.	*Less:* Realisable Value of security	(10.0)	(8.0)
		25.0	22.0
C.	*Less:* DICGC cover @ 40%	(10.0)	
	ECGC cover @ 50%		(11.0)
D.	Unsecured Amount	15.0	11.0
E.	Provision for Unsecured Portion (100%)	15.0	11.0
F.	Provision for Secured Portion (100%)	10.0	8.0
G.	Total Provision required	25.0	19.0

PROBLEM 11

In X Bank Ltd., the doubtful asset (more than 3 years) as on 31.3.2008 is ₹.1,000 lakhs. The value of security (including DICGC 100% cover of ₹.100 lakhs) is ascertained at ₹ 500 lakhs. How much provision must be made in the books of the Bank towards doubtful assets?

Solution

CALCULATION OF PROVISION

	(₹ in lakhs)
Doubtful Assets (more than 3 years)	1,000
Less: Value of security (excluding DICGC cover)	(400)
	600
Less: 100% DICGC cover of ₹.100 lakhs	100
Unsecured portion	500
Provision thereon:	
for unsecured portion @ 100%	500 lakhs
for secured portion @ 100%	400 lakhs
Total provision to be made	900 lakhs

PROBLEM 12

A loan account remains out of order as on the date of Balance Sheet of a Bank. The account has been classified as doubtful assets (upto 1 year).

Details of the accounts are:

Outstanding	₹ 6,73,000
ECGC coverage	25% (Limited to ₹ 1,00,000)
Value of security held	₹ 1,50,000

Compute the necessary provision to be made by a bank as per applicable rates.

Solution

COMPUTATION OF PROVISION

	₹
Doubtful Assets (upto 1 year)	6,73,000
Less: Value of security (excluding ECGC cover)	(1,50,000)
	5,23,000
Less: ECGC coverage (limited to ₹ 1,00,000)	(1,00,000)
Unsecured portion	4,23,000
Provision: for unsecured portion @100% on ₹ 2,23,000	4,23,000
for secured portion @ 25% on ₹ 1,50,000	37,000
Total provision to be made in the books of the bank	4,60,500

PROBLEM 13

A loan account remains out of order as on the date of Balance Sheet of a Bank. The account has been classified as doubtful assets (up to 3 years). Detail of the account is:

Outstanding	₹ 7,24,000
ECGC Cover	30% of outstanding (Subject to maximum of ₹ 1,50,000)
Value of security	
As per valuation on the date of grant of loan	2,25,000
As per realizable value as on date of Balance Sheet	1,75,000

Compute the necessary provision to be made by bank as per applicable rate.

Solution

Computation of provision to be made by a Bank

	₹
Outstanding Value of Doubtful Asset (up to 3 years)	7,24,000
Less: Value of security (excluding ECGC cover)	(₹ 1,75,000)
Sub Total	₹ 5,49,000
Less: ECGC Cover (subject to ₹ 1,50,000 maximum)	(₹ 1,50,000)
Unsecured Portion	₹ 3,99,000
Provision:	
For unsecured portion @ 100% of ₹ 3,99,000	₹ 3,99,000
₹For secured portion @ 40% of ₹ 1,75,000	₹ 70,000
Total Provision	₹ 4,69,000

CALCULATION OF REBATE ON BILL DISCOUNTED

PROBLEM 14

The following particulars are extracted from the (Trial Balance) Books of the M/s Commercial Bank Ltd. for the year ending 31st March. 2015:

	₹
(i) Interest and Discounts	1,96,62,400
(ii) Rebate on Bills Discounted (balance on 1.4.2014)	65,040
(iii) Bills Discounted and Purchased	67,45,400

It is ascertained that proportionate discount not yet earned on the Bills Discounted which will mature during 2015-2014, amounted to ₹ 92,760.

Pass the necessary Journal with narration adjusting the above and show:

(a) Rebate on Bill Discounted Account; and

(b) Interest and Discount Account in the ledger of the Bank.

Solution

(A) JOURNAL OF THE COMMERCIAL BANK LTD.

Date	Particulars		L.F.	Dr. (₹)	Cr. (₹)
1.4.12	Rebate on Bills Discounted A/c	Dr.		65,040	
	To Interest and Discount A/c				65,040
	(Being the amount of provision for unexpired discount brought forward from the previous year credited to Interest and Discount A/c)				
31.03.13	Interest and Discount A/c	Dr.		92,760	
	To Rebate on Bills Discounted A/c				92,760
	(Being provision for unexpired discount required at the end of the current year)				
31.03.13	Interest and Discount A/c	Dr.		1,96,34,680	
	To Profit and Loss A/c				1,96,34,680
	(Being transfer of balance to Profit & Loss A/c)				

Dr. **(B) REBATE ON BILLS DISCOUNTED ACCOUNT** Cr.

Date	Particulars	₹	Date	Particulars	₹
01.04.12	To Interest and Discount A/c	65,040	01.04.12	By Balance b/d	65,040
31.03.13	To Balance c/d	92,760	31.03.13	By Interest and Discount A/c (rebate required)	92,760
		1,57,800			1,57,800

Dr. **(c) Interest and Discount Account** Cr.

Date	Particulars	₹	Date	Particulars	₹
31.03.13	To Rebate on Bills Discounted A/c	92,760	01.04.12	By Rebate on Bills Discounted A/c (Opening Balance)	65,040
31.03.13	To Profit& Loss A/c (transfer)	1,96,34,680	2014-13	By Cash and Sundries	1,96,62,400
		1,97,27,440			1,97,27,440

PROBLEM 15

The following information is available in the books of X Bank Limited as on 31st March, 2015:

	₹
Bill discounted	1,37,05,000
Rebate on Bills discounted (as on 1.4.2014)	2,21,600
Discount received	10,56,650

Details of bills discounted are as follows:

Value of bill (₹)	*Due date*	*Rate of Discount*
18,25,000	5.6.2015	12%
50,00,000	12.6.2015	12%
28,20,000	25.6.2015	14%
40,60,000	6.7.2015	16%

Required: Calculate the rebate on bills discounted as on 31.3.2015 and give necessary journal entries.

Solution

STATEMENT SHOWING REBATE ON BILLS DISCOUNTED

Value of bill (₹)	*Due Date*	*Days after 31 March*	*Rate of discount*	*Discount Amount*
18,25,000	5 June	(30+31+5) = 66	12%	39,600
50,00,000	12 June	(30+31+12) = 73	12%	1,20,000
28,20,000	25 June	(30+31+25) = 86	14%	93,021
40,60,000	6. July	(30+31+30+6) = 97	16%	1,72,633
1,37,05,000		Rebate on bills discounted		4,25,254

JOURNAL

Particulars		*Dr. (₹)*	*Cr. (₹)*
Rebate on Bills Discounted A/c	Dr.	2,21,600	
To Discount on Bills A/c			2,21,600
(Being the opening balance of rebate on bills discounted account transferred to discount on bills account)			
Discount on Bills A/c	Dr.	4,25,254	
To Rebate on Bills Discounted A/c			4,25,254
(Being the provision made on 31st March 2008)			
Discount on Bills A/c	Dr.	8,52,996*	
To Profit and Loss A/c			8,52,966
(Being the transfer of discount on bills, of the year, to Profit and Loss Account)			

Note: * Credit to Profit and Loss A/c = ₹.10,56,650 + ₹ 2,21,600 – ₹.4,25,254

= ₹.8,52,996

PROBLEM 16

The following facts have been taken out from the records of Dee Bank Ltd. as on 31st March, 2015:

	Dr. (₹)	*Cr.* (₹)
Rebate on Bills Discounted (not due on March 31st, 2014)		45,800
Discount Received		2,02,500
Bills Discounted	12,25,000	

An analysis of the bills discounted is as follows:

	Amount ₹	*Due date* 2015	*Rate of discount*
(i)	3,75,000	April 8	12%
(ii)	1,50,000	May 5	14%
(iii)	2,20,000	June 12	14%
(iv)	4,80,000	July 15	15%

You are required to:

(i) Calculate rebate on bills discounted as on 31st March, 2015.

(ii) The amount of discount to be credited to the Profit and Loss Account.

(iii) Show necessary journal entries in the books of Dee Bank Ltd. as on 31st March, 2015.

Solution

(I) CALCULATION OF REBATE ON BILLS DISCOUNTED

S.No.	*Amount* (₹)	*Due date*	*No. of Days after 31st March*	*Rate of Discount*	*Rebate on bills Discounted* (₹,)
(i)	3,75,000	April 8	8 days	12%	986
(ii)	1,50,000	May 5	35 days	14%	2,014
(iii)	2,20,000	June 12	73 days	14%	6,160
(iv)	4,80,000	July 15	106 days	15%	20,910
			Rebate on Bills Discounted		30,070

(II) AMOUNT OF DISCOUNT TO BE CREDITED TO THE PROFIT AND LOSS ACCOUNT

Particulars	₹
Opening Rebate on bills discounted	45,800
Add: Discount received during the year	2,02,500
	2,48,300
Less: Closing Rebate on bills discounted	(30,070)
Discount credited to Profit and Loss Account	2,18,230

JOURNAL OF DEE BANK LTD.

Date	Particulars	Dr. (₹)	Cr. (₹)
(1)	Rebate on Bills Discounted A/c Dr. To Discount on Bills A/c (Being the transfer of opening balance of rebate on bills discounted account to discount on bills account)	45,800	45,800
(2)	Discount on Bills A/c Dr. To Rebate on Bills Discounted A/c (Being the unexpired portion of discount in respect of the discounted bills of exchange carried forward)	30,070	30,070
(3)	Discount on Bills A/c Dr. To Profit and Loss A/c (Being the amount of income for the year transferred from Discount on bills A/c Profit and Loss A/c)	2,18,230	2,18,230

PROBLEM 17

Given below is an extract from the trial balance of *T.K.* Bank Limited as on 31st December 2014:

Particulars	Debit ₹	Credit ₹
Bills Discounted	12,64,000	—
Rebate on Bills Discounted (Opening)	—	8,340
Discount received for the year		85,912

AN ANALYSIS OF THE BILLS DISCOUNTED IS SHOWN BELOW

Amount ₹	Due date in 2015	Rate of discount (% p.a.)
1,40,000	March 6th	5
4,36,000	March 12th	4.5
2,82,000	March 26th	8
4,06,000	April 6th	4

Show the workings, how the relevant items will appear in the bank's Profit and Loss account as on 31st December, 2014 and in bank's Balance Sheet as on 31st December, 2014.

Solution

AN EXTRACT OF PROFIT & LOSS ACCOUNT
for the period ending 31.12.2014

Particulars	₹
Opening 'Rebate on bills discounted'	8,340
Add: Discount for the year	85,912
Less: Closing Rebate on bills discounted	(13,274)
	80,978

AN EXTRACT OF BALANCE SHEET AS ON 31.12.2014

Liabilities	₹
Other Liabilities & Provisions:	
Rebate on bills discounted	13,274

Working Note:

STATEMENT OF REBATE ON BILLS DISCOUNTED AS ON 31.12.2014

Due date	*Amount (₹)*	*No. of days after 31 Dec.*	*Rate of discount (%)*	*Discount of the unexpired period*
March 6th	1,40,000	65	5	1,247
March 12th	4,36,000	71	4.5	3,816
March 26th	2,82,000	85	6	3,940
April 6th	4,00,000	96	4	4.271
		Total Rebate on bills discounted to be carried forward		13,274

PROBLEM 18

As on 31st March 2014, Strong Bank Ltd. has a balance of ₹ 27 crores in "Rebate on Bills Discounted" Account. The bank provides you the following further information:

(1) During the financial year ending 31st March 2015, Strong Bank Ltd. discounted bills of exchange of ₹ 4,000 crores charging interest @ 15% p.a. and the average period of discount being 146 days.

(2) Bills of exchange of ₹ 600 crores were due for realization from the acceptors/customers after 31st March 2015, the average period outstanding after 31st March 2015, being 73 days.

You are required to pass necessary journal entries in the books of Strong Bank Ltd. for the above transactions.

Solution

JOURNAL OF STRONG BANK LTD. [₹ in Crores]

Particulars		*Dr. (₹)*	*Cr. (₹)*
Rebate on Bills Discounted A/c	Dr.	27	
To Discount on bills A/c			27
(Being the transfer of opening balance in 'Rebate on bills discounted A/c' to 'Discount on bills A/c')			
Bills Purchased and Discounted A/c	Dr.	4,000	
To Discount on Bills A/c			240
To Clients A/c			3,760
(Being the discounting of bills of exchange during the year)			
Discount on Bills A/c	Dr.	18	
To Rebate on Bills Discounted A/c			18
(Being the unexpired portion of discount in respect of the discounted bills of exchange carried forward)			

Discount on Bills A/c Dr.	249	
To Profit and Loss A/c		249
(Being the amount of income for the year from discounting of bills of exchange transferred to Profit *and loss A/c)*		

Working Notes:

(i) Discount received = ₹ 4,000 crores $\times \frac{15}{100} \times \frac{146}{365}$ = Rs. 240 crores

(ii) Rebate on bill discounted = Rs. 600 crores $\times \frac{15}{100} \times \frac{73}{365}$ = Rs. 18 crores

(it is assumed that discounting rate of 15% is used for the bill of ₹ 600 crores also)

(iii) Income from bills discounted transferred to Profit and Loss A/c would be calculated by preparing Discount on Bills A/c

₹ in crores

Date	*Particulars*	*₹*	*Date*	*Particulars*	*₹*
31.03.13	To Rebate on Bills Discounted	18	1.04.12	By Rebate on bills Discounted	27
	To Profit and Loss A/c (b.f.)	249	2014-13	By Bills Purchased and Discounted	240
		267			267

PROBLEM 19

The following particulars are extracted from the records of Mis. Engco Bank Limited for the year ended 31st March, 2015:

	Amount (₹)
Rebate on bills discounted (not due on March 31st, 2014)	60,610
Discount received	6,10,800
Bills discounted	24,42,250

An analysis of the bills discounted is as follows:

Amount (₹)	*Due Date*
3,75,000	April 15, 2015
4,90,000	May6, 2015
2,45,000	June 1,2015
3,68,000	June 20, 2015
4,85,000	July 4, 2015

The rate of discount is 12% per annum. You are required to:

(i) Calculate rebate on bills discounted as on 31st March, 2015.

(ii) Determine the amount of discount to be credited to the profit and loss account for the year ended 31st March, 2015.

(iii) Show the necessary journal entries in the books of M/s. Engco Bank Ltd. as on 31st March, 2015.

Solution

(I) CALCULATION OF REBATE ON BILLS DISCOUNTED AS ON 31ST MARCH, 2015

Amount (₹)	*Due date*	*No. of days after 31st March*	*Product*
3,75,000	April 15, 2015	15	56,25,000
4,90,000	May06, 2015	36	1,76,40,000
2,45,000	June 01, 2015	62	1,51,90,000
3,68,000	June 20, 2015	81	2,98,08,000
4,85,000	July 04, 2015	95	4,60,75,000
19,63,000			11,43,38,000

Amount of rebate on bills = ₹ 11,43,38,000 × 12% × 1/365 = ₹ 37,591 (approx.)

(II) DETERMINATION OF AMOUNT OF DISCOUNT TO BE CREDITED TO THE PROFIT AND LOSS ACCOUNT FOR THE YEAR ENDED 31ST MARCH, 2015

Particulars	₹
Opening Rebate on Bills Discounted	60,610
Add: Discount received during the year	6,10,800
	6,71,410
Less: Closing Rebate on bills discounted	(37,591)
Amount transferred to Profit and Loss Account	6,33,819

JOURNAL OF ENGCO BANK LTD.

Date	*Particulars*	*Dr. (₹)*	*Cr. (₹)*
(i)	Rebate on bills discounted A/c Dr.	60,610	
	To Discount on bills A/c		60,610
	(Being transfer of Opening unexpired discoount on bills)		
(ii)	Discount on bills A/c Dr.	37,591	
	To Rebate on bills discounted A/c		37,591
	(Being the closing unexpired discount provided)		
(iii)	Discount on bills A/c Dr.	6,33,819	
	To Profits Loss A/c		6,33,819
	(Being the t/f of discount earned)		

PROBLEM 20

The following particulars are extracted from the Books of the Commercial Bank Ltd. for the year ending 31st March, 2014.

(i)	Interest and Discounts	1,98,64,800
(ii)	Rebate on Bills Discounted (opening balance)	70,080
(iii)	Bills discounted and purchased	77,46,400

It is ascertained that proportionate discount not yet earned on the Bills Discounted which will mature during 2014-2015 amount to ₹ 96,860.

Pass the necessary Journal entries with narration adjusting the above and show:
(a) Rebate on Bills Discounted Account; and
(b) Interest and Discount Account in the ledger of the Commercial Bank Limited.

Solution

(A) JOURNAL OF THE COMMERCIAL BANK LTD.

Date	Particulars		Dr. (₹)	Cr. (₹)
March 31	Rebate on Bills Discounted A/c	Dr.	70,080	
	To Interest and Discount A/c			70,080
	(Being the amount of provision for unexpired discount brought forward from the previous year credited to interest and Discount A/c)			
March 31	Interest and Discount A/c	Dr.	96,860	
	To Rebate on Bills Discounted A/c			96,860
	(Being provision for unexpired discount required at the end of the current year)			
March 31	Interest and Discount A/c	Dr.	1,98,38,020	
	To Profit & Loss A/c			1,98,38,020
	(Being transfer of balance to Profit and Loss A/c)			

Dr. **REBATE ON BILLS DISCOUNTED ACCOUNT** Cr.

Date	Particulars	₹	Date	Particulars	₹
March 31	To Interest and Discount A/c	70,080	April 1	By Balance b/d	70,080
March 31	To Balance c/d	9,860	March 31,	By interest and Discount A/c (Rebate carried forwarded)	96,860
		1,66,940			1,66,940

(B) INTEREST AND DISCOUNT ACCOUNT

Date	Particulars	₹	Date	Particulars	₹
March 31	To Profit & Loss A/c (transfer)	1,98,38,020	April 1	By Rebate on Bills Discounted A/c (opening balance)	70,080
March 31	To Rebate on Bills Discounted A/c	96,860	March 31	By Bills Discounted & purchased	1,98,64,800
		1,99,34,880			1,99,34,880

PREPARATION OF SCHEDULE 9: ADVANCES

PROBLEM 21

How will you disclose the following Ledger balances in the Final accounts of DVD bank:

	₹ in lacs
Current accounts	700
Saving accounts	500
Fixed deposits	700

	₹ in lacs
Cash credits	600
Term Loans	500
Bills discounted & purchased	800

Additional information:

(i) Included in the current accounts ledger are accounts overdrawn to the extent of ₹ 250 lacs.
(ii) One of the cash credit account of ₹ 10 lacs (including interest ₹ 1 lac) is doubtful.
(iii) 60% of term loans are secured by government guarantees, 20% of cash credits are unsecured, other portion is secured by tangible assets.

Solution

RELEVANT SCHEDULES (FORMING PART OF THE BALANCE SHEET) OF DVD BANK

SCHEDULE 3: DEPOSITS

	₹ in lacs
A Demand Deposits (700 + 250)	950
B Saving Bank deposits	500
C Term Deposits	700
	2,150

Schedule 9: Advances

	₹ in lacs
A. (i) Bills Discounted and Purchased	800
(ii) Cash Credits and Overdrafts (600 + 250)	850
(iii) Term Loans	500
	2.150
B. (i)Secured by tangible assets (bal. fig.)	1,730
(ii) Secured by Bank/Government Guarantees (500 × 60%)	300
(iii) Unsecured (600 × 20%)	120
	2.150

Schedule 5: Other Liabilities & Provisions

	₹ in lacs
Others (Provision for doubtful debts)	10

Profit and Loss Account (an extract)

	₹ in lacs
Less: Provision for doubtful debts*	10

***Note:** It is assumed that the cash credit has been in 'doubtful' category for more than three years

BILLS FOR COLLECTION ACCOUNT

PROBLEM 22

From the following details, prepare bills for collection (Asset) Account and Bills for collection (Liability) Account:

	₹
On 1.4.2014, Bills for Collection were	51,00,000
During the year 2014– 2015 Bills received for Collection amounted to	75,00,000
Bill collected during the year 2014– 2015	98,47,000
Bill dishonoured and returned during the year	27,10,000

Solution

(b) *Dr.* **BILLS FOR COLLECTION (ASSET) ACCOUNT** *Cr.*

Date	*Particulars*	₹	*Date*	*Particulars*	₹
1.4.2014	To Balance b/d	51,00,000	Apr-Mar	By Bills for collection (Liability) A/c	98,47,000
Apr-Mar	To Bills for collection	75,00,000		By Bills for collection (Liability) A/c	27,10,000
			31.3.2015	By Balance c/d	43,000
		1,26,00,000			1,26,00,000
1.4.2015	To Balance b/d	43,000			

Dr. **BILLS FOR COLLECTION (LIABILITY) ACCOUNT** *Cr.*

Date	*Particulars*	₹	*Date*	*Particulars*	₹
Apr-Mar	To Bills for collection (Asset) A/c	98,47,000	1.4.2014	By Balance b/d	51,00,000
	To Bills for collection (Asset) A/c	27,10,000	Apr-Mar	By Bills for collection (Asset) A/c	75,00,000
31.3.2015	To Balance c/d	43,000			
		1,26,00,000			1,26,00,000
				By Balance b/d	43,000

Note: ** Sub standard and doubtful assets have been treated as fully secured.

CALCULATION OF RISK-ADJUSTED AND RISK WEIGHTED ASSETS AND CAPITAL ADEQUACY RATIO

PROBLEM 23

A loan outstanding of ₹.50,00,000 has DICGC cover. The loan guaranteed by DICGC is assigned a risk weight of 50%. What is the value of Risk-adjusted asset?

Solution

Loan outstanding	₹	50,00,000
Guaranteed by DICGC – Risk weight		50%
Value of Risk Adjusted Asset = ₹.50,00,000 × 50% =	₹	25,00,000

PROBLEM 24

A commercial Bank has the following capital funds and assets. Segregate the capital founds into Tier-1 and tire-II Capitals. Found out the Risk-Adjusted and Risk Weighted Assets and Capital Adequacy Ratio:

Capital Funds:	₹
Paid up Equity Share Capital	750
Statutory Reserve	150
Securities Premium	150
Capital Reserve (of which Capital Funds ₹ 40 Crore were due to revaluation of assets and balance due to sale)	
Assets:	
Cash balance with RBI	60
Claims on Banks	170
Other investments	2,300
Loss and Advances:	
Guaranteed by Government of India/State Government	400
Granted to Staff of bank fully covered by Supper Annuation	
Benefits and mortgage of Flat/house	50
Other Loans and Advances	6,170
Premises, Furniture and Fixtures, Other Assets	3,925
Intangible Assets	15
Off-Balance Sheet Items;	
Acceptance, Endorsements and Letter of Credit, Guarantees and Other obligations.	1,550

Solution

CALCULATION OF CAPITAL FUNDS

Particulars	*₹ in crores*	*₹ in crores*
(i) Capital Funds – Tier I		
Equity Share Capital		750
Statutory Reserve		150
Securities Premium		150
Capital reserve (arising out of sale of assets) (90 – 40)		50
		1,100
Less: Intangible Assets		(15)
		1,085
Capital Funds – Tier II		
Capital reserve (arising out of revaluation of assets)	40	
Less: Discount to the extent of 55%	(22)	18
		1,103

CALCULATION OF RISK ADJUSTED ASSETS

Particulars	*₹ in crores*	*% in risk weight*	*₹ in Crores*
(ii) Risk Adjusted Assets			
Funded Risk Assets			
Cash balance with RBI	60	0	0
Claims on banks	170	20	34
Other investments	2,300	100	2,300
Loans and advances:			
(i) Guaranteed by the government	400	0	0
(ii) Granted to staff of bank, fully covered by super Annuation Benefits and mortgage of Flat/House	50	20	10
(iii) Other loans and advances	6,170	100	6,170
Other assets			
Premises, furniture and fixtures and other assets	3,925	100	3,925
			12,439
Off Balance Sheet Items:			
Acceptances, endorsements and Letters of credit, Guarantees and other obligations	1,550	100	1,550
			13,989

$$\text{Capital Adequacy Ratio} = \frac{\text{Capital fund}}{\text{Risk adjusted assets}} \times 100 = \frac{\text{Rs 1,103 crores}}{\text{Rs 13,989 crores}} \times 100 = 7.89\%$$

PROBLEM 25

A Commercial Bank has the following capital funds and assets. Segregate the capital funds into Tier I and Tier II capitals. Find out the risk adjusted asset and risk weighted assets ratio.

	(₹ in crores)
Equity Share Capital	500.00
Statutory Reserve	270.00
Capital reserve (of which ₹ 16 crores were due to revaluation of assets and the balance due to sale of capital asset)	78.00
Assets:	
Cash balance with RBI	10.00
Balance with other banks	18.00
Other investments	36.00
Loans and advances:	
(i) Guaranted by the Government	16.50
(ii) Others	5,675.00
Premises, furniture and fixtures	78.00
Off-Balance Sheet items:	
(i) Guarantee and other obligations	800.00
(ii) Acceptances, endorsements and letter of credit	4,800.00

Solution

CALCULATION OF CAPITAL FUNDS

	₹ in crores	*₹ in crores*
Capital Funds-Tier I		
Equity ShareCapital		500
Statutory Reserve		270
Capital Reserve (arising out of sale of assets) (78-16)		62
		832
Capital Funds-Tier II		
Capital reserve (arising out of revaluation of assets)	16	
Less: Discount to the extent of 55%	(8.8)	7.2
		824.8

	₹ in crores	*% of weight*	*₹ in crores*
(ii) Risk Adjusted Assets			
Funded Risk Assets			
Cash balance with RBI	10	0	0
Balance with other banks	18	20	3.60
Other investments	36	100	36
Loans and advances:			
(i) Guaranteed by the government	16.5	0	0
(ii) Others	5,675	100	5,675
Premises, furniture and fixtures	78	100	78
			5,792.60

	₹ in crores	*Credit conversion factor*	
Off-Balance Sheet items:			
Guarantees and other obligations	800	100	800.00
Acceptances, endorsements and letters of credit	4,800	100	4,800.00
			11,392.60

Risk Weighted Assets Ratio:

$$\frac{\text{Capital Fund}}{\text{Risk Adjusted Assets}} \times 100 = (824.88 / 11{,}392.60) \times 100 = 7.24\%$$

PROBLEM 26

A Commercial Bank has the following Capital Funds and Assets. Segregate the Capital Funds into Tier I and Tier II capitals. Find out the Risk Adjusted Asset and Risk Weighted Asset Ratio. State your observation on the Risk Weighted Asset Ratio.

Particulars	*₹ Crores*
Equity Share Capital	400.00
Statutory Reserve	250.00
Capital Reserve (of which ₹ 18 Crores were deu to Revaluation of Assets & balance due to Sale of Capital Assets)	86.00
Assets:	
Cash Balance with RBI	12.00
Balance with other Banks	20.00
Other Investments	40.000
Loans & Advances	
(a) Guaranteed by Government	14.50
(b) Others	5,465.00
Premises, Furniture & Fixtures	74.00
Off Balance Sheet Items	
(a) Guarantees and Other Obligations	700.00
(b) Acceptance, Endorsements and Letter of Credit	4,900.00

Solution

1. Computation of Tier I and Tier II Capital

Particulars		*₹ Crores*
Tier I – Capital:	Equity Share Capital	400.00
	Statutory Reserve	250.00
	Capital Reserve arising out of Surplus on Sale of Assets = Total 86 – Revaluation of Assets 18	68.000
	Total (A)	**718.00**

Tier II – Capital: Revaluation Reserve		18.00
Less: Discount at 55%		(9.90)
Total	**(B)**	**8.10**
Grand Total	**(A + B)**	**726.10**

2. Computation of Risk Weighted Assets

Particulars	*(%) Weight*	*₹ Crores*	*₹ Crores*
Cash Balance with RBI	0	12.00	0
Balance with Other Banks	20	20.00	4.00
Other Investments (assumed Other than Equikty Shares) 40.00		100	40.00
Loans and Advances:			
(i) Guaranteed by the Government	0	14.50	0
(ii) Others	100	5,465.00	5,465.00
Premises, Furniture and FIxtures	100	74.00	74.00
Off-Balance Sheet Items:			
(i) Guarantees and other Obligations	100	700.00	700.00
(ii) Acceptance, Endorsements and Letter of Credit	100	4,900.00	4,900.00
Total			**11,183.00**

3. Capital to Risk-Weighted Assets Ratio (CRAR)

$$= \frac{\text{Capital Funds}}{\text{Risk Adjusted Assets}} \times 100 = \frac{726.00}{11183.00} \times 100 = 6.49\%.$$

Inference: Benchmark CRAR is 9% whereas the Bank's CRAR is only **6.49%.**
Higher the CRAR – better stability – less risky, and lower the CRAR – lower stability – more risky.

LONG ANSWER PRACTICAL QUESTIONS

PREPARATION OF PROFIT AND LOSS ACCOUNT

PROBLEM 27

From the following information, calculate the amount of Provisions and Contingencies and prepare Profit and Loss Account of 'Hamara Bank Limited' for the year ending 31st March, 2015:

	₹ in lakhs		*₹ in lakhs*
Interest and discount	4,430	Interest expended	1, 360
Other Income	125	Operating Expenses	1,331
Interest accrued on Investments	10		

Additional Information:

	₹
(i) Rebate on bills discounted to be provided for	15
(ii) Classifications of Advances:	
Standard Assets	2,500
Sub-Standard Assets	560
Doubtful Assets not covered by security	255
Doubtful Assets covered by security	
For 1 year	25
For 2 years	50
For 3 years	100
For 4 years	75
Loss Assets	100
(iii) Make tax provisions @ 35% of the profit.	
(iv) Profit and Loss Account (Cr.) brought forward from the previous year	40

Solution

(A) CALCULATION OF PROVISIONS AND CONTINGENCIES

(i) Provision on Non-Performing Assets*

Particulars	*Amount*	*% of Provision*	*₹ in lakhs Provision*
Standard Assets	2,500	0.4	10
Sub-standard Assets	560	15	84
Doubtful Assets not covered by security	255	100	255
Doubtful Assets covered by security:			
For 1 Year	25	25	6.25
For 2 Years	50	40	20
For 3 Years	100	40	40
For 4 Years	75	100	75
Loss Assets	100	100	100
	3,665		590.25

Note: It is assumed that all sub standards assets are fully secured.

(ii) Calculation of Provision for tax = 35% of [Total Income – Total Expenditure (excluding tax)]

= 35% of [(4,415 + 125) – (1,360 + 1,331 + 590.25)] = ₹ 440.5625 lakhs

Total Provisions and contingencies = Provisions on NPAs + Provisions for tax

= 590.25 + 440.5625 = 1030.8125 lakhs

HAMARA BANK LIMITED P & L AC FOR THE YEAR ENDED 31ST MARCH, 2015

Particulars	Schedule No.	₹ lakhs
I Income		
Interest Earned	13	4,415
OtherIncome		125
		4,540
II Expenditures		
Interest Expended		1,360
Operating Expenses		1,331
Provisions & Contingencies		1030.8125
		3721.8125
III Profit/Loss		
Net Profit/Loss for the year		818.1875
Profit/Loss brought forward		40
		858.1875
IV Appropriations		
Transfer to Statutory Reserve @25%of 818.1875		204.5469
Balance carried over to Balance Sheet		653.6406
		858.1875
Schedule 13 - Interest earned		
I Interest & Discount (4,430 – 15 (Rebate) – 10 (Accrued Interest)		4405
II Income on Investments		10
		4,415

PROBLEM 28

The following are the figures extracted from the books of New Generation Bank Limited as on 31.3.2015:

	₹
Interest and discount received	37,05,738
Interest paid on deposits	20,37,452
Issued and Subscribed capital	10,00,000
Salaries and allowances	2,00,000
Directors fee and allowances	30,000
Rent and Taxes paid	90,000
Postage and Telegrams	60,286
Statutory reserve fund	8,00,000
Commission, exchange and brokerage	1,90,000
Rent received	65,000
Profit on sale of investments	2,00,000
Depreciation on Bank's properties	30,000
Statutory expenses	40,000
Preliminary expenses	25,000
Auditor's fees	5,000

The following further information is given:

(i) A customer to whom a sum of ₹ 10 lakhs has been advanced has become insolvent and it is expected only 50% can be recovered from his estate.

(ii) There were also other debts for which a provision of ₹ 1,50,000 was found necessary by the auditors.

(iii) Rebate on Bills discounted on 31.3.2014 was ₹ 12,000 and on 31.3.2015 was ₹ 16,000.

(iv) Provide ₹ 6,50,000 for Income-tax.
(v) The Directos desire to declare 10% dividend.

Required: Prepare the Profit and Loss account of New Generation Bank Limited for the year ended 31.3.2015 and also show, how the Profit and Loss account will appear in the Balance Sheet, if the Profit and Loss account opening balance was Nil as on 31.3.2014.

Solution

NEW GENERATION BANK LIMITED

Profit and Loss Account for the year ended 31st March, 2015

	Particulars	*Schedule*	*Year ended 31.03.2015*
I.	**Income:**		
	Interest earned	13	3,701.74
	Other income	14	455.00
	Total		4,156.74
II.	**Expenditure**		
	Interest expended	15	2,037.45
	Operating expenses	16	480.29
	Provisions and Contingencies (₹ 5,00,000 + 1,50,000 + 6,50,000)		1,300.00
	Total		3,817.74
III.	**Profits / Losses**		
	Net Profit for the year		339.00
	Profit brought forward		NIL
			339.00
IV.	**Appropriations**		
	Transfer to Statutory Reserve (25%)		84.75
	Proposed Dividend		100.00
	Balance carried over to Balance Sheet		154.25
			339.00

The Profit & Loss Account balance of ₹ ('000) 154.25 will appear in the Balance Sheet under the head 'Reserve and Surplus' in Schedule 2.

Schedule 13 – Interest Earned

		Year ended 31.03.2015 ₹ ('000)
I.	**Income:**	
	Interest earned	3,701.74
		3,701.74

Schedule 14 – Other Income

I.	Commission, exchange and brokerage	190.00
II.	Profit on sale of investments	200.00
III.	Rent received	65.00
		455.00

Schedule 15–Interest Expended

I.	Interests on Deposits	2,037.45

Schedule 16 – Operating Expenses

I.	Payment to and provisions for employees	200.00
II.	Rent, taxes and lighting	90.00
III.	Depreciation on Bank's property	30.00
IV.	Director's fees, allowances and expenses	30.00
V.	Auditor's fees	5.00
VI.	Law (statutory) charges	40.00
VII.	Postage and telegrams	60,29
VIII.	Preliminary expenses	*25.00
		480.29

*As per AS 26, preliminary expenses have been fully written off.

Working Note:

Interest/discount (net of rebate on bills discounted) (W.N. 1)	3,705.74
Add: Rebate on bills discounted on 31.3.2007	12.00
Less: Rebate on bills discounted on 31.3.2008	(16.00)
	3,701.74

PROBLEM 29

From the following information, you are required to prepare Profit and Loss Account of Zee Bank Ltd., for the year ending 31st March, 2015:

	₹		₹
Interest and Discount	44,00,000	Interest expended	13,60,000
Other Income	1,25,000	Operating expenses	13,31,000
Income on investments	5,000	Interest on balance with RBI	25,000

Additional information:

(a) Rebate on bills discounted to be provided for ₹ 15,000

(b) Classification of advances:

	₹
Standard assets	25,00,000
Sub-standard assets	5,60,000
Doubtful assets not covered by security	2,55,000
Doubtful assets covered by security	
For 1 year	25,000
For 2 years	50,000
For 3 years	1,00,000
For 4 years	75,000
Loss assets	1,00,000

(c) Make tax Provision @ 35%

(d) Profit and Loss A/c (Cr.) ₹ 40,000.

Solution

Form 'B'
ZEE BANK LTD.
PROFIT & LOSS ACCOUNT FOR THE YEAR ENDED 31ST MARCH, 2015

	Particulars	*Schedule No.*	*Year ended 31st March, 2015*
I.	**Income:**		
	Interest Earned	13	44,15,000
	Other Income	14	1,25,000
	Total		45,40,000
II.	**Expenditure**		
	Interest Expended	15	13,60,000
	Operating Expense	16	13,31,000
	Provisions and Contingencies		10,30,813
	Total		37,21,813
III.	**Profit/Loss**		
	Net profit for the year		8,18,187
	Profit brought forward		40,000
	Total		8,58,187
IV.	**Appropriations:**		
	Transfer to Statutory Reserve (@ 25% on ₹ 8,18,187)		2,04,547
	Balance carried forward to Balance Sheet		6,53,640
	Total		8,58,187

Schedule 13: Interest Earned

Particulars	₹
Interest and discount [44,00,000 – 15,000 (Rebate)]	43,85,000
Income on Investment	5,000
Interest on balance with RBI	25,000
Total	44,15,000

Working Notes:

(I) CALCULATION OF PROVISIONS ON ASSETS

Particulars	*Amount* ₹	*% of Provisions*	*Provision* ₹
Standard assets	25,00,000	0.40	10,000
Sub-standard assets (assumed all fully secured)	5,60,000	15	84,000
Doubtful assets not covered by security	2,55,000	100	2,55,000
Doubtful assets covered by security			
For 1 year	25,000	25	6,250
For 2 years	50,000	40	20,000
For 3 years	1,00,000	40	40,000
For 4 years	75,000	100	75,000
Loss assets	1,00,000	100	1,00.000
			5,90,250

(ii) Calculation of Provision for tax

Tax = 35% of [Total Income – Total Expenditure (excluding tax)].

Tax = 35% of [₹ 44,15,000 + ₹ 1,25,000 – (₹ 13,60,000 + ₹ 13,31,000 + ₹ 5,90,250)]

Tax = ₹ 4,40,563

(iii) Total Amount of Provisions and Contingencies

= Provision for non-performing assets + Provision for tax + Rebate on bills discounted

= ₹ 5,90,250 + ₹ 4,40,563 = ₹ 10,30,813

PROBLEM 30

From the following information prepare the Profit & Loss Account of Jawahar Bank Limited for the year ended 31st March, 2015. Also give necessary Schedules.

	Figures are in ₹ thousands
Interest earned on term loans	17.26
Interest earned on term loans classified as NPA	4.52
Interest received on term loans classified as NPA	2. 04
Interest on cash credits and overdrafts	38.54
Interest earned but not received on cash credit and overdraft treated as NPA	8.39
Interest on deposits	27.20
Commission	1.97
Profit on sale of investments	11.76
Profit on revaluation of investments	2. 76
Income from investments	15.53
Salaries, bonus and allowances	18. 75
Rent, taxes and lighting	1. 70
Printing and stationary	0. 75
Director's fees, allowances expenses	1.33
Law charges	0.22
Repairs and maintenance	0. 18
Insurance	0.30
Other information:	
Make necessary provision on risk assets:	
(i) Sub-standard	15.00
(ii) Doubtful for one year	7.00
(iii) Doubtful for two years	2.40
(iv) Loss assets	0.65
Investments	3700

Bank should not keep more than 25% of its investments as 'held-for-maturity' investment. The market value of its best 75% investments is ₹ 9,00,000 as on 31st March, 2015.

Solution

JAWAHAR BANK LIMITED
PROFIT & LOSS ACCOUNT FOR THE YEAR ENDED 31ST MARCH, 2015

Particulars	*Schedule*	*₹ '000s*
I. Income		
Interest earned	13	60.46
Other income	14	16.49
Total		76.95
II. Expenditure		
Interest expended	15	27.20
Operating expenses	16	23.23
Provisions & Contingencies (Refer W.N.)		1880.61
Total		1931.04
III. Profit/Loss		(1854.09)
IV. Appropriations		Nil

Schedule 13 - Interest Earned

	Rs'000s
Interest/discount on advances bills	
Interest on term loans [17.26 – (4.52 – 2.04)]	14.78
Interest on cash credits and overdrafts (38.54 – 8.39)	30.15
Income on investments	15.53
	60.46

Note: Interest on non-performing assets is recognized on receipt basis.

Schedule 14 - Other Income

	Rs'000s
Commission, exchange and brokerage	1.97
Profit on sale of investments	11.76
Profit on revaluation of investments	2.76
	16.49

Schedule 15 - Interest Expended

	Rs'000s
Interest on deposits	27.20

Schedule 16 - Operating Expenses

	Rs'000s
Payments to and provision for employees - salaries, bonus and allowances	18.75
Rent, taxes and lighting	1.70
Printing & stationery	0.75
Director's fee, allowances and expenses	1.33
Law charges	0.22
Repairs & maintenance	0.18
Insurance	0.30
	23.23

Working Note:

Provisions & Contingencies		₹ '000s
Provision for non-performing assets*		
Sub-standard (15 × 15%)		2.25
Doubtful for one year (7 × 25%)		1.75
Doubtful for two years (2. 40 x 40%)		0.96
Loss Assets (0.65 × 100%)		0.65
		5.61
Diminution in the value of current Investments:		
Cost 75% of ₹ 3,700 thousands**	27,75	
Less: Market value	(900)	1875.00
		1880.61

Note: It is assumed that all sub-standard and doubtful assets are fully secured.

**25% of investments classified as 'held for maturity' need not be marked to market as per RBI Guidelines. However, the remaining 75% investments have been marked to market according to RBI Guidelines.

PROBLEM 31

The following are the figures extracted from the books of KLM Bank Limited as on 31.3.2015:

	₹
Interest and discount received	38,00,160
Interest paid on deposits	22,95,360
Issued and Subscribed capital	10,00,000
Salaries and allowances	2,50,000
Directors fee and allowances	35,000
Rent and Taxes paid	1,00,000
Postage and Telegrams	65,340
Statutory Reserve Fund	8,00,000
Commission, Exchange and Brokerage	1,90,000
Rent received	72,000
Profit on sale of Investments	2,25,800
Depreciation on Bank's properties	40,000
Statutory Expenses	38,000
Preliminary Expenses	30,000
Auditor's Fees	12,000

The following further information is given:

(i) A customer to whom a sum of ₹ 10 lakhs has been advanced has become insolvent and it is expected only 55% can be recovered from his estate.

(ii) There were also other debts for which a provision of ₹ 2,00,000 was found necessary by the auditors.

(iii) Rebate on Bills discounted on 31.3.2014 was ₹ 15,000 and on 31.3.2015 was ₹ 20,000.

(iv) Provide ₹ 2,00,000 for Income-tax.

(v) The Directos desire to declare 5% dividend.

Required: Prepare the Profit and Loss account of KLM Bank Limited for the year ended 31.3.2015 and also show, how the Profit and Loss account will appear in the Balance Sheet, if the Profit and Loss account opening balance was Nil as on 31.3.2014.

Solution

KLM BANK LIMITED

PROFIT AND LOSS ACCOUNT FOR THE YEAR ENDED 31ST MARCH, 2015

	Particulars	*Schedule*	*Year ended 31.03.2015*
I.	**Income:**		
	Interest earned	13	37,95,160
	Other income	14	4,87,800
	Total		42,82,960
II.	**Expenditure**		
	Interest expended	15	22,95,360
	Operating expenses	16	5,70,340
	Provisions and Contingencies (₹ 4,50,000 + 2,00,000 + 2,00,000)		8,50,000
	Total		37,15,700
III.	**Profits / Losses**		
	Net Profit for the year		5,67,260
	Profit brought forward		NIL
			5,67,260
IV.	**Appropriations**		
	Transfer to Statutory Reserve (25%)		1,41,815
	Proposed Dividend		50,000
	Balance carried over to Balance Sheet		3,75,445
			5,67,260

The Profit & Loss Account balance of ₹ 3,75,445 will appear in the Balance Sheet under the head 'Reserve and Surplus' in Schedule 2.

Schedule 13 – Interest Earned

		Year ended 31.03.2015 ₹
I.	**Income:**	
	Interest earned	37,95,160

Schedule 14 – Other Income

I.	Commission, exchange and brokerage	1,90,000
II.	Profit on sale of investments	2,25,800
III.	Rent received	72,000
		4,87,800

Schedule 15–Interest Expended

I.	Interests on Deposits	22,95,360

Schedule 16 – Operating Expenses

I.	Payment to and provisions for employees	2,50,000
II.	Rent, taxes and lighting	1,00,000
III.	Depreciation on Bank's property	40,000
IV.	Director's fees, allowances and expenses	35,000
V.	Auditor's fees	12,000
VI.	Law (statutory) charges	38,000
VII.	Postage and telegrams	65,340
VIII.	Preliminary expenses*	30,000
		5,70,340

*As per AS 26 Preliminary Expenses have been fully written off.

Working Note:

Interest/discount (net of rebate on bills discounted) (W.N. 1)	38,00,160
Add: Opening Rebate on bills discounted	15,000
Less: Closing Rebate on bills discounted	(20,000)
	37,95,160

PREPARATION OF BALANCE SHEET

PROBLEM 32

From the following information, prepare a Balance Sheet of CANID Bank Ltd. as on 31st March, 2015 giving the relevant schedules and also specify at least four important Principal Accounting Policies:

(₹ in lakhs)

Particulars	*Dr. (₹)*	*Cr. (₹)*
Share Capital 19,80,000 Shares of ₹ 10 each		198.00
Statutory Reserve		231.00
Net Profit Before Appropriation		150.00
Profit and Loss Account		412.00
Fixed Deposit Account		517.00
Savings Deposit Account		450.00
Current Accounts	28.00	520.12
Bills Payable		0.10
Cash Credits	812.10	
Borrowing from other Banks		110.00
Cash on Hand	160.15	
Cash with RBI	37.88	
Cash with other Banks	155.87	
Money at Call	210.12	
Gold	55.23	
Government Securities	110.17	
Premises	155.70	
Furniture	70.12	
Term Loan	792.88	
	2,588.22	2,588.22

Additional Information:

Bills for collection		18,10,000
Acceptances and endorsements		14,12,000
Claims against the Bank not acknowledged as debt		55,000
Depreciation charge—	Premises	1,10,000
	Furniture	78,000

50% of the Term Loans are secured by Government guarantees. 10% of cash credit is unsecured. Also calculate cash reserves required and statutory liquid reserves required.

Note: *Cash reserve required 3% of demand and time liabilities; liquid reserves required 25% of demand and time liabilities.*

Solution

BALANCE SHEET OF CANID BANK LTD. AS ON 31ST MARCH, 2015

(₹ in lakhs)

Particulars	*Schedule No.*	*As on 31st March 2015 (₹ '000)*	*As on 31st March 2014 (₹ '000)*
Capital and Liabilities:			
Share Capital	1	1,98.00	
Reserves and Surplus	2	7,93.00	
Deposits	3	14,87.12	
Borrowings	4	1,10.00	
Other liabilities and provisions	5	0.10	
		25,88.22	

Assets:			
Cash and balances with RBI	6	2,04.76	
Balances with banks and money at call and short notice	7	3,59.26	
Investments	8	1,65.40	
Advances	9	16,32.98	
Fixed Assets	10	2,25.82	
Other Assets	11	—	
		25,88.22	
Contingent Liabilities	12	14.67	
Bills for Collection		18.10	

Schedule 1—Capital

Particulars	*As on 31st March, 2015 (₹ '000)*	*As on 31st March, 2014 (₹ '000)*
Authorized Capital		
Issued, Subscribed and Paid up Capital	19,800	
19,80,000 shares of ₹ 10 each	19,800	

Schedule 2—Reserves and Surplus

Particulars	*As on 31st March, 2015 (₹ '000)*	*As on 31st March, 2014 (₹ '000)*
(1) Statutory Reserve-Opening balance	2,31.00	
Additions during the year	37.50	
	268.50	
(2) Balance in Profit & Loss Account [Refer to Working Note (i)]	524.50	
	7,93.00	

Schedule 3—Deposits

Particulars	*As on 31st March, 2015 (₹ '000)*	*As on 31st March, 2014 (₹ '000)*
(i) Demand deposits from others	5,20.12	
(ii) Saving bank deposits	4,50.00	
(iii) Fixed Deposits	5,17.00	
	14,87.12	

Schedule 4—Borrowing

Particulars	*As on 31st March, 2015 (₹ '000)*	*As on 31st March, 2014 (₹ '000)*
Borrowing in India-Other banks	1,10.00	

Schedule 5—Other Liabilities and Provisions

Particulars	*As on 31st March, 2015 (₹ '000)*	*As on 31st March, 2014 (₹ '000)*
Other liabilities and provisions	0.10	

Schedule 6—Cash and balance with RBI

Particulars	*As on 31st March, 2015 (₹ '000)*	*As on 31st March, 2014 (₹ '000)*
(i) Cash in hand	1,60.15	
(ii) Balances with RBI-		
In current account [Refer to Working Note (ii)]	44.61	
	2,04.76	

Schedule 7—Balance with Banks and money at call and short notice

Particulars	*As on 31st March, 2015 (₹ '000)*	*As on 31st March, 2014 (₹ '000)*
I. In India		
(i) Balances with Banks		
(a) in current accounts		
[Refer to Working Note (iii)]	1,49.14	
(ii) Money at call and short notice	2,10.12	
	3,59.26	

Schedule 8—Investments

Particulars	*As on 31st March, 2015 (₹ '000)*	*As on 31st March, 2014 (₹ '000)*
(1) Investments in India in		
(i) Government securities	1,10.17	
(ii) Others—Gold	55.23	
	1,65.40	

Schedule 9—Advances

Particulars	*As on 31st March, 2015 (₹ '000)*	*As on 31st March, 2014 (₹ '000)*
A.(i) Cash credits, overdrafts	8,40.10	
(ii) Term Loans	7,92.88	
	16,32.98	
B.(i) Secured by tangible assets	11,52.53	
(ii) Secured by bank/govt. guarantees	3,96.44	
(iii) Unsecured	84.01	
	16,32.98	

Schedule 10—Fixed Assets

Particulars	*As on 31st March, 2015 (₹ '000)*	*As on 31st March, 2014 (₹ '000)*
1. Premises		
At cost on 31st March, 2014	156.80	
Depreciation to date	1.10	
	155.70	
2. Other Fixed Assets		
Furniture at cost on 31st March, 2014	70.90	
Depreciation to date	0.78	
	70.12	
Total (1 + 2)	2,25.82	

Schedule 11—Other Assets

Nil

Schedule 12—Contingent Liabilities

Particulars	*As on 31st March, 2015 (₹ '000)*	*As on 31st March, 2014 (₹ '000)*
(i) Claims against bank not acknowledged as debts	0.55	
(ii) Acceptances, endorsements	14.12	
	14.67	

Calculation of cash reserves and statutory liquid reserves

Total of demand & time liabilities (₹ 5,17.00 + ₹ 4,50.00 + ₹ 5,20.12)	14,87.12
Cash reserves (3% of above)	44.61
Statutory liquid reserves (25% of demand and time liabilities)	371.78

Working Notes:

(i) *Balance in Profit & Loss Account:*

Net Profit before appropriation	1,50.00
Add: Profit for the year	4,12.00
	5,62.00
Less: Transfer of Statutory Reserve (25% of 1,50.00)	37.50
	5,24.50

(ii) *Transfer from Cash with other banks to Cash with RBI*

Cash reserve required	44.61
Cash with RBI	37.88
Transfer needed to maintain cash reserve	6.73

(iii) *Liquid Assets:*

Cash on hand	1,60.15
Cash with other Banks (155.87 – 6.73)	1,49.14
Money at call and short notice	2,10.12
Gold	55.23
Government securities	1,10.17
	6,84.81
Excess Liquidity (6,84.81 – 371.78)	313.03

Principal Accounting Policies:

(a) *Foreign Exchange Transactions*

(i) Monetary assets and liabilities have been translated at the exchange rate prevailing at the close of the year. Non-monetary assets have been carried in the books at the historical cost.

(ii) Income and Expenditure in respect of Indian branches have been translated at the exchange rates on the date of transactions and in respect of foreign branches at the exchange rates prevailing at the close of the year.

(iii) Profit or Loss on foreign currency position including pending forward exchange contracts have been accounted for all the exchange rates prevailing at the close of the year.

(b) *Investments:*

Permanent category investments are valued at cost. Valuation of investment in current category depends on the nature of securities. While valuation of government securities held as current investments have been made on yield to maturity basis, the investments in shares of companies are valued on the basis of book value.

(c) *Advances:*

Advances due from sick nationalized units under nursing programmes and in respect of various sticky, suit filed and decreed accounts have been considered good on the basis of....

(i) Available estimated value of existing and prospective primary and collateral securities including personal worth of the borrowers and guarantors.

(ii) The proposed/on going revival/rehabilitation programmes.

(iii) The claim lodged/to be lodged under various credit guarantee schemes.

(iv) Pending settlement of claims by Govt.

Provisions to the satisfaction of auditors have been made and deducted from advances. Tax relief available when the advance is written off will be accounted for in the year of write-off.

(d) *Fixed Assets:*

The premises and other fixed assets except for foreign branches are accounted for at their historical cost. Depreciation has been provided on written down value method at the rates specified in the Income Tax Rules, 1962. Depreciation in respect of assets of foreign branches has been provided as per the local laws.

37 FINANCIAL STATEMENTS OF ELECTRICITY COMPANIES

PROBLEM 1

The CAS Electricity Company Ltd. decided to replace some parts of its plant by an improved plant. The plant to be replaced was built in 2012 for ₹ 27,00,000. It is estimated that it would now cost ₹ 40,00,000 to build a new plant of the same size and capacity. The cost of the new plant as per the improved design was ₹ 85,00,000 and, in addition, material belonging to the old plant valued at ₹ 2,75,000 were used in the construction of the new plant. The balance of the plant was sold for ₹ 1,50,000. Compute the amount to be written of to revenue and to be capatilised.

Required: Give the necessary journal entries and prepare Plant Account and Replacement Account.

Solution

Statement Showing the Computation of Amount to be Written off to Revenue Account

	Particulars		₹
A	Old Cost of Old Asset		27,00,000
B	Effect of increase in various Components of Old Cost		13,00,000
C	Current Cost of Old Assets (A + B)		40,00,000
D	*Less:* Recoveries from old Asset		
	(a) Sale Proceeds of Old Material	1,50,000	
	(b) Value of Old Materials Reused	2,75,000	4,25,000
E	Amount to be written off to Revenue A/c (C – D)		35,75,000

Statement Showing the Computation of Amount to be Capitalised

	Particulars	₹
A	Cash Cost of New Asset (Excluding the value of Old Material if any reused)	85,00,000
B	*Less:* Current Cost of Old Assets	(40,00,000)
C	Current Cash Cost to be Capitalised (A – B)	45,00,000
D	*Add:* Value of Old Materials Reused	2,75,000
E	Current Total Cost to be Capitalised (C + D)	47,75,000

Journal

Particulars		*L.F.*	*Dr. (₹)*	*Cr. (₹)*
Plant A/c	Dr.		45,00,000	
Replacement A/c	Dr.		40,00,000	
To Bank A/c				85,00,000
(Being the replacement of old plant by a new plant. The current cash cost of replacement being ₹ 40,00,000 and additional cost ₹ 45,00,000)				
Plant A/c	Dr.		2,75,000	
To Replacement A/c				2,75,000
(Being the old materials used in construction of the new plant)				

Particulars	L.F.	Dr. (₹)	Cr. (₹)
Bank A/c Dr. To Replacement A/c (Being the amount realised on account of sale of the old Materials)		1,50,000	1,50,000
Revenue A/c Dr. To Replacement A/c (Being the balance of replacement account transferred to revenue account)		35,75,000	35,75,000

Dr. **Plant Account** Cr.

Particulars	₹	Particulars	₹
To Balance b/d	27,00,000	By Balance c/d	74,75,000
To Bank A/c	45,00,000		
To Replacement A/c	2,75,000		
	74,75,000		74,75,000

Dr. **Replacement Account** Cr.

Particulars	₹	Particulars	₹
To Bank A/c	40,00,000	By Plant A/c	2,75,000
		By Bank A/c	1,50,000
		By Revenue A/c	35,75,000
	40,00,000		40,00,000

PROBLEM 2

C AMIC Ltd. an electricity company laid down a main at a cost of ₹ 50,00,000. Some years later, the company laid down an auxillary main for one-fifth of the length of the old main at a cost of ₹ 15,00,000. It also replaced the rest of the length of the old main at a cost of ₹ 60,00,000, the cost of materials and labour having gone up by 15 percent. Sale of old materials realised ₹ 80,000. In addition, Old materials valued at ₹ 1,00,000 were used in renewal and those valued at ₹ 50,000 were used in the construction of the auxillary main.

Required: Give the Journal entries for recording the above transactions.

Solution

Journal

Particulars	L.F.	Dr. (₹)	Cr. (₹)
New Main A/c Dr. Replacement A/c Dr. To Bank A/c (Being the current cost of replacement of 4/5th of the old main charged to Replacement A/c)		14,00,000 46,00,000	60,00,000
New Main A/c Dr. To Replacement A/c (Being the cost of old material used ₹ 1,00,000)		1,00,000	1,00,000

Particulars		L.F.	Dr. (₹)	Cr. (₹)
New Auxilliary Main A/c	Dr.		15,50,000	
To Bank A/c				15,00,000
To Replacement A/c				50,000
(Being the capitalisation of cost incurred on laying auxiliary main including old material worth ₹ 50,000)				
Bank A/c	Dr.		80,000	
To Replacement A/c				80,000
(Being the sale of old materials)				
Revenue A/c	Dr.		43,70,000	
To Replacement A/c				43,70,000
(Being the transfer of balance in Replacement A/c to Revenue A/c)				

Statement Showing the Computation of Amount to be written off to Revenue A/c

Particulars		₹
A. Old Cost of 4/5th of Old Asset (₹ 50,00,000 × 4/5)		40,00,000
B. Effect of increase in various Components of Old Cost [15% of ₹ 40,00,000]		6,00,000
C. Current Cost of Old Asset (A + B)		46,00,000
D. *Less:* Recoveries from Old Asset		
(a) Sale Proceeds of Old Material	80,000	
(b) Value of Old Materials Reused	1,50,000	2,30,000
E. Amount to be written off to Revenue A/c (C – D)		43,70,000

Statement Showing the Computation of Amount to be Capitalised

Particulars	₹
A. Cash Costs of New Asset (Excluding the value of Old Material if any reused)	60,00,000
B. *Less:* Current Cost of Old Asset	46,00,000
C. Current Cash Cost to be Capitalised (A – B)	14,00,000
D. *Add:* Value of Old Materials Reused	1,00,000
E. Current Total Cost to be Capitalised (C + D)	15,00,000

PROBLEM 3

CAMHI Power Supply Co. Ltd. has built a power station and the connecting lines during the year 2012. The following further particulars are furnished to you:

(i) In the year 2012, the company incurred an amount of ₹ 35,78,200, towards purchase of Machinery items and ₹ 3,97,500 towards labour expenses. The company also used stores worth ₹ 7,82,300 from its existing stock which was in the godown.

(ii) Extension and replacement was carried out to the power station in the year 2015 at a cost of ₹ 15,20,000, out of which material worth ₹ 30,000 was used from existing stock for replacement purposes. The extent of replacement was estimated at 20% of original cost.

(iii) The cost of materials and wages in 2015 have gone up by 25%.

(iv) The old material discarded in the process of extension and replacement was of the value of ₹ 1,42,000

(v) Out of the above, material valued at ₹ 75,000 was used for extension purposes and the balance not being used was sold for ₹ 67,000.

Required: Show the journal entries in respect of the above transactions for the year 2012 and 2015.

Solution

Journal

Date	*Particulars*		*L.F.*	*Dr. (₹)*	*Cr. (₹)*
2012	New Works A/c	Dr.		47,58,000	
	To Bank A/c				39,75,700
	To Stores A/c				7,82,300
	(Being the cost of power station & connecting lines—machinery ₹ 35,78,200 labour expenses ₹ 3,97,500 and stores ₹ 7,82,300, capitalised)				
2015	New Works A/c	Dr.		3,30,500	
	Replacement A/c	Dr.		11,89,500	
	To Bank A/c				14,90,000
	To Stores A/c				30,000
	(Being the cost of 20% replacement and extension cost of ₹ 3,30,500 capitalised)				
	Bank A/c	Dr.		67,000	
	New Works A/c	Dr.		75,000	
	To Replacement A/c				1,42,000
	(Being the cost of old material used in New Works ₹ 75,000 and balance sold for ₹ 67,000)				
	Revenue A/c	Dr.		10,47,500	
	To Replacement A/c				10,47,500
	(Being the balance of replacement account t/f to Revenue A/c)				

Working Notes:

(i) It has been assumed that total cost including purchase of Machinery in 2015 has gone up by 25%.

(ii) It has been assumed that the cost of old material used is not included in ₹ 15,20,000. Cost of new works given in the question.

(iii) Statement Showing the Computation of Amount to be written off to Revenue A/c

	Particulars		₹.
A	Old Cost of Old Asset 20% of [35,78,200 + 3,97,500 + 7,82,300]		9,51,600
B	Effect of increase in various Components of Old Cost [25% of 9,51,600]		2,37,900
C	Current Cost of Old Asset [A + B]		11,89,500
D	*Less:* Recoveries from Old Asset		
	(a) Sale Proceeds of Old Material	67,000	
	(b) Value of Old Materials Reused	75,000	1,42,000
E.	Amount to be written off to Revenue A/c (C – D)		10,47,500

(iv) Statement Showing the Computation of Amount to be Capitalised

	Particulars	₹.
A	Cash Cost of New Asset (Excluding the value of Old Material, if any, reused)	15,20,000
B	*Less:* Current Cost of Old Asset	11,89,500
C	Current Cash Cost to be Capitalised (A – B)	3,30,500
D	*Add:* Value of Old Materials Reused	75,000
E	Current Total Cost to be Capitalised (C + D)	4,05,500

PROBLEM 4

The CAMHA Electricity Company Limited decides to replace one of its old plants with a modern one with a larger capacity. The plant when installed in 2001 cost the company ₹ 24 lakhs, the components of materials, labour and overheads being in the ratio of 5 : 3 : 2. It is ascertained that the costs of materials and labour have gone up by 40% and 80% respectively. The proportion of overheads to total costs is expected to remain the same as before.

The cost of the new plant as per improved design is ₹ 60 lakhs and in addition, material recovered from the old plant of a value of ₹ 2,40,000 has been used in the construction of the new plant. The old plant was scraped and sold for ₹ 7,50,000.

The accounts of the company are maintained under the Double Account system.

Required: Indicate how much would be capitalised and the amount that would be charged to revenue. Show the ledger accounts.

Solution

Statement Showing the Computation of Amount to be written off to Revenue A/c

	Particulars		₹
A	Old Cost of Old Asset		24,00,000
B	Effect of increase in various Components of old Cost		
	(a) Increase in Material Cost [40% of ₹ 12,00,000]	4,80,000	
	(b) Increase in Labour Cost [80% of ₹ 7,20,000]	5,76,000	
	(c) Increase in Overheads [25% of (₹ 4,80,000 + ₹ 5,76,000]	2,64,000	13,20,000
C.	Current Cost of Old Asset (A + B)		37,20,000
D.	*Less:* Recoveries from Old Asset		
	(a) Sale Proceeds of Old Material	7,50,000	
	(b) Value of Old Materials Reused	2,40,000	9,90,000
E.	Amount to be written off to Revenue A/c (C – D)		27,30,000

Statement Showing the Computation of Amount to be Capitalised

	Particulars	₹
A	Cash Costs of New Assets (Excluding the value of Old Material, if any, reused)	60,00,000
B	*Less:* Current Cost of Old Asset	37,20,000
C	Current Cash Cost to be Capitalised (A – B)	22,80,000
D	*Add:* Value of Old Materials Reused	2,40,000
E	Current Total Cost to be Capitalised (C + D)	25,20,000

Dr. **Plant Account** Cr.

Particulars	₹	Particulars	₹
To Balance b/d	24,00,000	By Balance c/d	49,20,000
To Bank A/c (Cost of new plant capitalised)	22,80,000		
To Replacement A/c (old parts)	2,40,000		
	49,20,000		49,20,000

Dr. **Replacement Account** Cr.

Particulars	₹	Particulars	₹
To Bank A/c	37,20,000	By Plant A/c (old material used)	2,40,000
		By Revenue A/c (Transfer)	27,30,000
	37,20,000		37,20,000

PROBLEM 5

Messrs CANGB Gas Co. Ltd. rebuilds its works at a cost of ₹ 3,30,000. In the process, it completely replaces a part of the old works which had cost ₹ 1,30,000. In constructing the new works, old materials worth ₹ 4,600 has been used and the value is included in the cost of the new works. The balance of the material resulting from the old works which is replaced is sold for ₹ 10,000. In the cost of the works which is replaced, the cost of material was 70 per cent and of labour 30 per cent and the present cost of material and labour have increased by $12\frac{1}{2}$ per cent and 15 per cent respectively.

Assuming the accounts are maintained under the "Double Account System", determine the amount to be capitalised and the net charge to revenue.

Solution

Statement Showing the Computation of Amount to be written off to Revenue A/c

Particulars		₹
A. Old Cost of Old Asset		1,30,000
B. Effect of increase in various Components of Old Cost		
(a) Increase in Material Cost [12.5% of ₹ 91,000]	11,375	
(b) Increase in Labour Cost [15% of ₹ 39,000]	5,850	17,225
C. Current Cost of Old Assets (A + B)		1,47,225
D. *Less:* Recoveries from Old Asset		
(a) Sale Proceeds of Old Material	10,000	
(b) Value of Old Materials Reused	4,600	14,600
E. Amount to be written off to Revenue A/c (C – D)		1,32,625

Statement Showing the Computation of Amount to be Capitalised

Particulars	₹
A. Cash Costs of New Assets (Excluding the value of Old Material if any reused)	3,25,400
B. *Less:* Current Cost of Old Asset	1,47,225
C. Current Cash Cost to be Capitalised (A – B)	1,78,175
D. *Add:* Value of Old Materials Reused	4,600
E. Current Total Cost to be Capitalised (C + D)	1,82,775

PROBLEM 6

Power Electric Company decides to replace one of its old plant by an improved plant with larger capacity. The cost of the new plant is ₹ 16,00,000. Material and Labour earlier and now are in the ratio of 4 : 6. Original cost of the old plant is ₹ 3,00,000. Materials cost has gone up by 2½ times and Labour cost by 3 times since then. Old materials worth ₹ 10,000 were used in the construction of the new plant and ₹ 20,000 were realised from the sale of old materials.

Required: Give the ncesary Journal Entries for recordig the above transaction.

Solution

Journal

Particulars		*L.F.*	*Dr. (₹)*	*Cr. (₹)*
Plant A/c	Dr.		7,70,000	
To Bank A/c				7,60,000
To Replacement A/c				10,000
(Being the additional cost incurred and old materials utilised in new plant)				
Replacement A/c	Dr.		8,40,000	
To Bank A/c				8,40,000
(Being the current cost of replacement)				
Bank A/c	Dr.		20,000	
To Replacement A/c				20,000
(Being the old materials sold)				
Revenue A/c	Dr.		8,10,000	
To Replacement A/c				8,10,000
(Being the balance of replacement account transferred to revenue account)				

Working Note:

(i) *Calculation of Amount to be c/f to Revenue A/c*

			₹
A.	Cost of Materials increased by 250% = (3,00,000 × 4/10) × 250%		3,00,000
B.	Cost of labour increased by 300% = (3,00,000 × 6/10) × 300%		5,40,000
C.	Current cost of replacing old plant		8,40,000
D.	*Less:* Sale of old materials	20,000	
	Old materials utilised in new plant	10,000	30,000
E.	Amount to be transferred to Revenue Account		8,10,000

(ii) *Calculation of Amount to be Capitalised*

A.	Cash cost of the new plant	16,00,000
B.	*Add:* Old materials utilised	10,000
		16,10,000
C.	*Less:* Current cost of replacing old plant	8,40,000
D.	Amount to be capitalised	7,70,000

(iii) The cost of new plant given as ₹ 16,00,000, in the question has been assumed as cash cost.

PROBLEM 7

Electric Supply Ltd. rebuilt and re-equipped one of their Mains at a Cash cost of ₹. 40,00,000. The old Mains cost ₹ 15,00,000. The capacity of the new Main is double that of the old Main.
₹ 70,000 was realised from sale of old materials. Four old motors valued at ₹ 2,00,000 salvaged from the old Main were used in the reconstruction. The cost of Labour and Materials is respectively 30% and 25% higher now that when the old Main was built. The proportion of Labour to Materials in the Main then and now is 2 : 3.

Required: Show the Journal entries for recording the above transactions, if accounts are maintained under Double Account System.

Solution

Journal

Particulars	*L.F.*	*Dr. (₹)*	*Cr. (₹)*
New Main A/c Dr. Replacement A/c Dr. To Bank A/c (Being current cost of replacement charged to Replacement Account and the Balance Amount Capitalised		20,95,000 19,05,000	 40,00,000
New Main A/c Dr. To Replacement A/c (Being the value of motors salvaged from old main used in the reconstruction of main)		2,00,000	 2,00,000
Bank A/c Dr. To Replacement A/c (Being the amount realised from sale of old materials credited to replacement account)		70,000	 70,000
Revenue A/c Dr. To Replacement A/c (Being the net current cost of replacement transferred to revenue account		16,35,000	 16,35,000

Working Note:

(i) Current Cost of Replacement:

	Cost of existing main ₹	*Increase Rate*	*in Cost Amount* ₹	*Current cost* ₹
Materials (3/5 × ₹ 15 lacs)	9,00,000	25%	2,25,000	11,25,0000
Labour (2/5 × ₹ 15 lacs)	6,00,000	30%	1,80,000	7,80,000
Estimated current cost for replacement of present main (amount to be charged to replacement account)				19,05,000

(ii) Additional cost of reconstruction of amain (to be capitalised)

Cash cost of re-building new main	40,00,000
Less: Estimated current cost for replacement of existing old main	19,05,000
Additional cost in new main to be capitalised excluding old motors used	20,95,000

(iii) Dr. **Replacement Account** Cr.

Particulars	₹.	*Particulars*	₹.
To Bank A/c	19,05,000	By New Main A/c By Bank A/c By Revenue A/c (b/f)	2,00,000 70,000 16,35,000
	19,05,000		19,05,000

PROBLEM 8

'H' Electricity Company earned a profit of ₹. 60,00,000 (after tax) after paying ₹. 48,000 at 12% interest on debentures for the year ended 31.3.2015. The following further information is supplied to you:

	₹.
Share Capital	2,50,00,000
Reserve Fund Investment (invested in 8% Government Securities at par)	60,00,000
Contingencies Reserve Fund Investment (7%)	25,00,000
Loan from State Electricity Board	50,00,000
Develpment Reserve	16,00,000
Fixed Assets	6,00,00,000
Depreciation Reserve on Fixed Assets	60,00,000
Security Deposits of customers	80,00,000
Amount contributed by consumers towards cost of Fixed Assets	4,50,000
Intangible Assets	17,50,000
Tariffs and Dividends Control Reserve	22,00,000
Monthly average of Current Assets including amount due from Customers ₹. 5,00,000	36,00,000

Required: Show, how the profits of the company will be dealt with under the provisions of the Electricity Act, assuming the bank rate of the year was 8%. All working notes should from part of your answer.

Solution

Statement of Distribution of Profit for the year ended 31.3.2015

Capital Base	₹.	₹.
Fixed Assets as reduced by customers contribution (6,00,00,000 – 4,50,000)	5,95,50,000	
Intangible Assets	17,50,000	
Monthly average of Current Assets (Excluding amount due from customers i.e. 36,00,000 – 5,00,000)	31,00,000	
Contingencies Reserve Fund Investment	25,00,000	6,69,00,000
Deduct:		
Depreciation Reserve	60,00,000	
Loan from Electricity Board	50,00,000	
12% Debentures $\left(48,000 \times \frac{100}{12}\right)$	4,00,000	
Development eserve	16,00,000	
Security Deposits of Customers	80,00,000	
Tariffs and Dividends Control Reserve	22,00,000	2,32,00,000
Capital Base		4,37,00,000

Statement showing the computation of Reasonable Return

	₹.
10% (Bank Rate + 2%) on Capital Base	43,70,000
8% on Reserve Fund Investment	4,80,000
½% on Loan from Electricity Board	25,000
½% on Debentures	2,000
½% on Development Reserve	8,000
Reasonable Return	48,85,000

Statement showing the computation of Surplus and its Disposal

	₹.
A. Clear Profit	60,00,000
B. *Less:* Reasonable Return	48,85,000
C. Surplus	11,15,000
D. Less: 20% of Reasonable Return (to be disposed off)	9,77,000
E. Amount refundable to consumers	1,38,000

Statement showing the computation of Surplus of ₹. 9,77,000

		₹.
(i)	1/3 of surplus over clear profit limited to 5% of reasonable return will be at the disposal of the company i.e. ₹. 3,71,667 > ₹. 2,44,250	2,44,250
(ii)	Credit to Tariffs and Dividends Control Reserve (1/2 of remaining balance of 20% of Reasonable Return)	3,66,375
(iii)	Credit to Consumers' Suspense Account	3,66,375
		9,77,000

Statement showing the Total amount at the Disposal of the company

		₹.
(a)	Amount of reasonable return	48,85,000
(b)	Share in surplus	2,44,250
		51,29,250

Statement showing the Total Amount refunded to consumers

		₹.
(a)	Surplus in excess of 20% of reasonable return	1,38,000
(b)	Share in surplus	3,66,375
		5,04,375

PROBLEM 9

The Maduri Municipal Corporation replaces part of its existing water mains with larger mains at the cost of ₹. 150 lacs. The original cost of laying the old main was ₹. 30 lacs and the present cost of lying those mains would be three times the original cost. calculate the amount to be capitalized.

Solution

Amount to be capitalised = Total Cost of New Mains – Estimated current cost of Replacement
= ₹ 150 lacks – (₹ 30 lacs × 3) = ₹ 60 lacs

PROBLEM 10

ABC Electricity Company laid down a main at a cost of ₹. 24,00,000. Some years later the company replaced by improving the plant 2/3 portion of the main at a cost of ₹. 40,00,000. The cost of material and labour having gone up by 25%. Sale of old material realised ₹. 95,000. Old material value ₹ 1,05,000 were used in renewal (including in above).

Calculate the amount to be capitalised and show the journal entries for recording the transartion.

Solution

Statement showing amount to be capitalised

Particulars	₹.
Cash Cost of building new main	38,95,000
Add: Value of Old Material used in the construction of new main	1,05,000
	40,00,000
Less: Estimated Current Cost of replacing old plant	(20,00,000)
Total Amount to be capitalized	20,00,000

Journal Entries of ABC Electricity Company

Date	*Particulars*		*Dr. (₹.)*	*Cr. (₹.)*
	Replacement A/c	Dr.	20,00,000	
	To Bank			20,00,000
	(Being current cost of replacement)			
	New Main A/c	Dr.	20,00,000	
	To Bank A/c			18,95,000
	To Replacement A/c			1,05,000
	(Being additional cost of New Main to be capitalised)			
	Bank A/c	Dr.	95,000	
	To Replacement A/c			1,05,000
	(Being the sale of old materials)			
	Revenue A/c	Dr.	18,00,000	
	To Replacement A/c			18,00,000
	(Being the replacement cost to be written off to revenue)			

Working Note:

Statement showing amount to be written off to Revenue Account

Particulars		₹.
Cost of old plant		24,00,000
Replacement of 2/3 portion of old plant (₹.24,00,000 × 2/3)		16,00,000
Add: 25% increase in cost of material and labour		4,00,000
Current cost of old plant		20,00,000
Less: Cost of material used	1,05,000	
Cost of material sold	95,000	(2,00,000)
Amount to be written off to Revenue A/c		18,00,000

PROBLEM 11

The Super Electricity Company maintains accounts under the Double Accounts System. It decides to replace one of its old plant with a technologically advanced plant with a larger capacity. The plant when installed in 2000, cost the company ₹. 90,00,000, the components of materials, labour and overheads being in the ratio 5:3: 2.

It is ascertained that the costs of materials has gone up by 200% and the cost of labour has gone up by 300%. The proportion of material, labour and overheads has changed to 10:9:6.

The cost of the new plant is ₹. 2,80,00,000 and in addition, goods worth 12,60,000 have been used in the construction of the new plant. The old plant was scrapped and sold for A 19,00,000.

Find out the amount to be capitalized and also the amount to be charged to revenue. Draw the necessary Ledger Accounts.

Solution

Table showing calculation of Current Cost of Old Plant

	Old ratio	*Cost of existing plant*	*% increase*	*Current cost*	*New Ratio*
Material	5	45,00,000	200	90,00,000	10
Labour	3	27,00,000	300	81,00,000	9
Overhead	2	18,00,000		54,00,000*	6
Total		**90,00,000**		**2,25,00,000**	**25**

Amount to be Capitalized

	₹.
Cost of new plant (cash)	2,80,00,000
Add: Cost of old material used	12,60,000
	2,92,60,000
Less: Estimated Current Cost of replacing old plant	(2,25,00,000)
Amount to be capitalized	**67,60,000**
Amount to be charged to Revenue Afc	
Estimated Current Cost of Replacement	2,25,00,000
Less: Cash on sale of scrap	(19,00,000)
Less: Old material reused	12,60,000
Amount to be charged to revenue	**1,93.40,000**

Dr. **Plant Account** Cr.

Particulars	₹.	*Particulars*	₹.
To Balance b/d	90,00,000	By Balance c/d	1,57,60,000
To Bank A/c	55,00,000		
To Replacement A/c	12,60,000		
	1,57,60,000		1,57,60,000

$$\text{*Current cost of overhead} = \frac{(90,00,000 + 81,00,000)}{\left(\frac{10+9}{10+9+6}\right)} \times \frac{6}{25} = 54,00,000$$

Dr. **Replacement Account** Cr.

Particulars	₹.	*Particulars*	₹.
To Bank A/c	2,25,00,000	By Bank A/c	19,00,000
		By Plant A/c	12,60,000
		By Revenue A/c	1,93,40,000
	2,25,00,000		**2,25,00,000**

PROBLEM 12

Jaipur Electric Company Limited rebuilt and re-equipped a part of their power house at the cost of ₹ 85 lakhs. The part of the old power house thus superseded originally costed ₹ 50 lakhs, but if erected at the present time would cost 40% more, ₹ 3 lakhs is realized from the sale of old materials. Old materials worth ₹ 6 lakhs are used in the reconstruction and are included in the cost of ₹ 85 lakhs mentioned above.

Give necessary Journal Entries for recording the above transactions in the books of the company, indicating the allocations between amount to be capitalized and amount to be written off to Revenue Account.

Solution

Journal *[₹ in lakh]*

Date	*Particulars*	*Dr. (₹)*	*Cr. (₹)*
1.	Power House A/c Dr. To Replacement A/c To Bank A/c (Being the additional cost incurred and old materials utilized in new power house)	15	 6 9
2.	Replacement A/c Dr. To Bank A/c (Being the current cost of replacement)	70	 70
3.	Bank A/c Dr. To Replacement A/c (Being amount realised from the sale of materials of old power house)	3	 3
4.	Revenue A/c Dr. To Replacement A/c (Being transfer of balance of Replacement account to Revenue A/c)	61	 61

Working Notes:

(i) **Current Replacement Cost** = 50 + 40% = 70

(ii) **Amount Charged to Revenue Account** = 70 – (3 sale) – (6 Reused) = 61

(iii) **Amount to be Capitalised**

Cost of New Power-House	85
Less: Current Replacement Cost	(70)
Amount to be capitalised	15
Less: Materials Re-used	(6)
Cash amount to be capitalised	9

38 FINANCIAL STATEMENTS OF LIFE INSURANCE COMPANIES

SHORT ANSWER PRACTICAL QUESTIONS

PROBLEM 1

From the following figures of CAMJB Life Assurance Co. Ltd. prepare a Valuation Balance Sheet and Profit Distribution Statement for the year ended 31st March, 2015, also pass necessary Journal Entries to record the above transactions with narration.

(₹ in lacs)

Balance of Life Assurance Fund as on 1.4.2014	167.15
Interim Bonus paid for the valuation period	25.00
Balance of Revenue Account for the year ended 31.3.2015	240.00
Net Liability as per Valuer's certificate as on 31.3.2015	165.00

The company declared a reversionary bonus of ₹ 185 per ₹ 1,000 and gave the policyholders an option to take bonus in cash ₹ 105 per ₹ 1,000. Total business conducted by the company was ₹ 600 lacs. The company issued with profit policy only. 3/5 of the policy holders in value opted for cash bonus.

Solution

CAMJB LIFE ASSURANCE COMPANY LTD.
Valuation Balance Sheet as at 31st March, 2015

Particulars	₹ *(in Lakhs)*	*Particulars*	₹ *(in Lakhs)*
Net Liability	165.00	Life Assurance Fund as on 31.3.2015	240.00
Profit	75.00		
	240.00		240.00

Distribution Statement *(₹ in lakhs)*

Profit as per Valuation Balance Sheet	75.00	
Add: Interim Bonus Paid	25.00	100.00
Policy holders Share (95%)	95.00	
Less: Interim Bonus paid	(25.00)	70.00

JOURNAL *(₹ in lakhs)*

Particulars	*L.F.*	*Dr. (₹)*	*Cr. (₹)*
Life Assurance Fund A/c Dr.		75.00	
To Profit and Loss A/c			75.00
(Being profit transferred as per Valuation Balance Sheet)			

		Dr.	Cr.
Profit and Loss A/c To Bonus Payable in Cash A/c (Being Cash bonus payable @ 105 per thousand on 3/5 of 600 lakh)	Dr.	37.80	37.80
Profit and Loss A/c To Life Assurance Fund A/c (Being Bonus @ ₹ 185 per thousand on 2/5 of 600 lakhs transferred to Life Assurance Fund for reversionary Bonus)	Dr.	44.40	44.40

PROBLEM 2

The Life Assurance Fund of an Insurance Company was on 31.3.2015, ₹ 60 lakhs before providing for dividend of ₹ 20,000 for the year 2014-2015. While ascertaining the above fund figure, the following items were omitted:

(i) Interest received on investments ₹ 63,000 after deduction of tax at source 10%.
(ii) Bonus utilized for reduction of premium ₹ 14,000.
(iii) Death claim intimated, but not yet admitted ₹ 36,000.
(iv) Death claim covered under re-insurance ₹ 12,000.
(v) Consideration for annuities granted ₹ 9,000.

Interim bonus for the valuation period paid was ₹ 80,000.

Net liabilities as per valuation was ₹ 50 lakhs. It is now proposed to carry forward ₹ 2,70,000. The company declared a reversionary bonus of ₹ 12 per ₹ 1,000 and gave the policyholders an option to get the bonus in cash for ₹ 5 per ₹ 1,000. Total business of the company is ₹ 15 crores, 40% of the policyholders decided to get bonus in cash.

Prepare:

(i) Valuation Balance Sheet as at 31.3.2015.
(ii) Distribution Statement showing the amount due to the policyholders.

Also give journal Enries relating to reversionary bonus.

Solution

VALUATION BALANCE SHEET AS AT 31.3.2015

Particulars	₹	*Particulars*	₹
Net Liability	50,00,000	Life Insurance Fund	60,34,000
Net Profit	10,34,000	(adjused) (W.N. 1)	
	60,34,000		60,34,000

Distribution Statement

	₹
Net Profit as per Valuation Balance Sheet	10,34,000
Add: Interim bonus paid	80,000
	11,14,000
Less: Dividend provided	20,000
	10,94,000
Less: Carried forward	2,70,000
True Surplus	8,24,000
Share of Policy holders [₹ 8,24,000 × 95%]	7,82,800
Less: Interim bonus paid	80,000
Amount due to policy holders	7,02,800

JOURNAL

Particulars		L.F.	Dr. (₹)	Cr. (₹)
Profit and Loss A/c To Bonus payable in cash A/c (Being the bonus payable in cash)	Dr.		3,00,000	 3,00,000
Profit and Loss A/c To Life Insurance Fund A/c (Being transfer to Life Insurance Fund for nw liability)	Dr.		10,80,000*	 10,80,000

Working Notes:

(i) *Calculation of Adjusted Life Insurance Fund as on 31.3.2015*

			₹
Life Insurance Fund before adjustments			60,00,000
Add: Interest on investment (gross)			
$\frac{63,000 \times 100}{(100-10)}$	70,000		
Less: Tax deduced at source	7,000	63,000	
Consideration for annuities granted		9,000	72,000
			60,72,000
Less: Death claim intimated	36,000		
Add: Death claim covered under reinsurance	12,000	(24,000)	
Less: Bonus utilised in reduction of premium		(14,000)	38,000
Adjusted Life Insurance Fund			60,34,000

(ii) **Bonus**

₹ 15 crores × 4/10 × 5/1,000 = ₹ 3,00,000 payable in cash

₹ 15 crores × 6/10 × 12/1,000 = ₹ 10,80,000 transfer to fund

(iii) In the present case, the total of bonus payable in cash amounting ₹ 3,00,000 and the bonus by transfer to life insurance fund amounting 10,80,000 comes to ₹ 13,80,000 and the amount due to policyholders is ₹ 7,02,800.

The above solution has been worked out on the basis that the company has sufficient balance in Profit and Loss account for declaration of bonus.

PROBLEM 3

The Life Fund of Well-life Assurance Co. was ₹.90,00,000 as on 31st March 2015. The interim bonus paid during the valuation period was ₹.1,50,000. The periodical actuarial valuation determined the net liability at ₹.75,00,000. Surplus brought forward from the previous valuation was ₹.9,00,000. The directors of the company proposed to carry forward ₹.10,00,000 and to divide the balance between the shareholders and the policy holders. You are required to show:

(i) The Valuation Balance Sheet.
(ii) The Net Profit for the valuation period.
(iii) The Distribution of the Surplus.

Solution

WELL LIFE ASSURANCE CO. LTD.
Valuation Balance Sheet as at March 31, 2015

Particulars	₹	*Particulars*	₹
Net Liability as per actuarial valuation	75,00,000	Life Fund as per Balance Sheet	90,00,000
Surplus (Bal. Fig.)	15,00,000		
	90,00,000		90,00,000

Net Profit for valuation period:

	₹
A. Surplus as per valuation balance sheet	15,00,000
B. *Add:* Interim Bonus distributed	1,50,000
C. *Less:* Surplus in the beginning	(9,00,000)
D. Net Profit for the valuation period	7,50,000

Distribution of Surplus

A. Total Surplus	16,50,000
B. *Less:* Surplus to be carried forward	10,00,000
	6,50,000
C. Shareholders (5% of ₹.6,50,000)	32,500
D. Policy holders (95% of ₹.6,50,000)	6,17,500
E. *Less:* Interim bonus already distributed	1,50,000
F. Bonus still due to Policy holders	4,67,500

PROBLEM 4

The life fund of a life assurance company was ₹ 8,64,80,000 as on 31.3.2015. The interim bonus paid during the intervaluation period was ₹ 14,80,000. The periodical actuarial valuation determined the net liability at ₹ 7,42,50,000. Surplus brought forward from the previous valuation was ₹ 85,00,000. Calculate the net profit for the valuation period.

Solution

VALUATION BALANCE SHEET AS AT 31.3.2015

Particulars	₹	*Particulars*	₹
To Net Liability as per Actuarial Valuation	7,42,50,000	By Life Fund as per Balance Sheet	8,64,80,000
To Surplus (Bal. fig.)	1,22,30,000		
	8,64,80,000		8,64,80,000

CALCULATION OF NET PROFIT FOR THE VALUATION PERIOD

Particulars	₹
Surplus as per the Valuation Balance Sheet	1,22,30,000
Add: Interim bonus distributed	14,80,000
	1,37,10,000
Less: Surplus at the beginning of the period	(85,00,000)
Net Profit for the valuation period	52,10,000

PROBLEM 5

Domestic Assurance Co. Ltd. received ₹.5,90,000 as premium on new policies and ₹.1,20,000 as renewal premium. The company received ₹.90,000 towards reinsurance accepted and paid ₹.70,000 towards reinsurance ceded. How much will be credited to Revenue Account towards premium?

Solution

	₹
Premium received in respect of new policies	5,90,000
Add: Renewal premium	1,20,000
	7,10,000
Add: Re-insurance premium accepted	90,000
	8,00,000
Less: Re-insurance ceded	70,000
Premium amount to be credited to Revenue A/c	7,30,000

39 FINANCIAL STATEMENTS OF GENERAL INSURANCE COMPANIES

SHORT ANSWER PRACTICAL QUESTIONS

CALCULATION OF NET CLAIM

PROBLEM 1

From the following figures appearing in the books of Fire Insurance division of a General insurance Company, show the amount of claim as it would appear in the Revenue Account for the period ended 31st March 2015.

Particulars	Direct Business	Re-insurance
	₹	₹
Claim paid during the year	46,70,000	7,00,000
Claim Payable— 1st April, 2014	7,63,000	87,000
31st March, 2015	8,12,000	53,000
Claims received	—	
Claims receivable—1st April,2014	—	2,30,000
31st March, 2015	—	65,000
Expenses of Management (include ₹.35,000 Surveyor's Fee and ₹.45,000 Legal Expenses for settlement of claims	2,30,000	—

Solution

AN EXTRACT OF FIRE REVENUE ACCOUNT
for the year ended on 31st March, 2015

Particulars	*Schedule No.*	*Current Year (₹ '000)*	*Previous Year (₹ '000)*
Claim Incurred (Net)	2	5187	

Schedule 2 Claim incured (Net)

Particulars	*Current Year (₹ '000)*	*Previous Year (₹ '000)*
Claims paid on direct business	4799	
Less: Claims received on re-insurance ceded	(278)	
Add: Claim paid on re-insurance accepted	666	
Net Claim paid	5187	

Working Notes:

CLAIMS INCURRED

Particulars	*Direct Business (₹ '000)*	*Re-insurance Accepted (₹ '000)*	*Re-Insurance Ceded ₹ '000*
A. Paid / Received	4670	700	230
B. *Add:* Outstanding at end	812	53	113
C. *Add:* Exp. in connection with settlement of claim [35,000+45,000]	80		
D. *Less:* Outstanding at beginning	(763)	(87)	(65)
	4799	666	278

PROBLEM 2

Modern Insurance Company's Fire Insurance division provide the following information, show the amount of claim as it would appear in the Revenue Account for the year ended 31st March, 2015.

	Direct Business ₹	*Re-insurance* ₹
Claim paid during the year	35,30,000	8,20,000
Claim received		3,20,000
Claim payable		
1st April, 2014	8,23,000	58,000
31st March, 2015	8,75,000	87,000
Claim receivable:		
1st April, 2014	—	85,000
31st March, 2015	—	1,42,000
Expenses of management (Includes ₹ 38,000 Surveyor's fee and ₹ 42,000 Legal expenses for settlement of claims)	3,45,000	

Solution

CALCULATION OF NET CLAIMS INCURRED

Particulars		₹
Claims paid on direct business (35,30,000 + 38,000 + 42,000)		36,10,000
Add: Re-insurance	8,20,000	
Add: Outstanding at the end	87,000	
Less: Outstanding in the beg.	(58,000)	8,49,000
		44,59,000
Less: Claims received from re-insurance	3,20,000	
Add: Outstanding at the end	1,42,000	
Less: Outstanding in the beg.	(85,000)	(3,77,000)
		40,82,000
Add: Outstanding Direct Claims at the end of the year		8,75,000
Less: Outstanding Claims at the beginning of the year		(8,23,000)
Net Claims incurred		41,34,000

PROBLEM 3

From the following figures of Fire Insurance division of a General Insurance Company, show the amount of claim as it would appear in the Revenue Account for the year ended 31st March, 2015:

	Direct Business ₹	*Re-Insurance* ₹
Claims paid during the year	70,05,000	10,50,000
Claims payable		
1st April, 2014	11,44,500	1,30,500
31 March, 2015	12,18,000	79,500
Claims received	—	3,45,000
Claims receivable		
1st April, 2014	—	97,500
31st March, 2015	—	1,69,500
Expenses of management (includes ₹ 52,500 surveyor's fee and ₹ 67,500 legal expenses for settlement of claims)	3,45,000	

Solution

STATEMENT SHOWING THE AMOUNT OF CLAIMS FOR THE YEAR ENDED 31ST MARCH, 2015

Particulars	*(₹)*	*(₹)*
Claim paid on		
Claims paid on direct business (70,05,000 + 52,500 + 67,500)		71,25,000
Add: Re-insurance	10,50,000	
Add: Outstanding at the end	79,500	
Less: Outstanding in the beg.	(1,30,500)	9,99,000
		81,24,000
Less: Claims received from Re-insurance	3,45,000	
Add: Outstanding at the end	1,69,500	
Less: Outstanding in the beg.	(97,500)	(4,17,000)
		77,07,000
Add: Outstanding Direct Claims at the end		12,18,000
Less: Outstanding Direct Claims in the beg.		(11,44,500)
Net Claims incurred		77,80,500

CALCULATION OF NET PREMIUMS AND NET CLAIMS

PROBLEM 4

From the following information of Reliable of Marine Insurance Ltd. for the year ending 31st March, 2015 find out the

(*i*) Net Premiums earned
(*ii*) Net Claims incurred

	(₹) *Direct Business*	(₹) *Re-insurance*
Premium:		
Received	88,00,000	7,52,000
Receivable – 01.04.2014	4,39,000	36,000
Receivable – 31.03.2015	3,77,000	32,000
Paid	6,09,000	
Payable – 01.04.2014		27,000
Payable – 31.03.2015		18,000
Claims:		
Paid	69,00,000	5,54,000
Payable – 01.04.2014	89,000	15,000
Payable – 31.03.2015	95,000	12,000
Received		2,01,000
Receivable – 01.04.2014		40,000
Receivable – 31.03.2015		38,000

Solution

(i) Net Premiums earned

	(₹)	(₹)
Premium from direct business received	88,00,000	
Add : Receivable at the end	3,77,000	
Less: Receivable at the begnning	(4,39,000)	87,38,000
Add: Premium on Re-insurance accepted	7,52,000	
Add: Receivable at the end	32,000	
Less: Receivable at the begnning	(36,000)	7,48,000
		94,86,000
Less: Premium on Re-insurance ceded	6,09,000	
Add: Payable at the end	18,000	
Less: Payable at the begnning	(27,000)	(6,00,000)
Net Premium earned		**88,86,000**

(ii) Net Claims incurred

	(₹) *Direct Business*	(₹) *Re-insurance*
Claims paid on direct business		69,00,000
Add: Re-insurance	5,54,000	
Add: Outstanding at the end	12,000	
Less: Outstanding at the begnning	(15,000)	5.51,000
		74,51,000

Less: Claims received from Re-insurance	2,01,000	
Add: Outstanding at the end	38,000	
Less: Outstanding at the begnning	(40,000)	(1,99,000)
		72,52,000
Add: Outstanding direct claims at the end of the year		95,000
		73,47,000
Less: Outstanding claims at the beginning of the year		(89,000)
Net Claims incurred		**72,58,000**

UNEXPIRED RISK RESERVE ACCOUNT

PROBLEM 5

From the following information furnished to you by Ayushman Insurance Co. Ltd., you are required to pass Journal entires relating to unexpired risk reserve and show in columnar form "Unexpired Risks Reserve Account" for 2015.

(a) On 31.12.2014, it had reserve for unexpired risks amounting to ₹ 40 crores. It comprised of ₹.15 crores in respect of marine insurance business, ₹ 20 crores in respect of fire insurance business and ₹ 5 crores in respect of miscellaneous insurance business.

(b) Ayushman Insurance Co. Ltd. creates reserves at 100% of net premium income in respect of marine insurance policies and at 50% of net premium income in respect of fire and miscellaneous income policies.

(c) During 2015, the following business was conducted:

	(Amount in crores)		
	Marine	*Fire*	*Miscellaneous*
Premium collected from:			
(a) Insured in respect of policies issued	18.00	43.00	12.00
(b) Other insurance companies in respect of risks undertaken	7.00	5.00	4.00
Premium paid/payable to other insurance companies on business ceded	6.70	4.30	7.00

Solution

JOURNAL OF AYUSHMAN INSURANCE CO. LTD. *(₹ in crores)*

Date	*Particulars*		*Dr.*	*Cr.*
1.1.2015	Unexpired Risk Reserve (Fire) A/c	Dr.	20.00	
	Unexpired Risk Reserve (Marine) A/c	Dr.	15.00	
	Unexpired Risk Reserve (Miscellaneous) A/c	Dr.	5.00	
	To Fire Revenue A/c			20.00
	To Marine Revenue A/c			15.00
	To Miscellaneous Revenue A/c			5.00

	(Being unexpired risk reserve brought forward from last year)		
31.12.2015	Marine Revenue A/c Dr.	18.30	
	To Unexpired Risk Reserve A/c		18.30
	(Being Closing reserve for unexpired risk created at 100% of net premium income amounting to ₹.18.3 crores i.e. 18 + 7-6.70)		
	Fire Revenue A/c Dr.	21.85	
	To Unexpired Risk Reserve A/c		21.85
	(Being closing reserve for unexpired risk created at 50% of net premium income of ₹ 43.7 crores i.e. 43 + 5-4,30)		
	Miscellaneous Revenue A/c Dr.	4.50	
	To Unexpired Risk Reserve A/c		4.50
	(Being closing reserve for unexpired risk created at 50% net premium income of ₹ 9 crores i.e. 12+4-7)		

Dr. **UNEXPIRED RISK RESERVE ACCOUNT** *Cr.*

Date	*Particulars*	*Marine (₹)*	*Fire (₹)*	*Misc. (₹)*	*Date*	*Particulars*	*Marine (₹)*	*Fire (₹)*	*Misc. (₹)*
1.1.2015	To Revenue A/c	15.00	20.00	5.00	1.1.2015	By Balance b/d	15.00	20.00	500
31.12.2015	To Balance c/d	18.30	21.85	4.50	31.12.2015	By Revenue A/c	18.30	21.85	4.50
		33.30	41.85	9.50			33.30	41.85	9.50

PREPARATION OF FIRE INSURANCE REVENUE ACCOUNT

PROBLEM 6

Prepare the Fire Insurance Revenue A/c as per IRDA regulations for the year ended 31st March, 2015 from the following details:

	₹
Claims paid	4,90,000
Legal expenses regarding claims	10,000
Premiums received	13,00,000
Re-insurance premium paid	1,00,000
Commission	3,00,000
Expenses of Management	2,00,000
Provision against unexpired risk on 1st April, 2014	5,50,000
Claims unpaid on 1st April, 2014	50,000
Claims unpaid on 31st March, 2015	80,000

Solution

Since Rule 6 E of Income Tax Rules permits the insurance companies to claim a deduction of 50% of net premium income in respect of Fire and Miscellaneous Business. In view of this reserve has been created at the rates allowed under Income Tax act.

FORM B - RA

Name of the Insurer :

Registration No. and Date of Registration with the IRDA

FIRE INSURANCE REVENUE ACCOUNT

For the year ended 31st March, 2015

	Particulars	*Schedule*	*Amount*
1.	Premium earned	1	11,50,000
2.	Other income		—
3.	Interest, dividend and rent		—
	Total (A)		11,50,000
4.	Claims incurred	2	5,30,000
5.	Commission	3	3,00,000
6.	Operating expenses related to Insurance business	4	2,00,000
	Total (B)		10,30,000
	Operating Profit (A) – (B)		1,20,000

Schedule 1: Premium earned	₹
Premium received	13,00,000
Less: Re-insurance Premium	(1,00,000)
	12,00,000
Less: Change in provision for unexpired risk (Refer W.N.)	(50,000)
	11,50,000
Schedule 2: Claims Incurred	
Claims paid including legal expenses (4,90,000 + 10,000)	5,00,000
Add: Claims outstanding at the end of the year	80,000
Less: Claims outstanding at the beginnging of the year	(50,000)
Total claims incurred	5,30,000
Schedule 3: Commission	
Commission paid	3,00,000
Schedule 4: Operating Expenses	
Expenses of Management	2,00,000

Working Note: **Change in the provision for un-expired risk**

	₹
Unexpired Risk Reserve on 31st March, 2015 = 50% of Net Premium i.e. 50% of ₹ 12,00,000 =	6,00,000
Unexpired Risk Reserve on 1st April 2014	5,50,000
	50,000

Note: Alternatively, Reserve for unexpired risk may be taken @ 40% of net premium as per the provisions of the Insurance Act, 1938.

PROBLEM 7

Sunlife General Insurance Company submits the following information for the year ended 31st March 2015:

Particulars		Direct Business (₹)	Re-insurance (₹)
Premium received		65,75,000	9,50,000
Premium paid		—	4,75,000
Claims paid during the year		42,50,000	5,00,000
Claims payable	1st April, 2014	6,25,000	87,000
	31st March, 2015	7,18,000	60,0001
Claims received		—	3,25,000
Claims receivable	1st April, 2014		65,000
	31st March, 2015		1,10,000
Expenses of management		2,30,000	
Commission:			
On insurance accepted		1,50,000	11,000
On insurance ceded			14,000

The following additional information is also available:

(1) Expenses of management include ₹, 35,000 surveyor's fee and ₹ 45,000 legal expenses for settlement of claims.

(2) Reserve for unexpired risk is to be maintained @ 40% The balance of reserve for unexpired risk as on 1.4.2014 was ₹, 24,50,000.

You are required to prepare the Revenue Account for the year ended 31st March, 2015.

Solution

FORM B-RA (PRESCRIBED BY IRDA)
SUNLIFE GENERAL INSURANCE COMPANY
REVENUE ACCOUNT FOR THE YEAR ENDED 31ST MARCH, 2015

Particulars	Schedule	₹
Premium Earned (net)	1	66,80,000
Interest, Dividend and Rent		—
Other income		—
Total A)		66,80,000
Claims incurred (Net)	2	45,26,000
Commission	3	1,47,000
Operating Expenses related to insurance business	4	50,000
Bad Debts	—	
Total (B)		48,23,000
Operating Profit from insurance business (A – B)		18,57,000

Schedules forming part of revenue account

Schedule 1 : Premium Earned (Net)

Particulars	₹
Premium from direct business	65,75,000
Add: Premium on reinsurance accepted	9,50,000
Less: Premium on reinsurance ceded	(4,75,000)
Net Premium	70,50,000
Adjustment for change in reserve for unexpired risks	(3,70,000)
Total Premium earned (net)	66,80,000

Schedule 2 : Claims Incurred (Net)

Particulars	₹
Claims paid on direct business (W.N.1)	43,30,000
Add: Reinsurance accepted (W.N.1)	4,73,000
Less: Reinsurance ceded (W.N.1)	(3,70,000)
Net Claims paid	44,33,000
Add: Claims outstanding at the end of the year	7,18,000
Less: Claims outstanding at the beginning of the year	(6,25,000)
Total claims incurred	45,26,000

Schedule 3 : Commission

Particulars	₹
Commission paid on direct business	1,50,000
Add: Commission on reinsurance accepted	11,000
Less: Commission on reinsurance ceded	(14,000)
	1,47,000

Schedule 4 : Operating Expenses related to Insurance Business

Particulars	₹
Expenses of Management (2,30,000 – 35,000 – 45,000)	1,50,000
	1,50,000

Working Notes:

(i) Claims Incurred

Particulars	*Direct Business (₹)*	*Reinsurance Accepted (₹)*	*Reinsurance Ceded (₹)*
Paid/received	42,50,000	5,00,000	3,25,000
Add: Outstanding at the end of the year		60,000	1,10,000
Expenses in connection with settlement of claim (35,000 + 45,000)	80,000		
Less: Outstanding at the beginning of the year	(87,000)	(65,000)	
	43,30,000	4,73,000	3,70,000

(ii) Change in Reserve for Unexpired Risk

	₹
Opening Reserve	24,50,000
Less: Closing Reserve (₹ 70,50,000 × 40%)	28,20,000
Change in Reserve for Unexpired Risk	**3,70,000**

PROBLEM 8

From the following information of M/s. Bigfish Marine Insurance Co. Ltd., prepare the Revenue Account as per regulations of IRDA for theyear ended 31S* March, 2015:

Particulars	*Amount (₹)*
Premium received	18,75,000
Premium outstanding on March 31,2015	1,25,000
Premium paid on reinsurance ceded	2,28,000
Claimspaid	10,54,000
Estimated liability in respect of outstanding claims: On April 1,2014	1,89,000
On March 31,2015	2,25,000
Expenses of management (includes ₹ 45, 000 surveyor's fee and ₹ 65,000 legal expenses paid for settlement of claims)	4,85,000
Interest and dividend (Gross)	1, 65,250
Income tax on the above	49,575
Profit on sale of investments	46,000
Commission paid	1,94,000

Balance of fund on 1st April, 2014 was ₹ 18,50,000 including additional reserve of ₹ 1,80,000. Additional reserve has to be maintained at 10% of Net Premium for the year.

Solution

FORM B-RA NAME OF THE INSURER: M/S BIGFISH MARINE INSURANCE CO. LTD.
REVENUE ACCOUNT FOR THE YEAR ENDED 31ST MARCH, 2015

Particulars	*Schedule*	₹
Premium earned (Net)	1	16,72,800
Profit on sale of investment		46,000
Interest, dividend and rent (Gross)		1 ,65,250
Total (A)		18,84,050
Claims incurred (Net)	2	12,00,000
Commission	3	1,94,000
Operatinq expenses related to insurance business	4	3,75,000
Total (B)		17,69,000
Profit for Marine Insurance Business (A-B)		1,15,050

Schedule -1

Premium Earned (Net)	₹
Premium received	18,75,000
Add: Outstanding Premium at the end	1,25,000
Less: Premium on reinsurance ceded	(2,28,000)
Less: Adjustment for change in reserve for Unexpired Risk	(99,200)
Net premium earned	16,72,800

Schedule-2

Claim Incurred (Net)	₹
Claim paid	10,54,000
Add: Surveyor's fee & legal expenses paid for settlement of claim (₹ 45,000 + ₹ 65,000)	1,10,000
Add: Outstanding claims at the end	2,25,000
Less: Outstanding claims in the beg.	(1,89,000)
Claim incurred (Net)	12,00,000

Schedule-3

Commission	₹
Commission paid	1,94,000

Schedule-4

Operating expenses related to insurance business	₹
Expenses of Management	4,85,000
Less: Surveyor's fee & legal expenses	(1,10,000)
	3,75,000

Working Notes:

(I) CALCULATION FOR CHANGE IN RESERVE FOR UNEXPIRED RISK

		₹
Unexpired risk reserve at the beginning (including additional reserve)		18,50,000
Less: Reserve for unexpired risk as at the end (100% of ₹ 17,72,000)	17,72,000	
Additional reserve at the end (10% of ₹ 17,72,000)	1,77,200	(19,49,200)
Change in Provision for Unexpired Risk		99,200

(ii) Income tax on interest and dividend ₹ 49,575 is part of Profit & Loss Account, therefore, not given effect to in the Revenue Account.

PROBLEM 9

Prepare the Fire Insurance Revenue A/c as per IRDA regulations for the year ended 31st March, 2015 from the following details:

	₹
Claims paid	5,00,000
Legal expenses regarding claims	10,000
Premiums received	12,50,000
Re-insurance premium paid	50,000
Commission	3,00,000
Expenses of Management	2,00,000
Provision against unexpired risk on 1st April, 2014	5,75,000
Claims unpaid on 1st April, 2014	50,000
Claims unpaid on 31st March, 2015	80,000

Provision against unexpired risk @ 50% **less** Re-insurance

Solution

FORM B - RA

Name of the Insurer : Jasmine Fire Insurance Co. Ltd.

Registration No. and Date of Registration with the IRDA: ....

Fire Insurance Revenue Account
For the year ended 31st March, 2015

	Particulars	*Schedule*	*Amount*
1.	Premium earned	1	11,75,000
2.	Other income		—
3.	Interest, dividend and rent		—
	Total (A)		11,75,000
4.	Claims incurred	2	5,40,000
5.	Commission	3	3,00,000
6.	Operating expenses related to Insurance business	4	2,00,000
	Total (B)		10,40,000
	Operating Profit (A) – (B)		1,35,000

Schedule 1: Premium earned

	₹
Premium received	12,50,000
Less: Re-insurance Premium	(50,000)
	12,00,000
Less: Adjustment for Change in provision for un-expired risk (Refer W.N.)	25,000
	11,75,000

Schedule 2: Claims Incurred

Claims paid including legal expenses (5,10,000 + 10,000)	5,10,000
Add: Claims outstanding at the end of the year	80,000
Less: Claims outstanding at the beginnging of the year	(50,000)
Total claims incurred	5,40,000

Schedule 3: Commission

Commission paid	3,00,000

Schedule 4: Operating Expenses

Expenses of Management	2,00,000

Working Note:

Change in the Provision for Unexpired Risk

Closing Unexpired Risk Reserve [50% of ₹ 12,00,000]	₹6,00,000
Opening Unexpired Risk Reserve	₹(5,75,000)
	₹25,000

PROBLEM 10

From the following information of M/s. Bachao Insurance Co. Ltd., engaged in fire insurance business, prepare the Revenue Account reserving 40% of the net premiums for unexpired risks and an additional reserve of ₹ 3,50,000:

Particulars	*Amount (₹)*
Reserve for unexpired risk (opening)	7,50,000
Additional Reserve (opening)	1,50,000
Premium received	16,80,000
Re-insurance premium	1,12,500
Re-insurance recoveries	30,000
Claims paid	9,60,000
Estimated liability in respect of outstanding claims: On April 1,2014	97,500
On March 31,2015	1,35,000
Expenses of management (includes ₹ 45, 000 in connection with claims)	4,20,000
Interest and dividend	75,000
Profit on sale of investments	15,000
Commission	1,75,000

Solution

FORM B-RA NAME OF THE INSURER: M/S BACHAO INSURANCE CO. LTD.
REVENUE ACCOUNT FOR THE YEAR ENDED 31ST MARCH, 2015

Particulars	*Schedule*	₹
Premium earned (Net)	1	14,90,500
Profit on sale of investment		15,000
Interest, dividend and rent (Gross)		75,000
Total (A)		15,80,500
Claims incurred (Net)	2	10,12,500
Commission	3	1,75,000
Operatinq expenses related to insurance business	4	3,75,000
Total (B)		15,62,500
Operating Profit for Fire Insurance Business (A-B)		18,000

SCHEDULE -1

Premium Earned (Net)	₹
Premium received	16,80,000
Less: Premium on reinsurance ceded	(1,12,500)
Less: Adjustment for change in reserve for Unexpired Risk	(77,000)
Net premium earned	14,90,500

SCHEDULE-2

Claim Incurred (Net)	₹
Claim paid	9,60,000
Add: Surveyor's fee & legal expenses paid for settlement of claim	45,000
Add: Outstanding claims at the end	1,35,000
Less: Outstanding claims in the beg.	(97,500)
Claim incurred (Net)	10,12,500

SCHEDULE-3

Commission	₹
Commission paid	1,75,000

SCHEDULE-4

Operating expenses related to insurance business	₹
Expenses of Management	4,20,000
Less: Surveyor's fee & legal expenses	(45,000)
	3,75,000

Working Note:

CALCULATION FOR CHANGE IN RESERVE FOR UNEXPIRED RISK

		₹
Unexpired risk reserve at the beginning (including additional reserve)		9,00,000
Less: Reserve for unexpired risk as at the end (40% of ₹ 15,67,500)	6,27,000	
Additional reserve at the end	3,50,000	(9,77,000)
Change in Provision for Unexpired Risk		77,000

LONG ANSWER PRACTICAL QUESTIONS

PROBLEM 10

Prepare Revenue Account in proper form for the year ended 31st March, 2015, from the following particulars related to Krishna General Insurance Co. for the year ended 2014 – 2015:

	Related to Direct business (₹)	*Related to Reinsurance (₹)*
Premiums:		
Amount received	30,00,000	2,40,000
Receivable at the beginning	1,80,000	24,000
Receivable at the end	2,40,000	36,000
Amount paid	–	3,60,000
Payable at the beginning	–	30,000
Payable at the end	–	42,000
Claims:		
Amount paid	18,00,000	1,80,000
Payable at the beginning	60,000	12,000
Payable at the end	1,20,000	18,000
Amount recovered	–	1,20,000
Receivable at the beginning	–	18,000
Receivable at the end	–	12,000
***Commission*:**		
Amount paid	72,000	10,800
Amount received	–	14,400

Additional information:

(*i*) Interest, dividend and rent received 30,000

Income-tax in respect of above 6,000

(*ii*) Management expenses including ₹ 12,000 related to legal expenses regarding claims 1,32,000

(*iii*) Provision for income tax existing at the beginning of the year was ₹ 1,95,000, the income-tax actually paid during the year ₹ 1,68,000 and the provision necessary at the year end ₹ 2,07,000.

(*iv*) The net premium income of the company during the previous year was ₹ 24,00,000 on which reserve for unexpired risk @ 50% and additional reserve @ 7 ½% was created. This year, the balance to be carried forward is 50% of net premium on reserve for unexpired risk and 5% on additional reserve.

Solution

FORM B – RA

NAME OF THE INSURER : KRISHNA GENERAL INSURANCE COMPANY

REGISTRATION NO. AND DATE OF REGISTRATION WITH IRDA : ....

Revenue Account for the year ended 31.3.2015

Particulars	*Schedule*	₹
1. Premium earned (Net)	1	27,03,000
2. Profit/Loss on sales/Redemption of investment	–	–
3. Other	–	–
4. Interest, dividend & rent (Gross)	–	30,000
Total (A)		27,33,000
1. Claims incurred (Net)	2	19,44,000
2. Commission	3	68,400
3. Operating expenses related to insurance business	4	1,20,000
Total (B)		21,32,400
Operating profit/Loss from insurance business (C) = (A – B)		6,00,600

Schedule – 1 Premium Earned (Net)

Particulars	₹
Premium received from direct business	30,60,000
Add: Premium on reinsurance accepted (2,40,000 + 36,000 – 24,000)	2,52,000
	33,12,000
Less: Premium on reinsurance ceded (3,60,000 + 42,000 – 30,000)	3,72,000
Net Premium	29,40,000
Adjustment for change in reserve for unexpired risk	2,37,000
Total premium earned (Net)	27,03,000

Schedule – 2 Claims Incurred (Net)

Particulars	₹
Claims paid (Direct)	18,00,000
Add: Legal expenses regarding claims	12,000
	18,12,000
Add: Reinsurance Accepted	1,80,000
	19,92,000
Less: Reinsurance ceded (1,20,000 + 12,000 –18,000)	1,14,000
	18,78,000
Add: Claims outstanding at the end (1,20,000 + 18,000)	1,38,000
	20,16,000
Less: Claims outstanding at the beginning (60,000 + 12,000)	72,000
Total Claim incurred	19,44,000

Schedule –3 Commission

Particulars	₹
Commission paid Direct	72,000
Add: Re-insurance accepted	10,800
	82,800
Less: Re-insurance ceded	14,400
Net Commission	68,400

Schedule – 4 Operating Expenses related to Insurance Business

Particulars	₹
Expenses of management (1,32,000 – 12,000)	1,20,000
	1,20,000

Working Notes :

(i) Calculation of premium received from direct business

	₹
Premium on direct business	30,00,000
Add: Premium outstanding at the end	2,40,000
Less: Premium outstanding at the beginning	1,80,000
	30,60,000

(ii) Computation of change in reserve for unexpired risk

Closing Reserve for unexpired risk (29,40,000 × 50%)	14,70,000
Add: Closing Additional reserve for unexpired risk (29,40,000 × 5%)	1,47,000
Less: Opening Reserve for unexpired risk (24,00,000 × 50%)	12,00,000
Opening Additional reserve for unexpired risk (24,00,000 × 7.5%)	1,80,000
	2,37,000

PROBLEM 11

On 31[s1] March, 2015 the books ot Zee insurance company umuea, following particulars in respect of fire insurance:

Particulars	*Amount (₹)*
Reserve for unexpired risks on March 31, 2014	5,00,000
Additional reserve for unexpired risks on March 31, 2014	1,00,000
Premiums	11,20,000
Claims paid	6,40,000
Estimated liability in respect of outstanding claims:	
On March 31, 2014	65,000
On March 31, 2015	90,000
Expenses of management (including ₹.30,000 legal expenses paid in connection with the claims)	2,80,000
Interest and dividend	64,250
Income tax on the above	6,520
Profit on sale of investment	11,000
Commission paid	1,52,000

On 31st March, 2015 provide ₹ 5,60,000 as unexpired risk reserve and ₹ 75,000 as Additional reserve.

You are required to prepare the Fire Insurance Revenue account as per the regulations of IRDA, for the year ended 31st March, 2015.

Solution

FORM B- RA

Name of the Insurer: Zee Insurance Company Limited

Registration No. and Date of registration with IRDA:..........................

REVENUE ACCOUNT FOR THE YEAR ENDED 31ST MARCH, 2015

Particulars	*Schedule*	*Amount (₹)*
Premium earned (net)	1	10,85,000
Profit or loss on Sale/Redemption of Investments		11,000
Others	–	
Interest, Dividend & Rent (gross)		64,250
Total (A)		11,60,250
Claims incurred (Net)	2	6,95,000
Commission	3	1,52,000
Operating expenses related to insurance	4	2,50,000
Total (B)		10,97,000
Operating Profit/loss from insurance business (B) – (A)		63,250

Schedule -1 Premium earned (net)

Particulars	₹
Premium received	11,20,000
Less: Adjustment for change in Reserve for Unexpired risk (as per W.N.)	35,000
Total premium earned	10,85,000

Schedule -2 Claims incurred (net)

Particulars	₹
Claims paid	6,40,000
Add: Legal expenses regarding claims	30,000
	6,70,000
Add: Claims outstanding at the end	90,000
	7,60,000
Less: Claims outstanding at the beginning	65,000
Particulars	6,95,000

Schedule -3 Commission

Particulars	₹
Commission paid	1,52,000

Schedule-4 Operating Expenses related to Insurance Business

Expenses of management (₹.2,80,000 – ₹.30,000)	2,50,000

Working Note:

CALCULATION FOR CHANGE IN RESERVE FOR UNEXPIRED RISK

Particulars		₹
Opening Reserve for Unexpired Risk	5,60,000	
Opening Additional Reserve	75,000	6,35,000
Less: Closing Reserve for Unexpired Risk	5,00,000	
Closing Additional Reserve	1,00,000	(6,00,000)
		35,000

Note: *Interest and dividends are shown at gross value in Revenue account. Income tax on it will not be included in the Revenue account as it is the part of Profit and Loss account of an insurance company.*

PAPER–5: FINANCIAL ACCOUNTING

TULSIAN'S MODEL TEST PAPERS WITH SUGGESTED ANSWERS

ATTENTION PLEASE

Dear Students

Your Sincere and 100% Accurate Attempt of Tulsian's Model Test Papers under Examination conditions guarantees you 100% Sure Success in the Paper 5: Financial Accounting of Group 1

Best of Luck!

TULSIAN'S MODEL TEST PAPER 1
INTERMEDIATE EXAMINATION GROUP I
(SYLLABUS 2012)
PAPER – 5: FINANCIAL ACCOUNTING

Time Allowed: 3 Hours **Full Marks: 100**

The figures in the margin on the right side indicate full marks.
This paper contains seven questions. All questions are compulsory, subject to instruction provided against each question.
All working must form part of your answer.

1. Answer the following questions (Give workings): **2 × 10 = 20**

(a) The Stock was physically verified on 7th April and was valued at ₹ 2,00,000. Goods are normally sold by the trader at a profit of 25% on cost. On 1st April. goods of the sale value of ₹ 1,00,000 were sent on sale *or* return basis to a customer, the period of approval being two weeks. He returned 20% of the goods and approved 80% of the remaining on 6th April. Determine the value of stock to be taken to the Balance Sheet of PCT Ltd. as at 31st March.

(b) Cash Price—₹ 10,00,000, Cash Down Payment—20%, Four annual equal instalments of ₹ 2,50,000 each to be paid at the end of each year. Compute the payment of interest pertaining to each accounting year assuming that the sales were made at the beginning of the year.

(c) Following is the Balance Sheet of A,B,C and D who were sharing in the ratio of 3: 3: 2: 2 as at 31st March, 2015, when they decided to dissolve the firm:

Liabilities	₹	Assets	₹
Trade Creditors	1,21,000	Sundry Assets	1,70,000
A's Capital	60,000	C's Capital	48,000
B's Capital	49,000	D's Capital	18,000
General Reserve	20,000	B's Drawings	4,000
		Profit & Loss A/c	10,000
	2,50,000		2,50,000

After preparing the Balance Sheet as at 31st March, it was discovered that purchases amounting to ₹ 10,000 in March, were not recorded in books, though the goods were received during March. C is insolvent but ₹ 11,100 is realized from his estate. Sundry Assets realized 86%. Realization Expenses ₹ 2,200. State who will bear C's deficiency and in which ratio.

(d) Tulsian Ltd with its Head office in Delhi invoices goods to its Branch at Mumbai at 20% less than the catalogue price which is cost plus 50% with instructions that cash sales are to be made at invoice price and credit sales at catalogue price.

Opening Stock at Branch at its cost	₹ 12,000
Goods Sent to Branch (at cost to H.O)	₹ 1,40,000
Goods received by Branch till close of the year	₹ 1,38,000
Cash Sales	₹ 46,000
Credit Sales	₹ 1,00,000
Stock lost by fire (at Cost)	₹ 2,500

Required: Calculate the Closing Stock at Branch and Branch and Stock Reserve.

(e) How will you show the following items in General Ledger Adjustment Account in Debtors Ledger:

	₹
(a) Transfer from Debtors' Ledgers to Creditors' Ledger	1,100
(b) Transfer from Creditors' Ledger to Debtors' Ledger	1,900
(c) B/R endorsed to Creditors	4,000
(d) Endorsed Bills dishonoured	1,000
(e) Bad Debts written off (after deducting bad debts recovered ₹ 300)	2,200
(f) Provision for Doubtful Debts	550
(g) Provision for Discount on Debtors	1,000
(h) Bill Receivable Collected on maturity	5,000
(i) Bills Receivable discounted	6,000
(j) Discount allowed	1,500

(k) Discount allowed to debtors ₹ 500 was recorded as discount received from creditors.

(l) Closing Debtors Balance (as per General Ledger Adjustment Account) ₹ 60,000 (Cr.)

(f) M/s. SEA Ltd. recognized ₹ 5.00 lakhs on accrual basis income from dividend during the year 2014-2015, on shares of the face value of ₹ 25.00 lakhs held by it in Rock Ltd. as at 31st March, 2015. Rock Ltd. proposed dividend @ 20% on 10th April, 2015. However, dividend was declared on 30th June, 2015. Please state with reference to relevant Accounting Standard, whether the treatment accorded by SEA Ltd. is in order.

(g) Mr X sent 250 units costing ₹ 10,000 each to Mr Y. The goods were to be sold so as to yield a gross profit of 20% on sales. Mr Y sold 150 units @ ₹ 14,200 per unit on credit and 75 units @ ₹ 14,000 for cash. Mr Y entitled to a commission of ₹ 500 per unit sold *plus* one forth of the amount by which the gross sale proceeds less total commission thereon exceeded a sum calculated at the specified selling price.Calculate the commission due to Y.

(h) A and B enter into a joint venture sharing profit and losses in the ratio 3: 2. A purchased goods costing ₹ 2,00,000. B sold 95% goods for ₹ 2,50,000. A is entitled to get 1% commission on purchase and B is entitled to get 5% commission on sales. A drew a bill on B for an amount equivalent to 80% of original cost of goods. A got it discounted at ₹ 1,50,000. Calculate B's share of profit.

(i) A 3 month's bill of ₹ 5,00,000 dated 9.3.2015 was discounted @16% p.a. Give journal entries on 9.3.2015 and 31.3.2015.

(j) The Life Fund of Well-life Assurance Co. was ₹ 90,00,000 as on 31st March 2015. The interim bonus paid during the valuation period was ₹ 1,50,000. The periodical actuarial valuation determined the net liability at ₹ 75,00,000. Surplus brought forward from the previous valuation was ₹ 9,00,000. The directors of the company proposed to carry forward ₹ 10,00,000 and to divide the balance between the shareholders and the policy holders. Calculate Net Profit for the valuation period:

2. Answer any two questions: **4 × 2 = 8**

(a) The Trial Balance of Mr X failed to agree and the difference was put into Suspense Account pending investigation which discovered the following:

(a) Discount received ₹ 1,320 had been debited to Discount allowed as ₹ 132.

(b) Goods of the value of ₹ 200 returned by Kishan were entered in the Sales Day Book and posted therefrom to the credit of Krishan as ₹ 20.

(c) A credit purchase of ₹ 500 from N. Kumar was recorded as sale to M. Kumar for ₹ 50.

(d) A credit sale of machine to P. Dass for ₹ 600 recorded through Sales Day Book as sale to C. Dass for ₹ 60.

Required: Pass Rectifying Entries and prepare the Suspense Account.

(b) Calculate the value of raw materials and closing stock based on the following information:

Row material X	
Closing Balance	500 units
	₹ per unit
Cost price including excise duty	200
Exercise duty (Cenvat credit is receivalbe on the excise duty paid)	10
Freight inward	20
Unloading charges	10
Replacement cost	150
Finished good Y	
Closing Balance	1200 units
	₹ per unit
Material consumed	220
Direct labour	60
Direct overhead	40

Total Fixed overhead for the year was ₹ 2,00,000 on normal capacity of 20,000 units.

Calculate the value of the closing stock, when

(i) Net Realizable Value of the Finished Goods Y is ₹ 400.

(ii) Net Realizable Value of the Finished Goods Y is ₹ 300.

(c) From the following particulars, prepare a Bank Reconciliation Statement as on 31st March.

(a) Bank Balance as per Cash Book is ₹ 10,000

(b) A Cheque for ₹ 1,000 deposited but not recorded in the Cash Book.

(**Note:** Bank has collected and credited this cheque.)

(c) A Cash deposit of ₹ 200 was recorded in the Cash Book as if there is no Bank Column therein.

(d) A Cheque issued for ₹ 250 was recorded as ₹ 205 in the Cash Column. (Note: Bank has made the payment of this cheque.)

(e) The debit balance of ₹ 1,500 as on the previous day was brought forward as a credit balance.

(f) The payment side of the Cash Book (Bank column) was under cast by ₹ 100.

(g) A cash discount allowed of ₹ 112 was recorded as ₹ 121 in the Bank Column.

(h) A cheque of ₹ 500 received from a debtor was recorded in the Cash Book but not deposited in the Bank for collection.

(i) One outgoing cheque of ₹ 300 was recorded twice in the Cash Book.

3. Answer any two questions: **12 × 2 = 24**

(a) Tulsian Ltd. provides you the following information:

Date	Particulars
	The Machinery Account of Tulsian Ltd had a debit balance of ₹ 6,84,000 on 1st April, 2014
01.04.2012	Purchased 10 second hand Machines of the same type and incurred ₹ 70,000 towards freight & insurance, ₹ 20,000 towards carriage inward

01.01.2013	Incurred ₹ 7,000 towards Repairs and ₹ 3,000 on Installation of machines and ₹ 12,000 towards Annual Insurance Premium and commenced the commercial production.
01.10.2013	Sold one machine at a profit of 10%
01.01.2014	Incurred ₹ 10,000 on repairs of Machines
01.01.2015	Sold one machine at a loss of 10% and purchased a new machine for ₹ 90,000 and spent ₹ 10,000 on its installation

Depreciation was annually provided on 31st March @ 20% p.a on the written down value. On 31st March, 2015, it was decided to adopt the method of providing depreciation @ 20% p.a. on original cost.

Required: Prepare the Machinery A/c for the years 2012 – 2015.

(b) Following are the extracts from the Trial Balance of Mr. Bharat as at 31st March, 2015:

Particulars	₹	Particulars	₹
Purchases	5,25,000	Capital	5,19,000
Sales	6,30,000	Provision for Doubtful Debts	10,000
Trade Debtors	2,68,000	Provision for Discount on Debtors	1,800
Bad Debts	3,000	Bad Debt recovered	2,500
Discount Allowed	2,000	Income Tax paid	10,000
Building	60,000	Furniture and Fixtures	30,000
Plant and Machinery	2,10,000	Wages and Salaries	23,500
Outstanding Liabilities for Expenses (Dr.)	55,000	Salaries and Wages	11,200
Trade Creditors	10,000		

Additional Information:

1. Closing Stock : Cost ₹ 1,50,000,Market Value 80%,Realisable Expenses 5%
2. Write off further ₹ 4,000 as bad. Additional discount of ₹ 1,000 given to debtors. Maintain Provision for discount on Debtors@ 2%. Maintain a Provision for Doubtful debts @ 10%. Debtors also include Shyam for dishonoured bill of ₹ 10,000. Half the amount of Shyam's bills is irrecoverable. Remuneration of ₹ 2,000 paid to Sh. B. Barua, a temporary employee, stands debited to his personal account. Included amongst the Debtors is ₹ 3,000 due from Z and included among the Creditors ₹ 1,000 due to him.
3. On 31st March, Goods for ₹ 50,000 were sent to a customer on 'Sale or Return' basis at a profit of 25% on cost and recorded as actual sales.
4. Goods costing ₹ 20,000 (Sale Price ₹ 25,000) were taken by the proprietor for his personal use but not recorded .
5. Goods costing ₹ 30,000 (Sale Price ₹ 37,500) were distributed as free samples but not recorded.
6. On 31st March Goods costing ₹ 10,000 (Sale Price ₹ 12,500) were destroyed by fire it was fully insured but the insurance company admitted the claim to the extent of 60% only.
7. Wages include a sum of ₹ 4,000 spent on the erection of a cycle shed for employees and customers.
8. A Machine costing ₹ 1,90,000 was purchased on 1st July 2014. Wages₹ 10,000 paid for its Installation have been debited to Wages Account.
9. A Furniture costing ₹ 45,000 was purchased on 1st July 2014 but it was not recorded in the books as no payment was made of it. Wages ₹ 5,000 paid for its Installation have been debited to Wages Account.

10. Provide for depreciation on Plant & Machinery @ 10% p.a. Write 10% off the Furniture & Fixtures. Depreciate Buildings by 5%.
11. Printing and Stationery expenses of ₹ 55,000 relating to previous year had not been provided in that year but was paid in current year by debiting Outstanding Liabilities for Expenses.

Required: Show how these items will appear in the Financial Statements for the year ended 31st March, 2015

(c) Following is the Balance Sheet of A,B,C and D who were sharing in the ratio of 3: 3: 2: 2 as at 31st March, 2015, when they decided to dissolve the firm:

Liabilities	₹	Assets		₹
Trade Creditors	60,000	Cash at Bank		27,500
Bank Overdraft (Secured on Stock)	15,000	Sundry Debtors	50,000	
A's Loan	30,000	*Less:* Provision	(8,500)	41,500
Mrs. B's Loan	3,000	Stock		25,000
A's Capital	60,000	Prepaid Insurance		3,000
B's Capital	49,000	Goodwill		5,000
General Reserve	20,000	Tangible Fixed Assets		80,000
Employee's Provident Fund	5,000	B's Drawings		4,000
Machinery Replacement Reserve	20,000	C 's Capital		48,000
		D's Capital		18,000
		Profit & Loss A/c		10,000
	2,62,000			2,62,000

(a) After preparing the Balance Sheet as at 31st March, it was discovered that purchases amounting to ₹ 10,000 in March, were not recorded in books, though the goods were received during March.

(b) Half the Trade Creditors accepted the Net Tangible Fixed Assets at ₹ 24,000 [being 20% less than the book value] and cash in full settlement of their claims after allowing a discount of ₹ 2,000; Remaining Trade Creditors were paid ₹ 31,000 in final settlement including an investment worth ₹ 2,000 unrecorded in the books.

(c) Remaining Net Tangible Fixed Assets realised at a loss of 100% on net collection.

(d) 60% of Sundry Debtors realized 34% less; B is to take over 40% of the balance of Sundry Debtors at 70%. Further, he is to be allowed ₹ 800 to cover future losses and the remaining debtors (if any) were sold to a debt collecting agency at 70%.

(e) Stock was taken over by the banker, and it realised 80% of cost. Bank paid back ₹ 4,000 after recovering its overdraft and interest due thereon.

(f) There was a joint life policy for a sum assured of ₹ 90,000. The Joint Life Policy was surrendered to the insurance company. The company paid a sum of ₹ 4,000 after deducting an amount of ₹ 6,500 towards loan and interest thereon by B against the policy.

(g) A Debtor whose debt of ' 5,000 was written off as bad in the previous year paid 40% in full settlement.

(h) There was one unrecorded asset estimated at ₹ 40,000, half of which was handed over at an agreed valuation of 60% to an unrecorded liability of ₹ 26,000 in settlement of claim of ₹ 13,000 and remaining half was taken over by B at an agreed valuation of 42%.

(i) There was a bill for ₹ 21,000 under discount.The bill was received from Z. Z proved insolvent and a first and final dividend of 60% was received from his estate.

(j) B was appointed to realise the assets and to pay off the liabilities. He was entitled to receive 5% commission on the amount finally paid to other partners as capital. He was to bear the expenses of realisation. Expenses of realisation amounted to ₹ 1,600 which were met by B out of his private funds.

(k) The private position of the partners was as follows:

Particulars	A	B	C	D
Private Estate	1,00,000	2,00,000	3,00,000	4,00,000
Private Liabilities	89,200	1,94,000	2,88,900	3,70,000

Required: Prepare Realisation A/c, Partners' Capital A/cs and Bank A/c according to Garner vs. Murray Rule. (Ignore Commission while determining Realisation Loss)

4. Answer any two questions: **4 × 2 = 8**

(a) Following information is available from January 1 to March 31, 2011.

(i) Total Sales amounted to ₹ 60,000 including the sale of old furniture for ₹ 1,200 (Book Value ₹ 3,500). The total Cash Sales were 80% less than the total Credit Sales.

(ii) Cash collection from debtors amounted to 60% of the aggregate of the opening debtors and the Credit Sales for the period. Debtors were allowed Cash discounts for ₹ 2,600.

(iii) Bills Receivable drawn during the three months totalled ₹6,000 of which bills amounting to ₹ 3,000 were endorsed in favour of suppliers. Out of these endorsed B/R, a B/R for ₹ 600 was dishonoured for non-payment as the party became insolvent, his estate realizing nothing.

(iv) Cheques received from Sundry Customers for ₹ 6,000 were dishonoured; a sum of ₹ 500 is irrecoverable, Bad Debts written off in the earlier years realized ₹2,500.

(v) Sundry Debtors, as on 1st January 2011, stood at ₹ 40,000.

Prepare Debtors Ledger Adjustments Accounts in the General Ledger.

(b) Prepare Total Creditors Account for the year ended on 31.03.2013 from the data given below:

Particulars	₹
Creditors Balance on 01.04.2012	38,000
Credit Purchases during the year	2,67,000
Bills payable accepted	62,000
Cash paid to Creditors	1,37,000
B/R endorsed to creditors	16,000
Endorsed B/R dishonoured	3,000
B/P dishonoured	2,000
Purchase returns	11,000
Discount received	6,000
Transfer from Debtors ledger	7,000

(c) PCT Ltd. maintains self-balancing ledgers. On 31st March, 2014 the accountant of the company located the following errors in the books of account:

(i) An amount of 8,700 received from customer Meena was credited to Meenu, another customer.

(ii) The sales book for December, 2013 was undercast by ₹ 1,000.

(iii) Goods invoiced at 15,600 were returned to supplier, M/s BPO Ltd., but no entry was made in the books for this return made on 28th December, 2013.

Passs the necessary Journal entries to rectify the above mentioned errors.

5. Answer any two questions: **4 × 2 = 8**

(a) AQ Ltd., an investment company is finalizing its account for the Financial Year ending 2015 in the month of August 2015.

How will the following incomes be accounted for in the books of AQ Ltd.?

(1) X Ltd., has declared interim dividend which has not been received till 31-3-2015 but received on 25-4-2015.

(2) Y Ltd., has declared dividend on 8th May 2015 for the year ending 31-3-2015 which has been approved by the shareholders of the company on 30th June 2015.

(3) Z Ltd., a subsidiary of AQ Ltd., has declared dividend for the year ended 31-3-2015 on 25th May 2015 the AGM for which is to be held on September 2015.

(b) A firm of contractors obtain a contract for construction of a bridge across river Hindan. The following details are available in the records kept for the year ended 31st March, 2015:

Particulars	₹ in lakhs
Total Contract Price	2,000
Work Certified	1,400
Work Not Certified	400
Estimated Further Cost to Completion	700
Progress Payment: Received	1,000
To be Received	200

The firm seeks your advice and assistance in the presentation of accounts keeping in view the requirements of AS – 7.

(c) XYZ Company has taken a Transit Insurance Policy. Suddenly in the year 2014-2015 the percentage of accident has gone upto 10 % and company wants to recognize insurance claim as revenue in year 2014-2015 in accordance with relevant Accounting Standards. Comment.

6. Answer any two questions: **8 × 2 = 16**

(a) Arun and Anand were friends and in need of funds. On 1st Jan., Arun drew a bill for ₹ 2,00,000 for 3 months on Anand. On 4th Jan. Arun got the bill discounted at 10% p.a. and remitted half of the proceeds to Anand. At maturity, Anand could not meet the bill, instead, Arun accepted Anand's bill for ₹ 1,20,000 on 4th April for two months. This was discounted by Anand at 12% p.a. Out of this, ₹ 19,600 was paid to Arun after deducting ₹ 400 discounting charges. Due to financial crisis, Arun became insolvent and the bill drawn on him was dishonoured and his estate paid 50%. Days of grace for discount purposes may be ignored. Give journal entries in the books of Arun. Also prepare Anand's Account in Arun's books and Arun's Account in the books of Anand.

(b) On 1st September goods of the cost of ₹ 2,64,000 were consigned by Shri Shyamlal of Bangalore to his agent Shri Mahesh of Cochin at proforma invoice price of 20% profit on cost price. Shri Shyamlal paid insurance and other forwarding charges on consignment amounting to ₹ 10,000. Shri Mahesh was allowed ₹ 2,000 being establishment cost. He was entitled to 5% commission on gross sales and an additional 3% Delcredere commission on credit sales only. Shri Mahesh made an expense of ₹ 2,040 as landing charges.

Three fourth of the goods were sold at 33% profit on cost, half of which were credit sales. One half of the balance of goods were destroyed by fire and a claim lodged for ₹ 28,000 was settled at a discount of 10%. The balance of goods were in stock. Show the Consignment Account and the Stock Loss on Consignment Account as on 31st Dec. in the books of Shri Shyamlal.

(c) Ramda & Sons had taken out policies (without Average Clause) both against Loss of Stock and Loss of Profit, for ₹ 2,10,000 and ₹ 3,20,000 respectively. A fire occurred on 1st July 2013, and as a result of which sales were seriously affected for a period of 3 months.

TRADING AND PROFIT & LOSS A/C FOR THE YEAR ENDED ON 31ST MARCH 2013

Particulars	₹	Particulars	₹
To Opening Stock	96,000	By Sales	12,00,000
To Purchases	7,56,000	By Closing Stock	1,85,000
To Wages	1,58,000		
To Manufacturing Expenses	75,000		
To Gross Profit c/d	3,00,000		
	13,85,000		13,85,000
To Administrative Expenses	83,600	By Gross Profit b/d	3,00,000
To Selling Expenses (Fixed)	72,400		
To Commission on Sales	34,200		
To Carriage Outwards	49,800		
To Net Profit	60,000		
	3,00,000		3,00,000

Further detail provided is as below:

(a) Sales, Purchases, Wages and Manufacturing Expenses for the period 01.04.2013 to 30.06.2013 were ₹ 3,36,000, ₹ 2,14,000 ₹ 51,000 and ₹ 12,000 respectively.

(b) Other Sales figure were as follows:

From 01.04.2012 to 30.06.2012 ₹ 3,00,000

From 01.07.2012 to 30.09.2012 ₹ 3,20,000

From 01.07.2013 to 30.09.2013 ₹ 48,000

(c) Due to decrease in the Material Cost, Gross Profit during 2013-2014 was expected to increase by 5% on Sales.

(d) ₹ 1,98,000 were additionally incurred during the period after fire. The amount of policy included ₹ 1,56,000 for Expenses leaving ₹ 42,000 uncovered.

Required: Compute the Claim for Stock, Loss of Profit and Additional Expenses.

7. **Answer any two questions:** **8 × 2 = 16**

(a) From the following ledger balances, prepare Profit & Loss Account of a Tulsian Bank Ltd. for the year ending 31.3.2015. (The figures being in thousands)

Particulars	₹	Particulars	₹
Interest and Discount	8,880	Interest Expended	2,720
Other Income	220	Operating Expenses	2,662
Income from Investments	30		5,000

Additional Information:

(a)	Rebate on bills discounted: on 31.3.2014	₹ 15
	on 31.3.2015	₹ 45
(b)	Interest accrued on Investments	₹ 10
(c)	Classification of Advances:	₹
	Standard Assets	₹ 5,000

Sub-Standard Assets	₹ 1,120
Doubtful Assets not covered by security	₹ 510
Doubtful Assets covered by security	
for 1 year	50
for 2 years	100
for 3 years	200
for 4 years	150
Loss Assets	80
(d) Make Tax provision @ 35%	
(e) Profit and Loss A/c (Cr.) on 31.3.2014 ₹ 80	
(f) The Directors desire to recommend 5% Dividend.	
(g) Total Investments ₹ 800 of which 25% are held to maturity. The market value of Investment, is 80%.	

(b) Tulsian Fire Insurance Company submits the following information for the year ended 31st march 2015:

Particulars		Direct Business (₹)	Reinsurance (₹)
Premium received		75,25,000	8,25,000
Premium Receivable as on 01.04.2014		3,25,000	2,00,000
Premium Receivable as on 31.03.2015		5,00,000	3,75,000
Premium Paid			4,90,000
Premium Payable as on 01.04.2014			1,00,000
Premium payable as on 31.03.2015			4,50,000
Claims Paid during the Year		49,70,000	5,10,000
Claims Payable:	1st April 2014	6,85,000	95,000
	31st March 2015	7,38,000	70,000
Claims Received		–	3,95,000
Claims Receivable:	1st April 2014	–	75,000
	31st March 2015	–	1,25,000
Expenses of Management		2,90,000	–
Commission:	On Insurance Accepted	1,60,000	15,000
	On Insurance Ceded	–	18,000

The aollowing additional information are also available:

(i) Expenses of Management include ₹ 45,000 Surveyor's Fees and ₹ 55,000. Legal Expenses for settlement of claims.

(ii) Reserve for Unexpired Risk is to be maintained @ 40%. Additional Reserve is to be maintained @ 5%. The balance of Reserve for Unexpired Risk as on 01.04.2014 was ₹ 31,95,000 (including Additional Reserve ₹ 3,55,000)

(iii) Interest, Dividend & Rent Received (after TDS @ 10%) ₹ 34,200

You are required to make the Revenue Account for the year ended 31st March 2015.

(c) Tulsian Electricity Compamy which maintains accounts under the Double Account System laid down a main at a cost of ₹ 30 lacs. Some years later, the company laid down an auxillary main for one-fifth of the length of the old main at a cost of ₹ 15 lacs. It decides to replace the rest of the length of the old main at a cost of ₹ 60 lacs. It is ascertained that the proportion of Labour to materials in the main then and now is 3: 5 and overheads constitute 20% of total expenditure. The cost of materials and labours have gone up by 40% and 80% respectively.

Old materials valued at ₹ 2,40,000 were used in renewal and those value at ₹ 50,000 were used in the construction of the auxiliary main. Some old materials were sold for ₹ 7,50,000.

Required: Find out the amount to be capitalised and also the amount to be charged to Revenue. Pass the necessary journal entries.

TULSIAN'S MODEL TEST PAPER 2
INTERMEDIATE EXAMINATION GROUP I
(SYLLABUS 2012)
PAPER – 5: FINANCIAL ACCOUNTING

Time Allowed: 3 Hours **Full Marks: 100**

The figures in the margin on the right side indicate full marks.
This paper contains seven questions. All questions are compulsory, subject to instruction provided against each question.
All working must form part of your answer.

1. Answer the following questions (Give workings): **2 × 10 = 20**

(a) Balance as per Pass Book of Shri Krishan is ₹ 10,000. Bank collected a cheque of ₹ 500 on behalf of Shri Krishan but wrongly credited it to Shri Kishan's A/c (another customer). Bank recorded a Cash deposit of ₹ 1,589 as ₹ 1,598. Withdrawal column of the Pass Book undercast by ₹ 100. The credit balance of ₹ 15,121 as on page 5 of the Pass Book was recorded on page 6 as the debit balance of ₹ 15,112. The payment of a cheque of ₹ 350 was recorded twice in the Pass Book.The Pass Book showed a credit for a cheque of ₹ 50,000 deposited by Shri Kishan (another customer of the Bank). Calculate the Balance as per Cash Book on 31st March. Also Calculate the Bank Balance to be taken to the Balance Sheet.

(b) Bharat Tushar Ltd. which depreciates its machinery at 10% p.a. on diminishing balance method, had on1st April 2014 ₹ 29,160, to the debit of Machinery Account. On 31st March 2015, the company decided to change the method of depreciation to Straight Line Method with effect from 1st April 2011 being the date of purchase of machine and the rate of depreciation remaining the same. There was no purchase/sale of machine after1st April, 2011. Pass the necessary journal entry on account of change in method of depreciation

(c) H's Trial Balance contains the following information:

Bad debts ₹ 3,000,Discount allowed ₹ 3,000, Provision for discount on debtors ₹ 3,200, Provision for Doubtful Debts ₹ 13,500,Sundry Debtors ₹ 55,000.

Additional Bad Debts ₹ 4,000, Additional Discount allowed ₹ 1,000. At the end of the year, it is desired to maintain a provision for Doubtful Debts at 10% and Provision for Discount on Debtors at 2%. At what figure these items will appear in the Profit & Loss A/c?

(d) A, B, C and D were the partners in a firm sharing profits in the ratio of 3: 3: 2: 2. The firm was dissolved on 31.03.2015. There was one unrecorded asset estimated at ₹ 40,000, half of which was handed over at an agreed valuation of 60% to an unrecorded liability of ₹ 64,000 in settlement of claim of ₹ 32,000 and remaining half was taken over by B at an a greed valuation of 62%. Pass necessary journal entries in the books of the firm.

(e) How will you show the following items in General Ledger Adjustment Account in Creditors Ledger:

	₹
(a) Transfer from Debtors' Ledgers to Creditors' Ledger	1,100
(b) Transfer from Creditors' Ledger to Debtors' Ledger	1,900
(c) B/R endorsed to Creditors	4,000
(d) Endorsed Bills dishonoured	1,000
(e) Reserve for Discount on Creditors	2,000

(f) Bills Payable matured 7,000

(g) Discount received 600

(h) Allowances from Creditors 3,200

(i) Discount allowed to debtors ₹ 500 was recorded as discount received from creditors.

(j) Closing Creditors ₹ 30,000 (Dr.)

(f) XYZ Ltd. purchased goods on credit from ABC Ltd. for ₹ 250 crores for export. The export order was cancelled. XYZ Ltd. decided to sell the same goods in the local market with a price discount. ABC Ltd. was requested to offer a price discount of 15 %. The directors of ABC Ltd. want to adjust the sales figure to the extent of the discount requested by XYZ Ltd. Comment.

(g) X draws on Y a bill for ₹ 2,00,000 on 1st April for 3 months. Y accepts the bill and sends it to X who gets it discounted for ₹ 1,95,000. X immediately remits ₹ 97,500 to Y. On due date, X being unable to remit the amount due accepts a bill for ₹ 1,20,000 for 2 months which is discounted by Y for ₹ 1,17,600. Y sends ₹ 7,800 to X out of the same. How much discount will be borne by X at the time of remittance of ₹ 7,800?

(h) From the following, Calculate the amount of claim:

(a) Book value of Normal Stock ₹ 54,600

(b) Current value of Abnormal Stock ₹ 3,450

(c) Stock to the value of ₹ 8,700 was salvaged out of which one third was handed over to the Insurance Co.

(d) Sum Insured ₹ 50,000

(e) Fire Fighting expenses ₹ 2,750

(i) In X Bank Ltd., the doubtful assets (since Jan 2012) as on 31.3.2015 is ₹ 1,000 lakhs. The value of security (including DICGC 100% cover of ₹ 100 lakhs) is ascertained at ₹ 500 lakhs. How much provision must be made in the books of the Bank towards doubtful assets?

(j) The Life Fund of Well-life Assurance Co. was ₹ 90,00,000 as on 31st March 2015. The interim bonus paid during the valuation period was ₹ 1,50,000. The periodical actuarial valuation determined the net liability at ₹ 75,00,000. Surplus brought forward from the previous valuation was ₹ 9,00,000. The directors of the company proposed to carry forward ₹ 10,00,000 and to divide the balance between the shareholders and the policy holders. Show the Distribution of the Surplus:

2. Answer any two questions: **4 × 2 = 8**

(a) Pass the necessary journal entries to rectify the following errors:

(a) A cash sale of Goods to X ₹ 17,000 posted as ₹ 71,000

(b) A credit sale of Goods to Y ₹ 17,000 posted as ₹ 71,000.

(c) A credit sale of Furniture to Z for ₹ 17,000 posted as ₹ 71,000.

(d) Bills payable worth ₹ 3,000 accepted in favour of Murari, was passed through bills receivable book with ₹ 300 and Murari's account was debited with ₹ 3,000. Pass the Rectifying Entry.

(b) Cashier of A-One Limited embezzled cash amounting to ₹ 6,00,000 during March, 2013. However same comes to the notice of Company management during April, 2013 only. financial statements of the company are not approved by the Board of Directors of the company.

(a) With the help of provisions of AS 4 "contingencies and Event Occurring after the Balance Sheet Date" decide, whether the embezzlement of cash should be adjusted in the books of accounts for the ending March, 2013?

(b) What will be your replay, if embezzlement of cash comes to the notice of company management only after approval of financial statements by the Board Directors of the company?

(c) Determine the value of stock to be taken to the Balance Sheet of PCT Ltd. as at 31st March from the following information:

The stock was physically verified on 7th April and was valued at ₹ 4,00,000. After 31st March the following transactions had taken place till the date of stock taking.

(a) Purchases ₹ 2,00,0000 out of which 20% goods were returned.

(b) Sales of good units ₹ 2,00,000 out of which 20% goods were returned by the customers

(c) Sales of defective units ₹ 1,80,000 at 10% less than the normal selling price.

(d) On 26th March goods of the sale value of ₹ 2,00,000 were sent on sale or return basis to a customer, the period of approval being two weeks. He returned 20% of the goods and approved 80% of the remaining on 6th April.

(e) On 27th March goods of the sales value of ₹ 2,00,000 were sent on consignment basis. 80% of these goods had been sold on 6th April.

(f) On 28th March goods costing ₹ 2,00,000 were received for sale on consignment basis. 80% of these goods had been sold on 6th April.

Notes:

(i) Goods are sold by the trader at a profit of 25% on cost.

(ii) The sales referred to in (d), (e) & (f) are not included in (b) above.

3. Answer any two questions: **12 × 2 = 24**

(a) From the following information of TULSIAN CLUB, prepare the Restaurant Trading A/c, Income & Expenditure A/c for the year ended 31st March,2015 and Balance Sheet as on that date:

Receipts	₹	Payments	₹
Opening Balances:		Restaurant Purchases	2,04,800
Stamps	50	Wages (including ₹ 50000 for Restaurant).	92,300
Bank FD	10,000	Fuel	17,700
Bank Balance (as per Pass Book)	6,300	Supplier of Sports material	54,000
Restaurant Takings	3,61,600	Postage Expenses	200
Subscription:		Tournament Expenses	5,530
2012-2013	400	Rent	1,48,500
2013-2014	8,900	Rates & Taxes	300
2014-2015	1,34,400	Telephone charges	1,500
2015-2016	4,000	Affiliation Fee	2,400
2016-2017	1,200	Honorarium	12,000
Entrance Donation	1,00,000	Purchases of Books & Periodicals (including ₹.19,000 for Purchase of Books)	29,000
Donation for Prizes	2,800	Sundry Assets	8,000
Donation for Building	2,80,000	Prize awarded	2,000
Bank Interest received	1340	Expenditure on Building (31.3.2016)	2,00,000
Interest on Govt. Securities (after TDS @ 10%)	18,000	Expenditure on Pavilion	30,000
Sale of old Sports Assets	5,200	Closing Balances:	

Interest on Prize Fund Investment	600	Bank Balance (as per Pass Book)	1,96,535
Interest on Building Fund Investment	60,000	Stamps	25
Cash overspent	1,000	Bank FD	11,000
		10% Govt.Securities	1,80,000
	9,66,790		9,66,790

Additional Information:

(A) OPENING & CLOSING BALANCES

	01.04.2014	31.03.2015
Subscription Outstanding *(including 500 for 2012-2013)	*9,500	6,900
Advance Subscription *(including 200 for 2015-2016)	*3,000	?
Stock in Restaurant	3,900	4,500
China Glass Cutlery	2,500	?
Amt. due to suppliers of Sports material	15,000	9,750
Advances to supplier of Sports Material	5,000	3,250
Stock of Sports material	15,000	2,500
Rates & Taxes	?	?
Telephone charges	?	?
Entrance Donation received pending membership	1,00,000	
Cheques issued but not presented for Tournament Expenses	270	90
Pavilion at cost	87,000	1,17,000
Accumulated Depreciation on Pavilion	56,400	
Sundry Assets	44,000	43,200
10% Building Fund Investment	12,00,000	?
Building Fund	12,00,000	?
Prize Fund	12,000	?
10% Prize Fund Investment	12,000	?

(b) Boarding expenses - restaurant staff ₹ 20000, other staff ₹ 7,500.

(c) Subscription of ₹ 100 for 2012-2013 written off.

(d) 50% of Entrance Donation was to be capitalised. There was no pending membership as on 31.3.2015. A sum of ₹ 20,000 received in October 2014 as Entrance Donation was to be refunded. The refund was made on 3.6.2015.

(e) Interest accrued on Bank deposit but not received ₹ 200.

(f) Govt. Securities of ₹ 2,00,000 (cost ₹ 1,80,000) present investment in Endowment Fund.

(g) Cash overspent represents Honorarium not withdrawn due to cash deficit. Annual Honorarium ₹ 12,000.

(h) Depreciation on Pavilion is to be provided at 5% on WDV basis. Depreciation on China Glass Cutlery @ 20% is to be provided, Rate of Depreciation on Books 10%

(i) the Club was admitted as a member of All India Lawn Tennis Federation on 1.10.2014 when it paid subscription till 30.9.2015.

(j) Book value as on 1.4.2014 of Sports Assets sold was ₹ 4,000.

(k) Rent for 1 month is outstanding

(l) At 31.3.2015, rates & taxes were prepaid to the following 31 Jan., yearly charge ₹ 300.

(m) A quarter charge for telephone is outstanding, the amt accrued ₹ 300. The charge for each quarter is same.

(b) On 1.1.2013, X purchased 5 Machines from Y. Payment was to be made—20% down and the balance in four annual instalments of ₹ 2,80,000, ₹ 2,60,000, ₹ 2,40,000 and ₹ 2,20,000 commencing from 31.12.2013. The vendor charged interest @ 10% p.a. X, writes off depreciation @ 20% p.a. on the original cost. On X.'s failure to pay the instalment due on 31.12.2014, after negotiations on 1.1.2015 Y agreed to leave two machines with X adjusting the value of the other three machines against the amount due. The machines being valued at cost less 40% p.a. depreciation on W.D.V. basis, Y after spending ₹ 6,000 on repairs of each of such machines sold @ ₹ 70,000 on 30th June 2015. Prepare the relevant accounts in the books of X and Y

(c) TUSHAR Ltd. with its Head Office in Delhi invoices goods to its Branches at Mumbai and Kolkata at 20% less than the catalogue price which is cost plus 50% with instructions that cash sales are to be made at invoice price and credit sales at catalogue price less discount at 15% on prompt payments. Provision is to be made for discount to be allowed to debtors, at year end on the basis of year's trend of prompt payments. All branch expenses are paid by the Head Office and all branch collections are remitted daily to Head Office.

1. Opening Stock At Branch at its cost ₹ 12,000.
2. Opening Branch Debtors ₹ 10,000.
3. Goods Sent to branch (at cost to H.O.) ₹ 1,10,000.
4. Goods received by Branch till close of the year ₹ 1,27,000.
5. Transfer from Kolkata branch to Mumbai branch at catalogue price ₹ 75,000.
6. Transfer to Kolkata branch from Mumbai branch at catalogue price ₹ 30,000.
7. Goods purchased by Mumbai branch from local suppliers (cost) ₹ 30,000. Closing stock in hand at branch out of local purchases (cost) ₹ 6,000.
8. Cash Sales ₹ 74,800.
9. Credit Sales ₹ 1,45,000.
10. Goods returned by Credit Customers to branch ₹ 30,000.
11. Goods returned by Credit Customers directly to H.O. ₹ 15,000.
12. Goods returned by Branch to H.O. ₹ 24,000.
13. Cash remitted by Credit Customers directly to Branch ₹ 45,635.
14. Cash remitted by Credit Customers directly to H.O. ₹ 40,000.
15. Discount Allowed to Debtors ₹ 13,365.
16. Loss of Goods by fire (at invoice price) ₹ 3,000 against which 80% of cost was recovered from the insurance Company.
17. Loss of goods at Branch through normal pilferage (at catalogue price) ₹ 3,000.
18. Branch Expenses: Paid ₹ 9,000, Outstanding ₹ 741.
19. Branch Manager is entitled to a commission @ 6% of net profits after charging such commission.

Required: Prepare Mumbai Branch Stock Account, Mumbai Branch adjustment A/c, Mumbai Branch Expenses A/c and Mumbai Branch Profit & Loss A/c and Mubmai Branch Debtors A/c under Stock & Debtors Method.

4. Answer any two questions: **4 × 2 = 8**

(a) From the following information, prepare Total Debtors Account for the year ending on 31st March, 2015:

(a) Trade Debtors as on 1.4.2014 ₹ 2,00,000

(b) Gross Sales (including Cash Sales of ₹ 4,00,000) ₹ 16,20,000

(c) Return Inwards ₹ 20,000

(d) Discount Allowed ₹ 11,000 (of which later on ₹ 1,000 disallowed)

(e) Cash received from Debtors ₹ 2,20,000 (including ₹ 20,000 from a person to whom an old fixed asset was sold)

(f) Cheques received from Debtors ₹ 4,40,000 of which cheques amounting to ₹ 40,000 were dishonoured. Out of these dishonoured cheques a cheque for ₹ 10,000 was dishonoured for non-payment as the customer became insolvent and his estate realised nothing.

(g) Bills Receivables drawn during the year totalled ₹ 6,60,000 of which bills amounting to ₹ 60,000 were endorsed in favour of suppliers. Bills dishonoured ₹ 30,000 (including Bills of ₹ 10,000 endorsed to suppliers).

(h) Interest on Overdue Accounts ₹ 45,000

(i) Bad Debts written off in earlier years recovered ₹ 20,000

(j) Provision for Doubtful Debts on Debtors ₹ 25,000.

(k) Transfer to Bought Ledger ₹ 15,000.

(b) Pass the necessary journal entries using a Suspense Account presuming when the system of self-balancing is in use.

(a) Goods of the value of ₹ 500 returned by Mr Sharma were entered in the Sales Day Book and posted therefrom to the credit of his account.

(b) An amount of ₹ 300, entered in the Sales Returns Book, has been posted to the debit of Mr Philip, who returned the goods.

(c) A sale of ₹ 100 made to Mr Ghanshyam was correctly entered in the Sales Day Book but wrongly posted to the debit of Mr Radhesham as ₹ 10.

(d) Bad Debts aggregating ₹ 150 were written off during the year in the Sales Ledger but were not adjusted in General Ledger.

(e) The total of "Discount Allowed" column in the Cash Book for the month of Jan, amounting to ₹ 1,000 was not posted.

(c) From the following particulars, prepare the Creditors' Ledger Adjustment Account as would appear in the General Ledger of Mr. Sathish for the month of March 2015.

Date	Particulars
1	Purchased from Mr. Akash ₹ 7,500.
3	Paid ₹ 3,000 after adjusting the initial advance in full to Mr. Akash.
10	Paid ₹ 2,500 to Mr. dev towards the purchases made in February in full.
12	Paid advance to Mr. Giridhar ₹ 6,000.
14	Purchased goods from Mr. Akash ₹ 6,200
20	Returned goods worth ₹ 1,000 to Mr. Akash
24	Settled the balance due to Mr. Akash at a discount of 5%.
26	Goods purchased from Mr. Giridhar against the advance paid already.
29	Purchased from Mr. Nathan ₹ 3,500

30	Goods returned to Mr. Prem ₹ 1,200. The goods were originally purchased for cash in the month of February 2015.

5. Answer any two questions: 4 × 2 = 8

(a) B Ltd. entered into an agreement on 1st March, 2015 to buy computer spares from S Ltd. at prevailing market price for ₹ 1200 lakhs on which S Ltd. made a profit of 20% and received full advance payment. The transaction was concluded on 15th March, 2015. On the same day S Ltd. agrees to buy on 15th Sept., 2015 the same goods from B Ltd. at 20% over cost. The 20% mark up compensates B Ltd. for its inventory holding costs till sale date. You are required to show how both the buyer and seller account for the above transaction in the year 2015-2016 explaining in brief the justification for your treatment and also draft the Notes on Account on disclosure if any required in the annual accounts of year ended 31st March, 2015.

(b) PRARTHANA LTD, a firm of contractors provides the following details for the year ended 31st March, 2013:

	(₹ in lakhs)
Total Contract Price	₹ 1,000 lacs
Work Certified	500
Work not Certified	105
Estimated further Cost to Completion	495
Progress Payment Received	400
To be Received	140

Required: Show the relevant disclosures under AS 7.

(c) ABC Ltd. sells agriculture products to dealers. One of the condition of sale is that interest is payable at the rate of 2 % per month, for delayed payments. Percentage of intent recovery is only 10 % on such overdue outstanding due to various reasons. During the year 2014-2015 the company wants to recognize the entire interest receivable. Do you agree?

6. Answer any two questions: 8 × 2 = 16

(a) A of Agra and B of Kanpur entered into a joint venture for purchase and sale of C.D. players. The cost of each C.D. player was ₹ 3,600 and the fixed retail selling price ₹ 4,500. The following transactions were recorded between them:

2015	A purchased 100 C.D. players paying ₹ 72,000 in cash on account.
July 1	A raised a loan from Bank for ₹ 50,000 at 18% p.a. which is repayable with interest on 1.9.20X5. A forwarded 80 C.D. players to B incurring ₹ 2,880 as forwarding and insurance charges.
July 7	A received the consignment and paid ₹ 720 as clearing charges.
Aug. 1	A sold 5 mopeds for cash. B sold 20 mopeds for cash. A raised a loan of ₹ 1,50,000 from Bank, repayable with interest at 18% p.a. on 1.9.2015. B remitted ₹ 1,50,000 to A, incurring charges of ₹ 50. A paid the balance due for the C.D. players.
Aug.26	A sold the balance C.D. players for cash and paid selling expenses ₹ 5,000, B sold the balance C.D. players for cash and paid selling expenses ₹ 20,000.
Sept. 1	Accounts settled between the ventures and loans repaid, they shared profit equally. You are required to show: (i) The memorandum Joint Venture Account; (ii) Joint Venture with B account in A books; and (iii) Joint Venture with A Account in B books;

(b) Mr. A, a trader, dispatched goods costing ₹ 16,000 to his customer Mr B on sale or return basis after charging a gross profit of 25% on cost. Mr. A had treated the transaction as credit sale at the time of dispatch of the goods. Pass Journal entries in the books of Mr. A, if:

(i) the customer had approved the goods on 31st March.

(ii) the customer had rejected all the goods on 31st March:

(iii) the customer had retained half of the goods while rejecting the other half on 31st March.

(c) Blue-chip Equity Investments Ltd., wants to re-classify its investments in accordance with AS 13.

(i) Long term investments in Company A, costing ₹ 8.5 lakhs are to be re-classified as current. The comp0any had reduced the value of these investments to ₹ 6.5 lakhs to recognize a permanent decline in value. The fair value on date of transfer is ₹ 6.8 lakhs.

(ii) Long term investments in Company B, costing ₹ 7 lakhs are to be re-classified as current. The fair value on date of transfer is ₹ 8 lakhs and book value is ₹ 7 lakhs.

(iii) Current investment in Company C, costing ₹ 10 lakhs are to be re-classified as long term as the company wants to retain them. The market value on date of transfer is ₹ 12 lakhs.

(iv) Current investment in Company D, costing ₹ 15 lakhs are to be re-classified as long term. The market value on date of transfer is ₹ 14 lakhs.

7. Answer any two questions: **8 × 2 = 16**

(a) TULSIAN BANK Ltd provides you the following information:

1. Rebate on Bills Discounted as on 1st April, 2014,. ₹ 11.10 crores
2. An analysis of the bills discounted during the year

Date of Bill	Amount (₹ in Crores)	Term (Months)	Rate of Discount (% p.a)
27.12.2014	3,400	3	15%
09.03.2015	600	3	12%

Required:

(i) Pass the necessary journal entries for the year ended on 31st March, 2015

(ii) Prepare Rebate on Bills Discounted A/c and Discount on Bills A/c

(iii) Show how the relevant items will appear in the Bank's Financial Statements.

(b) Jalan Fire Insurance Company submits the following information for the year ended 31st march 2015:

Particulars		Direct Business (₹)	Reinsurance (₹)
Premium received		45,15,000	4,95,000
Premium Receivable as on 01.04.2014		1,95,000	1,20,000
Premium Receivable as on 31.03.2015		3,00,000	2,25,000
Premium Paid		—	2,94,000
Premium Payable as on 01.04.2014		—	60,000
Premium payable as on 31.03.2015		—	2,70,000
Claims Paid during the Year		29,82,000	3,06,000
Claims Payable:	1st April 2014	4,11,000	57,000
	31st March 2015	4,42,800	42,000
Claims Received		—	2,37,000
Claims Receivable:	1st April 2014	—	45,000

	31st March 2015	—	75,000
Expenses of Management		1,74,000	—
Commission:	On Insurance Accepted	96,000	9,000
	On Insurance Ceded	—	10,800

The aollowing additional information are also available:

(i) Expenses of Management include ₹ 27,000 Surveyor's Fees and ₹ 33,000. Legal Expenses for settlement of claims.

(ii) Reserve for Unexpired Risk is to be maintained @ 40%. Additional Reserve is to be maintained @ 5%. The balance of Reserve for Unexpired Risk as on 01.04.2014 was ₹ 19,17,000 (including Additional Reserve ₹ 2,13,000)

(iii) Interest, Dividend & Rent Received (after TDS @ 10%) ₹ 20,520

You are required to make the Revenue Account for the year ended 31st March 2015.

(c) The trial balance of Tulsian Electric Supply Ltd. For the year ended 31st March, 2015 is as below:

(₹ '000)

Particulars	Dr.	Cr.
Share Capital:		
Equity Shares of ₹.10 each		500,00
14% Preference Shares of ₹.100 each		150,00
Patents and trade mark	25,04	
15% Debentures		24,700
16% term loan		153,00
Land (additons during the year 20,50)	124,50	
Building (additions during the year 50,80)	351,34	
Plant & Machinery	570,58	
Mains	45,24	
Meters	31,50	
Electrical Instruments	15,30	
Office Rurniture	24,50	
Capital Reserve		40,20
Contingency Reserves		120,30
General Reserve		10,00
Transformers	164,40	
Opening Balance of Profit & Loss Account		350
Profit for the year 2014-2015 subject to adjustments		5,000
Stock in hand	120,50	
Sundry Debtors	62,46	
Contingency Reserve Investments:		
SBI Bonds-2020	100,10	
Other Investments	20,00	
Cash & Bank	32,54	

Public lamps	30,40	
Depreciation Fund		258,16
Sundry Creditiors		65,24
Proposed dividend		121,00
	1718,40	1718,40

During 2014-2015 1,00,000, 14% Preference Shares were redeemed at a premium of 10% out of proceeds of fresh issue of equity shares of necessary amounts at a premium of 10%

Adjustments:

1. Transfer to Contingency Reserve ₹.1,70,000 & to General Reserve ₹.2,00,000
2. Loss on Contingency Reserve Investment ₹.10,000
3. Make a Provision for debts considered doubtful of ₹.1,014,000

Required: Prepare Balance Bheet as at 31st March,2015 as per the Schedule III.

TULSIAN'S MODEL TEST PAPER 3 INTERMEDIATE EXAMINATION GROUP I (SYLLABUS 2012) PAPER – 5: FINANCIAL ACCOUNTING

Time Allowed: 3 Hours **Full Marks: 100**

The figures in the margin on the right side indicate full marks. This paper contains seven questions. All questions are compulsory, subject to instruction provided against each question. All working must form part of your answer.

1. **Answer the following questions (Give workings):** **2 × 10 = 20**

(a) Give two examples each of the Extra Ordinary Items and Prior Period Items.

(b). Cash Down Payment—₹ 1,58,500, Four Instalments of ₹ 2,21,900, ₹ 2,06,050, ₹ 1,90,200 & ₹ 1,74,350 at the end of the Ist year, 2nd year, 3rd year and 4th year respectively. Payment of cash price in each instalment—Uniform. Compute the amount of Interest.

(c) Tulsian Ltd provides you the following information:

Short Working B/f [₹ 6,000 for 2012, ₹ 10,000 for 2013]

Royalty @ ₹ 100 per unit produced subject to Minimum Rent of ₹ 1,00,000.

Sales of 2015: 950 units and Closing Stock: for 2014 300 units, for 2015 50 units.

In the event of strike, the minimum rent would be taken pro-rata on the basis of actual numbers of working days but in the event of lockout, the lessee would be enjoy a concession in respect of minimum rent of 50% of the period of lockout. There was strike for 73 days and lockout for 4 months during the year 2015. Recoumpent of short working of each year is allowed during the next 3 years subject to maximum of ₹ 5,000 p.a.Calculate the Actual Payment and Short Working C/F.

(d) A lease is purchased on 1st April, 2011 for 4 years at a cost of ₹ 40,000. It is proposed to depreciate the lease by the annuity method charging interest @ 5% p.a. A reference to the annuity table shows that to depreciate ₹ 1 by annuity method over 4 years charging interest at 5% p.a. one must write off a sum of ₹ 0.2820. ₹ 4,000 would also be refunded after 4 years. Calculate the Annual Depreciation Charge as per Annuity Method.

(e) Debtors List of ₹ 1,00,000 includes ₹ 1,000 owed by X and ₹ 500 by Y. Similarly, Creditors List of ₹ 2,00,000 covers ₹ 3,000 owed to X and ₹ 300 to Y. Give the necessary Journal Entries for the transfer under Self Balancing System.

(f) On 31st October, 2014, Bharat Construction Co. Ltd. undertook a contract to construct a Flyover for ₹ 215 crores. On 31st March, 2015, company found that its work certified is for ₹ 100 crores and work to be certified is for ₹ 35 crores. Prudent estimate of additional cost for completion was ₹ 90 crores. What amount should be charged to Revenue in the final accounts for the year ended 31st March, 2015 as per provisions of Accounting Standard 7 (revised).

(g) X invoiced goods to Y at 25% profit on cost. 40% of goods were lost in transit. 60% of goods received were sold by consignee at 25% above the invoice price. Rate of commission is 10% on sales at invoice price plus 50% of the surplus over invoice price. The amount of commission earned by consignee is ₹ 8,100. Calculate the cost of goods sent on consignment?

(h) Agreed G.P. Ratio 20%, Net Profit for the last accounting year 2,40,000, Standing Charges (out of which ₹ 80,000 have not been insured) ₹ 5,60,000, actual turnover during claim period ₹ 8,00,000. During the claim period, 50% of the total turnover of this period was maintained by incurring the additional expenses amounting to ₹ 1,50,000 and there was a saving in insured standing charges of 6.25% and in uninsured standing charges of ₹ 10,000. Turnover during 12 months preceding the date of fire ₹ 30,00,000. Agreed Increase 20%.Calculate the Net Claim for the increased Cost of Working.

(i) Interest and discount ₹ 8,850 lacs, Other Income ₹ 220 lacs, Income from investment ₹ 40 lacs, interest expended ₹ 2,720 lacs, Operating Expenses ₹ 2,662 lacs. Additional Information: Provision for NPA ₹ 1,060.50 lacs, Total Investments ₹ 800 of which 25% are held to maturity. The market value of Investment, is 80%. Tax to be provided @35%. Calculate the amount of Provision and Contingences.

(j) The company declared a reversionary bonus of ₹ 12 per ₹ 1,000 and gave the policyholders an option to get the bonus in cash for ₹ 5 per ₹ 1,000. Total business of the company is ₹ 15 crores, 40% of the policyholders decided to get bonus in cash. Pass the necessary journal entries.

2. Answer any two questions: **4 × 2 = 8**

(a) Pass the necessary journal entries to rectify the following errors:

(a) A credit sale of Goods of ₹ 4,230 to Krishan passed through the Purchase Book as ₹ 4,320 and posted therefrom to the credit of Kishan as ₹ 4,230.

(b) Goods (Cost ₹ 4,230, Sale Price ₹ 4,320) taken by Ganesh, the proprietor for his personal use recorded in the Sales Book.

(c) An amount of ₹ 8,000 owing by a customer had been omitted from the list of Sundry Debtors.

(d) A credit sale of old furniture to Rohan for ₹ 17,000 omitted to be posted.

(b) X Ltd. purchased machinery from Y Ltd. on 30/09/2014. The price was 522.50 lakhs after charging 10 % Vat and giving a trade discount of 5 % on the quoted price. Transport charges were 0.25 % on the quoted price and installation charges come to 1% on the quoted price.

A loan of ₹ 500 lakhs was taken from bank on which interest at 15 % per annum was to be paid.

Expenditure incurred on the trial run was: Material ₹ 50,000, wages ₹ 40,000 and overheads ₹ 30,000.

Machinery was ready for use on 01/12/2014. However it was actually put to use only on 01/05/2015. Find out the cost of the machine and suggest the accounting treatment for the expenses incurred in the interval between the dates 01/12/2014 to 01/05/2015. The entire loan amount remained unpaid on 01/05/2015. X Ltd. does not intend to utilize the input tax paid on capital good.

(c) Tulsian & Co. sold goods on credit to various customers. Details related to one of the customer, Shanker for the Quarter ending on 31st March, 2015, are given below:

(a) Trade Debtors as on 1.4.2015 ₹ 2,00,000

(b) Gross Sales (including Cash Sales of ₹ 4,00,000) ₹ 16,20,000

(c) Return Inwards ₹ 20,000

(d) Discount Allowed ₹ 11,000 (of which later on ₹ 1,000 disallowed)

(e) Cash received from Debtors ₹ 2,20,000 (including ₹ 20,000 from a person to whom an old fixed asset was sold)

(f) Cheques received from Debtors ₹ 4,40,000 of which cheques amounting to ₹ 40,000 were dishonoured. Out of these dishonoured cheques a cheque for ₹ 10,000 was dishonoured for non-payment as the customer became insolvent and his estate realised nothing.

(g) Bills Receivables drawn during the year totalled ₹ 6,60,000 of which bills amounting to ₹ 60,000 were endorsed in favour of suppliers. Bills dishonoured ₹ 30,000 (including Bills of ₹ 10,000 endorsed to suppliers).

(h) Interest on Overdue Accounts ₹ 45,000

(i) Bad Debts written off in earlier years recovered ₹ 20,000

(j) Provision for Doubtful Debts on Debtors ₹ 25,000.

(k) Transfer to Bought Ledger ₹ 15,000.

3. **Answer any two questions:** **12 × 2 = 24**

(a) Riots occurred and fire broke out on the evening of 31st March, 2015, destroying the books of accounts and factory shed (book value ₹ 20,000) of Bharat, a small trader. The cashier had absconded with the available cash. The following information was available:

1. Assets and Liabilities:

	31.03.2014 ₹	31.03.2015 ₹
Fixed Assets (after depreciation)	60,000	1,08,000
Stock	60,000	?
Trade Debtors	50,000	60,000
Bills Receivable	–	5,000
Cash	5,000	?
Bank	65,000	?
Prepaid Business Expenses	20,000	4,000
Outstanding Business Expenses	55,000	11,000
Trade Creditors for Goods	25,000	30,000
Bills Payable	–	25,000
Capital	?	1,01,000

2. Uniform Rate of Gross Profit – 20%.
3. Gross Profit for the year ended 31.03.2014 – ₹80,000.
4. Cash Sales 66-2/3% less than the net credit sales. Sales Returns – 1/7th of Gross Credit Sales.
5. Cash Purchases – 20% of Net Credit Purchases, Purchases Returns 1/7th of Gross Credit Purchases.
6. His sales for the year ended 21st March, 2015 were 20% higher than the previous year's.
7. On 1st April, 2014 the stock level was raised by ₹42,000 and stock was maintained at this new level all throughout the year.
8. Freight inwards ₹4,000 in cash.
9. Goods costing ₹9,000 were used as advertising materials.
10. Collections from Debtors (after 6% discount) were 80% in cash.
11. Payments to creditors (after 5% discount) amounted to ₹2,18,500 of which 80% were by cheques.
12. 80% of indirect Business Expenses were paid by cheques.
13. On 31.9.2014 Fixed Assets are purchased and paid by cheques. Depreciate Fixed Assets by 10%.

14. (a) Goods costing ₹ 1,000 were used by the proprietor for personal use.
    (b) Personal Drawings amounting to ₹1,00,000 of which 80% were in Cash.
15. 4% Govt. securities purchased by cheque (at 96% on 01.10.2014) for ₹9,600.
16. Cash deposited into the Bank ₹1,00,000.
17. During the year, acceptances amounting to ₹50,000 were discharged before maturity at a discount of 2% by means of a pay order and promissory notes amounting to ₹25,000 were also duly discharged at maturity by means of a pay order.
18. During the year, of the Bills drawn.
    (a) Some bills were endorsed in favour of creditors. Out of these endorsed bills, bills for ₹25,000 were dishonoured.
    (b) Bills amounting to ₹25,000 were discounted at a discount of 2% of which a bill for ₹12,500 was dishonoured.
    (c) Out of these dishonoured bills, drawees of bills of ₹18,750 became insolvent and paid 50% only by means of a bank draft.
    (d) Bills amounting to ₹10,000 were discharged by drawees before maturity at a rebate of 2% by means of a bank draft.
    (e) Bills amounting to ₹10,000 were collected at maturity by means of bank draft.
19. The amount defalcated by the cashier may be treated as recoverable from him.

Required: Prepare Trading & Profit & Loss Account for the year ended 31st March 2015 and the Balance Sheet as at 31st March, 2015.

(b) Following is the Balance Sheet of X, Y and Z who were sharing in the ratio of 2: 3: 5 as at 31st March 2013, when they decided to dissolve the firm:

Liabilities	₹	Assets	₹
X's Capital	18,00,000	Cash at Bank	60,000
Y's Capital	9,00,000	Sundry Assets	39,40,000
Z's Capital	3,00,000		
Reserves	10,00,000		
	40,00,000		40,00,000

Note: There was a bill for ₹ 10,000 due on 15th Aug. under discount.

The sundry assets were realised as follows:

1st April	₹ 7,70,000	Expenses	₹ 10,000
1st June	₹ 12,35,000	Expenses	₹ 40,000
1st July	₹ 7,80,000	Expenses	₹ 20,000
1st July	Z decided to take some sundry assets having book value of ₹ 1,00,000 at ₹ 4,40,000.		
15th Aug.	₹ 9,05,000	Expenses	₹ 20,000

Partners decided to keep a minimum cash balance of ₹ 10,000 in the first two months and ₹ 5,000 thereafter. The acceptor of the bill under discount met the bill on the due date.

Required: Prepare the Statement showing the distribution of cash among the partners according to (a) Maximum Loss Method (b) Proportionate Capital Method.

(c) TUSHAR Ltd. with its Head Office in Delhi invoices goods to its Branches at Mumbai and Kolkata at 20% less than the catalogue price which is cost plus 50% with instructions that cash sales are to be made at invoice price and credit sales at catalogue price less discount at 15% on prompt payments. Provision is to be made for discount to be allowed to debtors, at year end on the basis of year's trend of prompt payments. All branch expenses are paid by the Head Office and all branch collections are remitted daily to Head Office.

1. Opening Stock At Branch at its cost ₹ 12,000.
2. Opening Branch Debtors ₹ 10,000.
3. Goods Sent to branch (at cost to H.O.) ₹ 1,10,000.
4. Goods received by Branch till close of the year ₹ 1,27,000.
5. Transfer from Kolkata branch to Mumbai branch at catalogue price ₹ 75,000.
6. Transfer to Kolkata branch from Mumbai branch at catalogue price ₹ 30,000.
7. Goods purchased by Mumbai branch from local suppliers (cost) ₹ 30,000. Closing stock in hand at branch out of local purchases (cost) ₹ 6,000.
8. Cash Sales ₹ 74,800.
9. Credit Sales ₹ 1,45,000.
10. Goods returned by Credit Customers to branch ₹ 30,000.
11. Goods returned by Credit Customers directly to H.O. ₹ 15,000.
12. Goods returned by Branch to H.O. ₹ 24,000.
13. Cash remitted by Credit Customers directly to Branch ₹ 45,635.
14. Cash remitted by Credit Customers directly to H.O. ₹ 40,000.
15. Discount Allowed to Debtors ₹ 13,365.
16. Loss of Goods by fire (at invoice price) ₹ 3,000 against which 80% of cost was recovered from the insurance Company.
17. Loss of goods at Branch through normal pilferage (at catalogue price) ₹ 3,000.
18. Branch Expenses: Paid ₹ 9,000, Outstanding ₹ 741.
19. Branch Manager is entitled to a commission @ 6% of net profits after charging such commission.

Required: Prepare Mumbai Branch Account under Debtors Method.

4. Answer any two questions: **4 × 2 = 8**

(a) How will you show the following items in General Ledger Adjustment Account in Debtors Ledger and General Ledger Adjustment Account in Creditors Ledger:

	₹
(a) Transfer from Debtors' Ledgers to Creditors' Ledger	1,100
(b) Transfer from Creditors' Ledger to Debtors' Ledger	1,900
(c) B/R endorsed to Creditors	4,000
(d) Endorsed Bills dishonoured	1,000
(e) Bad Debts written off (after deducting bad debts recovered ₹ 300)	2,200
(f) Provision for Doubtful Debts	550
(g) Provision for Discount on Debtors	1,000
(h) Reserve for Discount on Creditors	2,000
(i) Cash Sales	3,000
(j) Cash Purchases	4,000

(k) Bill Receivable Collected on maturity	5,000
(l) Bills Receivable discounted	6,000
(m) Bills Payable matured	7,000
(n) Discount allowed	1,500
(o) Discount received	600
(p) Allowances from Creditors	3,200

(q) Discount allowed to debtors ₹ 500 was recorded as discount received from creditors.

(r) Closing Debtors Balance (as per General Ledger Adjustment Account) ₹ 60,000 (Cr.)

(s) Closing Creditors ₹ 30,000 (Dr.)

(b) X Ltd. maintains three Debtors Ledgers viz. (A-J) Debtors Ledger, (K-P) Debtors Ledger and (Q-Z) Debtors Ledger. Debtors list include ₹ 5,000 owed by Miss Kansal who became Mrs. Bansal after marriage. Give the necessary journal entries for transfer assuming Self Balancing System.

(c) Bharat Enterprise furnishes you the following information for the quarter Jan. to March. You are requested to draw up Debtors Ledger Adjustment account in the General Ledger:

(i) Total sales amounted to ₹ 2,20,000 including sale of old motor car for ₹ 10,000 (book value 5,000). Total credit sates were 80% higher than the cash sales.

(ii) Cash collection from debtors amounted to 60% of the aggregate of the opening debtors amounting to ₹ 40,000 and credit sales for the period. Debtors were allowed discount of ₹ 10,000.

(iii) Bills receivables drawn during the period totalled ₹ 20,000 of which one bill of ₹ 5,000 was dishonoured for non-payment as the party became insolvent and his estate realized 50 paise in a rupee.

(iv) A sum of ₹ 3,000 was written off as bad debts, ₹ 7,000 was realized against bad debts written off in earlier years and provision of ₹ 6,000 was made for doubtful debts.

5. Answer any two questions: **4 × 2 = 8**

(a) On 25th September, 2015, Planet Advertising Limited obtained advertisement rights to World Cup Hockey Tournament to be held in Nov./Dec., 2015 for ₹ 520 lakhs.

They furnish the following information:

1. The company obtained the advertisements for 70% of available time for ₹ 700 lakhs by 30th September, 2015.
2. For the balance time they got bookings in October, 2015 for ₹ 240 lakhs.
3. All the advertisers paid the full amount at the time of booking the advertisements.
4. 40% of the advertisements appeared before the public in Nov. 2015 and balance 60% appeared in the month of December, 2015.

You are required to calculate the amount of profit/loss to be recognized for the month November and December, 2015 as per Accounting Standard-9.

(b) The following information is extracted from the books of X Ltd. for the year ending 31st March, 2015.

Particulars	Contract			
	A	B	C	D
Contract revenue recognized during the year	50,000	1,25,000	1,00,000	2,00,000
Contract expense recognized during the year	50,000	1,00,000	1,20,000	1,50,000
Contract cost incurred during period	70,000	1,00,000	150,000	1,40,000

Expected loss		20,000		30,000
Progress billings	50,000	12,00,000	1,00,000	2,10,000
Advance received during year	20,000			10,000
Opening balance of contract work in progress			10,000	10,000
(Progress billing was not taken into consideration while determining this account)				

Required: How should this information should be disclosed as per AS – 7?

(c) Sale of goods costing ₹ 60,000 with a profit margin of 25 % on selling price is included in the inventory as delivery of goods was postponed at buyer's request. Comment.

6. Answer any two questions: **8 × 2 = 16**

(a) X of Calcutta on 15th January sent to Y of Bombay a consignment of 250 televisions costing ₹ 10,000 each. Expenses of ₹ 7,000 were met by the consignor. Y of Bombay spent ₹ 4,500 for clearance on 30th January and the selling expenses were ₹ 500 per television as and when the sale made by Y.

Y sold, on 4th March, 150 televisions @ ₹ 14,000 per television and again on 10th April, 75 televisions @ ₹ 14,400.

Mr Y was entitled to a commission of ₹ 500 per television sold plus one-fourth of the amount by which the gross sale proceeds less total commission there on exceeded a sum calculated at the rate of ₹ 12,500 per television sold. Y sent the account sale and the amount due to X on 30th April by bank demand draft.

You are required to show the Consignment Account and Y's account in the books of X.

(b) Monalisa & Co. runs plastic goods shop. Following details are available from quarterly sales tax return filed.

Sales	2009 ₹	2010 ₹	2011 ₹	2012 ₹
From 1st January to 31st March	1,80,000	1,70,000	2,05,950	1,62,000
From 1st April to 30th June	1,28,000	1,86,000	1,93,000	2,21,000
From 1st July to 30th September	1,53,000	2,10,000	2,31,000	1,75,000
From 1st October to 31st December	1,59,000	1,47,000	1,90,000	1,48,000
Total	6,20,000	7,13,000	8,19,950	7,06,000

Period	₹
Sales from 16-09-2011 to 30-09-2011	34,000
Sales from 16-09-2012 to 30-09-2012	Nil
Sales from 16-12-2011 to 31-12-2011	60,000
Sales from 16-12-2012 to 31-12-2012	20,000

A loss of profit policy was taken for ₹1,00,000. Fire occurred on 15th September, 2012. Indemnity period was for 3 months. Net Profit was ₹1,20,000 and standing charges (all insured) amounted to ₹43,990 for year ending 2011. Determine the Insurance Claim.

(c) From the following transactions, draw up an account current by means of product up to 31st December, 2015 to be rendered by X to Y and give the amount of interest charging @ 8% per annum.

Date 2015	Particulars	Amounts (₹ thousands)
July 01	Balance owing by Y	600
July 15	Goods sold to Y	900
Aug. 21	Goods bought from Y	700
Aug. 23	Cash received from Y	450
Oct. 23	Y accepted X's bill at 3 months	300
Nov. 01	Goods bought from Y	950
Dec.03	Accepted a bill drawn by Y at 3 months (due date of bill is on Sunday)	400

On 31st December, 2015, X and Y settled their account after considering the interest factor. Show the cash amount received or paid by X on that date.

7. **Answer any two questions:** **8 × 2 = 16**

(a) The following are the figures extracted from the books of IDFC Bank Limited as on 31.3.2015:

Particulars	₹
Interest and discount received	38,00,160
Interest paid on deposits	22,95,360
Issued and Subscribed capital	10,00,000
Salaries and allowances	2,50,000
Directors fee and allowances	35,000
Rent and Taxes paid	1,00,000
Postage and Telegrams	65,340
Statutory Reserve Fund	8,00,000
Commission, Exchange and Brokerage	1,90,000
Rent received	72,000
Profit on sale of Investments	2,25,800
Depreciation on Bank's properties	40,000
Statutory Expenses	38,000
Preliminary Expenses	30,000
Auditor's Fees	12,000

The following further information is given:

(i) A customer to whom a sum of ₹ 10 lakhs has been advanced has become insolvent and it is expected only 55% can be recovered from his estate.

(ii) There were also other debts for which a provision of ₹ 2,00,000 was found necessary by the auditors.

(iii) Rebate on Bills discounted on 31.3.2014 was ₹ 15,000 and on 31.3.2015 was ₹ 20,000.

(iv) Provide ₹ 2,00,000 for Income-tax.

(v) The Directos desire to declare 5% dividend.

Required: Prepare the Profit and Loss account of KLM Bank Limited for the year ended 31.3.2015 and also show, how the Profit and Loss account will appear in the Balance Sheet, if the Profit and Loss account opening balance was Nil as on 31.3.2014.

(b) Aggarwal Fire Insurance Company submits the following information for the year ended 31st march 2015:

Particulars		Direct Business (₹)	Reinsurance (₹)
Premium received		60,20,000	6,60,000
Premium Receivable as on 01.04.2014		2,60,000	1,60,000
Premium Receivable as on 31.03.2015		4,00,000	3,00,000
Premium Paid		—	3,92,000
Premium Payable as on 01.04.2014		—	80,000
Premium payable as on 31.03.2015		—	3,60,000
Claims Paid during the Year		39,76,000	4,08,000
Claims Payable:	1st April 2014	5,48,000	76,000
	31st March 2015	5,90,400	56,000
Claims Received		—	3,16,000
Claims Receivable:	1st April 2014	—	60,000
	31st March 2015	—	1,00,000
Expenses of Management		2,32,000	—
Commission:	On Insurance Accepted	1,28,000	12,000
	On Insurance Ceded	—	14,400

The aollowing additional information are also available:

(i) Expenses of Management include ₹ 36,000 Surveyor's Fees and ₹ 44,000. Legal Expenses for settlement of claims.

(ii) Reserve for Unexpired Risk is to be maintained @ 40%. Additional Reserve is to be maintained @ 5%. The balance of Reserve for Unexpired Risk as on 01.04.2014 was ₹ 25,56,000 (including Additional Reserve ₹ 2,84,000)

(iii) Interest, Dividend & Rent Received (after TDS @ 10%) ₹ 27,360

You are required to make the Revenue Account for the year ended 31st March 2015.

(c) From the following information Calculate

(a) Average Capital Cost, (b) Annual Depreciation as per Regulation 14 of the Central Electricity Regulatory Commission (Terms and Conditons of Tariff) Regulations, 2009.

1. Date of Commercial Operation of COD = 1st April 2011
2. Approved Opening Capital cost as on 1st April 2011 = ₹ 3,00,000
3. Weighted Average Rate of Depreciation: 5%
4. Details of allowed Additional Capital Expenditure as follows:

	1st year	2nd year	3rd year	4th year
Additional Capital Expenditure (Allowed)	20,000	6,000	4,000	4,000

ANSWERS TO TULSIAN MODEL TEST PAPER 1

Answer 1(a)

STATEMENT SHOWING THE VALUATION OF STOCK AS AT 31ST MARCH

	Particulars	₹
A.	Value of Stock as at 7th April	2,00,000
B.	*Add:* Cost of Goods Sent on approval and still with the customer	
	[80% of ₹ 1,00,000 – 20% of ₹ 80,000]	64,000
C.	Value of Stock as at 31st March	2,64,000
	Note: 20% of the goods is already included in given stock of 7th April.	

Answer 1(b)

Step 1: Hire Purchase Price = Down Payment + Instalments

= ₹ 2,00,000 + ₹ 10,00,000 = ₹ 12,00,000

Step 2: Total Interest = H.P. Price – Cash Price

= ₹ 12,00,000 – ₹ 10,00,000 = ₹ 2,00,000

Step 3:

CALCULATION OF RATIO OF HPP OUTSTANDING IN THE BEGINNING OF EACH YEAR

A Year	B Outstanding H.P.P., in the Beginning of each year	C Instalment Paid	D = B – C Outstanding H.P.P. at the end of each year
I	10,00,000	2,50,000	7,50,000
II	7,50,000	2,50,000	5,00,000
III	5,00,000	2,50,000	2,50,000
IV	2,50,000	2,50,000	Nil

Ratio of outstanding H.P.P. at the beginning of each year = 100: 75: 50: 25 *or* 4: 3: 2: 1

Step 4: Calculation of Interest for each year

Interest for 1st year — ₹ 2,00,000 × 4/10 = ₹ 80,000

Interest for 2nd year — ₹ 2,00,000 × 3/10 = ₹ 60,000

Interest for 3rd year — ₹ 2,00,000 × 2/10 = ₹ 40,000

Interest for 4th year — ₹ 2,00,000 × 1/10 = ₹ 20,000

Answer 1(c)

CALCULATION OF CAPITAL RATIO

Particulars	A ₹	B ₹
Capital	60,000	49,000
Less: B's Drawings	–	(4,000)
Less: Share of Debit balance of Profit & Loss A/c [10,000 + 10,000 (Ommited purchases)]	(6,000)	(6,000)

Add: Share of General Reserve	6,000	6,000
	60,000	45,000

C's deficiency is to be borne by A and B in the ratio of 60,000: 45,000 *or* 4: 3.

D will not bear C's deficiency since he had a debit balance in his Caoital Account.

Answer 1(d)

CALCULATION OF CLOSING STOCK AND STOCK RESERVE

	Particulars	₹
A.	Opening Stock	12,000
B.	*Add:* Goods received	1,38,000
C.	*Less:* Invoice Price of Cash Sales	(46,000)
	Invoice Price of Credit Sales [₹ 1,00,000 × 120/150]	(80,000)
	Abnormal Loss [₹ 2,500 + 20%]	(3,000)
D.	Closing Stock at Branch in hand	21,000
E.	Closing Stock in transit [₹ 1,68,000 – ₹ 1,38,000]	30,000
F.	Total Branch Stock	51,000
	Branch Stock Reserve = ₹ 51,000 × 20/120 = ₹ 8,500	

Answer 1(e)

Dr. GENERAL LEDGER ADJUSTMENT ACCOUNT (IN DEBTORS LEDGER) Cr.

Particulars	₹	Particulars	₹
To Debtors Ledger Adjustment A/c:		By Debtors Ledger Adjustment A/c:	
Discount Allowed (₹ 1,500 + ₹ 500)	2,000	Endorsed B/R dish.	1,000
Bad Debts (2,200 + 300)	2,500		
T/f from Drs Ledger to Crs. Ledger	1,100		
T/f from Cr. Ledger to Drs. Ledger	1,900		
To Balance c/d (60,000 – 500)	59,500		

Notes: The following items do not appear in GLA Account (in Debtors Ledger)

1. Cash Sales
2. Provision for Doubtful Debts
3. Provision for Discount on Debtors
4. Bad Debts Recovered
5. Bills Receivable matured/collected on maturity
6. Bills Receivable discounted
7. Bills Receivable endorsed

Answer 1(f)

PROVISION OF AS 9

As per AS 9 "Revenue Recognition" states that dividend from investments in shares are not recognized in the statement of Profit and Loss until the right to receive dividend is established.

ADVICE

The dividend is proposed on 10th April, 2015, while it was declared on 30th June, 2015. Hence, the right to receive dividend is established on 30th June, 2015 only. Therefore, on applying the provisions stated in the standard, income from dividend on shares should be recognized by Sea Ltd. in the financial year 2015-2016 only.

Therefore, the recognition of income from dividend of ₹ 5 iakhs, on accrual basis, in the financial year 2014-2015 is not in accordance with AS 9.

Answer 1(g)

Fixed Commission @ ₹ 500 = 225 × ₹ 500 = ₹ 1,12,500

Let the total Commission be X

Variable Commission = 1/4 [(₹ 31,80,000 – X) – (225 × ₹ 12,500)]

X – ₹ 1,12,500 = 1/4 [₹ 31,80,000 – X – ₹ 28,12,500]

X – ₹ 1,12,500 = 1/4 (₹ 3,67,500 – X)

X – ₹ 1,12,500 = 91,875 – 1/4 X

X – 1,12,500 = 91,875 –. 25 X

1.25 X = 2,04,375 X = ₹ 2,04,375/1.25 = ₹ 1,63,500

Answer 1(h)

Particulars	₹
Sales	250000
Closing Stock(5% of 200000)	10000
	260000
Less:	
Purchases	200000
A's Commission	2000
B's Commission	12500
Discount Charges	10000
	224500
Net Profit	35500
B's Share of Profit(35500 × 2/5)	14200

Answer 1(i)

JOURNAL

Date	Particulars	Dr. (₹)	Cr.(₹)
09.03.2015	Discounted Bills A/c Dr. To Discount A/c To Customer's A/c (Being bills discounted & purchased)	5,00,000	 20,000 4,80,000
31.03.2015	Discount A/c Dr. To Rebate on bill discounted A/c (₹ 80,000 × 73/365) To Profit & Loss A/c (Being unexpired discount carried over to Next Year & Balance T/f to P & L A/c)	16,000	 16,000 4,000

Answer 1(j)

VALUATION BALANCE SHEET AS AT 31ST MARCH, 2015

₹ in lakhs

Liabilities	₹	Assets	₹
To Net Liability as per actuarial valuation	75,00,000	By Life Insurance Fund	90,00,000
To Surplus (B/F)	15,00,000		
	90,00,000		90,00,000

STATEMENT SHOWING THE NET PROFIT FOR VALUATION PERIOD

Particulars	₹
A. Surplus as per Valuation Balance Sheet	15,00,000
B. *Add:* Interim Bonus already paid	1,50,000
C. *Less:* Surplus in the Beginning	(9,00,000)
D. Net Profit for the valuation period	7,50,000

Answer 2(a)

JOURNAL

Date	Particulars		L.F.	Dr. (₹)	Cr. (₹)
(a)	Suspense A/c	Dr.		1,452	
	To Discount Allowed A/c				132
	To Discount Received A/c				1,320
	(Being Discount Received wrongly posted to Discount Allowed A/c, now rectified)				
(b)	Krishan	Dr.		20	
	Sales A/c	Dr.		200	
	Sales Returns A/c	Dr.		200	
	To Kishan				200
	To Suspense A/c				220
	(Being sale returns recorded as sale with wrong amount and wrong posting therefrom, now rectified)				
(c)	Sales A/c	Dr.		50	
	Purchases A/c	Dr.		500	
	To N. Kumar				500
	To M. Kumar				50
	(Being the credit purchase recorded as sale, now rectified)				
(d)	P. Dass	Dr.		600	
	Sales A/c	Dr.		60	
	To Machine A/c				600
	To C. Dass				60
	(Being the credit sale of machine recorded as sale, now rectified)				

Answer 2(b)

Situation (i)

When Net Realisable Value of the Finished Goods Y is ₹ 300

NRV is greater than the cost of Finished Goods Y i.e. ₹ 330

Hence, Raw Material and Finished Goods are to be valued at cost

VALUE OF CLOSING STOCK

	Qty	*Rate*	*Amount (₹)*
Raw Material X	500	220	1,10,000
Finished Goods Y	1,200	330	3,96,000
Total Cost of Closing Stock			5,06,000

Situation (ii)

When Net Realisable Value of the Finsihed Goods Y is ₹ 300

NRV is less than the cost of Finished Goods Y i.e. ₹ 330

Hence, Raw Material is to be valued at replacement cost and Finished Goods are to be valued at NRV since NRV is less than the cost

VALUE OF CLOSING STOCK

	Qty	Rate	₹
Raw Material X	500	150	75,000
Finished Goods Y	1,200	330	3,60,000
Total Cost of Closing Stock			4,35,000

Note: It has been considered that Raw Material X is used for the production of Finished Goods Y.

WORKING NOTES:

Raw Materials X	₹
Cost Price	200
Less: Cenvat Credit	(10)
Add: Freight Inward	20
Unloading charges	10
Cost	220
Finished goods Y	*1*
Materials consumed	220
Direct Labour	60
Direct overhead	40
Fixed overhead (₹ 2,00,000/20,000 units)	10
Cost	330

Answer 2(c)

BANK RECONCILIATION STATEMENT AS AT 31ST MARCH ...

	Particulars		*Plus Items* ₹	*Minus Items* ₹
A.	Debit Balance as per Cash Book		10,000	
B.	*Add:*	(a) Error in carrying forward	3,000	
		(b) Cheque recorded twice in Cash Book	300	
		(c) Cash deposit but not recorded in Bank Column	200	
		(d) Cheque deposited but not recorded	1,000	
C.	*Less:*	(a) Under Casting of Payment Side		100
		(b) Cheque issued but not entered		250
		(c) A cash discount wrongly recorded in Bank Column		121
		(d) Cheque recorded but not deposited		500
			14,500	971
D.	Credit Balance as per Pass Book		13,529	

Answer 3(a)

Dr. **MACHINE ACCOUNT** **Cr.**

Date	Particulars	₹	Date	Particulars	₹
01.04.2012	To Bank A/c	9,00,000	31.03.2013	By Depreciation A/c [10,00,000 × 20% × 3/12]	50,000
01.04.2012	To Bank A/c	90,000		By Balance c/d	9,50,000
01.01.2013	To Bank A/c	10,000			
		10,00,000			10,00,000
01.04.2013	To Balance b/d	9,50,000	01.10.2013	By Depreciation A/c [95,000 × 20% × 6/12]	9,500
	To P & L A/c [Profit] [(95,000 – 9,500) × 10%]	8,550		By Bank A/c [(95,000 – 9,500) + 10%]	94,050
			31.03.2014	By Depreciation A/c [(9,50,000 – 95,000) × 20% × 12/12]	1,71,000
				By Balance c/d	6,84,000
		9,58,550			9,58,550
01.04.2014	To Balance b/d	6,84,000	01.01.2015	By Depreciation A/c [76,000 × 20% × 9/12]	11,400
01.01.2015	To Bank A/c	90,000		By Bank A/c [(76,000 – 11,400) – 10%)]	58,140
	To Bank A/c	10,000		By P & L A/c [Loss] [(76,000 – 11,400) × 10%)]	6,460

			31.03.2015	By P & L A/c (Short Depreciation)	8,000
				By Depreciation A/c:	
				Old [8,00,000 × 20%)]	1,60,000
				New [1,00,000 × 20% × 3/12]	5,000
				By Balance c/d:	
				Old 4,40,000	
				New 95,000	5,35,000
		7,84,000			7,84,000

Working Notes:

1. *Calculation of Excess/Short Depreciation on 8 Machines*

(A) Depreciation already provided on WDV basis @ 20% p.a.

= [8,00,000] – [8,00,000 × .95 × .80] = ₹ 1,92,000

(B) Depreciation which should have been provided on SLM basis @ 20% p.a.

= [8,00,000 × 20% × 15/12] = ₹ 2,00,000

(C) Short Depreciation still to be written off (A – B) = ₹ 8,000

2. Calculation of Purchase Price of 10 Machines as on 01.04.2012	₹
A. W.D.V. of 9 Machines as on 1.4.2014	8,64,000
B. *Add:* Depreciation during 2013-2014 (₹8,64,000 × 20/80)	1,71,000
C. W.D.V. of 9 Machines as on 1.4.2013	8,55,000
D. Book Value of 1 Machine (8,55,000 × 1/9)	95,000
E. W.D.V. of 10 Machines as on 1.4.2013	9,50,000
F. *Add:* Depreciation during 2012-2013 (₹ 9,50,000 × 5/95)	50,000
G. Total Cost of 10 Machines as on 1.1.2013	10,00,000
H. *Less:* Repairs and on Installation Incurred on 1.1.2013	10,000
I. *Less:* freight & insurance, and carriage inward Incurred on 1.4.2012	90,000
J. Purchase Price of 10 Machines as on 1.4.2012	9,00,000

Answer 3(b)

AN EXTRACT OF TRADING AND PROFIT AND LOSS ACCOUNT OF MR. BHARAT

Dr. *for the year ended 31st March, 2015* Cr.

Particulars		₹	Particulars		₹
To Purchases	5,25,000		By Sales	6,30,000	
Less: Goods for personal use	20,000		*Less:* Goods sent on approval	50,000	5,80,000
Less: Free Samples	30,000		By Closing stock	1,14,000	
Less: Goods destroyed by fire	10,000	4,65,000	*Add:* Cost of Stock with customer	40,000	1,54,000
To Wages & Salaries	23,500				
Less: Erection of a Cycle shed	4,000				
Less: Installation of Machine	10,000				
Less: Installation of Furnitures	5,000	4,500			

To Salaries & Wages	11,200		By Bad Debt recovered	2,500
Add: Salary to Barua	2,000	13,200		
To Sales Promotion Expenses		30,000		
To Loss of Stock by fire		4,000		
To Bad Debts	3,000			
Add: Further Bad Debts	4,000			
Add: New Provision	20,000			
Less: Old Provision	10,000	17,000		
To Discount Allowed	2,000			
Add: Further Discount Allowed	1,000			
Add: New Provision	3,600			
Less: Old Provision	1,800	4,800		
To Depreciation on New Plant & Machinery [₹ 2,00,000 × 10/100 × 9/12]		15,000		
To Depreciation on Old Plant & Machinery [₹ 20,000 × 10/100 × 12/12]		2,000		
To Depreciation on Furniture [₹ 80,000 × 10/100 × 12/12]		8,000		
To Depreciation on Buildings [₹ 64,000 × 5/100 × 12/12]		3,200		

AN EXTRACT OF BALANCE SHEET OF BHARAT AS AT 31ST MARCH, 2015

Liabilities		₹	Assets		₹
Capital Account:			**Fixed Assets:**		
Opening balance	5,19,000		Plant and Machinery (OB)	20,000	
Less: Goods for personal use	(20,000)		*Add:* Purchased	1,90,000	
Less: Income Tax	(10,000)		*Add:* Installation charges	10,000	
Less: O/s Liabilities for Expenses	(55,000)	4,34,000	*Less:* Depreciation	17,000	2,03,000
Supplier of Furniture		45,000	Furniture & Fixtures (OB)	30,000	
Trade Creditors	10,000		*Add:* Purchased	45,000	
Less: Due to Z	(1,000)	9,000	*Add:* Installation charges	5,000	
			Less: Depreciation	8,000	72,000
			Building (OB)	60,000	
			Add: Erection of a cycle shed	4,000	
			Less: Depreciation	3,200	60,800
			Closing Stock	1,14,000	
			Add: Stock with Customers	40,000	1,54,000
			Trade Debtors	2,68,000	
			Less: Due to Z	(1,000)	
			Less: Good sent on approval basis	50,000	
			Less: Further Bad debts [₹ 4,000 + ₹ 5,000 (Shyam)]	9,000	

		Less: Further Discount Allowed 1,000	
		Less: Salary to Mr B. Barua 2,000	
		2,05,000	
		Less: Provision for doubtful debts @ 10% (on ₹ 2,05,000 – ₹ 5,000) 20,000	
		1,85,000	
		Less: Provision for discount @ 2% (on ₹ 1,85,000 – ₹ 5,000) 3,600	1,81,400
		Insurance Company (claim)	6,000

Note: Depreciation on furniture has been charged for the full year because a flat rate of 10% (and not 10% p.a.) has been given, whereas depreciation on machinery has been charged for 9 months from 1st July to 31st Mar. No provision for discount on Debtors is required on Shyam's balance.

Answer 3(c)

Dr. **REALISATION ACCOUNT** **Cr.**

Particulars	₹	Particulars	₹
To Assets Transferred:		By Provision for Doubtful Debts	8,500
Stock	25,000	By Trade Creditors (60,000 + 10,000)	70,000
Debtors	50,000	By Bank Overdraft	15,000
Prepaid Insurance	3,000	By Mrs. B's Loan	3,000
Goodwill	5,000	By Employee's Provident Fund	5,000
Tangible Fixed Assets	80,000	By Machinery Replacement Reserve	20,000
To Bank A/c (Mrs B's Loan)	3,000	By Bank A/c:	
To Bank A/c (Trade Creditors) (9,000 + 29,000)	38,000	Tangible Fixed Assets [30,000 – (100/200 × 30,000)]	15,000
To Bank A/c (EPF)	5,000	Debtors (₹ 50,000 × 60% × 66%)	19,800
To Bank A/c (Unrecored Liability)	13,000	Debtors (₹ 20,000 × 60% × 70%)	8,400
To Bank A/c (Discounted B/R)	21,000	Stock	4,000
		Joint Life Policy	4,000
		Bad Debts recovered	2,000
		from Z	12,600
		By B's Capital A/c (Debtors) [(20,000 × 40% × 70%) – 800]	4,800
		By B's Capital A/c (JLP)	6,500
		By B's Capital A/c (Unrecored Asset)(₹ 20,000 × 42%)	8,400
		By Loss on Realisation t/f to:	
		A's Capital A/c	10,800
		B's Capital A/c	10,800
		C 's Capital A/c	7,200
		D 's Capital A/c	7,200
	2,43,000		2,43,000

Dr. **PARTNERS' CAPITAL ACCOUNTS** **Cr.**

Particulars	A	B	C	D	Particulars	A	B	C	D
To Balance b/d	—	—	48,000	18,000	By Balance b/d	60,000	49,000	—	—
To Drawings	—	4,000	—	—	By General Reserve	6,000	6,000	4,000	4,000
To P&L A/c (Goods)	3,000	3,000	2,000	2,000	By Bank A/c	10,800	4,400	11,100	25,200
To P&L A/c (Loss)	3,000	3,000	2,000	2,000	By A's Capital A/c	—	—	25,200	—
To Realisation A/c	—	6,500	—	—	By B's Capital A/c	—	—	18,900	—
To Realisation A/c	—	4,800	—	—	By A's Capital A/c	—	1,143	—	—
To Realisation A/c	—	8,400	—						
To Realisation A/c	10,800	10,800	7,200	7,200					
To C's Capital A/c	25,200	18,900	—	—					
To B's Capital A/c	1,143	—	—	—					
To Bank A/c	33,657	1,143	—	—					
	76,800	60,543	59,200	29,200		76,800	60,543	59,200	29,200

Dr. **BANK ACCOUNT** **Cr.**

Particulars	₹	Particulars	₹
To Balance b/d	27,500	By Realisation A/c (Trade Creditors)	38,000
To Realisation A/c (Assets)	65,800	By Realisation A/c (EPF)	5,000
To A's Capital A/c (Share of Loss on Realisation)	10,800	By Realisation A/c (Mrs B's Loan) By Realisation A/c (Dish. B/R)	3,000 21,000
To B's Capital A/c (Share of Loss on Realisation)	4,400	By Realisation A/c (Unrecorded Liability)	13,000
To C's Capital A/c	11,100	By A's Loan A/c	30,000
To D's Capital A/c (Including Share of Loss on Realisation)	25,200	By A's Capital A/c By B's Capital A/c	33,657 1,143
	1,44,800		1,44,800

Working Notes:

1. Total Trade Creditors = 60,000 + 10,000 (Ommited Purchases) =70,000
2. Book Value of Net Tangible Fixed Assets = Tangible Fixed Assets – Machinery Replacement Reserve = 80,000 – 20,000 = 60,000
3. Book Value of Net Tangible Fixed Assets taken over by Trade Creditors = 24,000 /80% = 30,000
4. Book Value of Net Tangible Fixed Assets sold = 60,000 – 30,000= 30,000

5. CALCULATION OF CAPITAL RATIO

Particulars	A ₹	B ₹
Capital	60,000	49,000
Less: B's Drawings	–	(4,000)
Less: Share of Debit Balance of Profit & Loss A/c [10,000 + 10,000 (Ommited Purchases)]	(6,000)	(6,000)
Add: Share of General Reserve	6,000	6,000
	60,000	45,000

C's Deficiency is to be borne by A and B in the ratio of 60,000: 45,000 *or* 4: 3.

A's Capital A/c [₹ 44,100 x 4/7]	Dr.	₹ 25,200	
B's Capital A/c [₹ 44,100 x 3/7]	Dr.	₹ 11,100	
To C's Capital A/c [₹59,200 – ₹ 11,100]			₹ 44,100

6. D will not bear nay portion of the loss due to C's insolvency since he had a debit balance in his capital account at the time of Insolvency.
7. Amount which B could brought in = [₹ 2,00,000 – (₹ 1,94,000 + ₹ 1,600 Expenses)] = ₹4,400
8. The amount due to A, before B 's commission is ₹ 24,000, ignoring the amount brought in by him on account of his share of the loss on realisation. Thus,B 's commission = ₹ 24,000 × 5/105 = ₹ 1,143

Answer 4(a)

DEBTORS LEDGER ADJUSTMENT ACCOUNT IN GENERAL LEDGER

Dr. Cr.

Particulars	₹	Particulars	₹
To Balance b/d	40,000	By General Ledger Adjustment A/c:	
To General Ledger Adjustment A/c. (In Sales Ledger) – Sales	49,000	(In Sales Ledger) – Cash	53,400
To Creditors A/c (B. R. dishonoured)	600	– Discount	2,600
To Bank (Cheques dishonoured)	6,000	By Bad Debts (₹ 500 + ₹ 600)	1,100
		By B/R	6,000
		By Balance c/d	32,500
	95,600		95,600

Workings:

1. *Computation of Credit Sales:*

   Let Credit sales = ₹100, cash sales = ₹20. Total sales = ₹120.

   Total Sales ₹ (60,000 – 1,200) = ₹ 58,800

   Credit sales = (58,800 × 100)/120 = ₹49,000
2. *Cash Received*

   Cash Received is 60% of opening Debtors + Credit Sales i.e. ₹ (40,000 + 49,000) = ₹ 89,000.

   So, Cash received = ₹ 89,000 × 60/100 = ₹ 53,400

Answer 4(b)

TOTAL CREDITORS ACCOUNT – FOR THE YEAR ENDED 31-03-2013

Date	Particulars	₹	Date	Particulars	₹
31-03-2013	To Bills payable accepted	62,000	01-04-2012	By Balance b/d	38,000
	To Cash paid to creditors	1,37,000	31-03-2013	By Purchases (Credit)	2,67,000
	To B/R endorsed	16,000		By Endorsed B/R Dishonored	3,000
	To Purchase returns	11,000		By B/P Dishonoured	2,000
	To Discount received	6,000		To Transfer from debtors Ledger	7,000
	To Balance c/d (Bal. fig.)	71,000			
		3,10,000			3,10,000

Answer 4(c)

JOURNAL

Date	Particulars		L.F.	Dr. (₹)	Cr. (₹)
(i)	Meena (In Sales/Debtors Ledger)	Dr.		8,700	
	To Meenu (In Sales/Debtors Ledger)				8,700
	(Being amount received from Meenu was wrongly credited to Meena, now rectified)				
(ii)(a)	Suspense A/c (In Sales/Debtors Ledger)	Dr.		1,000	
	To Sales A/c(In General Ledger)				1,000
(ii)(b)	Sales/Debtors Ledger Adjustment A/c (In General Ledger)	Dr.		1,000	
	To General Ledger Adjustment A/c (In Sales/Debtors Ledger)				1,000
	(Being rectification of the error resulting from under casting of the Sales Book)				
(iii)(a)	M/s. BPO Ltd. A/c (In Creditors/Bought Ledger)	Dr.		15,600	
	To Purchase Returns A/c (In General Ledger)				15,600
(iii)(b)	Creditors/Bought Ledger Adjustment A/c (In General Ledger)	Dr.		15,600	
	To General Ledger Adjustment A/c (In Creditors/Bought Ledger)				15,600
	(Being goods returned to supplier not recorded earlier, now recorded)				

Answer 5(a)

PROVISION OF AS-9

As per AS 9 "Revenue Recognition", dividends from investment in shares is recognized in the statement of Profit and Loss only when the owner's right to receive the payment is established.

ADVICE

(i) Since interim dividend was declared by X Ltd. before 31st March 2015 it means that the dividend had been vested (acrrued) to the shareholders of AQ Ltd. in the year 2014-2015. Therefore, though it is received on 25.4.2015 (before finalization of accounts) yet it should be recognized in the financial statements for the year ended 31st March, 2015.

(ii) Dividend declared by Y Ltd and approved by the shareholders of AQ Ltd. after balance sheet date but before finalization of accounts will be accounted for 2015-2016 as the right to receive dividend will arise when the AGM will approve the dividend i.e. on 30th June 2015. Since right to receive the dividend was not established on or before 31st March, 2015, it will not be accounted for in the books for the year ended 31st March, 2015.

(iii) Dividend declared by Z Ltd. will be approved in the AGM to be held on 30th September, 2015. Before that right to receive dividend cannot be established. Hence it will not be accounted for in the financial year ended on 31st March, 2015.

Answer 5(b)

AMOUNT TO BE DISCLOSED AS PER DISCLOSURE REQUIREMENTS OF AS – 7

	Particulars	₹ In Lakhs
A	Additions during the year	
	Cost Incurred during the year (1,400 + 400)	1,800
	Revenue recognized during the year (2,000 × 1,400)/2,500	1,120
	Total [A]	2,920
B	Deductions during the year	
	Expenses recognized during the year (Work certified)	1,400
	Expected loss [(₹ 1,400 lakhs + ₹ 400 lakhs + ₹ 700 lakhs)	
	₹ 2,000 lakhs] – [₹ 1,400 lakhs – ₹ 1,120]	220
	Total [B]	1,620
C	Balance [A – B] As per disclosure requirement of AS – 7]	1,300
D	Progress Billings	1,200
E	Amount due from customers for contract work [D – E]	100
F	Progress payment received	1,000
G	Retentions [D – F]	200

Answer 5(c)

PROVISION OF AS 9

As per AS 9 the revenue should be recognized if it can be measured reliably and there is not any significant uncertainty in its ultimate collection.

ADVICE

In the instant case it appears that these are uncertainties in measuring the claim and the settlement of the insurance claim. Hence, insurance claim can be recognized only if the amount can be measured reliably and ultimate collection is reasonably certain.

Answer 6(a)

JOURNAL OF ARUN

Date	Particulars		L.F.	Dr. (₹)	Cr. (₹)
Jan. 1	Bills Receivable A/c	Dr.		2,00,000	
	To Anand				2,00,000
	(Being the bill for ₹ 2,00,000 drawn on Anand)				
Jan. 4	Bank A/c	Dr.		1,95,000	
	Discount A/c	Dr.		5,000	
	To Bills Receivable A/c				2,00,000
	(Being the bill discounted @ 10% p.a.)				
Jan. 4	Anand	Dr.		1,00,000	
	To Bank A/c				97,500
	To Discount A/c				2,500
	(Being half the proceeds sent to Anand)				

Date	Particulars		L.F.	Dr. ₹	Cr. ₹
April 4	Anand	Dr.		1,20,000	
	To Bills Payable A/c				1,20,000
	(Being the bill of Anand accepted)				
April 4	Bank A/c	Dr.		19,600	
	Discount A/c	Dr.		400	
	To Anand				20,000
	(Being proceeds received from Anand)				
July 7	Bills Payable A/c	Dr.		1,20,000	
	To Anand				1,20,000
	(Being the bill dishonoured)				
	Anand	Dr.		1,20,000	
	To Bank A/c				60,000
	To Deficiency A/c				60,000
	(Being 50% payments made to Anand and unpaid balance transferred to Deficiency A/c)				

Dr. **ANAND'S ACCOUNT IN THE BOOKS OF ARUN** **Cr.**

Particulars	₹	Particulars	₹
To Bank A/c	97,500	By Bills Receivable A/c	2,00,000
To Discount A/c	2,500	By Bank A/c	19,600
To Bills Payable A/c	1,20,000	By Discount A/c	400
To Bank A/c	60,000	By Bills Payable A/c	1,20,000
To Deficiency A/c	60,000		
	3,40,000		3,40,000

Dr. **ARUN'S ACCOUNT IN THE BOOKS OF ANAND** **Cr.**

Particulars	₹	Particulars	₹
To Bills Payable A/c	2,00,000	By Bank A/c	97,500
To Bank A/c	19,600	By Discount A/c	2,500
To Discount A/c	400	By Bills Receivable A/c	1,20,000
To Bank A/c	1,20,000	By Bank A/c	60,000
		By Bad Debts A/c	60,000
	3,40,000		3,40,000

Answer 6(b)

Dr. **CONSIGNMENT ACCOUNT** **Cr.**

Particulars		₹	Particulars		₹
To Goods sent on Consignment (2,64,000 × 120/100)		3,16,800	By Mahesh A/c		
To Bank A/c (Insurance & Forwarding changes)		10,000	Cash Sales	1,32,000	
To Shri Mahesh A/c:			Credit Sales	1,32,000	2,64,000
Establishment Landing charges	2,040		By Stock Lost on Consignment A/c		
Landing charges	2,040	2,000	[1/2 × 1/4 × [2,64,000 + 10,000 + 2,040]		34,505

Del-credere Commission (3% on ₹ 1,32,000) 3,960	21,200	By Consignment Stock [1/2 × 1/4 × (3,16,800 + 10,000 + 2,040)]	41,105
To Profit on Consignment (transferred to P & L A/c)	37,810	By Goods sent on Consignment A/c (Total Load = (₹ 3,16,800 – ₹ 2,64,000)	52,800
To Stock Reserve A/c (Load = ₹ 52,800 × 1/8)	6,600		
	3,93,010		3,93,010

Dr. **STOCK LOST ON CONSIGNMENT ACCOUNT** **Cr.**

Particulars	₹	Particulars	₹
To Consignment A/c	34,505	By Insurance Company (claim) (90% of ₹ 28,000)	25,200
		By P&L A/c	9,305
	34,505		34,505

Answer 6(c)

COMPUTATION OF CLAIM FOR LOSS OF STOCK
1. MEMORANDUM TRADING ACCOUNT (1ST APRIL TO 30TH JUN 2013)

Particulars	₹	Particulars	₹
To Opening Stock	1,85,000	By Sales	3,36,000
To Purchases	2,14,000	By Stock on the date of fire(balancing figure)	2,26,800
To Wages	51,000		
To Manufacturing Expenses	12,000		
To Gross Profit @ 30%	1,00,800		
	5,62,800		5,62,800

Note: Normal GP Rate = 3,00,000/12,00,000 = 25%, Adjusted GP Rate = 25% + 5% = 30%

2. STATEMENT OF INSURANCE CLAIM

Particulars	₹
Value of Stock Lost on 30th June	2,26,800
Less: Salvaged Stock	Nil
Net Claim	2,26,800

COMPUTATION OF CLAIM FOR LOSS OF PROFIT

(i) Basic GP Rate = $\frac{\text{Net Profit} + \text{Insured Standing Charges}}{\text{Sales}} = \frac{60,000 + 1,56,000}{12,00,000} \times 100 = 18\%$

(ii) Adjusted GP Rate = 18% + 5% = 23%

(iii) Trend Precentage Increase in Sales = [(3,36,000 – 3,00,000)/3,00,000] × 100 = 12%

(iv) Insurable Amount = GP on Annual Adjusted Turnover = 23% (₹ 12,00,000 + 12%) = ₹ 3,09,120

(V) COMPUTATION OF SHORT SALES

Particulars	₹
Turnover from 1st July to 30th Sept. (previous year corresponding to Indemnity Period)	3,20,000
Add: Adjustment for Increase (₹ 3,20,000 × 12%)	38,400
Adjusted/Expected Turnover during Indemnity Period 3,58,400	
Less: Actual Turnover during Indemnity Period, i.e. from 01.07.2013 to 30.09.2013	(48,000)
Short Sales	3,10,400

(vi) Computation of Turnover for 12 months preceding the date of Fire is as under-

A. Sales from 1st Apr to 30th June (i.e. 3 mths of Year) is trend adjusted at 112% = 3,36,000 (Given)

B. After Trend Adjustment, Normal Value of Sales for 3 months of Year = 3,36,000/112% = 3,00,000

C. Sales from 1st July to 31st March (i.e. 9 months of Year) = 12,00,000/112% = 9,00,000

D. Normal Value of Sales for 12 months preceding the date of Fire (B + C) = 12,00,000

(VII) COMPUTATION OF ALLOWABLE ADDITIONAL EXPENSES

Particulars	₹
Actual Additional Expenses	1,98,000
GP on Sales generated by Additional Expenses (₹ 48,000 × 23%)	11,040
Additional Expenses × $\frac{\text{GP on Adjusted Annual Turnover}}{\text{GP on Adjusted Annual Turnover} + \text{Uninsured Standing Charges}}$ $= ₹1,98,000 \times \frac{23\% \times 12,44,000}{(23\% \times 12,44,000) + 42,000} = 1,98,000 \times \frac{3,09,120}{3,35,120}$	
Allowable Additional Expenses = Least of the above	11,040

(VIII) COMPUTATION OF CLAIM

Particulars	₹
Loss of Profit = Gross Profit on Short Sales = 23% on 3,10,400	71,392
Add: Allowable Additional Expenses	11,040
Less: Saving in Insured Standing Charges	Nil
Net Claim for Loss of Profit	82,432

Answer 7(a)

TULSIAN BANK LTD.
PROFIT & LOSS ACCOUNT

for the year ended 31st March, 2013

	Particulars	Schedule No.	year ended 31.3.2013 (₹'000)
I	Income:		
	Interest Earned	13	8,890

	Other Income	14	220
			9,110
II	Expenditure:		
	Interest Expended	15	2,720
	Operating Expenses	16	2,662
	Provisions & Contingencies (1180.50 + 891.625 W.Note)		2,072.125
			7,454.125
III	Profit/Loss:		
	Net Profit/Loss for the year		1,655.875
	Profit/Loss brought forward		80
			1,735.875
IV	Appropriations:		
	Transfer to Statutory Reserve @ 25% of 1,655.875		413.970
	Proposed Dividend		250.000
	Balance carried over to Balance-Sheet		1071.905
			1,735.875

SCHEDULE 13—INTEREST EARNED

	Particulars	₹ '000
I	Interest & Discount [8,880 + 15 (Opening Rebate) – 45 (Closing Rebate)]	8,850
II	Income on Investments (30 + 10)	40
		8,890

Working Notes:

1. PROVISION FOR NPA

Particulars	Amount (₹ '000)	% of Provision	Provision (₹ '000)
Standard	5,000	0.40	20.0
Sub Standard Assets	1,120	15	168.0
Doubtful Assets not covered by security	510	100	510.0
Doubtful Assets covered by security			
for 1 year	50	25	12.5
for 2 years	100	40	40.0
for 3 years	200	40	80.0
for 4 years	150	100	150.0
Loss Assets	80	100	80.0
			1060.5

2. CALCULATION OF THE AMOUNT OF PROVISION AND CONTINGENCES

A. Provision for Diminution in Value of Investments (other than Held to Maturity) = (₹ 800 – 25% of ₹ 800) – (80% of ₹ 600)	₹ 120
B. Provision for NPA	₹ 1,060.50
C. Provision & Contingencies (excluding tax) [₹ 1,060.50 + ₹ 120]	₹ 1,180.50
D. Tax = 35% of [Total Income – Total Expenditure (excluding tax)] = 35% of [(8,890 + 220) – (2,720 + 2,662 + 1180.50)]	₹ 891.625

Answer 7(b)

FROM–B–RA–REVENUE ACCOUNT OF TULSIAN FIRE INSURANCE CO. LTD

for the year ending 31st March 2015

Particulars	Sch.	Current Yr	Previous Yr
Premium Earned (Net)	1	75,18,000	
Interest, Dividend & Rent (Gross) (₹ 34,200 × 100/90)		38,000	
Total (A)		75,56,000	
1. Claims Incurred (Net)	2	51,63,000	
2. Commission	3	1,57,000	
3. Operating Expenses related to Insurance Business	4		
(2,90,000 – Legal Exps 55,000 – Surveyor Fees 45,000)		1,90,000	
Total (B)		55,10,000	
Operating Profit/(Loss) from Insurance Business (A – B)		20,46,000	
Appropriations		NIL	
Total (C)		20,46,000	

SCHEDULE 1 – PREMUM EARNED (NET)

Particulars	This Yr
Premiums from Direct Business written (75,25,000 + 5,00,000 – 3,25,000)	77,00,000
Add: Premium on Re-Insurance accepted (8,25,000 + 3,75,000 – 2,00,000)	10,00,000
Less: Premium on Re-Insurance ceded (4,90,000 + 4,50,000 – 1,00,000)	(8,40,000)
Total Premium Earned (Net)	78,60,000
Less: Adjustment for change in Unexpired Risk Reserve (Note)	(3,42,000)
Total Premium Earned (Net)	75,18,000

Note: Adjustment for Changes in Reserve for Unexpired Risks is computed as under:

Particulars	Reserve
Closing balance required [(40% of 78,60,000) + (5% of 78,60,000)]	35,37,000
Less: Opening Balance available(28,40,000 + 3,55,000)	31,95,000
Amt to be transferred to Reserve for the year	3,42,000

SCHEDULE 2 – CLAIMS PAID (NET)

Particulars	This Yr
Claims Paid – Direct (49,70,000 + 7,38,000 – 6,85,000)	50,23,000
Add: Claims on Re-Insurance accepted (5,10,000 + 70,000 – 95,000)	4,85,000
Less: Claims on Re-Insurance Ceded (3,95,000 + 1,25,000 – 75,000)	(4,45,000)
Add: Surveyor's Fees	45,000
Add: Legal Expenses	55,000
Total claims Incurred	51,63,000

SCHEDULE 3 – COMMISSION

Particulars	This Yr
Commision paid: Direct	1,60,000
Add: Commission on Re-Insurance accepted	15,000
Less: Commission on Re-Insurance ceded	(18,000)
Net Commission	1,57,000

Answer 7(c)

COMPUTATION OF AMOUNT TO BE CHARGED TO REVENUE ACCOUNT

Particulars		₹
A Old Cost of 4/5th of Old Asset [₹ 30,00,000 × 4/5]		24,00,000
B Effect of Increases in various components of old cost		
(a) Increase in Materials Cost 40% of (₹ 24 lacs – 20%) × 5/8]	4,80,000	
(b) Increase in Labour Cost 80% of (₹ 24 lacs – 20%) × 3/8]	5,76,000	
(c) Increase in Overheads [25% of (₹ 4,80,000 + ₹ 5,76,000]	2,64,000	13,20,000
C Current Cost of Old Asset (A + B)		37,20,000
D *Less:* Recoveries from Old Asset		
(a) Sale Proceeds of Old Materials	7,50,000	
(b) Value of Old Materials Reuses	2,40,000	9,90,000
E Amount to be written off to Revenue A/c (C – D)		27,30,000

COMPUTATION OF AMOUNT TO BE CAPITALISED

Particulars	₹
A. Cash Cost of New Asset (Excluding the Value of Old Materials, if any, reused)	60,00,000
B. *Less:* Current Cost of Old Asset	(37,20,000)
C. Current Cash Cost to be Capitalised (A – B)	22,80,000
D. *Add:* Value of Old Materials Reused	2,40,000
E. Current Total Cost to be Capitalised (C + D)	25,20,000

JOURNAL

Date	Particulars		L.F.	Dr. (₹)	Cr. (₹)
	New Main A/c	Dr.		22,80,000	
	Replacement A/c	Dr.		37,20,000	
	To Bank A/c				60,00,000
	(Being the current cost of replacement of 4/5th of the old main charged to Replacement A/c)				
	New Main A/c	Dr.		2,40,000	
	To Replacement A/c				2,40,000
	(Being the cost of old materials used in the main)				
	New Auxilliary Main A/c	Dr.		15,50,000	
	To Bank A/c				15,00,000
	To Replacement A/c				50,000
	(Being the capitalisation of cost incurred on laying auxiliary main including old materials worth ₹ 50,000)				
	Bank A/c	Dr.		7,50,000	
	To Replacement A/c				7,50,000
	(Being the sale of old materials)				
	Revenue A/c	Dr.		26,80,000	
	To Replacement A/c				26,80,000
	(Being the transfer of balances in Replacement A/c to Revenue A/c)				

ANSWERS TO TULSIAN MODEL TEST PAPER 2

Answer 1(a)

Bank Overdraft as per Cash Book = ₹ 10,000 + ₹ 500 + ₹ 30,233 + ₹ 350 – ₹ 9 – ₹ 100 – ₹ 50,000
= ₹ 9,026

Bank Overdraft to be taken to the Balance Sheet

= ₹ 10,000 + ₹ 500 + ₹ 30,233 + ₹ 350 – ₹ 9 – ₹ 100 – ₹ 50,000 = ₹ 9,026

Answer 1(b)

Cost as on 1.4.2014 = ₹ 29,160/(.90 × .90 × .90) = ₹ 40,000

A. Total Depreciation under Old Method = ₹ 40,000 – ₹ 29,160 = ₹ 10,840

B. Total Depreciation under New Method = ₹ 40,000 × 10% × 3 = ₹ 12,000

C. Short Depreciation to be provided = ₹ 1,160

JOURNAL ENTRY TO ADJUST SHORT DEPRECIATION

Profit and Loss A/c Dr. ₹ 1,160

To Machinery A/c ₹ 1,160

(Being the Short Depreciation provided on a/c of change in method of Depreciation)

Answer 1(c)

1. Profit & Loss A/c to be cr. with Excess Provision for Doubtful Debts ₹ 1,500
2. Profit & Loss A/c to be dr. with Short Provision for Discount on Debtors ₹ 1,700

Answer 1(d)

JOURNAL

Date	Particulars	L.F.	Dr. (₹)	Cr. (₹)
	B's Capital A/c Dr. To Realisation A/c [Being an unrecorded asset taken over by B (i.e. 62% of ₹ 20,000)]		12,400	12,400
	Realisation A/c Dr. To Bank A/c (Being the remaining unrecorded liability paid)		32,000	32,000

Answer 1(e)

Dr. GENERAL LEDGER ADJUSTMENT ACCOUNT (IN CREDITORS LEDGER) Cr.

Particulars	₹	Particulars	₹
To Creditors Ledger Adjustment A/c:		By Creditors Ledger Adjustment A/c:	
Endorsed B/R Dish.	1,000	T/f from Drs. Ledger to Crs. Ledger	1,100
		T/f from Crs. Ledger to Drs. Ledger	1,900
		B/R Endorsed to Crs.	4,000
		Discount received (₹ 600–₹ 500)	100
		Allowances	3,200
		By Balance c/d (30,000 + 500)	30,500

Notes: The following items do not appear in GLA Account (in Creditors Ledger)

1. Reserve for Discount on Creditors
2. Bills Payable matured / discharged

Answer 1(f)

PROVISION OF AS 9

As per AS 9 trade discounts and volume rebates are not encompassed within the definition of revenue. Trade discounts and volume rebates given should be deducted in determining the revenue.

ADVICE

However, the price discount of 15 % in the instant case, is not the discount given during the ordinary course of the trade. Hence, it cannot be treated in the nature of discount eligible for deduction from sales price, the better alternate is to treat the amount as bad debt, therefore the contentions of directors of XYZ Ltd. are not correct.

Answer 1(g)

Proportionate Discount to be borne by X = (₹ 2,400 × ₹ 1,07,800/ ₹ 1,17,600) = ₹ 2,200

Answer 1(h)

STATEMENT OF CLAIM

Particulars		₹
A. Estimated Value of Stock As at date of fire		
(a) Book-Value of Normal Items	₹ 54,600	
(b) Current Value of Abnormal Items	₹ 3,450	58,050
B. Value of Salvaged Stock [₹ 8,700 – ₹ 2,900 (handed over)]		5,800
C. Estimated Value of Stock Lost by fire (A–B)		52,250
D. Fire fighting expenses		2,750
		55,000
E. Amount of claim by applying Average clause: [(52,250 × 50,000)/58,050]		47,373

Answer 1(i)

Particulars	(₹ in lakhs)
Doubtful Assets (more than 3 years)	1,000
Less: Value of security (excluding DICGC cover)	(400)
Less: DICGC cover	(100)
Unsecured Portion	500
Provision for unsecured portion @100%	500
Provision for secured portion @100%	400
Total Provision to be made	900

Answer 1(j)

VALUATION BALANCE SHEET AS AT 31ST MARCH, 2015

₹ in lakhs

Liabilities	₹	Assets	₹
To Net Liability as per actuarial valuation	75,00,000	By Life Insurance Fund	90,00,000
To Surplus (B/F)	15,00,000		
	90,00,000		90,00,000

STATEMENT SHOWING THE DISTRIBUTION OF SURPLUS

Particulars	₹
A. Total Surplus after Taxation	16,50,000
B. *Less:* Surplus to be carried forward	(10,00,000)
C. Surplus Available for distribution (A – B)	6,50,000
D. Share of Shareholders @ 5%	32,500
E. Share of Policy holders @ 95%	6,17,500
F. *Less:* Interim Bonus already paid	(1,50,000)
G. Amount Due to Policy holders (E – F)	4,67,500

Answer 2(a)

JOURNAL

Date	Particulars		L.F.	Dr. (₹)	Cr. (₹)
(a)	Sales A/c	Dr.		5,400	
	To Suspense A/c				5,400
	(Being posting to Sales A/c, now rectified)				
(b)	Suspense A/c	Dr.		5,400	
	To X				5,400
	(Being the posting to X's A/c, now rectified)				
(c)	Furniture A/c	Dr.		5,400	
	To Z				5,400
	(Being error in posting, now rectified)				
(d)	Suspense A/c	Dr.		3,300	
	To B/R A/c				300
	To B/P A/c				3000
	(Being B/P recorded in B/R Book but Murari's A/c correctly posted, now rectified)				

Answer 2(b)

PROVISION OF AS 4

As per AS 4, Assets and Liabilities should be adjusted for events occurring after the balance sheet date that provide additional evidence to assist the estimation of amounts relating to conditions existing at the balance sheet date.

ADVICE

(a) Though the theft, by the cashier ₹ 6,00,000 was detected after the balance sheet date (before approval of financial statements) but it is an additional information materially affecting the determination of the cash amount relating to conditions existing at the balance sheet date. Therefore, it is necessary to make the necessary adjustments in the financial statements of the company for the ended 31st March, 2013 for recognition of the loss amounting ₹ 6,00,000.

(b) If embezzlement of cash comes to the notice of company management only after approval of financial statements by board of directors of the company, then the treatment will be done as per the provisions of AS 5. This being extra ordinary item should be disclosed in the Statement of Profit and Loss as a part of loss for the year ending March, 2013. The nature and the amount of prior period item should be separately disclosed on the Statement of Profit and Loss in a manner that its impact on current profit on loss can be perceived.

Answer 2(c)

STATEMENT SHOWING THE VALUATION OF STOCK AS ON 31ST MARCH

	Particulars	₹
A	Stock as per physical verification as at 7th April	4,00,000
B	*Less:* Cost of Net goods purchased after 31st March till stock taking [₹ 2,00,000 – 20% of ₹ 2,00,000]	(1,60,000)
C	*Add:* Cost of Net goods sold after 31st March till Stock taking	
	Good Units: [80% of (₹ 2,00,000 – 20% of ₹ 2,00,000)]	1,28,000
	Defective units: [80% of (₹ 1,80,000 + 1/9th of ₹ 1,80,000)]	1,60,000
D	*Add:* Cost of goods lying with others on our behalf as on 31st March	
	Goods sent as approval [80% of (₹ 2,00,000 – 20% of ₹ 2,00,000)]	1,28,000
	Goods sent on consignment [80% of ₹ 2,00,000]	1,60,000
E	*Less:* Cost of goods lying with as on behalf of others	
	Goods received for sale on consignment basis [20% of ₹ 2,00,000]	(40,000)
F	Stock as per books as at 31st March	7,76,000

Notes:

(i) No adjustment has been made in respect of goods returned by customers to whom goods were sent on approval basis since there goods are already included in the stock given as on 7th April.

(ii) No adjustment has been made in respect of goods sold out of those received for sale on consignment basis since these goods are not included in the stock given as on 7th April.

Answer 3(a)

RESTAURANT TRADING ACCOUNT

To Opening Stock	3,900	By Restaurant Takings	3,61,600
To Purchases	2,04,800	By Closing Stock	4,500
To Wages	50,000	By Boarding Expenses	27,500
To Fuel	17,700		
To Depreciation on China Glass Cutlery	500		
To Boarding Expenses of Restaurant Staff	20,000		

To Profit t/f to Income & Expenditure A/c	96,700		
	3,93,600		3,93,600

INCOME & EXPENDITURE ACCOUNT FOR THE YEAR ENDED 31.3.2015

Expenditure		₹	Income		₹
To Subscription w/o		100	By Entrance Donation		90000
To Boarding Expenses of other staff		7500	By Subscription		144000
To Sports material consumed		63000	By Bank Interest:	1340	
To Postage:			*Add:* Accrued	200	1540
Cash	175		By Profit from Restaurant		96700
Stamps	25	200	By Interest on Govt. Securities		
To Honorarium		12000	Received	18000	
To Tournament Expenses		5350	*Add:* TDS	2000	20000
To Depreciation on Books			By Profit on Sale of Sports Assets		1200
To Periodicals		1900			
To Depreciation on Premises [5% (87000 + 30000 – 56400)]		3030			
To Depreciation on Sundry Assets		4800			
To Rent (148500 + 13500)		162000			
To Wages		42300			
To Rates & Taxes:					
Paid	300				
Add: Prepaid in beg	250				
Less: Prepaid at end	250	300			
To Telephone Charges:					
Paid	1500				
Add: outstanding at end	300				
Less: Outstanding in beg	600	1200			
To Affiliation(2400 – 1200)		1200			
To Surplus		50460			
		353440			353440

CLOSING BALANCE SHEET AS AT 31.3.2015

Liablities.		₹	Assets		₹
Capital Fund	8500		Premises	87000	
Add: Entrance Donation	90000		Addition:	30000	
Add: Surplus	50460	148960	*Less:* Depreciation	59430	57570
Creditors for Sports Material		9750	Sundry Assets		43200
Entrance Donation refundable		20000	Subscription Outstanding:		
Subscription in Advance:			2013-2014	100	

2015-2016	4200		2014-2015	6800	6900
2016-2017	1200	5400	Govt Securities		180000
Prize Fund:	12000		Fixed Deposit		11000
Add: Donation	2800		T.D.S on Interest		2000
Add: Interest on PFI	1200		Stamps		25
Less: Prize Awarded	2000	14000	Accrued Bank Interest		200
Outstanding Rent(148500/11)		13500	Accrued Interest on Prize Fund		600
Outstanding Honorarium		1000	Advance Affiliation fee		1200
Outstanding telephone charges		300	Outstanding telephone charges		300
Bank overdraft		117985	Prepaid Rates & Taxes		250
			Stock in Restaurant		4500
			Advance for Sports Material		3250
			Stock of Sports Material		2500
			S.B. Account		
			Current Account		3700
			10% Prize Fund Investment		12000
			China Glass Cutlery	2500	
			Less: Depreciation	500	2000
		330895			331195

Working Notes:

1. OPENING BALANCESHEET AS AT 31.3.2014

Liablities	₹	Assets	₹
Entrance donation received in advance	100000	Sundry Assets	44000
Outstanding telephone charges	600	Prepaid Rates & Taxes	250
Creditors for Sports Material	15000	Advance to supplier of Sports Material	5000
Prize Fund	12000	Stock of Sports Material	15000
Accumulated Depreciation	56400	Premises	87000
Advance Subscription	3000	Stock in Restaurant	3900
Capital Fund(B.F)	8500	China Glass Cutlery	2500
		10% Prize Fund Investment	12000
		Subscription Outstanding	9500
		S.B. A/C	4200
		Current A/C	2100
		Stamps	50
		Bank F.D	10000
	195500		195500

2. CALCULATION OF ENTRANCE DONATION

A	Entrance donation received during year	100000
B	*Add:* Received in advance on 1.4.2014	100000
C	*Less:* Donation Refundable	20000
D	*Less:* 50% Capitalised	90000
E	Taken to Income & Expenditure A/C	90000

3. SUBSCRIPTION ACCOUNT

To Outstanding Subscription	9500	By Advance Subscription	3000
To Income & Expenditure a/c	144000	By Income & Expenditure w/o	100
To Advance Subscription	5400	By Bank	148900
		By Outstanding Subscription	6900
	158900		158900

4. CREDITORS FOR SPORTS MATERIAL ACCOUNT

To bal b/d	5000	By bal b/d	15000
To bank	54000	by Stock of Sports Material	50500
To bal c/d	9750	by bal c/d	3250
	68750		68750

5. STOCK OF SPORTS MATERIAL ACCOUNT

To bal b/d	15000	By Income & Expenditure a/c(consumed)	63000
To creditors for Sports Material	50500	By bal c/d	2500

6. PREMISES ACCOUNT

To bal b/d	87000	By depreciation on 1.4.09	56400
To Purchases	30000	By depreciation @ 5%	3030
		By bal c/d	57570
	117000		117000

7. SPORTS ASSETS ACCOUNT

To balance b/d	4000	By Bank a/c	5200
To Income & Expenditure(profit)	1200		
	5200		5200

8. SUNDRY ASSETS ACCOUNT

To Bal b/d (44000 – 4000)	40000	By depreciation	4800
To Bank	8000	By bal c/d	43200
	48000		48000

Answer 3(b)

COMPUTATION OF CASH PRICE AND PERIODIC INTEREST

A Instalment Number	B Closing Balance after the Payment of Instalment	C Instalment Amount	D = B + C Closing Balance before the payment of Instalment	E = D*R/(100 + R) Interest D* 10/110	F = D – E Opening Balance
IV	—	2,20,000	2,20,000	20,000	2,00,000
III	2,00,000	2,40,000	4,40,000	40,000	4,00,000
II	4,00,000	2,60,000	6,60,000	60,000	6,00,000
I	6,00,000	2,80,000	8,80,000	80,000	8,00,000

Let the cash price by 'X'

X = ₹ 8,00,000 + 20% of X (i.e. down payment)

0.8X = ₹ 8,00,000

X = ₹ 8,00,000/0.8 = ₹ 10,00,000

LEDGER ACCOUNTS IN THE BOOK OF X

Dr. MACHINERY ACCOUNT Cr.

Date	Particulars	₹	Date	Particulars	₹
01.01.2013	To Y	10,00,000	31.12.2013	By Depreciation A/c	2,00,000
				By Balance c/d	8,00,000
		10,00,000			10,00,000
01.01.2014	To Balance b/d	8,00,000	31.12.2014	By Depreciation A/c	2,00,000
				By Balance c/d	6,00,000
		8,00,000			8,00,000
01.01.2015	To Balance b/d	6,00,000	01.01.2015	By Y	2,16,000
				By P&L A/c (Loss on Default)	1,44,000
			31.12.2015	By Depreciation A/c	80,000
			31.12.2015	By Balance c/d	1,60,000
		6,00,000			6,00,000

Dr. Y 'S ACCOUNT Cr.

Date	Particulars	₹	Date	Particulars	₹
01.01.2013	To Bank A/c	2,00,000	01.01.2013	By Machinery A/c	10,00,000
	(Down Payment)		31.12.2013	By Interest A/c	80,000
31.12.2013	To Bank A/c [₹ 2,00,000 + ₹ 80,000]	2,80,000		[(₹ 10,00,000 – ₹ 2,00,000) × 10/100]	
	To Balance c/d	6,00,000			
		10,80,000			10,80,000

31.12.2013	To Balance c/d	6,60,000	01.01.2014	By Balance b/d	6,00,000
			31.12.2014	By Interest A/c [₹ 6,00,000 × 10/100]	60,000
		6,60,000			6,60,000
01.01.2015	To Machinery A/c	2,16,000	01.01.2015	By Balance b/d	6,60,000
	To Balance c/d	4,44,000			
		6,60,000			6,60,000

Working Notes:

1. *Calculation of Book value of Goods Repossessed*	
A. Cost [₹ 2,00,000 × 3]	₹ 6,00,000
B. *Less:* Depreciation for 2 years [₹ 6,00,000 × 20% × 2]	₹ 2,40,000
	₹ 3,60,000
2. *Calculation of Agreed value of Goods Repossessed*	
A. Cost [₹ 2,00,000 × 3]	₹ 6,00,000
B. *Less:* Depreciation for 1st year [40% of ₹ 6,00,000]	₹ 2,40,000
C. Book value in the beginning of 2nd year	₹ 3,60,000
D. *Less:* Depreciation for 2nd year [40% of ₹ 3,60,000]	₹ 1,44,000
E. Book Value at the end of 2nd year	₹ 2,16,000
3. Loss on default = Book value – Agreed value = ₹ 3,60,000 – ₹ 2,16,000 = ₹ 1,44,000	

LEDGER ACCOUNTS IN THE BOOKS OF Y

Dr. **X.'S ACCOUNT** **Cr.**

Date	Particulars	₹	Date	Particulars	₹
01.01.2013	To H.P. Sales A/c	10,00,000	01.01.2013	By Bank A/c (Down Payment)	2,00,000
31.12.2013	To Interest A/c [(₹ 10,00,00 – ₹ 2,00,000) × 10/100]	80,000	31.12.2013	By Bank A/c [₹ 2,00,000 + ₹ 80,000]	2,80,000
				By Balance c/d	6,00,000
		10,80,000			10,80,000
01.01.2014	To Balance b/d	6,00,000	31.12.2014	By Balance c/d	6,60,000
31.12.2014	To Interest A/c	60,000			
	[₹ 6,00,000 × 10/100]				
		6,60,000			6,60,000
01.01.2015	To Balance b/d	6,60,000	01.01X3	By H.P. Goods Repossessed A/c	2,16,000
				By Balance c/d	4,44,000
		6,60,000			6,60,000

Dr. **H.P. GOODS REPOSSESSED ACCOUNT** Cr.

Date	Particulars	₹	Date	Particulars	₹
01.01.2015	To X's.'s A/c	2,16,000	30.06.2015	By Bank A/c	2,10,000
	To Bank A/c (Repairs) (₹ 6,000 × 3)	18,000		By P&L A/c (Loss)	24,000
		2,34,000			2,34,000

Answer 3(c)

COST PRICE STRUCTURE

	₹
A. Cost Price	100
B. *Add:* Profit	20
C. Invoice Price (A + B)	120
D. *Add:* Extra Profit	30
E. Catalogue Price (C + D)	150

Dr. **MUMBAI BRANCH STOCK ACCOUNT** Cr.

Particulars	₹	Particulars	₹
To Balance b/d	12,000	By Goods sent to Branch A/c [₹ 30,000 × 120/150]	24,000
To Goods sent to Branch A/c [₹ 1,10,000 + 20%]	1,32,000	By Branch Cash A/c (Cash Sales)	74,800
To Goods sent to Branch A/c [₹ 75,000 × 120/150]	60,000	By Branch Debtors A/c (Credit Sales)	1,45,000
To Branch Debtors A/c (Returns)	30,000	By Goods sent to Branch A/c (Returns)	24,000
To Branch Debtors A/c (Returns)	15,000	By Goods sent to Branch A/c (Returns) [₹ 15,000 × 120/150]	12,000
To Branch Cash A/c [local purchases]	30,000	By Branch Adjustment A/c (Load)	500
To Branch Adjustment A/c [Load on local purchases]	6,000	By Branch Profit and Loss A/c (Stock destroyed by fire)	2,500
To Branch Adjustment A/c (Excess of catalogue price of Net Credit Sales over invoice price) (₹ 1,45,000 – ₹ 30,000 – 15,000) × 30/150]	20,000	By Branch Adjustment A/c [Invoice Price of Normal Loss] [₹ 3,000 × 120/150]	2,400
		By Balance c/d:	7,200
		Stock out of local purchases Stock in transit from H.O. [₹1,32,000 – ₹1,27,000]	5,000
		Stock in hand from H.O.(B. f.)	7,600
	3,05,000		3,05,000

Dr. **MUMBAI BRANCH ADJUSTMENT ACCOUNT** **Cr.**

Particulars	₹	Particulars	₹
To Stock Reserve A/c		By Stock Reserve A/c	
[₹ 19,800 × 20/120]	3,300	[₹ 12,000 × 20/120]	2,000
To Branch Stock A/c		By Branch Stock A/c	6,000
[load on abnormal Loss]	500	[Loading on local purchases]	
To Branch Stock A/c	2,400	By Branch Stock A/c	20,000
[Invoice Price of Normal Loss]		(Excess of catalogue price of Net Credit Sales over invoice price)	
To Branch Profit and Loss A/c (Gross profit)	43,800	By Goods sent to Branch A/c ; [Load on Net Goods sent] [₹ 1,32,000 + ₹ 60,000 – ₹ 24,000 – ₹24,000 – 12,000] [₹ 1,32,000 × 20/120]	22,000
	50,000		50,000

Dr. **MUMBAI BRANCH EXPENSES ACCOUNT** **Cr.**

Particulars	₹	Particulars	₹
To Branch Cash A/c	9,741	By Branch Profit & Loss A/c	23,106
To Discount Allowed A/c	13,365		
	23,106		23,106

Dr. **MUMBAI BRANCH PROFIT AND LOSS ACCOUNT** **Cr.**

Particulars	₹	Particulars	₹
To Branch Expenses A/c	23,106	By Branch Adjustment A/c (Gross Profit)	43,800
To Branch Stock A/c (Cost of Loss by fire)	2,500	By Insurance Claim	2000
To Provision for Discount A/c	1,485		
To Manager's Commission	1,059		
To General Profit and Loss A/c [₹ 18,709 × 6/106]	17,650		
	45,800		45,800

Dr. **MUMBAI BRANCH DEBTORS ACCOUNT** **Cr.**

Particulars	₹	Particulars	₹
To Balance b/d	10,000	By Branch Stock A/c	30,000
To Branch Stock A/c (Credit Sales)	1,45,000	By Goods sent to Branch A/c	15,000
		By Branch Cash/Bank A/c	45,635
		By Cash/Bank A/c	40,000

		By Discount Allowed A/c	13,365
		By Balance c/d (b.f.)	**11,000**
	1,55,000		1,55,000

Working Note: *Computation of Provision for discount*

(a) Prompt paying debtors who availed of discount = ₹ 13,365 × 100/15 = 89,100

(b) Total debtors who made payment during the year = ₹ 13,365 + 85,635 = ₹ 99,000

(c) Proportion of prompt payers to those who made payment = (89,100/99,000) × 100 = 90%

(d) Likely Prompt paying debtors included in closing Debtors = 90% of ₹ 11,000 = ₹ 9,900

(e) Provision for discount on the closing balance = 15% of ₹ 9,900 = ₹ 1,485

Answer 4(a)

Dr. **TOTAL DEBTORS ACCOUNT** **Cr.**

Date	Particulars	₹	Date	Particulars	₹
01.04.2014	To Balance b/d	2,00,000	31.03.2015	By Returns Inward	20,000
31.03.2015	To Credit Sales	12,20,000		By Discount Allowed	11,000
	To Discount disallowed	1,000		By Cash A/c	2,00,000
	To Bank A/c (Ch. dish.)	40,000		By Bank A/c	4,40,000
	To Bills Receivable A/c (B/R Dish)	20,000		By Bad Debts	10,000
	To Total Creditors A/c (Endorsed B/R Disc.)	10,000		By Bills Receivable	6,60,000
	To Interest	45,000		By Total Creditors A/c	15,000
				By Balance c/d	1,80,000
		15,36,000			15,36,000

Note: Cash Sales, Bad Debts Recovered and Provision for Doubtful Debts do not appear in the Total Debtors Account.

Answer 4(b)

JOURNAL

Date	Particulars		L.F.	Dr. (₹)	Cr. (₹)
(a)(i)	Sales A/c	Dr.		500	
	Sales Returns A/c	Dr.		500	
	To Suspense A/c (in Sales Ledger)				1,000
(a)(ii)	General Ledger Adjustment A/c (In Sales Ledger)	Dr.		1,000	
	To Sales Ledger Adjustment A/c (In General Ledger)				1,000

(b)	Suspense A/c Dr. To Mr Philips (In Sales Ledger)		600	 600
(c)	Mr Ghanshyam Dr. To Mr Radhesham To Suspense A/c (In Sales Ledger)		100	 10 90
(d)	Bad Debts A/c Dr. To Suspense (In Sales Ledger)		150	 150
(e)	Discount A/c Dr. To Suspense A/c (In Sales Ledger)		1,000	 1,000

Answer 4(c)

Dr. CREDITORS LEDGER ADJUSTMENT ACCOUNT IN GENERAL LEDGER Cr.

Date	Particulars	₹	Date	Particulars	₹
01.03.2015	To Balance b/d	4,500	01.03.2015	By Balance b/d	2,500
31.03.2015	To General Ledger		31.03.2015	By General Ledger	
	Adjustment A/c:			Adjustment A/c:	
	Cash paid {3,000 + 2,500 + 6,000 + 4,940 (5,200 – 5%)}	16,440		Purchases (7,500 + 6,200 + 6,000 + 3,500)	23,200
	Returns	1,000			
	Discount (5,200 × 5%)	260			
31.03.2015	To Balance c/d	3,500	31.03.2015	By Balance c/d	—
		25,700			25,700

Answer 5(a)

The transaction between S Limited and B Limited should be accounted for as financing transaction rather than as sale since S Ltd. concurrently agrees to repurchase the same goods from B Ltd. at a later date. Also, the repurchase price is predetermined and covers B Limited's purchasing and holding costs. Hence, the resulting cash inflow of ₹ 1,200 lakhs is not revenue as per AS-9 'Revenue Recognition'.

JOURNAL OF S LIMITED

Date	Particulars		Dr. (₹)	Cr. (₹)
15.3.2015	Bank A/c To Advance from B Limited A/c (Being amount received from B Ltd. as per sale and repurchasing agreement)	Dr.	1,200	 1,200
31.3.2015	Financing Charges A/c To Advance from B Ltd. A/c (Being the Financing charges 20% of ₹ 1200 lakhs for 1/2 month i.e. 240 × 0.5/6)	Dr.	20	 20
31.3.2015	Profit and Loss A/c To Financing charges (Being amount transferred to profit and loss account)	Dr.	20	 20

Disclosure in the Balance Sheet

1. An Extract of Balance Sheet of S Ltd. as at 31.3.2015

Particulars	(₹) in lakhs
Assets (Under the head "Current Assets")	
Short-term loans and advances	
Goods lying with B Limited (under sale and repurchase agreement)	1,000*
Liabilities (under the head "Secured Loans')	
Advance from B Limited	1,200
Add: Accrued finance charges	20
	1,220

2. Notes to accounts:

(a) Goods lying with B Limited costing ₹ 1,000 lakhs to be repurchased after 6 months at ₹ 1,440 lakhs.

(b) Goods sold to B Limited for ₹ 1,200 lakhs (cost ₹ 1,000 lakhs) on repurchase agreement. The difference between sale price and repurchase price is treated as financing charges and allocated proportionately in the current accounting period.

JOURNAL OF B LTD. ₹ in lakhs

Date	Particulars		Dr. (₹)	Cr. (₹)
15.3.2015	Advance from B Limited A/c	Dr.	1,200	
	To Bank A/c		1,200	
	(Being amount paid to S Ltd. as per sale and repurchase agreement)			
31.3.2015	Accrued Finance Income A/c	Dr.	20	
	To Finance income			20
	(Financing charges 20% of ₹1200 lakhs for 1/2 month i.e. 240 × 0.5/6)			
31.3.2015	Financing Income A/c	Dr.	20	
	To Profit and Loss A/c			20
	(Being financing charges received transferred to profit and loss account)			

Disclosure in the Balance Sheet

1. An extract of Balance sheet of B Ltd. as on 31.3.2015

Assets (Under the head 'Current Assets)'

Short-term loans and advances

Advance to S Ltd. (Under sale and repurchase agreement) ₹ 1,200 lakhs

Accrued Finance income ₹ 20 lakhs

(This advance is fully secured by goods of S Ltd. Market value of ₹ 1,200 lakhs lying with company as security)

2. Notes to Account

₹ 1,200 lakhs paid to S Limited against the sale and repurchase agreement against the security of goods of S Limited whose market value is ₹ 1,200 Lakhs.

The transaction is in the nature of a financing arrangement and hence is not recognized as a sale and hence the excess of repurchase price over sale price amounting to ₹ 240 lakhs have been treated as Finance charges allocated proportionately between accounting periods 2015-2016 and 2015-14. The value of the computer spares lying with B Ltd. on Balance Sheet date is considered as part of the company's inventory held as security for the Financing obligation.

Answer 5(b)

PROVISION OF AS 7

1. As per AS-7 when the outcome of a construction contract can be estimated reliably, contract revenue and contract costs associated with the construction contract should be recognised as revenue and expenses respectively by reference to stage of completion of the contract activity at the reporting date.
2. As per AS-7 an expected loss on the Construction contract should be recognized as an expense immediately irrespective of (i) whether or not the work has commenced on the contract; or (ii) the stage of completion of the contract: or (iii) the amount of profits expected to arise in other contracts.

ADVICE

A. Work Certified	500
B. Work Not Certified	105
C. Cost incurred till date/ Contract Expense[A + B]	605
D. Estimated Additional Cost	495
E. Estimated Total Cost [C + D]	1100
F. Contract Price	1000
G. Total Expected Loss [E – F]	100
H. % of Completion [(C/E)X 100]	55%
I. Contract Revenue to be recognised as Turnover [Contract Price × % of Completion]	550
J. Loss for the current year[I – C]	55
K. Expected Loss to be recognized immediately as per para 35 of AS 7[G – J]	45

DISCLOSURES AS PER AS – 7

Particulars	₹ Lakhs
Contract Revenue	550
Contract Expenses	(605)
Provision for Expected Loss	(45)

Progress Billings[Progress Payment Received + To be Received]	540
Retentions (billed but not received from Contractee)	140
Gross amount due to customers[605-100-540]	35

Answer 5(c)

PROVISION OF AS 9

As per AS 9 to recognize the revenue there should not be significant uncertainty in ultimate collection of the amount.

ADVICE

In the instant case it appears that there are uncertainties in the collection of interest. Therefore income can be recognized only if the amount can be measured reliably and ultimate collection is reasonably certain.

Answer 6(a)

MEMORANDUM JOINT VEBTURE ACCOUNT

Dr. *for the period from July 1 to Sept 1, 2015* Cr.

Particulars	₹	Particulars	₹
To A:		By Sales:	
Cost of Mopeds	3,60,000	(80 × 4,500) 3,60,000	
Forwarding & insurance	2,880	A (20 × 4,500) 90,000	4,50,000
Interest (for 2 months)	1,500		
Selling Expenses	5,000		
To B:			
Clearing Charges	720		
Interest (for the month)	2,250		
Sundry Expenses (Telegraphic transfer charges)	50		
Selling Expenses	20,000		
To Profit transferred to:			
A	28,800		
B	28,800		
	4,50,000		4,50,000

Dr. **JOINT VENTURE WITH B ACCOUNT IN THE BOOKS OF A** **Cr.**

Particulars	₹	Particulars	₹
To Bank A/c (part payment of cost)	72,000	By Bank A/c (sale proceeds)	22,500
To Bank A/c (balance cost of purchases)	2,88,000	By Bank A/c (remittance from Laxman)	1,50,000
To Bank A/c (forwarding charges)	2,880	By Bank A/c (sale proceeds)	67,500
To Bank A/c (selling expenses)	5,000	By Bank A/c (cash received	1,58,180
To Bank A/c (Interest)	1,500	in settlement)	
To Profit & Loss A/c (share of profit)	28,800		
	3,98,180		2,98,180

Dr. **JOINT VENTURE WITH A ACCOUNT IN THE BOOKS OF B** **Cr.**

Particulars	₹	Particulars	₹
To Bank A/c (clearing charges)	720	By Bank A/c (Sale proceeds of 20 mopeds)	90,000
To Bank A/c remittance excluding charges)	1,50,000	By Bank A/c (Sale proceeds of 60 mopeds)	2,70,000

To Bank A/c (selling expenses)	20,000		
To Bank A/c (interest)	2,250		
To Sundry Expenses	50		
To Profit & Loss A/c (share of profit)	28,800		
To Bank A/c (paid in settlement)	1,58,180		
	3,60,000		3,60,000

Answer 6(b)

JOURNAL

Date	Particulars		L.F.	Dr. (₹)	Cr. (₹)
	When goods are sent on approval:				
	Mr B's A/c	Dr.		20,000	
	To Sales A/c				20,000
	(Being goods sent on approval treated as credit sale)				
(i)	**When goods are approved by customer**				
	No Entry need to be passed				
(ii)	**When the customer rejects all the goods:**				
	Sales A/c	Dr.		20,000	
	To Mr B's A/c				20,000
	(Being entry for credit sale reversed on rejection of the goods by the customer)				
	Stock with customers A/c	Dr.		16,000	
	To Trading A/c				16,000
	(Being stock at the end recorded with the customers at cost price)				
(iii)	**When the customer retains half the goods while rejecting the other half:**				
	Sales A/c	Dr.		10,000	
	To Mr B's A/c				10,000
	(Being entry for credit sale reversed for the rejected portion i.e. half of the goods)				
	Stock with customers A/c	Dr.		8,000	
	To Trading A/c				8,000
	(Being stock at the end recorded with the customers at cost price)				

Working Note: Selling Price = Cost of goods sent + Gross Profit = ₹ 16,000 + 25% of ₹ 16,000
= ₹ 20,000

Answer 6(c)

As per AS 13 "Accounting for Investments", in case of reclassification of investment from long-term to current, transfer is to be made at lower of cost or carrying amount at the date of transfer. If investment is reclassified from current to long term, transfer is to be made at lower of cost and fair value. Keeping in view this provision, the answer is given below:

(i) Reclassification from Long term to Current: Cost is ₹ 8.5 Lakhs and carrying amount is ₹ 6.5 Lakhs. Hence transfer will be made at ₹ 6.5 Lakhs.

(ii) Reclassification from Long term to current: Cost is ₹ 7 Lakhs and carrying amount is ₹ 7 Lakhs. Hence transfer will be made at ₹ 7 Lakhs.

(iii) Reclassification from current to Long term: Cost is ₹ 10 Lakhs and Fair Value is ₹ 12 Lakhs. Hence transfer will be made at ₹ 10 Lakhs.

Answer 7(a)

JOURNAL (₹ in crores)

Date	Particulars	Dr.	L.F.	(₹)	Cr. (₹)
01.04.2014	Rebate on Bills Discounted A/c	Dr.		11.10	
	To Discount on bills A/c				11.10
	(Being the t/f of opening balance in Rebate on Bills Discounted A/c to Discount on Bills A/c)				
27.12.2014	Bills Purchased and Discounted A/c	Dr.		3,400	
	To Discount on Bills A/c [3,400 × 15% × 3/12]				127.50
	To Customers' A/c				3,272.50
	(Being the discounting of bills)				
30.03.2015	Cash/Bank A/c	Dr.		3,400.00	
	To Bills Purchased & Discounted A/c				3,400.00
	(Being the discounted Bills collected)				
09.03.2015	Bills Purchased and Discounted A/c	Dr.		600	
	To Discount on Bills A/c [600 × 12% × 3/12]				18
	To Customers' A/c				582
	(Being the discounting of bills)				
31.03.2015	Discount on Bills A/c [600 × 12% × 73/365]	Dr.		14.40	
	To Rebate on Bills Discounted A/c				14.40
	(Being the unexpired discount on discounted bills carried forward to next year)				
	Discount on Bills A/c	Dr.		145.50	
	To Profit and Loss A/c				145.50
	(Being the t/f of Income from Bills Discounting to Profit and Loss A/c)				

Ledger Accounts:

Dr. **1. DISCOUNT ON BILLS ACCOUNT** Cr.

Date	Particulars	₹	Date	Particulars	₹
31.03.2015	To Rebate on Bills Discounted A/c	14.40	01.04.2014	By Rebate on Bills Discounted A/c	11.10

31.03.2015	To Profit & Loss A/c	142.20	27.12.2014	By Bills Purchased and Discounted A/c	127.50
			09.03.2015	By Bills Purchased and Discounted A/c	18.00
		156.60			156.60

Dr. **2. REBATE ON BILLS DISCOUNTED ACCOUNT** **Cr.**

Date	Particulars	₹	Date	Particulars	₹
01.04.2014	To Discount on Bills A/c	11.10	01.04.2014	By Balance B/f	11.10
31.03.2015	To Balance c/f	14.40			
27.12.2014	By Discount on Bills A/c	14.40			
		25.50			25.50

AN EXTRACT OF PROFIT & LOSS ACCOUNT

for the period ending 3103.2015

Particulars	₹
Opening 'Rebate on Bills Discounted'	11.10
Add: Discount on Bills	145.50
Less: Closing Rebate on Bills Discounted'	(14.40)
	142.20

AN EXTRACT OF BALANCE SHEET AS AT 3103.2015

Liabilities	₹
Other Liabilities & Provisions:	
Rebate on bills discounted	14.40

Working Notes:

1. *Calculation of Date of Maturity & No. of Days After 31st March*

Date of Bill	Term of Bill in Months	Date of Maturity(including 3 days of grace)	No. of Days After 31st March
27.12.2014	3	30.3.2012	0
09.03.2015	3	12.6.2012	73

2. Discount Received = Amount of Bill × Discount Rate × Term of Bill

   On Bills of ₹ 3,400 = 3,400 × 15% × 3/12 = ₹127.50

   On Bills of ₹ 600 = 600 × 12% × 3/12 = ₹18

3. Rebate on Bills Discounted = Amount of Bill × Discount Rate × No. of Days After 31st March/365

   = 600 × 12% × 73/365 = ₹14.40

Answer 7(b)

FROM–B–RA–REVENUE ACCOUNT OF JALAN FIRE INSURANCE CO. LTD
for the year ending 31st March 2015

Particulars	Sch.	Current Yr	Previous Yr
Premium Earned (Net)	1	45,10,800	
Interest, Dividend & Rent (Gross) (₹ 20,520 × 100/90)		22,800	
Total (A)		45,33,600	
1. Claims Incurred (Net)	2	30,97,800	
2. Commission	3	94,200	
3. Operating Expenses related to Insurance Business	4	0	
(1,74,000 – Legal Exps 33,000 – Surveyor Fees 27,000)		1,14,000	
Total (B)		33,06,000	
Operating Profit/(Loss) from Insurance Business (A – B)		12,27,600	
Appropriations		NIL	
Total (C)		12,27,600	

SCHEDULE 1 – PREMUM EARNED (NET)

Particulars	This Yr
Premiums from Direct Business written (45,15,000 + 3,00,000 – 1,95,000)	46,20,000
Add: Premium on Re-Insurance accepted (4,95,000 + 2,25,000 – 1,20,000)	6,00,000
Less: Premium on Re-Insurance ceded (2,94,000 + 2,70,000 – 60,000)	(5,04,000)
Total Premium Earned (Net)	47,16,000
Less: Adjustment for change in Unexpired Risk Reserve (Note)	(2,05,200)
Total Premium Earned (Net)	45,10,800

Note: Adjustment for Changes in Reserve for Unexpired Risks is computed as under:

Particulars	Reserve
Closing balance required [(40% of 47,16,000) + (5% of 47,16,000)]	21,22,200
Less: Opening Balance available(17,04,000 + 2,13,000)	19,17,000
Amt to be transferred to Reserve for the year	2,05,200

SCHEDULE 2 – CLAIMS PAID (NET)

Particulars	This Yr
Claims Paid – Direct (29,82,000 + 4,42,800 – 4,11,000)	30,13,800
Add: Claims on Re-Insurance accepted (3,06,000 + 42,000 – 57,000)	2,91,000
Less: Claims on Re-Insurance Ceded (2,37,000 + 75,000 – 45,000)	(2,67,000)
Add: Surveyor's Fees	27,000
Add: Legal Expenses	33,000
Total claims Incurred	30,97,800

SCHEDULE 3 – COMMISSION

Particulars	This Yr
Commision paid: Direct	96,000
Add: Commission on Re-Insurance accepted	9,000
Less: Commission on Re-Insurance ceded	(10,800)
Net Commission	94,200

Answer 7(c)

TULSIAN ELECTRIC SUPPLY LTD.
BALANCE SHEET AS AT 31ST MARCH, 2015

Particulars	Note No.	(₹ in '000)
I. EQUITY AND LIABILITIES		
(1) Shareholders' Funds		
(a) Share Capital	1	65,000
(b) Reserves and Surplus	2	21,376
(2) Non-Current Liabilities		
(a) Long-term Borrowings	3	40,000
(3) Current Liabilities		
(a) Trade Payables		6,524
(b) Short-Term Provisions	4	121,00
Total		145,000
II. ASSETS		
(1) Non-Current Assets		
(a) Fixed Assets		
(i) Tangible Assets	5	109,960
(ii) Intangible Assets		2504
(b) Non-Current Investments	6	12,000
(2) Current Assets		
(a) Inventories		12,050
(b) Trade Receivables	7	5232
(c) Cash and Cash Equivalents		3254
Total		145,000

Notes To Accounts:

1. SHARE CAPITAL

Authorised Capital	
50,00,000 shares of ₹ 10 each	50,000
2,50,000 14% Pref. Shares of ₹ 100 each	25,000
	75,000

Issued & Subscribed Capital	
50,00,000 shares of ₹ 10 each	50,000
2,50,000 14% Pref. Shares of ₹ 100 each	25,000
Less: 1,00,000 14% Pref. Shares of ₹ 100 each	(10,000)
	65,000

2. RESERVES AND SURPLUS

Capital Reserve		4,020
Contingency Reserve (12,030 + 170 – 10)		12,190
Reserve (1000 + 200)		1,200
Profit & Loss Account		
Opening Balance	350	
Add: Profit for the period	5,000	
Less: Transfer to General Reserve	(200)	
Less: Transfer to Contingency Reserve	(170)	
Less: Provision for Doubtful Debts	(1,014)	3966
Total		21,376

3. LONG-TERM BORROWINGS

15% Debentures	24,700
16% Term Loan	15,300
	40,000

4. SHORT-TERM PROVISIONS

Proposed Dividend	12,100
	12,100

5. TANGIBLE ASSETS

Land (10,400 + 20,50)	124,50
Building (30,054 + 50,80)	351,34
Plant & Machinery	570,58
Mains	45,24
Meters	31,50
Electrical Instruments	15,30
Office Rurniture	24,50
Transformers	164,40
Public lamps	30,40
Less: Depreciation Fund	(258,16)
Total	109,960

6. NON-CURRENT INVESTMENTS

SBI Bonds-2020 (100,10 – 10)	100,00
Other Investments	20,00
	120,00

7. TRADE RECEIVABLES

Sundry Debtors	62,46
Less: Provision for Doubtful Debts	(10,14)
	52,32

ANSWERS TO TULSIAN MODEL TEST PAPER 3

Answer 1(a)

(i) Examples of Extraordinary items:

a. Loss due to earthquakes/fire/strike

b. Attachment of property of the enterprise by government

(ii) Examples of Prior period items:

a. Applying incorrect Rate of Depreciation in one *or* more prior periods.

b. Omission to account for Income *or* Expenditure in one *or* more prior periods.

Answer 1(b)

Difference between any two successive instalments represents the least amount of interest charged in the last year i.e. ₹ 2,21,900 – ₹ 2,06,050 = ₹ 15,850

Thus, Interest for 3rd year = Least amount of Interest × 2 = 31,700

Thus, Interest for 2nd year = ₹ 15,850 × 3 = 47,550

Thus, Interest for 1st year = ₹ 15,850 × 4 = 63,400

Thus, allocation of instalment between cash price and interest is as under:

Instalment (₹)	Interest (₹)	Cash Price (₹)
2,21,900	63,400	1,58,500
2,06,050	47,550	1,58,500
1,90,200	31,700	1,58,500
1,74,350	15,850	1,58,500
7,92,500	1,58,500	6,34,000

Total Cash Price = ₹ 6,34,000 + ₹ 1,58,500 = ₹ 7,92,500

Answer 1(c)

Minimum Rent for 2015 = 1,00,000 – [(1,00,000 × 73/365) + (1,00,000 × 2/12)] = 63,333

ANALYSIS OF ROYALTY PAYABLE AND SHORT WORKINGS

A Year	B Output (Units)	C = B X Rate Actual Royalty	D Minimum Rent	E = D – C Short Working	F Short Working Recouped	G = C + E – F Actual Payment	H Short Working W/O	$I_n = I_{n-1} + E - F -$ H Short Working C/F
2015	700	70,000	63,333	—	5,000	65,000	1,000	10,000

Answer 1(d)

CALCULATION OF ANNUAL DEPRECIATION CHARGE

A Cost of Lease paid	₹	40,000
B *Less:* Refundable amount	₹	4,000
C Depreciable amount (A – B)	₹	36,000
D Annuity Factor @ 5% interest for 4 years	₹	0.2820

E Fixed Depreciation Charge (C × D)	₹	10,142
F Interest on Salvage @ 5% on ₹ 2,000 for a year	₹	200
G Annual Depreciation Charge (E + F)	₹	10,352

Answer 1(e)

JOURNAL

Date	Particulars		L.F.	Dr. (₹)	Cr.(₹)
(a)	X (In Creditors' Ledger)	Dr.		1,000	
	To X (In Debtors' Ledger) (Being T/f of X's A/c from Debtors' Ledger to Creditors' Ledger)				1,000
(b)	Y (In Creditors' Ledger)	Dr.		300	
	To Y (In Debtors' Ledger) (Being t/f of Y's A/c from Creditors' Ledger to Debtors' Ledger)				300
(c)	General Ledger Adjustment A/c (In Debtors' Ledger)	Dr.		1,300	
	To Debtors Ledger Adjustment A/c (In General Ledger) (Being reduction in Total Debtors)				1,300
(d)	Creditors' Ledger Adjustment A/c (In General Ledger)	Dr.		1,300	
	To General Ledger Adjustment A/c (In Creditors' Ledger) (Being reduction in Total Creditors)				1,300

Answer 1(f)

PROVISION OF AS 7

1. As per AS-7 when the outcome of a construction contract can be estimated reliably, contract revenue and contract costs associated with the construction contract should be recognised as revenue and expenses respectively by reference to stage of completion of the contract activity at the reporting date.
2. As per AS-7 an expected loss on the Construction contract should be recognized as an expense immediately irrespective of (i) whether or not the work has commenced on the contract; or (ii) the stage of completion of the contract: or (iii) the amount of profits expected to arise in other contracts.

ADVICE

Particulars	₹ (crores)
A.Work Certified	100
B. Work Not Certified	35
C. Cost incurred till date/ Contract Expense[A + B]	135
D. Estimated Additional Cost	90
E. Estimated Total Cost [C + D]	225
F. Contract Price	215

G. Total Expected Loss [E – F]	10
H.% of Completion [(C/E)X 100]	60%
I. Contract Revenue to be recognised as Turnover [Contract Price × % of Completion]	129
J. Loss for the current year[I – C]	6
K. Expected Loss to be recognized immediately as per para 35 of AS 7[G – J]	4

DISCLOSURES AS PER AS – 7

Particulars	₹ (crores)
Contract Revenue	129
Contract Expenses Charged	(135)
Provision for Expected Loss	(4)

Answer 1(g)

Let Invoice price of Goods Sold = X

Total Commission = (10% of X) + (50% of 0.25X) = ₹ 8,100

8,100 = .X + 125X

X = ₹ 8,100/0.225 = ₹ 36,000

Cost of Goods Sold = ₹ 36,000/125% = ₹ 28,800

Cost of Goods received = ₹ 28,800/60% = ₹ 48,000

Cost of Goods Sent = ₹ 48,000/60% = ₹ 80,000

Answer 1(h)

1. Adjusted Turnover = ₹ 30,00,000 + 20% of ₹ 30,00,000 = ₹ 36,00,000
2. Net Claim for the increase cost of Working

   A. Gross claim for Increased Cost of Working (being the least of the following three amounts) ₹ 80,000

1. Actual Expenses ₹ 1,50,000
2. Proportionate Increased Cost of Working

$$= \text{Increased Cost of Working} \times \frac{\text{Gross Profit on Adjusted Turnover}}{\text{Gross Profit as above + Unisured Standing Charges}}$$

3. Maximum saving of liability of the insurer = Reduction in Turnover avoided through Increased Cost of Working × Agreed G.P. Ratio

   = ₹ 4,00,000 × 20% = ₹ 80,000

   B. *Less:* Saving In Insured Standing Charges (₹ 4,80,000 × 6.25%) ₹ 30,000

   C. Net Claim for Increased Cost of Working (A – B) ₹ 50,000

Answer 1(i)

CALCULATION OF THE AMOUNT OF PROVISION AND CONTINGENCIES

A. Provision for Diminution in Value of Investments (other than Held to Maturity) = (₹ 800 – 25% of ₹ 800) – (80% of ₹ 600)	₹ 120
B. Provision for NPA	₹ 1,060.50

C. Provision & Contingencies (excluding tax) [₹ 1,060.50 + ₹ 120]	₹ 1,180.50
D. Tax = 35% of [Total Income – Total Expenditure (excluding tax)]	
= 35% of [(8,890 + 220) – (2,720 + 2,662 + 1180.50)]	₹ 891.625

Answer 1(j)

JOURNAL

Date	Particulars		Dr. (₹)	Cr.(₹)
	Profit and Loss A/c	Dr.	3,00,000	
	To Bonus payable in cash A/c			3,00,000
	(Being the bonus payable in cash)			
	Profit and Loss A/c	Dr.	10,80,000	
	To Life insurance Fund A/c			10,80,000
	(Being transfer to Life Insurance Fund for liability)			

Answer 2(a)

JOURNAL

Date	Particulars		L.F.	Dr. (₹)	Cr. (₹)
(a)	Krishan	Dr.		4,230	
	Kishan	Dr.		4,230	
	Suspense A/c	Dr.		90	
	To Sales A/c				4,230
	To Purchases A/c				4,320
	(Being sale recorded as purchase with wrong amount and wrong posting therefrom, now rectified)				
(b)	Sales A/c	Dr.		4,320	
	Drawings A/c	Dr.		4,230	
	To Ganesh A/c				4,320
	To Purchases A/c				4,230
	(Being the goods taken by proprietor for his personal use reco. in sales book, now rectified)				
(c)	Sundry Debtors	Dr.		8,000	
	To Suspense A/c				8,000
	(Being a debtor omitted from the list now included) [**Note:** Debtor's A/c need not be posted again in the ledger in this case since it is already correctly balanced].				
(d)	No Journal Entry is to be passed as it has already been correctly passed in the Journal. Merely posting in both the accounts in the ledger is required.				

Answer 2(b)

CALCULATION OF COST OF MACHINE AS PER AS 10

	Particulars		₹ in lakhs
A	Quoted Price of machine		500.00
B	Trade Discount @ 5 % on ₹ 500		(25.00)
C	Price after discount [A – B]		475.00
D	VAT @ 10 % on ₹ 475		47.50
E	Selling Price [C + D]		522.50
F	Transportation charges [0.25 % of ₹ 500]		1.25
G	Installation charges [1 % of ₹ 500]		5.00
H	Borrowing cost [₹ 500 lakhs × 15% × 2/12]		12.50
I	Expenditure on Trial Run		
	Material:	0.50	
	Wages:	0.40	
	Overheads:	0.30	1.20
J	Total Cost of the Machinery to be capitalized [E + F + G + H + I]		542.45

As per AS – 16, the capitalization of interest should cease when substantially all the activities necessary for intended use are completed. Therefore, interest for the period 01/12/2014 to 01/05/2015 should be expensed.

Answer 2(c)

RECEIVABLE FROM SHIV – RECONCILIATION STATEMENT

Particulars	*Amount* (₹)
Opening Balance as on 1.1.2015	2,00,000
Credit Sales	12,20,000
Less: Goods returned by the Customer	20,000
Less: Cash received from Debtors	2,00,000
Less: Cheques received from Debtors of which cheques of ₹ 1,00,000 were dishonoured	4,40,000
Less: Bills Receivable drawn of which Bills of ₹ 1,00,000 were dishonoured	6,60,000
Less: Discount Allowed	11,000
Less: Bad Debts W/O (after deducting bad debts recovred ₹ 1,000)	10,000
Add: Cheques dishonoured	40,000
Add: Bills Receivable dishonoured	20,000
Add: Endorsed Bills Receivable dishonoured	10,000
Add: **Interest on Overdue Accounts**	45,000
Add: Discount Disallowed	1,000
Less: **Transfer to Bought Ledger**	15,000
Net Receivable from Customer	1,80,000

Note: Cash Sales, Bad Debts Recovered and Provision for Doubtful Debts do not appear in the Total Debtors Account.

Answer 3(a)

TRADING & PROFIT/LOSS ACCOUNT

Dr. *for the year ended 31st March, 2013* Cr.

Particulars		₹	Particulars		₹
To Opening Stock		60,000	By Sales		
To Purchases			Cash Sales	1,20,000	
Cash Purchases	72,000		Credit Sales	4,20,000	
Credit Purchases	4,20,000		*Less:* Sales Returns	(60,000)	4,80,000
Less: Purchase Returns	(60,000)		By Closing Stock		1,02,000
Less: Advertisement	(9,000)				
Less: Drawings	(1,000)	4,22,000			
To Freight Inward		4,000			
To Gross Profit		96,000			
		5,82,000			5,82,000
To Advertising		9,000	By Gross Profit B/d		96,000
To Bad Debts		9,375	By Discount Received		11,500
To Rebate Allowed		200	By Rebate Received		1,000
To Discount Allowed To Discount on bill		16,125 500	By Accrued Interest on Govt. Securities		200
To Loss by fire		20,000			
To Depreciation		12,000			
To Expenses (Balancing figure)		19,500			
To Net Profit		22,000			
		1,08,700			1,08,700

BALANCE SHEET OF BHARAT AS AT 31.03.2013

Liabilities		₹	Assets		₹
X's Capital Account			**Fixed Assets**		
Opening Balance	1,80,000		Opening Balance	60,000	
Add: Net Profit	22,000		*Less:* Loss Due to fire	(20,000)	
Less: Drawings	(1,01,000)	1,01,000	*Add:* Addition	80,000	
Creditors		30,000	*Less:* Depreciation	(12,000)	1,08,000
Outstanding Business Expense A/c		11,000	Closing Stock		1,02,000
Bank overdraft		1,39,700	Debtors		60,000
B/P		25,000	B/R		5,000
			Prepaid Business Expenses		4,000
			4% Govt.Securities		9,600

		Interest Accrued	200
		Due From Cashier	17,900
	3,06,700		3,06,700

Working Notes:

(i) *Calculation of Cash and Credit Sales during the current year:*	
	₹
A. Previous year's Total Sales (Gross Profit/GP Ratio) (₹80,000/.20)	4,00,000
B. *Add:* Increase in Sales during current year @ 20%	80,000
C. Current year's Total Sales (A + B)	4,80,000
D. *Less:* Cash Sales @ 25% of Net Sales (₹4,80,000 × 25%)	1,20,000
E. Net Credit Sales (C – D)	3,60,000
F. *Add:* Sales Returns (₹3,60,000 × 1/6)	60,000
G. Gross Credit Sales (E + F)	4,20,000
(ii) *Calculation of Cash and Credit Purchases during the current year:*	₹
A. Current year's Total Sales	4,80,000
B. *Less:* Gross Profit @ 20%	96,000
C. Cost of Goods Sold (A – B)	3,84,000
D. *Add:* Closing Stock (₹60,000 + ₹42,000)	1,02,000
E. *Add:* Material used in advertising	9,000
F. *Add:* Goods used as drawings	1,000
G. *Less:* Opening Stock	60,000
H. *Less:* Freight inward	4,000
I. Total Purchases	4,32,000
J. *Less:* Cash Purchases (₹4,32,000 × 1/6)	72,000
K. Net Credit Purchases	3,60,000
L. *Add:* Purchase Returns (₹3,60,000 × 1/6)	60,000
M. Gross Credit Purchases	4,20,000

Dr. (III) DEBTORS ACCOUNT Cr.

Particulars	₹	Particulars	₹
To Balance b/d	50,000	By Sales Returns A/c	60,000
To Sales A/c	4,20,000	By Bank A/c	9,375
To Creditors (Dish. of Endorsed B/R)	25,000	By Bad Debts A/c	9,375
To Bank A/c (Dish. of Discounted B/R)	12,500	By Discount Allowed A/c [₹2,68,750 × 6%]	16,125
		By Bank A/c [₹2,52,625 × 20%]	50,525
		By Cash A/c	2,02,100
		By B/R A/c	1,00,000
		By Balance c/d	60,000
	5,07,500		5,07,500

Dr. **(IV) CREDITORS ACCOUNT** **Cr.**

Particulars	₹	Particulars	₹
To Purchase Returns A/c	60,000	By Balance b/d	25,000
To Bank A/c	1,74,800	By Purchases A/c	4,20,000
To Discount Received A/c [₹2,18,500 × 5/95]	11,500	By Debtors A/c (Dish. of Endorsed B/R)	25,000
To Cash A/c	43,700		
To B/P	1,00,000		
To B/R [Endorsed B/R) (b.f.)	50,000		
To Balance c/d	30,000		
	4,70,000		4,70,000

Dr. **(V) BILLS RECEIVABLE ACCOUNT** **Cr.**

Particulars	₹	Particulars	₹
To Debtors A/c (B/R Drawn)	1,00,000	By Creditors A/c (Endorsed B/R)	50,000
(Balancing Figure)		By Bank A/c	24,500
		By Discounting Charges A/c	500
		By Bank A/c	9,800
		By Rebate Allowed	200
		By Bank A/c	10,000
		By Balance c/d	5,000
	1,00,000		1,00,000

Dr. **(V) BILLS PAYABLE ACCOUNT** **Cr.**

Particulars	₹	Particulars	₹
To Bank A/c	25,000	By Creditors A/c (B/P Accepted)	1,00,000
To Bank A/c	49,000	(Balancing Figure)	
To Rebate Received	1,000		
To Balance c/d	25,000		
	1,00,000		1,00,000

Dr. **(VII) FIXED ASSETS ACCOUNT** **Cr.**

Particulars	₹	Particulars	₹
To Balance b/d	60,000	By Loss by fire	20,000
To Bank A/c (Purchases) (Balancing Figure)	80,000	By Depreciation A/c (₹1,08,000 × 10/90)	12,000
		By Balance c/d	1,08,000
	1,40,000		1,40,000

(VIII) CALCULATION OF OPENING CAPITAL
BALANCE SHEET AS AT 31.03.2012

Liabilities	₹	Assets	₹
Outstanding Business Expenses	55,000	Fixed Assets	60,000
Trade Creditors for Goods	25,000	Stock	60,000
Capital (Balancing Figure)	1,80,000	Trade Debtors	50,000
		Cash	5,000
		Bank	65,000
		Prepaid Business Expenses	20,000
	2,60,000		2,60,000

(ix) Net Profit for current year = Closing Capital + Drawings – Opening Capital
= ₹1,01,000 + ₹1,01,000 – ₹1,80,000 = ₹22,000.

Dr. **(X) BUSINESS EXPENSES ACCOUNT** **Cr.**

Particulars	₹	Particulars	₹
To Prepaid Expenses A/c (Beg)	20,000	By Outstanding Exp A/c (Beg.)	55,000
To Bank A/c (80% of ₹ 47,500)	38,000	By Profit & Loss A/c	19,500
To Cash A/c (20% of ₹ 47,500)	9,500	By Prepaid Expenses A/c (End)	4,000
To Outstanding Exp A/c (End)	11,000		
	78,500		78,500

Dr. **(XI) CASH BOOK** **Cr.**

Particulars	Cash	Bank	Particulars	Cash	Bank
To Balance b/d	5,000	65,000	By Cash Purchases A/c	72,000	
To Cash Sales A/c	1,20,000		By Creditors A/c	43,700	1,74,800
To Debtors A/c	2,02,100	50,525	By Freight	4,000	
To Cash A/c(C)		1,00,000	By Fixed Assets A/c		80,000
To B/R A/c		24,500	By Business Exp.	9,500	38,000
To Debtors A/c		9,375	By Drawings A/c	80,000	20,000
To B/R A/c		9,800	By Bank A/c (C)	1,00,000	
To B/R A/c		10,000	By Debtor A/c (Dish of B/R)		12,500
To Balance c/d		1,39,700	By B/P		49,000
			By B/P		25,000
			By Govt. Securities		9,600
			By Balance c/d	17,900	
			(Defalcated by cashier)		
	3,27,100	4,08,900		3,27,100	4,08,900

Answer 3(b)

(A) STATEMENT SHOWING THE DISTRIBUTION OF CASH AMONG PARTNERS (ACCORDING TO MAXIMUM LOSS METHOD)

Particulars	Total	X (₹)	Y (₹)	Z (₹)
A. Capital as on 31st Mar. (including Reserves)	40,00,000	20,00,000	12,00,000	8,00,000
Maximum Loss (₹ 40,00,000–₹ 8,00,000)	32,00,000	6,40,000	9,60,000	16,00,000
		13,60,000	2,40,000	(8,00,000)
Deficiency of Z Charged to X, Y in 20: 12		(5,00,000)	(3,00,000)	8,00,000
		8,60,000	(60,000)	—
Deficiency of Y charged to X		(60,000)	60,000	—
B. Cash paid on 1st April	8,00,000	8,00,000	—	—
C. Balance Due (A–B)	32,00,000	12,00,000	12,00,000	8,00,000
Maximum Loss (₹ 32,00,000 – ₹ 12,00,000)	20,00,000	4,00,000	6,00,000	10,00,000
		8,00,000	6,00,000	(2,00,000)
Deficiency of Z charged to X and Y (20: 12)		(1,25,000)	(75,000)	2,00,000
D. Cash paid on 1st June	12,00,000	6,75,000	5,25,000	—
E. Balance Due (C–D)	20,00,000	5,25,000	6,75,000	8,00,000
Maximum Loss (₹ 20,00,000 – ₹ 7,60,000 – ₹ 4,40,000)	8,00,000	1,60,000	2,40,000	4,00,000
F. Balance Due	12,00,000	3,65,000	4,35,000	4,00,000
G. Cash brought in by Z (₹ 4,40,000 – ₹ 4,00,000)	40,000			40,000
H. Cash Paid to X and Y and Asset to Z	(12,40,000)	3,65,000	4,35,000	4,40,000
I. Balance due	8,00,000	1,60,000	2,40,000	4,00,000
J. *Add:* Profit on Realisation [₹ 9,05,000 + ₹ 5,000 (cash) – ₹ 10,000 (Exp.) – ₹ 8,00,000]	1,00,000	20,000	30,000	50,000
K. Cash Paid	9,00,000	1,80,000	2,70,000	4,50,000
L. Balance Due	Nil	Nil	Nil	Nil

(B) STATEMENT SHOWING THE DISTRIBUTION OF CASH (ACCORDING TO PROPORTIONAL CAPITAL METHOD)

Particulars	X	Y	Z
A. Capitals (including Reserves)	20,00,000	12,00,000	8,00,000
B. Amount distributed as on 1st April	(8,00,000)	—	—
C. Balance Due	12,00,000	12,00,000	8,00,000
D. Amount Distributed as on 1st June			
First ₹ 4,00,000	(4,00,000)	—	—
Next ₹ 8,00,000	(3,20,000)	(4,80,000)	—

E. Balance Due	4,80,000	7,20,000	8,00,000
F. Amount Distributed as on 1st July 1st ₹ 4,00,000	(1,60,000)	(2,40,000)	—
Cash brought in by Z	—	—	40,000
Balance ₹ 4,00,000 in 2: 3	(1,60,000)	(2,40,000)	—
Asset taken over by Z	—	—	(4,40,000)
G. Balance Due	1,60,000	2,40,000	4,00,000
I. *Add:* Profit on Realisation [₹ 9,05,000 + ₹ 5,000 (cash) – ₹ 10,000 (Exp.) – ₹ 8,00,000]	20,000	30,000	50,000
J. Cash Paid	1,80,000	2,70,000	4,50,000
K. Balance Due	Nil	Nil	Nil

Working Notes:

(I) STATEMENT SHOWING THE CALCULATION OF HIGHEST RELATIVE CAPITALS

Particulars	X	Y	Z
A. Capitals (including Reserves)	20,00,000	12,00,000	8,00,000
B. Profit Sharing Ratio (PSR)	2	3	5
C. Actual Capital / PSR	10,00,000	4,00,000	1,60,000
D. Proportionate Capitals taking Z's capital as base capital	3,20,000	4,80,000	8,00,000
E. Surplus Capitals (A–D)	16,80,000	7,20,000	—
F. Profit Sharing Ratio (PSR)	2	3	—
G. Surplus Capitals / PSR	8,40,000	2,40,000	—
H. Revised Proportionate Capital Taking Y's capital base capital	4,80,000	7,20,000	—
I. Revised Surplus Capital (E–H)	12,00,000	—	—

(ii) Scheme of Distribution of Cash: 1st instalment up to ₹ 12,00,000 will be paid to X, next instalment upto ₹ 12,00,000 will be distributed between X and Y in the ratio of 2: 3 and the balance among X, Y and Z in the ratio of 2: 3: 5

(III) STATEMENT SHOWING THE CALCULATION OF CASH AVAILABLE EACH MONTH

Particulars	April (₹)	June (₹)	July (₹)	Aug (₹)
A. Opening Balance	60,000	10,000	5,000	5,000
B. *Add:* Amount realised less expenses	7,60,000	11,95,000	7,60,000	8,85,000
C. *Less:* Amount reserved for discounted B/R	(10,000)	—	—	—
D. *Less:* Closing Minimum Balance	(10,000)	(5,000)	(5,000)	—
E. *Add:* Reserved amount released	—	—	—	10,000
F. Total Cash available for distribution	8,00,000	12,00,000	7,60,000	9,00,000

Answer 3(c)

Dr. MUMBAI BRANCH ACCOUNT UNDER DEBTORS METHOD Cr.

Particulars	₹	Particulars	₹
To Balance b/d: Opening Stock Opening Debtors	 12,000 10,000	By Goods sent to Branch A/c [₹ 30,000 × 120/150]	24,000
To Goods sent to Branch A/c [₹ 1,10,000 + 20%]	1,32,000	By Cash/Bank A/c(Remmitance) [₹ 74,800 + ₹ 45,635 + ₹ 40,000 + ₹ 2,000 – ₹ 30,000]	1,32,435
To Goods sent to Branch A/c [₹ 75,000 × 120/150]	60,000	By Goods sent to Branch A/c (Returns)	24,000
To Stock Reserve A/c [₹ 19,800 × 20/120]	3,300	By Goods sent to Branch A/c (Returns) [₹ 15,000 × 120/150]	12,000
To Cash/Bank A/c(Remmitance)	9,000	By Stock Reserve A/c [₹ 12,000 × 20/120]	2,000
To Balance c/d: Provision for Discount A/c Manager's Commission [₹ 18,709 × 6/106] Outstanding Expenses	 1,485 1,059 741	By Goods sent to Branch A/c [Load on Net Goods sent] [₹ 1,32,000 + ₹ 60,000 – ₹ 24,000 – ₹ 24,000 – 12,000] × 20/120	22,000
To General Profit and Loss A/c	17,650	By Balance c/d: Stock out of local purchases Stock in transit from H.O. [₹ 1,32,000 – ₹ 1,27,000] Stock in hand from H.O.(B. f.) Debtors	 7,200 5,000 7,600 11,000
	2,47,235		2,47,235

Working Notes:

1. COST PRICE STRUCTURE

	₹
A. Cost Price	100
B. *Add:* Profit	20
C. Invoice Price (A + B)	120
D. *Add:* Extra Profit	30
E. Catalogue Price (C + D)	150

Dr. 2. MUMBAI BRANCH STOCK ACCOUNT Cr.

Particulars	₹	Particulars	₹
To Balance b/d	12,000	By Goods sent to Branch A/c [₹ 30,000 × 120/150]	24,000
To Goods sent to Branch A/c [₹ 1,10,000 + 20%]	1,32,000	By Branch Cash A/c (Cash Sales)	74,800

To Goods sent to Branch A/c [₹ 75,000 × 120/150]	60,000	By Branch Debtors A/c (Credit Sales)	1,45,000
To Branch Debtors A/c (Returns)	30,000	By Goods sent to Branch A/c (Returns)	24,000
To Branch Debtors A/c (Returns)	15,000	By Goods sent to Branch A/c (Returns) [₹ 15,000 × 120/150]	12,000
To Branch Cash A/c [local purchases]	30,000	By Branch Abnormal Loss A/c (Stock destroyed by fire)	3,000
To Load on local purchases	6,000	By Normal Loss	2,400
To Excess of catalogue price of Net Credit Sales over invoice price (₹ 1,45,000 – ₹ 30,000 – 15,000) × 30/150]	20,000	By Balance c/d: Stock out of local purchases Stock in transit from H.O. [₹1,32,000 – ₹1,27,000] Stock in hand from H.O.(B. f.)	 7,200 5,000 7,600
	3,05,000		3,05,000

Dr. **3 MUMBAI BRANCH DEBTORS ACCOUNT** **Cr.**

Particulars	₹	Particulars	₹
To Balance b/d	10,000	By Branch Stock A/c	30,000
To Branch Stock A/c (Credit Sales)	1,45,000	By Goods sent to Branch A/c	15,000
		By Branch Cash/Bank A/c	45,635
		By Cash/Bank A/c	40,000
		By Discount Allowed A/c	13,365
		By Balance c/d (b.f.)	**11,000**
	1,55,000		1,55,000

4. COMPUTATION OF PROVISION FOR DISCOUNT

A. Prompt paying debtors who availed of discount [₹ 13,365 × 100/15]	₹ 89,100
B. Total debtors who made payment during the year [₹ 13,365 + 85,635]	₹ 99,000
C. Proportion of prompt payers to those who made payment [(89,100/99,000) × 100]	90%
D. Likely Prompt paying debtors included in closing Debtors [90% of ₹ 11,000]	₹ 9,900
E. Provision for discount on the closing balance [15% of ₹ 9,900]	₹ 1,485

Asnswer 4(a)

Dr. **GENERAL LEDGER ADJUSTMENT ACCOUNT (IN DEBTORS LEDGER)** **Cr.**

Particulars	₹	Particulars	₹
To Debtors Ledger Adjustment A/c:		By Debtors Ledger Adjustment A/c:	
Discount Allowed (₹ 1,500 + ₹ 500)	2,000	Endorsed B/R dish.	1,000
Bad Debts (2,200 + 300)	2,500		
T/f from Drs Ledger to Crs. Ledger	1,100		
T/f from Cr. Ledger to Drs. Ledger	1,900		
To Balance c/d (60,000 – 500)	59,500		

Dr. GENERAL LEDGER ADJUSTMENT ACCOUNT (IN CREDITORS LEDGER) Cr.

Particulars	₹	Particulars	₹
To Creditors Ledger Adjustment A/c:		By Creditors Ledger Adjustment A/c:	
Endorsed B/R Dish.	1,000	T/f from Drs. Ledger to Crs. Ledger	1,100
		T/f from Crs. Ledger to Drs. Ledger	1,900
		B/R Endorsed to Crs.	4,000
		Discount received (₹ 600–₹ 500)	100
		Allowances	3,200
		By Balance c/d (30,000 + 500)	30,500

Notes:

(i) The following items do not appear in GLA Account (in Debtors Ledger)

1. Cash Sales
2. Provision for Doubtful Debts
3. Provision for Discount on Debtors
4. Bad Debts Recovered
5. Bills Receivable matured/collected on maturity
6. Bills Receivable discounted
7. Bills Receivable endorsed

(ii) The following items do not appear in GLA Account (in Creditors Ledger)

1. Cash Purchases
2. Reserve for Discount on Creditors
3. Bills Payable matured / discharged

Asnswer 4(b)

JOURNAL

Date	Particulars		Dr. (₹)	Cr.(₹)
	Mrs. Bansal (In A-J Debtors' Ledger) To Miss Kansal (In K-P Debtors' Ledger) (Being transfer of A/c of Miss Kansal to A-J Debtors' Ledger)	Dr.	5,000	 5,000
	General Ledger Adjustment A/c (In K-P Debtors' Ledger) To (K-P) Debtors' Ledger Adjustment A/c (In G.L.) (Being reduction in total K-P Debtors)	Dr.	5,000	 5,000
	(A-J) Debtors' Ledger Adjustment A/c (In G.L.) To General Ledger Adjustment A/c (In A-J Debtors' Ledger) (Being increase in (A-J) Debtors)	Dr.	5,000	 5,000

Answer 4(c)

Dr. DEBTORS LEDGER ADJUSTMENT ACCOUNT IN THE GENERAL LEDGER Cr.

Date	Particulars	₹	Date	Particulars	₹
Jan. 1	To Balance b/d	40,000	Jan – Mar	By General Ledger	
Jan – Mar	To General.			Adj. A/c:	
	Ledger Adj A/c: Sales Bills Receivables dishonoured	 1,35,000 5,000		Collection from Debtors-bank [60% of (40,000 + 1,35,000)] Discount allowed	1,05,000 10,000
				Bills Receivables	20,000
				Bad debts (₹ 2,500 + 3,000)	5,500
			31st Mar	By Balance c/d	39,500
		1,80,000			1,80,000

Note: No entries are to be made:

(a) For 7,000 realised against bad debts written off in earlier years, and

(b) For provision of 6,000 made for doubtful debts.

Working Notes:

Credit Sales = (2,20,000 – 10,000) – (2,10,000 × 100/280) = ₹ 1,35,000

Answer 5(a)

PROVISION OF AS 9

As per AS 9 in a transaction involving the rendering of services, performance should be measured either under the completed service contract method or under the proportionate completion method, whichever relates the revenue to the work accomplished. Further, appendix to AS 9 states that revenue from advertising should be recognized when the service is completed. The service as regards advertisement is deemed to be completed when the related advertisement appears before the public.

ADVICE

In the given QUESTION, 40% of the advertisement appeared before the public in November, and balance 60% in December.

CALCULATION OF TOTAL PROFIT

Particulars	₹ in lakhs
Advertisement for 70% of available time obtained by 30th September, 2013	700
Advertisement for 30% of available time obtained in by October, 2013	240
Total	940
Less: Cost of advertisement rights	(520)
Profit	420

The profit amounting ₹ 420 lakhs should be apportioned in the ratio of 40: 60 for the months of November and December, 2015. Thus, the company should recognise ₹ 168 lakhs (i.e. ₹ 420 lakhs × 40%) in November, 2015 and rest ₹ 252 lakhs (i.e. ₹ 420 lakhs × 60%) in December, 2015.

Answer 5(b)

AMOUNT TO BE DISCLOSED AS PER DISCLOSURE REQUIREMENTS OF AS – 7

Particulars	₹
Contract revenue recognized as revenue in the period	4,75,000
Aggregate amount of costs incurred and recognized profits	4,85,000
(less recognized losses) upto the reporting date	
Amount of advances received	30,000
Gross amount due from customers for contract work as an asset	15,000
Gross amount due to customers for contract work as a liability	10,000

Working Note:

	Particulars	Contracts				
		A	B	C	D	Total
A	Opening Balance			10,000	10,000	20,000
B	Additions during the year					
	Cost Incurred during the year	70,000	1,00,000	1,50,000	1,40,000	4,60,000
	Revenue recognized during the year	50,000	1,25,000	1,00,000	2,00,000	4,75,000
	Total B	1,20,000	2,25,000	2,50,000	3,40,000	9,35,000
C	Deductions during the year					
	Expenses recognized during the year	50,000	1,00,000	1,20,000	1,50,000	4,20,000
	Expected loss	20,000		30,000		50,000
	Total C	70,000	1,00,000	1,50,000	1,50,000	4,70,000
D	Balance [A + B – C]	50,000	1,25,000	1,10,000	2,00,000	4,85,000
E	Progress billings	50,000	1,20,000	1,00,000	2,10,000	4,80,000
F	Amount due from customers	0	5,000	10,000	0	15,000
G	Amount due to customers	0	0	0	10,000	10,000

Answer 5(c)

PROVISION OF AS 9

As per AS 9 Revenue from sale of goods should be recognized if the seller has transferred to the buyer the property in the goods for a price or all significant risks and rewards of ownership have been transferred to the buyer and the seller retains no effective control of the goods transferred to a degree usually associated with ownership. The transfer of property in goods, in most cases, results in or coincides with the transfer of significant risks and rewards of ownership.

ADVICE

In this case, all significant risks and rewards of ownership have been transferred to the buyer and the seller retains no effective control of the goods transferred to a degree usually associated with ownership but delivery is postponed at the buyer's request. Hence this transaction should be recognized as revenue. Thus, ₹ 60,000 should be deducted from inventory, and the amount of ₹ 80,000 [i.e. ₹ 60,000 / (1.00 – 0.25)] should be included in sales with correspondence increase in Debtor's balances.

Answer 6(a)

Dr. **CONSIGNMENT TO BOMBAY ACCOUNT** **Cr.**

Particulars		₹	Particulars		₹
To Y's A/c:			By Y's A/c (Sales):		
Clearance	4,500		150 @ ₹ 14,000	21,00,000	
Selling Expenses	1,12,500	1,17,000	75 @ ₹ 14,400	10,80,000	31,80,000
To Goods sent on Consignment A/c		25,00,000	By Consignment Stock A/c:		
To Bank A/c (Expenses)		7,000	Cost of 25 TV @ ₹ 10,000	2,50,000	
To Y's A/c (Commission)		1,63,500	*Add:* Consignor's Exp. (7,000 × 25/250)	700	
To Profit & Loss A/c (Profit on Consignment)		6,43,650	*Add:* Consignee's Exp. (4,500 × 25/250)	450	2,51,150
		34,31,150			34,31,150

Dr. **Y 'S ACCOUNT** **Cr.**

Particulars	₹	Particulars		₹
To Consignment to Bombay A/c (Sales)	31,80,000	By Consignment to Bombay A/c:		
		— Clearance	4,500	
		— Selling Expenses	1,12,500	1,17,000
		By Cosignment to Bombay A/c (Commission)		1,63,500
		By Bank A/c		28,99,500
	31,80,000			31,80,000

Working Notes: *Calculation of Consignee's Commission*

(i) Fixed Commission @ ₹ 500 = 225 × ₹ 500 = ₹ 1,12,500

(ii) Let the total Commission be X

Variable Commission = 1/4 [(₹ 31,80,000 – X) – (225 × ₹ 12,500)]

X – ₹ 1,12,500 = 1/4 [₹ 31,80,000 – X – ₹ 28,12,500]

X – ₹ 1,12,500 = 1/4 (₹ 3,67,500 – X)

X – ₹ 1,12,500 = 91,875 – 1/4 X

X – 1,12,500 = 91,875 – .25 X

1.25 X = 2,04,375

X = ₹ 2,04,375/1.25 = 1,63,500

Answer 6(b)

1. **Gross profit ratio**	₹
Net profit in year 2011	1,20,000
Insured standing charges	43,990
Gross profit	1,63,990
Ratio of gross profit = 1,63,990/8,19,950 = 20%	
2. **Calculation of Short sales**	
Indemnity period: 16.9.2012 to 15.12.12	
Standard sales to be calculated on basis of corresponding period of year 2011	
	₹
Sales for period 16.9.2011 to 30.9.11	34,000

	Sales for period 1.10.2011 to 15.12.2011 (Note 1)	1,30,000
	Sales for period 16.9.2011 to 15.12.2011	1,64,000
	Add: upward trend in sales (15%) (Note 2)	24,600
	Standard Sales (adjusted)	1,88,600
	Actual sales of disorganized period	
	Calculation of sales from 16.9.12 to 15.12.12	
	Sales for period 16.9.12 to 30.9.12	Nil
	Sales for 1.10.12 to 15.12.12 (₹1,48,000 – ₹20,000)	1,28,000
	Actual Sales	1,28,000
	Short Sales (₹ 1,88,600 – ₹ 1,28,000)	60,600
3.	**Loss of gross profit**	
	Short sales × gross profit ratio = 60,600 × 20%	12,120
4.	**Application of average clause**	
	Net claim = Gross claim × [Policy Value/Gross Profit on Annual Turnover] = 12,120 × 1,00,000/1,79,860(Note 3)	
	Amount of claim = 6,738.57 (approx) i.e. ₹ 6,739 (round off)	

Working Notes:

1.	**Sales for period** 1.10.11 to 15.12.11	
	Sales for 1.10.11 to 31.12.11 (given)	1,90,000
	Sales for 16.12.11 to 31.12.11 (given)	60,000
	Sales for period 1.10.11 to 15.12.11	1,30,000
2.	**Calculation of upward trend in sales**	
	Total Sales in year 2009	6,20,000
	Increase in sales in year 2010 as compared to 2009	93,000
	% increase = [93,000(7,13,000 – 6,20,000)]/6,20,000 = 15%	
	Increase in sales in year 2011 as compared to year 2010	
	% increase = [1,06,950(8,19,950 – 7,13,000)]/7,13,000 = 15%	
	Thus annual percentage increase trend is of 15%.	
3.	**Gross profit on annual turnover**	
	Sales from 16.9.11 to 30.9.11	34,000
	1.10.11 to 31.12.11	1,90,000
	1.1.12 to 31.3.12	1,62,000
	1.4.12 to 30.6.12	2,21,000
	1.7.2012 to 15.9.2012 (1,75,000 – Nil)	1,75,000
	Sales for 12 months just before date of fire	7,82,000
	Add: 15% upward trend	1,17,300
	Adjusted sales of 12 months just before the date of fire	8,99,300
	Gross profit on adjusted annual sales @ 20%	1,79,860

Answer 6(c)

Dr. **Y IN ACCOUNT CURRENT WITH X FOR THE PERIOD FROM 1ST JULY, 2015 TO 31ST DECEMBER, 2015** **Cr.**

Date	Due Date	Particulars	Days upto 31st Dec.	Ami (₹ in 000s)	Product	Date	Due date	Particulars	Days upto 31st Dec.	Amt (₹ in 000s)	Product
2015	July 01	To Balance b/d	184	600	1,10,400	2015	Aug. 21	By Purchases A/c	132	700	92,400
July 15	July 15	To Sales	169	900	1,52,100	Aug. 23	Aug. 23	By Cash A/c	130	450	58,500
Dec. 03	Mar. 05	To Bills Payable	(64)	400	(25,600)	Oct. 23	Jan.25	By Bills Receivable	(25)	300	(7,500)
Dec. 31	Dec. 31	To Interest [36,500 × 8%/365]		8		Nov. 01	Nov.01	By Purchases A/c	60	950	57,000
Dec. 31	Dec. 31	To Cash A/c		492			Dec. 31	By Balance of Product			36,500
				2,400	2,36,900					2,400	2,36,900

Answer 7(a)

IDFC BANK LIMITED
PROFIT AND LOSS ACCOUNT FOR THE YEAR ENDED 31ST MARCH, 2015

Particulars	Schedule	Year ended 31.03.2015
I. Income:		
Interest earned	13	37,95,160
Other income	14	4,87,800
Total		42,82,960
II. Expenditure		
Interest expended	15	22,95,360
Operating expenses	16	5,70,340
Provisions and Contingencies (₹ 4,50,000 + 2,00,000 + 2,00,000)		8,50,000
Total		37,15,700
III. Profits / Losses		
Net Profit for the year		5,67,260
Profit brought forward		NIL
		5,67,260
IV. Appropriations		
Transfer to Statutory Reserve (25%)		1,41,815
Proposed Dividend		50,000
Balance carried over to Balance Sheet		3,75,445
		5,67,260

The Profit & Loss Account balance of ₹ 3,75,445 will appear in the Balance Sheet under the head 'Reserve and Surplus' in Schedule 2.

SCHEDULE 13 – INTEREST EARNED

I. Income:	
Interest earned	37,95,160

SCHEDULE 14 – OTHER INCOME

I. Commission, exchange and brokerage	1,90,000
II. Profit on sale of investments	2,25,800
III. Rent received	72,000
	4,87,800

SCHEDULE 15–INTEREST EXPENDED

I. Interests on Deposits	22,95,360

SCHEDULE 16 – OPERATING EXPENSES

I. Payment to and provisions for employees	2,50,000
II. Rent, taxes and lighting	1,00,000
III. Depreciation on Bank's property	40,000
IV. Director's fees, allowances and expenses	35,000
V. Auditor's fees	12,000
VI. Law (statutory) charges	38,000
VII. Postage and telegrams	65,340
VIII. Preliminary expenses*	30,000
	5,70,340

*As per AS 26 Preliminary Expenses have been fully written off.

Working Note:

Interest/discount (net of rebate on bills discounted) (W.N. 1)	38,00,160
Add: Opening Rebate on bills discounted	15,000
Less: Closing Rebate on bills discounted	(20,000)
	37,95,160

Answer 7(b)

FROM–B–RA–REVENUE ACCOUNT OF AGGARWAL FIRE INSURANCE CO. LTD

for the year ending 31st March 2015

Particulars	Sch.	Current Yr	Previous Yr
Premium Earned (Net)	1	60,14,400	
Interest, Dividend & Rent (Gross) (₹ 27,360 × 100/90)		30,400	
Total (A)		60,44,800	
1. Claims Incurred (Net)	2	41,30,400	
2. Commission	3	1,25,600	

3. Operating Expenses related to Insurance Business	4	—	
(2,32,000 – Legal Exps 44,000 – Surveyor Fees 36,000)		1,52,000	
Total (B)		44,08,000	
Operating Profit/(Loss) from Insurance Business (A – B)		16,36,800	
Appropriations		NIL	
Total (C)		16,36,800	

SCHEDULE 1 – PREMUM EARNED (NET)

Particulars	This Yr
Premiums from Direct Business written (60,20,000 + 3,00,000 – 2,60,000)	61,60,000
Add: Premium on Re-Insurance accepted (4,95,000 + 3,00,000 – 1,60,000)	8,00,000
Less: Premium on Re-Insurance ceded (3,92,000 + 3,60,000 – 80,000)	(6,72,000)
Total Premium Earned (Net)	62,88,000
Less: Adjustment for change in Unexpired Risk Reserve (Note)	(2,73,600)
Total Premium Earned (Net)	60,14,400

Note: Adjustment for Changes in Reserve for Unexpired Risks is computed as under:

Particulars	Reserve
Closing balance required [(40% of 62,88,000) + (5% of 62,88,000)]	28,29,600
Less: Opening Balance available (22,72,000 + 2,84,000)	25,56,000
Amt to be transferred to Reserve for the year	2,73,600

SCHEDULE 2 – CLAIMS PAID (NET)

Particulars	This Yr
Claims Paid – Direct (39,76,000 + 5,90,400 – 5,48,000)	40,18,400
Add: Claims on Re-Insurance accepted (4,08,000 + 56,000 – 76,000)	3,88,000
Less: Claims on Re-Insurance Ceded (3,16,000 + 1,00,000 – 60,000)	(3,56,000)
Add: Surveyor's Fees	36,000
Add: Legal Expenses	44,000
Total claims Incurred	41,30,400

SCHEDULE 3 – COMMISSION

Particulars	This Yr
Commision paid: Direct	1,28,000
Add: Commission on Re-Insurance accepted	12,000
Less: Commission on Re-Insurance ceded	(14,400)
Net Commission	1,25,600

Answer 7(c)

AVERAGE CAPITAL COST

Particulars	1st year	2nd year	3rd year	4th year
A. Opening Capital Cost	3,00,000	3,10,000	3,13,000	3,15,000
B. Additional Capital Cost	20,000	6,000	4,000	4,000
C. Closing Capital Cost (A + B)	3,20,000	3,16,000	3,17,000	3,19,000
D. Average Capital Cost [(A + C)/2]	3,10,000	3,13,000	3,15,000	3,17,000

1. COMPUTATION OF DEPRECIATION

Particulars	1st year	2nd year	3rd year	4th year
A. Average Capital Cost	3,10,000	3,13,000	3,15,000	3,17,000
B. Weighted Average Rate of Dep.	5%	5%	5%	5%
C. Annualized Depreciation (A × B)	15,500	15,650	15,750	15,850

PAPER–5: FINANCIAL ACCOUNTING

EXAMINATION PAPERS
WITH SUGGESTED ANSWERS

INTERMEDIATE EXAMINATION GROUP I (SYLLABUS 2012) DECEMBER 2014

PAPER-5: FINANCIAL ACCOUNTING

Time Allowed: 3 Hours **Full Marks : 100**

The figures in the margin on the right side indicate full marks.
This paper contains seven questions. All questions are compulsory, subject to instruction provided against each question.
All working must form part of your answer.
Assumptions, if any, must be clearly indicated.

1. Answer the following questions (Give workings): **2 × 10 = 20**

(a) A machine costing ₹ 13,75,000 is depreciated on straight line basis assuming 8 years working life and zero residual value. After third year machine's remaining useful life was reassessed at 7 years. Calculate the amount of depreciation charged for 4th year.

(b) Madhu purchased a machinery on hire purchase basis on 1st April, 2014. ₹ 75,000 was paid immediately and the remaining amount was to be paid in three annual instalments of ₹1,00,000 each. Interest rate is 15% per annum. Calculate the cash price.

(c) Gunnu and Chinu are partners. They are entitled for 9% interest on their capital contributions. The firm allowed ₹ 54,000 towards interest on capital to partners. Calculate the capital contribution of each partner if interest on Gunnu's capital is ₹13,500 more than the interest on Chinu's capital.

(d) State whether following transactions appear in Sales/Purchases Ledger Adjustment Account or not, when books are kept on self balancing ledger system:

(i) B/R discounted with bank for ₹ 15,000;

(ii) Old bad debts recovered ₹ 1,500;

(iii) Cash refunds to customers ₹ 4,500;

(iv) Provision made for bad debts ₹ 5,000.

(e) Ajay of Jaipur sent goods of ₹ 2,50,000 to Vijay of Mumbai on consignment. Ajay paid ₹8,500 as railway freight and ₹ 4,240 as insurance. 2% goods are damaged in the Vijay's godown due to normal circumstances. Vijay incurred cartage ₹ 5,140 and selling expenses ₹ 14,700. Calculate the value of stock of unsold 15% of goods sent to Vijay.

(f) The carrying amount of Plant and Machinery of X Limited on 31.3.2013 was ₹ 80 crores, where as the recoverable amount is ₹ 52 crores. The applicable Income Tax rate is 40%. For Income Tax purposes, the written down value is ₹ 40 crores. Compute the amount of Deferred tax asset/liability on Account of impairment as per AS 28.

(g) An IT enabled company supplied a software to a client at a fee of ₹ 50 lakhs during the year ended 30-09-2014 and also transferred the ownership. In November 2014, the Management of the company raised a supplementary bill on it's client for ₹ 10 lakhs, stating about additional features of the software supplied. While finalising the Accounts for the year ended 30-09-2014 in December 2014, how would the amount of ₹ 10 lakhs dealt?

(h) ₹ 3,25,000 is total cost of 6500 units, consignor's expenses are ₹ 65,000, units lost in transit was 700 units and consignee's nonrecurring expenses amounted to ₹ 4,300, what will be the value of stock?

(i) Human Life Insurance Company provides the following information:

Life Insurance Fund on 31st March, 2014	₹ 155 Lakhs
Net liability on 31st March as per actuarial valuation	₹ 132 Lakhs

Interim Bonus paid to Policy holders during inter valuation period ₹ 11 Lakhs

Prepare Valuation Balance Sheet.

(j) A loan account remains out of order as on date of Balance Sheet of MODERN Bank. The account has been classified as Doubtful asset (upto 1 year). Details of the account are as under:

Outstanding	₹ 6,73,000
ECGC Coverage	25% (limited to ₹ 1,00,000)
Value of security held	₹ 1,50,000

Compute the necessary provision to be made by the Bank in respect of this particular account.

2. Answer any two questions: $4 \times 2 = 8$

(a) Indicate whether the following items should be treated as ordinary activities, exceptional items arising out of ordinary activities or prior period items within the terms of AS-5:

(i) Cost ₹ 15,00,000 incurred in terminating production at one of the company's factories.

(ii) Currency exchange surplus accounting to ₹ 15,000 arising on remittance from an overseas depot.

(iii) An extra ₹ 2,00,000 contributions By the company to the employee's pension fund.

(iv) Profit of ₹ 3,00,000 on sale of machinery written-off in a previous year when production of the particular product ceased.

(v) Provision for an abnormally large bad debt of₹ 10,00,000 arising in a trading contract. [The turnover of the company is ₹ 1,20,00,000 and profits ₹ 20,00,000.]

(b) Pass necessary journal entries to rectify the following errors assuming that the errors were detected after the preparation of final accounts:

(i) Return inward book was under cast by ₹ 18,000.

(ii) Goods purchased for proprietor's use for ₹ 10,000 debited to purchase account.

(iii) ₹ 5,200 paid for freight on machinery was debited to freight account.

(iv) No adjustment entry Was passed for an amount of ₹15,000 relating to outstanding rent.

(v) Furniture of ₹13,000 purchased from Chandra Furniture House was entered in purchase book.

(vi) ₹ 10,000 received from Mohan has been credited to Sohan.

(c) From the following particulars, prepare the Bank Reconciliation Statement of Shri Krishan as on 31st March,

(i) Balance as per Pass Book is ₹ 10,000.

(ii) Bank collected a cheque of ₹ 500 on behalf of Shri Krishan but wrongly credited it to Shri Kishan's A/c (another customer).

(iii) Bank recorded a Cash deposit of ₹ 1,589 as ₹ 1,598.

(iv) Withdrawal column of the Pass Book under cast by ₹ 100.

(v) The credit balance of ₹ 1,500 as on page 5 of the Pass Book was recorded on page 6 as the debit balance.

(vi) The payment of a cheque of ₹ 350 was recorded twice in the Pass Book.

(vii) The Pass Book showed a credit for a cheque of ₹1,000 deposited by Shri Kishan (another customer of the Bank).

3. Answer any two questions: $12 \times 2 = 24$

(a) A company writes off depreciation at 10% P.A, on the diminishing balance. On 1st January, 2011 the machinery account showed a balance of ₹1,49,000. It was discovered in 2011 that—

(i) A heavy repairs effected to plant and machinery account (completed on 30th June, 2009), were debited to the machinery. The amount was ₹ 15,000; and

(ii) A machine cost ₹6,000 was entered in the purchases on 1st October 2009. The expenses on installation, ₹400 were debited to General Expenses Account. Necessary corrections were to be made in 2011. On 30th June 2011, a machine which had cost ₹ 20,000 on 1st January, 2009 was disposed of for ₹ 15,000 and a machine costing ₹ 30,000 was installed on the same date, the expenses on installing the same being ₹ 500.

Show Machinery Account for the year ended 31st December, 2011. Please show your working in detail.

(b) Doll and Dolly are in partnership sharing profits and losses equally. They keep their books by Single Entry System. No ready figures are available for the total sales but they maintain a steady gross profit rate of 25% on sales.

An abstract of their cash transactions for the year ended 30th June, 2011 is given below:

Receipts	₹	**Payments**	₹
Cash in hand	10,800	Salaries	22,000
Receipts from Customers	2,70,000	Rent	4,400
Cash Sales	32,000	Advertising	1,800
		Printing	1,600
		General Expenses	19,100
		Payment to Trade Creditors	2,24,000
		Doll's Drawings	4,000
		Cash in hand	35,900
	3,12,800		3,12,800

Following balances are available from their books as on 30th June, 2010 and 30th June, 2011.

Particulars	**As on 30-6-2010 ₹**	**As on 30-6-2011 ₹**
Stock in Trade	44,000	50,000
Sundry Debtors	?	70,000
Sundry Creditors	46,800	37,000
Furniture	6,000	?

Other Information:

(i) Discount allowed, ₹ 2,800.

(ii) Discount earned, ₹ 2,400.

(iii) Outstanding Printing, ₹ 500.

(iv) Capital of Doll as on 30th June, 2010 was ₹ 4,000 more than Capital of Dolly.

(v) Provide depreciation of Furniture @ 10% P.A.

From the above you are required to prepare in the books of Doll and Dolly:

(i) The Trading and Profit and Loss Account for the year ended 30th June, 2011 and

(ii) The Balance Sheet as on the date.

(c) TUSHAR Ltd. with its Head Office in Delhi invoices goods to its Branches at Mumbai and Kolkata at 20% less than the catalogue price which is cost plus 50% with instructions that cash sales are to be made at invoice price and credit sales at catalogue price less discount at 15% on prompt payments. Provision is to be made for discount to be allowed to debtors, at year end on the basis of year's trend of prompt payments. All branch expenses are paid by the Head Office and all branch collections are remitted daily to Head Office.

1. Opening Stock At Branch at its cost ₹ 12,000.
2. Opening Branch Debtors ₹ 10,000.

3. Goods Sent to branch (at cost to H.O.) ₹ 1,10,000.
4. Goods received by Branch till close of the year ₹ 1,27,000.
5. Transfer from Kolkata branch to Mumbai branch at catalogue price ₹ 75,000.
6. Transfer to Kolkata branch from Mumbai branch at catalogue price ₹ 30,000.
7. Goods purchased by Mumbai branch from local suppliers (cost) ₹ 30,000. Closing stock in hand at branch out of local purchases (cost) ₹ 6,000.
8. Cash Sales ₹ 74,800.
9. Credit Sales ₹ 1,45,000.
10. Goods returned by Credit Customers to branch ₹ 30,000.
11. Goods returned by Credit Customers directly to H.O. ₹ 15,000.
12. Goods returned by Branch to H.O. ₹ 24,000.
13. Cash remitted by Credit Customers directly to Branch ₹ 45,635.
14. Cash remitted by Credit Customers directly to H.O. ₹ 40,000.
15. Discount Allowed to Debtors ₹ 13,365.
16. Loss of Goods by fire (at invoice price) ₹ 3,000 against which 80% of cost was recovered from the insurance Company.
17. Loss of goods at Branch through normal pilferage (at catalogue price) ₹ 3,000.
18. Branch Expenses: Paid ₹ 9,000, Outstanding ₹ 741.
19. Branch Manager is entitled to a commission @ 6% of net profits after charging such commission.

Required: Prepare Mumbai Branch Stock Account, Mumbai Branch adjustment A/c, Mumbai Branch Expenses A/c and Mumbai Branch Profit & Loss A/c and Mubmai Branch Debtors A/c under Stock & Debtors Method.

4. Answer any two questions: **4 × 2 = 8**

(a) Following information is available from the books of a trader from January 1 to March 31, 2011.

(i) Total Sales amounted to ₹ 60,000 including the sale of old furniture for ₹ 1,200 (Book Value ₹ 3,500). The total Cash Sales were 80% less than the total Credit Sales.

(ii) Cash collection from debtors amounted to 60% of the aggregate of the opening debtors and the Credit Sales for the period. Debtors were allowed Cash discounts for ₹ 2,600.

(iii) Bills Receivable drawn during the three months totalled ₹6,000 of which bills amounting to ₹ 3,000 were endorsed in favour of suppliers. Out of these endorsed B/R, a B/R for ₹ 600 was dishonoured for non-payment as the party became insolvent, his estate realizing nothing.

(iv) Cheques received from Sundry Customers for ₹ 6,000 were dishonoured; a sum of ₹ 500 is irrecoverable, Bad Debts written off in the earlier years realized ₹2,500.

(v) Sundry Debtors, as on 1st January 2011, stood at ₹ 40,000. You are required to show the Debtors Ledger Adjustments Accounts in the General Ledger.

(b) Prepare Total Creditors Account for the year ended on 31.03.2013 from the data given below:

Particulars	₹
Creditors Balance on 01.04.2012	38,000
Credit Purchases during the year	2,67,000
Bills payable accepted	62,000
Cash paid to Creditors	1,37,000
B/R endorsed to creditors	16,000
Endorsed B/R dishonoured	3,000

B/P dishonoured	2,000
Purchase returns	11,000
Discount received	6,000
Transfer from Debtors ledger	7,000

(c) PCT Ltd. maintains self-balancing ledgers. On 31st March, 2014 the accountant of the company located the following errors in the books of account:

(i) An amount of 8,700 received from customer Meena was credited to Meenu, another customer.

(ii) The sales book for December, 2013 was under cast by ₹ 1,000.

(iii) Goods invoiced at 15,600 were returned to supplier, M/s BPO Ltd., but no entry was made in the books for this return made on 28th December, 2013.

Pass the necessary Journal entries to rectify the above mentioned errors.

5. Answer any two questions: 4 × 2 = 8

(a) On 25th September, 2013, PRARTHNA Advertising Limited obtained advertisement rights to World Cup Hockey Tournament to be held in Nov./Dec, 2013 for ₹ 520 lakhs.

They furnish the following information:

(i) The company obtained the advertisements for 70% of available time for ₹ 700 lakhs by 30th September, 2013.

(ii) For the balance time they got bookings in October, 2013 for 240 lakhs.

(iii) all the advertisers paid the full amount at the time of booking the advertisements.

(iv) 40% of the advertisements appeared before the public in Nov. 2013 and balance 60% appeared in the month of December, 2013.

Your are required to calculate the amount of profit/loss to be recognized for the month November and December, 2013 as per AS-9.

(b) Priyanshu Constructions obtained a contract for completion of a big factory building. The following details are available in the records kept the year ended 31st March, 2014:

Particulars	₹ in crores
Total Contract Price	45
Works Certified	23
Works not Certified	6
Estimated further cost	21
Progress payment received	20
Progress payment to be received	6

The company seeks your advice and assistance in presentation of accounts keeping in view the requirements of AS-7 "Accounting for Construction Contract".

(c) Write a note on Internally Generated Computer Software.

6. Answer any two questions: 8 × 2 = 16

(a) Jaipur Investment Ltd. hold 1,000 15%. Debentures of ₹100 each in Udaipur Industries Ltd. as on 1st April, 2010, at a cost of ₹ 1,05,000. Interest is payable on 30th June and 31st December each year. On 1st May, 2010, 500 Debentures are purchased cum-interest at ₹ 53,500. On 1st November, 2010, 600 Debentures are sold ex-interest at ₹ 57,300. On 30th November, 2010, 400 debentures are purchased ex-interest at ₹ 38,400. On 31st December, 2010, 400 Debentures are sold cum- interest for ₹ 55,000.

Prepare Investment Account valuing holding on 31st March, 2011 at cost (applying FIFO method).

(b) There was a serious fire in the premises of M/s Fortunate on 1st September, 2011. Their business activities were interrupted until 31st December, 2011, when normal trading conditions were re-established. M/s Fortunate are insured under the loss of profit policy for ₹ 42,000 the period of indemnity being six months.

You are able to ascertain the following information:

(i) The net profit for the year ended 31st December, 2010 was ₹ 20,000

(ii) The annual insurable standing charges amounted to ₹ 30,000 of which ₹ 2,000 were not included in the definition of insured standing charge under the policy.

(iii) The additional cost of working in order to mitigate the damage caused by the fire amounted to ₹ 600, and, but for this expenditure, the business would have had to shut down.

(iv) The saving in insured charges in consequence of the fire amounted to ₹ 1,500.

(iv) The turnover for the period of four month ended April 30, August 31 and December 31, for each of the years 2010 and 2011 was as under:

Particulars	₹	₹	₹
2010	65,000	80,000	95,000
2011	70,000	80,000	15,000

You are required to compute the relevant claim under the terms of the loss of profits policy.

(c) X and Y entered into a joint venture for purchase and sale of some household items. They agreed to share profits and losses in the ratio of their respective contributions. X contributed ₹ 10,000 in cash and Y ₹ 13,000. The whole amount was placed in a Joint Bank Account. Goods were purchased by X for ₹ 10,000 and expenses paid by Y amounted to ₹ 2,000. They also purchased goods for ₹ 15,000 through the Joint Bank Account. The expenses on purchase and sale of the articles amounted to ₹ 6,000 (including those met by Y). Goods costing ₹ 20,000 were sold for ₹ 45,000 and the balance were lost by fire.

Prepare Joint Venture Account, Joint Bank Account and the Ventures' Accounts closing the venture.

7. Answer any two questions: **8 × 2 = 16**

(a) Some of the items in the Trial Balance of CANHC Bank Limited as on March 31, 2012 were as follows:

Particulars	₹	Particulars	₹
Loans and Advances	71,50,000	Printing and Stationary	5,000
Current Accounts (including Overdrafts of ₹ 15,00,000)	66,00,000	Interest on Saving Bank Deposits Auditor's Fees	75,000 5,000
Bills Discounted and Purchased	19,20,000	Bad Debts	21,000
Interest on Fixed Deposits	1,55,000	Interest on Overdrafts	95,000
Discount (subject to unexpired discount ₹ 30,000)	/2,01,000	Provision for Doubtful Debts, April 1, 2011	42,000
Interest on Loans Interest on Cash Credits	2,25,000 1,05,000	Provision for Income tax, April 1, 2011	66,000
Commission earned	47,000	Income tax paid for 2011-2012	54,000
Loss on investment	34,000		
Salaries and Allowances	82,000		

Required: Prepare the Profit and Loss Account of the Bank maintaining the provision for Income tax at ₹ 84,000 and Provision for Doubtful Debts at ₹ 52,000 for the year ended March 31, 2012.

(b) Following information are provided by the Rashtriya Beema Company for the year ended 31st March, 2014:

(i) On 1st April, 2013, The unexpired risks reserve was in respect of marine insurance business ₹ 52.50 crores; in respect of fire insurance business ₹ 55 crores and in respect of miscellaneous insurance business ₹ 12.50 crores.

(ii) It is the practice of the company to create reserve at 100% of net premium income in respect of marine insurance policies and at 50% of net premium in respect of fire and miscellaneous insurance policies.

(iii) During the year 2013-2014 the following business was conducted:

(₹ in crores)

Particulars	Marine	Fire	Miscellaneous
Premium collected from:			
1. Insured in respect of policies issued	57	125	30
2. Other insurance companies in respect of risks undertaken	17.5	12.5	10
Premium paid/payable to other insurance companies on business ceded	21.50	16.50	8.50

You are required:

(i) Pass necessary journal entries relating to unexpired risks reserve.

(ii) Show unexpired risks reserve account (in columnar form) for the year ended 31st March, 2014.

(c) The Mettur Electricity Company Ltd. decides to replace one of its old plants with a modern one with a larger capacity. The plant when installed in 1950 cost the company ₹ 48,00,000, the components of materials, labour and overhead being in the ratio of 5:3:2.

It is ascertained that the cost of materials and labour have gone up by 40% and 80% respectively. The proportion of overheads to total costs is expected to remain the same as before.

The cost of the new plant as per improved design is ₹ 1,20,00,000 and in addition, materials recovered from the old plant of a value ₹ 4,80,000 have been used in the construction of the new plant. The old plant was scrapped and sold for ₹ 15,00,000.

The accounts of the company are maintained under Double Account System. Indicate how much would be capitalised and the amount that would be charged to revenue. Show journal entries and prepare necessary ledger accounts.

ANSWER TO EXAMINATION PAPER 5 [DECEMBER 2014]

Answer 1(a)

Cost of Machine ₹ 13,75,000
Less: Depreciation for first third years period = (1375000/8) × 3 = ₹ 5,15,625
Written down value at the end of third year ₹ 8,59,375
Remaining useful life = 7 years.
Depreciation for the fourth year onwards = 8,59,375/7 = ₹ 1,22,768

Answer 1(b)

Calculation of cash price of Machine

Balance of cash price at the time of III installment = 100000 – [100000 × (15/115)]
= 100000 – 13043 = 86957

Balance of cash price at the time of II instilment = (100000 + 86957) – [186957 × (15/115)]
= 186957 – 24386 = 162571

Balance of cash price at the time of I instilment = (100000 + 162571) – [262571 × (15/115)]
= 262571 – 34248 = 228323

Hence, Total cash price = 228323 + down payment 75000 = ₹ 303323

Answer 1(c)

Let interest on Chinu's capital 'x' then interest on Gunu's capital will be x + 13500
Total interest = x + 13500 + x = 54000
or x = (54,000 – 13,500)/2 = 20,250
Interest on Gunu's capital (x + 13500) = 20250 + 13500 = ₹ 33750 and her capital = 33750/9%
= ₹ 3,75,000
Interest on Chinu's capital (x) = ₹ 20250 and his capital = 20250/9% = ₹ 2,25,000

Answer 1(d)

Items will appear in Sales Ledger Adjustment A/c	Items will not appear
(iii) Cash refunds to customers ₹ 4,500	(i) B/R discounted with bank for ₹ 15000 (ii) Old bad debts recovered ₹ 1500 (iv) Provision made for bad debts ₹ 5000

Answer 1(e)

VALUATION OF CLOSING STOCK WITH AGENT

Particulars	₹
Goods sent on consignment	2,50,000
Share in Expenses incurred by Ajay (8,500 + 4,240)	12,740
Cartage paid by Vijay	5,140
Total	2,67,880

After Normal loss cost will be = 2,50,000 × 98% = ₹ 2,45,000

Unsold Stock = 2,50,000 × 15% = 37,500
Value of Unsold stock will be = 37,500 × (2,67,880 /2,45,000) = ₹41,002

Answer 1(f)

Particulars	Amount (₹ in Crores)
Impairment loss as per Income Tax purpose ₹(80-40)	40
Tax effect on above [40% of ₹40 Crores]	16
Impairment Loss ₹(80-52) Crores as per Accounting purpose	28
Income Tax effect on Impairment Loss [40% of ₹28 Crores]	11.2
Net Deferred Tax Liability	4.8

Answer 1(g)

As per As -9 revenue should be recognised only when there is no uncertainty about its ultimate collection. Revenue from software to be recognised on delivery. In this case delivery and transfer has been made by 30-9-2014 and the Revenue realised was ₹ 50 lakhs. About the additional bill of ₹10 lakhs., it cannot be concluded with certainty that the same will be realised in full or part or not at all. Hence the same cannot be considered as Revenue at this stage.

Answer 1(h)

A Cost of 6500 units (3,25,000 + 65,000)	₹ 3,90,000
B Cost of units lost in transit [(₹ 3,90,000 ÷ 6,500) × 700]	₹42,000
C Value of closing stock (A – B)	₹ 3,48,000
D *Add:* Non-recurring expenses	₹ 4,300
E Total cost price of 5800 units	₹ 3,52,30

Answer 1(i)

HUMAN LIFE INSURANCE CO.
VALUATION BALANCE SHEET AS AT 31ST MARCH, 2014

₹ in lakhs

Liability	₹	Assets	₹
To Net Liability as per actuarial valuation	132	By Life Insurance Fund	155
To Surplus	23		
	155		155

Answer 1(j)

COMPUTATION OF PROVISION

Particulars	₹
A Doubtful Assets (upto 1 year)	6,73,000
B. *Less:* Value of security (excluding ECGC cover)	(1,50,000)
	5,23,000
C. Less: ECGC coverage (limited to ₹ 1,00,000)	(1,00,000)
D. Unsecured portion	4,23,000

E. Provision: for unsecured portion @ 100% on ₹ 4,23,000	4,23,000
F. Provision for secured portion @ 25% on ₹ 1,50,000	37,500
G Total provision to be made (E + F)	₹ 4,60,500.

Answer 2(a)

(1) This is an exceptional item on account of size and arises from ordinary activities of the company. This should be separately disclosed.

(2) This surplus should be treated as part of the profit of the year from ordinary activities, since the amount is not material.

(3) The amount of ₹ 2,00,000 is stated to be 'extra' contribution, and it is material. It should, therefore, be disclosed as an exceptional item.

(4) The profit does not call for a prior period adjustment since there is no fundamental error. This should be disclosed separately as an exceptional item on account of its size and incidence.

(5) This loss arising out of ordinary activities, but since the amount is large it should be shown as an exceptional item.

Answer 2(b)

JOURNAL OF ....

Date	Particulars		Dr. (₹)	Cr. (₹)
(i)	Profit & Loss Adjustment A/c	Dr.	18000	
	To Suspense A/c			18000
(ii)	Capital (Drawings) A/c	Dr.	10000	
	To Profit & Loss Adjustment A/c			10000
(iii)	Machinery A/c	Dr.	5200	
	To Profit & Loss Adjustment A/c			5200
(iv)	Profit & Loss Adj. A/c	Dr.	15000	
	To Outstanding Rent A/c			15000
(v)	Furniture A/c	Dr.	13000	
	To Profit & Loss Adjustment A/c			13000
(vi)	Sohan's A/c	Dr.	10000	
	To Mohan's A/c			10000

Answer 2(c)

BANK RECONCILIATION STATEMENT AS AT 31 ST MARCH

Particulars			Plus (₹)	Minus (₹)
A.	Credit Balance as per Pass Book		10,000	
B.	*Add:*	(a) Cheque wrongly credited to another customers A/c	500	
		(b) Error in carrying forward	3,000	
		(c) Cheque recorded twice	350	
C.	*Less:*	(a) Excess credit for Cash Deposit		9
		(b) Under casting of withdrawal column		100
		(c) Wrong credit		1,000

	13,850	1,109
D. Debit Balance as per Cash Book	12,741	

Answer 3(a)

MACHINERY ACCOUNT

Date	Particulars	₹	Date	Particulars	₹
2011		2011			
Jan. 1	To Balance b/d	1,49,000	Jan.1	By Profit & Loss A/c (Machinery Repairs)	12,825
Jan. 1	To Profit & Loss A/c (Machinery purchased earlier)	5,616	June.30	By Bank	15,000
Jan.30	To Bank	30,500	June.30	By Depreciation A/c	810
			Dec.31	By Profit & Loss A/c (Loss)	390
				By Depreciation A/c	14,084
				By Balance c/d	1,42,007
		1,85,116			1,85,116

Working Note:

Particulars	₹
1. Machinery purchased on 1 -10-2009	
(₹6,000 + ₹400 Installation Expenses)	6,400
Less: Depreciation for 3 months	160
	6,240
Less: Depreciation for 2010	624
Amount debited to Machinery A/c and Credited to P. & L. A/c	5,616
2. Machine Account wrongly debited for repairs On 30-6-2009	15,000
Less: Depreciation for 6 months	750
	14,250
Less: Depreciation for 2010	1,425
Amount credited to Machinery A/c and debited to P. & L. A/c	12,825
3. Book value of Machinery on 1-1-2009	20,000
Less: Depreciation for 2009	2,000
	18,000
Less: Depreciation for 2010	1,800
Value on 1-1-2011	16,200
Depreciation for 6 months	810
Book value of machine on 30-6-2011	15,390
Less: Sale proceeds	15,000
Loss on sale of machinery	390

4. Depreciation:	
10% on ₹1,25,591 (i.e., ₹1,49,000 + ₹5,616 – ₹12,825 – ₹16,200)	12,559
10% on ₹ 30,500 for ½ year	1,525
	14,084

Answer 3(b)

IN THE BOOKS OF DOLL AND DOLLY TRADING AND PROFIT AND LOSS ACCOUNT

Particulars		₹	Particulars		₹
To Opening Stock		44,000	By sales: Cash	32,000	
To Purchase (Credit)		2,16,600	Credit	2,48,800	2,80,800
To Gross Profit c/d		70,200	By Closing Stock		50,000
		3,30,800			3,30,800
To Salaries		22,000	By Gross profit b/d		70,200
To Rent		4,400	By Discount earned		2,400
To Advertisement		1,800			
To Printing	1,600				
Add: Outstanding	500	2,100			
To General Expenses		19,100			
To Discount Allowed		2,800			
To Depreciation @ 10% on Furniture		600			
To Net profit transferred to Capital Accounts:					
Doll – ½ Share	9,900				
Dolly – ½ Share	9,900	19,800			
		72,600			72,600

BALANCE SHEET AS AT 30-6-2011

Liabilities		₹	Assets		₹
Printing Outstanding		500	Cash in Hand		35,900
Sundry Creditors		37,000	Sundry Debtors		70,000
Doll's Capital A/c (Opening)	56,000		Closing Stock		50,000
Add: Net Profit	9,900		Furniture	6,000	
Less: Drawing	4,000	61,900	*Less:* Depreciation	600	5,400
Dolly's Capital A/c as on 1-7-2010 (4)	52,000				
Add: Net Profit	9,900	61,900			
		1,61,300			1,61,300

Working Notes:

1. **Calculation of Credit Purchases**

SUNDRY CREDITORS ACCOUNT

Particulars	₹	Particulars	₹
To Cash	2,24,000	By Balance b/d	46,800
To Discount	2,400	By Purchases (Balancing Figure) (Credit Purchase)	2,16,600
To Balance c/d	37,000		
	2,63,400		2,63,400

2. CALCULATION OF CREDIT SALES

Opening Stock	44,000
Add: Credit Purchases	2,16,600
Less: Closing Stock	50,000
Cost of goods sold	2,10,600
Add: Gross Profit 331/3 % on cost of goods which is Equivalent to 25% of sales	70,200
Total Sales	2,80,800
Less: Cash Sales	32,000
Credit Sales	2,48,800

3. **Calculation of Debtors as on 1-7-2010**

SUNDRY DEBTORS ACCOUNT

Particulars	₹	Particulars	₹
To Balance b/d (Balance figure)	**94,000**	By Cash	2,70,000
To Credit Sales	2,48,800	By Discount	2,800
		By Balance c/d	70,000
	3,42,800		3,42,800

4. STATEMENT OF AFFAIRS AS AT 1-7-2010

Liabilities		₹	Assets	₹
Sundry Creditors		46,800	Cash in Hand	10,800
Combined Capital (Balancing figure)			Sundry Debtors	94,000
Doll's Capital			Stock-in-Trade	44,000
(₹ 4,000 more than Dolly's capital)	56,000		Furniture	6,000
Dolly's Capital	52,000	1,08,000		
		1,54,800		1,54,800

Calculation for Doll and Dolly's Capital:

Let Dolly's capital was = x and Doll's Capital was (x + 4,000).

The combined capital of Doll and Dolly which was derived from Statement of Affairs as on 01.07.2010 was ₹ 1,08,000.

Therefore,

(x + 4,000) + x = 1,08,000

Or, 2x + 4,000 = 1,08,000

Or, 2x = 1,08,000 – 4,000

Or, 2x = 1,04,000

Or, x = 1,04,000/2 = 52,000

So, Dolly's Capital was ₹ 52,000

And Doll's Capital was = (₹ 52,000 + ₹ 4,000) =₹ 56,000

Answer 3(c)

COST PRICE STRUCTURE

Particulars	₹
A. Cost Price	100
B. *Add:* Profit	20
C. Invoice Price (A + B)	120
D. *Add:* Extra Profit	30
E. Catalogue Price (C + D)	150

Dr. **MUMBAI BRANCH STOCK ACCOUNT** **Cr.**

Particulars	₹	Particulars	₹
To Balance b/d	12,000	By Goods sent to Branch A/c [₹ 30,000 × 120/150]	24,000
To Goods sent to Branch A/c [₹ 1,10,000 + 20%]	1,32,000	By Branch Cash A/c (Cash Sales)	74,800
To Goods sent to Branch A/c [₹ 75,000 × 120/150]	60,000	By Branch Debtors A/c (Credit Sales)	1,45,000
To Branch Debtors A/c (Returns)	30,000	By Goods sent to Branch A/c (Returns)	24,000
To Branch Debtors A/c (Returns)	15,000	By Goods sent to Branch A/c (Returns) [₹ 15,000 × 120/150]	12,000
To Branch Cash A/c [local purchases]	30,000	By Branch Adjustment A/c (Load)	500
To Branch Adjustment A/c [Load on local purchases]	6,000	By Branch Profit and Loss A/c (Stock destroyed by fire)	2,500
To Branch Adjustment A/c (Excess of catalogue price of Net Credit Sales over invoice price) (₹ 1,45,000 – ₹ 30,000 – 15,000) × 30/150]	20,000	By Branch Adjustment A/c [Invoice Price of Normal Loss] [₹ 3,000 × 120/150]	2,400
		By Balance c/d:	7,200
		Stock out of local purchases Stock in transit from H.O. [₹1,32,000 – ₹1,27,000]	5,000
		Stock in hand from H.O.(B. f.)	7,600
	3,05,000		3,05,000

Dr. **MUMBAI BRANCH ADJUSTMENT ACCOUNT** **Cr.**

Particulars	₹	Particulars	₹
To Stock Reserve A/c		By Stock Reserve A/c	
[₹ 19,800 × 20/120]	3,300	[₹ 12,000 × 20/120]	2,000
To Branch Stock A/c		By Branch Stock A/c	6,000
[load on abnormal Loss]	500	[Loading on local purchases]	
To Branch Stock A/c	2,400	By Branch Stock A/c	20,000
[Invoice Price of Normal Loss]		(Excess of catalogue price of Net Credit Sales over invoice price)	
To Branch Profit and Loss A/c			
(Gross profit)	43,800	By Goods sent to Branch A/c; [Load on Net Goods sent] [₹ 1,32,000 + ₹ 60,000 – ₹ 24,000 – ₹24,000 – 12,000] [₹ 1,32,000 × 20/120]	22,000
	50,000		50,000

Dr. **MUMBAI BRANCH EXPENSES ACCOUNT** **Cr.**

Particulars	₹	Particulars	₹
To Branch Cash A/c	9,741	By Branch Profit & Loss A/c	23,106
To Discount Allowed A/c	13,365		
	23,106		23,106

Dr. **MUMBAI BRANCH PROFIT AND LOSS ACCOUNT** **Cr.**

Particulars	₹	Particulars	₹
To Branch Expenses A/c	23,106	By Branch Adjustment A/c (Gross Profit)	43,800
To Branch Stock A/c (Cost of Loss by fire)	2,500	By Insurance Claim	2000
To Provision for Discount A/c	1,485		
To Manager's Commission	1,059		
To General Profit and Loss A/c [₹ 18,709 × 6/106]	17,650		
	45,800		45,800

Dr. **MUMBAI BRANCH DEBTORS ACCOUNT** **Cr.**

Particulars	₹	Particulars	₹
To Balance b/d	10,000	By Branch Stock A/c	30,000
To Branch Stock A/c (Credit Sales)	1,45,000	By Goods sent to Branch A/c	15,000
		By Branch Cash/Bank A/c	45,635
		By Cash/Bank A/c	40,000
		By Discount Allowed A/c	13,365

		By Balance c/d (b.f.)	**11,000**
	1,55,000		1,55,000

Working Note: *Computation of Provision for discount*

(a) Prompt paying debtors who availed of discount = ₹ 13,365 × 100/15 = 89,100

(b) Total debtors who made payment during the year = ₹ 13,365 + 85,635 = ₹ 99,000

(c) Proportion of prompt payers to those who made payment = (89,100/99,000) × 100 = 90%

(d) Likely Prompt paying debtors included in closing Debtors = 90% of ₹ 11,000 = ₹ 9,900

(e) Provision for discount on the closing balance = 15% of ₹ 9,900 = ₹ 1,485

Answer 4(a)

DEBTORS LEDGER ADJUSTMENT ACCOUNT IN GENERAL LEDGER

Dr. Cr.

Particulars	₹	Particulars	₹
To Balance b/d	40,000	By General Ledger Adjustment A/c:	
To General Ledger Adjustment A/c. (In Sales Ledger) – Sales	49,000	(In Sales Ledger) – Cash	53,400
To Creditors A/c (B. R. dishonoured)	600	– Discount	2,600
To Bank (Cheques dishonoured)	6,000	By Bad Debts (₹ 500 + ₹ 600)	1,100
		By B/R	6,000
		By Balance c/d	32,500
	95,600		95,600

Workings:

1. Computation of Credit Sales:
   Let Credit sales = ₹100, cash sales = ₹20. Total sales = ₹120.
   Total Sales ₹ (60,000 – 1,200) = ₹ 58,800
   Credit sales = (58,800 × 100)/120 = ₹49,000
2. Cash Received
   Cash Received is 60% of opening Debtors + Credit Sales i.e. ₹ (40,000 + 49,000) = ₹ 89,000.
   So, Cash received = ₹ 89,000 × 60/100 = ₹ 53,400

Answer 4(b)

TOTAL CREDITORS ACCOUNT – FOR THE YEAR ENDED 31-03-2013

Date	Particulars	₹	Date	Particulars	₹
31-03-2013	To Bills payable accepted	62,000	01-04-2012	By Balance b/d	38,000
	To Cash paid to creditors	1,37,000	31-03-2013	By Purchases (Credit)	2,67,000
	To B/R endorsed	16,000		By Endorsed B/R Dishonored	3,000
	To Purchase returns	11,000		By B/P Dishonoured	2,000
	To Discount received	6,000		To Transfer from debtors Ledger	7,000
	To Balance c/d (Bal. fig.)	71,000			
		3,10,000			3,10,000

Answer 4(c)

JOURNAL

Date	Particulars		L.F.	Dr. (₹)	Cr. (₹)
(i)	Meena (In Sales/Debtors Ledger)	Dr.		8,700	
	To Meenu (In Sales/Debtors Ledger)				8,700
	(Being amount received from Meenu was wrongly credited to Meena, now rectified)				
(ii) (a)	Suspense A/c (In Sales/Debtors Ledger)	Dr.		1,000	
	To Sales A/c (In General Ledger)				1,000
(ii) (b)	Sales/Debtors Ledger Adjustment A/c (In General Ledger)	Dr.		1,000	
	To General Ledger Adjustment A/c (In Sales/Debtors Ledger)				1,000
	(Being rectification of the error resulting from under casting of the Sales Book)				
(iii) (a)	M/s. BPO Ltd. A/c (In Creditors/Bought Ledger)	Dr.		15,600	
	To Purchase Returns A/c (In General Ledger)				15,600
(iii) (b)	Creditors/Bought Ledger Adjustment A/c (In General Ledger)	Dr.		15,600	
	To General Ledger Adjustment A/c (In Creditors/Bought Ledger)				15,600
	(Being goods returned to supplier not recorded earlier, now recorded)				

Answer 5(a)

PROVISION OF AS-9

As per AS 9 in a transaction involving the rendering of services, performance should be measured either under the completed service contract method or under the proportionate completion method, whichever relates the revenue to the work accomplished. Further, appendix to AS 9 states that revenue from advertising should be recognized when the service is completed. The service as regards advertisement is deemed to be completed when the related advertisement appears before the public.

ADVICE

In the given problem, 40% of the advertisement appeared before the public in November, 2013 and balance 60% in December, 2013.

CALCULATION OF TOTAL PROFIT

Particulars	₹ in lakhs
Advertisement for 70% of available time obtained by 30th September, 2013	700
Advertisement for 30% of available time obtained in by October, 2013	240
Total	940
Less: Cost of advertisement rights	(520)
Profit	420

The profit amounting ₹ 420 lakhs should be apportioned in the ratio of 40:60 for the months of November and December, 2013. Thus, the company should recognise ₹ 168 lakhs (i.e. ₹ 420 lakhs × 40%) in November, 2013 and rest ₹ 252 lakhs (i.e. ₹ 420 lakhs × 60%) in December, 2013.

Answer 5(b)

As per AS – 7 'Construction Contract', when it is probable that contract costs will exceed the total revenue, the expected loss should be immediately recognised as an expense. The amount of such a loss is determined irrespective of (a) Whether or not work has commenced on the contract, (b) the stage of completion of contract activity as per AS – 7.

COMPUTATION OF ANTICIPATED OR FORESEEABLE LOSS

Particulars	₹ in crores
Cost of Total Contract:	
Work certified	23
Add: Work not certified	6
Add: Estimated further cost to completion	21
	50
Less: Contract Price	45
Anticipated / Foreseeable Loss	5

Computation of percentage of completion:

[Work-in-progress/Cost of Total Contract] × 100 = (23 + 6)/50 × 100 = 58%

Recognition of Contract Revenue:

Total Contract Price × 58% = ₹ (45 × 58%) crores = ₹ 26.10 crores.

Current year's loss = ₹ (29 – 26.10) crores = ₹ 2.9 crores.

Provision to be made for balance of the anticipated loss i.e. ₹ (5 – 2.9) crores = ₹ 2.1 crores.

Therefore, anticipated/foreseeable loss amounting to ₹5 crores should be immediately recognised in the Profit and Loss account.

Answer 5(c)

Internally Generated Computer Software:

Internally generated computer software for internal use is developed or modified internally by the enterprise solely to meet the needs of the enterprise and at no stage it is planned to sell it.

The stages of development of internally generated software may be categorized into the following two phases:

(i) Preliminary project stage, i.e., the research phase.

(ii) Development stage.

(i) Preliminary project stage, i.e., the research phase:

At the preliminary project the internally generated software should not be recognized as on assets. Expenditure incurred in the preliminary project stage should be recognized as an expense when it is incurred. The reason for such a treatment is that at this stage of the software project an enterprise cannot demonstrate that an asset exists from which future economic benefits are probable.

(ii) Development stage.

Internally generated software arising at the development stage should be recognized as an asset if, and only if, an enterprise can find out all of the following:

The intention of the enterprise to complete the internally generated software and use it to perform the function needed.

Answer 6(a)

Dr. 15% DEBENTURES OF SIVA INDUSTRIES LTD ACCOUNT Cr.

Date	Particulars	FV	Int.	Cost	Date	Particulars	FV	Int.	Cost
01.04.11	To bal. b/d	1,00,000	3,750	1,05,000	30.06.11	By Bank A/c	---	11,250	---
01.05.11	To Bank A/c	50,000	2,500	51,000	01.11.11	By Bank A/c	60,000	3,000	57,300
30.11.11	To Bank A/c	40,000	2,500	38,400	01.11.11	By P&L A/c	---	---	5,700
31.12.11	To P&L A/c	---	---	10,000	31.12.11	By Bank A/c	---	6,750	---
31.03.12	To P&L -Int tfr	---	18,625	---	31.12.11	By Bank A/c	40,000	3,000	52,000
	(bal. fig.)				31.03.12	By bal. c/d	90,000	3,375	89,400
		1,90,000	27,375	2,07,400			1,90,000	27,375	2,07,400

Answer 6(b)

Short Sales = ₹ 95,000 – ₹ 15,000 = ₹ 80,000

Rate of Gross Profit = Net profit + Insured standing charges / Sales of the last accounting year × 100

= (₹ 20,000 + ₹ 28,000)/[₹ 65,000 + ₹ 80,000 + ₹ 95,000] × 100

= (₹ 48,000/ ₹2,40,000) × 100 = 20%

CALCULATION OF AMOUNT OF CLAIM FOR LOSS OF PROFIT

	₹
Loss of Profit on short sales of ₹ 80,000 @ 20%	16,000
Add: **Increased cost of working:**	
Increase in cost of working = $\frac{\text{Net Profit} + \text{Insured Standing Charges}}{\text{Net Profit} + \text{All Standing Charges}}$	
(₹ 20,000 + ₹ 28,000) / (₹ 20,000 + ₹ 30,000) × ₹600	576
	16,576
Less: Saving in insured charges as a result of fire	1,500
Gross Claim	**15,076**

APPLICATION OF AVERAGE CLAUSE

Sum Insured / Gross Profit on 12 months (Sales preceding the date of fire) × Gross claim

= ₹ 42,000 / 20% of ₹ 2,45,000(1) × 15,076 = ₹ 12,922

Claim for loss of profit to be lodged = ₹ 12,922.

Working Notes: (1)

Sales for 12 months preceding the date of fire i.e., September 1, 2011 is:

Particulars	₹
Sales for September 1, 2010 to December 31, 2010	95,000
Sales for January 1, 2011 to April 30, 2011	70,000
Sales for May 1, 2011 to August 31,2011	80,000
Sales from September 1,2010 to August 31,2011	2,45,000

(2) COMPUTATION OF ADDITIONAL EXPENSES TO BE CONSIDERED

Particulars	₹
(a) Actual expense incurred	600
(b) G.P on reduced turnover avoided ₹ 15,000 × 20%	3,000

(c) Increase in cost of working $= \frac{\text{Net Profit} + \text{Insured Standing Charges}}{\text{Net Profit} + \text{All Standing Charges}}$ i.e. ₹ 600 × (20,000 + 28,000)/(20,000 + 30,000) i.e. ₹ 576	576
Hence, least of (a), (b) and (c) i.e. ₹ 576 will be considered	

Answer 6(c)

JOINT VENTURE ACCOUNT

Particulars		₹	Particulars	₹
To X (Goods)		10,000	By Joint Bank A/c (Sales)	45,000
To Y (Expenses)		2,000		
To Joint Bank A/c (Goods)		15,000		
To Joint Bank A/c (Expenses)		4,000		
To Profit on Joint Venture transferred to:				
X (4/7 share)	8,000			
Y (3/7 share)	6,000	14,000		
		45,000		45,000

Profit of joint venture is to be divided in proportion to the contributions of X and Y. Their contributions are:

Particulars	X's Contribution ₹	Y's Contribution ₹
Amount contributed in cash	10,000	13,000
Expenses paid by Y		2,000
Goods purchased by X	10,000	
	20,000	15,000

Thus, profit sharing ratio between X and Y is 20,000 : 15,000, i.e., 4:3 or 4/7 and 3/7 respectively.

JOINT BANK ACCOUNT

Particulars	₹	Particulars	₹
To X	10,000	To Joint Venture A/c (Sales)	45,000
To Y	13,000	By Joint Venture A/c (Expenses)	4,000
		By Joint Venture A/c (Goods)	15,000
		By X	28,000
		By Y	21,000
	68,000		68,000

X ACCOUNT

Particulars	₹	Particulars	₹
To Joint Bank A/c	28,000	By Joint Bank A/c	10,000
		By Joint Venture A/c (Goods)	10,000
		By Joint Venture A/c (Profit)	8,000
	28,000		28,000

Y ACCOUNT

Particulars	₹	Particulars	₹
To Joint Bank A/c	21,000	By Joint Bank A/c	13,000
		By Joint Venture A/c (Expenses)	2,000
		By Joint Venture A/c (Profit)	6,000
	21,000		21,000

Answer 7(a)

CANHC BANK LTD.
PROFIT & LOSS A/C FOR THE YEAR ENDED 31ST MARCH, 2012

	Particulars	Schedule No.	Year ended 31st March 2012 (₹ '000)	Year ended 31st March 2011 (₹ '000)
I.	Income:			
	Interest earned	13	626	
	Other Income	14	13	
	Total		639	
II.	Expenditure:			
	Interest expended	15	230	
	Operating expenses	16	92	
	Provision and Contingencies [72+31+30]		133	
	Total		455	
III.	Profit/Loss:			
	Net profit for the year		184	
	Profit/Loss brought forward		---	
	Total		184	
IV.	Appropriations:			
	Transfer to Statutory Reserve @ 25%		46	
	Balance carried over to Balance Sheet		138	
	Total		184	

SCHEDULE 13-INTEREST EARNED

	Particulars	Year ended 31st March. 2012 (₹ '000)	Year ended 31st March 2011 (₹ '000)
I.	Interest/Discount [2.25 + 2.01 + 1.05 + 0.95] lakhs	626	
II.	Interest on Investment	---	
III.	Interest on Balance with RBI and Other inter bank fund	---	
		626	

SCHEDULE 14 – OTHER INCOME

	Particulars	Year ended 31st March. 2012 (₹ '000)	Year ended 31st March 2011 (₹ '000)
I.	Commission, Exchange and Brokerage	47	
II.	Loss on sale of Investment	(34)	
		13	

SCHEDULE 15 – INTEREST EXPENDED

	Particulars	Year ended 31st March. 2012 (₹ '000)	Year ended 31st March 2011 (₹ '000)
I.	Interest on Deposits [0.75 + 1.55]lakhs	230	
II.	Interest on RBI/inter bank borrowings	---	
		230	

SCHEDULE 16 – OPERATING EXPENSES

	Particulars	Year ended 31st March. 2012 (₹ '000)	Year ended 31st March 2011 (₹ '000)
I.	Payment to and provision for employees	82	
II.	Printing & Stationery	5	
III.	Auditors' fees	5	
		92	

PROVISION FOR DOUBTFUL DEBTS ACCOUNT

Dr. Cr.

Particulars	₹ '000	Particulars	₹ '000
To Bad Debts	21	By Balance b/d	42
To Balance c/d	52	By Profit & Loss A/c	31
	73		73

PROVISION FOR TAXATION ACCOUNT

Dr. Cr.

Particulars	₹ '000	Particulars	₹ '000
To Bank A/c	54	By Balance b/d	66
To Balance c/d	84	By Profit & Loss A/c	72
	138		138

Answer 7(b)

BOOKS OF RASHTRIYA BEEMA COMPANY

Date	Particulars		(₹ in crores)	(₹ in crores)
31.03.14	Marine Revenue A/c To Unexpired Risks Reserve A/c (Provision made for unexpired risks reserve on marine business is (53 – 52.50)]	Dr.	0.50	0.50
31.03.14	Fire Revenue A/c To Unexpired Risks Reserve A/c [Unexpired risks reserve made for fire business is (60.5 – 55)]	Dr.	5.50	5.50
31.03.14	Miscellaneous Revenue A/c To Unexpired Risks Reserve A/c [Unexpired Risks Reserve made for Miscellaneous business is(15.75 – 12.50)]		3.75	3.75

UNEXPIRED RISKS RESERVE ACCOUNT

(₹ in crores)

Dr. Cr.

Date	Particulars	Marine ₹	Fire ₹	Misc ₹	Date	Particulars	Marine ₹	Fire ₹	Misc ₹
31.3.14	To Revenue A/c	52.50	55.00	12.50	1.4.13	By Balance b/d	52.50	55.00	12.50
31.3.14	To balance c/d	53.00	60.50	15.75	31.3.14	By Revenue A/c	53.00	60.50	15.75
		105.50	115.50	28.25			105.50	115.50	28.25

Working Note: *Calculation of Account of Unexpired Risks Reserve as on 31.03.2014*

Particulars	(₹ in crores)		
	Marine (₹)	Fire (₹)	Misc (₹)
Premium collected from policy holders	57	125	30
Add: Premium collected from other Insurance Cos.	17.5	12.5	10
Less: Premium paid/payable to other Insurance Cos.	21.5	16.5	8.5
Net premium	53	121	31.5
Required % to create reserve	100%	50%	50%
Amount of Reserve will be on 31.03.2014	53	60.5	15.75
Less: Opening Balance of Reserve on 01.04.2013	52.5	55	12.50
Additional Reserve to be made	0.50	5.50	3.75

Answer 7(c)

Working notes:

Particulars	₹
1. Computation of total actual cost of new plant: Cost of new plant (as given)	1,20,00,000
Add: Value of materials of old plant used in construction of new Plant	4,80,000
	1,24,80,000

2. Split-up of cost of old Plant when acquired in 1950:	
Materials (48,00,000 × 5/10)	24,00,000
Labour (48,00,000 × 3/10)	14,40,000
Overheads (48,00,000 × 2/10)	9,60,000
	48,00,000

% of overheads to total cost = 9,60,000/48,00,000 × 100 = 20%

% of overheads to combined cost of material and labour = 9,60,000/38,00,000 × 100 = 25%

(b) Current Cost of Replacement:

(i) Material is (Increase by 40% over ₹24,00,000) (i.e., ₹ 24,00,000 + 40% increase 9,60,000)		33,60,000
Labour (increased by 80% over ₹14,40,000) (i.e., ₹14,40,000 + 80% increase ₹11,52,000)		25,92,000
Overheads (25% of combined cost of material and Labour i.e., 25% of (₹33,60,000 + 25,92,000)		14,88,000
		74,40,000
(ii) Computation of amount of replacement to be capitalized:		
Total actual cost of new Plant		1,24,80,000
Less: Estimated present cost of replacement		74,40,000
Amount to be capitalised		50,40,000
(iii) Computation of amount of replacement to be charged to Revenue A/c:		
Estimated present cost of replacement		74,40,000
Less: Value of old material used in construction of new plant	4,80,000	
Amount realized on sale of old Plant	15,00,000	19,80,000
Change to Revenue		54,60,000
(iv) Computation of actual amount of Cash spent on replacement:		
Total actual cost of new Plant		1,24,80,000
Less: Value of old materials used in construction of new Plant		4,80,000
		1,20,00,000

JOURNAL

Date	Particulars		L.F	Dr. (₹)	Cr. (₹)
1	Replacement A/c	Dr.		74,40,000	
	Plant A/c (Bal. Fig.)	Dr.		45,60,000	
	To Bank A/c				1,20,00,000
2	Bank A/c	Dr.		15,00,000	
	To Replacement A/c				15,00,000
3	Plant A/c	Dr.		4,80,000	
	To Replacement A/c				4,80,000
4	Revenue A/c	Dr.		54,60,000	
	To Replacement A/c				54,60,000

PLANT ACCOUNT

Particulars	₹	Particulars	₹
To Balance b/d	48,00,000	By Balance c/d	98,40,000
To Bank A/c	45,60,000		
To Replacement A/c	4,80,000		
	98,40,000		98,40,000

REPLACEMENT ACCOUNT

Particulars	₹	Particulars	₹
To Bank A/c	74,40,000	By Bank A/c	15,00,000
		By Plant A/c	4,80,000
		By Revenue A/c (Bal.Fig)	54,60,000
	74,40,000		74,40,000

INTERMEDIATE EXAMINATION GROUP I (SYLLABUS 2012) JUNE 2015

PAPER-5: FINANCIAL ACCOUNTING

Time Allowed: 3 Hours **Full Marks : 100**

The figures in the margin on the right side indicate full marks.
This paper contains seven questions. All questions are compulsory, subject to instruction provided against each question.
All working must form part of your answer.
Assumptions, if any, must be clearly indicated.

1. Answer all the questions: **2 × 10 = 20**

(a) MENZ LTD. purchased goods at the cost of ₹ 20 Lakh in Oct 2014. Till March 31,2015, 75% of the Stocks were sold. The company wants to disclose stock at ₹ 5 Lakh. The expected Sales Value is ₹ 5.5 Lakh and a Commission at 10% on sale is payable to the agent.

What is the correct Closing Stock to be disclosed as at 31.03.2015 as per AS-2?

(b) PARASH LTD. purchased a machine costing ₹ 72 Lakh on 01.04.2014 and the same was fully financed by foreign currency loan (US Dollars) payable in two annual equal instalments. Exchange rates were 1 US Dollar = ₹ 57.60 and ₹ 60.00 as on 01.04.2014 and 31.03.2015 respectively. First instalment was paid on 31.03.2015. What is the amount of difference to be charged to Profit and Loss Accounts for the year 2014-15 as per AS 11.

(c) GOPI purchased a plant on hire purchase system from GOPAL on 01.04.2015. The hire purchase rate was settled at ₹ 72,000, payable at ₹ 22,000 on 01.04.2015 and ₹ 25,000 at the end of two successive years. Interest was charged @ 5% P.A. [Given PVI FA (at 5%, 2 years) = 1.8594]

Ascertain the cash price of the plant.

(d) Compute the income from subscription for the year 2014 from the following particulars relating to TARUN CLUB:

Particulars	01.01.2014 ₹	31.12.2014 ₹
Outstanding subscription	9,500	7,000
Advanced subscription	2,800	5,200
Subscription received during the year 2014		₹ 1,45,000

(e) X,Y and Z are partners in the ratio of 3:2:1. W is admitted with 1/6th share in future profits. Z would retains his original shares. Find out the new profit sharing ratios of the partners.

(f) ANKIT LTD. provided the following particulars:

Debtor's ledger includes ₹ 5,000 due from Kumar & Co.

Creditor's ledger includes ₹ 3,000 due to Kumar & Co.

Give Journal Entry to record the above under Self-Balancing System.

(g) From the information of AMBA LTD. received from its branch -AB, **calculate** the invoice price of goods sent to branch and Profit included thereon.

Goods received from H.O. (AMBA LTD.) — ₹ 1,00,000

Goods in transit from H.O. — ₹ 50,000

Goods are invoiced to branch at cost plus 25%.

(h) NUPUR CONSTRUCTION LTD. obtained a contract for construction of a Fly-Over. Following information is available for the year ended March 31, 2015:

Particulars	₹ in Lakh
Total Contract Price	500
Work certified	300
Work not certified	50
Estimated further cost to completion	190
Progress payment received	200

What will be the foreseeable loss to be shown in the accounts of 2014-2015 as per AS-7.

(i) GRIZA LIFE INSURANCE CO. LTD. furnishes the following information:

Life Insurance fund as on 31.03.2014	₹ 26,56,000
Net Liability on 31.3.2014 as per actuarial valuation	₹ 10,34,000
Interim Bonus paid to Policy holders during inter valuation period	₹ 1,23,800
Amount proposed to carry forward amount of	₹ 2,55,000

What is the amount of share of Shareholders₹

(j) CHANDU purchased 2500,12% Debenture of MENZ LTD. on May 1, 2015 at ₹ 108 cum-interest (full value of debentures ₹ 100). Interest is paid on 30th June and 31st December in every year.

Ascertain the amount of interest and cost of debentures.

2. Answer any two questions (Carrying 4 marks each): **4 × 2 = 8**

(a) Journalise the following transactions in the books of SHIVA.

01.05.2015	—	Started business with ₹ 5,00,000 of which 50% amount was borrowed from SBI and 20 % amount was borrowed from his sister Patta.
05.05.2015	—	Purchased goods from Chinu Mart worth ₹ 1,60,000 at 25% trade discount and 40% amount paid in cash.
08.05.2015	—	Sold goods to Satish ₹ 60,000 at 20% trade discount and received 1/4 amount in cash.
15.05.2015	—	Paid to Chinu Mart ₹ 69,500 in full settlement of Account.

(b) The Cash book of PRARTHANA show ₹ 8,364 as the balance at bank as on 31st March, 2015 but you find that this does not agree with the balance as per the Bank Pass Book. On scrutiny, you find the following discrepancies:

(i) On 15th March, the payments side of the Cash Book was under cast by ₹ 100.

(ii) A cheque for ₹ 131 issued on 25th March, was recorded in the cash column.

(iii) One deposit of ₹ 150 was recorded in the Cash Book as if there is not Bank Column therein.

(iv) On 18th March, the debit balance of ₹ 1,526 as on the previous day, was brought forward as a credit balance.

(v) Of the total cheques amounting to ₹ 11,514 drawn in the last week of March, cheques aggregating ₹ 7,815 were encased in March.

(vi) Dividends of ₹ 250 collected by the Bank and subscription of ₹ 100 paid by it, were not recorded in the Cash Book.

(vii) One outgoing cheque of ₹ 350 was recorded twice in the Cash Book.

Required: Prepare a Bank Reconciliation Statement as on 31st March, 2015.

(c) JIMIRA LTD. bought a Machine on 30.09.2014 at a price of ₹ 248 Lakh after charging 6% Sales Tax and giving a trade discount of 1.3% on the quoted price. Transport charges and installation charges were 0.30% and 0.75% respectively on the quoted price. To meet machine purchase a loan of ₹ 240 Lakh was taken from the bank on which interest at 12% P.A. was to be paid. Expenditure incurred on trial run was materials, wages and overheads ₹ 24,000, ₹ 18,000 and ₹ 11,000 respectively. Machine was ready for use on 01-12-2014. However, it was actually put to use only on 01-05-2015. Entire loan amount remain unpaid on 01-05-2015.

Required: Find the cost of machine as per AS-10.

3. **Answer any two questions (Carrying 12 marks each):** **12 × 2 = 24**

(a) BAIDHNATH LTD. obtain a lease of marble mines for a period of 10 years, commencing from 1st April,2009. According to the lease terms being a royalty of ₹ 300 per tonne of marble blocks raised subject to a minimum rent of ₹ 15,00,000 per annum with a right of recoupment of short workings within the next two years following the year in which short workings arises. For the year of a Strike the minimum rent is to be reduced to 60%. The Sales and Closing Stock for the first 6 years are as follows:

Year Sales	(Tonnes) Closing	Stock (Tonnes)
2009-10	2000	500
2010-11	3600	1100
2011-12	5900	800
2012-13	6400	900
2013-14 (Strike)	3200	400
2014-15	7000	500

You are required to **prepare**:

(i) Royalty Account

(ii) Land Lord Account

(iii) Short workings Account — in the Book of Baidhnath LTD.

(b) A, B and C were equal partners in a firm. Their Balance Sheet as on 31st March, 2015 was as follows:

Liabilities	₹	Assets	₹
A's Capital	1,60,000	Building	4,00,000
C's Capital	1,00,000	Machinery	4,00,000
A's Loan	2,00,000	Furniture and Fixtures	1,60,000
Creditors	10,00,000	Stock	1,60,000
		Book Debts	2,00,000
		Cash at Bank	10,000
		B's Capital (Overdrawn)	1,30,000
	14,60,000		14,60,000

The firm was dissolved as all the partners were declared insolvent. The assets were realized as under:

Book Debts: 45% less; Building: ₹ 1,60,000; Stock: ₹ 1,00,000; Machinery: ₹ 2,00,000; and Furnitures and Fixtures: ₹ 40,000. Realization Expenses were ₹ 10,000.

The private assets and private liabilities of the partners were as follows:

Partner	Private Assets ₹	Private Liabilities ₹
A	2,50,000	2,50,000
B	2,00,000	1,80,000
C	2,30,000	2,50,000

You are required to prepare:

(i) Realisation Account, (ii) Bank Account,

(iii) Creditors Account, (iv) Partner's Capital Account, and

(v) Deficiency Account.

(c) ANSHU keeps his books under single entry system. On 31st March, 2014 his Balance Sheet was as follows:

Liabilities	₹	Assets	₹
Capital	4,50,000	Fixed Assets	2,25,000
Creditors	8,70,000	Stock	9,15,000
Bills Payable	1,87,500	Debtors	2,22,000
Expenses Outstanding	67,500	Bills Receivable	90,000
		Prepaid Insurance	3,000
		Cash/ Bank Balance	1,20,000
	15,75,000		15,75,000

(i) Following is the summary of cash and bank transaction for the year ended 31st March, 2015:

Cash Sales ₹ 1,10,70,000; Collection from Debtors ₹ 22,65,000; Payments to Creditors ₹ 1,12,60,500; Paid for Bills Payable ₹ 12,22,500; Sundry Expenses Paid ₹ 9,31,050; Drawings for Domestic expenses by Mr Anshu ₹ 3,60,000; Cash and Bank Balance as on 31-03-2015 ₹ 1,90,950.

(ii) Following further details are furnished:

Gross Profit on Sales @ 10%; Bills Receivable from Debtors during the year ₹ 6,52,500; Discount Allowed to Debtors ₹ 54,000; Discount Received from Creditors ₹ 42,000; Bills Receivable Endorsed to Creditors ₹ 22,500; Annual Fire Insurance Premium paid (This is paid on 1st August every year) ₹ 9,000; Depreciation on Fixed Assets @ 10%.

(iii) Balance as on 31-03-2015 are given below:

Stock in hand 19,75,000; Debtors ₹ 2,28,000; Bills Receivable ₹ 2,10,000; Outstanding Expenses ₹ 7,500; Bills payable ₹ 2,10,000.

You are required to prepare:

(1) Trading and Profit and Loss Account for the year ended March 31,2015; and

(2) Balance Sheet as on 31.03.2015.

4. Answer any two questions (Carrying 4 marks each): 4 × 2 = 8

(a) The summarized analysis of the accounts of the outstanding debtors of GANAPATHI LTD. at the date of 31.03.2015 (Annual Closing) of amount as under:

Debtors	Goods Sold during the year ₹	Goods returned during the year ₹	Cash and Cheques received during the year ₹	Discount allowed during the year ₹	Bill of Exchange received during the year ₹
A	6,000	—	4,000	1,000	—
B	4,000	1,000	2,000	—	—
C	10,000	—	6,000	—	—
D	20,000	2,000	12,000	1,000	2,000
F	24,000	3,000	16,000	2,000	2,000

Debtors' balance at the beginning of the year was ₹ 9,000. Out of the above receipts of a bill for ₹ 1,400 given by D was dishonoured, noting charges amounting to ₹ 40.

Required: Prepare General Ledger Adjustment Account in Debtors Ledger.

(b) MR. ANUBHAV GOYAL keeps his ledger on Self Balancing System.

The following particulars are extracted from his Books:

Date	Particulars
March, 2015	
1	Purchased from Mr. Akash ₹ 7,500.
3	Paid ₹ 3,000 after adjusting the initial advance in full to Mr. Akash.
10	Paid ₹ 2,500 to Mr. Dev towards the purchases made in February in full.
12	Paid advance to Mr. Giridhar ₹ 6,000.
14	Purchased goods from Mr. Akash ₹ 6,200.
20	Returned goods worth ₹ 1,000 to Mr. Akash
24	Settled the balance due to Mr. Akash at a discount of 5%.
26	Goods purchased from Mr. Giridhar against the advance paid already.
29	Purchased from Mr. Nathan ₹ 3,500.

Goods return to Mr. Prem ₹ 1,200. The goods were originally purchased for cash in the month of February, 2015.

You are required to **prepare** the Creditors Ledger Adjustment Account as would appear in Ledger for the month of March, 2015.

(c) M/s JAGGU & Co. maintains Ledger on Self-Balancing System on 31st March, 2015, the Ledger discloses the following Balances:

Debtors Ledger Adjustment Account	₹ 5,63,360 (Dr.)
Creditors Ledger Adjustment Account	₹ 2,31,615 (Cr.)

On scrutiny of ledgers the following errors were detected:

(i) An overcast of Bills Receivable Book by ₹ 5,000.

(ii) An under cast of Sales Book by ₹ 6,000.

(iii) Goods returned by Pankaj ₹ 4,600 have been entered in Sales Returns Book but not posted to Pankaj's Account in Debtors Ledger.

(iv) Cash discount allowed to customers amounting to ₹ 2,580 has not been taken into consideration while preparing Adjustment Accounts.

(v) An overcast of Purchases Book by ₹ 10,000.

(vi) Goods for ₹ 6,300 purchased on credit correctly entered in Purchases Book but wrongly posted as ₹ 3,600 in the Creditor's Personal Account in Purchases Ledger.

Required: Pass necessary Journal entries to rectify the Adjustment Accounts in different ledgers.

5. **Answer any two questions (Carrying 4 marks each):** **4 × 2 = 8**

(a) DAFALIBUILDCOM LTD. undertook a contract to construct a bridge across river Pennar for ₹ 1,500 Lakh on 1st July, 2014. The following details are available in the records kept for the year ended 31st March, 2015:

Particulars	(₹ in Lakh)
Works Certified	750
Works not Certified	207
Estimated further cost	638

Progress payment received	600
Progress payment to be received	210

Required: What is the additional provision for Foreseeable Loss which must be made in the final Accounts for the year ended 31 st March, 2015 as per provisions AS-7 on 'Accounting for Construction contract'?

(b) Write a Short Note on Project Accounting.

(c) PRARTHANA & PIYUSH Publication publishes a monthly magazine on the 15th of every month. It sells advertising space in the magazine to advertisers on the terms of 80% sale value payable in advance and the balance within 30 days of the release of the publication. The sale of space for the March 2015 issue was made in February 2015. The magazine was published on its scheduled date. It received ₹ 2,40,000 on 10.03.2015 and ₹ 60,000 on 10.04.2015 for the March, 2015 issue.

Discuss in the context of AS-9 the amount of revenue to be recognized and the treatment of the amount received from advertisers for the year ending 31.03.2015.

6. **Answer any two questions (Carrying 8 marks each):** **8 × 2 = 8**

(a) BABAI sold goods to KACHARI for ₹ 90,000 on 1st April,2014 for which the later accepted three bills of ₹ 30,000 each due respectively in 1,2 and 3 months. The first bill is retained by Babai and is duly met. The second bill was discounted (discount being ₹ 600) and is met in due course. The third bill is also discounted (discount being ₹ 900) and is dishonoured, the Noting charges being ₹ 150.

New arrangements were duly made whereby Kachari pays Cash ₹ 10,150 and accepts a new bill due in 2 months for the balance of the amount with interest at 15% P.A. The bill is retained. On due date the same is dishonoured, noting charges being ₹ 180. Kachari declared insolvent on 15th September 2014 and 35 paise in a rupee were received from his estate.

Required: Pass Journal entries in the Books of BABAI.

(b) On 15th December, 2014 the premises of NAGAR LTD. were destroyed by fire, but sufficient records were saved from which the following particulars were ascertained:

Particulars	₹
Stock at cost on 1st April, 2013	2,20,500
Stock at cost on 31st March, 2014	2,38,800
Purchases less returns, year ended 31st March, 2014	11,94,000
Sales less returns, year ended 31st March, 2014	14,61,000
Purchases less returns, 1st April, 2014 to 15th December, 2014	10,15,000
Sales less returns, 1st April, 2014 to 15th December, 2014	11,62,000

In valuing stock for Balance Sheet as at 31st March, 2014 ₹ 6,900 had been written off for certain stock which was a poor selling line, having cost of ₹ 20,700. A portion of these goods were sold in June, 2014 at a loss of ₹ 750 on the original cost of ₹ 10,350. The remainder of this stock was now estimated to be worth the original cost. Subject to the above exception, gross profit had remained at a uniform rate throughout. The stock salvaged was ₹ 17,500. The stock was insured for ₹ 2,50,000.

Required: Calculate the amount of claim to be lodged with the Insurance company for Loss of Stock.

(c) MR. NAITIK sends goods to the value of ₹ 9,37,500 at cost to MR. JATIN on consignment basis to be sold at 5% commission on sales on 01.01.2015. Jatin accepted a bill of ₹ 2,50,000 drawn by Naitik for 4 months on the same date. Naitik discounted the bill with his banker @ 15% P.A. on 04.02.2015. Naitik incurred ₹ 75,000 by way of freight and other expenses, whereas expenses of Jatin we ₹ 50,000 out of which 60% were nonrecurring. Jatin sent the final balance of ₹ 7,68,750 to Naitik on 31.03.2015 along with account sales. The Gross Profit margin is 25% on Sales and 10% of Goods Remained unsold with Jatin.

You are required to **prepare**:

(i) Consignment Account and

(ii) Jatin Account in the books of Mr. Naitik.

7. Answer any two questions (Carrying 8 marks each): 8 × 2 = 16

(a) On 1st April, 2014 NANU BANK LTD. had a balance of ₹ 45 Lakhs in 'Rebate on Bills Discount Account.'

During the year ended 31st March,2015, Nanu Bank Ltd. discounted bills of exchange of ₹ 51,000 Lakh charging interest at 15% per annum, the average period of discount being for 73 days. Out of these, Bill of Exchange of ₹ 3,067 Lakh were due for realization from the acceptor/customers after 31st March, 2015, the average period outstanding after 31st March, 2015 being 53 days.

You are required to pass the necessary Journal Entries and show the Ledger Accounts in the Books of NANU BANK LTD. pertain to

(i) Rebate on Bills Discounted Account

(ii) Interest and Discount Account

(b) LONG LIFE ASSURANCE CO. LTD. furnishes you the following information:

Particulars	₹
Life Assurance Fund on 31.03.2015	90,00,000
The interim bonus paid during the previous two-years period to Policyholders	1,50,000
Net Liability as per periodical Actuarial Valuation	75,00,000
Surplus brought forward from the previous valuation	9,00,000

The directors of the Company proposed to carry forward ₹ 10,00,000 and to divide the balance between the Policy holders and Shareholders.

You are required to show:

(i) The valuation Balance Sheet as on 31.3.2015

(ii) The Net profit for the two years (valuation period)

(iii) The distribution of the surplus (Profit)

(c) The following balances are extracted from the records of NARMODA ELECTRICITY CO. LTD. for the year ended March 31, 2015.

Particulars	(₹ in Lakh)	Particulars	(₹ in Lakh)
Balance as on 1st April, 2014:		Expenses of Management	14,400
Land	1,80,000	Cost of distribution	6,000
Machinery	7,20,000	Depreciation	24,000
Mains	2,40,000	Sale of energy for lighting	80,000
Share Capital–Ordinary shares	6,58,800	Sale of energy for Power	76,000
Debentures	2,40,000	Meter Rent	6,000
Expenditure during the year:		Interest on Debentures	12,000
Land	6,000	Interim Dividend	24,000
Machinery	6,000	Net Revenue Account as on 01.01.2014	34,200
Mains	61,200	Depreciation Fund	3,00,000
Sundry Creditors	1,200	**Sundry Debtors:**	

Cost of Generation	42,000	For Energy Supplied	48,000
Rent, Rates and Taxes	6,000	Others	600
		Cash Balance	6,000

You are required to prepare:

(i) Revenue Account and

(ii) Net Revenue Account for the year ended March 31, 2015

(iii) General Balance Sheet as at 31.03.2015.

(**Note:** Schedules/Note to Balance Sheet are not required)